Readings in Human-Computer Interaction:
A Multidisciplinary Approach

Other Titles in the Morgan Kaufmann Readings Series

Readings in Artificial Intelligence
Edited by Bonnie Lynn Webber and Nils J. Nilsson (1981)

Readings in Knowledge Representation
Edited by Ronald J. Brachman and Hector J. Levesque (1985)

Readings in Artificial Intelligence and Software Engineering
Edited by Charles Rich and Richàrd C. Waters (1986)

Readings in Natural Language Processing
Edited by Barbara J. Grosz, Karen Sparck Jones, and Bonnie Lynn Webber (1986)

Readings in Computer Vision: Issues, Problems, Principles, and Paradigms
Edited by Martin A. Fischler and Oscar Firschein (1987)

Readings in Nonmonotonic Reasoning
Edited by Matthew Ginsberg (Fall 1987)

Readings in Artificial Intelligence and Databases
Edited by John Mylopoulos and Michael Brodie (Spring 1988)

Readings in Human-Computer Interaction: A Multidisciplinary Approach

Written and Edited by
Ronald M. Baecker and William A. S. Buxton
University of Toronto

MORGAN KAUFMANN PUBLISHERS, INC.
SAN MATEO, CALIFORNIA

Editor and President *Michael B. Morgan*
Production Manager *Jennifer Ballentine*
Permissions Editor and
      Production Assistant *Todd R. Armstrong*
Cover Designer *Terry Earlywine*
Cover Picture *Robert Burns,*
      with the assistance of Ian Small, Leonard Slipp
      and many other students
Copy Editor *Lee Ballentine*
Research Assistant *Ilona R. Posner*
Research Assistant *Cynthia Wong*

Library of Congress Cataloging-in-Publication Data

Readings in human-computer interaction.

    Includes bibliographies and index.
    1. Interactive computer systems. 2. Human
engineering. 3. System design. I. Baecker, Ronald.
II. Buxton, William A. S.
QA76.9.I58R43 1987   004'.01'9   87-12512
ISBN 0-934613-24-9

Morgan Kaufmann Publishers, Inc.
2929 Campus Drive, San Mateo, California 94403
© 1987 by Morgan Kaufmann Publishers, Inc.
All rights reserved.
Printed in the United States of America

91 90 89   5 4 3 2

Brief Contents

Detailed Contents

Acknowledgments

The editors would like to thank the publishers and authors for permission to reprint copyrighted material in this volume.

M.C. Escher, *Belvedere*. Copyright, Escher estate, care of Cordon Art, Baarn, the Netherlands. Reprinted with permission of the copyright holder.

Robert Burns, the Cover Picture. Copyright from *The Dynamic Image* 1987. Reprinted with permission of the artist.

John D. Gould and Stephen J. Boies, "Speech Filing—An Office System for Principals," *IBM Systems Journal* 23(1):65-81, 1984. Copyright © 1984, International Business Machines Corporation. Reprinted with permission of the publisher and the authors.

John D. Gould and Stephen J. Boies, "Human Factors Challenges in Creating a Principal Support Office System—The Speech Filing System Approach," *ACM Transactions on Office Information Systems* 1(4):273-298, 1983. Copyright © 1983, ACM. Reprinted with permission of the publisher and the authors.

D. Boddy and D.A. Buchanan, "Information Technology and the Experience of Work," in Bannon, Barry, and Holst (Eds.), *Information Technology Impact on the Way of Life*, Dublin: Tycooly International Publishing, pp. 144-157. Copyright © 1982, D. Boddy. Reprinted with permission of the authors.

M.L. Markus, "Power, Politics, and MIS Implementation," *Communications of the ACM* 26(6):430-444. Copyright © 1983, ACM. Reprinted with permission of the publisher and the author.

H.K. Klein and R. Hirschheim, "Issues and Approaches to Appraising Technological Change in the Office: A Consequentialist Perspective," *Office: Technology and People* 2:15-42 (only pp. 15, 27-42 included here). Copyright © 1983, North Holland. Reprinted with permission of the publisher and the authors.

A.F. Westin, H.A. Schweder, M.A. Baker, and S. Lehman, "Office Technology and Managerial Excellence," *The Changing Workplace:* *A Guide to Managing the People, Organizational, and Regulatory Aspects of Office Technology,* White Plains, NY: Knowledge Industry Publications, Inc., pp. 15-1—15-10. Copyright © 1985, G.K. Hall Publishers. Reprinted with permission of the publisher and the authors.

Michael J. Smith, "Human Factors Issues in VDT Use: Environmental and Workstation Design Considerations," *IEEE Computer Graphics and Applications* 4(11):56-63. Copyright © 1984, IEEE. Reprinted with the permission of the publisher and the author.

S.L. Sauter, L.J. Chapman, and S.J. Knutson, "Preventing Back Strain" and "Lighting Control," *Improving VDT Work: Causes and Control of Health Concerns in VDT Use*, Madison, WI: University of Wisconsin, pp. 13-19 and 58-61. Copyright © 1985, Department of Preventive Medicine, University of Wisconsin. Reprinted with permission of the publisher and the authors.

Computer and Business Equipment Manufacturers Association, "Guide to the Draft American National Standard for Human Factors Engineering of Visual Display Terminal Workstations," *Computers and Standards* 4(2):113-116. Copyright © North Holland. Reprinted with permission of the publisher and the association.

T.J. Springer, "The Statutes and Standards Movement," *Office Ergonomics Review* 2(2):14-15. Copyright © 1985, Humantech, Inc. Reprinted with permission of the publisher and the author.

Andrew Monk, "How and When to Collect Behavioural Data" and "Statistical Evaluation of Behavioural Data," in Monk (ed.), *Fundamentals of Human—Computer Interaction*, London: Academic Press, pp. 69-79 and 81-87. Copyright © 1984, Academic Press Inc. (London) Ltd. Reprinted with permission of the publisher.

B. Curtis, E. Soloway, R. Brooks, J. Black, K. Ehrlich, and H. Ramsey, "Software Psychology: The Need for an Interdisciplinary Program," Proceedings of the IEEE 74(8):1092-1106. Copyright © 1986, IEEE. Reprinted with permission of the publisher and the authors.

Beau A. Sheil, "The Psychological Study of Programming," *ACM Computing Surveys* **13**(1):101-120. Copyright © 1981, ACM. Reprinted with permission of the publisher and the author.

Stuart K. Card, "Human Limits and the VDT Computer Interface," in Bennett, Case, Sandelin, and Smith (Eds.), *Visual Display Terminals: Usability Issues and Health Concerns*, Englewood Cliffs, NJ: Prentice Hall, pp. 117-155 (only pp. 124-143 plus Figures D-16 and D-17 included here). Copyright © 1984, S.K. Card. Reprinted with permission of the author.

S.K. Card, T.P. Moran, and A. Newell, "The Keystroke-Level Model for User Performance Time with Interactive Systems," *Communications of the ACM* **23**(7):396-410. Copyright © 1980, ACM. Reprinted with permission of the publisher and the authors.

S.K. Card, T.P. Moran, and A. Newell, "Computer Text-Editing: An Information Processing Analysis of a Routine Cognitive Skill," *Cognitive Psychology* **12**:32-74. Copyright © 1980, Academic Press. Reprinted with permission of the publisher and the authors.

Donald A. Norman, "Some Observations on Mental Models," in Gentner and Stevens (Eds.), *Mental Models*, Hillsdale, NJ: Erlbaum, pp. 7-14. Copyright © 1983, Lawrence Erlbaum Associates, Inc. Reprinted with permission of the publisher and the author.

Teresa L. Roberts and Thomas P. Moran, "The Evaluation of Computer Text Editors: Methodology and Empirical Results," *Communications of the ACM* **26**(4):265-283. Copyright © 1983, ACM. Reprinted with permission of the publisher and the authors.

Robert L. Mack, Clayton H. Lewis, and John M. Carroll, "Learning to Use a Word Processor: Problems and Prospects," *ACM Transactions on Office Information Systems* **1**(3):254-271. Copyright © 1983, ACM. Reprinted with permission of the publisher and the authors.

John M. Carroll and Robert L. Mack, "Learning to Use a Word Processor: By Doing, by Thinking, and by Knowing," in Thomas and Schneider (Eds.), *Human Factors in Computer Systems,* Norwood, NJ: Ablex, pp. 13-51. Copyright © 1984, Ablex Publishing Corporation. Reprinted with permission of the publisher and the authors.

Charles Bigelow and Donald Day, "Digital Typography," *Scientific American* **249**(2):106-119. Copyright © 1983, W.H. Freeman and Company, Publishers. Reprinted with permission of the publisher and the authors.

Aaron Marcus, "Graphic Design for Computer Graphics," *IEEE Computer Graphics and Applications* **3**(4):63-70. Copyright © 1983, IEEE. Reprinted with permission of the publisher and the author.

American Institute of Graphic Arts, "Symbol Signs: The System of Passenger/Pedestrian Oriented Symbols Developed for the U. S. Department of Transportation, New York: Hastings House, Publishers, pp. 60-61, 104-105, and 120-121. Copyright © 1981, American Institute of Graphic Arts. Reprinted with permission of the institute.

Gerald Murch, "Colour Graphics—Blessing of Ballyhoo?" *Computer Graphics Forum* **4**:127-135. Copyright © 1985, North Holland, Amsterdam. Reprinted with permission of the publisher and the author.

Robert F. Sproull, "Frame-Buffer Display Architectures," *Annual Review of Computer Science* **1**:19-46. Copyright © 1986, Annual Reviews Inc. Reprinted with permission of the publisher and the author.

William Buxton, "There's More to Interaction than Meets the Eye: Some Issues in Manual Input," in Norman and Draper (Eds.), *User Centered System Design: New Perspectives on Human-Computer Interaction*, Hillsdale, NJ: Erlbaum, pp. 319-337. Copyright © 1986, Lawrence Erlbaum Associates, Inc. Reprinted with permission of the publisher and the author.

W. Buxton, R. Hill, and P. Rowley, "Issues and Techniques in Tough-Sensitive Tablet Input," *Proceedings of Siggraph '85*, San Francisco, CA, pp. 215-224. Copyright © 1985, ACM. Reprinted with permission of the publisher and the authors.

Stuart K. Card, William K. English, and Betty J. Burr, "Evaluation of Mouse, Rate-Controlled Isometric Joystick, Step Keys, and Text Keys for Text Selection on a CRT," *Ergonomics* **21**(8):601-613. Copyright © 1978, Taylor & Francis Ltd., London. Reprinted with permission of the publisher and the authors.

C.A. Simpson, M.E. McCauley, E.F. Roland, J.C. Ruth, and B.H. Williges, "System Design for Speech Recognition and Generation," *Human Factors* **23**(2):115-141. Copyright © 1985, Human Factors Society. Reprinted with permission of the publisher and the authors.

Gadi Kaplan and Eric J. Lerner, "Realism in Synthetic Speech," *IEEE Spectrum* **22**(4):32-37. Copyright © 1985, IEEE. Reprinted with permission of the publisher and the authors.

W. Buxton, S.A. Bly, S.P. Frysinger, D. Lunney, D.L. Mansur, J.J. Mezrich, and R.C. Morrison, "Communications with Sound," *Proceedings of CHI '85*, pp. 115-119. Copyright © 1985, ACM. Reprinted with permission of the publisher and the authors.

J. Nievergelt and J. Weydert, "Site, Modes, and Trails: Telling the User of an Interactive System Where He Is, What He Can Do, and How to Get Places," in Guedj et al. (Eds.), *Methodology of Interaction,* pp. 327-338 (only pp. 327-332 included here). Copyright © 1980, North Holland, Amsterdam. Reprinted with permission of the publisher and the authors.

Elaine Rich, "Natural-Language Interfaces," *IEEE Computer*, September 1984, pp. 39-47. Copyright © 1984, IEEE. Reprinted with permission of the publisher and the author.

Gary Perlman, "Making the Right Choices with Menus," *Human-Computer Interaction — Interact '84*, Amsterdam: North Holland, pp. 317-321. Copyright © 1985, North Holland, Amsterdam. Reprinted with permission of the publisher and the author.

S.K. Card, M. Pavel, and J.E. Farrell, "Window-based Computer Dialogues," *Human-Computer Interaction — Interact '84,* Amsterdam: North Holland, pp. 239-243. Copyright © 1985, North Holland. Reprinted with permission of the publisher and the author.

Ben Shneiderman, "Direct Manipulation: A Step Beyond Programming Languages," *IEEE Computer*, August 1983, pp. 57-69 (only pp. 57-62 included here). Copyright © 1983, IEEE. Reprinted with permission of the publisher and the author.

E.L. Hutchins, J.D. Hollan, and D.A. Norman, "Direct Manipulation Interfaces," in Norman and Draper (Eds.), *User Centered System Design: New Perspectives on Human-Computer Interaction,* Hillsdale, NJ: Erlbaum, pp. 87-124 (only pp. 118-123 included here). Copyright © 1986, Lawrence Erlbaum Associates, Inc. Reprinted with permission of the publisher and the authors.

Ronald Baecker, "Towards a Characterization of Graphics Interaction," in Guedj et al. (Eds.), *Methodology of Interaction*, pp. 127-147. Copyright © 1980, North Holland, Amsterdam. Reprinted with permission of the publisher and the author.

Introduction

Computer systems have become pervasive in our society. From school children to university students and scholars, from secretaries to middle managers and executives, from factory workers to machine designers, from animators and printers to architects and planners, computers are changing roles and expectations, enhancing some careers while trivializing or eliminating others.

Although some computer systems are designed to run essentially autonomously, most have a *user interface* through which human users and computers interact. This interface is often the single most important factor in determining the success or failure of a system. It is also one of the most expensive. Sutton and Sprague (1978) gathered data on 22 interactive business applications in ten large organizations operating in a variety of industries, and found that the code required to support the user interface averaged 59 percent of the total code for the application. Smith and Mosier (1984) surveyed 201 people concerned with information systems design, mostly working in the industry, and many involved in human factors engineering. On the average, the 83 who replied to the survey estimated that 30 to 35 percent of operational software is required to support the user interface. Bobrow, Mittal, and Stefik (1986) report that the user interface often constitutes one third to one half of the code of typical expert, knowledge-based systems.

Yet, despite its importance, the user interface is one of the most poorly understood aspects of any system. Its success or failure is determined by a complex range of poorly understood and subtly interrelated issues, including whether the system is congenial or hostile, easy or difficult to learn, easy or difficult to use, responsive or sluggish, forgiving or intolerant of human error.

The capabilities and disciplines required to find an appropriate balance among these issues are as diverse as the issues themselves. Among others, they include the skills of the graphic designer and industrial designer, an understanding of organizational dynamics and processes, an understanding of human cognitive, perceptual, and motor skills, a knowledge of display technologies, input devices, interaction techniques, and design methodologies, and an aptitude for elegance in system design. Effective interface design is thus a multidisciplinary process requiring a holistic view of any design problem. It is also a task which requires more skills than any single individual is likely to possess.

But simply assembling a team of experts is no guarantee of success. Graphic design for computer displays, for example, is a very different exercise from that taught in most art and design schools. Analogous situations exist for the other disciplines involved. What's needed is a new specialist, trained to understand and improve the ways in which humans interact with computers.

What materials are available to assist in this process? There are increasing numbers of elementary books that summarize basic principles of human-computer interaction (Heckel, 1982; Rubinstein and Hersh, 1984; Nickerson, 1986; Shneiderman, 1986). Over a thousand papers relevant to the field are published annually. Although some of these may be found in journals of broad circulation, many of the best appear in a great variety of conference proceedings and books that are not widely avail-

1

able. There is also one professional research gathering, abstracting, indexing, and publishing service specializing in the field — *The Report Store* in Lawrence, Kansas. Despite this, we have been distressed by the lack of appropriate textbooks and teaching materials that integrate at an advanced level the rapidly increasing body of relevant results from the research community, from professional practice, and from real applications.

In 1982, along with John Arnott, we began developing a tutorial course presenting our view of some of the issues and techniques of user interface design. In the absence of any appropriate text, we assembled a comprehensive set of lecture notes to accompany this course. At a certain point, we discussed expanding these notes into a textbook appropriate for use at the advanced undergraduate, beginning graduate student, or practicing professional level. It was soon clear to us that the urgency of the need for such a book was inconsistent with the time it would take to complete the work. Thus we decided to address the immediate need and to gather, integrate, edit, and annotate a source book of outstanding papers in the field. The result, we hoped, would be a contribution that could rapidly fill the gap in teaching materials while still remaining useful in the future, when texts of other kinds are available.

What This Volume Is

This volume is organized into three major parts. Part I deals with *the context* — historical, socio-political, and physical, within which human-computer interaction takes place. Part II focuses on *the user and the usage* of interactive computer systems, on underlying cognitive processes, and on methods of modelling and evaluating users and systems. It also deals with the human sensori-motor systems through which a user interacts and with the technologies through which interaction takes place. In Part III we look at *the process of system design* — interaction techniques, design methodologies, tools to facilitate design and implementation, and issues to be considered in turning a design into a useful and usable system. The three parts are organized into thirteen chapters dealing with the above topics and four case studies analyzing specific systems and/or applications. Finally, we include a final chapter discussing research frontiers and unsolved problems, a guide to further study, and several indices.

Each of the chapters and case studies consists of an original introduction followed by a number of key articles selected and reprinted from the literature. The introductions explain why each paper was selected, what in it is of key importance, and how it relates to the other papers in the volume. In numerous cases, excerpts from

important papers that could not be reprinted in their entirety because of space limitations are included, either by themselves when the excerpt is lengthy, or within the introduction when it is brief.

Choosing these papers has been a difficult balancing act:

- We have tried to maintain a balance between the abstract and the concrete, between the universal and the application-specific, between theory and practice. This has led us to include among the theoretical papers some case studies of real systems and applications.
- We have included papers on the possibilities and constraints of technology, with others describing the capabilities and limitations of humans.
- We have tried to show the importance of the insights required for design and synthesis, as well as those needed in the more rigorous processes of analysis and evaluation.
- We have included articles dealing both with the individual user of a computer system and with the entire community of users, articles focusing on the user's dialogue with the computer and on the context within which the dialogue is carried out.
- Finally, we have included papers dealing with the past, the present, and the future of human-computer interaction, papers presenting approaches that are evolutionary as well as those that are revolutionary.

Despite the length of the volume, the sizeable number of contributions included, and the number of contributions excerpted, we make no claims to have included every desirable paper or to have made the *best* selection of papers in any absolute sense. We laboured under constraints of space and time, the need to provide balance, and the ever-expanding volume of relevant literature. The more we read and study, the more we find there is to know. Yet we feel that this volume, however imperfect, fills a gap in the literature and addresses the real needs cited above; our later editions, or similar volumes by others, will carry this effort further and improve upon the result. We welcome suggestions for papers our readers feel should be included in the next edition. We also invite comments on experiences in the use of this volume, and have included a form for this purpose at the end of the book.

Although the volume is intended as a source-book which brings together timely information, there is no central bibliography. First, several annotated bibliographies exist for the field (Ramsey, et. al., 1978; Atwood, et. al., 1979; Burch, 1984a; Burch, 1984b; Williams and Burch, 1985; McGee and Matthews, 1986; McGee,

1986). Second, many of the selected readings have good bibliographies. Finally, we felt it best to list additional readings at the end of the chapters, where they are in proximity to the relevant material. These end-of-chapter suggested further readings are also typically cited in context in the written introductions. Here particularly we had to be very selective. We biased our choices towards papers that were recent, to aid those using this volume to facilitate literature searches. We use the term bibliography broadly to include references to available video tapes, since a video tape record is in many ways a much more effective means of documenting, presenting, and explaining an interactive system than is a written record.

We hope that this volume will not only serve as a valuable free-standing collection but as a set of pointers and a guide to the rich and rapidly evolving literature of human-computer interaction.

What This Volume Is Not

The pace of technological development is increasing, and involving an ever-widening circle of computer scientists, behavioural scientists, engineers, and designers. The overwhelming mood among those involved in the development and delivery of this technology is one of optimism, ranging from mild pleasure at tangible advance to euphoria and belief in the liberating and enhancing effects of appropriate technology.

But what is appropriate technology? How should it be applied? Of what use is it to enhance a user interface if the purpose and the application are not ennobling and enriching?

The field of human-computer interaction as it is generally constituted does not usually deal with these issues in any depth. Their exploration is typically conducted under such rubrics as ''social implications of computing'' and ''computers and society.'' The focus in ''human-computer interaction'' is typically development and refinement, as opposed to critique and fundamental change in ''computers and society.'' Students of ''human-computer interaction'' are usually optimistic, whereas those who write on ''computers and society'' are often pessimistic.

The effect of computers on employment, on personal privacy, on our safety from an accidental nuclear holocaust, on the distribution of power and control in our society, and on our self image, to name some of the more serious issues raised by such scholars, are critical to the wise and humane use of computers and are issues that should be pondered and debated by all those active in the so-called ''computer revolution.''

On the other hand, despite the importance of these issues, this volume is intended to represent, insofar as is possible in 700 to 800 pages, the major results and research contributions in the field of human-computer interaction *as it is conventionally constituted today*. We must therefore refer those interested in a treatment of some of the above issues to books such as that by Weizenbaum (1976), who poses the issues most sharply, as well as those by Pylyshyn (1970), Taviss (1970), Gotlieb and Borodin (1973), Mowshowitz (1976), Dertouzos and Moses (1979), Forester (1980, 1985), Johnson (1985), Johnson and Snapper (1985), and Rosenberg (1986).

Acknowledgments

We have been privileged over the lifetime of this project to receive advice and assistance from many knowledgeable individuals, including John Arnott, Phil Barnard, Jack Carroll, Jim Foley, William Graves, John Gould, Heinz Klein, Rob Kling, Clayton Lewis, Gene Lynch, Tom Malone, Marilyn Mantei, Tom Moran, Neville Moray, S. Joy Mountford, Ray Nickerson, Jakob Nielsen, Niels Christian Nielsen, Don Norman, and Jim Rhyne. Tom Carey and Berney Williams were kind enough to give the manuscript particularly thorough readings and to provide us with insightful commentaries, as did our students Ralph Hill, Alison Lee, and Peter Rowley.

Despite this assistance, gratefully acknowledged and much appreciated, full responsibility for any errors and omissions lies with the editors. Although we are jointly responsible for all material, Bill Buxton is the primary author of Chapters 2, 3, 6, 8, 9, 12, and half of 14, and Ron Baecker is the primary author of the remaining chapters and the case studies.

Throughout the work, Ilona Posner provided skilled, tireless, and valued research, editorial, and clerical assistance. Cynthia Wong was also particularly helpful in these roles towards the end of the project.

We are grateful to Mike Morgan and to Jennifer Ballentine of Morgan Kaufmann Publishers for their support, their advice, and their forbearance through a lengthy series of missed deadlines and slipping schedules.

Global research support for our activities during this project has been provided by the Natural Sciences and Engineering Research Council of Canada.

Finally, and most importantly, we are deeply thankful to Karyn, and to Elizabeth, Blair, Adam, and Katie for their love and support during an effort which must have seemed to be a never-ending series of evening, late night, early morning, and weekend transformations into moody workaholics, or buzzy space cadets, or both.

References

Atwood, Michael E., Ramsey, H. Rudy, Hooper, Jean N., & Kullas, Daniel A. (1979). Annotated Bibliography on Human Factors in Software Development. *ARI Technical Report* P-79-1, Englewood, Colorado: Science Applications, Inc.

Bobrow, Daniel G., Mittal, Sanjay, & Stefik, Mark J. (1986). Expert Systems: Perils and Promise. *Communications of the ACM* 29(9), 880-894.

Burch, John L. (Ed.) (1984a). *Computers: The Non-Technological (Human) Factors*. A Recommended Reading List on Computer Ergonomics and User Friendly Design, Lawrence, Kansas: The Report Store.

Burch, John L. (Ed.) (1984b). *Ergonomics: The Science of Productivity and Health*, Capsule Reviews of the Principal Literature in Present-Day Ergonomics and Human Factors Engineering, Lawrence, Kansas: The Report Store.

Dertouzos, Michael L. & Moses, Joel (Eds.) (1979). *The Computer Age: A Twenty-Year View*, Cambridge, Mass.: MIT Press.

Forester, Tom (Ed.) (1980). *The Microelectronics Revolution*, Cambridge, Mass.: MIT Press.

Forester, Tom (Ed.) (1985). *The Information Technology Revolution*, Cambridge, Mass.: MIT Press.

Gotlieb, C.C. & Borodin, A. (1973). *Social Issues in Computing*, New York: Academic Press.

Heckel, Paul (1982). *The Elements of Friendly Software Design*, New York: Warner Books.

Johnson, Deborah G. (1985). *Computer Ethics*, Englewood Cliffs, N.J.: Prentice-Hall, Inc.

Johnson, Deborah G. & Snapper, John W. (1985). *Ethical Issues in the Use of Computers*, Belmont, CA.: Wadsworth Publishing Company.

Mowshowitz, Abbe (1976). *Conquest of the Will: Information Processing in Human Affairs*, Reading, MA.: Addison-Wesley Publishing Company.

McGee, Kate, & Matthews, Catherine (Editors) (1986a). *The Design of Interactive Computer Displays*, A Guide to the Select Literature, Lawrence, Kansas: The Report Store.

McGee, Kate (Editor) (1986b). *The Design of Interactive Computer Displays II*, A Guide to Selected Periodicals, Lawrence, Kansas: The Report Store.

Nickerson, Raymond S. (1986). *Using Computers: Human Factors in Information Systems*, Cambridge, Mass.: MIT Press.

Pylyshyn, Zenon W. (Ed.) (1970). *Perspectives on the Computer Revolution*, Englewood Cliffs, N.J.: Prentice-Hall.

Ramsey, H. Rudy, Atwood, Michael E., & Kirshbaum, Priscilla J. (1978). *A Critically Annotated Bibliography of the Literature of Human Factors in Computer Systems*. *Technical Report* SAI-78-070-DEN, Englewood, Colorado: Science Applications, Inc., available from NTIS.

Rosenberg, Richard S. (1986). *Computers and the Information Society*, New York: John Wiley & Sons.

Rubinstein, Richard & Hersh, Harry (1984). *The Human Factor: Designing Computer Systems for People*, Burlington, Mass.: Digital Press.

Shneiderman, Ben (1986). *Designing the User Interface: Strategies for Human-Computer Interaction*, Reading, Mass.: Addison-Wesley Publishing Company.

Smith, Sidney L. & Mosier, Jane N. (1984). The User Interface to Computer-Based Information Systems: A Survey of Current Software Design Practice. *Behaviour and Information Technology* 3(3), 195-203.

Sutton, Jimmy A. & Sprague, Ralph H., Jr. (1978). A Study of Display Generation and Management in Interactive Business Applications. *IBM Research Report* RJ2392(31804), Yorktown Heights, N.Y.

Taviss, Irene (Editor) (1970). *The Computer Impact*, Englewood Cliffs, N.J.: Prentice-Hall.

Weizenbaum, Joseph (1976). *Computer Power and Human Reason: From Judgment to Calculation*, San Francisco: W.H. Freeman.

Williams, Bernard O. & Burch, John L. (Editors) (1985). *Human Foundations of Advanced Computing Technology*, The Guide to the Select Literature, Lawrence, Kansas: The Report Store.

The Design of a Voice Messaging System

Our first case study is the design of a voice store-and-forward message system intended for direct use by "principals" (that is, for business people such as executives and professionals who rely upon secretaries to assist them in their work). It was developed by Stephen Boies, John Gould, and others at the IBM Thomas J. Watson Research Center. Our readings look at the design of this system, the Speech Filing System, from two points of view. Gould and Boies (1984) present the *design* of the system — the problem that it was intended to solve, the rationale and approach, the functionality, examples of the user-computer dialogue, advanced features, and a summary of the experiences with the results of developing the system. Gould and Boies (1983) focus on the *design process* — the general design methodology, the choice of technology, the development, testing, and refining of the user interface. Their emphasis is on the command language and the help system, and the processes of training and learning, and they give a more comprehensive summary of experiences and results with the system.

Several points can be made about these papers and the work they describe:

- The system is *real*, and is based on a decade of research and development (citations appear in the References within the two readings). The results were good enough to result in a commercial product.
- The work illustrates the *multidisciplinary* nature of interactive system design. The quality of the result is directly attributable to a happy synergy between computer scientists and behavioural scientists within a supportive and relaxed research and development environment.
- The papers illustrate the importance of the process of *iterative design*. The authors acknowledge that at each stage of their activities, there were imperfections in the then-current design, weaknesses that could not have been anticipated in advance and whose solutions could best be seen and developed in the process of iterative design and testing with real users.
- The work shows the importance of *behavioural analysis* and *empirical evaluation* in the design process. Solutions and improvements were not merely postulated and assumed, but were tested. Testing and experimentation was part of the decade of R&D cited above. The design methodology evolved by the IBM group in carrying out this work — an *early focus on users and tasks*, *empirical measurement*, and *iterative design*, is described in a paper by Gould and Lewis (1985) that is included in Chapter 11: Design Principles and Methodologies, of this volume.
- To make the process of iterative design economically feasible, a *rapid prototyping* system is needed. Such a system allows one to mock up and try a variety of interfaces and dialogues with ease. Richards, Boies, and Gould (1986) describe the interface toolkit used to develop both the Speech Filing System and a later similar voice messaging system known as the Olympic Messaging System (Gould and Boies, 1984; IBM, 1985; Gould, Boies,

Levy, Richards, and Schoonard, 1987). Tools to support such rapid prototyping are discussed in Chapter 12: Programming Techniques and Tools.

- This case study is of value in that the system is sufficiently far removed from mainstream computing applications that readers will hopefully recognize their existing biases in the process of going through it. At the same time, it is close enough that we can see that the issues are equally relevant to more "conventional" systems and designs.

- One example of this is in the technology that is applied. In many ways it is easier to think about fundamental issues in human-computer interaction and in user interface design in the context of the relative simplicity of a touch-tone telephone than in the seemingly more interesting high-resolution bit-mapped workstation with keyboard and mouse input.

- Another result is that the total change of context forces us to take a fresh look at some of our preconceptions. Take for example the current wisdom about the inadvisability of *moded* input (Tesler, 1981). Avoiding modes for a system with any significant complexity is virtually impossible on a touch-tone telephone, so one can ask what are perhaps more useful questions: How can we minimize modes when some are needed? How do we make them as cognitively accessible and acceptable as possible?

- The Gould and Boies papers are valuable in that they stress the critical issues of *training* and *learning*, and the related importance of good *documentation* and where possible, self-documentation.

- The issues of *individualization* and *personalization* of the interface were raised in the work and dealt with very effectively. The designers were able to provide a system that could interact differently and appropriately with novices and with experts.

- Finally, there is a hint of some of the political and economic realities that are often ignored in discussions of ideal systems and interfaces in the abstract. The authors are able to demonstrate that their system is highly attractive, and eventually even essential to its users. They are also able to argue in a back-of-the-envelope calculation that a speech filing system is economically justifiable, in other words, that it saves money. It is therefore not surprising that the work led to the introduction of a product, the Audio Distribution System (ADS).

On the other hand, the system was not without its flaws, and its introduction into a real customer's environment was not always smooth and did not always lead to successful usage. One study that documented

this is that of Roemer, Pendley, Stempski, and Borgstrom (1986a). They administered a questionnaire to a randomly-selected sample of 200 subscribers and 50 ex-subscribers from among the 3,000 users of ADS at a development and manufacturing plant. Of these, "121 subscribers and 26 ex-subscribers rated overall level of satisfaction with the product, its usability, usefulness of various functions and features, reaction to possible nuisance situations, and preferences for alternative methods of communication."

User satisfaction as measured by the questionnaire was mixed:

- 65% of subscribers and 100% of ex-subscribers responded "using the low end of the scale" on a "percent satisfied" measure.

- 31% of subscribers and 52% of ex-subscribers rated "ease of learning" negatively.

- 61% of subscribers rated "ease of use after learning" positively, but 60% of ex-subscribers rated "ease of use after learning" negatively.

What accounts for the negative reactions? Roemer et al. (1986a, 1986b) cite a number of reasons:

- A person calling someone's number would not automatically be connected to the system if that person failed to answer her phone. This was later corrected in the ADS system that is marketed today in Europe.

- Four different systems were required to support the user population at this site, in other words, it scaled up awkwardly.

- Users cited the "need for exact spelling," a somewhat paradoxical complaint, since the system would also complete names from partial input where possible.

- The system was found by some to be "difficult" or "cumbersome," or "have too many keystrokes." An example of why this may have been can be seen in Figure 3 of Gould and Boies (1983).

- The ability to tailor the system to the users worked against it in this particular case, in that the new system prompts created for that particular installation were lengthy, difficult, and poorly recorded (Roemer, 1987).

It appears that the subscribers on the whole did not make sufficient use of the system for it to achieve critical mass — consider, for example, how the effectiveness of electronic mail deteriorates when a substantial part of the population is not using it. Why did this particular installation not achieve critical mass and general user satisfaction when most installations did? In addition to the reasons cited above, Roemer et al. (1986a) list some environmental, organizational, and social factors:

- Individuals didn't use the system because the people they wanted to communicate with didn't use it.

- The assignment of users to the four systems reflected the functional organization of the plant, not the "communication requirements."

- The availability of related resources and facilities reduced system usage. All managers had secretaries, who all used an electronic mail system, so managers perceived no need for the system.

- The lack of resources also played a role. Prior to the system's installation, centrally located message centers took phone messages for professional employees. Elimination of most of these centers to reduce costs happened at about the same time that the voice mail system was introduced. Many employees thought that the two events were related. The result was "some hostility towards the voice mail system," exacerbated by the difficulties experienced in using it.

- Initial training, which consisted of "a presentation of the system's features and functions to several hundred people at a time," was "probably not very effective."

- Finally, the intended use or application of the system, which was for a means of noninteractive communication, did not meet the plant's requirement, which was for telephone answering.

In summary, the case study shows how system quality can be improved by adopting the design approaches described, and that there must be extensive testing of usefulness and usability in a variety of real customer environments. It also shows that these approaches are not sufficient to guarantee that the system will work well in all contexts. This raises many issues to which we shall return later in this volume.

Finally, it leads us to think about broader issues such the role of voice messaging in office automation (Teger, 1983), other possible applications of voice technology (Aucella, 1987), and the ways in which voice can be utilized more effectively in enhancing human-computer communication (Schmandt, 1985). More of these latter topics can be found in Chapter 9: The Audio Channel, and in Chapter 14: Research Frontiers and Unsolved Problems.

Readings

Gould, John D. & Boies, Stephen J. (1984). Speech Filing — An Office System for Principals. *IBM Systems Journal* 23(1), 65-81.

Gould, John D. & Boies, Stephen J. (1983). Human Factors Challenges in Creating a Principal Support Office System — The Speech Filing System Approach. *ACM Transactions on Office Information Systems* 1(4), 273-298.

References

Aucella, Arlene (Organizer) (1987). Voice: Technology Searching for Communication Needs. *Proceedings of the 1987 Conference on Human Factors in Computing Systems, CHI + GI '87*, New York: ACM, 41-44.

Gould, John D., Boies, Stephen J., Levy, Stephen, Richards, John T., & Schoonard, Jim (1987). The 1984 Olympic Message System — A Test of Behavioral Principles of System Design. To appear in the September, 1987 issue of the *Communications of the ACM*.

Gould, John D. & Boies, Stephen J. (1984). Human Factors of the 1984 Olympic Message System. *Proceedings of the 28th Annual Meeting of the Human Factors Society*, 547-551.

Gould, John D. & Boies, Stephen J. (1984). Speech Filing — An Office System for Principals. *IBM Systems Journal* 23(1), 65-81.

Gould, John D. & Boies, Stephen J. (1983). Human Factors Challenges in Creating a Principal Support Office System — The Speech Filing System Approach. *ACM Transactions on Office Information Systems* 1(4), 273-298.

Gould, John D. & Lewis, Clayton (1985). Designing for Usability: Key Principles and What Designers Think. *Communications of the ACM* 28(3), 300-311.

IBM (1985). Olympic Messaging System. *SIGGRAPH Video Review* 19, New York: ACM.

Richards, John T., Boies, Stephen J., & Gould, John D. (1986). Rapid Prototyping and System Development: Examination of an Interface Toolkit for Voice and Telephony Applications. *Proceedings of the 1986 Conference on Human Factors in Computing Systems*, New York: ACM, 216-220.

Roemer, Joan M. (1987). Private communication.

Roemer, Joan M., Pendley, Wayne L., Stempski, Mark O., & Borgstrom, Mark C. (1986a). Field Study of a Voice Mail System: Design and Design-Process Implications. *SIGCHI Bulletin* 18(2), 60-61.

Roemer, Joan M., Pendley, Wayne L., Stempski, Mark O., & Borgstrom, Mark C. (1986b). Case Study of a Voice Mail System: Environmental Considerations in the Design Process. In Brown, J.O. & Hendrick, H.W. (Eds.) (1986). *Human Factors in Organizational Design and Management II*, Amsterdam: Elsevier Science Publishers, 681-686.

Schmandt, Christopher (1985). Voice Communication with Computers. In Hartson, H. Rex (Ed.), *Advances in Human-Computer Interaction*, Norwood, N.J.: Ablex, 133-159.

Teger, Sandra L. (1983). Factors Impacting the Evolution of Office Automation. *Proceedings of the IEEE* 71(4), 503-511.

Tesler, Larry (1981). The Smalltalk Environment. *Byte*, August 1981.

Speech filing—An office system for principals

by J. D. Gould
S. J. Boies

Business people spend most of their time communicating, or attempting to communicate, with others. We briefly describe our ideas about these communication activities and their resulting problems, and then discuss an experimental tool we developed to help business people solve some of their communication problems. This tool, called the Speech Filing System, allows users to send messages to anybody in the world and receive messages from anybody in the world. The system offers powerful editing, filing, retrieval, and message distribution and control functions, using pushbutton telephones as the terminals.

There is currently much interest in creating new work tools for business people, or so-called office principals, e.g., "white-collar" professionals, managers, executives, salesmen, etc. This interest in principal-support tools is stimulated by increasing white-collar costs, the need for greater principal productivity, potential decreases in secretarial services, and the absence of computerized tools for principals today.

Since 1973, we have been doing research on principal-support tools. This paper first describes the way we structured the problems to be solved and the experimental system we designed to solve them. The main part of the paper then describes what a principal can do with this new system, or tool.

The tool is called the Speech Filing System (SFS). It was developed at IBM Research in Yorktown Heights, New York, from 1973 to 1975. In 1975 principals began to use SFS in their own work, and informal evaluation with users began.[1,2] At the same time, formal human factors laboratory experiments related to SFS were underway.[3,4] For the next six years, about 750 IBM principals around the world used SFS in their daily work. This six-year period allowed us to con-

centrate on improving the user interface (including training, documentation, and help facilities) through a series of experiments, field studies, and major changes and the subsequent empirical evaluations of the interface.[5] In September 1981, IBM announced that the IBM Audio Distribution System (ADS), a direct outgrowth of SFS, would be available as a commercial product. The first customer installation was in February 1982. Other companies, including AT&T, Electronic Communications Systems (ECS), and Wang, have announced audio systems that have some functions in common with ADS.

Many of the audio functions described here are implemented in ADS. A description of the functions contained in ADS is contained in the "subscriber's guide."[6] We also describe some functions that we have designed or incorporated in research prototypes only, including message composition and transmission of nonaudio messages. The user interfaces for these functions and for ADS were jointly developed to make them compatible.

Whereas this paper provides a functional description of SFS, a related human factors paper[5] describes the design challenges and how we addressed them by drawing upon the behavioral literature to understand what principals actually do and by the empirical research we carried out through laboratory experiments, simulations, and prototype studies.

The problem

Communicating with other people is the main activity of principals, as well as of most other people. Communicating takes a lot of time. Studies show principals spend about 25 percent of their time in *noninteractive* communication, i.e., reading and writing,[7-9] and they spend over 40 percent of their time in *interactive* communication, i.e., face-to-face conversations, meetings, and telephone conversations.[7] If these percentages do not seem intuitively obvious, it may be because principals overestimate the amount of time they spend in noninteractive communication (42 percent estimated versus 26 percent actual) and underestimate the amount of time they spend in interactive communication (28 percent estimated versus 42 percent actual).[7] Interactive communication is the source of major frustrations for principals, e.g., inability to get the desired person on the telephone, inability to get to the point in a conversation, and inability to be understood.

Noninteractive communications provide a permanent record and have traditional distribution methods (e.g., U. S. Mail, public libraries). But these require very expensive, time-consuming typing and editing. Multiple copies are often required, and distribution is very slow. The increasing use of electronic mail and electronic message systems[10] is still pretty much limited to people using computer systems and terminals which are cost-justified for other purposes.

Interactive communications usually have speed advantages over noninteractive communications. Most interactive communication makes use of voice, and the intonation of speech carries information. But interactive communication has become increasingly difficult, in part as a consequence of having to locate a person in both space and time. Principals are unavailable over half the time because of being on the telephone, out of their offices, or in meetings. Principals make 15 or so telephone calls each day, completing only half of them to the parties they want to talk with.[11] They almost never leave a content message with a secretary but rather a message to "call me back." And, of course, when the call-back is made, the same statistics apply. (Incidentally, secretaries spend ten percent of their time handling these telephone messages.[8]) Principals often volunteer that this telephone roulette is their main pet peeve at work. Because people are frequently away from their desks and may be traveling, the caller may not know where to reach the called person. Thus, locating a person at a particular time has become an increasingly difficult task.

The problem, then, is to help principals with their communications needs. The solution lies in understanding these needs and developing a tool that addresses them.

Our solution

Required behavioral characteristics. From our behavioral analyses of principals' communication patterns, we decided that the solution involved many critical characteristics:

1. It must address principals' *communication* problems because communicating is the main activity of principals.
2. It must be a communication *system* that many principals will use.
3. It must be able to be used *directly* by a principal. Direct use is required to avoid the cost and potential errors of a human intermediary specialist and to identify displaceable costs that customers may need to justify the expense of buying the system.
4. It must be able to be used *anywhere* because principals work in many places—their offices, other people's offices, conference rooms.
5. It must be *sufficiently powerful* to be *useful* in addressing the necessary broad range of principals' communication needs.
6. It must communicate with *people*, not things (e.g., machines and traditional computer data bases) because principals communicate mainly with people.
7. It must handle *soft* information (opinions, attitudes, predictions, emotions, etc.) as well as hard information (facts, numbers, propositions, etc.) because principals almost always take into account soft information in making decisions.
8. It must handle information with a *short* lifetime as well as information with a *long* lifetime. Much office information has a short, but critical, lifetime, often of less duration than it typically takes to update most data bases, e.g., "the meeting has been postponed for 15 minutes" or "we have to go now."
9. It must *automatically* update itself.
10. It must be *easy to learn* and *easy to use*. This is the *sine qua non*. Principals say they do not want to read documentation or spend much time being trained. Some critics find it hard to reconcile this position with the fact that principals have spent many years in school learning from books and going to classes. The key insight has to do with the difference between learning to *do*

something, and learning *about* something. People learn to *do* things by *doing* them (walking, riding a bike, playing a game, speaking a foreign language, aerobics, typing, swimming, giving talks, cooking, successfully interacting with people, etc.), not by reading about how to do them.

These criteria led to severe challenges at the beginning of our work in the early 1970s. Office principals did not use computer typewriter or video terminals or computer systems, and there was a general belief that they would not. Computer systems communicated with things, not people, and contained hard,

SFS contains the best features of both noninteractive and interactive communication systems.

not soft, information. Computer terminals were used only by specialists. Data bases were updated periodically, and only by specialists. Computer systems required extensive training to learn. It was hard then, just as it is now almost ten years later, to predict the rate at which these facts will change. However, we believed then—and now—that the manner in which they will change depends upon providing systems that are more useful and easy to learn and use.

Summary of the system. SFS contains the best features of both noninteractive and interactive communication systems. Figure 1 shows a conceptual schematic of SFS. As shown, users can send and receive messages using standard pushbutton telephones. Messages are stored in a computer (an IBM Series/1 computer in ADS), which is connected to the telephone network and can be dialed from anywhere. Starting from the lower left of the figure and going clockwise, users can get or send messages from telephone booths, from their office, from conference rooms (where several people can use SFS at once), or from motels and home. A user's secretary can, via the secretary password, assist the principal.

SFS allows a person to *compose* (edit, review, insert, delete, annotate, and format) messages, *distribute*

these to any person in the world, and *receive* messages from any person in the world. (There is no distinction between messages, memos, documents, mail, notes, letters, etc. in SFS.) To do all this, SFS uses a pushbutton telephone (or its equivalent) as the terminal. The telephone was selected because it is the most ubiquitous terminal in the world, and users can thus send messages at almost any time and from almost any place. All principals have telephones in their offices and at home (but need not use their own telephones). Telephones are also in most other places where principals work, or else nearby, e.g., phone booths. With SFS, unlike with most other computer message systems, users need not seek out a special-purpose terminal. A principal gives commands to SFS via the pushbuttons on the telephone. Audio messages (as well as other media documents) are stored and modified in digital form but can be received or played out in analog or digital form.

Key results. Our research in the last six years shows that principals use SFS directly (from our interviews and observational data), use it at all hours of the day (from interviews, observations, and usage analyses), find it is easy to learn (ADS customers tell us that new users often learn it with no training), find it very useful in their work (from self-reports, interviews, and surveys), and send content messages (from observations and self-reports). If it is unavailable for even a short period of time, they are disturbed (self-reports and survey data). These results are elaborated upon elsewhere.[5,12] SFS is a cost-effective way of communicating and can pay for itself in less than one year (based upon displaceable costs and not counting any increase in principal productivity; see below).

What a person can do with SFS

Message creation or editing. A person, using only a pushbutton telephone as a terminal, can (1) create an audio message, (2) review and replace all or part of it, and (3) insert, delete, move, and edit segments of it. Although most of our work so far emphasizes spoken messages, we have used SFS to compose and distribute handwritten and typed messages as well. Figure 2 is an example of how a user calls SFS, records a message, and transmits it.

A person can annotate audio, written, printed, or pictorial messages received from other people. Figure 3 shows an example of a user listening to a message from his manager, adding the answer to her question, listening to both voices now in the message, and

Figure 1 Conceptual diagram of SFS (from original rendition by Jennifer Howard)

returning it to his manager as well as to the sales manager. Note that it is equally easy for a user to annotate a message anywhere in that message or to start over. Experience has shown that annotation is often used, and users often like to send both the initial inquiry and the response.

Unlike a tape recorder or conventional dictating system, SFS is voice-activated. A person does not turn it off and on while recording. In effect, SFS records only when a person is talking. For subsequent ease of listening, as well as storage compaction, pauses between words are encoded and automatically compressed by SFS.[13] Encoding and storing pauses, rather than simply deleting them, allows users to put the pauses back in if they want to.

Users create messages quickly, usually in a minute or two.[12] Because of this, and because of a terminal (the telephone) almost always being nearby, users indicate they can compose a message under almost any circumstances, including during a meeting with other people. Users volunteer that they like being able to send someone a message when "it occurs to me."

As SFS has evolved over the years, it has been used by principals much more as a message system (super-telephone) than as an enhanced dictation system (see Gould and Boies[5]): Our laboratory experiments showed that it is easier and more efficient for people to speak the contents of documents (whereby the recipient will listen to them) than to dictate the documents (whereby the recipient will read them).[14,15]

Message distribution. A user can send a message to any person in the world who has access to a push-button telephone (or device to convert a dial telephone into a pushbutton telephone) and who knows how to use a telephone. Most often, users send messages to other "registered" users, i.e., users whose names ("user IDs") are stored in SFS and are played out. Messages are sent by key-pressing the last name of a registered user, as shown in Figure 2. In the case

Figure 2   Example of a user calling SFS, recording a message, and transmitting it. Pressing 00 means "do it," or transmit it

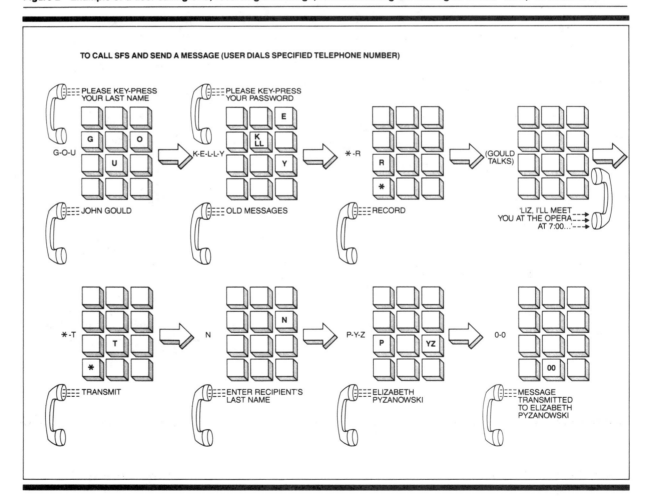

Figure 3 Example of a user (Jim) listening to a message, replying to it, and sending the reply back to the sender (Faye Hindery, his manager) and a copy of it to another person (Stephen Boies, the sales manager)

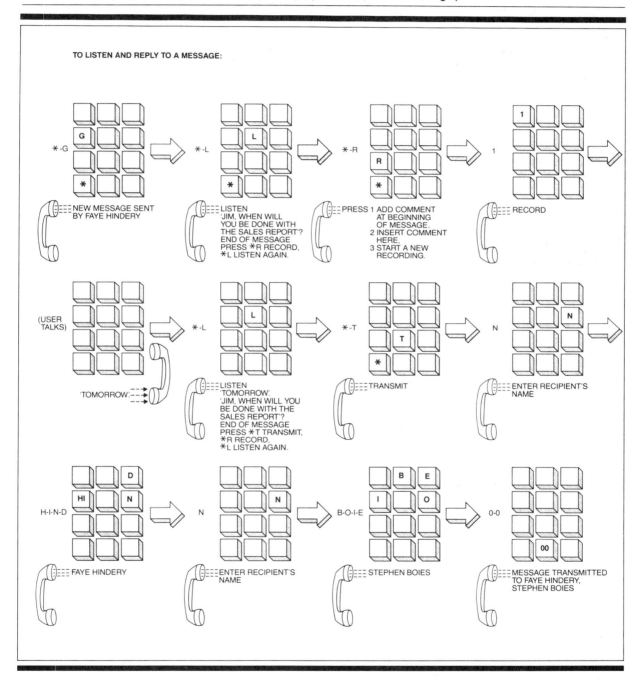

of ambiguities with names (e.g., several Smiths), SFS asks the user which Smith.

A user can send a message to more than one person at once, as shown in Figure 3, or to people on user-

Figure 4   Example of a user sending a message to a predefined distribution list. Users can give any name they choose to their distribution lists and can play out those names if they have forgotten them

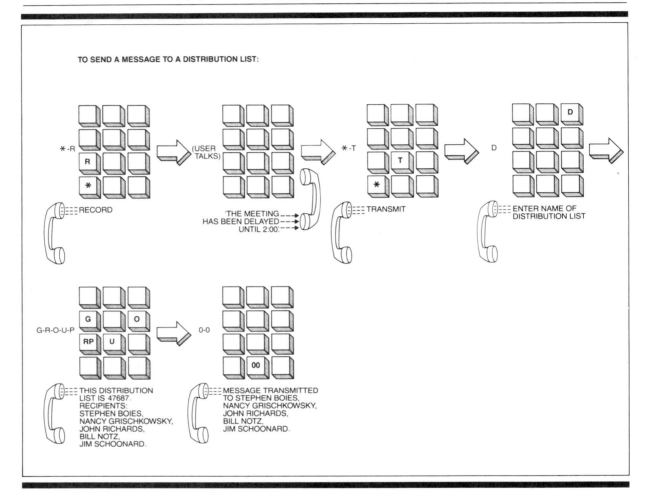

defined distribution lists. Figure 4 is an example of a user sending a message to a distribution list. Users can play out the names of their distribution lists and the names of the people on them. The concept of distribution lists is further enhanced by SFS, which can store defined sets of people, e.g., group members and organizational charts, and automatically update these.

A user can actually send a message to *any* person in the world who has a telephone number, or receive a message from any such person. Figure 5 is an example of a user sending a message to a nonregistered person. In this case, the user key-presses the telephone number of the recipient. If a message is sent to a telephone number, the security may not be as great as when it is sent to a person's name because the message can be heard by anyone answering the telephone.

A user may send a request to several people, and as they respond, SFS notes this. SFS will make additional reminder calls to the remaining people, reminding them of overdue replies.

A user can page other people via radio in conjunction with a telephone.

Note that a recipient can receive a message at *any* telephone, which is very useful while traveling. The

Figure 5   Example of transmitting a message to a nonuser. Should a user make a mistake in keying a telephone number, he or she can key that number in again to delete it and then key in the correct number

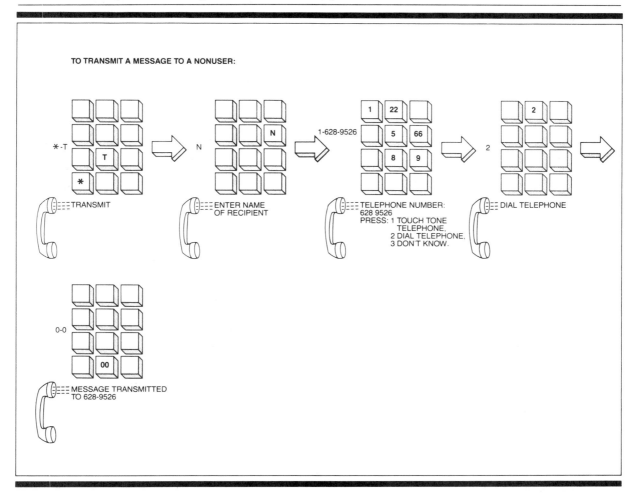

sender need not know where a registered recipient is or will be. Users can call SFS from any telephone, or be called by SFS at any telephone number included in the list of numbers where SFS can reach him or her. These numbers can correspond to a recipient's office phone, laboratory phone, and off-hours phone, for example. Users can easily change their numbers (from any telephone), which allows SFS to call them no matter where they are. The order and number of times SFS calls each number depends upon the hour of the day and whether the sender has assigned a special classification (e.g., urgent) to the message. SFS will call back in a few minutes if the recipient's phone is busy; it will try alternative numbers that the recipient has specified; and it will retry later if the phone is unanswered.

When a message is sent, SFS calls the recipient and notifies him about this. This call may be made at a time designated by SFS, or it may be made at times designated either by the sender or the recipient. SFS will automatically retry should a recipient be unavailable or should the number be busy.

A person can send a message to himself or herself to be delivered at any time (i.e., make his or her own phone ring at any time). Since one can send messages to oneself, SFS provides a reminder service. Figure 6 shows an example of a user sending himself a personal reminder, which in this case serves as a wake-up call as well. If the user makes a mistake keying in a time or date, he or she simply keys it in again.

Figure 6   Example of John Gould sending himself a personal reminder wake-up call. SFS will call him at home, his off-hours location, because of the time of day he entered

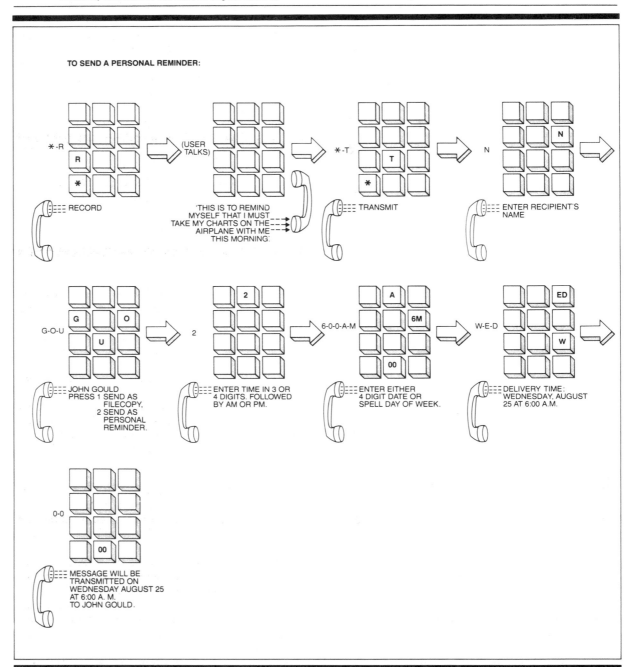

A user can send a message to a recipient and ask SFS to automatically notify him or her once the recipient has listened to it. Or, a user can ask SFS if a particular individual has listened to a message that he or she sent to that individual. This is in contrast to other forms of noninteractive communication. Although people can verify through the U. S. Post Office's Registered Mail system whether someone at the recipient's (presumed) location has *accepted* a document, this does not tell whether the intended recipient has actually *read* it. With SFS a user can learn whether a message he or she sent has actually been listened to. This information has proven valuable in reducing user uncertainty about whether a recipient, especially one who is traveling and whose whereabouts are unknown, has received a crucial message. SFS provides this information immediately, whereas U. S. Registered Mail, for example, requires several days, and even some electronic message systems have network delays.

A user can amend or cancel a message that has already been sent if the facts have changed or the information is no longer needed. We have adopted the policy that if the message is sent to several people, and if one or more people have listened to it, then the message cannot be amended or canceled.

A user can solicit a reply to his or her message, and both the sender and recipient can be automatically notified the day this reply is due, as well as if it is overdue. SFS automatically tells the user of the overdue status, and then plays out the text of the message.

Besides a New Message Box, an Old Message Box, and an Outgoing Message Box, each user has a Pending Message Box. The Pending Message Box contains a list of people who are overdue in replying to a user, as well as the people to whom that user owes replies. Users skip from one box to another with a two-key command. The most important box is activated when SFS calls a user or a user calls SFS. For example, if users have new messages, their New Message Box is automatically activated. If there are no new or pending messages, their Old Message Box is automatically activated when a user calls SFS (but in this case, SFS would not call a user).

There is a private bulletin board or shared message facility. If, for example, over a period of weeks a group of users wanted names of potential recruits for a new job, each user could send messages to this central collection point so that each member could hear the entire set (i.e., the messages from all group members) as it grows.

Message filing and retrieval. Each audio message has associated with it relevant statistics (e.g., time and date of creation, author's name, list of recipients, time at which each has heard it, and actions they

have taken on it). Upon retrieving a message, a user can play out these statistics (by pressing the W-key, i.e., the Who, What, When key).

A valuable application is filing a message to yourself containing important information that you use only occasionally but which is critical when you need it, e.g., the social security numbers of your children, project numbers, passbook numbers, credit card

A user can tailor SFS to his or her own needs.

numbers, zip code numbers, where to call if you lose your traveler's checks, automobile license numbers, and other hard-to-remember facts. These can be accessed at any time and from anywhere, e.g., if you should lose your credit cards while traveling.

A sender or a recipient can classify or label a message with any heading he or she chooses. The recipient can give the message a coded name, via pushbutton telephone key presses, and can associate a spoken name with this coded name to provide a mnemonic name. Users can scan through the names of the files they have stored.

A person can retrieve a message by sender's name, by recipient's name, by file name, by date of origin, or by classification (e.g., personal, confidential, or secret).

Recipients can erase messages they receive. SFS also erases messages that have been saved past a certain time—unless a user requests otherwise. This time is set by a "customer" (i.e., the owner of the entire system). Retention dates can be limited by the sender. SFS provides an audit trail that may be retained indefinitely.

A person has great control over the message he or she sends. A person can *classify* a message (e.g., confidential, secret, or personal). A person can regulate what others may do with the message (e.g., listen only, listen and comment on it, listen, com-

Figure 7   Example of SFS calling a user and the secretary answering. With default options, SFS does not allow the secretary to listen to the messages, only learn who they are from

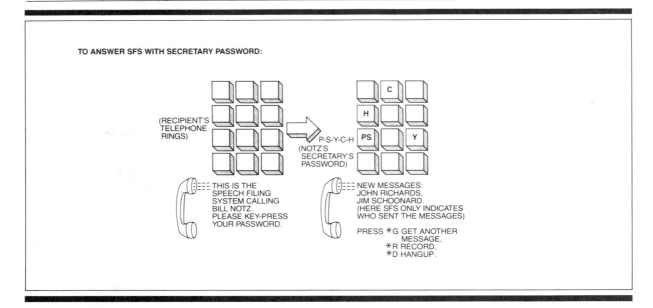

ment, and forward it, etc.), and how long they may retain it. A person can request responses to a message.

All these functions are accomplished by the user pressing the telephone pushbuttons.

Listening to messages. A user can listen to his or her messages from anywhere. Messages, of course, are heard in the voice of their creator. Pauses are automatically encoded when a message is recorded, so they can be contracted or expanded while listening. Listening to messages without pauses is much preferred over listening to messages containing the pauses of the author (as with traditional tape recorders or dictating equipment). Experiments have shown that comprehension of material heard via SFS's pause-deleted speech is equal to or better than that for the same material heard via careful reading or via extemporaneous speech.[4] The limiting factor in listening to SFS messages is the quality of the telephone lines. A user can change listening speed, increasing it several times over the rate it normally plays out. Other listening aids are described below.

Personalization. A user can tailor SFS to his or her own needs via pushbutton telephone key-press commands. A user has four passwords: personal, secretary, family, and guest. A user can use all SFS func-

tions with his or her personal password. Initially, SFS assigns a subset of the functions to the other passwords.

Figure 7 is an example of what happens when SFS calls and a secretary answers. With the secretary password, a secretary can learn who the principal's messages are from, but not listen to their content. A principal can modify what his or her secretary's password (as well as the others) can do, assigning more function to it. For example, a principal may want the secretary to be able to listen to all nonconfidential messages.

Special attention, in the form of a special password and priorities, is given to a user's family. (Ever try calling home at 4:30 p.m. and get a busy signal?) With the family password, one accesses only the messages designated for the family, e.g., "I'll be home late tonight."

A user has three telephone numbers where SFS will call him or her. Users can call SFS and set these numbers from any telephone anywhere, which is useful when a user is at another location and wants SFS to call there. These numbers are usually the user's office number, secondary work number, and off-hours or home number.

Figure 8   The user command language that evolved from SFS and now runs on the ADS product

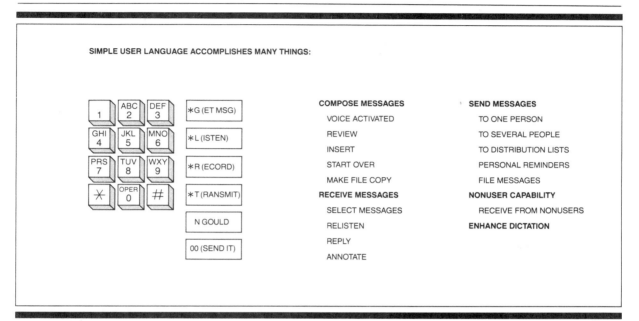

SIMPLE USER LANGUAGE ACCOMPLISHES MANY THINGS:

COMPOSE MESSAGES
- VOICE ACTIVATED
- REVIEW
- INSERT
- START OVER
- MAKE FILE COPY

RECEIVE MESSAGES
- SELECT MESSAGES
- RELISTEN
- REPLY
- ANNOTATE

SEND MESSAGES
- TO ONE PERSON
- TO SEVERAL PEOPLE
- TO DISTRIBUTION LISTS
- PERSONAL REMINDERS
- FILE MESSAGES

NONUSER CAPABILITY
- RECEIVE FROM NONUSERS

ENHANCE DICTATION

Several user interface languages are available, and the user can select the one he prefers. A new user, for example, may choose to use the system-driven, prompted language that experience has shown requires no user training.[5] The experienced user, on the other hand, may not want the prompted, or audio menu, approach, but would rather choose to key-press the commands based upon his recollection of them.

Users can select the rate at which system messages automatically play out, making pronunciation faster or slower than originally recorded. It has been found that with experience, users like messages to play out faster.

SFS is designed to be able to monitor automatically user behavior and to provide feedback and help appropriate to the user's knowledge.

Results of using SFS

Useful functions. The two major user interface issues in any system are identifying the required useful functions and making these easy to learn and use. The first issue was initially accomplished with our behavioral analyses of principals' needs. The suc-

ceeding years of empirical research that studied the functions principals actually used and the additional functions they wanted led to major refinements (see Gould and Boies[5]) which proved ultimately to be successful, as mentioned earlier under "Key results."

Learning SFS. The second basic behavioral challenge was to make SFS easy to learn and use. The main problem centered on mapping the 100–200 different SFS functions onto the 12-key telephone set. The basic commands arrived at after several years of empirical and experimental research[5] are shown in Figure 8. They are *G to get a message, *L to listen to a message, *R to record a message, and *T to transmit a message. Each of these commands is, in effect, a command mode. For example, within the Transmit mode the N key is the prefix for a user's Name. With these basic commands, a user can do all the things shown in Figure 8. In addition, there is a Customize mode (*C) that allows users to personalize SFS for themselves, e.g., set their passwords and telephone numbers. The Customize mode is entirely prompted—after pressing *C a user selects from a series of three-choice alternatives—because it contains much function that is only infrequently used.

The solution that evolved included identification of the basic functions people wanted, a small number of commands to accomplish these functions (with only a few key-presses), feedback messages after every key-press, selective prompting messages, and almost no need for documentation. Experience has shown that users now require only a few minutes of training to learn these basic functions. Getting to

---

Users learn the basic functions in a few minutes.

---

this point, however, took years of human factors empirical research and several major iterations on the user interface.[5]

The self-help tools on SFS have in fact proven helpful primarily because they are integrated with the command languages and are easy to use. Pressing the # key causes suggestions about what the user might want to do next, conditioned by the user's context, to play out. Pressing the W key (i.e., 9 key) answers who, what, when, and where questions about a message a user is listening to or creating. The aim of this help system is not merely to aid the user in using SFS, but to aid the user with the general problem he or she is trying to solve.

From novice to experienced user. We have attempted to solve the general problem in SFS, found in all user-oriented interactive computer systems, of how to help a person use additional features of the system as he or she becomes more experienced. One simple method that new users in some customer locations have liked is to play out a "Helpful Hint of the Week" to a user upon first using SFS that week. In another approach, after a (programmable) number of uses by a given user, the SFS user interface can be automatically changed for that user. This approach has worked well in the case of automatically speeding up the rate of system message playout after a user uses SFS a certain number of times.

Handicapped users. SFS would seem to have advantages for the blind, who can listen to documents that might otherwise be available only in printed form. SFS ordinarily plays messages at about 200 words per minute, without being much affected by the rate at which they are recorded. The sped-up speech facilities of SFS allow messages to play out at about twice this rate, which approaches the maximum rate of speech perception.[16,17] The few manual controls and possibility of voice commands (see below) make SFS potentially attractive for the manually handicapped also.

Some observations on SFS usage. The following summarizes some qualitative observations on SFS usage. Users learn the basic functions in a few minutes. They require little or no documentation. SFS is truly principal-oriented. Principals use it directly. We know of no example in which a principal has asked his secretary to send a message for him or her. Much more is accomplished by noninteractive communication than we had initially imagined. Principals send content messages (as opposed to simply asking the recipient to return a telephone call). SFS appeals to a wide range of users, including those who dislike gadgets and had no intention of ever using a computer terminal. SFS is especially used by managers. SFS is used remotely (at night, while traveling, in other offices, etc.). Perhaps of most relevance, experience shows that users miss SFS if it is unavailable for a short time—as was occasionally the case with the research prototypes. All these observations are elaborated upon in Gould and Boies.[5]

What SFS does for principals. The following is a summary of informal positive comments we have heard from users of SFS over the last several years. Users like to be able to communicate with people at any time, from any place, and are especially appreciative of this when they do not know where other people are. It solves the time-zone problems, e.g., California to New York, Europe to U.S. (The fact that all times are based upon the SFS installation location does not seem to be a problem, probably because few timed deliveries are sent across several time zones.) Users say SFS relieves their anxieties about certain types of communication, and relieves what would otherwise be a larger (human) memory load. It helps them to control their interruptions and to communicate on relevant matters without getting into other, unwanted subjects. They like the personal touch of voice messages. SFS is said to eliminate the burden of routine matters. Users do not have to hunt around for people, and they can inform several people at once. It is easier and quicker to compose spoken messages than to compose written, dictated, or text-edited messages.[14,15,18,21,22] Users say that SFS improves their intragroup and intergroup communication.

Table 1   Estimated ADS displaceable costs

Operating Expense	Cost Savings*
Reduction in long-distance telephone costs	$15.00
(Assumes 6 fewer long distance calls/mo.)	
Reduction in memos—saved secretary time	51.60
(Assumes 8 fewer memos/mo.)	
Reduction in secretary message handling	26.65
(Assumes 5 fewer messages/day)	
TOTAL PER USER PER MONTH	$93.25
COST OF ADS PER USER PER MONTH	−$10.00
NET COST SAVINGS WITH ADS PER USER PER MONTH	$83.25

*Estimates are based upon unpublished studies available to the authors from IBM sources of what principals do without ADS and informal studies of what principals did with SFS prototypes. The ADS cost per user assumes users already have a paid-for telephone and at least 200 users on an ADS, and includes maintenance charges.

Cost of SFS. An estimate of the costs of SFS can be obtained from the commercially available IBM Audio Distribution System. ADS costs about $10.00 per month per user for an average system configuration,[5] which is much less expensive than electronic message systems used from video terminals.[19]

ADS is a principal-support system. Generally such systems can be cost-justified only in terms of increased principal productivity, which is difficult to estimate or measure. However, given the way ADS impacts principals' behavior, it can, fortunately, be cost-justified in terms of displaceable costs (so-called "hard dollars") as well. Three normal operating costs, shown in Table 1, can be reduced by ADS. First, long-distance telephone costs can be reduced because customers can lease a single 800 number for ADS. Second, typing costs can be reduced because fewer typed memos are required. Third, telephone message handling can be reduced because of fewer missed telephone calls. As shown in Table 1, we estimate these displaceable costs to be currently $93.25 per user per month in a typical office. Thus, the net cost saving is $83.25 per user per month.

Additional SFS features

What has been described so far are the general characteristics and main functions of SFS, and how and why people are using them. In this last section we describe some additional SFS features not yet mentioned.

Feedback. SFS provides the user with stored voice prompts, hints, suggestions, and menu choices for accomplishing useful work. SFS also responds to the

SFS has enhanced dictation facilities.

user with stored-voice confirming messages when key-presses are appropriate. When key-presses are inappropriate, SFS responds with stored-voice error messages, warnings, and helpful hints.

If the user is stuck or still does not know what to do after prompting, SFS aids in other ways. First, if a user, during a work session, has not done anything for a prescribed length of time (which is usually tens of seconds and depends upon what the user is trying to do), SFS detects this and tells the user about his or her options. What SFS tells the user is entirely dependent upon where the user is in the system. Second, a user presses the # key and SFS lists the options. Again, this is entirely context-dependent. A user can also press the W key. SFS then plays out answers to who, what, when, and where questions. Finally, a user can select a completely prompted language to guide him or her through the basic functions. This selection is made by changes in the user's profile (i.e., the user presses *C to get into the Customize mode).

Mnemonics. There are many levels of mnemonics, or memory aids, designed to make SFS easy to learn and use. The command names shown in Figure 8 illustrate verbal memory aids, e.g., G for Get, L for Listen. There are verbal mnemonics within a mode also. For example, in Transmit mode, the "D" key is the prefix for Distribution lists, the "N" key is the prefix for a user's Name, and the "W" key provides Who, What, When, and Where information.

An example of a spatial mnemonic is illustrated in Figure 9. SFS allows a person to skip around within a message. Imagine a person's forefinger resting on the 5 key. To go to the beginning, or *top*, of a message, a user presses 5 and then moves his finger *up* to press the 2 key. To go to the end, or *bottom*, of the message, a user presses 5 and then moves his finger *down* to press the 8 key. To skip back a little bit (several seconds of speech), a user presses 5 and then moves his finger to the left to press the 4 key. To skip forward a little bit, a user presses 5 and then moves his finger to the right to press the 6 key.

Enhanced dictation. SFS has enhanced dictation facilities, both for creating a long document and for listening to it or another one. With traditional dictating equipment, authors cannot copy, move, or delete segments of speech. With SFS, however, they can do these operations anywhere in the document. They can also insert material anywhere in the document. (Of course, they can record over the last several words of what they said, as with traditional dictating equipment.) They can listen to a document (theirs or somebody else's) in sped-up speech. They can attach audio format markers, through keypresses, to various parts of the document. We conceive of these markers as sentence, paragraph, and topic markers. When pressed, each causes an audio tone of a different frequency to be heard by the user. They are hierarchically organized, provide listeners clues to document structure analogous to what punctuation and indentation provide readers, and facilitate listening. The user, again through key-presses, can, for example, skip to a new paragraph, or listen only through a particular topic.

Voice commands. Presently SFS does not include any speech recognition. Users give SFS commands by pressing buttons on their telephones. The SFS input stream contains pushbutton signals mixed together with voice signals. SFS automatically separates these two, and interprets the frequencies corresponding to the telephone button presses as commands. SFS could be controlled with voice commands instead of key-presses, as our early feasibility experiments demonstrated. SFS would recognize and separate out the speech patterns corresponding to the voice commands. A special dictionary might be needed for each user, however. Further, users could not use SFS command names or user names in their messages, unless other precautions were taken. The programming underlying SFS makes it possible to switch between command modalities.

Coded data collection. When SFS is used as a voice message system, it is storing and manipulating so-called *noncoded information.* SFS can also collect

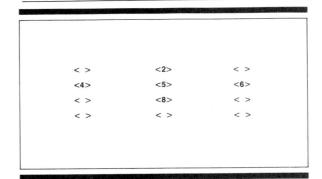

Figure 9   Example of a spatial mnemonic, or memory aid, in the Listen mode

```
   < >        <2>        < >
   <4>        <5>        <6>
   < >        <8>        < >
   < >        < >        < >
```

coded information. That is, people can enter actual coded data remotely, through the telephone, e.g., social security numbers, customer orders, and research data. There are many important SFS applications of this function. In a study conducted by Eric Goldwasser in 1978 (unpublished), IBM field engineers called SFS, often from a customer's location, just after completing a service call. These field engineers were immediately prompted with a series of questions, e.g., the customer's name, the serial number of the machine repaired, etc. They were asked to key in part numbers that needed to be ordered, and the quantity required. (Appropriate branching was included here so that as many part numbers could be ordered as needed.) These data were automatically transferred, on a computer network, to the appropriate departments in IBM. This operation allowed quick processing of orders, without the errors introduced by delayed data entry. Further, it also provided fast and accurate tracking of the performance of the new computer processors that these field engineers were servicing. After entering the data, the field engineers could make voice comments about the customer or the new processors they were servicing, and these comments were relayed to product people.

Language for coded application design. Creating these prompting sequences for new applications was easily done using the SFS computer-assisted instruction facility designed for applications people by Jim Schoonard.[20]

Remote control. SFS is designed in such a way that it could be used to remotely control analog and digital instruments and appliances, given appropriate telephone interfaces. To cite examples relating to the home, one could raise his home temperature just before leaving work in the evening, or turn on a microwave oven from any telephone. Since most principals have irregular work hours, this feature has advantages over preset controls. SFS is also designed in such a way that it could be used in connection with biofeedback applications and other health-related instrumentation.

Mixed media. SFS, as mentioned earlier, is a document distribution system that can accept as input and distribute all media, e.g., written, spoken, typed, graphic, and facsimile. Users can edit and annotate other media documents just as they can edit and annotate audio messages.

Telephone answering. If SFS is attached to a telephone exchange (either public or private, as ADS is in Europe), incoming calls can be automatically transferred to SFS when a person does not answer the telephone. The caller can hear the recorded SFS message and then can leave a message which will be placed by SFS in the user's New Message Box.

SFS is basically different from conventional telephone-answering devices[5] in that it has much more function. In addition, with telephone-answering devices, callers generally *expect* to talk directly with a person and are disappointed when they hear a taped message instead. In using SFS, users have no such violated expectations.

Generating automatic documentation. SFS provides automatic user documentation of itself, thus eliminating the errors that often occur when user documentation of a system is not kept in step with how the system actually operates. We keep documentation and system in step by using a virtual machine (VM) simulator to generate the documentation. The code (in the form of the command tables) that controls SFS (on an IBM Series/1 computer) is put into this VM simulator. The 12 function keys on the IBM 3270 display terminal are arranged in the same spatial array as the keys on a pushbutton telephone. A person uses the SFS simulator with these keys. Printed (rather than audio) system messages appear on the video screen. A user types, rather than speaks, his messages. As the document designer uses the simulator, the results can be printed, thus supplying the final documentation.

Summary

Communication is the main activity of business people. SFS was designed to improve communication.

Using a pushbutton telephone as the terminal, users can send messages to anyone in the world and receive messages from anyone in the world. Because of the years of human factors research that led to several iterative improvements in the user interface (described more fully in Gould and Boies[5]), SFS includes useful functions that are easy to learn and use. An IBM product, the Audio Distribution System, is based upon the SFS research and is now commercially available.

Acknowledgments

The work described in this paper is not just that of the authors. SFS was a team effort, with Stephen J. Boies serving as the leader. Other members of the group who contributed significantly over several years were John Gould, Nancy Grischkowsky, Bill Notz, John Richards, David Zeheb, and Jack Duffy. We thank Clayton Lewis, Bill Notz, and Mary Beth Rosson for their comments on earlier versions of the manuscript.

Cited references

1. S. J. Boies, "A computer based audio communication system," *AIIE Conference on Automating Business Communications,* (January 23–25, 1978), pp. 369–372. (Paper can be obtained from Management Education Corporation (MEC), Box 3727, Santa Monica, CA 90403.)
2. D. Zeheb and S. J. Boies, "Speech filing migration system," in H. Inose (Editor), *Proceedings of the International Conference of Computer Communication* (September 1978), pp. 571–574.
3. J. D. Gould, *An Experimental Study of Writing, Dictating, and Speaking,* Research Report RC-6186, IBM Corporation, Thomas J. Watson Research Center, P.O. Box 218, Yorktown Heights, NY 10598 (1976).
4. D. Nix, *Two Experiments on the Comprehensibility of Pause-Depleted Speech,* Research Report RC-6305, IBM Corporation, Thomas J. Watson Research Center, P.O. Box 218, Yorktown Heights, NY 10598 (1976).
5. J. D. Gould and S. J. Boies, "Human factors challenges in creating a principal support office system—The speech filing system approach," *ACM Transactions on Office Information Systems* (1983, in press).
6. *IBM Audio Distribution System Subscriber's Guide,* SC34-0400-1, IBM Corporation, 4111 Northside Parkway N.W., Box 2150, Atlanta, GA 30056; also available through IBM branch offices.
7. E. T. Klemmer and F. W. Snyder, "Measurement of time spent communicating," *Journal of Communication* **22,** 142–158 (1972).
8. G. H. Engel, J. Groppuso, R. A. Lowenstein, and W. Traub, "An office communications system," *IBM Systems Journal* **18,** No. 3, 402–431 (1979).
9. H. Mintzberg, *The Nature of Managerial Work,* Harper and Row, New York (1973).
10. R. R. Panko, "The EMS revolution (A survey of electronic message systems)," *Computerworld* (August 25, 1980).

11. R. Lowenstein, IBM Stamford, CT, personal communication based upon the results of an extensive unpublished field study of principals conducted at a large corporate headquarters building (1979).

12. J. T. Richards, *The IBM Research Speech Filing System: Analysis of the System 7/S370 Prototype,* Research Report RC-9114, IBM Corporation, Thomas J. Watson Research Center, P.O. Box 218, Yorktown Heights, NY 10598 (1981).

13. S. J. Boies, W. A. Notz, and D. Zeheb, "Encoding and decoding digital speech," *IBM Technical Disclosure Bulletin* **19,** No. 6, 2357–2359 (1976).

14. J. D. Gould, "An experimental study of writing, dictating, and speaking," in J. Requin (Editor), *Attention and Performance VII,* Lawrence Erlbaum Associates, Hillsdale, NJ (1978), pp. 299–319.

15. J. D. Gould, "How experts dictate," *Journal of Experimental Psychology: Human Perception and Performance* **4,** No. 4, 648–661 (1978).

16. R. P. Carver, "Effects of increasing the rate of speech presentation upon comprehension," *Journal of Educational Psychology* **65,** 118–126 (1973).

17. E. Foulke and T. G. Sticht, "Review of research on the intelligibility and comprehension of accelerated speech," *Psychological Bulletin* **72,** 50–62 (1969).

18. J. D. Gould, "Writing and speaking letters and messages," *International Journal of Man-Machine Studies* **16,** 147–171 (1982).

19. R. E. Rice, "The impacts of computer-mediated organizational and interpersonal communication," in M. Williams (Editor), *Annual Review of Information Science and Technology* **15,** Knowledge Industry Publications, White Plains, NY (1981), pp. 221–249.

20. J. W. Schoonard, *How to Use Speakeasy,* unpublished manuscript (1979). (Obtainable from the author at the IBM Thomas J. Watson Research Center, P.O. Box 218, Yorktown Heights, NY 10598.)

21. J. D. Gould and S. J. Boies, "Writing, dictating, and speaking letters," Science **201,** 1145–1147 (1978).

22. J. D. Gould, "Experiments on composing letters: Some facts, some myths, and some observations," in L. Gregg and I. Steinberg (Editors), *Cognitive Processes in Writing,* Erlbaum and Associates, Hillsdale, NJ (1980), pp. 98–127.

John D. Gould *IBM Research Division, Thomas J. Watson Research Center, P.O. Box 218, Yorktown Heights, New York 10598.* Dr. Gould is a psychologist and research staff member at the Research Center. He has been interested in human factors and offices for almost a decade. He was responsible for the user interface on the Speech Filing System. Among his achievements was to help Stephen Boies.

Stephen J. Boies *IBM Research Division, Thomas J. Watson Research Center, P.O. Box 218, Yorktown Heights, New York 10598.* Dr. Boies is a psychologist and senior manager of office systems applications at the Research Center. He has been interested in human factors and offices for almost a decade. He managed and led the Speech Filing System project. Among his achievements is that John Gould works for him.

Reprint Order No. G321-5210.

Human Factors Challenges In Creating a Principal Support Office System— The Speech Filing System Approach

JOHN D. GOULD and STEPHEN J. BOIES
IBM Thomas J. Watson Research Center

This paper identifies the key behavioral challenges in designing a principal-support office system and our approaches to them. These challenges included designing a system which office principals would find useful and would directly use themselves. Ultimately, the system, called the *Speech Filing System* (SFS), became primarily a voice store and forward message system with which users compose, edit, send, and receive audio messages, using telephones as terminals. Our approaches included behavioral analyses of principals' needs and irritations, controlled laboratory experiments, several years of training, observing, and interviewing hundreds of actual SFS users, several years of demonstrating SFS to thousands of potential users and receiving feedback, empirical studies of alternative methods of training and documentation, continual major modifications of the user interface, simulations of alternative user interfaces, and actual SFS usage analyses. The results indicate that SFS is now relatively easy to learn, solves real business problems, and leads to user satisfaction.

Categories and Subject Descriptors: H.1.2 [Models and Principles]: User/Machine Systems; H.4 [Information Systems Applications]; H.4.1 [Information Systems Applications]: Office Automation; H.4.3 [Information Systems Applications]: Communications Applications

General Terms: Human Factors

Additional Key Words and Phrases: Principal support system, office of the future

1. INTRODUCTION

1.1 Purpose of this Paper

The intent of this paper is to highlight the key *behavioral* challenges we faced in designing a principal-support office system, the approaches we took toward addressing them, and our general results. (Principals are business people, including executives, managers, professionals, and salespeople who rely upon secretaries to assist them in their work, especially through typing.) This paper describes the close coupling between continually on-going behavioral research and the way this motivated changes in the design and development of a prototype office system, called the *Speech Filing System* (SFS). The significance of focusing upon behavioral challenges is that we believe behavioral factors, and not technical factors, limit the arrival of the excellent offices of the future. Useful functions must be identified and easy-to-use human interfaces must be created. Both can be imple-

mented, tested, and improved upon with the behavioral methodology and systems technologies already in existence (see [11]).

1.2 Key Issues

The goal of the work, which began in 1973, was to create a useful computer-based principal-support office system. We had the intuitive belief that this was possible, and that successful solutions would not only lead to more productive and happier principals but would, in the long run, move toward reducing stagnating U.S. productivity and health-related work-stress problems.

Issue 1. What should the system do? Computing was being increasingly extended to offices through word processing, database, and electronic mail systems. Secretaries were receiving new tools, but principals were not. The key reason was not the lack of economic opportunity; indeed, 15 million U.S. principals represented an attractive marketing potential. Rather, nobody could figure out what principals needed. Traditional analytic attempts to identify isolated, repeatable principal activities which could then be automated were unsuccessful. On the useful side, activity analyses revealed that principals spent nearly all of their time in communicating interactively and that the second largest amount of time was spent in composing and reading documents (e.g., [16], [19]). These findings and our own initial behavioral analyses of principals' activities, needs, and irritations suggested the importance of improving the efficiency and quality of document composition and principal interpersonal communication. To do this, we focused first upon enhancing dictation as a method of composition and, second, on creating a noninteractive voice communication system.

Issue 2. Could dictation be significantly enhanced? We observed that handwriting was the main method by which principals composed. We had the intuitive belief that dictation was a potentially superior method of composition. Dictating is potentially five times faster than writing, on the basis of estimates of maximum writing and speaking rates when composition is not required (see [6]). Dictation may also be qualitatively superior: potentially faster transfer of ideas from limited capacity human working memory to a permanent record may reduce forgetting attributable to interference or decay.

Issue 3. Would noninteractive communication be useful? At the beginning there was no strong evidence that it would be. In 1973 noninteractive communication involved delays, usually of days, in communicating and feedback. It involved printed material (e.g., the U.S. mail). It was, and still is, often a formal medium, with emphasis upon historical record. Principals, on the other hand, communicate interactively and informally [16]. There were no audio noninteractive communication systems (except that people occasionally mailed audio cassettes), and computer-based electronic mail was barely around and not used by office principals. (In universities, electronic video mail systems were just beginning to come into use, e.g., ARPANET mail, HERMES, EDUMAIL, and EIES, see [25]).

Issue 4. Would principals actually—and directly—use a computer system, even though it was useful to do so? Office principals did not use computers in their work in 1973, and there was a general belief that they would not. The challenge was to get principals to directly use SFS, rather than have their

Authors' address: IBM Thomas J. Watson Research Center, Yorktown Heights, NY 10598.

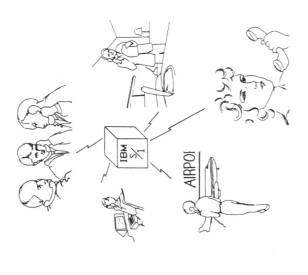

Fig. 1. Conceptual diagram of SFS. Users can send and receive messages using standard pushbutton telephones. Messages are stored in an IBM S/1 computer, which is connected to the telephone network and can be dialed from anywhere. Starting from the lower left and going clockwise, users can get or send messages from telephone booths, from their offices, from conference rooms (where several people can use SFS at once), or from motels and homes. A user's secretary can, with the secretary password, assist the principal via ADS.

secretaries use it for them. This was important if content messages were to be sent regularly, if the maximum potential of SFS was to be realized, and if there were to be clear displaceable costs (as opposed to only value-added, or "more productive principals," see [10]).

Issue 5. Would principals send content messages? Telephone "yellow slip" messages rarely contain content—only the name and number of the person who called. Further, people generally do not leave content messages on traditional telephone answering devices. We were concerned that principals might use SFS only as a secondary or backup system (i.e., only when they could not get hold of a person on the telephone). Perhaps even here a user would not send a content message, but only ask a recipient to call back. We believed that content messages were important, however, if noninteractive communication was to be useful. A content message in a user's own voice and words would be very useful, we thought, since this would eliminate the potential communication errors introduced by intermediaries and the need for transcription, as well as eliminating telephone roulette.

1.3 What Is SFS?

SFS is a voice store and forward office system intended to augment communication among principals—which is their main activity [16]. With SFS a principal can create a voice message by calling a designated telephone number, keypressing his or her last name and password, and speaking into the telephone (see [10] for a fuller description). Principals can listen to and edit their messages by keypressing commands on the telephone, and can send them to other users or to predetermined distribution lists by keypressing those names. Feedback and prompts have been developed over the years to make SFS easy to learn and use, to eliminate mistakes, and to make users feel comfortable. The recipient hears the message in the sender's own voice, with the actual prosody and inflections. Unfilled pauses are automatically compressed. A principal can send or listen to messages from any pushbutton telephone anywhere, as illustrated conceptually in Figure 1. A principal can review and annotate messages, have them typed, and control what recipients can do with them.

SFS contains enhanced dictation facilities for creating, formatting, reviewing, editing, and listening to audio documents.

SFS is one of the few office systems designed to be used directly by office principals. The services it provides can increase white collar productivity, substantially decrease the time delays associated with many office communications, and reduce the frustrations commonly experienced when attempting to interact with one's colleagues. Telephones are the terminals that make SFS convenient to use from just about anywhere and at almost any time. However, these services are only valuable if the principal is willing to use the system directly for important business communications.

1.4 History of SFS

SFS started as a research project at the IBM Thomas J. Watson Research Center in 1973, under the leadership of Stephen Boies. The first running prototype was

made available to users in 1975. Four people could use it at once. From 1975–1981 about 750 IBM principals, mainly in the U.S., used various SFS prototypes in their daily work. For seven years we modified and enhanced prototypes on the basis of informal observations, interviews, studies of users and through helping users with their problems. These SFS prototypes ran on an IBM System/7 computer attached to VM370 for additional storage. A unique feature of the SFS project was the interdisciplinary nature of the research group, with emphasis upon behavioral expertise. (Half of the group of ten had PhDs in experimental psychology.)

We began work on a Series/1-based prototype in 1978. In September 1981, IBM announced this project as the *Audio Distribution System* (ADS). Each ADS can support up to 1000 principals (with up to ten people using it at once). In this paper we describe our work up to, and including, the ADS product. During 1982 we unplugged the SFS prototype and now use ADS in our work. Other companies, including AT&T, Electronic Communications Systems (ECS), and Wang, have announced audio systems which have some functions in common with ADS.

Table I. SFS Function Compared to Traditional Telephone-Answering Device Functions*

Recording	Filing System
+Voice activated	Selective retrieval
Insert	Statistics
Delete	Scan descriptions
Move, Copy	Able to group messages
Review	
Combine messages	Access
Erase selectively	Name-oriented
Audio markers	+Remote
+Messages from anyone	Automatic notification
	Other
	User profile
	+Dictation
Listening	Multiple simultaneous users
Sped speech	Call divert
Review (replay)	Usage analysis
Skip around	Automatic roll-over
Annotation capability	Password security
+Erase	++Message light
Selective erase	++Music when busy
	Growth
	Uses digital computer
Distribution	Integrate to PBX
One person	Integrate with text, pictures
Several people	Data entry and processing
Distribution lists	Combine with speech recognition
Timed transmit	User networks
Personal reminder	
Status of messages	Present Estimated Costs
Reply	$200-2000/user total cost
	$10/user/month

* SFS functions are listed in this table. The SFS functions which typical telephone-answering devices have are preceded by a + sign. Functions which telephone-answering devices have and SFS does not have are preceded by ++.

1.5 General Methodology

Our approach was fivefold:

(1) Our initial design relied upon our intuition and behavioral analyses of principals' work activities.

(2) From 1975–1981 we conducted informal field studies of how principals used SFS, with the view of learning what was needed to make SFS more useful, and then implementing these requirements, regardless of the difficulties.

(3) At the same time we investigated related issues in controlled laboratory experiments on composition [4, 5, 8, 9, 10]; listening [20]; and impression formation [26].

(4) We often simulated possible new versions of SFS in informal laboratory studies, sometimes with an experimenter sitting behind a curtain and pretending that he or she was SFS. At other times (1978–1980) we used the VM Simulator because it was easier to change the messages and user interface control flow on it than on the small IBM S/7 (or, later, S/1). This allowed us to simulate a user interface before an actual new one existed.

(5) During the same period we gave talks and live demonstrations to thousands of potential users, and received their reactions about what they believed should be included in SFS to make it useful as a noninteractive message system. Here we also began to understand better some necessary commercial factors, that is, the need for displaceable costs.

While working on this project, we followed (and recommend to others) several principles of system design [11]:

(1) Focus initially on important user characteristics.

(2) Make intended users part of the initial design team.

(3) Empirically measure, through simulations and prototype experiments, how people use the system, with the aim of modifying the user interface, training procedure, and reading material.

(4) Create a system architecture so that the user interface can be changed easily on the basis of empirical results. The user interface should be as easy to change as the documentation. This iterative design philosophy may seem expensive, but, with the present state of understanding of user interface design, it is the only way to ensure excellent systems. It is not just a trivial, expensive matter of "fine-tuning," but a basic design philosophy to be contrasted with other principled design philosophies [11].

(5) Put one person in charge of all aspects of usability—user interface, reading materials, training approach, hot line, etc.

Although these principles may seem intuitive, results show that they are not typically recommended or followed [11].

1.6 Limitations of the Data

The work reported here is mainly informal, and lacks the rigor of controlled laboratory experiments. Often, we studied a question only until we became convinced of a better alternative, then implemented and tested it. We publish this work because perhaps no office system has been studied as extensively as SFS and because we would like to contribute to a beginning in the publication of such case histories.

2. SFS FUNCTIONS

The main functions of SFS are shown in Table I. They are summarized under composing (recording), listening, filing, and distributing documents. As described more fully in [10], SFS is voice activated, recording only when a user is speaking. While recording a message, a user can insert, delete, move, or copy speech signals. A user can attach audio markers, through key presses, to various parts of the document, which then provide listeners with clues to the document's format and structure and allow listeners to skip to a new paragraph, or listen only through a particular topic. While listening, a user can review, scan, or skip around in a message. A user can annotate a message, return it to the sender and/or send it to someone else also. A user can send a message to one person, to several people, or to user defined distribution lists. A user can send personal reminders, requesting a telephone to ring at a designated time. A user can inquire whether his or her messages have been heard. A user can file and retrieve a message on the basis of the sender's name, date, or topic. Users send messages to people's names, not to their telephone numbers or other arbitrary designations. Each user has several telephone numbers at which SFS will call after new messages arrive. Each user has not only a personal password but also secretary, family, and guest passwords—each of which has limited, appropriate functions. A user can alter these and other items of personal profile information from pushbutton telephones anywhere. SFS can be used with coded information as well, for example in remote data entry or in service repair applications.

3. TERMINALS

3.1 Why Telephones?

Our behavioral analyses suggested that telephones should be the terminals for a principal support system rather than, for example, typewriters or CRTs. Telephones are located nearly everywhere and are available 24 hours per day, which is important because principals work in many places and at many different times of the day. Telephones were chosen because many people must be on a communication system in order for it to be useful; the fact that all principals have telephones makes it possible for this to happen just as soon as SFS is installed. New users can be immediately joined to SFS without having to cost justify new terminals or wait for delivery, wiring, and installation. Telephones were already present and cost justified for other purposes. Further, telephones, not video terminals, were the terminals principals were actually using.

The challenge was to map the many functions of SFS onto the 12-key pushbutton telephone so that SFS would be easy to learn and use. Laboratory development and marketing people were skeptical that we would ever be successful. For example, they would watch demonstrations, be impressed with the useful function, but volunteer that most people would never bother to learn the finger dances required. There was a strong opinion that a special purpose terminal with a different, labelled key for each of the 40-50 functions was needed, perhaps with a visual display. To this end, we verified that commercially available Touchamatic telephones could serve as a special purpose terminal [7]. (Touchamatic telephones are "one-button dialing" devices which contain a panel of buttons each of which when pressed ordinarily causes a different telephone number to be dialed.) We labelled each of the thirty separate keys and set each to execute a different SFS function.

We resisted this one-key-one-function approach for two reasons: the ubiquity of the telephone, allowing for remote, convenient use and its very low entry cost. We knew that the user interface problems would be much harder to solve using the 12-key pad.

System messages that are heard raise issues which do not come up with system messages that are read. A voice system requires pronouncing the names of symbols which ordinarily go unnamed. Should the #-key on the telephone be called the "number sign key," the "tic tac toe sign," the "hash mark," or the "pound sign" key? Should the *-key be called the "asterisk key" or the "star"? We settled on the last alternative in each set after years of observing what other people called them and of trying various alternatives ourselves. Should a person be told to "enter," "dial," "type," or "keypress" his or her last name? We settled on the last alternative after trying the others as well. Should voice messages be of the form "To insert here, press the 1-key" or, alternatively, of the form "Press the 1-key to insert here"? Initially we composed all messages in the former way, since this first identified what a person wanted to do and then said how to do it. However, we gradually switched most of the messages to the latter format, which seemed to lead the less novice confusion. The alphabetic labels on the 12-key pad omit the letters Q and Z. When these letters appear in a user's name (e.g., Quinones, Zeheb), users keypress the 7 key for Q (PQRS) and the 9 key for Z (WXYZ).

3.2 Keypressing vs. Voice Commands

Why not voice commands? The state of the art of speech recognition over telephone lines was not good enough when we started. Errors would have been made in recognizing voice commands in the stream of other words a user was saying; such errors could rarely occur in recognizing pushbutton tones in the stream. Each user would probably need his or her own stored set of commands for speech recognition to work reliably. Results of controlled experiments satisfied us, however, that voice commands do not interfere with composing [9]. Over the years, users did not ask for voice commands, even though this would have reduced the inconvenience of using dial telephones when pushbutton telephones were not available.

3.3 Results

We learned over the years that the telephone was an excellent choice as a terminal, particularly as we improved ease of use (see Section 4). Field studies and interviews with potential customers indicated that they would be less disposed to put large groups of people on SFS if they had to cost justify terminals (in addition to the system itself). Principals used SFS from many different places and at all hours of the day and night. Our observations indicated that prospective users felt the need for hardcopy, but once they became actual users they rarely asked for this, or used the available facility to get it. Uhlig [27] has also noted the value of the telephone in being able to send a message whenever and from wherever one wants to. His project's solution, however, was to have people carry with them "very lightweight portable computer terminals" that attach to telephones so users could get and send printed and video messages.

4. USER INTERFACE

4.1 Multifunction Mapping

Modes. Our basic approach to the multifunction mapping problem was to organize SFS functions into command modes. Partitioning a command language into modes involves a trade-off. The benefits include simplification, reduced (human) memory load, and a helpful structure with which users could think about system

Key			
1-key	Press 1 Immediate Delivery, Quick-Ring Notification, Special Notification, Normal Notification	2 Time Delivery, Enter Time, Enter Date	
C-key	Press 1 Classify Messages, Unclassified, Internal Use Only, Confidential, Personal, Personal and Confidential	2 Limit Access, Unlimited, Append and Forward, Listen Only	3 Limit Retention, Retain 180 Days, Retain 90 Days, Retain 60 Days, Retain 30 Days, Retain 2 Weeks
D-key	Precedes Name of Distribution List		
4-key	Undefined Key		
5-key	Undefined Key		
N-key	Precedes Recipient's Name		
R-key	Press 1 Request Reply, Reply Requested, Specify Deadline Time, Enter Time, Enter Date, Use Standard Deadline	2 Request Approval, Approval Requested, Specify Deadline Time, Enter Time, Enter Data, Use Standard Deadline	
T-key	Press 1 Call Me when Received, Specify Notify Time, Enter Time, Enter Date, Use Standard Notify Time	2 Call Me when Action Taken, Specify Notify Time, Enter Time, Enter Date, Use Standard Notify Time	
W-key	Answers Who, What, Where Questions		
*-key	Changes Modes		
#-key	Activates Help System		

Fig. 3. Specialized function in Transmit mode.

Simple ADS User Language Accomplishes Many Things

*R (ecord)   *T (transmit)   *G (et)   *L (isten)
N Gould
00 (Send it)

Compose Messages	Receive Messages
Voice Activated	Select Messages
Review	Relisten
Insert	Reply
Start Over	Annotate
Make File Copy	
Send Messages	**Nonuser Capability**
To One Person	Receive from Nonusers
To Several People	Enhanced Dictation
To Distribution Lists	
Personal Reminders	
File Messages	

Fig. 2. Basic ADS commands are shown at the top, and the functions they accomplish are listed next. The command language is designed to minimize the number of commands required to accomplish the most frequently used SFS functions, as identified over the years by observation of people's usage patterns. Users compose messages by recording (*R), send messages by transmitting (*T), and receive messages by getting (*G), and listening (*L) to them.

functions. The potential costs are that users must keep track of which mode they are in, and they are limited in what they can do in that mode.

Initially we had 13 modes. This worked fine to identify the functions users preferred, but our field studies showed that this number was too many for novices' preferences. We gradually reduced the number to four basic modes. This approach has worked well. However, even with only a few modes, novices occasionally made mistakes, for example, in trying to send a message from the Listen mode instead of the Transmit mode.

As shown in Figure 2, the basic mode commands of ADS are now *R, *T, *G, and *L. There is also a Customize mode (*C). With these mode selection commands one can execute the basic functions shown in the lower part of Figure 2.

As shown in Figure 3, in Transmit mode a user can Classify a message (C-key), send a message to a Distribution list (D-key), or to a person's Name (N-key). Inside each mode each key can stand for a different function. Users were taught to think about these intramode commands as prefixes or alternative selectors (see Section 4.2).

We made the mode approach easier to use by reducing needless distinctions, adding mnemonics, improving feedback messages, adding the concept of selector keys, developing partially and fully prompted user languages, and adding a help system. These were added and continually modified and improved on the basis of user requests, feedback, and simulations.

Reduction of Some Distinctions. In initial versions of SFS it was thought necessary, for example, to have an "Edit" mode separate from a "Record" mode. Another example was having separate commands for an unformatted Listen mode and a formatted Listen mode. In the formatted Listen mode, beeps played out where audio format markers were located, whereas in the unformatted Listen mode, beeps did not play out [24]. Through empirical studies we learned that this and several other distinctions were not important to users, and we eliminated them.

For several years the SFS command language had a neutral command (the user pressed the *-key), which explicitly took users out of the mode they were in and put them in a neutral state. Figure 4 is an example scenario, as shown in an early (1977) Examples-of-Use card. We learned this neutral concept could be dropped by combining the * with the next command mode to be selected. For example, the user learned to press *R to record a message, rather than pressing * to leave a mode and then pressing R to activate the Record mode. Figure 5 shows an example scenario of this improvement. The important point here is that in both cases users pressed exactly the same keys—they just thought about it differently in the two cases. Whereas in the first case they thought of neutral

To Compose and Transmit a Message (with 1977 User Interface)

*	
NEUTRAL	Return to Neutral
71	Confirming Message
RECORD	Select Record Mode
"John, I will be in	System Prompt
Washington this week."	
*	
NEUTRAL	Return to Neutral
82	Confirming Message
TRANSMIT	Select Transmit Mode
5 Gould ##	Confirming Message
JOHN GOULD	Define Recipient
ADDED TO LIST	Confirming Message
00	Confirming Message
	Send Message
BEEP, BEEP	System is working
AUDIO SLATE TRANSMITTED	Confirming Message
*	Return to Neutral
NEUTRAL	Confirming Message

Fig. 4. Example of a user composing and transmitting a message with the 1977 user interface. Note the lack of alphabetic mnemonics and the separation of the * and mode commands. (Compare to Fig. 5 to see the improvement in the command language.)

To Compose a Message and Transmit It (Final User Interface)

```
*R
 R
 RECORD
 "Bill, what is the
   part number that..."
*T
 T
 TRANSMIT
 N
 ENTER RECIPIENT'S NAME
 notz
 BILL NOTZ
 00
 MESSAGE TRANSMITTED TO BILL NOTZ
```

Fig. 5. Example of a user composing a message and sending it to Bill Notz. (This may be compared with an earlier version of the user interface shown in Fig. 4.)

```
( )   (2)   ( )
(4)   (5)   (6)
( )   (8)   ( )
( )   ( )   ( )
```

Fig. 6. Example of a spatial mnemonic, or memory aid, in the Listen mode. Imagine that your forefinger pivots on the 5-key. To go to the beginning, or top, of a message, move your finger up and press the 2-key. To go to the end, or bottom, of a message, move your finger down and press the 8-key. To skip back a little in the message, move your finger to the left and press the 4-key. To skip ahead a little in the message, move your finger to the right and press the 6-key.

(memory aids). As shown in Figure 2, users pressed *R to record a message, *L to listen to it, and *T to transmit it. We were initially worried that mixing alphabetically and numerically represented commands might be confusing to users, especially in print. This was not the case, however.

We also incorporated spatial mnemonics, and applied consistency in this regard across modes [10]. An example of spatial mnemonics is illustrated in Figure 6. SFS allows a person to skip around within a message. Imagine a person's forefinger resting on the 5 key. To go to the beginning or top of a message, a user presses 5 and then moves his finger up and presses the 2 key. To go to the end or bottom of the message, a user presses 5 and then moves his finger down and presses the 8 key. An analogous arrangement was provided for selecting messages in queues in the Get mode.

Feedback Messages. Years of empirical studies were aimed at improving SFS prompting, feedback, helping, and confirming messages. (Message consistency was of course incorporated. Consistency was not the problem that it often is, since one person was in control of all messages.) A message played out after every user-action. Sometimes a small study would be directed at the exact wording of a single message. On the VM simulator we changed the message set literally thousands of times. In ADS there are about 565 messages. Customers can reword any of these voice messages—and in any language.

Selector Keys. We observed that Atari was able to design a system of several hundred video games which children (and adults) play with no instruction. One principle is that a player simply holds down a switch until he or she reaches the desired game. We incorporated this concept into SFS. For example, a user might want to classify a message he or she is sending as company confidential, and, in addition, limit in other ways what a recipient can do with it. Thus, as shown in Figure 7, the user would press the C-key (mnemonic for message Control) and then answer the questions SFS asks until the right alternatives are selected.

4.2 Partially Prompted Language

Gradually, we moved away from an entirely self-produced command language to one that under some circumstances presented users with audio menus (no more than three choices per item). This relieved some of the user's memory burden

and mode selection as two separate commands, in the second case they thought of mode selection as only one command (in which they pressed two keys).

To be able to make these changes consistently and to evaluate them quickly meant that we had to introduce them simultaneously in the user interface, in reading materials, and in the training procedure. A fragmented development procedure with no single focus for usability would not allow this easy coordination. In eliminating other needless distinctions, we dropped much general, generic terminology (e.g., "items," "parameters," "lists").

Mnemonics. Initially, all commands were numbers, that is, a user pressed the number 72 to record a message. Gradually, we began using alphabetic mnemonics

To Classify a Message and to Restrict What Can Be Done With It

```
*T
TRANSMIT
C
PRESS 1 CLASSIFY MESSAGE, 2 LIMIT ACCESS, 3 LIMIT RETENTION
1
UNCLASSIFIED
PRESS 1 CHANGE CLASSIFICATION, 2 DON'T CHANGE CLASSIFICATION
1
INTERNAL USE ONLY
PRESS 1 CHANGE CLASSIFICATION, 2 DON'T CHANGE CLASSIFICATION
1
CONFIDENTIAL
PRESS 1 CHANGE CLASSIFICATION, 2 DON'T CHANGE CLASSIFICATION
2
CONFIDENTIAL
C
PRESS 1 CLASSIFY MESSAGE, 2 LIMIT ACCESS, 3 LIMIT RETENTION
2
PRESS 1 UNLIMITED, 2 APPEND AND FORWARD, 3 LISTEN ONLY
3
LISTEN ONLY
N
ENTER RECIPIENT'S NAME
Boies
STEPHEN BOIES
00
MESSAGE TRANSMITTED TO STEPHEN BOIES
```

Fig. 7. Example of a person using a selector key to send a confidential message that will allow Stephen Boies to only listen to the message (and not alter it or send it to someone else).

and allowed another level of function without increasing the number of key presses required.

4.3 Entirely Prompted User Language

As SFS became increasingly easier to learn—through years of observation of users and resulting improvements in the user interface, training approach, and training material—we decided to try to design the ultimate in ease of learning, namely, a user interface requiring no user training whatsoever. If we fell short of this goal, we would at least know how close we were to the ideal. One approach we took, beginning in 1979, was to design and experimentally study through simulations an entirely prompted SFS language containing only the basic subset of SFS functions shown at the bottom of Figure 2. It made command selection a recognition task rather than a recall task. Figure 8 shows an example scenario with the prompted language. All prompts are context sensitive. People were never prompted for things they could not do or that were inappropriate (e.g., prompted to get a new message when there was none). Futher, for the first time we began to use system messages that did not stand alone but relied on context, that is, contained demonstrative pronouns.

To Compose and Transmit a Message With the Fully Prompted Language

```
PRESS *G GET A MESSAGE, *R RECORD A MESSAGE
*R
RECORD
"Nancy, are you coming to...?"
*
PRESS *L LISTEN, *T TRANSMIT, *R RECORD
*T
TRANSMIT
PRESS N TO SPECIFY A NAME
N
ENTER RECIPIENT'S NAME
Gris
NANCY GRISCHKOWSKY
PRESS 00 TRANSMIT MESSAGE, N SPECIFY ANOTHER NAME BEFORE TRANSMIT-
TING
00
MESSAGE TRANSMITTED TO NANCY GRISCHKOWSKY
PRESS *R RECORD, *G GET MESSAGE, *L LISTEN, *T TRANSMIT TO ADDITIONAL
PEOPLE
```

Fig. 8. Example of a person using the fully prompted language to compose a message and send it to Nancy Grischkowsky. (Compare this to Fig. 2.)

In informal experiments involving about 100 new users we found that most novices could use this prompted language with no training. In these experiments we simply told participants that SFS allowed them to send messages to people and to receive messages from people, and that they should try to use it to carry out some test problems which we gave them. When problems did occur, they usually involved the three concepts mentioned in "Induction of Concepts From Examples" in Section 5.3.

4.4 Three ADS Languages

Like others who design systems, we felt that novices might need a "menu" system (the entirely prompted language), but that experienced users would want a non-menu system. As a result, ADS has both. ADS has a fully prompted language containing mainly the basic functions shown in Figure 2. The motivation here was to give users a simple, basic system with a very easy to learn command language. Here, users are always given a menu of choices (three or less) after each action. The drawbacks to any fully prompted language are that (a) users must take the time to go through the menus, and (b) learning a menu-oriented language may not transfer well to learning a non-menu oriented language—which is what we believed our full function language should be and we wanted users to eventually migrate to it. We addressed the first problem by letting users interrupt the audio menus or prompts any time they wished. We addressed the potential transfer of learning problem by offering a second basic command language for new users, functionally equivalent to the fully prompted one. (Users have the option of which language they want to use.) This language appears to the user to be exactly like the full function language (in prompts and feedback), except that it contains less function. (Here, if a user presses a key which would trigger

Table II. Some SFS Features that Are Called User Friendly by Users

Name oriented
Voice activated
Mnemonic
Multiple user languages
Adaptive system
Context sensitive system messages
Safeguards against possible user errors
Anticipates likely user errors
Help key
W-key
Automatic system message playout when user is stuck
Forgiving system (e.g., dates, times)
Prompted customize mode
Multiple passwords
Optional notification when recipient listens to message

To Check if Recipient Has Listened To Your Message

```
*G
NEW MESSAGES
  STEPHEN BOIES
55
OLD MESSAGES
  JOHN GOULD
55
OUTBOUND MESSAGES
  NANCY GRISCHKOWSKY
  JIM SCHOONARD
  STEPHEN BOIES
PRESS *L TO LISTEN TO THE MESSAGE TO NANCY GRISCHKOWSKY
W
SENT TODAY SEPTEMBER 26 AT 6:32 p.m.
W
TO NANCY GRISCHKOWSKY. NOT RECEIVED.
```

Fig. 9. Example of a user checking whether Nancy Grischkowksy has listened to a message the user sent to her. Note that after the user enters his Outbound Message Box, he presses the W-key to learn what has happened to the message.

advanced function in the full function language, he or she is told that the key is undefined and is then prompted as to what is allowable in that context.) Both are basic languages and are true subsets of the full function language. The full function language is the third language, and is a combination of prompted and self-produced commands. (Self-produced commands are those which a user emits without being given a menu of choices.) As already mentioned, within each mode of the full function language each key generally has a specialized function (see Figure 3 for the Transmit mode; see the *IBM ADS Subscriber's Guide* [15] for a complete description of all ADS function).

4.5 Help System

To help novices get started and to help experienced users learn additional functions, we implemented a help system on ADS. We have been told by ADS customers that it contributes significantly to ease of learning the full function language, and that their users require little training and little documentation (a telephone template and a wallet-sized card containing the basic commands).

Help Key. The important concept here is the designation of the #-key as a help key. If a user is stuck, he or she can press the #-key and SFS plays out the user's alternatives in that context.

Automatic Help. In addition, if the user does nothing for many seconds, then ADS plays a prompt to the user. The length of these pauses is variable, being tuned to what the user is trying to do.

W-Key. With the W-key (i.e., the 9-key) a user can get answers to the who, what, when questions, that is, who sent the message, when was it sent, who else was it sent to, who else already listened to it and when (see Figure 9).

Other Significant User Interface Features. Table II provides a list of SFS features which users have described as "user friendly." For example, users key-in their last name rather than a telephone number or other identification code. Thus, SFS is telephone-independent, and users can send messages to others without worrying about which telephone number to send them to. As a result of years of study, SFS will anticipate likely user errors; for instance, if a user presses a zero instead of the letter "O" while keying a person's name, SFS will tell the user that. SFS safeguards against possible user errors (e.g., if a user leaves Transmit mode without actually transmitting a message, SFS will ask the user whether he or she forgot to transmit that message). SFS can notify a user when a recipient has listened to (and/or replied to) an important message, which frees the user from anxiously calling SFS to hear a reply.

5. TRAINING AND LEARNING

There was no office system in 1973 which principals themselves used. Thus, our early attempts at training had to be both motivational and instructional. We had the general belief that principals did not want to spend much time being trained, nor did they want to read much documentation. Designing a powerful audio system (using only the telephone as a terminal) to meet these requirements seemed much more difficult than designing an electronic mail video system, with large keyboards, screens, printers, and a decade of experience in using such terminals and editors.

5.1 Initial Tutorial Approach

At the beginning (1975), small groups of new users (5 people) were taught SFS through an audio-visual orientation lecture and a subsequent followup lecture. Users were given printed material to take back to their offices, including telephone templates. Some of this material was instructional, via manuals on how to use SFS, and some was motivational, indicating how SFS could help them in their everyday work.

This approach did not work well. People did not transfer what they learned in the lecture to actual use of SFS in their offices. Second, principals confirmed our beliefs about their desire for minimal training and documentation.

do much better. By 1978 novices typically learned to use SFS with about one hour of training. Grishkowsky [12] provided recommendations for such training. By 1982 the need for this much training was reduced. ADS customers now indicate that formal training classes are often not needed. New users are simply told that they have been added to ADS, and are given documentation, sometimes consisting of only a wallet-sized card or a telephone template. If a learning problem arises, it is sometimes handled by using the third-party add-on facility of a PBX. ADS is added to a telephone conversation between a novice and the system supervisor. Either party can control ADS with pushbuttons.

This is a far cry from usability results in 1975. The biggest gains over seven years have been in the improvement of the user interface, so that now novices can experience immediate success, and in the careful integration of the help system, the minimal printed material, and the improvements in the user interface. Clearly, any development process that separates education, training materials, and interface design could not have worked as well. Recent reports show that even with the improved computer-based electronic mail systems of today, users require 1 to 2 hours [25], at least several hours [27], about one day [21], or more [18] of introductory training to do basic functions. In addition, users are also given much documentation. Even after training, a significant fraction of office principals do not *directly* use electronic mail systems, but instead use them through intermediaries [2, 13]. (Usability should be little affected by the number of users on a network.)

Induction of Concepts From Examples. We designed the Examples-of-Use card with the hope that users would inductively derive SFS from it. In general, this approach worked very well. However, it fell a little short of complete success for some first-time users with no training. When some of these people made a mistake in following the examples, they were not always able to infer the proper recovery action. They could press the *.-key to escape from the mode they were in, or start over, but this fell short of a magic "undo key" which they would have preferred.

A few concepts seemed to be the sticklers. We learned that these had to be explained to some users. We found that a 8-page comic book (written by John Conti) together with a 1- to 2-page printed description was satisfactory.

One sticky concept was that of the audio slate, which is a temporary work or storage area where the current message being composed or listened to resides. Novices did not need to be told about this until they made a mistake. Often, however, an understanding of why this temporary storage area existed was required for a novice to recover. Involved here was the concept that two copies of the same message existed when a person was listening to a message: one on the audio slate and the other in the user's Old Message Box.

Another difficult concept was how to retrieve and relisten to a message which a user had listened to somewhat earlier in that session. This involved the concept of the audio slate, as well as the concept that this message had been transferred from the user's New Message Box to his or her Old Message Box as a result of being listened to. The following example illustrates what makes this problem particularly complicated for the novice. Assume the novice has four messages called A, B, C, and D in his or her New Message Box; and two messages called E

5.2 Training with Examples

We addressed this lack of transfer in two ways. First, we installed four telephones in a small room and asked people to actually practice using SFS for most of the first hour of training. Second, we designed an Examples-of-Use card which contained printed examples of the most frequently used SFS scenarios, such as those shown in Figure 5. Novices would follow these during their hour of training and then take the card back to their offices.

Hands-On Training. The approach of having new users practice using SFS during most of the first hour of training worked well. Seeing other participants achieve success and/or make mistakes was helpful to novices and reduced their anxiety. We were able to learn of problems novices were having with the user interface (e.g., pressing zero instead of the letter "Oh" when keying a last name such as Owens) and with SFS concepts. We mixed secretaries and principals in the same group. Although we were sometimes warned not to do this, it worked well.

The first hour of training provided many insights into how to modify the Examples-of-Use card, our tutorial about SFS, and ultimately the user interface itself. For example, we modified the layout and order of examples based upon how people searched for and used them.

Users came back in about two weeks for a second hour of training in advanced SFS functions. This second hour was dropped after about one year because of users' lack of interest and because we increasingly learned what the most typically used functions were and covered them in the first hour.

Examples-of-Use Card. By 1977, our Examples-of-Use card and a telephone template were the only documentation we gave most users. The Examples-of-Use card was a 4-fold fan card that conveniently fit in a suit-coat pocket. It contained about 20 examples of SFS use, plus one page of additional information. By combining the card with hands-on training, the transfer problem, that of novices leaving the training session and being actually able and willing to use SFS on their own, was substantially solved.

Principals did indeed use the Examples-of-Use card in everyday business. In individual interviews conducted by John Conti with about twenty high-level principals who had used SFS for a year or more, each one reported using the card in everyday business. As a further test, each was asked where his card was. To assess the accuracy of recall, each principal was then asked to show the interviewer where the card was, and each one was successful at finding it quickly.

Gradually, the Examples-of-Use approach became the way we thought about adding new function. That is, it became part of the design process. We would work out new scenarios and rationalize them with already existing examples. If a new scenario appeared to be cumbersome, we then redesigned the relevant part of the command language, which had already been established. Ultimately, about 100 Examples-of-Use served as an initial functional specification in 1979 for what became IBM's ADS.

5.3 Results

The important point here is that SFS was initially usable, requiring much less time than that required to learn today's text editors (e.g., [17]). But we wanted to

and F in his or her Old Message Box. Assume that the novice has listened to message A. Now the Old Message Box contains A, E, and F, in the order last in, first out. Assume the novice is now recording a message of his own. He wants to relisten to message A. To do this he must get into the Old Message Box, which requires skipping over the remaining new messages. Further, the novice wonders what will happen to his partially recorded new message.

The third difficult concept was that of modes. The notion that specific actions could only be done within specific modes (e.g., send a message from Transmit mode only) had to sometimes be explained to a first-time user.

6. SYSTEM USE

6.1 What Was SFS Used For?

Principals could use SFS to replace or displace five types of communications: (1) dictated documents intended to be typed and read; (2) "yellow slip" messages; (3) memos and letters; (4) interactive telephone conversations; and (5) face-to-face conversations. Results show that SFS was used mainly as a voice message system. New users typically used it when they were unable to reach a person on the telephone, and to respond to SFS messages that others sent them. However, they always left content messages, rather than simply asking that person to call back. A typical user then used SFS to gradually replace some memos, letters, and interactive conversations.

This usage pattern points at displaceable cost savings, separate from any claim about improved principal productivity. Three normal operating costs can be reduced: long-distance telephone costs, because ADS customers can use a single 800-number; typing costs due to fewer written memos; and human telephone message handling costs due to fewer missed calls. We estimate the costs savings here to be about $90 per user per month in a typical office. This cost savings is based upon the assumption of 6 fewer long-distance calls ($15 savings), 8 fewer memos ($50 savings), and 100 fewer telephone messages ($25 savings) per user per month. Assuming that ADS costs about $10 to $15 per user per month, the net cost saving is about $75 to $80 per user per month. If these estimates are approximately right, ADS pays for itself in less than one year, which is very unusual for a computer system.

People did not much use SFS for dictation. This was true even when users were told that they would receive a typed version within an hour or so after they dictated their letters (and their own secretaries would not have to do the typing). (Most did not use any other dictation system either.) Our laboratory studies began to show the superiority of noninteractive speaking over other methods of composition. (With speaking an author assumes the recipient will listen to the resulting letter, whereas with dictation an author assumes the recipient will read the letter.) Speaking was faster than dictating and writing [4, 5, 7] and using text-editors [9], with no reduction in quality [4]. People composed spoken messages in laboratory experiments [7] about four times faster than did users of a video electronic mail system (EIES), who composed at a rate of 6 to 8 words per minute (wpm) [14]. Actual users of SFS compose even faster, typically at about 120 wpm [23]. People found speaking easier because listeners are more tolerant of mistakes, poor syntax, false starts, and inexact wording than are readers, and no spelling is involved. In laboratory experiments [7] new SFS users did not experience the same anxieties as did people new to dictation [5].

Users typically sent short messages on SFS (often less than one minute long [23]). Laboratory experiments showed that the pause-compressed speech on SFS was at least as comprehensible as extemporaneous speech, based upon tests of subjective understanding, listenability, and comprehension [20]. The important listening features turned out to be those valuable for listening to short messages (e.g., automatic pause compression). Thomas [26] conducted experiments suggesting that an automatic pause-compression facility would lead listeners to form more positive impressions of callers than if callers were heard to talk slowly with many pauses. Audio quality and reliability had to be, and now are, as good as the telephone system's. SFS surpasses the telephone system in some matters of convenience that are important to users, for example, SFS answers after one ring; (almost always) has no busy signals when a user calls it; and plays out messages quickly when it calls a user. Compared to electronic video mail systems, composing and listening on SFS appear to be more efficient and easier.

6.2 Noninteractive Communication

The value of noninteractive SFS communication has exceeded our expectations of a decade ago. It fulfills basic communication needs of principals by giving them the ability to communicate with people when they want to, to communicate across time zones, to communicate without knowing where a recipient is, to communicate without need for irrelevant conversation, to communicate under a variety of circumstances (which otherwise would be prohibitive), to formulate a reply without the pressures of interactive communication, to eliminate telephone roulette, and to control interruptions.

We began to realize that a significant percentage of all interactive telephone calls (and some interactive conversations) were "one way," and thus were easily displaced by SFS. Our initial view of the usefulness of noninteractive communication was colored by the technology then available. But, relatively rapid noninteractive communication through SFS (or printed electronic mail systems with terminals convenient to principals see [21] and [22] for reviews) has altered our view.

Hardcopy Record and Audit Trail. Before people became users of SFS, they generally believed that a hardcopy record would be essential for them to use SFS. Sometimes this belief was based upon the suspicion that they would rather read their SFS messages than listen to them. At other times it was based upon the tradition of having a printed historical record from noninteractive communication. Once people became users, however, this perceived need disappeared. From 1976-77 users could have any of their audio documents typed by sending them to a user called "typist," but they rarely did so. For the most part, users do not even retrieve an audio message which they filed earlier [23], although some want the possibility of doing so.

A related perceived need was for an audit trail indicating the history of each message, who listened to it, and when. We have found that users do want to know the current status of a just sent message (e.g., has the recipient listened to

Table III.   What Users Volunteer that SFS Does For Them

Saves My Time
5:1 faster composition time
Fewer handwritten memos
Less proofreading
Less telephone roulette
Reduction in looking-up telephone numbers
Able to and does leave content messages
Able to get content messages
More control over working environment
Reduced need to interrupt on-going activities to communicate with people
Less need to organize activities around other people's (presumed) schedules
Adds useful time to workday
More powerful, flexible dictation

Makes Me More Effective
Solves real problems
Does not interrupt regular office procedures
More timely information
Faster communications
Reduces errors in messages
Provides better telephone coverage
Fewer missed telephone calls
Controls interruptions
No need to hunt around for people
Solves time zone communication problems
Able to locate people to communicate effectively
Able to send messages from any place at any time
Able to get messages at any place at any time
Unique advantages in multinational companies

Makes Me Happier
Satisfies major annoyances
Reduces interpersonal communication problems
Less need to come to office during off hours

it yet, or taken action?) We have incorporated a detailed audit trail into ADS, and we await the results of its usage.

6.3 Content Messages

Principals did send content messages. In seven years of field studies and interviews we did not learn of a single example of a user sending a message which only asked the recipient to call back. With experience, users began to use SFS as an alternative communication means, often using it rather than calling a person directly. For example, users sometimes suggested in conversation that a person should send them a SFS message, rather than call them, to resolve some matter. Users did not receive junk mail from other users, as happens with video electronic mail systems (e.g., [14]). The tone of the messages we have heard was almost always businesslike. We were initially concerned that principals might not use SFS for important content messages because they might be afraid that their emotions would show through in their voices. However, users have not expressed this concern and have themselves heard only a few emotionally intoned messages.

Many factors contributed to principals sending content messages.

(1) The composing facility was easy to learn and use, as already discussed.
(2) SFS contained useful functions, and users perceived these as making a positive contribution to their worklives. Table III summarizes some of the positive statements made by users about SFS. Users believe SFS saves them time, makes them more effective, and happier.

In a field study conducted by Epstein [1] on 80 principals in a corporate headquarters location, most users were satisfied with SFS, felt they were more productive with it, and felt that they would be unhappy if it were taken away (see Table IV). The same principals indicated that their satisfaction and productivity would improve more if up to five more key people of their choice were added to the system. One of the most effective ways of learning about the value of a discretionary use system is to take it away from people. Seventy-five per cent of these principals reported they would be dissatisfied if they were removed from SFS—which is perhaps the ultimate test of user satisfaction. We found that, over the years, if SFS was unavailable for a short time, even in the middle of the night, at least one user would complain to us the next day. From 1977–1981 we had a waiting list of several hundred people who wanted to be on SFS.

Electronic mail (video or printed media) systems also report increased principal happiness, effectiveness, and productivity. Uhlig [27] reports that users communicate more frequently and more effectively, and that they like the ability to communicate whenever and from wherever they want. A survey of 210 users of another electronic mail system (Darcom) showed that, as a result of using it, over half the managers and professionals felt they were more productive and had better long distance communication [21]. Most managers, but not professionals or secretaries, felt they had more flexibility in their working hours as a result of using an electronic mail system.

(3) Principals sent content messages because they quickly developed confidence that recipients would listen to their messages. Several factors contributed to this confidence. First, SFS was reliable. Almost perfect reliability was necessary not only during transmission but also while composing (so that a half-composed message would not be lost at this stage). Second, the message was available to recipients immediately after it was sent, unlike some other electronic mail systems. Third, users addressed a message with a recipient's own name, rather than with the recipient's telephone number or some other arbitrary number. This gave users confidence that the right person would listen to the message (rather than just anyone at that telephone number). Fourth, users generally expected recipients to listen to their messages soon after they sent them, and this usually happened. If a message was sent in the morning, the median amount of time until a recipient listened to it was 4.3 hours [23]. Recipients usually called SFS, but if they did not, and they had new messages, then SFS called them. Fifth, users could easily check whether a recipient had listened to a message. Figure 9 shows an example of this. Users could also be automatically notified when a recipient had listened to a message. Sixth, users were given some control over when the recipient's phone would ring. They could make a recipient's telephone ring

that they *expect* to talk with the person directly. With SFS the "caller" has already made the decision not to talk directly with the other person. Traditional telephone answering devices have only a few SFS functions, as shown in Table I.

(6) We, as systems administrators and trainers, were supportive of user concerns.

(7) Users sent content messages because a top-down sociology set in, whereby senior managers sent messages to people reporting to them, thereby encouraging them to use SFS similarly (see also [23]). (It was also possible that workers and professionals would be the first users of SFS, and then convince their managers of its value, i.e., "bottom-up" sociology.) In our early field studies we let the senior manager of a new group of users assign those who should be on SFS. He or she would assign as many new users as we would allow. This, however, did not work out as well as assigning a subset of users initially and then letting the net grow. The latter approach insured that a higher percentage of users would opt to take advantage of SFS.

6.4 Direct Use

Principals used SFS directly. We did not find a single example where principals asked a secretary or other support person to send a message for them. SFS was not viewed by users as a computer but, rather, as a tool to help them communicate. This is in contrast to the findings that some principals use electronic video mail systems by having their secretaries send the messages for them [2, 13].

7. GENERAL CONCLUSIONS

A voice store and forward system, as implemented in SFS, contains useful functions, solves real user problems, leads to user satisfaction and to the user perception of increased productivity, and is relatively easy to learn. New users used it when they were unable to reach a person on the telephone, or to respond to messages that others sent them. They used SFS directly, and always sent content messages. A typical user gradually used SFS in place of some written memos and interactive conversations.

A second set of conclusions has to do with methodology. We developed a process which worked successfully in identifying useful systems functions and in making these functions easy to learn and use. This process includes four critical steps:

(1) early focus upon the characteristics and needs of the intended user population (in this case, office principals);

(2) participative design in which the intended users become part of the design team;

(3) empirical and experimental measurement of how simulated and early prototypes are actually used;

(4) iterative design during which the user interface, training procedures, and reading material are modified based upon earlier and on-going measurements, and are then measured again.

This design philosophy is not an expensive, unprincipled fine-tuning, but is a principled approach which is necessary if progress toward significantly easier to

Table IV. Results of a Survey of User Satisfaction*

User Satisfaction (in Percent)	
Very dissatisfied	1
Dissatisfied	0
Neutral	29
Satisfied	58
Very satisfied	9
No response	4

How Users Would Feel if SFS were Taken Away (in Percent)	
Satisfied	5
Neutral	19
Mildly dissatisfied	28
Somewhat dissatisfied	19
Very dissatisfied	28
No response	2

Estimated Productivity Gains (in Percent)	Users Estimating Productivity Gains Due to SFS (in Percent)	Users' Estimates of Their Productivity Gains if Five People of Their Choice Were Added to SFS (in Percent)
Negative	5	1
Zero	35	15
1–3	24	24
4–10	20	26
11–20	11	23
Over 20	3	1
No response	1	1

* Results from a survey of 80 principals who used SFS in a corporate office for 1 to 4 months during a field study [1]. The entries are the percentages of the 80 users who selected various alternative answers.

immediately, if desired, or at any other time. Seventh, users wanted SFS to be available 24 hours a day, and it was.

(4) Users sent content messages because SFS was perceived as being secure. Users frequently sent sensitive messages, for instance about personnel matters. We learned from our demonstrations to thousands of potential users that they were more concerned about security when they were potential users than when they became actual users. Security included password features, message classification features, and name-orientation. The password system on SFS was typical of the security on most computer systems, but users were given multiple passwords, each of which had a different power associated with it. For example, the secretary password allows one's secretary to obtain the names of people sending a principal new messages, but not to listen to the messages' content. The message classification system lets a user tag a message, for example, as personal or confidential. In addition, users could limit what a recipient could do with a message, that is, not alter it.

(5) Users sent content messages because SFS had to be—and was—sufficiently different from traditional telephone answering devices so that users would (a) like SFS and (b) leave content messages. One reason many callers do not leave *any* message (content or otherwise) on traditional telephone answering devices is

learn and more useful systems is to be achieved. While we thought we had an excellent system several years ago, we concede that ADS is better today as a result of continual iterations of this methodology. Indeed, we continue to use it in our research on new office systems.

ACKNOWLEDGMENTS

This paper does not describe just the authors' work. SFS was a team effort. Stephen J. Boies was the leader throughout. The other group members who contributed significantly over several years are John Gould, Nancy Grischkowsky, Bill Notz, John Richards, and David Zeheb. The authorship reflects who wrote the paper.

We thank Mary Beth Rosson, Bob Mack, Jim Schoonard, Nancy Grischkowsky, and Clayton Lewis for commenting on drafts of this manuscript, and two anonymous reviewers for their thoughtful comments on the manuscript originally submitted.

REFERENCES

1. EPSTEIN, A. A user survey of SFS. Personal communication, 1981.
2. GOODWIN, N.C., AND HOSMER, S.W. A user-oriented evaluation of computer-aided message handling. MME Final Rep. volume VI, part 1, MTR 3920, Mitre Corp., Bedford, Mass., 1980.
3. GOULD, J.D. An experimental study of writing, dictating, and speaking. In *Attention and Performance VII*. J. Requin, Ed, Lawrence Erlbaum Associates, Hillsdale, N.J., 1978, pp. 299–319.
4. GOULD, J.D., AND BOIES, S.J. How authors think about their writing, dictating, and speaking. *Hum. Factors 20* (1978), 495–505.
5. GOULD, J.D. How experts dictate. *J. Experimental Psychol. Hum. Perception Perform. 4*, 4(1978), 648–661.
6. GOULD, J.D., AND BOIES, S.J. Writing, dictating, and speaking letters. *Science 201* (1978), 1145–1147.
7. GOULD, J.D. Writing and speaking letters and messages. *Int. J. Man Mach. Stud. 16* (1982), 147–171.
8. GOULD, J.D. Experiments on composing letters: some facts, some myths, and some observations. In *Cognitive Process in Writing*. L. Gregg and I. Steinberg, Eds, Lawrence Erlbaum and Associates, Hillsdale, N.J., 1980, pp. 98–127.
9. GOULD, J.D. Composing letters with computer-based text editors. *Hum. Factors 23* (1981), 593–606.
10. GOULD, J.D., AND BOIES, S.J. Speech filing—an office system for principals. IBM Res. Rep. RC-9769, Dec. 1982.
11. GOULD, J.D., AND LEWIS, C. H. Designing for usability—key principles and what designers think about them. In preparation, 1983.
12. GRISCHKOWSKY, N.L. Training users on the Audio Distribution System. IBM Res. Rep. RA-136, 1981.
13. HERSH, H.M. Electronic mail usage analysis. In *Proc. Human Factors in Computer Systems*. Sponsored by the Institute for Computer Sciences and Technology, the NBS, and the Washington Chapter of the ACM, 1982, pp. 278–280.
14. HILTZ, S.R., AND TUROFF, M. The evolution of user behavior in a computerized conferencing system. *Commun. ACM 24*, 11 (Nov. 1981), 739–751.
15. IBM AUDIO DISTRIBUTION SYSTEM SUBSCRIBER'S GUIDE. SC34-0400-1. (Can be obtained from IBM, 4111 Northside Parkway N. W., Box 2150, Atlanta, GA 30056).
16. KLEMMER, E.T., AND SNYDER, F.W. Measurement of time spent communicating. *J. Commun. 22*, (1972), 142–158.
17. MACK, R., LEWIS, C., AND CARROLL, J. Learning to use word processors: problems and prospects. *ACM Trans. Office Inf. Syst. 1*, 3 (July 1983), 254–272.
18. MILLER, D.G. Military message experiment—final training report. Mitre Tech. Rep. MTR 3919, Mitre Corp., Bedford, Mass., 1980.
19. MINTZBERG, H. *The Nature of Managerial Work*. Harper and Row, New York, 1973.
20. NIX, D. Two experiments on the comprehensibility of pause-depleted speech. IBM Res. Rep. RC-6305, 1976.
21. PANKO, R.R. The EMS revolution (a survey of electronic message systems). *Computerworld* (Aug. 25, 1980), 1–12.
22. RICE, R.E. The impacts of computer-mediated organizational and interpersonal communication. In *Annual Review of Information Science and Technology, 15*, M. Williams, Ed., Kowledge Industry Publications, White Plains, N.Y., 1981, pp. 221–249.
23. RICHARDS, JOHN T. The IBM Research Speech Filing System: analysis of the System 7/S 370 Prototype. IBM Res. Rep. RC-9114, 1981.
24. SCHOONARD, J.W., AND BOIES, S.J. *Speech Filing System Reference Manual*. Unpublished manuscript, 1975. (Can be obtained from the authors at the IBM Research Center, Yorktown Heights, NY 10598).
25. TAYLOR, J. Evaluation of the terminals for managers (TFM) program at Stanford University. A report from the Center for Information Technology, Stanford Univ., Stanford, CA 94305, 1981.
26. THOMAS, J.C. Office communications studies: I. Effects of communication behavior on the perception of described persons. IBM Res. Rep. RC-7572, 1979.
27. UHLIG, R.P. Human factors in computer message systems. *Datamation 23*, 5 (1977), 120–126.

Part I

The Context of Human-Computer Interaction

Human-computer interaction is the set of processes, dialogues, and actions through which a human user employs and interacts with a computer. The computer is a tool, a complex man-made artifact that can stretch our limits and can extend our reach. The purpose of the discipline of human-computer interaction is to apply, systematically, knowledge about human purposes, human capabilities and limitations, and machine capabilities and limitations so as to extend our reach, so as to enable us to do things we could not do before. Another goal is simply to enhance the quality of the interaction between human and machine.

More generally, the attempt to enhance the quality of man's use of his artifacts is the domain of the discipline of *human factors*, also known as *ergonomics* (Sanders and McCormick, 1987; Kantowitz and Sorkin, 1983; McCormick and Sanders, 1982; Van Cott and Kinkade, 1972). McCormick and Sanders (1982) define human factors as follows:

> The central *focus* of human factors relates to the consideration of human beings in carrying out such functions as (1) the design and creation of man-made objects, products, equipment, facilities, and environments that people use; (2) the development of procedures for performing work and other human activities; (3) the provision of services to people; and (4) the evaluation of the things people use in terms of their suitability for people.
>
> The *objectives* of human factors in these functions are twofold, as follows: (1) to enhance the effectiveness and efficiency with which work and other human activities are carried out; and (2) to maintain or enhance certain desirable human values (e.g., health, safety, and satisfaction). The second objective is essentially one of human welfare and well-being.
>
> The central *approach* of human factors is the systemic application of relevant information about human abilities, characteristics, behaviour, and motivation in the execution of such functions.

Human factors is therefore a branch of applied psychology and a discipline to guide and enhance the processes of design. But before we look in detail at the emerging applied psychology of the computer user and at the art of user interface design, we need to understand something of the context and the environment in which human-computer interaction takes place. There are three major aspects of the context — historical, socio-political, and physical.

This book is being published in 1987. The computer user of 1987 does not exist in a vacuum. On the contrary, the beliefs and expectations with which she sits down at her terminal or personal computer are a direct result of her concept of what the computer is like and what the computer has become. We need therefore look briefly at the development of interactive computing over the past forty years, and at the paradigms (Kuhn, 1970) which have become dominant. The historical overview of Chapter 1: A Historical and Intellectual Perspective, will also serve to put into context many of the results and contributions to be presented throughout the book.

Another crucial aspect of the environment in which people interact with computers is the socio-political context. For whom and for what purpose is the computer to be used? Who has the power? Who is in control? How are decisions being made? Is the user motivated, indifferent, alienated, or hostile? What are the determinants of the quality of her working life? How does the structure of an organization affect the use and effectiveness of computers, and how does the introduction of new technology affect the functioning of an existing organization? Such questions, often overlooked in a narrow view of the interface between human and machine, will be examined in Chapter 2: The Socio/Political Environment.

Of equal importance and again often overlooked is the physical environment in which human-computer interaction takes place. This includes such issues as display quality, lighting, noise, air quality, and the suitability of furniture. Is the environment healthy? Is it safe? How can it be made healthier, safer, more comfortable, and more satisfying? These and other related questions are the topic of Chapter 3: The Physical Environment.

References

Kantowitz, Barry H. & Sorkin, Robert D. (1983). *Human Factors: Understanding People-System Relationships*, New York: John Wiley & Sons.

Kuhn, Thomas S. (1970). *The Structure of Scientific Revolution*, Second Edition, Enlarged, Chicago: University of Chicago Press.

McCormick, Ernest J. & Sanders, Mark S. (1982). *Human Factors in Engineering and Design*, Fifth Edition, New York: McGraw-Hill Book Company. © 1982, McGraw-Hill Book Company, reprinted with permission.

Sanders, Mark S. & McCormick, Ernest J. (1987). *Human Factors in Engineering and Design*, Sixth Edition, New York: McGraw-Hill Book Company.

Van Cott, H.P. & Kinkade, R.G. (Editors) (1972). *Human Engineering Guide to Equipment Design*, Revised Edition, Washington, D.C.: American Institutes for Research.

Chapter 1

A Historical and Intellectual Perspective

There is a tendency when dealing with technology always to look for hope in the future. We are often too quick to forget the past. The much heralded introduction of systems with "advanced" user interfaces (such as the Xerox Star in 1981 and the Apple Macintosh in 1984) are a case in point. Much of the groundwork for these systems was laid in the 1960s and 1970s.

In this chapter, we provide some historical perspective, introducing a few of the seminal ideas, contributors, and systems. However, our objective is not a detailed, historically complete recitation of names, places, and dates. Our emphasis is intellectual, with a focus on the history of ideas. We repeat a question asked by Alan Kay in a speech given at SIGGRAPH '84: Why in the 1980s do we consider implementing the ideas introduced by these seminal systems as a measure of our success rather than as a starting point?

The MEMEX

Although the modern digital computer is grounded in ideas developed in the 18th and 19th centuries, important concepts and the technology required to implement the ideas in systems only became available in the 1930s and the 1940s. The motivation was to speed the routine and laborious calculations required for ballistic and atomic energy computations.

Perhaps the first person to see beyond these uses and conceive of the computer as a fundamental tool for transforming human thought and human creative activity was Vannevar Bush (1945). In his classic paper, "As We May Think," he described the increasing difficulties mankind was having in managing and disseminating the results of research:

> Professionally our methods of transmitting and reviewing the results of research are generations old and by now are totally inadequate for their purpose. If the aggregate time spent in writing scholarly works and in reading them could be evaluated, the ratio between these amounts of time might well be startling. Those who conscientiously attempt to keep abreast of current thought, even in restricted fields, by close and continuous reading might well shy away from an examination calculated to show how much of the previous month's efforts could be produced on call. Mendel's concept of the laws of genetics was lost to the world for a generation because his publication did not reach the few who were capable of grasping and extending it; and this sort of catastrophe is undoubtedly being repeated all about us, as truly significant attainments become lost in the mass of the inconsequential.
>
> The difficulty seems to be not so much that we publish unduly in view of the extent and variety of present-day interests but rather that publication has been extended far beyond our present ability to make real use of the record. The summation of human experience is being expanded at a prodigious rate, and the means we use for threading through the consequent maze to the momentarily important item is the same as was used in the days of square-rigged ships.

To solve this problem, he sketched the outlines of a device he called the MEMEX:

> Consider a future device for individual use which is a sort of mechanized private file and library. It needs a name, and, to coin one at random, "MEMEX" will do. A MEMEX is a device in which an individual stores all his books, records, and communications, and which is mechanized so that it may be consulted with exceeding speed and

flexibility. It is an enlarged intimate supplement to his memory.

It consists of a desk, and while it can presumably be operated from a distance, it is primarily the piece of furniture at which he works. On the top are slanting translucent screens, on which material can be projected for convenient reading. There is a keyboard and sets of buttons and levers. Otherwise it looks like an ordinary desk.

In one end is the stored material. The matter of bulk is well taken care of by improved microfilm. Only a small part of the interior of the MEMEX is devoted to storage, the rest to mechanism. Yet if the user inserted 5,000 pages of material a day it would take him hundreds of years to fill the repository, so he can be profligate and enter material freely.

Most of the MEMEX contents are purchased on microfilm ready for insertion. Books of all sorts, pictures, current periodicals, newspapers, are thus obtained and dropped into place. Business correspondence takes the same path. And there is provision for direct entry. On the top of the MEMEX is a transparent platen. On this are placed longhand notes, photographs, memoranda, all sorts of things. When one is in place, the depression of a lever causes it to be photographed onto the next blank space on a section of the MEMEX film, dry photography being employed.

There is, of course, provision for consultation of the record by the usual scheme of indexing. If the user wishes to consult a certain book, he taps its code on the keyboard, and the title page of the book promptly appears before him, projected onto one of his viewing positions. Frequently used codes are mnemonic, so that he seldom consults his code book; but when he does, a single tap of a key projects it for his use. Moreover, he has supplemental levers. On deflecting one of these levers to the right he runs through the book before him, each page in turn being projected at a speed which just allows a recognizing glance at each. If he deflects it further to the right, he steps through the book ten pages at a time; still further at one hundred pages at a time. Deflection to the left gives him the same control backward.

A special button transfers him immediately to the first page of the index. Any given book of his library can thus be called up and consulted with far greater facility than if it were taken from a shelf. As he has several projection positions, he can leave one item in position while he calls up another. He can add marginal notes and comments, taking advantage of one possible type of dry photography, and it could even be arranged so that he can do this by a stylus scheme, such as is now employed in the telautograph seen in railroad waiting rooms, just as though he had the physical page before him.

All this is conventional, except for the projection forward of present day mechanisms and gadgetry. It affords an immediate step, however, to associative indexing, the basic idea of which is a provision whereby any item may be caused at will to select immediately and automatically another. This is the essential feature of the MEMEX. The process of tying two items together is the important thing.

When the user is building a trail, he names it, inserts the name in his code book, and taps it out on his keyboard. Before him are the two items to be joined, projected onto adjacent viewing positions. At the bottom of each there are a number of blank code spaces, and a pointer is set to indicate one of these on each item. The user taps a single key, and the items are permanently joined. In each code space appears the code word. Out of view, but also in the code space, is inserted a set of dots for photocell viewing; and on each item these dots by their positions designate the index number of the other item.

Thereafter, at any time when one of these items is in view, the other can be instantly recalled merely by tapping a button below the corresponding code space. Moreover, when numerous items have been thus joined together to form a trail, they can be reviewed in turn, rapidly or slowly, by deflecting a lever like that used for turning the pages of a book. It is exactly as though the physical items had been gathered together from widely separated sources and bound together to form a new book. It is more than this, for any item can be joined into numerous trails.....

Wholly new forms of encyclopedias will appear, ready made with a mesh of associative trails running through them, ready to be dropped in the MEMEX and there amplified. The lawyer has at his touch the associated opinions and decisions of his whole experience and of the experience of friends and authorities. The patent attorney has on call the millions of issued patents, with familiar trails to every point of his client's interest. The physician, puzzled by a patient's reactions, strikes the trail established in studying an earlier similar case and runs rapidly through analogous case histories, with side references to the classics for the pertinent anatomy and histology. The chemist, struggling with the synthesis of an organic compound, has all the chemical literature before him in his laboratory, with trails following the analogies of compounds and side trails to their physical and chemical behaviour.

The historian, with a vast chronological account of a people, parallels it with a skip trail which stops only on the salient items, and can follow at any time contemporary trails which lead him all over civilization at a particular epoch. There is a new profession of trail blazers, those who find delight an the task of establishing useful trails through the enormous mass of the common record. The inheritance from the master becomes, not only his additions to the world's record, but for his disciples the entire scaffolding by which they were erected.

Bush's vision was remarkable. He not only foresaw the application of the computer to information storage and retrieval, and the value of associative indexing in that activity, but he also correctly anticipated the multimedia nature of computer use in the future. He predicted the development of ''a machine which types when talked to,'' and speculated on the possibility of some day establishing a path from the written word to the brain that is ''more direct'' than the senses — tactile, oral, and visual. Now that the emergence of the technology of CD/ROM (Lambert and Ropiequet, 1986) makes a fully digital MEMEX possible, it will be interesting to watch the extent to which Bush's dream becomes a reality.

Man-Computer Symbiosis

These ideas were far ahead of their time. However others in the 1950s also began to see the potential of the computer as a facilitator of aspects of human creativity and problem solving. One such individual was J.C.R. Licklider (1960), who conceived of a synergistic coupling of human and machine capabilities that he labeled "man-computer symbiosis":

> The fig tree is pollinated only by the insect *Blastophaga grossorum*. The larva of the insect lives in the ovary of the fig tree, and there it gets its food. The tree and the insect are thus heavily interdependent: The tree cannot reproduce without the insect; the insect cannot eat without the tree; together, they constitute not only a viable but a productive and thriving partnership. This cooperative "living together in intimate association, or even close union, of two dissimilar organisms" is called symbiosis.
>
> "Man-computer symbiosis" is a subclass of man-machine systems. There are many man-machine systems. At present, however, there are no man-computer symbioses. The purposes of this paper are to present the concept and, hopefully, to foster the development of man-computer symbiosis by analyzing some problems of interaction between men and computing machines, calling attention to applicable principles of man-machine engineering, and pointing out a few questions to which research answers are needed. The hope is that, in not too many years, human brains and computing machines will be coupled together very tightly and that the resulting partnership will think as no human brain has ever thought and process data in a way not approached by the information-handling machines we know today.

Licklider outlines how the then-current generation of computers is not suited to facilitating man-computer symbiosis:

> Present-day computers are designed primarily to solve preformulated problems or to process data according to predetermined procedures. The course of the computation may be conditional upon results obtained during the computation, but all the alternatives must be foreseen in advance. (If an unforeseen alternative arises, the whole process comes to a halt and awaits the necessary extension of the program.) The requirement for preformulation or predetermination is sometimes no great disadvantage. It is often said that programming for a computing machine forces one to think clearly, that it disciplines the thought process. If the user can think his problem through in advance, symbiotic association with a computing machine is not necessary.
>
> However, many problems that can be thought through in advance are very difficult to think through in advance. They would be easier to solve, and they would be solved faster, through an intuitively guided trial-and-error procedure in which the computer cooperates, turning up flaws in the reasoning or revealing unexpected turns in the solution. Other problems simply cannot be formulated without computing-machine aid. Poincaré anticipated the frustration of an important group of would-be computer users when he said, "The question is not 'What is the answer?' The question is 'What is the question?'" One

of the main aims of man-computer symbiosis is to bring the computing machine effectively into the formulative parts of technical problems.

> The other main aim is closely related. It is to bring computing machines effectively into processes of thinking that must go on in "real time," time that moves too fast to permit using computers in conventional ways. Imagine trying, for example, to direct a battle with the aid of a computer on such a schedule as this. You formulate your problem today. Tomorrow you spend with a programmer. Next week the computer devotes 5 minutes to assembling your program and 47 seconds to calculating the answer to your problem. You get a sheet of paper 20 feet long, full of numbers that, instead of providing a final solution, only suggest a tactic that should be explored by simulation. Obviously, the battle would be over before the second step in it planning was begun. To think in interaction with a computer in the same way that you think with a colleague whose competence supplements your own will require much tighter coupling between man and machine than is suggested by the example and than is possible today.

Licklider goes on to justify his belief that computers integrated effectively into the thought process would improve or facilitate thinking and problem-solving:

> Despite the fact that there is a voluminous literature on thinking and problem-solving, including intensive case-history studies of the process of invention, I could find nothing comparable to a time-and-motion-study analysis of the mental work of a person engaged in a scientific or technical enterprise. In the spring and summer of 1957, therefore, I tried to keep track of what one moderately technical person actually did during the hours he regarded as devoted to work. Although I was aware of the inadequacy of the sampling, I served as my own subject.
>
> It soon became apparent that the main thing I did was to keep records, and the project would have become in infinite regress if the keeping of records had been carried through in the detail envisaged in the initial plan. It was not. Nevertheless, I obtained a picture of my activities that gave me pause. Perhaps my spectrum is not typical — I hope it is not, but I fear it is.
>
> About 85 per cent of my "thinking" time was spent getting into a position to think, to make a decision, to learn something I needed to know. Much more time went into finding or obtaining information than into digesting it. Hours went into the plotting of graphs and other hours into instructing an assistant how to plot. When the graphs were finished, the relations were obvious at once, but the plotting had to be done in order to make them so. At one point, it was necessary to compare six experimental determinations of a function relating speech intelligibility to speech-to-noise ratio. No two experimenters had used the same definition or measure of speech-to-noise ratio. Several hours of calculating were required to get the data into comparable form. When they were in comparable form, it took only a few seconds to determine what I needed to know.
>
> Throughout the period I examined, in short, my "thinking" time was devoted mainly to activities that were essentially clerical or mechanical: searching, calculating, plotting, transforming, determining the logical or

dynamic consequences of a set of assumptions or hypotheses, preparing the way for a decision or an insight. Moreover, my choices of what to attempt and what not to attempt were determined to an embarrassingly great extent by considerations of clerical feasibility, not intellectual capability.

The main suggestion conveyed by the findings just described is that the operations that fill most of the time allegedly devoted to technical thinking are operations that can be performed more effectively by machines than by men. Severe problems are posed by the fact that these operations have to be performed upon diverse variables and in unforeseen and continually changing sequences. If those problems can be solved in such a way as to create a symbiotic relation between a man and a fast information-retrieval and data-processing machine, however, it seems evident that the cooperative interaction would greatly improve the thinking process.

In a later paper, Licklider and Clark (1962) outline applications of man-computer communication to military command and control, mathematics, programming, war gaming and management gaming, planning and design, education, and scientific research. They report on some early experiments and prototype systems that demonstrate the potential of using computers in these applications. Then, showing remarkable foresight, they list ten problems whose solutions are prerequisites for true man-computer symbiosis. The first five they term ''immediate,'' the next one ''intermediate,'' and the last four ''long-term'':

- time sharing of computers among many users
- an electronic input-output surface for the display and communication of correlated symbolic and pictorial information (This capability, as well as that of a computer-driven wall display, had been cited as essential in the earlier paper.)
- an interactive, real-time system for information processing and programming
- systems for large scale information storage and retrieval designed to make possible concurrent, cooperative problem solving in many disciplines
- the facilitation of human cooperation in the design and programming of large systems
- combined computer speech recognition, hard-printed character recognition, and light-pen editing
- natural language understanding, including syntactic, semantic, and pragmatic aspects
- recognition of the speech of arbitrary computer users (The earlier paper had also stressed the need for automatic production of speech.)
- the theory of algorithms — discovery, development, and simplification
- heuristic programming

Time Sharing and Networking

Even before Licklider's papers, John McCarthy and Christopher Strachey independently had proposed the development of a system of time-sharing as a means of allowing the computer to work on several jobs simultaneously and to give each user the illusion, up to a point, that she had the machine to herself. The concept was soon validated by experimental systems built in the early 1960s at Bolt Beranek and Newman, Inc., MIT, and System Development Corporation, among others (Davis, 1966; Fano and Corbato, 1966; Licklider, 1968).

The viability and rapid development of time-sharing advanced the art of human-computer interaction significantly:

- It dramatically increased the accessibility of computers and the size of their user communities.
- Because the user could now afford to think while at the terminal and not simply carry out preconceived actions, designers of interactive programs were encouraged to pay more attention to the user's behaviour at the terminal and to methods for making him maximally productive. One way in which this began to happen was through the development of new "interaction languages" such as JOSS (Shaw, 1964), which facilitated on-line control and programming of the machine (Davis, 1966; Licklider, 1968).
- Because each computer now had a community of users who could interact with each other both directly through messages and indirectly through a shared file system, human-computer interaction and computer-mediated human interaction were significantly enriched.

The latter phenomenon was further accelerated beginning in the middle 1960s by the development of wide area computer networks, linking machines and users located in geographically remote sites (Roberts, 1986).

Sketchpad

Some of the earliest computers, such as MIT's Whirlwind and the SAGE air-defense command and control system, had displays as integral components in the early 1950s (Machover, 1978; Bell, 1986; Ross, 1986). Thus by the middle 1950s it was obvious that the computer could be used to manipulate pictures as well as numbers and text. A number of investigators therefore began exploring the potential for enhanced graphical communication between human and machine. No one was as successful as Ivan Sutherland, whose pioneering work at MIT Lincoln Laboratory was the Sketchpad system (1963; MIT, 1963). In developing Sketchpad, he introduced many powerful new ideas and concepts:

- the concept of the internal *hierarchic* structure of a computer-represented picture and its definition in terms of subpictures
- the concept of a *master* picture and of its *instances* which are transformed versions of the master, a concept which helped lay the foundation for modern object-oriented programming
- the concept of the *constraint* as a method of specifying details of the geometry of a picture, for example, a horizontal constraint applied to a line, and a equal distance constraint applied to two pairs of points
- the ability to display and manipulate *iconic* representations of constraints
- the ability to copy as well as instance both pictures and constraints
- some elegant techniques for picture construction using a light pen
- the separation of the coordinate system in which a picture is defined from that on which it is displayed
- recursive operations such as ''move'' and ''delete'' applied to hierarchically defined pictures

Computer Aided Design

Others were active at the same time exploring additional possibilities suggested by the new interface technology. The intensity and excitement surfaced perhaps most intensely at the same 1963 Spring Joint Computer Conference where Sutherland reported on the Sketchpad work. Work described there also included a general outline of the requirements for a computer-aided design (CAD) system (Coons, 1963), a presentation of the requirements for CAD in terms of languages and data structures (Ross, 1963), a description of hardware requirements for CAD (Stotz, 1963), and a method of generalizing Sketchpad to allowing input and manipulation of three dimensional line drawings (Johnson, 1963).

New Display and Input Technologies

Realizing the tremendous potential of computer graphics that was suggested by Sutherland and the early CAD pioneers required advances in graphics hardware and software.

The earliest graphics hardware was very expensive, requiring costly memory to store image representations and costly circuitry to refresh cathode ray tube (CRT) displays without annoying flicker. An invention of the 1950s called the direct view storage tube (Preiss, 1978) would by the early 1970s make low-cost graphics possi-

ble and thus provide a tremendous stimulus to the industry. Work was also underway on enhancing the expressive potential of the technology. This led to two kinds of innovations, more powerful display processors (Myer and Sutherland, 1968) capable of real-time manipulations of simple line drawings, and new input technologies, such as data tablets (Davis and Ellis, 1964), which would accept real-time input of sketches and gestures.

On the software front there was progress in two major directions. Investigators at Lincoln Laboratory and other sites developed operating systems capable of supporting interactive graphics under time-sharing, another step towards making the technology more cost-effective (Sutherland, Forgie and Morello, 1969). Simultaneously there were developed a number of languages with embedded graphics support that facilitated the production of graphics applications (Rovner and Feldman, 1968).

New Graphics Applications

These advances in the supporting technology led to a flourishing of new applications to mathematics, science, engineering, and art. Culler and Fried, for example, pioneered in the development of computer-aided mathematical laboratories (Culler, 1968). Typical of the new scientific applications was the use of 3D computer graphics in molecular modelling, begun by Levinthal (1966) and later refined by several groups such as that of Brooks (1977). On the artistic front, and following the pioneering work of Knowlton (1966) and others in allowing animated pictures to be defined by program, Baecker (1969) provided a convincing example of how artists could specify and refine movies through an interactive language of sketches, direct actions, and real-time playback. Davis (1966), Licklider (1968), and a special issue of readings from *Scientific American* (1971) are good sources describing some of these early developments.

Computer Aided Document Creation

The most pervasive application of interactive computing was soon to become word processing and the computer-aided production of documents.

Two of the dominant influences in suggesting the potential of the technology have been Doug Engelbart (1963, 1982, 1986; Engelbart and English, 1968) and Ted Nelson (1965, 1973, 1974, 1981). Both took Bush's concept of the MEMEX and elaborated it in various imaginative ways. Both elaborated the role of the computer in building and manipulating richly structured complexes of structured, interconnected, and interlinked bodies of text, which Nelson termed *hypertext*. Both realized, as Bush had not, that most information would eventually be stored in purely digital form rather than on microfilm.

The approaches of Engelbart and Nelson also differed in various substantive ways. Whereas Engelbart focused primarily on hierarchic structure in documents, Nelson was more interested in the links and interconnections. Whereas Engelbart focused primarily on group creation and problem solving, Nelson was excited by the individual exploration of document structures that would ultimately include contributions from remote participants not part of the same organization. Whereas Engelbart has for twenty-five years been elaborating his concepts with substantial government and industry support into a real working system now known as "Augment," Nelson has had to content himself with meager support inadequate to realize anything more than prototypes of his hypertext system, which he now calls "Xanadu."

Engelbart (1963) conceived of his work as the "augmentation of man's intellect":

> By "augmenting man's intellect" we mean increasing the capability of a man to approach a complex problem situation, gain comprehension to suit his particular needs, and to derive solutions to problems. Increased capability in this respect is taken to mean a mixture of the following: the comprehension can be gained more quickly; that better comprehension can be gained; that a useful degree of comprehension can be gained where previously the situation was too complex; that solutions can be produced more quickly; that better solutions can be produced; that solutions can be found where previously the human could find none. And by "complex situations" we include the professional problems of diplomats, executives, social scientists, life scientists, physical scientists, attorneys, designers — whether the problem situation exists for twenty minutes or twenty years. We do not speak of isolated clever tricks that help in particular situations. We refer to a way of life in an integrated domain where hunches, cut-and-try, intangibles, and the human "feel for a situation" usefully coexist with powerful concepts, streamlined terminology and notation, sophisticated methods, and highly-powered electronic aids.....

> Our culture has evolved means for us to organize and utilize our basic capabilities so that we can comprehend truly complex situations and accomplish the processes of devising and implementing problem solutions. The ways in which human capabilities are thus extended are here called *augmentation means*, and we define four basic classes of them:

> 1. *Artifacts* — physical objects designed to provide for human comfort, the manipulation of things or materials, and the manipulation of symbols.
> 2. *Language* — the way in which the individual classifies the picture of his world into the concepts that his mind uses to model that world, and the symbols that he attaches to those concepts and uses in consciously manipulating the concepts ("thinking").
> 3. *Methodology* — the methods, procedures, and strategies with which an individual organizes his *goal-centered* (problem-solving) activity.
> 4. *Training* — the conditioning needed by the individual to bring his skills in using augmentation means 1, 2 and 3 to the point where they are operationally effective.

> The system we wish to improve can thus be visualized as comprising a trained human being together with his artifacts, language, and methodology. The explicit new system we contemplate will involve as artifacts computers and computer-controlled information-storage, information-handling, and information-display devices. The aspects of the conceptual framework that are discussed here are primarily those relating to the individual's ability to make significant use of such equipment in an integrated system.

> Pervading all of the augmentation means is a particular structure or organization.....

Twenty years later, in reviewing his progress, Engelbart (1982) asserted that he had been successful in facilitating "almost all phases of any simple to complex document production process," and in providing a "dialogue support system" consisting of electronic mail and remote shared screen capabilities. Echoing Licklider, he stresses the importance of synergy (Engelbart, 1982, pp. 306-307):

> It is extremely important to note the multiple levels of synergism at work here:

> (a) The synergistic effect of integrating many tools into one coherent workshop makes each tool considerably more valuable than if it were used alone — for instance, the value of teleconferencing is very much greater when the participants are already doing a large proportion of their everyday work on line, so that any of the working material is available for selective citing and accessing, and when the users are already at home with the basic techniques of preparing and studying on-line material and of organizing and finding related passages.

> (b) And at another level, the synergistic effect of integrating many augmented individuals into one coherent community makes each element of augmentation considerably more valuable than if it were applied just to support its one individual — this is derived from the collaborative communication capabilities as applied through extended organizational methods to integrate the augmented capabilities of individuals into augmented teams and communities.

> And finally, for any application of significant power — of which augmentation of an engineering project would be a good example — the adaptability and evolutionary flexibility of the computer-communication system is extremely important. The working methods of individuals will shift markedly as they settle into use of a comprehensive workshop, and with these new methods and skills will come payoff potential for changes and additions to their workshops — a cycle that will be significantly active for many years to come. A similar cycle will be even more dramatically evident at the organizational level.

Nelson (1965) began his work with an investigation of file structures suitable for implementing hypertext:

> The kinds of file structures required if we are to use the computer for personal files and as an adjunct to creativity are wholly different in character from those customary in business and scientific data processing. They need to provide the capacity for intricate and idiosyncratic arrangements, total modifiability, undecided alternatives, and thorough internal documentation.....
>
> Systems of paper have grave limitations for either organizing or presenting ideas. A book is never perfectly suited to the reader; one reader is bored, another confused by the same pages. No system of paper — book or programmed text — can adapt very far to the interests or needs of a particular reader or student.
>
> However, with the computer-driven display and mass memory, it has been possible to create a new, readable medium, for education and enjoyment, that will let the reader find his level, suit his taste, and find the parts that take on special meaning for him, as instruction or entertainment.
>
> Let me introduce the word *hypertext* to mean a body of written or pictorial material interconnected in such a complex way that it could not conveniently be presented or represented on paper. It may contain summaries, or maps of its contents and their interrelations; it may contain annotations, additions and footnotes from scholars who have examined it. Let me suggest that such an object and system, properly designed and administered, could have great potential for education, increasing the student's range of choices, his sense of freedom, his motivation, and his intellectual grasp. Such a system could grow indefinitely, gradually including more and more of the world's written knowledge. However, its internal file structure would have to be built to accept growth, change and complex informational arrangements.

Sixteen years later (1981), in presenting the concept and design of Xanadu, at that time still unimplemented, he states pessimistically:

> This book presents a dream, a wild surmise that perhaps many have had but most have kicked under the bed as unfit for daytime contemplation. I have tried to capture it, a ludicrous butterfly-hunter scampering through unknown territory.
>
> Okay, maybe it will turn out to be impossible. But if not the details, if not our valiant try, perhaps the *vision* may endure — and perhaps also some readers may achieve an expanded realization of what it means to make simplicity happen.

Doug Engelbart was one of the first to recognize the need for experiments to test various approaches to the user interface (English and Engelbart, 1967). Nelson shares Engelbart's concerns about the quality of the interface, but takes a more passionate and less scientific approach. Typical of his style, for example, is his invention of the term "cybercrud," which he defines as "putting things over on people using computers" (1973):

> The myth of technical determinism seems to hold captive both the public and the computer priesthood. Indeed, the myth is believed both by people who love, and by people who hate, computers. This myth, never questioned because never stated, holds that whatever is to come in the computer field is somehow preordained by technical necessity or some form of scientific correctness. This is cybercrud.
>
> Computers do what people want them to do, *at best*. Figuring out what we should want, in full contemplation of the outspread possibilities, is a task that needs us all, laymen no less. There is something right about the public backlash against computers: things don't have to be this way, with our bank balances unavailable from computers, the immense serial numbers of our drivers' licenses generated by computers, the unstaunchable rivers of junk mail sent to us by computers. And it is the duty of the computer-man to help demythologize, to help the intelligent layman understand the specifics of systems he must deal with, and to help the public explore the question, *what do we want?*.....
>
> I can now state what I believe to be the central problem of screenworld design, and indeed of design of man-machine *anything* — that is, psychic architecture.
>
> By the psychic architecture of a system, I mean the mental conceptions and space structures among which the user moves: their arrangements and their qualities, especially clarity, integration and meshing, power, utility and lack of clutter.
>
> It should be noted that these notions are much like those by which we judge regular architecture, and indeed the relationship would seem very close. An architectural grand design — say, of a capitol building — embraces the fundamental concepts a user will have to know to get around: main places, corridor arrangement (visualization and symmetries), access structure. These concepts are the very same in a screenworld or other complex man-made virtual structure: main places, corridors or transition rules (and their visualization and symmetries), access structure. It is a virtual space much like a building (though not confined to three "normally" connected dimensions), and susceptible to the same modes of spatial understanding, kinds of possible movement within, and potential appreciation and criticism.....
>
> The psychic engineering of fantic fields — adult's hyperspaces of word and picture, child's gardens of verses — is our new frontier. We must look not to Asimovian robotics and the automated schoolmarm and librarian, but to the penny arcade and the bicycle, the clever diagram and the movie effect, to furnish this new realm.

Bravo! Happily, Nelson has had a profound effect on many young people interested in computers through this lively and deeply humanistic vision of the creative potential of appropriate computer technology. One example of his influence is the widely-known Nelson (1974, p. DM58) *Ten Minute Rule*, perhaps the strongest formulation of the goal of congenial interface design: "Any system which cannot be well taught to a layman in *ten minutes*, by a tutor in the presence of a responding setup, is too complicated." It is unfortunate that much of his writing such as that contained in his *Computer Lib* and *Dream Machines* (Nelson, 1974) are self-published and are effectively unavailable.

In the mainstream of text processing development, the 1960s and 1970s have seen the evolution of interactive text editors from the IBM MTST magnetic tape Selectric typewriter through the interactive line editors of the early time sharing systems, context-driven line editors, variable-length line editors, and stream editors to what are variously called full-screen or display editors (Meyrowitz and van Dam, 1982). Another step in the trend towards more congenial environments for document creation has been the kind of system known as WYSIWYG, "What You See Is What You Get," in which the user sees and manipulates on the screen a representation of the document that is intended to look identical to the ultimate printed page (Thacker, 1986; Lampson, 1986). More recently (Yankelovich and Meyrowitz, 1985), effective microcomputer-based hypertext systems have started to become available. Perhaps Nelson's dream is soon to be realized.

Early Experiments on Interface Quality

Engelbart and English were not the only ones to pose the question of empirical confirmation of optimal design choices and quantitative validation of interface quality. This can be seen, for example, in some issues that captured research attention in the middle 1960s:

- comparisons of batch processing and time sharing computer use, off-line and on-line problem solving (Grant and Sackman, 1967; Lampson, 1967, a critique of that paper; Nickerson, Elkind, and Carbonell, 1968; Gold, 1969)
- understanding how the efficacy of problem solving in a time-shared environment depends upon the response time provided to the user (Miller, 1968; Grossberg, Wiesen and Yntema, 1976)
- the nature of human-computer cooperative problem solving (Yntema and Torgerson, 1961; Carbonell, Elkind, and Nickerson, 1968; Miller, 1969)

An influential book, the first dealing with methods of psychological research on programming, was that of Sackman (1970). After reviewing past work on human problem solving using computers both off-line and on-line, Sackman presents detailed results and analyses of a new set of experiments dealing with these issues. Of particular interest is the attention he pays to individual differences and the recommendations he makes for a "scientific study of man-computer problem solving."

Psychologists and human factors specialists also began at that time looking more broadly at issues in human-computer interaction where they could play a useful role. Shackel (1969) and Nickerson (1969) are two representative and influential papers outlining proposals for such a role. Bennett (1972) reviews some of the resulting early work.

The Psychology of Computer Programming

Even more significant than the Sackman book was one published the following year by Weinberg (1971). It dealt very broadly with programming as human performance, with programming as an individual activity, and with programming as a social activity. More than any other single work up to that time, the book focused attention on the human factors of programming and described the actual behaviour and thought processes of programmers as they carried out their daily activities. By encouraging programmers to think about how they could improve their own interface to their computerized tools, and thereby to increase their productivity and enhance program reliability and maintainability, it naturally led them to more general considerations of improving everyone's interface to the machine. A book summarizing the first decade of this activity is that by Shneiderman (1980). Other work is cited in Case Study B: The Psychology of Computer Programming.

The Design of Man-Computer Dialogues

A landmark event in the consolidation and popularization of human-machine interface issues was the publication of a book entitled "Design of Man-Computer Dialogues" by James Martin (1973), one of the most widely published and influential consultants and lecturers in the data processing industry. The scope of his work includes the following:

- categorization of terminal operators
- alphanumeric dialogues, including natural language dialogues, programming dialogues, display techniques, and supporting hardware
- dialogues using sound and graphics, including the uses of pictures, the role of symbolic presentation, and the technology of voice answerback systems
- psychological considerations, including response time requirements, human channel and buffer capacity considerations, display encoding, and the role of creativity
- operators with training, including the totally naive operator, computer assisted instruction, information control rooms, and terminals for management
- implementation considerations, including control of user errors, techniques for dealing with failures, "bullet proofing" of systems, security and privacy, dialogue program generators, and simulation of the human-machine interface

Three other influential works of that period were a paper by Hansen (1971) entitled ''User Engineering Principles for Interactive Systems,'' the chapters on interactive graphical techniques and command languages in the first edition of the textbook by Newman and Sproull (1973), and a paper by Foley and Wallace (1974) entitled ''The Art of Natural Graphic Man-Machine Conversation.'' While Martin's work did much in acquainting the commercial data processing world with the issues and importance of good user interface design, the Newman and Sproull book and the two papers cited above helped to raise the human factors consciousness of the computer science academic community.

The Personal Workstation

Returning to system and technology development, we now turn our attention to the Xerox Palo Alto Research Center (PARC), formed in 1971. An incredible concentration of computer science talent converged on PARC just as the evolution of memory and processor technology offered new opportunities in computer design and implementation. This resulted by the mid 1970s in several major contributions (Pake, 1985; Perry and Wallich, 1985), although most were not published until late in the decade.

- Xerox developed the Alto, a prototype of a new kind of computer called a ''personal workstation'' (Thacker et al., 1979; Thacker, 1986), a computer intended for use by one individual with significant local processing power and memory, a high resolution bit-mapped display, a keyboard, and a pointing and drawing device called the mouse, which originally had been developed by Engelbart's group at Stanford Research Institute.

- Xerox pioneered the development of congenial graphical interfaces to such workstations and to applications such as text editing, creation of illustrations, document creation, and electronic mail which could be supported within the workstation (Lampson, 1986). These user interfaces incorporated various kinds of windows, menus, scroll bars, mouse control and selection mechanisms, and views of abstract structures, all presented to the user and integrated in a consistent manner.

- Xerox pioneered methods for the local area networking of such workstations (Metcalfe and Boggs, 1976; Lampson, 1986). The result was that users could have both the advantages of their own personal machines and the advantages of access to shared resources such as a central file system and high-speed printers.

It should be noted that other earlier computers, for example, the Whirlwind, the TX-0, the TX-2, the DEC PDP-1s, and the Linc (Clark, 1986), were often used as ''personal computers'' (Bell, 1986). However, it was only with the Alto and its successors that the concept of a computer which could be dedicated to the use of a single individual became technologically and economically realizable, although this was at first only possible in highly capitalized, advanced research and development laboratories.

The Dynabook

Perhaps the single most compelling vision amidst the excitement of the many new ideas and applications at Xerox was that of Alan Kay — his concepts of the ''Reactive Engine'' (Kay, 1969) and the ''Dynabook'' (Kay and Goldberg, 1977):

''Devices'' which variously store, retrieve, or manipulate information in the form of messages embedded in a medium have been in existence for thousands of years. People use them to communicate ideas and feelings both to others and back to themselves. Although thinking goes on in one's head, external media serve to materialize thoughts and, through feedback, to augment the actual paths the thinking follows. Methods discovered in one medium provide metaphors which contribute new ways to think about notions in other media.

For most of recorded history, the interactions of humans with their media have been primarily nonconversational and passive in the sense that marks on paper, paint on walls, even ''motion'' pictures and television, do not change in response to the viewer's wishes. A mathematical formulation — which may symbolize the essence of an entire universe — once put down on paper, remains static and requires the reader to expand its possibilities.

Every message is, in one sense or another, a simulation of some idea. It may be representational or abstract. The essence of a medium is very much dependent on the way messages are embedded, changed, and viewed. Although digital computers were originally designed to do arithmetic computation, the ability to simulate the details of any descriptive model means that the computer, viewed as a medium itself, can be *all* other media if the embedding and viewing methods are sufficiently well provided. Moreover, this new ''metamedium'' is *active* — it can respond to queries and experiments — so that the messages may involve the learner in a two-way conversation. This property has never been available before except through the medium of an individual teacher. We think the implications are vast and compelling.

A *dynamic medium for creative thought*: the *Dynabook*. Imagine having your own self-contained knowledge manipulator in a portable package the size and shape of an ordinary notebook. Suppose it had enough power to outrace your senses of sight and hearing, enough capacity to store for later retrieval thousands of page-equivalents of reference materials, poems, letters, recipes, records, drawings, animations, musical scores, waveforms, dynamic simulations, and anything else you would like to remember and change.

We envision a device as small and portable as possible which could both take in and give out information in quantities approaching that of human sensory systems. Visual output should be, at the least, of higher quality than what can be obtained from newsprint. Audio output should adhere to similar high-fidelity standards.

There should be no discernible pause between cause and effect. One of the metaphors we used when designing such a system was that of a musical instrument, such as a flute, which is owned by its user and responds instantly and consistently to its owner's wishes. Imagine the absurdity of a one-second delay between blowing a note and hearing it!

These "civilized" desires for flexibility, resolution, and response lead to the conclusion that a user of a dynamic personal medium needs several hundred times as much power as the average adult now typically enjoys from timeshared computing. This means that we should either build a new resource several hundred times the capacity of current machines and share it (very difficult and expensive), or we should investigate the possibility of giving each person his own powerful machine. We chose the second approach.

The Role of Artificial Intelligence

As Kay was prototyping his Dynabook, Nicholas Negroponte (1969) in the Architecture Machine Group at MIT was developing an even more radical view of the ultimate human-computer interaction:

Computer-aided design cannot occur without machine intelligence — and would be dangerous without it. In our area, however, most people have serious misgivings about the feasibility and more importantly, the desirability of attributing the actions of a machine to intelligent behaviour. These people generally distrust the concept of machines that approach (and thus why not pass?) our own human intelligence. In our culture an intelligent machine is immediately assumed to be a bad machine. As soon as intelligence is ascribed to the artificial, some people believe that the artifact will become evil and strip us of our humanistic values. Or, like the great gazelle and the water buffalo, we will be placed on reserves to be pampered by a ruling class of automata.

Why ask a machine to learn, to understand, to associate courses with goals, to be self-improving, to be ethical — in short, to be intelligent?

The answer is the underlying postulate of an architecture machine. A design machine must have an artificial intelligence because any design procedure, set of rules, or truism is tenuous, if not subversive, when used out of context or regardless of context. It follows that a mechanism must recognize and understand the context before carrying out an operation. Therefore, a machine must be able to discern changes in meaning brought about by changes in context, hence, be intelligent. And to do this, it must have a sophisticated set of sensors, effectors, and processors to view the real world directly and indirectly.

Negroponte goes on to describe the need for a rich language of interaction between human and machine and for the evolution of dialogues idiosyncratic to particular humans and particular machines and evolving based on the context of their past dialogues:

You are in a foreign country, do not know that language, and are in desperate need of help. At first your hand movements and facial expressions carry most of your meaning to the silent observer. Your behaviour uses a language of gestures and strange utterances to communicate your purpose. The puzzled listener searches for bits of content he can understand and link to his own language. You react to his reactions, and a language of pantomime begins to unfold. This new language has evolved from the mutual effort to communicate. Returning to the same person a second time, let us say with a new need, the roots of a dialogue already exist. This second conversation might be gibberish to a third party brought into the exchange at this time.

A designer-to-machine introduction should have a similar linguistic evolution. Each should track the other's design maneuvers, evoking a rhetoric that cannot be anticipated. "What was mere noise and disorder or distraction before, becomes pattern and sense; information has been metabolized out of noise" (Brodey and Lindgren, 1967). The event is circular inasmuch as the designer-machine unity provokes a dialogue and the dialogue promotes a stronger designer-machine unity. This progressively intimate association of the two dissimilar species is the symbiosis. It evolves through mutual training, in this case, through the dialogue.

Such man-machine dialogue has no historical precedent. The present antagonistic mismatch between man and machine, however, has generated a great deal of preoccupation for it. In less than a decade the term "man-machine communication" has passed from concept to cliché to platitude. Nevertheless, the theory is important and straightforward: in order to have a cooperative interaction between a designer of a certain expertise and a machine of some scholarship, the two must be congenial and must share the labor of establishing a common language. A designer, when addressing a machine, must not be forced to resort to machine-oriented codes. And in spite of computational efficiency, a paradigm for fruitful conversations must be machines that can speak and respond to a natural language.

With direct, fluid, and natural man-machine discourse, two former barriers between architects and computing machines would be removed. First, the designers, using computer-aided design hardware, would not have to be specialists. With natural communication, the "this is what I want to do" and "can you do it" gap could be bridged. The design task would no longer be described to a "knobs and dials" person to be executed in his secret vernacular. Instead, with simple negotiations, the job would be formulated and executed in the designer's own idiom. As a result, a vibrant stream of ideas could be directly channeled from the designer to the machine and back.

The second instruction overcome by such close communion is the potential for reevaluating the procedures themselves. In a direct dialogue the designer can exercise his proverbial capriciousness. At first a designer may have only a meager understanding of his specific problem and thus require machine tolerance and compatibility in his search for the consistency among criteria and form and method, between intent and purpose. The progression from visceral to intellectual can be articulated in subsequent provisional statements of detail and moment-to-moment reevaluations of the methods themselves.

But, the tete-à-tete must be even more direct and fluid; it is gestures, smiles, and frowns that turn a conversation into a dialogue. "Most Americans are only dimly aware of this silent language even though they use it everyday. They are not conscious of the elaborate patterning of behaviour which prescribes our handling of time, our spatial relationships, our attitudes towards work, play, and learning" (Hall, 1959). In an intimate human-to-human dialogue, hand-waving often carries as much meaning as text. Manner carries cultural information: the Arabs use their noses, the Japanese nod their heads. Customarily, in man-machine communication studies, such silent languages are ignored and frequently are referred to as "noise." But such silent languages are not noise; a dialogue is composed of "whole body involvement — with hands, eyes, mouth, facial expressions — using many channels simultaneously, but rhythmized into a harmoniously simple exchange" (Brodey and Lindgren, 1968).

Imagine a machine that can follow your design methodology and at the same time discern and assimilate your conversational idiosyncrasies. This same machine, after observing your behaviour, could build a predictive model of your conversational performance. Such a machine could then reinforce the dialogue by using the predictive model to respond to you in a manner that is in rhythm with your personal behaviour and conversational idiosyncrasies.

What this means is the the dialogue we are proposing would be so personal that you would not be able to use someone else's machine, and he would not understand yours. In fact, neither machine would be able to talk directly to the other. The dialogue would be so intimate — even exclusive — that only mutual persuasion and compromise would bring about ideas, ideas unrealizable by either conversant alone. No doubt, in such a symbiosis it would not be solely the human designer who would decide when the machine is relevant.

The elaboration of Negroponte's vision can be found in Negroponte (1975) and in the two decades of work of the Architecture Machine Group, now the Media Laboratory, of MIT, some of which we review in Chapter 14: Research Frontiers and Unsolved Problems. To date, much of the vision is still unrealized.

The Personal Computer

About the time that Kay was building and elaborating his Interim Dynabook, an article in Popular Electronics (Roberts and Yates, 1975) triggered a veritable revolution in the computing industry. The resulting personal computer not only increased the availability of compute power at an incredible rate, but also significantly

broadened the usefulness of the computer. No longer was it primarily the purvey of a technical and mathematical priesthood. Instead, there were now rapidly growing numbers of computer users who were doctors and lawyers, teachers and librarians, business people and shopkeepers. Some were professional users, some amateurs, some hobbyists. But independent of vocation or motivation, a common element among the new class of computer user is a need and desire for an interface that is more congenial, more forgiving, more "user-friendly" than that required by the mathematical and technical user of the past. The strength of this phenomenon resulted in the reception afforded the Apple Macintosh (Williams, 1984), which was the first commercially successful personal computer implementation of the Xerox-style human interface. (See also Case Study D: The Star, the Lisa, and the Macintosh.)

Studying and Modelling the Interface

In the late 1960s there were relatively few scientific and behavioural studies of interfaces, other than those of Nickerson, Sackman, and Yntema and their colleagues at Bolt Beranek and Newman, System Development Corporation, and MIT Lincoln Laboratory. The pace of effort began to pick up in the 1970s. An early and influential group has been that begun around 1971 by John Gould at IBM Research, Yorktown Heights, which soon grew to include Stephen Boies, John Thomas, and Lance Miller. One of their first contributions was to study the interface to Moshe Zloof's (1975, 1976) new concept of "Query by Example" before a single line of code had been written (Thomas and Gould, 1975).

Another influential group has been the Applied Information Processing Psychology Project of Allen Newell, Stu Card, and Tom Moran, begun at Xerox PARC in 1974. This approach grew out of a field which arose in the 1950s and 1960s and which is called "information processing psychology" (Lindsay and Norman, 1977), The approach is to build models of human information processing expressed as computer programs or as other formal descriptions or processes such as state transition diagrams or production rules.

Newell, Card and Moran developed a model of the human user of computer systems called the Model Human Information Processor (see Chapter 5: Models of Computer User and Usage) and a methodology for calibrating the model and applying it as predictive tool. Even though the resulting work, *The Psychology of Human-Computer Interaction* (Card, Moran and Newell, 1983), raises more questions than it answers, it is a landmark contribution to the field, for it is the first major body of work that attempts to develop an underlying applied science of human-computer interaction. A paper that places much of this work in its historical context is Card and Moran (1986).

A Developing Community of Scholars

By the late 1970s and early 1980s numerous other corporations were joining IBM and Xerox in mounting major efforts to study and improve the human factors of computing systems. Work also began on the academic front. In England, Professor Brian Shackel, who in the late 1950s began working on the ergonomics of computers (Shackel, 1962), founded in 1970 the influential Research Group on Human Sciences and Advanced Technology (HUSAT) at the University of Loughborough. Other prominent university scholars included Allen Newell at Carnegie-Mellon University, Don Norman at the University of California at San Diego, James Foley at George Washington University, Ben Shneiderman at the University of Maryland, Thomas Green and Max Sime at the Medical Research Council Social and Applied Psychology Unit at the University in Sheffield, England, and Phil Barnard, John Long, John Morton, and Patricia Wright at the Medical Research Council Applied Psychology Unit in Cambridge, England.

Communication among these individuals became easier as there were created in the 70s and 80s a series of forums for technical discussion, interchange, and publication among members of the profession:

- International Symposium on Man-Machine Systems, held in Cambridge, England, in 1969 (IEEE, 1969)
- International Journal of Man-Machine Studies, begun in 1969
- Software Psychology Society, based in Washington, D.C., which has met monthly since 1976 (Shneiderman, 1986)
- Technical Group on Computer Systems within the Human Factors Society, formed in 1971
- Conference on Easier and More Productive Use of Computing, held at the University of Michigan in 1981
- annual ACM Special Interest Group on Computers and Human Interaction (SIGCHI) Conference on Human Factors in Computing Systems, begun with the surprisingly successful 1982 meeting in Gaithersburg, Maryland
- journal Behaviour and Information Technology, begun in 1982
- IFIP Conference entitled Interact, held first in 1984 and again in 1987

- British Computer Society Conference entitled HCI, held annually since 1985
- International Conference on Human-Computer Interaction, held first in 1985 and again in 1987
- journal Human-Computer Interaction, begun in 1985

Recently, historical reviews of the field have begun to appear (Gaines, 1985; Shackel, 1985). The study of human-computer interaction has arrived. Now the really hard work begins.

References

Baecker, R.M. (1969). Picture-Driven Animation. *AFIPS Conference Proceedings* 34, 273-288.

Bell, Gordon (1986). Toward a History of Personal Workstations. *Proceedings of the Conference on the History of Personal Workstations*, New York: ACM, 1-17.

Bennett, John L. (1972). The User Interface in Interactive Systems. *Annual Review of Information Science and Technology* 7, 159-196.

Brodey, W.M. and Lindgren, N. (1967). Human Enhancement Through Evolutionary Technology. *IEEE Spectrum* 4(9), September 1967, 87-97.

Brodey, W.M. and Lindgren, N. (1968). Human Enhancement: Beyond the Machine Age. *IEEE Spectrum* 5(2), February 1968, 79-93.

Brooks, F.P., Jr. (1977). The Computer "Scientist" as Toolsmith — Studies in Interactive Computer Graphics. *IFIP Conference Proceedings*, 625-634.

Bush, Vannevar (1945). As We May Think. *The Atlantic Monthly*, Vol. 176, July 1945, 101-108.

Carbonell, J.R., Elkind, J.I., & Nickerson, R.A. (1968). On the Psychological Importance of Time in a Time Sharing System. *Human Factors* 10(2), 135-142.

Card, S.K., Moran, T.P., & Newell, A. (1983). *The Psychology of Human-Computer Interaction*, Lawrence Erlbaum Associates.

Card, S.K. & Moran, T.P. (1986). User Technology: From Pointing to Pondering. *Proceedings of the Conference on the History of Personal Workstations*, New York: ACM, 183-198.

Clark, Wesley (1986). The LINC was Early and Small. *Proceedings of the Conference on the History of Personal Workstations*, New York: ACM, 133-155.

Coons, S.A. (1963). An Outline of the Requirements for a Computer-Aided Design System. *AFIPS Conference Proceedings* 23, 299-304.

Culler, Glen C. (1968). Mathematical Laboratories: A New Power for the Physical and Social Sciences. Reprinted in *Proceedings of the Conference on the History of Personal Workstations*, New York: ACM, 1986, 59-72.

Davis, M.R. & Ellis, T.O. (1964). The Rand Tablet: A Man-Machine Graphical Communication Device. *AFIPS Conference Proceedings* 24, 325-331.

Davis, Ruth M. (1966). Man-Machine Communication. In Cuadra, C.A. (Ed.) *Annual Review of Information Science and Technology* 1, Interscience, New York, 221-254.

Engelbart, D.C. (1963). A Conceptual Framework for the Augmentation of Man's Intellect. In Howerton & Weeks (Eds.), *Vistas in Information Handling*, Vol. 1, Washington, D.C.: Spartan Books, 1-29.

Engelbart, D.C. & English, W.K. (1968). A Research Center for Augmenting Human Intellect. *AFIPS Conference Proceedings* 33, 395-410.

Engelbart, D.C. (1982). Integrated, Evolutionary, Office Automation Systems. In Landau & Bair (Eds.), *Emerging Office Systems*, Ablex.

Engelbart, Doug (1986). The Augmented Knowledge Workshop. *Proceedings of the Conference on the History of Personal Workstations*, New York: ACM, 73-83.

English, W.K., Engelbart, D.C., & Berman, M.L. (1967). Display-Selection Techniques for Text Manipulation. *IEEE Transactions on Human Factors in Electronics* HFE-8(1), March 1967, 5-15.

Fano, R.M. & Corbato, F.J. (1966). Time-Sharing on Computers. *Scientific American* 214(9), September 1966, 129-140.

Foley, J.D. & Wallace, V.L. (1974). The Art of Natural Graphic Man-Machine Conversation. *Proceedings of the IEEE* 62(4), April 1974, 462-470.

Gaines, Brian R. (1985). From Ergonomics to the Fifth Generation: 30 Years of Human-Computer Interaction Studies. *Human-Computer Interaction — Interact '84*, Elsevier Science Publishers B.V.: North-Holland, 3-7.

Gold, Michael M. (1969). Time-Sharing and Batch-Processing: An Experimental Comparison of Their Values in a Problem-Solving Situation. *Communications of the ACM* 12(5), May 1969, 249-259.

Grant, Eugene E. & Sackman, Harold (1967). An Exploratory Investigation of Programmer Performance Under On-Line and Off-Line Conditions. *IEEE Transactions on Human Factors in Electronics* 8(1), March 1967, 33-48.

Grossberg, Mitchell, Wiesen, Raymond A., & Yntema, Douwe B. (1976). An Experiment on Problem Solving with Delayed Computer Responses. *IEEE Transactions on Systems, Man, and Cybernetics*, March 1976, 219-222.

Hall, E.T. (1959). *The Silent Language*, New York: Doubleday.

Hansen, Wilfred J. (1971). User Engineering Principles for Interactive Systems. *AFIPS Conference Proceedings* 39, Fall Joint Computer Conference, Montvale, N.J.: AFIPS Press, 523-532.

IEEE (1969). *IEEE Transaction on Man-Machine Systems: Special Issue* , 10 Part II (4).

Johnson, T.E. (1963). Sketchpad III: Three Dimensional Graphical Communication with a Digital Computer. *AFIPS Conference Proceedings* 23, 347-353.

Kay, A. (1969). The Reactive Engine. Ph.D. Thesis, University of Utah.

Kay, A. & Goldberg, A. (1977). Personal Dynamic Media. *IEEE Computer* 10(3), March 1977, 31-42.

Knowlton, K.C. (1966). Computer-Produced Movies. *Science* 150, November 1965, 1116-1120.

Lambert, Steve and Ropiequet, Suzanne (Eds.) (1986). *CD ROM: The New Papyrus*, Redmond, WA.: Microsoft Press.

Lampson, Butler W. (1967). A Critique of "An Exploratory Investigation of Programmer Performance Under On-Line and Off-Line Conditions." *IEEE Transaction on Human Factors in Electronics* 8(1), March 1967, 48-51.

Lampson, Butler (1986). Personal Distributed Computing: The Alto and Ethernet Software. *Proceedings of the Conference on the History of Personal Workstations*, New York: ACM, 101-131.

Levinthal, C. (1966). Molecular Model-building by Computer. *Scientific American* 214(6), June 1966, 42-52.

Licklider, J.C.R. (1960). Man-Computer Symbiosis. *IRE Transactions of Human Factors in Electronics* HFE-1(1), March 1960, 4-11.

Licklider, J.C.R. & Clark, Welden E. (1962). On-Line Man-Computer Communication. *AFIPS Conference Proceedings* 21, 113-128.

Licklider, J.C.R. (1968). Man-Computer Communication. *Annual Review of Information Science and Technology* 3, 201-240.

Lindsay, P. & Norman, D. (1977). *Human Information Processing: An Introduction to Psychology*, Second Edition, Academic Press.

Machover, Carl (1978). A Brief, Personal History of Computer Graphics. *IEEE Computer* 11(11), November 1978, 38-45.

Martin, J. (1973). *Design of Man-Computer Dialogues*, Prentice-Hall, Inc.

Metcalfe, R.M. & Boggs, D.R. (1976), ETHERNET: Distributed Packet Switching for Local Computer Networks. *Communications of the ACM* 19(7), July 1976, 395-404.

Meyrowitz, Norman & Van Dam, Andries (1982). Interactive Editing Systems: Part 1. *ACM Computing Surveys* 14(3), 321-352.

Miller, R.B. (1968). Response Time in Man-Computer Conversational Transactions. *AFIPS Conference Proceedings* 33, 267-277.

Miller, R.B. (1969). Archetypes in Man-Computer Problem Solving. *IEEE Transaction on Man-Machine Systems* 10 PartII(4), 219-241.

MIT (1963). Sketchpad. "Reprinted in" *SIGGRAPH Video Review* 13, New York: ACM, 1984.

Myer, T.H. & Sutherland, I.E. (1968). On the Design of Display Processors. *Communications of the ACM* 11(6), June 1968, 410-414.

Negroponte, Nicholas (1970). *The Architecture Machine: Towards a More Humane Environment*, Cambridge, Mass.: The MIT Press.

Negroponte, Nicholas (1975). *Soft Architecture Machines*, Cambridge, Mass.: The MIT Press.

Nelson, T.H. (1965). A File Structure for the Complex, the Changing, and the Indeterminate. *Proceedings of the ACM National Conference*, 84-100. Copyright 1965, Association for Computing Machinery, by permission.

Nelson, T.H. (1973). A Conceptual Framework for Man-Machine Everything. *Proceedings of the National Computer Conference*, M21-M26.

Nelson, T.H. (1974). *Computer Lib* and *Dream Machines*, The Distributors, South Bend, Indiana.

Nelson, T.H. (1981). *Literary Machines*, Project Xanadu, 8400 Fredericksburg, #138, San Antonio TX 78229.

Newman, William M. & Sproull, Robert F. (1973). *Principles of Interactive Computer Graphics*, First Edition, 1973, Second Edition, 1979, New York: McGraw-Hill.

Nickerson, Raymond S., Elkind, Jerome I., & Carbonell, Jaime R. (1968). Human Factors and the Design of Time Sharing Computer Systems. *Human Factors* 10(2), 127-134.

Nickerson, R.S. (1969). Man-Computer Interaction: A Challenge for Human Factors Research. *Ergonomics* 12 (4), 501-517.

Pake, George E. (1985). Research at Xerox PARC: A Founder's Assessment. *IEEE Spectrum* 22(10), 54-61.

Perry, Tekla S. & Wallich, Paul (1985). Inside the PARC: The 'Information Architects'. *IEEE Spectrum* 22(10), 62-75.

Preiss, R.B. (1978). Storage CRT Terminals: Evolution and Trends. *IEEE Computer* 11(11), November 1978, 20-26.

Roberts, H.E. & Yates, W. (1975). ALTAIR 8800: The Most Powerful Minicomputer Project Ever Presented — Can Be Built For Under $400. *Popular Electronics*, January 1975, 33-38.

Roberts, Larry (1986). The Arpanet and Computer Networks. *Proceedings of the Conference on the History of Personal Workstations*, New York: ACM, 51-58.

Ross, Douglas (1986). A Personal View of the Personal Work Station: Some Firsts in the Fifties. *Proceedings of the Conference on the History of Personal Workstations*, New York: ACM, 19-48.

Ross, D.T. & Rodriguez, J.E. (1963). Theoretical Foundations for the Computer-Aided Design System. *AFIPS Conference Proceedings* 23, 305-322.

Rovner, P.D. & Feldman, J.A. (1968). The LEAP Language and Data Structure. *IFIP Conference Proceedings*, 579-585.

Sackman, Harold (1970). *Man-Computer Problem Solving: Experimental Evaluation of Time-Sharing and Batch Processing*, Princeton: Auerbach Publishers.

Scientific American (1971). *Readings from Scientific American: Computers and Computation*, W.H.Freeman & Co., San Francisco.

Shackel, B. (1962). Ergonomics in the Design of a Large Digital Computer Console. *Ergonomics* 5, 229-241.

Shackel, B. (1969). Man-Computer Interaction — The Contribution of the Human Sciences. *IEEE Transactions on Man-Machine Systems* 10 Part II (4), 149-163.

Shackel, B. (1985). Ergonomics in Information Technology in Europe — A Review. *Behaviour and Information Technology* 4(4), 263-287.

Shaw, J.C. (1964). JOSS: A Designer's View of an Experimental On-Line Computing System. *Proceedings — Fall Joint Computer Conference* 26, 455-464.

Shneiderman, Ben (1980). *Software Psychology: Human Factors in Computer and Information Systems*, Cambridge, Mass.: Winthrop Publishers.

Shneiderman, Ben (1986). No Members, No Officers, No Dues: A Ten Year History of the Software Psychology Society. *SIGCHI Bulletin* 18(2), 14-16.

Stotz, R. (1963). Man-Machine Console Facilities for Computer-Aided Design. *AFIPS Conference Proceedings* 23, 323-328.

Sutherland, I.E. (1963). Sketchpad: A Man-Machine Graphical Communication System. *AFIPS Conference Proceedings* 23, 329-346.

Sutherland, W.R., Forgie, J.W., & Morello, M.V. (1969). Graphics in Time-sharing: A Summary of the TX-2 Experience. *AFIPS Conference Proceedings*, 34, 629-636.

Thacker, Chuck (1986). Personal Distributed Computing: The Alto and Ethernet Hardware. *Proceedings of the Conference on the History of Personal Workstations*, New York: ACM, 87-100.

Thacker, C.P., McCreight, E.M., Lampson, B.W., Sproull, R.F., & Boggs, D.R. (1979). Alto: A Personal Computer. In Siewiorek, Bell, & Newell, *Computer Structures: Principles and Examples*, Second Edition, McGraw-Hill, 549-572.

Thomas, John C. and Gould, John D. (1975). A Psychological Study of Query By Example. *AFIPS Conference Proceedings* 44, 439-445.

Weinberg, Gerald (1971). *The Psychology of Computer Programming*, New York: Van Nostrand Reinhold.

Williams, Gregg (1984). The Apple Macintosh Computer. *Byte* 9(2), February 1984, 30-54.

Yankelovich, Nicole and Meyrowitz, Norman (1985). Reading and Writing the Electronic Book. *IEEE Computer* 18(10), October 1985, 15-30.

Yntema, D.B. & Torgerson, W.S. (1961). Man-Computer Cooperation in Decisions Requiring Common Sense. *IRE Transactions on Human Factors in Electonics*, March 1961, 20-26.

Zloof, Moshe M. (1975). Query By Example. *AFIPS Conference Proceedings* 44, 431-437.

Zloof, Moshe M. (1976). Query By Example — Operations on Hierarchical Data Bases. *AFIPS Conference Proceedings* 45, 845-853.

Chapter 2

The Socio/Political Environment

In this chapter, we address issues that fall outside of what is normally considered the user interface. Our concern is the interplay between the design of a system and the sociological and organizational context in which it exists.

The bulk of the literature on this aspect of computing looks outwards, toward the social impacts of technological change (Bannon, Barry and Holst, 1982; Bjørn-Andersen and Rasmussen, 1980; Gotlieb and Borodin, 1973; Kiesler, Sproull, and Eccles, 1985; Morgall, 1983; Kling, 1980; Zuboff, 1981; Marcus, 1983; Hirschheim, 1986). All this is descriptive in nature. Since our main concern is with design, we are most interested in developing a prescriptive understanding of these issues.

User interface design is generally thought of in terms of technical issues, such as comparing menu versus command-based interaction. Seen in a larger context, however, such issues are of only secondary or tertiary importance. Systems exist within a social/political, or organizational context. No matter how well the mechanics of interaction are designed, if a system does not fulfill its intended role and expectations within that context, it can fail. And since most organizations are made up of a number of diverse groups, each with its own (and often conflicting) agenda and expectations, there are a number of ways in which such failure can occur.

Tools are not neutral: they affect how work is done. When we design an information system, we are designing an organizational structure for doing work, not just a technology. But like a technology, if all components of the design are not carefully planned and considered, the success of the design is at risk.

An Introductory Case Study

Kling (1980) discusses a study, undertaken by Albrecht (1979), of a system for tracking cases in a southern court. It is an excellent example of why concern for socio/political issues is important to the systems designer.

The system was intended to serve two different groups of users: the court's legal staff and its probation officers. While both groups were employed in the same court and served the same clients, their objectives were different. Since the system did not take these differences into account, it failed.

The legal staff members were concerned that cases be processed through the courts in an orderly manner and emphasized due process. In contrast, the probation staff emphasized rehabilitating individuals to become productive and trusted members of the community. When the information system was being designed, each group proposed a reporting structure which minimized its accountability and maximized its visibility and possible control over its other group. An automated system, which included a compromise set of data, was built and operated for four years. During this time it was primarily used as a record-keeping system and rarely used to enhance the control of either group of court administrators. Finally it was removed, and the court reverted to a manual record-keeping system

Albrecht considered this information system to have been used as an instrument in the power struggle between the legal staff and probation staff. Neither group was able to gain sufficient power to force the other to submit to its form of measurement and management. Since neither group could tightly manage the other and thus provide ''objective'' data about the productivity and efficacy of court activities, the automated system was a sterile tool. This case also highlights the close coupling of management control systems and the exercise of power in organizations. (Kling, 1980, pp. 86-87).

The key point to recognize with this case study is that *the system would have failed regardless of how well the dialogues, response time, hardware, or documentation had been designed and implemented.* The basic flaw was that the conflicting goals of the users were not taken into account during the design process. As a result, it was virtually guaranteed that there would be no trust in the integrity of the data base. The problem was socio/political. The fatal flaw was at the organizational level and it could have been foreseen had a different approach to design been adopted.

This example compels us to start questioning our traditional technology-driven perspective on systems design. Technology can provide new options, but the fundamental problem is one of designing to reflect the social structures of the organization. The technology employed should be chosen and/or designed to support that structure. Technology should not be the tail which wags the organizational dog, and design methods which help minimize the danger of this happening are beginning to emerge.

Two Approaches to Social Analysis

One of the best introductions to the analysis of the social impact of computing was written by Kling (1980). While the article is too long to fit into the current volume, it is highly recommended.

In addition to an excellent review of the literature, Kling establishes some theoretical perspectives on the field based upon a body of empirical research. One of the main concepts of his analysis is the identification of two different approaches that has been taken in the literature.

The *systems rationalist* approach takes the perspective of rationalizing the introduction of technology on the basis of improved cost or efficiency of operation. It assumes that there is a problem in an organization and looks at the technology as a means of addressing the problem and then getting on with business. From this perspective, technology is a solver of problems, rather than a creator of new approaches, *per se*.

The *segmented-institutionalist* approach takes a broader stance. It assumes that organizations are characterized by factions and conflicts of interest. Technology, besides serving its purported role within an organization, also serves hidden agendas for the different segments of the institution, or organization.

The court reporting example that opened the chapter provides one example that can be used to illustrate the difference in perspective of these two views. In this case, a systems-rationalist view was adopted. Efficiency through having two groups with common clients share the same system dominated the design. The conflict between the two groups that corrupted the system would only have been considered by a segmented-institutionalist approach.

A current example results from the introduction of local area network (LAN) technology to interconnect personal computers in the workplace. The systems-rationalist would view this as an advance for two reasons. First, one central file server could be set up to service a number of PCs, thereby facilitating software maintenance and ensuring general access to software resources. Second, due to the existence of a remote file server, less expensive ''diskless'' PCs could be used in the network, thereby saving money, or enabling more people to have access to a PC.

However, from another perspective, this technological ''advance'' could have serious consequences. What the segmented-institutionalist approach might anticipate, is that the introduction of diskless PCs could result in a conflict between the interests of management and the PC users. By centralizing file service, management has also centralized control. Users may possibly no longer be able to determine what software is available nor how it is organized. They have less control over their own computing environments, and may even be susceptible to computer usage being monitored by management.

The problems that may result from these differences in perspective are not insurmountable. However, if they are not anticipated and taken into account as the technology is being introduced, serious problems may result.

Often there is a tendency to automate the work that we are able to do, as opposed to the work that is our primary concern. In a stock-broker's office, for example, it is more likely that routine tasks such as word-processing will be implemented *before* the introduction of a decision support system to aid in stock acquisitions. Routine, highly proceduralized tasks have been characterized as *Type I* by Panko and Sprague (1982) and Panko (1984), whereas non-routine, loosely structured tasks have been called *Type II*. One of the challenges of research in human-computer interaction is to develop a better understanding of problem solving and human needs in the performance of Type II tasks so as to better enable us to provide support for both types of work. This is one area where the introduction of expert systems may have a strong impact on the next generation of workstations (Luconi, Malone and Morton, 1986).

If we were looking at an organization which involved both types of work, the argument of the systems rationalist would be that even if we can't effectively automate the Type II tasks, by automating the Type I tasks, we may free resources to better address more complex Type II activities. In looking at another example from Kling (1980), however, we see that this need not be true, especially if explicit procedures are not introduced by management.

> If there is any kind of task for which computer systems ought to pay off, it is the support of routine operations such as billing and airline reservations. Most of the system successes reported by managers or designers of computer-based systems were written from a system-rationalist perspective. The typical report describes how goals were set and how the author and his co-workers successfully designed a computer-based system to meet them. All the drama focuses on the battles faced by the implementors in getting a "successful" system designed on time, priced within budget, and loved by its users.
>
> There are relatively few careful studies of computer use in organizations, and few of these focus on routine operations. The better quality evaluations are less triumphant and report complex or ambiguous results. Many routine systems, such as traffic ticket processing, do help increase organizational efficiency (Colton, 1978; Kraemer, Dutton & Northrup, 1980). Systems may fail because they are technically unsound (e.g., response time is too slow in a demanding decision-making environment) or because they do not contain terribly useful or accurate information (Kling, 1978). Most important, the criteria adopted for success may strongly influence one's evaluations. Laudon (1974), Colton (1978) and Kraemer et al. (1980) have all studied police patrol support systems that provide information about wanted persons, stolen property, and criminal records to patrol officers in the field. Colton and Kraemer et al. examined the use of these systems by patrolmen and found the systems to be "successful" with respect to two measurers: response time and job effectiveness. Colton contrasts a "successful" system in which the mean response time is 5-10 seconds with a nearly worthless system in which the mean response time was 10 minutes. Patrolmen made about four times as many inquiries per capita with the better automated system. Kraemer et al. found that police who used a local automated information system were much more likely to find people with outstanding arrest warrants and to locate stolen vehicles than were police who had access only to statewide and national systems. These are the kinds of internal efficiencies that systems rationalists identify as major values of computing use.
>
> However, as one enlarges the array of activities and subjects included in an evaluation, the picture can alter dramatically. For example, Colton also reported that the (ex)chief of the Kansas City Police Department at times lamented the enhanced efficiency of Kansas City's system in helping patrolmen find stolen cars, unpaid parking tickets, and unregistered vehicles. His feelings stemmed from the increased field stops patrol officers made for these relatively minor offenses, which displaced time from other important police tasks. Laudon adopted a frame of reference that included the network of criminal justice agencies from police through courts. He argued that the increasing success of police in locating stolen vehicles and citing minor traffic offenders further clogged the already jammed courts. Furthermore, Kraemer et al. found that at locally automated sites police were more likely to detain people who should not have been detained and to arrest people who should not have been arrested. (Kling, 1980, p. 83).

The Effect of A Priori Views

The examples discussed above, and papers such as Kling's, make the importance of social implications abundantly clear. But today, when the design of information systems is largely carried out by people with a technological focus, there are problems. To begin with, there is little in the educational background of the typical engineer or computer scientist that equips them to deal with these issues. To make matters worse, the literature in these areas is widespread and diffuse. (A look at the bibliography of Kling's 1980 paper is a good illustration of this.)

Before delving into this literature, the motivated reader should realize that there are some pitfalls that may only be evident to the expert. These are articulated in another excellent survey paper by Hirschheim (1986). This paper is highly recommended, and was not included as a reading only because of its length.

Hirschheim describes the literature as highly inconclusive. His major thesis is that the conflicting results encountered are the result of bias imposed by the *a priori* views of researchers. He identifies three basic stances which have served as the point of departure for the studies reported in the literature:

- *Optimist:* Sometimes referred to as the "technological imperative," this view sees technology as solving many of the problems that arise in a complex, rapidly changing environment.

- *Pessimist:* The subscriber to this view is concerned about how technology brings increased control, and degrades quality of life.

- *Relativist:* Between these two extremes is the view that the impact of technology can go either way, and that it is a matter of design (or lack thereof) and implementation which determines the actual effect.

Hirschheim's study focussed on office information systems, but his conclusions can be reasonably expected to apply in the more general context. What he does is use these three stances as a basis for comparing attitudes, positions, and results concerning a number of issues, including:

- productivity
- employment
- the nature of work
- communications
- quality of working life
- power
- personal privacy

These are some of the key factors according to which the social impact of computing is determined. The benefit of Hirschheim's survey is the guidance that it provides in seeing various authors' findings in these areas in a larger context.

Methodology

Understanding the social impact of technology is extremely problematical. How, for example, can one ever "prove" cause and effect relations given the complexity of organizational and social dynamics? And if we can't identify causes, how can we use analytical data for predictive and design purposes? Clearly, converting a concern about the social aspects of computing into a methodology for the design of socially responsible systems involves crossing some major methodological hurdles. It should not be surprising, therefore, that the papers by Kling and Hirschheim are greatly concerned with methodology.

The perennial problem in developing disciplines, however, is determining how to approach today's design problems while we wait for the discipline to mature to the point that reliable methodologies are in place. Clearly awareness of the issues and involvement of specialists trained in the social sciences provides a starting point.

Other methodologies are being suggested, however, that may provide a means of supporting a segmented-institutionalist / relativist approach. One, in particular, is included as a reading to this chapter. This is the excerpt from Klein and Hirschheim (1983). The basis of their approach is a group role-playing exercise. Each stake holder in the population being studied is identified and representative groups or individuals play the role of arguing and supporting that particular stake holder's interests. The underlying belief at play in this approach is that populations are driven by different groups pursu-

ing their individual goals, goals which are often different and in conflict with those of others. Due to its goal-oriented focus, the approach is said to be *hermeneutic*. The assumption is that if the players in the role-playing exercise are well trained and imaginative, the exercise will bring to light potential problems, conflicts and benefits while there is still time to correct them.

In the reading, the authors discuss the problems of identifying the appropriate predictor groups. They then work through an example in which the roles of a number of players are discussed:

- top management
- middle management
- clerks and their union
- technologists

In cases where this book is being used in a class situation, a highly recommended exercise is to undertake a similar role-playing exercise which covers some other domain of work. In the readings, there are a number of case studies presented. Boddy and Buchanan (1982) discuss the introduction of word processing into an engineering firm, and the automation of a biscuit making firm. The problems encountered in the two situations are typical of many real-world situations. Another such example is discussed in the reading by Markus (1983), which develops theories to explain resistance to the introduction of management information systems. In each of these cases, one can ask, "How could better design practice and methodology be applied to reduce the problems encountered? To what extent can approaches such as the role-playing exercise be applied?" Finally, after the Klein and Hirschheim (1983) reading, already discussed, we include the final chapter from an excellent book by Westin, Schweder, Baker and Lehman (1985). They take a *socio/technical* approach to the introduction of office technology, providing a guide to managing its people, organizational, and regulatory aspects. This is a view also developed in considerable detail in many of the references cited in the bibliography, especially those of Mumford.

Conclusions

We have seen a number of cases which illustrate that unless the real (inherently long-term) needs of the organization *and* individuals are taken into account, no amount of design effort at other levels will bring about an effective system. What is disturbing in the short-term is the general lack of training of technologists to deal with these types of issues.

While there is a large literature on the analyses of the social impacts of computing, there is little that specifically addresses the issue of design. What is clear is that we must exercise careful design and control over what technologies are used, how they are introduced, the structure of the target organization, and the design of the technology itself.

We have to adjust the current skewing of attention towards technological issues within the discipline of human-computer interaction, and take better account of these socio/political issues. There are clear educational, managerial, and methodological implications in this.

Readings

Boddy, D. & Buchanan, D.A. (1982). Information Technology and the Experience of Work. In L. Bannon, U. Barry, & O. Holst (Eds.), *Information Technology Impact on the Way of Life*, Dublin: Tycooly International Publishing, 144-157.

Markus, M.L. (1983). Power, Politics, and MIS Implementation. *Communications of the ACM* 26(6), 430-444.

Klein, H.K. & Hirschheim, R. (1983). Issues and Approaches to Appraising Technological Change in the Office: A Consequentialist Perspective. *Office: Technology and People* 2, 15-42 (excerpt).

Westin, A.F., Schweder, H.A., Baker, M.A. & Lehman, S. (1985). Office Technology and Managerial Excellence. In *The Changing Workplace: A Guide to Managing the People, Organizational, and Regulatory Aspects of Office Technology*, White Plains, N.Y.: Knowledge Industry Publications, Inc., 15-1—15-10.

References/Bibliography

Albrecht, G. (1979). Defusing Technical Change in Juvenile Courts: The Probation Officer's Struggle for Professional Autonomy. *Sociology of Work and Occupation* 6(3), 259-282.

Anderson, M. (1980). Human Factors Analysis of Business Computer Systems. *Proceedings of the 13th Annual Meeting of the Human Factors Association of Canada*, 62-67.

Attewell, P. & Rue, J. (1984). Computing and Organizations: What we Know and Don't Know. *Communications of the ACM* 27(12), 1184-1192.

Bannon, L. (1986). Issues in Design: Some Notes. In D. Norman & S. Draper, (Eds.), *User Centered System Design: New Perspectives on Human-Computer Interaction*, Hillsdale, NJ: Lawrence Erlbaum Associates, 25-29.

Bannon, L, Barry, U. & Holst, O. (Eds.) (1982). *Information Technology Impact on the Way of Life*, Dublin: Tycooly International Publishing.

Bikson, T.K. & Gutek, B.A. (1983). Advanced Office Systems: An Empirical Look at Use and Satisfaction. *Proceedings of the AFIPS National Computer Conference*, 319-327.

Bjørn-Andersen, N. (Eds.)(1980). *The Human Side of Information Processing*, Amsterdam: North-Holland Publishing Company.

Bjørn-Andersen, N. & Rasmussen, L.B. (1980). Sociological Implications of Computer Systems. In Smith, H.T. & Green, T.R.G. (Eds.), *Human Interaction with Computers*, London, Academic Press, 97-123.

Bowen, W. (1986). The Puny Payoff from Office Computers. *Fortune*, May 26, 20-24.

Carlopio, J. (1986). Macroergonomics: A New Approach to the Implementation of Advanced Technology. In O. Brown & H.W. Hendrick (Eds.). *Human Factors in Organizational Design and Management*, Amsterdam: North-Holland Publishing Company, 581-591.

Cass, C. (1985). Creativity and Automation. *Computer Graphics World*, November 1985, 33-36.

Chambers, A.B. & Negel, D.C. (1985). Pilots of the Future: Human or Computer? *Communications of the ACM* 28(11), 1187-1199.

Colton, K. (Ed.) (1978). *Police Computer Technology*, Lexington MA: Lexington Books.

Cullen, J. (1982). Impact of Information Technology on Human Well-Being. In L. Bannon, U. Barry, & O. Holst (Eds.), *Information Technology Impact on the Way of Life*, Dublin: Tycooly International Publishing, 73-79.

Davis, L.E. & Cherns, A.B. (Eds.) (1975). *The Quality of Working Life, Volume One: Problems, Prospects, and the State of the Art*, London: The Free Press.

Eason, K. (1982). The Process of Introducing Information Technology. *Behaviour and Information Technology* 1(2), 197-213.

Eason, K. (1987). *Information Technology and Organizational Change*, London: Taylor & Francis.

Fallik, F. (1987). *Managing Organizational Change: Case Studies in Ergonomics Practice* Volume 3, London: Taylor & Francis.

Giuliano, V. (1982). The Mechanization of Office Work. *Scientific American* 247(3), 148-164.

Gotlieb, C.C. & Borodin, A. (1973). *Social Issues in Computing*, New York: Academic Press.

Hedge, A. & Crawley, R.C. (1982). Employee and Organizational Responses to Information Technology: A Socio-Psychological Approach to Systems Design. In L. Bannon, U. Barry, & O. Holst (Eds.), *Information Technology Impact on the Way of Life*, Dublin: Tycooly International Publishing.

Helander, M. (1985). Emerging Office Automation Systems. *Human Factors* 27(1), 3-20.

Hirschheim, R.A. (1986). The Effect of A Priori Views on the Social Implications of Computing: The Case of Office Automation. *Computing Surveys* 18(2), 165-195.

Ives, B. & Olson, M. (1984). User Involvement and MIS Success: A Review of Research. *Management Science* 30(5), 586-603.

Johnson, D.G. & Snaper, J.W. (Eds.)(1985). *Ethical Issues in the Use of Computers*, Belmont, CA: Wadsworth Publishing Company.

Kiesler, S., Sproull, L. & Eccles, J.S. (1985). Poolhalls, Chips, and War Games: Women in the Culture of Computing. *Psychology of Women Quarterly* 9, 451-462.

Klein, H.K. (1986). Organizational Implications of Office Systems: Towards a Critical Social Action Perspective. In A.A. Verrijn-Stuart

& R.A. Hirschheim (Eds.). *Office Systems,* Amsterdam: North Holland Publishing Company.

Klein, H.K. & Hirschheim, R. (1983). Issues and Approaches to Appraising Technological Change in the Office: A Consequentialist Perspective. *Office: Technology and People* 2, 15-42.

Klein, H.K. & Hirschheim, R. (1987). Social Change and the Future of Information Systems Development. In R.J. Boland Jr. & R.A. Hirschheim (Eds.), *Critical Issues in Information Systems Research,* New York: John Wiley & Sons, 275-304.

Kling, R. (1978). Automated Welfare Client Tracking and Service Integration: the Political Economy of Computing. *Communications of the ACM* 21(6), 484-493.

Kling, R. (1980). Social Analyses of Computing: Theoretical Perspectives in Empirical Research. *ACM Computing Surveys* 12(1), 61-110. Copyright 1980, Association for Computing Machinery, Inc., by permission.

Kling, R. (1984). Assimilating Social Values in Computer-Based Technologies. *Telecommunications Policy,* June 1984, 127-147.

Kraemer, K., Dutton, W. & Northrup, A. (1980). *The Management of Information Systems,* New York: Columbia University Press.

Laudon, K.C. (1974). *Computers and Bureaucratic Reform: The Political Functions of Urban Information Systems,* New York: John Wiley & Sons.

Lucas, H.C. (1975). *Why Information Systems Fail,* New York: Columbia University Press.

Luconi, F.L., Malone, T.W. & Morton, M.S. (1986). Expert Systems: The Next Challenge for Managers. *Sloan Management Review,* Summer 1986, 3-14.

Malone, T.W. (1985). Designing Organizational Interfaces. *Proceedings of CHI '85,* 66-71.

Malone, T.W. (1987). Computer Support for Organizations: Towards and Organizational Science. In J. Carroll (Ed.), *Cognitive Aspects of Human-Computer Interaction,* Cambridge, MA.: MIT Press.

Markus, M.L. (1983). Power, Politics, and MIS Implementation. *Communications of the ACM* 26(6), 430-444.

Morgall, J. (1983). Typing our Way to Freedom: Is it True that New Office Technology can Liberate Women? *Behaviour and Information Technology* 2(3), 215-226.

Mowshowitz, A. (Ed.)(1980). *Human Choice and Computers* 2, Amsterdam: North-Holland Publishing Co.

Mumford, E. (1986). *Using Computers for Business Success,* Manchester: Manchester Business School.

Mumford, E. & Henshall, D. (1979). *A Participative Approach to Computer Systems Design,* New York: John Wiley & Sons.

Mumford, E., Hirschheim, R.A., Fitzgerald, G. & Wood-Harper, T. (Eds.)(1985). *Research Methods in Information Systems,* Amsterdam: North-Holland Publishing Company.

Mumford, E. & Sackman, H. (Eds.)(1975). *Human Choice and Computers,* Amsterdam: North-Holland Publishing Company.

Panko, R. (1984). 38 Offices: Analyzing Needs in Individual Offices. *ACM Transactions on Office Systems* 2(3), 226-234.

Panko, R. & Sprague, R.H. Jr. (1982). Toward a New Framework for Office Support. *Proceedings of SIGOA Conference on Office Information Systems,* ACM, NY, 82-92.

Pew, D. (Moderator)(1986). Socio-Tech: What is it (and Why Should We Care)? Introduction to panel discussion. *Proceedings of CHI '86,* 129-130.

Sandberg, A. (1985). Socio-Technical Design, Trade Union Strategies and Action Research. In E. Mumford, R.A. Hirschheim, G. Fitzgerald & T. Wood-Harper (Eds.), *Research Methods in Information Systems,* Amsterdam: North-Holland Publishing Company, 79-92.

Stewart, T. (1985). Ergonomics of the Office. *Ergonomics* 28(8), 1165-1177.

Turoff, M. & Hiltz, S.R. (1982). Computer Support for Group Versus Individual Decisions. *IEEE Transactions on Communications* 30(1), 82-91.

Van Cott, H.P. (1985). High Technology and Human Needs. *Ergonomics* 28(8), 1135-1142.

Westin, A., Schweder, H., Baker, M & Lehman, S. (1985). *The Changing Workplace: A Guide to Managing the People, Organizational and Regulatory Aspects of Office Technology,* White Plains, NY: Knowledge Industry Publications, Inc.

Zuboff, S. (1981). Psychological and Organizational Implications of Computer-Mediated Work. *CISR No. 71,* Sloan WP No 1224-81, Cambridge MA.: Sloan School of Management.

Information Technology and the Experience of Work

David Boddy and David A. Buchanan

Department of Management Studies, University of Glasgow, UK

INTRODUCTION

THE APPLICATIONS of information technology are described and analysed here in two case studies. The first case, completed in 1980, concerns the development of word processing in an engineering consultancy organization. The second, completed in 1981, looks at the application of computerized production measurements and controls in a biscuit-making factory.

Information technologies are distinguished from mechanical and electro-mechanical devices by their ability to combine the following features in single or closely linked pieces of equipment:

(1) capture information — gather, collect, monitor, detect and measure information;

(2) store information — convert information to digital form and retain it in some form of permanent memory which allows the information to be retrieved when required;

(3) manipulate information — rearrange and perform calculations;

(4) distribute information — transmit, move and display information electronically;

(5) control operations — which happens in three ways:

(a) the equipment gives the operator rapid and relevant feedback information to make control of the equipment or process more effective;

(b) the equipment is taken, under computer control,' through a predetermined sequence of operations;

(c) deviations from equipment or process performance standards are measured and corrective action initiated by the computer.

Information storage, manipulation and distribution happen inside the equipment, without human intervention beyond activating the procedures, and operate with high degrees of predictability and reliability. Information capture, the receipt and interpretation of distributed information, and operations control — all have different characteristics. They concern the links between the device and the world beyond it. They rely on conventional engineering technologies and on human intervention; they constitute sources of unreliability, error and flexibility; and they are areas of choice in work organization design.

The aim of this discussion is to generate tentative answers to the following questions:

(1) What factors influence management decisions to use informatioin technologies?

(2) What factors influence management decisions about the organization of work around the new technology?

(3) How do these decisions affect the roles of operators of the new technology?

Data were collected in each case from three main sources. Firstly, relevant company documents were studied. Secondly, semi-structured interviews were held with employees at all levels concerned with the new technology. And finally, the research findings were fed back to the respondents to check their accuracy, completeness and emphasis.

INFORMATION TECHNOLOGY IN THE OFFICE

THIS CASE STUDY concerns the development of word processing in an engineering consultancy firm. Word processors have three main components:

(a) a video-display screen with a keyboard;

(b) a central processing unit with internal and external memory; and

(c) a printer (called a 'daisy wheel' printer from the shape of the print element).

There are five distinct capabilities of word processing which are as follows:

Information capture: as the video typist (the term used here, in preference to 'word processor operator') hits the terminal keys, the words appear temporarily on the video-display screen and are sent by the central processor to the machine's storage device.

Information storage: text is stored either in the machine or on some form of portable storage medium (usually magnetic disc, tape or card) and the text can then be retrieved and reproduced any number of times without retyping.

Information manipulation: once stored, the text can be edited before it is committed to paper; the typist can correct mistakes as they appear on the screen and can edit the draft once the author has checked it.

Information distribution: information stored for one machine can be read, edited and printed on another compatible machine and text entered on one device may be transmitted by telephone line or other wiring directly to other machines.

Operations controls: all typing, or printing, is done under computer control; the typist gives the computer instructions on what to type and how to type it, by entering page format and other print instructions along with the text.

In larger installations, several typists can share one or more printers and one or more central processing units. These are called 'shared logic' systems, where the central processor controls the queue of materials waiting to be typed.

The organization studied in this case was a Glasgow engineering consultancy which had developed its own shared logic, word-processing system. The company employed about 500 people. Consultancy work was presented to clients in written technical reports, which usually had several authors and went through several revisions. Before the introduction of word processing, each group of specialist consultants had a secretary and one or two copy typists. Reports were typed on conventional electric typewriters; secretaries and copy typists worked close to each other and to the authors of the reports.

The company formed a 'Typing Services Working Party' in 1977 to examine the benefits of word processing. The minutes of the Working Party indicated that the decision to adopt word processing had been influenced by three factors:
(1) the objective of increasing typists' productivity and reducing the number and cost of the typing staff;
(2) the enthusiasm of two managers closely concerned with computing and typing for the word-processing technology;
(3) the need to replace obsolescent typesetting equipment.

Pressures arising within the company were more powerful than those arising outside. The decision was not prompted by competition and the equipment that was obsolescent in 1977 was still operating in 1980. The role of 'champions' or 'promotors' in stimulating interest in, and encouraging adoption of, technological change was a key factor.

The Working Party decided to establish two word-processing centres in which all the video typists would be grouped, with a supervisor in each. The centres were the responsibility of a Technical Services Manager, whose line of authority extended down through a word-processing Section Head, a Typing Services Co-ordinator and the two Supervisors to the nine video typists. This arrangement was strongly influenced by the perceived need to control more effectively the flow of work to and from the typists. Other advantages of grouping were easier training, flexible staffing, less cable and fewer printers. It was recognised that typists would lose contact with authors who would not easily be able to follow the progress of their typing through the system. This re-organization of the typists was therefore determined by management objectives for the control of typing work. There was nothing in the technology of word processing that dictated this pooling arrangement.

Copy-typing and word-processing staff, as a percentage of technical staff, fell from 8.3 to 4.5 per cent between December 1975 and June 1980; 28 typists worked for 338 authors in 1975 and 16 worked for 352 authors in 1980. The overall reduction in support staff, however, was small and their percentage of the company's salary bill did not fall. The typists' output increased dramatically. Copy typists produced 5.8 pages a day on average whereas the video typists produced 40.5 pages a day. The overall effect on typing productivity was difficult to assess. The typists' output had risen but the time that authors waited for reports to be typed was not reduced; they also felt that more time was spent correcting drafts.

The two centre supervisors and nine video typists were interviewed to discover how their jobs had been affected by the word-processing equipment. Their individual experience with the system ranged from three weeks to two years. All were internally recruited, trained copy typists. Training on word processing was informal and on the job.

In some respects, video typing was less skilled than conventional copy typing. Little or no paper handling was required. The keyboard touch was light. Corrections were simple and the fear of making mistakes at the bottom of a page, which slows the conventional typist, did not arise. The video typist did not have to be concerned about the paper edges and line lengths as the computer positioned text on the paper. The keys on modern terminals are closer together, involving less finger stretching, and the keyboard is flatter, more comfortable and less painful on the wrists. The terminals are quieter than typewriters and, although the printers are noisy, they were kept in a separate room. Through experience with a group of authors, the copy typist build up knowledge of their handwriting, technical terms and report-layout needs and preferences. The video typists in the word-processing centres could neither acquire nor exploit this knowledge.

But the video-typing job required more skill and knowledge than conventional typing in three respects. Firstly, the video typist had to learn the codes for formatting and editing text and be able to assess the appearance of printed text from the format codes attached to the input. As the system developed, this knowledge had to be updated. Secondly, the job required more concentration and was physically more demanding than conventional typing. Thirdly, the system editor on the computer could cause files to be lost and erase the work of others if not used carefully, thus much of the training concerned file management procedures. The overall pattern of skill and knowledge required by the typist had therefore changed.

Overall, the variety of the video typists' job was less than they had experienced as copy typists. Each video typist worked for several different groups of authors who had different report styles and preferences. In this respect, variety had increased. But the video typists spent almost all of their time in one location, entering and editing text. Most of the preparatory and auxiliary tasks concerning the operation of the printers, the collating and delivering of work to the authors, were carried out by the supervisors. The typists could vary their work by switching between input and editing tasks, and by dividing long and monotonous reports between them. But the copy typists could vary the pace and intensity of work to a greater extent. There were

usually know which typist was doing their work and the typists no longer controlled those aspects of the typing that were interesting to the authors: the amount and timing of the work done. The formal rules and re-allocation of control led the authors to the Supervisors and higher levels of management.

There were also physical and technological barriers between typists and authors. The typists were geographically remote from the authors, who did not know what the video typists' job involved and were uncertain about the capabilities and constraints of the new equipment. Rather than checking spelling and format problems with authors, typists would 'have a go' because corrections were easy. The capabilities of the equipment reduced the need to get the typing right first time.

The combination of these organizational, physical and technological barriers meant that authors and typists did not develop or retain the personal, informal working relationships of the previous copy-typing system. This loss of contact was regretted by both typists and authors.

INFORMATION TECHNOLOGY IN BISCUIT-MAKING

THE SECOND CASE STUDY concerns applications of computerised production measurements and controls in a biscuit-making factory. The organization studied in this case was the Glasgow branch of one of the largest biscuit manufacturers in Britain, employing about 2,000 people in 1981. The factory had 15 production lines, each making a different type of biscuit. This case concerns the 'Number 4' line which made one of the company's most popular and profitable products.

Management were constantly looking for ways to improve the performance of all the lines in the factory and the company had a specialist group whose function was to monitor developments in process control which could be applied in biscuit-making. Biscuits were made in three stages: mixing, baking and wrapping. The mixing stage was controlled by computer. Flour arrived in bulk tankers and was pumped into storage silos. Recipes for each biscuit-type were stored on computer paper tape. The required amounts and types of flour were pumped from the silos into automatic weighing vessels and the computer controls then fed the flour, along with the correct amounts of water and sugar, to the appropriate mixing machine.

The operators in the computer control room had an illuminated wall display called a 'mimic board', showing a plan of the process for each line. At the start of each shift, the 'doughman' (or mixer operator) checked with the control-room operators that the correct recipe tape was loaded and made sure that enough sundries — ingredients added in small quantities — were available. The doughman then pressed a call button to start the mixing cycle. When the computer had delivered the water and flour to his mixing machine, a light

natural breaks for setting-up the typewriter and contacting authors to clarify their requests. One video typist stated that "there is now pressure to keep working" and another said that she felt like a "zombie", constantly typing with infrequent breaks. The system was interactive, prompting responses from the typist, and the screen was always 'live'. The video typist was thus subjected to a form of machine-pacing and was likely to work for longer periods than a copy typist without a change of activity. Apart from lunch, the video typists had two official 15-minute breaks, in the morning and afternoon, and the lighting and seating in the centres were carefully planned.

Copy typists, working for one group of authors, normally followed a job through to completion. The video typists felt that it was satisfying, after they had done a long job, to watch the printer producing perfect copy; but this rarely happened in the video centres as successive drafts were often done by different typists. This loss of identity with the whole job was reinforced when a large job was divided among several typists, when the typist did not know the author whose work was being typed and when the typist did not know when she was typing the final copy.

The copy typists had dealt directly with the authors. To give a particular job priority was a matter for negotiation between the author, the group and the copy typist. These negotiations had become a major component of the jobs of the centre Supervisors, the Typing Services Co-ordinator and the Section Head. Although typists could share longer jobs, control over work scheduling passed to management, who acted as a buffer between typists and authors. The typists felt, however, that they had more control over the quality and appearance of the end product through the word-processing system. An item that was 're-typed' carried its corrections without the introduction of fresh errors, as may be the case with conventional re-typing of a document. Producing better quality reports was evidently a source of satisfaction.

Feedback to the video typist was limited because she could not see on the screen the precise format of the copy to be typed and had to judge the appearance of the printed text from the accompanying format codes. There was no instant 'hard' copy. The typist had to wait until the printout was complete to check that the text and format instructions had been entered correctly. The printers were in a room separate from the centres and typists did not always see their work being printed. The centre Supervisor often collated the printouts and delivered them to their authors. This lack of feedback on performance impeded learning the system. Feedback from authors was also absent when editing was not given to the typist who did the input.

Management tried to encourage interaction between typists and authors but the equipment and the change in work organization inhibited this. Authors were given written instructions which declared that all discussions about their requirements should take place with either the Supervisor or the Typing Services Co-ordinator. Negotiations over job priority often involved the Section Head and sometimes managers and directors. At this stage, the Supervisor would not normally know which typist was going to do the job. The instructions encouraged authors to contact their typists, but authors did not

came on to tell him he could start the mixer. The sundries (including salt, syrup and various chemicals) were added by the doughman during the process which was interrupted by the computer at the required times. Each mix took about 20 minutes, with three interruptions. During each mix, the computer refilled the storage units above the mixing machine and the cycle was ready to start again as soon as the previous mix was over. A dough sample was then passed through the oven to test it. If the dough passed the 'oven test', it was emptied into a trough and taken by conveyor to the cutting machine. The dough was flatted to the correct thickness by passing it through rollers, adjusted by a machine operator. The flat dough sheet then passed through a cutter which stamped out the biscuits. The biscuits were baked as they travelled on conveyor through a 100-metre-long oven for about 4 minutes. As they came out, an ovenman checked the thickness or 'bulk' of each batch. If the bulk was wrong, the ovenman would adjust the oven temperature to correct it. He could also control the colour and moisture content of the biscuits. Too much moisture reduced the shelf-life of the biscuits; too little made them fragile. After leaving the oven, the biscuits went through several loops on the conveyor to cool them.

The biscuits were next fed into an automatic wrapping machine which counted a pre-set number of biscuits, wrapped them and sealed the packet. Each packet then passed, still on the conveyor, over a checkweigher which pushed light-weight packets off the line. The wrapping-machine operator saw an instant digital display of the weight of each packet as it crossed the checkweigher. If the weight was wrong, she could adjust, within limits, the number of biscuits that the wrapping machine put into each packet. Summary information about packet weights also appeared on a video display unit in the ovenman's area. Packets were finally boxed and loaded on pallets for despatch.

To achieve the highest quality and lowest cost of the end product, therefore, several production variables had to be controlled, such as the composition of the dough, the biscuit bulk, shape, colour, moisture content and the final packet weight. The company's policy was to develop ways of controlling these variables by machine, and in particular by computer, to reduce human error and labour costs. Local management had considerable freedom to use the computerised systems they felt appropriate to improve productivity. Managers throughout the company, however, avoided the word 'computer' and used specific machine names or the term 'process control equipment'.

The company's first production computer was installed in 1971 to control the mixing process. The computer also recorded the amounts of raw materials used, which allowed management to accurately calculate stock losses; it also displayed information about faults in the weighing equipment and blockages in the pipework. Thus, the system had the information capture, storage, manipulation and distribution features discussed earlier. This is also an example of operations control by the computer, taking the equipment through a predetermined sequence, with human intervention restricted to activating the cycle and assisting the transfer of materials to the next stage of the process.

In this case, the jobs most radically affected by information technology over the past ten years in the biscuit factory were those of the doughman and the ovenman. The doughman was previously responsible for getting the flour, with the help of other manual workers. Mixing was done in open 'spindle' mixers, which were vats with devices resembling domestic food mixers. When he could see and hear the dough, the doughman could tell by the appearance, sound and feel whether it 'was too dry or too wet, or lacking some other ingredient, in which case he could simply add what was required. This job used to be done by time-served master bakers.

With the introduction of the computer, the doughman's job became repetitive, with a cycle time of around 20 minutes, and was classed as semi-skilled. His main tasks were now to start the mixing machine (by pressing a button when the light came on), to add the sundries when the computer interrupted the mix, to pass a sample of each mix to the ovenman and to empty the finished mix into the trough and onto the conveyor for the machineman. The mixing vessel was enclosed and the doughman had to leave it only to collect more sundries. When the mixing machine or any of its control gear failed, electronic technicians were needed to track down the cause and repair it. The doughman sometimes forgot to add the sundries, such as syrup or fat, and this was only discovered when the mixing was over or past the oven test.

The skilled and varied craft of the doughman had thus been replaced by the computer and management preferred the job title 'mixer operator'. The comments of some production managers illustrate this change:

There used to be more variation in the things they did. Now they seem to lose all interest. There are some who have been here longer than the computer and they've really switched off. I've seen it happening to new people coming in as well.

We found that one of the reasons they forgot to add sundries was that they were talking to 'visitors' from other parts of the factory. So now we keep people out of their area unless they're there for a reason.

It affects our ability to get foremen and managers from the operators. They don't want to get out of the rut.

The problem with the whole mixer set-up seems to be that the new generation of operators don't appreciate as fully as before the consequences of what they do. It's all so automatic, they have difficulty visualizing the effects of, say, half-a-minute extra mixing time on later stages in production.

Talking about their work and how it had changed, two doughmen stated:

It's very repetitive. The computer controls it. We just press the button. If something goes wrong, it's more difficult to fix.

We used to have much more humour. You had your own group of manual workers with you doing the manhandling and this gave a lot more fun. The computers make it much easier, but if it breaks down, we can't do it by hand.

It also takes the responsibility off us. They can't blame the doughmen. If we had to weigh it ourselves, it would be our fault if anything went wrong.

It's much less interesting, more routine, very little scope for human error now. Initially, it's more skilled, till you get to know the set-up, then there's a fair amount of boredom. Except when something goes wrong.

The ovenman was responsible for baking biscuits that had the correct bulk, weight, moisture content, colour, shape and taste. This was complex because action to correct a deviation from standard on one of these variables affected the others. The job, therefore, was to balance these biscuit features so that they were acceptable at all times. The training time for ovenmen was 12 to 16 weeks. Every mix had different properties. Some flours absorbed more moisture than others; some doughs were soft and others were tough. Constant checking was necessary to ensure consistency of output. The ovenman checked the biscuit bulk and weight manually, at least once during the baking of every mix, and checked their colour and shape visually.

Biscuits are sold in packets by weight, which is stamped on the packet. Legislation allowed the company to sell a small proportion of packets that were light in weight, down to a standard minimum. Legislation did not prevent the sale of heavy packets, which gave the customer free biscuits. The amount of excess biscuit going to the customer was called 'turn of scale'. This term reflects the time when biscuit packets were weighed by hand on a scale with a pointer which could be deflected from the vertical (turned) by heavy packets. A computer-controlled 'turn-of-scale package' was installed in the Glasgow factory in 1979 to reduce the turn of scale on Number 4 line, which was over 3 per cent. The conventional electromechanical checkweigher that it replaced worked slowly and kept no records of packet weights. Operators and managers knew whether packets were over or under weight but not by how much. The problem with the conventional checkweigher was that it did not give the operators direct and rapid feedback nor did it indicate the degree of deviation from performance standard.

The turn-of-scale package was developed by the company's engineers. For one line, the cost of the package was about £20,000 at 1978 prices; it consisted of four components:

(a) a checkweigher with a microprocessor controller;
(b) a mini computer which recorded the packets' weights and controlled the display of information;
(c) a visual-display unit to display packet weight information for the individual ovenman's line; and
(d) a printer with keyboard for requesting and printing out information.

In the new system, packets still passed over a checkweigher. The weight of each packet appeared on a light-emitting diode display on the front of the machine and the computer recorded the weights of all packets. The computer analysed this information in various ways. Management had access to production-performance information that was not previously available and production, quality control and cost-office records were produced automatically. The computer also gave summary information on the state of production to the ovenman through the video-display unit next to his oven-control panel. This information was updated every two minutes and included:

(a) the average weight and standard deviation of accepted packets for the past two minutes of production;
(b) a graph plotting the number of packets produced against standard weight;
(c) the number of accepted packets for the shift so far;
(d) the number of rejected packets for the shift so far; and
(e) the average packet weight for the shift so far.

Most of the deviations from standard were controlled by the ovenman who could change the characteristics of the biscuits being baked by carefully adjusting the oven-temperature controls. The turn-of-scale package gave him information that he did not have before, at a speed and in a format that enabled him to take rapid corrective action. The turn-of-scale package thus incorporated information capture, storage, manipulation and distribution capabilities.

The ovenman felt that the new system had reduced the pressure on him. When production was running smoothly, management kept out of his way. The new package was also used to settle disputes about responsibility for turn of scale; the ovenman felt that it protected him from unfair accusations. He also felt that the package had increased the challenge and interest in his job because it gave him a goal that he could see and influence. This was reflected in the bonus-payment system and he felt that he had the additional satisfaction of knowing that he was cutting waste and costs. One of the process supervisors explained the effects of these changes as follows:

There is now no need for a physical check. The new package highlights problems, making it easier to make corrections quicker. The operators are continually on top of the job. The pressures on the operators have been reduced. The package acts as a double check for the ovenman. It's an assistant, a second opinion. More people can now see what is happening and are aware of the state of production and level of performance. The checkweigher is an instant reminder of the need to take corrective action. If things start to go wrong, we can regain the situation faster. Before, those unforgiving minutes were lost. Another effect of this spread of information is that nobody can fiddle because everybody has a clearer idea of where the problem lies when things go wrong.

Commenting on how his job had changed, the ovenman said:

Management want a straight graph on the video, showing minimum turn of scale. We're working to finer tolerance now. That's what our job is really all about. The equipment does all the work and our job is essentially to make sure that it is doing everything correctly. But when everything is computer-

controlled and the computer breaks down, the manual skills will still be needed and there will be nobody around who has them. And when everything is interlocked, in the way that this plant already is, problems arise when things start to break down.

Technological innovation in the plant had led to more consistent output, quantity and quality, by reducing product-handling and the opportunities for human error. The turn-of-scale package was not justified beforehand solely on financial grounds. One of the main argument for its introduction was a 'theoretical' one, based on its potential to improve production control by generating performance information quickly. Turn of scale on the Number 4 line fell from 3.5 per cent in 1977 to 1.8 per cent at the end of 1980.

CONCLUSIONS

WHAT FACTORS INFLUENCE management decisions to use information technologies? Firstly, the role of promoters or champions in encouraging technological change was important in both cases. Internal pressures for technological change were thus more significant than events in the organizations' environments. Secondly, all the changes discussed were justified at some stage on cost and productivity grounds. Thirdly, there appears to have been a management desire to reduce human intervention and contribution by replacing people, their knowledge and skills with machinery. Along with the economic objectives therefore, information technologies were perhaps introduced to increase the predictability, reliability, consistency, controllability or manageability of operations. Fourthly, different management levels and functions appear to accept new technology for different reasons. Top management seek return on investment; middle management seek improved operating control; supervisors want smoother work flow, fewer problems and less frustration. The information that a computerised system produces can be used in different ways by production and quality-control management and by accountants.

What factors influence management decisions about the organization of work around the new technology? The re-organization of the typists into two word-processing centres was determined strongly and directly by management's perceived need to control the flow of work to and from the typists; weakly and indirectly, it was influenced by the technology of word processing. It was felt that typing support would thus become more flexible, with supervisors handling competing priorities for typing work between different groups. These advantages were felt to outweigh the problems created by the loss of contact between typists and authors.

Although the roles of individual biscuit-making operators had changed, the overall organization of their work remained substantially intact. Their case is however comparable with that of the typists in one respect. The equipment that gave the operators more control over the baking process also gave management more control over the operators. The doughman had less discretion and influence over the mixing process and any errors made by the ovenman were revealed faster than before.

How do these decisions affect the roles of operators of the new technology? The assumption, 'as technology does more, people do less' is not generally true. Technology can either replace or complement people. Robots and automatic washing machines replace, musical instruments and conventional metal-working lathes complement human abilities.

The ovenman's case demonstrates complementarity. The turn-of-scale package gave him accurate and rapid information about the state of production that enabled him to control the baking line more effectively. This is described as complementarity because:

(1) The ovenman still had to decide what corrective actions were necessary to control the line, using information not previously available.
(2) The information capture, storage, manipulation and distribution features of the turn-of-scale package helped him to improve performance in his area of discretion — operations control.
(3) The ovenman was given a visible goal that he could influence and which made his job more interesting and challenging.

The video typists demonstrate unfulfilled complementarity. The word processor is a tool that complements the skills of the typist in the presentation of text. The video typist can visualize, create and experiment with different ways of presenting a given piece of text. In the case described here, however, the form of work organization that accompanied the introduction of word processing disrupted this complementarity in the following ways:

(1) Although the typing operations were computer controlled, the information-handling features of the system gave the typist the ability to develop a new area of discretion — information manipulation.
(2) Typists were remote from authors who were not fully aware of the facilities and constraints of the technology.
(3) Typists were not able to develop and use knowledge of individual authors' needs and preferences.
(4) Control over work scheduling was transferred to management.
(5) Typists did not follow jobs through to completion.

So while the typists enjoyed working with the new technology, they felt that the work re-organizaton had considerably reduced their job satisfaction. The authors were also unhappy about the new arrangements.

The doughman suffered a radical loss of craft skills as the computer replaced the need for human intervention in the mixing process, leaving him with the 'residual' tasks of pressing a button to start the cycle, adding small ingredient quantities and emptying the dough out at the end of the cycle. Overall process control was supervised by control-room operators remote from the mixing area and the doughman was thus left with no area of discretion. This led to what may be described as a distancing effect which had the following

operations of biscuit baking;

(b) unfulfilled complementarity, where video typists were unable to fully exploit the information manipulation capabilities of word processing because of the form of work organization;

(c) replacement, where the craft skills of the doughman were made redundant with the introduction of computerised mixing control.

(7) The residual role of the operator in a nearly automated system can be a 'distanced' one in which:

(a) the operator has no understanding of the equipment and machinery;

(b) the operator cannot assist with repairs or give manual backup: and

(c) operators become apathetic, deskilled and unpromotable.

characteristics:

(1) operators had no understanding of the machinery or the process;

(2) operators could not visualize the consequences of personal action or inaction;

(3) operators could not trace sources or diagnose causes of process and equipment faults;

(4) specialised maintenance staff were required;

(5) there was no manual or mechanical back-up system;

(6) operators became bored, apathetic and careless;

(7) operators rejected responsibility for breakdowns;

(8) operators developed no knowledge or skills through their work experience that made them promotable, thus management lost a source of supervisory recruitment.

These may be features of many computerised and 'nearly automated' tasks. This distancing effect may be overcome, however, by reconsidering the organization of work around the biscuit-making process as a whole. One option would be the establishment of a 'line team' to replace the existing rigid and fragmented task allocations. It may also have been possible at an earlier stage of technological development to consider siting the computer mixing-control equipment in the mixing area, to be operated by the doughman. The point is that, as with the video typists, the information technology did not uniquely determine the organization of work that accompanied it.

Summary of Conclusions

(1) Promoters within organizations are a necessary prerequisite of process innovation.

(2) Information technologies are introduced to meet several management objectives concerning costs, productivity and system reliability.

(3) Different management levels and functions accept and use information technologies for different reasons.

(4) The organization of work around information technology is determined more by management orientations than by the technology itself. The two components of management thinking that appear to have the strongest influence in this respect are:

(a) the desire to reduce human intervention and error, and

(b) the desire to control work flow and operators more closely.

(5) Technology can be used either to replace or to complement human capabilities. The consequences of a particular application depend partly on the capabilities of the technology and partly on the way in which work is organized around the technology.

(6) The three applications described here illustrate:

(a) complementarity, where the ovenman was given information not previously available that enhanced his ability to control the

Social Impacts
of Computing

Rob Kling
Editor

Power, Politics, and MIS Implementation

M. LYNNE MARKUS *Alfred P. Sloan School of Management,*
Massachusetts Institute of Technology

*M. Lynne Markus specializes in
the organizational issues that
surround the use of advanced
information technologies.
Among these are the impacts of
computer-based technology,
resistance to systems,
requirements analysis for office
automation, structuring and
managing the information
systems resource in
organizations, and strategic
planning for information
technology. She also has
experience in organizational
development, primarily in
manufacturing and health care
organizations. M. Lynne Markus
is the author of Bugs and
Features: An Organizational
Perspective on Systems (Pitman
Publishing, 1984) and articles in
such journals as Human
Relations, Computerworld
Office Automation,
Organizational Dynamics, and
Computer Decisions. She is a
member of the editorial board of
a new journal on office
automation: Office Technology
and People.*
Author's Present Address:
M. Lynne Markus,
Alfred P. Sloan School of
Management, Massachusetts
Institute of Technology, E53-
311, 50 Memorial Drive,
Cambridge, MA 02139.

INTRODUCTION

No one knows how many computer-based applications, designed at great cost of time and money, are abandoned or
expensively overhauled because they were unenthusiastically
received by their intended users. Most people who have
worked with information systems encounter at least mild resistance by those who are designated to input data or use the
output to improve the way they do their jobs.

Many explanations have been advanced to account for people's resistance to change in general, to technological change
in particular, and most specifically to management information systems (MIS) implementation efforts. Some of these explanations are informal rules of thumb that practitioners rely
on in the heat of action; others are purportedly based on
social scientific theories or research findings. Some are said to
apply in every situation; others are contingent upon a variety
of prevailing conditions. Some are mental models that form
the basis for actions but are rarely articulated or explicitly
examined for consistency and completeness; others are more
formal models with clearly spelled-out connections. Familiar
comments regarding resistance are:

1. To avoid resistance, get top management support and obtain user involvement in the design process [16];
2. Technically sound systems are less likely to be resisted
   than those with frequent downtime and poor response
   time [1];
3. Users resist systems that are not "user friendly" (assertions
   by EDP equipment vendors);
4. All other things being equal, people will resist change (received wisdom);
5. People will resist an application when the costs outweigh
   the benefits (received wisdom).

Explanations of resistance are important because, however
informal or implicit, they guide the behavior and influence
the actions taken by managers and systems analysts concerned with implementing computer-based applications. The
premise of this paper is that better theories of resistance will
lead to better implementation strategies and, hopefully, to
better outcomes for the organizations in which the computer
applications are installed. This suggests the need to examine
commonly used explanations and the assumptions underlying
them in some detail.

*ABSTRACT: Theories of resistance
to management information systems (MIS) are important because
they guide the implementation
strategies and tactics chosen by implementors. Three basic theories of
the causes of resistance underlie
many prescriptions and rules for
MIS implementation. Simply stated,
people resist MIS because of their
own internal factors, because of
poor system design, and because of
the interaction of specific system
design features with aspects of the
organizational context of system
use. These theories differ in their
basic assumptions about systems,
organizations, and resistance; they
also differ in predictions that can
be derived from them and in their
implications for the implementation
process. These differences are described and the task of evaluating
the theories on the bases of the differences is begun. Data from a case
study are used to illustrate the theories and to demonstrate the superiority, for implementors, of the interaction theory.*

Critical examination of implementors' theories regarding the causes of resistance is a process that, according to at least one view of resistance (cost versus benefits), implementors themselves may be expected to resist. Such examination is hard work, and the examiner runs the risk of discovering (a) that his or her mental models are just fine, in which case the effort appears wasted, or (b) that the explanations need changing, which is uncomfortable and requires more hard work. In addition, it is not likely that the commonly held heuristics mentioned earlier (e.g., top management support) can be very far from wrong: in the first place, there is some academic research to support each one of them, and second, many analysts and managers have found that the heuristics have prevented them from making blunders in everyday situations. Consequently, many readers may decide that the uncertain benefits of examining their personal models of resistance are outweighed by the costs of doing so. This paper is written either for those who compute the costs and benefits differently or for those whose behavior is describable by a different explanation of resistance to change.

The argument of the paper follows this format: Three basic theories of resistance are presented and contrasted in terms of their underlying assumptions about information systems, organizations, and resistance itself. Several bases for evaluating the theories are enumerated, including the applicability of basic assumptions, the accuracy of predictions drawn from the theories, and the utility for implementors of the strategies and prescriptions derived from the theories. The paper then proceeds to evaluate the theories using logic and the limited data of a single case. The paper concludes with recommendations for implementors.

TYPES OF THEORIES

Kling [13] has provided a very helpful starting point for examining theories of resistance. He identified six distinct theoretical perspectives: Rational, Structural, Human Relations, Interactionist, Organizational Politics, and Class Politics. Kling shows how these perspectives differ on a variety of dimensions, such as their view of technology and of the social setting into which it is introduced, their key organizing concepts, their ideologies of the workplace and of "good" technology, and their implied theories of the dynamics of technical diffusion. For ease of comparison, he groups the first three perspectives into the category of Systems Rationalism and the latter three into Segmented Institutionalism.

This paper builds upon Kling's work by exploring different theoretical perspectives as they relate to one small aspect of computing in organizational life—the introduction and implementation of computer-based information systems, and the human resistance that so often accompanies them. Since this paper emphasizes the perspectives from the viewpoint of their implications for action, that is, for the implementation strategies of managers and systems analysts, rather than of their theoretical differences per se, this paper may group Kling's perspectives differently while liberally drawing on his insights.

Three Theories

An implementor trying to decide what to do about resistance of individuals or organizational subunits may hold one of three divergent theories about why that resistance occurred. First, the person or subunit may be believed to have resisted because of factors internal to the person or group. These factors may be common to all persons and groups or unique to the one being examined. Examples of explanations compatible with this theory are: people resist all change; people with

analytic cognitive styles accept systems, while intuitive thinkers resist them.

Second, the person or group may be believed to have resisted because of factors inherent in the application or system being implemented. Examples of compatible explanations are people resist technically deficient systems, systems that are not ergonomically designed, and systems that are not user friendly. A fair amount of research has been done to support the contention that technical and human factors problems are associated with resistance and system failure. For example, Ginzberg [6] reviewed much of the (then) existing literature on OR/MS/MIS research and noted that several studies identified technical problems as a factor related to system failure (over 100 factors were mentioned at least once in the studies reviewed). Alter [1] studied 56 systems and reported that technical problems were related to implementation problems in several cases.

These two theories are clearly divergent, because the first assumes that a person's (group's) behavior is determined internally, and the second assumes that behavior is determined externally by the environment or by technology. Nevertheless, implementors often implicitly hold both theories simultaneously, believing that behavior is determined both from within and from without. An example of such a compound theory is: there is always a tendency for people to resist systems, but, other things being equal, they are less likely to resist ones that are well designed.

The third theory holds that people or groups resist systems because of an interaction between characteristics related to the people and characteristics related to the system. This theory is difficult to define, but easier to describe. The theory is not the same as a simultaneous belief in the two previously mentioned theories. The operant word in the definition is "interaction." Examples of explanations derived from the interaction theory are: systems that centralize control over data are resisted in organizations with decentralized authority structures, systems that alter the balance of power in organizations will be resisted by those who lose power and accepted by those who gain it, and resistance arises from the interaction of technical design features of systems with the social context in which the systems are used.

Several distinct variations of the interaction theory can be identified. One, which may be called the sociotechnical variant, focuses on the distribution of responsibility for organizational tasks across various roles and on the work-related communication and coordination around this division of labor. New information systems may prescribe a division of roles and responsibilities at variance with existing ones; they may structure patterns of interaction that are at odds with the prevailing organizational culture. In this light, systems can be viewed as a vehicle for creating organizational change. The greater the implied change, the more likely the resistance. Similar articulations of a variant of the interaction theory can be found in Keen [9], Ginzberg [7], and Kling [13].

It should be noted that this explanation identifies neither the system nor the organizational setting as the cause of resistance, but their interaction. The system-determined theory would predict that a given system be accepted or resisted in every setting because of its design features. The interaction theory can explain different outcomes for the same system in different settings. Similarly, the people-determined theory would predict the rejection of all systems in a setting in which any one system is resisted. The interaction theory can explain different responses by the same group of users to different settings. Compared with a concatenated people-plus-system-determined theory, the interaction theory allows for more precise explanation and predictions of resistance.

A second variant of the interaction theory can be called the political version. Here, resistance is explained as a product of the interaction of system design features with the intraorganizational distribution of power, defined either objectively, in terms of horizontal or vertical power dimensions, or subjectively, in terms of symbolism. The appendix provides additional details on the political variant of the interaction theory and compares it briefly with other variants. The case analysis given in this paper employs the political variant exclusively.

How are we to evaluate these theories? This is a difficult thing to do, if for no other reason than that there are several ways to do it, each of which may yield different results. Scientists are generally agreed that theories cannot be tested directly, which in our case means that it is impossible to say without doubt that people resist computer applications because of internal factors, external factors, or interaction effects. But the basic assumptions underlying the theories can be examined and compared with facts in the "real world," predictions derived from theories can be tested against observed occurrences, and the implications for action derived from theories can be tested for their usefulness to implementors. This last test may be conducted indepenently of the first two, and implementors may prefer this. Because this paper assumes that good implementation strategies derive from good theories, we attempt to address all three types of evaluations.

BASIC ASSUMPTIONS OF THE THEORIES

In order to perform the first type of evaluation, it is necessary to identify the assumptions that underlie the theories. Kling's list of theoretical perspectives yields two that are especially relevant for comparing theories of resistance with computer-based applications: assumptions about the nature of technology (in this case, information systems) and assumptions about the nature of the setting in which the applications are introduced. A third assumption can be added—beliefs about the nature of resistance. The first two dimensions, the people-determined and system-determined theories of resistance, are similar and easily contrasted with the interaction theory.

Assumptions about Information Systems

Information systems can be described and categorized in many ways: by type of processing technology—interactive or batch; by type of data (numbers, text, graphics, audio, video); by degree of centralization, distribution, or decentralization. One analytic scheme that proves especially fruitful for examining resistance is that of system "purpose," which refers to the intentions of system designers. Purpose is a tricky thing to pin down, because systems can be viewed from many angles, and users may describe a system's purpose differently than designers. Rather than haggle about whose view is right, one can infer system purpose from system design features and other clues to the designer's goals, values, and intentions.

Generally speaking, system purposes can be lumped into two classes, depending upon whether the purposes are consistent with the Rational Theory of Management. Very briefly summarized, the Rational Theory of Management holds that organizations have goals and that they behave in ways that are consistent with achieving these goals. For many businesses, a major goal is to achieve a specified profit subject to certain constraints. System purposes that are consistent with the Rational Theory are: to rationalize work (achieve predictable outputs with consistent units of input—a goal of many operational systems), to enhance managerial decision-making and planning, to control and motivate the performance of employees toward agreed-upon goals, and to improve communication and coordination among people in the organization or between the organization and aspects of its environment (customers, suppliers, competitors, etc.).

Without denying the existence of these Rational purposes for systems, some researchers and theoreticians have pointed out that other purposes of systems can be identified. Kling [10] and Markus and Pfeffer [19] have described systems whose purpose is to appear as though they were intended to rationalize work or to improve decision-making without having any real impact on organizational procedures or outcomes. Systems with this purpose can be useful in attracting outside funding or in discouraging external intervention. Another non-Rational purpose of systems is to change the balance of power inside a firm. The system described later in this paper can be argued to have had the purpose of creating a power shift among organizational subunits, although great pains were taken to make the system appear as if the only motivations for it were Rational ones. Still another non-Rational purpose is to gain control over or reduce dependence on members of a different occupational group. Noble [22] has described particular designs of numerically controlled machine tools whose purpose, he argues, was for managers to wrest control over production from the hands of shop floor machinists. These purposes are not consistent with the Rational Theory, and hence are called non-Rational; there is considerable evidence to suggest that at least some systems are partly, if not totally, intended to achieve non-Rational purposes [12, 13].

Assumptions about Organizational Contexts of Use

The organizations in which information systems are used can be described by

Structure: functional, divisional, matrix, centralized, decentralized;
Culture: power-oriented, cooperative, Theory Z;
Employment contracts: professional, bureaucratic, semiprofessional.

For purposes of understanding resistance, it is most useful to describe organizations in terms of the degree to which the people and subunits affected by the proposed information system are believed to have congruent goals and values or divergent ones.

The view of organizations that most frequently coexists with the Rational Theory of Management and with beliefs in the Rational purposes of information systems is that all organizational members share common goals for the organization and that, generally speaking, they will collaborate to achieve these objectives. In contrast, the non-Rational view assumes that different individuals or subgroups in the organization have different objectives depending upon their location in the hierarchy and that, in general, they can be expected to try to achieve these local goals rather than global organizational goals whenever differences exist. Some empirical work has described the existence of competing intraorganizational goal systems (Dalton [5] and Crozier [4] are classics), and analysts of the "class politics" persuasion take chronic conflicts of interest between workers and managers as an article of faith [3]. Thus, there is reason to believe that, at least in some organizations at certain times, there are situations that do not conform to the Rational perspective.

Assumptions about the Nature of Resistance

Quite apart from one's view of the cause of resistance, people can hold different assumptions about the nature of resistance and the role it plays in organizations. As used in this paper, resistance is defined as behaviors intended to prevent the implementation or use of a system or to prevent system designers from achieving their objectives. However, careful inspection of the trade press and even some MIS scientific literature will reveal that the term is also applied to behaviors that may not have these intentions. For example, the label "resistance" is frequently applied to all cases of nonuse of a system, even when nonuse may reflect ignorance of the system's existence, inadequate training in system operation, or personal fear of the computer. This author would make the following distinction: where one individual's use of a system is not critical to the operation of a system, that individual's choice not to use the system cannot be considered resistance. Data entry is a use critical to the operation of a system; use of a decision support system to evaluate a stock portfolio by one analyst in a department of 20 is not. Resistance is easiest to identify when a person engages in behavior that may result in the disruption or removal of a system that is interdependently used by others as well as by that person.

Social scientists are justifiably leery of any concept that requires an attribution of intention, for two reasons. First, behaviors can be observed, but intentions cannot. Second, the act of attributing intention often indicates more about the person doing the attributing than about the person to whom the intention is attributed. In other words, many people who identify a behavior as resistance are really saying, "they are not doing things the way I want them to." This implies that resistance is a relative rather than an absolute behavior. It can only be defined in the context of two or more parties, each with desires and intentions. Party A intends to introduce a change of certain design; party B intends to prevent this from happening. Consequently, resistance can only be believed to be bad or undesirable if the intentions of the designer or implementor are accepted as good or desirable.

In the people-determined and the system-determined theories of resistance, the objectives and intentions of designers and implementors are never identified or analyzed. The implicit assumptions are either that designers' objectives are good, or that, whether good or bad, the intended users of a system do or should accept these objectives. Consequently, both of these theories tend to regard resistance as a negative result, which must be avoided or overcome.

In contrast, the interaction theory does not examine resistance out of the context of designer's intentions. The interests and intentions of both users and designers are identified and compared. When these interests are very similar, resistance rarely occurs. As the difference between their interests widens, the possibility of resistance increases. Resistance is viewed as neither good nor bad, unless you align yourself with the interests of either party. Resistance can be destructive, because it generates conflict and ill-will and consumes time and attention. But resistance can also be functional for organizations, by preventing the installation of systems whose use might have on-going negative consequences (e.g., stress, turnover, reduced performance).

Table I summarizes the underlying assumptions about information systems, organizations, and resistance for each of the three theories. One basis for evaluating the theories is the degree to which data from real-world cases can be found to be consistent with the assumptions of the theories. If the assumptions are shown to be unrealistic or inoperative in natural settings, the theories may be rejected on this account. One case study from the author's research is presented to illustrate the application of the theories and to serve as a basis for preliminary evaluation.

Background of the FIS Case Study

The methodology employed in this case research study was historical reconstruction of the initiation, design process, design content, installation, and use of information systems in large manufacturing firms [18]. Sources of data included interviews with over 30 designers and users of the systems and documentary evidence about the systems and the organizations. The documentary evidence included corporate annual reports (spanning, in the case of a financial information system (FIS), 15 years from 1964 to 1979), organizational charts, system training manuals and design documents, and internal correspondence about the systems. Our account is organized

TABLE I. Theories of Resistance: Underlying Assumptions.

	People-Determined	System-Determined	Interaction Theory
Cause of resistance	Factors internal to people and groups	System factors such as technical excellence and ergonomics	Interaction of system and context of use
	Cognitive style Personality traits Human nature	Lack of user-friendliness Poor human factors Inadequate technical design or implementation	*Sociotechnical variant*: Interaction of system with division labor *Political variant*: Interaction of system with distribution of intra-organizational power
Assumptions about purposes of information systems	Purposes of systems are consistent with Rational Theory of Management, can be excluded from further consideration	Purposes of systems are consistent with Rational Theory of Management, can be excluded from further consideration	*Sociotechnical variant*: Systems may have the purpose to change organizational culture, not just workflow *Political variant*: Systems may be intended to change the balance of power
Assumptions about organizations	Organizational goals shared by all participants	Organizational goals shared by all participants	*Sociotechnical variant*: Goals conditioned by history *Political variant*: Goals differ by organizational location; conflict is endemic
Assumptions about resistance	Resistance is attribute of the intended system user; undesirable behavior	Resistance is attribute of the intended system user; undesirable behavior	Resistance is a product of the setting, users, and designers; neither desirable nor undesirable

as follows. The system is briefly described. Then the context of system use is examined to see whether the three theories apply. First, are there differences between resistors and non-resistors? Second, are there technical problems with the system? Third, what is the political context of system use? Subsequently, we evaluate the theories in the light of case data.

The FIS System

A financial information system collects and summarizes financial data for the Golden Triangle Corporation (GTC) (see Figure 1). The inputs to the system are transactions involving revenues and expenditures, assets and liabilities. The outputs are monthly profit and loss statements for each division and for the Corporation as a whole; balance sheets are produced by the system. The information managed by FIS is primarily used for external reporting purposes (to the SEC), although profit and loss information is relevant to managerial decision-making.

Obviously, financial reporting was not a new function at GTC, but FIS, installed in 1975, incorporated some innovative features. Prior to FIS, divisional accountants collected and stored transaction data however they saw fit, but reported summary data to corporate accountants in a standardized format (see Figure 2). With FIS, divisional accountants entered their transactions into the system (identified and retrievable by a 24-digit account code) which specified the type of transaction (asset-office furniture, expense-travel) and place of origin (group, division, plant). FIS automatically summarized these data into reports for corporate accountants and for the relevant division (see Figure 3).

The idea for FIS originated in the corporate accounting department around 1971. A task force was formed to evaluate the need for such a system and to estimate its costs and benefits. This task force was composed entirely of people from within the corporate accounting group, some of whom had considerable data processing experience.

In 1972, after the necessary investigations and approvals, the task force arranged for the purchase of a financial accounting package from a software vendor (much to the chagrin of GTC's internal data processing department who would have preferred to build it themselves). The package purchased was designed so that it mirrored almost exactly the way in which financial accounting was then performed at GTC (see Figure 2), except that formerly manual databases were computerized, inconsistent summarization procedures were standardized, and consolidation was automated. Nevertheless, the FIS task force decided to modify the package, ostensibly to make use of modern database management techniques. In the process of modification, however, which took over 2½ years, the design team also replaced separate divisional databases with a single corporate database (see Figure 3).

The task force members did not solicit information from divisional accountants about the design of FIS until 1974, when it was time to set up the database. Divisions were, however, invited to attend presentations describing the need for FIS and the benefits to be derived from it. Implementation of the system was to be done in phases. FIS task force members had decided to solicit a volunteer for the first division to "go up" on FIS. After the initial division had found it workable, the other divisions would be required to use it. FIS was meant to be the corporate financial system.

Resistance to FIS

The largest division of GTC volunteered to pioneer FIS in January 1975. In October 1975, an accountant from this division wrote a memo complaining that

...Except for providing more detailed information, the FIS system has not been beneficial to us.

In response to complaints from this person and other individuals in several divisions, a study team was created to explore problems related to "system inefficiency." The study team

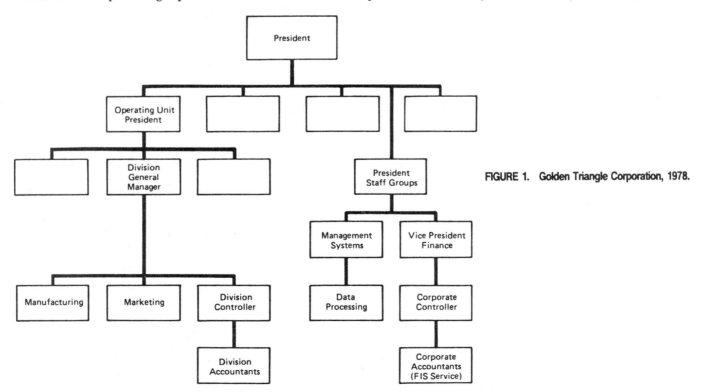

FIGURE 1. Golden Triangle Corporation, 1978.

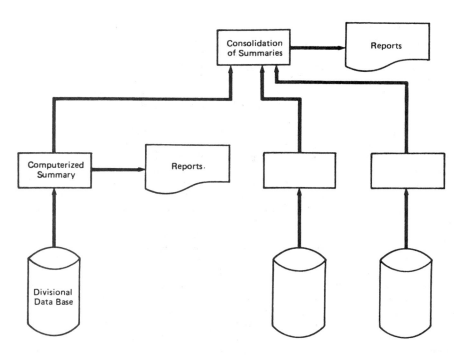

FIGURE 2. FIS Purchased Package Design.

met for several months and made technical recommendations to the data processing department. These changes proceeded slowly, and were set back in early 1977, when the data processing project leader quit.

In the meantime, other divisions had started up on the new system; all major divisions were using FIS by the end of 1975. This was surprising in light of the problems experienced by the initial FIS-using division, especially since participation in the system was supposed to be voluntary. Many accountants on the central corporate staff later pointed to this fact with pride as evidence of the success of FIS, but one person explained the incongruity as follows:

Participation was voluntary on the surface, but there was a hidden inducement to participate. Those who wanted to wait to join FIS could do so, but they had to provide the same information manually. This would have been quite burdensome. So it really wasn't all that voluntary.

There is evidence that later divisional users were no happier about the new system than the original division. One division kept on using its old accounting methods after it started using FIS, even though this required twice the effort. There were frequent discrepancies between the two sets of books, and the staff of this division claimed that its system (thick manual ledger books!) was accurate and that FIS was at fault. The staff of this "recalcitrant" division persisted in this behavior for two years, until a member of the corporate accounting staff actually carried the old ledgers away. Some divisional accountants also admitted to slight "data fudging" to circumvent the technical and human factors problems with the system.

If it turned out that an account we needed had not already been defined to FIS, rather than wait for the special account creation run, we might change the plant code, just to get the data in. After all, we knew what the numbers really were!

At the same time, corporate accountants, who used the system for corporate consolidation, were delighted with it. FIS automatically performed tedious tasks of calculation and re-

porting that they had formerly done by hand. In addition, FIS provided several totally unanticipated benefits for them, such as automated tax accounting. Corporate accountants could not account for the resistance of the divisions' staff members. They bitterly denounced the "troublemakers." One said:

I can't understand why the divisions don't like FIS. There are so many benefits.

But the divisional accounting staff apparently did not perceive these benefits, even after substantial experience with FIS. Here is an excerpt from another memo written by the accountant who first complained about the system in October 1975. This memo is dated August 1977.

After being on FIS for several months, I expressed the opinion that the system was basically of little benefit. After two years and seven months, my opinion has not changed. Even worse, it seems to have become a system that is running people rather than people utilizing the system.

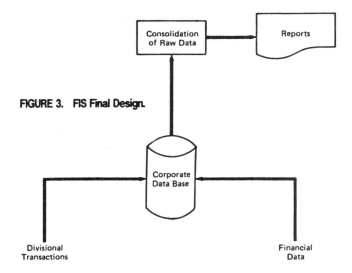

FIGURE 3. FIS Final Design.

When this author visited GTC, well over one year after that memo was written, many divisional accountants reported that they were still very unhappy with FIS.

Differences Between Resistors and Nonresistors

From the preceding description, it can be seen that those who could be said by their behavior to resist FIS were divisional accountants; those who accepted it and liked it were corporate accountants. According to the people-determined theory of resistance, resistors and acceptors should differ psychologically or cognitively in some significant way. In fact, several corporate accountants interviewed in 1979 subscribed to this notion: their stated explanation for the resistance was the personality characteristics of the resistors, who were "troublemakers." Although this author did not administer any psychological tests, there are some factors that lend credibility to the hypothesis that differences between the groups accounted for the resistance.

First, corporate accountants performed tasks that can be described as "financial accounting." They dealt with historical data, largely for purposes of external reporting. In contrast, divisional accountants, who reported to divisional general managers, can be described as "managerial accountants." They saw their role as one of providing future- and profit-oriented information to managers. Second, prior to 1975, there was little mobility between corporate and divisional accounting groups. Mobility would probably have encouraged more homogeneity in outlook; lack of it undoubtedly led to greater differences in outlook.

These differences, however, are not the inherent cognitive style differences usually studied by information systems theorists [26]. Rather, they are cognitive differences derived from status and functional location within a firm's hierarchy and division of labor.

Technical Problems with FIS

According to the system-determined theory, resistance can be traced to human factors and technical design features. Evidence can be found in the FIS case to support the reasonableness of this contention.

Part of the reason for the complaints of early FIS users can be found in a series of technical and human factors problems with the system. The database management system chosen for this application did not work well with the computer's operating system, and there was insufficient main storage to meet the applications requirements. Consequently, downtime

was frequent and reports were often late. At the same time, the schedules of monthly closings were not relaxed to accommodate the problems. In addition, the data entry procedures were cumbersome. For example, FIS represents accounts with 24-digit account codes; the system it replaced had 8-digit codes. New accounts had to be created almost daily, but to do so required a special computer run. In the special run, once weekly, the new account had to be related to the other accounts in the hierarchy. This was not quite as difficult as might be inferred from the 10^{24} possible accounts, but the rules for doing it were difficult to learn and not documented in a user manual. Transactions were entered into the system daily; those intended for an as-yet-undefined account wound up in a suspense account. Given the weekly periodicity of the account creation run, the suspense accounts often grew to staggering amounts.

Political Context of FIS at GTC

According to the interaction theory, resistance can be attributed to an interaction between the design features of the system and features of its organization and social context of use. One aspect of this context is the intraorganizational politics and power dynamics between corporate and division accountants. Sufficient data exist in the FIS case to provide a basis for the plausibility of the interaction theory.

GTC is a major chemical and energy products manufacturing concern, with sales from its international operations exceeding $3 billion. It is currently decentralized into a staff group that includes corporate accounting and four operating groups with relative autonomy over marketing strategy and investment decisions for their product lines (see Figure 1). Within each operating group are several divisions, headed by general managers. Divisional accountants report directly to these general managers with only a "dotted line relationship" to the corporate accounting group, whose role is to provide "broad policy guidelines."

This organizational structure dated back to about 1968. In 1967, Golden Chemical Company had merged with two energy product concerns to form GTC. In the restructuring, the old parent company was subjugated to a new corporate entity. This subjugation was reflected in the creation of a new staff group, corporation accounting, interposed between corporate management (which was disproportionately staffed with non-Chemical Company people) and the Chemical Divisions (see Figure 4). A Chemical Company manager (Howard) was chosen to head the corporate controller's office. Whether by

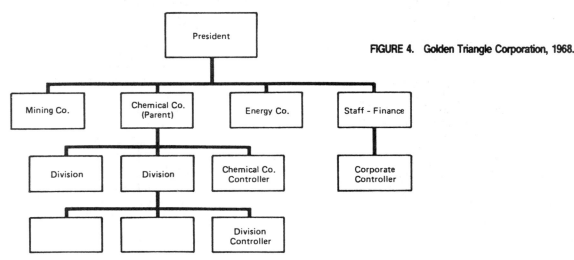

FIGURE 4. Golden Triangle Corporation, 1968.

TABLE II. Theories of Resistance: Predictions.

	People-Determined	System-Determined	Interaction Theory (Political Variant)
Facts needed in real-world case for theory to be applicable	System is resisted, resistors differ from nonresistors on certain personal dimensions	System is resisted, system has technical problems	System is resisted, resistance occurs in the context of political struggles
Predictions derived from theories	Change the people involved, resistance will disappear	Fix technical problems, resistance will disappear	Changing individuals and/or fixing technical features will have little effect on resistance
	Job rotation among resistors and nonresistors	Improve system efficiency Improve data entry	Resistance will persist in spite of time, rotation, and technical improvements Interaction theory can explain other relevant organizational phenomena in addition to resistance

accident or by design is unknown, but Howard was the rival of the head controller for the Chemical Company divisions (Spade). (Spade had hired Howard many years before.) Respondents described the relationship between the two men as "strained at best," especially during 1972–1973, about the time that FIS was initiated and designed.

Howard found himself in an unenviable position. He had before him the task of creating an important and influential staff group where none had previously existed. Furthermore, his charter called for him to provide broad policy guidelines to all divisional accounting units, but he had no authority over them other than dotted-line relationships. Finally, because of his bad relationship with the Chemical Company controller, Howard was uncertain whether he had an accurate picture of reality: all data came to him through Spade.

> Corporate accountants felt the divisions were lying to them. And maybe there was some withholding of data on our side.
> *Divisional Accountant*

Howard felt that the divisions were doing things behind his back, and that he needed a better way of ferreting out how the knaves were doing in the trenches. A large part of the reason for initiating FIS was to provide this information.

> *Corporation Accountant*

All three theories, then, appear at least plausible in the context of FIS since some data can be found to support their basic assumptions. It remains to demonstrate how well predictions drawn from each theory account for subsequent events in the case.

PREDICTIONS DERIVED FROM THE THREE THEORIES
The people-determined theory leads to the prediction that replacing individual resistors or coopting them by allowing them to suggest improvements to the system might reduce or eliminate resistance. The system-determined theory predicts that if the technical features and human factors of a resisted system are changed, then resistance will disappear. The political variant of the interaction theory argues that neither of these changes will have much effect on the intensity of resistance if the resistance was generated by patterned interactions among competing groups. These predictions are summarized in Table II.

Actual evidence from the FIS case supports the political variant of the interaction theory and gives no support to the other two. The test of a single case is not a strong proof, nor is it so intended here. But it can be a useful illustration. Conse-

quently, the reader is invited to try out any version of the interaction theory on any familiar situation to test its ability to account for events. However, our exposition of the case does not stop with demonstrating the utility of the interaction theory in accounting for events; we now show the assumptions of the interaction theory to be useful in helping an implementor to predict, to gather data, to explain resistance, and to develop strategies for implementation.

Changing the People
The people-determined theory predicts, among other things, that if some acceptors were moved into positions occupied by the resistors, resistance among divisional accountants would diminish or vanish. While hardly a scientific test of this prediction, such an event did take place accidentally within GTC.

After 1975, GTC encouraged more mobility among corporate and divisional accountants for career development purposes. Under this policy, one of the corporate accountants who had participated in the design of FIS in the original design task force became the controller in one of the divisions. According to one informant, this accountant rapidly became convinced of the problems with FIS (at least as seen by divisional accountants) and became an active and critical member of the second efficiency task force formed in December 1977 to improve FIS.

Further, while it surely does not conclusively refute the people-determined theory, behavioral evidence and interview reports show that resistance continued. It persisted in 1979, four years after the introduction to FIS. Evidence to support this statement will be given shortly.

Fixing Technical Problems
The system-determined theory predicts that fixing technical problems eliminates resistance. The second FIS efficiency task force was formed in December 1977, composed of several "resistors" (divisional accountants) in addition to data processing specialists. This task force made technical recommendations similar to those of the first task force, but also speculated about whether FIS should be scrapped and replaced. Before it could complete its deliberations on the latter issue, the second task force was disbanded in March 1978.

This date coincided with the completion of the technical recommendations from the two task forces. The Data Processing Department had purchased and installed a larger computer with a more powerful operating system. This technical change improved the efficiency of FIS. In addition, the processing mode of the system had been changed from a batch to a transaction (on-line) basis; together, these changes reduced downtime to an acceptable level. Changes were made to the method of data entry, from remote batch to on-line, and the method of creating new accounts was simplified.

In spite of all these improvements in technical features and human factors, divisional resistance to FIS did not disappear. In fact, when data were collected for this study, about one year after the last of these changes was installed, informants in the divisions still spoke resentfully of FIS. Many felt strongly that the system should be replaced because FIS was inadequate as a tool for managerial accounting, even though it (now) functioned adequately as a tool for performing financial accounting. (Managerial accounting was the chief concern of divisional accountants.) Corporate accountants, however, maintained that FIS was more than adequate for managerial accounting (not their specialty), and they were increasingly pressuring divisional accountants to use FIS for this additional purpose.

Organizational Politics

The interaction theory predicts that neither changing people (by removing them, by educating them, or by attempting to coerce them), nor changing technical features of the system will reduce resistance as long as the conditions which gave rise to it persist. Resistance-generating conditions are mismatches between the patterns of interaction prescribed by a system and the patterns that already exist in the setting into which the system is introduced. According to the political version of the interaction theory (see the appendix), the existing political setting can be identified as follows.

Corporate accounting had little formal organizational power and no independent information on which to base its attempts to develop and administer broad policy guidelines. An obvious solution to this problem was to develop a system by means of which the necessary information would flow directly to Corporate Accounting without the intermediate step of manipulation by the divisions. This is precisely what FIS did, as can be seen in Figures 2 and 3.

The way in which FIS was designed implied a major gain of power for corporate accountants relative to their prior position vis á vis the divisional accountants. Prior to FIS, divisional accountants summarized raw data on the transactions in their divisions and sent the summaries to the corporate accountants for consolidation. Divisions retained control of their own data and exercised substantial discretion in summarizing it. This allowed them to "account for" unusual situations before reports reached corporate accountants or divisional general managers. After FIS, however, all financial transactions were collected into a single database under the control of corporate accountants. The divisional accountants still had to enter data, but they no longer "owned" it. FIS automatically performed the divisional summaries that both divisional and corporate accountants received. At any time, corporate accountants had the ability to "look into" the database and analyze divisional performance.

Corporate accountants designed and used FIS to create a substantial change in the distribution of, or access to, financial data, a valued resource. It is not surprising that those who gained access (corporate accountants) were pleased with the system and that those who lost control (divisional accountants) resisted it by writing angry memos, maintaining parallel systems, engaging in behavior that jeopardized the integrity of the database, and participating in a task force with the public objective of eliminating FIS and replacing it with another system.

Given the details of the design of FIS, it is likely that

divisional accountants would have resisted it even if the loss of power implied for the divisions had been accidental. But there is some evidence that the corporate accountants acted deliberately in their design of the new financial accounting system. First, as mentioned above, they had sufficient motive to try to shift the power balance. Second, they clearly felt powerless in their dealings with the divisions. They staffed the FIS project team without any representatives from the divisions, who might voice objections to its design details. This group selected a package, which conformed in overall design principles to the existing information flows at GTC, and modified it deliberately[1] into a design that would alter the power balance between the two groups. Furthermore, some observers with GTC were willing to ascribe the motivation behind FIS to political reasons. For example, the man who was Data Processing Manager in 1975 (long since gone to another company when interviewed in 1979) said,

> FIS was definitely established for political reasons ... Howard wanted to take over the whole world ... Therein started the wars between the Chemical Company and Corporate.

A design for FIS that entailed a power loss for one group and a power gain for the other could be expected to strongly affect power dynamics between the groups. Once the resistance of the divisional accountants is understood in this way, it is common sense as well as derivation from theory to hypothesize that changing human factors and even replacing a few key actors would do little to resolve the resistance. In fact, changing them did not eliminate the resistance.

UTILITY OF THE INTERACTION THEORY TO IMPLEMENTORS

At this point, the superiority of the political variant of the interaction theory has been established based upon the ability of predictions drawn from it to account for the resistance to a system in one case. Rather than stop at this point, the case example can be extended a bit further to show what additional facts and data can be uncovered and explained by an analyst who uses this theory. These additional facts and data may be useful in designing an implementation effort. In the case of FIS, there are two additional relevant "events": a reorganization of accounting within GTC that occurred in mid-1975, shortly after the start-up of FIS, and the on-going (in 1979) debate about what (else) should be done to or done about FIS.

In 1974, Spade retired. In the next year, his old position as Chemical Company Controller was first moved under the direct line control of corporate accounting and then eliminated the following year (see Figure 5). Similar changes were *not* made in the Energy Group of GTC. A member of the corporate controller's staff cited this as an example of what FIS was intended to accomplish:

> If (the corporate reorganization in 1975 which eliminated Spade's job as Chemical Company Controller) had occurred several years previously, FIS might never have been instigated. The reorganization eliminated much of the need for FIS.
>
> *Corporate Accountant*

It may seem as though FIS caused this structural change. But it is probably more accurate to view the reorganization as

---

[1] The modification was optional, not mandatory, since the package was quite operational as purchased. The modification required a negotiated agreement with the vendor and was originally estimated to take six months to complete. (It actually took over two years.) To proceed in this way was, therefore, a deliberate decision on the part of the project team.

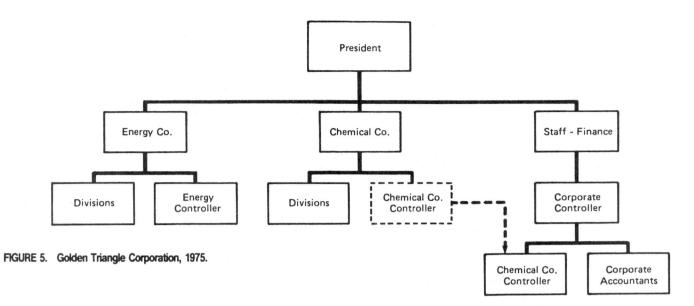

FIGURE 5.   Golden Triangle Corporation, 1975.

an outgrowth of the same political situation that created the "need" for FIS. The political variant of the interaction theory, then, helps an analyst understand this event and to explain the resistance it generated.

The political variant of the interaction theory also helps an analyst understand the dynamics of the intraorganization debate about FIS, which continued long after technical problems with the system were fixed. As interviews in 1979 disclosed, resistance to FIS had not disappeared but had changed its form: no longer were the divisions protesting the technical problems with the system (now solved); they were complaining that the corporate accountants were insisting they use FIS for tasks for which the system was inappropriate, namely, managerial accounting.

An administrator reporting to the President of one of GTC's operating groups summarized the feelings of many divisional accountants when he said:

> I think it's about time they realized that FIS is really an operational tool. It just can't do everything.

In this remark, he summarized the view that FIS had been grudgingly accepted by divisional accountants as a tool for performing financial accounting (balance sheets, taxes, and corporate consolidations), but that it was still being resisted as a managerial accounting tool. Divisional accountants argued strenuously that FIS was not useful for managerial accounting.

> FIS does not provide us with the data we need to prepare profit center reports. To prepare profit center reports we must maintain a separate system, the PGP system . . . They tell us we can use FIS for profit center reports! That's garbage! You *could* do it, but I've already told you how you have to enter data into FIS. To get a profit center report, you'd have to enter each transaction by commodity code. There are a thousand commodity codes. This would be a horrendous job. Besides, PGP is our product gross profit report. We've had this system unchanged for almost ten years . . . Naturally, the profit figures from this and FIS should reconcile, but they never do, so we have to make the necessary adjustments . . . .

But an analysis of interview notes, internal memos, and task forces minutes, covering the period from 1975 to 1979, indicates that the difficulty of using FIS was only a secondary complaint; proposed changes in the way managerial accounting would be done was the real issue, one that no amount of technical fixing would solve. Further, this real issue was one of potential loss of power for divisional (managerial) accountants. Consider the following evidence.

First, an early memo about FIS (outlining a presentation to GTC's top management) explained "the direction we are heading" in the design of FIS. This direction represented a major shift in the way GTC did managerial accounting, that is, reporting to management about profit performance on specific products as opposed to the manipulation of aggregated, historical data. The intended shift in direction is clear in this excerpt from a 1972 memo:

> The last item of deficiencies that we list is the inability to analyze results on a total variance basis by business unit or corporate wide. By that, we mean a lack of sales information by principal product and the lack of product line profitability. What was the volume of a given product? What was its price for a given period? What did that product contribute at the gross profit level? To me, the guts of our operation is what we do on a product line basis. In addition, we do not report on a given plant profitability. We feel that all this type of information, as was indicated, should all be part of a Financial Information System and available to management when needed.

Thus, corporate accountants had intended from the very beginning that FIS be used for managerial accounting, not just, as its name implies, for financial accounting.

Second, corporate accountants did not immediately reveal these intentions to the divisions. When the staff in the divisions first heard about it they were surprised. In an October 1975 memo complaining about FIS, the divisional writer noted:

> I think we have to take a good look at what we have right now and improve it before we take *any additional tasks* proposed for the FIS system.

The "additional tasks proposed" referred to product profit (managerial) accounting.

Third, corporate accountants were quite well aware that

the divisions did not see eye to eye with them on the issue of managerial accounting. The second FIS task force was created, it will be recalled, in December 1977 in response to another angry memo written by the accountant in the first FIS-using division. Responding to that memo, a highly placed corporate accountant referred to the heart of the resistance issue in this memo written in August 1977:

> I must say that I am not surprised that your attitude toward the FIS system has not changed . . . That same attitude is shared by the entire financial [sic] staff of your division, and hence, FIS will never be accepted nor will it be utilized fully as an analysis tool by your division.

"Analysis tool" here means a tool to be used in the analysis of managerial-oriented profit data. (Note the use of the term "financial" to refer to the duties of divisional accountants.)

Finally, the divisional accountants themselves were quite explicit in distinguishing between operational and ease of use problems and use of the system for managerial accounting purposes. When the second task force was formed, it was partly "to improve things from a public relations point of view as well as from a technical point of view," according to one corporate accountant. But the divisional members of the committee did not intend to settle for symbolic gestures. "It was never really stated as such but one question we were looking at was: should we look for a new system?" Task force minutes in December 1977 confirm this:

> During the sessions we have had thus far, one complex question already surfaced: is the system capable of being any more than a giant bookkeeping system, e.g., can it ever effectively serve divisional needs for budgeting, reporting, allocations, etc.? Therefore, we see two related issues we will attempt to offer recommendations on: (1) ways to deal with problems so the system can be counted on to operate effectively during month-end over the short-term, and (2) what, if anything, must be done to assure us that, for the long-term, we will have a system usable as more than a consolidator.

Since the task force was disbanded before they could tackle the second question, we will never know what they decided, but interview data suggests that the divisions remained very negative both toward FIS and toward the corporate accountants' proposed "additional" uses for it.

Here is the situation in summary. From the perspective of the divisional accountants, financial accounting is the legitimate domain of corporate accountants. A system intended primarily for financial accounting would have no real impact on the divisions, provided, of course, that it was reasonably easy to use. The FIS system was not easy to use, but it was also not just a financial accounting system. It was intended to encroach upon the legitimate domain of the divisional accountants, that is, managerial accounting. Divisional accountants would resist the use of FIS for managerial accounting

even if it were easy to use, and, in fact, their resistance continued beyond March 1978.

Who won? Did the corporate accountants succeed in their attempt to alter the balance of power between themselves and the divisions? The answer is not altogether clear. The corporate accountants did succeed in having the second task force disbanded (the axe man was the Vice-President of Finance) in March 1978, after the technical problems had been solved but before the committee could decide to replace FIS. The divisional accountants succeeded in redressing the more egregious faults of FIS, but failed in having it removed. In all likelihood, the net result was something of a draw: the corporate accountants had better information than before, an important power advantage in their dealings with the divisions, but not quite the total victory they had wished; the divisional accountants had regrouped and entrenched themselves to prevent any further losses.

IMPLICATIONS OF THE THEORIES FOR IMPLEMENTATION

The preceding analysis may have convinced an implementor that the interaction theory, at least in its political variation, has superior explanatory and predictive power. But the true test of the theories for the implementor will lie in their implications for implementation. Interaction theories are distinctly different from the people-determined, the system-determined, and the people-plus-system-determined views of resistance in their implications for action. An implementor holding the people-determined theory of resistance, for example, would find certain tactics appropriate. Among these are: carefully selecting the people who will use a new system or allowing users to self-select after careful explanations about the system; training and educating users to change their cognitive styles or attitudes about computing; getting users to participate in the design process so that they will feel more committed to the outcome; gaining support of the users' bosses who will encourage or demand compliance of recalcitrant users; changing organizational structures or reward systems to conform to the features of the system.

An implementor who believes that systems determine people's behavior will consider some different tactics and some of the same tactics for different reasons. Among these are: modifying packages to conform to the ways people think, work, or do business; training system designers to improve technical efficiency, ergonomic excellence, and a smooth man–machine interface; involving users in the design process so that the design is better than that which would have been developed without user input.

Implementors who hold both people- and system-determined theories simultaneously will pick and choose among the tactics. To these people, user participation in design is the most desirable tactic, because it is consistent with both theories, albeit for different reasons. In the face of prolonged or intense resistance, however, they are often forced to choose between changing people or organizational structures and

TABLE III. Theories of Resistance: Recommendations for Implementation.

People-Determined	System-Determined	Interaction Theory
Educate users (training)	Educate designers (better technology)	Fix organizational problem before introducing systems
Coerce users (edicts, policies)	Improve human factors	Restructure incentives for users
Persuade users	Modify packages to conform to organizational procedures	Restructure relationships between users and designers
User participation (to obtain commitment)	User participation (to obtain better design)	User participation is not always appropriate

modifying the system; and in the process, they reveal their theory of last resort.

Implementors who hold the interaction theory of resistance find that no tactics are useful in *every* situation. User participation in the design process, for example, is clearly contraindicated in cases where powerful authorities have decided that a specific change, unpopular with users, *will* take place (see Markus [17]). In such situations, users are likely to resent strongly a tactic that is meant to make them feel as though they have some say in the matter, when they obviously do not.

One major implication of the interaction theory is that computer-based systems alone cannot accomplish the task of radical organizational change. If radical change is desired, a thorough analysis of the existing situation should be conducted to identify factors that will facilitate or hinder the change. Examples of such factors can be inappropriate reporting relationships among individuals or groups, incentive schemes that do not reward the desired behavior or punish undesired behavior, unclear allocation of responsibility for certain tasks. Changes in these areas should be made before a system is implemented, and the system should be designed to be consistent with the revised organizational procedures. In cases like this, the organizational changes may generate resistance, but once they have been implemented, a system that supports them is unlikely to be the target of resistance itself.

Another implication of the interaction theory is that the specific designs of systems are in part a product of the relationships between users and designers. In the case of FIS, the designers were also systems users, as opposed to systems professionals. But similar cases of resistance have occurred where design objectives and specifics have been set by supposedly "neutral" parties such as operations researchers and systems analysts. According to the interaction theory, no designers are ever completely neutral. Consequently, a great deal of thought and attention should be given to the tasks of structuring the relationships between users and designers and of developing methodologies for designing and implementing systems. For example, many organizations with centralized computing facilities have deliberately decentralized systems development to improve relationships between users and designers.

The most important implication of the interaction theory is that the best prescriptions for an implementation strategy and for the specific design content of a system will follow from a thorough diagnosis of the organizational setting in which the system will be used. At present, system builders are using methods such as structured systems analysis which allow them to describe and analyze only the technical features of a setting which is to be automated. To design systems that will not be resisted or to devise ways to modify resisted systems, this technical systems analysis must be augmented with a social or political analysis of the sort performed for FIS. Table III summarizes these conclusions.

CONCLUSION

The final evaluation of the interaction theory (in whatever variation) is to show how it is useful to the implementor of systems. The theory leads to a model of organizational analysis and diagnosis that can be used to design systems that do not generate resistance or to devise strategies to deal with settings in which resistance has already occurred.

In the case of FIS, an analysis of this sort could have been performed prior to the system analysis and development effort to identify where resistance was likely to occur. Given the facts presented in this paper, the analyst would probably have concluded that divisional accountants would certainly resist design features such as (a) the ability of the corporate accountants to retrieve and analyze raw (unsummarized) data, and (b) the necessity to do profit analysis at a level of aggregation that was meaningless to them. Knowing this and his/her own motives, the analyst could decide upon a course of action that may have included

(1) Altering the design of the system in ways that would be more palatable to divisional accountants;
(2) Sacrificing some of the corporate accountants' objectives for the system;
(3) Allowing divisional accountants to participate in selected aspects or all aspects of the system design process;
(4) "Buying" acceptance of the system by giving divisional accountants some other concessions valued by them;
(5) Touting the system from the start as the ultimate "managerial accounting information system";
(6) Terminating the proposed project.

Once FIS was designed and resistance already apparent, an analysis could have been performed to determine precisely why the resistance occurred and what could be done about it. This analysis would also be useful in helping plan future system implementations involving one or more of the parties affected by the original system. In the case of FIS, one would conclude that for corporate accountants to persist in pressing their view of managerial accounting is probably organizational folly. Furthermore, relations between the two groups are now badly strained. Successful future implementations of financial systems will necessitate either improving these relationships or providing solutions to problems perceived by the divisional accounting group.

The interaction theory has the apparent disadvantage of providing no universal, noncontingent advice to systems analysts and management implementors of systems. But it is more useful than other theories for predicting resistance and for generating varied and creative strategies that will help both to prevent it and to deal with it when it arises. Two observations on the use of the theory are in order.

First, one key to the successful use of the interaction theory is that the implementor consider himself or herself as one of the parties in the analysis. Self-examination of interests, motives, payoffs, and power bases will lend much to the implementor's ability to understand other people's reactions to the systems the implementor is designing and installing.

Second, the analyst should recognize that the goal of the exercise is not to "overcome" resistance, but to avoid it, if possible, and to confront it constructively, if not. In some cases, this indicates that the implementor may have to lose the battle and sacrifice a pet system project in order to win the war. Resistance is not a problem to be solved so that a system can be installed as intended: it is a useful clue to what went wrong and how the situation can be righted. If the implementor can divorce the need to see a system up and working from the need to achieve a particular result, many more degrees of freedom exist. In conclusion, although the process is difficult and time-consuming, the results produced from the application of the interaction theory of resistance are often substantially better than those produced from the application of the universal heuristics derived from other theories.

APPENDIX. DETAILS OF THE POLITICAL VARIATION OF THE INTERACTION THEORY
Several variations of interaction theories are possible; the basic constraint is the notion that resistance is caused by an interaction between organization and system. The specific or-

ganizational concepts an analyst uses may vary. The set used in this paper are concepts of intraorganizational power and politics. Other sets of concepts are also consistent with the interaction theory. One example involves concepts of organizational learning and change (see Keen [9], Ginzberg [7], and Kling [13] for details).

The primary assumption of the political variant of the interaction theory is that information systems frequently embody a distribution of intraorganizational power among the key actors affected by its design. Intraorganizational power is an attribute of individuals or subgroups, such as departments, within the organization; it can be defined as the ability to get one's way in the face of opposition or resistance to those desires [25]. There are a number of ways by which an individual or subgroup can come to have power in an organization, including personal characteristics, such as being an expert or being charismatic, but position in the formal structure of the organization often provides greater access to specific power resources and the legitimacy required to use them. Pfeffer [25] describes the major determinants of power: dependence of others on the power holder, ability of the power holder to provide resources, ability of the power holder to cope with uncertainty and irreplaceability, and ability to affect a decision-making process. All of these determinants of power are relevant to an understanding of MIS implementation, but the most frequently cited is ability to cope with uncertainty.[2] The raison d'etre of MIS is to provide managers with useful information, presumably so that they can cope better with variances arising from their production technologies and from the external units that supply inputs to and distribute outputs from the core technology.

The information required to cope effectively with uncertainty is distributed throughout organizations in a nonrandom way; some people/groups have more access to this than others, and this gives them power. Many management information systems are designed in ways that redistribute nonrandomly the information required to cope with uncertainty; thus an MIS can alter bases of power. For example, a relatively stable balance of power will develop in the relationships between the purchasing, engineering, operations, and production control departments in any manufacturing organization. Sometimes engineering will call the shots, sometimes manufacturing. The introduction of a new logistics system may funnel all key information through the production control department, thus giving them an unaccustomed power edge in their dealings with other groups. The result might be a permanent redistribution in the balance of intraorganizational power,[3] unless something happens to prevent it. The sufficiently powerful "something" is resistance by those parties who stand to lose in the reallocation of power.

The political variant makes some precise predictions about where resistance is likely to occur around the implementation of information systems. Power, as it has been defined here, is a valuable resource. People and organizational subunits may differ in the extent to which they actively seek to gain power, but it is unlikely that they will voluntarily give it up. When the introduction of a computerized information system specifies a distribution of power which represents a loss to certain participants, these participants are likely to resist the system. Conversely, when the distribution of power implied in the design of an information system represents a gain in power to

participants, these participants are likely to engage in behaviors that might signify acceptance of it: frequent use and/or positive statements about the system. In general, one would not expect people who are disadvantaged in their power position by a system to accept it (gracefully), nor would one expect people who gain power to resist.

Testing these propositions might involve comparing distributions of power bases before a system is installed with the distributions implied in a system's design, that is, identifying the winners and losers if the system were to be used exactly as designed. Clearly, however, there are some problems with this procedure. Necessary conditions for resistance (acceptance) in the hypotheses as stated are that people perceive the system to represent a power loss (gain) and that people's behavior adequately represents their feelings. In some cases, people may misperceive the loss (gain) they receive as a result of the system. In other cases, people may feel it is not to their advantage to engage in behaviors that could be labeled resistance: criticizing the system, avoiding it, trying to bring out changes [25]. Most of these factors argue that, of the people or subunits who lose power in an objective comparison of new system with former conditions, only some of these are likely to resist, or to resist with any strength. Strength of resistance would appear to be strongly related to size of the loss and its perceived importance.

Some of the specific conditions in the design of an MIS that will spell objective losses or gains in power can be spelled out. It is important to note that a single system can represent a power loss for several individuals or subunits, and at the same time, a power gain for several others. Access to information is probably less important as a basis of power than is the ability to *control* access to information or to define what information will be kept and manipulated in what ways [10, 14, 23, 24]. When a system centralizes control over data, the individual or subunit who gains the control is likely to accept the system readily, while those units losing control are likely to resist, even if they receive access to larger amounts of data in return. Similarly, decentralization of control over data is likely to be resisted by the formerly controlling unit and to be accepted by units gaining control.

If control over data (whether centralized or local) has prevented certain groups from obtaining needed or desired access to it, distribution of data, even unaccompanied by control over it, will provide those receiving it significant power gains. Their dependence on the controlling group will be reduced, since they will have an alternative source of data. They are likely to accept a system which accomplishes this distribution. On the other hand, those whose data monopoly is threatened in the process are likely to resist. Distribution of data that makes the performance of a subunit more visible, hence subject to control attempts by other units, is likely to be resisted by the group whose performance is exposed [15] and accepted by those who would like to influence the others' performance.

The strength of resistance is also likely to be affected by the organizational position of the person or subunit to whom one loses power. If the "winner" is located in a vertically superior position in the hierarchy, resistance is much less likely than if the winner is a peer. Formal authority relationships tend to make power differences between superiors and subordinates more legitimate than similar differences among groups at the same horizontal level in the organization.

At this point, the philosophical stance of the political variant toward resistance should be clear. Resistance is neither good nor bad in and of itself; whether or not it is so labeled usually depends on the vested interests of the person or group

_____

[2] The ways in which information systems affect the organizational balance of power either through their symbolic aspects or through their effect on the decision process is described in detail in Markus and Pfeffer [19].

[3] Such redistributions have been documented by Kling [11], Hedberg et al. [8]; research on this topic has been reviewed by Bariff and Galbraith [2].

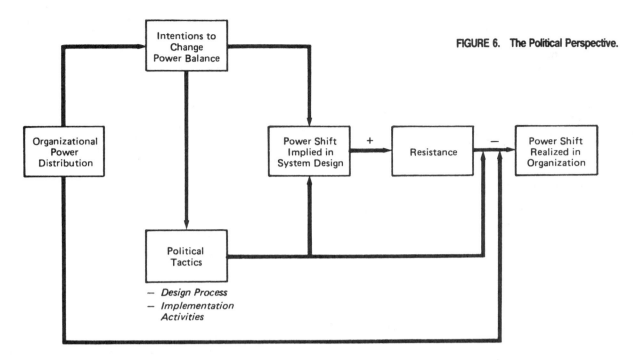

FIGURE 6. The Political Perspective.

doing the labeling. Resistance can be an important, even organizationally healthy, phenomenon by signaling that an information system is altering the balance of power in ways that might cause major organizational dysfunctions. The political variant assumes that systems have no inevitable impacts on the organizations which employ them; ultimately, impacts will depend upon the choices made by people about how to use them. Some of these choices are exercised in the design process; others are expressed in the form of resistance, when previously unforeseen consequences that negatively affect a legitimate group of users come to light. Noble [22] makes a similar point about the impact of technological change generally. Specifically, people can alter management information systems as they use them and thus prevent the realization of implied power distributions by sabotaging the system, providing inaccurate data, not using the system at all, keeping other sets of records, circumventing the intent of the system while obeying the letter, and many other ways. Mechanic [20] describes some of the bases of power available even to people very low in the organizational hierarchy that could give the ability to affect the final outcomes of an MIS, and Strauss [27] describes other tactics that have been used laterally between horizontally related subunits.

The degree of resistance generated by the introduction of a computerized information system is seen, then, in the political variant as a variable intervening between the degree of change in the intraorganization balance of power designed into a system and the degree of power shift actually realized in the organization. Obviously, resistance is not the only factor that could intervene here. Systems in practice rarely match perfectly the intentions of designers, partly because of imperfections in the translation and partly because use contributes to learning about how the system ought to have been designed in the first place. Even more important is the degree to which powerful organizational actors, who may directly benefit from others' loss in power and who may actually intend such loss, are motivated to try to overcome the resistance. The preexisting balance of power and the relative adeptness of various groups at the use of political tactics for

avoiding and overcoming resistance will largely affect the net outcome for the organization. These considerations are summarized diagrammatically in Figure 6.

The fact that the political version of the interaction theory is only one of several raises the question, when is the political variant more likely than others to be appropriate for understanding MIS implementation? Pfeffer [25] has discussed the circumstances under which organizational decision-making is likely to be accompanied by politics. While the process of designing information systems is not the same as organizational decision-making, it is probably a special case; at least, some of the decision-making processes reported by Mintzberg et al. [21] bear a strong resemblance to the front-half of the information system life cycle. This implies that the political variant is most appropriate when conditions likely to produce political decision-making obtain: when there is disagreement about organizational goals and values; when uncertainty exists about the means required to produce the desired objectives; when resources are scarce; when the decisions are important [25].

Translating these factors into the information systems context suggests that the political variant is the most appropriate analytical framework when organizational participants disagree about the nature of the problem that a system is proposed to solve, when there exists uncertainty about whether a particular proposed system will solve the problem, and when the power bases allocated are highly valued and in short supply. These conditions are most likely to be met when the information system cuts horizontally across several diverse organizational subunits and has many different types of users. Thus the political variant may be more relevant to understanding the implementation of integrated operational information systems, whereas some other perspective, such as one based on concepts of organizational learning, may apply better to single-user decision support systems. However, although the political variant may not be most appropriate for every case, it considerably enhances the ability to explain and predict events surrounding the introduction of management information systems into complex organizations.

Acknowledgment.   The author wishes to thank the many people who have made comments on the multiple incarnations of this paper and the ideas contained in it, especially Rob Kling and Jeffrey Pfeffer.

REFERENCES

1. Alter, S.L. A study of computer aided decision-making in organizations. Unpublished doctoral dissertation, Massachusetts Institute of Technology, Cambridge, Mass., 1975.
2. Bariff, M.L., and Galbraith, J.R. Intraorganizational power considerations for designing information systems. *Accounting Organizations and Society 3* (1978), 15–27.
3. Braverman, H. *Labor and Monopoly Capital.* Monthly Review Press, New York, 1974.
4. Crozier, M. *The Bureaucratic Phenomenon.* Univ. Chicago Press, Chicago, 1964.
5. Dalton, M. *Men Who Manage.* Wiley, New York, 1959.
6. Ginzberg, M.J. A detailed look at implementation research. Rept. CISR-4, Center for Information Systems Research, Massachusetts Institute of Technology, Cambridge, 1974.
7. Ginzberg, M.J. Implementation as a process of change: A framework and empirical study. Rept. CISR-13, Center for Information Systems Research, Massachusetts Institute of Technology, Cambridge, 1975.
8. Hedberg, B., Edstrom, A., Muller, W., and Wilpert, S.B. The impact of computer technology on organizational power structures. In E. Grochla and N. Szyperski (Eds.), *Information Systems and Organization Structure,* New York, 1975, pp. 131–148.
9. Keen, P.G.W. Information systems and organizational change. Rept. CISR-46, Center for Information Systems Research, Massachusetts Institute of Technology, Cambridge, 1980.
10. Kling, R. Automated information systems as social resources in policy making. *Proceedings of the Association for Computing Machinery,* 1978, pp. 666–674.
11. Kling, R. Automated welfare client tracking and service integration: The political economy of computing. *Comm. ACM* (June 1978), 484–493.
12. Kling, R. Defining the boundaries of computing in complex organizations: A Behavioral approach. Working Paper, Univ. California, Irvine, 1982.
13. Kling R. Social analyses of computing: Theoretical perspectives in recent empirical research. *Comput. Surv. 12,* 1 (1980), 61–110.
14. Laudon, K.C. *Computers and Bureaucratic Reform.* Wiley, New York, 1974.
15. Lawler, E. and Rhode, J.G. *Information and Control in Organizations.* Goodyear, Palisades, Calif., 1976.
16. Lucas, H. *Why Information Systems Fail.* Columbia Univ. Press, New York, 1975.
17. Markus, M.L. Implementation politics—Top management support and user involvement. *Systems, Objectives, Solutions* (1981), 203–215.
18. Markus, M.L. Understanding information systems use in organizations: A theoretical explanation. Unpublished doctoral dissertation, Case Western Reserve Univ., Cleveland, Ohio, 1979.
19. Markus, M.L., and Pfeffer, J. Power and the design and implementation of accounting and control systems. *Accounting, Organizations and Society.* In press.
20. Mechanic, D. Sources of power of lower participants in complex organization. *Administrative Sci. Quart.* (Dec. 1962), 349–364.
21. Mintzberg, H., Raisinghani, D., and Theoret, A. The structure of "unstructured" decision processes. *Administrative Sci. Quart. 21,* 246–275.
22. Noble, D.F. Social choice in machine design: The case of automatically controlled machine tools, and a challenge for labor. *Monthly Rev.* (1979).
23. Pettigrew, A.M. Information control as a power resource. *Sociology* (May 1972), 187–204.
24. Pfeffer, J. *Organizational Design.* AHM Publ. Corp., Arlington Heights, Ill., 1978.
25. Pfeffer, J. *Power in Organization.* Pitman Publ. Co., Marshfield, Mass., 1981.
26. Robey, D., and Taggart, W. Measuring managers' minds: The assessment of style in human information processing. *Acad. Manag. Rev. 6* (3), 1981.
27. Strauss, G. Tactics of lateral relationship: The purchasing agent. In Kolb et al. (Eds.), *Organizational Psychology: A Book of Readings,* 2nd ed., Prentice-Hall, Englewood Cliffs, N.J. 1974.

CR Categories and Subject Description: K.4.3 [**Computers and Society**]: Organizational Impacts
   General Terms: Human Factors, Management
   Additional Key Words and Phrases: resistance, intraorganizational power, politics, implementation.

ISSUES AND APPROACHES TO APPRAISING TECHNOLOGICAL CHANGE IN THE OFFICE: A CONSEQUENTIALIST PERSPECTIVE

H.K. Klein

ISRAM, McMaster University, Faculty of Business, Hamilton, Ontario (Canada)

and R. Hirschheim

London School of Economics, Houghton Street, London (U.K.)

SUMMARY

Offices have always been complex social systems. With the growth of office automation they will have to be recognized as socio-technical systems. The problems of prediction of consequences of change — in particular, technological change — in such systems are examined in some length and the limitations of causal analysis noted. A distinction between causal and hermeneutic modes of prediction is drawn. Hermeneutic modes of prediction are advocated as necessary in addition to predictions based on causal models in order to overcome the shortcomings of the latter. The results of a hermeneutic predictive exercise are reported which shed some light on the possible impact of future technological change in the office.

4. A HERMENEUTIC ROLE-PLAYING EXERCISE: THE PREDICTION OF CONFLICTS ABOUT OFFICE TECHNOLOGY

A hermeneutic role-playing exercise should proceed in four phases: (1) Identification of the predictor group, and assessment of its hermeneutic pre-understanding relevant to the phenomena to be predicted. (2) The improvement of the pre-understanding and the identification of tools to support the imagination of the predictor group(s). If there is a lack of understanding or motivation to play, a hermeneutic role-playing exercise must fail. In phase two these conditions must be carefully assessed. (3) The prediction exercise as such resulting in some documented results — opinions, observed behaviors, etc. (4) The critical evaluation and discussion of these results. Each of these four steps completes a major hermeneutic cycle by which the understanding accomplished in the previous cycle is used as a basis to improve one's knowledge of the situation as a whole. In each major cycle, various minor cycles may exist as will become evident in the example to be reported.

4.1 The first hermeneutic cycle: identification of qualified predictor groups

The experiment described below was part of a workshop, and was not preplanned. In fact, the theoretical basis suggested here for explaining the effectiveness of the exercise was not fully understood by the participants at the time when the exercise was performed. This should not be viewed as a disadvantage, because it safeguards against an unwanted "researcher bias". But as a result of this, the first phase of a hermeneutic role playing was replaced by a general discussion of how to proceed with the workshop.

Essentially, the exercise began with identifying the stakeholder interests by a discussion. Clearly, in practice this part can be improved by applying a proper stakeholder analysis. Under the given circumstances it was decided, after some discussion, that the following stakeholder groups needed consideration: Top Management, Middle Management, Clerks and their Union, and Technologists. The outcome of the experiment is very sensitive to the correct identification of stakeholders — witness the split of management into two distinct groups. Clearly, this phase, like some

Excerpted from Klein, H.K. and Herschheim, R. (1983). Issues and Approaches to Appraising Technological Change in the Office: A Consequentialist Perspective. *Office: Technology and People 2.* Amsterdam, the Netherlands: Elsevier Scientific Publishing Co.

parts of the next, benefited from the familiarity of the work group with the general issues and technology of office automation. In the case of another application, the pre-conditioning of the participants could be achieved in other ways (such as more extensive briefings or a preceding instructional workshop), and might need more attention than in this pilot study.

Next, the working group was split into four sections, each serving as a predictor group for one of the stakeholder sets. Top and middle management were each represented by 2 participants, and the clerks and technologists each by 5. The essential features of phase two, the "conditioning" of the hermeneutic "pre-understanding" of the situation of the predictor group, are described next.

4.2 Improving the hermeneutic pre-understanding of the predictor group

In order to prepare each predictor group for the role-playing exercise, it was agreed that each group identify and list the possible technological tools of the future, their functions in the office, and their possible consequences. Some groups chose to tabulate this information in the form of a matrix. The essential purpose of this was to support the imagination of the role players in the absence of "a real system to play with". One could think of various means to improve this part, such as using a simulation laboratory, but chosen is hard to beat. It is important to note that each group originally constructed its own matrix, thereby focusing on a description of technological components (the matrix rows) in a language that is most relevant to its professional view, and filling in the consequences (in the columns) as seen from the viewpoint of the stakeholder target group.

In order to facilitate discussion, each group put its material on flip-charts, which were posted next to each other on a wall during the role-playing session (a similar device is employed by the META-PLAN technique).

4.3 Description of the role-playing exercise and hermeneutic results

The results of the previous phase was that a mental set was created which focused attention on the following three topics:

(1) Identify and list the office technologies of the future;
(2) Identify their functions or applications in the future;
(3) Identify the possible consequences of applying these technologies.

This prepared the way for engaging in the principle stage of the predictive exercise. It is described best by explaining how the four predictor groups interpreted their role.

Top management

This group interpreted the exercise in terms of how new office technologies could enhance the profitability of the company. The individuals playing the roles of top management were concerned with corporate growth and stability. They made assumptions regarding what would be a reasonable rate of return on investment, and how this rate could (or would) be enhanced by any new office technology. Consideration was given to how a new technology might affect the amount of work obtainable from the clerks. Increased throughput was envisaged, as efficient, predictable automation could replace, or at least enhance, inefficient and unpredictable humans. Additionally, top management gave thought to the benefits of technology to areas of the organization other than the office. Considerable attention was given to other types of technology, such as Prestel and teleconferencing, and how these technologies could be useful to the organization (see Fig. 1). In summary, top management's primary concern was with increasing profits; whether this would be done at the expense of the firm's clerks was not an issue. It must be added, however, that top management did *not* consciously avoid the worker issue or see it as not important; rather it was not perceived by top management as an issue. In fact, no mention was ever made as to how the clerks might react to a change in their jobs brought about by any new office technology.

Middle management

In contrast to top management's lack of consideration of worker reactions to office technology, middle management was concerned with how implementing new technology might cause reactions from the clerks, and also the clerks' union. On the one hand, middle management had to be concerned with the firm's profitability, as this would be the primary yardstick of their worth to the firm in the eyes of top management. On the other, they had to be concerned with the people who they managed. Basically, they perceived themselves as a buffer between top management and the clerks; as such their role was one of conflict resolution. Middle management, in their attempt to address the possible new office technologies and their impact on the firm, had appeared to be keenly aware of the impending worker problems inherent in any large scale automation implementation and hence were a bit reticent in recommending anything major. But they also recognized the value of some of the new technology. They therefore took a somewhat "middle-of-the-road" approach in their attempt to keep both top management and the clerks and their union satisfied.

Clerks and their union

The clerks and their union took a totally different view of office technology from top management. They recognized that new technology might be valuable to the firm, but this would not be a primary consideration for them. The clerks' major interest was that of job satisfaction, and how their job satisfaction needs could be met (see Fig. 2). It followed that they would be concerned with how the technology might affect their jobs and thus them. For this reason the clerks wanted some say in how the technology would be used. They desired to be part of any design team which would consider the implementation of any new office technology.

The clerks did not address the various types of new office technologies available. In essence, they did not care; their concern was not with any specific technology, only with how the technology, when implemented, would affect them. Therefore, the overall design of how the technology would be used was their major concern.

Technologists

Unlike their counterparts, who were concerned with company profitability or dehumanized jobs, the technologists addressed the issue of new technologies and their possible applications in the office. The technologists viewed themselves as externals, i.e., salesmen, whose task was to produce a suitable marketing plan to sell management on the virtues of new technology. They developed a listing of various new technologies, where they could be used in the office, and why they should be obtained. The strategy was obviously geared for management as issues such as possible effects on workers' jobs were not raised. Instead, the technologists produced a document which reflected management's concern with profitability and stability.

The squeezing of middle management and other conflicts

The role-playing session then followed where each group got up in front of the others and acted out what had been discussed and agreed in each group's private sessions. The order of presentation is important. The session began with top management describing their views. Their presentation centered on how the firm's first and foremost consideration must be with profitability. Therefore, if new office technology would enhance the firm's financial position it should be considered seriously. Top management pleaded ignorance when it came to concrete new technology recommendations; it was up to middle management to "know about these things". Top management concluded by stating that new office technology could be beneficial to the firm, and that middle management should begin a program to see in what areas the new technology would be useful.

The technologists followed. Having listened to top management's openness, and, in fact, desire for new technology, the technologists seized this opportunity and oriented their presentation exactly around the issues raised by top management. They went step by step through the various technologies available, where and how they could be used in the firm, and how they would save the firm money in the long run. Obviously this was exactly what top management wanted to hear, and a rather pronounced dialogue developed between these two groups. Middle management would occasionally add a word of caution to top managements' optimism, but one wonders whether it had any impact.

Middle management next presented their discussions. Right from the very beginning a sense of pressure could be felt. It appeared as though what had been discussed in private sessions had to be somewhat modified. Middle management had sensed top management's enthusiasm for the new office technology, and thus had to temper their remarks to keep their enthusiasm fueled. On the other hand, middle management knew the clerks had to be considered in any new technology decision but were unclear on how to bring this point to the attention of top management without drawing their wrath. This had a definite squeezing effect on middle management. They wanted to show the clerks that they had been considered by middle management but they did not want top management to think they were not concerned with the firm's profitability. The resulting presentation was one of ambiguity, tension, and conflict. Clearly middle management was thrust into a no-win situation. Pro-top management support would be viewed with anger by the clerks, pro-clerk support would be viewed with contempt by top management, and a noncommittal approach would risk the distrust of both top management and the clerks. Middle management unquestionably had a dilemma which they could neither solve nor ignore.

The clerks then followed. Sensing the uneasy environment, they attempted to make known their concern over any new office technology implementation, but they attempted to present their case in what they thought would

be the least offensive manner. They brought up some concerns which they had about what constituted reasonable working conditions, and what kinds of opportunities they desired. It was clear that they were concerned with the human aspects of work, and not about any particular kinds of technology. All they really wanted was to be considered and involved in any technological innovation which would affect their working environment, or more specifically, their jobs. To this end the clerks drew up a design principle (see Fig. 2), which addressed this need. Unfortunately, the clerks' presentation fell on deaf ears. Middle management was busy planning how they could convince top management that they *were* concerned about the firm's profitability and not allied with the clerks' union. Top management really did not *understand* what the clerks were worried about since they felt they had always had concern for their employees even though it had not always been explicitly stated. They therefore felt the clerks' presentation was inaccurate and thus irrelevant. The technologists were interested in selling their technology. Since it was not the clerks who were buying the technology they had little reason to listen to the clerks. The clerks presentation was thus *irrelevant* as far as they were concerned.

Synthesis

The above information represents one level of hermeneutic understanding. It provides the basis for a possible further iteration when the information which each group produces is fed back to the other groups and a conscious attempt made to evaluate it and see its wider implications. In the case at hand, this led to three major insights: (1) Major technology changes in the office will inevitably spark conflict due to the different goals and needs of the stakeholders. (2) The question why conflict is inevitable led to the identification of three antagonistic views of the nature of technological change in modern society. (3) These general insights led to a commonly recognized need for the development of conflict handling methods and managerial strategies which would minimize destructive side-effects of conflicts about technological change.

1. The inevitability of conflict

The message which arose as a result of the role-playing exercise is that conflict inevitably arises due to the different goals and needs of the different interest groups. Each group had determined what was important for it and that is what it would strive to attain. Unfortunately, these needs and goals which are deemed important by the group's members do not always match those of other groups; in fact, they rarely do. Therefore conflict is inevitable. How a firm handles or deals with this conflict can have an impact on how successfully the firm operates. The choice of looking at office technology is only one example of an almost infinite number of possible conflict-producing situations.

The realization that a great deal of the role-playing exercise involved the raising of conflicts led to the discussion and subsequent need to include conflict-solving methods in the office design process. It was suggested as a preliminary conclusion that technology will only be effectively used if it is adaptive enough to meet the needs and interests of all the different interest groups in the situation. Therefore, if power is distributed, then strategies to influence the acceptance of new technology will essentially be negotiating and conflict resolving rather than the traditional planning approach, the latter assuming that a specific rationality serves all parties best.

An assumption embedded in the preliminary conclusion was that power is "somehow" distributed in offices (or companies in general). Nothing was said of the evenness or fairness of distribution, however. This led one of the participants to state that "... there is an overshadowing power relationship between workers and entrepreneurs that also covers the dialectics of introducing new technology". From this evolved the spelling out of three views of consequences of applying new technologies in the office (or in general).

2. Technological consequences: three views

The *optimistic view* stated that with growing technological advancement (as in our time of tremendous computer development), technology is — or will be — flexible enough to be used to the advantage of the entire society, including all groups affected. Moreover, the existence of a flexible technology will ensure that the flexibility is actually used for this purpose.

With a *pluralistic view* a critique was launched against the optimistic view as to its lack of taking into account the existence of conflicting interests and of non-uniform power distribution. Although technologists themselves may want to promote "positive" ways of using technology, other groups usually decide what specific technologies to develop and to apply, and how to implement and use them. In other words, specific characteristics of a society, such as its level of technology and its distribution of power, will greatly influence the manner in which technology will be used.

Participants claiming a *repressive view* pointed to what they perceived as the actual power distribution between workers and owners of the means of production in the western capitalist societies. From this, they concluded a great danger of new technologies being used as a repressive tool against workers, not for the sake of repression itself, but as a means of increasing profit and control over the working process. Flexibility is two-sided, and it is a power question if such technological flexibility will be used for improving working conditions whenever this does not at the same time improve cost.

3. Strategies to promote the optimistic view

Neither of the three proposed views could possibly be unanimously adhered to by all participants. There was no doubt, however, as to what direction the group wanted the actual use of technology to be changed. Actions to promote the design and use of technology as suggested by the optimistic view were considered. The four major strategies that were assumed to give positive contributions in this direction, are listed below.

(1) Participation in technological choice and design.
(2) Experimentation, in particular with new forms of work organization.

(3) Increasing workers' consciousness about technological change. This is also a prerequisite for successful participation. Research conducted by or controlled by workers and their unions is part of this strategy.

(4) Increasing systems analysts' consciousness about human and social consequences.

It was underlined, though, that what can be reached through these strategies is to take into account certain non-used degrees of freedom already embedded in the existing societal structures. Both the humanization approach and the democratization approach can only operate within certain fixed limits given by the power distribution. Neither of the four strategies listed will be sufficient to move these limits, beyond which there exist technologies and technological applications that will serve workers and society better, but that will not be developed under the present conditions.

5. DISCUSSION AND CRITICAL EVALUATION

As is the case with the results of a causal model, the information generated by the application of hermeneutic skills should be carefully evaluated to check for possible sources of errors. This part is in no way different from the critical evaluation of the results of a formal model. This, too, relies entirely on the judgemental skill of the researchers. This section summarizes our conclusions in this regard, with a view towards stating some recommendations on how the hermeneutic prediction method could be improved by recognizing possible error sources and some comments on the "efficiency" of the approach.

5.1 The question of trustworthiness

How much confidence can we have that the results produced in this study are "real" and therefore worth paying attention to? The same question must be asked about any

model-based predictions. Even if the model is accurate, in the sense that the relationships which were used in its construction are "empirically true", the predictions still need not be true because of the issue of self-falsifying predictions: if I predict that my car is on a crash course then I will take purposeful corrective action and the prediction will hopefully turn out false. Let us focus on some characteristics of the process by which the predictions were made and see if they inspire confidence.

As was described in subsection 4.3, it was agreed as a starting point that each group should address three topics: the technologies, their functions, and the consequences of application. It turned out that the technologists stuck very closely to this original plan, while some other groups deviated quite a bit from this. Figures 1 and 2 contain some of the workshop notes of the Top Management and the Clerks/Union predictor groups. From these notes it is evident that as far as these two groups were concerned they "emancipated" themselves so far from the original instructions that one might be inclined to say they redefined their mandate. If this can happen, what light does this shed on the trustworthiness or validity of the results, and if it reduces our confidence, then what safeguards could be taken in future versions of hermeneutic exercises to prevent this from recurring?

An answer to the question of trustworthiness seems to depend on one's assumptions of the reasons why some groups deviated while others stuck with the original plan. Two interpretations seem possible: (1) The original plan was wrong and the subgroups modified it as their understanding of the problems involved increased in the course of the hermeneutic procedure. So in this case it is good that the groups emancipated themselves from misleading instructions and made the best of them as they saw fit. But why then did at least one group — the technologists — stay with it, and what does this mean for the trustworthiness of the information generated by this subgroup? One obvious answer is that the technologists were more loyal to the original plan and made it more of an unquestionable assumption than the other groups.

This would be in line with the observation that the training of technologists is generally more conformist than the training of philosophers or social scientists. It would mean that the information generated by the technologists is less trustworthy because it rests on assumptions that were not critically evaluated. There is, however, a second interpretation which we feel is more likely the correct one. (2) The original plan was dominated by the way technologists tend to think. To express it differently: the technologists' world view was the one on which the first pre-understanding of the problem rested. It provided the anchoring point. If this is the case one would hope that the results should be independent of the anchoring point. That is, no matter what the first pre-understanding is, over the course of the several hermeneutic circles

TOP MANAGEMENT

Assumptions:

— we, as the senior management for this organisation, have assumed the following objectives:
- 5—8% growth in profit yearly
- increase market share to 12% by 1985
- minimize risk whenever possible, this leads us to be interested in increasing efficiency (Technology might be appropriate in this case)

— more competition
— uncertainty caused by resource scarcity, e.g. energy raw materials, etc.
— high labour turnover
— increased awareness of unionization
— difficulty in recruiting good quality staff
— already had computerised many d.p. functions, but still had many to go
— d.p. budget is 3.4% of turnover
— stagnate customer growth
— overheads rising as a proportion of costs

Technical opportunities:

EFTS
— direct debit looks promising in the short run
— improvements in cash flow can reduce our indebtedness to approximately 3 or 4 days from the present 10
— there may be a risk however in the loss of goodwill

Marketing through PRESTEL
— we perceive our catalogue to be on Prestel which could then expand the number of customers available
— we would like a preliminary study done, however, and possibly some experiment
— the general feeling is we would like access to a larger market; Prestel may offer us this

Word processing
— may provide us the opportunity to produce multiple catalogues for special markets
— connection with databases could allow us to reorganise the way we handle customers. This could lead to a more personalised service

Computerised warehouse
— seems like a good idea. Previously this was looked at and was deemed not economical; now however, we should look again in light of the recent micro technology

In general:

— we, as senior management, are happy with our computing services. We view them in a 'line' capacity rather than 'service' and are more than happy to let them deal with technical innovations. They have the authority to call in consultants if they feel this is necessary

Fig. 1. Transcript of notes from the top management predictor group.

CLERKS AND UNION GROUP

General design principle

Organizations need to think out their values and their goals and ensure that the design of technology fits these values and goals.

We as clerks expect that our organizations will have humanistic values and make our job satisfaction one of their important goals.

Clerks job satisfaction needs

Knowledge needs   Use skills
                      Learn new skills

Psychological needs   Job security
                      Adequate pay
                      Status
                      Social contact/relationships
                      Shorter work hours/year — Overtime
                                                Restrict.

ended and unbureaucratic style of leadership is preferable for the management of innovation (cf. [42]). This style of leadership encourages the growth and development of human creativity: independent thought, sharing of ideas, initiative and responsibility taking in spite of substantial risks of failure. A mechanistic style of management encourages defensive behaviors, but may nevertheless be more productive for well-defined and clearly structured tasks.

But then what could be more ill-defined than to predict the future consequences of technological change in the offices of complex organizations? Instead of ending up with a list of technological applications and their possible consequences spelled out in detail, the hermeneutic procedure came up with a better understanding of the conflict-laden nature of changing office technology — a qualitatively totally different kind of knowledge, but one which nevertheless is highly pertinent to the issue at hand. This shift in perspective should be a credit and not a debit of the procedure which was able to bring it about. (We do not wish to deny that the same sort of result can also be triggered by a model-based experiment.)[3] To some extent this also spells out that problem-solving methods must be consistent with the kind of problem to be solved: traditional planning and causal models of prediction for purely technical problems, dialectical inquiry, participatory group techniques and conflict-handling procedures for dealing with complex issues involving multiple human interests.

[3] Witness the consequences of the historical Michelson-Morley experiment in physics, the outcome of which questioned the universality of Newtonian physics (because it showed that the speed of light is independent of the reference frame) and thereby contributed to the shift in perspective eventually brought about by Einstein. For further discussion of the related methodological issues see Kuhn [43].

Task needs	Clerks control machines (not vv)
	No machine recording of human performance
	To take decisions (creative)
	Judgement
	Discretion
	Routine work: reduce, distribute optimally
Organizational needs	Flexi-structure
Personnel policies	Equity
	Influence on what personal data to be recorded
Legislation T.U./Empl. Agreements	To protect our interests

Fig. 2. Transcript of notes from the clerks and union predictor group.

an iterative convergence towards the "truth" should occur. Under this interpretation it seems very natural that the technologists were unable to transcend their own view. The onus of the convergence rests primarily on the shoulders of the other groups.

Under this interpretation one would be led to believe that it is confidence inspiring that the other groups managed to emancipate themselves from the original instructions, because it shows that these subgroups managed to switch their thinking towards the beliefs and interests of those whom they were to represent. If this is accepted then any advice to tighten the hermeneutic procedure by imposing controls on the flexibility of the predictor groups, e.g. to prevent them from redefining their mandate as they see fit, would seem to be counterproductive.

5.2 Implications for procedure

There is some external evidence that this latter interpretation is the correct one. In the literature on the rationality of organic management it has been shown that an open-

6. CONCLUSIONS

The application of new information technology in the office provides the potential for numerous benefits — both for the employees of the organization, and the organization as a whole. The realization of these benefits through the appropriate application of new technology, however, will not be easy. The consequences of introducing office automation could be very great indeed. It has, therefore, become apparent that we need a better understanding of what these consequences might be. Unfortunately, predicting these consequences is not straightforward. Our present method of prediction, mechanistic causal analysis, has been shown to be deficient in the social sciences, and thus this paper has proposed a new approach — hermeneutic analysis. The application of hermeneutic analysis has been documented in the form of a role-playing exercise, and the results were promising. A much better understanding of the potential consequences of office automation, and how to deal with them, was gained. It is thus contended that hermeneutic analysis is a much better vehicle for understanding and predicting the human consequences of new technology introduction than any of those currently in use.

ACKNOWLEDGEMENT

We would like to thank Hakon Finne for his contribution to Section 4 of this paper.

REFERENCES

1 H.K. Klein, I.S.G. Meadows and R.J. Welke, Improving the quality of working life (QWL) through information systems development. Proc. Int. Congr. on Appl. Syst. Res. and Cybernetics, Acapulco, Mexico, Dec. 2—16, 1980, Vol. 1, pp. 420—428.

2 H.C. Lucas, Behavioral factors in system implementation, in: Implementing Operations Research/Management Science, R.L. Schultz and Slevin (Eds.), Elsevier, New York, 1975.

3 C. Argyris, Interpersonal barriers to decision making, Harvard Business Review, 44(2) March—April 1966, 84—97.

4 C. Argyris, Management information systems: the challenge to rationality and emotionality, Management Science, 17 (1971) B—275.

5 C. Argyris, Theories of action that inhibit individual learning, American Psychologist, 39 (1976) 638—654.

6 R.W. Zmud, Individual differences and MIS success: a review of the empirical literature, Management Sc., 25 (10) (Oct. 1979) 966—979.

7 M.J. Ginzberg, Early diagnosis of MIS implementation failure, Management Science, 27(4) (1981) 459—478.

8 S. Alter, Decision Support Systems, Addison-Wesley, (Don Mills, 1980).

9 P.G.W. Keen, Information systems and organizational change, CACM, 24(1) (Jan. 1981) 24—33.

10 I. Kant, Groundwork of the Metaphysic of Morals, Harper Torchbooks, New York, 1964.

11 W.C. Churchman, Challenge to Reason, McGraw Hill, New York, 1968.

12 H.K. Klein, Design ideals and their critical reconstruction, Invited paper presented at the TIMS College on Management Philosophy, May Session MB04.2, 1981, Toronto; McMaster University, Hamilton, Ontario, 1981.

13 K. Kumar, Participant values and their role in the system development process, draft for a thesis proposal, McMaster University, Hamilton, 1982.

14 D. Hume, A treatise of human nature, 1739 and 1740, in: David Hume on Human Nature and the Understanding, A. Flew (Ed.), Collier Classics in the History of Thought, McMillan, London, 1962, p. 167.

15 D. Hume, An inquiry concerning human nature, in: David Hume on Human Nature and the Understanding, A. Flew (Ed.), Collier Classics in the History of Thought, McMillan, London, 1962, p. 21.

16 H. Wold, Causality and econometrics, Econometrica, 22 (1954) 162—177.

17 H. Wold, Possibilités et limitations des systèmes à chaine causale, in: Cahiers Du Seminaire D'Econométrie, 3, Service des Publications du C.N.R.S., 13 Quai Anatole, Paris, 1955, pp. 81—101.

18 H. Wold, Case study of interdependent versus causal chain systems, Rev. Int. Stat. Inst., 26 (1958) 5—25.

19 H.A. Simon, Causal ordering and identifiability, in: Studies in Economotric Method, W.C. Hood and T.C. Koopmans (Eds.), J. Wiley, New York, 1953.

20 H.A. Simon, Causality and econometrics, Comment in Econometrica, 23 (1955) p. 193.

21 T. Koopmans, Identification problems in econometric method, in: Studies in Econometric Method, W.C. Hood and T.C. Koopmans (Eds.), J. Wiley, New York, 1953.

22 F.M. Fisher, The Identification Problem in Econometrics, McGraw-Hill, 1966.

23 J. Manninen and R. Tuomela (Eds.), Essays on Explanation and Understanding, Dordrecht-Holland, 1975.

24 K.-O. Apel, The Explanation: Understanding Controversy in Transcendental—pragmatic Perspective (title translated from German), Theorie-Diskussion, Suhrkamp, Frankfurt, 1979.

25 K. Popper, The Logic of Scientific Discovery, Hutchinson, London, 1965.

26 M. Lessnoff, The Structure of Social Science, A Philosophical Introduction, Allen & Unwin, London, 1974.

27 H.A. Simon, Theories of decision making in economics and behavioral science, Am. Econ. Rev., 49 (1959) 253—283; here quoted from Managerial Economics, G.P.E. Clarkson (Ed.) Penguin Modern Economics, Harmondsworth, 1968, pp. 13—49.

28 H.A. Simon, Administrative Behavior, New York, 1957.

29 H.A. Simon, Motivational and emotional controls of cognition, Psych. Rev., 74(1) (1967) 29.

30 E. Durkheim, The Rules of Sociological Method, The Free Press, New York, 1964.

31 A. Newell, J.C. Shaw and H.A. Simon, Elements of a theory of problem solving, Psych. Rev., 65 (1958) 151—166.

32 A. Newell and H.A. Simon, Human Problem Solving, Prentice Hall, Englewood Cliffs, 1972.

33 J.R. Searle, Expression and Meaning. Studies in the Theory of Speech Acts, Cambridge University Press, London, 1979.

34 J.G. March and H.A. Simon, Organizations, J. Wiley, New York, 1958, p.151.

35 R. Welke, Information Systems Effectiveness Evaluation (ISEE), paper presented at IFIP TC8 WG8.2 Meeting, London 1977; McMaster University, Hamilton, Ontario (mimeographed).

36 G.H. von Wright, Explanation and Understanding, London, 1971 (German translation Königstein 1973).

37 H.G. Gadamer, Philosophical Hermeneutics, (Edited and translated by D.E. Linge.) University of California Press, Berkeley, 1976.

38 J. Habermas, Theory of Communicative Action (title translated from German: Theory des Kommunikativen Handelns), Suhrkamp, Frankfurt, 1981.

39 H.-G. Gadamer and G. Boehm (Eds.), Seminar: Philosophical Hermeneutics (title translated from German), Suhrkamp, Frankfurt, 1979.

40 R. Mason and I. Mitroff, Strategic Assumption Analysis, J. Wiley, London, 1981.

41 R.P. Bostrom and S. Heinen, MIS Problems and failures: a sociotechnical perspective, MIS Quarterly, Sept.—Dec. 1977, pp. 17—32 and 11—28.

42 T. Burns and Stalker, The Management of Innovation, Tavistock, London, 1961.

43 T.S. Kuhn, The Structure of Scientific Revolutions, Univ. of Chicago Press, Chicago, 1970.

44 B. Langefors, Hermeneutics, Infology, and Information Systems, TRITA-IBADB no. 1052, University of Stockholm, June 1977.

Conclusion:
Office Technology and
Managerial Excellence

Many of the organizations described in this book are paying attention to the impact that office automation is having on their work forces, often using innovative approaches to manage these concerns. Other organizations have experienced serious employee and labor relations problems when people-technology issues have been ignored or handled poorly by management. In addition, we have seen instances in which organizational problems existing prior to or apart from the advent of OA may surface or become exacerbated when new technology is introduced. In these situations, OA can provide an opportunity to address such issues and reshape management practices which may be outmoded or inappropriate for VDT work environments.

SOCIO-TECHNICAL APPROACH

As emphasized in preceeding chapters, effective people-technology planning requires a socio-technical approach to managing change. For employees who spend the majority of their time in front of a terminal, a complex set of factors influences how they experience OA. These aspects, in turn, contribute to or detract from truly successful implementation. Furthermore, VDT operators experience the impact of management decisions with regard to training, job design, work monitoring, ergonomics, and health and safety issues holistically. Work stress, visual and musculoskeletal discomfort, degree of social interaction, etc., are all interlinked with the tool, task, individual and workstation. These elements are also set in the context of a specific work group, organizational setting and external environment (see Figure 15.1).

Thus, a socio-technical approach entails careful consideration of hardware and software choices, integration of office systems with other computer-based technology and attention to new people, organizational and social issues generated by technological change (see Figure 15.2). *However, in over 75% of the 110 organizations we visited during 1982-84, "people, organizational and social issues" were not being addressed in any comprehensive and systematic way and were not the assigned responsibility of any particular staff group or department.*

Excerpted from Westin, A.F., Schweder, H.A., Baker, M.A. and Lehman, S. (1985). Office Technology and Managerial Excellence. In *The Changing Workplace: A Guide to Managing the People, Organizational, and Regulatory Aspects of Office Technology*. White Plains, N.Y.: Knowledge Industry Publications, Inc.

Figure 15.1: Factors Affecting VDT Operator Work Experience

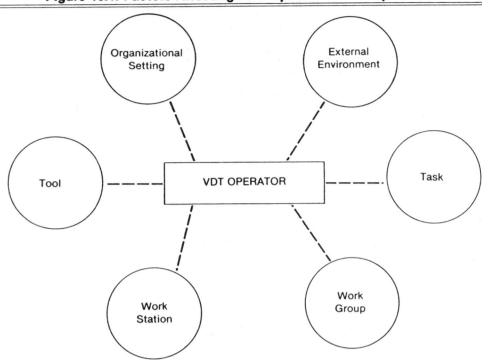

During the first wave of office automation (1978-1983), mastering the technical dimensions of new office systems technologies was the dominant concern of most of the organizations studied. Most have found implementing OA more difficult than the development and implementation of computerized mainframe systems that occurred during the EDP era. Hence, problems associated with rapidly changing OA hardware/software, inter-system incompatibilities, integration of OA with mainframe computers, etc., have been the first priority of many MIS/EDP/OA departments.

In addition, interdepartmental planning and co-ordination for transitions to VDT work environments has generally been lacking. Few organizations have developed centralized, master OA plans to bring together all the players and provide a framework for integrating both the technical and human dimensions of office automation. Some managers we interviewed commented that "in the early days of word processing it was like buying typewriters"—a loose, piecemeal effort with individual departments placing orders for new equipment purchases. Consequently, systems and hardware have frequently been chosen by information experts with little user input or consultation.

Ergonomics—in the broad sense of planning suitable workstations and work environments for VDT users—has been the responsibility of facilities planners accustomed to the lighting, electrical and other requirements of more traditional office layouts. Training, often provided by vendors, has had a narrow "how to key" focus with insufficient follow-up support for users. Finally, participation by the personnel department in the entire OA effort has been highly limited in most organizations. Many human resources staff were themselves uninformed and ill-prepared to anticipate the human impact of intensive OA work, both for clerical and professional/technical users. As a result, important employee relations implications were often not perceived during transitions to office automation.

KEY PEOPLE-TECHNOLOGY ISSUES

At the same time, as described in Chapter 3, a small number of the sites we visited have developed comprehensive and innovative approaches to people-technology planning in order to address problems stemming from inattention to important "people" issues. While these organizations were highly diverse in terms of industry, size of work force, manage-

Figure 15.2: Socio-Technical Approach to Adopting New Office Systems Technology

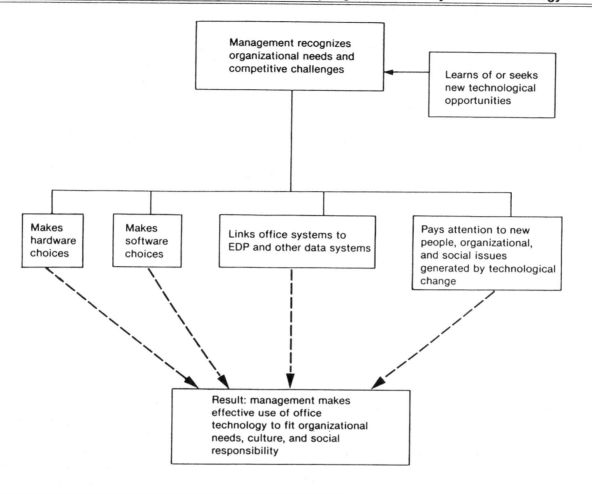

ment style, extent of OA, etc., they each paid close attention to a number of key *process* and *substantive* issues associated with the introduction of new office technology. These issues, which have been discussed in detail in earlier chapters, include:

(1) *Strategic Planning.* Top management must have a commitment to:

• Anticipating people-technology issues associated with new office technologies and integrating these into overall OA planning on both a short- and long-term basis;

• Developing an interdisciplinary approach to translate changing internal and external OA forces and trends affecting VDT operators into organizational policies and practices.

(2) *OA "Ownership."* This entails the identification and involvement of all participants significantly affected by and affecting the OA process, including:

• Functional support groups. For example: MIS/EDP/OA technical staff; human resource/personnel executives (including health and safety, labor relations, Equal Employment Opportunity/Affirmative Action staff); facilities planners; legal counsel; and public affairs departments;

• End-users. These include: clerical, data-entry, customer service, word processing operators; secretarial, administrative end-users; professional/technical staff; and managers/executives.

Effective "ownership" may be facilitated by formal and informal structures to provide interaction and coordination among different groups through the use of task forces, professional staff units, joint management-labor committees, ad hoc task teams, quality circles, periodic meetings, etc. Obviously, the roles and responsibilities of each group of participants will shift in terms of emphasis and initiative at different times during the process of adopting new technology.

(3) *Employee Involvement and Participation.* There needs to be a conscious management decision to actively solicit input and feedback from users *on an ongoing basis* concerning decisions and changes affecting their jobs and work units during and after the transition to VDT work environments. Such employee involvement provides management with valuable information on technical problems and work organization issues. In addition, the lack of user participation in an OA project can sabotage employee acceptance and use of new technology after equipment has been installed. Specific channels for employee involvement and feedback include periodic surveys and questionnaires, individual and focus group interviews, quality circles, and formal and informal management/employee discussions.

(4) *Communications/Problem-Resolution.* Ongoing efforts are needed to maintain open management/employee communication to actively keep employees informed about OA plans and decisions and to solicit employee complaints. This may include:

• Developing in-house brochures, videotapes, newsletters, etc., to communicate management policy on health and safety issues, ergonomics and job security, as well as information about organizational plans for future OA activities and projects;

• Providing both formal and informal mechanisms to discover and resolve user problems with VDTs and complaints about the ways in which policies are being implemented.

(5) *Training.* New VDT users frequently need more extensive training than many managers and vendors think is necessary. Providing both employees and managers with sufficiently broad-based skills and information to *integrate* the use of new office technologies effectively into their jobs and work units is essential in order to obtain maximum benefits from OA. This involves:

• Educating nontechnical users to articulate software needs to systems analysts in the early planning stages;

• Tailoring training approaches to the needs of different types of users as well as providing sufficient follow-up support to initial training sessions;

• Incorporating ergonomic and health and safety concerns into training sessions;

• Training managers and supervisors to oversee VDT work environments and support employees during the transition period. Also, managers and supervisors often need to overcome their own resistance to innovation and develop *realistic* OA expectations in terms of how quickly employees learn to use new equipment.

(6) *Job Redesign.* During and after the transition to a VDT work environment, it is important to address the impact of office systems technologies on both incumbent and newly hired employees' job satisfaction, in order to maintain or increase productivity and quality of work life. This includes:

• Reviewing job tasks with employees to obtain input for designing systems that meet the VDT user's job task needs and to avoid designing the job around the system;

• Establishing appropriate management practices with regard to work breaks, social interaction, etc.;

• Evaluating hiring and placement criteria, career path opportunities, etc., for long-range human resource planning;

• Restructuring job tasks when necessary to maintain sufficient autonomy, variety, etc., in order to "keep jobs whole" and provide employees with a sense of identity with their work. Task variety also helps avoid visual and muscle fatigue in jobs requiring extensive VDT use.

(7) *Work Monitoring and Performance Standards.* Developing both meaningful and fair qualitative and quantitative measurements of VDT operators' job performance standards is essential. This involves:

• Incorporating both technical expertise and meaningful employee participation and input (through surveys, employee rap sessions, etc.) during the process of establishing both individual operator and group production standards;

• Openly informing employees about work monitoring policies and of their right to see records compiled and contest evaluations they feel are unfair;

• Periodically reviewing performance standards for fairness and appropriateness to specific work settings (e.g., allowing for downtime, processing orders of different length and complexity);

• Training supervisors to motivate rather than "police" employees when evaluating VDT operators' work performance;

• Emphasizing customer service and quality of work as essential aspects of producing a "whole product" in addition to *quantitative* measurements of production. Such emphasis is essential to minimize error rate and provide greater employee pride and identification with the products produced.

(8) *Health and Safety.* Managements must assess the overall VDT operator work environment in terms of organizational health and safety practices and determine appropriate organizational policies. This includes:

• Monitoring current scientific research on: (a) VDT health and safety issues, such as radiation, stress, pregnancy, vision and musculoskeletal discomfort; and (b) monitoring office health in general, especially the problems of noise and air quality;

• Communicating this research information with candor to employees;

• Reviewing the scope of employee health-related record-keeping and organizational policies affecting VDT user physical comfort (e.g., rest breaks, exercise, vision policies);

• Providing special channels to solicit employee complaints, questions and experiences with regard to health-related concerns.

(9) *Ergonomics.* A sound plan must focus on ergonomic problems affecting end-user work performance, physical comfort and job satisfaction. This entails:

• Observing work sites and soliciting employee input to evaluate the fit among individual needs, job design, hardware, workstations and software; paying particular attention to sites with older equipment and to settings that mix VDT and "paper" work;

• Altering and upgrading equipment in light of growing recognition that there is no "best" solution —flexibility and individual adjustability are key elements;

• Training employees to recognize ergonomic problems and make maximum effective use of available workstation, terminal and software features;

• Developing and piloting software that responds to user needs and preferences by involving users in the development and evaluation processes;

• Establishing ergonomic standards for longer-term planning and for expansion and modernization of work sites;

• Periodically monitoring the ergonomics of current workstations to uncover changes in work conditions and development of new problems that require adjustments.

(10) *Labor Relations Issues.* During the past five years, union interest in the impact of office automation on the work force has grown considerably. The result is a broad range of collective bargaining positions, including: how new technology is introduced, work training and retraining programs, health and safety concerns, ergonomics, VDT work monitoring, job design and work reorganization. Many unionized firms are pursuing cooperative rather than confrontational approaches to addressing these issues through joint management/union committees, quality-of-work-life circles, etc. Cooperation has been particularly effective in the areas of ergonomic specifications, coping with harmful stress, better training in using VDTs and alleviation of physical discomforts.

(11) *Women's Quality-of-Work-Life and Discrimination Issues.* Since the great majority of VDT-related jobs are filled by women, and they have a virtual monopoly on clerical, customer service and secretarial jobs, it is important that managers pay attention to the growing issues of

women's pay equity and opportunities for promotion. This involves:

• Recognizing that women have unique needs and that long-established patterns of labor market and economic discrimination have to be actively addressed to be overcome;

• Conducting focus group interviews and organizational audits or assessments of management policies and practices, in terms of hiring and promotion patterns, career path and educational opportunities for women;

• Making organizational and technological changes with an awareness of emerging social and legal expectations concerning equality for women and minorities.

(12) *Legal/Regulatory Trends*. Managers need to appreciate that there is a rapidly developing legal milieu and potential regulatory intervention with regard to VDT use which calls for anticipative management in this area. For example:

• Worker compensation suits and tort lawsuits related to VDT use are proliferating, making attention to ergonomics in VDT work settings a legal as well as a "good job/good practices" concern.

• Current state legislative efforts to regulate VDT-related management practices (ergonomic standards, frequency of rest breaks, etc.) will require organizations to demonstrate their responsible practices. This will have to occur both in the public arena (through testimony, media coverage, etc.) and through efforts to develop industry and government sector standards that upgrade management practices beyond a few innovative leaders. How individual firms respond will probably determine whether there will be extensive legislative intervention in the future.

TRANSITIONS TO VDT WORK ENVIRONMENTS

As noted earlier, the most effective approach for integrating these issues into an overall people-technology strategy will vary with each organization and individual OA project. At the same time, without developing some general guidelines, important issues and concerns can easily be overlooked—creating problems which could otherwise be avoided or minimized.

It is difficult to easily categorize the dynamics of any complex organizational process into discrete steps. However, it is useful from a management perspective to think about the process of adopting new technology as entailing four functions or stages that can be used as a framework for integrating the technical and human dimensions of office automation. (See Figure 15.3.) While these tend to occur sequentially, in some instances more than one function or stage may be happening at once. These stages apply to small or large scale OA efforts; professional/technical, administrative, clerical or customer service applications; and to first-time or expanding use of automated systems. They are:

(1) *Planning*. This function includes: determining departmental, work unit, or organizational systems and hardware needs; anticipating effects on the work force through an organizational-impact analysis; developing technical systems plans; and selecting hardware and software with "people" considerations incorporated.

(2) *Piloting or Pre-implementation*. Piloting entails the small-scale use of new equipment for demonstration purposes and/or to assess impact on individual users and the work unit as a whole. Piloting a new application provides immediate feedback and early assessment of potential problems from employees directly involved in the pilot and from others who may be indirectly affected. In some situations, piloting may not be feasible or appropriate. However, in the pressure to get OA projects "up and running," the pilot stage is often omitted, creating problems later on.

(3) *Implementation*. At this stage, systems hardware is installed throughout the work unit, department or organization on a full-scale basis. This transition stage is a period of intensive learning for new users, disruption of established work routines and reorganization of work procedures. Managers also must be aware that employee attitudes toward new systems and hardware are likely to change considerably during this period as users "unlearn" established work routines and, over time, become proficient with new equipment and systems.

(4) *Integration*. During the final stage systems are fully integrated into users' jobs and are functioning smoothly with minimal disruption in work routines. New processes and work procedures are in place and long-term impacts on jobs, career paths, performance standards, etc., can be assessed.

Figure 15.3: Transition to VDT Work Environment

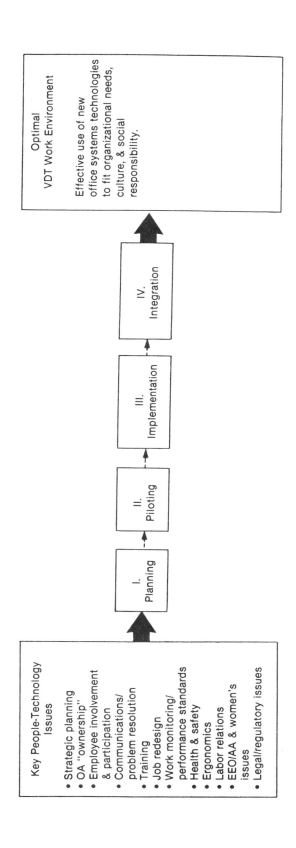

Key People-Technology
Issues

- Strategic planning
- OA "ownership"
- Employee involvement
  & participation
- Communications/
  problem resolution
- Training
- Job redesign
- Work monitoring/
  performance standards
- Health & safety
- Ergonomics
- Labor relations
- EEO/AA & women's
  issues
- Legal/regulatory issues

I.
Planning

II.
Piloting

III.
Implementation

IV.
Integration

Optimal
VDT Work Environment

Effective use of new
office systems technologies
to fit organizational needs,
culture, & social
responsibility.

Each of the 12 people-technology issues outlined earlier needs to be addressed at some point during the planning, piloting, implementation or integration stages. Some issues may be critical during one particular stage, such as establishing strategic planning objectives and OA ownership during the planning period. Others, such as employee involvement and communication/problem-resolution need to be an integral part of all four functions. In still other instances, the process by which substantive issues are handled may be especially important, e.g., communicating health and safety information to VDT users. Each organization, of course, needs to determine the most appropriate sequence and timing for addressing these issues on both a short- and long-term basis.

STRATEGIES FOR INNOVATION

During our field study of organizations undergoing extensive change due to the adoption of new office systems technologies, we observed several strategies that the most effective organizations were using both to encourage innovation and to manage the impact of organizational change. These include:

• Conducting special OA-impact assessments;

• Creating people-technology staff units;

• Recognizing critical staff and middle management roles.

We will briefly discuss each in turn.

Conducting Special OA-Impact Assessments

Many of the organizations highlighted in Chapter 3, as well as others with similar comprehensive approaches to people-technology issues, conducted extensive individual and focus group interviews with a broad cross-section of employees to assess the impact of office technology applications on their work force. In some cases, these organizations used an outside consulting firm to provide greater objectivity. In other instances, trained in-house human resource/personnel staff were used. Organizations that used this type of interviewing to assess employee reactions and perceptions of new technology were able to develop highly accurate profiles of organizational successes and "pressure points" in terms of how technology was affecting employee job satisfaction, adequacy of training,

health and safety concerns, special women's issues, etc. This information was then incorporated into existing programs to correct weak areas, enhance positive aspects and help improve planning and piloting of new applications. In no instance did we hear of employee relations problems or negative reactions to conducting such interviews. In fact, employees were generally pleased to participate in an evaluation of OA in their jobs and work units, and to be "consulted."

Creating People-Technology Staff Units

Some of the innovative organizations we visited had established special people-technology staff units to provide a unifying focus on these issues. The model developed by Aetna Life and Casualty (described in Chapter 3) is an example of a small professional staff unit drawn from both the human resource and MIS/EDP functions. The unit connects the organization with the outside world on these issues and evaluates external trends and developments. In addition, the unit serves both an educational and catalytic function for managers and employees within the company. Finally, the unit helps provide coordination *across* departments on issues such as ergonomics that may require planning by several different functions.

IBM's VDT Ergonomics Project Office is another example of a people-technology unit, staffed with a variety of technical and professional specialists. The function of the unit is to integrate all the information IBM needs to develop sound VDT policies and to channel this information to top management, operating units, the personnel function and legal/public affairs units.

Recognizing Critical Staff and Middle Management Roles

There is some tendency to say that "what doesn't come from the top, isn't regarded as important," and we have stressed that senior management support for the adoption of a socio-technical approach is critical. However, this emphasis should not obscure the essential role of professional staff and middle managers, who are often the first to grasp the need for simultaneous attention to people, technological and organizational aspects in the OA process.

In many of the sites visited, it was clear that the entire OA effort might have gone better if those managers and staff had been allocated the time and resources with which to act on their understanding of what needed to be done. Their interest in the "people aspects" of OA often stemmed from two perceptions:

(1) Understanding that employees wanted to work with new technology, and that this basically positive orientation represented an opportunity to be grasped;

(2) Recognizing that OA provided a strategic opening for organizational change, including the addressing of longstanding problems, that could not be opened up without the fluid atmosphere created by a large-scale OA effort.

In some organizations, the human resources/personnel function provided leadership in reaching out to coordinate and involve other functions in developing an overall socio-technical approach within the company. In others, the data processing and MIS staff were both concerned with and knowledgeable about the "people aspects" of systems and automated work environments. Wherever located in the organizational structure, however, such staff were catalysts for thoughtful innovation, for coordination across units, and for identifying potential people-technology problems.

Experienced middle managers and staff also served a vital role as "shock absorbers" during periods of major technological change, e.g., during the actual implementation of new systems. Their own familiarity with organizational priorities and practices enabled them to guide employees and supervisors through the transition period to new equipment and systems with a minimum of disruption in overall work routines.

LONG-TERM CONCERNS FOR MANAGEMENT

In addition to managing the short-term transition to VDT work environments effectively, managers also need to be concerned with the long-term implications of the way in which they handle people-technology issues. The basic theme of this book has been that managements can and must choose how they will apply office systems technology in their organizations. We do not accept the view held by some enthusiasts and critics alike that OA applications are basically dictated by the logic of micro-electronics and the efficiency needs of bureaucratic organizations, and that as managements realize

what is "required," a uniform pattern of automated office work will emerge.

Our position is that managements have wide zones of choice in using office systems technologies, that these choices will exert powerful influences on the organizational effectiveness and employee acceptance of automation in office work, and that how such choices are made will largely determine the degree of social and legal intervention that will be applied to office automation by American society in the next decade. These judgments flow from our empirical studies, from our reading of the literature on organizational behavior, from our analysis of technology-society relations and from our conception of the professional and social responsibilities of managers in a democratic society.

This is not to say that certain broad trends in applications and certain discernible effects on workplaces have not been taking place. Throughout this guide we have noted some emerging trends among the organizations studied in the application of office automation to various types of work. Among the most significant are:

• A major shift to telecommunications services for regional and national handling of customer and client relations;

• Incorporation of low-level decision making into the software system for many types of high-volume transaction processes in organizations;

• Growing automation of technical and professional tasks;

• Efforts to fuse office automation, data processing and telecommunications into an integrated approach to overall information processes and top management strategic planning.

We also noted that the extent of such applications is still quite varied among units of the same organization, among organizations in the same field and across different organizational sectors.

MANAGING FOR EXCELLENCE

Having studied application trends, workplace impacts and types of management strategies for office automation unfolding in 1982-1984, we set out in this guide to provide a handbook for managers who believe—or whom we can convince—that they have important choices to make. One point is worth underscoring. In one sense, effective people-technology planning is an aspect of good strategic planning in general, in the tradition of recent scholarly and popular literature about managing for excellence.

Paying attention to good job design, equitable work standards and performance appraisal; training people well to use new tools; providing comfortable and efficient workplaces that minimize physical and psychological stress; protecting workers against health hazards; meeting legal and regulatory standards; involving employees in the planning, implementation and evaluation of new projects; and providing meaningful problem-resolution procedures to deal with employee concerns—these are not policies that are special to office automation. They are good general policies that, when applied to office automation, will produce the same kind of high payoffs for management, employees and society that they do when applied to other aspects of work in America.

Viewed another way, the arrival of office systems technology, along with other information technology processes being applied in organizations, offers managements interested in pursuing excellence the chance to revitalize established organizational structures and processes and to experiment with new techniques and systems. Inertia is a powerful force in organizations, however, and improvements in important aspects of work—job design, working conditions, employee commitment—do not happen if top managements believe that the "priorities" lie elsewhere.

However, the fact that enormous sums of money are being invested in office technology, that new staff groups are being organized and new task forces are being created to develop office automation policies, and that potential legal and regulatory interventions might take place if proper policies are not installed all contribute to the prospect that office automation can supply the motivating force for large-scale organizational innovation in the late 1980s.

If there is one common theme that echoes throughout much of the thoughtful literature about office automation—by promoters, early users and critics alike—it is the idea that office technology is a "two-edged sword," "an opportunity and a danger," a "Jekyll and Hyde" force. Recognizing the great truth that lies behind this characterization, American managers have a critical role to play, along with many others in a democratic society, in seeing that wise choices are made. To that end, we hope this book will be a useful contribution to managers and key staff groups undertaking this critical role.

Chapter 3

The Physical Environment

The physical environment has a strong influence upon the quality of human-computer interaction. As with the socio-political environment, the issues concerning the physical environment are low-tech. Nevertheless, a bad physical environment can render the most technologically advanced system useless. Conversely, and often ignored by management and technologists alike, it is in this low-tech area that we can often get the greatest improvement in human performance and satisfaction, and for the lowest cost!

The issues affecting the physical environment can be considered under six main topics:

- workstation ergonomics
- lighting
- air quality
- noise
- health and safety issues
- standards

Each of these will be discussed independently.

In going through the literature, it is often difficult to find the right level to match our needs. For example, articles on room design may be directed at architects, decorators, industrial engineers, or at the people actually working or living in rooms. Similarly, articles on furniture range from those discussing design and manufacturing issues to consumer awareness.

In this chapter, we try to address the issues at the level of the user, from the perspective of what users and management can do about improving their environment. For further discussion on interactive technologies, the reader is directed to Chapters 6: Cognition and Human Information Processing, Chapter 7: The Visual Channel, and Chapter 8: The Haptic Channel.

Finally, note that citations in the References/Bibliography section of this chapter are grouped together by topic under sub-headings.

Measurement and Anthropometrics

The literature in human factors, industrial engineering, and ergonomics is full of quantitative information. It sometimes seems that researchers in these fields are in love with measurement. Many of the measurements are important and useful *when appropriately applied*. However, they are easily subject to misinterpretation by non-specialists, and often convey an air of authority, or rigor, that is not warranted.

One branch of human factors, *anthropometrics*, is concerned with the measurement of the human body: issues such as height and reach. Here one should be very careful in using numbers as the basis for design. Are the measurements from a population representative of that to which the design is being targeted? For example, North American men are not the same size now as they were 40 years ago when some of the commonly used measurements were taken. Also, measurements for males in the military are not representative for males in general. Issues such as reach, zone of visual comfort, and desk height are important. The literature helps make this clear, but one must be careful to know the users and apply the metrics with care and discretion.

One example of excessive reliance on statistics and not enough on actual observation in the field comes to light in a study by Grandjean, Hunting and Pidermann (1983). They conducted a field study to observe operators' actual posture and how they adjusted their ergonomic chairs. What was discovered was that operators did not sit in the erect posture recommended by the ergonomics literature. Rather, operators generally adopted a sitting posture in which they leaned further back than recommended. The effect of this was that the position of hands and eyes to the VDT keyboard and screen was not what had been predicted, and standards that were calculated under the assumption of the recommended erect posture were inappropriate for the actual posture used. The lesson to be learned from this is that effective user interface design must incorporate a healthy balance between theory and field work.

Workstation Ergonomics

Here by "workstation" we mean the terminal as well as the furniture employed by the operator. The design concern is to match these physical devices to the operator's body dimensions and physical capabilities.

The introduction of ergonomically designed furniture can result in significant improvements in the workplace (Dainoff, Fraser and Taylor, 1982; Shute and Starr, 1984). However, while attention to human needs is important, there is a tendency to get carried away by all of the studies and advertising concerning furniture and design.

Ergonomic furniture may make things worse: The design philosophy of much current furniture design is that since we are all different, furniture should be designed to be able to be adjusted to our individual needs. As a result, one of the prime characteristics of "ergo" furniture is that it is highly adjustable. But this adjustability can cause problems.

After a recent trade show of office furniture, a colleague who is an industrial designer pointed out that virtually all of the furniture being demonstrated was adjusted incorrectly. That is, the sales staff themselves did not understand the reasons behind the adjustable features, and consequently, were not able to adjust it properly.

Another issue to consider in selecting office furniture is that what is appropriate for short-term comfort may lead to ailments in the long term. (A soft stuffed chair may result in bad sitting posture, for example.) In order to yield the hoped-for gains, an investment in adjustable furniture must be accompanied by an investment in educating users how to evaluate it properly.

Ergonomic furniture may not be needed: Many of the issues which have motivated the design for ergonomic furniture have grown out of a concern for workers who are doing repetitive tasks for extended periods of time. Lack of mobility or variation of work for extended periods certainly causes problems which need serious attention. However, these are the extreme cases, and are not typical of many office tasks. In confusing the demands of different types of work, some efforts to install ergonomic furniture are excessive for the context. Again, the key to making decisions is knowing who the workers are, what the nature of the work involved is, what the potential problems are, and what causes them.

Once the problem is understood in context, it may turn out that a simpler solution is possible. In many cases, for example, what the operator needs is not an adjustable chair or desk. What is required is a chair and desk that fit. If furniture need not be shared, then often simple inexpensive solutions can achieve the desired fit. Tables can be lowered, chairs exchanged, and monitors elevated, all with minimal expense. (Even inexpensive office chairs, for the most part, can be adjusted for height.) Just as in buying clothes, one must learn how to determine if furniture fits. And, if there are minor problems, simple alterations can often be made. If one understands the *cause* of a problem, then one is better equipped to tailor an individual solution.

There are a number of books and articles dealing with workstation ergonomics. A general introduction can be found in Van Cott and Kinkade (1972), Kantowitz and Sorkin (1983), Frome (1984), and Sanders and McCormick (1987). More specific information can be found in other sources, such as Cakir, Hart and Stewart (1980), Eastman Kodak (1983), and the reading by Smith (1984). An excellent, clearly written introduction that should be read by anyone interested in these issues is Sauter, Chapman, and Knutson (1985). We include as a reading an excerpt from this discussing the prevention of back strain.

Lighting

In our observations of work-places using CRTs, the most common environmental problem is glare on the surface of a CRT caused by poorly controlled lighting. One way to address this problem is to use an anti-glare filter. There are a number of different filter types, including optical coating (generally the best), etched, polarized, and mesh mounted over the screen surface. Comparative studies of some of these filter techniques can be found in Beaton and Snyder (1984) and Morse (1985).

While such filters can reduce glare, they also diffuse the light emitted from the CRT and can spawn other artifacts affecting visual performance (such as blurring). The artifacts introduced are less problematic than the glare eliminated, and are minimal with the better filters. But even with excellent filters, the problem should still be attacked at the source: lighting.

While comprehensive lighting design is complex, and includes colour, drapes, furniture layout, and possible major structural design, there are many less drastic steps that can be taken by workers directly, or by management. The second excerpt from the outstanding booklet by Sauter, Chapman and Knutson (1985) presents some of these strategies, such as baffles on fluorescent lights, alignment of desks to lights and windows, and the value of vertical venetian blinds.

Control of lighting is greatly neglected, but it is an area where management and workers, alike, can reap significant improvements for minimal investment.

Temperature and Air Quality

One of the trends in information processing is a switch-over from simple terminals to personal workstations, or computers. This transition is accompanied by a need to cope with the added heat and noise that these workstations generate.

The heat issue is important since even moderate changes in temperature can affect performance. With added heat, drowsiness becomes a common problem, and concentration is reduced.

In a previous era, all computers were relegated to the "computer room," and suitable air conditioning was installed. With the problem distributed throughout the workplace, new types of demands are made on the heating and ventilation systems of buildings. In particular, it is increasingly important to be able to exercise local control over the air temperature and circulation so that areas of need can be adjusted without adversely affecting other regions of the workplace.

Temperature and humidity are the immediately obvious aspects of air quality. However, other factors are also important, and can directly affect health. In particular, the type and quality of the filtering system installed affects the performance of humans and computers.

Some of the problems of air temperature and quality can be dealt with at the source. The amount of heat (and noise) radiated by a piece of equipment should be one of the parameters seriously considered before it is acquired. While air conditioning can be added, consideration should be given to minimizing the amount that the ambient noise is increased. Air filters can often be retrofitted on an existing air circulation system, or set up free-standing in the workplace.

Noise

Most people have had the experience of sitting in a restaurant and having the air conditioner switch off. Invariably, our response is surprise at how quiet it is, and how loud the air conditioning was, despite our not having been conscious of it.

There are at least two lessons to be learned from this example. First, we seem not to be conscious of steady-state sounds, as long as they are not overwhelming. (There is a corollary to this: we are very sensitive to transient sounds, even at moderate levels.) The second point is that even noises we are unconscious of can cause stress. Think about how relieved you generally are after the air conditioner has shut off.

The sound environment has an important influence on concentration, level of stress, and other aspects of performance. However, the interaction between the sound environment and these aspects of human performance is complex and confused by the conflicting results of many of the studies in the literature.

In extreme cases, however, the individual can exercise control over the acoustic environment simply by using ear protectors. These can be in the form of ear plugs or headphone-type protectors. While this results in a noise vs comfort trade-off, effective relatively comfortable ear protectors are available. Quality ear plugs, for example, reduce noise by about 20 dB, yet still permit normal conversation in person or on the telephone. Supplying ear protectors to employees is an excellent yet inexpensive investment by management.

While ear protectors are a useful tool for self-preservation, they are no substitute for proper acoustic control. One of the ironies in acoustic design is that an all-too-common strategy for controlling noise is to introduce more noise! This technique, borrowed from psychoacoustics, is known as *masking*. By distributing relatively low-level broad-band noise (something like the sound of the ocean), other sounds will be hidden, or muffled. Hence, you will still be able to hear your neighbour's voice, for example, but it won't be as loud, relative to the general ambient noise, and you won't be able to make out any of the words. As a result, the likelihood of distraction is greatly reduced.

The technique of introducing noise is discussed in Eastman Kodak (1983), as is the observation that in very quiet environments we are most sensitive to, and disturbed by, intermittent sounds — even if they are at quite a low level. Steady-state noise is subliminal, and fatigueing, while quiet ambience is very susceptible to interruption by intermittent sounds. Such is the dilemma of acoustic design, a dilemma which is aggravated by open-concept type offices.

The bibliography contains a number of readings in the area of noise and the acoustic environment. Kryter (1970) presents a very detailed account of the effects of noise on man. Koelega and Brinkman (1986) present an excellent summary of the literature of the effects of noise on vigilance tasks. Propst and Wodka (1975) is an understandable and practical handbook for dealing with acoustic problems in open plan offices. Besides the citations found in the bibliography of this chapter, the reader is also referred to the bibliography of Chapter 9: The Audio Channel, which cites several references on hearing and psychoacoustics.

Health and Safety Issues

With the introduction of any technology into the workplace or the home, health and safety issues must be considered. Within the context of the office, for example, there has been a great deal of debate concerning the effects on the worker of using the technology. These issues are becoming important in collective bargaining and in the legislation of standards.

Two excellent surveys of these issues can be found in Smith (1984), included as a reading, and Sauter, Gottlieb, Jones, Dodson and Rohrer (1983). NRC (1983) is a comprehensive investigation of health, safety, and standards issues pertaining to video displays, work and vision. See also Peters (1983).

One point which is increasingly being recognized is that a large number of problems are more appropriately attributed to inappropriate *usage* of technology as opposed to the technology itself. From this, the importance of training should be evident.

Readers interested in investigating health and safety issues in more detail are strongly recommended to review Hedge (1987). This paper presents an excellent, up-to-date annotated bibliography covering technology-related health issues in office systems.

Standards

Largely because of health and safety issues, there are numerous efforts at several levels of national and international organizations to set standards for the ergonomics of the workplace. Most of these efforts are well motivated. However, there is a great deal of controversy surrounding them. For an example of standards being adopted in Germany, see HGB (1980). A commentary on the draft ANSI standards for VDT workstations (ANSI, 1986) is included as one of the readings for this chapter (Computer and Business Equipment Manufacturers Association, 1985). Although simplified, this reprint gives the flavour, nature and breadth of the standards being proposed.

In the right place, standards are a good thing. However, in order to standardize, one must first understand the issues. One must also be sure that standards, once adopted, are not applied out of context.

Europe has lead the way in much of the standards efforts. Based on scientific studies, standards for phosphors on CRTs have been established. The problem is that conflicting standards are evolving because the studies on which they are based are in conflict. There is a clear danger here in legislating prematurely. There are other, political issues, which have influenced some of the standards efforts. Some of the pressure to standardize early in Europe can reasonably be interpreted as having to do with protecting the European market from imports.

Designers and consumers should not assume that equipment that ''meets the X standard'' is automatically the most appropriate for their use. In doing so, one runs the risk of not looking for, and discovering, a far more innovative and appropriate solution. The reading by Springer (1985) makes some of these points and shows how wide-spread (and potentially chaotic) are current standardization efforts.

Readings

Smith, M.J. (1984). Human Factors Issues in VDT Use: Environmental and Workstation Design Considerations. *IEEE Computer Graphics and Applications* 4(11), 56-63.

Sauter, S.L., Chapman, L.J. & Knutson, S.J. (1985). Preventing Back Strain (pp. 13-19) and Lighting Control (pp. 58-61). Excerpted from *Improving VDT Work: Causes and Control of Health Concerns in VDT Use*, Madison: University of Wisconsin, Distributed by the Report Store, 910 Massachusetts St., Suite 503, Lawrence, Kansas 66044.

Computer and Business Equipment Manufacturers Association (1985). Guide to the Draft American National Standard for Human Factors Engineering of Visual Display Terminal Workstations. *Computers and Standards* 4(2), 113-116.

Springer, T.J. (1985). The Statutes and Standards Movement. *Office Ergonomics Review* 2(2), 14-15.

References/Bibliography — General

Cakir, A., Hart, D.J. & Stewart, T.F.M. (1980). *Visual Display Terminals: A Manual Covering Ergonomics, Workplace Design, Health and Safety, Task Organization*, New York: John Wiley & Sons.

Dainoff, M., Fraser, L. & Taylor, (1982). Visual, Musculoskeletal and Performance Differences Between Good and Poor VDT Workstations: Preliminary Findings. *Proceedings of the Human Factors Society's 26th Annual Meeting*, Seattle, WA.

Eastman Kodak (1983). *Ergonomic Design for People at Work*, Belmont CA.: Lifetime Learning Publications.

ERGOLAB (Ed.)(1983). *Ergonomic Principles in Office Automation*, S-16183 Bromma, Sweden: Ericsson Information Systems AB.

Forest, G. (1970). *The Office - Environmental Planning*. Ottawa: Design Canada.

Frome, F. (1984). Improving Color CAD Systems for Users: Some Suggestions from Human Factors Studies. *IEEE Design & Test* 1(1), 18-27.

Grandjean, E. (1980). *Fitting the Task to the Man: An Ergonomic Approach*, London: Taylor & Francis.

Grandjean, E. (Ed.) (1984). *Ergonomics and Health in Modern Offices*, London: Taylor & Francis.

Grandjean, E. (Ed.)(1986). *Ergonomics in Computerized Offices*, London: Taylor & Francis.

Grandjean, E., Hunting, W. & Pidermann, M. (1983). VDT Workstation Design: Preferred Settings and their Effects. *Human Factors* 25(2), 161-175.

IBM (1984). *Human Factors of Workstations with Visual Displays*, Third Edition, San Jose: IBM Corp. Human Factors Center P15, Bldg 078, 5600 Cottle Road, San Jose, CA. 95193.

Kantowitz, B.H. & Sorkin, R.D. (1983). *Human Factors: Understanding People-System Relationships*, New York: John Wiley & Sons.

Koffler, *Office Systems Ergonomics Report*, The Koffler Group, 3029 Wilshire Blvd., Suite 200, Santa Monica, CA. 90403.

Sanders, M.S. & McCormick, E.J. (1987). *Human Factors in Engineering and Design (6th Edition)*, New York: McGraw-Hill Book Company.

Sauter, S.L., Chapman, L.J. & Knutson, S.J. (1985). *Improving VDT Work: Causes and Control of Health Concerns in VDT Use*, Madison: University of Wisconsin, Distributed by the Report Store, 910 Massachusetts St., Suite 503, Lawrence, Kansas 66044.

Shute, S. & Starr, S. (1984). Effects of Adjustable Furniture on VDT Users. *Human Factors* 26(2), 157-170.

Smith, M.J. (1984). Human Factors Issues in VDT Use: Environmental and Workstation Design Considerations. *IEEE Computer Graphics and Applications* 4(11), 56-63.

Van Cott, V.P. & Kinkade, R.G. (Eds.) (1972). *Human Engineering Guide to Equipment Design*, Washington: Supt. of Documents, U.S. Government Printing Office, Washington, D.C., 20402.

Noise and the Acoustic Environment

Note: Additional readings on psychoacoustics and audition can be found in the bibliography of Chapter 9: The Audio Channel.

ACGIH (1982). Threshold Limit Values for Chemical Substances in Workroom Air Adopted by ACGIH for 1982, Cincinnati: American Conference of Government Industrial Hygienists, 82-83.

Beaton, R.J. & Snyder, H.L. (1984). The Display Quality of Glare Filters for CRT Terminals. *SID 84 Digest*, Society for Information Display, 298-301.

Beranek, L.L., Blazier, W.E. & Figwer, J.J. (1971). Preferred Noise Criterion (PNC) Curves and their Application to Rooms. *Journal of the Acoustical Society of America* 50(5.1), 1223 - 1228.

Broadbent, D.E. (1957). Effects of Noise on Behaviour. In Harris, C. (Ed.), *Handbook of Noise Control*, New York: McGraw-Hill, 10:1-10:34.

Cohen, A. (1969). Effects of Noise on Psychological State. In American Speech and Hearing Association, *Noise as a Public Health Hazard* , ASHA Reports 4, 74-88.

Corliss, E.L.R. & Jones, F.E. (1976). Method for Estimating the Audibility and Effective Loudness of Sirens and Speech in Automobiles. *Journal of the Acoustical Society of America* 60(5), 1126-1131.

Fidell, S., Pearsons, K.S., & Bennet, R. (1974). Prediction of Aural Detectability of Noise Signals. *Human Factors* 16(4), 373-383.

Grandgean, E. (1961). Musik und Arbeit. *Zeitscrift fur Praventivmedizin,* 6, 65-70.

Harris, C.M. (Ed.) (1957). *Handbook of Noise Control*, New York: McGraw-Hill.

Koelega, H.S. & Brinkman, J. (1986). Noise and Vigilance: An Evaluative Review. *Human Factors* 28(4), 465-481.

Kryter, K.D. (1970). *The Effects of Noise on Man*, New York: Academic Press.

Miller, J.D. (1971). Noise and Performance. In NTID, *Effects of Noise on People*, Washington D.C.: Environmental Protection Agency, Supt. of Documents.

Morse, R.S. (1985). Glare Filter Preference: Influence of Subjective and Objective Indices of Glare, Sharpness, Brightness, Contrast and Color. *Proceedings of the Human Factors Society - 29th Annual Meeting,* 782-786.

Nemecek, J & Grandgean, E. (1973). Noise in Landscaped Offices. *Applied Ergonomics* 4(1), 19-22.

NIOSH (1972). *Criteria for a Recommended Standard - Occupational Exposure to Noise*, Cincinnati: U.S. Department of Health, Education and Welfare, National Institute for Occupational Safety and Health.

Pew, R.W. (1974). Human Perceptual-Motor Performance. In H. Kantowitz, H. (Ed.), *Human Information Processing: Tutorials in Performance and Cognition*, Hillsdale, N.J.: Lawrence Erlbaum Associates, 1-38.

Propst, R. & Wodka, M. (1975). *The Action Office Acoustic Handbook: a Guide for the Open Plan Facility Manager, Planner, and Designer* , Ann Arbor: Herman Miller Research Corp., 3970 Varsity Drive, Ann Arbor, Michigan 48104.

Webster, J.C. (1969). Effects of Noise on Speech Intelligibility. In American Speech and Hearing Association. *Noise as a Public Health Hazard*, ASHA Reports 4, 49-73.

Health and Safety Issues

Hedge, A. (1987). Office Health Hazards: an Annotated Bibliography. *Ergonomics* 30(5), 733-773.

NRC (1983). *Video Displays, Work, and Vision*, Washington, D.C.: National Academy Press.

Peters, T. (1983). Health and Safety Aspects. In ERGOLAB (Ed.) *Ergonomic Principles in Office Automation*, S-16183 Bromma, Sweden: Ericsson Information Systems AB. 99-114.

Sauter, S.L., Gottlieb, M.S., Jones, K.C., Dodson, V.N. & Rohrer, K.M. (1983). Job and Health Implications of VDT Use: Initial Results of the Wisconsin-NIOSH Study. *Communications of the ACM* 26(4), 284-294.

Smith, M.J. (1984). Health Issues in VDT Work. In Bennett, J., Case, D., Sandelin, J. & Smith, M. (Eds.), *Visual Display Terminals: Usability Issues and Health Concerns*, Englewood Cliffs, N.J.: Prentice-Hall, 193-228.

Standards

ANSI (1986). *Draft Standard for Visual Display Terminal Workstations* , Human Factors Society, Box 1369, Santa Monica, CA 90406.

Computer and Business Equipment Manufacturers Association (1985). Guide to the Draft American National Standard for Human Factors Engineering of Visual Display Terminal WorkStations. *Computers and Standards* 4(2), 113-116.

HGB (1980). *Safety Regulations for Display Work Places in the Office Sector*, Fachausschuss "Verwaltung", 2000 Hamburg 60, Uberseering.

Springer, T.J. (1985). The Statutes and Standards Movement. *Office Ergonomics Review* 2(2), 14-15.

VDTs and humans: mismatch of the century? Not if designers consider particular job characteristics and modify designs accordingly.

Human Factors Issues in VDT Use: Environmental and Workstation Design Considerations

Michael J. Smith

University of Wisconsin-Madison

The increased use of video display terminals for general office applications such as data entry/retrieval and word processing has brought to light human factors problems associated with VDT use. These problems are epitomized by the complaints of VDT users about visual and musculoskeletal strain and discomfort.[1,2] A number of studies have been conducted in field settings and in laboratory simulations to determine the causes of these complaints. Human factors considerations regarding environmental and workstation design have been shown to be significant determinants of the quantity and quality of visual and muscular complaints in VDT operators. This article reviews research that has examined these human factors considerations.

VDT operator physical complaints

Concerns about VDTs and their potential health implications originated in Europe during the 1970's. Some of the first research examining VDT operator health problems was performed in Austria by Haider and his colleagues.[3,4] They demonstrated that VDT operators performing in laboratory simulations showed increased myopia,* which became more profound with increased viewing time. Laubli,[5] in Switzerland, showed that VDT employee visual complaints, such as eyestrain, carried over from one day to the next. This demonstrated a potential for chronic impact of VDT viewing on the visual system. In addition, Laubli found that VDT operators performing different kinds of work activities displayed different levels of visual problems. Operators performing record-retrieval tasks (interactive) had more visual complaints, such as eyestrain, than those VDT operators performing data entry tasks or typists using standard electric typewriters. His colleague, Hunting[6] found that VDT operators' muscular complaints (sore shoulder, back pain, sore wrist) also showed a different pattern for different work activities. In this case, the data entry VDT operators had higher levels of muscular complaints than the interactive VDT operators or standard typists. These results demonstrate the influence of job requirements in defining the potential health problems of VDT work.

*Myopia, often referred to as nearsightedness, is a condition of the eye in which parallel rays are focused in front of the retina, resulting in the individual having decreased visual ability when objects are far from the eye.

In Sweden, Gunnarsson and Ostberg[7] found that older VDT operators at an airline reservation facility reported higher levels of visual problems than younger VDT operators when both were given more intensive VDT job tasks. In Germany, Cakir[8] and his colleagues conducted a large-scale study of over 1000 VDT operators and a number of comparison occupations. This study corroborated previous findings of increased visual and muscular problems for VDT operators, but more importantly, it defined a number of workstation design and environmental features that could have been responsible for the problems observed. Some examples of these features were screen glare, nonoptimal illumination levels, poorly designed furniture, and screen flicker.

In the United States, health concerns about VDTs were first investigated in 1977 by the National Institute for Occupational Safety and Health when ionizing radiation measurements were taken on terminals at

---

**Results indicated
that the clerical VDT operators
reported higher levels
of visual complaints
than either the professionals
using VDTs
or the nonoperators.**

---

workplaces.[9] One NIOSH field evaluation examined the potential radiation hazards and human factors problems for VDT operators.[10,11] This evaluation used a questionnaire survey to examine employees' health complaints and a field evaluation of basic ergonomic features of a sample of VDTs. Factors such as screen size, glare, lighting, postural requirements, and machine/worker incompatibilities were examined. In addition, radiation measurements were made on a sample of VDTs to identify the levels of sources of ionizing and nonionizing radiation.

The radiation testing measured no levels of radiation that exceeded current US occupational radiation standards.[11] The questionnaire results indicated that the clerical VDT operators reported higher levels of visual complaints than either the professionals using VDTs or the nonoperators. These visual complaints included burning eyes, itching and tearing eyes, blurred vision, and eyestrain. Most of these complaints were symptoms of visual fatigue that could have been produced by prolonged viewing, glare from the VDT, and/or improper illumination levels. The clerical VDT operators also reported more muscular complaints than either the professionals using the VDTs or the nonoperators. These complaints showed a generalized effect ranging from back pain to sore necks, wrists, and fingers. Such complaints could be related to the keying requirements of the VDT work and possibly to poor posture that could be due to improper seating or incorrect visual viewing distance or angle.

In summarizing some of the research findings regarding VDT health issues, I found that visual problems have

predominated in the studies both in Europe and in the US (see Table 1). The evidence from these studies indicates that VDT operators, as a group, suffer from a high incidence of visual disturbances, including visual fatigue, visual irritation, and headache.[1,2] In addition, it is clear that the type of VDT work activity, such as data entry versus word processing, and the specific visual demands imposed by that activity, influence the incidence of visual complaints. VDT workers at visually demanding jobs (for example, records retrieval) have a much higher rate of visual complaints than those at less visually demanding jobs (for example, word processing). Furthermore, almost all types of VDT work activity produce higher levels of visual complaints than traditional office work that is also visually demanding.[1,2]

The same sort of pattern holds true for muscular problems. As with the visual complaints, muscular problems vary with the type of VDT work activity, but generally almost all types of VDT work produce more muscular complaints than other types of traditional office work. These muscular complaints are of a diverse nature affecting the neck, shoulders, back, arms, hands, and fingers, which demonstrates an effect on the total musculature.

Design deficiencies contributing to complaints

Both the workstation and the work environment can contribute to the health complaints of VDT users.

Environmental design. Three of the most often cited causes of vision problems are improper illumination, glare on the VDT screen, and improper contrasts in luminance. These environmental problems usually occur together, although any one could conceivably produce visual disturbances. Hultgren and Knave[12] found that lighting levels at 76 percent of the workstations examined exceeded 700 lux (30 percent were over 1000 lux), while at 53 percent of the workstations VDT operators reported trouble reading images on their VDT screens. Findings similar to these have been shown by Cakir[8] and Laubli.[5] However, variations have been observed in some studies. For instance, Gunnarsson and Ostberg[7] found that illumination levels varied between 150 and 500 lux. In the NIOSH San Francisco study[13] over 85 percent of the workstations had illumination levels between 300 and 700 lux. As with the other studies, bothersome glare was observed with 85 percent of the VDT operators citing screen glare. In addition, 70 percent of the operators reported problems with character brightness, 69 percent with readability of screen, 68 percent, screen flicker, and 62 percent, screen brightness. Coe[14] found that 90 percent of the workstations examined had illumination levels 500 lux or lower. In this study, it was observed that there were more visual complaints when the lighting level was below 500 lux than when it was above 500 lux. Again glare was a significant problem (in 42 percent of the VDTs).

These findings indicate that VDT operators still complain about visual problems when illumination levels are between 200 lux and 500 lux, levels considered adequate for VDT work.[7,8] Thus, it would appear that glare and/or contrast problems are more critical elements in VDT operator visual complaints than illumination level. Of course, higher illumination levels can increase the possibility of the sources of screen glare. Laubli[5] found a correlation between the measured intensity of glare reflections and reported annoyance by the VDT operators but no relationship between the luminance of the reflections and reported visual impairment. Stammer-john[13] also found a clear relationship between glare and visual complaints.

Other environmental factors. Temperature and humidity have always seemed to evoke complaints from office workers. Dissatisfaction with these workplace features can influence worker perception of the overall job situation. However, it is not known whether office atmospheric conditions can have a direct influence on worker health.

Cakir[8] found that in nonair-conditioned offices about 50 percent of the VDT operators complained of the heat, while in air-conditioned offices about 30 percent complained of the heat. In addition, almost two thirds of the VDT operators complained that the air was too dry, even though the relative humidity in their workplace was between 30 and 40 percent. In the NIOSH San Francisco study,[13] 63 percent of the employees rated summer

---

It would appear that glare and/or contrast problems are more critical elements in VDT operator visual complaints than illumination level.

---

temperatures as too high, while 41 percent rated winter temperatures as too low, even though measurements of the temperatures and relative humidities at the work sites were within established limits for comfort (between 21°C and 25°C and 35 percent and 80 percent relative humidity). Coe[14] found that 80 percent of the VDT

Table 1.
Health complaints reported by VDT operators in select field studies.

Study, Country	VDT Population and Control Group	Types of Health Complaints	Comments
Gunnarsson & Ostberg, 1977, Sweden	89 airline reservations clerks	Muscular problems: pains in neck, shoulders, lower back, arms, hands, legs Visual problems: eye fatigue, eye irritation, blurred focus, headache	The major health complaints were sore shoulders, lower back pain, visual fatigue, and eye irritation.
Cakir et al., 1978, Germany	548 data acquisitions clerks 473 dialogue operators (clerks, editors, programmers) 16 data acquisition clerks not using VDTs	Muscular problems: back strain, back pain, and neck pain Visual problems: eye pressure, focusing difficulties, burning eyes, eyestrain	The major health complaints were neck pain, back pain, and eyestrain. Data acquisition VDT operators had higher levels than dialogue VDT operators for all health complaints.
Hunting et al., 1980, Laubli et al., 1980, Switzerland	53 data entry clerks 109 dialogue clerks 78 typists not using VDTs 55 clerical workers not using VDTs	Muscular problems: painful neck, shoulder, arms, and hands Visual problems: eye fatigue, shooting eye pains, burning eyes, red eyes, blurred vision, headache	The major health complaints were neck pain, arm pain, eye fatigue, burning eyes, and blurred vision. Dialogue VDT operators had more visual complaints than the data entry VDT operators and the nonusers of VDTs. The reverse was true for muscular complaints, where the data entry VDT operators had more complaints than dialogue VDT operators and nonusers of VDTs.
Smith et al., 1981, United States	125 newspaper editors and reporters 129 data entry and retrieval clerks 157 data entry and retrieval clerks not using VDTs	Muscular problems: back pain, painful or stiff shoulders or neck, neck pressure, sore shoulders, sore wrists, weakness in arms or hands, swollen muscles or joints Visual problems: headache, eyestrain, burning eyes, blurred vision, irritated eyes	The major health complaints were eyestrain, burning eyes, irritated eyes, blurred vision, back pain, painful or stiff shoulders or neck, and sore shoulders. The clerical VDT operators had the greatest levels of visual and muscular complaints, with editors and reporters having the next highest level, followed by nonusers of VDTs.

operators and 75 percent of the nonoperators reported that the temperature of their work areas was uncomfortable.

Workstation design. A host of features of the VDT, the desk, and the chair have been examined to determine relationships to health complaints. Figure 1 illustrates the various aspects of the workstation that have significance for worker comfort.

In terms of the screen, the issue of adequate contrast between the characters and screen background is of concern. In many of the field studies,[12] these contrast ratios were found to be much less than optimal (7:1 to 10:1 is considered acceptable) and, in some cases, were less than adequate (3:1 is considered adequate).[13,15] Grandjean[16] demonstrated that the quality of the screen characters can influence the level of health complaints with poorer quality images producing more visual complaints. Gould[17] indicated that blurred and/or flickering characters can be a contributing factor in the ability to read a video display. Thus, character quality may also be a factor in VDT operator visual complaints.

Although most field studies have found that the large majority of VDTs examined have the capabilities to meet minimum requirements for contrast ratios, many VDTs do not achieve these minimum requirements in the field, because of screen glare.[1,2] Screen color and positive versus negative contrast (dark characters on light background versus light characters on dark background) are

additional factors that have been suggested as potential influences on VDT operator complaints. To date, there is no evidence to suggest that these factors have an effect on visual performance or health complaints.[1]

The workstation has been implicated in a number of the studies as a significant factor contributing to both visual and muscular health complaints.[1,2] In particular, the height of the working surface has an impact on the height of the arms, wrists, and hands, as well as wrist and neck angles.[2] In addition, the height of the chair and the amount of support that it provides for the lumbar region of the back have been postulated as factors contributing to worker muscular complaints.[1,2]

Stammerjohn[13] found that over one half of the VDT operators he studied were working at VDT keyboard heights that exceeded the US military standards for keyboard height. He also found that over 80 percent of the male and 40 percent of the female VDT operators had viewing angles that were greater than 40 degrees (which is considered excessive[1,8,13]). Hunting[6] also reported excessive keyboard heights in VDT operators (750-790 mm). He found that these higher keyboard levels were associated with more arm and hand complaints but with less shoulder complaints. It was hypothesized that higher keyboard levels allowed VDT operators the opportunity to rest their hands and wrists on the keyboard and thus reduce strain on the shoulders. Reports by the VDT operators indicated that those operators who were able to rest their arms had fewer muscular complaints.

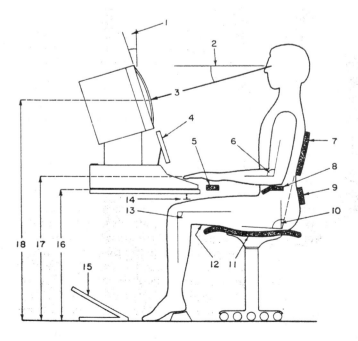

1. Screen tilt angle
2. Visual angle between the horizontal and the center of the display
3. Eye-screen distance
4. Document holder and source document
5. Wrist rest
6. Elbow angle
7. Backrest
8. Elbow rest
9. Lumbar support
10. Seat back angle (from horizontal)
11. Seat pan angle (from horizontal)
12. Clearance between leg and seat
13. Knee angle
14. Clearance between leg and table
15. Footrest
16. Table height
17. Home row (middle row height)
18. Screen height to center of screen

Figure 1. Definitions of VDT workstation terminology. (Taken from M. Helander,[23] NIOSH, 1984).

Coe[14] found that most of the VDTs he examined had nondetachable keyboards. This was related to excessive gaze angle (over 40 degrees) in over three fourths of the VDT operators studied. He also found that two thirds of the VDT operators had chairs that could not be adjusted and that over one third complained of seating discomfort.

Sauter[18,19] carried out a photographic analysis and performed ergonomic measurements of VDT operator workstations. The findings were correlated with VDT operator health complaints. Two factors stood out as significant predictors of VDT operator strain: the view-

---

VDT operators showed improved performance under good ergonomic workstation design conditions.

---

ing angle and the keyboard. The VDT operator's viewing angle was associated with neck, back, and shoulder strain; and nondetachable keyboards were associated with increased arm and hand strain.

Dainoff[20] conducted a series of laboratory simulation studies to determine the influences of environmental factors and workstation design on VDT operator health complaints and performance. The results of his studies indicate that workstation design that provided proper keyboard and seating height, wrist support, and a copyholder showed reduced back, neck, and shoulder pain and less pain in arms and wrists than a suboptimal workstation design. In addition, VDT operators showed improved performance under good ergonomic workstation design conditions.

Ergonomic solutions to VDT design problems

Given the research findings on VDT problems, it is possible to establish a framework from which appropriate ergonomic interventions for various types of VDT work activity can be examined. First of all, four basic points must be considered in ergonomic issues that relate to the basic functions of VDT use and thus the VDT work system. The first point deals with the work environment. Where is the VDT located? Where is it being utilized? What are the conditions of the work environment? The second point deals with the extent of use. How long is the VDT used: four hours a day? eight hours a day? The third consideration centers on the types of tasks. How are the tasks done in terms of the perceptual and motor requirements? And fourth, what are the psychological loads imposed on the individual in carrying out this work? Is the work boring? Does the work present a challenge? Does the work have meaning to the individual?

These points provide the basis for examining four areas of health issues in relation to VDT work. These areas include the visual load, the muscular load, the postural load, and the emotional stress load. The visual load is reflected in visual fatigue, eye irritation, and possibly headache. Muscular load problems show up in muscular fatigue, sore muscles, and sore joints of the manipulative components of the body, such as the arms, the hands, the wrists, the fingers, and the neck. Postural load problems, on the other hand, produce muscular fatigue and sore muscles and joints related to the major body musculature that keeps one seated upright, such as the back muscles and the leg muscles. The emotional load is reflected in emotional distress, such as anxiety, depression, irritability, and fatigue, and in such reactions as job dissatisfaction. This framework for examining the various load aspects of VDT work and the strains they impose helps designers determine where they might intervene in the different VDT tasks. We can look at these modifications in the context of four types of tasks: data entry, data acquisition, interactive, and word processing.

Data entry tasks. Typically, data entry jobs are oriented toward work with hard copy; thus the operator spends little time looking at the screen but performs a high rate of keying. An example of a typical data entry operation would be a claims clerk at an insurance company. Many such jobs limit the clerk solely to entering information about the insurance claims into the computer system and require the clerk to look at the screen only when a mistake has been perceived. This type of job is similar to traditional keypunching, with the addition of a video display screen that tends to attract the eyes away from the hard copy.

In examining the categories of physical strain, that is visual, muscular, and postural loads, in such a job, it is obvious that the visual load is not related to the screen, since it is not a screen-intensive job. In this case, the visual load is related to the hard copy, which may create as much visual fatigue as the VDT screen itself because the quality of the hard copy can often be poor. Because the hard copy is the major factor that relates to the visual issues in data entry jobs, it is the factor that must be addressed. Such hard copy should meet the minimum character contrast, size, and quality requirements that have been suggested for VDTs.[21] Lighting recommendations that have been proposed for this type of job would be 500 lux (approximately 50 footcandles) of illumination.[22]

In terms of the muscular load, these jobs impose a heavy load on the hands, wrists, fingers, and arms owing to the number of keystrokes involved. An ergonomic solution for dealing with this situation is to take the load off the fingers and the wrists by providing something for the arms and wrists to rest on, such as the arms of a chair, a wrist rest, or the worktable.[1] Additionally, it is important that the position of the wrists and the arms for these individuals be correct, and thus adjustable keyboard height and position become very important. A VDT with a detachable keyboard and an adjustable worktable should be provided for data entry workers.

When examining the postural load, it has been observed that these job tasks produce a great load on the backs and shoulders of VDT operators.[6,8,13] For this situation, the most important feature is a proper chair. The chair must provide adequate lumbar support and the chair height should be adjustable, as should the backrest tension. In addition, data entry jobs require handling and looking at hard copy, which produce a good number of postural adjustments and head and neck movements. In order to limit the number of neck problems, it is important to have a document holder to reduce the number and extent of head and neck movements. To summarize, for data entry jobs, the screen is a secondary concern, while the workstation adjustability is the primary concern. Therefore, these workers need to be provided with a good chair, an adjustable keyboard, and a proper surface for source documents, as well as high-quality source documents.

Data acquisition tasks. Data acquisition tasks are almost the opposite of data entry tasks in terms of the load characteristics. The kinds of jobs in this category include telephone directory operations, air traffic controllers, and postal clerks working on a computer mail forwarding system. In these jobs operators spend most of their time looking at the screen to retrieve information. Such jobs can be as visually demanding as they are screen intensive. The best available VDT screen with good character quality, high character-to-screen contrast, and glare control are essential.[21] In addition, environmental factors such as lighting and glare must be controlled. In terms of illumination, it has been suggested that this work activity requires about 300 lux (approximately 30 footcandles) of illumination.[22] Glare control approaches include proper VDT positioning, covering glare sources, and providing glare filters.[1]

In terms of muscular load, it is difficult to offer a general specification for data acquisition VDT operators, since job tasks differ considerably. Telephone directory operators appear to have high muscular and postural loads because of repetitive work performed at a very quick pace. On the other hand, air traffic controllers work in a completely different type of situation with a high cognitive and perceptual load but with a smaller muscular load. In those job tasks where the muscular load is high as a result of a high number of repetitive motions, arm and/or wrist support and an adjustable keyboard should be provided. Almost all data retrieval VDT jobs place a high demand on the postural load and therefore require a good chair as well as adjustable screen height.

Interactive tasks. Interactive types of VDT operators have an astounding variety of job tasks. The jobs vary from computer programmers and computer-aided design engineers (who work at very creative activities where they are able to get up and move around at will) to reservation clerks (who sit continuously for hours without moving). Thus, a huge difference exists in terms of the job demands and the resulting loads that are put on various types of interactive operators.

For a programmer, the visual load makes the greatest demand, while the muscular load and the postural loads become secondary demands. In terms of reservation clerks, a dual load exists: a visual load because of the need to be able to interact with the screen and a muscular load because of the need to process information in a very rapid manner with many keystrokes. As for the postural load, both programming and design engineering have relatively high requirements.

> **The main point
> of ergonomic controls
> is that the job task characteristics
> define the necessary interventions
> that should be applied.
> The major applications
> need to be directed
> to the area
> where the greatest loads
> are imposed.**

For a very visually demanding job, good screen characteristics are needed as discussed earlier.[21] In addition, a good visual environment with approximately 300 to 500 lux (30 to 50 footcandles) of illumination and good glare control is best.[22]

For most interactive jobs the muscular load is not as intense as it is for operators who do nothing but enter data. However, this load may still be relatively high and may make arm and/or wrist support vital. In terms of the postural load, an adjustable chair is required. Depending on the need to interact with the screen and the amount of screen-viewing time, an adjustable screen height may be necessary. For particular applications, a document holder should be provided, particularly for the people using resource materials.

Word processing tasks. Here again, the loads will vary depending on the tasks that are being conducted. Word processing jobs vary from those of typists (who spend most of their time keying with very little of their time looking at the screen) to those of editors (who spend most of their time looking at the screen and very little time keying).

Ergonomic controls. The main point of ergonomic controls is that the job task characteristics define the necessary interventions that should be applied. The major applications need to be directed to the area where the greatest loads are imposed by the job tasks. Some jobs will impose loads on both the visual and the muscular/skeletal system; some jobs will affect only the visual system or only the muscular system. In essence, the loads must determine the types of interventions in a VDT work situation.

Summary

An existing body of evidence indicates that working with VDTs can produce a variety of health complaints, including visual fatigue and discomfort, muscular aches and pains, emotional disturbances, psychosomatic symptoms, and job dissatisfaction. A number of factors, such as improper lighting, environmental glare, poor workstation design, inadequate chairs, poor job design, unreasonable organizational demands, poor supervison, and inadequate training, have been identified as contributing to these problems.

Table 2 illustrates those factors related to physical design considerations and suggests some solutions. All of these influences are modified by the type of VDT activity being undertaken and by the amount of load each puts on the visual, muscular, and emotional mechanisms of the operator. However, all can be controlled through the application of ergonomic principles for environmental, workstation, job and organizational design. ∎

References

1. M. J. Smith, "Health Issues in VDT Work," in *Visual Display Terminals*, J. Bennett, D. Case, J. Sandelin, and M. J. Smith, eds., Prentice-Hall, Englewood Cliffs, New Jersey, 1984, pp. 193-228.

2. M. J. Dainoff, "Occupational Stress Factors in Visual Display Terminal (VDT) Operation: A Review of Empirical Research," *Behaviour and Information Technology,* 1982, Vol. 1, No. 2, pp. 141-176.

3. M. Haider, J. Hollar, M. Kundi, H. Schmid, A. Thaler, and N. Winter, "Stress and Strain on the Eyes Produced by Work with Display Screens: Report on a Work-Physiological Study Performed for the Union of Employees in the Private Sector," Austrian Trade Union Assoc., Vienna, Austria, 1975.

4. M. Haider, M. Kundi, and M. Weissenbock, "Worker Strain Related to VDUs with Differently Colored Characters," in *Ergonomic Aspects of Visual Display Terminals,* E. Grandjean and E. Vigliani, eds., Taylor and Francis, Ltd., London, 1980, pp. 53-64.

Table 2.
Comfort problems of VDT operators, some contributing factors and solutions.

Health Complaint	Contributing Factors	Suggested Interventions
Visual fatigue, eye irritation, and focusing problems	Improper lighting	Keep room illumination between 300-700 lux.
	Glare and reflections	Position VDTs parallel to windows and luminaries and between luminaries rather than underneath. Use glare shields as needed.
	Poor character definition	Control screen glare and reflections. Use contrast enhancing filters. Adjust character brightness and contrast.
Musculoskeletal—back	Poor chair	Provide a chair that gives adequate lumbar (back) support and is adjustable (height, back tension, back angle).
	Inadequate leg room	Provide worktable that is large enough to allow the operator to shift posture without bumping legs.
Neck, shoulders, and arms	Improper desk height	Provide a worktable that is height adjustable and allows for independent adjustment of VDT screen height and VDT keyboard height.
		Have VDT keyboard detachable from screen.
Wrists	Improper wrist angle	Have a chair with armrests. Provide a wrist rest.
	Too many keystrokes	Set keystrokes rate according to principles of time and motion analysis.
		Provide periodic breaks from keying tasks.

5. T. Laubli, W. Hunting, and E. Grandjean, "Visual Impairments Related to Environmental Conditions on VDU Operators," in *Ergonomic Aspects of Visual Display Terminals,* E. Grandjean and E. Vigliani, eds., Taylor and Francis, Ltd., London, 1980, pp. 85-94.

6. W. Hunting, T. Laubli, and E. Grandjean, "Constrained Postures of VDU Operators," in *Ergonomic Aspects of Visual Display Terminals,* E. Grandjean and E. Vigliani, eds., Taylor and Francis, Ltd., London, 1980, pp. 175-184.

7. E. Gunnarsson and O. Ostberg, "The Physical and Psychological Working Environment in a Terminal-Based Computer Storage and Retrieval System," National Board of Occupational Safety and Health, report 35, Stockholm, Sweden, 1977.

8. A. Cakir, D. J. Hart, and T. F. M. Stewart, *The VDT Manual,* Ince-Giej Research Association (IFRA), Darmstadt, West Germany, 1979.

9. C. E. Moss, W. E. Murray, W. H. Parr, J. Messite, and G. J. Karches, "An Electromagnetic Radiation Survey of Selected Video Display Terminals," pub. no. 78-129, National Institute for Occupational Safety and Health, Cincinnati, Ohio, 1978.

10. M. J. Smith, B. G. F. Cohen, L. Stammerjohn, and A. Happ, "An Investigation of Health Complaints and Job Stress in Video Display Operations," *Human Factors,* Vol. 23, 1981, pp 387-400.

11. W. D. Murray, C. E. Moss, W. H. Parr, and C. Cox, "A Radiation and Industrial Hygiene Survey of Video Display Terminal Operations," *Human Factors,* Vol. 23, 1981, pp. 413-420.

12. G. Hultgren and B. Knave, "Discomfort and Disturbances from Light Reflections in an Office Landscape with CRT Display Terminals," *Applied Ergonomics,* Vol. 17, 1974, pp. 2-8.

13. L. Stammerjohn, M. J. Smith, and B. G. F. Cohen, "Evaluation of Work Station Design Factors in VDT Operations," *Human Factors,* Vol. 23, 1981, pp. 401-412.

14. J. B. Coe, K. Cuttle, W. C. McClellon, N. J. Warden, and P. J. Turner, "Visual Display Units," New Zealand Dept. of Health, report W/1/8, Wellington, New Zealand, 1980.

15. ANSI A132.1, "American National Standard Practice for Office Lighting," American National Standards Institute, New York, 1973.

16. E. Grandjean, "Ergonomics Related to the VDT Workstation," in *Proc. Zurich Seminar on Digital Comm.,* Federal Institute of Technology, Zurich, Switzerland, 1982.

17. J. D. Gould, "Visual Factors in the Design of Computer-Controlled CRT Displays," *Human Factors,* Vol. 10, 1968, pp. 359-376.

18. S. L. Sauter, M. S. Gottlieb, and K. C. Jones, "A General Systems Analysis of Stress-Strain in VDT Operations," *Conf. on Human Factors in Computer Systems,* Gaithersburg, Maryland, 1982. (Copies available from S. Sauter at Dept. of Preventive Medicine, University of Wisconsin, Madison, Wisconsin 53706.)

19. S. L. Sauter, M. S. Gottlieb, K. M. Rohrer, and V. A. N. Dodson, "The Well-Being of Video Display Terminal Users," Dept. of Preventive Medicine, University of Wisconsin, Madison, Wisconsin, 1983.

20. M. J. Dainoff, L. Fraser, and B. J. Taylor, "Visual, Musculoskeletal and Performance Differences Between Good and Poor VDT Workstations: Preliminary Findings," *Proc. Human Factors Society 26th Annual Meeting,* Santa Monica, California, 1982.

21. H. Snyder, "Optimizing the Equipment and Operator," *Proc. on Health and Ergonomic Considerations for Visual Display Units,* American Industrial Hygiene Association, Akron, Ohio, 1983, pp. 21-28.

22. W. Cushman, "Illumination Considerations for VDT Work," *Proc. on Health and Ergonomic Considerations of Visual Display Units,* American Industrial Hygiene Association, Akron, Ohio, 1983, pp. 73-86.

23. M. G. Helander, "Ergonomic Design of Office Environments for Visual Display Terminals," National Institute for Occupational Safety and Health (DTMD), Cincinnati, Ohio, 1982.

Michael J. Smith is an associate professor of industrial engineering at the University of Wisconsin-Madison. From June 1974 to August 1984 he served as chief of the Motivation and Stress Research Section, Applied Psychology and Ergonomics Branch, National Institute for Occupational Safety and Health. His research interests include the human factors aspects of person/computer interaction with emphasis on workplace design, job design, and the management and organization of work processes to minimize job stress.

Smith received the BA in psychology and the MA and PhD in industrial psychology with a minor in behavioral cybernetics, from the University of Wisconsin at Madison. He is a member of the Human Factors Society.

Smith may be contacted through the Industrial Engineering Dept., University of Wisconsin-Madison, 1513 University Ave., Madison, WI 53706.

Preventing Back Strain

How the Back Works

The back is a very complex structure and back problems can result from many different sources. In order to realize how VDT work can result in back strain and the importance of the solutions we prescribe, it is necessary to have a basic understanding of the construction of the back and the physiological basis for back pain.

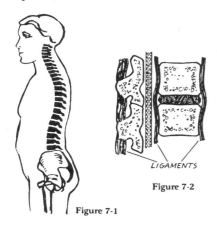

Figure 7-1

Figure 7-2

The backbone (spine) is the major framework or support structure for your body. As seen in figure 7–1, the spine is really a series of separate bones (vertebrae) reaching from the neck to the hip area. The vertebrae are held together in a vertical column by tough, somewhat elastic tissues, called ligaments, which attach from one vertebra to the next (figure 7–2).

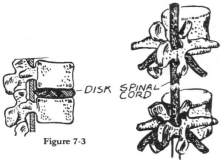

Figure 7-3

Figure 7-4

The hard vertebral bones are separated by softer compressible material called discs (figure 7–3). Discs prevent the vertebrae from grinding against one another, allow

flexibility of the spine, and act as cushions to absorb shocks or jolts to the spine.

In addition to providing support for the body, the spine also houses and protects the spinal cord (figure 7–4). Nerves to various parts of the body branch out from the spinal cord in the space between the adjacent vertebrae.

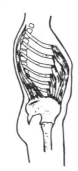

Figure 7-5

Finally, the muscles of the back and of the stomach area (figure 7–5) support the back in different postures and create motion. Much as "stays" support the mast of a sailboat, the muscles of the stomach connect from the hip area to the ribs in front, and from the hip area to the vertebrae in back. All movements of the back such as bending and twisting, and even maintaining a stationary upright standing or sitting position, require muscular effort.

Basis for Back Problems in VDT Work

Figure 7-6

Back pain or discomfort is one of the most common complaints of VDT users. One potential source is muscle fatigue result-

ing from muscular efforts to hold particular postures for long periods. To avoid or relieve discomfort from muscular fatigue, VDT operators sometimes adopt a slouched sitting position (figure 7–6). While a slouched posture requires little muscular effort, discomfort may now result from increased tension placed upon the ligaments which connect the vertebrae and which now must take over the responsibility for supporting the back.

Probably a less prevalent but more serious cause of back pain in VDT use or office work results from direct mechanical wear of the structures of the spinal column. Unlike muscle fatigue, this type of problem may take years to develop. The chance of this type of damage increases whenever the standing or seated posture causes a change in the position of the spine away from its natural position.

The natural position of the spine, seen from the side, is an S-shaped curve with an inward curve at the neck, an outward curve at the mid-back and an inward curve at the lower back. These curves are shown in figure 7–1.

When the shape of the back is changed away from this position (such as when slouching) abnormal forces are placed upon the discs separating the vertebrae (figure 7–7), as well as the ligaments connecting the vertebrae.

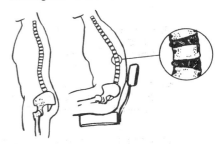

Figure 7-7

Flattening of the lower curve of the back occurs to some degree whenever we sit down. Figure 7–8 shows why. As seen, when we sit down, the bottom of the hip bone contacts the chair first. As the sitting process is completed, the hip actually rotates backward, thereby flattening the curve in the lower part of the back. A good low back support can help reverse this effect.

Excerpted from Sauter, S.L., Chapman, L.J., and Knutson, S.J. (1985). *Improving VDT Work: Causes and Control of Health Concerns in VDT Use*, Madison: University of Wisconsin.

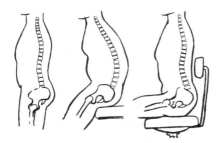

Figure 7-8

Years of abnormal forces on discs caused by poor spinal alignment may hasten their degeneration. As this happens, the vertebrae will collapse more tightly upon one another, increasing back stiffness and the opportunity for painful pinching of nerves exiting the vertebrae, or irritating contact between adjacent vertebrae. Abnormal tension upon ligaments connecting the vertebrae also leads to these problems by stimulating abnormal bone growth around the edges of the vertebrae.

Workplace Causes and Control of Back Problems

The Chair

The design of the chair is a crucial factor in preventing back strain in VDT work.

There are three main principles to keep in mind when selecting a chair from the standpoint of preventing back strain. These are:

- Lumbar (low back) support to preserve the normal alignment of the lower spine.

- Full back support and tilt-back capabilities to allow VDT users to incline backwards slightly; thereby relieving muscular efforts and fatigue in sitting. A slight backward incline also helps reduce the flattening of the lower spine when sitting.

- The chair must not be so confining that it restricts movement while sitting. While movement is needed to avoid fatigue, it also promotes the circulation of nourishing fluids through the discs.

The following examples indicate violations of some of these principles which are commonly observed in VDT workplaces.

Problems

A straight back chair (figure 7-9) provides little or no support to the lower back, and even relatively poor upper back support. Sitting in this type of chair for extended periods can result in muscle fatigue from efforts to sit erect, and the lack of lower back support results in poor posture of the lower spine.

Figure 7-9   Figure 7-10

As needed, lumbar support can be improved by using a pillow or increased padding in the lower back area. It is even possible to purchase a specially designed lower back support (figure 7-10). However, this procedure is not recommended as a long term solution or alternative to a well-designed chair.

When the chair height is too low (often caused by a worktable surface that is too low), the elevation of the legs causes the pelvis to tilt further backward resulting in increased flattening of the lower spine (figure 7-11).

Figure 7-11

It should be pointed out, however, that for some people with low back problems a straight back chair and sitting with the legs slightly elevated is more comfortable and is sometimes prescribed by a physician or therapist.

Figure 7-12 shows the traditional secretarial chair which is commonly used in

Figure 7-12

VDT work. It is designed to provide support to the lower back and preserves the contour of the spine by pushing the lower spine forward, thereby counteracting the flattening tendency which occurs with sitting. Of course, this requires that the tension and fore-aft position of the backrest be properly adjusted. Figure 7-13 depicts an all-too-common case of poor backrest adjustment. Still, like the straight back chair, the traditional secretarial chair provides little support for the upper part of the back, and can therefore lead to fatigue or slouched posture with long periods of sitting.

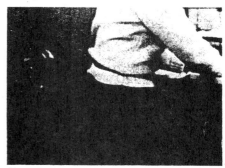

Figure 7-13

When chairs are too soft, people sink in too far and their ability to move or adjust their posture is impaired. Fatigue is then accelerated. Alternately, when the chair is too hard, an individual may adopt an awkward posture to relieve discomfort from pressures to the thighs and buttocks.

Because smooth vinyl covered seats are more slippery than chairs with textured cloth coverings, the effort of upright sitting and chances of sliding into a slumped posture are increased when the chair has a smooth vinyl covering.

Solutions: Positive Design Features for a VDT Chair

Now that we have identified some of the common shortcomings in chair design and use from the standpoint of preventing back strain in VDT use, what are the appropriate features and adjustments? The type of chair recommended for VDT users looks something like the composite shown in figure 7-14.

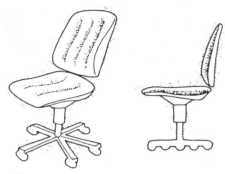

Figure 7-14

Important design features which are readily apparent include the following:

- Full backrest (usually tilts back) with a low backrest protrusion for lumbar support.
- A pan (seat) which tilts back only slightly as the backrest tilts back.
- A porous fabric upholstery.
- Chair controls (for height and back and seat angle adjustment) which can be easily manipulated from the seated position.
- Adjustable height.
- 5-legged base.
- Optional armrests.

Appendix A provides a detailed checklist giving design specifications for VDT chairs and how they vary with different applications of the chair. Appendix A also describes procedures for selecting and evaluating chairs. Some of the information contained in Appendix A is not directly related to the prevention of back strain per se, but is important for the prevention of other types of musculoskeletal problems discussed further on.

The Worktable
Problems

Common worktable-related situations which contribute to back strain include:

- Displays which are too low.
- Using VDT tables for non-VDT work.
- Stand-up VDT work.

It is often recommended that the keyboard for a VDT or typewriter be at about elbow height. (However, current research suggests that this level may not be as crucial as conventionally believed.) For this reason, the table surface for a typewriter or VDT table is usually several inches lower than the height of a conventional office desk. But when the video display is positioned at this level, it may be too low for comfortable viewing while sitting erect. This is especially likely when the display is attached to the keyboard and thus cannot be independently elevated. This arrangement may cause operators (especially taller individuals) to either lower their chairs, stoop forward, or slouch down in the chair to improve their viewing of the display (figure 7-15). The result in any of these cases is poor back posture.

Figure 7-15

When performing desk work not involving use of the VDT, poor back posture also results as individuals bend forward to a table top set at a lowered level for keyboard operation.

Figure 7-16

Operating a VDT while standing can also contribute to poor back posture. If the VDT is positioned on a conventional office desk, the operator has to stoop forward excessively to operate the keyboard and view the display (figure 7-16).

Standing up straight for long periods can also result in poor back posture which is just the opposite of that occurring when the display is too low. As fatigue sets in, the abdominal area may sag forward. The result is an excessive forward curvature of the lower spine (figure 7-17). Obesity and shoes with high heels can contribute to this effect.

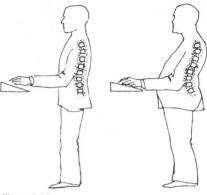

Figure 7-17

Solutions

Refer to Appendix B for a detailed checklist of design specifications for VDT worktables.

Height of the Table/Display. Solutions to table height problems are identified below. Key factors in determining the suitability of the different solutions are:

- The number of individuals using the worktable.
- The variety of tasks performed at the worktable.
- The type of VDT used.

Adjustable *multi-surface* VDT tables enable good posture by allowing the keyboard and display to be independently adjusted to appropriate heights for different users (figure 7-18).

However, three potential drawbacks may make this table impractical:

- Many stand-alone models provide only limited workspace for documents and work materials.
- It is difficult to use the table for tasks other than VDT use.
- Cannot be used for VDTs without separate displays and keyboards.

Figure 7-18

DETACHED KEYBOARDS:

A detached keyboard helps to avoid a compromise between preferred keyboard and display position, and is therefore advisable for most VDT applications. However, in some tasks, either the keyboard or the display may be seldom used. For example, some data entry operators only look infrequently to the display. In such cases, the need for separation of the display and keyboard is relaxed since the entire VDT can be positioned for comfortable viewing or keyboarding, according to task requirements.

Note

Non-adjustable multi-surfacce tables are not recommended. They offer no advantage over the following options:

Figure 7-19

- A common or a basic VDT table used in combination with a tabletop pedestal for elevation of the display enables comfortable display viewing without compromising back posture (figure 7-19). Workspace and flexibility for materials arrangement may be increased over that offered with some multi-surface tables. The system may also be relatively inexpensive. However, without ready adjustablity of table and display height, this approach is practical for single-user applications only. Even

for single users, at least *one-time* adjustment of table and display height is necessary. One-time display height adjustment is possible using a commercial or fabricated support (figure 7-20), or readily available objects such as books or lumber to support the display (figure 7-21).

Figure 7-20

Figure 7-21

- A readily adjustable single surface table (figure 7-22) in combination with an adjustable pedestal (figure 7-23) offer flexible keyboard and display height adjustment for *multiple* users, and more workspace and flexibility in materials arrangement than some multi-surface tables. The table height can also be adjusted to be suitable for conventional office work. User adjustable single surface tables and height adjustable pedestals are relatively uncommon, but are commercially available.

Figure 7-22

Figure 7-23

What range of height adjustability is needed for the display support? From the standpoint of preventing back strain, the crucial thing is that the display be adjusted high enough so that the user doesn't need to stoop or slouch to view the display comfortably. Recent research shows that preferred display heights (from floor to center screen) range from about 33 inches to about 43 inches for most people. Screen center is commonly about 10 inches above tabletop (depending upon brand of VDT). This suggests that the support surface for the display should be adjustable up to 33 inches, assuming that heights below the preferred result in a compromise in back posture.

Minimum table height is more critical from the standpoint of neck and arm-hand comfort. If the display support doesn't adjust low enough, short operators will have an uncomfortable upward gaze to the display. If the keyboard support is too high, discomfort in keyboard operation may result. A low point of about 23 inches should be suitable for the keyboard. For multi-surface tables, it would be helpful for the display support surface to be adjustable to an inch or two lower yet to accommodate tall displays.

WHAT TABLE-DISPLAY HEIGHT IS RIGHT FOR YOU?

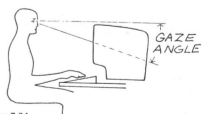

Figure 7-24

Recent data on user preferences indicates that the display should be positioned so that the viewing or "gaze" angle (an angle subtended by the horizon and a line intersecting the operator's eye and center screen—see figure 7-24) is not much in excess of 15–20 degrees, nor much less than 5–10 degrees. It would seem appropriate that source material be similarly positioned.

WHAT IF THE KEYBOARD IS NOT DETACHABLE FROM THE DISPLAY?

In dialogue tasks, this arrangement forces a compromise between preferred keyboard and display positions or heights. The best solution is to replace the VDT with one having a detachable keyboard. However, because there is little evidence of musculoskeletal discomfort with the limbs elevated so long as they can be supported, a *short-term* solution might be to raise the entire VDT somewhat to avoid a severe gaze angle. And at the same time provide wrist supports as needed (figure 7-25).

Figure 7-25

HOW TO MAKE A NON-ADJUSTABLE TABLE SUITABLE WHEN ADJUSTMENT IS REQUIRED (figure 7-26):

Figure 7-26

Use a fairly tall table (to make sure taller people can get their legs under) in combination with a height adjustable chair and footrest. Raise the chair until the keyboard is at a comfortable working level. The footrest is necessary if the chair adjustment raises the feet off the floor or puts uncomfortable pressure beneath the thighs. Then adjust the display height for a comfortable viewing angle.

Note: *This is not a good long-term solution.* A footrest is one more piece of equipment to contend with, and movement is restricted because placement of the feet is limited to the position of the footrest.

Tables for Non-VDT Work. When a VDT table is also used for lengthy periods of non-VDT work, its height will have to be readily adjustable. Alternately, a separate work surface about 28–29 inches high can be used.

Stand-up Work. First, long periods of stand-up VDT work are best avoided. Even at correct working heights, the relatively immobile or passive nature of VDT work may result in rapid fatigue—if not of the back, in the legs.

Perhaps the bulk of stand-up VDT work is performed at service counters. Where VDTs are used for long periods at counters, it is recommended that:

- Operators rotate frequently between the VDT task and other tasks which involve movement and sitting.
- The workstation be designed to allow the operator to sit, or alternately sit and stand.

Sitting, or alternate standing and sitting is sometimes used to avoid fatigue at counters. A work routine involving alterations between standing and sitting tasks is highly desirable because standing offsets the stresses of sitting and vice versa. However, sitting, or alternate sitting and standing at counters may be problematic for the following reasons:

- Mounting and dismounting a tall chair or stool may present a safety hazard.
- It is difficult to adequately position or reposition a tall chair/stool when seated.
- Stool design features may present problems. Footrests which commonly consist of a ring at the bottom of the stool are often unadjustable in height, and stool backrests are not well designed for long periods of sitting.

For these reasons, sitting or alternate standing-sitting may be less preferable a control measure for avoiding back strain in VDT counter work than to minimize the period of continuous stand-up VDT operation through job redesign. A good solution would be rotation between stand-up counter tasks and sit-down VDT tasks or non-VDT work at desks.

Elevating one foot slightly on a support while standing can help reduce stress to the back (figure 7-27). This posture causes the hips to rotate backwards slightly, reducing the excessive forward curve that may occur in the lower spine as the muscles of the abdomen fatigue.

Figure 7-27

Care must be taken, however, that the support doesn't present a tripping hazard!

Counters are often 40–42 inches high. Forty-two inches is about elbow height for an adult of average stature. Placing a VDT on the countertop may result in an uncomfortably high keyboard for most users when they are standing. However, assuming the period of continuous work at the counter is fairly short, this may present no problem. A recess in the counter which allows the keyboard to be lowered a few inches may help.

Assuming preferred gaze angles during stand-up VDT work are the same as sitting, a good height for the display center for each person would be about the level of the mouth. This provides a gaze angle of about 10 degrees at a viewing distance of about 20 inches from the display. A height adjustment range for the display support between 43–57 inches (assuming screen center height of about 10 inches) will allow a viewing angle of about 10 degrees for most people. (Note: the assumption that an appropriate gaze angle for stand-up VDT work is the same as the preferred gaze angle for sit-down VDT work at a table may not be valid. Some people may prefer to have the display positioned lower in stand-up work, particularly if documents are placed and manipulated on the counter top. Lowering the display in this case reduces the angle in looking between the document and display. There has been no research, and little or no discussion on appropriate VDT positioning at counters.)

For multiple users, ideally the display height should be readily adjustable. But again, adjustment to suit people of different stature may be unnecessary with limited periods of continuous stand-up work. For a non-adjustable display support, a height of about 48 inches may be a good choice for multiple users. At this height, a small-to-average stature woman looks almost straight ahead to the display, and the gaze angle of an average-to-large man should not exceed 30 degrees.

Placement of Work Materials
Problems

Poor positioning or alignment of display screens, keyboards, source documents, and other work materials may contribute to stress to the back, and also to the neck and shoulder as explained in the following chapter. Familiar examples include long reaches to work materials, placing loads on the muscles of the back and stresses on the spine (figure 7-28). Stresses to the spine result from twisting toward work materials (figure 7-29).

Figure 7-28

Figure 7-29

Solutions

To prevent these problems, consideration must be given to:

* The primary task performed.
* Reach and viewing distances.
* Environmental factors—especially lighting.

Alignment of Materials. Equipment and material placement needs to be prioritized according to the primary tasks performed. For example, in data or text entry tasks which may require only modest amounts of screen inspection or viewing, the keyboard and source document should take precedence, and be positioned immediately in front of the VDT user (figure 7-30).

Figure 7-30

In editing, programming, or other tasks which involve extensive screen viewing, the position of the keyboard and display takes priority (figure 7-31). Obviously, the hard copy takes precedence when the VDT is seldom used. Further direction on alignment of the document and display is provided in the following chapter on preventing neck strain.

Figure 7-31

Reach and Viewing Distances. For easy manipulation of the keyboard (without causing the operator to bend or reach forward excessively), the home row should be no more than about 7–10 inches away from the front of the desk. Frequently accessed materials need to be carefully placed. They should be accessible without excessive twisting or reaching. A good rule is that at most they should be no further away than the distance to a few inches short of the end of the thumb when sitting at the worktable with the arm outstretched. In the table area directly in front of the person, this is a maximum of about 14–18 inches from the front of the desk.

Suitable reading distances for paper documents and the video display depend upon their legibility. Preferred reading distances for paper materials are usually less than 20 inches. As explained further in the chapter on preventing eyestrain, the character size with many VDTs (usually not in excess of 3 millimeters—about one-eighth inch) may make viewing difficult as the display gets much beyond 24 inches away. As the document and display are placed beyond these distances, VDT users may need to lean forward to see the display clearly. With poor display or document quality, it may be necessary to reduce viewing distances for easy reading with good posture.

Lighting Control. Poor posture or poor placement of displays or documents commonly results from efforts to minimize glare from these sources. Can you recall ever having to assume an uncomfortable or awkward reading position to prevent light from a lamp or the sun from reflecting off the page and making reading difficult? Thus both lighting and the reflective quality of work materials need to be carefully controlled. (More on this subject is presented in the chapter on preventing eyestrain.)

Influence of Personal Characteristics on Back Strain

Visual Problems with Aging

A common problem is the VDT user with bifocals or reading glasses who leans forward to view a display or source document (figure 7-32). The bifocal user is at an additional disadvantage since the head must be tilted back (to see the display through the lower lens) and thus neck strain as well as back strain is likely.

Figure 7-32

As we age, the lens of the eye grows progressively larger and becomes more rigid. This has the effect of making near-vision difficult. For example, by the age of 40-50, many people cannot read a newspaper without holding it at arms' length. To correct for this effect, reading glasses or bifocals are prescribed. But when looking through reading glasses or the lower lens of a bifocal, objects in excess of about 18 inches may be blurry. Because a video display is commonly positioned at this distance or further away, a middle-aged VDT user wearing glasses may have to lean forward uncomfortably to see the display clearly.

Solutions to this problem include:

- Adjusting the distance of the display and work materials.

- Obtaining a more appropriate type of eyewear.

The chapter on preventing eyestrain goes into greater detail on the nature of different types of visual deficiencies, how they can affect eye and musculoskeletal comfort in VDT work, and how they can be corrected or workstation adjustments made to improve comfort.

Pre-existing Back Conditions

Since chronic back problems are such a common malady, it can be expected that a significant proportion of VDT users will begin their jobs with some prior history of back problems. These individuals might be particularly susceptible to back strain with VDT use, and may therefore require special attention in terms of:

- Assignment of work that minimizes stress to the back.

- Ensuring that proper chairs and work-tables are utilized, and that they are properly adjusted. In the implementation of new "ergonomic" furniture, individuals with a history of back problems should be among the first to receive this equipment.

- Surveillance, to be sure that back problems are not worsening.

- Encouragement in terms of pursuing appropriate exercise or treatment regimens.

Personal Habits and Activities

One of the most familiar problems is poor sitting posture at the VDT. Improper posture frequently indicates fatigue resulting from poor equipment design or adjustment. But in other cases poor posture is more indicative of habitual behavior of individuals than it is work-related. Training in proper sitting posture and in workstation adjustment to enable correct postures is critical for avoiding poor postural habits.

There are many off-the-job circumstances which may initiate or contribute to back strain at work:

- Poor lifting techniques (e.g., stooping instead of bending at the knees with the back straight) is a common habit.

- Poor quality household furniture or a sagging bed might result in the same type of distortion of the spine as a poorly-designed office chair.

- Obesity is another important personal characteristic which increases the load to the spine.

We mention these factors not to downplay the role of good workplace design, but simply to direct attention to some common personal matters that should not be neglected in controlling or trouble-shooting the causes of back strain at work.

Lighting Control

From the standpoint of preventing eyestrain, the primary objectives in the design of VDT workplace lighting are to:

- Keep bright lights or reflections out of the field of view of the operator

- Keep the brightness of scenes in the foreground of the operator in balance with the brightness of the display. Most important is preventing a foreground that is excessively brighter than the display. A darker foreground is both less likely and of lesser concern from the standpoint of operator comfort and display visibility.

- Keep light from windows and light fixtures from shining directly or reflecting into the display.

- Ensure that sufficient light is available for non-VDT tasks.

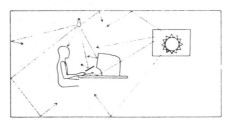

Figure 12-61

The sources of light at VDT workstations and hence points of control, are illustrated in figure 12-61. In summary, they include:

- Light coming directly from windows or light fixtures.

- Indirect (reflected light) from
  —walls or partitions
  —ceiling
  —floor
  —workstation materials (VDT, document and holder, personal effects)
  —furniture (tabletop)
  —the operator (operator's apparel)

Controlling light from these sources requires attention to:

- Design of lighting fixtures in terms of directional control of lighting and the amount of light they produce.

- Window coverings.

- Placement of lighting fixtures and windows in relation to the workstation.

- The reflectance of materials in the workplace.

Design of Lighting Fixtures
Overhead Lights

A major concern in VDT workplace lighting is the horizontal dispersion of light. Because the gaze of the VDT operator is directed toward a relatively dim display at a near horizontal angle, lighting fixtures which disperse light horizontally create the opportunity for discomfort glare. Disability glare is also possible if the light is intense and close enough to the line of sight, though such an arrangement would be rare in the VDT workplace. Controlling horizontal dispersion of light is also important for preventing screen reflections since the near vertical orientation of the screen causes it to reflect horizontally travelling light rays back to the operator.

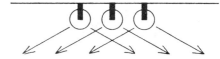

Figure 12-62

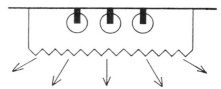

Figure 12-63

The use of unshielded lamps is never a good idea in a VDT workplace since light is dispersed at wide angles (figure 12-62). Similarly, light fixtures enclosed with a refractor-type lens—for example, the

roughened plastic panel commonly used
with a fluorescent tube fixture—also creates a broad spread of light (figure 12-63).

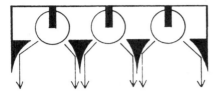

Figure 12-64

One of the most effective ways to control the spread of light is to install a parabolic (sometimes called "para-wedge")
louver beneath light fixtures. The function
of the parabolic louver is illustrated in figure 12-64. The openings or cells in the
parabolic louver have a "dished" (parabolic) shape, as seen from the side. This
shape causes incident light rays to be
directed principally downward.

Figure 12-65

Figure 12-65 provides a dramatic demonstration of the effectiveness of this type
of louver. Figure 12-65 shows a perspective of a ceiling in which the nearest light
fixture is covered by a parabolic louver,
whereas the more distant one contains the
more conventional refractor. In fact, the
near (parabolic) fixture appears far dimmer than the more distant fixture.

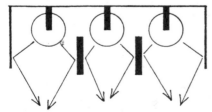

Figure 12-66

Another solution to the control of horizontal dispersion of light from fixtures is
the use of traditional louvers or baffles
(figure 12-66). Light at wide angles is
blocked, but the effect is less pronounced
than with the parabolic louver. A variant
of this technique is to hang or erect a partition between an offending fixture and
the operator (figure 12-67).

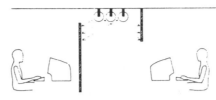

Figure 12-67

Finally, indirect lighting is sometimes
recommended for VDT facilities. With
indirect lighting, light from the fixture is
reflected and diffused from the ceiling
(figure 12-68). This effectively removes
light fixtures as a source of direct glare or
sharp reflections to operators, but the
broad spread of light from the illuminated
ceiling can contribute to diffuse reflections from the VDT.

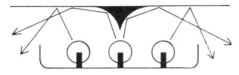

Figure 12-68

Task Lighting

"Task" lighting refers to localized lighting
at the workstation to replace or supplement "ambient" lighting systems (usually
overhead fixtures) used for more generalized lighting of the workplace. Task lighting is handy for lighting source documents whose visibility may suffer as
ambient lighting is controlled to reduce
direct glare and screen reflections. But
because task lamps are usually in close
proximity to the source document—which
is close to the line of sight in viewing the
display, they represent a potential source
of discomfort glare. And if the task lamp
(and thus the document) is very bright,
display visibility may be momentarily
impaired as the operator looks from the
document to the display (while the sensitivity of the visual system adjusts to the
dimmer display). Another potential problem is that excessive light spread from the
task lamp will contribute to diffuse reflections from the display.

To prevent these problems, task lamps
should be no more powerful than necessary, and carefully shaded. Some task
lamps are equipped with baffles or parabolic louvers to help control light spread.

UNSTEADY LIGHT SOURCES

Fluorescent tubes are intrinsically unsteady.
They dim and brighten (flicker) somewhat at the
frequency of the electrical current supplying the
fixture. Though the rate is relatively high (60
cycles/second), it is perceptible and annoying to
some people.

Most fluorescent fixtures are equipped with
two or four tubes. In these fixtures, pairs of
tubes usually work together so that one tube is
brightening while the other is dimming. This
reduces the ability to perceive the flicker of a
single tube. A "high capacitance ballast" is an
important design feature of a florescent fixture
which helps to assure that the two tubes are out
of phase with one another in turning off and on.

Sometimes one bulb of a pair is removed to
dim the fixture to help control glare or screen
reflections. In most cases (but not always,
depending upon how the fixture is designed to
function) this will cause the fixture to cease to
operate. However, a "phantom" tube can be
installed to cause a fixture to operate with one
tube. This is never a good idea since the flicker
of the remaining tube is now more likely to be
perceptible. Removing two paired tubes from a
four-tube fixture is acceptable, but never
remove one tube from a pair.

Sometimes a fluorescent fixture will flicker
noticeably at a low rate as a tube begins to fail.
The tubes should be replaced immediately in
these cases.

Window Coverings

Since light entering through windows
travels in a horizontal path, it is a potential source of discomfort glare and screen
reflections for VDT users. Disability glare
might result when VDTs are positioned
directly before windows.

Light entering through windows can
be controlled by the use of:

- Curtains which are fairly opaque.
- Awnings.
- A dark film covering (neutral density filter).
- Blinds.

In worst cases, it may be necessary to
completely occlude windows altogether
with building materials. However, this
measure should be a last resort since dissatisfaction is likely to result if VDT users
lose the opportunity to look outside.

When using curtains or blinds for large
expanses of the window, it is better to use
several small sections of curtains or blinds
rather than a few large systems. This
arrangement increases the flexibility in
adjusting light according to needs at different locations in the workplace.

Figure 12-69

Vertical blinds (in comparison to horizontal blinds) hold a distinct advantage (figure 12-69). They can be oriented to obstruct troublesome light for someone sitting before the window or in the path of the incoming light, while someone to the side of the window or path of light can still see outside. Horizontal blinds obstruct the view for everyone.

Window covering is important even for night work at VDTs in order to prevent window reflections of interior office lights.

Placement of Lights and Windows

Ambient Lighting

Ideally, bright overhead light fixtures should be placed so that they are far from the line of sight of the VDT user. Figure 12-70 shows how the critical intensity needed for a light source to produce discomfort decreases as the source moves closer to the line of sight. The values given are approximate figures for an office with an overall lighting level appropriate for VDT use (see "A Note on Office Illumination Level" below).

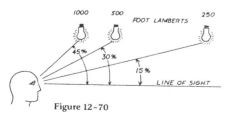

Figure 12-70

At the same time, problems can result when the fixture is placed directly above or behind a workstation. Overhead placement may result in troublesome reflections from the document or work surface. And screen reflections can result from placement behind the workstation (figure 12-71).

Figure 12-71

A more satisfactory placement is just to the side of the workstation, or when workstations are arranged in rows (front-to-front, front-to-back, or back-to-back), between the rows (figure 12-72). The lateral separation of light fixtures from the workstation minimizes direct glare as well as reflections off the screen and work surface into the line of sight of the operator.

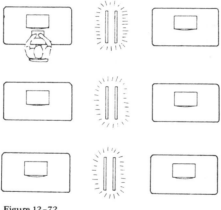

Figure 12-72

Figure 12-72 shows fluorescent fixtures with the tubes oriented parallel to the line of sight. It is usually better to orient fluorescent fixtures so that they are viewed from the side rather than the ends (tubes perpendicular to the line of sight). However, when the fixtures can be placed away from the line of sight as in figure 12-72, this requirement is less critical.

Fixtures that are connected end-to-end in continuous strips can produce continuous reflection lines across a VDT screen.

The reflections from fixtures that are discontinuous or spaced (as in figure 12-72) may be less objectionable.

Flexibility is a key consideration in the design of ambient lighting systems in VDT facilities. To cope with unanticipated lighting problems or adjust to changing lighting needs or individual lighting preferences, the system should allow:

- Removal or relocation of lighting fixtures.
- Individual fixtures or small groups of fixtures to be separately controlled.

It would also be helpful if the amount of light delivered by fixtures could be controlled—for example, by adjustment of the number or power of bulbs, or possibly the use of dimmer systems.

Task Lighting

The placement of task lamps should be adjustable to enable the VDT user to effectively illuminate documents and control the spread of light onto the display screen or other reflective surfaces of the workstations. Lamps affixed rigidly to the workstation (commonly mounted beneath a shelving unit above the table) are restrictive in this regard. Lamps supported by an articulated arm, similar in design to the conventional architect's lamp, should be fairly effective for most VDT applications.

Placement of Workstations in Relation to Windows

VDTs and worktables that are oriented so that the operator faces a window invite discomfort or disability glare from light entering the window. Similarly, positioning the display screen so that it faces a window creates the opportunity for troublesome screen reflections. Unless the window can be covered to effectively prevent the transmission of light to the operator or VDT screen, the VDT should be positioned so that the line of sight of the operator is parallel to the window pane (the display screen at a right angle to the window pane). Even so, it is wise to position the VDT well away from the window.

Similarly, the VDT should be positioned so that the line of sight is parallel and the screen surface perpendicular to highly reflective walls or partitions in the workplace.

Control Over Reflectance

The reflectance of an object refers to its

capacity to reflect light. Light colored surfaces reflect more light (and thus have a higher reflectance) than dark colored surfaces. As with a VDT screen, glossy surfaces tend to produce the more objectionable sharp, distinct reflections, whereas reflections from matte or textured surfaces are soft and diffuse. For this reason it is important to avoid very light and glossy finishes in the interior design of VDT workplaces. Materials and objects of special concern include:

- Walls or workstation partitions.
- The floor.
- The ceiling.
- Worktable tops.
- VDT keyboard keys and the keyboard chassis.
- The display chassis.
- The document holder.
- Personal effects at the workstation—for example, pictures, and even the attire of the operator.

The document, of course, must reflect a fair amount of light to be readily visible, and therefore should be light colored. However, glossy paper should be avoided.

The colors of objects in the VDT workplace don't have to be extremely dark to prevent reflection problems. In fact, very dark colors will create a dissatisfying gloomy appearance and hamper visibility. Following are some approximate values for the percentage of incident light reflected by surfaces of different colors:

Dull or flat white	75–90%
Light green	70–75%
Light beige	70%
Tan	55%
Light grey	35–50%
Pumpkin orange	35%
Cocoa brown	25%
Medium green	20%
Medium grey	20%
Forest green	5%

Colors with reflectance values of about 50 percent or somewhat less will probably suffice to minimize reflection problems and at the same time assure a reasonably pleasant surround with good visibility. This assumes, of course, that the amount of light falling on workplace surfaces is appropriate (see "A Note on Office Illumination Level" below).

"Flat" paints should always be used in order to minimize sharp reflections. Carpeted floors and fabric covered partitions are particularly effective for this purpose. They also have the added benefit of helping to control noise.

A Note on Office Illumination Level

"Illuminance" refers to the amount of light *falling upon* a surface. Illuminance is readily measured with an instrument called a light meter. The unit of measurement in the English system is the "footcandle" (ft.c). To put this measure in perspective, the amount of light falling upon a desk top directly beneath a conventional four bulb fluorescent ceiling fixture will be in the neighborhood of 50–60 footcandles (assuming no other light sources are close by). Illuminance is also commonly expressed in metric units. "Lux" (Lx) is the metric measure. For conversion purposes, one footcandle is equivalent to approximately 10.8 Lux.

The more light which falls upon an object or surface, the brighter it will appear (the greater its "luminance"). From the standpoint of display viewing alone, there is little need for much light to be cast upon objects in the workplace. The VDT emits its own light, and as illumination levels increase and surfaces around the VDT become brighter, the opportunity for troublesome glare and reflections increases. However, if illumination levels are too low, the workplace will appear gloomy, and visibility of paper documents will suffer.

Satisfaction with lighting in general office work does not improve much at illuminance levels (values at the desk top) in excess of 50–70 ft.c., unless the reflectance of work materials is quite low. However, levels much below 50 ft.c. are likely to produce a sharp decline in satisfaction. Thus when paper documents are used, office illumination levels should be in this range.

At the same time, however, generalized office illumination levels of 50–70 ft.c., and certainly anything in excess of these values, runs the risk of producing glare or reflection problems in display viewing. Twenty to 30 ft.c. may be more appropriate from the standpoint of display viewing alone.

One solution to this dilemma is to use task lighting to illuminate documents at 50–70 ft.c. in an ambient environment of 20–30 ft.c. Ambient illumination below 20–30 ft.c. can result in a dreary workplace.

On the other hand, depending upon reflectances and the directional control of light in the workplace, and the ability of the display to resist reflections, an ambient illumination of 50 ft.c. may be quite satisfactory for VDT tasks involving use of documents.

Guide to the Draft American National Standard for Human Factors Engineering of Visual Display Terminal Workstations

CBEMA Computer and Business Equipment Manufacturers Association

311 First Street, N.W., Washington, D.C. 20001, USA

Note: The following guide has been developed by the Computer and Business Equipment Manufacturers Association (CBEMA) to help non-engineers understand the "Draft American National Standard for Human Factors Engineering of Visual Display Terminal Workstations." This guide is not a Human Factors Society document and has not been approved by the committee that drafted the standard. It has, however, been reviewed for accuracy by Committee Chairman Gene Lynch of Tektronix, Inc.

Formal comments to the drafting committee on the standard must be based on the official draft of the standard, which is *not* available from the Human Factors Society. This Guide is not connected in any way with the official ANSI canvass process.

This document may be quoted or copied if attribution is given to CBEMA. Additional copies are available for $10 by writing to: VDT GUIDE CBEMA, 311 First St. NW. Suite 500, Washington, D.C. 20001.

What is the American National Standards Institute?

The American National Standards Institute (ANSI), headquartered in New York, is the nationally recognized coordinator of voluntary national and international consensus standards relating to information processing and to many other industries in the United States. ANSI standards are not laws. Rather they serve as guidelines to American industries that want to better serve customers through standardized products while at the same time maintaining high levels of competition and technological innovation.

How was this Draft Standard Developed?

In 1982, a committee of the Human Factors Society undertook the task of drafting a standard on VDT workstations. Committee membership was solicited from the Human Factors Society (HFS). The HFS Executive Council selected the members to engage in the long and difficult task of developing the standard. The Committee had 17 members, including eleven from the computer industry, one from government, four from the academic community and one from the furniture industry.

What VDT Applications are Covered?

The standard is limited to three VDT applications: text processing, data entry and data inquiry. The standard covers only applications done from a seated position.

Why is the Draft Standard Limited to These Applications?

The Committee based its standard on empirical evidence available from scientific tests conducted on VDTs and workstations. The draft does not include specifications for applications or workplace designs for which the amount of available scientific evidence was insufficient to ensure the development of an adequate standard.

Under What Circumstances can an Organization Say It Conforms to a Standard?

Organizations conform to standards if they meet all the parts of the standard in which the word

"shall" is used. For example, if the current draft were to be accepted as a standard, an organization would comply by having no workstations surface temperatures above 122 degrees Fahrenheit. However, an organization does not have to meet the parts of the standard in which the word "should" is used in order to be in compliance. For instance, the draft says that "the width of the seat back should be sufficient to permit the operator to assume different working postures." This is a suggestion, not a requirement.

What Happens If Organizations Don't Conform to the Standard?

ANSI standards are voluntary. They do not have the force of law.

Organizations that use VDTs will be encouraged to conform because the standard aims at enhancing productivity and organizational effectiveness in workplaces. Organizations that fail to comply will in general find themselves less effective and less competitive than organizations that do.

Manufacturers will be encouraged to conform because failure to do so seriously limits the marketability of their products.

What Does the Draft Provide?

The draft provides a technical base of information with which to evaluate individual workstations and general-purpose equipment. It also provides a set of standard measuring tools through which manufacturers can provide information to their customers.

What Does the Draft Require?

Working Environment:

- Room lighting shall not be so high that users cannot see the characters on the screen (defined technically in the standard).
- Forced air exhausts shall not be directed toward the user.
- Surface temperatures shall not exceed 122 degrees Fahrenheit.

Visual Display Design:

- Screens shall have adequate resolution and luminance (defined technically in the standard).
- The contrast ratio between characters and background shall be at least 3:1. Small characters must have a higher minimum contrast (defined technically in the standard).
- Jittering displays (defined technically in the standard) shall be avoided.
- Characters must appear solid to the viewer; discrete dots that make up the character should not be perceived. (This is defined technically in the standard.)
- If legibility (rapid identification of single characters) is important, a minimum character size shall be 16 minutes of arc. If readability (the ability to recognize words in context) is important, then in addition the maximum character size shall be 24 minutes of arc.
- Height to width character ratios shall be between 1:0.7 and 1:0.9 for fixed column presentations. (However, if more than 80 characters on a line are required, ratios can go as low as 1:0.5. And proportional spacing presentations should permit ratios of 1:1 for some characters.)
- Tasks that require continuous reading shall require 7–9 character matrices. Smaller matrices may be used for numeric and upper-case-only presentations.
- Space between characters shall be a minimum of one strokewidth. Two strokewidths are required between lines. A minimum of one character width is required between words.
- The minimum viewing distance between the eyes and the screen is 12 inches.
- The angle between the line of sight and a line perpendicular to the screen shall be less than or equal to 40 degrees.

Workstation Design:

- There shall be adequate room under the work-surface for legs and feet. (The amount of space is defined technically in the standard.) The minimum width shall be thigh breadth. Leg clearance shall be at least equivalent to the highest point on the thigh or knee.
- The keyboard shall permit the user seated in an upright position to keep the angle between the

upper arm and forearm at 70 to 90 degrees. If the operator is leaning back, then the angle may increase; but the maximum angle should not exceed 135 degrees.

- The primary viewing area shall be 0 to 60 degrees below the horizontal line of sight.
- Chairs shall allow the user to place the feet firmly on a support surface.
- Seat depth shall permit contact between the lumbar area and the seat back.
- Minimum seat width shall be the thigh breadth of the seated user.
- If the chair design has the user placing feet flat on the floor, the seat pan angle shall keep the angle between upper and lower leg between 60 and 100 degrees.
- The angle between the seat pan and back shall permit the user to assume a working posture in which the torso-thigh angle is not less than 90 degrees. (100 degrees is preferable.)
- Chairs shall have back rests with lumbar support. If they have arms, the distance between the armrests shall be a minimum of 17.2 inches.

Keyboard Design:

- The QWERTY layout is required. (See ANSI Standard X4.23.)
- Numeric keypads shall be provided if the entry of numeric data from the keyboard.
- Text processing applications require a two-dimensional dedicated cursor control that is spatially related to the way the cursor moves. (For instance, a control that moves the cursor to the left should be located to the left of a control that moves the cursor to the right.)
- Keyboard slope shall be between 0 and 25 degrees.
- Key cap reflectance shall not be a source of glare (defined technically in the standard).
- Key spacing shall be reasonable, with reasonable displacement levels and reasonable response to pressure (defined technically in the standard).
- Actuation of the key shall be accompanied by either tactile or auditory feedback (or both).
- The keyboard shall be stable for normal keying functions.

What Does the Draft Recommend?

Working Environment:

- Minimizing glare. (The standard contains suggestions.)
- Avoiding intense sources of light in the user's peripheral field of vision.
- Avoiding high-gloss surfaces on or near the workstation.
- Reducing noise to a maximum of 55 decibels and avoiding sporadic noises above normal ambient sound levels.
- Keeping temperatures between 67.1 and 73.4 degrees Fahrenheit in winter and between 72.7 and 78.8 degrees in summer, with corresponding ranges in humidity.
- Avoiding drafts.
- Keeping temperature gradations at the workstation to a minimum (under 9 degrees Fahrenheit vertically and under 18 Farenheit degrees horizontally).
- Maintaining floor temperature between 65 and 84 degrees Fahrenheit.
- Avoiding heat buildup under the desk of more than 5.5 degrees Fahrenheit.

Visual Display Design:

- Avoiding saturated blue on a dark background for text, thin lines or high resolution information.
- Avoiding red in displays. (This is to help "color-blind" people read displays.)
- Providing adequate differentiation among colors used in color coding and between colored symbols and their background (defined technically in the standard). The standard also gives guidance on using various intensities of one color for coding.
- Limiting blink rates to two different ones.
- Keeping characters in rows and columns on the screen, rather than letting them seem "out of position", and keeping the sizes of characters such that users perceive size as constant.
- Keeping luminance from one part of the screen to another such that the user perceives luminance as uniform (defined technically in the standard).
- Avoiding flicker.
- Maintaining minimum character size at 10 minutes of arc. (See standard for conditions.)
- Making strokewidth a minimum of 1/12 of character height.
- Making controls obvious, easily accessible, clear and not easily actuated accidentally.

Workstation Design:

- Making sure that, when the leg is perpendicular to the floor, minimum leg clearance depth under the worksurface (distance, for instance, to the wall against which a desk is placed) is 60% of the buttock-to-knee length.
- Making workstation adjustment controls convenient and easy to use.
- Accommodating the size of the worksurface to the task being done.
- Avoiding pressure on the back side of the lower leg as a result of seats that are too deep.
- Keeping the angle between upper and lower legs at 140 degrees or less for chairs that provide support to the lower leg.
- Keeping seat back widths at a minimum of 12.5 inches in the lumbar region.
- Providing footrests when needed.
- Providing appropriate chair castors.

Keyboard Design:

- Keeping the height of the home row of keys such that the angle between the user's lower arm and forearm is between 70 and 135 degrees.
- Allowing easy repositioning of the keyboard on the worksurface.
- Providing adequate size and contrast for key nomenclature (defined technically in the standard).

How Will Most People Know If Their Workstation Meets These Standards?

The measurement techniques used in the draft are not easily understood or performed by the non-engineer. While one of the major contributions of this standard will be the standardization of certain measurements that have not previously been standardized, the fact remains that most people will have to ask their equipment vendors about the extent to which current equipment meets the draft provisions.

However, users will be able to determine the non-technical measurements and more easily understood requirements (such as whether their workstations allow their feet to be placed firmly on a support).

In the future, if the draft becomes a standard, manufacturers will commonly supply information about the conformance of their products to the ANSI standard.

How Can I Comment on the Standard?

You must first obtain a copy of the draft by sending $15 to:

The Human Factors Society
Box 1369
Santa Monica, CA 90406

Anyone may comment. Contents must be received by October 1, 1985. Objections should be accompanied by recommendations that would remove the objection, and should also be accompanied by documentation and/or references establishing the technical validity of the objection and recommendation.

Does CBEMA Support the Standard?

CBEMA is a canvassee, and has just received its official copy of the draft. We are a consensus organization, and there has not yet been time to poll our 40 members and develop a consensus position.

However, CBEMA strongly supports the voluntary standards *process*. Through the development of voluntary standards, we enable our industry to develop the highest calibre of products while maintaining incentives for technological innovation.

The Statutes and Standards Movement

Dr. T.J. Springer

The trend toward government definition, specification, recommendation and guidance regarding the work, worker and workplace of VDT use is growing rapidly everywhere. Often, opposition to "health and safety" statutes and standards is akin to denouncing Mom and apple pie.

Everyone seems to have concerns. Some sectors of organized labour view the VDT Health issue as a key to the unplumbed membership of white — collar workers. Some politically powerful industries, (e.g. eye care) see the business potential in mandatory eye exams for VDT workers. Individuals and organizations seeking support from information workers make pursuasive emotional appeals regarding health and safety.

Some would argue where there's smoke there's fire and call Smokey the Bear before it's too late. They contend that imperfect protection is better than no protection at all. They maintain that legislation can be easily updated to reflect current state of knowledge regarding the myriad of issues covered by proposed statutes to date.

Manufacturers of VDT devices have sponsored numerous studies to prove or disprove the hypothesis that VDT's are not harmful. Opponents contend the research is designed to protect products and investments and thus is suspect.

Scientists continue to explore the questions of health, safety, comfort, and productivity surrounding the use of VDTs. To date nearly all findings have either demonstrated directly or were shown to later uphold the assumption that VDTs were not inherently hazardous. Most physical, psycho-social and productivity problems are traced to improper matching between the work environment, tools techniques, support equipment and worker. Further a number of studies show real benefit from careful and skillful integration of the many elements comprising a workplace.

Certainly there are concerns associated with the use of VDTs. However, it is equally important to include the following when discussing statutes and standards.

CONSTITUENCY

Who is best served by the bill as proposed? Generally the loudest support or the most generous contributions come from those who stand to gain or lose the most. In this case, that group includes organized labour, political groups such as NOW, 9 to 5, the eye care industry, etc.

COST OF COMPLIANCE

From a business perspective, what is the additional costs for compliance with multiple sets of guidelines and regulations? The fire safety and wiring code problems one encounters from city to city bespeak the difficulties of operating under and entrophic regulatory environment.

EMPIRICAL EVIDENCE

Many of the "hazards" from which the proposed legislation or regulations would protect workers either do not exist or are not caused by the VDT. Radiation has been consistently shown to be lower from a VDT than from many other electronic devices and materials and orders of magnitude lower than the most stringent health/safety hazard levels.

REPRODUCTIVE CONCERNS

Many of the more recent bills include language dealing with pregnant workers. Most suggest a reasonable approach to dealing with this concern — transferring pregnant workers to equivalent jobs not involving a VDT. However certain bills go so far as to include recommendations that pregnant workers be provided lead aprons to protect against emissions. Aside from the potential distress of unwelcomed additional weight, the source and path of what measurable emissions eminate from a VDT are from the flyback transformer at the back and move tangentially to the rear of the device. While "pockets" of miscarriages and birth related problems have been reported, no evidence exists showing higher than normal frequency of problems A longitudinal study by NIOSH will be finished in 1987.

VISUAL FATIGUE

Before anyone blames CRTs and VDTs for increasing eyestrain, deteriorating vision or generally being a pain in the eye, consider-

* 30 to 60% of the adult population requires visual correction
* The eyeglass has changed relatively little since Benjamin Franklin invented the bifocal. It is a paper handling aid.
* 4% of the adult population will develop incipient cataracts.
* Eye fatigue is reported by non-VDT users about as often as VDT users.
* Most workplaces in which VDTs are used are inappropriate for paper based information processing let alone electronic information processing.

POSTURAL STRESS

Pain in muscles, joints, back and neck are most often caused by a combination of the position of the VDT on the desk, the chair and the task.

FATIGUE AND REST

Dictated work rest intervals as proposed do not do as much good as shorter, more frequent rest intervals. Better still is giving the employee freedom to choose and structure work and rest intervals to conform with the work flow.

MEDIOCRITY

Once an official position is taken, the trend is away from innovation and creativity and toward conformity and compliance.

ENFORCEMENT

Who will be charged with enforcing the laws? What will that cost? What penalties and fines are reasonable?

INCENTIVE

The evidence of direct, positive economic benefit from the sound application of ergonomic principles offers enormous incentives to businesses. The combination of competition, rising labour costs, slowed economic growth, unemployment, and an aging labour force puts pressure on management to find ways in which business operations can be improved.

We know far too little and it is far too early in the evolution of technology to begin regimenting the equipment and environment and ways in which VDTs are used. Rapidly advancing technology promises to resolve many of the present and perceived problems with today's VDTs. Flat panel display technology, quiet printers, reduced size, weight and power requirements will all increase the ease with which the technology is assimilated into the work environment.

The Canadian Scene.

Jim Wiley of the **Canadian Standards Association** provided the following update on the Office Ergonomics Guidelines presently in preparation.

"The guidelines are presently past the first draft stage and are ready for a second draft review. We are anticipating a preliminary public review period in the near future. We should emphasize that we view the guidelines as a useful educational tool for the specifier, planner, and purchasing officer. These are guidelines intended for general use — they are not legislation."

Dr. T.J. Springer is President of Springer and Associates, an ergonomics consulting firm servicing the office sector.

PROPOSED UNITED STATES VDT-RELATED LEGISLATION OR REGULATIONS
September, 1984

STATE LEGISLATURES

ST	Bill No./Version	Adjustable Equipment	Chemical Agents	Eye Exams	Further Study	Glare Screens	Heat & Noise	Limit on VDT Work	Monitored Keystrokes	Other Proposals	Proper Lighting	Pregnancy Transfer	Rest Breaks	Radiation Shielding	Stress Reduction	Terminal Lenses	Testing & Maintenance	Technology Refusal	Upgrade Notification
CA	A 3175 5/21 Hearing 9/84	X	X			X	X			4	X	X	X	X		X			X
CA	A 3256 2/16 Withdrawn		X			X					X	X	X			X			
CT	S 811 Passed 83 Rpt due 2/23/84		X	X						1			X						
CT	Nonleg agreement after 6/19 meet																		
HI	HR 137 2/17 Tabled				X														
HI	HR 387 PASS 4/17 Commend CBEMA									1									
IL	H 274 2/16/83 Tabled	X	X			X	X			1	X		X			X	X		
IL	H 2397 2/8/84 Hrng Jul Au Sp	X	X	X	X	X	X	X	X	4	X	X	X	X		X	X		
IA	Regulatory inq.																		
LA	Legislative inq.																		
ME	HP 1265/LD 1675 Passed 6/2/83				X														
ME	Lbr Bur Stdy 831 regs rejected 4/25	X	X							1			X				X		
MD	HJR 47 2/3 Comm tabld 3/16				X														
MA	H 2658-1983 Died in comm	X	X			X		X	X	2	X	X	X	X		X	X		
MA	H 2291 1/84	X	X			X		X	X	2	X	X	X	X		X	X		
MA	H 2300 1/84	X	X			X		X	X	2	X	X	X	X		X	X		
MA	H 3079 1/84	X	X			X		X	X	2	X	X	X	X		X	X		
MA	S 90 1/84 Hearings 3/14	X	X			X		X	X	2	X	X	X	X		X	X		
MA	H 3023 1/84	X	X					X		4	X	X	X	X		X	X	X	
MA	H 3024 1/84		X	X												X			
MA	H 3025 1/84		X							1				X		X			
MA	H 3026 1/84		X							5				X		X	X		
MA	H 3600 1/84				X														
MA	H 4537 1/84	X	X	X	X	X	X	X	X	5	X	X	X	X		X	X		X
MA	S 94 1/84 Workmen Comp		X							1									
MI	Regulatory inq																		
MN	H 2333 4/18 Fall hearings	X	X	X				X		1	X	X	X			X			
MN	S 2217 4/17 Fall hearings	X	X	X				X		1	X	X	X			X			
MO	Regulatory inq.																		
NV	Legislative inq.																		
NJ	Reg inquiry under NJ Pub Empl OSHA																		
NM	Regs pending on NM St VDT buys & workplace health																		
NY	A 3175 Defeated 39-20																		
NY	A 7158A 3/28/83	X	X			X		X		2	X	X	X	X		X	X	X	
NY	S 6528A 5/10/83 In W & M Comm													X					
NY	A 6260 3/24/83																		
NY	S 4314 3/15/83																		
NY	S 4689 3/24/83 In Labor Comm													X					
NY	A 10536 3/28/83																		
NY	S 5012 3/28/83 In Labor Comm													X					
NY	A 10951A 3/30/84 In Labor Comm				X														
NY	A 11078 3/30/84 In Comm	X				X				4									
NY	S 3014 Withdrew																		
NY	S 6074 4/26/83 In Labor Comm	X	X			X		X		4	X	X	X	X		X	X		X
OH	H 552 10/14/83 hearings 4/84	X	X	X		X		X		2	X	X	X	X		X	X		
OR	S 568 6 hearings by 1/85	X	X			X	X	X		2	X	X	X	X		X			
PA	S 1450 6/25 in comm; St emp	X	X	X		X	X	X	X	3	X	X	X	X	X	X	X		
PA	S 1451 6/25 in comm; all emp	X	X	X		X	X	X	X	3	X	X	X	X	X	X	X		
RI	H 7012 5/18/84 PASSED	X	X	X		X	X	X		2	X		X	X		X	X		
RI	HRes 7718 2/28 in comm; students				X					1									
RI	H 7832 2/29 Died in comm																		
WA	Reg. action on U of Wash rept																		
WI	A 1076 2/28	X	X			X		X		1	X	X	X			X	X		

Part II

The User and the Usage
of Interactive Computer Systems

Viewed somewhat narrowly, the young field of human-computer interaction (as well as the more mature discipline of human factors) is a branch of applied psychology. As such, and as a discipline that guides and enhances the processes of design, it must make statements about user capabilities and preferences and about the determinants of quality in a user interface. How can it do so?

One can of course resort to empirical measurement, to the careful running of experiments which compare and quantify differences in performance, usability, and learnability among interfaces, input-output devices, interaction techniques, and the like. The design and execution of such experiments is the domain of experimental design and statistical evaluation, an immense topic we can only touch on briefly in Chapter 4: Empirical Evaluation of User Interfaces.

Unfortunately, it is difficult to define and carry out meaningful experiments. We illustrate this by reviewing methodological problems that have been observed in the literature of ''the psychology of programming.'' These problems are presented in the context of a brief review of this important aspect of human-computer interaction which appears as Case Study B: The Psychology of Computer Programming.

Even when carried out with the best methodology, there are narrow limits to the empirical approach. It is literally impossible to test even a tiny subset of the possible variations in an interactive computer application. These include variations in interface style and command language, in interface technology and in the design of specific devices, in screen organization, choice of names or icons, and error messages, to name just a few of the variables.

Far more important, therefore, is the progress towards developing a science of human-computer interaction, a family of analytic models that can be used to make quantitative predictions about a user's performance with an interface even before it is built. These models will minimize the need to build multiple versions and carry out lengthy experiments. Although this science is in its infancy, there are a number of seminal works that are already required reading for any serious student. Chapter 5: Models of Computer User and Usage, presents some information processing models of the human user and her usage of interactive computer systems.

Information processing models, however, do not span the full range of the cognitive aspects of computer use. Chapter 6: Cognition and Human Information Processing presents a body of literature concerned with the relationship of perception to cognition, with the issue of limited *cognitive resources*, with methods of characterizing tasks by their resource utilization, and with the concepts of *cognitive load* and *interference*. We look at the nature of *problem solving*, at the role of human *mental models* (sometimes also called *user's models*) of a computer system, and at the role of *metaphor* in the understanding of a computer system. We consider *learning* and *skill acquisition*, the nature of *routine cognitive skills*, the process of *skill transfer*, the concept of *stimulus-response compatibility*, and the nature of *errors*.

One of the areas in which observational studies, empirical evaluation techniques, and predictive information processing models have been applied most effectively is in the study of text editors and word processors. We review this work in Case Study C: Text Editors and Word Processors. It will demonstrate how far we have come in our understanding of the human user of interactive computer systems, and, more importantly, how much of the rich complexity of human behaviour we do not yet understand.

We must also examine the channels through which human-computer communication takes place. We consider the three primary channels in use today — in Chapter 7: The Visual Channel, the transmission of visual displays from computer screens through to the human visual system; in Chapter 8: The Haptic Channel, the transmission of manual movements and gestures through a variety of input devices to the computer; and, in Chapter 9: The Audio Channel, the transmission of sound and speech from the computer to the human user and of speech from the human user to the computer.

Each presentation looks at the channel from two different points of view. We examine the human perceptual or motor system that uses the channel, specifically, visual perception, auditory perception, and manual motor skill. We also look at the kinds of devices available for mediating human-computer dialogues that ideally should exploit the properties and characteristics of the human sensori-motor systems. In the case of the visual system, we additionally review some of the insights that the field of graphic design offers to the structuring of effective human-computer communication.

There are certain characteristics of the human sensori-motor system which apply regardless of the modality. One of these is the difference between the magnitude of a physical stimulus and the magnitude of the psychological sensation of that stimulus. Thus we shall see that we must distinguish between visual intensity and brightness, between wavelength and hue, between aural intensity and loudness, and between frequency and pitch. Research in *psychophysics* has concluded that psychological magnitude is related to physical stimulus by a power law which applies across a wide variety of sensory phenomena with exponents ranging from 0.33 for visual brightness to 3.5 for the subjective strength of electric current applied to the finger (Stevens, 1961).

The science of psychophysics also contributes a number of other useful concepts (Van Cott and Warrick, 1972), including:

- sensitivity range along a stimulus scale from minimum perceivable to maximum tolerable for a human observer
- relative discrimination sensitivity, measuring an observer's ability to distinguish between two stimuli or to detect a change in one stimulus, also known as the Just Noticeable Difference (JND)
- ability to make absolute judgments of stimuli or of their magnitude along some scale, expressed as a number of distinguishable values (Miller, 1956)

Absolute judgements are typically much more difficult than relative judgements. Thus, although we can distinguish several hundred different intensities of light or sound on a relative basis, we can only reliably identify three to five different absolute stimuli along the same scale.

The process of organizing sensations into perception also shares common elements independent of sensory modality (Lindsay and Norman, 1977, Chapter 1). Perhaps the most important of these is the brain's attempt to organize sensory messages into meaningful *patterns* and *structures*. It does this by applying rules which summarize its model of the way the world is organized and the way it should appear in various contexts. This allows us to integrate often incomplete and sometimes inconsistent sensations into a plausible perception and concept of the structure of the source of the sensations.

The interested reader is referred especially to a superb recent publication that presents a comprehensive and encyclopedic survey of perception and human performance (Boff, Kaufman, and Thomas, 1986).

References

Boff, K.R., Kaufman, L., & Thomas, J.P. (1986). *Handbook of Perception and Human Performance*, 2 Volumes, New York: John Wiley & Sons.

Lindsay, Peter H. & Norman, Donald A. (1977). *Human Information Processing: An Introduction to Psychology*, Second Edition, New York: Academic Press.

Miller, G.A. (1956). The Magical Number Seven, Plus or Minus Two: Some Limits on Our Capacity for Processing Information. *Psychological Review* 63, 81-97.

Stevens, S.S. (1961). The Psychophysics of Sensory Function. In Rosenblith, Walter A. (Ed.), *Sensory Communication*, Cambridge, MA: MIT Press, 1-34.

Van Cott, H.P. & Warrick, M.J. (1972). Man as a System Component. In *Human Engineering Guide to Equipment Design*, Revised Edition, Washington, D.C.: American Institutes for Research, 17-39.

Chapter 4

Empirical Evaluation of User Interfaces

The complexity of modern user interfaces makes it difficult to intuit the answers to many questions about the consequences of design variations. Are general or specific terms better for the names of commands? Is it preferable to use colour, shape, size, and/or text to encode and present data? Is a mouse faster than a tablet? Which is more important, consistency in command syntax or compatibility of a command language with English usage? Which of three interface designs do users prefer? What problems do naive, casual, and expert users have in working with a real application system under highly pressured conditions?

With a little work, these sentences could be turned into precise, well-formed, meaningful research questions. Assuming that we ask the right questions, how do we design and carry out valid research to obtain useful answers? How do we ensure that the answers we obtain are generalizable, that they reflect and illuminate the complex, subtle, real usage of interactive computer systems?

A particularly lucid and relevant introduction to these topics in the more general context of human factors research is that by Chapanis (1959). Ray and Ravizza (1986) suggest that we can characterize possible research approaches in terms of three continuous dimensions:

- *Naturalistic observation* versus *true experiments*. The former is the attempt to describe an ongoing process as it evolves over time; the latter is the process of studying relationships by manipulating one or more independent variables directly and observing the effect on one or more dependent variables.

An advantage of observation is that we do not need a preconceived notion of what we are looking for. This often leads to insights which can later be pursued through experiments.

- *Field research* versus *laboratory research*. The latter gives us more control over environmental factors. With the former, the subject is more likely to be behaving in a natural, realistic, ecologically valid manner.

- *Scientist as participant* versus *scientist as observer*. This approach deals with the extent to which the scientist is herself a part of the study or is a "passive" recorder of data.

A fourth dimension should be added:

- *Few* or *many* subjects. Possibilities range from the detailed study of one special individual to experiments on surveys of hundreds of individuals.

There is therefore a rich space of possible research procedures. Different points in this space have unique advantages and disadvantages. A recurring theme as we explore the space is the tradeoff between *internal* and *external validity*. *Internal validity* concept describes our confidence that we have found "the" explanation for our experimental results, that we are not aware of other plausible explanations which can equally well account for them. *External validity*, sometimes known as *generalizability*, describes the degree to which our research results have applicability to explaining other situations or phenomena. Ray and Ravizza (1986, p. 248) note that "we are always faced with a trade-off between (1) precision and direct control over experimental design and (2) desire for maximum generalizability and relevance to real-life situations.'' We strive for research that is both sound *and* relevant.

Although we shall return to this topic again briefly in Chapter 11: Design Principles and Methodologies, we shall now look at some of the most useful techniques for observing and evaluating user interfaces, and for studying the quality of human-computer interaction (Ray and Ravizza, 1986; Anderson and Reitman Olson, 1985, excerpts of which appear later in this volume). These are:

- gathering reports and evaluations from users of real systems
- detailed observations of users working with a system
- field tests on users working with real systems
- ''quasi-experimental'' designs
- controlled experiments

Surveys of users are appropriate means of eliciting reports and evaluations of real systems once they have been introduced in the field. They employ naturalistic observation, are carried out in the field by scientists acting as observers, and require many subjects. An example is the survey evaluating the Audio Distribution System cited in Case Study A: The Design of a Voice Messaging System, Roemer et al. (1986).

Detailed observations of users working with a system allow us to examine their behaviour microscopically under idealized conditions. They employ naturalistic observation, often aided by the computer recording of keystrokes and the timing of keystrokes, audio taping, and video taping. They are typically carried out in the laboratory by scientists acting as observers, although they may occasionally use themselves as subjects. They are valuable even if done with only a few subjects. A good example is ''thinking aloud'' and ''protocol analysis'' in the studies of users of text editors by Mack, Lewis and Carroll (1983) and Carroll and Mack (1984), included as readings later in this volume. For a discussion of some of the controversy and methodological issues involved in the use of ''verbal reports'' as data, the reader is referred to Nisbett and Wilson (1977) and Ericsson and Simon (1980).

Field tests are observational studies on real systems in complex use. They employ naturalistic observation, are carried out in the field by scientists acting as observers, and typically require an intermediate number of subjects. A good example is the work evaluating nine text editors by Roberts and Moran (1983), included as a reading later in this volume.

Quasi-experimental designs are used to study a system as it evolves over time. They employ technique that

falls midway in the spectrum of observation to experiment, are often carried out in the field by scientists acting as observers, and require an intermediate number of subjects. Good examples are some of the evaluation studies carried out on the Speech Filing System that are reported in Gould and Boies (1983), and the ''Graphics Test'' reported in Bewley, Roberts, Schroit and Verplank (1983), both included as readings in this volume.

Controlled experiments are carried out in the laboratory by scientists acting as observers and using many subjects. Good examples are Perlman (1985) and the ''Selection Scheme'' and ''Icon Shape'' tests reported in Bewley, Roberts, Schroit and Verplank (1983), both included as readings in this volume.

Monk (1985a), which we include as a reading, asserts the value of doing controlled experiments, then provides a competent overview of key issues involved in conducting them properly. Of particular interest is his discussion of the pros and cons of ''within-subject'' and ''between-subjects'' design. In a companion piece, also included as a reading, Monk (1985b) cogently summarizes some of the key ideas of the process of statistical evaluation of behavioural data.

One important point not made by Monk is the importance of developing *predictive models and theories* which can suggest and explain empirical results. We return to this topic, with appropriate examples, in Chapter 5: Models of Computer User and Usage.

Experimental design and statistical evaluation are complex subjects. Readers are referred to Snedecor and Cochran (1980) and to Kirk (1982) for comprehensive surveys, and to a useful paper by Hammer (1984). The difficulty of meaningful empirical evaluation, even with accepted designs and proper statistical procedure, is illustrated by the paper by Sheil (1981) included in the next section, a Case Study of the ''Psychology of Programming.''

Readings

Monk, Andrew (1985a). How and When to Collect Behavioural Data. In Monk, Andrew, *Fundamentals of Human—Computer Interaction*, London: Academic Press, 69-79.

Monk, Andrew (1985b). Statistical Evaluation of Behavioural Data. In Monk, Andrew, *Fundamentals of Human—Computer Interaction*, London: Academic Press, 81-87.

References

Anderson, Nancy S. & Reitman Olson, Judith (Eds.) (1985). *Methods for Designing Software to Fit Human Needs and Capabilities*, Proceedings of the Workshop on Software Human Factors, Committee on Human Factors, Commission on Behavioural and Social Sciences and Education, National Research Council, Washington, D.C.: National Academy Press.

Bewley, W.L., Roberts, T.L., Schroit, D. & Verplank, W.L. (1983). Human Factors Testing in the Design of Xerox's 8010 "Star" Office Workstation. *Proceedings of CHI '83 Conference on Human Factors in Computing Systems*, 72-77.

Carroll, John M. & Mack, Robert L. (1984). Learning to Use a Word Processor: By Doing, by Thinking, and by Knowing. In Thomas and Schneider (Eds.), *Human Factors in Computer Systems*, Ablex Publishing Company, 1984, 13-51.

Chapanis, A. (1959). *Research Techniques in Human Engineering*, Baltimore: The Johns Hopkins Press.

Gould, John D. & Boies, Stephen J. (1983). Human Factors Challenges in Creating a Principal Support Office System — The Speech Filing Approach. *ACM Transactions on Office Information Systems* 1(4), 273-298.

Ericsson, K. Anders & Simon, Herbert A. (1980). Verbal Reports as Data. *Psychological Review* 87(3), 215-251.

Hammer, John H. (1984). Statistical Methodology in the Literature on Human Factors in Computer Programming. In Salvendy, G. (ed.), *Human—Computer Interaction*, Amsterdam: Elsevier Science Publishers B.V., 189-193.

Kirk, R.E. (1982). *Experimental Design: Procedures for the Behavioural Sciences*, Second Edition, Belmont, CA.: Wadsworth Publishing Company.

Mack, Robert L., Lewis, Clayton H. & Carroll, John M. (1983). Learning to Use Word Processors: Problems and Prospects. *ACM Transactions on Office Information Systems* 1(3), July 1983, 254-271.

Monk, Andrew (1986a). How and When to Collect Behavioural Data. In Monk, Andrew, *Fundamentals of Human—Computer Interaction*, London: Academic Press, 69-79.

Monk, Andrew (1986b). Statistical Evaluation of Behavioural Data. In Monk, Andrew, *Fundamentals of Human—Computer Interaction*, London: Academic Press, 81-87.

Nisbett, Richard E. & Wilson, Timothy D. (1977). Telling More Than We Can Know: Verbal Reports on Mental Processes. *Psychological Review* 84(3), 231-259.

Perlman, G. (1985). Making the Right Choices with Menus. *Human-Computer Interaction — Interact '84*, Amsterdam: North-Holland, 317-321.

Ray, William J. & Ravizza, Richard (1986). *Methods Toward a Science of Behavior and Experience*, Second Edition, Belmont, CA.: Wadsworth Publishing Company.

Roberts, Teresa L. & Moran, Thomas P. (1983). The Evaluation of Computer Text Editors: Methodology and Empirical Results. *Communications of the ACM* 26(4), 265-283.

Roemer, J.M., Pendley, W.L., Stempski, M.O., & Borgstrom, M.C. (1986). Field Study of a Voice Mail System: Design and Design-Process Implications, *SIGCHI Bulletin* 18(2), 60-61.

Sheil, B.A. (1981). The Psychological Study of Programming. *ACM Computing Surveys* 13(1), 101-120.

Snedecor, G.W. & Cochran, W.G. (1980). *Statistical Methods*, Seventh Edition, Ames, Iowa: Iowa State University Press.

How and When to Collect Behavioural Data

Andrew Monk

5.1 THE VALUE OF BEHAVIOURAL DATA

Imagine that you have been asked to lead a team of software engineers who are going to automate the system for collating information 'monitored' from private telephone conversations at a secret defence establishment. You have been provided with a sketch of the function of the system and you have some idea of the hardware available. From your initial deliberations a number of questions arise. One might be whether to use colour. It is necessary to display complex graphs representing communication pathways. You could indicate the nature of a pathway by using different coloured lines, or alternatively and much more cheaply, by using different kinds of broken line on a monochrome display. You remember reading somewhere that colour is an effective way of identifying the elements of a graph. A search of the literature reveals that many of the recommendations are based on little more than anecdote. There are recommendations based on well-documented experience and properly controlled experiments but none quite fit the circumstances of your application. The literature reveals that colour can often lead to considerably improved user performance, but that this is not necessarily the case.

Another question might concern more cognitive considerations. The initial specification you are working from gives the critical attributes which are to be used to classify the conversations. It does not specify how the attributes are related. Would a hierarchical scheme work and if so how would it be ordered?

The best way to answer the questions whether to use colour and how to organise the classification of conversations is to collect some behavioural data. The first question can be answered in a controlled experiment comparing two otherwise similar set ups. The second can be answered by careful questioning and observation of users of the present paper-based system your system is to replace.

The above scenario illustrates the problems faced by the designer. It is rarely the case that the human factors literature will precisely answer the questions asked of it. It should help to define the problems a user will have and it may suggest some ways that these problems may be minimised but the most appropriate solution will rarely be obvious and the designer will need additional information. Behavioural data should be the major source of additional information used in making a design decision.

5.2 WHEN TO COLLECT BEHAVIOURAL DATA

The scenario developed in the last section will be extended to illustrate the different points in the design process where behavioural data may be usefully collected, starting at the beginning when the old system to be replaced is being studied.

System Analysis

Part of the design team is sent to the defense establishment to find out how the existing paper-based system works. The manager of the department concerned in fact designed the present system. You interview him at length but suspect that what he is telling you is what he expects the users to be doing rather than what they are actually doing. You go on to interview the rest of the department and study the behaviour of two operators in some detail. You find that while the manager views the classification of conversations as essentially hierarchically structured the operators have difficulty using his scheme and have adopted all sorts of tricks to get round the limitations it imposes. Further discussions with operators and the manager together result in a potentially better scheme. At the same time you have identified those parts of the operators' task which are seen to be boring or too demanding so that the new system can avoid these problems if possible.

efficiency will pay for the development of the system in four months. It is thus worth their while to pay for the development of two systems and then to choose between them on the basis of efficiency. The client sets up a controlled experiment in his own human factors laboratory. Of course your system which was designed with careful attention to the needs of the user is shown to be 40% more efficient than the system it replaces and 20% more efficient than the opposition's system. Your company wins the contract and you are promoted to the board of directors!

Current design practice may be somewhat distant from the scenario sketched above, however, as time goes by, more companies are moving in the direction indicated. The remainder of this chapter explains how to collect behavioural data, how to select the users from whom you collect it and how to design effective experiments. As well as permitting you to collect your own data this chapter will make it possible for you to evaluate the data of others and the conclusions they draw.

5.3 BEHAVIOURAL MEASURES

It is a relatively simple matter to build monitoring functions into one's prototyping set up. An instrumented prototype can record errors made (how many, where they were made) and times (time to complete the task, time to recover from an error, and so on). The most important measures of overall efficiency are time to complete the task and some quantification of correctness.

From this point of view errors detected by the system and which the user recovers from are important only in so far as they contribute to the total time taken to complete the task. This assumes that there is no large systems cost associated with some errors. Errors which go undetected by the user are more serious as they indicate the task has not been completed correctly and must somehow be incorporated into one's measure of overall efficiency.

Instrumentation of the kind described above provides objective measures of user performance. More subjective measures may also be useful. In particular you will need to observe users at work and debrief them at the end of an experimental session.

Observation may be very informal and simply involve sitting in on one or two sessions. At a more formal level you may decide to videorecord the users as they perform his task. Another technique is to have the user verbalise his thoughts as he performs the task. This commentary on the

Specification

The system specification incorporates 'usability specifications' of the kind advocated by Carroll and Rosson (In Press). An example might be

"A skilled operator will be able to enter the classification for a conversation in less than 10 seconds for 50% of conversations classified and less than 20 seconds for 90% of conversations classified."

The figures in the above specification are based on observation of the present system. Notice that the specification includes details of the user population and the margin for error (50% of conversations).

Some of the more important design decisions are made with the aid of small experiments. For example, communication pathway graphs are displayed in monochrome or colour. Tests are performed to see which kind of display results in the best user performance. The tests utilise artificial experimental tasks which are designed to capture the essence of the tasks the operators will perform with these displays in the real system. These experiments show that the colour display results in 30% less errors as well as slightly faster responses than the monochrome one so you decide the additional expense is justified.

Implementation

Having fully specified the system it is emulated at your Human Factors Evaluation Centre and several users with the appropriate background and experience are taught to use it. The centre videotapes the users working with the system and the emulation is instrumented so that a time stamped record of every user-computer transaction is available. In addition the users are interviewed at length. On the basis of this data the Human Factors Evaluation Centre suggests a number of weak points in the design and you make changes to sort them out. Further testing reveals that your changes were effective.

Human Factors Evaluation

Your client has calculated that, in terms of the manpower required and the results obtained, a 10% improvement in

user's own actions is recorded and transcribed and can then be subjected to what is known as 'protocol analysis'(see Mack, Lewis and Carroll 1983 for a representative study using this technique). Both video recording and protocol analysis are very tedious to score and expensive to do and can probably only to be used to a limited extent. There is also the problem that both these techniques may themselves affect the behaviour of the user. Having the user keep a diary of his experiences with a system is a possible alternative to protocol analysis for long term studies (see Naur 1983 for an example of such a study).

Useful insights into the strengths and weaknesses of a system can often be obtained by the careful debriefing of users after they have performed the experiment. Informal questioning may be appropriate as long as care is taken to avoid leading the user into giving you the answers that you want. Being this objective is not as easy as it might seem and if you have some specific questions to ask you might consider constructing some sort of questionnaire. This could take the form of written questions with open answers or it might be some sort of attitude scale. The latter is useful for assessing the user's feelings towards the system.

Table 5.1 gives some examples of items from attitude scales. Normally one would have more than six items in each scale, there should be an equal number of statements expressing positive and negative attitudes to the system and the items should cover a range of attitudes. Clearly if all the 'Yes' responses in the questionnaire count towards one outcome and all the 'No' responses to the other, the final result could reflect more the user's bias to say 'Yes' than the question one was originally concerned with. A. is scored by counting the number of positive items ticked and subtracting the number of negative items ticked. B. is scored similarly by adding up the ratings for positive items and subtracting the ratings for negative items. As well as computing an overall 'favourability' it may be revealing to examine the scores for individual items. Repertory grids may also be used to explore users' attitudes to a system (see Shaw, 1980).

TABLE 5.1 Examples of items from two types of attitude scale.

A. Tick the statements you agree with.

'This system is a real pleasure to use.'
'This system is very tiring to use.'
'Some of the commands are rather obscure.'
'I had no difficulty learning to use the system.'
'This system is an improvement on previous systems I have used.'
'The system does not have a good 'feel' to it.'

B. Give each statement a rating between 1 and 5.
   5 = I strongly agree.
   4 = I agree with reservations.
   3 = I do not agree or disagree.
   2 = I disagree to some extent.
   1 = I strongly disagree.

'I had considerable difficulty learning to use the system.'
'The commands are all straight forward to use.'
'Using the system requires a lot of concentration.'
'The replies given by the system are very 'business like'.'
'The system takes a long time to answer.'
'The system messages are easy to understand.'

5.4 SELECTING SUBJECTS

Behavioural scientists refer to the people who take part in their experiments as subjects. Choosing the users who are going to be subjects in your experiment is one of the most important parts of the design of that experiment.

Let us say that in the course of designing some word processing software we have to decide between two methods of cursor control, say a touch screen as opposed to special function keys. A poor way of doing this would be to set up an instrumented prototype and run several members of the design team through a series of standard word processing tasks. The results of such an experiment are very unlikely to generalize to the secretaries who will be the users of the final product. First of all the designers will have had more experience of computer systems in general than the computer naive secretary. This will lead to quite different expectancies and thus to quite different patterns of behaviour. Of course, if the design team has been involved with this particular project their expectations will be even more atypical. Secondly, the design team will know less about the task (formatting documents) than a secretary and may use a rather different vocabulary to describe it. More importantly, this will make the way they conceptualise the task quite different. Thirdly, and not least, the secretaries will be skilled typists and the way they use the

aim of this methodology is to control all the different 'variables' which may affect the results of the experiment. For our discussion of this subject we will take as an example the experiment considered above which compares two methods of cursor control.

A useful first step when designing an experiment is to make a list of all the variables which might affect the results of the experiment. Table 5.2 contains some headings you might use in constructing such a list.

TABLE 5.2

Subject	Environment	Procedural
Experience with computers	Noise	Within/Between subjects design
Experience of the task	Other distractions	Training/Practice
Typing ability	Lighting, seating	Scoring
Intelligence/Flexibility		
Anxiety/Motivation		

We have already considered the category Subject Variables under the heading of 'Selecting Subjects'. This whole category of variables is 'controlled' by making the subjects as representative of the target population as possible. The sample should be representative in range as well as mean value. Thus, for example, the range of intelligence to be expected in the target population should be matched in the range of intelligence of your subjects. Technically this procedure is described as declaring subjects to be a 'random' variable.

Environmental variables are controlled by fixing them at levels typical of the environments in which the final product will be used. For example, the results obtained in a quiet laboratory may be quite different to those obtained in the more realistic situation of an open plan office.

Finally we come to the most difficult class of variables, those that have to do with the way the experiment is conducted i.e., the experimental procedure adopted. We have discussed 'scoring' under the heading 'Behavioural Measures'. We have also briefly discussed the problem of training and practice in the last section. How the experiment is structured is discussed in the next section.

keyboard may be quite different. For example, using special function keys may allow them to maintain their 'home keys' position so that this method may result in less disruption of typing behaviour. This would not be the case with less skilled typists.

In general, the principles of sampling subjects for an experiment are the same as those applied in sampling consumers in marketing exercises. For important experiments, where generalization to a target population is important, for example the comparison of your product with others, you may wish to employ marketing organizations to do the sampling for you. For experiments where generalization is less important it is often sufficient to choose subjects who roughly match the target population in terms of experience under the three categories which arose in the example above: experience with the task, general experience with computer systems and (if you are using keyboard input) typing ability.

While we are considering the topic of user expertise we should consider the problem of practice. The knowledge a user has of a task depends both on prior experience and how practised he or she is at using this particular system. In general, when evaluating a system, one will be interested both in ease of use and ease of learning. Ease of learning is measured in terms of the time required to achieve some asymptotic level of performance. Ease of use is measured in terms of how high that asymptote is. A system which is easy to use may not be the easiest to learn, though experience suggests this is often the case.

5.5 DESIGNING EXPERIMENTS

Some of the behavioural data collected in human factors work is purely observational in the sense that one is simply looking for evidence of problems with the user interface. To collect such data it is necessary carefully to consider the subjects tested and the measures taken as discussed in the previous two sections. When one is designing an experiment - our original example was to compare a coloured display with a monochrome version - there are additional considerations to be taken account of.

Experimental Control

Behavioural science like any other scientific discipline has developed its own methodology for doing experiments. The

TABLE 5.3 Examples of between- and within-subjects designs. The scores given are solution times in seconds.

A. Between-Subjects

Group I (System A)		Group II (System B)	
Subject 1	735	Subject 2	425
Subject 3	623	Subject 4	367
Subject 5	791	Subject 6	276
Subject 7	798	Subject 8	548
Subject 9	562	Subject 10	418
Subject 11	752	Subject 12	391

B. Within-Subjects

	System A	System B
Subject 1	651	452
Subject 2	438	321
Subject 3	859	657
Subject 4	672	653
Subject 5	712	752
Subject 6	546	444

The latter, where this is not the case and one has groups of subjects, is said to be a between-subjects design. Examples of data from these two experimental designs are given in Table 5.3.

Each type of design has its advantages and disadvantages. Within-subjects designs can be more efficient than between-subjects designs because you get more information from each subject you test and each subject acts as his own control. It may be necessary to run a large number of subjects in a between-subjects design before a stable picture of what is happening emerges. However, even with a between-subjects design a large effect should be apparent after running seven or eight subjects. Between-subjects designs score over within-subjects designs in that they are much less liable to order effects and range effects.

Consider the experiment on menu length as a within-subjects design. Clearly the two experimental systems will have elements in common and it is likely that there are practice effects so that whichever task is performed last will be performed better (although it is also possible to get order effects due to fatigue). In an attempt to control this, one might have half the subjects use System A then System B and half System B then System A. However, this will only be effective if the practice effects are symmetrical. If, for example, practice on System A is useful when you use System B but not the other way round then the result may be seriously biased. Some statisticians argue that this kind of range effect, where doing one task affects how you do another, is always a possibility and within-subjects designs should never be used. This is probably an extreme position but care should be taken when using within-subjects designs. The menu length experiment, for example, should be done as a between-subjects design.

When using a between-subjects design you must ensure that the groups selected are matched or are randomly selected. If, for example, subjects are allowed to select which group they perform in, or even if the whole of one group is tested before the other, there is the strong possibility of bias.

5.6 SUMMARY

'Know your user' is a commonly quoted slogan. The message of this chapter is that you will only achieve such knowledge by systematic study of the users' behaviour. This may take various forms including user performance measures, interviews, protocol analysis and so on. Behavioural data can be utilised as observations which indicate how the

Within- and Between-subjects Designs

Typically any experiment will have a 'dependent variable' and an 'independent variable'. The dependent variable is the thing you measure, the independent variable is the thing you manipulate. For example, consider an experiment to compare System A which uses long menus with System B which uses a larger number of shorter menus. The question is whether the subjects can achieve a number of trial goals faster using System A or System B. The dependent variable here is time in seconds to complete the test. The independent variable is menu length or system type. The different levels of the independent variable, in this case long and short or A and B, can be combined with the variable subjects in two ways. Every subject can provide scores from all the levels or conditions, or each level can be represented by a different group of subjects who only provide scores for that condition. The former design, where one can make comparisons between conditions within each subject's scores, is said to be a within-subjects design.

system is used and where its strengths and weaknesses lie. Alternatively in the context of a controlled experiment it can be used to answer specific questions.

Effective experimental design is a relatively straight forward matter as long as one is aware of the different variables and factors which may affect the outcome of the experiment. Whenever you are designing an experiment and whenever you read about someone else's experiment, you should always be trying to think of alternative ways of explaining the results. If you can think of the alternative explanation is generally possible to control it out. Variables can be controlled by fixing them at some representative level (e.g., distraction due to noise) or declaring them as random variables and then sampling from some representative population (e.g., subjects). If your experiment has an independent variable (e.g., menu length) then the appropriate design must be selected (within- or between-subjects). Finally dependent variables (what you measure) must be selected to capture the aspects of the task you are interested in. It is often a good idea to use several dependent variables to measure different aspects of performance (e.g., time taken, number of errors, rated ease of use).

5.7 FURTHER READING

For a useful treatment of experimental design including suggestions about how to format a report on an experiment see Robson (1973). Robson is writing for psychology students. An alternative which may be more closely tailored to the needs of designers and engineers is Shneiderman's book (1980). His chapters 1 to 3 are relevant to this chapter.

For further information about psychometric tests and attitude measurement see Anastasi (1982). Shaw (1980) explains how to use repertory grids.

REFERENCES

Anastasi, A. (1982) Psychological Testing. 5th edition. Macmillan, New York.

Shaw, M. (1980). On Becoming a Personal Scientist. Academic Press, New York.

Statistical Evaluation of Behavioural Data

Andrew Monk

6.1 INTRODUCTION

Chapter 5 explained how to collect behavioural data. One unfortunate characteristic of behavioural measures, in comparison with physical measures, is that they are much more subject to chance influences. Within a group of subjects there will be differences due to background, experience, age and so on. Even within the performance of a given subject there will be variations due to uncontrolled changes in the environment, minute by minute changes in alertness and so on. It is thus advisable when reporting some measure of central tendancy, such as a mean performance time, also to report a measure of dispersion such as the variance or the range of times. This allows the reader of the report to estimate the precision of the result.

When it comes to assessing the results of experiments a similar problem arises. Given there is some chance variation in the results, any difference observed between experimental conditions could be due to these chance fluctuations rather than the experimental manipulation. Inferential statistics of the kind described below allow us to test against this possibility.

6.2 TESTING FOR DIFFERENCES BETWEEN MEANS

Rationale

Any experiment will have some chance element to it. For example, consider the experiment described in Chapter 5, the aim of which was to compare two systems. System A is controlled by making choices from menus of a certain length. System B works on the same basis but uses more, shorter menus to achieve the same result. Let us say that a between-subjects design is used, so one group of subjects uses System A and the other System B. After a suitable amount of practice both groups are given five specific problems to solve and the total time taken is measured. Subjects are selected to be representative of the population of potential users of the systems.

To assess the effect of the manipulation of menu length we need to compare the solution times for the two groups.

The individuals within each group will differ in a number of ways and so will their scores (time to solve all the problems). In a sense they have been chosen to do so as the groups are supposed to be representative. Thus when we compute a mean score for each group there is always the possibility that the means differ, not because of our manipulation but by chance. Table 6.1 gives two sets of results. Both have the same mean scores but it is clear that in only case A. is likely to be a reliable finding. In case B. the variability within the groups is very large, in fact easily large enough to account for the difference between the groups.

The null-hypothesis

The business of inferential statistics is to quantify the above arguments. This is done by computing the probability that the result obtained (or one that is in some sense better) could have arisen by chance. If that probability is very small then the result is said to be 'significant'. This computation is achieved by setting up a 'null-hypothesis' which is in effect a definition of what we mean by chance.

As another example take an experiment where users are exposed to a white on black CRT display as well as an equivalent black on white CRT display. The subjects in this experiment are simply asked which display they prefer. A reasonable null-hypothesis for this task would be that each subject has an equal probability of choosing each display. On that basis one can see it is a relatively simple matter to compute the probability of say 10 out of 10 subjects choosing the black on white display. The probability is small (<0.002) and so we can reject the null-hypothesis and accept that the result 10 out of 10 is a reliable one.

The computation required for our 'menu length' experiment is different but the logic is the same. This time the null-hypothesis is that there is no effect of system type on the scores. All the variance in the scores is assumed to arise from the subject variables. This variance can be estimated from the within-group variance. Using certain statistical techniques it is then possible to estimate the probability that the difference between groups arose from this same source of 'error' variance.

TABLE 6.1 Two sets of Hypothetical Results. The scores are solution times in seconds. Each score is contributed by a different subject.

A.	Group I	Group II
	623	367
	791	276
	798	548
	562	418
	752	391
	651	452
Mean	696.2	408.7

B.	Group I	Group II
	312	1276
	456	142
	1548	330
	125	303
	561	131
	1175	270
Mean	696.2	408.7

Significance Levels

Having computed the probability of getting our result, or something better, assuming the null-hypothesis is true (i.e., by chance) the next step is to decide whether that probability is small enough for us to reject the null-hypothesis. Arbitrary levels are set for this purpose; if the probability is less than this the result is said to be significant at that level. The critical levels are known as significance levels. In behavioural science the most commonly used significance level is the .05 level. That is if the probability of getting your result, or something better, by chance is less than .05 the result is deemed reliable; otherwise it is not. The significance level represents an error rate. If you habitually set a significance level of .05 then in five percent of your experiments where the manipulation really had no effect you will wrongly conclude that there was an effect. Of course, if one sets a very high significance level to avoid these false positives one runs an increasing risk of making errors in the opposite direction and rejecting real results. The .05 level has been arrived at by balancing the costs of the two kinds of errors. If, as is likely, these costs are different in your situation then a different significance level may be used. Returning to our menu length example, it may be that System A is already well established and is being used in a number of your installations. In that case one would want to be sure that the difference in performance between systems A and B was large and could not be attributed to chance before changing over to system B.

What Test to Use

Three statistical tests are listed below. They have been chosen because they are simple to use and make no strong assumptions about the nature of the dependent variable. Which test you use depends primarily on the experimental design.

(i) Mann-Whitney U test-
Used for between-subjects designs where there are two groups of subjects. The dependent variable must be a score of some kind that can at least be ranked.

(ii) Wilcoxon Matched Pairs Signed Ranks test-
Used for within-subjects designs where each subject gives you two scores, one for each of two experimental conditions. The dependent variable is a score of some kind so that the differences can at least be ranked.

(iii) Sign Test (also known as the binomial test)-
Used when each subject can be classified as supporting or not supporting your hypothesis. Useful as a quick check but it may ignore a lot of the information you have collected.

Procedures for performing the tests will be found in Robson (1973). More complicated designs are beyond the scope of this chapter. Some reference books are given in the bibliography.

6.3 CORRELATION

The tests given in the previous section are for comparing experimental conditions. A rather different kind of statistic is needed to measure an association or correlation. Consider an experiment to see how easily operators can adapt from one system to another. Each operator is presented with the new system and after some suitable amount of practice his performance is measured. Let us say that as well as this score we also have some measure of his familiarity with the old system, say the number of months he has used it. Figure 6.1 is a graph representing this data. Each subject is represented by a point giving his performance and experience. The cloud of points is elliptical and its major axis has a negative slope. This indicates that in general the more experience with the old system you have the worse you are with the new one. Pearson's product-moment correlation, signified r, will quantify this trend. If r is near to 1 there is a strong positive relationship. If it is near to -1 there is a strong negative relationship. If it is near to 0 there is no relationship. The significance of r depends on the number of subjects as well as the strength and refers to the probability of getting a relationship of the same sign.

There are all sorts of pitfalls to be encountered when interpreting correlations. The three most common are given below:

(i) Attributing causality - You cannot attribute causality on the basis of a correlation. Take the example above, it is not possible to say that experience with the old system caused difficulties with the new one because there is always the possibility there is some third factor causing the difficulty which is correlated with experience (for example, age).

If in doubt contact an expert. There are particular problems inherent in interpreting correlations when there are several dependent variables.

6.4 SUMMARY

Statistical tests for assessing the reliability of differences between means and a test of correlation have been discussed. These tests allow one to determine the significance of a result. Significance is achieved if the probability of getting that result, or better, by chance is less than some arbitrary significance level.

6.5 FURTHER READING

Robson (1973) can be recommended as a cheap and easy-to-read text on the principles of experimental design and statistics. All the tests he covers are described with step-by-step procedures accompanied by worked examples. He covers all the tests mentioned in this chapter and a few more. As an alternative to Robson try Shneiderman (1980).

For further technical detail, including tests for use with experimental designs more complex than those considered here and in Chapter 5, consult Kirk (1968) or Ferguson (1981).

REFERENCES

Ferguson, G.A. (1981). Statistical Analysis in Psychology and Education. 5th edition. McGraw-Hill, London.

Kirk, R.E. (1968). Experimental Design: Procedures for the Behavioural Sciences. Brooks/Cole, Belmont, California.

Robson, C. (1973). Experimental Design and Statistics in Psychology. Penguin, Harmondsworth, Middx.

Shneiderman, B. (1980). Software Psychology. Winthrop Publishers Inc., Cambridge, Mass.

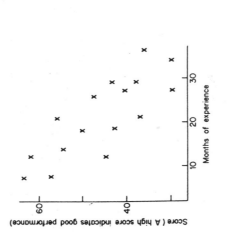

FIG. 6.1 Scattergram of experience on old system against ability to use the new one.

(ii) Drawing strong conclusions from small numbers of subjects - Correlation coefficients are notoriously unreliable when the number of subjects is small. Be wary of accepting any thing more than the direction of the correlation unless you have at least 40 subjects.

(iii) Confusing significance with strength - The significance of a correlation depends on the number of subjects as well as its strength. With large numbers of subjects quite small correlations are significant. This only means that the direction of the correlation is reliable. The strength of the correlation is given by r. For most purposes, anything over .6 is a strong correlation.

Case Study B

The Psychology of Computer Programming

Our second case study deals with the application of human factors to enhance the process of computer programming itself, rather than to improve the interface for those using the computer to write, make music, design circuits, or carry out some other task. We have seen in Chapter 1: A Historical and Intellectual Perspective, how the pioneering studies of Sackman (1970) and the classic book by Weinberg (1971) served to raise the consciousness of the computer community so that they began to believe their own productivity and satisfaction could be enhanced by the appropriate application of behavioural science. Since then, several thousand papers have explored aspects of this ongoing research effort.

Three early reviews of this voluminous literature are Atwood, Ramsey, Hooper, and Kullas (1979), Shneiderman (1980), and Curtis (1981). Recent reviews are provided by Curtis (1986a), Curtis et. al. (1986), Basili, Selby and Hutchens (1986), and Shneiderman (1986). A workshop dedicated to the subject was recently conducted by Soloway and Iyengar (1986). A follow-on workshop is planned for December, 1987.

It is possible to approach the subject from a number of points of view. Both Curtis (1986a) and Shneiderman (1986) talk about enhancing human performance in the various phases of the programming process, the *software life cycle*, which typically is described in terms of such stages as requirements definition, design, coding, debugging and verification, and maintenance. Shneiderman (1986) focuses on critical areas in which programmers can be made more productive, for example, improving programming languages, and developing more powerful programming tools and methods. What makes this particularly difficult is the great diversity of programming situations, program size and complexity, and programmer skill levels. Another point of view articulated by Shneiderman (1986) is in terms of the methodology with which one can study the programming process, approaches that we have already enumerated in the preceding chapter.

The most interesting recent work is that which is *theory-based*, incorporating a cognitive model of the programming process. Of particular consequence is the excellent work of Ruven Brooks (1977, 1983), of John R. Anderson and students (Anderson, Farrell, amd Sauers, 1984; Anderson and Jeffries, 1985; Anderson and Skwarecki, 1986), and of Elliot Soloway and students (Soloway and Ehrlich, 1984; Soloway, 1986). Their work is well represented in Curtis (1986a) and Soloway and Iyengar (1986).

The interested student should begin study with the two books previously mentioned and with Curtis et. al. (1986), included as a reading. The paper reviews past work in the psychology of programming, and then sketches a research agenda for future work in software psychology. But one must approach the literature with a critical mind, for much of the empirical work is laden with problems — problems of technique, problems of methodology, and problems in concept. Two articles which examine these difficulties are Brooks (1980), and Sheil (1981), the latter included as a reading.

Brooks (1980) looks at the task of studying programmer behaviour experimentally and notes that the work will ultimately be judged according to the same standards of methodological rigor that are applied to the behavioural sciences. He then focuses on three topics of methodological concern: the selection of subjects, the development of experimental materials, and the choice of empirical measures of performance.

- He emphasizes the problems caused by the huge individual differences in programming skills, problems which cannot simply be solved by using students in programming classes, who themselves vary greatly in ability and are not representative of professional programmers, and which cannot be solved by stratifying subjects according to ability, since it is difficult to define and apply an appropriate measure. He then recommends use of a "within subjects" design as the best way of dealing with subject variability.

- Secondly he discusses the tendency to do experiments using beginning programmers working on tiny artificial programs (see also Curtis, 1986b), and notes the difficulty of preparing stimulus materials (programs) that are matched across all respects except those being studied experimentally, a difficulty that is particularly serious for within subject designs which require a great deal of stimulus material.

- Finally, he discusses the pro's and con's of a variety of program construction, debugging, modification, memorization-recall, reconstruction, question answering, and hand execution measures, and asserts the need for an underlying theory to guide the choice of experimental measures.

Sheil (1981) is even more critical of much of the past work on the psychology of programming. He discusses the problems of designing an experiment so that it generalizes to an interesting class of real-world situations, the interference caused by practice effects, the problem of high individual variability, the questionable choice of significance level used in some of the studies, the problem of effects that are *significant* but not of great enough size to be *relevant*, and the lack of a theoretical orientation behind much of the work.

In reading the literature of the psychology of programming, one should look for implications pertaining to the broader study of human-computer interaction. One should also keep in mind that the literature reports on and describes programming as it has been carried out in the past. Yet the processes of programming are now changing dramatically. One source of insight into these changes is a set of videos on novel programming environments, for example, Xerox (1983; 1985), Lieberman (1985), and Tektronix (1985).

Readings

Curtis, Bill, Soloway, Elliot M., Brooks, Ruven E., Black, John B., Ehrlich, Kate & Ramsey, H. Rudy (1986). Software Psychology: The Need for an Interdisciplinary Program. *Proceedings of the IEEE* 74(8), 1092-1106.

Sheil, B.A. (1981). The Psychological Study of Programming. *ACM Computing Surveys* 13(1), 101-120.

References

Anderson, J.R., Farrell, R., & Sauers, R. (1984). Learning to Program in LISP. *Cognitive Science* 8(2), April-June 1984, 87-129.

Anderson, J.R. & Jeffries, R. (1985). Novice LISP Errors: Undetected Loss of Information from Working Memory. *Human-Computer Interaction* 1(2), 107-131.

Anderson, John R. & Skwarecki, Edward (1986). The Automated Tutoring of Introductory Computer Programming. *Communications of the ACM* 29(9), September 1986, 842-849.

Atwood, Michael E., Ramsey, H. Rudy, Hooper, Jean N., & Kullas, Daniel A. (1979). Annotated Bibliography on Human Factors in Software Development, *ARI Technical Report* P-79-1, Englewood Cliffs, Colorado: Science Applications, Inc.

Basili, V.R., Selby, R.W. & Hutchens, D.H. (1986). Experimentation in Software Engineering. *IEEE Transactions on Software Engineering* SE-12(7), July 1986, 733-743.

Brooks, Ruven (1977). Towards a Theory of the Cognitive Processes in Computer Programming. *International Journal of Man-Machine Studies* 9, 737-751.

Brooks, Ruven E. (1980). Studying Programmer Behavior Experimentally: The Problems of Proper Methodology. *Communications of the ACM* 23(4), 207-213.

Brooks, Ruven (1983). Towards a Theory of the Comprehension of Computer Programs. *International Journal of Man-Machine Studies* 18, 543-554.

Curtis, Bill (Ed.) (1981). *Tutorial: Human Factors in Software Development*, First Edition, Washington, D.C.: IEEE Computer Society.

Curtis, Bill (Ed.) (1986a). *Tutorial: Human Factors in Software Development*, Second Edition, Washington, D.C.: IEEE Computer Society.

Curtis, Bill (1986b). By the Way, Did Anyone Study Any Real Programmers? Appears in Soloway and Iyengar, 256-262.

Curtis, Bill, Soloway, Elliot M., Brooks, Ruven E., Black, John B., Ehrlich, Kate & Ramsey, H. Rudy (1986). Software Psychology: The Need for an Interdisciplinary Program. *Proceedings of the IEEE* 74(8), 1092-1106.

Lieberman, H. (1985). ZStep: A Stepper for Lisp Based on Visual Inspection. *SIGGRAPH Video Review* 19, New York: ACM.

Sackman, Harold (1970). *Man-Computer Problem Solving: Experimental Evaluation of Time-Sharing and Batch Processing*, Princeton: Auerbach Publishers.

Sheil, B.A. (1981). The Psychological Study of Programming. *ACM Computing Surveys* 13(1), 101-120.

Shneiderman, Ben (1980). *Software Psychology: Human Factors in Computer and Information Systems*, Cambridge, Mass.: Winthrop Publishers.

Shneiderman, Ben (1986). Empirical Studies of Programmers: The Territory, Paths, and Destinations. Appears in Soloway and Iyengar, 1-12.

Soloway, Elliot (1986). Learning to Program = Learning to Construct Mechanisms and Explanations. *Communications of the ACM* 29(9), September 1986, 850-858.

Soloway, Elliot & Ehrlich, Kate (1984). Empirical Studies of Programming Knowledge. *IEEE Transactions on Software Engineering* SE-10(5), September 1984, 595-609.

Soloway, Elliot & Iyengar, Sitharama (Eds.) (1986). *Empirical Studies of Programmers*, Norwood, N.J.: Ablex Publishing Corp.

Tektronix Inc. (1985). Magpie. *SIGGRAPH Video Review* 19, New York: ACM.

Weinburg, Gerald (1971). *The Psychology of Computer Programming*, New York: Van Nostrand Reinhold.

Xerox Corp. (1983). Smalltalk. *SIGGRAPH Video Review* 8, New York: ACM.

Xerox Corp. (1985). Cedar Programming Environment. *SIGGRAPH Video Review* 19, New York: ACM.

Software Psychology: The Need for an Interdisciplinary Program

BILL CURTIS, SENIOR MEMBER, IEEE, ELLIOT M. SOLOWAY, RUVEN E. BROOKS, JOHN B. BLACK, KATE EHRLICH, AND H. RUDY RAMSEY

Invited Paper

Research issues concerning human interaction with computers have become crucial because of dramatic increases in the number of computer users who have no formal mathematical, engineering, or computer science training. This review focuses on the state of the art in Software Psychology—the study of human factors in computer systems. One area of software psychology, the psychology of programming, is picked for an in-depth discussion of research results. This area was selected for its interest to the readers of the PROCEEDINGS OF THE IEEE. The review then discusses the methodological issues involved in performing experimental research in software psychology. Future trends are discussed both for the programming research reviewed here and for the whole field of software psychology. The conclusions identify multidisciplinary training and research as critical to further progress in this field.

I. SOFTWARE PSYCHOLOGY: DEFINITION AND SCOPE

"The increasing power of computer hardware has extended the complexity of applications of computers, while the decreasing cost of technology has made the computer available to a much wider variety of users. These trends have brought some unanticipated problems, focusing attention on human factors in the process of system development as well as in the performance of the end user of computer systems. The life cycle cost of major systems has shifted

Manuscript received March 22, 1985; revised February 13, 1986. This paper is drawn from work originally performed for the National Science Foundation under Requisition 82-SP-1011 (Ruven Brooks, Principal Investigator). The opinions expressed in this paper are not necessarily those of the National Science Foundation.
B. Curtis is with the Microelectronics and Computer Technology Corporation (MCC), Austin, TX 78759-6509, USA.
E. M. Soloway is with the Department of Computer Science, Yale University, New Haven, CT 06520, USA.
R. E. Brooks is with Schlumberger-Doll Research Inc., Ridgefield, CT 06877, USA.
J. B. Black is with Teachers College, Columbia University, New York, NY 10027, USA.
K. Ehrlich was with Honeywell Information Systems, Billerica, MA 01821. She is now with Symbolics Inc., Cambridge, MA 02142, USA.
H. R. Ramsey is at 8 Grand Place, Newton, CT 06470, USA.

away from hardware to the personnel associated with system development, maintenance and use.

The importance of research on human factors in computer systems is clear: whether the user of a computer is a programmer or analyst, military command and control expert, sales clerk, applications user, or office worker, we must develop mechanisms for harnessing the power of our computer systems to extend and complement the user's capabilities" [97, p. iii].

This statement opened the first Conference on Human Factors in Computer Systems held in Gaithersburg, MD, in March of 1982. While the conference proceedings from which this quotation was taken are very recent, interest in the scientific study of human interaction with computer systems dates back almost two decades. The term, "software psychology," was coined by Tom Love to describe those aspects of human–computer interaction that are particularly concerned with the way humans interact with software structures and systems and with the effect different structures and systems have on human behavior [117]. Examples of the topics studied within this area include how users':

- performance in writing or debugging programs is affected by programming language constructs,
- conceptual models of the structure of a database affect their formulation of queries to it,
- previous experiences with text editing systems affect learning a new one,
- intellectual traits affect their performance with different user interfaces.

Software psychology differs from related areas of software engineering, such as programming language design or user interface management systems, in that it stresses the scientific study, modeling, and measurement of human behavior in creating or using software systems [116]. Software psychologists try to avoid the commercial or project deadline pressure to provide informal, nonempirical judgements of "what people will like" or what is "easier to use." Rather, they employ rigorous methods of behavioral research to provide an experimental foundation for their opinions [47].

In contrast to other areas of psychology, software psychology emphasizes developing models and theories of behavior that specifically describe human interaction with software, regardless of their usefulness in describing other kinds of behavior [95]. It also differs from traditional human factors or ergonomics, in that it is not concerned with the physical design of equipment such as keyboard layouts, or about the arrangement of the physical environment in which equipment is used. The emphasis in software psychology is on cognitive factors in software development and use.

In this paper, we will begin by reviewing some selected results in one area of software psychology, the psychology of programming, and will then analyze the methodologies used to obtain these results. We will argue for what we believe to be the most profitable directions for future research in software psychology. Finally, we will argue the need for interdisciplinary collaboration for progress in this research.

II. SOFTWARE PSYCHOLOGY: THE STATE OF THE ART

Software psychology is now more than 15 years old. Its beginnings can be seen in books like *Man–Computer Problem Solving* by Harold Sackman in 1970 [103], *The Psychology of Computer Programming* by Gerald Weinberg in 1971 [138], and *Design of Man–Computer Dialogues* by James Martin in 1973 [87]. Several thousand articles in the field have already appeared; their range can best by grasped by reading the edited books that have recently appeared (e.g., [10], [28], [44], [51], [71], [75], [105], [110], [120], [125], [133]), the textbooks (e.g., [11], [36], [98], [117]), or conference proceedings. There are three journals dedicated to this area: *Human–Computer Interaction*, *The International Journal of Man–Machine Studies*, and *Behavior and Information Technology*. In addition, journals such as IEEE TRANSACTIONS ON SOFTWARE ENGINEERING, IEEE COMPUTER GRAPHICS AND APPLICATIONS, IEEE COMPUTER, *Communications of the ACM*, *ACM Transactions on Office Information Systems*, and *ACM Computing Surveys* often publish relevant research papers.

Originally, researchers who took a cognitive approach to the use of computers stressed the psychological properties of software development tools such as programming languages over the study of the products developed with those tools (e.g., the user interface). The basis for this emphasis has been three-fold. First, the substantial costs of producing software and the problems of making it reliable were recognized in the early 1970s and motivated research on the behavioral aspects of software development, particularly in the evaluation of programming language features. If behavioral methods could lead to significant improvement in software production, there would be strong justification for work in the field.

Second, since a large proportion of software is embedded in products at a level not directly seen by users, the behavioral issues in software creation were seen as more general than those in software use. For example, the software that controls the automatic pilot in commercial jetliners performs many operations that, although once done manually, can now be accomplished without pilot intervention.

Third, a distinction was made between the populations of those who were programmers and those who were users. Since the behavior of the former was seen to be more complex that that of the latter, it was more attractive for study. (Later, we shall argue that the programmer–user distinction is no longer valid.)

In order to give the flavor of work in the field, the following sections will review the current state of the art of selected topics in software psychology. As the previous discussion indicates, the emphasis will be on research in software development. These topics were selected because of their impact on the performance of programmers in developing and using computer systems. They include:

- individual differences in programming
- problem solving in unstructured domains
- the design of programming languages
- knowledge representation in programmers
- how program comprehension relates to text comprehension
- the terminology used for commands.

A. *Individual Differences in Programming*

One of the primary problems in psychological studies of programming has been the large individual difference variation among participants. Sackman, Erickson, and Grant [114] produced data displaying a 28:1 range in performance. However, their data were confounded by the use of different programming languages. Curtis [48] reported debugging data collected with his colleagues at GE which displayed 23:1 differences without confounding factors. Boehm [25] reported that differences in team and personnel capability were the most significant factor affecting programming productivity in his multi-year cost-modeling study. McGarry [89] found a similar effect in the data from the NASA Software Engineering Laboratory.

Individual differences among programmers have been related to a number of factors. Sheppard, Curtis, Milliman, and Love [113] found that the breadth of relevant experience was a better predictor of performance than was the length of experience. This occurs because broader experience produces a broader knowledge base. Moher and Schneider [94], however, found years of experience to be a better predictor of performance than a variety of measures of academic achievement and ability. The magnitude of these correlations is typically in the 0.3 to 0.4 range, a modest level of prediction at best.

Better prediction of programmer performance has been achieved with tests of cognitive skills related to programming. The Computer Programmer Aptitude Battery (Science Research Associates) consists of vocabulary, arithmetic word problems, letter series, results estimation, and decision structure problems. The tests which have proven to be the most consistently predictive are the arithmetic word problems and the decision structure problems. The predictive validities are typically in the 0.4 to 0.5 range. The Berger Aptitude for Programming Test (Psychometrics, Inc.) requires participants to learn a small language of less than 15 commands and then use it to solve problems of increasing complexity. Predictive validities as high as 0.7 have been obtained by its developers for this test with both training and job performance.

The available correlates of programming skill provide benefit not only to the employer, but also to researchers who need a way to reduce the impact of individual difference variation in their results. Carefully developed correlates of aptitude and/or experience can be used as covariates in experimental studies to remove some of the individual differences variation from the error variance. Further research on good correlates should provide a more complete picture of which cognitive skills are crucial to different programming tasks.

B. Problem Solving in Unstructured Domains

Most problem solving research has been performed on well-defined problems with finite solution states. In problems such as the Towers of Hanoi, there is an optimal path to the solution. The path to a successful solution in chess is not so clearly defined. Nevertheless, in chess there are a finite number of moves which can be chosen at any time and a well-defined solution state. In a semantically rich domain such as programming, neither are the options from which one can choose limited nor is there a clearly defined solution state. Therefore, problem solving in programming is a qualitatively different task than most of those used in problem solving research.

A series of studies by Carroll and his associates at IBM's Watson Research Center identified several factors that affected the design process. Carroll, Thomas, and Malhotra [41] argued that solving unstructured problems could not be explained with existing theory. They began their investigations of the design process by studying how analysts and clients interact in establishing the requirements for a system. Carroll, Thomas, and Malhotra [40] observed that client/analyst requirements sessions are broken into cycles which represent the decomposition of the problem. However, these cycles do not decompose the problem in a top-down fashion as recommended by structured programming practices. Rather, these cycles represent a linear or sequential decomposition of the problem in which the subproblem to be attacked in the next cycle is cued by the results of the last cycle.

The only a priori structure placed on the content of these client/analyst cycles is determined by the initial goal structure of the client. The problem in moving from the idea for a system to its final implementation is in transforming a linearly derived sequence of desired components into a hierarchical arrangement of functions or data transformations. Once the requirements have been delineated, they must be organized so that the inherent structure of the problem becomes visible. The next step is to construct a solution structure which matches the problem structure. To the extent that these structures are logically organized and matched, the system will possess a structural integrity which will expedite its implementation.

In a subsequent study, Carroll et al. [41] demonstrated differences in problem analysis based on differences in the application attempted. Problem solving research has consistently shown that people do not transfer solution structures across problem isomorphs. Isomorphs are problems with the same structural characteristics, but whose cover stories (or subject areas) differ. The structure of the cover story affects the difficulty people experience in reaching a solution.

Carroll et al. [41] observed that people had more difficulty solving a problem that involved temporal relations (designing a manufacturing process) than an isomorph which involved spatial relations (arranging an office layout). The difference arose in part because the spatial problem lends itself to graphical representation. However, the temporal isomorph does not present spatial cues and participants had difficulty representing it to themselves. Many retreated to a verbal description of the problem. When a graphical aid was provided for solving this temporal problem, it appeared to make the problem easier to understand, but not easier to solve.

The structuring of the requirements also seems to have an impact on the characteristics of the problem solution. Presenting the requirements in clusters based on their inherent structure assisted participants in designing solutions which better reflected the problem structure and were more stable when new requirements were added [42]. Greater structure in the original problem statement seems to reduce the amount of iteration through design cycles. Thus a critically important focus of the structured programming movement should be on methods of structuring the statement of requirements. Far less attention has been paid to this problem than to areas, such as coding, that have less impact on system integrity and costs.

C. The Use of Programming Languages

One way of characterizing languages for interacting with computers is the extent to which they force one to write in machine level procedures versus natural language. This continuum runs all the way from machine languages and assemblers through high-level programming languages on to query languages and finally to natural language. As one progresses up this continuum the structures in the language hide more and more of the details of integrating the software with the hardware. Languages at the upper end of this scale make computers accessible to more people, because users are not forced to understand the intricacies of the hardware in order to interact with the machine. However, many higher level languages usually make working at the machine level, as in real-time microprocessor-based programming, extremely difficult or impossible. Some languages, such as C, have been designed to be a hybrid that integrate the advantages of high-level programming languages with the ability to get at the machine.

An early program of research on languages was initiated by Lance Miller and his associates at IBM's Watson Research Center. Miller studied the use of natural language commands by people who were not familiar with a computer language. Miller [91] found that "or" problems were more difficult to handle than "and" problems, and that negation increased the difficulty of writing a solution to the problem. In a second study, Miller [92] investigated how nonprogrammers expressed procedural specifications in English. He observed that people used a characteristic personal approach to solving different problems, even when the structure of the problem was inappropriate for the approach. People also had difficulty being explicit about procedures and assumed that abstract references to an object were clear from the context of their paragraph.

One of Miller's most important observations in this study was that people used a limited vocabulary in developing their specifications. Only 610 unique words were used in the 84 protocols he collected. The size of this vocabulary could be reduced even further when redundancies and synonyms were removed or replaced. He believed that a vocabulary of 100 words would have been sufficient to express the specifications developed in his study. This finding was similar to the determination by Kelly and Chapanis [80] that a vocabulary of 300 words was sufficient for a computer-aided problem solving task.

Miller [92] observed that people spent much more time describing data manipulations than control flow. This is an important point since programming languages provide for the development of massive control structures in which data manipulations are embedded. Yet, the natural human tendency seems to start with data manipulations and add control flow as a qualification to the action. Miller concluded that natural language was not adequate for procedural specifications, but that a limited and structured subset of natural language might be more effective.

Interest in the design of specific language control structures began when Dijkstra assailed the GO TO statement in 1968 [58]. He argued that having the control paths created by the structure of the program's logic wander throughout the program, as it often did with the GO TO branching structure, made programs difficult to develop correctly and even more difficult to understand. This argument is psycholinguistic in that it assumes an interaction between human problem solving and language structure.

Over the next few years the structured programming movement emerged, calling for greater discipline in developing program logic by limiting the conditional structures allowed in the program.

Early studies on structured control constructs were conducted by Weissman [139] and Lucas and Kaplan [86]. The first program of research on language structures was initiated by Max Sime, Thomas Green, and their associates at the University of Sheffield [70], [72], [121], [122]. Through research publications that have spanned a decade, the Sheffield group has demonstrated:

- the superiority of IF THEN ELSE (a structured conditional) over the GO TO branching structure,
- possible advantages of using scope markers to delineate the boundaries of the code governed by a conditional expression,
- how the benefits of a programming technique may vary with the nature of the programming task,
- a standard (perhaps automated) procedure for generating the syntax of a conditional statement can improve coding speed and accuracy.

Subsequent research by Sheppard, Curtis, Milliman, and Love [113] at GE suggested that it was the discipline of a top-down flow of control that was important, rather than the specific conditionals employed. They found that Dijkstra's rigid prescriptions for structured code could be violated in ways that made the control flow more natural for the language being used (i.e., Fortran), without damaging the comprehensibility of the program. The empirical evidence favoring structured control flow has been consistent, although discussion still continues on the most appropriate forms for control constructs. In fact, Gannon [66] found that although changes in language structures could eliminate specific problems related to these structures, an overall decrease in errors may not necessarily result.

Finally, Soloway, Bonar, and Ehrlich [126] found, in an empirical study with novice, intermediate, and advanced student programmers, that a loop construct which permits a jump from the middle of the loop (e.g., Ada's LOOP ... EXIT construct) facilitates increased performance (correctness of a written program) when compared with the performance of those using a construct that does not permit such an exit (e.g., Pascal's WHILE loop). In fact, the latter two groups of programmers improved by 25 percent. Soloway et al. argued that the basis for the performance difference was cognitive. When the problem requires the reading and processing of successive data values until some sentinel value is encountered, then the natural cognitive strategy is to read an element, test for the stopping condition (and exit if necessary), and then process the element. This strategy is facilitated by a loop construct that permits a mid-loop exit. In contrast, Pascal's WHILE loop requires the actions in the loop to be out of synchronization; on the ith pass through the loop, the ith element is processed, and the ith + 1 element is read. These results are consistent with those of Sheppard et al. [113].

Gannon has moved beyond control structures and investigated how data affect programming. In studying a statically typed versus a typeless language, Gannon [67] found little evidence that the compile-time checking of data types in the statically typed language aided the performance of experienced programmers. Rather, the value of the statically typed language stemmed from the increased power it provided by supporting a broader range of data types. These additional data types freed a programmer from worrying about machine level representations of data. This finding was similar to Miller's observation that people would rather think of manipulating large data structures en masse.

In a further investigation of data referencing, Dunsmore and Gannon [59] found that programs in which the programmer had kept only a moderate number of variables "live" at any given point in the program were easier to produce. A variable was "live" from its first to its last reference in a procedure. A moderate level of variable referencing was found to be between 0.57 and 2.06 variables per statement.

Two primary themes have emerged in research on language structures. First, structuring the control flow assists programmers in understanding a program. Rather than geographically dispersing the statements governed by a control construct, structured control flow organizes these control episodes into groups. This organization allows these segments of code to be fused more easily into a recognizable chunk [53], [123].

Structured control flow also allows programmers to direct more of their cognitive resources to the semantic content of the program. They are able to do this because structuring allows them to develop expectations about the control flow, rather than having to actively track its direction.

Cognitive resources are freed when expectations about flow are cued by the language structure, rather than existing as a phenomenon separate from the design of the language.

The second theme emerging from this research is the importance of the data structure. Gannon found that the advantage of strongly typed languages was in the enhanced data structures they supported. Miller argued that people tend to think in terms of data manipulations rather than control structures. The area of data structures has only been lightly considered in behavioral research. In one of the few such studies, Durding, Becker, and Gould [60] demonstrated that people are quite capable of organizing data into structures which maintain the relations inherent among the elements. These results suggest that data structuring capability and data structure documentation may be strong determinants of programming performance.

D. Knowledge Representation in Programmers

Experienced programmers view programs in mental chunks [53], [123] that are much larger than the single statement or line. The lines of code in the program listing:

```
SUM := 0;
COUNT := 0;
READ (N);
WHILE N < )999 DO;
  BEGIN
  SUM := SUM + N;
  COUNT := COUNT + 1;
  READ (N);
  END;
```

would be fused by an experienced Pascal programmer into the chunk "calculate the sum of an array." The programmer can now think about working with an array sum, a single entity, rather than the various unique instructions in the program above. When it is necessary to deal with the procedural implementation, the programmer can call these four statements from long-term memory as underlying the chunk "calculate an array sum."

Much of a programmer's maturation involves observing more patterns and building larger chunks. Soloway and Ehrlich [127] argue that programming knowledge consists both of plans for accomplishing specific computations and of the rules of discourse enforced in a particular programming language. These are the elements from which the "chunks" of programming knowledge are constructed. The scope of the concepts that programmers have been able to build into chunks provides one indication of their programming ability. The particular elements chunked together have important implications for educating programmers. Educational materials and exercises should be presented in ways that maximize the likelihood of building useful chunks.

Long-term memory is usually treated as having limitless capacity for storing information [24]. This information is interrelated and indexed such that:

1) items in short-term memory can quickly cue the recall of appropriate chunks of information from long-term memory;

2) items in short-term memory can be linked into and transferred quickly to long-term memory for retention;

3) information retrieved from long-term memory can cue the retrieval of additional chunks of information when appropriate.

The effects of both experience and education are most prominent in the knowledge base they construct in long-term memory. The construction of this base involves more than accumulating facts, it involves organizing them into a rich network of semantic material.

Shneiderman and Mayer [119] have characterized the structure of knowledge in long-term memory in a syntactic/semantic model. In their model, syntactic and semantic types of knowledge are organized separately in memory. Semantic knowledge concerns general programming concepts or relationships in the applications domain which are independent of the programming language in which they will be executed. Syntactic knowledge involves the procedural idiosyncrasies of a given programming language.

An important implication of the Shneiderman and Mayer model is that the development of skill in writing programs requires the integration of knowledge from several different knowledge domains. For instance, the programming of an on-board aircraft guidance system may require knowledge of:

- aeronautical engineering,
- radar and sensors technology,
- mathematical algorithms,
- the design of on-board microprocessors,
- the development machine and support tools,
- a high-level programming language,
- an assembly language.

Each of these is a separate field of knowledge, some of which require years of training and experience to master. Thus programming skill is specific to the application being considered. One can be a talented avionics programmer, and still be a novice at programming concurrent multi-user business databases.

Several efforts have been made to model the structure of programming knowledge at a level deeper than that of Shneiderman and Mayer. Brooks [31] used Newell and Simon's [96] production system approach to model the rules a programmer would use in writing the code for a program. These rules are of the type, "If the following conditions are satisfied, then produce the following action." Based on analysis of a verbal protocol, Brooks identified 73 rules which were needed to model the coding process of a single, and relatively simple, problem solution. Brooks estimated that the number of production rules needed to model the performance of an expert programmer was in the tens to hundreds of thousands.

Atwood and Ramsey [8] modeled a programmer's understanding of a program using Kintsch's (1974) model of text comprehension. Their approach treats a program as a text base composed of propositions. A microproposition is a simple statement composed of a relational operator and one or more arguments (operands). Comprehension occurs when elementary, or micropropositions, are fused into macropropositions which summarize their meaning or content. This process is similar to chunking. The result of this process is a hierarchy of macropropositions built from the micropropositions at the bottom of the tree.

Atwood, Turner, Ramsey, and Hooper [9] demonstrated

that a program design could be broken into a hierarchical structure of propositions. They observed that after studying a design, experienced programmers were able to recall propositions at a greater depth in the hierarchy than novices. The experienced programmers had more elaborate structures in long-term memory for use in encoding such designs. Thus they were able to retain propositions at greater depth because

1) the higher level macropropositions in the design did not represent new information, and thus could be referenced by existing knowledge structures,

2) the propositions representing new information could be linked into the existing knowledge structures and shifted into long-term memory.

This propositional hierarchy is only one of the proposed representations of how knowledge is structured in long-term memory.

The study of expert–novice differences in programming has generated information on how the programming knowledge base is developed. Both Adelson [2] and Weiser and Shertz [140] demonstrated that novices comprehend a program based on its surface structure, that is, the particular applications area of the program such as banking or avionics. Experts, however, analyze a program based on its deep structure, the solution or algorithmic structure of the program. Similarly, McKeithan, Reitman, Rueter, and Hirtle [90] observed that experts are able to remember language commands based on their position in the structure of the language. Novices often use mnemonic tricks to remember command names.

On the basis of the above work in showing that expert programmers do have and use deep structure knowledge, Soloway and his colleagues at Yale have taken the next step and attempted to codify programming knowledge and test whether programmers actually have these specific types of knowledge structures. Their research is similar to that by Barstow [15] and Rich [101] who are trying to identify the elementary structures from which programs are synthesized in order to support the technology of automatic programming. In their empirical studies, Soloway and his colleagues at Yale [3], [126], [127], [129] showed that programmers have and use programming plans (i.e., generic stereotypic action sequences found in programming) and rules of programming discourse (i.e., tacit rules shared by programmers which allow one programmer to write code that another programmer can read and understand).

Further, Soloway and his colleagues are also attempting to build a process model that explains why novices generate program bugs. Building on the *repair theory* model of bug generation developed by Brown and VanLehn [33], Bonar and Soloway [27] suggest that when novices hit a gap in their understanding of programming, they attempt to bridge it by drawing on related knowledge of how they would specify the solution in nonprogramming terms. Unfortunately, use of this alternate knowledge base invariably leads the novice to create a bug.

For instance, novices have been observed substituting the English language meaning of *while* for the Pascal WHILE statement. In Pascal, the WHILE construct carries out the stopping test once, each time through the loop. In contrast, however, the English language connotation of *while* conveys a sense of continuous testing. Thus novices who bridge their understanding of the Pascal WHILE construct by drawing on related knowledge of English vocabulary, suspect that the computer is constantly monitoring the test condition and will immediately exit the loop once the test condition is met. Although this type of demon control structure is possible, it is not the structure instantiated in Pascal. Their *plan* for using the WHILE loop must be altered before they can create a correct program using it.

Sporher, Soloway, and Pope [131] have observed specific bug-prone patterns. For instance, when novices attempt to merge two programming plans that have a similar goal structure into one piece of code, they often leave off the final goal for one of the plans. Sporher *et al.* conjecture that working memory limitations may be at least partially responsible for this type of bug. Anderson and Jeffries [6] have provided empirical evidence that bugs may arise due to overloading of a novice's working memory.

Recently, a number of researchers have carried out protocol studies with software designers of varying levels of expertise [3], [76], [79]. Broadly speaking, their goal was to identify the key skills that differentiated an expert from a novice. They observed, for example, that experts continually executed their designs either on specific examples or using more symbolic data. These simulations apparently were used to detect unwanted interactions, inconsistencies, weaknesses, and incompleteness in their designs. Moreover, it appeared that designers carried out these simulations at all levels in the design process. For example, they would simulate even an abstract, sketchy design. Such studies begin to point out how designers actually go about the task of design. They also suggest problem areas where tools might be built to facilitate design.

Results of the expert–novice differences research in programming agree with the results of similar research on other subject areas, such as thermodynamics [20], physics [85], and chess [43] conducted by Herbert Simon and his associates at Carnegie-Mellon. This research indicates that developing technical skill is not merely a matter of learning a long list of facts. Rather, developing technical skill in an effort to learn the underlying structure of the knowledge domain. McKeithan *et al.* [90] found that the programming knowledge structures developed by experts were much more similar to each other than they were those of intermediates or novices. Thus programmers tend to gravitate toward a similar understanding of the language structure with experience. The development of this structure enhances the ability of experienced programmers to assimilate new information.

E. Connections Between Programming and Text Research

A program is actually a form of text. In particular, it is a conceptually connected group of statements that can be understood and executed by a computer, while also being understood by other programmers who might want to modify it. Thus we would expect parallels between research on program comprehension and on natural language text understanding. Both because text has been around longer and is easier to investigate, text research is more fully developed than programming research [30], [55] [134]. Thus text research gives clues about factors, research methods, and theoretical frameworks that ought to be considered for programming.

Text research has gone through three phases of development. Programming research has gone through the first two of these and is now on the threshold of the third. The first phase focused on quality metrics that use formulas involving surface characteristics of texts or programs. In text research these are the readability formulas (e.g., [61]) and in programming they are software metrics [26], [46], [62], [74]. A typical readability formula involves a weighted combination of the number of syllables and number of words per sentence. Similarly, Halstead's [74] system of software metrics involves the number of unique operators and operands, and the total usage of operators and operands. Both readability formulas and software metrics offer statistically significant prediction of performance when averaged over a large sample of texts or programs [52], [102]. However, what they cannot do is indicate why a given text or program is easy to understand, or indicate how to turn one that is hard into one that is easy [26], [128]. Readability formulas have been used to guide revision of children's reading texts for years. Yet, recent research indicates that this guidance has been harmful rather than helpful [54]. A similar expose on software metrics may occur in the future.

Following the quality metric phase is the propositional network phase as represented by Kintsch [83] for text and Atwood and Ramsey [8] for programs. Here the text or program is divided into propositions (i.e., a predicate (or operator) plus its arguments (or operands)) and the propositions connected if they contain common arguments (operands). A hierarchy is formed from this network by placing the proposition that first mentions an argument in a superordinate position dominating the other propositions that contain that argument. The hierarchical level of a proposition has been shown to be correlated with the probability of recall in text and the difficulty of finding a bug in a program [8].

Text research has now entered a third phase, the knowledge-based processing phase. This new phase emerged after realizing that propositional networks could not explain why some interpropositional connections were so much stronger than others [1], [21]; why some texts were more predictable than others [93]; and the variety of inferences that readers make as part of understanding a text [109]. This research phase is characterized by a concern for the inferences made as part of understanding, the knowledge schemas used to make those inferences, and the memory indexing schemes used to organize what has been understood. The first signs of this knowledge-based phase is beginning to appear in programming research. The work of Soloway and his colleagues draws directly on the schemata-based theories of understanding developed in AI [106] and evaluated experimentally in cognitive psychology [29]. For example, Soloway and Ehrlich [127] show that when programs are unschemata-like they are difficult for programmers to comprehend. This result parallels those obtained in text understanding research [18], [29].

F.   The Terminology Used for Commands

The issue of how to choose the best terminology for commands has been investigated mostly using interactive-command languages, but it is also an important issue for programming languages. The initial research in this area started with the intuition shared by many system users that

if system designers had only chosen more common names for commands, then systems would be much easier to learn and use. However, when Black and Moran [23] asked a naive group of subjects to provide names for text editor commands, the subjects disagreed about the names to use. Even in the optimum case, only 40 percent of the subjects agreed on the name. Thus the highest probability that any two people would choose the same name for a command was only 0.16 (i.e., 0.4 squared). Similarly, Furnas, Landauer, Gomez, and Dumais [64] found agreement ranging only from 0.10 to 0.20 over four different domains. Further, when Black and Moran [23] tried out a command language using the names most frequently produced by the subjects, other subjects did not find this language easier to learn and use than a language that used infrequently produced names. Thus system designers cannot select the best command names to use for systems by blindly asking a group of people what to use.

More useful results have been obtained from research that investigated how various factors affect the learnability and usability of commands. For example, Black and Moran [23] found that the best command names are verbs that clearly discriminate among the operations performed, while being fairly infrequent in English as a whole, and specific rather than general letter patterns that were not words.

In addition to choosing the best names for the command operators, it is also important to identify how objects or operands are associated with the operators. Barnard, Hammond, Morton, Long, and Clark [14] investigated factors that affected the best order for operands and found that it is always best to put the same kind of operands in the same position (i.e., follow expectations from natural English). Further, they found that it was best to put first the operands used most frequently in the system.

Instead of examining commands in isolation, Carroll [37] investigated the effects of providing an overall framework or "command paradigm" and found that having the command names follow a consistent framework aided user learning and performance on a variety of tasks. Similarly, Mayer [88] found that providing a "mental model" helped people learn the BASIC programming language and a database query language. Thus providing users with frameworks or mental models as guides seems to be the key to making systems easier to learn and use. In fact, if a framework had been provided to the subjects in the command name production studies described earlier, they may have agreed more about the names to use (studies are needed to test this contention). The Carroll and Mayer studies are initial efforts that leave many unanswered questions, but they do promise that research on this topic will produce gains in user performance. Further research on using consistent mental models to guide system design and training should be a priority.

III.   The Methodology of Software Psychology

In the preceding section, we discussed some of the results that have been obtained in one area of software psychology. In this section, we shall discuss the methodologies used to conduct this research. Recently, a number of critical reviews of the field have appeared [24], [32], [47], [94], [111] which have focused on shortcomings in the methodology of the experimental research. The thrust of these reviews is that many of the existing results suffer from being unreplicable, poorly controlled, and open to alternative and often uninteresting explanations. While this problem may be substantially due to issues of the training and background of the researchers, there are also some serious issues stemming from research strategies and the methodologies themselves.

A. Experimental Techniques

There are, broadly speaking, two approaches that can be taken to empirical research on programming. One approach is to design tightly controlled experiments that are rigorous, systematic, and narrow in scope. Sheppard, Kruesi, and Curtis [114] employed a particularly complex, repeated measures, multifactor, experimental design to evaluate the impact of different attributes of software documentation. Their repeated measures on participants allowed them to gain control over the ravaging impact of individual differences in the data. At the same time, their use of a randomized block, multifactor design afforded them great statistical power to investigate several factors in documentation with a minimum number of experimental participants. Reducing the number of participants was important, because of the cost of using professional programmers in the experiment.

The second approach is to design exploratory experiments that are less tightly controlled, allow for collection of a wider and richer range of data, and whose interpretations may be broad in scope. Black, Galambos, and Reiser [22] have called these two approaches verification and discovery research. They argue for the necessity of employing both approaches in research on text comprehension. In software psychology it is even more important to adopt differing experimental techniques so that the full range of programming and user behavior is available for study.

The techniques that might be adopted for discovery research include videotaped interviews, verbal protocols, and naturalistic observation. For instance, Carroll and Mack [39] have made extensive use of videotaped protocols to find the range of errors that people make while learning to use a text editor. Similarly, research on cognitive factors in programming carried out by Soloway and his colleagues [27], [77], [130], [131] has sought to expose the range of errors that novice programmers make, by collecting all the programs written by an entire class of students over the course of a semester. Neither the collection nor the analysis of these data are simple. Nevertheless, it is important to obtain data which reveal both quantitative and qualitative characteristics of the errors that people make. For instance, one of the incidental pieces of information to emerge from the data collected by Soloway and his colleagues was that not only is there great variability in performance among programmers of differing levels of experience, but also even for the same programmer writing different programs. None had demonstrated how this variability might impact the actual code that was written.

If the research question concerns the variability in behavior among different subjects or over different tasks, then it may be appropriate to adopt a more discovery-oriented approach to research. In analyzing data they had collected

to test the predictive value of software metrics, Basili and Hutchens [19] instead identified characteristic relationships for individual programmers between the amount of complexity they created in a module and the number of changes that had to be made to it. That is, some programmers could create relatively stable modules of great complexity, while others lost the integrity of their modules if coding them required even moderate levels of complexity as measured by the number of logical decisions involved.

In contrast, there are times when it is important to adopt a more confirmatory approach in order to explain the source of some behavior. For instance, if the goal of a research project is to examine why people make errors in writing computer programs, it would be more appropriate to design a controlled experiment in which the variables hypothesized to effect the error rate were systematically varied. An example of this second kind of study comes from Soloway, Bonar, and Ehrlich [126]. In this study it was argued that one source of error in writing programs in Pascal comes from a mismatch between the strategy facilitated by the language and the strategy that people prefer. The study examined this hypothesis by systematically varying the language construct so that it was consistent or inconsistent with people's preferred strategy. The experiment was run with three groups of subjects. Each group represented a different level of programming experience. The experiment demonstrated that subjects at all levels of experience wrote fewer correct programs when they used the construct facilitated by Pascal rather than the construct that matched their cognitive model.

B. Experimental Design

Many of the early experiments in software psychology sought to demonstrate that one language, language feature, or system is better than another. A more profitable way to pursue research is to design experiments which explore the limitations as well as the advantages of a particular language feature. One of the ways in which research tools can be honed to produce sharper and more robust results is by designing experiments that seek to demonstrate effects that are dependent on the interaction of two critical variables rather than by designing experiments that seek to demonstrate the effect of a single variable. This difference can, perhaps, best be described with an example.

Expert programmers are assumed to have more programming knowledge than novices. Thus in a task that elicits programming knowledge, experts should perform better than novices. A result which merely demonstrated better performance by expert programmers might not be very informative, because it would not explain how superior knowledge is translated into superior performance. In order to develop a better understanding of programming knowledge, it is important to design experiments that seek to examine conditions under which this knowledge fails to contribute to performance.

A common approach that has been adopted by experimenters in the past [43], [56] is to vary the kind of problem the subject is given in addition to selecting subjects with differing levels of expertise. For instance, if subjects are asked to recall the layout of chess pieces that have been placed randomly on the board, then knowledge of chess cannot help them organize their recall. In this case, experts perform no better than novices. Similar results have been demonstrated in the domain of programming, where expert programmers performed no better than novices when asked to recall a program consisting of random lines of code [90], [115]. In both the chess studies and the programming studies, however, the experts did perform better than the novices when given legitimate games or legitimate programs to recall. In terms of the experimental design, these studies demonstrate an interaction between expertise and problem type in that experts perform better than novices only on problems that elicit the relevant knowledge. This interpretation goes beyond restating that experts know more than novices.

Soloway and Ehrlich [127] have taken this approach a step further. Based on their plan-based theory of programming knowledge, they were able to construct programs that were either plan-like (i.e., that represented typical programming solutions) or unplan-like. The unplan-like programs ran, but used atypical programming solutions to sólve the problem. These unplan-like programs served the same methodological function as the scrambled programs used in previous studies, but because they were executable programs, the results demonstrated subtle aspects of programming knowledge. Results obtained from interactions rather than from main effects are often more informative, because they show the limits of the interpretations that can be made of the factors studied.

A similar design could be adopted if the intention of the experiment was to demonstrate some of the consequences of individual differences. For instance, if a researcher wanted to demonstrate that people with high imagery skills were better able to perform certain text editing tasks, it would be more convincing to show that the high imagery group did better on tasks that had a hypothesized visual manipulation, but that they performed no better or even worse than the comparison group on another set of tasks for which there was no hypothesized visual component. An alternative approach might be to demonstrate just that the high imagery people performed better than another group of subjects. The first experiment is designed to show an interaction between characteristics of the user and characteristics of the task. The second experiment is designed to demonstrate only effects that are dependent on the characteristics of the user. The first design is more interesting and robust, because it can be used to demonstrate the limits of a particular kind of ability.

IV. THE CHANGING NATURE OF PROGRAMMING

In the previous sections, we have reviewed some of the past achievements of software psychology research and some of the problems in the methodology used to obtain these results. In this section, we discuss the future of computing technology, particularly in regard to those developments that will impact the selection of important issues for behavioral research.

For research in software psychology to have significant practical impact, it must produce results that are reliable and generalizable beyond the particular details of an experiment. The results must be representative of those that would be expected across a broad class of tasks, user populations, and systems. We have also suggested that such

results are best obtained by a cognitive approach in which a variety of experimental methodologies are employed to provide converging evidence on the phenomena or behaviors under investigation.

A. Plan-Based Programming

Over the past two decades, a major focus of software engineering research has been on how to develop new programs rapidly and accurately. A key to increasing programming productivity in the future will be the reuse of existing software components. In the past, the main approach to reusability has been the construction of libraries of fixed routines whose internal structure is never modified or seen by the programmers who use them. These modules are then used by adding additional code to call them and combine their results together. For example, a programmer doing matrix manipulation might first write the code to read in the matrix from an external device and then call a matrix inversion routine from a scientific subroutine library without any need to look at its source code.

Even though the notion of building libraries of fixed modules dates back more than 25 years, it has only been in the past six to eight years that programming language features besides object module libraries and INCLUDE libraries have been developed to specifically support reusing existing modules. Two examples of these newer tools are the object-oriented and "pipe" constructs.

Object-oriented programming [45] is the basis for the Smalltalk language [69] and also appears in the Ada "package" construct. The goal is to permit a set of functions to access common data structures without requiring them to be aware of how the data structures are implemented, or having to explicitly pass information among themselves. This permits the construction of module collections while reducing the special code needed to connect them together.

The Unix "pipe" construct [81] allows the output of one whole program to be fed directly into another program without making one program a subroutine of the other and without any kind of intervening file manipulation. Thus to provide an editing capability for data to be fed to a processing program, an existing editor can be "piped" in front of the data-reading program, so that the output of the editor becomes the input for the data-reading program. This construct facilitates the reuse of entire, existing programs without requiring that they be converted into subroutine form.

While aids to closed module and program reuse will continue to play a role in future programming, their importance will be less than that of reusing program schemas or plans. The term *plan* is used here to indicate the underlying structure of a function apart from the particular form of its expression in a programming language. The reuse of these plans can take several different forms. For domains which are well-understood, it is possible to construct program generators which use these plans as skeletons around which to assemble code customized for a particular application. Two examples of such generators are compiler compilers and report generators for database management systems. Compiler compilers take as input the syntax specification for a programming language such as Fortran and generate lexical and syntax analyzers. Although the part of the compiler that generates the instructions for a specific computer must still be hand-coded, a substantial part of the needed compiler code is automatically generated.

Report generators are systems that are used to create special-purpose programs to produce reports from databases. An example of the program that is generated is a monthly financial statement from a database of ledger entries. Such report generators can frequently produce the special-purpose programs without any direct programmer coding. However, even when the report program that they produce is not the desired one, it often can be easily modified to produce the desired output.

Both compiler compliers and report generators are already in widespread, practical use. When domains such as office automation become well understood, program generators will appear for them as well. For applications that never become widespread enough to justify program generators, the reuse of program plans will still play an important role in the form of systems to facilitate the combination and tailoring of code fragments. In this approach, a "rough draft" of a program is created by assembling pieces of existing code which are then edited by the programmer to create the program. While programmers have used this method informally for decades, tools to aid this approach have only recently emerged. Systems for doing source to source transformations [12], [13], [16] and code-fragment-based editors [136], [137] are examples of the tools that will appear in the future to aid in reusing program plans for special applications. These and other "power tools for programmers" [112] will play an increasing role in future programming activity. Thus software psychological research must shift more of its emphasis to how programmers design a system and how these designs are decomposed to the level that can be supported by reusable code tools and program generators [49]. Design activities have received far too little attention in the behaviorial research on programming.

B. New Programming Languages

Conventional, algorithmic languages such as Fortran and C will continue to play an important role in the future, because of the large amount of code already written in them. A substantial portion of the new code written in the future, however, may be written in languages with non-traditional control structures, most notably Lisp and the applicative languages. The ease with which rich programming environments can be constructed around these languages, their tractable formal properties, and the possibilities of developing hardware architectures for them using very large scale integrated circuits have extended their use far outside of their traditional applications. This will be especially true where there is a closer match between the structure of these languages and the problem to be solved. It will be important to determine how the model of computation supported by new languages can be best matched with a programmer's mental model of how to solve programming problems.

C. Programming Environments

Another factor affecting future programmer activity will be the trend toward putting more computing power in the hands of individual programmers, resulting in the creation of ever richer programming environments [15], [17]. Many of the features of these environments will be aimed toward "programming in the large" [57] and coordinating the work of programming teams. Examples include source code control and configuration management systems, project and resource management tools, and requirements tracking systems. It will become important for software psychologists to help in defining the behavioral attributes of cooperative team activity and how it can best be supported by advanced technology.

Other tools will alter the work of the individual programmer more directly. Currently, programs are written by first using a text editor to enter or modify the program in a linear string format. The syntactic analysis performed by the compiler or interpreter converts this string to an internal syntax-tree format. If the compiler has optimization capabilities, they are used to manipulate this syntax tree. The syntax tree is then used to generate code that is tested with the help of source language level debuggers and tracers.

In future systems, however, the activities of program entry, compilation, and debugging are likely to be much less distinct. Thus structure editors will permit programmers to directly enter the program in syntax tree form, largely eliminating the syntactic analysis phase of compilation. The use of source language transformations on those trees will cause more of the optimization activity to take place at the source language level and under the direct control of the programmer. The possibility of systems which infer code from "watching" the programmer perform the desired manipulations on sample data [135] open the possibility of merging even the debugging and program entry phases. Software psychologists can play an important role in helping adapt such tools to the range of programming styles displayed by different programmers.

D. The Expanding Need to Program

As mentioned earlier, it has been a convention in software psychology to distinguish between the programmers and the users of computer systems, and to discuss the tools and behavior of these two groups separately. Because of the steady growth in the availability of programmable devices of all kinds, we see this distinction disappearing. The growing diversity of computer applications, from automatic bank teller machines to microwave ovens to automobiles, will make casual users out of everyone. While individual users might become experts in using one system, there will be other systems they use only infrequently. In order to communicate their needs to the computer, all users will need to become programmers to some degree. As the second author is fond of saying, "All God's children gonna program."

The need to support both expert and novice users in the same system is already at hand. A Pascal or Fortran programmer may be expert in using the editor and language compiler, since they are used constantly. However, the same programmer may use a database query system or statistical package only infrequently. Thus the interface to these systems will need to facilitate use by both experts and casual users. Powerful new techniques such as direct manipulation [118] appear to solve interaction problems for both classes of users.

The user interface issue leads directly to our second implication: the need to learn to program and the redefinition of the term "programming." Current applications programs, such as text editors and statistical packages, initially attempted to provide a simple, nonprocedural command language for the user. However, such canned packages, with their limited functionality, quickly evolved additional features that enabled the user to write "little programs" in order to provide increased capabilities. For example, it is frustrating to use an editor that permits searches for only one occurrence of a string. Instead, the user should be allowed to compose small search procedures. Thus to convert a set of decimal numbers into percentages, the user might write a procedure to search for all occurrences of the pattern "decimal point followed by two numbers" and replace that string with "the two numbers followed by a percent sign."

Deciding whether or not composing such search procedures is "programming" and whether the person who does this is a "programmer" is difficult. Are managers who have workstations on their desk, and who write query routines to a database, "programming"? Is the using of computer-based spread sheets, programming? Clearly, this level of programming is not as complex as writing a real-time flight control system, but the user is nevertheless telling the system how to carry out a complicated calculation. Papert [99] has coined the term "semi-programmer" to refer to casual users who use computer systems in this manner.

In summary, more and more people are directly interacting with computers. Rather than moving towards "programmerless" computer use, we see the future as one in which every user is to some extent a programmer, able to customize the behavior of computer systems to suit their needs. In the next section, we shall describe the implications that this change has on directions for software psychology research.

V. THE FUTURE OF SOFTWARE PSYCHOLOGY RESEARCH

A. Goals of Research in Software Psychology

The design of effective communication between humans and computers calls for behavioral research. We believe that the goal of this research should be to develop theoretical models of human cognitive activities in the computing milieux, rather than merely obtaining results relevant to one particular design decision. These models should, however, be presented in a form that can generate design principles for particular situations and explain why they work using basic cognitive processes (cf. [63], [82], [100]). These goals demand experimental results tied to theoretical models so that they can be generalized beyond the particular situation used in the experiment. Such experiments and models should take into account both the characteristics of the user population and an analysis of the task.

However, many existing cognitive models are inadequate for our purposes. The cognitive psychology texts present numerous theoretical models that do not seem applicable to human–computer interaction, because they were developed from oversimplified laboratory tasks. Models are needed which are complex enough to deal with human–computer interaction.

An example of the kind of research we are advocating has been performed by Card, Moran, and Newell [34], [35]. They provide an analysis of a routine cognitive skill, such as text editing, by describing the sequence of keystrokes that the user executes and the mental preparations that precede the keystrokes. A model based on data they have collected is sophisticated enough to be able to predict the performance of an expert user working on a particular system. That is, if given details of the user and some parameters of the task the user is to perform, the model can predict how long it will take to perform that task.

In many ways, the research of Card et al. exemplifies many of the points we have made about experimental methodology. In particular, they have combined different experimental techniques, such as data gathering and formal modeling. They have designed their research to be sensitive to differences between users, even users at the same level of expertise. They have provided a systematic analysis of the task domain. Finally, they have been careful to design experiments in which the limitations of the results are made explicit. The strength of this research is perhaps best illustrated by its ability to make both a theoretical contribution to psychology [34], as well as provide a tool for the design of interactive systems [35].

B. Research Issues

Communication between humans and computers will proceed smoothly when the demands of the communication language, whether it be a command, programming, or visual language, match the characteristics of the user and the tasks that the user is performing [7]. That is not to say that computer systems should be slavishly designed to conform to the current skills of every user. In particular, it is a mistake to design systems primarily for the naive user. People are extremely adaptable and have great capability for learning new systems and new techniques. Indeed, one of the advantages of computers is that they encourage and support people in developing new skills. Nevertheless, there are limits to this adaptability and flexibility. If we are to provide general principles for the design of human–computer communication, we should first understand how people develop and perform various cognitive skills [4].

We need to understand how people conceptualize a task or knowledge domain (i.e., mental models; [68]), what kinds of limitations there may be on the amount and way information is encoded and retrieved (i.e., psychological factors, [24]), how skills are learned [5], and the preferred communication medium (e.g., linguistic versus visual, written versus spoken, static versus dynamic) for expressing different kinds of messages [107], [132]. Experimental results in these areas should have implications for the design of automated advisors, tutorials, or manuals [38], [65]; for the design of future programming languages, command languages, tools and environments [84]; as well as for curricula development [108]. Some of the research questions we feel are relevant to these practical goals are clustered as follows:

1) Conceptual Models and Mental Models

- What concepts do people have of the task they are to perform?
- What concepts do people have of the machine?
- What concepts do novices bring to a new domain such as programming?
- Do analogies help people to learn command languages or programming languages?

2) Psychological Factors

- How do people chunk information to make the most effective use of their limited short-term memory capacity?
- What role does prior knowledge play in the way people encode programming and command languages?
- What effect on the ease of learning a new skill such as programming or text editing do individual differences such as level of experience, age, sex, verbal skills, math skills, level of education, and perceptual skills such as imagery have?
- How do the properties of a system that facilitate learning interact with those that facilitate performance? Is there a tradeoff between the size and versatility of a language or command system and its learnability and ease of use?

3) Transfer of Skills

- What kind of skills are transferred from one knowledge domain to another? For instance, do skills in programming transfer to other domains such as mathematics?
- What kind of skills are transferred from one application area to another? Is it easier to learn text editing if one has already mastered some other computer-based task?
- What kind of skills are transferred from one application system to another? Is it easier or harder to master a new text-editing system if one has already learned another text-editing system, or is there negative transfer? Is it easier or harder to learn text editing on the computer for people who are experienced typists? What is the effect of the first programming language learned on later language learning and on programming style?

4) Medium of Communication

- How do people process information from different media? Linguistically, visually, auditorily, or by some combination of these and/or other media? What are the additional factors that need to be considered such as whether the information should be chromatic or monochromatic, animated or static, etc.
- How do people combine information from different sources? For instance, would people find it easier to learn text editing if they were given auditory instructions while doing examples, rather than by reading written instructions prior to the task?

5) Problem Solving Representation

- How does the use of procedural versus nonprocedural programming or command languages affect problem solving?
- How does programming with data structures differ from programming with control structures?
- How does the task of specifying requirements for a program or system differ from the task of actually writing the programs? How should an optimal representational system for the two kinds of tasks differ?

C. The Need for Interdisciplinary Research

In the preceding section, we argued for a future software psychology which identifies fundamental characteristics of human behavior involved in interacting with software. In this section, we shall address the profile of the research community needed to create such a science. We shall argue that substantial contributions are needed from both psychologists and computer scientists.

The needed contributions from psychologists lie in two areas: methodology and connection to other areas of psychology. The scientific study of any kind of human behavior requires formal recording and analysis of behavior, even if that observation takes place under informal conditions. If the observation is part of a formal experiment, then skills in the statistical design of experiments and the preparation of stimulus materials are also needed. These skills are not easily learned. A typical doctoral program in psychology includes numerous advanced courses in statistics and several years of apprenticeship to learn the hueristic skills of conducting psychological studies. Yet, without these skills, software psychology becomes only the advocacy of personal taste in software properties.

Furthermore, the involvement of psychologists in the methodology of software psychology must extend beyond mere consultancy on the design of particular experiments. Most psychological research methodology has evolved from controlled laboratory experimentation. For many important issues in software psychology, however, the nature of the technology involved makes controlled laboratory study economically impossible. Consider, for example, the cost in subject time of having two groups of 20 programmers each write four 10 000-line programs. Addressing some of these issues will require new observational methods, experimental designs, and statistical analysis techniques.

The second major contribution of psychologists will lie in establishing connections between software psychology and research in other areas of psychology, as exemplified in the strong relationship between understanding text and understanding programs. Again, the level of involvement by psychologists must be deep. A theory of the role of punctuation markers in programming languages, for example, is not likely to be of much value if the widespread use of structure editors eliminates the need of inserting punctuation. Tracking software technology is not just a matter of reading the trade journals and looking for product announcements. It involves understanding the concepts that underlie the technology and the directions research in them is likely to take. Such an understanding is not easily achieved with a few programming courses or some experience using systems. It must be based on a deep exposure to research issues in computer science.

The role of computer scientists in guaranteeing relevance extends beyond guidance in selecting research areas, into participation in the actual construction of studies or experiments. If the results of such work is to generalize, it is important that the materials used in such studies share specific characteristics of those used in situations outside the study. Constructing such materials can be a difficult business. In one software metrics study, 27 different versions of the same program had to be constructed [52]. Unless those designing the studies are aware of the necessary characteristics of the research materials, there is a danger that the materials used will be those that are easy to construct, not those relevant to the actual research issue.

The second basis for the participation of computer scientists in software psychology research lies in the application of the results of such research to software construction and use. If the kind of software psychology we advocate here succeeds, the results will take the form of models and principles of human behavior in interacting with software. In order to apply them, the constructors of new software tools and systems will have to understand the models, particularly their boundary conditions and limitations. Achieving such an understanding may not be easy, particularly if the models are subtle and sophisticated. If computer scientists are active participants in the research leading to those models, there is less danger that the models will be misunderstood and misused.

Collaboration between computer scientists and psychologists is more than an idealistic goal. Much of the best research described earlier was performed by interdisciplinary collaborations, such as those at General Electric Space Division, Yale University, the University of Maryland, Xerox Palo Alto Research Center, and IBM Watson Research Laboratory. Encouraging enough collaboration to achieve the results we have advocated earlier requires dedication from both disciplines. The result of such collaborations will be the much needed unification of the behavioral and mathematical aspects of computer science and software engineering practice.

ACKNOWLEDGMENT

The authors would like to thank the Microelectronics and Computer Technology Corporation (MCC) for its support of the final manuscript preparation.

REFERENCES

[1] V. Abbott and J. B. Black, "A comparison of the memory strength of alternative text relations," in 1982 Annual Meeting of the American Education Research Association. New York: Amer. Educ. Res. Assoc., 1982.
[2] B. Adelson, "Problem solving and the development of abstract categories in programming languages," Memory Cogn., vol. 9, no. 4, pp. 422–433, 1981.
[3] B. Adelson and E. Soloway, "The role of domain experience in software design," IEEE Trans. Software Eng., vol. SE-11, no. 11, pp. 1351–1360, 1985.
[4] J. R. Anderson, Ed., Cognitive Skills and Their Acquisition. Hillsdale, NJ: Erlbaum, 1981.
[5] J. R. Anderson, R. Farrell, and R. Sauers, "Learning to program in Lisp," Cogn. Sci., vol. 8, no. 2, pp. 87–129, 1984.
[6] J. R. Anderson and R. Jeffries, "Novice Lisp errors: Undetected losses of information from working memory," Human–Computer Interact., vol. 1, no. 2, pp. 107–131, 1985.
[7] M. E. Atwood, "A report on the Vail Workshop on Human Factors in Computer Systems," IEEE Comput. Graph. Appl., vol. 4, no. 12, pp. 48–66, 1984.
[8] M. E. Atwood and H. R. Ramsey, , "Cognitive structures in the comprehension and memory of computer programs: An investigation of computer program debugging," Tech. Rep. TR-78-A21, U.S. Army Res. Ins. For the Behavioral and Social Sciences, Alexandria, VA, 1978.
[9] M. E. Atwood, A. A. Turner, H. R. Ramsey, and J. N. Hooper, "An exploratory study of the cognitive structures underlying the comprehension of software design problems," Tech. Rep. ARI-TR-79-392, U.S. Army Res. Ins. For the Behavioral

and Social Sciences, Alexandria, VA, 1979.
[10] A. Badre and B. Shneiderman, Eds. Directions in Human Computer Interaction. Norwood, NJ: Ablex, 1982.
[11] R. W. Bailey, Human Performance Engineering: A Guide for System Designers. Englewood Cliffs, NJ: Prentice-Hall, 1982.
[12] R. Balzer, "Transformational implementation: An example," IEEE Trans. Software Eng., vol. SE-7, no. 1, pp. 3–14, 1981.
[13] ____, "A 15 year perspective on automatic programming," IEEE Trans. Software Eng., vol. SE-11, no. 11, pp. 1257–1268, 1985.
[14] P. J. Barnard, N. V. Hammond, J. Morton, J. B. Long, and I. A. Clark, "Consistency and compatibility in human-computer dialogue," Int. J. of Man-Machine Studies, vol. 15, 87–134, 1981.
[15] D. R. Barstow, Knowledge-Based Program Construction. New York: Elsevier, 1979.
[16] ____, "Domain-specific automatic programming," IEEE Trans. Software Eng., vol. SE-11, no. 11, pp. 1321–1336, 1985.
[17] D. R. Barstow, H. E. Shrobe, and E. Sandewall, Eds., Interactive Programming Environments. New York: McGraw-Hill, 1984.
[18] F. C. Bartlett, Remembering. Cambridge, UK: Cambridge Univ. Press, 1932.
[19] V. R. Basili and D. H. Hutchens, "An empirical study of a syntactic complexity family," IEEE Trans. Software Eng., vol. SE-9, no. 6, pp. 664–672, 1983.
[20] R. Bhaskar and H. A. Simon, "Problem solving in semantically rich domains: An example from engineering thermodynamics," Cogn. Sci., vol. 1, pp. 193–215, 1977.
[21] J. B. Black and H. Bern, "Casual coherence and memory for events in narratives," J. Verbal Learn. Verbal Beh., vol. 20, pp. 267–275, 1981.
[22] J. B. Black, J. A. Galambos, and B. J. Reiser, "Coordinating discovery and verification research," in D. Kieras and M. Just, Eds., New Methods in the Study of Immediate Processes in Comprehension. Hillsdale, NJ: Erlbaum, 1983.
[23] J. B. Black and T. P. Moran, "Learning and remembering command names," in Proceedings of Human Factors in Computer Systems. New York: Assoc. Comput. Mach., 1982, pp. 8–11.
[24] J. B. Black and M. M. Sebrechts, "Facilitating human-computer communication, Appl. Psycholingu., vol. 2, pp. 149–177, 1981.
[25] B. W. Boehm, Software Engineering Economics. Englewood Cliffs, NJ: Prentice-Hall, 1981.
[26] B. W. Boehm, J. R. Brown, H. Kaspar, M. Lipow, G. J. McLeod, and M. J. Merritt, Characteristics of Software Quality. New York: North-Holland, 1978.
[27] J. Bonar and E. Soloway, "Pre-programming knowledge: A major source of misconceptions in novices," Human–Comput. Interact., vol. 1, no. 2, pp. 133–161, 1985.
[28] L. Borman and B. Curtis, Eds., Human Factors in Computer Systems—II. New York: North-Holland, 1985.
[29] G. H. Bower, J. B. Black, and T. J. Turner, "Scripts in memory for text," Cogn. Psychol., vol. 11, pp. 179–230, 1979.
[30] B. K. Britton, J. B. Black, Eds., Understanding Expository Text: A Theoretical and Practical Handbook for Analyzing Explanatory Text. Hillsdale, NJ: Erlbaum, 1985.
[31] R. Brooks, "Towards a theory of the cognitive processes in computer programming," Int. J. of Man-Machine Studies, vol. 9, pp. 737–751, 1977.
[32] ____, "Studying programmer behavior experimentally: The problem of proper methodology," Commun. ACM, vol. 23, no. 4, pp. 207–213, 1980.
[33] J. S. Brown and K. VanLehn, "Repair theory: A generative theory of bugs in procedural skills," Cogn. Sci., vol. 4, pp. 379–426, 1980.
[34] S. K. Card, T. P. Moran, and A. Newell, "Computer text-editing: An information-processing analysis of a routine cognitive skill," Cogn. Psychol., vol. 12, pp. 396–410, 1980.
[35] ____, "The keystroke-level model for user performance time with interactive systems," Commun. ACM, vol. 23, pp. 396–410, 1980.
[36] ____, The Psychology of Human-Computer Interaction. Hillsdale, NJ: Erlbaum, 1983.

[37] J. M. Carroll, "Learning, using, and designing command paradigms," *Human Learn.*, vol. 1, pp. 1–34, 1982.

[38] J. M. Carroll and C. Carrithers, "Training wheels in a user interface," *Commun. ACM*, vol. 27, no. 8, pp. 800–806, 1984.

[39] J. M. Carroll and R. Mack, "Actively learning to use a word processor," in *Proc. 4th Annu. Conf. of the Cognitive Science Society* (Ann Arbor, MI, University of Michigan Cognitive Science Program), 1982.

[40] J. M. Carroll, J. C. Thomas, and A. Malhotra, "Clinical-experimental analysis of design problem solving," *Des. Studies*, vol. 1, pp. 84–92, 1979.

[41] ____, "Presentation and representation in design problem-solving," *Brit. J. Psychol.*, vol. 71, pp. 143–153, 1980.

[42] J. M. Carroll, J. C. Thomas, L. A. Miller and H. P. Friedman "Aspects of solution structure in design problem solving," *Amer. J. Psychol.*, vol. 92, pp. 269–284, 1980.

[43] W. C. Chase and H. Simon, "Perception in chess," *Cogn. Psychol.*, vol. 5 no. 1, pp. 55–81, 1973.

[44] M. J. Coombs and J. L. Alty, Eds., *Computing Skills and the User Interface.* London: Academic Press, 1981.

[45] B. J. Cox, "Message/object programming: An evolutionary change in programming technology," *IEEE Software*, vol. 1, no. 1, pp. 50–61, 1984.

[46] B. Curtis, "In search of software complexity," in *Proceedings of Quantitative Software Models for Reliability, Complexity, and Cost.* Washington, DC: IEEE Computer Soc., 1979, pp. 95–106.

[47] ____, "Measurement and experimentation in software engineering," *Proc. IEEE*, vol. 68, no. 9, pp. 1144–1157, 1980.

[48] ____, "Substantiating programmer viability," *Proc. IEEE*, vol. 69, no. 7, p. 846, 1981.

[49] ____, "Cognitive issues in reusability," in *Proc. Workshop on Reusability in Programming* (Stratford, CT, ITT Programming Technology Center), 1983.

[50] ____, "Fifteen years of psychology in software engineering: Individual differences and cognitive science," in *Proc. 7th Int. Conf. on Software Engineering* (Washington, DC, IEEE Computer Soc.), pp. 79–106, 1984.

[51] ____, *Human Factors in Software Development*, 2nd ed. Washington, DC: IEEE Computer Soc., 1986.

[52] B. Curtis, S. B. Sheppard, and P. Milliman, "Third-time charm: Stronger prediction of programmer performance by software complexity metrics," in *Proc. 4th Int. Conf. on Software Engineering* (Washington, DC: IEEE Computer Soc.), pp. 356–360, 1979.

[53] B. Curtis, E. Soloway, I. Forman, K. Ehrlich, and R. Brooks, "Cognitive perspectives on software science," *Informat. Process. Manag.*, vol. 28, no. 1, pp. 81–96, 1984.

[54] A. Davison, R. N. Kantor, J. Hannah, G. Hermon, R. Lutz, and R. Salzillo, "Limitations of readability formulas in guiding adaptations of text," Rep. 162, Urbana, IL, Univ. of Illinois, Center for the Study of Reading, 1980.

[55] R. de Beaugrande, *Text, Discourse, and Process: Toward a Multidisciplinary Science of Texts.* Norwood, NJ: Ablex, 1980.

[56] A. DeGroot, *Thought and Choice in Chess.* Paris: Mouton, 1965.

[57] F. DeRemer, and H. Kroa, "Programming-in-the-small," *ACM Sigplan Notices*, vol. 10 no. 6, 114–121, 1975.

[58] E. W. Dijkstra, "Go to statement considered harmful," *Commun. ACM*, vol. 11, pp. 147–148, 1968.

[59] H. E. Dunsmore and J. D. Gannon, "Data referencing: An experimental investigation," *Computer*, vol. 12, no. 12, pp. 50–59, 1979.

[60] B. M. Durding, C. A. Becker, and J. D. Gould, "Data organization," *Human Factors*, vol. 19, no. 1, pp. 1–14, 1977.

[61] R. Flesch, *The Art of Readable Writing.* New York: Harper & Row, 1949.

[62] A. Fitzsimmons and T. Love, "A review and evaluation of software science," *ACM Comput. Surv.*, vol. 10, no. 1, pp. 3–18, 1978.

[63] J. D. Foley, V. L. Wallace, and P. Chan, "The human factors of computer graphics interaction techniques," *IEEE Comput. Graph. Appl.*, vol. 4 no. 11, pp. 13–47, 1984.

[64] G. W. Furnas, T. K. Landauer, L. M. Gomez, and S. T. Dumais, "Statistical semantics: Analysis of the potential per-

[65] J. A. Galambos, M. M. Sebrechts, E. Wikler, and J. B. Black, "A diagrammatic language for instruction of a menu-based word processing system," in S. Williams, Ed., *Linguistics, Humanism and Computers.* Hillsdale, NJ: Erlbaum, 1983.

[66] J. D. Gannon, "An experimental evaluation of language features," *Int. J. Man-Machine Studies*, vol. 8, pp. 61–73, 1976.

[67] ____, "An experimental evaluation of data type conventions," *Commun ACM*, vol. 20, no. 8, pp. 584–595, 1977.

[68] D. Gentner and A. L. Stevens, Eds. *Mental Models.* Hillsdale, NJ: Erlbaum, 1982.

[69] A. Goldberg and D. Robson, *Smalltalk-80: The Language and Its Implementation.* Reading, MA: Addison-Wesley, 1983.

[70] T. R. G. Green, "Conditional program statements and their comprehensibility to professional programmers," *J. Occup. Psychol.*, vol. 50, pp. 93–109, 1977.

[71] T. R. G. Green, S. V. Payne, and G. C. van der Veer, Eds., *The Psychology of Computer Use.* London: Academic Press, 1983.

[72] T. R. G. Green, M. E. Sime, and M. J. Fitter, "The problems the programmer faces," *Ergonomics*, vol. 23, pp. 894–907, 1980.

[73] ____, "The art of notation" in M. J. Coombs and J. L. Alty, Eds., *Computing Skills and the User Interface.* London: Academic Press, 1981, pp. 221–251.

[74] M. H. Halstead, *Elements of Software Science.* New York: Elsevier, 1977.

[75] H. R. Hartson, Ed. *Advances in Human-Computer Interaction: Vol. 1.* Norwood, NJ: Ablex, 1985.

[76] R. Jeffries, A. A. Turner, P. G. Polson, and M. E. Atwood, "The processes involved in designing software," in J. R. Anderson, Ed., *Cognitive Skills and Their Acquisition.* Hillsdale, NJ: Erlbaum, 1981, pp. 255–283.

[77] W. L. Johnson, E. Soloway, B. Cutler, and S. Draper, "Bug catalogue I," Tech. Rep. TR-286, Dep. Comput. Sci., Yale Univ., New Haven, CT, 1983.

[78] W. L. Johnson and E. Soloway, "PROUST: Knowledge-based program understanding," in *Proc. 7th Int. Conf. on Software Engineering* (Washington, DC: IEEE Comput. Soc.), pp. 369–380, 1984.

[79] E. Kant and A. Newell, "Problem solving techniques for the design of algorithms," *Inform. Process. Manage.*, vol. 28, no. 1, pp. 97–118, 1984.

[80] M. J. Kelly and A. Chapanis, "Limited vocabulary natural language dialogue," *Int. J. Man–Machine Studies*, vol. 9, pp. 479–501, 1977.

[81] B. W. Kernighan and J. R. Mashey, "The Unix programming environment," *IEEE Computer*, vol. 14, no. 4, pp. 12–24, 1981.

[82] D. Kieras and P. G. Polson, "An approach to the formal analysis of user complexity," *Int. J. of Man-Machine Studies*, vol. 22, no. 4, pp. 365–394, 1985.

[83] W. Kintsch, *The Representation of Meaning in Memory.* Hillsdale, NJ: Erlbaum, 1974.

[84] E. Kruesi, "The human engineering task area," *IEEE Computer*, vol. 16, no. 11, pp. 86–93, 1983.

[85] J. Larkin, J. McDermott, D. P. Simon, and H. A. Simon, "Expert and novice performance in solving physics problems," *Science*, vol. 208, pp. 1335–1342, 1980.

[86] H. C. Lucas and R. B. Kaplan, "A structured programming experiment," *Comput. J.*, vol. 19, no. 2, pp. 136–138, 1974.

[87] J. Martin, *Design of Man–Computer Dialogues.* Englewood Cliffs, NJ: Prentice Hall, 1973.

[88] R. E. Mayer, "The psychology of how novices learn computer programming," *ACM Comput. Surv.*, vol. 13, pp. 121–141, 1981.

[89] F. E. McGarry, "What have we learned in the last six years?" in *Proc. 7th Annu. Software Engineering Workshop* (SEL-82-007) (Greenbelt, MD: NASA Goddard Space Flight Center), 1982.

[90] K. B. McKeithen, J. S. Reitman, H. H. Rueter, and S. C. Hirtle, "Knowledge organizations and skill differences in computer programmers," *Cogn. Psychol.*, vol. 13, pp. 307–325, 1981.

[91] L. A. Miller, "Programming by non-programmers," *Int. J.*

Man-Machine Studies, vol. 6, pp. 237–260, 1974.

[92] ____, "Natural language programming: Styles, strategies, gies, and contrasts," *IBM Syst. J.*, vol. 20, pp. 184–215, 1981.

[93] J. R. Miller and W. Kintsch, "Readability in recall of short prose passages," *Text*, vol. 1, pp. 33–54, 1982.

[94] T. Moher and G. M. Schneider, "Methods for improving controlled experimentation in software engineering," in *Proc. 5th Int. Conf. on Software Engineering* (Washington, DC: IEEE Computer Society), pp. 224–233, 1981.

[95] T. Moran, "Guest editor's introduction: An applied psychology of the user." *ACM Comput. Surv.*, vol. 13, pp. 1–11, 1981.

[96] A. Newell and H. A. Simon, *Human Problem Solving*. Englewood Cliffs, NJ: Prentice-Hall, 1972.

[97] J. A. Nichols, "Forward," in *Proc. Human Factors in Computer Systems*. New York: Assoc. Comput. Mach., 1982, p. iii.

[98] D. A. Norman and S. W. Draper, Eds., *User Centered System Design: New Perspectives in Human-Computer Interaction*. Hillsdale, NJ: Erlbaum, 1986.

[99] S. Papert, *Mindstorms: Children, Computers, and Powerful Ideas*. New York: Basic Books, 1980.

[100] H. R. Ramsey and J. D. Grimes, "Human factors in interactive computer dialogue," *Annu. Rev. Informat. Sci. Technol.*, vol. 18, pp. 29–59, 1983.

[101] C. Rich, "Inspection methods in programming," Tech. Rep. AI-TR-604, AI Laboratory, MIT, Cambridge, MA, 1981.

[102] E. Z. Rothkopf, "Structured text features and the control of processes in learning from written materials," in J. Carroll and R. Freedl, Eds., *Language Comprehension and the Acquisition of Knowledge*. Ann Arbor, MI: UMI, 1972.

[103] H. Sackman, *Man-Computer Problem Solving*. Princeton, NJ: Auerbach, 1970.

[104] H. Sackman, W. J. Erickson, and E. E. Grant, "Exploratory and experimental studies in comparing on-line and off-line programming performance," *Commun. ACM*, vol. 11, pp. 3–11, 1968.

[105] G. Salvendy, Ed., *Human-Computer Interaction*. New York: Elsevier, 1984.

[106] R. C. Schank and R. Abelson, *Scripts, Plans, Goals and Understanding*. Hillsdale, NJ: Erlbaum, 1977.

[107] M. M. Sebrechts, J. G. Deck, and J. B. Black, "A diagrammatic approach to computer instruction for the naive user," *Behav. Res. Methods Instrum.*, vol. 15, 1983.

[108] R. J. Seidel, R. E. Anderson, and B. Hunter, Eds., *Computer Literacy*. New York: Academic Press, 1982.

[109] C. M. Seifert, P. Robertson, and J. Black, "Online processing of pragmatic inferences," Tech. Rep. CS-TR-15. Dep. Psychol., Yale Univ., New Haven, CT, 1982.

[110] B. Shackel, Ed., *Man-Computer Interaction: Human Factors Aspects of Computers & People*. Alphen aan din Ryn, Netherlands: Sythoff & Noordhoff, 1981.

[111] B. A. Sheil, "The psychological study of programming," *ACM Comput. Surv.*, vol. 13, no. 1, pp. 102–120, 1981.

[112] ____, "Power tools for programmers," *Datamation*, vol. no. 2, pp. 131–144, 1983.

[113] S. B. Sheppard, B. Curtis, P. Milliman, and T. Love, "Modern coding practices and programmer performance," *IEEE Computer*, vol. 12, no. 12, pp. 41–49, 1979.

[114] S. B. Sheppard, E. Kruesi, and B. Curtis, "The effects of symbology and spatial arrangement on the comprehension of software specifications," in *Proc. 5th Int. Conf. on Software Engineering*. (Washington, DC: IEEE Comput. Society, 1981), pp. 207–214.

[115] B. Shneiderman, "Exploratory experiments in programmer behavior," *Int. J. Comput. Informat. Sci.*, vol. 5, pp. 123–143, 1976.

[116] ____, "Human factors experiments in designing interactive systems," *IEEE Computer*, vol. 12, no. 12, pp. 9–19, 1979.

[117] B. Shneiderman, *Software Psychology: Human Factors in Computer and Information Systems*. Cambridge, MA: Winthrop, 1980.

[118] ____, "Direct manipulation: A Step beyond programming languages," *IEEE Computer*, vol. 16, no. 8, pp. 57–69, 1983.

[119] B. Schneiderman and R. E. Mayer, "Syntatic/semantic interactions in programmer behavior: A model and experimental results," *Int. J. Comput. Informat. Sci.*, vol. 8, no. 3, pp. 219–238, 1979.

[120] M. E. Sime, and M. J. Coombs, Eds., *Designing for Human-Computer Communication*. London: Academic Press, 1983.

[121] M. E. Sime, T. R. G. Green, and D. J. Guest, "Psychological evaluations of two conditional constructions used in computer languages," *Int. J. Man-Machine Studies*, vol. 5, pp. 105–113, 1973.

[122] M. E. Sime, A. T. Arblaster, T. R. G. Green, "Reducing programming errors in nested conditionals by prescribing a writing procedure," *Int. J. Man-Machine Studies*, vol. 9, pp. 119–126, 1977.

[123] H. A. Simon, "How big is a chunk?" *Science*, vol. 183, pp. 482–488, 1974.

[124] ____, "Information processing models of cognition," *Annu. Rev. Psychol.*, vol. 30, pp. 363–396, 1979.

[125] H. T. Smith and T. R. G. Green, Eds., *Human Interaction with Computers*. London: Academic Press, 1980.

[126] E. Soloway, J. Bonar, and K. Ehrlich, "Cognitive strategies and looping constructs: An empirical study," *Commun. ACM*, vol. 26, pp. 853–860, 1983.

[127] E. Soloway and K. Ehrlich, "Empirical studies of programming knowledge," *IEEE Trans. Software Eng.*, vol. SE-10, no. 5, pp. 595–609, 1984.

[128] E. Soloway, K. Ehrlich, and J. B. Black, "Beyond numbers: Don't ask "how many"…ask "why"," in *Proceedings of CHI'83: Human Factors in Computer Systems*. New York: ACM, pp. 240–246, 1983.

[129] E. Soloway, K. Ehrlich, J. Bonar, and J. Greenspan, "What do novices know about programming?" in A. Badre and B. Schneiderman, Eds., *Directions in Human-Computer Interaction*. Norwood, NJ: Ablex, 1982, pp. 27–54.

[130] J. Spohrer, E. Pope, M. Lipman, W. Sack, S. Freiman, D. Littman, W. L. Johnson, and E. Soloway, "Bug Catalogues II, III, IV," Yale Univ., Comput. Sci. Dep., Tech. Rep. TR-386, New Haven, CT, 1983.

[131] J. Spohrer, E. Soloway, and E. Pope, "A goal/plan analysis of buggy Pascal programs," *Human-Comput. Interact.*, vol. 1, no. 2, pp. 163–207, 1985.

[132] J. C. Thomas and J. M. Carroll, "Human factors in communication," *IBM Syst. J.*, vol. 20, pp. 237–263, 1981.

[133] J. Thomas and M. L. Schneider, Eds., *Human Factors in Computer Systems*. Norwood, NJ: Ablex, 1984.

[134] T. A. van Dijk and W. Kintsch, *Strategies of Discourse Comprehension*. New York: Academic Press, 1983.

[135] D. A. Waterman, "A rule-based approach to knowledge acquisition for man-machine interface programs," *Int. J. Man-Machine Studies*, vol. 10, pp. 693–711, 1978.

[136] R. C. Waters, "The programmer's apprentice: Knowledge-based program editing," *IEEE Trans. Software Eng.*, vol. SE-8, no. 1, pp. 1–12, 1982.

[137] ____, "The programmer's apprentice: A session with KBEmacs," *IEEE Trans. Software Eng.*, vol. SE-11, pp. 1296–1320, 1985.

[138] G. M. Weinberg, *The Psychology of Computer Programming*. New York: Van Nostrand Reinhold, 1971.

[139] L. Weissman, "Psychological complexity of computer programs: An experimental methodology," *ACM SIGPLAN Notices*, vol. 9, no. 6, pp. 25–36, 1974.

[140] M. Weiser and J. Shertz, "A study of program problem representation in novice programmers," *Int. J. Man-Machine Studies*, vol. 17, 1983.

The Psychological Study of Programming

B. A. SHEIL

Cognitive and Instructional Sciences, Xerox Palo Alto Research Center, 3333 Coyote Hill Road, Palo Alto, California 94305

Most innovations in programming languages and methodology are motivated by a belief that they will improve the performance of the programmers who use them. Although such claims are usually advanced informally, there is a growing body of research which attempts to verify them by controlled observation of programmers' behavior. Surprisingly, these studies have found few clear effects of changes in either programming notation or practice. Less surprisingly, the computing community has paid relatively little attention to these results. This paper reviews the psychological research on programming and argues that its ineffectiveness is the result of both unsophisticated experimental technique and a shallow view of the nature of programming skill.

Keywords and Phrases: programming, cognitive psychology, programming languages, programming methodology, human factors, software engineering

CR Categories: 4.0, 4.29

CONTENTS

INTRODUCTION

As practiced by computer science, the study of programming is an unholy mixture of mathematics (e.g., DIJK76), literary criticism (e.g., KERN74), and folklore (e.g., BROO75). However, despite the stylistic variation, the claims that are made are all basically psychological; that is, that programming done in such and such a manner will be easier, faster, less prone to error, or whatever. How compelling we find such formal, stylistic, and anecdotal arguments reflects primarily the degree to which they appeal to our own "common sense" model of the cognitive processes involved in programming. However great their appeal, though, the methodological recommendations of computer science should be recognized as *empirically testable, psychological hypotheses*. Unlike mathematics, literary criticism, or folklore, a discipline of computer science has an obligation to validate these claims.

The results of psychological experiments have, indeed, often been used as ammunition in disputes over computing practice. One of the earliest contributions was Sackman's study of time sharing [SACK70], conducted in response to the then current debate on the relative efficacy of batch and time-shared processing. Weinberg's well-known book, *The Psychology of Computer Programming* [WEIN71], in addition to making a forceful claim for the importance of psychological considerations in computing, accommodates the then current debate on programmer team organization by treating the sociology of programming groups at length. More recently, much of the work on programming language constructs and practices discussed both in this review and in Sneiderman's book, *Software Psychology* [SHNE80], is clearly motivated by the structured programming movement.

Sadly, however, psychological data have been at best a minor factor in these debates.

Sackman's inability to find decisive advantages for time sharing did little to slow its spread. Although one could certainly find points to object to in his studies, the unfortunate fact is that they were largely ignored by a discipline that did not want to hear about them. Despite the greater acceptance now than then of the relevance of experimental results, little of the work on the psychology of programming shows any sign of challenging computer science's established wisdom on programming and programming methodology. Much of what follows is an attempt to explore why this is so.

1. PSYCHOLOGICAL THEORY AND BEHAVIORAL EVALUATION

Before considering the behavioral evaluations of programming technology, one might ask whether the relevant insights could be obtained from conventional psychological *theory*. An analysis based on a psychological theory which has been validated in a different domain would have the considerable authority of independent grounding, as opposed to the somewhat ad hoc flavor of technology-driven experimentation. Unfortunately, although some psychological theory is very suggestive, it usually lacks the robustness and precision required to yield exact predictions for behavior as complex as programming. As a result, the psychological work on programming consists mainly of atheoretical evaluations motivated directly by the concerns of contemporary computing practice.

Such evaluations might, at first sight, seem to be a straightforward matter of comparing the performance of groups of similar programmers using different programming techniques. Unfortunately, the complexity of programming behavior makes the execution and interpretation of such comparisons anything but straightforward. A rudimentary appreciation of these difficulties is necessary to motivate the methods used, lest they seem pointlessly abstruse.

The empirical methods span a spectrum defined by the tension between the conflicting goals of *reliability* and *generalizability*. Reliability (or *control*) is the degree to which observed relationships are systematic rather than circumstantial, whereas generalizability is the degree to which such relationships occur or are significant in situations other than the one observed. Observations made in real-world situations are at one extreme, in that any findings are known to apply to at least *one* real-world situation. Their generalizability to others, however, is clouded by the fact that real-world programming performance varies in too many uncontrolled ways to allow reliable interpretation of its causes. Intervention to control these extraneous influences (e.g., by reassigning programmers within working groups to equalize the level of ability across the groups) is apt to disrupt the organization, with totally unpredictable effects on the phenomenon being observed. Indeed, the very act of introducing some technical innovation for the purposes of evaluating it may cause changes of behavior

TABLE 1. ERROR DATA FOR PROGRAMMING TASK[a,b]

	Language			
	Jump	Nested	Repeated	p-level
Semantic errors	0.40	0.07	0.04	.01
Syntactic errors	0.20	0.85	0.13	.05
Error lifetimes	1.06	1.60	0.09	.02

[a] From SIME77.
[b] The first two lines give the number of the indicated type of error per problem. The last line gives the number of additional attempts after an initial error. All entries are medians.

that are unrelated to any properties of the innovation, a phenomenon known as the *Hawthorne effect*. These difficulties are common to most *in situ* investigations of complex behavior, and a variety of specialized techniques (for a discussion of which see, e.g., CAMP79) are required to circumvent them.

The alternative to real-world experimentation is to construct artificial experimental situations in which extraneous influences can be either eliminated or controlled. The construction of realistic experimental programming situations that differ in only (a few) controlled ways is, however, both difficult and subject to its own forms of bias. Creating two or more similar programming environments by altering an existing environment can cause interference effects among programmers familiar with the status quo. Completely novel environments, on the other hand, whether specially constructed for the experiment or obtained by studying programmers with no experience of some existing environment, require that the programmers being studied be thoroughly trained for their new environment, lest learning transients dominate the results. Similar issues arise with respect to the type and size of the programming task used. Failures of either realism or control can result in any differences between technologies being concealed by extraneous variation.

The difficulty of reliable experimentation using complete programming tasks suggests experiments which focus on either isolated aspects of the programming task or the psychological claims that implicitly underlie different programming techniques. Thus one might evaluate the suitability of using different control to express conditional action by investigating how well people can formulate and understand simple procedures in various stylized natural languages, such as those commonly used to express sets of instructions such as recipes. Differences in behavior could be used to support claims about the appropriateness of certain uses of transfer of control within programming languages. The attractiveness of this approach is that its distance from real-world programming permits much easier and more tightly controlled experimenta-tion. That same distance, however, makes the argument from experimental findings to normal programming practice very perilous. Not only must it be shown that the experimental situation taps psychological processes which occur during programming, but those processes must also be shown to account for a significant proportion of programming effort. Neither of these demonstrations, needless to say, is at all straightforward.

2. SCOPE OF THIS REVIEW

The behavioral research on programming can be roughly separated into studies of

- *programming notation*, which includes the effects of programming language features such as control structures;

- *programming practices*, such as programming methodologies, tools, and aids, such as the use of comments, indentation, and flowcharting;

- *programming tasks* or behavior specific to certain aspects of programming, such as learning a programming language, coding, and debugging;

- *programming management*, which includes issues relating to the management, review, and organization of programming groups.

In addition, a variety of other studies have investigated such factors as the programmer's physical environment, personality, and motivation, and the predictive value of various measures of program complexity. While all of these are potentially significant, this review concentrates exclusively on studies in the first three areas, which form a coherent body of research on the *cognitive* processes underlying programming. The other studies cover a very different and very diverse range of topics, such as the social context in which the programming takes place.

Even within the area of cognitive psychology this review is not exhaustive. In addition to the usual caveats of unintentional oversight and limited space, a detailed enumeration of work in this area has recently been published [SNHE80]. The intent here is to explore its overall direction, current state, and future prospects.

3. STUDIES OF PROGRAMMING NOTATION

As one might expect, given the diversity of programming languages and the intensity of feeling about them in the computing community, the study of programming notations is both the largest and the most controversial area. As one might further expect in light of the structured programming debate, choice of control constructs dominates as subject matter.

3.1 Conditionals

The use of GOTOs to express conditional and loop structures was one of the first targets of the structured programming critique [DIJK68], so it is not surprising that notation for conditionals was one of the first subjects of psychological study. An early study by Sime, Green, and Guest [SIME73] compared a nested IF-THEN-ELSE notation with one that used explicit transfers of control. In this experiment non-programmers were asked to compose several sets of instructions for a simple mechanical device using one of the two notations. Each set of instructions was to select the appropriate action (a method of cooking) to be applied to an input object (a vegetable, texture, etc.). For each problem the subjects were presented with a specification in the form of a set of action-attributes pairs, and measures were taken of both the amount of time and number of errors required to produce a correct program. On both counts the IF-THEN-ELSE notation was found to be superior to test-and-jump. They later [SIME77] replicated this result in an experiment which included a third notation wherein the predicate was repeated in each clause of the conditional (i.e., IF *pred action*$_1$, NOT *pred action*$_2$, END *pred*, as shown in Figure 1). Their results presented in Table 1 indicate that, for the simple (one-word) predicates they used, the repeated predicate form is slightly superior to the IF-THEN-ELSE form, although their version of the latter is a little prolix in its use of BEGIN ... END pairs.

Similar results were later obtained by Green [GREE77] for two comprehension tasks using the same notations. Experienced professional programmers were presented with programs written in one of the three different languages and asked to specify either the action that would be carried out for an input with given properties or what those properties would have to have been given that the program performed some given action. An example of the forward reasoning task, using the programs in Figure 1, would be to specify the action to be taken (grill) if the input were hard and not green; the backward reasoning task would be to specify what properties the input must have had given that it was grilled. The amount of time taken to answer these questions for each of the three languages is shown in Table 2. Both types of questions were answered faster for nested language programs than for jump programs. In addition, a smaller difference was found between the two nested languages for reasoning backward from effect to precondition.

These studies make a reasonable case for the superiority of nested conditional structures over those using jumps. The authors explain this difference in terms of redundant perceptual encoding (specifically, that the indentation of nested programs provides a secondary clue to their logical structure). This seems reasonable, although it is puzzling that no direct test of this explanation (e.g., by comparing jump and nest programs, both unformatted) has ever been reported.

By contrast, the explanation of the difference between the repeated predicate and the IF-THEN-ELSE notations in terms of the latter requiring the reader to negate predicates when reasoning backward from

number and positioning of symbols provide more than sufficient reason to expect differences in performance.

GREE77 also provides an example of another very striking effect which is often found in behavioral studies of programming. Each participant in this experiment attended three sessions held on consecutive days. The reaction time data presented in Table 2 show large practice effects (improvement in performance across sessions) for all three languages in both experiments. Whereas the effect of the different languages is to change the mean reaction time by amounts which range from 4 to 15 percent, the effect of a single session of practice ranges from 13 to 27 percent! Even though these practice effects do not interact with those due to language, their size relative to the effects of notation provides one measure of the importance of those notational differences.

Practice and experience effects like this have been noted in other studies, often interacting with or extinguishing the linguistic effects being studied. Sime et al. [SIME73] reported that with practice the differences between the two languages they studied became nonsignificant. A study of the FORTRAN arithmetic and logical IF statements [SHNE76] found the logical IF to be significantly easier for novices but found no such differences for more experienced programmers. These interactions between notation and experience suggest that the effects of notation being measured in these experiments may be somewhat evanescent.

3.2 Control Flow

The evidence for the structured programming position on control structures other than the conditional is considerably more mixed, possibly because of the difficulty of developing experimental materials that differ only in the degree to which they are structured. Weissman [WEIS74] used two PL/I programs, each written at three levels of structuring, and found that the structured version led to greater confidence on the programmer's part, but no reliable differences in performance on either comprehension measures or debugging performance, although most of these measures were

tending to favor the structured version. He speculated that the effects would have become clearer with larger programs than those he used (50 and 100 lines, respectively) but points out that such programs would be difficult to use in the necessarily restricted time of an experiment.

Lucas and Kaplan [LUCA76] contrasted performance on composing one program and modifying another using GOTO-less and standard PL/I. On their performance and attitudinal measures, the only reliable differences between the two groups were that writing GOTO-less programs required more test runs (and, perhaps not incidentally, was thought to be less easy) but no more programming time, whereas modifying the GOTO-less programs took less programming time but no fewer test runs (see Table 3). This asymmetry may reflect the fact that no explicit training in GOTO-less programming was provided, and its sudden imposition as a constraint may have disrupted the participants' established programming styles in the composition task.

Sheppard et al. [SHEP79] studied the performance of professional programmers on small (~50 statements) FORTRAN programs that were structured in a number of different ways, including chaotically. The latter were significantly more difficult both to memorize and modify, but no differences were found, either for these tasks or for debugging, between "naturally" structured programs and versions that were more strictly structured, flow-graph reducible, or written in FORTRAN77 (a dialect with structured programming constructs such as IF...THEN...ELSE...).

All told, this is fairly poor support for

TABLE 3. RESULTS FROM STRUCTURED PROGRAMMING STUDY[a,b]

| | Composition | | Modification | |
	Structured	Unstructured	Structured	Unstructured
Test runs	14.63	8.87	10.06 =	10.25
Time taken	14.75 =	11.69	9.13 =	13.06
Easy to write	4.00	5.19	5.13 =	4.63

[a] From LUCA76.

[b] Time units were not reported. "Easy to write" is a subjective evaluation with higher scores indicating greater ease. Differences are significant at .05 level unless marked by =.

ELSE alternatives is much less convincing. The use of secondary visual clues to explain the superiority of nested structures suggests that the effectiveness of these notations will be very sensitive to differences in formatting conventions. Nested languages, however, permit many variations both of indentation and choice of delimiters, and this factor is neither systematically varied nor controlled in these studies. Specifically, the superiority of the repeated predicate conditional over the standard IF-THEN-ELSE form might simply be an effect of the formatting used for the latter. Simply glancing at Figure 1 shows that the two nested languages are not matched in terms of number of symbols, the amount of space they occupy, or the relative spatial displacement of related clauses. Intuitively, reading programs in the IF-THEN-ELSE language seems to require a significant amount of effort to climb over the forest of redundant BEGIN...END brackets. Neither can it be claimed that these uncontrolled differences are inherent in the two types of nesting, as a variety of more concise techniques has been used in various programming languages to delimit the clauses of IF-THEN-

ELSE constructs. Without experiments that control for these alternative sources of variation, there is simply no evidence for the claim that the difference between the two nested languages is due to the mental overhead of the implicit negation required for ELSE clauses. The differences between the two nested languages in terms of the

```
Test and jump

         IF hard GOTO L1
         IF tall GOTO L2
         IF juicy GOTO L3
              roast STOP
    L1   IF green GOTO L4
         peel grill STOP
    L2   chop fry STOP
    L3   boil STOP
    L4   peel roast STOP
```

```
Nested

IF hard THEN
BEGIN peel
IF green THEN
BEGIN roast
END
ELSE
BEGIN grill
END
END
ELSE
BEGIN
IF tall THEN
BEGIN chop fry
END
ELSE
BEGIN
IF juicy THEN
BEGIN boil
END
ELSE BEGIN roast
END
END
END
```

```
Repeated conditions

IF hard peel
IF green roast
NOT green grill
END green
NOT hard
IF tall chop fry
NOT tall
IF juicy boil
NOT juicy roast
END juicy
END tall
END hard
```

FIGURE 1. Three notations for conditionals (from SIME77).

TABLE 2. CONDENSED REACTION TIME DATA ON TWO COMPREHENSION TASKS[a,b]

Language	Session 1	2	3	Mean	p Level
	Forward Reasoning Task				
Jump	7.415	6.050	5.135	6.200	.032
Nested	7.095	5.670	4.760	5.842	
Repeated	7.470	5.870	4.860	6.067	ns
Mean	7.327	5.863	4.918		
	Backward Reasoning Task				
Jump	10.090	7.590	6.510	8.063	<.001
Nested	9.345	7.040	6.120	7.502	
Repeated	8.825	6.605	5.675	7.037	.011
Mean	9.420	7.078	6.085		

[a] From GREE77.

[b] One factor (number of conditionals) has been collapsed out. Times are in seconds. Probability levels contrast Jump with both nested forms, and Repeated with Nested.

computer science's dominant programming paradigm. Shneiderman's review is more sanguine, stating "These controlled experiments and a variety of informal field studies indicate that the choice of control structure does make a significant difference in programmer performance. Evidence supports the anecdote that the number of bugs in a program is proportional to the square of the number of GOTOs ..." [SHNE80, p. 81]. Unless the (uncited) "informal studies" which are alluded to are very compelling, the evidence suggests only that deliberately chaotic control structure degrades performance. These experiments provide virtually no evidence for the beneficial effect of any specific method of structuring control flow.

On the other hand, one could argue that the results of these experiments simply do not bear on the methodology of structured programming that they purport to test. As Dijkstra points out in his book, *A Discipline of Programming* [DIJK76], any reasonable programming methodology is a *discipline*, a way of thinking, not just a collection of programming constructs. The empirical claim of structured programming is that a programmer who approaches problems in a certain way will be more effective. The syntactic constructs are appropriate to that approach, but they are not themselves that approach. Therefore there is no reason to believe that their presence or absence will, by itself, have any significant impact. Either the programmer understands the structured approach to programming, in which case her code will reflect it (whether or not structured control constructs are available), or the programmer does not, in which case the presence of syntactic constructs is irrelevant.

The experimental manipulations of LUCA76 are quite inappropriate from this point of view. Simply outlawing the use of a language feature without providing any motivation or alternative strategies may replicate some of the foolishness of the early days of the structured programming movement but is hardly likely to produce much else other than resentment. The same assumption, that the value of a program's being well structured is independent of the person reading it, also

underlies the investigation of the tractability of differently structured programs in SHEP79. Since their programmers were not trained in any particular programming methodology, their finding that strictly structured programs were no easier to deal with than "naturally" structured ones may reflect only that such "natural" structuring was most familiar to their participants. Likewise, the result that FORTRAN77 programs were no better understood than "naturally" structured ones is not at all surprising given that less than 10 percent of their participants had had any exposure to FORTRAN77.

3.3 Data Types

One of the major distinctions among programming languages is whether the objects in the language are required to be known to be of a certain *type* (e.g., integer, string), either *statically* (at compile time, as in PASCAL), *dynamically* (at run time, as in LISP), or not at all (as in BCPL). This is a particularly critical issue for system programming languages, where both reliability and expressive freedom are highly desirable.

Gannon conducted an experiment designed to compare the error proneness of statically typed and typeless languages [GANN77]. His method was to provide both statically typed (with integer and string types) and typeless (e.g., arbitrary subscripting of memory) extensions to a common language core, thus generating two languages which were essentially matched except for differences in the type conventions. A class of 38 students programmed the same problem in both languages, with half doing it in each order. Gannon's careful analysis makes a strong case for the superiority of the statically typed language in controlling errors.

Unfortunately for the argument for static typing, Gannon's analysis of the source of the errors makes it clear that few of the errors made in the typeless language had to do with the lack of static checking, but mostly reflected problems with data representation. This, as Gannon points out, is an inherent confound, as a statically typed language must provide a basic set of operations

on the data types it supports. Although Gannon took pains to minimize the extent of the built-in semantics, his error analysis clearly shows the bulk of errors made in the typeless language to be in the code that provided the operations on strings that were built into the statically typed language. This certainly affords evidence for extending the facilities offered by programming languages, but little evidence for the value of static typing.

Gannon's study also provides another instance of the experience effects noted in the studies of conditionals, as the differences between the two languages were much reduced for both more competent (as measured by course grades) and more experienced (as measured by number of programming languages known) participants.

3.4 Everything at Once

Perhaps the most ambitious attempt to contrast programming language designs empirically is Gannon's thesis [GANN75, GANN76]. Flush with the confidence of the structured programming movement at its height, Gannon and Horning took an existing language that was in use as a teaching language at the University of Toronto and made nine separate modifications based on their analysis of its deficiencies. The resulting language was constrasted with its predecessor in a two-group (stratified by ability) experiment using student programmers, who were asked to complete two moderate size (75–200 line) programming problems in their assigned language. The evaluation measure was the error rate for those participants who completed both problems (an astonishingly low 49 percent of the original group).

Unfortunately, the overall error rates of the two languages were not significantly different, leaving Gannon the unrewarding task of tracing the source of each of the 3937 errors (!!) in an attempt to construct causal interpretations by *post hoc* analysis. The language features found to be more prone to error (as measured by either error counts, occurrences, or persistence) included untraditional operator precedence, assignment being an operator rather than a statement, semicolon being a separator rather than a statement terminator, use of

bracketing to close both compound statements and expressions, and the inability to use named constants.

The problem with this analysis is that it is very unclear how to interpret the results. For example, Gannon and Horning argue that the persistence of assignment errors in the original language "calls into serious question the treatment of the assignment symbol := as 'just another operator'" [GANN75, p. 19]. These results, however, are open to far too many plausible alternative explanations. One such alternative is that the errors may result from confusion due to the use of an assignment symbol which closely resembles another valid operator (=) which is itself the assignment operator in other well-known languages, one of which (PL/I) is mentioned as being familiar to some of the students. This, possibly compounded by the use of nonstandard precedence, may well be a specifically deadly combination of language features. Gannon and Horning claim that use of a different symbol (such as ←) might "probably avoid some of these errors, but provide no better error detection." Then again, it might avoid all of them. One just cannot tell on the basis of a single observation.

3.5 Summary

Our discussion of the effects of various programming notations has raised two significant general issues. First, given the small sizes of and inconsistencies among the reported effects, it is not even clear that notation is a major factor in the difficulty of programming. The study of programming languages has been central to computer science for so long that it comes as a shock to realize how little empirical evidence there is for their importance. Second, many of these effects tend to disappear with practice or experience. This raises some doubt as to whether these results reflect stable differences between notations or merely learning effects and other transients that would not be significant factors in actual programming performance.

4. STUDIES OF PROGRAMMING PRACTICES

Programming "practices" include such things as flowcharting, prettyprinting, variable naming, and commenting. The empirical investigation of their efficacy has been prompted both by their frequent recommendation by textbooks on programming (e.g., KERN74) and by their apparent accessibility to simple experimental test. A claim that some such practice as extensive use of comments will significantly improve some measure of programming effectiveness is easily tested, as the practice can be imposed in any appropriate existing programming environment. The study of notations, by contrast, not only requires the construction of quite elaborate experimental environments, but it is much more difficult to vary aspects of the notation independently, as such changes tend to interact with other aspects of the environment.

4.1 Flowcharting

Shneiderman et al. carried out a series of experiments designed to determine which kinds of programming tasks were most enhanced by use of detailed flowcharting [SHNE77b]. Five successive experiments, with different tasks and measures, failed to reveal any reliable advantage of flowchart use. As Brooks pointed out [BROO80], one can explain the lack of results in two of these studies as "ceiling" effects (i.e., the scores of both experimental groups were so close to the maximum that there was no room for differences to occur). One could also explain away the lack of results in the remaining studies by objecting to the choice of materials, language, and/or participants. However, in so doing, the claim for the utility of flowcharting is being restricted so as not to include some class of situations of which these experiments are instances. The strong form of the flowcharting hypothesis having failed (and the results of Shneiderman et al. have demonstrated that flowcharting is not invariably useful), it is incumbent on those who advocate flowcharts to formulate *and empirically validate* a more limited hypothesis.

The addendum on empirical validation is significant. Even if one's stylistic preference is for debates on programming practice to be carried out on the basis of intuition rather than data, one's intuition in some area is surely somewhat suspect after one's

previous claims in that area have failed empirically. Yet, as Shneiderman sadly notes in a retrospective review of this work, "Flowchart critics cheered our results as the justification of their claims, while adherents found fault and pronounced confidence in the utility of flowcharts in their own work" [SHNE80, p. 82]. It is in response to reactions like this that the use of psychology in computer science debates was earlier characterized as "ammunition."

4.2 Indenting (Prettyprinting)

The use of indentation to indicate program structure is another practice for which there is little behavioral evidence. Weissman once again found positive self-evaluations but no performance improvements for either modifying, hand simulating, or answering questions about indented versus unindented versions of programs written in ALGOL W and PL/I [WEIS74]. Shneiderman and McKay (reported in SHNE80) contrasted ability to locate single bugs in indented and unindented versions of two PASCAL programs and found no performance improvement in the indented versions. Love also found no reliable improvement in a reconstruction task for indented and unindented short FORTRAN programs [LOVE77]. This lack of support leads Shneiderman to conclude that, like flowcharting, "the advantage of indentation may not be as great as some believe" [SHNE80, p. 74].

There is, however, a critical difference between flowcharting and indenting concerning the range of phenomena to which it is reasonable to generalize these negative experimental results. "Flowcharting" refers to the use of a supplementary graphical representation of program control flow. As no instance of any such technique has ever been demonstrated to enhance programming performance, it is reasonable to generalize the negative experimental results to the entire class of such techniques. "Indenting," on the other hand, refers to the use of white space formatting to indicate program structure. There is strong reason to believe that such techniques can be effective in some circumstances. One example is the superiority of nested over test-and-jump structures for conditionals discussed

earlier. A sweeping conclusion that program layout has no effect would require another explanation for that finding. More intuitively, the most rudimentary use of white space to indicate program structure is the use of a line break between statements in languages such as FORTRAN. Clearly, it would be rash to claim that these studies show that programs in these languages would be as easy to work with if they were laid out without line breaks (or with them placed every n characters without reference to the statement structure). The existence of both positive and negative results suggests a search for some set of principles which indicate how and when program formatting techniques will be effective.

Any such principles must be shaped primarily by empirical evaluation rather than by appeals to intuition. However, it seems suggestive that, as opposed to the relative consensus on flowcharting techniques (as reflected, for example, in the existence of standards), program layout schemes are hotly disputed, even within relatively homogeneous programming communities. One can draw one of two conclusions from this lack of agreement. The view of the disputants is that there are decidedly good and bad ways of formatting programs. Alternatively, one could conclude that individuals differ as to what attributes they find it useful for the layout to emphasize. This, in turn, could be a function of individual differences, such as personality factors, or, much more likely, simply reflects the formatting scheme that the individual is accustomed to using. Intuitively, the latter seems reasonable because the value of a standardized program layout is in being able to use its (rapidly available) perceptual cues to skip over code that would otherwise have to be at least partially understood as it is scanned. It is unlikely that this would be an effective strategy unless the perceptual operation were highly practiced.

From this point of view indenting is not an inherent attribute of a program. What is indented for one person may seem to be very poorly arranged on the page for another. Any given program formatting scheme might actually degrade the per-

formance of a programmer accustomed to work with programs laid out in another style. At the very least, it seems premature to conclude that indentation is an ineffective technique until it has been demonstrated that neither variation in the formatting style nor practice using some (any) systematic formatting scheme has any effect.

4.3 Variable Naming

There is only scattered research on the oft-claimed benefits of using names with mnemonic properties. Several of Weissman's experiments [WEIS74] addressed this question, but the results are unclear except for the usual improvement of programmer self-evaluation. Shneiderman [SHNE80, pp. 70-72] reports two experiments—a comprehension experiment which showed mnemonic names to be more effective and a debugging experiment that found no such effects. Sheppard et al. [SHEP79] found no evidence that mnemonic names helped professional programmers to memorize ~50 line FORTRAN programs. The overall pattern is unclear. It seems plausible that mnemonic variable names would be less useful in smaller or better understood programs, as they offer less chance for confusion and hence less need for mnemonics. For the same reason one might expect mnemonic names to be more useful for programs with which the programmer is less familiar. Such program/programmer variability would account for the inconclusive results, but needs independent experimental confirmation.

4.4 Commenting

The judicious use of comments is almost universally considered to be good practice. Just as for the use of mnemonic variable names, however, empirical evidence for this position is both sparse and equivocal. Weissman found that appropriate comments caused hand simulation to proceed significantly faster, but with significantly more errors [WEIS74]. Shneiderman contrasted students' modification and recall of FORTRAN programs with either high-level (overall program description) or low-level (statement description) comments

[Shne77a]. The programs with the higher level comments were found to be significantly easier to modify. Sheppard et al. found that neither high- nor low-level comments had any reliable effect on either the accuracy of or the time taken to modify small FORTRAN programs [Shep79].

Although the evidence for the utility of comments is equivocal, it is unclear what other pattern of results could have been expected. Clearly, at some level comments *have* to be useful. To believe otherwise would be to believe that the comprehensibility of a program is independent of how much information the reader might already have about it. However, it is equally clear that a comment is only useful if it tells the reader something she either does not already know or cannot infer immediately from the code. Exactly which propositions about a program should be included in the commentary is therefore a matter of matching the comments to the needs of the expected readers. This makes widely applicable results as to the desirable amount and type of commenting so highly unlikely that behavioral experimentation is of questionable value.

5. STUDIES OF PROGRAMMING TASKS

Programming "tasks" include activities such as learning a language, debugging, coding, and testing. The work reviewed in this section typically explores a single phase of programming activity in depth, rather than evaluate the effects of some manipulation (such as the effects of a language feature) which might cut across several different phases. Rather than be driven by hypotheses drawn from computing, this work also tends to be more exploratory and descriptive in nature. Perhaps as a result, it is more influenced by psychological theory and is far less normative.

5.1 Learning

Mayer [Maye75, Maye81] addressed the question of what students actually learn when learning how to program. He conjectured that students learn the semantics of programming languages by likening their actions to physical or mechanical models, from which they abstract the programming language semantics. Consequently, he reasoned that instruction that provides explicit concrete models (e.g., an erasable chalkboard for memory) for the basic operations of the language would facilitate learning. His 1975 study confirmed this conjecture in the context of teaching BASIC to introductory programming students. More recently [Maye79], he proposed a detailed decomposition of the knowledge required for BASIC programming into a number of different levels, such as statement, prestatement, or transaction. He further claims that translation between these levels is a critical component of the programmer's skill. However, while this is certainly *one* way to categorize programming knowledge, Mayer has yet to provide any evidence that it is either the only way or the way that programmers actually use.

5.2 Coding

Brooks [Broo77] noted the enormous variation in performance between different programmers of comparable experience for the same tasks (estimates vary between factors of 5 and 100). Such large individual differences, he pointed out, suggest that different programmers might be using quite different strategies, in which case the detailed study of individuals would be more revealing than the aggregated behavior of several individuals as observed in classical experimental studies. He therefore gathered detailed protocols of one experienced programmer working on 23 different programming problems. Using these protocols, he developed a very detailed model of the coding process (the translation from an abstract program to the target computer language) expressed as a production system.

The primary value of such detailed models is that they force the researcher to give a complete account for at least one specific set of actual behavior in all its complexity. For reasonably complex skill, providing any sufficient model at all is a considerable challenge. The amount of information (Brooks estimates $\sim 10^4$ rules) required to account for the detailed behavior in these coding protocols is very compelling. Brooks makes a strong case not only for the necessity of this level of complexity in any descriptively adequate model but also for the necessity of some kind of structure to organize this knowledge.

5.3 Debugging

Debugging is generally considered to be the most expensive phase of software production and has been explored empirically in several studies. Some of the studies discussed earlier that used error detection measures could also be considered studies of debugging.

The earliest systematic behavioral exploration of debugging [Youn74] contrasted the debugging behavior of novice and expert programmers in several different languages. In addition to a detailed breakdown of the observed errors by the type of the statement in which they appeared, Youngs presents data which indicate that, although both groups made about the same number of errors in their original programs, the experts removed their errors much more quickly. Apparently this is due not so much to the experts' generally superior diagnostic skills, but to their ability to correct the more superficial semantic inconsistencies quickly, so they could concentrate on the more subtle logical ones.

Two studies of expert programmers detecting artificially placed bugs in FORTRAN programs from the IBM Scientific Subroutine Package [Goul74, Goul75] classified the bugs by the type of statement in which the bug was placed. Bugs placed in assignment statements were considerably harder to find than those in iterations or array subscripts. This is, however, a somewhat unsatisfying result in that one's intuition is that the "same" bug can often manifest itself in statements of quite different syntactic type, and vice versa. Atwood and Ramsey [Atwo78] further suggest that a variety of quite shallow techniques could have been used to detect many of the array and iteration bugs (e.g., scanning for incommensurate bounds of arrays and indices) but that some of the assignment bugs required a much more complete analysis of the program (including, in some cases, knowledge of its subject matter). They propose instead a representation scheme for the knowledge required to understand such programs and predict that difficulty of debugging will reflect primarily depth of embedding of the buggy component within this representation. They partially confirmed this analysis in a replication of Goul74, although the interpretation of their findings is clouded by strong differences in the results obtained for the two different programs they used.

6. CRITIQUE AND EVALUATION

This section takes up the question of how compelling a body of research these behavioral studies of programming are, considered both as a guide to computing practice and as a psychological investigation of an interesting complex skill. Unfortunately, as a group they are unsatisfactory in that they are methodologically weak, the effects they report are small, and yet they are presented as if they establish claims that go far beyond their data. These failings can, in turn, be traced to an underlying naive view of programming skill which has been shaped more by the fashions of contemporary computing practice than by any reasonable appreciation of the complexity of the behavior.

6.1 General Methodology

As a body of psychological studies, the research on programming is very weak methodologically. One of the reasons for this is that, as discussed earlier, programming is a very difficult topic on which to do experimental work. Brooks [Broo80] provides a thoughtful review of many of the technical problems associated with carrying out effective research on programming. In particular, he points out the problems associated with selecting participants, test materials, and performance measures, and how one's choices of these can affect one's findings. Brooks also alludes to the established methodological practices of other behavioral sciences and warns that

Researchers in these other behavioral disciplines have come to expect the use of such tools as an integral part of behavioral research and to judge research, in part, by the skill with which these tools are used. Behavioral research, even if done in a computer science context, will inevitably be judged by these same standards of methodological rigor. In order to maintain credibility with behavioral researchers in other areas, behavioral researchers in computer science must pay close attention to methodological issues [Broo80, p. 208].

The real issue, however, is not one of our credibility to social scientists, but the fact that methodological sloppiness introduces artifact and error into both the experimental results and the conclusions that we draw from them.

Apart from the issues raised by Brooks, the empirical research on programming is plagued by a variety of technical flaws of experimental design and analysis. Although some of these have already been discussed in the context of specific studies and further study by study treatment would be tedious, some of them are significant enough to warrant separate discussion.

6.2 Experimental Treatments

The point of an experiment is to generalize to some other (real-world) situation. Consequently, one's experimental treatments should, in some sense, be representative of that other situation both in type and in strength. Excessively forceful or weak experimental treatments limit this generalizability, as they are not representative of conditions to which programmers are subject in the real world. Overly forceful treatments bias results not simply by distorting their magnitude, but by being so salient that participants modify their behavior in response to what they believe the treatment tells them about what the experimenter wants (from which these effects have come to be known as "demand characteristics" [Orne69]). One commonly used experimental situation which lends itself to this artifact is a classroom experiment in which students are given tests or problem sets on topics which are (or are perceived to be) part of the subject matter of the class. Students in such circumstances are, understandably, very sensitive to any indications as to the "correct" response, and their behavior can easily be determined by this perception rather than by any characteristic of the task. For example, Basili and Reiter [Basi79] contrasted the amount of computer resources used to construct one moderate-size program by structured and unstructured groups in two programming courses. Students in the "structured" condition, however, were being taught techniques whose mastery was *supposed* to result in early error detection and thus reduced computer usage. Therefore, especially since all the students knew that their computer usage was being monitored, it is not at all surprising that those in the "structured" condition held their computer usage to a minimum. The situation demanded that they do so. Needless to say, it does not at all follow either that the structured methodology reduced the amount of "effort" or even that the amount of computer usage would be similarly reduced were these techniques applied in a more neutral setting.

Excessively weak manipulations simply result in no effects being observed. How weak a treatment has to be before it is unrealistic to expect it to have any effect is a matter of judgment. On the other hand, Sheppard et al., noting that less than 10 percent of their participants had had any exposure to FORTRAN77, comment that "... a lack of familiarity with the new constructs may have slowed their debugging. However, we conducted a short training session on these constructs shortly before the experiment, so lack of familiarity was probably not a significant factor," [Shep79, p. 46]. But what kind of model of programming competence makes it reasonable to expect that such a "short training session" would have any effect on performance?

6.3 Practice Effects

Many of the studies on programming have found strong, persistent practice effects. Some amount of improvement over a series of similar tasks is inevitable as the participants adapt to the experimental environment and task. For that reason it is standard practice to provide a "warm-up" period to allow this transient to dissipate. If the improvement persists strongly beyond such a warm-up period, however, it is clear that the participants are *learning* during the experiment. Generalizing to stable performance from results obtained in a learning phase is dubious, as there is usually no reason to believe either that the different behaviors being contrasted are at similar points on the learning curve or that their relative performance will remain unchanged with further learning. On the other hand, one thing that the existence of strong practice effects *does* establish is that the task is *not* one in which the participants are expert. If it were, they would be well practiced before the experiment began. Specifically, for expert programmer participants, strong practice effects indicate that the experimental task is *not* a substantial component of real-world programming. This is a very serious problem for studies like GREE77 whose main claim for generalizability to real-world programming is that the participants were expert programmers and that the experimental task is "evidently, a substantial component of 'real' programming." [GREE77, p. 108].

6.4 Individual Variability

The high degree of variability among programmers makes simple experimental designs (in which different participants are used for each condition) prone to negative conclusions, as slight systematic differences between conditions tend to be washed out by large within-condition variation. One of the standard techniques for controlling this is the use of "repeated-measures" designs, in which each participant is observed in more than one condition. However, because of the need to correct for the systematic variance between conditions that share participants, these designs require special analysis techniques. Failure to use these can both create spurious "effects" and mask real ones. Unfortunately, their interpretation is clouded in the presence of strong practice effects, such as those found in some studies of programming (see, e.g., WINE71, pp. 517 ff). Intuitively, this is because in a repeated-measures design each participant is observed in several conditions so that the idiosyncrasies of individual participants (such as prior experience) are shared by conditions across which comparisons are made. But if these idiosyncrasies are changing during the experiment, this "control" becomes a source of confounds. Counterbalancing techniques may be an effective remedy, depending on the nature of the practice effects, but less is usually known about these than about any other aspect of the behavior.

One of the more striking symptoms of high individual variability is that one occasionally finds a small number of participants whose scores on some measure are far outside the range for the group to which they belong. Such individuals are called "outliers." Their presence not only invalidates the common statistical techniques, but it can both mask real differences (by increasing the variance) and create illusory ones (if they all happen to fall in the same group). Although nonparametric statistics and/or data recoding can be used to avoid the technical problems, it is far preferable simply to discard outliers before the analysis. The reason for this is that very extreme observations strongly suggest that the individual is not typical of those to whom the results are to be generalized. For example, such an individual might be doing something quite different from the other participants, possibly as a result of having misunderstood the instructions. (The classic example is the participant who falls asleep during a reaction time experiment.) Therefore, although examining the outliers separately can often be very illuminating, their data should not be included in standard group analyses. Without the raw data it is impossible to determine to what extent outlier effects might have contaminated published behavioral studies of programming. However, very few studies make any reference to outliers having been discarded.

6.5 Significance Tests

Another technical issue in experimental analysis concerns the use of statistical tests of significance and the criteria by which one decides whether an observed difference is reliable. Psychology has adopted the standard that the probability of the null hypothesis should be below .05 in order for a researcher to conclude that an observed effect is not simply the result of chance variation. Although one can argue with the choice of this particular value, studies of programming have reported "effects" which have been demonstrated at no better than the $p < .20$ level. The problem with this practice is that significance measures are not estimates of the *size* of an effect, but estimates as to *whether one occurred* at all. Thus raising the *p* level at which effects are judged to be worthy of explanation has the effect of cluttering the literature with spurious results. The problem is particularly acute in studies which use large numbers of variables. GANN75, for example, reports over 45 tests of significance. BASI79 reports 346! One would expect 69 of these to be significant at the $p < .20$ level, even if none of their manipulations had any effect at all! Nor can one take comfort in the fact that more than 69 such effects were found. It simply raises the question of how many of them were spurious.

6.6 Effect Sizes

By far the most critical problem with the research on programming, related to the misuse of statistical tests of significance, is the weakness of its findings in terms of their size, reliability, and generalizability beyond the experimental contexts in which they were gathered. We have already pointed out that the probability level obtained from a test of significance is not a measure of effect size. Sophisticated data analysis techniques are available, with any desired level of confidence, minute systematic differences between sets of observations. For this reason methodologists have long urged *all* behavioral researchers to use (or at least report) measures of effect size. They are, however, especially important for applied research, such as that on programming, because the value of some practice is not determined by whether its use is *detectable* but by *how much difference* it makes.

Various different techniques are available to measure the size of an effect [FLEI69]. The most straightforward is the use of ratios or differences between the mean or median values of the different conditions. Although immediate, these measures are weak because they are not invariant under linear transformations of the raw data. Measures of performance are often subject to linear transformation simply by the choice of measure or data collection method. Task completion times, for example, vary substantially with changes in the required error rate, and vice versa. Therefore, unless the data measure is directly interpretable (dollars, for example), it is preferable to measure effect size by the *proportion of the observed variability accounted for* (PVA) by the effect. The merit of this measure is that it indicates to what extent the observed behavior was determined by the experimental manipulation and how much it varied freely. On the other hand, PVA is a very hard standard of evaluation. Human behavior is sufficiently complex that even the most reliable psychological phenomena rarely account for very large proportions of the variance.

The weakness of PVA as a measure of effect size is not a question of the details of the experiment itself but of what class of situations the experiment is considered to represent. One can vary the PVA in an experiment simply by varying the amount of extraneous variance. A tightly controlled experiment in which very few factors are allowed to vary will produce much higher PVAs than one in which extraneous factors vary freely. The evaluation of an experimental PVA thus involves determining (or judging) the relative importance of the factors that were controlled and those that were left free to vary. Then there is the separate question of how significant (in terms of practical value) a given real-world PVA is considered to be.

Virtually none of the studies on programming report either PVA estimates of effect size (SHEP79 is an exception) or the information which would allow them to be computed. Even when expressed as mean differences or ratios, the effects reported are generally weak. When one further considers how well they would survive the introduction of other sources of variation, the outlook is bleak indeed. Many of them did not! Of those that did, we have already commented on the size of some of them relative to "incidental" effects such as practice. The apogee of control over generalizability is reached in the Sime et al. studies on conditionals [SIME73, SIME77]. These were carried out using experimental tasks that involved "programming" a mechanical rabbit because their nonprogrammer participants were so intimidated by the idea of interacting with a computer that their nervousness dominated any effects of notation. The conclusion seems inescapable that the notation for expressing conditionals can hardly be a leading term in novice programming performance.

6.7 Theoretical Orientation

One of the most salient characteristics of the psychological research on programming is its preoccupation with the issues of contemporary computing practice. While the practical concern is understandable, many of the studies are so narrowly focused in an attempt to settle some debate among computer scientists that they are of dubious scientific value. GANN75 is the most extreme example. Varying nine independent factors simultaneously is an absurd way to do empirical research and it is inconceivable that such a design could have come from any motivation other than to make a point to the programming community. Unfortunately, the demonstration failed. As a scientific experiment it could never have succeeded.

Another consequence of this dependency on computing is that behavioral researchers tend, possibly in an attempt to make their work appeal to computer scientists, to generalize far beyond their data. We have already had cause to remark on several instances of this. The most damaging, because it will undoubtedly influence many computer scientists' ideas about behavioral research, is Shneiderman's review [SHNE80]. Detailed discussions of experimental results are interleaved with totally (empirically) unsupported opinions on programming style (e.g., sections 4.3.2 and 4.3.3 and the summaries on pages 77 and 81). Much of this material would be quite legitimate, intuitively based argument in a computer science debate. However, its presentation as part of a discussion of empirical research completely blurs the distinction between data and intuition, inviting readers to reject data that do not support their preconceptions. This makes the entire empirical enterprise moot.

6.8 Summary

Methodological critiques are of limited appeal. The reason for this one is that most of this work has never been critically reviewed *as behavioral research*. Considered as such, it has serious flaws. Unfortunately, much of it has been taken at face value and is cited, in one-sentence summary form, as having established positions for which the studies provide only slight evidence when examined closely. The absence of a critical review process, coupled with the very considerable difficulty of research in this area and the constant tendency to drift into intuitively based argument and generalize far beyond what has been established, has created a pseudopsychology of programming. At one time that might have been healthy—after all, the bulk of Weinberg's book was simply a plea for computer scientists to *consider* behavioral issues. Now, however, most computer scientists are quite sophisticated armchair psychologists. It is therefore appropriate that these psychological discussions now be established on a rather more solid footing.

7. A CHARACTERIZATION OF PROGRAMMING SKILL

The unimpressive results of behavioral research on programming could simply be the results of sloppy methodology, of a poor choice of hypotheses from computer science, and of the considerable practical difficulty of investigating complex behavior. While all of these have had their impact, the basic problem is a fundamental misunderstanding of the nature of programming skill. Specifically, most psychological research on programming assumes (usually implicitly) that different programming tasks (produced, for example, by differences in notation or practice) vary in difficulty and that the level of difficulty is an attribute of the task. Further, the motivation for (and generalizations made from) much of this work is the belief that the difficulty of large tasks is an aggregation of the difficulties of many component tasks, such as inverting a logical predicate when reasoning backward through an ELSE clause. These assumptions have formed the basis for many successful human factors investigations for a variety of different skills and are thus certainly a reasonable starting point in the absence of more specific knowledge. The role of the psychologist, in this view of the world, is to evaluate the difficulties of different aspects of the programming task so that the more difficult can be eliminated from programming systems.

The problem is that these assumptions are simply false for programming. Most notably, they give no account of the most salient single fact about programming, which is that the difficulty of programming is a very nonlinear function of the size of the problem. The primary requirement of any psychological account of programming is that it give an account of this nonlinearity. However, the simple aggregation of difficulty model provides no mechanism by which such a nonlinearity could be generated. Further, no program of research predicated on a simple composition of component task difficulties is likely to even consider this question.

More fundamentally, programming is clearly a learned skill and, therefore, what is easy or difficult is much more a function of what skills an individual has learned than of any inherent quality of the task. While some of the lower level component behaviors may vary reliably in difficulty across individuals, most programming behavior is dominated by higher level skills and knowledge whose plasticity simply does not allow such reliable differences. This simple observation casts the existing psychological research on programming in a completely different light. High individual variances, strong practice effects, and (consequently) weak findings are exactly what one would expect from studying the average performance of highly learned skills across diverse collections of individuals. Studying naive or semitrained programmers in this way does not avoid this problem but merely measures the common tendencies that result from the use of shared cultural skills. In the course of learning to program, however, these are rapidly displaced by the special-

purpose skills that constitute expertise in a particular environment. To characterize the (slight) differences found between groups of novices as deep principles of programming skill (or major sources of variance in expert performance) is simply foolish.

The evidence for a characterization of programming as a "learned skill" is mainly negative, as such a characterization says more about what a skill is not than about what it is. Experimental demonstrations of the plasticity of programming performance with training would provide direct support. However, the most compelling subjective demonstration for the experienced programmer is to introspect (an old psychological technique now fallen into disfavor) while formulating a procedure which, given a set of N positive numbers, finds the largest. Nearly all experienced programmers will immediately produce the following procedure, notational variants aside.

$$m \leftarrow 0$$
$$\text{for } i \text{ from } 1 \text{ to } N \text{ do (if } a_i > m \text{ then } m \leftarrow a_i)$$

Consider how that procedure could have been generated or understood. One way, the way that you might believe it was done if you read the literature on programming that is written by computer scientists, is by formulating a loop invariant. For this loop the appropriate invariant is that, at the end of the kth pass through the loop, $m \geq a_j$ for $j \in [1, k]$. Once formulated, that invariant can be proved by induction. Having been proved for $k = N$ and now constitutes a proof that m is a maximum of the set, which is the desired result.

The problem is that nobody does it that way. And the reason nobody does it that way, except in introductory programming courses, is that it takes too long and is far too complicated. If you know how to program, you would neither generate this program nor synthesize an understanding of it. You would *know* the answer. You would *recognize* the problem, key directly into that knowledge, and pull out a working procedure. The compelling subjective evidence for this, alluded to above, is the complete absence of any introspective trace whatsoever!

The immediacy with which the expert programmer "solves" problems of this sort indicates that the programmer's expertise is made up of an enormous number of interrelated pieces of knowledge. The primary piece of direct behavioral evidence for this position is Shneiderman's replication [SHNE76] for programming of Chase and Simon's classic study on memory for chess positions [CHAS73]. In both these studies it was found that experts in a particular domain could memorize information from that domain (i.e., a program or a chess position) far better than novices, provided that the information was appropriately structured. If the structure were made random (by shuffling the statements of the program or rearranging the chess pieces), the advantage of the expert would be greatly reduced. The standard interpretation of this result is that the expert has no better memory than the novice, but rather an elaborate knowledge structure in terms of which correspondingly structured items can be very efficiently encoded. Further support for the notion of a large knowledge base comes from Brooks' study of coding discussed earlier [BROO77], in which he estimated that ~10^4 elementary rules would be required to capture the knowledge used in his protocols.

While there is currently little evidence as to how these knowledge structures are organized, some recent work in automatic programming based on "natural deduction" techniques (e.g., BARS79, RICH78) and programming methodology (e.g., FLOY79) is suggestive. This work shares the notion that programming knowledge can be thought of as a collection of units ("frames," "paradigms," "schemata"), each of which is organized as a program fragment, abstracted to some degree, together with a set of propositions about its behavior and rules for combining it with others, and indexed in terms of the problem classes for which it is appropriate. The *maximum* procedure discussed above, if not stored directly, can be derived by (or described as) a single transformation of a *reduction* schema (so called after the APL operator) or a two-step transformation of various *bounded iteration* schemata. The descriptive econ-

omy and structuring power of this basic idea make it attractive to programming theorists. There is currently no direct empirical evidence for it as a behavioral theory of programming. On the other hand, it does provide a theory which is plausible and sufficient (in that the automatic programming systems which represent their knowledge of programming this way demonstrate that this representation can be used to write programs) and can account for the nonlinear growth of difficulty with size in terms of the behavior of the appropriate deduction algorithms.

However programmers' knowledge bases are actually organized, their existence and size seem clear. Hypotheses which posit differences in either individual aptitude or task difficulty are therefore, at best, extremely difficult to investigate, as the enormous size of the knowledge bases being drawn on imply that different individuals approach the "same" task with vastly different resources. Comparing their behavior is like contrasting the work of two tile layers, each of whom has covered an equivalent wall, working with radically different sizes and colors of tiles. Similarity of pattern is unlikely.

8. HOW TO PROCEED

The diversity of goals which motivate the behavioral exploration of "programming" suggests that programming may be an equally diverse collection of skills. Most studies of programming difficulty are prefaced, by way of justification, with allusions to the "software crisis" or the need for widespread procedural literacy. These, however, are quite different concerns, much better addressed by targeted research than by a vague assault on the "difficulty of programming."

If one's concern is the software crisis and the rapidly increasing cost of program development, the appropriate strategy is to determine whence that cost is coming, rather than assume that it is the performance of the individual programmer. Determining the source of the cost requires detailed studies of large programming projects—a job for a "cost anthropologist," not a psychologist. Such studies are expensive, difficult, and subject to the caveats mentioned earlier that apply to all *in situ* studies, which is why so little work of this type has been done.

On the other hand, if one's concern is procedural literacy, the key question is the determinants of the learning behavior of novices. There is no reason to believe that these have anything to do with the determinants of expert performance. As novices do not have the specialized knowledge and skills of the expert, one might expect their performance to be largely a function of how well they can bring their skills from other areas to bear [SHEI80]. MAYE75 can be interpreted as providing some support for this point of view.

Finally, given that the performance of the expert programmer is the topic of interest, the appropriate approach at this stage of our knowledge is the detailed study of individual expert performance (in the style of BROO77) in an attempt to identify the components of expert skill. Our primary need at the moment is for a theory of programming skill that can provide both general guidance for system designers and specific guidance to psychologists selecting topics for detailed study. The experimental investigation of such factors as the style of conditional notation is premature without some theory which gives some account of why they might be significant factors in programmer behavior. The existing literature of attempts to provide complete performance models of complex skills (e.g., CARD80, BROW78) suggests that even broad theories will have to be very much more complex than the simplistic hypotheses that have guided the work on programming so far.

ACKNOWLEDGMENTS

Many people have helped shape this paper. In particular, I would like to express my gratitude to Ron Kaplan, Joanne Martin, and the referees for their comments; to Tom Moran, the editor of this special issue, for both detailed commentary and extraordinary editorial patience; and to my colleagues at Cognitive and Instructional Sciences at Xerox PARC for the supportive, yet critical, environment without which topics of this complexity would seem more intimidating than exciting.

REFERENCES

ATWO78   Atwood, M. E., and Ramsey, H. R. "Cognitive structures in the comprehension and memory of computer programs: An investigation of computer debugging." Tech. Rep. TR-78-A21, U.S. Army Research Institute for the Behavioral and Social Sciences, Alexandria, Va, 1978.

BARS79   Barstow, D. *Knowledge based program construction*, North-Holland, Amsterdam, 1979.

BASI79   Basili, V. R., and Reiter, R. W. "An investigation of human factors in software development," *Computer* 12 (1979), 21-40.

BROO75   Brooks, F. P. *The mythical man-month*, Addison-Wesley, Reading, Mass., 1975.

BROO77   Brooks, R. E. "Towards a theory of the cognitive processes in computer programming," *Int. J. Man-Mach. Stud.* 9 (1977), 737-751.

BROO80   Brooks, R. E. "Studying programmer behavior experimentally: The problems of proper methodology," *Commun. ACM 23*, 4 (April 1980), 207-213.

BROW78   Brown, J. S., and Burton, R. R. "Diagnostic models for procedural bugs in basic mathematical skills," *Cognitive Sci.* 2 (1978), 155-192.

CAMP79   Campbell, D. T., and Cook, T. D. *Quasi-experimentation: Design and analysis for field settings*, Rand McNally, Chicago, Ill., 1979.

CARD80   Card, S. K., Moran, T. P., and Newell, A. "Computer text editing: An information processing analysis of a routine cognitive skill," *Cognitive Psychol.* 12 (1980), 32-74.

CHAS73   Chase, W. G., and Simon, H. A. "Perception in chess," *Cognitive Psychol.* 4 (1973), 55-81.

DIJK68   Dijkstra, E. W. "GOTO statement considered harmful," *Commun. ACM 11*, 3 (March 1968), 147-148.

DIJK76   Dijkstra, E. W. *A discipline of programming*, Prentice-Hall, Englewood Cliffs, N.J., 1976.

FLEI69   Fleiss, J. L. "Estimating the magnitude of experimental effects," *Psychol. Bull.* 72 (1969), 273-276.

FLOY79   Floyd, R. W. "The paradigms of programming," *Commun. ACM 22*, 8 (Aug. 1979), 455-460.

GANN75   Gannon, J. D., and Horning, J. J. "The impact of language design on the production of reliable software," *IEEE Trans. Softw. Eng. SE-1* (1975), 179-191.

GANN76   Gannon, J. D. "An experiment for the evaluation of language features," *Int. J. Man-Mach. Stud.* 8 (1976), 61-73.

GANN77   Gannon, J. D. "An experimental evaluation of data type conventions," *Commun. ACM 20*, 8 (Aug. 1977), 584-595.

GOUL74   Gould, J. D., and Drongowski, P. "An exploratory investigation of computer program debugging," *Hum. Factors* 16 (1974), 258-277.

GOUL75   Gould, J. D. "Some psychological evidence on how people debug computer programs," *Int. J. Man-Mach. Stud.* 7 (1975), 151-182.

GREE77   Green, T. R. G. "Conditional program statements and their comprehensibility to professional programmers," *J. Occup. Psychol.* 50 (1977), 93-109.

KERN74   Kernighan, B. W., and Plauger, P. J. *The elements of programming style*, McGraw-Hill, New York, 1974.

LOVE77   Love, T. "Relating individual differences in computer programming performance to human information processing abilities," Ph.D. dissertation, Univ. Washington, 1977.

LUCA76   Lucas, H. C., and Kaplan, R. B. "A structured programming experiment," *Comput. J.* 19 (1976), 136-138.

MAYE75   Mayer, R. E. "Different problem solving competencies established in learning computer programming with and without meaningful models," *J. Educ. Psychol.* 67 (1975), 725-734.

MAYE79   Mayer, R. E. "A psychology of learning BASIC," *Commun. ACM 22*, (Nov. 1979), 589-593.

MAYE81   Mayer, R. E. "The psychology of learning computer programming by novices," *Comput. Surv.* 13 (March 1981), 121-141.

ORNE69   Orne, M. T. "Demand characteristics and the concept of quasi-controls," in *Artifact in behavioral research*, R. Rosenthal and R. L. Rosnow, Eds., Academic Press, New York, 1969.

RICH78   Rich, C., and Schrobe, H. "Initial report on a Lisp programmer's apprentice," *IEEE Trans. Softw. Eng. SE-4* (1978), 456-467.

SACK70   Sackman, H. *Man-computer problem solving*, Auerbach, Princeton, N.J., 1970.

SHEI80   Sheil, B. "Teaching procedural literacy," in *Proc. ACM Annual Conf.*, 1980, pp. 125-126.

SHEP79   Sheppard, S., Curtis, B., Milliman, P., and Love, T. "Modern coding practices and programmer performance," *Computer* 12 (1979), 41-49.

SHNE76   Shneiderman, B. "Exploratory experiments in programmer behavior," *Int. J. Comput. Inf. Sci.* 5 (1976), 123-143.

SHNE77a Shneiderman, B. "Measuring computer program quality and comprehension," *Int. J. Man-Mach. Stud.* 9 (1977), 465-478.

SHNE77b Shneiderman, B., Mayer, R., McKay, D., and Heller, P. "Experimental investigations of the utility of detailed flowcharts in programming," *Commun. ACM 20*, 6 (June 1977), 373-381.

SHNE79   Shneiderman, B., and Mayer, R. "Syntactic/semantic interactions in programmer behavior: A model and experimental results," *Int. J. Comput. Inf. Sci.* 7 (1979), 219-239.

SHNE80   Shneiderman, B. *Software psychology*, Winthrop, Cambridge, Mass., 1980.

SIME73   Sime, M. E., Green, T. R. G., and Guest, D. J. "Psychological evaluation of two conditional constructs used in computer languages," *Int. J. Man-Mach. Stud.* 5 (1973), 123-143.

SIME77   Sime, M. E., Green, T. R. G., and Guest, D. J. "Scope marking in computer conditionals—A psychological evaluation," *Int. J. Man-Mach. Stud.* 9 (1977), 107-118.

WEIN71   Weinberg, G. M. *The psychology of computer programming*, Van Nostrand Reinhold, New York, 1971.

WEIS74   Weissman, L. "A methodology for studying the psychological complexity of computer programs," Ph.D. dissertation, Univ. Toronto, Canada, 1974.

WINE71   Winer, B. J. *Statistical principles in experimental design*, McGraw-Hill, New York, 1971.

YOUN74   Youngs, E. A. "Human errors in programming," *Int. J. Man-Mach. Stud.* 6 (1974), 361-376.

Chapter 5

Models of Computer User and Usage

We have seen that many of the empirical studies of interactive computer use lack a theoretical orientation — data is collected, but there is no underlying model of the process being studied, to confirm or refute. The branch of modern psychology that attempts to correct this failing is *information processing* psychology (Lindsay and Norman, 1977; Gardner, 1987). It views man as an information processing system which is a component of a larger system consisting of some collection of human beings and physical entities. Man is in turn viewed as consisting of perceptual or sensing, cognitive or processing, memory, and motor or response subsystems. An understanding of the basic characteristics, strengths, and weaknesses of these subsystems and of the methods of describing and measuring their characteristics is essential to the understanding of human-computer interaction and to the appropriate design of human-computer interfaces. Van Cott and Warrick (1972) introduces some of the key concepts, as do the human factors references listed earlier.

Man as an Information Processor

The deepest and most comprehensive application of information processing psychology to the study of human-computer interaction has been carried out by Stuart K. Card, Thomas P. Moran, Allen Newell, and their co-workers. Their work has been documented in a series of papers published over the last ten years and at length in book form in Card, Moran, and Newell (1983). We include in this volume, excerpts from one paper and complete reprints of two others. In doing so, we present some of the major results and themes from the book.

The authors state in their preface (p. vii) that their purpose is "to help lay a scientific foundation for an applied psychology concerned with the human users of interactive computer systems." They insist that this psychology be "theory-based, in the sense of articulating a mechanism underlying the observed phenomena" (p. 13). But one of their ultimate goals is a pragmatic one, to develop an applied psychology that is "relevant to design," for "design is where the action is in the human-computer interface" (p. 11). They illustrate what they have in mind with the following scenario (p. 9):

> A system designer, the head of a small team writing the specifications for a desktop calendar-scheduling system, is choosing between having users type a key for each command and having them point to a menu with a light-pen. On his whiteboard, he lists some representative tasks users of his system must perform. In two columns, he writes the steps needed by the "key-command" and "menu" options. From a handbook, he culls the times for each step, adding the step times to get total task times. The key-command system takes less time, but only slightly. But, applying the analysis from another section of the handbook, he calculates that the menu system will be faster to learn; in fact, it will be learnable in half the time. He has estimated previously that an effective menu system will require a more expensive processor: 20% more memory, 100% more microcode memory, and a more expensive display. Is the extra expenditure worthwhile? A few more minutes of calculation and he realizes the startling fact that, for the manufacturing quantities anticipated, training costs for the key-command system will exceed unit manufacturing costs! The increase

in hardware costs would be much more than balanced by the decrease in training costs, even before considering the increase in market that can be expected for a more easily learned system. Are there advantages to the key-command system in other areas, which need to be balanced? He proceeds with other analyses, considering the load on the user's memory, the potential for user errors, and the likelihood of fatigue. In the next room, the Pascal compiler hums idly, unused, awaiting his decision.

Card, Moran, and Newell then go on to argue that a useful applied information processing psychology must be based on *task analysis*, *calculation*, and *approximation* (p. 10). It must be based on task analysis because human users "attempt to adapt to the task environment to attain their goals." It must be based on calculation because "the ability to do calculations is the heart of useful, engineering-oriented applied science." It must be based on approximation because "if calculations are going to be made rapidly, they are necessarily going to be oversimplified."

The Model Human Processor

Card, Moran and Newell begin their work by reviewing and codifying the existing scientific base that is relevant to their applied psychology. The central idea is that of the *Model Human Processor*, an idealized information processing model of the human perceptual, motor, and cognitive systems. They then proceed to demonstrate its utility with a set of "finger exercises" applying the Model Human Processor to the prediction of human performance in areas of perception, motor skill, simple decisions, learning, and retrieval that they view as bearing potential relevance to human-computer interaction. Both the Model Human Processor and the examples of typical applications are summarized in our excerpts from Card (1984), as is some empirical data on the performance of a number of text selection devices including the mouse which originally appeared in longer form in Card, English, and Burr (1978), a paper included as a reading in Chapter 8: The Haptic Channel. A far more detailed presentation of this material is Card, Moran, and Newell (1983).

The Analysis of a Routine Cognitive Skill

The view of man as an information processing system leads naturally to attempts to formalize his procedures in carrying out certain tasks interactively with a computer. Card, Moran, and Newell (1980b) shows that such attempts, however preliminary and however crude, can already lead to models with some predictive power. The task is text editing, which they categorize as a *routine cognitive skill*. The model they develop is known as GOMS; it is a representation of a user's cognitive struc-

ture in terms of *goals*, *operators*, *methods* for achieving the goals, and *selection rules* for choosing among different possible methods. Their results include predictions both of the *methods* that a user employs to carry out certain tasks and the *time* that it takes to accomplish those tasks. The work is particularly profound in that it describes text editing at a number of levels of detail, starting at a gross level and progressing to finer representations and analyses. They refer (Card, Moran, and Newell, 1983, p. 162) to the levels as the *unit-task* level, the *functional* level, the *argument* level, and the *keystroke* level. The surprising and important result is that in many cases the model's accuracy is independent of the granularity of analysis.

This important paper is discussed further and included as a reading in Chapter 6: Cognition and Human Information Processing.

The Keystroke-Level Model

The level that the experimenters studied in the greatest detail could be termed the *lexical* level: the individual keystrokes, mouse movements, and other motor activities of which a dialogue is ultimately comprised. Our next reading, Card, Moran, and Newell (1980a), is a thorough theoretical and empirical study of keystroke-level models and methods for predicting *user performance time* with interactive systems. The keystroke-level model assumes a task, a system's command language, estimates of motor skill parameters of the user and response time parameters of the system, and methods to be used for the task. Given this, it allows one to predict the time it will take an expert user to perform the given task using these methods on this system. Their paper is perhaps the best example of a development of the kind of "cognitive engineering" tools that they seek, tools that allow them to predict performance time, to define system performance benchmarks, to perform a parametric analysis and express a prediction as a function of particular task variables, and to perform a sensitivity analysis and derive how changes in predictions depend upon changes in task or model parameters. Another interesting aspect of the study is the investigation of how successively greater approximations in the model affects the predictive power of the result.

Allen and Scerbo (1983) provide additional data, based on applying the model to a text editor, as well as a critique of the model. Some of their objections seem to be based on a misunderstanding of the original work and how it is to be applied. However, they make a number of useful suggestions dealing with ways in which it should be possible to increase the model's predictive accuracy. These proposals need to be evaluated in the light of the original supposition of Card, Moran and Newell (1980a, p.409), that a technique must be "quick and easy to use" in order to be "useful to practicing computer system designers."

Other Modeling Paradigms

The paradigms of Card, Moran, and Newell are not the only ones that have been proposed. We now take a brief look at some other important approaches.

The predictive power of simple BNF grammatical models of dialogue syntax was investigated in some early and influential studies by Reisner (1977, 1981, 1984). Her goal was to show that formal descriptions of the "action languages" of interactive system users have "psychological validity" in that they could be used to predict the relative ease of learning and remembering particular command sequences, the relative times required to carry them out, and the relative likelihood of making errors. She noted that such endeavors, if successful, would have value for a number of different reasons (Reisner, 1981, p. 237):

- We would have an analytical tool with which we could analyze a paper and pencil representation of a system in advance of building it.

- Use of the formalism for expressing interface designs would force us to be precise.

- Use of a formal description would help us "in formulating clear, testable hypotheses about design decisions."

- Use of the formalism may help us to discover "quantifiable, general, intrinsic properties of easy-to-use systems."

- We can automatically manipulate descriptions of designs expressed in a formal notation.

- The formalism may help us to explain user errors.

An even more ambitious attempt carried out in this spirit is the Command Language Grammar (CLG) of Moran (1981). CLG describes the user interface of an interactive computer system in terms of six levels, each level being a refinement of the previous level. These are:

- Task Level, listing the set of tasks the system is intended to accomplish.

- Semantic Level, specifying the conceptual objects manipulated by the system, and the conceptual actions the system can perform.

- Syntactic Level, defining the command language with which the user communicates to the system.

- Interaction Level, specifying the physical actions associated with each element of the Syntactic Level.

- Spatial Layout Level, describing the arrangement of the input and output devices and the graphics display.

- Device Level, specifying "all the remaining physical features."

Moran (1981) illustrates this formalism by a detailed presentation of the first four levels of a system designed to help a user manage a file of electronic mail messages. He closes by listing a set of weaknesses and remaining problems with CLG as presented, and by arguing the significance of the approach in terms of three points of view: linguistic, psychological, and design.

Another approach to the linguistic description of command languages is that of Payne and Green (1983; Green and Payne, 1984). Their goal is a formal representation of what they call the "grammar in the head." They argue that any notation that is proposed must reflect the importance of *consistency* as an organizing principle of effective command languages. Towards this end, they propose a new formalism, *set-grammars*, in which the re-write rules operate upon sets of similar grammatical objects rather than individual nonterminals or terminal symbols. They show how such representations can explain a number of empirical results relating to the learning and remembering of command languages. Some of these results were previously reported, and some were new. In more recent work (Payne and Green, 1986), they extend their formalism into a new system called *task-action grammars*, one which has a deeper concept of the semantics of tasks than does the previous approach, and which can therefore make a more comprehensive set of predictions about the relative learnability of different task languages.

Kieras and Polson (1983, 1985) propose an approach to the formal analysis of *user complexity*, "the complexity of a device or system from the point of view of the user." Two different models are required, a *production system* model to describe the user's knowledge of how to use the device, and a *generalized transition network* model to represent the device itself. Polson and Kieras (1985, 1987) show how a production system model can be used to predict empirical results about text editing learning, performance, and skill transfer.

John, Rosenbloom, and Newell (1985) apply procedural descriptions of computer command abbreviation techniques expressed in a programming pseudo-language and a GOMS theory of stimulus-response compatibility (see Chapter 6: Cognition and Human Information Processing) to predict times to type the first letter of an abbreviation and to complete the typing of an abbreviation. More recent work by John and Newell (1987) extends the analysis to predicting the time to recall computer command abbreviations.

Finally, Norman (1984, 1985, 1986) presents a model of the performance of a task in terms of various sequences chosen from among seven stages of user activities: 1) establishing a goal; 2) forming an intention; 3) specifying an action sequence; 4) executing the action; 5) perceiving the system state; 6) interpreting the state; and, 7) evaluating the system state with respect to the goals and intentions. Although not currently expressed in quantitative terms, the model is used qualitatively to provide useful insights throughout the recent book edited by Norman and Draper (1986).

Summary and Conclusions

The work by Card, Moran, and Newell is a landmark achievement in the study of human-computer interaction. It is the first comprehensive attempt at a quantitative theory of human-computer interaction. It is also a theory aimed at assisting the process of design, for, as Stu Card expressed so eloquently in a panel at SIGGRAPH '87, "Theory adds wings to intuition." Yet perhaps more significant than what has been achieved is what remains to be done. Card, Moran, and Newell focus typically on routine cognitive skills, whereas much of computer use consists of *problem solving* behaviour in which the appropriateness of the user's *mental model* is essential to success. They look primarily at expert users, whereas many of the most difficult issues arise with *novices*, for whom considerations of the ease of *learning* and *skill acquisition* are paramount, or with *casual users*, for whom *memory* can be the bottleneck on performance. Card, Moran and Newell usually study error-free use, despite the significance of *errors* in almost all computer use. They have also typically worked with text editing applications, leaving generalizability of the results to other domains of interactive computer use an open question.

Despite the promise of the more recent work by Payne and Green, Kieras and Polson, and John, Rosenbloom, and Newell, formal models have thus far contributed little to our understanding of deeper cognitive issues such as problem solving, learning, and memory as they manifest themselves in human-computer interaction. Yet cognitive psychologists understand a great deal about these areas. We shall therefore review some of this knowledge in Chapter 6: Cognition and Human Information Processing. After doing so, we shall in Case Study C: Text Editors and Word Processors return to the study of text editing, for it illustrates the role of models, the application of empirical evaluation, and the relevance of the key issues from modern cognitive psychology.

Readings

Card, S.K. (1984). Human Limits and the VDT Computer Interface. In Bennett, John, Case, Donald, Sandelin, Jon, & Smith, Michael (1984), *Visual Display Terminals: Usability Issues and Health Concerns*, Englewood Cliffs, N.J.: Prentice-Hall, 117-155, only pp. 124-143 plus Figures D-16 and D-17 included here.

Card, S.K., Moran, T.P., & Newell, A. (1980a). The Keystroke-Level Model for User Performance Time with Interactive Systems. *Communications of the ACM* 23(7), 396-410.

References

Allen, R.B. & Scerbo, M.W. (1983). Details of Command-Language Keystrokes. *ACM Transactions on Office Information Systems* 1(2), April 1983, 159-178.

Card, S.K. (1984). Human Limits and the VDT Computer Interface. In Bennett, John, Case, Donald, Sandelin, Jon, & Smith, Michael (1984), *Visual Display Terminals: Usability Issues and Health Concerns*, Englewood Cliffs, N.J.: Prentice-Hall, 117-155.

Card, S.K., English, W.K., & Burr, B.J. (1978). Evaluation of Mouse, Rate-controlled Isometric Joystick, Step Keys, and Text Keys for Text Selection on a CRT. *Ergonomics* 21, 601-613.

Card, S.K., Moran, T.P., & Newell, A. (1980a). The Keystroke-Level Model for User Performance Time with Interactive Systems. *Communications of the ACM* 23(7), 396-410.

Card, S.K., Moran, T.P., & Newell, A. (1980b). Computer Text-Editing: An Information Processing Analysis of a Routine Cognitive Skill. *Cognitive Psychology* 12, 32-74.

Card, S.K., Moran, T.P., & Newell, A. (1983). *The Psychology of Human-Computer Interaction*, Hillsdale, N.J.: Lawrence Erlbaum Associates.

Gardner, H. (1987). *The Mind's New Science*, Second Edition, New York: Basic Books.

Green, T.R.G. & Payne, S.J. (1984). Organization and Learnability in Computer Languages. *International Journal of Man-Machine Studies* 21, 7-18.

John, Bonnie E. & Newell, Allen (1987). Predicting the Time to Recall Computer Command Abbreviations. *CHI + GI '87 Proceedings*, 33-40.

John, Bonnie E., Rosenbloom, Paul S., & Newell, Allen (1985). A Theory of Stimulus-Response Compatibility Applied to Human-Computer Interaction. *CHI '85 Proceedings*, 213-219.

Kieras, David & Polson, Peter G. (1983). A Generalized Transition Network Representation for Interactive Systems. *CHI '83 Proceedings*, 103-106.

Kieras, David & Polson, Peter G. (1985). An Approach to the Formal Analysis of User Complexity. *International Journal of Man-Machine Studies* 22, 365-394.

Lindsay, P.H. & Norman, D.A. (1977). *Human Information Processing: An Introduction to Psychology*. Second Edition, New York: Academic Press.

Moran, Thomas P. (1981). The Command Language Grammer: A Representation of the User Interface of Interactive Computer Systems. *International Journal of Man-Machine Studies* 15, 3-50.

Norman, D.A. (1984). Stages and Levels in Human-Machine Interaction. *International Journal of Man-Machine Studies* 21, 365-375.

Norman, D.A. (1985). Four Stages of User Activities. *Human-Computer Interaction — Interact '84*, 507-511.

Norman, D.A. (1986). Cognitive Engineering. In Norman, D.A. & Draper, S.W. (1986), *User Centered System Design*, Hillsdale, N.J.: Lawrence Erlbaum Associates, 31-61.

Norman, D.A. & Draper, S.W. (1986). *User Centered System Design*, Hillsdale, N.J.: Lawrence Erlbaum Associates.

Payne, S.J. & Green, T.R.G. (1983). The User's Perception of the Interaction Language: A Two-Level Model. *CHI '83 Proceedings*, 202-206.

Payne, Stephen J. & Green, T.R.G. (1986). Task-Action Grammars: A Model of the Mental Representation of Task Languages. *Human-Computer Interaction* 2(2), 93-133.

Polson, Peter G., Bovair, Susan, & Kieras, David (1987). Transfer Between Text Editors. *CHI + GI '87 Proceedings*, 27-32.

Polson, Peter G. & Kieras, David E. (1985). A Quantitative Model of the Learning and Performance of Text Editing Knowledge. *CHI '85 Proceedings*, 207-212.

Reisner, Phyllis (1977). Use of Psychological Experimentation as an Aid to Development of a Query Language. *IEEE Transactions on Software Engineering* SE-3(3), May 1977, 218-229.

Reisner, Phyllis (1981). Formal Grammar and Human Factors Design of an Interactive Graphics System. *IEEE Transactions on Software Engineering* SE-7(2), March 1981, 229-240.

Reisner, Phyllis (1984). Formal Grammar as a Tool for Analyzing Ease of Use: Some Fundamental Concepts. In Thomas, J.C. & Shneider, M.L. (Eds.), *Human Factors in Computer Systems*, Norwood, New Jersey: Ablex Publishing Corp.

Van Cott, Harold P. & Warrick, Melvin J. (1972). "Man as a System Component." In Van Cott, H.P. & Kinkade, R.G. (Eds.), *Human Engineering Guide to Equipment Design*, Revised Edition, American Institutes for Research, 1972, 17-39.

USER INFORMATION-PROCESSING MECHANISMS

Anyone who has ever tried to improve his design effort by perusing the experimental psychology literature knows what a frustrating experience that can be. Four main difficulties stand out:

1. Relevant results are widely scattered.
2. They often apply with confidence only to certain narrow experimental paradigms.
3. The worth of a model is often assessed only by fitting it with parameters derived from the data itself.
4. Models are assessed in terms of statistically significant differences between theory and data.

On the contrary, for application in computer science:

1. We need a unified model of the human.
2. The model should be applicable across various tasks.
3. It should allow the calculation of new results using tables of parameters already in hand.
4. We want to know how good an approximation the model is to the observable behavior.

It is especially important to understand that "statistical significance" has only a limited, secondary role in evaluating system designs and theories. After all, if the number of trials or the number of subjects is but increased sufficiently, a significant difference between one thing and another will almost always ensue. On the other hand, a difference between two systems significant at $p < 0.0001$ might only be a matter of 1% and might easily be irrelevant; a matter (and here is the important part) to be decided on the basis of the content of a problem rather than on the statistics alone. The proper role of statistics is to make sure that a certain magnitude of effect, interesting itself in the context of a particular problem, is not an artifact due to chance variation. Statistics cannot tell us mechanically, without regard to content, what is interesting and what is not. For example, a theory that could predict within $\pm 50\%$ at design time the number of hours required to learn a new computer system, for some appropriate technical specification of the system and intended class of users, would be a great scientific advance of considerable practical use. Yet the theory would surely fail all devisable statistical tests for being "significantly different from the data."

It is in this spirit of task analysis, calculation, and approximation that the following model of human information processing is presented. The model is not intended as a detailed model of what is really "in the head" so much as an engineering approximation from which constraints and properties of human-computer interfaces can be derived. For these reasons, accuracy has purposefully been traded for simplicity and wider coverage.

The Model Human Processor

Consider the human processor from the point of view of a computer scientist understanding a complicated computer system. The computer scientist often finds it helpful to suppress the details of computer systems in order to be able to understand how the larger system fits together. One way to do this is to employ a technique such as the PMS notation (Siewiorek, Bell, and Newell, 1981) that conceives the system in terms of processors, memories, and switches. In a similar spirit, we can give a description, which we shall call the Model Human Processor, in terms of processors, memories, and principles of operations. The processors and memories, Figure D-6(a), summarize properties of the human functional information-processing architecture. The principles of operation, Figure D-6(b), give some additional principles for predicting human performance that are not easily expressible architecturally.

In this view, the human contains three processors—a Perceptual Processor, a Cognitive Processor and a Motor Processor—all operating in "pipelined parallel." That is, a person can read one word while saying the previously read word, both at the same time but only under the right circumstances. We can also distinguish four memories. Two of the memories are sensory buffers for the eyes and ears. To continue the computer metaphor, they are the sample-and-hold circuits and the analogue-to-digital converters for the eyes and ears. Another memory is the Working Memory, a sort of cache memory—the place where recently experienced and currently active information is quickly accessible. And finally there is Long-Term Memory, in which the user holds his general store of knowledge. We should not think of Working Memory and Long-Term Memory as separate sets of storage registers; it is closer to current opinion in psychology to consider Long-Term Memory as a directed graph of semantically linked nodes and of Working Memory as a small subset of those which are "activated" at any given moment.

To illustrate the model, the boxes in Figure D-7 trace how a user is supposed to do the simple task of pressing a button whenever a certain letter appears on his VDT: a letter appears on the screen. One Perceptual Processor cycle later, the letter has been transmitted to the Visual Image Store, in which it is represented as some physical code (that is, in some form affected by the intensity of the light and other physical variables) and very quickly thereafter (at a rate below the time grain of the model) a symbolic (not affected by physical intensity) version of the letter appears in Working Memory. It requires one Cognitive Processor cycle for the user to make the decision to push the Yes button and one Motor Processor cycle actually to push it.

Processor Parameters

In addition to the qualitative description of the human processor we have just given, the Model Human Processor includes a few quantitative parameters. We can characterize the processors by their cycle time, and the

Excerpted from Card, S.K. (1984). Human Limits and the VDT Computer Interface. In Bennett, John, Case, Donald, Sandelin, Jon, and Smith, Michael (Eds.) Visual Display Terminals: Usability Issues and Health Concerns. Englewood Cliffs, N.J.,

P1. Variable Perceptual Processor Rate Principle. The Perceptual Processor cycle time τ_P varies inversely with stimulus intensity.

P2. Encoding Specificity Principle. Specific encoding operations performed on what is perceived determine what is stored, and what is stored determines what retrieval cues are effective in providing access to what is stored.

P3. Discrimination Principle. The difficulty of memory retrieval is determined by the candidates that exist in the memory, relative to the retrieval clues.

P4. Variable Cognitive Processor Rate Principle. The Cognitive Processor cycle time τ_C is shorter when greater effort is induced by increased task demands or information loads; it also diminishes with practice.

P5. Fitts's Law. The time T_{pos} to move the hand to a target of size S which lies a distance D away is given by

$$T_{pos} = I_M \log_2(D/S + .5), \text{ where } I_M = 100 \,[70 \sim 120] \text{ msec/bit.}$$

P6. Power Law of Practice. The time T_n on perform a task to the nth trial follows a power law:

$$T_n = T_1 n^{-\alpha}, \text{ where } \alpha = .4 \,[.2 \sim .6].$$

P7. The Uncertainty Principle. Decision time T increases with uncertainty about the judgment or decision to be made,

$$T = I_C H,$$

where H is the information-theoretic entropy of the decision and $I_C = 150 \,[0 \sim 157]$ msec/bit. For n equally probably alternatives (Hick's Law),

$$H = \log_2(n + 1).$$

For n alternatives with different probabilities of occurring p_i,

$$H = \sum_i p_i \cdot \log_2(1/p_i + 1).$$

P8. Rationality Principle. A person acts so as to attain his goals through rational action, given the structure of the task and his inputs of information and bounded by limitations on his knowledge and processing ability:

Goals + Task + Operators + Inputs + Knowledge + Process-Limits → Behavior.

P9. The Problem Space Principle. The rational activity in which people engage to solve a problem can be described in terms of (1) a set of states of knowledge, (2) operators for changing one state into another, (3) constraints on applying operators, and (4) control knowledge for deciding which operator to apply next.

Figure D–6(b). The Model Human Processor.

simplification of the psychological literature. The full review is contained in Card, Moran, and Newell (1983). Here I will simply summarize the major points.

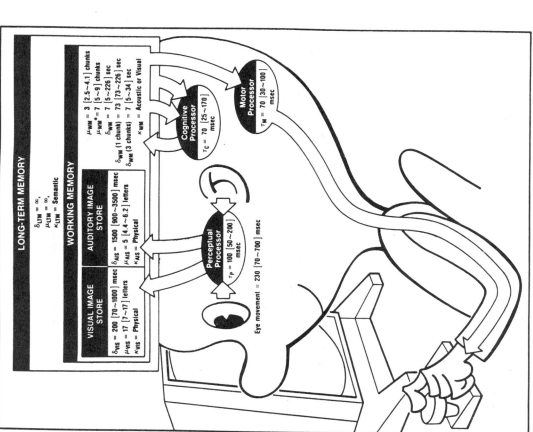

Figure D–6(a). The Model Human Processor.

memories by their decay rates, their capacities, and the codings they use. All of these parameters, summarized in Figure D–6 (a), arise from a review and

as the duration of a flashed light is less than about 100 milliseconds (msec), in our terms one Perceptual Processor cycle, one light will look the same as another light twice as intense but only one half as long. This is a special case of the more general observation that two perceptual events occurring within about 100 msec of each other will under most conditions be combined into a single perceptual event. Another line of evidence concerns what is known as perceptual masking. A person shown a briefly flashed letter and then 100 msec later shown a circle surrounding the letter will not register the letter. Intriguingly, the alpha rhythm of the brain, varying between 77 ~ 125 msec (Harter, 1967), is also in this range.

These experiments, and others, lead us to two conclusions. First, a number of quite different techniques converge to produce numbers which tend to be a little less than 0.1 sec per cycle. Second, various ways of estimating these numbers give somewhat different values as a result of second-order effects ignored by the Model Human Processor, or as a result of individual differences among subjects, or even because the experiments measure slightly different things. The values we shall give our parameters will reflect both of these facts. On the one hand, we shall give our best estimate for the parameter. In this case the Perceptual Processor cycle time will be set at $\tau_P = 100$ msec, approximately the average of the values from a number of experiments reviewed. On the other hand, we will also include a range in rounded numbers, in this case 50 ~ 200 msec, of the reasonable experimental values reported. In compact form, we shall write these two together as

$$\tau_P = 100 \ [50 \sim 200] \ \text{msec}.$$

We should also note that a user must move the 1 ~ 2 degree high-resolution center of his visual field so that it covers what he wishes to examine. The visual system is organized so that this high-resolution part moves quickly to some location and then remains fixed for a while before moving to some new location. Each of these fixations (including movement time) lasts

$$230 \sim 700] \ \text{msec}.$$

The Cognitive Processor also gives values on the order of 0.1 sec/cycle. One set of relevant experiments derives from a paradigm called memory scanning invented by Sternberg (1966) at Bell Laboratories. A user read a set of items, such as the letters B, A, C, G, is asked if some letter, say A, is in the list. The response time has been found to be a linear function of the number of items in the list. In our terms, the user must scan down the list using one Cognitive Processor cycle for each item. The time per cycle, varies in these experiments from as low as 27 msec for numbers to as much as 93 msec for random forms.

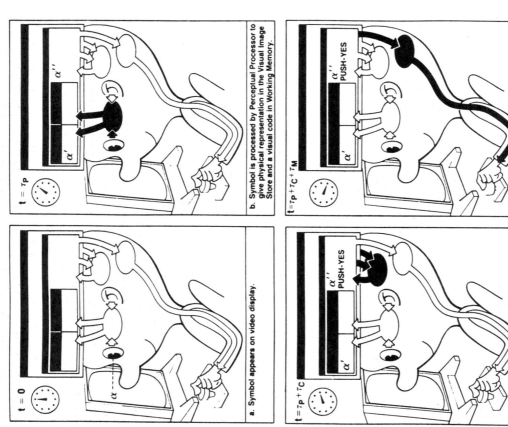

Figure D-7. Simple reaction time analysis using the Model Human Processor.

Let us start with the cycle time of the Perceptual Processor. There are a number of experiments which have established Bloch's Law (1885): as long

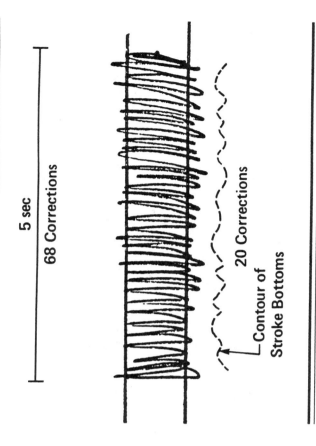

Figure D-8. Scribbling as rapidly as possible for 5 sec while trying to stay between two lines.

Memory Parameters

Now let us consider the memory parameters of the Model Human Processor as illustrated in Figure D-1(a). There are three such parameters of interest: memory capacity, code type, and decay rate.

Capacity

The most important memory capacity, that for Working Memory, seems to be about 3 ~ 4 items:

$$\mu_{WM} = 3 \,[2.5 \sim 4.1]\ \text{msec.}$$

Of course, if one were to give a subject a seven digit telephone number and ask him to repeat it, he probably could. The reason is that he is using not only Working Memory, but also some Long-Term Memory in the process. Since these two are closely packaged together as a system, the number of items that can be repeated back is the famous 7 ± 2 number. To distinguish this number from the capacity of Working Memory proper, we say that the user has an *effective Working Memory size of*

In another task, first measured by Jevons (1871), the experimenter shows the subject some number of objects and ask him how many there are. Again the time required for the subject to answer is linearly proportional to the number of items with time/item of around 40 msec for four or fewer dots (Chi and Klahr, 1975) to 94 msec (individuals ranged from 40 to 172 msec) for four or fewer 3-dimensional objects (Akin and Chase 1978). Yet another task has the subject count silently to himself as fast as possible, producing times on the order of 167 msec/digit (Landauer, 1962). From these studies and others, we can derive the cycle time of the Cognitive Processor to be

$$\tau_C = 70 \,[25 \sim 170]\ \text{msec.}$$

Finally, experiments on the rate at which people can move their hand or foot or tongue also give numbers around 0.1 sec/movement. For example, tapping takes 35 ~ 65 msec/movement. Repeating a key in typing for a good typist takes about 90 msec. So the Motor Processor cycle time is

$$\tau_M = 70 \,[30 \sim 100]\ \text{msec.}$$

Now we can return to our example in Figure D-7 and ask how long should the response take. As the figures shows, the task requires one cycle each of the Perceptual Processor, the Cognitive Processor, and the Motor Processor for a total time of $\tau_P + \tau_C + \tau_M$, or

Perceive stimulus	$\tau_P = 100\,[50 \sim 200]$	msec
Decide to respond	$\tau_C = 70\,[25 \sim 170]$	msec
Respond	$\tau_M = 70\,[30 \sim 100]$	msec
	Total　$240\,[105 \sim 470]$	msec.

As another example, consider the task of scribbling as fast as possible between two parallel lines. Figure D-8 shows a typical result. Two kinds of periodicity are evident in this scribble: one very rapid and another shown by the slower adjustments made by the user attempting to stay between the lines. In terms of the Model Human Processor, these periodicities correspond to two processing routes through Figure D-6(a): The fast scribbles are the maximum output rate of the Motor Processor. According to our model, there should be a direction change every 70 [30 ~ 100] msec. In fact there are 68 corrections in 5 sec or 5/68 = 74 msec/correction. The slower adjustments require the scribbler to notice that his scribbles are the wrong size (one Perceptual Processor Cycle), to decide which way to adjust them (one Cognitive Processor Cycle), and to respond with an adjustment (one Motor Process or Cycle)—all of which should take 240 [105 ~ 470] msec as computed above. In Figure D-8 there are 20 such corrections in 5 sec, or 5/20 = 250 msec/correction.

$$\mu^*_{WM} = 7 \, [5 \sim 9] \text{ msec.}$$

But if one were to read a long string of digits to a subject, then unexpectedly in the middle ask him to repeat as many back as possible, the number of digits he could repeat would be closer to $3 \sim 4$ than to 7.

The capacity of Long-Term Memory is indefinitely high, so while there must be some limit, we can express the fact that Long-Term Memory capacity does not seem to play a practical role in limited user performance by

$$\mu_{LTM} = \infty.$$

Code type

The type of coding used to store information in memory is a complicated topic, but for our purposes it is only necessary to distinguish a few major types of codes. The sensory buffers, that is the Visual Image Store (VIS) and the Auditory Image Store (AIS), use some sort of physical code. If a light is brighter, it takes longer to decay (Fig. D-9):

$$\kappa_{VIS} = \text{Physical};$$
$$\kappa_{AIS} = \text{Physical}.$$

This is not the case for Working Memory. If a subject is given a set of letters to remember, one of the mistakes he is likely to make when repeating it is to give a wrong letter that sounds similar to the correct letter. This is a clue that the code in Working Memory for the letter is acoustic; in other cases it is possible to demonstrate that the user employs visual codes. But the codes are not physical, and therefore:

$$\kappa_{WM} = \text{Acoustic or Visual}.$$

For Long-Term Memory the confusions are likely to be semantic, not between two things which look or sound alike, but between two things which have similar meanings:

$$\kappa_{LTM} = \text{Semantic}.$$

Decay rate

The decay rate of an item in Working Memory or the sensory memories seems to depend on the number of items in memory. One way of measuring the decay rate, developed by Sperling (1960) and Averbach and Coriell (1961) at Bell Laboratories, is to flash subjects a set of letters in some sort of array where the number of letters in the array is larger than the effective Working

Memory capacity, μ^*_{WM}. The subjects are only able to report back μ^*_{WM} of them, although they claim to have seen them all. To get around this Working Memory limit for reporting, subjects are given some cue shortly after the letters have been presented that tells them which part of the display to report. For example, a tone might indicate which row to report. If there are four rows of four letters each, and if the subject could report correctly three of the four letters of the row on which he was cued, then he is supposed to have $3/4 \times 16 = 12$ letters available in the Visual Image Store at that time, or $12 - 7 = 5$ letters available in excess of Working Memory capacity. By varying the time between the flash and the reporting cue, it is possible to trace the decay of the Visual Image Store. Figure D-9 plots log letters available in excess of Working Memory capacity as a function of time for three experiments on the Visual Information Store and one experiment on the Auditory Image Store. The curves show that the decay plotted this way is exponential (a straight line in semi-log coordinates) and that it depends on the number of items. From the slope of these lines, we can compute the half-life, δ, and use this to define the decay. From these and other experiments we derive:

$$\delta_{VIS} = 200 \, [70 \sim 1000] \text{ msec, and}$$
$$\delta_{AIS} = 1500 \, [900 \sim 3500] \text{ msec.}$$

One method to measure Working Memory decay, is to give the subject some items to remember and then to prevent him in some way from rehearsing them. After a certain period of time, he is asked for the item. Figure D-10 gives the results from this sort of experiment. Again, the decay rate depends on the number of items to be remembered. More technically, it depends on the number of "chunks" to be remembered, that is, the number of meaningful units:

$$\delta_{WM}(1 \text{ chunk}) = 200 \, [70 \sim 1000] \text{ msec, and}$$
$$\delta_{WM}(3 \text{ chunks}) = 1500 \, [900 \sim 3500] \text{ msec.}$$

Notice that the decay rate is about the same for three consonants or for three words. Here I add a caveat. The most serious cause of forgetting in Working Memory is thought to be interference between new items and items already in memory. However, it is difficult, even in the laboratory, to differentiate cleanly this kind of decay from the decay that would be obtained if pure time was the variable. Even though this is a difficult problem for experimental psychology, the very fact of the difficulty means it is possible, for engineering purposes, to simplify the analysis by acting as though time were the independent variable.

Sample calculations

Now let us perform some sample calculations to give further illustration of the Model Human Processor's application.

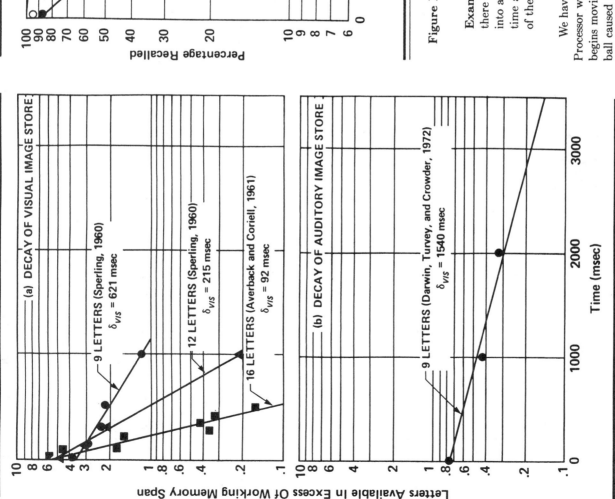

Figure D-10. Working Memory decay rate.

Example 1. In a graphic computer simulation of a pool game, there are many occasions upon which one ball appears to bump into another ball, causing the second one to move. What is the time available, after the collision, to compute the initial move of the second ball, before the illusion of causality breaks down?

We have said that events which occur within one cycle of the Perceptual Processor will tend to be perceived as a single percept. So if the second ball begins moving within $\tau_P = 100$ msec of the collision, it will appear the first ball caused the second to move. If we want to be very sure, since 100 msec is the time at which the causality will break down, we should use the lower bound of $\tau_P = 50$ msec. Figure D-11 shows the results of an experiment, in which one ball appeared to collide with a second ball that moved after various delays. Subjects were asked to judge whether they perceived a single causal

Figure D-9. Time decay of Visual and Auditory Image Stores. **(a)** Decay of Visual Image Store. **(b)** Decay of Auditory Image Store.

$$(1 \text{ saccade/word})(230 \text{ msec/saccade}) = 261 \text{ words/minute},$$

a rate, incidentally, closer to being typical. Finally, it has been found that 13 characters is about the most people can perceive within a fixation. If by some means the reader could read so that he saw 13 new characters (= 2.5 words) each time, his reading rate would be

$$(1/2.5 \text{ saccade/word})(230 \text{ msec/saccade}) = 652 \text{ words/minute}.$$

In other words, speed readers who claim to read 2000 or 5000 words/minute are actually skimming.

Example 3. Show that a user will probably remember the meaningful file name CAT longer than the arbitrary name TXD.

The solution to this problem can be approached using the Working Memory decay-rate parameter. The user will probably remember a meaningful file name like "CAT" as one chunk, whereas a meaningless name like "TXD" will require 3 chunks, one for each letter. As we have noted (Figs. D–6(a) and 10), a single chunk decays much more slowly (half-life $\delta_{WM} = 73$ [73 ~ 226] msec) than three chunks ($\delta_{WM} = 7$ [5 ~ 34] msec). In fact, there should be an order of magnitude, $73/7 \cong 10$ difference in the decay time.

INTERFACE COMPONENTS

Now that we have discussed human information-processing generally, let us turn to an examination of several computer interface components. Here we can see characteristics of the human processor reflected in system user performance. As examples, I shall discuss the design of keyboards, pointing devices, and expert dialogues.

Keyboards

Keystroking Rate

Good typists can type 60 ~ 100 words/minute. This imposes a substantial limitation on the rate a user can communicate with a computer system. From whence does it arise? Could people type at infinite speed with enough practice? A simple calculation based on the Model Human Processor shows approximately where the upper bound in human keying performance lies.

Example 4. How fast can a person type?

A keystroke consists of two actions: raising the finger and lowering the finger. According to our model, each should take about one Motor Processor

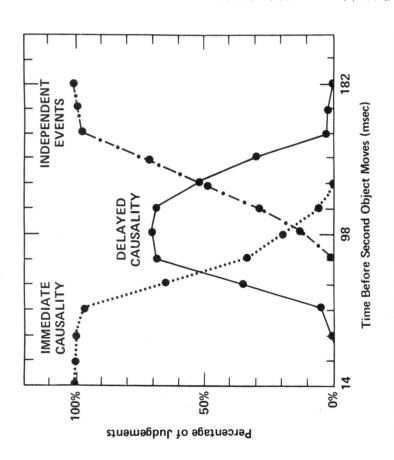

Figure D–11. Perceived causality as a function of inter-event time.

event, two independent events, or a third category called delayed causation. The figure shows that the dividing point between causation and independent events was near the 100 msec predicted; furthermore, events which occurred with a delay of less than 50 msec were almost always perceived as causal.

Example 2. How fast can a person read text?

Suppose that when people read they need to use one eye movement for every letter. If, as in Figure D–6(a), the fixation time could be taken as 230 msec/fixation, that would imply a reading rate of

$$(5 \text{ saccade/word})(230 \text{ msec/saccade}) = 52 \text{ words/minute}.$$

On the other hand, suppose people on the average require only one eye-movement per word. That would give

Cycle or 2 × 70 msec = 140 msec, about 78 words/minute. Actually, the user can at least partially overlap one keystroke with the next. If he could completely overlap the downward part of one stroke with the upward part of the next, then the typing rate would be twice this, or 156 words/minute. The actual performance of fast typists, where some but not all keystrokes overlap, would be expected to be in this region. Indeed 90 ~ 110 words per minute is considered excellent typing performance and 130 words/minute is typing speed-competition performance.

Speed of Keyboards

Now let us consider the performance consequences of the arrangement of the keys on the keyboard for expert performance. While this might, at first glance, seem a simple matter for experiment, in fact convincing experimental demonstrations of key arrangements are difficult and expensive due to the large amount of learning required of the subject. Subjects must be recruited and trained for months until they reach expert speed, during which time they must not use the standard Sholes arrangement so that they are not already contaminated by standard keyboard experience. The designer cannot, practically speaking, fiddle with experiments on 16 different key arrangements and choose the best. With the help of some additional keystroking data such as the digraph times in Figure D-12 from Kinkead (1975), however, it is possible to make rapid calculations in the spirit of the Model Human Processor that approximate the results to be expected. Figure D-12 gives data for the times to type some key, for example, the letter g, if the previous key was from the alternate hand (example: k), the same hand (example: a), the same finger (example: r), or the same key (the letter: g). Let us consider an example.

Example 5. A manufacturer is considering whether to use an alphabetic keyboard (see Fig. D-13) on his small business com-puter system. Among several factors influencing his decision is the question of whether experienced users will find the keyboard slower for touch typing than the standard Sholes (QWERTY) keyboard arrangement. What is the relative typing speed for expert users on the two keyboards?

We can compute the nominal typing rate with the proposed keyboard by using a table of all the digraphs in English (such as Underwood and Schulz, 1960) and multiplying the frequency of occurrence of each digraph by the time from Figure D-12 required for that digraph. When we do this for the alphabetic keyboard in Figure D-13, we get 164 msec/keystroke = 66 words/min. When we do the same exercise with a standard Sholes keyboard, we get 152 msec/keystroke = 72 words/min. In other words, the alphabetic keyboard is calculated to be about 8% slower than the standard keyboard. Depending on one's purpose, this may or may not be a reasonable penalty to pay for an alphabetic keyboard.

The design of keyboard arrangements is of some current interest. The argument usually goes that there are so many keyboards out in the world that it is impractical to change from the standard Sholes arrangement once the enormous expense of retraining is considered. Hence, consideration of new keyboard designs is a waste of time. But there is a counterargument (for which I am indebted to David Thornburg) that runs like this: At just this point there is a technology window that is about to open, during which it is practical to consider new keyboards. In consequence of the mass proliferation of computer devices now just beginning, the number of keyboards in the world is expected to increase by an order of magnitude greater than what exists today. Furthermore, these keyboards will go especially to people

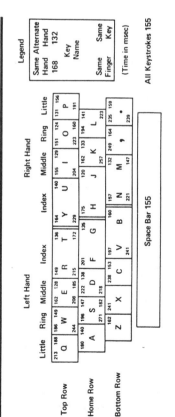

Figure D-12. Inter-keystroke times.

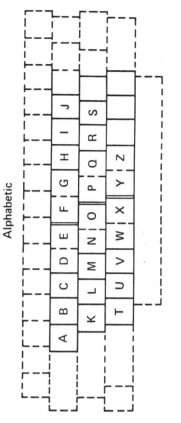

Figure D-13. Proposed arrangement of letters on typewriter.

without touch-typing skills, for example, business executives and grade-school children. In a few years, of course, the expansion will have occurred; these people will be accustomed to typing on whatever keyboards were available and the technology window will close. So there is a limited time during which a new keyboard arrangement could emerge and have a reasonable opportunity for technological diffusion. Calculations like this are the simplest way of exploring the performance consequences of different arrangements since answers are available within seconds instead of months.

Pointing Devices

The trend for the future is clearly for the graphics interface to dominate in human-computer interaction. An important component of this interface is the device the user employs to select some object on the VDT screen. Again, the characteristics of the human information processor set constraints on the design and use of such devices. As examples of these constraints, we can examine the minimum time required to point to an object on the screen and how this varies with alternative pointing devices.

Minimum pointing time

Let us consider the task of pointing to some target with a pencil or a finger (Fig. D-14). A little experimentation shows that the time to point to a target decreases if the target is located closer or if it is larger.

Example 6. What is the minimum time for pointing to a target S cm wide that is D cm distant?

According to the Model Human Processor, the user makes such a movement through a series of discrete micromovements. The user moves his hand (one Motor Processor Cycle), observes how well it is moving as it moves (one Perceptual Processor Cycle), and decides how to correct the motion (one Cognitive Processor Cycle). Let us assume that each micromovement of the hand brings the hand towards the target subject to a certain constant error, say 7%. The user keeps going around this cycle until finally he perceives that the hand is within the target area and so stops. As we have seen previously, each of these cycles ought to take nominally $\tau_P + \tau_C + \tau_M = 240$ msec. If this is so, then the time to point to the target is just $240n$ msec, where n is the number of cycles. The question of how long it takes to get within the target. We can compute this number by referring to Figure D-14 and by assuming a constant error. Suppose the user starts X_0 cm from the target. After the first cycle he will be

$$X_1 = \epsilon X_0 = \epsilon D$$

away from the target, where ϵ is the error. After the next cycle he will be

$$X_2 = \epsilon X_1 = \epsilon(\epsilon D) = \epsilon^2 D$$

away. After the nth cycle, he will be

$$X_n = \epsilon^n D$$

away. The hand will stop when

$$\epsilon^n D \leq S/2,$$

that is, when the finger is somewhere within the target. Solving for n, we get

$$n = \frac{\log_2\left(\frac{2D}{S}\right)}{\log_2 \epsilon}.$$

Thus the minimum movement time is:

$$\begin{aligned}
\text{Movement time} &= (\tau_P + \tau_C + \tau_M)n \\
&= (\tau_P + \tau_C + \tau_M)\frac{-\log_2\left(\frac{2D}{S}\right)}{\log_2 \epsilon} \\
&= -\left[\frac{\tau_P + \tau_C + \tau_M}{\log_2 \epsilon}\right]\log_2\left(\frac{2D}{S}\right).
\end{aligned}$$

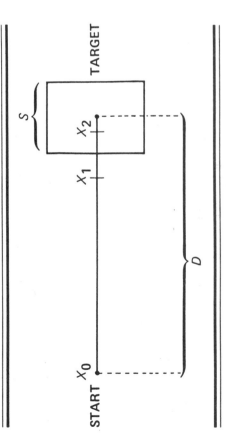

Figure D-14. Analysis of the movement of a user's hand to a target.

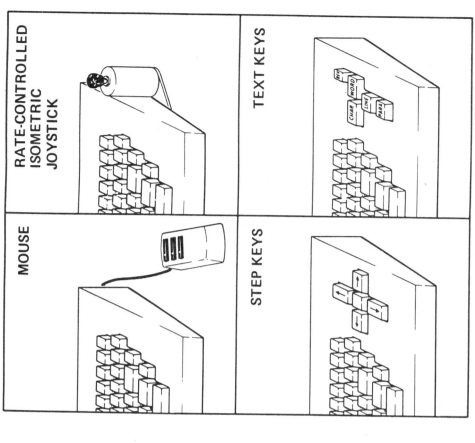

Figure D–15. Some devices used in pointing to a place on the VDT screen.

Substituting for the cycle times of the processors and taking the $\epsilon = .07$ from the literature, gives

$$\text{Movement time} = .1 \log_2 \left(\frac{2D}{S} \right).$$

This result is known as Fitts's Law. Welford (1968) has shown that it can be improved slightly by the addition of a constant within the log, so the version we shall use for movement time (see Figure D–1(b)) is

$$\text{Movement time} = .1 \log_2 \left(\frac{2D}{S} + .5 \right). \qquad \text{Eq. (1)}$$

We can now proceed to use this result, together with our results on keystroking, to consider the speed of different pointing devices.

Speed of pointing devices

Figure D–15 contains examples of several pointing devices. The device in Figure D–15(a) is a mouse. Figure D–15(b) shows a sort of joystick designed to be mounted as a key on a keyboard. When the knob on the top of the device is pushed in some direction, the knob itself moves very little, but a strain gauge senses the force and moves the cursor with a rate proportional to the square of the force. Figure D–15(c) shows a standard set of step keys. Figure D–15(d) shows a set of text keys with keys to advance the cursor by a character, a word, a line, or a paragraph and a shift key, which when depressed, reverses the direction of the cursor.

Experiments on the speed with which users can use each of these devices to point to a text target show that the mouse is superior to the other devices in speed (and accuracy, too) and that the step keys are particularly deficient (Figs. D–16(a) and (b)). The differences in the times for the devices can can be accounted for by the Model Human Processor. Pointing time for the step keys and text keys is proportional to the number of keystrokes required, as seen in Figure D–17(a). The constants of proportionality—74 msec/keystroke for the step keys and 209 msec/keystroke for the text keys—are in the general range of keystroke times discussed earlier. The step key rate is faster partially because it had a high-speed automatic repetition feature and partially because the sequence of keystrokes is simpler. But while the step keys are faster, keystroke per keystroke, many more keystrokes are required than for the text keys; hence the step keys are slower.

Both the mouse and the joystick have pointing times given by Fitts's Law (Fig. D–17(b)). In the case of this particular joystick, apparently the fact that the control was nonlinear made the device suboptimal. The mouse is able to achieve the .1 sec/bit expected from our derivation from the Model Human Processor in Eq. (1). This fact has important implications. The limitation on pointing time with the mouse is not the design of the device itself, but the information-processing rate of the user's eye-hand coordination system. This in turn means that, using the same set of muscles at least, it is probably impossible to build a pointing device which does pointing substantially faster than the mouse, although there may be a number of devices equally as good.

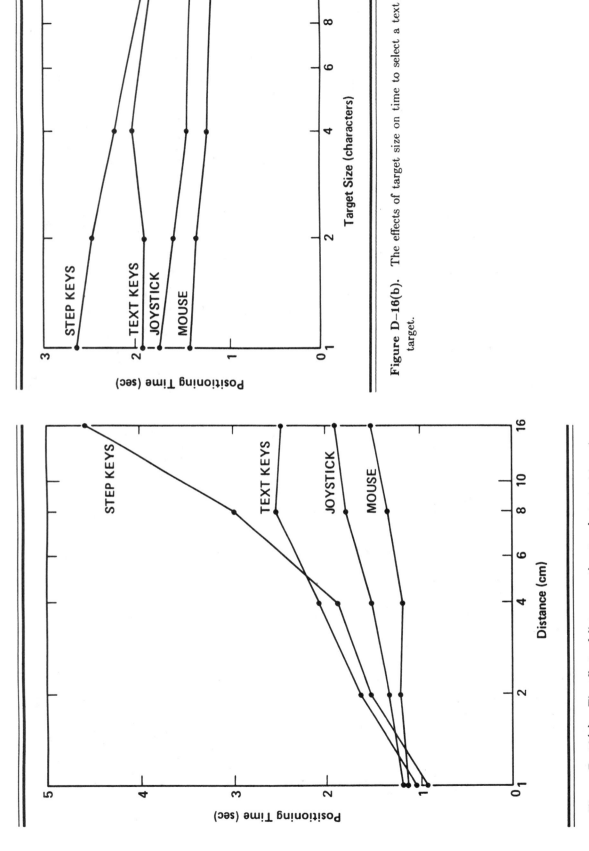

Figure D–16(b).   The effects of target size on time to select a text target.

Figure D–16(a).   The effects of distance on time to select a text target.

REFERENCES

Akin, O., and Chase, W. 1978. Quantification of three-dimensional structures. *Journal of Experimental Psychology* 4:397–410.

Averbach, E., and Coriell, A. S. 1961. Short-term memory in vision. *Bell System Technical Journal* 40:309–28.

Bloch, A.M. 1885. Expérience sur la vision. *Comptes Rendus de Seances de la Société de Biologie* (Paris) 34:493–95.

———. 1983. *The psychology of human-computer interaction.* Hillsdale, N.J.: Lawrence Erlbaum Associates.

Chi, M. T., and Klahr, D. 1975. Span and rate of apprehension in children and adults. *Journal of Experimental Child Psychology* 19:434–39.

Harter, M. R. 1967. Excitability and cortical scanning: a review of two hypotheses of central intermittency in perception. *Psychological Bulletin* 68:47–58.

Jevons, W. S. 1871. The power of numerical discrimination. *Nature* 3: 281–2.

Kinkead, R. 1975. Typing speed, keying rates, and optimal keyboard layouts. *Proceedings of the 19th Annual Meeting of the Human Factors Society*, pp. 159–61.

Landauer, T. K. 1962. Rate of implicit speech. *Perception and Psychophysics* 15:646.

Siewiorek, D.; Bell, G.; and Newell, A. 1981. *Computer structures.* New York: McGraw-Hill.

Sperling, G. 1960. The information available in brief visual presentations. *Psychological Monographs* 74 (11, Whole No. 498).

Sternberg, S. 1966. High-speed scanning in human memory. *Science* 153:652–54.

Underwood, B. J., and Schulz, R. W. 1960. *Meaningfulness and verbal learning.* Philadelphia: Lippincott.

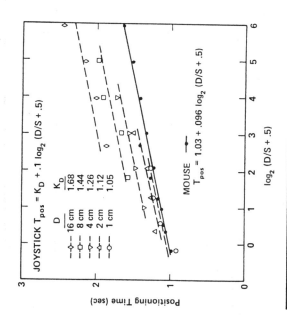

Figure D–17(b). Positioning time analogue devices as a function of Fitts's Index of Difficulty.

Figure D–17(a). Positioning time key-operated devices as a function of the number of keystrokes required.

The Keystroke-Level Model for User Performance Time with Interactive Systems

Stuart K. Card and Thomas P. Moran
Xerox Palo Alto Research Center

Allen Newell
Carnegie-Mellon University

There are several aspects of user-computer performance that system designers should systematically consider. This article proposes a simple model, the Keystroke-Level Model, for predicting one aspect of performance: the time it takes an expert user to perform a given task on a given computer system. The model is based on counting keystrokes and other low-level operations, including the user's mental preparations and the system's responses. Performance is coded in terms of these operations and operator times summed to give predictions. Heuristic rules are given for predicting where mental preparations occur. When tested against data on 10 different systems, the model's prediction error is 21 percent for individual tasks. An example is given to illustrate how the model can be used to produce parametric predictions and how sensitivity analysis can be used to redeem conclusions in the face of uncertain assumptions. Finally, the model is compared to several simpler versions. The potential role for the Keystroke-Level Model in system design is discussed.

Key Words and Phrases: human-computer interface, human-computer interaction, user model, user performance, cognitive psychology, ergonomics, human factors, systems design

CR Categories: 3.36, 4.6, 8.1

Authors' present addresses: S.K. Card and T.P. Moran, Xerox Corporation, Palo Alto Research Center, 3333 Coyote Hill Road, Palo Alto, CA 94304; A. Newell, Department of Computer Science, Carnegie-Mellon University, Pittsburgh, PA 15213.

1. Introduction

The design and evaluation of interactive computer systems should take into account the total performance of the combined user-computer system. Such an account would reflect the psychological characteristics of users and their interaction with the task and the computer. This rarely occurs in any systematic and explicit way. The causes of this failure may lie partly in attitudes toward the possibility of dealing successfully with psychological factors, such as the belief that intuition, subjective experience, and anecdote form the only possible bases for dealing with them. Whatever may be true of these more global issues, one major cause is the absence of good analysis tools for assessing combined user-computer performance.

There exists quite a bit of research relevant to the area of user-computer performance, but most of it is preliminary in nature. Pew et al. [14], in a review of 40 potentially relevant human-system performance models, conclude "that integrative models of human performance compatible with the requirements for representing command and control system performance do not exist at the present time." Ramsey and Atwood [15], after reviewing the human factors literature pertinent to computer systems, conclude that while there exists enough material to develop a qualitative "human factors design guide," there is insufficient material for a "quantitative reference handbook."

This paper presents one specific quantitative analysis tool: a simple model for the time it takes a user to perform a task with a given method on an interactive computer system. This model appears to us to be simple enough, accurate enough, and flexible enough to be applied in practical design and evaluation situations.

The model addresses only a single aspect of performance. To put this aspect into perspective, note that there are many different dimensions to the performance of a user-computer system:

—*Time.* How long does it take a user to accomplish a given set of tasks using the system?
—*Errors.* How many errors does a user make and how serious are they?
—*Learning.* How long does it take a novice user to learn how to use the system to do a given set of tasks?
—*Functionality.* What range of tasks can a user do in practice with the system?
—*Recall.* How easy is it for a user to recall how to use the system on a task that he has not done for some time?

The authors of this report are listed in alphabetical order. A. Newell is a consultant to Xerox PARC. This paper is a revised version of [3]. For a view of the larger research program of which the study described in this paper is a part, see [5].

—*Concentration.* How many things does a user have to keep in mind while using the system?

—*Fatigue.* How tired do users get when they use the system for extended periods?

—*Acceptability.* How do users subjectively evaluate the system?

Next, note that there is *no single kind of user.* Users vary along many dimensions:

—Their *extent of knowledge* of the different tasks.

—Their *knowledge of other systems*, which may have positive or negative effects on the performance in the system of interest.

—Their *motor skills* on various input devices (e.g., typing speed).

—Their general *technical ability* in using systems (e.g., programmers vs. nonprogrammers).

—Their *experience* with the system, i.e., whether they are *novice users*, who know little about the system; *casual users*, who know a moderate amount about the system and use it at irregular intervals; or *expert users*, who know the system intimately and use it frequently.

Finally, note that there is *no single kind of task.* This is especially true in interactive systems, which are expressly built around a command language to permit a wide diversity of tasks to be accomplished. The number of qualitatively different tasks performable by a modern text editor, for instance, runs to the hundreds.

All aspects of performance, all types of users, and all kinds of tasks are important. However, no uniform approach to modeling the entire range of factors in a simple way appears possible at this time. Thus, of necessity, the model to be presented is specific to one aspect of the total user-computer system: *How long it takes expert users to perform routine tasks.*

The model we present here is simple, yet effective. The central idea behind the model is that the time for an expert to do a task on an interactive system is determined by the time it takes to do the keystrokes. Therefore, just write down the method for the task, count the number of keystrokes required, and multiply by the time per keystroke to get the total time. This idea is a little too simplistic. Operations other than keystrokes must be added to the model. Since these other operations are at about the same level (time grain) as keystrokes, we dub it the "Keystroke-Level Model." (The only other similar proposal we know of is that of Embley et al. [9], which we discuss in Section 6.1.)

The structure of this paper is as follows: Section 2 formulates the time prediction problem more precisely. Section 3 lays out the Keystroke-Level Model. Section 4 provides some empirical validation for the model. Section 5 illustrates how the model can be applied in practice. And Section 6 analyzes some simpler versions of the model.

2. The Time Prediction Problem

The prediction problem that we will address is as follows:

Given: A task (possibly involving several subtasks); the command language of a system; the motor skill parameters of the user; the response time parameters of the system; the method used for the task.

Predict: The time an expert user will take to execute the task using the system, providing he uses the method without error.

Several aspects of this formulation need explication, especially the stipulations about execution, methods, and the absence of error.

2.1 Unit Tasks and Execution Time

Given a large task, such as editing a large document, a user will break it into a series of small, cognitively manageable, quasi-independent tasks, which we call *unit tasks* [4; 5, ch. 11]. The task and the interactive system influence the structure of these unit tasks, but unit tasks appear to owe their existence primarily to the memory limits on human cognition. The importance of unit tasks for our analysis is that they permit the time to do a large task to be decomposed into the sum of the times to do its constituent unit tasks. Note that not all tasks have a unit-task substructure. For example, inputting an entire manuscript by typing permits a continuous throughput organization.

For our purposes here, a unit task has two parts: (1) *acquisition* of the task and (2) *execution* of the task acquired. During acquisition the user builds a mental representation of the task, and during execution the user calls on the system facilities to accomplish the task. The total time to do a unit task is the sum of the time for these two parts:

$$T_{task} = T_{acquire} + T_{execute}$$

The acquisition time for a unit task depends on the characteristics of the larger task situation in which it occurs. In a manuscript interpretation situation, in which unit tasks are read from a marked-up page or from written instructions, it takes about 2 to 3 seconds to acquire each unit task. In a routine design situation, in which unit tasks are generated in the user's mind, it takes about 5 to 30 seconds to acquire each unit task. In a creative composition situation, it can take even longer.

The execution of a unit task involves calling the appropriate system commands. This rarely takes over 20 seconds (assuming the system has a reasonably efficient command syntax). If a task requires a longer execution time, the user will likely break it into smaller unit tasks.

We have formulated the prediction problem to predict only the execution time of unit tasks, not the acquisition time. This is the part of the task over which the system designer has most direct control (i.e., by manipulating the system's command language), so its prediction suffices for many practical purposes. Task acquisition times are highly variable, except in special situations (such as the manuscript interpretation situation); and we can say little yet about predicting them.

Two important assumptions underlie our treatment of execution time. First, execution time is the same no matter how a task is acquired. Second, acquisition time and execution time are independent (e.g., reducing execution time by making the command language more efficient does not affect acquisition time). These assumptions are no doubt false at a fine level of detail, but the error they produce is probably well below the threshold of concern in practical work.

2.2 Methods

A *method* is a sequence of system commands for executing a unit task that forms a well-integrated ("compiled") segment of a user's behavior. It is characteristic of an expert user that he has one or more methods for each type of unit task that he encounters and that he can quickly (in about a second) choose the appropriate method in any instance. This is what makes expert user behavior routine, as opposed to novice user behavior, which is distinctly nonroutine.

Methods can be specified at several levels. A user actually knows a method at all its levels, from a general system-independent functional specification, down through the commands in the language of the computer system, to the keystrokes and device manipulations that actually communicate the method to the system. Models can deal with methods defined at any of these levels [4, 11]. The Keystroke-Level Model adopts one specific level—the keystroke level—to formalize the notion of a method, leaving all the other levels to be treated informally.

Many methods that achieve a given task can exist. In general such methods bear no systematic relationship to each other (except that of attaining the same end). Each can take a different amount of time to execute, and the differences can be large. Thus, in general, if the method is unknown, reasonable predictions of execution time are not possible. For this reason, the proper prediction problem is the one posed at the beginning of the section: Predict the time given the method.

2.3 Error-Free Execution

The Keystroke-Level Model assumes that the user faithfully executes the given method. The user deviates from a postulated method when he makes an error. Up to a fourth of an expert's time can be spent correcting errors, though users vary in their trade-off between speed and errors. We are simply ignoring the tasks containing errors and only predicting the error-free tasks, for we do not know how to predict where and how often errors occur. But, if the method for correcting an error is given, the model can be used to predict how long it will take to make the correction. Indeed, experts handle most errors in routine ways, i.e., according to fixed, available methods.

3. The Keystroke-Level Model

We lay out the primitive operators for the Keystroke-Level Model and give a set of heuristics for coding methods in terms of these operators. Then we present a few examples of method encoding.

3.1 Operators

The Keystroke-Level Model asserts that the execution part of a task can be described in terms of four different physical-motor operators: **K** (keystroking), **P** (pointing), **H** (homing), and **D** (drawing), and one mental operator, **M**, by the user, plus a response operator, **R**, by the system. These operators are listed in Figure 1. Execution time is simply the sum of the time for each of the operators.

$$T_{execute} = T_K + T_P + T_H + T_D + T_M + T_R. \qquad (1)$$

Most operators are assumed to take a constant time for each occurrence, e.g., $T_K = n_K t_K$, where n_K is the number of keystrokes and t_K is the time per keystroke. (Operators **D** and **R** are treated somewhat differently.)

The most frequently used operator is **K**, which represents a keystroke or a button push (on a typewriter keyboard or any other button device). **K** refers to keys, not characters (e.g., hitting the SHIFT key counts as a separate **K**). The average time for **K**, t_K, will be taken to be the standard typing rate, as determined by standard one-minute typing tests. This is an approximation in two respects. First, keying time is different for different keys and key devices. Second, the time for immediately caught typing errors (involving BACKSPACE and rekeying) should be folded into t_K. Thus, the preferred way to calculate t_K from a typing test is to divide the total time taken in the test by the total number of nonerror keystrokes, which gives the *effective* keying time. We accept both these approximations in the interest of simplicity.

Users can differ in their typing rates by as much as a factor of 15. The range of typing speeds is given in Figure 1. Given a population of users, an appropriate t_K can be selected from this range. If a user population has users with large t_K differences, then the population should be partitioned and analyzed separately, since the different classes of users will be likely to use different methods.

The operator **P** represents pointing to a target on a display with a "mouse," a wheeled device that is rolled around on a table to guide the display's cursor. Pointing time for the mouse varies as a function of the distance to the target, d, and the size of the target, s, according to Fitts's Law [2]:

$$t_P = .8 + .1 \log_2 (d/s + .5) \text{ sec.}$$

The fastest time according to this equation is .8 sec, and the longest likely time ($d/s = 128$) is 1.5 sec. Again, to keep the model simple, we will use a constant time of 1.1 sec for t_P. Often, pointing with the mouse is followed by pressing one of the buttons on the mouse. This key press is not part of **P**; it is represented by a **K** following the **P**.

Fig. 1. The Operators of the Keystroke Model.

Operator	Description and Remarks	Time (sec)
K	Keystroke or button press. Pressing the SHIFT or CONTROL key counts as a separate K operation. Time varies with the typing skill of the user; the following shows the range of typical values:	
	Best typist (135 wpm)	.08[a]
	Good typist (90 wpm)	.12[a]
	Average skilled typist (55 wpm)	.20[a]
	Average non-secretary typist (40 wpm)	.28[b]
	Typing random letters	.50[a]
	Typing complex codes	.75[a]
	Worst typist (unfamiliar with keyboard)	1.20[a]
P	Pointing to a target on a display with a mouse. The time to point varies with distance and target size according to Fitts's Law. The time ranges from .8 to 1.5 sec, with 1.1 being an average time. This operator does *not* include the button press that often follows (.2 sec).	1.10[c]
H	Homing the hand(s) on the keyboard or other device.	.40[d]
$D(n_D, l_D)$	Drawing (manually) n_D straight-line segments having a total length of l_D cm. This is a very restricted operator; it assumes that drawing is done with the mouse on a system that constrains all lines to fall on a square .56 cm grid. Users vary in their drawing skill; the time given is an average value.	$.9n_D + .16l_D$[e]
M	Mentally preparing for executing physical actions.	1.35[f]
$R(t)$	Response of t sec by *the system*. This takes different times for different commands in the system. These times must be input to the model. The response time counts only if it causes the user to wait.	t

[a] See [8].

[b] This is the average typing rate of the nonsecretary subjects in the experiment described in Section 4.1.

[c] See [2].

[d] See [2, 4].

[e] The drawing time function and the coefficients were derived from least squares fits on the drawing test data from the four MARKUP subjects. See Sections 3.1 and 4.1.

[f] The time for M was estimated from the data from experiment described in Section 4.1. See Section 4.2.1.

The mouse is an optimal pointing device as far as time is concerned; but the t_P is about the same for other analog pointing devices, such as lightpens and some joysticks [2].

When there are different physical devices for the user to operate, he will move his hands between them as needed. This hand movement, including the fine positioning adjustment of the hand on the device, is represented by the H ("homing") operator. From previous studies [2, 4], we assume a constant t_H of .4 sec for movement between any two devices.

The D operator represents manually drawing a set of straight-line segments using the mouse. D takes two parameters, the number of segments (n_D) and the total length of all segments (l_D). $t_D(n_D, l_D)$ is a linear function of these two parameters. The coefficients of this function are different for different users; Figure 1 gives an average value for them. Note that this is a very specialized operator. Not only is it restricted to the mouse, but also it assumes that the drawing system constrains the cursor to lie on a .56 cm grid. This allows the user to draw

straight lines fairly easily, but we would expect t_D to be different for different grid sizes. We make no claim for the generality of these times or for the form of the drawing time function. However, inclusion of one instance of a drawing operator serves to indicate the wide scope of the model.

The user spends some time "mentally preparing" to execute many of the physical operators just described; e.g., he decides which command to call or whether to terminate an argument string. These mental preparations are represented by the M operator, which we estimate to take 1.35 sec on the average (see Section 4.2.1). The use of a single mental operator is, again, a deliberate simplification.

Finally, the Keystroke-Level Model represents the system response time by the R operator. This operator has one parameter, t, which is just the response time in seconds. Response times are different for different systems, for different commands within a system, and for different contexts of a given command. The Keystroke-Level Model does not embody a theory of system response time. The response times must be input to the model by giving specific values for the parameter t, which is a placeholder for these input times.

The **R** times are counted only when they require the user to *wait for the system*. For example, a system response counts as an **R** when it is followed by a **K** and the system does *not* allow type-ahead, and the user must wait until the response is complete. However, when an **M** operation follows a response, the response time is not counted unless it is over 1.35 sec, since the expert user can completely overlap the **M** operation with the response time. Response times can also overlap with task acquisition. When a response is counted as an **R**, only the nonoverlapping portion of the response time is given as the parameter to **R**.

3.2 Encoding Methods

Methods are represented as sequences of Keystroke-Level operations. We will introduce the notation with examples. Suppose that there is a command named PUT in some system and that the method for calling it is to type its name followed by the RETURN key. This method is coded by simply listing the operations in sequence: **MK**[P] **K**[U] **K**[T] **K**[RETURN], which we abbreviate as **M 4K**[P U T RETURN]. In this notation we allow descriptive notes (such as key names) in square brackets. If, on the other hand, the method to call the PUT command is to point to its name in a menu and press the RED mouse button, we have: **H**[mouse] **MP**[PUT] **K**[RED] **H**[keyboard].

As another example, consider the text editing task (called T1) of replacing a 5-letter word with another 5-letter word, where this replacement takes place one line below the previous modification. The method for executing task T1 in a line-oriented editor called POET (see Section 4) can be described as follows:

Method for Task T1-Poet:

Jump to next line	**MK**[LINEFEED]
Call Substitute command	**MK**[S]
Specify new 5-digit word	**5K**[word]
Terminate argument	**MK**[RETURN]
Specify old 5-digit word	**5K**[word]
Terminate argument	**MK**[RETURN]
Terminate command	**K**[RETURN]

Using the operator times from Figure 1 and assuming the user is an average skilled typist (i.e., $t_K = .2$ sec), we can predict the time it will take to execute this method:

$$T_{execute} = 4t_M + 15t_K = 8.4 \text{ sec.}$$

This method can be compared to the method for executing task T1 on another editor, a display-based system called DISPED (see Section 4):

Method for Task T1-Disped:

Reach for mouse	**H**[mouse]
Point to word	**P**[word]
Select word	**K**[YELLOW]
Home on keyboard	**H**[keyboard]
Call Replace command	**MK**[R]
Type new 5-digit word	**5K**[word]
Terminate type-in	**MK**[ESC]

$$T_{execute} = 2t_M + 8t_K + 2t_H + t_P = 6.2 \text{ sec.}$$

Fig. 2. Heuristic rules for placing the **M** operations.

Begin with a method encoding that includes all physical operations and response operations. Use Rule 0 to place candidate Ms, and then cycle through Rules 1 to 4 for each M to see whether it should be deleted.

Rule 0. Insert Ms in front of all Ks that are not part of argument strings proper (e.g., text strings or numbers). Place Ms in front of all Ps that select commands (not arguments).

Rule 1. If an operator following an M is *fully anticipated* in the operator just previous to M, then delete the M (e.g., PMK → PK).

Rule 2. If a string of MKs *belong to a cognitive unit* (e.g., the name of a command), then delete all Ms but the first.

Rule 3. If a K is a *redundant terminator* (e.g., the terminator of a command immediately following the terminator of its argument), then delete the M in front of the K.

Rule 4. If a K *terminates a constant string* (e.g., a command name), then delete the M in front of the K; but if the K terminates a variable string (e.g., an argument string), then keep the M.

Thus, we predict that the task will take about two seconds longer on POET than on DISPED. The accuracy of such predictions is discussed in Section 4.

The methods above are simple unconditional sequences. More complex or more general tasks are likely to have multiple methods and/or conditionalities within methods for accomplishing different versions of the task. For example, in a DISPED-like system the user often has to "scroll" the text on the display before being able to point to the desired target. We can represent this method as follows:

.4(**MP**[SCROLL-ICON] **K**[RED] **R**(.5)) **P**[word] **K**[YELLOW].

Here we assume a specific situation where the average number of scroll jumps per selection is .4 and that the average system response time for a scroll jump is .5 sec. From this we can predict the average selection time:

$$T_{execute} = .4t_M + 1.4t_K + 1.4t_P + .4(.5) = 2.6 \text{ sec.}$$

For more complex contingencies, we can put the operations on a flowchart and label the paths with their frequencies.

When there are alternative methods for doing a specific task in a given system, we have found [4] that expert users will, in general, use the most efficient method, i.e., the method taking the least time. Thus, in making predictions we can use the model to compute the times for the alternative methods and predict that the fastest method will be used. (If the alternatives take about the same time, it does not matter which method we predict.) The optimality assumption holds, of course, only if the users are familiar with the alternatives, which is usually true of experts (excepting the more esoteric alternatives). This assumption is helped by the tendency of optimal methods to be the simplest.

3.3 Heuristics for the M Operator

M operations represent acts of mental preparation for applying subsequent physical operations. Their occurrence does not follow directly from the method as defined by the command language of the system, but from the specific knowledge and skill of the user. The Keystroke-Level Model provides a set of rules (Figure 2) for placing M's in the method encodings. These rules embody psychological assumptions about the user and are necessarily heuristic, especially given the simplicity of the model. They should be viewed simply as guidelines.

The rules in Figure 2 define a procedure. The procedure begins with an encoding that contains only the physical operations (**K, P, H,** and **D**). First, all candidate M's are inserted into the encoding according to Rule 0, which is a heuristic for identifying all possible decision points in the method. Rules 1 to 4 are then applied to each candidate M to see if it should be deleted.

There is a single psychological principle behind all the deletion heuristics. Methods are composed of highly integrated submethods ("subroutines") that show up over and over again in different methods. We will call them *method chunks* or just *chunks*, a term common in cognitive psychology [17]. The user cognitively organizes his methods according to chunks, which usually reflect syntactic constituents of the system's command language. Hence, the user mentally prepares for the next chunk, not just the next operation. It follows that in executing methods the user is more likely to pause between chunks than within chunks. The rules attempt to identify method chunks.

Rule 1 asserts that when an operation is fully anticipated in another operation, they belong in a chunk. A common example is pointing with the mouse and then pressing the mouse button to indicate a selection. The button press is fully anticipated during the pointing operation, and there is no pause between them (i.e., **PMK** becomes **PK** according to Rule 1). This anticipation holds even if the selection indication is done on another device (e.g., the keyboard or a foot pedal). Rule 2 asserts that an obvious syntactic unit, such as a command name, constitutes a chunk when it must be typed out in full.

The last two heuristics deal with syntactic terminators. Rule 3 asserts that the user will bundle up redundant terminators into a single chunk. For example, in the POET example in Section 3.2, a RETURN is required to terminate the second argument and then another RETURN to terminate the command; but any user will quickly learn to simply hit a double RETURN after the second argument (i.e., **MKMK** becomes **MKK** according to Rule 3). Rule 4 asserts that a terminator of a constant-string chunk will be assimilated to that chunk. The most common example of this is in systems that require a terminator, such as RETURN, after each command name; the user learns to immediately follow the command name with RETURN.

It is clear that these heuristics do not capture the notion of method chunks precisely, but are only rough approximations. Further, their application is ambiguous in many situations, e.g., whether something is "fully anticipated" or is a "cognitive unit." What can we do about this ambiguity? Better general heuristics will help in reducing this ambiguity. However, some of the variability in what are chunks stems from a corresponding variability in expertise. Individuals differ widely in their behavior; their categorization into *novice, casual,* and *expert* users provides only a crude separation and leaves wide variation within each category. One way that experts differ is in what chunks they have (see [6] for related evidence). Thus, some of the difficulties in placing M's is unavoidable because not enough is known (or can be known in practical work) about the experts involved. Part of the variability in expertise can be represented by the Keystroke-Level Model as encodings with different placements of M operations.

4. Empirical Validation of the Keystroke-Level Model

To determine how well the Keystroke-Level Model actually predicts performance times, we ran an experiment in which calculations from the model were compared against measured times for a number of different tasks, systems, and users.

4.1 Description of the Experiment

A total of 1,280 user-system-task interactions were observed, comprised of various combinations of 28 users, 10 systems, and 14 tasks.

Systems. The systems were all typical application programs available locally (at Xerox PARC) and widely used by both technical and nontechnical users. Some of the systems are also widely used nationally. Three of the systems were text editors, three were graphics editors, and five were executive subsystems. The systems are briefly described in Figure 3.

Together, these systems display a considerable diversity of user interface techniques. For example, POET, one of the text editors, is a typical line-oriented system, which uses first-letter mnemonics to specify commands and search strings to locate lines. In contrast, DRAW, one of the graphics systems, displays a menu of graphic icons on the CRT display to represent the commands, which the user selects by pointing with the mouse.

Tasks. The 14 tasks performed by the users (see Figure 4) were also diverse, but typical. Users of the editing systems were given tasks ranging from a simple word substitution to the more difficult task of moving a sentence from the middle to the end of a paragraph. Users of the graphics systems were given tasks such as adding a box to a diagram or deleting a box (but keeping a line which overlapped it). Users of the executive subsystems were given tasks such as transferring a file between computers or examining part of a file directory.

Task-system methods. In all there were 32 task-system combinations: $4 \times 3 = 12$ for the text editors, $5 \times 3 = 15$ for the graphics systems, and one task each for the five executive subsystems. For each task-system combination, the most efficient "natural" method was determined (by consulting experts) and then coded in Keystroke-Level Model operations. For example, the methods for T1-POET and T1-DISPED are given in Section 3.2. (A complete listing of all the methods can be found in [3].)

Experimental design. The basic design of the experiment was to have ten versions of each task on each system done by four different users, giving 40 observed instances per task-system. No user was observed on more than one system to avoid transfer effects. Four tasks were observed for each of the text-editing systems, five tasks for each of the graphics systems, and one task for the executive subsystems.

Subjects. There were in all 28 different users (some technical, some secretarial): 12 for the editing systems, 12 for the graphics systems, and 4 for the executive subsystems. All were experts in that they had used the systems for months in their regular work and had used them recently.

Experimental procedure. Each user was first given five one-minute typing tests to determine his keystroke time, t_K. In addition, users of MARKUP (the only system requiring manual drawing) were given a series of drawing tasks to determine the parameters of their drawing rate (as discussed in Section 3.1).

After the preliminary tests, the user was given a small number of practice problems of the sort to be tested and was told the method to use (see above). In most cases, the methods presented were those users claimed they would have used anyway; in other cases, the method was easily adopted. Users practiced tasks until they were judged to be at ease with using the correct method; this was usually accomplished in three or four practice trials on each task type.

After practicing, the user proceeded to the main part of the experiment. The user was given a notebook containing several manuscript pages with the tasks to be done marked in red ink. Text-editing and graphics tasks appeared in randomized order. Executive subsystem tasks were always in the order T11, T12, T13, T14. All ten instances of task T10 were done in succession.

Each experimental session, lasting approximately 40 minutes, was videotaped and the user's keystrokes recorded automatically. Time stamps on the videotaped record and on each keystroke allowed protocols to be constructed in which the time of each event was known to within .033 sec. These protocols are the basic data from which the results below are derived.

4.2 Results of the Experiment

Each task instance in the protocols was divided into acquisition time and execution time (see Section 2.1) according to the following definitions. Acquisition time began when the user first looked over to the manuscript to get instructions for the next task and ended when the user started to perform the first operator of the method. Execution time began at that point and ended when the

Fig. 3. Systems measured in the experiment.

System	Description
Text Editors	
POET[a]	Line-oriented with relative line numbers.
SOS[b]	Line-oriented with "sticky" line-numbers.
DISPED[e]	Display-oriented; full-page; uses mouse for pointing.
Graphics Systems	
MARKUP[c]	Uses mouse to draw and erase lines on a bitmap display; commands selected from a hidden menu, which must be re-displayed each time.
DRAW[e]	Lines defined by pointing with mouse to end points; commands selected with mouse from a menu.
SIL[e]	Lines defined by pointing with mouse to end points; boxes defined by pointing to opposite vertices; commands selected by combinations of mouse buttons.
Executive Subsystems	
LOGIN[d]	TENEX command for logging in.
FTP[e]	Program for transferring files between computers.
CHAT[e]	Program for establishing a "teletype" connection between two computers.
DIR[d]	TENEX command for printing a file directory; has a subcommand mode.
DELVER[d]	TENEX command for deleting old versions of a file.

[a] POET is a dialect of the QED editor [7].
[b] See [16].
[c] See [13, ch. 17].
[d] See [12].
[e] Experimental systems local to Xerox PARC, designed and implemented by many individuals, including: Roger Bates, Patrick Baudelaire, David Boggs, Butler Lampson, Charles Simonyi, Robert Sproull, Edward Taft, and Chuck Thacker.

Fig. 4. Tasks for the experiment.

Editing Tasks (used for POET, SOS, DISPED)

T1. Replace one 5-letter word with another (one line from previous task).

T2. Add a 5th character to a 4-letter word (one line from previous task).

T3. Delete a line, all on one line (eight lines from previous task).

T4. Move a 50-character sentence, spread over two lines, to the end of its paragraph (eight lines from previous task).

Graphics Tasks (used for MARKUP, DRAW, SIL)

T5. Add a box to a diagram.

T6. Add a 5-character label to a box.

T7. Reconnect a 2-stroke line to a different box.

T8. Delete a box, but keep an overlapped line.

T9. Copy a box.

Executive Tasks

T10. Phone computer and log in (4 char name, 6 char password).

T11. Transfer a file to another computer, renaming it.

T12. Connect to another computer.

T13. Display a subset of the file directory with file lengths.

T14. Delete old versions of a file.

user looked over to the notebook for the next task. (On the protocol the first measured time at the beginning of an execution is always the end of the first **K** of the method. Thus, operationally, the beginning of execution time was estimated by subtracting from this first **K** time the operator times for this first **K** plus all the operators that preceded it.)

Those tasks on which there were significant errors (i.e., other than typing errors) or in which the user did not use the prescribed method were excluded from further consideration. After this exclusion, 855 (69 percent) of the task instances remained as observations to be matched against the predictions. No analysis was made of the excluded tasks.

The resulting observed times for task acquisition and execution were stable over repetition. There was no statistical evidence for task times decreasing (learning) or increasing (fatigue) with repetition.

4.2.1 Calculation of execution time.

Execution time was calculated using the method analysis for each task-system combination together with estimates of the times required for each operator. All times, except for the mental preparation time, were taken from sources outside of the experiment. Pointing time, t_P, and homing time, t_H, were taken from Figure 1. Typing time, t_K, and drawing time, $t_D(n_D, l_D)$, were estimated from the typing and drawing tests by averaging the times of the four users involved in each task-system. System response time, T_R, for each task-system was estimated from independent measurements of the response times for the various commands required in each method. For task T10, logging in to a computer, a telephone button-press was assumed to take time t_K. Moving the telephone receiver to the computer terminal modem was estimated to take .7 sec, using the MTM system of times for industrial operations [10].

Mental preparation time, t_M, was estimated from the experimental data itself. First, the total mental time for each method was estimated by removing the predicted time for all physical operations from the observed execution time. Then t_M was estimated by a least-squares fit of the estimated mental times as a function of the predicted number of **M** operations. The result was $t_M = 1.35$ sec ($R^2 = .84$, standard error of estimate = .11 sec, standard error about the regression line = 2.48 sec). A rough estimate of the SD of t_M is 1.1 sec, which indicates that the **M** operator has the characteristic variability of mental operators [4].

Execution times for each task-system combination were calculated by formula (1) in Section 3. The calculations of the execution times are summarized in Figure 5, which also gives the observed execution times from the experiment for comparison.

4.2.2 Execution time.

The predicted execution times are quite accurate. This can be seen in Figure 6, which plots the predicted versus the observed data from Figure 5. The scales are logarithmic, since prediction error appears to be roughly proportional to duration. The root-mean-square (RMS) error is 21 percent of the average predicted execution time. This accuracy is about the best that can be expected from the Keystroke-Level Model, since the methods used by the subjects were controlled by the experimental procedure. The 21 percent RMS error is comparable to the 20–30 percent we have obtained in other studies on text-editing with more elaborate models that also predict the method [4].

The distribution of percentage prediction errors is fairly evenly spread, as an analysis of Figure 6 will show. No particular systems or tasks make excessively large contributions. Predictions are not consistently positive or negative for systems or tasks, except that all the executive subsystem tasks were overpredicted. Examination of the individual observations does not reveal any small set of outliers or particular users that inflate the prediction error.

Prediction accuracy is related to the duration of the attempted prediction. The results above are for individual unit tasks. Since unit tasks are essentially independent, prediction of the time to do a sequence of tasks will tend to be more accurate. This can be seen directly in the present data, since each user ran all the tasks for a given system. For example, consider predicting by the model how long it took to do *all four* editing tasks. The average RMS error is only 5 percent. The corresponding RMS error for the graphics editors over the five tasks is only 6 percent.

Ideally, all of the parameters of the model should be determined independently of the experimental situation. This was achieved for all the physical operation times, but not for the mental operation time, t_M. We did not have available an appropriate independent source of data from which to determine t_M. The accuracy of the model is somewhat inflated by the determination of one of its parameters from the data itself. The substantial variability of t_M indicates that this inflation is probably not too serious, which is to say that small changes in the value of t_M do not make much difference. For example, if a t_M as small as 1.2 sec or as large as 2.0 sec were used in the predictions, the RMS error for the Keystroke-Level Model would only increase from 21 to 23 percent. It should be noted that the t_M estimated from this experiment is now available as an independent estimate for use by others.

The variability of the observed task times is of interest per se, since user behavior is inherently variable. In our data the average coefficient of variation (CV = SD/Mean) of the individual observations over each task is .31, which is the normal variability for behavior of this duration [4]. In comparing the predictions of the model against any actual behavior, the prediction error will always be confounded with some error from the process of sampling the behavior. The sampling error for each of our observed task times is indicated in the SE column of Figure 5. The average standard error is 9 percent.

Fig. 5. Calculated and Observed Execution Times in the Experiment.

Task-System	t_K[b] (sec)	Calculated[a]								Observed $T_{execute}$ M ± SE(N)[c] (sec)(sec)	Pred. Error[d]
		n_M	n_K	n_H	n_P	n_D	l_D (cm)	T_R (sec)	$T_{execute}$ (sec)		
T1-POET	.23	4	15	--	--	--	--	--	8.8[e]	7.8 ± 0.9(27)	11%
T1-SOS	.22	4	19	--	--	--	--	--	9.6	9.6 ± 0.8(31)	1%
T1-DISPED	.23	2	8	2	1	--	--	--	6.4[e]	5.7 ± 0.3(31)	11%
T2-POET	.28	4	14	--	--	--	--	--	9.4	8.9 ± 0.7(17)	5%
T2-SOS	.23	4	18	--	--	--	--	--	9.5	9.7 ± 0.8(32)	– 3%
T2-DISPED	.24	2	4	2	1	--	--	--	5.6	4.1 ± 0.3(32)	26%
T3-POET	.19	3	12	--	--	--	--	--	6.3	6.3 ± 0.4(24)	0%
T3-SOS	.23	2	7	--	--	--	--	--	4.3	4.0 ± 0.3(37)	8%
T3-DISPED	.23	1	2	1	1	--	--	--	3.3	3.5 ± 0.2(38)	– 7%
T4-POET	.19	13	92	--	--	--	--	--	35.3	37.1 ± 4.3(20)	– 6%
T4-SOS	.23	12	47	--	--	--	--	--	26.8	32.7 ± 1.8(16)	–22%
T4-DISPED	.24	2	6	1	3	--	--	3.8	11.6	14.3 ± 1.1(33)	–23%
T5-MARKUP	.25	--	3.2	--	2.5	4	24.9	--	11.1	10.5 ± 1.1(27)	6%
T5-DRAW	.25	7.6	12.6	--	5	--	--	--	18.9	12.5 ± 3.0(22)	34%
T5-SIL	.27	1	4	0.4	2	--	--	--	4.8	5.4 ± 0.7(32)	–12%
T6-MARKUP	.26	1	7	2	1	--	--	--	5.0	6.2 ± 0.4(34)	–23%
T6-DRAW	.25	1	7	1	1	--	--	--	4.6	5.9 ± 0.4(34)	–29%
T6-SIL	.27	--	6	1.4	1	--	--	--	3.3	3.6 ± 0.3(19)	– 9%
T7-MARKUP	.24	--	8.6	--	4.8	6	13.6	--	15.1	15.0 ± 2.1(29)	2%
T7-DRAW	.19	5	13	--	8	--	--	--	18.0	18.2 ± 1.9(9)	– 1%
T7-SIL	.28	1	8	--	5	--	--	--	9.1	12.3 ± 2.1(23)	–36%
T8-MARKUP	.26	--	8	--	8	1	4.0	--	12.3	9.3 ± 0.4(22)	24%
T8-DRAW	.21	1	5	--	3	--	--	--	5.7	5.3 ± 0.3(25)	7%
T8-SIL	.27	1	5	0.7	2	--	--	--	5.2	4.1 ± 0.2(33)	20%
T9-MARKUP	.25	2	8	--	6.5	--	--	3.5	15.4	13.0 ± 2.5(26)	15%
T9-DRAW	.22	--	5.7	--	5.7	--	--	--	7.5	10.5 ± 1.0(25)	–40%
T9-SIL	.28	--	5	0.3	3	--	--	--	4.8	6.0 ± 1.0(28)	–24%
T10-LOGIN	.29	2	28	--	--	--	--	15.9	27.4[f]	25.1 ± 0.7(29)	9%
T11-FTP	.30	5	31	--	--	--	--	10.1	26.1	19.7 ± 0.7(29)	24%
T12-CHAT	.31	1	11	--	--	--	--	8.3	13.1	11.5 ± 0.6(36)	12%
T13-DIR	.30	2	20	--	--	--	--	0.5	9.2	6.6 ± 0.3(32)	28%
T14-DELVER	.32	2	20	--	--	--	--	0.4	9.4	7.5 ± 0.4(33)	20%

[a] The calculations are done according to formula (1) using the operator times in Figure 1, except for t_K.

[b] t_K is the average time from the typing tests for the subjects on a given system. Each subject's time is weighted by the correct number of instances for that subject on a given task (see Section 4.2.1).

[c] SE is the standard error of estimation of the population mean for samples of size N.

[d] The prediction error is given as a percentage of the calculated time, $T_{execute}$.

[e] The calculated times for these tasks are different from the calculated times in the examples in Section 3.2, because different t_K are used.

[f] The execute time for this task also includes .7 sec for the operation of moving the telephone receiver (see Section 4.2.1).

That the prediction error of the Keystroke-Level Model is over two times larger than this indicates that most of the prediction error is due to the inaccuracy of the model and not just unreliable observations.

4.2.3 Acquisition time. Turning from the execution part of the task to the acquisition part, the data shows that it took users 2 sec, on the average, to acquire a task from the manuscript. This number may be refined by breaking the tasks into three types: (a) those tasks that the user already had in memory (the executive subsystem tasks that were done each time in the same order); (b) those tasks for which the user had to look at the manuscript each time (all the graphics tasks, the POET and SOS tasks, and task T11); and (c) those tasks for which the

user had to look at the manuscript, then scan text on the CRT to locate the task. The times for these three types of acquisition are given in Figure 7. Users took only .5 sec when the task was in memory, 1.8 sec to get the task from the manuscript, and 4.0 sec to get the task from the manuscript and scan the CRT. These times are similar to results obtained in previous experiments [4]. It is interesting to note that, although display editors are generally faster to use, they impose a 2 sec penalty by requiring the user to visually scan the text on the display.

We can use the acquisition times in Figure 7, along with the predicted execution times in Figure 5, to predict the total task times. The RMS error of these predictions is 21 percent, which is just as accurate as predicting the execution times alone.

Fig. 6. Predicted vs. observed execution times in the experiment.

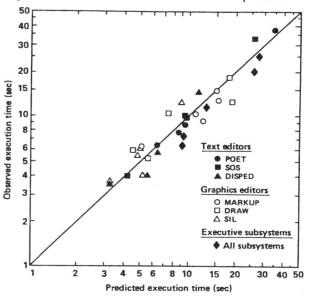

Text editors
● POET
■ SOS
▲ DISPED

Graphics editors
○ MARKUP
□ DRAW
△ SIL

Executive subsystems
◆ All subsystems

5. Sample Applications of the Keystroke-Level Model

The experiment has provided evidence for the Keystroke-Level Model in a wide range of user-computer interactions. Given the method used, the time required for experts to perform a unit task can be predicted to within about 20 percent by a linear function of a small set of operators. This result is powerful in permitting prediction without having to do any measurements of the actual situation and in expressing the prediction as a simple algebraic expression. Its limitation lies in requiring that the method be completely specified at the level of keystrokes and in being limited to error-free expert behavior.

In this section we illustrate how the Keystroke-Level Model can be used, both to exploit its power and to work within its restrictions. The basic application—to predict a time for a specific situation by writing down a method and computing the value—has been sufficiently illustrated in the course of the experiment, where such point predictions were made for 32 different tasks involving 10 highly diverse systems. We now show three further uses: (1) calculated benchmarks for systems; (2) parametric analysis, where predictions are expressed as functions of task variables; and (3) sensitivity analysis, where changes in the predictions are examined as a function of changes in task or model parameters.

5.1 Calculated Benchmarks

Given the ability to predict tasks, it is possible to calculate the equivalent of a benchmark for a system and hence to compare systems. This has obvious cost advantages over obtaining actual measurements. More importantly, it permits benchmarking at design time, before the system exists in a form that permits measurement.

The analysis for the experimental data lets us illustrate this easily.

Consider the three text editors, POET, SOS, and DISPED. Let the benchmark be the four tasks T1 to T4. We can use the Keystroke-Level Model to compute the total time to do the benchmark for each system. The answer comes directly from Figure 5 by summing the calculated $T_{execute}$ for T1–T4 for each editor. This gives 59.8 sec, 50.2 sec, and 26.9 sec as the predicted execution times, respectively, for POET, SOS, and DISPED. Taking the POET time (the slowest) as 100, we get ratios of 100:84:45. Thus, as we might have expected, the two line-oriented editors are relatively close to each other and the display editor is substantially faster. Since we have also done the experiment, we can compare these calculated benchmarks with the observed benchmarks (by summing the observed $T_{execute}$ from Figure 5). We get 60.1 sec, 56.0 sec, and 27.6 sec, respectively. This gives experimentally determined ratios 100:93:46, which is essentially the same result. This agreement between the calculated and observed benchmark provides confidence only in using the calculated benchmark in place of a measured one. It does not provide evidence for the validity of the particular benchmark (tasks T1–T4) or whether benchmarks are generally a valid way to compare editors.

A similar analysis can be performed for the three graphics systems, using tasks T5–T9 as the benchmark. This yields predicted ratios of 100:93:46 for MARKUP, DRAW, and SIL, respectively, with observed ratios of 100: 97:58. MARKUP and DRAW are close enough to raise the question of whether the predicted difference between them is too small to be reliable. The calculated difference between MARKUP and DRAW on the benchmark is 59.0 –54.7 = 4.3 sec or 7 percent. The model has an RMS prediction error of 21 percent for a single unit task. Since this benchmark is essentially an independent sum of five unit tasks, the RMS error should theoretically be 21 percent/SQRT(5) = 9 percent. Thus, the predictions for the two systems are within the RMS error of the model, and so the predicted difference between them can hardly

Fig. 7. Observed acquisition times in the experiment.

Task Type	Task numbers	Acquisition Time $M \pm SE^a$ (N) (sec) (sec)
All tasks	T1–T14	2.0 ± 2.0 (885)
Repeated task, recalled from memory	T10, T12, T13, T14	0.5 ± 0.3 (130)
Task acquired by looking at manuscript	T1–T4 (POET, SOS), T5–T9, T11	1.8 ± 1.9 (621)
Task acquired by looking at manuscript, then scanning for task on display	T1–T4 (DISPED)	4.0 ± 1.9 (134)

* SE is the standard error of estimation of the population mean for samples of size N.

be reliable. The fact that the model correctly predicted that DRAW was slightly faster than MARKUP was lucky—there is no reason to expect the Keystroke-Level Model to make such close calls.

5.2 Parametric Analysis

We illustrate the notions of parametric analysis and sensitivity analysis with a new example. Consider the following task: A user is typing text into an editor and detects a misspelled word n words back from the word he is currently typing. How long will it take to correct the misspelled word and resume typing?

In DISPED there are two methods for making the correction, which we wish to compare. Since the methods may behave quite differently depending on how far back the misspelled word is, we need to determine how long each method takes as a function of n. The first method makes use of the Backward command (called by hitting the CTRL key and then W), which erases the last typed in word:

Method W (Backword):

Set up Backword command	MK[CTRL]
Execute Backword n times	$n((1/c)$MK[W]$)$
Type new word	5.5K[word]
Retype destroyed text	5.5$(n - 1)$K

$$T_{execute} = (1 + n/c)t_M + (1 + 6.5n)t_K$$
$$= 1.6 + 2.16n \ sec. \qquad (2)$$

The execution time is a function not only of n, but also of another parameter, c. When a user has to repeat a single-keystroke command several times, such as the Backword command in the above method, he will tend to break the sequence into small bursts or *chunks*, separated by pauses, which are represented as **M** operations, according to Rule 2 in Figure 2. Thus, we postulate a chunk size, c, which is the average number of Backword commands in a burst. This is used in the second step in the above method, where we count $1/c$ **M** operations for each call of the Backword command. An exact value for c is unknown, but we use a "reasonable" value, $c = 4$, in our calculations (we will return to this decision in Section 5.3). In the calculations we also assume an average nonsecretary typist ($t_K = .28$ sec) and an average word length of 5.5 characters (including punctuation and spaces).

The second method is to get out of type-in mode, use the Replace command to correct the word, and then get back into type-in mode, so that input can be resumed:

Method R (Replace):

Terminate type-in mode	MK[ESC]
Point to target word and select it	H[mouse] P[word] K[YELLOW]
Call Replace command	H[keyboard] MK[R]
Type new word	4.5K[word]
Terminate Replace command	MK[ESC]
Point to last input word and select it	H[mouse] P[word] K[YELLOW]
Reenter type-in mode	H[keyboard] MK[I]

$$T_{execute} = 4t_M + 10.5t_K + 4t_H + 2t_P$$
$$= 12.1 \ sec.$$

The predicted time for each method as a function of n is plotted as the solid lines in Figure 8(a). As the figure shows, it is faster to use the Backword method up until a certain crossover point, n_{WR}, after which it becomes faster to use the Replace method. Under the above assumptions, the crossover from the Backword method to the Replace method is found to be at 4.9 words.

Suppose a designer wants to add a feature to DISPED to improve performance on this task. We wish to determine, *before* implementation, whether the proposed feature is likely to be much of an improvement.

The designer proposes two new commands. The first is a Backskip command (CRTL S), which moves the insertion point back one word without erasing any text. The second is a Resume command (CTRL R), which moves the insertion point back to the end of the current type-in (where Backskip was first called). These commands allow:

Method S (Backskip):

Set up Backskip command	MK[CTRL]
Execute Backskip $n - 1$ times	$(n - 1)((1/c)$MK[S]$)$
Call Backward command	MK[W]
Type new word	4.5K[word]
Call Resume command	M2K[CTRL R]

$$T_{execute} = (3 + (n - 1)/c)t_M + (n + 7.5)t_K \qquad (3)$$
$$= 5.8 + .62n \ sec.$$

The predicted time for the Backskip method is plotted as the dashed line in Figure 8(a). With the addition of this method there are two additional crossover points, n_{WS} and n_{RS}, between it and the other two methods. As can be seen, the Backskip method is faster than both of the other methods between n_{WS} and n_{RS}, i.e., from 2.7 to 10.2 words. Thus, a brief analysis provides evidence that the proposed new feature probably will be useful, in the sense that it will be the fastest method over a region of the task space.

5.3 Sensitivity Analysis

How sensitive to variations in the parameters of the methods are the aforementioned calculations? The question of interest is whether, over such variations, there is still a region in the task space in which the Backskip method is the fastest. An important parameter is the user's typing speed, t_K. How much does the crossover between the Backword method and the Backskip method change as a function of typing speed? Setting eq. (2) equal to (3) and solving for n as a function of t_K gives $n = 1.2 + .43/t_K$. The crossover increases with faster typists (decreasing t_K), going up to $n = 6.6$ words for the fastest typist ($t_K = .08$ sec). That is to say, faster typists should prefer the old Backword method (which involves more typing) for larger n before switching to the new Backskip method (which involves less typing, but more mental overhead).

We can plot the crossover boundary between the two methods in the space of the two parameters: n (characterizing different tasks) and t_K (characterizing different users). The two boundaries of the new Backskip method are plotted in Figure 8(b). These boundaries define the

Fig. 8(a). Execution time for three methods as a function of *n*.

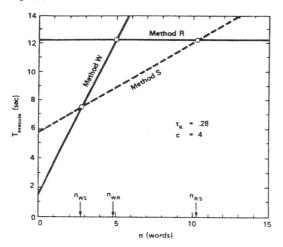

Fig. 8(b). Phase diagram for the fastest method.

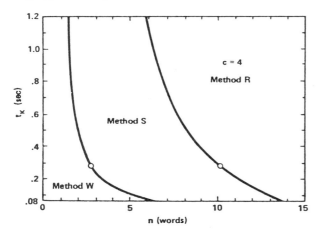

Fig. 8(c). Phase diagram adjusted for different chunk sizes.

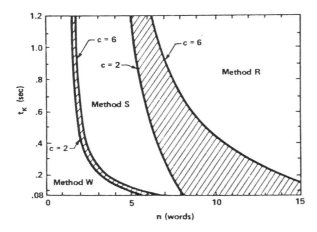

regions in the parameter space where each method is fastest. The circles mark the crossover points corresponding to the ones in Figure 8(a) (i.e., at $t_K = .28$ sec). This diagram clearly shows the shift of crossovers for fast typists. It also shows that, for any speed of typist, there are some tasks for which the Backskip method is the fastest.

We are not sure of the exact chunk size, c, and so we must check whether our conclusions about the usefulness of the Backskip method are sensitive to the choice of a value for c. To do this, we rederive the crossover between the Backword and Backskip methods by setting eq. (2) equal to (3) and solving for n as a function of both c and t_K; this gives $n = 1.2 + .49/t_K - .24/ct_K$. Although we do not know an exact value for c, we can be reasonably confident that it will be between 2 and 6. With $t_K = .28$ sec, for example, the crossover varies between 2.5 and 2.8 words as c varies between 2 and 6; so the value of c does not seem to have a great effect at this point.

The best way to see the overall affect of the value of c is to replot Figure 8(b) using the reasonable extreme values of c. The two crossover boundaries for the Backskip method are plotted in Figure 8(c) as "fat" lines defined by setting c to 2 and 6 in the crossover equations. This diagram clearly shows that the value of c affects one boundary more than the other. The boundary between the Backword and Backskip methods is not affected much by c, because the chunk size is involved in both methods in exactly the same way. But the boundary between the Backskip and Replace methods is greatly affected by the value of c, since c is not involved in the Replace method at all. Small chunk sizes, especially, penalize the Backskip method. Overall, however, varying c does not squeeze out the region for the Backskip method; and our basic conclusion—that the new method is a useful addition—still holds.

There are other aspects of the above methods for which we could do a sensitivity analysis. (For example, if the last two **M** operations of the Backskip method were eliminated according to Rule 1, how much would the value of the Backskip method increase?) However, the sensitivity analyses above illustrate how the Keystroke-Level Model can be used to evaluate design choices—even when many aspects of the calculation are uncertain—for the principal conclusions are often insensitive to many of the uncertainties.

6. Simplifications of the Keystroke-Level Model

The question naturally arises as to whether further simplifications of the Keystroke-Level Model might do reasonably well at predicting execution time. One could (a) count only the number of keystrokes, (b) count just the physical operators and prorate the time for mental activity, or (c) use a single constant time for all operators. We show below that such simplifications substantially degrade accuracy. However, they provide useful approximations where the lowered accuracy can be tolerated.

6.1 Keystrokes Only

With this simplification, execution time is proportional to the number of keystrokes:

$$T_{execute} = \kappa n_K + T_R.$$

We separate out the system response times, T_R, so as not to confound the comparison. The constant of proportionality, κ, should be distinguished from t_K, the typing speed, which is determined from standard typing tests. Estimating the value of κ from a least-squares fit of the values of n_K and the observed $T_{execute}$ in Figure 5 gives $\kappa = .49$ sec/keystroke. The correlation between the times predicted by this model and the observed times is .87, and the RMS error is 49 percent. The statistics for comparing all models are presented in Figure 9. As can be seen, using keystrokes only is substantially less accurate than the full Keystroke-Level Model. This simplification is inappropriate for tasks that are not dominated by keystroking. For example, it only predicts about a third of the observed time for the MARKUP tasks, which are dominated by pointing and drawing operations.

The above estimate of κ is held down by one outlying point in the data, T4-POET ($n_K = 92$). Estimating κ with this one point removed gives $\kappa = .60$ sec, a value close to another estimate obtained in an earlier benchmark study [1; 5, ch. 3]. T4-POET is the only task that requires any input-typing of text. One obvious refinement of the keystrokes-only model would be to distinguish two kinds of keystrokes: mass input-typing (at t_K sec/keystroke) versus command-language keying (at κ sec/keystroke). For this purpose, a κ of .60 sec is the more reasonable value.

The model of Embley et al. [9] is formally similar to our keystrokes-only version. However, their model is conceptually different from ours. The Keystroke-Level Model is based on the notion of a unit task structure; Embley et al. use commands instead. Our model is restricted to skilled expert behavior, whereas they attempt to model all kinds of users (essentially, by varying their versions of the parameters $T_{acquire}$ and κ). Unfortunately, they did not compare their model against any empirical performance data, so we cannot compare our results to theirs. The keystrokes-only model can, perhaps, be taken as an indicator of the accuracy of their model for expert behavior.

6.2 Prorated Mental Time

According to this simplification, execution time is the time required for the physical operations multiplied by a factor to account for the mental time:

$$T_{execute} = \mu(T_K + T_H + T_P + T_D) + T_R.$$

The idea is that the physical operations will require a certain average overhead of mental activity. Thus, instead of trying to predict exactly how many mental operations there are, we can do fairly well by just using a multiplicative mental overhead constant, μ.

Using a least-squares analysis to determine μ from the sum of the calculated times for the physical opera-

Fig. 9. Comparison of the keystroke model with simpler variations.

Model Variation	Parameters	Correlation (r)[a]	RMS Error[b]
Keystrokes Only	κ = .49 sec/keystroke[c]	.87	49%
Prorated Mental Time	μ = 1.67	.81	45%
Constant Operator Time	τ = .43 sec/operator[c]	.92	34%
Keystroke Model	(See Figure 1)	.95	22%

[a] The correlations are between the execution times predicted by each of the models and the observed execution times from Figure 5.

[b] The RMS error is given as a percentage of the observed execution time, 11.0 sec.

[c] More useful parameter values are κ = .60 sec and τ = .49 sec (see Sections 6.1 and 6.3).

tions and the observed values of $T_{execute}$ in Figure 5 gives $\mu = 1.67$; i.e., there is a 67 percent overhead for mental activity. The correlation between predicted and observed times is .81, and the RMS error is 45 percent.

This simplification is also less accurate than the Keystroke-Level Model, as can be seen in Figure 9. This suggests that the extra detail in the Keystroke-Level Model, involving the placements of the mental preparedness operator, **M**, is effective. It is this operator that qualifies the Keystroke-Level Model as a genuine psychological model and not simply as an analysis of the physical operations.

There is an interesting relation between these two simpler models and the rules for placing occurrences of **M** in the Keystroke-Level Model (Figure 2). The initial placement of **M**'s, by Rule 0, with certain **K**'s and **P**'s is essentially an assumption that mental time is proportional to a subset of the physical operators. If Rule 0 had specified all physical operators, Rule 0 by itself would have been equivalent to prorating mental time. If the other physical operators (**P**, **H**, and **D**) had been ignored, this would have been equivalent to counting keystrokes only. Therefore, the deletion of the **M**'s according to Rules 1 to 4 constitutes the ways in which the Keystroke-Level Model departs from these simpler models. The evidence for the superiority of the Keystroke-Level Model presented in Figure 9 is also evidence that Rules 1 to 4 had a significant effect. In fact, each of the rules individually makes a significant contribution, in the sense that its removal leads to a decrease in the accuracy of the Keystroke-Level Model.

6.3 Constant Operator Time

According to this simplification, execution time is proportional to the *number* of Keystroke-Level operations:

$$T_{execute} = \tau(n_M + n_K + n_P + n_H + n_D) + T_R.$$

The idea here is the statistical observation [18] that the accuracy of linear models is not sensitive to the differential weighting of the factors—equal weighting does nearly as well as any other weighting. Thus, we disregard the different operator times and use a single time, τ, for all operators. Note that the constant-operator-time model is formally similar to the keystrokes-only model; the latter can be viewed as using n_K as a crude estimate of the total number of operators.

Estimating τ by a least-squares fit of the data in Figure 5 gives $\tau = .43$ sec/operator. The correlation between predicted and observed times is .92, and the RMS error is 34 percent. (For the reason discussed in Section 6.1, it is useful to estimate τ with the T4-POET task removed, getting $\tau = .49$ sec/operator.)

The constant-time model is quite a bit more accurate than the keystrokes-only model, which tells us that taking into account operators other than **K** is useful. In fact, most of the action in the constant-time model (over the set of data in Figure 5, at least) comes from counting only the **K**, **P**, and **M** operators. In any particular task, of course, any of the operators can be dominant. On the other hand, the constant-time model is still less accurate than the Keystroke-Level Model, showing that taking into account accurate estimates of each operator's time yields another increment of accuracy.

In summary, all of the simplifications presented in this section are less accurate than the Keystroke-Level Model. However, these simplified models are probably good enough for many practical applications, especially for "back-of-the-envelope" calculations, where it is too much trouble to worry about the subtleties of counting the **M**'s that the full Keystroke-Level Model requires.

7. Conclusion

We have presented the Keystroke-Level Model for predicting the time it will take a user to perform a task using a system. We view this model as a *system design tool*. We have shaped it with two main concerns in mind. First, the tool must be quick and easy to use, if it is to be useful *during the design* of interactive systems. The existing strengths of psychology and human factors methods are primarily in the design and analysis of experiments; but experiments are too slow and cumbersome to be incorporated into practice. Ease of use implies that the tool be analytical—that it permit calculation in the style familiar to all engineers. Second, the tool must be useful to practicing computer system designers, who are not psychologists. This implies that the entire tool must be packaged to avoid requiring specialized psychological knowledge. We think that the Keystroke-Level Model satisfies these concerns, along with the primary consideration of being accurate enough to make design decisions. We believe that the Keystroke-Level Model belongs in the system designer's tool-kit.

It is possible to formulate more complicated and refined models than the Keystroke-Level Model by increasing its accuracy or by relaxing some of its serious restrictions (e.g., models that predict methods or that predict errors). One of the great virtues of the Keystroke-Level Model, from our own perspective as scientists trying to understand how humans interact with computer systems, is that it puts a lower bound on the effectiveness of new proposals. Any new proposal must do better than the Keystroke-Level Model (improve on its accuracy or lessen its restrictions) to merit serious consideration.

The Keystroke-Level Model has several restrictions: The user must be an expert; the task must be a routine unit task; the method must be specified in detail; and the performance must be error-free. These restrictions are important and must be carefully considered when using the model. Yet, we believe that the Keystroke-Level Model model represents an appropriate idealization of this aspect of performance and that it is a flexible tool allowing the system designer to deal systematically with this aspect of behavior.

The Keystroke-Level Model predicts only one aspect of the total user-computer interaction, namely, the time to perform a task. As we discussed at the beginning of this paper, there are many other important aspects of performance, there are nonexpert users, and there are nonroutine tasks. All of these must be considered by the system designer. Designing for expert, error-free performance time on routine tasks will not satisfy these other aspects. We would like to see appropriate models developed for these other aspects. However, even with a collection of such models, the designer still must make the inevitable trade-offs. Scientific models do not eliminate the design problem, but only help the designer control the different aspects.

Acknowledgments. We thank J. Farness, who ran the experiments described in this report, and T. Roberts, who helped in some of our early explorations of the keystroke-counting idea and provided extensive comments on earlier drafts of this paper.

References

1. Card, S.K. Studies in the psychology of computer text-editing systems. Ph.D. Th., Dept. of Psychol., Carnegie-Mellon Univ., Pittsburgh, Pa., May 1978.
2. Card, S.K., English, W.K., and Burr, B.J. Evaluation of mouse, rate-controlled isometric joystick, step keys, and text keys for text selection on a CRT. *Ergonomics 21* (1978), 601–613.
3. Card, S.K., Moran, T.P., and Newell, A. The keystroke-level model of user performance time with interactive systems. Rep. SSL-79-1, Xerox, Palo Alto Res. Ctr., Palo Alto, Ca., March 1979.
4. Card, S.K., Moran, T.P., and Newell, A. Computer text-editing: An information-processing analysis of a routine cognitive skill. *Cognitive Psychol. 12* (1980), 32–74.
5. Card, S.K., Moran, T.P., and Newell, A. *Applied Information Processing Psychology: The Human-Computer Interface.* Erlbaum, Hillsdale, N.J. (in preparation).
6. Chase, W.G., and Simon, H.A. Perception in chess. *Cognitive Psychol. 4* (1973), 55–81.
7. Deutsch, P.L., and Lampson, B.W. An online editor. *Comm. ACM 10*, 12 (Dec. 1967), 793–799.

8. Devoe, D.B. Alternatives to handprinting in the manual entry of data. *IEEE Trans. HFE-8* (1967), 21–32.

9. Embley, D.W., Lan, M.T., Leinbaugh, D.W., and Nagy, G. A procedure for predicting program editor performance from the user's point of view. *Internat. J. Man-Machine Studies 10* (1978), 639–650.

10. Maynard, H.B. *Industrial Engineering Handbook.* McGraw-Hill, New York, 3rd ed., 1971.

11. Moran, T.P. The command language grammar: A representation for the user interface of interactive computer systems. *Internat. J. Man-Machine Studies* (in press).

12. Myer, T. H., and Barnaby, J.R. Tenex executive language manual for users. Bolt, Beranek, and Newman, Inc., Cambridge, Mass., 1973.

13. Newman, W., and Sproull, R. *Principles of Interactive Computer Graphics.* McGraw-Hill, New York, 2nd ed., 1979.

14. Pew, R.W., Baron, S., Feehrer, C.E., and Miller, D.C. Critical review and analysis of performance models applicable to man-machine systems evaluation. Bolt, Beranek, and Newman, Inc., Cambridge, Mass., 1977.

15. Ramsey, H.R., and Atwood, M.E. Human factors in computer systems: A review of the literature. Science Applications, Inc., Englewood, Colorado, 1979.

16. Savitsky, S. Son of STOPGAP. Rep. SAILON 50.1, Stanford Artif. Intell. Lab., Stanford, Ca., 1969.

17. Simon, H.A. How big is a chunk? *Science 183* (1974), 482–488.

18. Wainer, H. Estimating coefficients in linear models: It don't make no nevermind. *Psychol. Bull. 83* (1976), 213–217.

Chapter 6

Cognition and Human Information Processing

The objective of this chapter is *not* to provide a short-course in cognitive psychology, but rather, to introduce a few of the key cognitive issues and terms that play a role in user interface design, and which a reader might encounter in the literature. If the chapter meets our objectives, it will also provide a catalyst for the reader to pursue these issues more deeply. Good sources for additional information are Neisser (1967); Lindsay and Norman (1977); Lachman, Lachman, and Butterfield (1979); Norman (1982); Anderson (1985); and, Gardner (1987).

An Information Processing Model

The discussion that follows will treat human cognition from the perspective of the human being as an information processor, using concepts such as input/output, memory, processing power, and critical resources. This is a convenient metaphor, since most readers of this volume will have some information processing background. It is also convenient because it is a metaphor used in cognitive psychology, captured, for example, in the title of a standard introductory text on psychology, *Human Information Processing: An Introduction to Psychology* (Lindsay and Norman, 1977).

Using this metaphor, however, does *not* imply that the brain's functioning is analogous to that of a computer, or that we are all walking around with Von Neumann machines in our heads. What we *are* saying is that the concepts and vocabulary of information processing help in describing many current theories of human cognition.

Perception and Cognition

Perception and cognition are considered by many people to be more or less separate processes. Folk wisdom imagines the perceptual mechanism as a kind of preprocessor that captures signals from the outside world, identifies tokens and their attributes, and passes them on for cognitive processing. This pre-processor view of perception is simplistic and misleading.

While the ear is peripheral to the brain, it is incorrect to infer that the sensory processing of acoustic stimuli is also peripheral. The perceptual mechanism is not a sponge that simply soaks up stimuli. It is an active process that involves cognition. In listening to music, for example, there is a great deal of processing that must take place before we can even begin to determine what pitch each of two different instruments is playing. We can't hear without listening, and we can't see without looking.

Figure 1 illustrates the active nature of perception. One has to look, postulate hypotheses, and use real-world knowledge to interpret the scene. So it is, to a greater or lesser degree, in all perception. Later in this chapter, we will see how this fact has important design implications, especially as concerns audio and visual stimuli.

Although perception is intimately linked to cognition, we defer the subject of perception to Chapters 7-9, dealing with the visual, haptic, and audio channels, respectively.

Figure 1: Perception as an Active Process.
What is this a figure of? To understand this scene, viewers must actively use their knowledge of the world to infer some structure. It is unlikely that anything other than a pattern of black shapes will be perceived by the passive observer. Successful interpretation of the scene, a Dalmation dog in a park, will generally be accomplished only by active viewing (from Lindsay and Norman, 1977, p. 12).

The Issue of Limited Resources

There are two concepts from information processing that are of particular importance in understanding current theories of cognition:

- critical resources
- limited resources

Critical resources are resources that are required to perform a particular task, or to execute a particular process. *Limited resources* are resources that are in short supply relative to their need. In cognition, as in operating systems, problems arise when critical resources are limited, and supply cannot meet the demand. One quality of the human information processor, compared to the typical computer system, is that performance generally degrades gracefully when resources become so saturated.

The Resource Utilization of Tasks

Various tasks and cognitive activities can be discussed in terms of the resources that they consume: both in type and in quantity. This is developed, for example, in Norman and Bobrow (1975), in which processes are characterized as being limited by either

- the processing resources available, or
- the quality of data available

The issue of available processing *resources* has to do with memory, processing "cycles," and internal communications channels. If additional resources will improve performance, then the task is said to be *resource limited.*

Data quality has to do with what is being processed, rather than what is doing the processing. Once we reach a point at which adding processing resources does not improve performance, the process is said to be *data limited.* That is, no improvement in performance can be achieved without improving the quality of the data available for processing.

Data limited processes can be further divided into two categories, having either

- signal data limits, or
- memory data limits

Signal data limits have to do with the quality of input. In audio terms, we would describe such cases as having a poor "signal-to-noise" ratio. One example would be trying to hold a conversation with a jack-hammer running right beside you. Clearly, unless something is done about the ambient noise, you are never going to get beyond a certain level of communication, regardless of how closely you listen. Similarly, if text is presented on a CRT in a terrible typeface and with a lot of glare on the screen, your reading speed will be limited despite your best efforts to the contrary.

Memory data limits are less straightforward, but equally important. In an earlier section we discussed the relationship between perception and active processing. Memory data limits have to do with this processing. Consider the preceding example of trying to read poorly presented text on a CRT. One of the processes at play in this situation is your use of "world knowledge," your knowledge about what an "A" is, for example. Your ability to use this kind of "previous experience" affects your effectiveness at reading in this situation. It is reasonable to assume that someone using this terminal for the first time will not be able to read as fast as someone who has experience with it. This illustrates the idea that the paradigms, or the bases of stored past experience, used can differ in quality. Furthermore, the quality of the stored paradigm influences the quality of the data available for processing. The quality of these stored paradigms is an example of a memory data limit.

The relationship between resource and data limitation in the performance of a sample task is shown in Figure 2. Once a minimum number of resources have been allocated (point R_{min}), performance improves as resources are added, up to the point R_{dl}. To this point, the task is resource limited. Beyond R_{dl}, the task is data limited. Unless the data is improved, performance beyond this point will not improve, despite any additional resources that may be allocated.

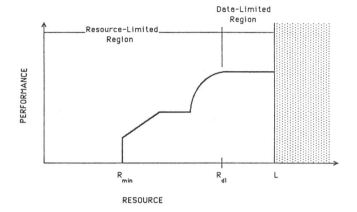

Figure 2: Data and Resource Limitation
Resource and data limitation in performing a sample task. Increase in performance is shown on the vertical axis. Increase in resources is shown along horizontal axis. Certain minimal resources (R_{min}) are required to initiate the task. Performance levels off at a certain point, when the task becomes data limited (R_{dl}) (from Norman and Bobrow, 1975).

In the sample task illustrated in Figure 2, the quality of data is constant, and the resources allocated are increased. However, if the quality of the data were improved, the same performance would likely be achievable using fewer resources (or better performance achieved utilizing the same resources.) There is a trade-off between resources and data quality. In virtually all cases a primary design objective should be to *minimize resource consumption by improving the quality of the data.* Improved display quality and graphic design are techniques for pushing back signal data limits. Training and the use of appropriate mental models are means to push back memory data limits.

Cognitive Load

Why do we need to minimize the cognitive resources required to perform a task or complete a given quantum of work? Cognitive resources are in short supply, and there is a high demand. Hence, there is a cost associated with their use.

A good measure of the complexity, or difficulty of a task is the number of resources it uses (Moray, 1977; Kramer, Wickens and Donchin, 1983; Berlyne, 1960; Sheridan, 1980; Welford, 1978; Hartman, 1961). This measure is known as *cognitive load.* The concept of cognitive load is important, since it correlates directly with factors such as:

- learning time
- fatigue
- stress
- proneness to error, and
- inability to "timeshare"

Cognitive load is an important consideration in the design of both isolated tasks and large systems. At the individual task level, for example, one could consider the different load imposed in making a selection with a mouse having one, two, or three buttons respectively. This is an example that has been studied experimentally. (See Bewley, Roberts, Schroit and Verplank, 1983, included as a reading in Case Study D: The Star, the Lisa, and the Macintosh.) By testing individual cases, it may turn out that the one-button case has the lowest load, since there is no overhead in determining which button to select. However, in the larger context, it may turn out that there is a penalty "down the road" resulting from having only a one-button mouse. Consequently, rather than having reduced the overall load of the system, we may have just redistributed it to another place or time for the user to deal with.

We leave it to the reader, as an exercise, to debate whether this is the case with the one-button mouse on the Apple Macintosh computer. For our purposes, suffice it to say that the example illustrates how complexity and design must always be considered in context, since almost every decision has side-effects.

Interference

Given that resources are limited, sometimes a critical resource cannot be allocated. This may occur when performing a single task with a particularly high cognitive load. More often, it occurs when simultaneous demands are being made on the same resource by two or more different tasks. An everyday example of this is the experience of a parent listening to two children who are talking at once.

There are some situations, however, in which we can do more than one thing at a time, when there are enough resources to go around. Listening to a radio program while driving would be one example. But what happens in an extreme case, such as when the car goes into a skid? It is very likely that the driver will stop listening to the radio, and concentrate on getting the vehicle back under control. Full attention will be focussed on the driving task, and no surplus resources will be available to concentrate on the radio, no matter how interesting the program may be.

Degradation in the performance of one task due to competition for critical resources with another is known as *interference*. In some cases, processes will mutually interfere, resulting in a degradation in the performance of each. As with the driving example, however, what seems to happen more often is that some priority mechanism is invoked that determines which of the competing tasks is more important. This mechanism then allocates the resources under contention accordingly. Thus, the performance of the task with higher priority continues at the expense of the other.

Since many of the tasks that are performed using a computer have a high cognitive load, they are susceptible to interference. One of the goals of the designer is to reduce the likelihood of this occurring. Reducing the load associated with task performance is one approach. As discussed earlier, another way is to improve the quality of data available to the user.

Yet another way to reduce interference is to take steps to minimize the likelihood of competition. Different sensory modalities utilize different resources (Wickens, Sandry and Vidulich, 1983). Processes using them are less susceptible to interference than those using a common modality. For example, while tracking a moving target on a display (using a mouse, for example), you are more likely to be able to perform a simultaneous verbal task than another visual/manual one.

An area in which this might be applied is in the design of help mechanisms. We could base a design on the hypothesis that presenting help messages using the audio channel will not interfere with an application which is presented *via* the visual channel. This may or may not be an improvement, but it is an example of how an understanding of the underlying cognitive structures can help suggest design ideas.

Problem Solving

At this point, there is a strong temptation to enter a long discussion about the nature of problem solving, and all of the current theories that relate to it. But this is an involved topic, one for which we do not have the space, and which others (such as Lindsay and Norman, 1977) have already treated excellently. We will restrict ourselves here to making a few key points.

First, problem solving requires one's attention. It exhibits what is known as *attentive* behaviour. Second, problem solving uses a relatively large number of resources. Consequently, problem solving and its accompanying attentive behaviour are highly susceptible to interference.

In working with a computer system, there are two classes of problems that confront the user: *operational*

and *functional*. Operational problems have to do with the *means* of performing work. Functional problems have to do with the *content* of that work. Imagine you are composing music with an interactive editor for musical notation. "How do I delete that note?" is an operational problem. "Should I orchestrate this note with a flute or saxophone?" is a functional one.

One objective of user interface design should be to minimize operational problem solving. All resources consumed at this level are being diverted from the primary application for which the computer was adopted in the first place. That is, *they are wasted*, insofar as the primary task is concerned. Design features such as consistency and careful documentation are critical in reducing this diversion of resources.

The overhead of functional problem solving can also be reduced by careful design. The key here is to recognize the influence of representation on the relative difficulty of solving a problem. This goes back to the old notion that "representation is a tool of thought," or "a problem properly represented is 3/4 solved."

If a computer is adopted to help perform a particular task, the chances are that the task has already taxed a human's problem solving ability. This being the case, it is critical that the system be designed so that the user can get to the heart of the problem by the most effective path, using a minimum of valuable cognitive resources along the way.

Cognitive Skills

We have all encountered people who seemed to perform tasks effortlessly that we find exceedingly difficult. For us, if it can be done at all, the task clearly involves attentive, problem solving behaviour. Playing piano, sailing a boat, writing computer programs, or solving math problems are all possible examples. While experts in such activities are likewise performing complex tasks, they exhibit behaviour which is very different from our own. What characterizes their behaviour is that they are *skilled* in that particular activity.

A useful and important point made by Card, Moran and Newell (1983) is their contrasting problem-solving *vs* skilled behaviour as two extremes along a continuum. Similarly, Rasmussen (1983) describes three levels of task performance: *knowledge-*, *rule-*, and *skill*-based performance.

Unlike the attentive nature of problem solving, skilled task performance is *automatic*. Skilled task performance consumes negligible cognitive resources, compared to problem solving. Consequently, skilled performance is less susceptible to interference. Also, the resources thus released can sometimes be allocated to some other task which may be performed synchronously with the skilled task. One visible clue that a subject is exhibiting skill is the execution of two or more complex tasks in parallel. (Of course, the extent to which this is possible is very task dependent).

Many of the properties of skilled and unskilled (i.e., problem solving) behaviours can be observed in a simple experiment in a Chinese restaurant. Have a meal with someone who has never used chopsticks, someone who has used chopsticks since childhood, and someone else whose skill level lies in between. Eating will occupy the novice's full attention. The slightest distraction will result in spilled food. The subject who is slightly beyond the level of a beginner may seem to eat effortlessly, but if you ask her a difficult enough question (i.e., one that generates enough interference) she too will drop her food. With the expert, it is unlikely that any task that you present, that doesn't interfere with the use of hand or mouth, will interfere with their eating. Expert chopstick users can talk, read, recite poetry, or answer calculus questions while eating, without problems. They are skilled.

One way to gain insights into the nature of skill is to observe people who are experts at a particular task. This is precisely what is done by Card, Moran and Newell (1980) in the reading describing their study of computer text editing. What they discovered was that experts had built up a repertoire of techniques, or *methods*, for dealing with the standard situations encountered in editing a document by computer. One can think of these methods as the cognitive equivalent of macros, or subroutines. All of the individual steps, or *operators*, required to perform a particular learned task are bound together. In text editing, the expert need only recognize the problem, *select* the most appropriate method for dealing with it, and invoke it.

Because experts are highly practiced, and recognize each situation that they have seen before, the recognition and selection tasks impose minimal loading, and the execution of a task can be automatic.

The metaphor of a cognitive subroutine is a fairly functional description of skilled performance. Like a program calling a subroutine, the expert considers the performance of the skilled task as a single act. By contrast, the novice has to "write" and "debug" the solution to each text-editing task on a step-by-step basis. Neves and Anderson (1981) have described the acquisition of cognitive skills as the process of *compilation* and *proceduralization* of these individual steps (what Card, Moran and Newell call *unit tasks*) into debugged, higher-level structures.

Skill Acquisition

Achieving a skilled level of proficiency in any task is difficult. It seems that skills — cognitive and sensori-motor — are learned through simple practice and repetition. This is seen in a classic study by Crossman (1959), who studied the acquisition of skills in cigar making. It is also discussed in Newell and Rosenbloom (1981), who discuss a "power law of practice." Obviously, not all skills have the same difficulty of acquisition. Most of us can master riding a bicycle. Fewer, even if given the opportunity, can learn to fly a helicopter or become a virtuoso on violin. The *learning curve* for a number of diverse skills is shown in Figure 3.

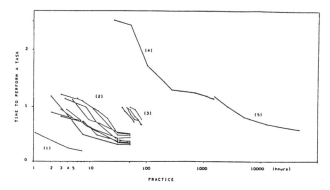

Figure 3: Learning Curves
Learning curves for a number of diverse tasks are presented (Bösser and Melchior, 1985). (1) Reading inverted text (minutes/text); Average 6 subjects (Kolers, 1976). (2) Text Processing with Wordstar-editor (minutes/CET); Benchmark test with 50 core editing tasks (CET; 9 subjects). (3) Typing alpha numeric code material (seconds/keystroke); Average of 18 employees each group (Baddeley and Longman, 1978). (4) Mail sorting (seconds/letter); Average of 30 employees. (5) Cigar-making (minutes/cigar); Average of several employees (Crossman, 1959).

The study of the acquisition of cognitive skills is an important and developing field. The interested reader is referred, in particular, to Anderson (1981) and to Schneider (1985). The reader is also referred to the somewhat larger literature on sensory/motor skills, since much of it applies equally to cognitive skill. Welford (1976) is a good place to start.

Training procedures are part of the user interface, and their design should encourage the development of skills in an isolated, controlled, and non-threatening way. For example, at Xerox Palo Alto Research Center, a program was developed to acclimate users to a mouse. It was a simple pursuit-tracking task with a twist: the target being tracked was represented as a fly, and the tracking symbol was a fly-swatter. The instructions given to the user were to kill the moving fly by getting the swatter over top of it and clicking the mouse button. As a result of this training, users were able to proceed to other tasks without any overhead being consumed by the operational problems of the mouse. Similar training methods were used by Buxton and Myers (1985) to rapidly train novices to simultaneously perform a continuous task with each hand.

The general rule here is that many skills developed in isolation transfer well to situations where the skill is used in conjunction with the performance of other tasks. There is also some evidence that the skill is acquired more rapidly in this isolated situation (Schneider, 1985). As with all rules, however, this one does not always hold. For individual cases, field testing is the final proving ground.

Skill Transfer and Consistency

We now encounter a bit of a dilemma. Skilled performance has the desirable property of minimal loading during task execution. On the other hand, skill acquisition has been shown to be expensive. Is this not just a case of transferring the loading from execution time to learning time? Is there a net improvement, especially in the current climate that suggests that systems should be easy to learn as well as to use?

We can sidestep some of these questions by being clearer about what we want to accomplish. Let's stop talking about vague concepts like ''ease of use'' and ''user friendly.'' A clearer formulation of our goal is to *accelerate the process whereby novices begin to perform like experts.* This implies a recognition that the qualitative difference between novice and expert performance is the exhibition of skilled behaviour.

While skills *are* difficult to acquire, new users don't come to a system completely unskilled. Life has equipped us with a large repertoire of highly developed skills, and the more specialized we are in any aspect of our work or pleasure, the more specialized those skills are likely to be.

The skills required to operate a system need not be learned from scratch. Generally, the more specialized the application, the easier it is to design around existing skills. For example, accountants can touch-type on numerical keypads and draftsmen can work a drafting machine with one hand while using a pencil in the other. These are both skills that can form the basis for a powerful *and appropriate* design. Analyzing the target population with respect to possible exploitable skills gives a whole new direction and bite to the platitude, ''know the user.''

In some cases, however, a new skill may be required. We may be able to get a head-start in training by using an existing skill as a point of departure. The use of metaphor is one aspect of this. However, metaphors can go beyond the use of icons, to incorporate control functions based on existing motor skills.

The use of existing skills as the basis for performing new tasks is known as *skill transfer*. Here are four dicta for successfully designing an interface to maximize this transfer:

- build upon the users' existing set of skills
- keep the set of skills required by the system to a minimum
- use the same skill wherever possible in similar circumstances
- use feedback to effectively reinforce similar contexts and distinguish ones that are dissimilar.

The idea is that by keeping the repertoire of skills small, the skills are used more often. This is consistent with the method of practice, whereby a novice attains a skilled level of proficiency.

Using the same skill in similar circumstances is a critical part of this. Beyond the issue of practice, an underlying cognitive principle here is that if interfaces are *consistent* in the choice of skills to be required in a particular context, then the exploitation of in-system skills will be maximized. That is, in a well designed system, when the user is confronted with a new situation, all of the feedback mechanisms will shout ''this is like this other task which you have done before,'' and the user will be able to transfer what has already been learned to the new situation.

As a means of confronting the issues of consistency and transfer, we suggest the following exercise. Analyze the direct manipulation systems at your disposal, and consider the degree of consistency that exists among dragging, selection from pop-up menus, and drawing with rubber-band lines. (See Chapter 10: Interaction Styles and Techniques if these are new concepts.) Are these the same basic transactions? How so? Can and should they be performed using the same motor skills? In what way is loading reduced if they are? Our view of some of these issues is discussed in Chapter 8: The Haptic Channel, especially in the reading, ''Chunking and Phrasing in the Design of Human-Computer Dialogues,'' (Buxton, 1986).

Crossman (1959) is an important early paper on skills acquisition. By its emphasis on methods and their selection, it laid much of the ground-work for the GOMS model of Card, Moran and Newell (1980, 1983). Payne and Green (1983) and Green and Payne (1984) are a source of discussion of issues pertaining to interface design, learnability, and consistency. Polson, Muncher and Engelbeck (1986) present a model of transfer, and therefore a theoretical definition of consistency. In the paper, they make quantitative predictions of transfer effects, and test them experimentally. This paper is interesting for its approach as well as its results. Polson and Kieras (1985) is a related paper that discusses learning and performance in text editing. A study based on this work, which investigates transfer between different text editors is that by Karat, Boyes, Weisgerber and Schafer (1986). Transfer between two different tasks, text editing and graphics editing, is discussed in Zieger, Hoppe and Fahnrich (1986).

Mental Models, Analogy, and Metaphor

Intimately linked to performance in using interactive systems is the *mental model* which the user applies in trying to understand and predict system behaviour. Mental models, according to Carroll (1984a), are ''structures and processes imputed to a person's mind in order to account for that person's behaviour and experience.'' An influential discussion of mental models is that of Norman (1983), included here as a reading. In a more recent work, Norman (1986, pp. 46-47) elaborated further on the nature and role of mental models in the design and usage of interactive systems:

> ...The problem is to design a system so that, first, it follows a consistent, coherent conceptualization — a design model — and, second, so that the user can develop a mental model of that system — a user model — consistent with the design model...
>
> There really are three different concepts to be considered: two mental, one physical. First, there is the conceptualization of the system held by designer; second, there is the conceptual model constructed by the user; and, third, there is the physical image of the system from which the users develop their conceptual models. Both of the conceptual models are what have been called ''mental models,'' but to separate the several different meanings of that term, I refer to these two aspects by different terms. I call the conceptual model held by the designer the *Design Model*, and the conceptual model formed by the user the *User's Model*. The third concept is the image resulting from the physical structure that has been built (including the documentation and instruction). I call that the *System Image*.
>
> The Design Model is the conceptual model of the system to be built. Ideally, this conceptualization is based on the user's tasks, requirements, and capabilities. The conceptualization must also consider the user's background, experience, and the powers and limitations of the user's information processing mechanisms, most especially processing resources and short-term memory limits.
>
> The user develops a mental model of the system — the User's Model. Note that the user model is not formed from the Design Model: It results from the way the user

interprets the System Image. Thus, in many ways, the primary task of the designer is to construct an appropriate System Image, realizing that everything the user interacts with helps to form that image: the physical knobs, dials, keyboards, and displays, and the documentation, including instruction manuals, help facilities, text input and output, and error messages. The designer should want the User's Model to be compatible with the underlying conceptual model, the Design Model. And this can only happen through interacting with the System Image. These comments place a severe burden on the designer. If one hopes for the user to understand a system, to use it properly, and to enjoy using it, then it is up to the designer to make the System Image explicit, intelligible, consistent. And this goes for everything associated with the system. Remember too that people do not always read documentation, and so the major (perhaps entire) burden is placed on the image that the system projects.

In addition to the above, the interested student should look at Young (1981), Young (1983), and Halasz and Moran (1983), which analyze and apply users' conceptual models of calculators. Another useful reference is a comprehensive recent survey by Carroll (1984b).

Learners make use of *analogy* (Rumelhart and Norman, 1981) between the system being learned and systems previously experienced. The interpretation and use of analogy is based upon the *metaphor* with which the system is conceptualized. Thus, in understanding a word processor, we often think of it as something like a typewriter, and the text being edited as something like the characters on a sheet of paper.

Carroll and Thomas (1982) present a series of recommendations concerning learning through the use of metaphor:

> Find and use appropriate metaphors in teaching the naive user a computer system.
>
> Given a choice between two metaphors, choose the one which is most congruent with the way the system really works. The more aspects of the system that can be ''covered'' by a single metaphor, the better.
>
> Take care to ensure that the emotional tone of the metaphor is conducive to the desired emotional attitude of the user.
>
> When it is necessary to use more than one metaphor for a system, choose metaphors drawn from a single real-world task domain (i.e., similar enough) but do not choose objects or procedures which are exclusive alternatives from within that domain (i.e., not too similar).
>
> Consider the probable *consequences* to users and system designers of each metaphor used.

They follow with some recommendations that pertain to the experienced user:

> When introducing a metaphor, explicitly point out to the user that it is not a perfect representation of the underlying system and point toward the limits of the metaphor.
>
> Keep in mind from the beginning that any metaphors presented to the user are to give an overview of the system and that there may be a time, at least for the continual user, that the metaphor is no longer useful.

Provide the user with exciting metaphors for routine work and eventually present the user with a variety of scenarios which present different views and require different actions but whose underlying structure is identical.

Since metaphors may be helpful in some respects and misleading in other respects, Halasz and Moran (1982) have argued the perhaps extreme position that "analogy be considered harmful." A subsequent paper by Carroll and Mack (1985) responds to this position and attempts to present a balanced view of the complementary roles of metaphors and of models.

Compatibility

When the cause-and-effect behaviour encountered in working with a system matches the user's expectations, it is said to have good *stimulus-response (S-R) compatibility*. Having good spatial congruence between items in a menu and the layout of function keys used for making selections is a good example of S-R compatibility. Since the pairing between menu items and function keys is clear, we can expect that training time and operating load will be reduced.

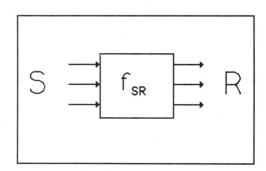

Figure 4: Compatibility as a Mapping Function
We can consider S-R compatibility in terms of a function that maps stimuli onto responses. Compatibility varies with the inverse of the complexity of the mapping function.

A good way to think of compatibility is in terms of a transfer function, f_{sr}, that maps stimuli onto responses (Figure 4). Essentially, compatibility varies inversely with the complexity of this mapping function.

There are two main forces that drive compatibility: *spatial congruence*, as was seen in the menu-function key example, and *custom*. That much of compatibility *is* custom, and is learned, can be seen from the example of a toggle light-switch. In North America, the rule is generally "up is on, down is off." However, in many other countries, such as England, the convention is just the opposite. There are many comparable learned conventions, or *stereotypes*, that may be used in the design of a user interface. The meaning of colours or words are examples. Like the light-switch, these are usually cul-

turally or professionally dependent. Their meanings can vary widely, and the designer must be aware of potential problems.

Some examples can help us develop a better understanding of other aspects of compatibility and stereotypes.

Suppose that we are running an acoustics simulation and we want to increase the frequency of a waveform. The controls that we might use are shown in Figure 5. For each, in what direction would you move the control to increase the frequency? Try to formulate a concise rule that states how to increase and decrease the parameter being controlled using each type of controller.

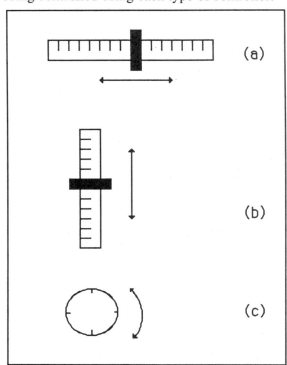

Figure 5: Three Potentiometers
For each type, indicate which direction increase the parameter being controlled. Formulate a general rule for each case.

There will probably be a fairly high consensus that "increase" corresponds to a right, up, and clockwise motion, respectively. However, the choice of the parameter to be thought of as increasing must be consistent with the user's expectations. For example, if the user is interested in the waveform's *period*, rather than its frequency, then the control's effect on the waveform should be reversed (period being the inverse of frequency). Subtle differences can have a strong affect on compatibility. Understanding the user's mental model is critical.

Water faucets introduce another concept about compatibility. Look at the faucets illustrated in Figure 6. Which faucet is for hot water and which is for cold? What direction should each faucet be turned in order to turn on the water? Try to generalize the rules that you

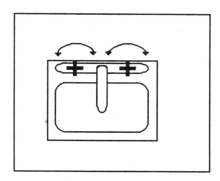

Figure 6: Water Faucets
Which faucet is for hot water and which is for cold? Indicate what direction each faucet is turned to turn the water on (from Smith, 1981).

use in answering each of these questions.

In North America, there will be fairly strong consensus that the hot water tap is on the left. However, there will likely be some disagreement on which direction to turn the tap to get the water flowing, especially with the hot water tap. The degree of consensus is a good indicator of the strength of the S-R stereotype.

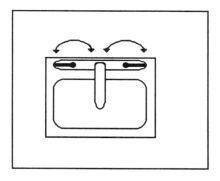

Figure 7: Lever-Type Faucets
If the faucets shown in Figure 6 are replaced by lever-type faucets, how are your expectations affected? Is the direction that you would turn the taps to turn the water on affected? (from Smith, 1981).

What happens if the faucets of the previous example are replaced, as they are in Figure 7, by lever-type faucets? Are our expectations the same with respect to how to turn the water on? From the previous example, most North Americans would have formulated the rule: ''Faucets are closed by clockwise motion and are opened by counter-clockwise motion.'' We now have to qualify this rule. The supplement is: ''If the faucet has lever-type controls, it is opened by pulling and closed by pushing.''

Seemingly simple changes can affect our expectations and behaviour. As with changing the tap handles in the previous example, minor changes in graphical presentation or input devices can have a strong effect on user's expectations about system behaviour. As a designer you

must understand these effects so that they work for you, rather than against you.

The next example illustrates this type of error in an actual system. On the Apple Macintosh there is a rotary potentiometer to control the screen brightness. Its position with respect to the computer is illustrated in Figure 8.

Before reading further, look at the figure, then close your eyes and mentally turn up the intensity of the display. Which way did you turn the potentiometer?

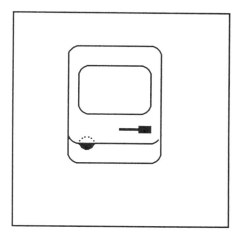

Figure 8: The Macintosh Intensity Control
A rotary pot is used to control intensity. Which way should the pot be turned to increase the intensity of the screen?

Since a rotary potentiometer was used, the designers automatically assumed that the ''rotate clockwise to increase'' rule applied. While well intentioned, this wiring conflicts with our expectations and is wrong. Why? The problem arises because only the bottom half of the potentiometer is exposed. Therefore, the rule that the user applies is one that we saw with the horizontal linear potentiometer: ''move right to increase, left to decrease.''

For further information on compatibility, the reader is encouraged to read Smith (1981). This paper has many good examples, several of which have been used in this chapter. Fitts and Seeger (1953) and Fitts and Deininger (1954) are important early papers. Barnard, Hammond, et al. (1981) discuss compatibility with respect to the ordering of elements in command languages. Finally, an interesting attempt to refine the theory of compatibility can be found in John, Rosenbloom and Newell (1985) and Rosenbloom (1985).

Summary

The use of computing systems makes heavy demands on our cognitive systems. Performing many tasks imposes a high cognitive load. This can be partially dealt with by adopting training procedures that develop skills appropriate for the application. Training, however, imposes its own cost in time and effort that must be invested before expert performance can be achieved.

Taking a broader perspective, we see that every system can be characterized by the skills that are required to utilize its full functionality. This we will call the *prescriptive model* (PM) (Bösser 1986, personal communication). Similarly, we can characterize users by the set of skills with which they approach the system. This we will call the *descriptive model* (DM).

Typically, the descriptive model is a subset of the prescriptive model. These two concepts provide a means of illustrating the relationship between the two main components of *cognitive engineering:* training and design.

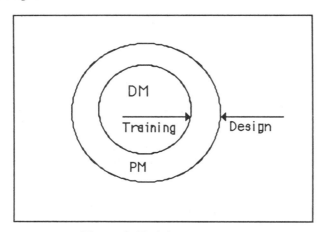

Figure 9: Training and Design
The gap between system demands and user capabilities are shown by the difference between the prescriptive model (PM) of the system and the descriptive model (DM) of the user. In the ideal system, PM = DM. The objective of training is to push the DM outwards. The objective of design is to push the PM inwards.

In Figure 9 we see that the role of design is to minimize the difference between the PM and the DM. In this context, training is seen to be a necessary evil which compensates for the shortcomings of the design.

Good design will take serious account of the cognitive issues discussed in this chapter. It will minimize the operational hurdles that users must overcome in order to achieve their primary task. Where there are shortcomings in design, cognitive principles must again be employed to develop effective training procedures. While not providing an exact science, the cognitive principles discussed will hopefully help suggest good design alternatives. The theory should provide a starting point. But testing and evaluation must always serve as the final proving ground.

Readings

Card, S., Moran, T. & Newell, A. (1980). Computer Text-Editing: An Information Processing Analysis of a Routine Cognitive Skill. *Cognitive Psychology* 12, 32-74.

Norman, Donald A. (1983). Some Observations on Mental Models. In Gentner, Dedre & Stevens, Albert L. (Eds.), *Mental Models*, Hillsdale, N.J.: Lawrence Erlbaum Associates, pp. 7-14.

References/Bibliography

Allen, R. (1982). Cognitive Factors in Human Interaction with Computers. In A. Badre & B. Shneiderman (Eds.), *Directions in Human/Computer Interaction,* Norwood, N.J.: Ablex, 1-26.

Anderson, J.R. (Ed.) (1981). *Cognitive Skills and their Acquisition,* Hillsdale, N.J.: Lawrence Erlbaum Associates.

Anderson, J.R. (1983). *The Architecture of Cognition,* Cambridge, MA: Harvard University Press.

Anderson, J.R. (1985). *Cognitive Psychology and its Implications,* Second Edition, New York: W.H. Freeman.

Baddeley, A.D. & Longman, D.J.A. (1978). The Influence of Length and Frequency of Training Session on the Rate of Learning to Type. *Ergonomics* 21(8), 627-635.

Barnard, P. Hammond, N. Morton, J. & Long, J. (1981). Consistency and Compatibility in Human-Computer Dialogue. *International Journal of Man-Machine Studies* 15, 87-134.

Berlyne, D. (1960). *Conflict, Arousal, and Curiosity,* New York: McGraw-Hill.

Bewley, W., Roberts, T., Schroit, D. & Verplank, W. (1983). Human Factors Testing in the Design of Xerox's 8010 "Star" Office Workstation. *Proceedings of CHI '83,* 72-77.

Boff, K.R., Kaufman, J.P. & Thomas, J.P.(Eds) (1986). *Handbook of Human Perception and Performance,* Vol. I & II, New York: John Wiley & Sons.

Bösser, T. (1985). *Learning in Man-Computer Interaction,* to appear shortly, Springer Verlag.

Bösser, T. (1986). Personal communication.

Bösser, T. & Melchior, E. (1985). Learning to Control Complex Technical Systems. In H.P. Willumeit (Ed.), *Human Decision Making and Manual Control,* Amsterdam: North Holland.

Buxton, W. (1986). There's More to Interaction than Meets the Eye: Some Issues in Manual Input. In Norman, D.A. and Draper, S.W. (Eds.), *User Centered System Design: New Perspectives on Human-Computer Interaction,* Hillsdale, N.J.: Lawrence Erlbaum Associates, 319-337.

Buxton, W. & Myers, B. (1985). A Study in Two-Handed Input. *Proceedings of CHI '86,* 321-326.

Card, S., Moran, T. & Newell, A. (1980). Computer Text-Editing: An Information Processing Analysis of a Routine Cognitive Skill. *Cognitive Psychology,* 12, 32-74.

Card, S., Moran, T. & Newell, A. (1983). *The Psychology of Human-Computer Interaction,* Hillsdale, N.J.: Lawrence Erlbaum Associates.

Carroll, J.M. (1984a). Minimalist Training. *Datamation,* November 1, 1984, 125-136.

Carroll, J.M. (1984b). Mental Models and Software Human Factors: An Overview. Research Report RC 10616 (#47016), Yorktown Heights, N.Y.: IBM Watson Research Center.

Carroll, J.M. & Mack, R.L. (1985). Metaphor, Computing Systems, and Active Learning. *International Journal of Man-Machine Studies* 22, 39-57.

Carroll, J.M. & Thomas, J.C. (1982). Metaphor and the Cognitive Representation of Computing Systems. *IEEE Transactions on Systems, Man, and Cybernetics* 12(2), 107-116.

Carswell, C. M. & Wickens, C. D. (1985). Lateral Task Segregation and the Task-Hemispheric Integrity Effect. *Human Factors* 27(6), 695-700.

Chapanis, A. (1965). Words, Words, Words. *Human Factors* 7, 1-17.

Crossman, E.R.F.W. (1959). A Theory of the Acquisition of Speed-Skill. *Ergonomics* 2(2), 153-166.

Eysenck, M. (1984). *A Handbook of Cognitive Psychology,* Hillsdale, N.J.: Lawrence Erlbaum Associates.

Fitts, P.M. & Deininger, R.L. (1954). S-R Compatibility: Correspondence Among Paired Elements Within Stimulus-Response Codes. *Journal of Experimental Psychology* 48, 483-492.

Fitts, P.M. & Seeger, C.M. (1953). S-R Compatibility: Spatial Characteristics of Stimulus and Response Codes. *Journal of Experimental Psychology* 46, 199-210.

Gardner, H. (1987). *The Mind's New Science,* Second Edition, New York: Basic Books.

Green, T.R.G. & Payne, S.J. (1984). Organization and Learnability in Computer Languages. *International Journal of Man-Machine Studies* 21(1), 7-18.

Halasz, F. & Moran, T.P. (1982). Analogy Considered Harmful. *Proceedings of the Conference on Human Factors in Computing Systems,* Gaithersburg, Maryland, 383-386.

Halasz, Frank & Moran, Thomas P. (1983). Mental Models and Problem Solving in Using a Calculator. *Proceedings of CHI '83,* 212-216.

Hartman, B.O. (1961). Time and Load Factors in Astronaut Proficiency. In B. E. Flatery (Ed.), *Symposium on Psychophysiological Aspects of Space Flight,* New York: Columbia University Press.

John, B., Rosenbloom, P. & Newell, A. (1985). A Theory of Stimulus-Response Compatibility Applied to Human-Computer Interaction. *Proceedings of CHI '85,* 213-219.

Karat, J., Boyes, L., Weisgerber, S. & Schafer, C. (1986). Transfer Between Word Processing Systems. *Proceedings of CHI '86,* 67-71.

Kantowitz, H. (Ed.) (1974). *Human Information Processing: Tutorials in Performance and Cognition,* Hillsdale, N.J.: Lawrence Erlbaum Associates.

Kolers, P.A. (1976). Reading a Year Later. *Journal of Experimental Psychology* 2, 554-565.

Kramer, A., Wickens, C. & Donchin, E. (1983). An Analysis of the Processing Requirements of a Complex Perceptual-Motor Task. *Human Factors* 25(6), 597-621.

Lachman, R., Lachman, J.L., & Butterfield, E.C. (1979). *Cognitive Psychology and Information Processing: An Introduction,* Hillsdale, N.J.: Lawrence Erlbaum Associates.

Lindsay, P. & Norman, D. (1977). *Human Information Processing: An Introduction to Psychology,* Second Edition, New York: Academic Press.

Miller, G.A. (1956). The Magic Number Seven, Plus or Minus Two: Some Limits on our Capacity for Processing Information. *Psychological Review* 63, 81-97.

Moran, T.P. (1981). Guest Editor's Introduction: An Applied Psychology of the User. *Computing Surveys* 13(1), 1-11.

Neisser, U. (1967). *Cognitive Psychology,* New York: Appleton-Century-Crofts.

Moray, N. (1977). *Workload Measurement,* New York: Plenum.

Neves, D.M. & Anderson, J.R. (1981). Knowledge Compilation: Mechanisms for the Automatization of Cognitive Skills. In J. R. Anderson, *Cognitive Skills and their Acquisition,* Hillsdale, N.J.: Lawrence Erlbaum Associates, 57-84.

Newell, A. & Rosenbloom, P. (1981). Mechanisms of Skill Acquisition and the Law of Practice. In J. R. Anderson (Ed.), *Cognitive Skills and their Acquisition,* Hillsdale, N.J.: Lawrence Erlbaum Associates, 1-55.

Norman, D.A. (1982). *Learning and Memory,* New York: W.H. Freeman.

Norman, D.A. (1983). Some Observations on Mental Models. In Gentner, Dedre & Stevens, Albert L. (Eds.), *Mental Models,* Hillsdale, N.J.: Lawrence Erlbaum Associates, pp. 7-14.

Norman, D.A. (1986). Cognitive Engineering. In D.A. Norman & S.W. Draper (Eds.), *User Centered System Design,* Hillsdale, N.J.: Lawrence Erlbaum Associates, 31-61.

Norman, D. & Bobrow, D. (1975). On Data-Limited and Resource-Limited Processes. *Cognitive Psychology* 7, 44-64.

Payne, S.J. & Green, T.R.G. (1983). The User's Perception of the Interaction Language: A Two-Level Model. *Proceedings of CHI '83,* 202-206.

Polson, P. & Kieras, D. (1985). A Quantitative Model of the Learning and Performance of Text Editing Knowledge. *Proceedings of CHI '85,* 207-212.

Polson, P., Muncher, E. & Engelbeck, G. (1986). A Test of Common Elements Theory of Transfer. *Proceedings of CHI '86,* 78-83.

Rasmussen, J. (1983). Skills, Rules, and Knowledge; Signals, Signs, and Symbols, and Other Distinctions in Human Performance Models. *IEEE Transactions on Systems, Man, and Cybernetics* 13(3), 257-264.

Rasmussen, J. (1986). *Information Processing and Human-Machine Interaction: An Approach to Cognitive Engineering,* Amsterdam: North Holland Publishing.

Rosenbloom, P.S. (1985). The Chunking of Goal Hierarchies: A Model of Practice and Stimulus-Response Compatibility, Doctoral Dissertation, Dept. of Computer Science, Carnegie Mellon University.

Rumelhart, David E. & Norman, Donald A. (1981). Analogical Processes in Learning. In J.R. Anderson (Ed.), *Cognitive Skills and Their Acquisition*, Hillsdale, N.J.: Lawrence Erlbaum Associates, 335-360.

Schneider, W. (1985). Training High-Performance Skills: Fallacies and Guidelines. *Human Factors*B 27(3), 285-300.

Sheridan, T. (1980). Mental Workload — What is it? Why Bother with it? *Human Factors Society Bulletin* 23, 1-2.

Sheridan, T. (1980). Human Error in Nuclear Power Plants. *Technology Review* 82(4), 22-33.

Smith, S.L. (1981). Exploring Compatibility with Words and Pictures. *Human Factors* 23(3), 305-315.

Welford, A. T. (1976). *Skilled Performance: Perceptual and Motor Skills*, Glenview, Illinois: Scott, Foresman and Co.

Welford, A. T. (1978). Mental Workload as a Function of Demand, Capacity, Strategy and Skill. *Ergonomics* 21, 151-167.

Wickens, C., Sandry, D. & Vidulich, M. (1983). Compatibility and Resource Competition between Modalities of Input, Central Processing, and Output. *Human Factors* 25(2), 227-248.

Wickins, C., Vidulich, M. & Sandry-Garza, D. (1984). Principles of S-C-R Compatibility with Spatial and Verbal Tasks: The Role of Display-Control Location and Voice-Interactive Display-Control Interfacing. *Human Factors* 26(5), 533-543.

Young, R.M. (1981). The Machine Inside the Machine: Users' Models of Pocket Calculators. *International Journal of Man-Machine Studies* 15, 51-85.

Young, R.M. (1983). Surrogates and Mappings: Two Kinds of Conceptual Models for Interactive Devices. In Gentner, Dedre & Stevens, A. L. (Eds), *Mental Models*, Hillsdale, N.J.: Lawrence Erlbaum Associates.

Zieger, J.E., Hoppe, H.U. & Fahnrich, I. (1986). Learning and Transfer for Text and Graphics Editing with a Direct Manipulation Interface. *Proceedings of CHI '86*, 72-77.

Computer Text-Editing: An Information-Processing Analysis of a Routine Cognitive Skill

Stuart K. Card and Thomas P. Moran
Xerox Palo Alto Research Center

AND

Allen Newell
Carnegie–Mellon University

An information-processing model is presented that describes how a person uses an interactive computer text-editing system to make modifications to a manuscript. It is demonstrated that the behavior of an expert user can be modeled by giving his goals, operators, methods, and selection rules for choosing among method alternatives. The paper assesses the predictions of such a model with respect to (1) predicting user behavior sequences, (2) predicting the time required to do particular modifications, and (3) determining the effect on accuracy of the detail with which the modeling is done (the model's "grain size"). Chronometric task protocols from several users are examined in some detail. Users' choices between alternative methods are predicted about 80% of the time by a few simple rules. Accuracy of the model is little affected by the detail of modeling. The manuscript-editing task is discussed as an example from the larger class of tasks called "routine cognitive skills."

The current attempt to understand man as a symbolic information processing system has concentrated on certain domains of behavior: recall and recognition tasks, which reveal the mechanisms of learning and the structure of short-term and long-term memory; discrete symbolic puzzles and mathematical exercises, which reveal the nature of search in problem solving; discrete symbolic induction tasks, which reveal elementary concept acquisition; tasks of elementary sentence comprehension, decision, and arithmetic, which reveal the nature of the immediate processor; and simple tasks that occur in child development. Most of this work is summarized by Anderson and Bower (1973), Lindsay and Norman (1977), Klatzky (1975), and Newell and Simon (1972). There remain, however, important domains of behavior for which we do not yet have any reasonable detailed theory nor any verification that the theory of man as a symbolic information processor provides an appropriate theoretical base.

We wish in this paper to consider an example task from one such domain of behavior which we shall call *routine cognitive skill*. Such behavior occurs in situations that are familiar and repetitive, and which people master with practice and training, but where the variability in the task, plus the induced variability arising from error, keeps the task from becoming completely routine and requires cognitive involvement. The example task is the *manuscript-editing task*: making corrections from a marked-up manuscript in a text file stored in a computer system through an on-line editor.

Our motives for studying the manuscript-editing task are both to extend the theory of man as a symbolic information processing system and to apply the theory of human information processing in practical task domains. The consideration of tasks with real application is important as a check on the often-noted tendency for psychological research to become paradigm-bound, as a way of testing the power of theoretical ideas against the complexity of real-world behavior, and as a means of fostering progress in the application domain.

This paper focuses on the basic structure of behavior in a close laboratory analogue of the natural manuscript-editing task environment: We consider the behavior of people under laboratory conditions (free from interruptions) employing a computer text-editing program commonly used in their daily work. They work from manuscripts with legible instructions to perform straightforward, single-line, but otherwise typical, modifications. We shall be concerned with several issues: Is it possible to describe the behavior of a person in a reasonably complex workaday task, like computer text-editing, as the repeated application of a small set of basic information processing operators? Is it possible to predict the actual sequence of operators a person will use and the time required to do any specific task? Finally, in attempting to describe behavior in this way, the issue of the level of analysis is critical. How does the model's ability to describe and predict a person's behavior change as we vary the grain size of the analysis?

THE MANUSCRIPT-EDITING TASK

It will be helpful for our later discussion to describe the manuscript-editing task in concrete detail. A person (the "user") sits before an on-line computer terminal, which has a keyboard for input and a CRT display for output. In the computer is a text file. To the user's left is a manuscript, a printout of the text-file, marked with modifications. The user, working

The authors are listed in alphabetical order. We would like to acknowledge George Baylor, University of Montreal, for helping us formulate the method selection issue and for running some pilot experiments. We would like to thank Donald Norman, Richard Young, Daniel Bobrow, and Jerome Elkind for comments on an earlier report (Card, Moran, & Newell, 1976) on which this paper is based. We would also like to thank Janet Farness for assistance for running the experiments and Richard Lyon for help with the matching algorithm.

Reprint requests should be sent to S. K. Card or T. P. Moran at Xerox Palo Alto Research Center, 3333 Coyote Hill Road, Palo Alto, CA. 94304.

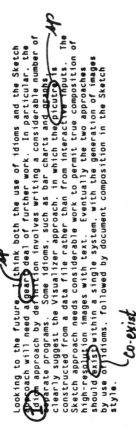

Looking to the future, I think both the use of idioms and the Sketch approach will need a geart deal of further work. In particular, the idiom approach by definition involves writing a considerable number of separate programs. Some idioms, such as bar charts and graphs, clearly suggest the Visualizer approach, in which the picturts is constructed from a data file rather than from interactive inputs. The Sketch approach needs considerable work to permit true composition of high-resolution images with text. Eventually the two approaches should exist within a single system, with the generation of images by use of idioms, followed by document composition in the Sketch style.

FIG. 1. Sample fragment of the manuscript used in experiment.

through a text-editor computer program, is to effect each of the modifications marked on the manuscript in the text file, thus producing an updated file. The task is daily routine for thousands of workers using equipment ranging from small "word-processors" to large general-purpose time-sharing computers. Variations of the task occur with variations in the nature of the computer, the editor, the terminal, the size of the manuscript, the type and number of corrections, the physical layout, and the familiarity of the user with the manuscript and with the editor.

To bring the details of the task into focus, let us consider the problem of making the corrections indicated in Fig. 1 with the system we will use for our analysis—a system called POET (Russell, 1973). The first instruction on the manuscript indicates the word "great" has been mistyped in the manuscript as "geart." A typical dialogue between the system and the user is as follows.[1]

```
SYSTEM:    #              (Prompts user for a command)
USER:      "geart"        (The user indicates the line he wants by typing between
                           quotation marks some characters that identify the line)
```

The system responds internally by finding the next line that contains the sequence of characters "geart" and making that its "Current Line."

```
SYSTEM:    #
USER:      /              (This command requests the system to display its Cur-
                           rent Line. The user issues the command to make sure
                           the system is attending to the line he intended.)
```

The system displays the Current Line on the bottom line of the display screen.

[1] Ellipsis "..." is used to shorten long typeouts by the system; carriage returns typed by the user are indicated as ⟨CR⟩, linefeed characters by ⟨LF⟩; the dialogue proceeds by adding new lines to the bottom of the CRT, "scrolling" the rest of the lines up and eventually off the top.

SYSTEM: approach will need a geart deal of further work...

The user decides to make the change by using the system's Substitute command to substitute the characters "grea" for the characters "gear."

```
SYSTEM:    #              (Tells system to use the substitute command)
USER:      s
SYSTEM:    ubstitute      (System completes typing of command name)
USER:      grea⟨CR⟩       (Types new text followed by a carriage return)
SYSTEM:    (for)          (Prompts user for second argument)
USER:      gear⟨CR⟩       (Types text to be replaced followed by a carriage return)
SYSTEM:    [OK]           (Asks user to confirm that the command is correct be-
                           fore system will execute it)
USER:      ⟨CR⟩           (Types carriage return to confirm)
```

The system makes the substitution as many times as it can and responds by printing the number of substitutions it made—in this case only one is made.

```
SYSTEM:    1
SYSTEM:    #
```

Again, the user wishes to look at the Current Line to see if, in fact, the modification was made as he intended.

```
USER:      /
SYSTEM:    approach will need a great deal of further work...
SYSTEM:    #
```

The modification was correct. The user now proceeds to the next task.

In the next task, the word *idiom* is to be capitalized. The user decides he will do this by substituting *Idi* for *idi*. This time he uses the "linefeed method" rather than the "quoted string method" to locate the line to be changed.

```
USER:      ⟨LF⟩           (This is the command to print the next line and to make
                           it be the Current Line)
SYSTEM:    idiom approach by definition involves writing a...
SYSTEM:    #
USER:      s
SYSTEM:    ubstitute
USER:      Idi⟨CR⟩
SYSTEM:    (for)
USER:      idi⟨CR⟩
SYSTEM:    [OK]
USER:      ⟨CR⟩
SYSTEM:    1
SYSTEM:    #
USER:      /
SYSTEM:    Idiom approach by definition involves writing a...
SYSTEM:    #
```

In this manner, the user proceeds, modification by modification, through the manuscript.

THE GOMS MODEL

The account we shall give of behavior in the manuscript-editing task is an application of the general theory of humans as symbolic processors to this particular task environment (for more general treatment, see Card, Moran, & Newell, in preparation). The models we shall describe hypothesize that the user's cognitive structure consists of four components: a set of Goals, a set of Operators, a set of Methods for achieving the goals, and a set of Selection rules for choosing among a goal's competing methods. For short, we shall call a model specified by such components a GOMS model.

Example Model

As an example of the basic concepts of a GOMS model and the notation used, let us consider a particular model, called M4B, of the manuscript-editing task. According to the model, the user begins with the top-level goal:

GOAL: EDIT-MANUSCRIPT

It is a characteristic of manuscript-editing that the larger task of editing the manuscript is composed of a collection of small *unit tasks* which are almost completely independent of each other. The obvious method for accomplishing the top level goal is to do each of the individual unit tasks one at a time:

GOAL: EDIT-MANUSCRIPT
- GOAL: EDIT-UNIT-TASK   *repeat until no more unit tasks.*

The indentation above indicates that EDIT-UNIT-TASK is a subgoal of EDIT-MANUSCRIPT, and the annotation in italics says that the subgoal is to be invoked repeatedly until no more unit tasks remain.

To edit a unit task, the user must first get the unit task from the manuscript and then do what is necessary to accomplish the unit task:

GOAL: EDIT-UNIT-TASK
- GOAL: GET-UNIT-TASK
- GOAL: DO-UNIT-TASK

Each subgoal will itself evoke appropriate methods. There is a simple method for getting a task:

GOAL: GET-UNIT-TASK
- GET-NEXT-PAGE   *if at end of manuscript page*
- GET-UNIT-TASK

The operator GET-NEXT-PAGE is invoked only if there are no more edit instructions on the current page of the manuscript. The bulk of the work toward the goal—looking at the manuscript, finding an editing instruction, and interpreting the instruction as an edit task—is done by the operator GET-UNIT-TASK.

To do a unit task in POET there is a two-step method:

GOAL: DO-UNIT-TASK
- GOAL: LOCATE-LINE
- GOAL: MODIFY-TEXT

The Current Line of the POET editor must first be set to the line where the correction is to be made. Then the appropriate text on that line can be modified.

To locate POET at a line, there is a choice of two methods:

GOAL: LOCATE-LINE
- [select: USE-LF-METHOD
             USE-QS-METHOD]

To use the LF-METHOD, the linefeed key is pressed repeatedly, causing the editor to advance one line each time. To use the QS-METHOD, a string in quotation marks is typed which identifies the line. Usually the LF-METHOD is selected when the new unit task is within a few lines of the current unit task, and the QS-METHOD is selected when the new unit task is farther away.

Once the line has been located, there is a choice of how to modify the text:

GOAL: MODIFY-TEXT
- [select: USE-S-COMMAND
             USE-M-COMMAND]
- VERIFY-EDIT

That is, either POET's Substitute command or Modify command can be used to alter text on a line. An example has already been given of the Substitute command. The Modify command allows the user to invoke a series of subcommands for moving forward and backward and for making modifications within a line. In either case a VERIFY-EDIT operation is evoked to check what actually happened against the user's intentions.

Putting all the pieces together into one tree structure, we have:

GOAL: EDIT-MANUSCRIPT
- GOAL: EDIT-UNIT-TASK   *repeat until no more unit tasks*
- - GOAL: GET-UNIT-TASK
- - - GET-NEXT-PAGE   *if at end of manuscript page*
- - - GET-UNIT-TASK
- - GOAL: DO-UNIT-TASK

TABLE 1

Trace of Model M4B during Performance of a Unit Task

Step	Contents of goals stack[a]	Operator executed	User action
1	(EDIT-MS)[b]		
2	(EDIT-MS) (EDIT-UT)		
3	(EDIT-MS) (GET-UT) (EDIT-UT)		
4	(EDIT-MS) (GET-UT) (EDIT-UT)	GET-UT	(*Looks at manuscript*)
5	(EDIT-MS) (GET-UT)		
6	(EDIT-MS) (GET-UT) (DO-UT)		
7	(EDIT-MS) (GET-UT) (DO-UT) (LOCATE-LINE)		
8	(EDIT-MS) (GET-UT) (DO-UT) (LOCATE LINE)	USE-LF-METHOD	(*Types* ⟨LF⟩)
9	(EDIT-MS) (GET-UT) (DO-UT)		
10	(EDIT-MS) (GET-UT) (DO-UT) (MODIFY-TEXT)		
11	(EDIT-MS) (GET-UT) (DO-UT) (MODIFY-TEXT)	USE-S-COMMAND	(*Types* sIdi⟨CR⟩idi⟨CR⟩⟨CR⟩)
12	(EDIT-MS) (GET-UT) (DO-UT) (MODIFY-TEXT)	VERIFY-EDIT	(*Types* /)
13	(EDIT-MS) (GET-UT) (DO-UT)		
14	(EDIT-MS) (GET-UT)		
15	(EDIT-MS)		

[a] The top of stack (the current goal) is at the right.

[b] To save space, the word GOAL: has been dropped from the beginning of goal expressions, MANUSCRIPT has been abbreviated MS, and UNIT TASK has been abbreviated UT.

```
•  •  •  GOAL: LOCATE-LINE
•  •  •  •  [select:  USE-QS-METHOD
                      USE-LF-METHOD]
•  •  •  GOAL: MODIFY-TEXT
•  •  •  •  [select:  USE-S-COMMAND
                      USE-M-COMMAND]
•  •  •  •  VERIFY-EDIT.
```

The dots at the left of each line show the depth of the goal stack. To complete this model of manuscript-editing, we must add method selection rules that would determine the actual submethods at the two occurrences of "select."

The step-by-step behavior of the model in performing a unit task is traced in Table 1. The user is imagined to have a goal stack with the current goal at its top. New subgoals are pushed onto the stack and completed goals (whether satisfied or abandoned) are popped off the stack. The goals eventually cause operators to be executed. It is during the execution of the operators that interactions with the physical world take place. The user executes the operator GET-UNIT-TASK by turning to the manuscript, reading the instructions, and turning back to the terminal. The user executes the operator USE-S-COMMAND for the second task in Fig. 1 by typing **sIdi⟨CR⟩idi⟨CR⟩⟨CR⟩**, as described in the previous section.

Components of the GOMS Model

Goals. A goal is a symbolic structure that defines a state of affairs to be achieved and determines a set of possible methods by which it may be accomplished. In the example, the goals are GOAL: EDIT-MANUSCRIPT, GOAL: EDIT-UNIT-TASK, GOAL: GET-UNIT-TASK, GOAL: DO-UNIT-TASK, GOAL: LOCATE-LINE, and GOAL: MODIFY-TEXT. The dynamic function of a goal is to provide a memory point to which the system can return on failure or error and from which information can be obtained about what is desired, what methods are available, and what has been already tried.

Operators. Operators are elementary motor or information-processing acts, whose execution is necessary to change any aspect of the user's memory or to affect the task environment. In the example, the operators are: GET-NEXT-PAGE, GET-UNIT-TASK, USE-QS-METHOD, USE-LF-METHOD, USE-S-COMMAND, USE-M-COMMAND, and VERIFY-EDIT. The behavior of the user is ultimately recordable as a sequence of these operations. In the example traced in Table 1, the sequence of behavior is GET-UNIT-TASK, USE-LF-METHOD, USE-S-COMMAND, VERIFY-EDIT. The model does not deal with any fine structure of concurrent operation.

An operator is defined by a specific effect (output) and by a specific duration. The operator may take inputs, and its outputs and duration may be a function of its inputs. An obvious example is the typing operator, whose input is the text to be typed, whose output is the keystroke sequence to the keyboard, and whose duration is (approximately) a linear function of the number of characters.

For a specific model the operators define the grain of analysis. In general, they embody an indeterminate mixture of basic psychological mechanisms and learned organized behavior, the mixture depending on the level at which the model is cast. The finer the grain of analysis, the more the operators reflect basic psychological mechanisms. The coarser grain of analysis, the more the operators reflect the specifics of the task environment, such as the terminal, the physical arrangement, and the editor.

Methods. A method describes a procedure for accomplishing a goal. The description of the procedure is cast as a conditional sequence of goals and operators, with conditional tests on the contents of the user's immediate memory and on the state of the task environment. In the example above, one of the methods was

GOAL: GET-UNIT-TASK
- GET-NEXT-PAGE   *if at end of manuscript page*
- GET-UNIT-TASK

This method is associated with the goal GET-UNIT-TASK. It will give rise to either the operator sequence GET-NEXT-PAGE followed by GET-UNIT-TASK or the single operator GET-UNIT-TASK, depending on whether the test "*at end of manuscript page*" is true of the task environment at the time the test is performed.

In the manuscript-editing task, the methods are sure of success, up to the possibility of having been misselected, the occurrence of errors of implementation, and the reliability of the equipment. By contrast, in problem-solving tasks, such as the task faced by a novice in the Tower of Hanoi puzzle, methods have a chance of success distinctly less than certainty due to the user's lack of knowledge or appreciation of the task environment. This uncertainty is a prime contributor to the problem-solving character of a task; its absence is a characteristic of a routine cognitive skill.

Methods are learned procedures which the user has at performance time. They are not plans that are created during a task performance. They constitute one of the major ways in which familiarity (skill) expresses itself. The particular methods that the user builds up from prior experience, analysis, and instruction reflect the detailed structure of the task environment. In the manuscript-editing task, they reflect knowledge of the exact sequence of steps required by the editor to accomplish specific tasks.

Control structure: selection rules. When a goal is attempted, there may be more than one method available to the user to accomplish the goal. The selection of which method is to be used need not be an extended decision process, for it may be that the task environment features dictate only one method is appropriate. On the other hand, a genuine decision may be required. The essence of skilled behavior is that these selections are not problematical, that they proceed smoothly and quickly and without the eruption of puzzlement and search characteristic of problem-solving behavior.

In the GOMS model, method selection is handled by a set of *selection rules*. Each selection rule is of the form "if such and such is true in the current task situation, then use method M." Selection rules for the LO-CATE goal of the example model might read: *If the number of lines to the next modification is less than 3, use the* LF-METHOD; *otherwise use the* QS-METHOD. Such rules allow us to predict from knowledge of the task environment (in this case the number of lines to the target) which of several possible methods will be selected by the user in a particular instance.

Limitations of the GOMS Model

For error-free behavior, the GOMS model provides a complete dynamic description of behavior, measured at the level of goals, methods, and operators. Given a specific task (i.e., a specific manuscript), this description can be expanded into a sequence of operations (operator occurrences). By associating times with each operator, such a model will make total time predictions. If these times are given as distributions, it will make statistical predictions. But, without augmentation, the model will not make predictions if errors occur. Yet, errors exist in routine cognitive skilled behavior. Indeed, error rates may not even be small, in the sense of having negligible frequency, taking negligible time, or having negligible consequences. What is true of skilled behavior is that the detection and correction of errors is mostly routine. It cannot be entirely routine, since the occurrence of rare types of errors for which the user is unprepared is always possible (the terminal catching fire, the editor performing incorrectly). But, in the main, errors are quickly detected and converted to the additional time to correct the error. The final result of the behavior remains relatively error free and can be characterized solely by the time to completion. Thus, errors can be converted to variance in operator times, so that the GOMS theory can be applied to actual behavior at the price of degraded accuracy. For a general treatment of errors and interruptions of the user, the hierarchical control structure of the GOMS model is inadequate; a more general control structure, such as a *production system* (Newell & Simon, 1972; Newell, 1973), is required. The

GOMS model should be taken as a simplified approximation to this more general theory of the human information processing system, especially appropriate for skilled cognitive behavior.

Design of Experiments

The purpose of the experiments that follow is to describe a practical, workaday task, the manuscript-editing task, in information-processing terms. The general technique is to observe a user in a close laboratory analogue of the task he commonly performs, to describe his behavior using the GOMS model, and to evaluate in various ways the adequacy of the description. The experiments are directed specifically at three elements of this analysis: (1) description of how the user decides which method to use for a task, (2) description of the time course of events, and (3) an investigation of how the adequacy of the description varies as a consequence of the grain of analysis.

EXPERIMENT I: SELECTION RULES

The purpose of this experiment was to discover how users choose which of several alternative methods to use and to determine if the method choices could be gracefully described in terms of the selection rules of the GOMS model.

We have already seen two places where, for a given goal, the user has a choice of methods. The first method selection came in deciding how to "locate the line" (the LOCATE-LINE goal), that is, how to make the Current Line of the editing system be the line containing the text to be modified:

GOAL: LOCATE-LINE
- [select: USE-LF-METHOD
            USE-QS-METHOD]

The second method selection came in choosing between commands for making the text modification (the MODIFY-TEXT goal).

GOAL: MODIFY-TEXT
- [select: USE-S-COMMAND
            USE-M-COMMAND]
- VERIFY-EDIT

What we seek is a set of selection rules describing the conditions under which the user will choose one rather than the other of these methods.

Method

Users were given a manuscript, marked with corrections, and asked to use the POET text editor to make the corrections. Although the experiment was performed in the laboratory, an effort was made to make the situation seem naturalistic from the user's point of view: The physical surroundings, the task, the terminal, and the editor were all familiar as part of the user's daily activities. The manuscript and the modifications to be made on it were selected to be typical.

Users. Users were two professional secretaries and a Ph. D. computer scientist. All had at least one year of daily experience using the editor.

Manuscript. The manuscript was an 11-page memo. Each page was 8.5 by 11 in., with 55 lines of text and 70 characters per line, printed unjustified in a 10-point fixed-pitch font. There were 73 different modifications marked with a red pen, giving an average density of one modification every 8.3 lines, or 6.6 modifications per page (from 3 to 11 on any one page). An effort was made to vary the number of lines between consecutive modifications and to place an equal number of modifications in each of the left, right, and middle portions of the page. The marked modifications were relatively short: four of them were deletions (of an average of 5.5 characters), 26 were insertions (of an average of 2.9 characters), and 40 were replacements (of an average of 4.1 characters by 4.4 characters). The paragraph of Fig. 1 was taken from the manuscript and illustrates the style in which modifications were indicated to the user.

Terminal. Two terminals were used in the experiment: a Texas Instruments (TI) Silent 700 (prints on paper at 30 characters/sec) and a CRT display 8.5 in. wide by 10.75 in. high (42 lines, 72 characters per line, maximum display rate about 6 lines/sec). The display was programmed to operate according to a simple scrolling discipline (the same discipline used on the hardcopy terminal): Each new line was displayed at the bottom of the screen with the other lines scrolling up to make room. The last 42 lines of an interaction were visible on the screen.

Procedure. The user was seated before the terminal with the manuscript to his left. He first performed editing tasks on a one-page manuscript for warm-up and to insure that he understood what to do. Then he edited the manuscript described above. One user was run on the TI terminal alone; one on the CRT terminal alone; and one was run twice, first on the CRT and 2 weeks later on the TI. For two of the experimental sessions, the users were instructed to proceed through the manuscript inserting an asterisk at the beginning of the line (since these sessions were run to investigate only methods for locating the target line). In the other two experimental sessions, the users were instructed to edit the 11-page manuscript. Editing the manuscript required approximately 20 min.

Keystrokes typed by the users and the system's responses were recorded on a computer file. These data were used to infer the methods used on a task and the reasons for using them.

Results

Typescripts of the four experimental sessions were examined to identify the methods employed by the users. Table 2 gives the methods observed and the frequencies with which the methods were selected. QS-METHOD and LF-METHOD are the methods previously described for the LOCATE-LINE goal. S-COMMAND and M-COMMAND are the methods previously described for the MODIFY-TEXT goal. The others are additional methods that were used less frequently and may be described as follows:

+N-METHOD. The user estimates the number of lines, n, to the next unit task then types the command $+n/$, which causes POET to advance n lines and print the line. It is assumed that a correction may be needed: The user may have to type a few linefeeds (each of which moves him down a line), ↑'s (each of which moves him up a line), or may even have to repeat the $+n/$ command with a new n.

TABLE 2
Frequency of Method Selections, Experiment I

		User		
	S1 (Computer scientist)	S4 (Secretary)		S22 (Secretary)
Terminal	TI	TI	CRT	CRT
LOCATE methods				
LF-METHOD	11 (16)[a]	14 (21)	45 (68)	25 (38)
QS-METHOD	44 (65)	2 (02)	0	40 (62)
+N-METHOD	2 (03)	51 (77)	20 (30)	0
AN-METHOD	11 (16)	0	2 (02)	0
MODIFY methods				
S-COMMAND	—[b]	48 (73)	—	57 (86)
M-COMMAND	—	18 (27)	—	9 (14)

[a] Percentages given in parentheses.
[b] No MODIFY method data were collected.

AN-METHOD. The user selects an easily specified "anchor" line near the target line, such as a blank line (specified by the empty string " "), the last line of a page (which has the special symbol $), or a line that has a short unique string, such as a paragraph number. Then the target line is reached by using linefeeds or ↑'s. For example, the command " " ⟨LF⟩ locates POET at the first line of the next paragraph.

TABLE 3
Frequency of Use of Locate Methods as a Function of Number of Lines to Target, Experiment I

User	Method	Number of lines from current line to line containing target (D)										
		1	2	3	4	5	6	7	8	9	10–14	15+
S1 (TI)	LF	8	3									
	QS		2	4	5	2		1	3	4	8	15
	+N		1	1								
	AN											
S4 (TI)	LF	8	4	1						1		1
	QS							1				
	+N			5	5	1	1	1	4	4	11	17
	AN											
S4 (CRT)	LF	6	7	6	5	3		1	3	2	2	10
	QS											
	+N					1			1	2	9	7
	AN											1
S22 (CRT)	LF	6	5	6	5	1		1	4	4	10	18
	QS	1	1	6	1	2		1				
	+N											
	AN											
MS total[b]		8	6	6	6	5	4	0	1	4	11	19

[a] The vertical bar indicates where LF-METHOD stops being the preferred method.
[b] Frequency of D's taking the tasks over the whole manuscript in order. Since users usually did some edits in a different order, totals for different experiments in the same column are not necessarily equal.

A striking feature of the frequencies in Table 2 is how each user clearly has a dominant method. By knowing only the dominant method of the user, his method selection can be predicted correctly about 66% of the time for the LOCATE-LINE goal and 80% of the time for the MODIFY-TEXT goal. Apparently, the user will use this dominant method unless it is obviously inefficient (as in linefeeding a line at a time through 10 pages of text to get the next task).

That a user's selection of methods depends systematically upon the features of the task environment is illustrated by the choice of method for the LOCATE-LINE goal. The most important characteristic of the task environment for this goal is the number of lines D between the Current Line and the line with the text to be next modified. As is clear from Table 3, all users used the LF-METHOD if the next line was close enough. Where users differed was in the threshold for how far away the target had to be before they shifted to other methods. The time required to use the LF-METHOD was sensitive to the speed of the terminal. (Each time the user types linefeed, the system prints out the new Current Line.) It was not surprising, therefore, that the LF-METHOD was used less frequently by user S4 on the slower TI than with the faster CRT terminal (21% of the time on the TI vs 68% of the time on the CRT according to Table 2) or that the threshold for when to abandon the LF-METHOD was lower when S4 was using a slow terminal than when she was using a fast one ($D = 3$ lines for the TI vs $D = 10$ lines for the CRT).

Tables 2 and 3 make it clear that there are important individual differences in how users decide which method to use. Keeping the terminal and the task the same, S22 uses the QS-METHOD 62% of the time, but S4 never uses it. Averaging together the data for all users and attempting to write rules to describe the choices of the group would, therefore, produce inaccurate predictions, as well as being quite misleading. Yet, despite the existence of significant individual differences in methods for accomplishing this goal, each user's behavior was highly structured and amenable to a GOMS description. The complete prediction of which method each user employed for the LOCATE goal is organized as a set of Selection Rules in Table 4. Each row gives the results of the accumulation of Rule 1 to Rule n

adding rules one at a time. The Hits column shows the total number of cases correctly predicted, the Misses column shows the number of cases in which the prediction was wrong (Hits + Misses = the total number of method selections). As each rule is added, the set of rules taken together predicts more cases correctly, but a few individual cases which were predicted correctly may now be missed. For example, adding Rule 2 in the second line of the table correctly predicts 11 method selections of the 24 that had been missed using Rule 1 alone, but at the cost of missing 2 of the 44 that were previously hits—a net gain of 9. As the table shows, using from two to four simple rules, it is possible to predict accurately the method selection for users an average of 90% of the time.

EXPERIMENT II: CHRONOMETRIC PREDICTIONS

Experiment I showed that it was possible, using the GOMS model, to give an information processing description of which methods a user would choose. Experiment II was designed to examine chronometrically how users combine selection rules with methods and operators into sequences to accomplish a task. The technique was to observe directly and to record (1) the sequence in which operators occurred for a task and (2) the duration of each operator occurrence. These data allow testing of task time predictions calculated from the model.

Method

Users. Users were two secretaries and two computer scientists familiar with POET. The terminal was similar to the CRT of the previous experiment.

Measurement apparatus. The terminal was connected to a large computer running the POET editor under the TENEX time-sharing system. For this experiment the terminal was modified to time-stamp and record all input events on a data file. It should be noted that the accuracy of the timing of events did not depend on the response of the time-sharing system. Accuracy of time-stamping was to within 32 msec of the actual time of the event at the terminal. The average response time of the editor to commands during the experiment was 0.8 sec ($SD = 0.6$ sec).

Two television cameras were directed at the user, one camera giving an overall view of the user and terminal, the other closely focused on the user's face, from which it could be determined whether he was looking at the manuscript, the keyboard, or the CRT. The user wore a lapel microphone, recording onto the soundtrack of the videotape. A digital clock was electronically mixed with the video picture, time-stamping each frame. The times measured from video frames were accurate to 33 msec (one video frame).

Procedure. The procedure was similar to that for the previous experiment. The user was first given a test to determine his typing rate, then several editing tasks as a warm-up. Finally, he edited the same manuscript as in Experiment I.

Data sets. The first three unit tasks were discarded before analysis to minimize any warm-up effect. The remaining 70 unit tasks were partitioned into two comparable data sets: a *Derivation* data set, consisting of the 34 unit tasks on the odd-numbered pages, and a *Crossvalidation* data set consisting of the 36 unit tasks on the even-numbered pages. This partition allowed basic operator statistics to be computed on the Derivation data, while

TABLE 4

Selection Rules for LOCATE Goal, Experiment I

User	Rule	This rule		Cumulative		Hits (%)
		Gain	Loss	Hits	Misses	
(TT)	1: Use the QS-METHOD unless another rule applies	44	0	44	24	65
	2: If $D < 3$, use the LF-METHOD	11	2	53	15	78
	3: If the target line is the last line of the page, use the AN-METHOD (with $)	5	0	58	10	85
	4: If the current method is to use paragraph numbers for search strings and the target line is near a paragraph number, then use the AN-METHOD.	2	0	60	8	88
(TT)	1: Use the +N-METHOD unless another rule applies	51	0	51	15	77
	2: If $D < 3$, use the LF-METHOD	12	1	62	4	94
(CRT)	1: Use the LF-METHOD unless another rule applies	45	0	45	21	68
	2: If $D > 9$, use the +N-METHOD.	16	12	49	17	74
	3: If the target line is on the next page of the manuscript, use the LF-METHOD	56	10	56	10	85
2 (CRT)	1: Use the QS-METHOD unless another rule applies	40	0	40	25	62
	2: If $D < 5$, use the LF-METHOD	22	2	60	5	92
	Average final hits (%)					90

USE-M-COMMAND. Use of the Modify Command to modify the text. Starts when the user types the first keystroke of the command; ends when the final character of the command string is typed.

VERIFY-EDIT. Act of examining output on terminal to check for correct modification. Starts when the final character of the previous command is typed; ends when the eyes move to the manuscript for the next task.

Results

Operator Sequences

Selection rules. Results replicated those in Experiment I. One or two selection rules (Table 6) were sufficient to predict 88% of the method choices in the Derivation data and 80% in the Crossvalidation data. Accuracy of the rules was about the same for different goals. Interestingly, the rules were better at predicting the secretaries (90% of choices predicted) than the computer scientists (77%).

Accuracy of sequence predictions. In addition to wrong method choices, there are other possible ways in which the model might make errors in the prediction of operator sequences. Ultimately, these will be registered as the intrusion into the observed data of unpredicted operators or the nonoccurrence of predicted operators.

Model M4B was used to calculate the sequence of operators for each task, and this sequence was matched against the sequence actually observed. There is no standard statistical technique for indexing how well one sequence matches another, so the following method was used. The sites of mismatches because of operator insertions, deletions, or replacements were determined using a simple dynamic programming algorithm (based on Hirschberg, 1975, and Sakoe & Chiba, 1978) to optimize the number of matches. Then the percentage of predicted operator occurrences matching observed operator occurrences was computed (see Appendix for details). Sequences generated by the model were in generally good agreement with those observed (Table 7). The percentage of matches varied from 79 to 98% with an average of 88%. There were no differences between the Derivation and the Crossvalidation data, but again, the model did better at calculating sequences for secretaries (94% of operators in sequences matched) than for computer scientists (83%). Except for the above noted method selection errors, the only other error made by the model was to predict that users would always perform a VERIFY-EDIT operation, whereas users sometimes omitted it.

Time Prediction

The protocols contain times from which it is possible to compute chronometric statistics for each operator in each model. Estimates of the time to perform a specific unit task were computed in two ways: (1) *Given* the observed sequence of operators, sum the mean times for each

TABLE 5
Derivation and Crossvalidation Datasets for Experiment II

	User				
	S34 (Computer scientist)	S53 (Computer scientist)	S50 (Secretary)	S95 (Secretary)	Mean
Number of error-free tasks					
Derivation data (36 tasks)	25	27	28	21	25.3
Crossvalidation data (34 tasks)	23	25	27	24	24.8
Mean error-free task time (sec)					
Derivation data	9.0	15.3	15.1	13.4	13.2
Crossvalidation data	8.5	14.7	17.0	14.0	13.2

Note. All differences between mean number of error-free tasks or mean error-free tasks time for Derivation data vs Crossvalidation data and computer scientists vs secretaries were nonsignificant by Mann–Whitney U test, $p > .05$.

preserving the Crossvalidation data for an attempt at prediction in a matched situation, no statistical advantage having been taken of chance.

The data were also partitioned into the set of *error-free* unit tasks and the set of *error* unit tasks, each of the latter containing at least one identifiable error. The criterion for identifying an error was that the user took some *overt corrective action,* defined as some action that undid the effect of a preceding action. All of the analyses below will use the error-free data. The analysis of errors, while partially within the competence of the GOMS model (most errors being routine), requires a separate analysis (see Card et al., 1976, for the beginnings of a GOMS analysis of errors).

Table 5 gives statistics on the derivation and crossvalidation data sets and shows that both the derivation and crossvalidation data were comparable with respect to the number of tasks having errors and in the mean time/task for error-free tasks.

Protocols. The videotaped record of the user's behavior and the time-stamped file of keystrokes were coded into a protocol of operator occurrences according to the following operational definitions of the operators:

GET-NEXT-PAGE. Turning the manuscript page. Starts when the user's eyes begin to turn toward the manuscript; ends when the page falls flat.

GET-UNIT-TASK. The act of looking over to the manuscript to get the next task. Starts when the user's eyes begin to turn toward the manuscript; ends when the user types a keystroke for the next operation or begins to look back, whichever comes first.

USE-LF-METHOD. Use of the LF-METHOD for indicating the target line. Starts when the user's eyes begin to turn toward the screen or the user types the first keystroke for the next operation, whichever comes first; ends when the last linefeed is typed.

USE-QS-METHOD. Use of the QS-METHOD for indicating the target line. Starts when the user's eyes begin to turn toward the screen or the user types the first keystroke for the next operation, whichever comes first; ends when the final character of the search command is typed.

USE-S-COMMAND. Use of the Substitute Command to modify the text. Starts when the user types the first keystroke of the command; ends when the final character of the command string is typed.

TABLE 6

Selection Rules for **LOCATE** and **MODIFY** Goals, Experiment II

		Hits (%)	
User	Rule	Derivation data	Crossvalidation data
LOCATE goal			
S34	1: Use the **QS-METHOD** as default 2: If $D < 3$, then use the **LF-METHOD**	84	74
S50	1: Use the **QS-METHOD** as default 2: If $D < 3$, then use the **LF-METHOD**	96	93
S53	1: Use the **QS-METHOD** as default 2: If $D < 3$, then use the **LF-METHOD**	63	72
S95	1: Always use the **LF-METHOD**	95	71
MODIFY goal			
S34	1: Use the **M-COMMAND** as default 2: If a word is to be replaced not at the very beginning or very end of the line, then use the **S-COMMAND**	85	83
S50	1: Use the **S-COMMAND** as default 2: If the correction is at the very beginning or the very end of the line, then use the **M-COMMAND**	84	83
S53	1: Use **S-COMMAND** as default 2: If the correction is at the very beginning or the very end of the line or is a double task or involves only punctuation, then use the **M-COMMAND**	93	60
S95	1: Always use the **S-COMMAND**	100	100
	Mean	88	80

Note. Mean accuracy (percentage Hits) of the rules is: greater for Derivation data than for Crossvalidation data, Mann–Whitney $U (8,8) = 9$ $p = .014$; greater for secretaries (90%) than for computer scientists (77%), $U (8,8) = 12.5, p < .025$; no different for the **LOCATE** (81%) and **MODIFY** (86%) goals, $U (8,8) = 25, p = .253$.

operator in the sequence. This estimate, which we shall call a *reproduction* of the data, corresponds with how well the models would do were there no sequence prediction errors. (2) Using the sequence of operators *predicted by the models*, sum the mean times for each operator in the sequence. This latter estimate, which we shall call a *prediction*, should correspond more with what we might expect to find applying the models in practice. Error can enter into the estimates either because an operator actually takes longer in some contexts than others or, in the prediction case, because the model predicts the wrong sequence of operators and this sequence takes a different amount of time than the correct sequence actually requires.

Operator times. The durations of all occurrences of each operator type in the Derivation data were used to estimate the operator times (Table 8). Since the data come from a quasi-naturalistic situation and since a rare method may appear only once in the data, there is a fair chance that some radically extreme times may show up in the distributions of operator times. Though these must be accepted in any prediction test, it is appropriate to avoid them in estimating the characteristics of the operators. Consequently, in Table 8 we have dropped two outliers that lie beyond two SD's from the raw mean and then recomputed the mean and coefficient of variation CV ($= SD$/mean) for each operator.

While there are moderate differences between users in their operator times, the variation in times between users is comparable to the variation of times within a user. The average CV between users is .36, whereas the average CV within a user is .40.

Accuracy of time predictions. Comparing the time/task calculated from the model with the times observed gives a root mean square (rms) error of 33% (expressed as a percentage of the mean observed time). As shown in

TABLE 7

Percentage of Operators in Observed Sequence Matching Predicted Sequence, Experiment II

	User (%)				
Dataset	S34 (Computer scientist)	S53 (Computer scientist)	S50 (Secretary)	S95 (Secretary)	Mean
Derivation data	79	81	98	94	88
Crossvalidation data	89	83	92	93	89

Note. Secretaries were matched better (94%) than computer scientists (83%), $U (4,4) = 0$, $p = .014$; but Derivation data was matched as well (83%) as Crossvalidation data (89%), $U (4,4) = 8, p = .56$.

TABLE 8

Operator Statistics for All Users, Experiment II

Operator	S34 (Computer scientist) Mean (sec)	CV	N	S53 (Computer scientist) Mean (sec)	CV	N	S50 (Secretary) Mean (sec)	CV	N	S95 (Secretary) Mean (sec)	CV	N	All[a] Mean (sec)	CV
Typing rate (sec/keystroke)	.16			.30			.16			.12				
GET-NEXT-PAGE	2.50	.23	5	1.18	.45	4	1.81	.41	5	3.31	—	1	2.20	.42
GET-UNIT-TASK	1.29	.41	25	2.11	.41	27	2.07	.46	28	1.25	.44	21	1.68	.28
USE-QS-METHOD	2.07	.24	18	3.32	.37	12	4.48	.36	22	—	—	—	3.29	.37
USE-LF-METHOD	2.10	.76	4	1.85	.53	4	3.47	.49	5	—	—	—	3.21	.51
USE-+N-METHOD	2.10	.40	3	4.07	.48	8	—	—	—	5.40	.53	17	3.09	.45
USE-AN-METHOD	—	—	—	8.18	.33	2	—	—	—	10.06	.21	3	9.12	.15
USE-S-METHOD	2.94	.29	5	6.60	.34	12	6.78	.40	21	4.66	.35	21	5.25	.35
USE-M-METHOD	4.38	.29	20	8.12	.44	15	8.52	.45	7	—	—	—	7.01	.33
VERIFY-EDIT	.64	.30	11	.96	.31	21	.76	.37	28	.85	.68	18	.80	.17 / .36[b]
Mean CV		.37			.41			.38			.44			.40[c]

[a] Based on user means.
[b] Average between-subjects CV.
[c] Average within-subjects CV.

TABLE 9

Root Mean Square of Prediction Error as a Percentage of Mean Task Time in Table 5, Experiment II

	S34 (Computer scientist)	S53 (Computer scientist)	S50 (Secretary)	S95 (Secretary)	Mean
Derivation data					
Reproduction	32	31	29	29	30
Prediction	31	32	29	34	32
Crossvalidation data					
Reproduction	35	35	36	35	35
Prediction	33	36	37	39	36

Note. Error is less for Derivation data (31%) than for Crossvalidation data (36%), $U(8,8) = 0$, $p = .01$; but there is no difference between Reproduction (33%) and (34%), $U(8,8) = 24$, $p > .25$; or between computer scientists (33%) and secretaries (34%), $U(8,8) = 26$, $p > .40$.

Table 9, there were no differences in prediction accuracy between computer scientists and secretaries or between reproduction and prediction, but the Derivation data was more accurately predicted (rms error 31% of mean task time) than the Crossvalidation data (36%).

If the rms error measure is interpreted as the average model error, 33% error may seem to be high. But predicting editing times unit task by unit task for a single user is a very stringent test. If the unit of prediction were the whole manuscript rather than the unit task, then the prediction error would drop considerably, since the high and low predictions of the various unit tasks would tend to cancel each other. The rms error approximately obeys a square root of n law,[2] where n is the number of unit tasks. So the rms error for predicting the time to edit the whole manuscript (70 tasks) would be $(33\%)(70)^{-1/2} = 4\%$ (neglecting, of course, the effects of users' mistakes, which aren't addressed by this model). The error for these models of variable sequence, cognitive activity would thus seem to be in the same range (about 5%) as that sometimes cited for predetermined time system predictions of invariable sequence, physical activity by industrial engineers (Maynard, 1971).

[2] rms error $= (\Sigma e_i^2/n)^{\frac{1}{2}}$, where e_i is the prediction error $pred_i - obs_i$ on the ith unit task. The rms error is the standard deviation SD of e about zero, instead of the actual mean of e, $M(e)$, and thus rms error $\geq SD(e)$. If $M(e) = 0$, then rms error $= SD(e)$, and rms error is equivalent to the standard error. The square root law argument should actually be made for $SD(e)$ about $M(e)$, but the use of rms error is approximately correct if $M(e)$ is close to zero.

TABLE 10

Description of GOMS Models Tested, Experiment III

Level 16 model	
M16A	Constant time per unit task. Only one operator: EDIT-UNIT-TASK.
Level 4 models	
M4A	Single operator for each functional step in unit task sequence: GET-UNIT-TASK, LOCATE-LINE, MODIFY-TEXT, VERIFY-EDIT.
M4B	Like M4A but with operators LOCATE-LINE and MODIFY-TEXT broken into separate cases based on methods used to accomplish them.
Level 2 models	
M2A	Like M4B, but with operators at the level of typing a system command (SPECIFY-COMMAND) or typing an argument to a command (SPECIFY-ARG).
M2B	Like M2A but with SPECIFY-COMMAND and SPECIFY-ARG broken into separate cases according to whether they involve an implicit need to get information from manuscript (suffix /G) or not (suffix /NG).
M2C	Like M2A but with SPECIFY-COMMAND and SPECIFY-ARG broken into separate cases according to four method contexts: quoted string method (/Q), first argument to substitute command (/S1), second argument to substitute command (/S2), or modify command (/M).
M2D	Like M2A but with all the distinctions in both M2B and M2C combined multiplicatively.
Level 0.5 models	
M0.5A	Like M2B but with operators at the level of basic perceptual, cognitive, and motor actions: LOOK-AT, HOME, TURN-PAGE, TYPE, and MOVE-HAND. All mental actions not overlapped with motor operations represented as MENTAL operator.
M0.5E	Like M0.5A but with MENTAL broken down into SEARCH-FOR, COMPARE, CHOOSE-COMMAND, and CHOOSE-ARG.

EXPERIMENT III: GRAIN OF ANALYSIS

The model discussed above is not the only possible GOMS model for the manuscript-editing task. Models could be constructed with either more or less detail. Thus, there is an important issue of the appropriate *grain* of the analysis.

A priori, it is not possible to know which grain size is appropriate. As the grain of the analysis becomes finer, the model successively accumulates opportunities for conditional behavior (either optional application of some method or differentiation into cases). Thus, from one point of view, models at a finer grain should be more accurate. But opposing forces are also at work. At a finer grain, operators will be likely to appear in a larger number of contexts. Combining low-level operators to form functional units that a coarser grain would reflect directly may miss set-up or other operations that are properties of the unit as a whole. The duration of operations may depend on other operators in the sequence (Abruzzi, 1956). And finally, there is typically greater error in the measurement of finer grain operators than of coarser grain operators. So a finer grain analysis might actually be less accurate.

A direct test of how the grain of analysis affects the accuracy of the GOMS model is to recast the analysis at several levels of detail. There appear to be two essentially independent dimensions along which the grain of analysis can be made finer or coarser. The primary dimension involves duration of the operators. Given that the duration of human primitive operators is something less than a third of a second (people can count silently at about 0.1 sec/digit, for example), many levels of time aggregation are possible. The second dimension involves the amount of differentiation between operators, i.e., the degree to which conditionality is suppressed and alternative operators (or sequences of operators) are considered to be the same operator. Such case-analysis aggregation can happen within any level of time aggregation.

We will explore variations of GOMS models along both of these dimensions. Table 10 describes the family of nine manuscript-editing models we will consider and Table 11 lays out the models themselves. Each model is given a name of the form M*l*d. The *l* indicates the *level*, i.e., the order of magnitude time grain of the model in seconds. For convenience, we consider models which increase roughly in powers of 2 sec. Thus, M16A has operators whose durations are on the order of 16 (2^4) sec; M0.5A has operators closest to 0.5 (2^{-1}) sec.

Within each level we consider various degrees of differentiation. There is no convenient metric here, nor do differentiations at the different levels correspond, so we simply assign arbitrary letter labels—the *d* in the model name. However, we do adopt the convention that model M*l*A is the most aggregated model at level *l*, i.e., the one that collapses conditional se-

quences into each other as much as possible or has the fewest number of operators.

At the most aggregated level, Model M16A (see Table 11) consists of a single operator, EDIT-UNIT-TASK. The goal of manuscript editing is accomplished by repeating this operator for each unit task. With a single operator, M16A always predicts that it takes the same amount of time to do a unit task. Level 4 models come from decomposing the unit task into its functional cycle: (1) get the next edit task, (2) locate the editor at the line on which the modification is to be made, (3) make the modification, and (4) verify that the edit was done correctly. The model used to analyze Experiment II is a Level 4 model (M4B). Level 2 models arise by decomposing the methods used at Level 4 into the individual steps of specifying commands and arguments.

TABLE 11

Methods for Models, Experiment III

Model M16A
GOAL: EDIT-MANUSCRIPT
▪ EDIT-UNIT-TASK   ▪ *repeat until no more unit tasks*

Model M4A
GOAL: EDIT-MANUSCRIPT
▪ GOAL: EDIT-UNIT-TASK   ▪ *repeat until no more unit tasks*
▪ ▪ GOAL: GET-UNIT-TASK   ▪ ▪ *if task not remembered*
▪ ▪ ▪ GET-NEXT-PAGE   ▪ ▪ ▪ *if at end of manuscript page*
▪ ▪ ▪ GET-UNIT-TASK
▪ ▪ GOAL: DO-UNIT-TASK   ▪ ▪ *if any edit task was found*
▪ ▪ ▪ LOCATE-LINE   ▪ ▪ ▪ *if task not on current line*
▪ ▪ ▪ MODIFY-TEXT
▪ ▪ ▪ VERIFY-EDIT

Model M4B
GOAL: EDIT-MANUSCRIPT
▪ GOAL: EDIT-UNIT-TASK   ▪ *repeat until no more unit tasks*
▪ ▪ GOAL: GET-UNIT-TASK   ▪ ▪ *if task not remembered*
▪ ▪ ▪ GET-NEXT-PAGE   ▪ ▪ ▪ *if at end of manuscript page*
▪ ▪ ▪ GET-UNIT-TASK
▪ ▪ GOAL: DO-UNIT-TASK   ▪ ▪ *if an edit task was found*
▪ ▪ ▪ GOAL: LOCATE-LINE   ▪ ▪ ▪ *if task not on current line*
▪ ▪ ▪ [select USE-QS-METHOD
            USE-LF-METHOD]
▪ ▪ ▪ GOAL: MODIFY-TEXT
▪ ▪ ▪ [select USE-S-COMMAND
            USE-M-COMMAND]
▪ ▪ ▪ VERIFY-EDIT

Model M2A
GOAL: EDIT-MANUSCRIPT
▪ GOAL: EDIT-UNIT-TASK   ▪ *repeat until no more unit tasks*
▪ ▪ GOAL: GET-UNIT-TASK   ▪ ▪ *if task not remembered*
▪ ▪ ▪ GET-NEXT-PAGE   ▪ ▪ ▪ *if at end of manuscript page*
▪ ▪ ▪ GET-FROM MANUSCRIPT
▪ ▪ GOAL: DO-UNIT-TASK   ▪ ▪ *if an edit task was found*
▪ ▪ ▪ GOAL: LOCATE-LINE   ▪ ▪ ▪ *if task not on current line*
▪ ▪ ▪ [select GOAL: USE-QS-METHOD
▪ ▪ ▪ ▪ SPECIFY-COMMAND   ▪ ▪ ▪ ▪ *repeat until at line*
▪ ▪ ▪ ▪ SPECIFY-ARG
▪ ▪ ▪ GOAL: USE-LF-METHOD
▪ ▪ ▪ ▪ SPECIFY-COMMAND]
▪ ▪ ▪ VERIFY-LOC
▪ ▪ ▪ GOAL: MODIFY-TEXT
▪ ▪ ▪ [select GOAL: USE-S-COMMAND
▪ ▪ ▪ ▪ SPECIFY-COMMAND
▪ ▪ ▪ ▪ SPECIFY-ARG
▪ ▪ ▪ ▪ SPECIFY-ARG

TABLE 11—*Continued*

▪ ▪ ▪ ▪ GOAL: USE M-COMMAND
▪ ▪ ▪ ▪ SPECIFY-COMMAND
▪ ▪ ▪ ▪ SPECIFY-COMMAND   ▪ ▪ ▪ ▪ *repeat until at text*
▪ ▪ ▪ ▪ SPECIFY-ARG
▪ ▪ ▪ ▪ SPECIFY-COMMAND]
▪ ▪ ▪ VERIFY-EDIT

Model M2B: as in M2A but substitute
SPECIFY-COMMAND/G or SPECIFY-COMMAND/NG *for* SPECIFY-COMMAND
SPECIFY-ARG/G or SPECIFY-ARG/NG   *for* SPECIFY-ARG

Model M2C: as in M2A but substitute
SPECIFY-ARG/Q or SPECIFY-ARG/M or
SPECIFY-ARG/S1 or SPECIFY-ARG/S2   *for* SPECIFY-ARG

Model M2D: as in M2A but substitute
SPECIFY-COMMAND/G or SPECIFY-COMMAND/NG *for* SPECIFY COMMAND
SPECIFY-ARG/Q/G or SPECIFY-ARG/Q/NG or
SPECIFY-ARG/M/G or SPECIFY-ARG/M/NG or
SPECIFY-ARG/S1/G or SPECIFY-ARG/S1/NG or
SPECIFY-ARG/S2/G or SPECIFY-ARG/S2/NG   *for* SPECIFY-ARG

Model M0.5E
GOAL: EDIT-MANUSCRIPT
▪ GOAL: EDIT-UNIT-TASK   ▪ *repeat until no more unit tasks*
▪ ▪ GOAL: GET-UNIT/TASK   ▪ ▪ *if task not remembered*
▪ ▪ ▪ GOAL: TURN-PAGE*   ▪ ▪ ▪ *if at end of manuscript page*
▪ ▪ ▪ GOAL: GET-FROM-MANUSCRIPT*
▪ ▪ GOAL: DO-UNIT/TASK   ▪ ▪ *if an edit task was found*
▪ ▪ ▪ GOAL: LOCATE-LINE   ▪ ▪ ▪ *if task not on current line*
▪ ▪ ▪ CHOOSE-COMMAND
▪ ▪ ▪ [select GOAL: USE QS-METHOD   (see below for expansion of
                                               goals ending in *)
▪ ▪ ▪ ▪ GOAL: SPECIFY-COMMAND*
▪ ▪ ▪ ▪ GOAL: SPECIFY-ARG*   ▪ ▪ ▪ ▪ *repeat until at line*
▪ ▪ ▪ GOAL: USE-LF-METHOD
▪ ▪ ▪ ▪ GOAL: SPECIFY-COMMAND*]
▪ ▪ ▪ GOAL: VERIFY-LOCATION*
▪ ▪ ▪ GOAL: MODIFY-TEXT
▪ ▪ ▪ CHOOSE-COMMAND
▪ ▪ ▪ [select GOAL: USE-S-COMMAND
▪ ▪ ▪ ▪ GOAL: SPECIFY COMMAND*
▪ ▪ ▪ ▪ GOAL: SPECIFY-ARG*
▪ ▪ ▪ ▪ GOAL: SPECIFY-ARG*
▪ ▪ ▪ GOAL: USE-M-COMMAND
▪ ▪ ▪ ▪ GOAL: SPECIFY COMMAND*
▪ ▪ ▪ ▪ GOAL: SPECIFY COMMAND*   ▪ ▪ ▪ ▪ *repeat until at text*
▪ ▪ ▪ ▪ GOAL: SPECIFY-ARG*
▪ ▪ ▪ ▪ GOAL: SPECIFY-COMMAND*]
▪ ▪ ▪ GOAL: VERIFY-EDIT*

(Expansion of goals appearing several times)
*GOAL: TURN-PAGE

TABLE 11—Continued

- LOOK-AT-MANUSCRIPT   ▪ *repeat twice*
- ACTION
- MOVE-HAND   ▪ *repeat twice*
- TURN-PAGE
- *GOAL: GET-FROM-MANUSCRIPT
- LOOK-AT-MANUSCRIPT
- SEARCH-FOR
- LOOK-AT-DISPLAY   ▪ *optional*
- *GOAL: SPECIFY-COMMAND
- GOAL: GET-FROM-MANUSCRIPT*   ▪ *if not already selected*
- CHOOSE-COMMAND   ▪ *if not already selected*
- GOAL: TYPE-STRING*
- *GOAL: SPECIFY-ARG
- GOAL: GET-FROM-MANUSCRIPT*   ▪ *optional*
- CHOOSE-ARG
- GOAL: TYPE-STRING*
- *GOAL: VERIFY
- LOOK-AT-DISPLAY   ▪ *optional*
- GOAL: GET-FROM-MANUSCRIPT*
- COMPARE
- *GOAL: TYPE-STRING
- HOME   ▪ *optional*
- LOOK-AT-DISPLAY   ▪ *optional*
- TYPE-STRING   ▪ *optional*

(typing rate 103 words/min) with 2 years experience on the POET editor, much of it with the type of terminal used in this experiment.

Procedure. The procedure was similar to that of Experiment II.

Protocol. A protocol of the user's behavior was coded directly from the videotape and the time-stamped keystroke file using a set of descriptive operators not related a priori to any model. The overwhelming bulk of behavior was coded by the operators TYPE, LOOK-AT, and MENTAL defined as follows:

TYPE (*char1, char2, . . .*). A burst of typewriting starting with the beginning of the finger trajectory toward the first key and ending when the last key makes contact. A "burst" is defined as a sequence of keystrokes with no more than 0.30 sec between successive key contacts and is based on studies (Kinkead, 1975) showing that keystrokes for skilled typists doing straight typing usually do not take more than this time.

LOOK-AT (*place*). Act of looking from one place to another. A *place* is either the CRT, the keyboard, or the manuscript. LOOK-AT includes the physical head movement and gross eye movement, but does not include any perceptual scanning within a place (such as searching a manuscript page for a new task).

MENTAL. Generic operator for mental activity that does not overlap with physical operations.

Other operators, used infrequently, were HOME (*hand, place*) for moving a hand to the keyboard preparatory to typing, MOVE-HAND (*hand, place*) for other hand movements, TURN-PAGE, ACTION (*description*), and EXPRESSION (*description*). The last two were miscellaneous categories for recording other behavior.

Data sets. As in Experiment II, the first 3 tasks were discarded and the remaining 70 tasks were partitioned into a Derivation data set and a Crossvalidation data set. The two data sets were found to be comparable with respect to time/unit task (Mann–Whitney $U(19,26) = 180.5$, $p > .05$).

Fitting the models to the data. The protocol record for the error-free Derivation unit tasks was recoded into a sequence of operators for each model. To encode each operator requires a recognizer that determines whether the operator occurs in the data and, if so, what its boundary times are. Such recognizers are insensitive to many of the details of what happens. An odd MENTAL operator in a SPECIFY-COMMAND (at Level 2), a USE-QS-METHOD (at Level 4), or an EDIT-UNIT-TASK (at Level 16) is consistent and is accepted by the recognizers for these operators. Thus, it is possible—and indeed it is the case—that the higher-level models account for all of the descriptive operators in the protocol. But these odd descriptive operators (e.g., the odd MENTAL) are not without consequence; they may show up as sequence errors in the lower-level models and, in chronometric analysis, as variance in the higher-level operator times.

The Level 0.5 models, on the other hand, must map one-to-one onto the protocol, since the Level 0.5 operators are at the same level of aggregation as the protocol operators. Many of the protocol operators (such as TYPE) are identical to the Level 0.5 operators and are identified directly, whereas other protocol operators (such as MENTAL) must be relabeled (e.g., SEARCH-FOR or CHOOSE-COMMAND in M0.5E) to fit the models. The possibility then exists that there will be descriptive operators in the protocol that are not accounted for by the models. More often, a descriptive operator, though a possible operator type in the model, may not correspond to any possible operator produced by the model at that point. This happens for 78 of the 581 operator instances in the protocol. The most significant kind of unaccounted-for operators are instances of MENTAL that cannot be interpreted as one of the M0.5E operators and are labeled UNKNOWN. These mostly arise from our stringent rule of coding the occurrence of a mental operator whenever there is a pause in the protocol

Both Levels 4 and 2 are driven by the structure of the POET commands. These are themselves reflections of the demands of the task as it is defined in the manuscript. At Level 0.5 an entirely different set of operators comes into view, defined not by their functional role in a command language, but by reference to the basic physical and mental actions of the user: typing, looking, moving a hand, and various mental operations. These operators, unlike the operators at other levels, are task free.

The cost of obtaining the estimates of all the different operators and selection rules increases as the size of the operators decreases, because the more data is required for a given level of robustness and because the observation and measurement problems increase at the lower levels. A possible compensation for the greater cost of using the Level 0.5 operators is that, unlike the larger operators, it may not be necessary to determine lower level operators for each new application.

Method

User. A single user (S13) was employed for this experiment, because of the amount of data analysis required at the fine-grained levels. The user was a highly skilled secretary

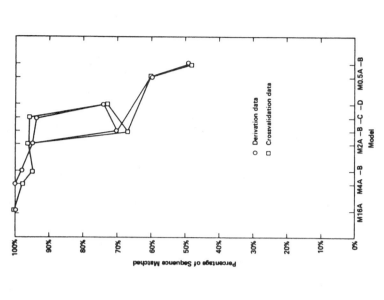

FIG. 2.   Accuracy of operator sequence predictions, Experiment III.

her hand to her mouth and lick her fingers before turning the page. In fact, she would usually also lick her fingers one task too early (a true case of fractional anticipatory goal response *in vivo*). This action was not in the model and so caused mismatched operators. Second, the UNKNOWN operators counted as mismatches.

Time Prediction

Operator times. Durations of the operators for all models, as empirically determined from the Derivation data, appear in Table 12 along with the percentage of the time spent in each operator. Since manuscript-editing has the appearance of a motor-intensive task, it is interesting that 60% of the time for the manuscript-editing task was mental time; only 22% was actually spent typing.

All operators except the TYPE operator are assumed to take constant time. While it is obvious that TYPE should be parameterized by the number of characters to be typed, we must be able to predict the search

---

longer than 0.30 sec. The mean time of the UNKNOWN operators is only 0.28 sec. Of the unaccounted-for operators, 71 are UNKNOWNs, 6 are MOVE-HANDs, and 1 is an AC-TION.

It sometimes happens that two mental operators (such as **VERIFY-LOC** and **SPECIFY-COMMAND** in M2A) are predicted by the model to occur in succession. There is then a problem determining the boundary between them, for there is no overt indication in the data. Each operator type involved in such cases (e.g., **VERIFY-LOC**) was compared to instances of the operator where the boundaries were observable (instances where it was surrounded by nonmental operators). This comparison showed clearly that the operator times of these adjacent mental operators were not additive. These cases are listed in Table 12 as if they were separate operator types, and they are given combined names like V+SC. In all, there are four different combined operator types, two at Level 2 and, correspondingly, two at Level 0.5. For purposes of predicting task times, the values of the noncombined versions of these operators were used, thus counting their nonadditivity against the models.

Results

Operator Sequences

Selection rules. Analysis of the Derivation data yielded selection rules for the user very similar in form and in accuracy to those of users in the previous experiments:

Selection rules for LOCATE *goal:*
  Rule 1. Use the QS-METHOD as default.
  Rule 2. Use the LF-METHOD if $D < 5$ lines.
Selection rules for MODIFY *goal:*
  Rule 1. Use the S-COMMAND as default.

The selection rules for the LOCATE goal were correct 88% of the time. The rule for the MODIFY goal was correct 92% of the time.

Accuracy of sequence predictions. For some of the models it was necessary to fix the conditions under which the "optional" operators would be invoked. These operators mainly center around the question of when to invoke extra GET-FROM-MANUSCRIPT operations, either implicitly (the /G versions of the SPECIFY operators in models M2B and M2D, see Table 11) or explicitly (the GET-FROM goal in M0.5E). Since the conditions which cause extra GET-FROM-MANUSCRIPT operations were not clear from the data, each option was decided such that exactly one extra GET-FROM was predicted for each unit task.

The match between predicted and observed sequences was comparable to that obtained in Experiment II for the comparable model M4B (96% in the present experiment vs 88% in Experiment II). As expected, the match declined as the grain of analysis became finer (see Fig. 2). The decline in accuracy for Models M2B and M2D resulted mainly from the models' inabilities to predict (1) the exact sites at which the users would glance back at the manuscript for more information and (2) how often users would consult the manuscript. Models at Level 0.5 encountered two other difficulties as well. First, it happened that this user would always move

TABLE 12

Operator Statistics for All Models, Experiment III (S13)[a]

Operator	Mean (sec)	CV	N	Percentage of total time in operator								
				M16A	M4A	M4B	M2A	M2B	M2C	M2D	M0.5A	M0.5E
EDIT-UNIT-TASK	11.38	.30	26	100	—	—	—	—	—	—	—	—
GET-NEXT-PAGE	2.14	.64	5	—	3	3	3	3	3	3	—	—
GET-UNIT-TASK	1.92	.33	24	—	16	16	—	—	—	—	—	—
LOCATE-LINE	3.98	.29	24	—	32	—	—	—	—	—	—	—
MODIFY-TEXT	3.85	.40	26	—	35	—	—	—	—	—	—	—
VERIFY-EDIT	1.49	.57	26	—	14	14	4	4	4	4	—	—
USE-QS-METHOD	3.94	.30	21	—	—	28	—	—	—	—	—	—
USE-LF-METHOD	4.27	.25	3	—	—	4	—	—	—	—	—	—
USE-S-COMMAND	3.63	.37	24	—	—	29	—	—	—	—	—	—
USE-M-COMMAND	9.72	.63	2	—	—	6	—	—	—	—	—	—
GET-FROM-MANUSCRIPT	2.06	.44	5	—	—	—	4	4	4	4	—	—
GFM + SC	1.80	.22	18	—	—	—	12	12	12	12	—	—
VERIFY-LOC	1.94	.45	17	—	—	—	12	12	12	12	—	—
VL + SC	2.00	.44	7	—	—	—	4	4	4	4	—	—
SPECIFY-COMMAND	1.47	.77	28	—	—	—	13	—	—	—	—	—
SPECIFY-ARG	1.46	.57	76	—	—	—	38	—	—	—	—	—
SPECIFY-COMMAND/NG	.40	.88	11	—	—	—	—	2	—	2	—	—
SPECIFY-COMMAND/G	2.03	.49	17	—	—	—	—	11	—	11	—	—
SPECIFY-ARG/NG	1.29	.54	63	—	—	—	—	29	—	—	—	—
SPECIFY-ARG/G	2.28	.45	13	—	—	—	—	10	—	—	—	—
SPECIFY-ARG/Q	2.07	.28	21	—	—	—	—	—	14	—	—	—
SPECIFY-ARG/S1	1.34	.70	24	—	—	—	—	—	12	—	—	—
SPECIFY-ARG/S2	.94	.31	24	—	—	—	—	—	8	—	—	—
SPECIFY-ARG/M	2.04	.67	7	—	—	—	—	—	5	—	—	—
SPECIFY-ARG/Q/NG	1.94	.22	14	—	—	—	—	—	—	9	—	—
SPECIFY-ARG/Q/G	2.29	.33	7	—	—	—	—	—	—	5	—	—
SPECIFY-ARG/S1/NG	1.12	.65	21	—	—	—	—	—	—	9	—	—
SPECIFY-ARG/S1/G	2.79	.34	3	—	—	—	—	—	—	3	—	—
SPECIFY-ARG/S2/NG	.93	.32	23	—	—	—	—	—	—	8	—	—
SPECIFY-ARG/S2/G	1.20	—	1	—	—	—	—	—	—	0	—	—
SPECIFY-ARG/M/NG	2.05	.59	5	—	—	—	—	—	—	3	—	—
SPECIFY-ARG/M/G	2.02	1.13	2	—	—	—	—	—	—	1	—	—
MENTAL	.62	.88	260	—	—	—	—	—	—	—	60	—
TYPE	.39	.31	173	—	—	—	—	—	—	—	22	22
LOOK-AT	.31	.32	139	—	—	—	—	—	—	—	13	13
HOME	.52	.22	9	—	—	—	—	—	—	—	2	2
TURN-PAGE	.67	.32	5	—	—	—	—	—	—	—	1	1
MOVE-HAND	.19	.91	17	—	—	—	—	—	—	—	1	1
ACTION	.13	1.56	6	—	—	—	—	—	—	—	0	0
EXPRESSION	.23	—	1	—	—	—	—	—	—	—	0	0
SEARCH-FOR	.72	.71	28	—	—	—	—	—	—	—	—	7
SF + CM	1.07	.52	20	—	—	—	—	—	—	—	—	7
CHOOSE-METHOD	.74	.57	8	—	—	—	—	—	—	—	—	2
CHOOSE-ARGUMENT	.41	.81	56	—	—	—	—	—	—	—	—	9
COMPARE	1.01	.82	69	—	—	—	—	—	—	—	—	22
C + CM	1.14	.60	18	—	—	—	—	—	—	—	—	7
UNKNOWN	.28	.92	71	—	—	—	—	—	—	—	—	8

[a] Outliers greater than ±2 SD removed.

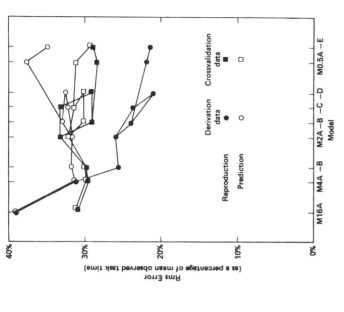

FIG. 3. Accuracy of time/task predictions, Experiment III.

strings and the substitution strings the user will employ in order to capitalize on the parameterization. The time for TYPE was parameterized by the number of shift characters N_{shift}, carriage returns N_{cr}, and other characters N_{other}, according to the equation:

$$T = .05 + .17 N_{shift} + .19 N_{cr} + .11 N_{other} \text{ sec.}$$

The equation is based on the regression fit of 157 short typing bursts from the experiment (1 to 18 characters in a burst, mean 3.8 characters). The equation explained 92% of the variance, all terms making a significant ($p < 10^{-4}$) contribution. The operator times of this user for Model M4B were comparable to the times for the same operators observed in Experiment II.

Accuracy of time predictions. The main result is that, except for M16A on the Derivation data, time calculations based on any of the models were about equally accurate. Accuracy of the model was comparable to that obtained in Experiment II. There, rms error was 33%; here, for the comparable model M4B, it was 29%. Various combinations of models, data set, and calculation method varied in the range of rms error 20 to 40% (Fig. 3). Finer grain models did better on reproduction, but not on prediction, of the Derivation data. The finer grain models were no better at either reproduction or prediction of the Crossvalidation data; in fact, prediction of the Crossvalidation data is worse at Level 0.5 than at Level 2. This occurs because, in one of the tasks, the user compares information on the display with the manuscript much more than the model predicts, resulting in a large underprediction. Recomputation of the points in Fig. 3 using the mean absolute deviation, an index not as sensitive to single outliers as the rms error, gave a graph similar to Fig. 3, but with the prediction of the Derivation data indistinguishable from the curves for the Crossvalidation data, confirming the general stability of the results.

A study of the prediction errors on unit tasks with different task environment features revealed that the only task environment feature that allowed gain in prediction was when the unit task shared the same line with another unit task. There were two tasks with this feature in the Derivation data, and they were the reason why M16A predicted more poorly on that data. Conversely, the lack of such features in any of the Crossvalidation unit tasks allowed M16A to do better on that data.

DISCUSSION

Assessment of the Models

Description of behavior. From the three experiments, it is apparent that descriptions of a user's behavior in the manuscript-editing task can be constructed from a reasonably small number of components. Depending on the grain of analysis, the behavior of each of the seven users observed

in these experiments has been described by 1–20 goals, 1–13 operators, 4–6 methods, and 1–4 selection rules. Moreover, this description is a reasonably accurate account of each user's behavior in the task. The selection rules were able to predict the user's choice of methods about 90% of the time using the data on which they were derived and 80% of the time on new data. The GOMS models were able to predict 80–100% of the operator sequences for the manuscript editing task down to Level 2. But models which attempted to predict the exact site and number of looks at the manuscript or which attempted to account for pauses on the order of a quarter of a second were considerably less accurate. Recent work on visual feedback for skilled keying (Long, 1976) indicates that users routinely look to the manuscript for information concerning errors and to the keyboard to locate unfamiliar keys. Undoubtedly, users also look to the manuscript because they forget what they are supposed to do. Successful modeling of this behavior would either require (1) models contingent on the contents of the text, such as the familiarity of the user with certain words or the clarity of particular editing instructions, or (2) stochastic models (see Card, 1978, Chap. 7).

Prediction of task times. The GOMS models likewise provide a reasonable prediction for the amount of time a task consumes. In Experiment II, the models were able to predict the time for a single task to within about 25% on new data (Table 9, Crossvalidation), where the models had to predict the times for all the operators as well as the operator sequence. In Experiment III, the equivalent prediction on Crossvalidation data was within 20-25%.

Even when the model fails to predict exactly the sequence of operators, the resulting time prediction may sometimes not be far off. The reason is that there is a certain amount of continuity in the space of methods. If the model predicts the user will look to the manuscript and he doesn't actually look until after the next operation, the time prediction will not suffer since the frequencies of the operators remain unchanged. If the user inserts one extra operator in a sequence of 15, the time prediction will be degraded, but slightly. Even if the wrong method is chosen, there is a reasonable chance the substituted method will not be wildly different in time, because it is in choosing among methods whose time is comparable that the model is most likely to err. Robustness of time prediction across minor variations in method is a very useful characteristic for applied work.

Grain of analysis. How do the abilities of the GOMS models to predict the behavior of the user vary as a function of the grain of analysis? In the current experiment, the rather surprising answer is that accuracy was essentially independent of the grain.

Two factors seem to be at work. First, the gain in chronometric predic-tive power arising from new opportunities for conditional behavior in the finer grain models seems to have been cancelled by the difficulties in refining the grain of operations (Fig. 2). Second, there seems to have been insufficient variability in the tasks which could be exercised by the finer grain models to their advantage. With respect to the latter, if the models could predict operator sequences perfectly, then the prediction curve in Fig. 3 for the Derivation data would drop to the reproduction curve. That the prediction curve is essentially horizontal implies that refining the grain of analysis did not tap the sources of time variability. In the models, variability is expressed in the method selection rules and optionality conditions, which are triggered by features of the task environment. Thus, either the models didn't capitalize on all the available features in the task environment, or there were no task environment features that gave clues to the variability. In the case of the Crossvalidation data, the gains made by the finer grain models were not sufficient to overcome the error in predicting operator duration arising from the determination of operator times from independent data (this is why, in a few instances, the prediction is actually slightly better than the reproduction) and both the reproduction and prediction curves are essentially flat.

It is important to note that the variability in the set of unit tasks in the experiment is quite small, both with respect to the user's performance times and with respect to the possible range of editing tasks—all are small edits of about the same complexity. This low variance comes about because we were not trying to manipulate the task environment, but were trying to assess the natural variability in the data and the ability of various models to deal with it. It appears that while the models, as a whole, were not bad at predicting the average time per unit task, there was insufficient variation within the editing tasks to trigger increased responsiveness from the finer grain models.

General Issues of Model Structure

What psychological reality is to be ascribed to the various components and features of the GOMS model?

Goals. The occurrence of goals in the GOMS model is one of its primary cognitive features. Goals are required in generating the model and in supporting its rational character as behavior directed toward the end of editing the manuscript. As it stands, however, the goals do not make any distinguishable contribution to the time calculations of the various models. Technically, this arises from a confounding of goals and methods/operators, so that any time assigned to creating a goal or to cleaning up and disposing of a goal would not be distinguishable from additional time in the associated operators. Goal-manipulation operations should not take longer than about 0.5 sec, so that goal operators should not show up at the Level 2 or above in any event.

The confounding of goal manipulation times results in part from GOMS being a model of error-free skilled behavior, so that the overt record contains evidence only of the sequence of effective actions. This can be confirmed from the verbal expressions made during manuscript editing. For our users, there are essentially no verbal expressions that indicate goal activity. However, protocols from inexperienced users are sprinkled with goal statements that correspond to the goals in the GOMS model. In one such experiment, when the model predicted the processing of GOAL: USE-QS-METHOD, the user would almost invariably make comments like: ''Okay, I want to get down to a line that starts with 'Food store.' '' When the model predicted GOAL: USE-S-COMMAND, the user would say: ''Now I want to substitute '30' for '39.' '' But in line with this view, no verbalizations occurred related to operator actions like TYPE.

Operator variability. The order of precision of our operators, as measured by the CV, ranges from about .9 at Level 0.5 to .3 at Level 16. In general, CVs should be expected to decrease with increasing mean when operators are composed of suboperators, a relationship that might be called ''Abruzzi's Law'' (Abruzzi, 1952, 1956). It is easy to see why such a relationship is reasonable. Suppose a composite operator, mean dura-

periment are roughly what would be expected from the size of the operations alone.

As CV increases, the number of observations needed to estimate the mean operator duration to a fixed precision also increases (see Abruzzi, 1956). This is reflected in the figure as greater dispersion for operators having small durations and in the fact that many of the points on the outlying edge are those with the lowest Ns. As the time for the operators becomes shorter, approaching the grain of characteristic physiological events, the operators tend to become more purely physical or mental. Since the physical operators are easier to identify and measure, these should have lower CVs. In Fig. 4, the outlying points below the regression line are mostly simple physical acts (indicated by squares) such as LOOK and TURN-PAGE. The outlying points above the line are mostly mental actions (indicated by triangles) such as CHOOSE-COMMAND or VERIFY-EDIT. If the purely physical and purely mental operators are ignored, the slope of the line becomes $-.433$, even closer to the $-.5$ of Eq. 2.

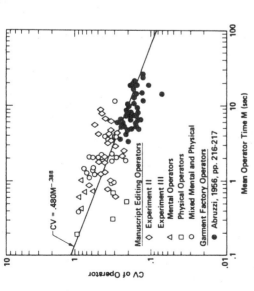

FIG. 4. Coefficient of variation for operators as a function of mean operator duration.

tion M, were simply composed of a sequence of n identical elementary operators, mean duration m. Then, $M = nm$ and

$$var(M) = n \, var(m). \tag{1}$$

Recasting Eq. 1 in terms of the CV gives

$$CV_M = \alpha M^{-0.5}, \text{ where } \alpha = m^{0.5} CV_m. \tag{2}$$

That is, the CV is inversely proportional to the square root of the mean operator time. The actual decrease is illustrated in Fig. 4, which plots CV against operator mean (M). Each point on the graph is based on multiple observations of a single person. The open symbols are manuscript editing operators from Tables 8 and 12 that occurred more than five times (excluding combination operators, TYPE, ACTION, and UNKNOWN). The solid circles are operators in a ladies' garment factory, such as cutting and stitching clothing patterns, from Abruzzi (1956, pp. 216–217). In log–log coordinates the relationship between mean and CV is essentially linear. A regression fit of the points in Fig. 4 gives

$$\ln CV = -.735 - 0.388 \ln M,$$

($R^2 = .55$, $SE = .38$, coefficient $\neq 0$ at $p < 10^{-8}$), or

$$CV = 0.480 M^{-0.388}.$$

Figure 4 suggests that, in absolute terms, the CVs observed in our ex-

ROUTINE COGNITIVE SKILL

Our analysis of user behavior in the manuscript-editing task leaves little doubt about its characterization as a routine cognitive skill, however that phrase is ultimately defined. The *cognitive* apparatus is much in evidence, epitomized by the GOMS model: selection of courses of action in accordance with the demands of the task mediated by hierarchical goal structures. The GOMS model gives a reasonable account of the user's behavior, at least during the error-free portion of it, the only part we have examined here in detail.

The notion of *routine* refers both to the absence of extreme demands for performance and to the user's expectation of being able to meet whatever demands are made without difficulty. The routine character of manuscript editing becomes evident in part by the absence of certain types of behavior. No trace of problem-solving behavior reveals itself, either by search behavior or by puzzlement and uncertainty of what to do next. Errors get uniformly and routinely converted to successful performance with increased time so that total performance is error free. Informal examination of the error-containing unit tasks reveals substantial problem-solving behavior only on rare occasions.

The notion of *skill* encompasses that of routine in general, for people generally become skilled in whatever becomes routine for them (though interesting counterexamples can be imagined). But there are many skilled performances that are far from routine, such as a championship runner setting a new record. Applied to physical motions, skill connotes smoothness, control, economy of effort (Bartlett, 1958; Welford, 1968). One indicator is the time taken to perform the same task by those who are obviously unskilled. In pilot experiments, we have observed that lack of experience with the specific editor (but with general on-line editor experience) degrades performance time per unit task by a factor of at least two.

The absence of significant learning during performance can often be taken as a characteristic of skilled routine performance. In Experiment III, S13 seems to be engaged in a steady-state performance. Within the experimental session, there is no evidence of learning. If anything, there is a slight slowdown over the course of the 20-min experimental session. Nor is there evidence of learning over extended time. Five months earlier, S13 used the same terminal and system to edit a different manuscript at the rate of 11.0 sec per task compared with 11.8 sec in this experiment.

The assertion that absence of learning characterizes routine skilled behavior must be qualified. Though there is no appearance of skill learning over a single session, it is only through repeated sessions that a user becomes skilled, and much of this happens after the user already gives the appearance of being skilled in many ways. Furthermore, substantial learning does take place within a single session about the specific manuscript being edited (which is, of course, entirely new to the user).

Dimensions of Routine Cognitive Skill

Manuscript editing is simply a single example of a routine cognitive skill, and the theory we have presented for it (GOMS), however successful it becomes for manuscript editing, is only a specialization of the theory of routine cognitive skills to the special characteristics of the manuscript-editing task environment. Although it is not possible to state a general theory of routine cognitive skill at this point, it is possible to note some ways in which manuscript editing appears to be specialized, and thus to indicate where the general theory might be significantly different from the one presented here. We do this by listing some dimensions on which routine cognitive skills can vary:

(1) *Unit task structure.* Manuscript editing is structured into a sequence of almost totally independent unit tasks, each about 12 sec duration (with the POET editor). This provides an extremely short time horizon for the integration of behavior. There are routine cognitive skill tasks with even shorter unit tasks, such as making change. More often, the relevant task duration is much longer, such as cataloguing a book for a library. However, it is most important to note that many routine cognitive skills, such as typing (Shaffer, 1976), do not have any unit task structure at all, but are essentially continuous activities.

(2) *Activity role of the task environment.* In manuscript editing, the task environment is not passive, as in the task of writing a business letter by hand, but responsive to the user's actions. Yet neither does the task environment initiate new action. By contrast, in the task of taking airline travel reservations over the phone, the task environment is the major agent of initiation.

(3) *Payoff characteristics.* The usual trade-off between speed and accuracy is reflected in this dimension. Consider the difference between typing a rough draft and typing a final copy. Both speed and accuracy are important in manuscript editing, with absolute priority given to accuracy. The emphasis on accuracy, plus the detectability of errors, leads to the conversion of most errors to time.

(4) *Input to LTM.* With respect to knowledge in long-term memory, a distinction may be drawn between memory for the components of the skill itself, and memory for the objects in the environment being processed by the skill. It is this latter to which we refer here. There is little long-term task-specific information to remember in manuscript editing other than the assimilated knowledge of the skill of the specific editor. By contrast, in the game of bridge, the task-specific knowledge players must input into LTM is fairly large: the bidding and all the cards played.

(5) *Retrieval from LTM.* Only modest amounts of information need to be retrieved from LTM for manuscript editing. A security guard must draw on LTM frequently and rapidly to recognize many faces, whereas the information needed by an elevator operator is provided by the task environment.

(6) *Type of cognitive activity.* In manuscript editing the primary type of cognitive activity is interpretation: interpretation of the instructions of the manuscript as commands and interpretation of the feedback from the editor in terms of successful performance of the modifications to be made. There are no forms of routine reasoning, design, or evaluation activity in manuscript editing. In contrast, the electrician's task of installing a new fixture may require considerable routine inference to discover the connections for circuits only partially seen. (What differentiates the electrician's task from problem solving is that the problems are familiar and the solution schemata previously stored.)

(7) *Degree of motor involvement.* This dimension lies along the major axis of discrimination between motor skills and cognitive skills. Motor involvement in many cases implies the lightening of the cognitive load, since the motor activity may not demand too much cognitive involvement. Copying digits has greater motor involvement and lesser cognitive load than multiplying the digits together. In the manuscript editing task, 40% of S13's time was spent in motor operations.

(8) *Requirement for inventing plans.* The issue here is whether a goal hierarchy (created from a limited stock of goal types) is sufficient to control behavior or whether new plans have to be constructed and then interpreted. Simple manuscript editing, such as we have been discussing, requires no planning; the goal structure provides adequate control. But if

the editing task were made more complex—say, by requiring shuffling of manuscript sections—then planning would be required to decide on a correct and efficient order in which to make the changes.

(9) *Conditionality.* Conditionality is the extent to which the operators recombine in different sequences. At one extreme are the single, repetitive, assembly-line sequences studied by industrial engineers. At the other end of the scale is the short-order cook, simultaneously processing a random mixture of pancakes, eggs, and home-fries. His behavior is highly conditional, deriving from the large number of different combinations of orders that can come from even a small menu. Manuscript editing sits in the middle, having only a moderate amount of conditionality, expressed mainly in the selection of methods and in the optional choices of operators within methods.

CONCLUSION

It is possible to describe the behavior of a person using a computer to edit a manuscript by a cognitive theory composed of a small number of goals, operators, methods, and selection rules. In this paper we have exhibited models composed of these elements which give a reasonable quantitative account of the behavior:

(1) The GOMS model for the manuscript-editing task predicted the sequences of user actions in the task fairly well. It was possible to predict a user's choices of methods, about 80–90% of the time. Sequences of operators were predicted 80–100% of the time in models cut at the level of 4 sec per operator. But ability to predict sequences was reduced at the most detailed levels by the model's inability to predict when the user would glance at the manuscript, mannerisms of the user, and difficulty accounting for very small pauses.

(2) The model also made reasonably good predictions for the amount of time necessary to make individual modifications to the text. It was able to predict the time to within about 33% on new (Crossvalidation) data. This was comparable to achieving 4% accuracy on the whole 20-min task of editing the manuscript (neglecting user mistakes).

It is important to consider at what level of behavior a model will operate—the issue of the grain size of the analysis. In this paper we have attacked the issue of grain size directly, repeating our analyses at nine different grain sizes. While accuracy in predicting the sequences of user actions fell off as the model grain became finer, finer grain models were no less accurate than coarser grain models at predicting task times.

The methods of analysis employed on this task should generalize to other situations where an experienced person faces a task in which variability in behavior along routine lines is demanded. In particular, informal observation suggests that a large number of computer interaction tasks share, with manuscript editing, a get-locate-modify-verify unit task cycle. The analysis in this paper could be used to make zero-parameter predictions of user performance in a novel computer system.

Finally, the methods reported here lay the ground work for the study of routine cognitive skill and provide a start toward a chronometric analysis study of practical cognitive tasks.

APPENDIX

The problem is to put two strings of operators, which, in general, are of different lengths, into correspondence and then to compute the degree of match. For example, if GFM, SC, SA, etc., are acronyms for operators, the algorithm to be described will take a Predicted sequence and an Observed sequence,

Predicted: GFM SC SC VL SC SA SA VE   (1)
Observed: GFM SC SA SC SA SA VE,

and insert dummy X operators to bring them into correspondence,

Predicted: GFM SC SC VL SC SA SA VE   (2)
Observed: GFM SC SA X SC SA SA VE.

There are now six matches out of a possible eight or 75%. The algorithm inserts Xs in such a way as to maximize the number of matches.

The following procedure is a translation of the INTERLISP function that was used for computations in the paper into an informal Algol-like notation. The algorithm is based on Hirschberg (1975) and Sakoe & Chiba (1978). It takes as input predicted and observed sequences like (1) and returns the percentage of matches and new versions of the input sequences resulting from the addition of dummy X operators, like (2).

```
procedure matchSeqs (PredSeq, ObsSeq):
Step 1. Initialize
  PredLength ← length(PredSeq);
  ObsLength ← length(ObsSeq);
  array PredSeq[1:PredLength],   ... Predicted sequence of operators
    ObsSeq[1:ObsLength],         ... Observed sequence of operators
    Score[0:PredLength, 0:ObsLength]←0, ... Working space
    PredSeqResult[1:PredLength + ObsLength],
    ObsSeqResult[1:PredLength + ObsLength];
Step 2. Compute scores for a matrix with one row for every operator in the
  predicted sequence and one column for every operator in the observed sequence.
  for i from 1 to PredLength do
    for j from 1 to ObsLength do
      if (PredSeq[i] = ObsSeq[j]) then
        Score[i,j]← Score[i-1,j-1] + 1;
      else Score[i,j] ← max(Score[i-1,j], Score[i,j-1]);
Step 3. Traverse the matrix backward along the path of highest scores.
  i ← PredLength; j ← ObsLength; k ← 1;
  until (i=0 and j=0) do
```

```
if (i≠0 and (j=0 or (Score[i−1,j] > Score[i−1,j−1])) then
    PredSeqResult[k] ← PredSeq[i];
    ObsSeqResult[k] ← "X";
    k ← k+1; i ← i−1;
else if (j≠0 and (i=0 or (Score[i,j−1] > Score[i−1,j−1])) then
    PredSeqResult[k] ← "X";
    ObsSeqResult[k] ← ObsSeq[j];
    k ← k+1; j ← j−1;
else
    PredSeqResult[k] ← PredSeq[i];
    ObsSeqResult[k] ← ObsSeq[j];
    k ← k+1; i ← i−1; j ← j−1;
%Match ← Score[PredLength, ObsLength] / (k−1);
return(%Match, PredSeqResult, ObsSeqResult); end;
```

REFERENCES

Abruzzi, A. *Work measurement*. New York: Columbia Univ. Press, 1952.

Abruzzi, A. *Work, workers, and work measurement*. New York: Columbia Univ. Press, 1956.

Anderson, J. R., & Bower, G. H. *Human associative memory*. Washington, D.C.: Winston, 1973.

Bartlett, F. *Thinking*. New York: Basic Books, 1958.

Card, S. K. *Studies in the psychology of computer text-editing systems*. Ph.D. Dissertation, Department of Psychology, Carnegie-Mellon Univ., 1978.

Card, S. K., Moran, T. P., & Newell, A. *The manuscript editing task: A routine cognitive skill* (Technical Report SSL-76-8). Palo Alto, CA: Xerox Palo Alto Research Center, 1976.

Card, S. K., Moran, T. P., & Newell, A. Hillsdale, NJ: Erlbaum, book in preparation.

Hirschberg, D. S. A linear space algorithm for computing maximal common subsequences. *Communications of the ACM*, 1975, **18**, 341–343.

Kinkead, R. Typing speed, keying rates, and optimal keyboard layouts. *Proceedings of Annual Meeting of the Human Factors Society*, 1975, 159–161.

Klatzky, R. L. *Human memory: structures and processes*. San Francisco: Freeman, 1975.

Lindsay, P. H., & Norman, D. A. *Human information processing: An introduction to psychology*. New York: Academic Press, 1977. 2nd ed.

Long, J. Visual feedback and skilled keying: Differential effects of masking the printed copy and the keyboard. *Ergonomics*, 1976, **19**, 93–110.

Maynard, H. B. *Industrial engineering handbook*. New York: McGraw–Hill, 1971. 3rd ed.

Mills, R. G., & Hatfield, S. A. Sequential task performance: Task module relationships, reliabilities, and times. *Human Factors*, 1974, **16**, 117–128.

Newell, A. Production systems: Models of control structures. In W. G. Chase (Ed.), *Visual information processing*. New York: Academic Press, 1973.

Newell, A., & Simon, H. A. *Human problem solving*. Englewood Cliffs, NJ: Prentice–Hall, 1972.

Russell, D. S. POET: A page oriented editor for TENEX. University of Utah, Computer Science Division, 1973.

Sakoe, H., & Chiba, S. Dynamic programming algorithm optimization for spoken word recognition. *IEEE Transactions on Acoustics, Speech, and Signal Processing*, 1978, ASSP-26(1), 43–49.

Shaffer, L. H. Intention and performance. *Psychological Review*, 1976, **83**, 375–393.

Welford, A. T. *Fundamentals of Skill*. London: Methuen, 1968.

(Accepted May 14, 1979)

Some Observations on Mental Models

Donald A. Norman
University of California, San Diego

One function of this chapter is to belabor the obvious; people's views of the world, of themselves, of their own capabilities, and of the tasks that they are asked to perform, or topics they are asked to learn, depend heavily on the conceptualizations that they bring to the task. In interacting with the environment, with others, and with the artifacts of technology, people form internal, mental models of themselves and of the things with which they are interacting. These models provide predictive and explanatory power for understanding the interaction. These statements hardly need be said, for they are consistent with all that we have learned about cognitive processes and, within this book, represent the major underlying conceptual theme. Nonetheless, it does not hurt to repeat them and amplify them, for the scope of the implications of this view is larger than one might think.

In the consideration of mental models we need really consider four different things: the *target system*, the *conceptual model* of that target system, the user's *mental model* of the target system, and the *scientist's conceptualization* of that mental model. The system that the person is learning or using is, by definition, the *target system*. A *conceptual model* is invented to provide an appropriate representation of the target system, appropriate in the sense of being accurate, consistent, and complete. Conceptual models are invented by teachers, designers, scientists, and engineers.

Mental models are naturally evolving models. That is, through interaction with a target system, people formulate mental models of that system. These models need not be technically accurate (and usually are not), but they must be functional. A person, through interaction with the system, will continue to modify the mental model in order to get to a workable result. Mental models will be

constrained by such things as the user's technical background, previous experiences with similar systems, and the structure of the human information processing system. The *Scientist's conceptualization* of a mental model is, obviously, a model of a model.

Some Observations on Mental Models

My observations on a variety of tasks, with a wide variety of people, lead me to a few general observations about mental models:

1. Mental models are incomplete.
2. People's abilities to "run" their models are severely limited.
3. Mental models are unstable: People forget the details of the system they are using, especially when those details (or the whole system) have not been used for some period.
4. Mental models do not have firm boundaries: similar devices and operations get confused with one another.
5. Mental models are "unscientific": People maintain "superstitious" behavior patterns even when they know they are unneeded because they cost little in physical effort and save mental effort.
6. Mental models are parsimonious: Often people do extra physical operations rather than the mental planning that would allow them to avoid those actions; they are willing to trade-off extra physical action for reduced mental complexity. This is especially true where the extra actions allow one simplified rule to apply to a variety of devices, thus minimizing the chances for confusions.

Let me now expand upon these remarks. In my studies of human error and human-machine interaction, I have made reasonably extensive observation of people's interactions with a number of technological devices. The situations that I have studied are quite diverse, including such tasks as the use of calculators, computers, computer text editors, digital watches and cameras, video cameras and recorders, and the piloting of aircraft. Some of these have been studied extensively (the computer text editor), others only in informal observation. I conclude that most people's understanding of the devices they interact with is surprisingly meager, imprecisely specified, and full of inconsistencies, gaps, and idiosyncratic quirks. The models that people bring to bear on a task are not the precise, elegant models discussed so well in this book. Rather, they contain only partial descriptions of operations and huge areas of uncertainties. Moreover, people often feel uncertain of their own knowledge—even when it is in fact complete and correct—and their mental models include statements about the degree of certainty they feel for different aspects of their knowledge. Thus, a person's mental model can include knowledge or beliefs that are thought to be of doubtful validity. Some of this is characterized as "superstitious"—rules that "seem to work," even if they make no sense. These doubts and superstitions govern behavior and enforce extra caution when performing operations. This is especially apt to be the case when a person has experience with a number of different systems, all very similar, but each with some slightly different set of operating principles.

Observations of Calculator Usage

Let me briefly review some of my observations on people's use of calculating machines. I observed people using hand-held versions of four-function, algebraic, and stack calculators while they were solving a series of arithmetic problems. They were asked to "think aloud" as they did the problems and I watched and recorded their words and actions. When all problems were complete, I questioned them about the methods they had used and about their understanding of the calculator.[1] Although the people I observed were all reasonably experienced with the machines on which I tested them, they seemed to have a distrust of the calculator or in their understanding of the details of calculator mechanics. As a result, they would take extra steps or decline to take advantage of some calculator features, even when they were fully aware of their existence. Most of the people I studied had experience with several different calculators, and as a result they mixed up the features. They were often unsure which feature applied to which calculator, and had various superstitions about the operations of the calculator. Finally, their estimation of the amount of mental workload required by various strategies often determined their actions; they would perform extra operations in order to reduce the amount of mental effort. Let me provide some examples.

One of the subjects I studied (on a four-function calculator) was quite cautious. Her mental model seemed to contain information about her own limitations and the classes of errors that she could make. She commented: "I always take extra steps. I never take short cuts." She was always careful to clear the calculator before starting each problem, hitting the clear button several times. She wrote down partial results even where they could have been stored in the machine memory. In a problem involving "constant sums," she would not use the calculator's memory because:

> I would not have done that because often when you play with the memory and the clear button, if you are not really clear about what it actually clears you can clear out the memory and it—it—I'm too cautious for that. I would be afraid that I'd mess up the memory.

All the people I observed had particular beliefs about their machines and about their own limitations, and as a result had developed behavior patterns that made them feel more secure in their actions, even if they knew what they were doing was not always necessary. A major pattern that seemed to apply to all my calculator studies was the need for clearing the registers and displays. The four-function calculator did need to be cleared before starting new problems, but the stack and algebraic calculators did not. Yet, these people always cleared their calculators, regardless of the type. Moreover, they would hit the clear button several times saying such things as "you never know—sometimes it doesn't register," or, explaining that "there are several registers that have to be cleared and sometimes the second and third clears do these other registers." (The four-function calculator that I studied does require two depressions of the CLEAR button to clear all registers.)

In an interesting complement to the excessive depressing of CLEAR to ensure that everything got cleared, during a problem with the four-function calculator where it became necessary to clear the display during the solution of a problem, one person balked at doing so, uncertain whether this would also clear the registers. All the people I observed expressed doubts about exactly what did and did not get cleared with each of the button presses or clear keys (one of the algebraic calculators has 3 different clear keys). They tended toward caution: excessively clearing when they wanted the calculator to be restarted, and exhibiting reluctance to use CLEAR during a problem for fear of clearing too much.

A similar pattern applied to the use of the ENTER button on the stack calculator. They would push it too much, often while commenting that they knew this to be excessive, but that is what they had learned to do. They explained their actions by saying such things as "It doesn't hurt to hit it extra" or "I always hit it twice when I have to enter a new phrase—its just a superstition, but it makes me feel more comfortable."

These behaviors seem to reflect some of the properties of mental models, especially the ease of generating rules that have great precision and of keeping separate the rules for a number of very similar, but different devices. The rule to hit the CLEAR button excessively allows the user to avoid keeping an accurate count of the operation. Moreover, it provides a rule that is functional on all calculators, regardless of design, and that also makes the user resistant to slips of action caused by forgetting or interference from other activities. All in all, it seems a sensible simplification that eases and generalizes what would otherwise be a more complex, machine specific set of knowledge.

When people attribute their actions to *superstition* they appear to be making direct statements about limitations in their own mental models. The statement

---

[1]The inspiration for these studies came from Richard Young's analyses of calculator operation, presented at the conference that led to this book. However, his work did not include any studies of what people actually believed of the calculators or how they used them: hence my investigations. I made up problems that required only simple arithmetic operations—addition, subtraction, multiplication, and division—but some required storage registers, writing down of partial results, or planning of the sequence to avoid the need for writing or storage.

Since performing these studies and writing the paper I have learned of the closely related observations and analyses made by Mayer and Bayman (1981).

implies uncertainty as to mechanism, but experience with the actions and outcomes. Thus, in this context, superstitious behavior indicates that the person has encountered difficulties and believes that a particular sequence of actions will reduce or eliminate the difficulty.

Finally, there seemed to be a difference in the trade-off between calculator operations and mental operations that the people I studied were willing to employ. For problems of the sort that I was studying, the four-function machine was the most difficult to use. Considerable planning was necessary to ensure that the partial answers from the subparts of the problem could be stored in the machine memory (most four-function calculators only have one memory register). As a result, the users seemed to prefer to write down partial sums and to do simple computations in their heads rather than with the machine. With the stack machine, however, the situation is reversed. Although the machine is difficult to learn, once it is learned, expert users feel confident that they can do any problem without planning: They look at the problem and immediately start keying in the digits.

On Modeling a Mental Model

Consider the problem of modeling some particular person's mental model of some particular target system. Let the particular target system be called t. Before we can understand how a person interacts with a target system, we need to have a good conceptualization of that system. In other words, we need a conceptual model of the system: call the conceptual model of t, $C(t)$. And now let the user's mental model of that target system be called $M(t)$.

We must distinguish between our conceptualization of a mental model, $C(M(t))$, and the actual mental model that we think a particular person might have, $M(t)$. To figure out what models users actually have requires one to go to the users, to do psychological experimentation and observation.[2]

In order to effectively carry out such observation and experimentation, we need to consider both representational and functional issues. Let me discuss three of the necessary properties: belief systems, observability, and predictive power.

These three functional factors apply to both the mental model and our conceptualization of the model, to both $M(t)$ and $C(M(t))$. They can be summarized in this way:

Belief System. A person's mental model reflects his or her beliefs about the physical system, acquired either through observation, instruction, or inference. The conceptual model of the mental model $C(M(t))$, should contain a model of the relevant parts of the person's belief system.

Observability. There should be a correspondence between the parameters and states of the mental model that are accessible to the person and the aspects and states of the physical system that the person can observe. In the conceptual model of the mental model, this means that there should be a correspondence between parameters and observable states of $C(M(t))$ and the observable aspects and states of t.

Predictive Power. The purpose of a mental model is to allow the person to understand and to anticipate the behavior of a physical system. This means that the model must have predictive power, either by applying rules of inference or by procedural derivation (in whatever manner these properties may be realized in a person); in other words, it should be possible for people to "run" their models mentally. This means that the conceptual mental model must also include a model of the relevant human information processing and knowledge structures that make it possible for the person to use a mental model to predict and understand the physical system.

On the Relationship between Conceptual and Mental Models

Conceptual models are devised as tools for the understanding or teaching of physical systems. Mental models are what people really have in their heads and what guides their use of things. Ideally, there ought to be a direct and simple relationship between the conceptual and the mental model. All too often, however, this is not the case.

That a mental model reflects the user's beliefs about the physical system seems obvious and has already been discussed. What is not so obvious is the correspondence that should hold between the mental model and a conceptual model of the physical system, that is, between $M(t)$ and $C(t)$.

In the literature on mathematical learning models, Greeno and Steiner (1964) introduced the notion of "identifiability." That is, they pointed out that a useful model will have a correspondence between the parameters and states of the model and the operation of the target system. I find that these remarks apply equally well to the problems of mental models. It is important that there be a

---

[2]Let me warn the nonpsychologists that discovering what a person's mental model is like is not easily accomplished. For example, you cannot simply go up to the person and ask. Verbal protocols taken while the person does a task will be informative, but incomplete. Moreover, they may yield erroneous information, for people may state (and actually believe) that they believe one thing, but act in quite a different manner. All of a person's belief structures are not available to inspection, especially when some of those beliefs may be of a procedural nature. And finally, there are problems with what is called the "demand structure" of the situation. If you ask people why or how they have done something, they are apt to feel compelled to give a reason, even if they did not have one prior to your question. They are apt to tell you what they believe you want to hear (using their mental models of your expectations). Having then generated a reason for you, they may then believe it themselves, even though it was generated on the spot to answer your question. On-line protocols generated while in the act of problem solving and that give descriptions of activities rather than explanations are much more reliable.

correspondence between the parameters and states of one's model and the things one is attempting to describe. This restriction does pose some strong constraints upon the nature of the mental model. Certain kinds of mental models will be ruled out if the identification cannot be easily made.

A major purpose of a mental model is to enable a user to predict the operation of a target system. As a result, the predictive power of such a model is of considerable concern. Although great stress is laid in this book to the notion of "running" a conceptual or mental model, it should also be possible to make predictions by straightforward inference, a declarative form of predictability, rather than the implied notion of procedural running of a model. Whatever the mechanism, it is clear that prediction is one of the major aspects of one's mental models, and this must be captured in any description of them.

The System Image

In the ideal world, when a system is constructed, the design will be based around a conceptual model. This conceptual model should govern the entire human interface with the system, so that the image of that system seen by the user is consistent, cohesive, and intelligible. I call this image the *system image* to distinguish it from the conceptual model upon which it is based, and the mental model one hopes the user will form of the system. The instruction manuals and all operation and teaching of the system should then be consistent with this system image. Thus, the instructors of the system would teach the underlying conceptual model to the user and, if the system image is consistent with that model, the user's mental model will also be consistent.

For this to happen, the conceptual model that is taught to the user must fulfill three criteria:

Learnability
Functionality
Usability

What good is a conceptual model that is too difficult to learn? Or a model that has little functionality, failing to correspond to the system image or failing to predict or explain the important aspects of the target system? Or what of a conceptual model that cannot easily be used, given the properties of the human information processing structure with its limited short-term memory and limited ability to do computations?

Alas, all too often there is no correspondence among the conceptual model of the system that guided the designer, the system image that is presented to the user, the material in the instructional manuals that is taught to the user, and the mental models of the user. Indeed, for many target systems, there is no single conceptual model that was followed in the design. The stack calculator gives us a good positive instance where a conceptual design was neatly implemented into a consistent physical device, with the operations and instructions all based around the same basic model. It should be no surprise, therefore, that in my studies, users of this calculator were most confident of their abilities.

Summary

The moral of this story is that it is important for us to distinguish among several different kinds of models and conceptualizations. Our conceptualization of a target system should not be confused with the mental model that a user creates of that system. The designer's conceptualization may also differ from the image that the system itself presents to the user. In the ideal world, the system image will be consistent with the designer's conceptualization, and the user's mental model will thereby be consistent with both.

People's mental models are apt to be deficient in a number of ways, perhaps including contradictory, erroneous, and unnecessary concepts. As designers, it is our duty to develop systems and instructional materials that aid users to develop more coherent, useable mental models. As teachers, it is our duty to develop conceptual models that will aid the learner to develop adequate and appropriate mental models. And as scientists who are interested in studying people's mental models, we must develop appropriate experimental methods and discard our hopes of finding neat, elegant mental models, but instead learn to understand the messy, sloppy, incomplete, and indistinct structures that people actually have.

ACKNOWLEDGMENT

This research was conducted under Contract N00014-79-C-0323, NR 157-437 with the Personnel and Training Research Programs of the Office of Naval Research, and was sponsored by the Office of Naval Research and the Air Force Office of Scientific Research. I thank Sondra Buffett for her suggestions for the manuscript.

REFERENCES

Greeno, J. G., & Steiner, T. E. Markovian processes with identifiable states: General considerations and applications to all-or-none learning. *Psychometrika*, 1964, 29, 309–333. (An easier treatment is provided in the chapter on identifiability in Restle, F., & Greeno, J. G., *Introduction to mathematical psychology*. Reading, Mass.: Addison-Wesley, 1970.)

Mayer, R. E., & Bayman, P. Psychology of calculator languages: A framework for describing differences in users' knowledge. *Communications of the ACM*, 1981, 24, 511–520.

Text Editors and Word Processors

No area of computer application has been as widely studied in terms of its human factors aspects as that of text editing and word processing. An early overview of the technology is that of Rice and van Dam (1971). A survey of behavioural research appears in Embley and Nagy (1981). Two somewhat later surveys (Meyrowitz and van Dam, 1982a, 1982b; Furuta, Scofield, and Shaw 1982) focus primarily on design approaches, functionality, and implementation, but also discuss issues of usability. Two videos on the subject of text editors are IBM (1985) and Xerox (1985). The interested reader should also consult a series of newsletters which for 15 years have been providing sensitive observations and evaluations of both the functionality and interfaces of commercial word processors and publishing systems (Seybold, 1971-87).

The Evaluation of Text Editors

One of the more valuable and comprehensive studies has been carried out by Roberts (1979; Roberts and Moran, 1982). Roberts and Moran (1983) summarize this work in an article included as a reading. It presents a multidimensional methodology for evaluating and comparing text editors. The dimensions studied are the time it takes experts to perform a set of fundamental benchmark editing tasks, the time used by experts to make and correct errors while carrying out these tasks, the rate at which novices learn the tasks, and the functionality of editors in handling tasks ranging from the simple to the complex. Time, errors, and learning are measured empirically;

functionality is estimated analytically. Time is also predicted analytically using the Keystroke-Level Model (see Chapter 5: Models of Computer User and Usage). The methodology is applied to nine diverse text editors, including both keyboard- and mouse-based systems; systems that run on dedicated workstations and those than run in a time-shared environment; so-called "modeless" systems and those that are clearly very moded; "What You See Is What You Get" (WYSIWYG) systems and those that are not; and, systems that are experimental prototypes and those that are commercial products.

The nine editors when compared along the four dimensions studied showed differences by factors ranging from 2 to 5, only some of which were statistically significant. Use of too few subjects, and the large individual differences between subjects were major sources of the difficulty in establishing results that were reliable. The Keystroke-Level Model was reasonably successful in predicting error-free execution time on the set of core editing tasks. Perhaps the most interesting results were those aspects of the "conventional wisdom" that were not substantiated in the study. Those who worked faster did not in general make more errors, in other words there was no consistent tradeoff between speed and accuracy. Furthermore, there was no tradeoff between ease of learning by novices and efficiency of use by experts. On the contrary, there was a high positive correlation between the score measuring ease of learning and the score measuring ease of use.

The Roberts and Moran study was carried out methodically and carefully. Nonetheless, there are many subtle issues involved in the design of an appropriate experimental methodology (see Chapter 4: Empirical Evaluation of User Interfaces). Allen (1985) criticizes the statistical methodology used in the Roberts and Moran study, although Roberts and Moran (1985) argue that it is adequate in the context in which it was used. Allen then presents some new statistical analyses of the time data reported in the original study, but these do not result in conclusions quantitatively different from those in the original study. Finally, Allen notes the problem, also implicit in the original study, of the non-random assignment of subjects to editors, since each subject had to be "experts" in the use of one particular editor, and there was no guarantee that these subjects had comparable levels of expertise.

Borenstein (1985) is a second critical review of the Roberts and Moran methodology based on new experiments. He evaluated three text editors, one being another version of a system included in the original nine. His results generally support the approach taken by Roberts and Moran and provide additional experimental evidence of its value. Nonetheless, he does note four "minor flaws" in their methodology:

- The use of a stopwatch does not always provide sufficient accuracy in measurements of execution time.
- Small errors in execution cannot be ignored.
- The concept of "expert user" must be refined when a variety of skills are involved and subjects may be expert in some and non-expert in others.
- Descriptions of functionality need to be more sophisticated when dramatically different kinds of applications are involved, such as the text editing of documents and the text editing of programs.

The Borenstein paper is valuable reading for those seeking to become more sensitive to the subtleties of good behavioural experimentation and to the difficulties in developing effective methodologies for evaluating real and complex computer systems.

These two papers substantively advance the state-of-the-art. Despite this, it is interesting to reflect on what has *not* been accomplished, for this points the way to needed future work:

- Problems with the classification of users. Although Roberts recognizes that there are casual users in addition to novice and expert users, and that expert technical users are different from expert nontechnical users, she does very little with these categories and distinctions. Folley and Williges (1982) present some rudimentary results showing how expert and novice users differ in their mastery of subsets of a text editing command language.

- Problems with the error paradigm. Roberts deals primarily with errors made by experts in routine use, and only slightly with the issue of disaster analysis. She ignores errors made by novices, errors made by casual users, and errors due to interruptions.

- Problems with the learning paradigm. Roberts justifies the use of a human instructor in one-to-one contact because there would be too many artifacts and uncontrollable events in learning only from the system and the documentation. But this is the way, perhaps with occasional questions to a nearby human, that many or most people learn a system. We shall return to the question of how one might evaluate learning as it normally occurs. (Mack, Lewis, and Carroll, 1983; Carroll and Mack, 1984).

- Problems with the classification of functionality. Roberts's taxonomy of 212 editing tasks and her proposal for benchmark tasks are significant steps towards a more consistent method of comparing systems. Yet it fails to distinguish two kinds of tasks, those specialized for different kinds of editing, a point made by Borenstein, and those appropriate to low end, medium end, and high end systems (Brown, 1985). These problems are highlighted by the work of Whiteside, Archer, Wixon, and Good (1982), who present empirical data based on logging keystrokes from several hundred hours of the usage of two word processors, one experimental, one commercial. The percentages of time spent by users in such states as typing, moving the cursor, erasing, and editing are dramatically different from the data of users carrying out the Roberts benchmark tasks. Gould (1981) and Allen (1982) also present results describing how people actually use text editors to input and revise manuscripts.

- The issue of product tiers. Brown (1985) suggests that commercial products are now being positioned in one of three tiers, the high, the middle, and the low. This can lead to meaningful differences among the three tiers in terms of functionality (as discussed above), ease of use, ease of learning, and susceptibility to errors.

- The issue of subjective evaluations. Individuals have very strong opinions about text editors. There is also an emerging literature of quality product evaluations and reviews, as for example in the various Seybold (1971-87) reports. What is the role of subjective evaluations? Should they be integrated into the evaluation methodology, and, if so, how can this be done?

- The issue of correlations between various measures of "goodness." As noted above, ease of use and ease of learning are correlated in the systems that Roberts has evaluated. There is need for a great deal of research on the relationships among various measures.

- The issue of documentation (see Chapter 13: Enhancing System Usability). Although Roberts mentions the issue of documentation, she does little with it. But documentation in the broad sense, including tutorial guides, reference manuals, principles of operation manuals, command summaries, on-line documentation, on-line help, error messages, and the like, are critically important to the success or failure of a system. They also serve different functions, including teaching novices how to do it, enabling casual users to look up how to do it, and aiding all users in discovering what they did wrong.

- The issue of technology. Borenstein mentions the importance of input technology such as the keyboard and the mouse, and the use of appropriate technology with each system. We shall return to this topic in Chapter 8: The Haptic Channel.

- The issue of individual differences, and their impact on one's success in using and learning text editors (see for example, Gomez et al., 1983). One determinant of success is that of skill transfer between text editors (Singley and Anderson, 1985).

The Learning of Word Processing

The issues involved in novices' learning word processors have been investigated and reported in Mack, Lewis, and Carroll (1983) and Carroll and Mack (1984), both included in our readings. Another report on the same research with some interesting insights is Lewis and Mack (1982). The authors employed *thinking aloud* protocols (Lewis, 1982) in observing ten office temporaries with little or no word processing experience as they learned either the text editing plus formatting tools on a large general-purpose computer system, or the capabilities of a commercially available word processor. The subjects were encouraged to report (Carroll and Mack, 1984):

> questions that were raised in their minds, plans and strategies they felt they might be considering or following out, and inferences and knowledge that might have been brought to awareness by ongoing experiences.

Mack, Lewis, and Carroll (1983) summarize their major results as follows:

> (1) Learning is difficult. Learners experience frustration and blame themselves. Learners take longer than expected, and learners have trouble applying what they know after training.

(2) Learners lack basic knowledge. Learners are naive about how computers work (e.g., do not understand computer jargon). Learners do not know what is relevant to understanding and solving problems.

(3) Learners make ad hoc interpretations. Learners try to construct interpretations for what they do or for what happens to them. Learners' interpretations can prevent them from seeing that they have a problem.

(4) Learners generalize from what they know. Learners assume that some aspects of text editors will work like typewriting (especially functions that simply move the typing point on a typewriter). Learners assume that text-editing operations will work consistently.

(5) Learners have trouble following directions. Learners do not always read or follow directions. Learners do not always understand or correctly follow directions even when they do try.

(6) Problems interact. Learners have trouble understanding that one problem can create another.

(7) Interface features may not be obvious. Learners can be confused by prerequisites and side effects of procedures. Learners can be confused by feedback messages and the outcome of procedures.

(8) Help facilities do not always help. Learners to not always know what to ask for. Help information is not always focused on the learner's specific problem.

The other two papers develop conceptual frameworks to assist in understanding the above results. Lewis and Mack (1982) analyze and classify the problems in terms of the interaction among three factors: (1) the training method (self study in this case); (2) the interface design; and, (3) the learner. Carroll and Mack (1984) characterize learning as consisting of three very different kinds of activity:

- *Learning by Doing*. Users want to try things out rather than read about them. They have a tendency to jump the gun. One reason for doing so is that it is in fact very difficult to follow written sequences of instructions — they are usually so fragile that the slightest deviation from the correct procedure leads to a failure from which there is no obvious or easy recovery.

- *Learning by Thinking*. Despite their tendency to wander off into the unknown, users do try to construct interpretations to make sense of their experiences. They set goals for themselves, and engage in purposeful problem solving activity (see Chapter 6: Cognition and Human Information Processing).

- *Learning by Knowing*. Finally, learning does not occur in a vacuum. On the contrary, one's success depends in great part on the ability to make use of prior knowledge. Learners about word processing make use of the metaphor of the typewriter and expectations based on past work experience as they attempt to integrate bits and pieces of knowledge into an effective model of how to use a new system.

In other words, learning is an *active process — learning by discovery* (Carroll and Mack, 1984, p. 17):

> is that people are so busy trying things out, thinking things through, and trying to relate what they already know (or believe they know) to what is going on that they often do not notice the small voice of structured instruction crying out to them from behind the manual and the system interface.

Following up on these insights, Carroll and his group have begun to develop training materials more suited to exploration and independent discovery (Carroll et al., 1985; Carroll et al., 1986), and system interfaces that are more forgiving in that they are guaranteed to prevent the user from making certain kinds of errors that would have very serious consequences or would be difficult to recover from (Carroll and Carrithers, 1984a, 1984b; Carroll and Kay, 1985). Carroll (1984) is an overview of their approach, which they term *minimalist design*. (See also Chapter 13: Enhancing System Usability.)

In summary, we include the two papers not only because of the value of their conceptualizations of learning but also because they contain numerous examples with sensitive observations about the behaviour of real users experiencing real systems. The insights to be derived have relevance to all interactive systems, not just to text editors.

On the other hand, one can ask questions about the validity of the results. The first is the extent to which the results have been affected by the abysmal quality of the user interfaces of the systems studied. Although the authors insist that the systems and manuals were "state-of-the-art" (Carroll and Mack, 1984, p. 15), the prevalence of jargon, obscure modes, awkward dialogue sequences, needless complexity, and lack of consistency led to a multitude of user problems and confusion that seems almost artificially extreme. A deeper question, acknowledged by the authors in some of their writings, is the extent to which the thinking aloud methodology and the sometimes intrusive questions of the experimenter could have substantially modified the behaviour of the subjects and introduced artifacts not present in the normal learning of word processing (see also Chapter 4: Empirical Evaluation of User Interfaces).

Further experimentation, ideally in independent laboratories, is required to answer these questions.

Readings

Roberts, Teresa L. & Moran, Thomas P. (1983). The Evaluation of Computer Text Editors: Methodology and Empirical Results. *Communications of the ACM* 26(4), 265-283.

Mack, Robert L., Lewis, Clayton H., & Carroll, John M. (1983). Learning to Use Word Processors: Problems and Prospects. *ACM Transactions on Office Information Systems* 1(3), July 1983, 254-271.

Carroll, John M. & Mack, Robert L. (1984), Learning to Use a Word Processor: By Doing, by Thinking, and by Knowing. In Thomas, John C. & Schneider, Michael L. (Eds.), *Human Factors in Computer Systems*. Norwood, N.J.: Ablex Publishing Company, 13-51.

References

Allen, Robert B. (1981). Composition and Editing of Text. *Ergonomics* 24(8), 611-622.

Allen, Robert B. (1982). Patterns of Manuscript Revisions. *Behaviour and Information Technology* 1(2), 177-184.

Allen. Robert B. (1985). The Evaluation of Text Editors: Methodology and Empirical Results. *Communications of the ACM* 28(3), 324-325.

Borenstein, Nathaniel S. (1985). The Evaluation of Text Editors: A Critical Review of the Roberts and Moran Methodology based on New Experiments. *CHI '85 Proceedings*, 99-106.

Brown, Eric (1985). Word Processing and the Three Bears. *PC World* 3(12), December 1985, 192-201.

Card, Stuart K. & Moran, Thomas P. (1980). The Keystroke-Level Model for User Performance Time with Interactive Systems. *Communications of the ACM* 23(7), 396-410.

Carroll, John M. (1984). Minimalist Training. *Datamation* 1, 1 November 1984, 125-136.

Carroll, John M. & Carrithers, Caroline (1984a). Training Wheels in a User Interface. *Communications of the ACM* 27(8), August 1984, 800-806.

Carroll, John M. & Carrithers, Caroline (1984b). Blocking Learner Error States in a Training Wheels System. *Human Factors* 26(4), 377-389.

Carroll, John M. & Kay, Dana S. (1985), Prompting, Feedback and Error Correction in the Design of a Scenario Machine. *CHI '85 Proceedings*, 149-153.

Carroll, John M. & Mack, Robert L. (1984). Learning to Use a Word Processor: By Doing, by Thinking, and by Knowing. In Thomas, John C. & Schneider, Michael L. (Eds.), *Human Factors in Computer Systems*, Norwood, N.J.: Ablex Publishing Company, 13-51.

Carroll, John M., Mack, Robert L., Lewis, Clayton H., Grischkowsky, Nancy L., & Robertson, Scott R. (1985). Exploring Exploring a Word Processor. *Human-Computer Interaction* 1, 283-307.

Carroll, John M., Smith-Kerker, Penny L., Ford, Jim R., & Mazur, Sandra A. (1986). The Minimal Manual. IBM Research Report RC 11637 (#52295), January 1986.

Egan, Dennis E., Bowers, Cheryll, & Gomez, Louis M. (1982). Learner Characteristics that Predict Success in Using a Text-Editor Tutorial. *Proceedings of the Conference on Human Factors in Computing Systems*, New York: ACM, 337-340.

Embley, David W. & Nagy, George (1981). Behavioral Aspects of Text Editors. *ACM Computing Surveys* 13(1), March 1981, 33-70.

Folley, Lisa J. & Williges, Robert C. (1982). User Models of Text Editing Command Languages. *Proceedings of the Conference on Human Factors in Computing Systems*, New York: ACM, 326-331.

Furuta, Richard, Scofield, Jeffrey, & Shaw, Alan (1982). Document Formatting Systems: Survey, Concepts, and Issues. *ACM Computing Surveys* 14(3), September 1982, 417-472.

Gomez, Louis M., Egan, Dennis E., Wheeler, Evangeline, A., Sharma, Dhiraj K., & Gruchacz, Aleta M. (1983). How Interface Design Determines Who Has Difficulty Learning To Use a Text Editor. *CHI '83 Proceedings*, 176-181.

Gould, John D. (1981). Composing Letters with Computer-Based Text Editors. *Human Factors* 23(5), 593-606.

IBM Corp. (1985). Designing a ''No Surprise Editor'' Prototype. *SIGGRAPH Video Review* 18, New York: ACM.

Lewis, Clayton (1982). Using Thinking Aloud Protocols to Study the ''Cognitive Interface.'' *Research Report* RC 9265, Yorktown Heights, N.Y.: IBM Thomas J. Watson Research Center.

Lewis, Clayton & Mack, Robert (1982). Learning to Use a Text Processing System: Evidence from ''Thinking Aloud'' Protocols. *Proceedings of the Conference on Human Factors in Computing Systems*, New York: ACM, 387-392.

Mack, Robert L., Lewis, Clayton, H., & Carroll, John M. (1983). Learning to Use Word Processors: Problems and Prospects. *ACM Transactions on Office Information Systems* 1(3), 254-271.

Meyrowitz, Norman & van Dam, Andries (1982a), Interactive Editing Systems: Part I. *ACM Computing Surveys* 14(3), September 1982, 321-352.

Meyrowitz, Norman & van Dam, Andries (1982b), Interactive Editing Systems: Part II. *ACM Computing Surveys* 14(3), September 1982, 353-416.

Rice, D.E. & van Dam, A. (1971). An Introduction to Information Structures and Paging Considerations for On-line Text Editing Systems. In Tou, J. (Ed.) (1971). *Advances in Information System Science*, New York: Plenum Press, 93-159.

Roberts, Teresa L. (1979). Evaluation of Computer Text Editors. *Xerox Palo Alto Research Center Report* SSL-79-9, November 1979.

Roberts, Teresa L. (1983). The Evaluation of Text Editors: Methodology and Empirical Results. *Communications of the ACM* 26(4), 265-283.

Roberts, T.L. & Moran, T.P. (1982). Evaluation of Text Editors. *Proceedings of the Conference on Human Factors in Computing Systems*, New York: ACM, 136-141.

Roberts, T.L. & Moran, T.P. (1983). The Evaluation of Computer Text Editors: Methodology and Empirical Results. *Communications of the ACM* 26(4), 265-283.

Roberts, T.L. & Moran, T.P. (1985). Author's Response. *Communications of the ACM* 28(3), 326-327.

Seybold Publications (1971-87). *The Seybold Report on Publishing Systems* (since 1971), *The Seybold Report on Office Systems* (since 1979), and *The Seybold Report on Professional Computing* (since 1982), PO Box 644, Media PA 19063.

Singley, Mark K. & Anderson, John R. (1985). The Transfer of Text-Editing Skill. *International Journal of Man-Machine Studies* 22, 403-423.

Whiteside, John, Archer, Norman, Wixon, Dennis, & Good, Michael (1982). How Do People Really Use Text Editors? *SIGOA '82 Proceedings*, New York: ACM, 29-40.

Xerox Corp. (1985). Multilingual Typing. *SIGGRAPH Video Review* 18, New York: ACM.

The Evaluation of Text Editors: Methodology and Empirical Results

Teresa L. Roberts *Xerox Office Systems Division*

Thomas P. Moran *Xerox Palo Alto Research Center*

Thomas J. Moran's major research interests are in mental models of systems, the learning of systems, and the nature of expertise in using systems, as well as the formalization of the issues and processes of designing systems. Teresa L. Roberts received her Ph.D. in Computer Science from Stanford University in 1979.

Authors' Present Addresses:
Teresa Roberts,
Xerox Office Systems
Division,
3333 Coyote Hill Road,
Palo Alto, CA 94304
Arpanet Roberts.
PA @ PARC-MAXC;
Thomas Moran,
Xerox Palo Alto Research
Center,
3333 Coyote Hill Road,
Palo Alto, CA 94304
Arpanet Moran.
PA @ PARC-MAXC.

1. INTRODUCTION

Text editors are the most heavily used programs on interactive computing systems since the advent of time-sharing systems (e.g., [1]). Text editing, or word processing, is also a very pervasive use of personal computers [15]. There are probably hundreds of different text editors in use today: many computation centers have their own local editors, and new computers often come with their own text editors. System programmers cannot seem to resist the temptation to design a better text editor. Heated debates rage over computer networks about text editor design. Yet, remarkably little objective information is known about the relative advantages of different kinds of editing paradigms.

Systematic study of text editors is hampered, at least partially, by the complex of issues surrounding text editor usage. Text editors are flexible tools that are used for a wide variety of purposes, since many kinds of human communication are done by text. Simple informal notes, letters and memoranda, structured text (such as lists and tables), reports and specifications (requiring sophisticated formatting and layout), and program code (structured differently from narrative text) are all applications for which text editors are regularly used. There are many different kinds of editor users—first-time novices, hardened experts, occasional users, and users with specialized applications that lead them to know how to perform some tasks well and other tasks not at all. Finally, there are many different measures of the quality of user–editor interaction, including both objective measures of performance, such as time and errors, and subjective measures of acceptability, such as feelings of enjoyment, clumsiness, and so forth.

The study of text editors up to now has been dominated by functional descriptions of editors, both by proponents of particular systems (e.g., [16]) and by neutral

ABSTRACT: This paper presents a methodology for evaluating text editors on several dimensions: the time it takes experts to perform basic editing tasks, the time experts spend making and correcting errors, the rate at which novices learn to perform basic editing tasks, and the functionality of editors over more complex tasks. Time, errors, and learning are measured experimentally; functionality is measured analytically; time is also calculated analytically. The methodology has thus far been used to evaluate nine diverse text editors, producing an initial database of performance results. The database is used to tell us not only about the editors but also about the users—the magnitude of individual differences and the factors affecting novice learning.

evaluators (e.g., [10, 14, 8]). These reports mainly present subjective opinions as the basis for comparing different systems, either by deciding **a priori** what features are desirable or by informally trying out the systems to get a feel for what works well and what is lacking. Various arguments, which on the surface seem reasonable, are also used to defend the conclusions in these reports, but the validity of these arguments is seldom tested. The purpose of the present study is to obtain objective, replicable results. A survey of related behavioral studies done up to this time is given in [6].

Our purpose in this paper is to present a **standardized evaluation** of text editors. This kind of evaluation may be contrasted with a **specific evaluation**, which is tailored to a particular purpose or situation, such as the evaluation of a set of editors to determine their utility in a particular working environment. A standardized evaluation does not make assumptions about the particulars of any given situation, nor does it cover all of the various aspects of editor usage. It focuses on the common properties of text editors rather than on the idiosyncracies of particular editors. A standardized evaluation attempts to address the most fundamental issues and is thus applicable to a variety of editors. A familiar example of a standardized evaluation is the EPA rating of automobile gasoline mileage. While the conditions used to obtain the EPA rating do not match the driving conditions of any specific car, the ratings do relate to common driving situations. Thus, the ratings can be used to compare different cars and, to some extent, can be adjusted to tell about specific driving situations.

A benefit of using a standardized evaluation over a period of time is the accumulation of a database of consistent information about editors. This gives a standard for interpreting the results of any new evaluation, a critical factor missing from many specific evaluations (e.g., [7]). One of our goals in proposing a standarized evaluation is to initialize a database of information about the population of existing editors.

The methodology we present here evaluates computer text editors from the viewpoint of the performance of their users—from novices learning the editor for the first time to dedicated experts who have mastered the editor. Objectivity, thoroughness, and ease-of-use were the criteria used in creating this methodology. **Objectivity** implies that the methodology not be biased in favor of any particular editor's conceptual structure. **Thoroughness** implies that multiple aspects of editor usage be considered. The methodology focuses on four dimensions of editor usage that are behaviorally fundamental and practically important.

The **Time** to perform basic editing tasks by experts.
The **Error** cost for experts.
The **Learning** of basic editing tasks by novices.
The **Functionality** over a wide range of editing tasks.

Ease-of-use means that the methodology should be usable by editor designers, managers of word processing centers, or other nonpsychologists who need this kind of evaluative information, but who have limited time and equipment resources.

The structure of this paper is as follows: In Sec. 2, we describe the evaluation methodology. In Sec. 3, we apply the methodology to nine different text editors, presenting and discussing the empirical results, and assessing the methodology itself. In Sec. 4, we turn the empirical results around to gain some insight into user performance with computers, particularly in the areas of individual differences and novice learning.

2. DESCRIPTION OF THE METHODOLOGY
The methodology is based on the specific kinds of tasks involved in text editing. It consists of experimentally measuring user performance on three dimensions—Time, Error, and Learning—and on an analysis of Functionality. Also, expert performance time can be calculated analytically.

2.1 Taxonomy of Editing Tasks
An evaluation scheme for editors needs to have a common ground on which to compare different kinds of editors. Editor design features (e.g., "modeless" insertion of new text vs. having an "insert mode") and design concepts (e.g., table creation using sequential text with formatting characters such as tabs vs. using a two-dimensional structure) cannot serve this role, since the features and concepts differ so much from editor to editor. There is no evidence that one feature is always better than another. In fact, the overall consistency in how well the different design features of the editor fit together may well be more important than any individual feature in determining the quality of the editor.

What is constant across all text editors, in contrast to design features, is the editing tasks they permit their users to accomplish. Thus, the methodology here is based on a taxonomy of 212 editing tasks that can potentially be performed by a text editor. These tasks are specified in terms of their effect on a text document, independent of any specific editor's conceptual model [9]. The organization of the task taxonomy, along with a sample of tasks in each category, is given in Figure 1. The Functionality dimension of an editor is measured with respect to the set of tasks in this taxonomy, by assessing how many of the tasks the editor can perform.

Comparisons between editors on the performance dimensions (Time, Error, and Learning) must be based on tasks that all editors can perform. For this purpose, we identify a small set of **core editing tasks** (see Figure 2). The core tasks are the ones that all text editors, by definition, can perform; they are also the most common editing tasks in normal text-editing applications. Most of the core tasks are generated by applying basic text editing operations (e.g., **insert, delete, replace**) to basic text entities (e.g., **characters, words, lines**). Also included in the core set are the tasks of accessing and saving documents and the simplest text-display and text-addressing operations.

A lengthy specification is required to instruct an evaluator to carry out this methodology. In this paper we can give only enough information to make clear the basic structure and procedure of the methodology and the resulting measures. Full instructions and materials for running the evaluation tests and analyses may be found in the report by Roberts [11].

2.2 The Time Dimension
The time it takes expert users to accomplish routine text modifications is measured by observing expert users as they perform a set of **benchmark tasks**, which are drawn from the core tasks.

Benchmark.   There are 53 editing tasks in the benchmark, embedded in four documents: a short interoffice memo, two two-page reports, and a six-page chapter from

FIGURE 1. Taxonomy of Editing Tasks on which the Evaluation Methodology is Based.

Modify Document
  Content and structure of text
     Characters, words, numbers, sentences , paragraphs, lines, sections, document
     References [e.g., keep up-to-date references to section numbers in the document]
     Sources for text or attributes [e.g., make the text layout be the same as in another document]
  Layout of running text and structure
     Inside paragraphs [e.g., indent the first line of a paragraph so far from the left margin]
     Headings, random lines [e.g., center]
     Interparagraph layout [e.g., leave so much space between paragraphs]
     General [e.g., lay out document in so many columns]
  Page layout
     Every page [e.g., print a page heading that includes the current section number]
     Non-mainline text [e.g., position footnotes at the bottom of the page]
  Attributes of characters
     Line break [e.g., automatic hyphenation]
     Shape [e.g., boldface]
  Tables
     Column beginning [e.g., columns are equally spaced]
     General alignment [e.g., align the column on the decimal points]
     Modify alignment [e.g., swap the positions of two columns]
     Treatment of table entries [e.g., line up the left and right edges of (justify) each table entry]
  Summary of text [e.g., table of contents]
  Special applications [e.g., mathematical formulas]

Locate Change (Addressing)
  Text [e.g., find text which has specified content]
  Structure [e.g., find the next section heading]
  Layout/Attributes [e.g., find a boldface character]
  Misc.

Program Edits (Control)
  Command sequences [e.g., invoke a sequence of commands with parameters]
  Control structure [e.g., repeat a sequence of commands a specified number of times]
  Tests [e.g., compare strings for alphabetical order]
  Storage [e.g., store pointers to places in documents]
  User control [e.g., ask user for parameters during execution]
  Preexisting composite commands [e.g., sort a sequence of text strings]

Find Task or Verify Change (Display)
  Display text and layout [e.g., show the outline structure of the text]
  Display system state [e.g., show where the selection is relative to the whole document]

Miscellaneous
  Hardcopy
       Draft copy [e.g., print with extra space between lines]
       Misc. [e.g., print on envelopes]
  Intermediate Input/Output [e.g., save away the current version of a document]
  Other [e.g., perform arithmetic on numbers in the document]

a philosophy book. The types of tasks in the benchmark are randomly drawn from the core tasks, and the locations and complexities of the benchmark tasks are also randomly distributed. The distribution of tasks in the benchmark is more uniformly distributed than one would observe in normal text-editing work, the benchmark giving more emphasis to the more complex kinds of tasks (most real-world editing tasks are simple text modifications involving a small number of characters). For example, tasks involving "tricky" boundary conditions are over-represented in order to identify special cases, such as insertion at the beginning of a paragraph, which an editor may treat awkwardly. The benchmark also under-represents the typing of lengthy new text, since such typ-

ing performance is more a reflection of the skill of the user than of the quality of the editor. We will discuss later how to relate this benchmark to other distributions of tasks.

Subjects.   Four expert users were tested individually on the benchmark. The evaluator should select the set of subjects to represent the diversity of the expert user community: at least one user should be **nontechnical** (i.e., with no programming background) and at least one should be **technical** (i.e., know how to program). Four is the absolute minimum number of subjects needed to get any reliability of measurement and to get some indication of individual user variation.

FIGURE 2. Core Editing Tasks used in the Methodology for Expert Time Performance and Novice Learning.

Core tasks consist mainly of the cross-product (except for a few obvious semantic anomalies) of the following basic editing operations applied to the following basic text objects:

Operations:	*insert*	Objects:	*character*
	delete		*word*
	replace		*line*
	move		*sentence*
	copy		*paragraph*
	transpose		*section*
	split		
	merge		

For example:

—*insert character(s)*
—*insert word(s)*
—*delete character(s)*
etc.

Core tasks also contain the following miscellaneous tasks:

—*display a continuous chunk of text*
—*address a specified place*
—*address according to content*
—*make a document available for editing*
—*put a document away*
—*start a new document*

Note. The formal definition of the core in the task taxonomy also includes operations on the object *number*; however, no tasks using numbers were included in the experiments. The learning experiments omitted the operation *transpose* since it can be regarded as an optimization of two *moves*.

Measurement. The evaluator measures the performance in the test sessions with a clock and a stopwatch, measuring the overall performance time with the clock and the times spent in error with the stopwatch. The evaluator also notes whether or not each task is performed correctly. When the subject is finished with the tasks, the evaluator asks the subject to make a second pass to complete any incorrectly done tasks. This relatively crude method of measurement is used because it is easy for anyone to run (not everyone has an instrumented editor or a videotape setup, but anyone can acquire a stopwatch) and because stopwatch accuracy is sufficient.[1]

Error-free and Error Time. The benchmark typically takes about 30 minutes of steady work to complete. The elapsed time in the experiment is partitioned into error-free time and error time, according to two types of observed behavior. The **error time** is the time the user spends dealing with errors (see below for more detail), and the **error-free time** is the elapsed time minus the error time.

Scoring. The individual user's Time score is the average error-free time to perform each task (i.e., the total error-free time divided by the number of tasks). The overall Time score is the average score for the four subjects.

2.3. The Error Dimension

The effect of errors in an editor is measured by the **error time**, which is the time cost of errors on the benchmark tasks. The course of a typical error includes committing the error, discovering it, correcting it, and then resuming productive behavior. Error time consists of all the activity up to the resumption of productive activity [4]. Only those errors that take more than about 15 seconds to correct are counted by the evaluator (which is the best that can be done with a stopwatch). Thus, the time for typographical and other simple errors is not included in the error time. We do not know exactly how close this method approximates the true error time, but the true error time is not likely to be dominated by the time in these small errors. In addition to the time for the immediately corrected errors, the time for the second-pass corrections is also counted in the error time.

Scoring. The individual Error score for each user is the user's error time expressed as a percentage of his/her error-free Time score.[2] The overall Error score is the average score for the four expert users.

2.4 The Learning Dimension

The ease of learning of an editor is tested by actually teaching four novice subjects, individually, to perform the core editing tasks.

Subjects. Each subject must be a **novice** to computers (defined as someone with **no** previous experience with computers or word processors). This gives us an easily defined baseline measure of learning, that is, from zero experience.[3]

Teaching Paradigm. The learning tests are performed in a one-on-one, oral teaching paradigm, with an instructor individually teaching each novice the editor. Although more expensive than group-teaching or self-teaching paradigms, this paradigm has the crucial advantage that it is adaptable to the individual learner. The other paradigms are more rigid and may tend to magnify the differences between different learners, which obscures the learnability of the editor itself. For example, in a self-teaching paradigm using the editor's documentation, a learner can easily get confused on a point because of a short lapse of attention or because of the particular wording of the documentation and not because the point is inherently difficult. In the one-on-one paradigm, on the other hand, the instructor can respond to the particular difficulties of each learner by explaining things in a different way, by correcting misconceptions, and so forth.

Teaching Procedure. The teaching procedure is structured as a series of five instruction–quiz cycles. In each cycle, the instructor first instructs the learner on some new tasks or corrects the learner's difficulties, and during this time the learner is allowed to practice performing tasks on the system; finally, the learner is given a quiz to test what tasks s/he can do independently. The learner paces the session, deciding how much to practice, when to take the quiz, and so on.

The methodology includes a standard syllabus specify-

---

[1] The reliability of the measurements is determined more by the small number of subjects than by the accuracy of measurement.

[2] Thus, the total time to perform an average benchmark task is $T + Te$, where T is the error-free Time score and e is the Error score.
[3] More and more people today have some exposure to computers, and it may become more important to look at the learning users experienced in other systems. However, this would present difficult methodological problems in assessing their degree of experience and the similarity of their experience to the editor to be learned.

ing what core tasks are to be taught on each cycle. However, it is up to the instructor to determine which specific editor commands and facilities to teach in order for the subject to be able to accomplish the core tasks. The structure of a particular editor might also make it necessary to slightly alter which tasks are taught in which cycle. The teaching procedure is strongly method-oriented; by "teaching tasks" we mean teaching methods to accomplish the tasks.

The quizzes consist of documents marked with changes to be made (similar to the benchmark performed by the expert users). Only a sample of the core tasks appears on each quiz. Not all tasks on a quiz have necessarily been taught up to that point, which allows learners to figure out, if possible, how to do tasks that have not been explicity taught. During the quizzes, the learners are given access to a one-page summary sheet listing all the editor commands taught. Thus, a learner is not hung up a long time on a quiz because of a simple difficulty, such as not being able to remember the name of a particular command.

Scoring. The amount that a subject learns is measured by counting the number of different task types the subject is able to perform on the quizzes. Only half-credit was given if the subject performed a task incompletely or had to look at the summary sheet. The individual Learning score is the amount of time taken for the learning session divided by the total number of tasks learned, that is, the average time it takes to learn how to do a task. The overall Learning score is the average Learning score for the four novice learners.

2.5 The Functionality Dimension
The range of functionality available in an editor is measured by analyzing the editor against a checklist of tasks covering the full task taxonomy (Figure 1).

The Analyst. The editor is rated on the functionality checklist by a very experienced user of the editor, the ***analyst***, who uses whatever documentation material is necessary to ensure accuracy.

Rating Criteria. Rating the functionality of an editor on a task involves deciding whether the task can or cannot be done with the editor. This is not a simple binary decision. Almost any task can be performed on almost any editor with enough effort. Consequently, the editor is given full credit for a task only if the task can be done efficiently with the editor. It is given half-credit if the task can be done awkwardly, which can appear in several guises: repetition of commands, excessive typing of text, limitations in parameter values to the task, interference with other functions, substantial planning required of the user, etc. The editor is given no credit for a task if it cannot be done at all (such as trying to specify an italic typeface on a system designed for a line printer) or if doing the task requires as much effort as retyping all the affected text (such as having to manually insert page numbers on every page).

Scoring. The overall Functionality score is the percentage of the total number of tasks in the task taxonomy that the editor can do, according to the rating criteria. This score may be broken down into subscores according to the classes of tasks in the taxonomy, to show the strengths and weakness of the editor.

2.6 Calculation of Expert Performance Time
The error-free performance time of an expert using an editor can be calculated analytically, using the Keystroke-Level Model [3, 4]. This model predicts expert performance time by counting the number of physical and mental operations required to perform a task and by assigning a standard time for each operation. The model counts operations at the grain-level of keystrokes: typing, pointing at a location on the display with a pointing device, homing the hands onto a device, mentally preparing for a group of physical operations, and waiting for system responses. The Keystroke-Level Model analysis gives a precise characterization of methods for accomplishing tasks.

When the model is applied to the set of benchmark tasks, it produces a calculated performance time for a "standard expert" that can be compared to the experimentally measured times. However, making this calculation requires the evaluator to predict what methods an expert user would use to perform the benchmark tasks, since the model requires that the methods be specified as input. In the absence of knowledge about the style of expert user interaction, the most useful heuristic is to first identify the common, frequently used commands of the editor and to pick the optimal method for each task within that set of commands. The fact that the experimental subjects sometimes use methods different from those predicted, plus other differences between the assumptions of the Keystroke-Level Model and the test conditions in this methodology (e.g., the inclusion of small errors) leads us to expect small-to-moderate differences between the calculated performance and the experimental results.

3. EVALUATION OF NINE TEXT EDITORS
Nine text editors have been evaluated using this methodology, both as a test of the methodology and for the inherent interest in the results. The results of these evaluations provide the beginnings of a database of empirical results giving us behavioral data on user performance, as well as the basis for comparing editors.

3.1 Description of the Editors
The nine text editors evaluated are: TECO [20], WYLBUR [24], EMACS [23], NLS [18, 19], BRAVOX [21], BRAVO [22], a WANG word processor [26], STAR [27], and GYPSY [25]. These represent a wide variety of text editors and word processors, some in wide use around the country and some experimental. The first two of these editors were designed for teletypelike terminals, and the rest were designed for display-based terminals or personal computers. The intended users of these editors range from devoted system hackers to publishers and secretaries who have had little or no contact with computers.

Text editors are complex interactive systems. Thus, it is difficult to succinctly describe the design of these nine editors. Figure 3 attempts to characterize the editors according to a set of commonly discussed design features. For example, the Command Invocation column describes the design feature concerned with the ways in which a user designates commands to the system. The nine editors cover a wide range of choices for this feature: (1) type all or part of an English verb, (2) type a one-letter mnemonic for the command name, (3) hold down a control key while typing a one-letter mnemonic, (4) type a one-letter mnemonic on a chordset, (5) press a special function key, (6) select a command from a menu on the display.

FIGURE 3. Feature Description of Nine Text Editors.

Editor [Ref.]	Feature								
	Display	Auto Line Wrap[a]	Strong Line Concept[b]	Text Units	Command Invocation	Insert Mode	Means of Addressing[c]	Addressing Hardware	Computer Processor[d]
TECO [20]	TTY[e] style	No	Yes	Characters, lines	1-letter mnemonic	Yes	Relative to current position	Keyboard	PDP-10 equivalent, via 3Mb net
WYLBUR [24]	TTY[e] style	No	Yes	Characters, lines	English-like, abbreviated	Yes	Absolute line numbers	Keyboard	IBM 370, 1200 baud
EMACS [23]	Partial page	Yes	Yes	Characters, words, lines, sentences, paragraphs	1-letter mnemonic, control keys	No	Relative to current position	Keyboard	PDP-10 equivalent, approximately 1200 baud
NLS [18, 19]	Partial page	Yes	No	Characters, words, paragraphs	1-letter English-like on keyboard or 5-key chordset	Yes	Screen position	Mouse	PDP-10 with local processor
BRAVOX [21]	Full page	Yes	No	Characters, words, lines, paragraphs	1-letter mnemonic, menu, function keys	No	Screen position	Mouse	Xerox Alto personal computer
BRAVO [22]	Partial page	Yes	No	Characters, words, lines, paragraphs	1-letter mnemonic	Yes	Screen position	Mouse	Xerox Alto personal computer
WANG [26]	Partial page	Yes	No	Characters	Function keys	Yes	Screen position	Step keys[f]	Stand-alone Wang word processor
STAR [27]	Full page	Yes	No	Characters, words, sentences, paragraphs	Function keys, menus	No	Screen position	Mouse	Xerox 8000 processor
GYPSY [25]	Partial page	Yes	No	Characters, words, paragraphs	Function keys	No	Screen position	Mouse	Xerox Alto personal computer

[a] Automatic line wrap means that during type-in a new line is automatically begun when a word overflows the old line, without any intervention from the user.

[b] This refers to editors that require the user to type RETURN at the end of each line of text. Usually, this also means that there is an explicit CARRIAGE-RETURN character at the end of each line in the internal representation of the document.

[c] This refers to the primary means of addressing (all editors have the ability to search).

[d] Time-sharing computers were used under conditions of light load. Terminals and computer displays were all CRTs, except that one WYLBUR user preferred her own hardcopy terminal.

[e] A TTY (teletype) style display is one that does not continuously show the state of the document, but only shows the sequence of commands entered by the user. Snapshots of pieces of the document are displayed when the user explicitly asks for them.

[f] Four keys with arrows on them, which move the cursor up, down, left, and right (see [2]).

Figure 3 also gives the conditions under which the editors were used for the experiments. For example, TECO was run on a time-sharing machine connected to a terminal over a 3-megabit local network, while the WANG word processor was run on its own stand-alone hardware. Note that the methodology does not provide an evaluation of an editor in the abstract, but only of a particular implementation under a particular set of conditions. It is possible that the particular conditions (e.g., the quality of the terminal or the bandwidth of its connection to the central processor) dominate the abstract characteristics of the editor (e.g., its command language conventions) in determining an expert's performance. Therefore, an attempt was made to run each editor under reasonably optimal conditions, in order to make the overall evaluation results as generally useful as possible.[4]

Figure 4 gives a different characterization of the editors. It shows in detail how a user would go about performing a specific word-replacement task in each of the editors, using the notation of the Keystroke-Level Model (the footnote to the figure lists the different types of Keystroke-Level Model operations). For example, it can be seen that the editors described in Figure 3 as having an insert mode (TECO, WYLBUR, NLS, BRAVO, and WANG) all require the typing of a special character (preceded by a mental operation) after the insertion to terminate the insertion of new text. On the other hand, the "modeless" editors (EMACS, BRAVOX, STAR, and GYPSY) do not require any operations after typing in new text. These methods also show where moving the hands from the keyboard to the pointing device and back (homing) add extra motions to the methods used with editors which have a mouse or step keys (NLS, BRAVOX, BRAVO, WANG, STAR, and GYPSY).

This Keystroke-Level Model analysis can be used to calculate the expected expert performance time for each editor, and to give a detailed quantitative decomposition of the times for each type of operation in each editor. To do this, the Keystroke-Level Model analysis was applied to all the benchmark tasks for each of the nine editors. The calculated task times thus obtained were averaged over the 53 benchmark tasks to give times for an "average editing task" for each editor. Figure 5 presents these first empirical (not experimental) results.

Figure 5(a) gives the calculated average task times for each editor. This leads us to expect a certain pattern of experimental results, for example, for there to be an overall factor of 2.5 between the fastest and the slowest editors. The figure also shows how each average task time is decomposed into the times for each operator type. For instance, the cost of slow system response stands out clearly. If EMACS had been run on a fast terminal, its speed would be faster than NLS's; STAR would be the fastest editor of all if system response times for all editors could be effectively reduced to zero. A weak point of the WANG, on the other hand, is the pointing time required by the step keys; it would be improved at least 2 sec/task (over 10 percent) by using a mouse.

The task time decomposition can also be considered as a percentage of total task time, as shown in Figure 5(b). This shows, for example, that homing time between the keyboard and pointing device is not a major problem (except perhaps with the WANG, which relies heavily on

function keys that are separate from the main typing array). An interesting contrast exists between TECO and WYLBUR. Both use the same set of operations: Acquire, Keying, Mental time, and system Response. But TECO, with its emphasis on minimal typing, only spends one-third of its user's time in typing, while WYLBUR spends over half. This is paid for, however, in Mental time, where the ratios are reversed.

3.2. Overall Evaluation Results

All nine editors were run through all the evaluation tests. According to the methodology, the overall evaluation of a text editor is a four-tuple of numbers, one numeric score from each dimension. The overall evaluation scores for the nine editors are presented in Figure 6.

Differences were found between the editors on all dimensions. The expert Time results show, for instance, that TECO, WYLBUR, and EMACS are the slowest editors and that GYPSY and STAR are the fastest. Most of the display-based systems are about twice as fast to use as the non-display systems. The difference between the fastest and slowest system was a factor of 2.5, as the Keystroke-Level Model analysis led us to expect. The Error dimension shows a range of a factor of 5 in the cost of errors between systems. On the Learning dimension, TECO is clearly the slowest to learn, with the next system being a factor of 2 faster to learn, and the rest of the editors ranging over another factor of 2 in learning speed. We also see large differences in the Functionality dimension, with scores ranging smoothly from under 40 percent of the tasks to almost 80 percent.

We see that no editor is superior on all dimensions, indicating that tradeoffs must be made in deciding which editor is most appropriate for a given situation. For example, consider the editor BRAVOX, which was developed at Xerox as an extension to the earlier editor BRAVO. Its purpose was to increase functionality and speed and to try out fashionable design features such as command menus and modeless text insertion. Is BRAVOX really an improvement over BRAVO? From Figure 6 we see that BRAVOX is indeed an improvement over BRAVO in Functionality; it is also faster to learn, possibly justifying the design innovations that were incorporated. The analysis in Figure 5 shows that BRAVOX should be faster than BRAVO, but that improvement does not materialize in the experimental Time score (the reason for this is unknown).

Reliability.[5]   Thus far we have only been considering the mean evaluation scores for each editor without considering the variability associated with these scores. Figure 6 expresses the variability of each experimentally measured score by the Coefficient of Variation (CV),[6] which represents the between-user variability. We see that the variability is very high for the Error scores, but quite moderate for the Time and Learning scores. However, the statistical reliability of the scores depends on the number of subjects as well as on the variability. Since we ran only four subjects, only large differences between scores are statistically reliable. For example, we can say that WYLBUR is reliably faster to learn than TECO, but we cannot say

---

[4] EMACS was the only system for which optimal conditions were not found. The workstation used was actually a personal computer running a rather slow terminal-emulation package. This cut the effective communication rate between the main computer and the workstation to around 1200 baud, which is much slower than is often available with EMACS.

[5] In this paper we use the term "reliability" instead of the more usual term "(statistical) significance," since we are trying to emphasize the difference between *statistical* and *substantive* significance, the latter of which we call "importance."

[6] We use the CV, which is the Standard Deviation normalized by the Mean, instead of the Standard Deviation, because CVs are more constant across the different scores. That is to say, the absolute size of the variation is approximately proportional to the mean.

FIGURE 4. Example of the Use of each Text Editor: An Illustrative Method for Accomplishing the Specific Task of Replacing the Word "European" with the Words "Far Eastern".

Editor	Method (informal)	Method (Keystroke-Level Model encoding)[a]
TECO	Get task. Place pointer after old word. Delete previous 8 characters. Insert new words. Display line to verify.	**A**[task] **MK**[s] 9**K**[European] **MK**[ESC] **M** 3**K**[−8d] **MK**[i] 13**K**[Far Eastern] **MK**[ESC] **M** 2**K**[v ESC] **R**(0.4)

WYLBUR	Get task.
	Get number of line with old word
	  (system returns line 11).
	Change old word
	  to new words.
		A[task]
		M 2**K**[L⌴] 10**K**[' European] **M** 3**K**[' RETURN]
		R(1.0)
		M 3**K**[ch⌴] 10**K**[' European] **M** 6**K**[' ⌴to⌴]
		  14**K**[' Far Eastern] **M** 6**K**[' ⌴in⌴] 2**K**[11] **MK**[RETURN]

EMACS	Get task and find it on display. Place pointer in old word. Back up to beginning of word. Call Delete Word command. Type new words.	**A**[task] **S**[European] **M** 4**K**[CTRL S e u] **R**(2.0) 2**K**[META B] **M** 2**K**[META D] 13**K**[Far Eastern]
NLS	Get task and find it on display. Call Replace Word command. Point to old word. Type new words.	**A**[task] **S**[European] **H**[chordset and mouse] **MK**[r] **MK**[w] **P**[European] **K**[OK] **H**[keyboard] 13**K**[Far Eastern] **MK**[OK]
BRAVOX	Get task and find it on display. Point to old word. Delete old word. Type new words.	**A**[task] **S**[European] **H**[mouse] **P**[European] **K**[BUTTON2] **H**[keyboard] **MK**[DEL] 13**K**[Far Eastern]
BRAVO	Get task and find it on display. Point to old word. Call Replace command. Type new words.	**A**[task] **S**[European] **H**[mouse] **P**[European] **K**[BUTTON2] **H**[keyboard] **MK**[r] 13**K**[Far Eastern] **MK**[ESC] **R**(2.7)
WANG	Get task and find it on display. Call Replace command. Select ends of old word. Type new words.	**A**[task] **S**[European] **H**[function keys and step keys] **MK**[REPLACE] **P**$_s$[E] **K**[EXECUTE] **P**$_s$[n] **K**[EXECUTE] **H**[keyboard] 13**K**[Far Eastern] **H**[function keys] **MK**[EXECUTE]
STAR	Get task and find it on display. Point to old word. Delete old word. Type new words.	**A**[task] **S**[European] **H**[mouse and function keys] **P**[European] 2**K**[SELECT SELECT] **MK**[DELETE] **H**[keyboard] 14**K**[Far Eastern⌴]
GYPSY	Get task and find it on display. Point to ends of old word. Type new words.	**A**[task] **S**[European] **H**[mouse] **P**[E] **K**[BUTTON1] **P**[n] **K**[BUTTON1] **H**[keyboard] 13**K**[Far Eastern]

[a] Methods are encoded in the Keystroke-Level Model [3] as a sequence of primitive operations that the user must perform. All operations are encoded as one of the following types of operations:

A	Acquire a task by looking at the manuscript (1.8 sec).
S	Search the display for the location of the task (2.2 sec).
K	Type a key or press a button (measured by typing tests; .23 sec used here).
P	Point to a location with a mouse (1.1 sec).
P$_s$	Point to a location with step keys (2.3 sec).
H	Home the hands on a physical device (.4 sec).
M	Mentally prepare for physical actions (1.35 sec).
R(n)	Wait n seconds for a system response (measured for each system).

The notation in square brackets after each operation is an informal comment telling, e.g., what keys are pressed. All operations, except A, S, and P$_s$, are the same as in [3]. The A and S operations used here simply encode [3]'s notion of task acquisition into new operations. P$_s$ represents a type of pointing not covered in [3]. The time attributed to P$_s$ comes from [2].

that it is reliably faster to use.[7] We also see that the Learning difference noted above between BRAVOX and BRAVO is reliable,[8] but the Time difference in the other direction is not. None of the differences in the Error di-

mension are reliable, because the between-subject variation is so high.

The reliability of the scores can be improved by increasing the number of subjects tested.[9] For example, consider the Time difference between WANG and STAR. Al-

---

[7] Quantitative formulas for computing which differences between scores are reliable (derived from the standard statistical concept of confidence limits) are given in the notes to Figure 6.
[8] This result was obtained using the actual variances of the BRAVOX and BRAVO data, rather than by using the general formulas given in Figure 6.

[9] Reliability, as measured by the confidence interval around a score, is approximately inversely proportional to the square root of the number of subjects used to determine the score.

FIGURE 5. Decomposition of the Calculated Editing Times into the Different Types of Keystroke-Level Model Operations.

(a) Average time (in seconds) per core editing task in each type of operation.

Editor	Operation Type								Total Task
	A	S	K	P	P$_S$	H	M	R	
TECO	4.1	—	15.3	—	—	—	20.3	2.8	42.5
WYLBUR	2.7	—	18.3	—	—	—	10.1	1.4	32.5
EMACS	2.0	2.5	4.6	—	—	—	7.8	6.9	23.8
NLS	2.5	3.0	4.3	2.0	—	1.0	4.9	1.3	19.0
BRAVOX	1.9	2.3	2.7	2.0	—	0.7	2.6	3.5	15.7
BRAVO	2.1	2.6	2.5	2.2	—	0.4	3.0	5.6	18.4
WANG	2.3	2.8	2.0	—	4.6	2.0	3.1	2.4	19.2
STAR	2.2	2.7	2.2	2.3	—	0.4	2.1	8.3	20.2
GYPSY	2.1	2.6	2.2	2.6	—	0.7	2.8	3.3	16.3

(b) Percentage of task time in each type of operation.

Editor	Operation Type							
	A	S	K	P	P$_S$	H	M	R
TECO	10%	—	34%	—	—	—	48%	7%
WYLBUR	8%	—	56%	—	—	—	31%	4%
EMACS	8%	10%	19%	—	—	—	33%	29%
NLS	13%	16%	22%	11%	—	5%	26%	7%
BRAVOX	12%	15%	17%	13%	—	5%	17%	22%
BRAVO	12%	14%	14%	12%	—	2%	16%	30%
WANG	12%	15%	11%	—	24%	10%	16%	13%
STAR	11%	13%	11%	11%	—	2%	10%	41%
GYPSY	13%	16%	14%	16%	—	5%	17%	20%

though the Time difference between these editors is not reliable with only four subjects per editor, this difference would be reliable if it had been found with ten subjects for each editor.

Importance. We want to emphasize the obvious fact that reliability is quite different from importance. Any observed difference between scores, however small, can be made reliable by running enough subjects. The real question is whether the observed difference is ***important***, which is a substantive, not a statistical, question. For example, small differences between editors on the Error dimension, even if they were reliable, may not be as important as the fact that the user population is highly variable; even large differences in the Time dimension would not be important in a situation where there were not many dedicated expert users.

In practical situations, small differences are usually not important, for they will be washed out by a host of interacting factors in the larger context. Thus, the fact that small observed differences are unreliable (except in extensive, expensive tests) is of little consequence. The utility of a relatively cheap test, such as the methodology proposed in this paper, is that it reveals potentially important (i.e., large) differences. Once a potentially important difference is identified, then it is a cost–benefit issue to determine how reliable the difference needs to be. But even if the difference is found to be reliable, it is not as important to be certain that there is some difference as to

be certain that the difference is reliably large enough to matter.

One reason that the reliability issue arises is that only overall scores are being considered. Often, an informal visual inspection of the more detailed data comprising the overall scores can tell us more than a formal reliability analysis.

3.3 A Closer Look at the Data

The next several figures present breakdowns of the overall evaluation scores in Figure 6. Note that the editors in each of the figures are shown in different orders, corresponding to the order of scores on the different dimensions.

3.3.1. Time. Figure 7 is a scatter graph showing each individual expert user's error-free Time score. This graph shows the actual spread of user performance for each editor. The greater the overlap of the performance ranges of two editors, the less likely that the editors are reliably different. The individual points also allow us to identify outliers among the users. An outlier can penalize an editor's score compared to editors that were not unlucky enough to get an unusual user. For instance, the BRAVO outlier suggests that our mean is higher than it would be if the population of subjects had been larger and thus more evenly representative.

Also playing a part in the data is the mix of technical and nontechnical users run on each editor, since the technical users were on the average somewhat faster than the nontechnical users (this will be discussed in Sec. 4.1). We can adjust the overall editor scores to compensate for the different mix of technical and nontechnical users in each editor, but this adjustment does not change any score by more than 2 sec/task and turns out not to change the rank ordering of the editors.

CALCULATED TIME. The task times calculated with the Keystroke-Level Model [Figure 5(a)] are also shown in Figure 7. These calculated times correlate quite well with the empirical Time scores (R = .90). The calculated times are on average about 75 percent of the error-free Time scores (the worst case is 54 percent for BRAVOX, and the best case is 96 percent for STAR). The reader will note that there are two calculated times shown for TECO. The original prediction (shown in parentheses) predicted only about 49 percent of the actual error-free time. Because this calculation was so low and because we had time-stamped keystroke records of the users' actual behavior with TECO, we recalculated the task times using the actual methods that the subjects used (rather than trying to predict the methods, as we did for the original calculation).

This second calculated time is 87 percent of the actual time. The discrepancy between the method predictions in the two calculations was due to the fact that the users were much more conservative, hence, less optimal, than predicted. The predicted methods used a minimum of searching, displaying, and verifying, while three of the four users were much more careful in their use of this nondisplay-based system. One user was much more daring, and the original calculation was about 70 percent of the actual time for that user—an outcome similar to the calculation results for the other editors.

The reasons for the rather consistent disparity between the Keystroke-Level Model calculations and the actual editing times have to do with the differences between the assumptions of the Keystroke-Level Model and the conditions of our experiments, as noted in Sec. 2.6. There are several differences: (1) The Keystroke-Level Mode assumes that the user's method for performing each task is known. However, we cannot always predict the methods, as we saw with TECO. We can usually predict the shorter, easier methods; but the longer, more complex methods are more difficult to predict. Since predicted methods are nearly optimal methods, when a user deviates from a

FIGURE 6. Overall Evaluation Scores for Nine Text Editors.

Editor[a]	Time[b] M ± CV[f] (sec/task)	Error[c] M ± CV (% Time)	Learning[d] M ± CV (min/task)	Functionality[e] (% tasks)
TECO	49 ± .17	15% ± .70	19.5 ± .29	39%
WYLBUR	42 ± .15	18% ± .85	8.2 ± .24	42%
EMACS	37 ± .15	6% ± 1.16	6.6 ± .22	49%
NLS	29 ± .15	22% ± .71	7.7 ± .26	77%
BRAVOX	29 ± .29	8% ± 1.03	5.4 ± .08	70%
BRAVO	26 ± .32	8% ± .75	7.3 ± .14	59%
WANG	26 ± .21	11% ± 1.11	6.2 ± .45	50%
STAR	21 ± .18	19% ± .51	6.2 ± .42	62%
GYPSY	19 ± .11	4% ± 2.00	4.3 ± .26	37%
M(M) M(CV)[g]	31 .19	12% .98	7.9 .26	54%
CV(M)[g]	.31	.49	.53	.25

a The evaluations for TECO, WYLBUR, NLS, and WANG are from the first author's thesis [11]; the first author also evaluated STAR. The evaluations of the other editors were done in the second author's laboratory.

b The Time score is the average error-free expert performance time per benchmark task on the given editor. A difference between editors with mean values M_1 and M_2 is statistically reliable (95% confidence) if $|M_1 - M_2| > 0.33 \cdot (M_1 + M_2)/2$.

c The Errors score is the average time, as a percentage of the error-free performance time, that experts spend making and correcting errors on the given editor. A difference between editors with mean values M_1 and M_2 is statistically reliable (95% confidence) if $|M_1 - M_2| > 20\%$. Thus, no differences between editor means are reliable in this data.

d The Learning score is the average time for a novice to learn how to do a core editing task on the given editor. A difference between editors with mean values M_1 and M_2 is statistically reliable (95% confidence) if $|M_1 - M_2| > 0.45 \cdot (M_1 + M_2)/2$.

e The Functionality score is the percentage of the tasks in the task taxonomy (Figure 1) that can be accomplished with the given editor.

f The Coefficient of Variation (CV) = Standard Deviation / Mean is a normalized measure of variability. The CVs on the individual scores indicate the amount of between-user variability.

g The M(CV)s give the mean between-user variability on each evaluation dimension, and the CV(M)s give the mean between-editor variability on each dimension.

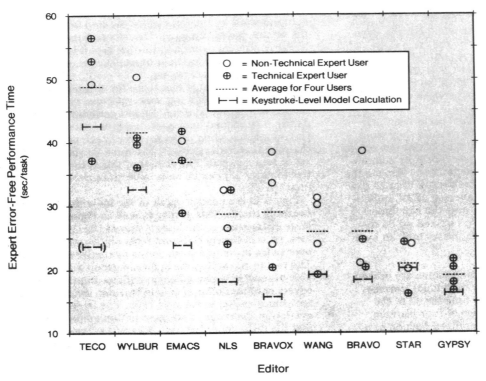

FIGURE 7. Error-Free Time Scores for Individual Expert Users. The editors are ordered by descending Time score.

predicted method, it is usually in the direction of using a slower method. (2) Some of the users may have had to engage in problem-solving to perform some of the more complex tasks in some editors (e.g., to transpose phrases with TECO) and their behavior would not be the simple method-execution behavior assumed by the model. (3) The error time for small errors is included in the experimental error-free time, but is not considered in the calculated time. (4) The experimental time includes all the time **between** tasks. Some of this time is not considered in the model, such as page turning time, pauses for rest, etc. But even without such differences, it should be remembered

that the Keystroke-Level Model is an approximate model, and we should not expect its calculations to be perfect.

The data for individual users show that, for most editors, one user comes very close to the level of performance represented by the Keystroke-Level Model calculation. Since the calculations were based on predictions of optimal methods, this suggests that only a minority of users are likely to approach optimal performance.[10]

[10] The one exception to this observation is in STAR, which had one user who performed much better than the Keystroke-Level Model calculation. We believe that that is because the user constantly overlapped his actions with STAR's long system response times; he often did not wait for the machine to catch up with him between tasks, but typed ahead whenever possible.

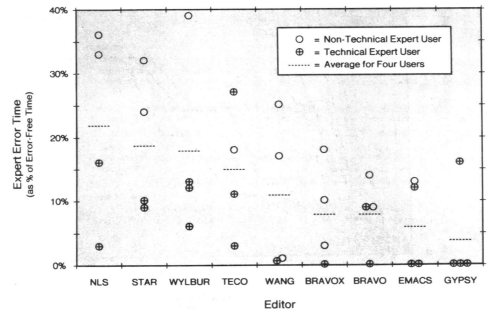

FIGURE 8. Error Time Scores for Individual Expert Users. The editors are ordered by descending Error score.

3.3.2. Error. Figure 8 is a scatter plot of the individual expert users' Error scores. This data shows a factor of 5 difference between the best and the worst editors; even so, these differences are swamped by the large ranges of error within editors. The relative variabilities are summarized in Figure 6: the between-editor *CV* is .49, whereas the between-user *CV* averages .98. Thus, no conclusions can be drawn about the differences between editors in error cost.

It might be noted that the individual users who have large Error scores do not have them because they were unfortunate enough to be struck by rare, disastrous errors; rather, these users merited their Error scores by committing several errors throughout the experiment. Among the seven users whose Error scores were greater than 20 percent, the error time came from an average of 7.4 individual errors: 3.1 during the first pass over the benchmark and 4.3 incomplete tasks that had to be fixed up on the second pass. The errors during both passes took an average of over 70 seconds each.

3.3.3 Learning. The overall Learning scores are broken down in two ways: by time and by individual learners. Figure 9 gives learning curves over time for all of the editors, each curve being the average of four learners. Each learning curve is drawn in a stylized fashion as a series of five steps, one step for each cycle in the learning session. The instruction part of a cycle is represented by the sloped part of the step, and the quiz part of the cycle is represented by the flat part of the step (as if no learning occurs during the quiz). These curves can be seen to be fairly straight overall, indicating that it is reasonable to summarize them using their overall slopes, which is just what the Learning scores are.

The reader will note that there are two learning curves for TECO. The learning test was replicated for TECO with a second instructor, who ran the test completely independently. The second instructor, using only the materials in [11], taught a slightly different set of TECO commands than the first instructor and of course taught a different set of four subjects. The results of this second evaluation test (marked JF) can be seen to be quite close to the first (marked TR).

Figure 10 is a scatter graph of the individual novices' Learning scores. This graph, as well as Figure 9, shows large differences in the learnability of the different editors. TECO is clearly different from all the others, taking over twice as long to learn as the next editor (WYLBUR). The rest of the editors lie in a tight group with considerable overlap between adjacent editors. But this group still covers another factor of two in learning time, so GYPSY is four times as fast to learn as TECO. The large amounts of overlap in the range of learners within editors indicate that the differences between adjacent editors are mostly not reliable. The difference in Learning scores between TECO and WYLBUR is reliable, as are the differences be-

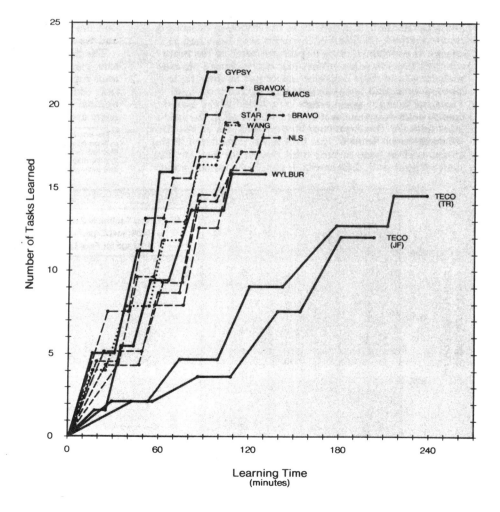

FIGURE 9. Average Learning Curves over all Learners on each Editor. The two TECO curves were produced by different instructors.

tween GYPSY and each of TECO, WYLBUR, NLS, and BRAVO.

Figure 10 allows us to identify outlier learners, as we did with the Time scores. One such outlier is a STAR learner, which suggests that the mean Learning score for STAR might be slightly lower from a more representative subject sample. In addition, there was one subject who was completely unable to learn TECO at all (that subject's partial data is not included in any of our data or graphs). The fact that the only learning failure of the whole set of learning experiments occurred with TECO reinforces the notion that TECO is more difficult to learn than the rest.

INSTRUCTOR EFFECTS.   The instructor plays a strong role in the learning experiments—s/he decides what subset of commands to teach, and s/he tries to maximize the learning rate by keeping the subject from getting bogged down in nonproductive efforts. Thus, the instructor could have a potentially strong effect on the learning results. To show instructor effects, the specific instructors are noted in Figure 10. Since the scores for the different editors overlap so much, it seems that no instructor is consistently faster or slower than the others. This can be seen most clearly in the cases where the learning tests have been replicated. In the TECO case (mentioned above), the second instructor obtained a mean Learning score within 12 percent of the score obtained by the first instructor. In the second case, the EMACS learning tests were replicated in a different laboratory, obtaining a virtually identical overall Learning score [13].

The differences in teaching style of the different in-

structors can, on the other hand, be seen in the between-subject variations. The two TECO data sets show this difference most clearly—the second instructor has very much less between-subject variation. This can also be seen in the between-subject CVs in the editor evaluations run by TR and BS, the two instructors who ran most of the tests. TR's CVs range from .24 to .45, while BS's CVs range from .08 to .26. The instructors seem to be exerting different amounts of control over the learners. However, this does not seem to affect the mean Learning scores.

3.3.4. Functionality.
Figure 11 gives a breakdown of the Functionality scores by the different categories in the task taxonomy. These functionality results show that most of the editors can perform about half of the tasks in the task taxonomy. Each system has its areas of strength and weakness. To show this, the scores are broken down into subscores in Figure 11. For instance, EMACS is excellent in programming capability, while NLS and BRAVOX are especially good in formatting and layout tasks. Because the number of tasks in the taxonomy was weighted more toward text layout than programming, the document-oriented editors generally scored somewhat better overall than EMACS. But NLS, which tries to cover all needs, is clearly superior in overall functionality.

We can question the reliability of these Functionality scores, as well as the other scores generated by this methodology. An analyst's rating of the functionality of an editor is partly a matter of judgment, as was noted in Sec. 2.5, and partly a matter of detailed knowledge of the edi-

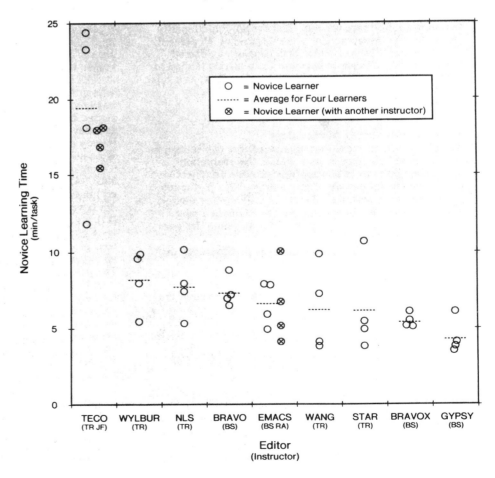

FIGURE 10. Learning Scores for Individual Novice Learners. The editors are ordered by descending Learning score. The instructors are noted below each editor.

FIGURE 11. Functionality Subscores for the Nine Text Editors.

Task Category[a] (No. of Tasks)[b]	Editor[c]									All Editors[d] M±CV
	NLS	BRAVOX	STAR	BRAVO	WANG	EMACS	WYLBUR	TECO	GYPSY	
TOTAL (212)[b]	77%	70%	62%	59%	50%	49%	42%	39%	37%	54%±.25
Modification										
Content (66)	94%	89%	93%	90%	87%	74%	63%	88%	80%	84%±.13
Text Layout (19)	89%	71%	66%	71%	37%	37%	26%	3%	26%	47%±.56
Page Layout (25)	74%	62%	56%	40%	34%	2%	6%	4%	4%	31%±.85
Characters (21)	43%	76%	57%	62%	38%	14%	21%	0%	17%	36%±.66
Other (16)	53%	59%	50%	22%	34%	0%	16%	3%	0%	26%±.84
Addressing (22)	68%	36%	30%	30%	16%	61%	34%	25%	18%	35%±.48
Control (23)	56%	37%	24%	20%	24%	89%	61%	48%	9%	41%±.58
Display (8)	94%	94%	63%	69%	19%	81%	62%	38%	50%	63%±.42
Misc. (12)	100%	88%	100%	71%	71%	46%	71%	25%	42%	68%±.38

[a] The Task Categories are described in the task taxonomy shown in Figure 1.

[b] The number in parentheses after the task category name gives the total number of tasks in that task category. The Functionality scores and sub-scores are given as a percentage of the total number of tasks in each task category. The scores in the TOTAL row are the same as in Figure 6.

[c] The editors are ordered in descending order of their overall Functionality scores.

[d] The numbers in the All Editors column tell how well the task categories are handled by the whole collection of editors and the amount of between-editor variability there is.

tor (e.g., knowing about limitations that may not be apparent from the documentation). To quantify the variation between analysts, three different analysts were asked to independently rate WYLBUR. The overall Functionality scores for the three analysts were 42 percent, 45 percent, and 39 percent. Scores within task categories differed more, but the differences between the analysts tended to be averaged out over the total set of tasks. Thus, as a rule of thumb, we can consider the overall Functionality scores to be accurate to around 10 percent.

3.4 Assessment of the Methodology

The above results show that diverse editors can indeed be evaluated and compared. As a whole, the evaluation methodology seems to successfully provide an objective, multidimensional picture of text editors. This methodology is also quite practical. For an experienced evaluator, about one week of time is required to evaluate a new editor. Thus, it should be practical for a system designer or a potential buyer.

Several other issues surrounding the methodology deserve discussion.

3.4.1. *Reliability*.

The main drawback in the use of this methodology is that the small number of subjects used for each of the tests makes the results very coarse. In addition, the results point out that the Error dimension needs a more reliable measure to differentiate editors, which will have to take into account the effect of large differences among the users.

Another way to increase reliability, besides increasing the number of subjects, is to decrease the between-user variability by homogenizing the subject sample. For instance, potential subjects could take a pretest, and only people who scored within a certain range could be used. This, however, specializes the results so that they only

represent a small segment of the user population, decreasing the generality of the methodology.[11]

Given that the methodology accepts a wide range of subjects, we can check whether the methodology is being applied to a restricted sample. If the between-user variance is ever substantially less than in the data here, the reason may be that the evaluator has picked a restricted sample of subjects. This is a useful caution for designers who are testing their own systems and who especially have to guard against bias. For example, in the data presented here, we note that the Time data for GYPSY does in fact have a lower than normal *CV*, which in this case is largely explained by the fact that only technical subjects were used.

3.4.2. *Coverage*.

Although the methodology covers several basic aspects of editor usage, there are still aspects not covered. When this methodology was being developed [11], a variety of easy-to-obtain measures of other aspects were explored. Some examples are: (1) The error-proneness of an editor was measured by putting external stress on expert users while they performed editing tasks. (2) The possibility of disastrous errors in an editor was measured by a procedure for analyzing the editor's command language. (3) The display capabilities of an editor were measured by users performing proofreading tasks. (4) The learning and use of advanced features was addressed by using a questionnaire to measure experts' knowledge of how to perform complex editing tasks. Unfortunately, all of these attempts turned out to be too crude to be reliable and too unproductive in differentiating systems. The tests presented in this paper are the only ones we know currently that work well enough to be included in a methodology.

---

[11] Another way to increase reliability is to use all the subjects, but to use the pretest scores to normalize the overall results. This would require a model of the relation between pretest scores and performances results.

3.4.3. Representativeness.

TIME. A general criticism of benchmark testing is that the items in the benchmark are not appropriate or appropriately weighted for any particular application. Specifically, the benchmark used in the present methodology has been criticized for not representing the true mix of tasks in real text-editing situations [17]. This is true, as we noted in Sec. 2.2. However, we are skeptical that there is a single benchmark set representing the majority of text-editing situations. This is an empirical issue, and we know of no data currently that settles it. But there remains the issue of how to use the results of the present methodology if one is interested in a particular situation that has a different mix of tasks from the benchmark.

We propose an analytic procedure for adjusting the Time score from the benchmark test to correspond to a new situation, which is characterized as a new set of tasks (weighted by the frequency of the individual tasks). This adjustment procedure is based on the assumption that there is a constant ratio between the experimentally measured Time score and the time calculated with the Keystroke-Level Model. This can be expressed in a formula:

$$T/C = T'/C'$$

where T is the Time score on the benchmark, C is the calculated time on the same benchmark (as in Figure 5), C' is the calculated time for the new mix of tasks, and T' is the Time score we would expect from an experimental test on the new mix of tasks. T and C are given by the present methodology. T' is the desired result. It can be estimated by calculating C', which is done by using the Keystroke-Level Model on the new (weighted) set of tasks. One must be cautious about the assumption behind this adjustment procedure, especially if the new task set contains many complex editing tasks, for the assumptions behind the Keystroke-Level Model (see [3]) might be violated (such as was our experience with the first TECO calculation).

LEARNING.   The particular set of tasks chosen for the learning experiments undoubtedly affects the results obtained here, but it is likely to be less influential than which teaching paradigm is used. For example, we would expect the results of a self-teaching paradigm to be mostly determined by the quality of documentation. We do not in general know how teaching paradigms differ, but there is one preliminary result in a recent study by Robertson and Akscyn [13] comparing different teaching paradigms. They applied the present learning methodology to the ZOG frame editor, using an instructor and using two self-teaching paradigms by substituting online and offline documentation for the instructor. They found that the instructor produced about 13 percent faster learning than the self-teaching documentaton; and they found that the offline documentation was about 6 percent faster than the online documentation. The reason for the small difference caused by mode of documentation was that all the learners used the documentation in the same way in both cases—by reading through it at the beginning of the session. The lesson here is that real learners do not necessarily follow the paradigms laid out for them by the system documenters.

FUNCTIONALITY.   Finally, the issue of representativeness also applies to the checklist of tasks for testing functionality: the tasks in the checklist do not represent the needs of any particular situation. The degree of elaboration of the tasks in the task taxonomy was influenced by the capabilities of the editors existing or being envisioned at the time the taxonomy was being created. Thus, there are eight tasks relating to the layout of paragraphs but only one about the ability to typeset mathematical formulas properly. An editor that performs both functions equally well gets far more credit for one than the other. This problem is best addressed by using the functionality subscores; for a given application more weight can be given to the areas relevant to the application.

3.4.4. Applicability.

EXTRAPOLATION TO A LARGER CONTEXT. All of the data we have gathered have been from people performing a small number of preset tasks in a laboratory environment. What relationship do these results have to productivity in an office where the tasks may be different (e.g., proofreading and editing one's own work) and the environmental conditions may be different (e.g., a receptionist with constant small interruptions from people walking by)? A 20 percent improvement in the Time score for this methodology would not necessarily translate into a 20 percent improvement in overall office productivity. This is because an improvement in editing speed may not be accompanied by a proportional improvement in the speed of other activities that the user is doing along with editing, such as thinking about the proper wording of the text, typing in large amounts of new text, or proofreading for errors. Another possible factor is that the intense concentration on the editing task allowed by laboratory conditions, but often not allowed by real situations, may differentially affect the performance of different editors. Such problems beset all laboratory work, and the questions raised can only be answered when laboratory studies are supplemented by on-site studies to determine the relationship between the two.

USE BY EDITOR DESIGNERS.   The full methodology requires an implemented text editor that has been running long enough to have at least a few expert users, which suggests that the methodology is not useful for a designer of a new editor. However, the designer can use parts of the methodology to get an early indication of how well the proposed editor compares with existing editors and where the strengths and weaknesses of the new editor lie. Two of the evaluation measures, Time and Functionality, can be obtained analytically, when the design is still on paper. Learning can be measured experimentally on a prototype (that need only be complete enough to cover the core tasks). The Error measure is the only one that cannot be obtained easily; this should pose no problem, since editors cannot be differentiated on this dimension anyhow.

On the Time dimension, the Keystroke-Level Model can be used to produce a calculated task time, along with a decomposition of the time into the times for the different operations. These times can be compared to the calculated task times for other editors in Figure 5 to see whether the times are in line with similar editors and to reveal possible bottlenecks on some operations. (The calculated task time can also be adjusted, by multiplying by 1.3, to compensate for the model's tendency to underpredict the experimental Time scores. The adjusted time can then be compared to the Time scores in Figure 6). In this analysis, the only parameters which must be estimated

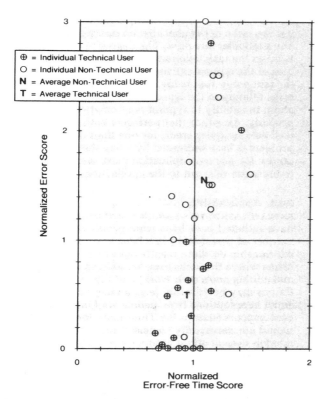

FIGURE 12. Normalized Time and Error Scores for all Expert Users. A user's score is normalized by dividing it by the average score in the editor.

are the system response times. If these are not available, this analysis can be turned around to provide the designer with a specification for acceptable limits for the response times (by showing how different response times make the proposed editor compare to other editors). Finally, if a prototype system is available, experimental benchmark tests can be run using the designers and implementors themselves as subjects. These data would be useful to provide a check on the calculated times and the predicted methods that the times are based on.

4. BEHAVIORAL RESULTS

The database of results from the experimental studies gives us information not only about the specific editors, but about user behavior in general, such as the gross levels of user performance in text editing. The data show that the core editing tasks require about 20–45 seconds per task for most expert users on most systems, and it shows that a period of about two hours of one-on-one training is enough to teach novice users about 20 core tasks in most editors. These results should be of interest to researchers in office productivity, for example, to measure the cost-effectiveness of word processing. More detailed results are interesting in two principal ways: for the light they shed on (1) the individual differences in performance between users and (2) the factors influencing novice learning.

4.1 Individual User Differences

4.1.1. Magnitude of Individual User Differences. The greatest individual differences by far are found in Error time scores (ranging from 0 to 39 percent), which reflects a wide variation among expert users in how careful they

are in avoiding errors and in performing tasks completely. There is much less variation among experts in speed of editing—about a factor of 1.5 to 2 between the fastest and slowest users' Time scores within each editor. This range is much smaller than the factor of 3.5 reported in [4]. However, [4] tested a more diverse sample of users, including casual users as well as dedicated expert users.

A somewhat surprising result is that the variation among novice learners is not much greater than among expert users. Learners exhibit about the same range of variation (up to a factor of 2.5 between the fastest and slowest learners within an editor) and *CV* (.19 for experts and .26 for novice learners). This is partly due, no doubt, to the fact that the learning tests are designed to minimize variation due to idiosyncratic learners (e.g., the command summary sheet and the always present instructor). A self-teaching paradigm is likely to yield much more variation among learners.

4.1.2. Time vs. Errors. It is common wisdom that there is a speed–accuracy tradeoff: that when people work faster, they make more errors. Our data can be used to investigate whether the users who spend more time in error do so because they are working faster, that is, whether users with higher Error time scores have lower error-free Time scores. We cannot directly compare scores of users on different editors, however, unless we normalize over editors. A user's score on an editor can be normalized by dividing it by the overall (mean) score for the editor. That is, a normalized score of 1.0 indicates an average user, and a score of .5 indicates a user twice as good as the average. Figure 12 plots the normalized Time vs. Error scores for all the expert users. What is immediately obvious from this plot is the much larger variation on the Error dimension than on the Time dimension. However, we do not see the tradeoff between Time and Error scores that a speed–accuracy tradeoff would suggest, but rather a modest positive correlation between them ($R = .58$). Some users tend to be better than others on both dimensions.

4.1.3. Technical vs. Nontechnical Expert Users. The individual users plotted in Figure 12 are marked as being technical or nontechnical. The technical users are clearly the better users on both Time and Error (clustering in the lower left quadrant). Also plotted in the figure is the average technical user and the average nontechnical user. These two fictitious average users account for the major features of the plot. The average nontechnical user is 15 percent slower than the average technical user (.94 vs. 1.08) and spends a factor of 3 more time in error (.50 vs. 1.56).[12] The factor 1.15 difference between technical and nontechnical users on the Time dimension is comparable to the factor of 1.3 reported in [4].

The underlying reason for the difference between technical and nontechnical users is not known. It is not due to physical skill factors, such as typing proficiency, for which nontechnical users are superior.[13] It could just be

---

[12] This data allows us to calculate an adjustment for the effects of using different proportions of technical and nontechnical subjects in different editors. As mentioned in Sec. 3.3.1, such an adjustment does not change the rank ordering of the editors of the Time dimension. A similar adjustment on the Error dimension also makes little difference in the results: the range of Error scores becomes a factor of 4 instead of a factor of 5, and differences between editors are still not statistically reliable.

[13] The nontechnical users were 1.4 times faster than the technical users. Given that an average of about 22 percent of the time is spent in typing [Figure 5(b)], this would give the nontechnical users about a 7 percent advantage over the technical users.

due to a difference in general intelligence or education, rather than anything due to technical experience per se. (The programmers we used as technical subjects have been preselected to be very bright and highly educated, whereas the secretarial and support personnel we used as nontechnical subjects have undergone less of such preselection.) Other possible factors, suggested by a recent study [5], are that technical users might have more spatial ability or be younger than nontechnical users. These two factors have been shown to affect editor learning rates, and they are also likely to apply to expert performance.

4.2. Novice Learning

Learning behavior is less well understood than expert performance. The Keystroke-Level Model [3] (along with its theoretical underpinnings [4]) provides a usefully accurate account of the time performance of expert users. However, we have no similar account of why some editors are easier for novices to learn than others. Our learning data provide the opportunity to test some ideas about the main factors affecting learnability.

4.2.1. Factors Affecting Editor Learnability.   How does the structure of an editor affect its learnability? Perhaps the most obvious hypothesis to consider is that the command languages of some editors are more complex. One measure of command language complexity is the number of distinct commands in an editor. According to this hypothesis, the editors with fewer commands should be faster to learn. (This might be called the "weigh-the-manual" theory of learnability, since most reference manuals consist of an enumeration of the different commands.) In this methodology, since only commands necessary to do core editing tasks are taught, we restrict our measure to the number of these "core commands." Figure 13 shows that this measure correlates poorly ($R = .37$) with the Learning scores.[14]

FIGURE 13. Correlations of Learning Scores with Various Measures.

Measure	Correlation (R)	
	All Nine Editors	All Editors except TECO[a]
Number of Core Commands in Editor	.37	.19
Number of Physical Operations per Task	.68	.58
Number of Method Chunks (M's + A's) per Task	.93	.65
Expert Time Score	.79	.67

[a] Since the Learning score for TECO is an extreme value, it has a large influence on the correlations. Hence, it is useful to present a separate set of correlations with the influence of the TECO score removed.

The crucial point missed by this hypothesis is that commands are not useful in isolation, rather they are used in the context of methods or procedures to accomplish editing tasks. Thus, the second hypothesis to consider as a predictor of learnability is that learning is related to the *procedural complexity* of a command language. This is quite different from command language complexity. For example, a "simple" command language with only three commands might require lengthy and intricate procedures to accomplish editing tasks, whereas an editor with a

large variety of commands might only require a couple of those commands to do any one task. The procedural complexity hypothesis says that a user must learn not just what each command does, but how each command is used in various ways in different methods. This leads us to consider the number of distinct uses of commands, which is related to the length of the methods (rather than the length of the list of commands).

One way to approximate the procedural complexity of an editor is to compute the average number of steps in the methods for accomplishing a representative set of tasks, such as the benchmark used in the Time and Error dimensions of our methodology.[15] The physical operations in the Keystroke-Level Model encodings of methods (see Figure 4) provide a simple, unambiguous set of steps to count. Figure 13 shows that the average number of physical operations per task correlates substantially better with the Learning scores ($R = .68$) than do the commands, although the correlation is still modest.

The length (in physical operations) of a method, although it may correlate with procedural complexity, can be a misleading indicator. For example, a method requiring the user to type D E L E T E RETURN is not seven times more complex than a method requiring only D to be typed. Thus, we see that procedural complexity has more to do with the *mental* "chunking" of physical steps into coherent fragments than the physical steps themselves. To operationalize this notion, let us return to the Keystroke-Level Model encoding of methods. This model has two kinds of mental operations, A's and M's. When a large editing task is broken into subtasks, the subtasks are each preceded by an A operation, representing the user's having to acquire a mental representation of the subtask. Within a subtask, the sequence of physical operations is punctuated with M operations, which represents small mental preparations for the upcoming physical operations (rules for placing M operations are given in [3]). The A and M operations have the effect of breaking the sequence of physical operations into procedural chunks. For example, consider the method encodings of the example task in Figure 4. The method for WYLBUR is:

A M 12K M 3K R M 13K M 20K M 8K M K

Here the physical operations are divided into seven chunks by the A's and M's. The methods for the same task in EMACS and STAR contain only three and two chunks, respectively.

A S M 4K R 2K M 15K

A S H P 2K M K H 14K

The number of chunks in a method, which can be estimated by simply counting the A's and M's, should be a better indicator of the procedural complexity of the method than the physical operations we counted before. In fact, the mental chunking measure correlates better with the Learning scores ($R = .93$) than do the physical operations, as Figure 13 shows. It is the best correlate we have of Learning time.

This notion of procedural complexity as determined by mentally defined chunks is an instance of the "zeroth-order theory of learning" [4]: that learning time is proportional to the number of chunks of information that must

---

[14] One problem with this measure is deciding what a command is (e.g., is a preselection a command itself or just an argument to a command that follows it?). This issue can be sidestepped somewhat by counting parts of commands, such as commands names, arguments, terminators, etc. However, this "finer" measure does no better than just counting "whole" commands (see [11]).

[15] It may seem paradoxical that we are using the expert benchmark test to measure learnability by novices. But note that we are only using the benchmark test as a convenient sample of tasks to get at the procedural complexity *required by the core functions of the editor*. Since the novices are trying to acquire this same expertise, it represents the *target competence* they are trying to achieve.

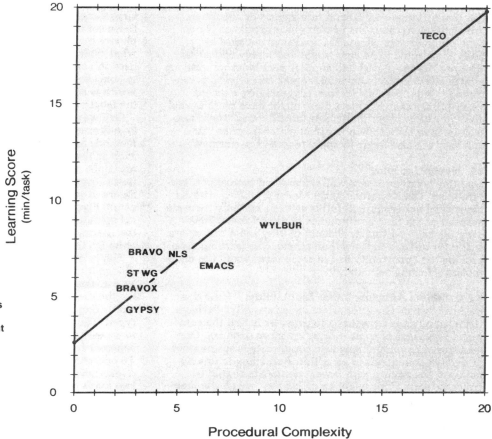

FIGURE 14. Plot of Learning Scores vs. the Mental-Chunks Measure of Procedural Complexity. (Note that STAR is abbreviated as ST and WANG as WG.)

be learned. To make this theory operational, we must be able to specify what the chunks are. In this case, the chunks are the procedural fragments bounded by mental operations.

Figure 14 shows a plot of the mental-chunking measure of procedural complexity against the Learning scores. This plot shows how raw correlations must be interpreted with caution, for we see that the learning score for TECO, which lies far out from the others, has great leverage on the correlation (which is why we also give the correlations excluding TECO in Figure 13). What we see in Figure 14 is that procedural complexity accounts for the difference between the fastest and slowest editors, but that it tells us little about the observed differences among the set of fastest editors. Procedural complexity is not the only factor affecting learnability; in fact, it seems to be dominated by other factors among fast editors.[16] However, procedural complexity may be the most dominant factor in learning overall, statistically accounting for about half the variance between editors.

4.2.2. Learning vs. Time. The conventional wisdom among designers is that there is a tradeoff between systems that are easy to learn by novices and systems that are efficient to use by experts. However, if we correlate

the Learning scores with the Time scores, we see exactly the opposite. The data from our study shows a high positive correlation ($R = .79$, Figure 13) between the Time and Learning scores.[17] The concept of procedural complexity introduced in the last section explains this correlation. It says that the same factor—procedural complexity—underlies both expert performance (longer methods take longer to execute) and novice learning (longer methods imply that there are more chunks to learn).[18]

5. CONCLUSION

A standardized four-dimensional methodology for evaluating text editors has been presented and applied to nine different editors. The methodology seems to be an effective tool for the empirical evaluation of text editors along the dimensions of Time, Error, Learning, and Functionality. Of course, the methodology has limitations—having to do with reliability, coverage, representativeness, and applicability—which is the price of keeping the methodology simple to use. It is obvious that the methodology could be improved by both refinement and extension.

---

[16] A candidate for one of the other factors is what we might call "conceptual unfamiliarity," which taps how well novice users understand, a priori, the conceptual constructs involved in an editor. This notion is currently being explored by the second author and Sally Douglas in *Learning to Text Edit: Semantics in Procedural Skill Acquisition*. Ph.d dissertation, Stanford University, March '83.

[17] This is the only substantial correlation between scores on the methodology's dimensions. Correlations between the other dimensions range between .24 and .36. All of these correlations are positive, in the sense that editors tend to improve in the two dimensions together, with the exception that there is a tradeoff between Error and Functionality.

[18] We can use this result to conjecture that the main reason for the superiority of display-based systems, on both the Time and Learning dimensions, over nondisplay systems is not the display itself, but rather that the display-based systems permit much less complex procedures.

However, even in its present form, it provides for the generation of a valuable user–editor performance database of objective measures. We would urge others who need to do evaluations of editors to use this methodology. Its main advantage is that the numbers produced can be put in the context of the database of already evaluated editors (without such a context, numbers are difficult to interpret). At the same time, the additional evaluations (either replications of existing evaluations or evaluations of new editors) would be contributing to extending the database, allowing our knowledge of editor performance to systematically accumulate.

We have also shown how the database of results can help us understand user performance, by making clear the magnitude of individual differences of both experts and novices, and by providing a testing ground for understanding the factors affecting learning. Although we presently favor a theory of learning based on the notion of procedural complexity, a larger database will show whether this theory holds up. Finally, we have shown that Keystroke-Level Model calculations of editor performance, which also belong in the database, are useful analyses against which to compare and interpret the experimental results.

Acknowledgements.   We thank Betsey Summers for organizing and running many of these evaluation studies and for helping us analyze the data. We thank Allen Newell and Stu Card for many helpful discussions and Allen Newell for commenting on drafts of this paper.

This paper is based in part on the first author's thesis research (reported in [11]) which was done under the supervision of the second author, and on continuing research by the second author. A short, preliminary version of this paper was published as [12]. The authors are listed in reverse-alphabetic order.

REFERENCES

1. Boies, S. J. User behavior in an interactive computer system. *IBM Systems Journal 13* (1974) 1–18.
2. Card, S. K., English, W. K., and Burr, B. J. Evaluation of mouse, rate-controlled isometric joystick, step keys, and text keys for text selection on a CRT. *Ergonomics 21* (1978) 601–613.
3. Card, S. K., Moran, T. P., and Newell, A. The Keystroke-Level Model for user performance time with interactive systems. *Comm. ACM 23, 7* (July 1980) 396–410.
4. Card, S. K., Moran, T. P., and Newell, A. *The Psychology of Human-Computer Interaction.* Lawrence Erlbaum Associates, Hillsdale, NJ, 1983.
5. Egan, D. E., Bowers, C., and Gomez, L. M. Learner characteristics that predict success in using a text-editor tutorial. *Proc. Conference on Human Factors in Computer Systems,* Gaithersburg, MD, (March 1982), 337–340.
6. Embley, D. W., and Nagy, G. Behavioral aspects of text editors. *Computing Surveys 13,* 1 (March 1981) 33–70.
7. Good, M. An ease of use evaluation of an integrated document processing system. *Proc. Conference on Human Factors in Computer Systems,* Gaithersburg, MD, (March 1982), 142–147.
8. Meyrowitz, N., and van Dam, A. Interactive editing systems. *Computing Surveys 14,* 3 (Sept. 1982) 321–415.
9. Moran, T. P. The Command Language Grammar: A representation for the user interface of interactive computer systems. *Int. Journal of Man-Machine Studies 15,* 1 (July 1981) 3–50.
10. Riddle, E. A. *Comparative Study of Various Text Editors and Formatting Systems.* Report AD-A029 050, Air Force Data Services Center, The Pentagon, Washington, D.C., (Aug. 1976).
11. Roberts, T. L. *Evaluation of Computer Text Editors.* Ph.D. dissertation, Department of Computer Science, Stanford University, Stanford, Calif., (1980). Available as Report AAD 80-11699 from University Microfilms, Ann Arbor, Mich.
12. Roberts, T. L., and Moran, T. P. Evaluation of text editors. *Proc. Conference on Human Factors in Computer Systems,* Gaithersburg, MD, (March 1982), 136–141.
13. Robertson, C. K., and Akscyn, R. Experimental evaluation of tools for teaching the ZOG frame editor. Computer Science Department, Carnegie-Mellon University, Pittsburgh, PA, (1982).
14. *The Seybold Report on Office Systems* (through 1981 called *The Seybold Report on Word Processing*). Media, PA.
15. *The Seybold Report on Word Processing.* 4, 4, (April 1981). Issue on Personal Computers: Word Processing Packages.
16. Smith, D. C., Irby, C., Kimball, R., Verplank, W., and Harslem, E. Designing the Star user interface. *Byte 7,* 4 (April 1982) 242–282.
17. Whiteside, J., Archer, N., Wixon, D., and Good, M. How do people really use text editors? *Proc. SIGOA Conference on Office Information Systems,* Philadelphia, (1982) 29–40.

References (for Editor Documentation)
18. Augmentation Research Center. *NLS-8 Command Summary.* Stanford Research Institute, Menlo Park, Calif., (May 1975).
19. Augmentation Research Center. *NLS-8 Glossary.* Stanford Research Institute. Menlo Park, Calif., (July 1975).
20. Bolt, Beranek, and Newman, Inc. *TENEX Text Editor and Corrector* (Manual DEC10-NGZEB-D). Cambridge, Mass. (1973). (Documents TECO.)
21. Garcia, K. *Xerox Document System Reference Manual.* Xerox Office Products Division, Palo Alto, Calif, (1980). (Documents BRAVOX.)
22. Lampson, B. Bravo manual. *Alto User's Handbook.* Xerox Palo Alto Research Center, Palo Alto, Calif., (1979).
23. Stallman, R. M. *EMACS Manual for ITS Users.* AI Lab Memo 554, MIT, Cambridge, Mass., (1980).
24. Stanford Center for Information Processing. *Wylbur/370 The Stanford Timesharing System Reference Manual,* 3rd ed. Stanford University, Stanford, Calif., (1975).
25. Tesler, L. The Smalltalk environment. *Byte 6,* 8, (Aug. 1981) 90–147. (There is no available GYPSY documentation. This paper describes the Smalltalk editor, which is based on many of the same design ideas as GYPSY.)
26. Wang Laboratories, Inc. *Wang Word Processor Operator's Guide,* 3rd release. Lowell, Mass., (1978).
27. Xerox Corporation. *8010 Star Information System Reference Guide.* Dallas, Texas, (1981). (See also [16].)

CR Categories and Subject Descriptors: H.1.2 [**Models and Principles**]: User/Machine Systems—*human factors*; I.7.1 [**Text Processing**:] Text Editing—*languages*; I.7.2 [**Text Processing**]: Document Preparation—*languages*
   General Terms: Experimentation, Human Factors.
   Additional Key Words and Phrases: human–computer interface, human–computer interaction, user model, user performance, user psychology, ergonomics, human factors, system design, system evaluation, text editing.

Learning to Use Word Processors: Problems and Prospects

ROBERT L. MACK, CLAYTON H. LEWIS, and JOHN M. CARROLL
IBM Thomas J. Watson Research Center

Computer text editors are powerful, but complex, tools. Particularly in the early stages of learning, the complexity of these tools can cause serious problems for users who are not experienced with computers. The problems of new users were studied by asking the users to think out loud while learning to use word-processing systems. In this paper several of the most typical and debilitating problems these users had understanding and following directions in using training manuals, as well as problems understanding and using interface functions to accomplish word processing tasks, are taxonomized and analyzed. Approaches for improving design features of the interface functions and the training methods used for learning are discussed.

Categories and Subject Descriptors: H.1.2 [Models and Principles]: User/Machine Systems—human factors; human information processing; H.4.1 [Information Systems Applications] Office Automation—equipment; word processing; I.2.6 [Artificial Intelligence]: Learning—analogies; concept learning

General Terms: Human Factors

Additional Key Words and Phrases: Behavioral science, cognitive psychology, protocol methodology, instruction, novices, text editors, human-computer interface

1. INTRODUCTION

One problem challenging designers of office systems today is developing text-processing systems that are easy to learn and use. As we show in this paper, learning to use text-processing systems can be difficult, time consuming, and frustrating. Learning difficulties can have serious practical impact on the use of office systems. For example, these learning difficulties can be costly when they require tutorial help from trained personnel (e.g., [21]).

How can we make using office systems easier to learn? The first step in answering this question is to have a better understanding of how people learn to use computer systems and what problems they have. In this paper, we report research aimed at providing insight into both issues, see [12, 17, 22]. (For further discussion of behavioral issues in interactive text editing, see [12, 17, 22].

Authors' address: IBM Thomas J. Watson Research Center, Computer Science Department, P.O. Box 218, Yorktown Heights, NY 10598.

2. STUDYING TEXT PROCESSING SYSTEMS

Our approach to studying learning has been to bring office temporaries into the laboratory and ask them to "think aloud" as they go about learning to use text-processing equipment. This approach has given us insight not only into specific problems with the systems we studied, but also into general mechanisms of learning and reasoning on the part of new users. In this paper we discuss generalizations about these problems, illustrating each with our observations and suggesting ways we believe training and interface design might be improved.

2.1 The Thinking-Aloud Method of Studying Learning

The method we used to study learning is called the "thinking-aloud" protocol method. We asked learners to verbalize as they worked, describing what questions were raised in their mind and what plans, strategies, inferences, or knowledge they were currently aware of. These comments were tape-recorded, and what happened on the computer screen was video-recorded for later analysis.

We remained with participants to prompt them to continue verbalizing, but did so nondirectively to avoid suggesting what they should think about. We only intervened to help if it appeared that the participant would give up if we did not do so. Our presence with participants detracted somewhat from the realism of the task, but this is an unavoidable aspect of the thinking-aloud technique. Of course, virtually all empirical methods of studying behavior involve some interaction with people participating. (We believe that participants soon became accustomed to the thinking-aloud task and to the routine of verbalizing. Those participants who were unable or unwilling to verbalize fluently were not forced to do so: we simply accepted sketchy verbalizations in these cases.) Finally, many of our observations are based on observing participants' overt behavior and not on verbalizations, spontaneous or prompted.

We used the thinking-aloud method because it has proved to be a useful tool in cognitive psychology for studying in depth a new task domain without imposing the limitations of more traditional experimental methods. It has been used in pioneering work on problem solving by Newell and Simon (e.g., [18]) and is now applied routinely to investigate many kinds of psychological problems, including the study of person-computer interaction. Bott ([4]), for example, has used it to study how college students learned commands for a line editor.

Thinking-aloud protocols produce qualitative data that can provide a broad survey of phenomena and problems in a task domain. This is in contrast to controlled experimental studies, which typically examine the influence on behavior of only a few factors in terms of some quantitative measure of performance (see, e.g., [1, 22] for examples and discussion of experimental methodology applied to the study of person-computer interaction). Further discussion of the usefulness of thinking-aloud protocols, as well as their advantages and disadvantages, can be found in [11, 13, 19].

2.2 The Participants and Their Task

We gave ten office temporaries four half-days to learn one of two possible text-processing systems: four worked at learning a subset of text-editing and formatting functions on a large general-pupose computer system in use at the Watson Research Center, and six worked at learning a commercially available dedicated word-processing system. The participants worked in a laboratory setting, which included the text-processing system and recording equipment.

2.2.1 *Participants.* Participants had varied work and educational backgrounds, which are summarized in Table I. Five of the participants were between 20 and 35 years of age, the other five over 40 years. Nine of them were women. As can be seen from the table, six participants had data entry experience, one a course in word processing, and two no experience with computers. All of the participants had worked in an office situation and knew how to type letters.

2.2.2 *The Training Task.* We were interested in how well participants could learn by unaided self-study, so we asked them to imagine that they were working in an office situation where no one else knew anything about the system and where all that was available for learning was a self-study manual. Unaided self-study, incidentally, is not necessarily representative of how people learn to use the text-processing systems we studied, each of which supports multiple work stations (and hence a potential community of users). But it is a *strategy* for operator training that has obvious practical interest.

Participants spent varying amounts of time learning, but we generally stopped the learning phase after about 12 hours (regardless of where they were in the training materials) so that they had time to try typing and revising a simple letter on their own without explicit instructions and time to answer questions about their experience. Participants had varying amounts of time to type the one-page letter, depending on how long they needed to complete the training materials, but all had at least an hour.

Four temporaries were asked to learn a subset of the commands for a full-screen editor on the general-purpose computer system and some basic formatting instructions. This system has a command-based interface (as opposed to providing menus). The functions studied were sufficient for creating, printing, and revising simple letters, as well as for creating simple form letters with symbols standing for variable information. Participants were given a self-study manual, which we wrote but patterned after the existing self-study manual for the commercial word-processing system (described below).

The other six were asked to learn basic text-editing operations for a dedicated word-processing computer. This system is menu driven: users select tasks (e.g., print or create a document) by typing in command abbreviations listed on selection menus, and then fill in menus corresponding to the selected task (e.g., the name of a to-be-created document). There are, of course, several function keys for cursor movement, deleting, underscoring, and so on.

We asked the participants to cover material in four topic chapters of the self-study manual provided for the commercially available word processing system. The first three of these covered basic letter entry and revision skills, the use of menus, interpretation of messages, and the use of an on-line help facility. A fourth chapter introduced more advanced document composition skills, including form letters with variables and symbols and building documents from parts using document merge operations.

Both self-study manuals combined explanations about how to do things with the system and structured step-by-step practice. Figure 1 illustrates this design

Table I. Summary of Ten Participants' Background

(1) H.S., some college but no secretarial training; 1 year typing for psychiatrist; data entry (keypunch) but no experience with magnetic card typewriter or word processor

(2) H.S.; 30 years in office work; data entry with video display terminal (VDT) but no experience with magnetic card typewriter or word processor

(3) H.S., 3 years college; 30 years office work, including own business; NCR bookkeeping, data entry with VDT but no magnetic card typewriter or word processor

(4) No data (information about participants' background was voluntary)

(5) H.S., some college, 2 years secretarial school; 6 months office experience; word processor course but no on-the-job experience or magnetic tard typewriter

(6) College graduate (science); 5-6 years office temporary; data entry and introductory FOR-TRAN, but no magnetic card typewriter or word processor

(7) M.A. music; 10 years office temporary; no magnetic card typewriter or word processor

(8) H.S., business course; 2 years office experience; data entry but no magnetic card typewriter or word processor

(9) H.S.; 15 years office experience; data entry but no magnetic card typewriter or word processor

(10) H.S., some college, 1 year secretarial school; 1 year and summer work in office; no experience with magnetic card typewriter or word processor

---

Exercise Preview

You have now finished typing the two-page memo.

Normally, you would finish a job; then print it. For this exercise, though, you will practice revising it before it gets printed.

The short exercise below will use the TOP command to move you back to the beginning of the document.

Exercise Four-Page Return

1. Press the BACKWARD key five times.
   * You are now at the "top" of your document. The "current line" should be the "TOP-OF-FILE" line.

2. Press the FORWARD key five times.
   * You are now at the "bottom" of your document. The "current line" should be the "END-OF-FILE" line.

3. Type TOP.

4. Press ENTER.
   * You are again at the "top" of your document. The "current line" should be the "TOP-OF-FILE" line.

Exercise Preview

In this exercise you will practice moving through two pages of text to make deletions and additions. You will also "print" the document on the display before printing it on paper.

Fig. 1. A sample of the self-study manual.

Table II. Summary of Major Results

(1) Learning Is Difficult
    Learners experience frustration and blame themselves
    Learning takes longer than expected, and learners have trouble applying what they know
    after training

(2) Learners Lack Basic Knowledge
    Learners are naive about how computers work (e.g., do not understand computer jargon)
    Learners do not know what is relevant to understanding and solving problems

(3) Learners Make Ad Hoc Interpretations
    Learners try to construct interpretations for what they do or for what happens to them
    Learners' interpretations can prevent them from seeing that they have a problem

(4) Learners Generalize from What They Know
    Learners assume that some aspects of text editors will work like typewriting (especially
    functions that simply move the typing point on a typewriter)
    Learners assume that text-editing operations will work consistently

(5) Learners Have Trouble Following Directions
    Learners do not always read or follow directions
    Learners do not always understand or correctly follow directions even when they do try

(6) Problems Interact
    Learners have trouble understanding that one problem can create another

(7) Interface Features May Not Be Obvious
    Learners can be confused by prerequisites and side effects of procedures
    Learners can be confused by feedback messages and the outcome of procedures

(8) Help Facilities Do Not Always Help
    Learners do not always know what to ask for
    Help information is not always focused on the learner's specific problem

---

with a page from the self-study manual we wrote. Practice exercises are set off from explanation with boxes, and the exercises contained both descriptions of explicit actions and commentary about the action (the asterisked information in Figure 1).

2.3 How the Data Were Analyzed

Thinking-aloud protocols produce a large amount of nonquantitative observational data. (An example can be found in the Appendix.) For example, we have accumulated roughly 96 hours for the commercial system alone. Thus, we must necessarily be selective in the discussion to follow.

Our approach is both clinical and inductive. It is clinical in that we make hypotheses about the possible cause of some behavior or learning problem and illustrate it with examples. It is inductive when we infer generalizations from multiple examples and use the most typical examples to illustrate the generalizations. We did not count frequency of a particular problem, nor can we provide rigorous criteria for the problem categories we identify. Our goal was exploratory, intended to identify a broad range of problems encountered by learners. The qualitative results might be used to design classificatory schemes for more quantitative surveys, but that is not our goal in this paper.

3. RESULTS AND DISCUSSION

The generalizations we discuss in this paper (and summarize in Table II) focus on the activities of the learner, but our discussion has implications for understanding the role of training materials and interface design in the learning situation as a whole. We try to suggest what aspect of the training or interface design might explain the learning difficulty, and we discuss how these problems might be solved.

3.1 Learning Is Difficult

It is generally conceded that people who are not experienced with computers have trouble learning to use text-processing equipment. This is not surprising given the complexity and power of these systems, but it is a challenge for efforts to expand the market for office automation. Both systems we studied provide examples of how frustrating learning can be for people not experienced with computers.

For example, one participant who tried to sign on (without reading how to do so) immediately got into trouble and concluded: "I'm lost already." A participant frustrated while trying to solve a problem finally exclaimed: "Stupid stuff!" We ultimately had to intervene to solve her problem.

Other participants complained about the amount of material to read and remember: "So much to read and nothing to reinforce it!" or "How much can I remember? So much going through my head!" or "Too much information to take in at one time. Confusing." The problems they had with learning also led them to lose sight of what they were trying to learn: "What did we do?" or "I know we did something but I don't know what it is!"

These kinds of comments also arose during preliminary field interviews with office workers who learned text editing in a real work environment. As one person

put it: "It makes me feel stupid." Others who had come to value the particular text editor we had studied nevertheless admitted that they had considered quitting because of frustrating training experiences.

Learners also took longer to learn than expected and had problems applying what they had learned following training. Participants took about 8 hours and 15 minutes to learn basic text-editing skills on the commercially available word processor as compared to designer estimates of about 4 to 5 hours. Of course, these estimates may be unrealistic, and participants were asked to verbalize as they worked. But even with this extra time, participants still made many errors in transcribing, printing, retrieving, and revising a one-page letter after training.

For example, only three participants were able to control pagination of text (i.e., rearranging text to justify right margins). Of four major commands needed to complete the letter task (create, revise, print, and paginate the document), two participants ran out of time to get to revising and paginating, while the other four had problems with one or more of these four tasks (albeit ultimately solving them). All participants also had trouble using delete functions to make corrections or understanding the effect of carrier return on text (it inserts blank lines). Participants had had practice with all of these basic text-editing tasks during training.

Our laboratory data probably underrepresent these problems because we tried to be supportive when participants had problems (e.g., we emphasized that they should not be surprised if they had problems and should not blame themselves). In real work situations these difficulties (and those we discuss below) may contribute to job stress when learners and supervisors have unrealistic expectations about how quickly people can learn and increase their productivity.

A short-term way to help learners cope with difficulties is to give them and their supervisors more realistic expectations about the difficulty of, and time required for, learning. These expectations should result in a more supportive environment for learning, since the learners know they face a challenging learning task and should not blame themselves for problems.

3.2 Learners Lack Basic Knowledge

Computer-naive learners lack general knowledge about how computers work, as well as specific knowledge of text-editing systems. They fail to readily understand basic ideas and jargon, they entertain implausible possibilities, and they have trouble identifying what is relevant to solving or understanding problems.

One participant, for example, wondered what the cursor was after several hours of using the system. Another wondered "who" the printer was. Yet a third wondered if she was using the printer. These examples of learners' "innocence" about basic concepts in using computers are reminiscent of Bott's study [4] of problems college students had learning to use a line editor: for example, many of his learners thought that a "command" was something the computer wanted them to do!

Participants also lacked familiarity with technical jargon. They had trouble with terms such as "parameter" (or "perimeter" as one learner put it), "queue," "reversed video," "background," "pagination," and "default." Learners often invoked misleading associations; for example, "default" can have a negative (legal) connotation.

Participants' lack of knowledge about text processing can make it hard for them to interpret what happens accurately. One participant, who finally succeeded in executing an operation after several attempts, wondered if her earlier failures were somehow due to her having hit the ENTER key incorrectly. To an experienced user this is a nonsensical possibility: how can one hit a key incorrectly? But new users simply do not know enough to rule out interpretations that seem obviously wrong to an experienced user.

During sign-on, another participant made an error that disabled the keyboard. Unbeknown to the learner, only a key called RESET would remedy this condition. The learner pressed various keys, eventually trying RESET. But before discovering the effect of this, she also pressed a switch that placed the system in a test mode, giving a garbled but recognizable version of the normal display. Noting that the system was now responding to the keys, the learner concluded that the critical action had been pressing the test switch, not the RESET key, and continued to operate the system in a test mode for some time.

Learners also have trouble finding or selecting information relevant to their concerns and problems. Because they do not know what is relevant, they are easily influenced by superficial and specious connections between what they do or perceive and the problems they are trying to solve.

One editor studied has separate input and command modes, so that a command typed in input mode becomes a line of text. One participant entered the command FILE to store her text but neglected to leave input mode first, so the command was not executed. But the learner concluded it *had* been executed, for two reasons. First, when she entered the command at the bottom of the screen, the system seemed to respond by moving it up the screen to join previous lines of input. Part of the system indicated that it was paying attention. Second, she noticed a message had been on the screen for some time, unnoticed, and had nothing to do with the FILE command, but now it looked relevant (it indicates she is in a mode for inputting text). Here is what the learner said: "I think it possibly did [store the file] because I had it [the "command"] down here and it went up here. So my input mode is file. That's the status area which I assume means file, file one, which would probably be important."

Another example of finding spurious relevance is illustrated in the protocol excerpt in the Appendix. At one point the participant inadvertently inserted a blank line between two sentences. Wishing to "bring back" the second sentence to its former position under the first, she chose a key marked REQUIRED RETURN. Unfortunately, RETURN here means CARRIAGE RETURN, not "bring back," so the effect of her action was to add another unwanted blank line between the two sentences.

Learners' innocence and the problems stemming from it may not yield to frontal attack. Giving learners more explanatory material to master may not work well because they do not like this kind of material and read it carelessly if at all. One of our participants turned quickly through some pages of background text saying dismissively, "This is just information." It may be more fruitful to reduce the amount of knowledge needed to operate the system.

Better screening for jargon is an area where we can reduce what learners need to understand. User testing can reveal unfamiliar terms in manuals and messages. Many can be replaced or, failing that, introduced with suitable examples. A related approach may be to conceal information from learners and make it available only after they are experienced or present it only on demand. For example, many menu displays for the commercial word processor contained technical details or options that are useful for experienced users but were not used or readily understood by the participants.

3.3 Learners Make Ad Hoc Interpretations

Learners may lack knowledge about computers, but we have evidence that this does not deter them from trying to make sense of what they experienced by constructing and elaborating ad hoc interpretations of their experiences.

Sometimes these interpretations are constructed to explain things that seem puzzling about the system. In one system the keys that normally moved the cursor could not be used when a menu was displayed. A participant explained this by taking as an example the key that normally moved the cursor from one line of text to the next. Since there could be more than one menu field on one line of the screen, this key could not be used to move the cursor between menu fields.

One may accept this reasoning or not: the point here is that the participant spontaneously developed this explanation. She was troubled by an apparent inconsistency and developed an analysis satisfactory to herself to account for it, rather than simply accepting the facts about the system uncritically.

where the top, bottom, and margins were, since the screen was smaller than a complete page. They wondered how to set the margins, since the familiar mechanical controls of the typewriter were missing. There was message information on the screen that they had not typed, and they wondered whether this would appear on their finished printed document.

In building new ideas on old knowledge, learners also draw on things they have just learned. They expect consistency: in learning a new operation that is similar or related to one they have already learned, they expect it to be carried out in a similar or related way. Unfortunately, participants did not always agree with designers about what operations were similar or related. Participants seemed to have a less sharply focused view, so that operations the designers treated as distinct tended to be blurred together by the learners.

In the menu system the keys that moved the cursor when entering text did not work on menu screens, as we have mentioned earlier. To the designers these were two distinct sets of operations: moving a reference point through a text string, and selecting a field on a menu. There is no a priori reason to suppose that these operations should be performed similarly, any more than sharpening a pencil should be similar to filling a pen. Empirically, however, it was clear that participants saw both operations as moving one thing, the cursor, around on the screen, and they made errors both by using menu operations on text and by using text operations on menus.

Learners spontaneously try to relate text editors to what they already know about typewriting. Where the correspondence works, it saves time and confusion in learning. Where it fails, it causes trouble. It may be possible to exploit more analogies between text editing and typewriters in designing office systems (we return to this point later).

Achieving consistency is difficult, and it is clear that designers already work hard to achieve it. But it appears that they cannot always anticipate how learners will group the operations provided or what they will expect to be consistent with what. User testing may be required to determine what relationship users see among the functions of the system.

3.5 Learners Have Trouble Following Directions

Participants made many kinds of errors in following seemingly clear instructions in the manuals. It was common for them to jump the gun, trying to do things before reaching the instructions that were provided. Half of the participants on the commercial system tried to sign on after seeing a quick demonstration but before reading the detailed instructions at the very beginning of the training manual; all failed. The protocol excerpt in the Appendix shows a learner trying to correct a typing error before reaching the relevant exercises in the manual. Participants sometimes tried to execute operations described in exercise previews, which were intended only to introduce the detailed, step-by-step instructions.

When the step-by-step instructions were used, other problems appeared. If an instruction, however clearly stated, conflicted with the learner's view of what was appropriate, it might be modified or abandoned. For example, one participant refused to use BACKSPACE as directed in an exercise, because she saw that some characters needed to be deleted, and she was sure that BACKSPACE would

In explaining away puzzles participants can convince themselves that all is well when the odd happenings they have noticed are really the evidence of disaster. One learner misread the instructions for typing in a letter and found herself moving the cursor from place to place on the screen, but not entering the actual text of the letter. She concluded that she was constructing a sort of template on the screen and that the text she was expecting would appear later. She carried on with the exercise rather than backing up and starting again.

Another participant was preparing a lease by replacing symbols in a form lease with names and addresses. She made a number of errors, so that some symbols were left in place, others were replaced by blanks, and the like. The learner was happy with this result, however, because a lease is a legal document, and one has to expect legal documents to look strange. She did not detect or correct any of the errors she had made.

Despite their unfamiliarity with computers, these learners were working hard to construct their own ideas about what they saw happening. Unfortunately, their ideas often diverged from what designers and manual writers intended (see [7, 14]). These spurious interpretations may be a response to a sort of knowledge vacuum: if learners knew more about what they were doing, they would construct more accurate interpretations of events.

But what can designers or writers do to help? We see no specific remedy. Exercises could give a clearer picture of the results learners should expect, in order to cut down on the number of errors that are just explained away. A style of training in which learners can test their own developing conceptions, rather than follow predetermined action sequences, might help as well. We discuss this further below.

3.4 Learners Generalize from What They Know

Not surprisingly, many ad hoc interpretations are adaptations of ideas learners already have. Prior experience with typewriters provides a ready source of expectations about how the text-processing system operates (see [4] for discussion of other sources). Other sources include the learner's evolving knowledge of text-editing procedures.

It is natural that learners try to relate how the text-processing system works to what they know about typewriters. On the positive side, participants did not have trouble typing basic alphanumeric characters, nor did they have trouble with the fact that characters appear on a video display rather than on paper. Other functions, however, reveal inappropriate expectations about how the text-processing system operates.

Participants were surprised that the SPACE bar, BACKSPACE, and RETURN keys not only moved the typing point, but also changed material they had already typed (see the example in the Appendix). The word-processing system we studied is always in insert mode, so that pressing SPACE inserts blank spaces, and RETURN inserts blank lines. On a typewriter these functions simply move the typing point. One participant was explicit about her expectations: "I wanted to move the cursor and . . . the old typewriter . . . I hit the SPACE BAR."

Participants also tried to relate the screen into which text was entered to a blank sheet of paper in a typewriter, but had trouble doing so. They wondered

not do this (actually, BACKSPACE on her system did delete characters, unlike typewriter BACKSPACE). She substituted another operation, which drastically disrupted the later flow of the exercise. Similar disruption often followed from simple oversight: a step skipped or repeated in general resulted in the remainder of an exercise producing errors or other unexpected results from which the learner could not recover.

These problems aside, the basic coordination of information required to carry out and learn from instructions was difficult for some participants. It was necessary to read instructions, find keys on the keyboard, follow the action on the screen, and think about what was going on. Though these demands may seem obvious, they were new to some participants. As one said: "You have to get used to looking at the monitor to see what happens when you press a key." Other participants did not examine output from exercises to see what they had just done.

One consequence of these difficulties may be that learners lose track of what they are trying to do or what they have learned. Evidence for this comes from statements participants made while working on exercises. Earlier we referred to examples like "What did we do?" or "I know I did something but I don't know what it is!" Others include "I'm getting confused because I'm not actually doing anything except following these directions!" or "Did that make any sense to you? It didn't to me!" Their questions were justified. As described earlier, performance on a simple transfer task, requiring only simple operations they had often carried out in exercises, was poor.

These misuses of instructions have complex causes. Some seem to arise from the participants' impatience with explanations and their eagerness to learn by doing rather than reading, and others from a mismatch between the participant's agenda of questions and the writer's planned sequence of answers. These difficulties might be eased if participants had greater control over the training activities.

3.6 Problems Interact

Earlier we discussed the learner who did not know about the critical RESET key: her keyboard was disabled, and so the keys she pressed had no effect. This problem was bad enough in itself, but it spawned others. She did not know that the keyboard was disabled, and as she tried out various keys she chalked up false conclusions about their ineffectiveness.

Another participant was trying to get a report on a recently completed task. She tried to type "yes" into a menu field to indicate that she wanted the report, but the system refused to accept her entry. She then tried typing capital "YES", despite having been told that the case of her entries was not important. When this failed, she concluded that she could not type "yes" because there was no report, and the system would therefore not allow her to request it. The real problem here was that the learner was not clearing the previous contents of the field, as was required by the system. She never recognized this problem because she could conceive of too many other things that could have gone wrong.

As these examples illustrate, problems are seldom encountered in tractable isolation, but rather tend to crop up in groups and form muddles. A problem that

looks utterly trivial to the designer may go unsolved because the learner cannot get the problem into a corner by itself. This has an important implication for design: the impact of problems cannot be fairly assessed in isolation. Designers apparently need to be aggressive in eliminating even seemingly minor rough spots, if they involve extra things the learner has to know or figure out.

3.7 Interface Features May Not Be Obvious

Many problems we have discussed, including how problems can interact, can be triggered by features of interface design that are not obvious or intuitive to learners. Prerequisite steps and feedback are particular occasions for error and misunderstanding.

In one system some menu fields could not be modified without pressing a special key before typing. Participants tended to go ahead and try to type in the field without pressing this key. On the other hand, once they understood what the cursor was they rarely tried to type without positioning the cursor. Both of these examples involve prerequisite steps to typing, yet one caused trouble and the other did not. Why?

We can speculate that learners accepted that cursor positioning was logically necessary to accomplish their goal. If they did not position the cursor, the system could not determine where they wished to type. On the other hand, there is no logical reason why they could not type directly into menu fields. The requirement to press the special key is arbitrary in that it cannot be derived from the goal of typing into the field but has to be learned as a requirement imposed by the system.

Feedback at best can fall short of being informative, and at worst can invite misleading interpretations. When participants selected the SIGN OFF option on a menu on one system, they immediately saw the SIGN ON menu on the screen. "But I wanted to sign off!" What happened was this: since signing off does not call for any information to be supplied by the system, there is no need for a SIGN OFF menu, and the system signs the participant off as soon as the request is made. Once the learner is signed off, the system is ready for the next user, so it puts up the SIGN ON menu.

Once one understands the sequence of events, one can interpret the SIGN ON menu as the signal that one has signed off: if one does not know what is happening, the feedback is quite misleading. Some learners thought they were being required to sign on again.

In the other system the feedback from a command is a READY message. This indicates that the command has been carried out but conveys no information about what it did. One participant was uncertain what the FILE command did, so she tried it out (it stored the document file she had been working on). The only response from the system was a new blank display with the message READY, leaving her none the wiser.

Other operations do not provide direct feedback but require users to press a key to get it. When a document is printed, for example, one system returns the display to a general selection menu and sends a print confirmation message to a message queue. The user has to press a key to display the message. This is convenient for an experienced user who may want to go to something else while his or her document is being printed in parallel. But new users, like some of our participants, did not realize that they had to request feedback by pressing a key. Moreover, the fact that the system presented them with the selection menu from which they started led them to question whether printing had been carried out. We can speculate that they expected something direct and obvious to indicate that their document had been printed.

These kinds of feedback are adequate for experienced users, since it is logically possible to infer what has happened, but they are of little help to the novice. The learner needs feedback that can be interpreted without much knowledge and without complex reasoning.

3.8 Help Facilities Do Not Always Help

Can a help facility solve these user problems? The experiences of the participants in this study make us doubtful. The commercially available word processor had a state-of-the-art help facility. For example, it had some sensitivity to the problem context from which it was called (thus relieving users, at least in principle, of having to describe what help they wanted). Thus users can position the cursor in a field of a menu (e.g., the field for naming a document in a menu for creating or revising a document) about which they want information and request help. Or they can get help for a current error message on the display by requesting help when it is on the screen without having to describe the problem.

Despite these features, the help facility did not prove useful. Sometimes no help was provided for a given operation, such as signing on. Sometimes learners could not understand the information provided, because of jargon, or could not find the particular points they needed among the many that were discussed. For example, one learner wanted to know how long a document name could be. When she requested help, she got a screen full of facts about naming documents, including the permitted length. But she could not find this piece of information without reading most of the screen, which she was unwilling to do.

Other failures reflect deeper problems. Learners often could not describe their problems well enough to use help, or they chose descriptions that did not match the categories offered. The participant in the Appendix, for example, wanted to bring two lines of text back together, rather than delete the blank line she had accidentally inserted between them. But there was no help on "bringing lines together." Later in this episode, after the participant had inserted more blank lines and spaces in her document (trying to move the cursor around inappropriately by using SPACE and RETURN), she considered requesting help but did not because "I'm not really sure which key I can get help for because it [the text] is all over the place."

Help is easiest to give for specific questions of information, but learners do not typically confront this kind of question. As we have seen, problems form muddles in which the apparent problem is often not the real one. The help system can not discern what the real confusion is.

One participant was having trouble retrieving a document. She was trying to do this using the menu for creating documents, but the system would not allow her to create a document that already existed. The help system suggested she try to delete the existing document and create a new one of the same name, but this

would have destroyed what she was trying to retrieve. Ironically, the participant was saved by another problem with the system. When she tried to delete the document, she was prevented from doing so because she had retrieved it successfully earlier in her session and had not properly filed it away again. Thus the help information, even had it been correct, could not be used because of a circumstance the help system could not anticipate. In general, it is very hard to provide suggestions that do not depend in a detailed way on context, and the help system cannot diagnose the context shrewdly enough.

As Clark [10] argues, designers of help systems have to decide whether they are providing tutorial information for the learner or reference information for the skilled user: they cannot effectively do both. The problems we observed were so serious that we doubt that help intended for learners is feasible for experienced users and the systems we studied.

4. GENERAL DISCUSSION

Learning to use a text editor on one's own is very difficult. The growth of specialized word-processing training services (e.g., [2]), as well as the concern expressed in trade journals (e.g., [21]) and media stories (e.g., [15]), testifies to the practical implications of these problems. The research reported here gives us insight into why these problems occur and suggestions for how to solve them.

New users lack knowledge about text editing. This is expressed in naive questions about, or implausible interpretations for, things they experience. Yet, at the same time, new users try to learn with energy and intelligence: we conclude that new users are *active* learners (see [7] for further discussion). They work hard to make sense out of what they are seeing. They build on what they know about typing, and they try to understand why the system does what it does and what patterns connect the parts of the interface.

Learners are also active in that they do not like to read explanations, but prefer to learn things by trying them out on their own. Moreover, even when they try to follow instructions that might seem to let them bypass explanations, they have trouble doing so. It is easy to get sidetracked and hard to recover. Trying to do so often forces them to figure things out on their own after all.

How can we design a text editor for new users who learn actively, that is, by trying things out rather than by reading? This is a challenge whose solution we can only speculate on at this point. But we close by sketching two key ideas that we hypothesize could help solve this problem.

4.1 Let the Learner Help

It may be possible to mobilize the energies of the learners themselves to solve some of the problems. Training materials might be devised that give the learners a framework for learning by exploring the system (trying things out on their own), rather than by reading explanations or following detailed rote instructions.

For example, we might reinforce active involvement in learning with materials that provide only information that the learner could not figure out from trying to use the system. This would reduce the amount of reading required and encourage the learner's interest in, and attention to, the training materials. We might also present information about key subtasks in an *unordered* way (perhaps on separate cards rather than on bound pages) in order to encourage the learner to do more organizing of the steps in a task, rather than passively following a prescribed sequence of steps.

We hypothesize that these changes could help with the problem of not learning from instructions. If learning tasks are self-generated, less energy may go into the mechanics of following instructions, and more into thinking that more closely resembles that needed to peform real work. Preliminary research indicates that such an approach can facilitate learning (see [8]), although these hypotheses remain to be fully tested.

4.2 Reduce the Need to Teach

Whether we change our approach to training along these lines, along different lines, or not at all, we believe that progress will require reducing the sheer quantity of material that users must be taught. Reducing the amount of material may in turn require that the text-editing interface itself be simplified so that less must be explained. Our results point to three areas in which designers might work to simplify interface design (see [5, 6] for further discussion of these issues).

4.2.1 *Replace Teaching by Knowing.* As we have seen, learners try to use what they know about typing when they encounter a text editor. This can be useful because learners do not need to learn what they already know. We should try to design in more analogies between the editor and the typewriter. A parallel can be drawn with Zloof's Query-by-Example [25], a system that successfully exploits the familiar concept of tables as a representation for data. (See also [23] for other examples of user models in designing a professional work station.)

On the other hand, there are obviously limits to the extent to which a new tool can usefully mimic an old one. New concepts will inevitably be needed, and users need to know where familiar concepts leave off and new ones take over. For further discussion see [4], [9], [20], [3], [16], and [24].

4.2.2 *Replace Teaching by Guessing.* If users can guess how to do something, they do not have to be told. We have described earlier some design features that make guessing hard. When functions that the learner thinks are related must be done in unrelated ways, the learner will guess wrong. If a function requires a prerequisite operation that is not obvious, it will be missed. User testing is probably the only way to determine where users expect consistency and what operations they find obvious.

4.2.3 *Replace Teaching by Exploration.* If learners' first guesses are not correct, they may still be able to figure out what to do. To do so, they have to be able to tell what happened when they tried out their guesses, and they have to be able to recover from the effects so they can try something else. Today, messages and other feedback from the system may be too difficult to interpret or may not actually say what has happened, as in the case of the system that indicated when an operation was complete but not what it had done. Having figured out what has happened, the learner will often need to repair some damage. New design ideas are badly needed in this area, since at present error recovery usually requires considerable knowledge of the system, just what the learner does not have.

5. CONCLUSION

This study was an exploratory survey of major problems computer-naive people have learning to use text editors. The burden of our results is partly negative: learning is hard, and it is hard for many reasons. As designers or writers we may find it hard to grasp the complexity of the task. But seeing the reasons in detail should allow us to deal with them and help us to allocate our energy to the crucial areas in the design of interfaces and training materials.

APPENDIX. AN EXAMPLE OF PROTOCOL DATA

We present below an excerpt from a thinking-aloud protocol. It has been transcribed from a video recording of a participant beginning a practice exercise on cursor movement. The exercise involves typing two paragraphs and then following instructions for moving the cursor around the file. (Interpretations and descriptions of what the learner is doing are given in parentheses.)

The excerpt illustrates three typical problems. First, the participant is uncertain about the purposes of the practice exercise. She wants to correct typing errors, but the exercise is about cursor movement (a prerequisite for revising, which comes later in the chapter). This is an example of how participants' goals can mismatch the order of topics in the manual.

Second, when the participant makes an error, she decides to try to figure out how to correct it on her own (at the end of the first sentence, which is the third line of the file, she types a comma instead of the required period).

Finally, the participant gets into trouble by trying to move the cursor around with the space bar and return key, rather than the appropriate cursor movement keys. Unlike the corresponding typewriter keys, these function keys not only move the cursor but insert spaces and blank lines. (The experimenter's comments are indicated by "E;".)

E: What are you thinking?

P: I'm trying to figure out what [this] exercise is supposed to be [for]—for line advance? [It is] supposed to be an exercise on errors. But am I supposed to be trying to make errors and then move back?

P: (Participant types two lines. At the end of the second line, she types a comma instead of a period and then presses return which positions the cursor at the beginning of a new blank line. Participant notices the typing error.)

P: Oh. I see. So now . . . .

E: What are you thinking?

P: I made a mistake up here. Now if I want to go back, I guess I would . . . (looks in manual for information.)

E: What are you looking at? Page 3–4? (Participant says nothing.) What is that telling you?

P: Well, I'm trying to figure out how to go back to correct that mistake. Am I supposed to correct my mistakes yet? Or am I supposed to just not worry about the mistakes? Or . . . I'm going to try to go back.

P: (Participant presses backspace and incurs an error which is signaled by a beep. This is because backspace will not move the cursor beyond the left edge of the screen.)

P: Woo! It didn't like that!

P: (Participant presses correct key to move cursor up to line with typing mistake.)

E: Okay. What did you hit?

P: I pressed (identifies key).

E: On page 3–4 again? What's that telling you?

P: I'm still trying to figure out ... (reads instructions) "press and hold down (cursor key) until the cursor moves to first line." That's a step but ... (Participant seems to be trying to adapt manual instructions to her problem.)

P: (Hits the space bar which inserts a space at the beginning of the line. Then uses backspace which deletes space.)

E: You hit a space and backspace?

P: Yes. I'm just going to leave that mistake and press return.

P: (The cursor is at the beginning of the line. When participant presses return a new blank line is inserted between that line and the previous one, in effect "splitting" her lines.)

P: Whoa!

E: What are you thinking?

P: I didn't know it was going to do that. Wonder how I can bring it back? (Hits a key labeled "code".)

E: Okay. What are you thinking?

P: I pressed code ... (does not continue talking).

E: What are you thinking?

P: I'm going to try to bring it back to where it was.

E: Bring what back?

P: Bring back the line, although I'm not really sure if it matters ... [there is a] space in between there. I press return ....

P: (Participant presses a coded version of the return key which inserts yet another blank line.)

P: It went even further. I'm having difficulty because I'm trying to bring it back up.

P: (Participant uses cursor key to move cursor back down to the line of text that she wants to rejoin with the previous line.)

P: I'm trying to remember how to bring it back. I don't even know if it matters if it has a space in between. I can just continue typing.

P: (Participant advances to the next empty line and continues to type without correcting either the typing error or the blank line problem.)

ACKNOWLEDGMENTS

We thank John Gould and Stephen Boies for their useful comments on earlier drafts of this paper, and three anonymous reviewers for comments that helped improve the final version.

REFERENCES

1. BARNARD, P., HAMMOND, N., MORTON, J., LONG, J., AND CLARK, I. Consistency and compatability in human-computer dialogue. *Int. J. Man-Mach. Stud. 15*, 1 (1981), 87–134.
2. BENDER, D. Meeting a new demand. *Gannett Westchester Newspapers*, April 25, 1982, p. B1-B3.
3. BLACK, J., AND SEBRECHTS, M. Facilitating human-computer communication. *J. Appl. Psycholinguist. Res. 2*, 2 (1981), 150–177. 1982.
4. BOTT, R. A study of complex learning: Theory and methodology. CHIP Rep. 82, Center for Human Information Processing, Univ. of Calif. at San Diego, La Jolla, Calif, 1979.
5. CARROLL, J.M. Learning, using, and designing command paradigms. *Human Learning: J. Pract. Res. Appl. 1* (1982), 31–62.
6. CARROLL, J.M., AND MACK, R. Learning to use a word processor: By doing, by thinking, and by knowing. In *Human Factors in Computer Systems*, J. Thomas and M. Schneider (Eds.). Ablex, Norwood, N.J., 1983.
7. CARROLL, J.M., AND MACK, R. Actively learning to use a word processor. In *Cognitive Aspects of Skilled Typewriting*, W. Cooper (Ed.). Springer-Verlag, New York, 1983.
8. CARROLL, J.M., AND MACK, R. Learning to use a word processor by guided exploration. Presented at the Psychonomic Society Conf. Minneapolis, Minn. Nov. 11-13, 1982.
9. CARROLL, J.M., AND THOMAS, J.C. Metaphor and the cognitive representation of computing systems. *IEEE Trans. Syst. Man Cybern. SMC-12* (1982), 107–116.
10. CLARK, I.A. How to help 'HELP' help. Tech. Rep. HF022, IBM United Kingdom Laboratories, Hursley Park, Winchester, Hampshire, England, 1982.
11. ERICSSON, K., AND SIMON, H. Verbal reports as data. *Psychol. Rev. 87* 3 (1980), 215–251.
12. GALITZ, W. *Human Factors in Office Automation*. Life Office Management Association, Atlanta, Ga, 1980.
13. LEWIS, C. Using the "Thinking aloud" method in cognitive interface design. Res. Rep. RC 9265, IBM Thomas J. Watson Research Center, Yorktown Heights, N.Y., Feb. 1982.
14. LEWIS, C., AND MACK, R. The role of abduction in learning to use text-processing systems. Presented at the annual meeting of the American Educational Research Association, New York, Mar. 19-24, 1982.
15. LINSCOTT, J. Here's the word on word processing. *New York Daily News*, March 9, 1982.
16. MAYER, R.E. The psychology of how novices learn computer programming. *ACM Comput. Surv. 13*, 1 (Mar. 1981), 121–141.
17. MILLER, L., AND THOMAS, J. Behavioral issues in the use of interactive systems. *Int. J. Man-Mach. Stud. 9*, 5 (1977), 509–536.
18. NEWELL, A., AND SIMON, H. *Human Problem Solving*. Prentice-Hall, Englewood Cliffs, N.J., 1972.
19. NISBETT, R., AND WILSON, T. Telling more than we can know: Verbal reports on mental processes. *Psychol. Rev. 84*, 3 (1977), 231–259.
20. RUMELHART, D., AND NORMAN, D. Analogical processes in learning. In *Cognitive Skills and Their Acquisition*, J. Anderson (Ed.). Lawrence Erlbaum, Hillsdale, N.J., 1981.
21. SEYBOLD, J. Training and support: Shifting the responsibility. *Seybold Rep. on Word Processing 4*, 1 (Jan. 1981).
22. SHNEIDERMAN, B. *Software Psychology: Human Factors in Computer and Information Systems*. Winthrop Publishers, Cambridge, Mass, 1980.
23. SMITH, D., IRBY, C., KIMBAL, R., VERPLANK, B., AND HARSLEM, E. Designing the Star user interface. *Byte* (Apr. 1982), 242–282.
24. YOUNG, R. The machine inside the machine: Users' models of pocket calculators. *Int. J. Man-Mach. Stud. 15* (1981), 51–85.
25. ZLOOF, M. Query-by-Example: A data base language. *IBM Syst. J. 16*, 4 (1977), 324–343.

Learning to Use a Word Processor: By Doing, by Thinking, and by Knowing

JOHN M. CARROLL
ROBERT L. MACK

Learning to use a word processor provides a study of real complex human learning that is fundamentally "active," driven by the initiatives of the learner—which are, in turn, based on extensive domain-specific knowledge and skill, and on reasoning processes which are systematic yet highly creative. State-of-the-art application systems and their training materials presuppose "passive" learners and are—to that extent—unusable. Some general design implications of active learning were discussed.

Suppose that people learned "passively." That is, suppose that designers of systems and of their training materials could place new users in a carefully programmed learning environment with confidence that through this experience new users would become skilled experts. These passive learners would presumably read descriptions and explanations of the system's functional capabilities; they would carefully follow exercises to drill and develop their skill and understanding; and gradually these experiences would converge on a mature stereotype of skill and understanding.

In point of fact, the above is pretty much what designers of state-of-the-art application systems and training material have supposed. Were this supposition correct, the human factors of computer systems would be in good shape today: the technology for "passive" learning of systems is well developed. But unfortunately, the supposition is almost totally wrong. As we will argue here, people learn *actively* not passively. The problems new users have with existent systems and training are testimony to this contention. That people do learn to use such systems via such training programs is testimony to the adaptability and intellectual tenacity of people. This point will also be amply illustrated in our discussion.

In order to be more usable, future application systems and their training support will need to accommodate the real (= "active") learner, rather than what might have been—from the perspective of the system designer and manual writer—the ideal (= "passive") learner. Toward the end of this chapter we will sketch some general design proposals along these lines and attempt to theoretically bring our work to bear on the analysis of human behavior and experience in realistic situations that is developing in current Cognitive Science (Norman, 1981).

METHOD AND OVERVIEW

The research discussed consists of studies of office personnel learning to use word processing equipment. In this chapter, we are not concerned with issues regarding particular systems (see Mack, Lewis, & Carroll, 1983). Our principal focus will be on the learning strategies (actually the classes of learning strategies) we have identified in the course of this work. The three classes of strategies we address are learning by doing, learning by thinking, and learning by knowing.

Our view is that these are natural—albeit complex—strategies for people to adopt when confronted by a learning task of nontrivial complexity. The learners we have studied are almost entirely "innocent" with respect to computer technology. In the context of learner innocence, we argue, these "natural" strategies entail severe and wide ranging learning problems. Analysis of these problems, in turn, suggests research directions for the analysis of real human learning within contemporary cognitive science and practical directions in which computer systems, and the educational technologies that support their training and use might evolve.

The Learners and Their Task

In this research project, ten office temporaries spent four half-days learning to use one of two possible word processing systems in our laboratory. Four were given a subset of the word processing operations for a general purpose, command-based system. The other six were asked to learn basic functions of a commercially available word processor which was menu-based.

These people were highly experienced in routine office work, but quite naive with respect to computers in general and word processing systems in particular. We asked them to imagine a scenario in which a word processing system had recently been introduced to their office, and they had been asked to be the first to learn it (to then pass this knowledge on to colleagues). The point was that they were to learn to use the system using the training materials that accompany it as their only resource. The manual we used was designed to be used as the nucleus of a "self-study" training method, although, in fact, such material is rarely used in complete isolation from other methods such as tutorial assistance (which is not surprising in light of our results, see below).

The materials we asked our learners to study addressed basic letter entry and revision skills (including formatting, printing, document retrieval, and document merging) and, in the case of the commercially available system, the use of command menus, the interpretation of messages, and the use of the on-line Help facility.

Learners spent varying amounts of time with this task, but we stopped them in any case after about 12 hours in order to ask them to try a simple "transfer task," involving typing in, revising, formatting, and then printing out a one-page letter. This transfer task was not part of the self-study manual; it served as a sort of benchmark achievement test. Finally, we asked learners about their prior work background, about specific queries that occurred to us during the course of the learning sessions, and about their overall impressions of the system and the experience.

Our concern here is not to detail the results of the project; they can be found in Mack et al. (1983). Suffice it to say that a great many problems cropped up during the sessions and that even after the 12 hours or so of self-study learning not a single learner was able to complete the transfer task without some kind of serious difficulty in editing subtasks such as document creation, retrieval or printing, or in actually entering and revising text.

Two very general points should be stressed about this project. First, the domain in which we studied learning is drawn from the real world of actual learning that real people must cope with: we studied real word processing systems, real training books, and users drawn from the population to whom the system and the books were targeted. We take this project to constitute an "ecologically valid" investigation of human learning. Second, the systems and the manuals which were our materials for this work are state-of-the-art. Thus, our findings—especially those pertaining to learner problems—are not abstract effects of "materials," but rather have immediate and specific practical implications for the design of technology in the word processing domain (see Mack et al., 1983).

Thinking Aloud

Our method involved prompting learners to "think aloud" as they worked through the training materials. They were to report questions that were raised in their minds, plans and strategies they felt they might

be considering or following out, and inferences and knowledge that might have been brought to awareness by ongoing experiences. We remained with the learners to keep them talking and to intervene, if at any time it appeared that a problem was so grave that a learner might leave the experiment if we did not help out. Our prompting remained nondirective, and indeed once learners got going we needed to prompt very infrequently at all. We had to actually intervene rarely.

Throughout the learning sessions, video and sound recordings were made (in what we hoped was an unobtrusive manner). Our analysis consisted first of an enumeration of "critical incidents" which were cataloged and classified in various ways. This was constrained by the consensus of the three experimenters (the authors and Clayton Lewis) The chief goal of this was to form a picture of the typical experience of a learner, and it is this induced "prototype" learning experience to which we will refer in what follows (for details, see Mack et al., 1983). Our method of reporting will be to cite induced generalizations and to illustrate these by concrete examples transcribed from our audio recordings.

We are aware that the thinking aloud technique has been of great methodological interest recently, but this topic lies outside the scope of the present study (see Ericsson & Simon, 1980; Nisbett & Wilson, 1977).

How People Learn

Perhaps the most apt description of the world of the new user of a word processor is that often quoted phrase of William James: "a bloomin' buzzin' confusion." People in this situation see many things going on, but they do not know which of these is relevant to their current concerns. Indeed, they do not know if their current concerns are the appropriate concerns for them to have. The learner reads something in the manual; sees something on the display; and must try to connect the two, to integrate, to interpret. It would be unsurprising to find that people in such a situation suffer conceptual—or even physical—paralysis. They have so little basis on which to act.

And yet people do act. Indeed, perhaps the most pervasive tendency we have observed is that people simply strike out into the unknown. If the rich and diverse sources of available information cannot be interpreted, then some of these will be ignored. If something *can* be interpreted (no matter how specious the basis for this interpretation), then it will be interpreted. Ad hoc theories are hastily assembled out these odds and ends of partially relevant and partially extraneous generalization. And these "theories" are used for further prediction. Whatever initial confusions get into such a process, it is easy to see that they are at the mercy of an at least partially negative feedback loop: things quite often get worse before they get better.

TABLE 1
Signing on the Word Processing System

(1) *Learner has been trying to type the letter string "abc" on display in order to observe cursor movement and practice backspacing. She is typing this string on the operator name field for the sign-on menu. Due to a number of errors which include prematurely trying to sign-on with "abc" as the incorrect—and inadvertent—operator name, the learner decides to simply start over.*

L: So now let's see. Could I turn it off and start all over? That's what I would do. Will it hurt anything?
E: You're in control.
L: Let's see what happens. If I were all alone that's what I would do.
E: Yup! You're all alone!

Powers off, and immediately back on. A new sign-on menu display appears.

(2) *Correctly types operator name "learner6" in the sign-on menu field labeled "operator name."*

L: Uh, the six [i.e., of "learner6"] was right next to it [i.e., no space] and it entered without typing anything. Do I have to make it, press "enter" to make it stay? No. Didn't say anything about that so we will forget about that.

Reference unclear, but she does not "enter" the filled-in sign-on menu. Instead, she continues with the next exercise, involving typing the letters "abc" and backspacing. This is intended to be done on the sign-on menu to illustrate how one can correct mistakes made while filling in menu parameters.

(3) L: Okay now we are off. [Reads aloud] "If you have worked with this type "abc" and watch the cursor move."

Now she types "abc" right after the operator name which causes an error signalled several ways: audio message, a message about exceeding the length of the menu field, an indicator light signaling the need to take corrective action (labeled "reset/help"), and a locked keyboard which can only be unlocked by pressing a reset key.

L: Whoops!
E: What do you think happened then?
L: A bell rang. A buzzer or something.

(4) L: *Reads instructions on Sign-on menu display.* "Enter to finish" Okay let's see what happens. [Presses the enter key]

E: You pressed enter?
L: I pressed enter and nothing happened. [The keyboard is locked]

Reads more fragments of manual, stops at: "Ask your training administrator for help." How do I get the menu? Request the menu again. All right. Press request, cancel.

Presses keys labeled request and cancel, to no effect because of the locked keyboard. Reference to "the menu" is not clear but may reflect her current understanding that she has not signed on yet or that she needs some other kind of display to proceed.

Okay. I didn't get the original menu to press anything.

Learner believes she needs a different menu, one which lists the tasks or commands available (e.g., create or retrieve or print a document). It appears after one completes sign-on.

Oh "enter" it. Nothing.

Designers of word processors and training technology probably would have liked things to have been different. The easiest way to teach someone something is, after all, to tell them. However, what we see in the learning-to-use-a-word-processor situation is that people are so busy trying things out, thinking things through, and trying to relate what they already know (or believe they know) to what is going on that they often do not notice the small voice of structured instruction crying out to them from behind the manual and the system interface.

What's wrong? We would argue that the learning practices people adopt here are typical, and in many situations adaptive. The problem in this particular learning situation is that new learners of word processors are *innocent* in the extreme. Each feature of a word processing system may indeed have a sensible design rationale from the viewpoint of the systems' engineer, but this rationale is frequently far beyond the grasp of the new user. "Word processor," so far as we know, is not a natural concept. People who do not know about word processors have little, possibly nothing, to refer to in trying to actively learn to use such things. Innocence turns reasonable learning strategies into learning problems. This is what this study is about.

LEARNING BY DOING

Our learners relentlessly wanted to learn by trying things out rather than by reading about how to do them. In part this was impatience: they were reluctant to read a lot of explanation or get bogged down following meticulous directions. But it also devolved from mismatched goals: Learners wanted to discover how to do specific things at particular times, and this did not always accord with the sequence in which topics were treated in the manual.

Jumping the Gun

Half of our learners impatiently tried to sign on to the system before reading how to do so. Table 1 presents highlights of one such learner. The learner had reached a point in the manual which showed the sign on display. This was intended as orientation and included no instruction about how to sign on.

The learner immediately incurs a number of errors which prevent her from signing on easily, and she is forced to try out various actions on her own initiative in order to deal with these ancillary problems. Indeed, it is only after considerable exploration of keys and commands that she is able to sign on. The specific character of her errors, and the exploration

TABLE 1—*Continued*

Presses enter, which would have the effect of bringing up another display, but to no effect because of locked keyboard.

Now presses request key which is not relevant to anything here.

E: You pressed request?

L: Request and enter, trying to find that menu page because this page is not; I don't know how to get off this page. *Not clear what she is referring to here, but clearly she believes that she must have a different display to work on.*

All right. Come on. *Reads more fragments of manual referring to functions which advance and return the function from one menu parameter field to another.*

Okay. Pressed that.

E: Variable advance?

L: Right. "Watch the cursor . . ." Nothing. [*Keyboard is still locked.*] Great!

E: Okay what are you pressing there?

L: Variable Advance. [*then*] "Enter" to see if anything different might happen. Okay. Let's try it once more. Nothing!

(5) Still nothing. Okay. If I wanted to go back I would use the . . . ". . . look on the front . . ." Where is the "code" key? Now I'm trying the variable advance key and the code key to see if anything happens. Nothing happens! For all the punching I'm doing nothing at all is happening.

E: Do you have any idea why that might be?

L: Ah, I can't understand why it isn't entering, even entering the mistakes if I'm making mistakes. It's coming up with nothing. They did not tell me to get off this page.

New Audio Tape—some interaction may have been lost.

Now I'm touching the backspace key and it is not erasing anything. [*because keyboard remains locked*] So I have made some kind of error that has locked everything in here.

E: Nothing seems to be working?

(6) L: Right. Reset/Help? [*Presses the reset key, which is the correct remedy*]

E: Pressing reset?

L: I pressed reset/help to see what would happen there.

E: What do you think happened?

L: Nothing, really. [*In fact, the reset/help indicator light went off, signaling the unlocking of keyboard.*]

E: Why did you press that?

L: I'm trying to get back to a beginning. To start over.

All right. What would happen if I put it on "test"? *Referring to a button on the display unit which is labelled "test status." It is used to diagnose problems with the unit. It is totally irrelevant here.*

Turns test status "on" and a diagnostic pattern overlays screen.

Beautiful!

E: What happened?

TABLE 1—*Continued*

L: I decided to put it on test. Status is "test" rather than normal. Now let's see what happens if you backspace.

Backspace works and she does so, deleting the incorrect string "learner6abc."

Oh, my gosh, are you sure this isn't hurting everything. Oh, hey, hurrah! Good! Very good! Now we are in business.

Now if we backspace, it takes it off. Okay. Fine. Now where did it tell me that I should have started at "test"?

(7) [*Sometime later the learner is reading the manual.*]

E: Can you summarize what you were just doing there?

L: Well I was looking at this [*page*] 1–8. I was looking at this diagram and it says "The reset/help indicator is on." So then I figured out that these are indicators. I didn't know that before this. *Summarizes what other indicator lights mean.*

Now I pressed the correct key and nothing happened, which is exactly what they tell you in the directions will happen. "When you are in a reset [*condition*] you cannot move the cursor or type anything." Now this was my probem before. But I wasn't up to page 1–9 so I didn't know that if the reset/help key, uh indicator is on the machine is going to do nothing. So you need to press . . .

E: Was that your problem before?

L: Yes.

E: Huh?

L: I didn't realize that it would not act as long as that was on, that I have to do something to get it back to acting again. Okay. To be able to continue you need to press the reset key. So I press that. Now the . . . did they call it a code? An indicator. The indicator went off. The reset/help indicator went off. So evidentally we are back in business.

(8) Well, um. Do you want . . . maybe I should go back and put it on normal and see if I could do the same thing?

E: Well, you're in control.

Puts test status button on "normal" setting. Now it's on "normal." Let's do everything we did and see if it will work on this because we may still have been on the reset/help button over there. I don't know.

We'll type the "abc" [*types "abc" in the operator name sign-on menu field*] and see what happens. Then we'll try to backspace [*does so, deleting the "abc" she has just typed*] Does that alright. We'll go backwards and do the things they told us to do.

Tries function to advance the cursor to a new menu field. Which moves the cursor. Now they want us to move back. We'll code it in and we're back. [i.e., when user uses cursor advance function in conjunction with a code key, the cursor returns or moves up to the next menu field]

Okay. I'm running back through the instructions and it is working with it set on "normal." [*Reads fragments of manual—repeats exercise on making "invalid key" errors and pressing reset*] Okay I could have done the exercise on "normal."

E: Is that what you concluded?

L: That's what I concluded. Evidently when I heard the bell before and I didn't

TABLE 1—Continued

know that the reset/help indicator was on or didn't realize what was happening in that column. In other words I got into trouble before I got to [page] 1–8! So now we know why nothing was registering because I hadn't read on page 1–9 that I had to press the reset key.

Okay. Now I am going on to exercise two. We're going to find out how to sign on.

At this point begins following directions to sign-on.

TABLE 2
Correcting a Typing Mistake Prematurely

(1) E: What are you thinking?
L: I'm trying to figure out what exercise is supposed to be for [*pause*] line advance? Supposed to be an exercise on errors, but am I supposed to be trying to make errors and then move back?

Types first three lines of file. At end of third line, types comma instead of a period. Realizes her mistake after she has already carrier returned. Wants to know how to move the cursor back to make the correction.

(2) Oh, I see, so now . . .
E: What are you thinking?
L: I made a mistake up here, now if I want to go back I guess I would. . . . *Looks in the manual for information.*
E: What are you looking at, page 3–4? [*Pause*] What is that telling you?
L: Well, I'm trying to figure out how I can go back to correct that mistake. Am I supposed to correct my mistake yet, or am I supposed to just not worry about the mistakes or . . . I'm going to try to go back.

(3) *Backspaces with the cursor at the beginning of current line in order to move cursor back to immediately preceding line. This is not allowed and incurs a beep error message.* Oh! It didn't like that.

(4) *Presses line return, which moves the cursor to the beginning of the previous sentence with the comma which she wants to correct.*
E: OK, what did you hit?
L: I pressed line return.

A function that moves the cursor up one line
E: On page 3–4 again, what's that telling you?
L: I'm still trying to figure out . . . press and hold down line return until the cursor moves to the first line . . . that's a step but. . . . *Trying to adapt the manual instructions to her situation.*

(5) *Hits the space bar to move the cursor to the right through the line, which puts a space at the beginning of the line. Then immediately backspaces, which deletes it.*
E: You hit a space then a backspace?
Pressing backspace deletes the unintended spaces at the beginning of the line.
L: Yes. I'm just going to leave that mistake and press return.

(6) *The cursor is at the beginning of the third line, so when she presses return she inserts a blank line above it.*
Whoa!
E: OK, what are you thinking?
L: I didn't know it was going to do that. Wonder how I can bring it back.

(7) *Hits code key.*
E: What did you hit?
L: I pressed code . . . .

For example, in segment 2 the learner has typed her operator identification but she does not immediately realize that she must press the "enter" key to execute the sign on task. When she later tries the enter key (segment 4) she has in the meantime incurred an additional error that has locked the keyboard (segment 3). Hence, enter has no effect after all. In segment 5 she begins to appreciate that there is a problem after trying out a number of other function keys to no avail (e.g., a backspace to delete the erroneous typed parameter entry). Finally, in segment 6 the learner manages to solve the locked keyboard problem, but she confuses that action with an immediately following—and perhaps some salient—operation (involving a "Test Status" key) and so misinterprets the solution to her problem.

Jumping the gun is not always traceable to "mere" impatience. Often learners strike out on their own because their specific goals do not match those implied by the manual designers. As the first few segments of Table 2 reveal, the learner is not certain of the point of the exercise. She wants very much to learn how to correct typing errors but this topic is not covered until later. The current practice exercise is about a prerequisite cursor movement skill.

The learner's uncertainty about the exercise and her own specific concerns encourage her to try correcting a typing error on her own (beginning of segment 2). However, her attempt fails because she has not yet learned how to correct typing errors (it involves positioning the cursor and using backspace or delete keys), and is not able to work out how to do so from what she already has learned or can guess. Indeed, the learner ultimately inserts blank lines into her text (segment 6) and botches the exercise. These errors arise because she incorrectly tries to move the cursor using the space and return keys (segments 5 and 6, respectively) which are not appropriate on the word processing system (i.e., these keys actually change what one has typed because the system is always in insert mode, that is, spaces and line breaks are inserted into the text line wherever the cursor happens to be).

Passive Learning

When learners do not, or cannot, follow directions the problems that arise can result in their losing track of what they are trying to do. It is likely, of course, that this loss of task orientation contributes to the overall failure of learning—as indicated by the trouble all learners had applying their learning experiences to the routine typing "transfer task" after training.

What is more surprising perhaps is that even when learners were able to successfully follow instruction sequences out, they still seemed to experience a loss of task orientation, as evidenced by comments like: "What did we do?" "I know I did something, but I don't know what it is!" or "I'm getting confused because I'm not actually doing anything except following these directions." For these subjects, the overall orientation toward accomplishing meaningful tasks (e.g., type a letter, print something out) has been subverted by a narrower orientation toward following out a sequence of instructions.

This is ironic, since self-study educational technology is predicated upon learning-by-doing mix of exposition and practice. The materials we used provided expository information about how to do things with the word processing system along side of step-by-step practice with those procedures. The problem seems to be that "learning by doing" means different things to manual designers and new users: following programmed exercises is "active" from the viewpoint of the designers but "passive" from the viewpoint of the learners. Unfortunately for the learners, their innocence about computers prevents them from actively learning by doing on their own with much success—at least given state-of-the-art system/training constellations.

LEARNING BY THINKING

Just as learners take the initiative to try things on their own, so also are they active in trying to make sense of their experience with the system. Learning passively by rote assimilation of information is atypical. Rather, learners actively try to develop hypotheses about why it operates the way it does. These quests after meaning can be triggered by new and salient facts. They can be forced by discrepancies between what is expected and what actually happens. They can be structured by the learner's personal agenda of goals and queries, referred to as new problems arise. And they can be resolved by analysis into elementary procedures in the context of some word processing goal. In each case, learners' lack of knowledge about word processing makes it difficult for them to rea-

TABLE 2—*Continued*

E: What are you thinking?
L: I'm going to try to bring it back to where it was.
E: Bring what back?
L: Bring back the line, although I'm not really sure if it matters ... space in between there. [*points to blank line*] I press return ...

(8) *Presses required return and inserts yet another empty line. Don't go any further! I'm having difficulty because I'm trying to bring it back up.*

Uses line advance to move cursor down to the line that needs to be "moved back up."

I'm trying to remember how to bring it back. I don't even know if it matters if it has a space in between. I can just continue typing.

Instruction Sequences Are Fragile

Learning by trying things out according to a personal agenda of needs and goals is not merely a preference. Learners who try to follow out manual instructions are often unable to do so. The instruction sequences are fragile in the sense that it is easy to get sidetracked and there is no provision in them for recovery. One example is a learner who inadvertently paginated (reformatted) a document at the beginning of an exercise on revising documents. This not only rearranged the lines in the file to make right margins even, it also stored the document away. The learner had not yet learned how to retrieve documents and the manual itself provided no recovery information for this type of error. Accordingly, she was forced to try to discover how to retrieve the document on her own. She was ultimately unable to do so and we had to intervene.

Once we restored the document to her display, she was faced with an equally staggering problem: the pagination operation had rearranged the lines of her file so that the revising instructions did not refer to the same document. An experienced user who understood reformatting could have reinterpreted the instructions and adapted them to this rearranged text. But this learner had no idea what she had done, and thus was hopelessly puzzled by the fact that the instructions seemed to be wrong.

The fragility of instruction sequences, coupled with the propensity of learners to try to recover by initiating exploratory forays, can result in problem tangles: Learners, who may not even fully understand the individual operations, have little basis for appreciating the subtle interdependence of clusters of word processor operations. They may be unable to diagnose or even recognize the problems they encounter.

son out coherent solutions that accurately represent the objective operation of the word processor.

Constructing Interpretations

Because learners have no basis for recognizing and ruling out irrelevant connections, their interpretations of word processing systems are often influenced by spurious connections between what they think they need and what they perceive. The protocol example in Table 3 provides an example.

A learner is trying to find some way of using a "create document" command to retrieve a document (beginning of segment 2). The command is initiated by filling in parameters of a create document task menu. However, "create document" won't retrieve a document that already exists. Hence, when she fills in the name of the stored document (toward the end of segment 2), she incurs an error. Because the learner does not know what is relevant to getting a document back, she grasps for other possibilities (segments 6–8). The word "number" in a menu parameter called "document charge number" suggests to her that typing in page numbers will retrieve those pages for her. The word "originator" in the parameter called "document originator" suggests that typing in her operator name might somehow tell the system she wants her document. Neither parameter has anything to do with document retrieval, and both merely evoke further errors.

Learners are often faced with situations where they perceive a need to interpret some fact or observation in order to make sense of it. Often these interpretations are not necessary for understanding how to do something, but simply reflect their desire to *make sense of their experience.* For example, more than one learner was troubled by an inconsistency in the functions which are used to move the cursor around the screen. One set of functions is used to move the cursor within a menu display, while another set is used to move it around a typing display. The learner reconciled herself to the distinction by reasoning that a cursor movement function which moved the cursor from one line of a document file to another would not work in a menu display, because there could be more than one field on a line of a menu and she decided the function would not be able to move from one field to another *within* a line of a menu. In both cases, the learners could have simply accepted the way things were accomplished. Instead, they tried to construct rationales for why things were done the way they were.

In other cases, learners are faced with the need to *interpret discrepancies* between what happens to them, and what they think should happen. Because they lack knowledge about how the system operates, these ex-

---

TABLE 3
Not Knowing What Is Relevant to Retrieving a Document

(1) L: Did that make any sense to you? It didn't to me. I don't know why we had to do that, that was ridiculous. Now, let's see how do we get the pages back, that's going to be fun.

(2) *In a selection menu listing things users can do, learner presses enter to bring up a menu which when filled in and entered will create a new document file.*
You know what it's probably going to do now, it's going to tell me that there is a memo in there already. [*She is correct: i.e., she has already created a document named "Memo"; she wants to retrieve, not create this*]

Looks in manual for help.

E: What are you thinking?
L: Well, they were supposed to tell me anyway how to get these pages that I just lost.

In the create document menu she types the name of the document that she wants to get back. A message, "document name already exists," appears.

Document name already exists, I knew that was going to happen because I just typed it in.

(3) *Presses some other keys.*
I don't know how to do this.
E: What did you just press there?
L: Reset.
E: And before that?
L: This again, cancel [*which has no effect when the selection menu for tasks like create or revise is on the display, because there is nothing to cancel*].
Request. Presses request, cursor in now on "request line."
I'm just going to type "memo1" and press page return to see if it comes up [*"memo1" is the name of the document*]
Presses request. Looks in manual for help.
E: What are you looking up?

(4) L: I might have to look it up in one of these documents [*referring to tasks listed on the menu. The task or command she needs is listed there*]
I don't remember which one it was. [*Because she has not learned it yet*] Create a document... I can't use that.

(5) E: Why don't you think about it a little bit more, and if you still can't figure it out we'll help.

Reads the manual. Presses an invalid key.

L: Invalid key...
E: What were you looking for there?
L: Some solution to this problem.... We're at a stand still here....

(6) E: You pressed reset a couple of times there?

Without answering presses request, types "create," and the create document menu appears.

"input mode 1 file" which indicates that she is in the text input mode. However, the word "file" matched her file command, and this was enough to suggest some kind of feedback that her "file" (as in store document) command had worked.

Table 4 illustrates a slightly different kind of reasoning in which a learner copes with a number of problems as she tried to sign on to a command-based word processing system we studied. For example, in segment 1 she is trying to decide where to enter the password. The correct point is the command line on the bottom of the display (where other commands have been entered). However, the explanation of signing on that she is following is not explicit about this, and the learner fills in by trying to type the password at the top of the display next to the "password:" prompt (perhaps she thought of this as a blank line of a form that one might fill out). This area of the display is a protected area and her attempt to type locks the keyboard and cursor. But in segment 3 she hypothesizes that inability to move the cursor at that point means the cursor is already in the right location to type! Finally, in segment 4 the learner seems to conclude that the lack of response to her password is the result of heavy load on the system!

How can we characterize these reasoning processes? In some cases, reasoning appears to consist in *adducing* factual support to a premise the learner would like to hold as true. Table 4 shows that the learner began with the hypothesis that she had stored the document file away, and sought evidence to confirm that this was the case. Her adduction here was incorrect because she did not know which facts were relevant to verifying the premise. She was persuaded that the superficially relevant word "file" in the status message signaled successful storing of the file.

In other cases, reasoning appears to consist in *abducing* (Peirce, 1958) a hypothesis when it, together with other assumptions the learner may already hold, is consistent with some fact or observation. An example in Table 4 (segment 1) is the learner's hypothesis the password is entered like an item in a form, that is, after the password prompt with the colon (rather than on the command line like other entries into the system). Other examples of abduction and a fuller discussion can be found in Lewis and Mack (1982).

Abductions and adductions are often incomplete and partial: people do not test them against all potentially relevant data. In particular, people tend to reason only from confirming evidence—and to overlook potentially disconfirming evidence (see Nisbett & Ross, 1980). As a consequence, learners are able to construct and verify ad hoc interpretations of what happens which may misrepresent the situation they are actually in.

Nevertheless, adductive and abductive reasoning processes are important in that they afford net growth in knowledge without requir-

TABLE 3—*Continued*

(7) E: What are you thinking?
   L: Would this be, "document charge number," would that be the page number? [*It has nothing to do with page number—she is still in effect trying to create a document*] Maybe I have to look it up by the page number.
   E: What are you thinking?
   L: Last time I wrote the document name in there it didn't take it the way I wanted it to take it.

Advances cursor to the "document charge number" parameter.

   E: What did you conclude from that, what you just read there?
   L: No, No, I didn't read this. [*i.e., she had not noticed the "document charge number" parameter before in the menu for creating a new document*]

Deletes the "001" charge number and types in "0002" page number but overflows the menu field limits and gets an error message to this effect.

Doesn't fit. [*Presses reset to acknowledge error*]

   E: Press reset there?

Deletes the "0002."

(8) L: [*Reads*] "document originator," would that be me?

Advances cursor to yet another menu parameter, this one called "document originator." This is where one indicates whose document one is typing, e.g., in an office, one's boss.

She types "learner1", presses enter to enter the create document menu; but because she has not specified a name for this "new" document, she incurs an error "Parameter omitted or not valid." The actions are irrelevant to retrieving a document anyway.

(9) E: What are you thinking?

Learner realizes that she has "paginated" document prematurely rather than after she has completed the exercise she was about to begin. That they should explain that it was going to be done later on. [i.e., paginate or cause the rearranging of lines of text to right justify] Cause they said before you do all of this you have to paginate. You will also, oh, no before printing it. So, in other words I assumed that I was supposed to do it right at the beginning, but where as I like wiped myself out. [*In fact, she has not deleted anything—she simply does not know how to retrieve the document file*] But it was done much later on, down here.

planations often are not accurate representations of what is really happening. In one case, a learner tried to decide if a "file" command has stored a document file away. It was not stored because the command was entered in a text input mode where all typed strings are interpreted as text, and not executed as commands. But she assumed that the file had been stored, and adduced evidence to confirm this premise. Not knowing what is really relevant, the learner found two features of the screen that were superficially similar to what one might hypothesize if the file command had been successful and the learner concluded the document had been stored. For example, at one point she notices a status message

ing extensive prerequisite knowledge. In contrast, both classical methods of reasoning—deductive and induction—impose this requirement. Deduction requires an extensive knowledge base of principles from which univocal predictions can be derived. Induction requires an extensive and systematic empirical data base—and in any case cannot guarantee the validity of its conclusions. Neither of these two methods would be appropriate for our learners. This is because the information they have available about the system is typically too impoverished to allow them to build up representations by systematic induction and deduction, even assuming that people are sophisticated and motivated enough to do this. Abduction and adduction provide means of generating and supporting hypotheses from limited information.

Setting Goals and Solving Problems

Beyond merely trying to interpret experiences, learners often set goals which they actively pursue by trying to solve problems. They are hampered in this by not knowing the appropriate problem space, or domain of possible actions and interpretations relevant to accomplishing goals and addressing queries. Accordingly, their strategies are often local and fragmentary; they have difficulty integrating information or other experiences, and in formulating their concerns in ways that map transparently onto system functions. Learners appear to construct a personal agenda of goals and queries as they go along. As situations arise, this agenda is referred to opportunistically: fragmentary aspects of the local situation are assimilated to some standing goal or query.

Table 3 provides an example of the local and fragmentary character of setting goals and solving problems. Recall that the learner in this example is trying to retrieve a document she has inadvertently stored, but does not yet know how to do this. Segments 2 and 4 suggest that the learner has a relatively accurate general idea of what her problem is and what goal she should pursue: retrieve a document. In segment 4 she even tumbles to a relatively good strategy for solving the problem, namely, look for a command listed on the selection menu which could retrieve her document. Unfortunately, the correct command, while listed there in fact, evidently does not have a suggestive name and the learner drops that strategy without trying anything out.

Instead, beginning in segment 6, the learner tries to exploit a create document task with which she is already quite familiar. While the learner again reveals partial insight into her strategy by suggesting (correctly) the she will incur an error using the create task (users cannot "recreate" existing files), she nevertheless incurs an error when she tries to retrieve her document using this command.

TABLE 4
Abductive Inferences in Signing On to the Text-Processing System

(1) L: OK, let's try it again. [*i.e., type password*] I'm on the wrong keys. Password, now type in your password. Now I can only type by going up correct? It's not telling me that. I'm assuming I can take the cursor up there.

I.e., learner does not know where to put cursor. In fact, it is already on the command line where the password should be entered. But the learner decides to move the cursor up the display right after the password prompt at the top of the screen.

(2) *After moving the cursor up the screen, she tries to type password, but this is a protected area of display which causes the keyboard to lock until a reset key is pressed. An "input inhibited" light also comes on.*

I expected it to come out. I expected to see the word. [*i.e., password*] but it's . . .

E: What happened?
L: It probably fed it and I made, umm, contact without showing it here, because it is a password and not everybody knows it generally. So it's sort of a secret between me and the computer.

Rereads description of password.

"The password will not print what you typed. If you are correct the display will blink and in a moment a few lines of greeting messages . . ." and evidently it's not right.

E: OK, what makes you think it's not right?
L: Cause it's not blinking. OK, do I? Ok, let's see the display will, at this point the display will . . . the word will appear, um.

The keyboard is locked, the cursor is in a protected area to the right of the password prompt.

(3) I assume maybe I should space one [*after the password*] Would that maybe [*work*]?

Tries moving cursor one space to the right of colon using space bar, cursor movement blocked because of locked keyboard condition.

Well it doesn't even space so I'm in my right position.

Tries typing password again

E: Ok, you just typed it again.
L: Shouldn't I hit enter?

(4) *Notices the input inhibited light on the display.* What do you think that means?

E: What were you pointing at?
L: The input inhibited [*light on the display*]. Is that possibly why that's not accepting that at the moment?

[*After brief digression*] I've seen that all too often. *She had had some experience using terminals for data entry.*

E: Well, what do you think that means?
L: So it's being held up temporarily. I don't think there's anything you can do at the moment until the light goes off. Oh it might be accepting my, it could be accepting my . . . what I put in and it will go off as soon as it's um . . . When you put information on there now maybe it . . . the input, the fact that you're putting in . . .
The learner is unable to develop any hypothesis as to why the system will not respond or accept input. The experimenters later were forced to intervene.

earlier problem: indeed, when she next had the opportunity, she performed the appropriate deletion.

In light of these experiences, segments 7 and 8 are especially interesting. Despite her interpretation of the inappropriateness of the "create document" task for retrieving the document (segments 2 and 4), the learner returns to this menu and hypothesizes that other parameters of the task might be relevant to getting her document back. As we discussed in the preceding subsection, the learner does not know what is relevant to her goal, and so can entertain even specious hypotheses about what might be relevant based on very superficial resemblances. For example, the learner fills in the page number in a menu field labeled "document charge number" because the word "number" suggests page numbering.

Table 2 describes another example of how difficult it is for learners to formulate goals, and find information relevant to solving them. In segment 8 the learner tried to delete a blank line she had inadvertently inserted between two sentences. However, she did not describe her problem in this way, but thought of it as one of bringing the bottom sentence back under the first one (segment 6). The relevance problem arises during her search for some way to "bring the sentence back": the learner "Required Return" on a carrier return key seemed to be relevant to this problem. In fact, the connection is specious. The Required Return function is just another version of the return key and resulted in the learner inserting yet another blank line.

When learners cannot solve a problem or resolve some query immediately, it may be saved away on a task agenda—with the hope that an answer will be found later. The goals and queries on this task agenda are typically addressed opportunistically rather than through systematic problem solving. (See Hayes-Roth and Hayes-Roth, 1979, for related views of planning behavior.) An example is the learner who initially misinterpreted why the word processing system did not let her sign on (i.e., in segment 6 of Table 1, the learner thinks she must be in a "Test Mode" to work on the system). Later (segment 7), when she dealt with a similar problem situation it occurred to her that her current (correct) interpretation was probably applicable to her earlier difficulty. Not only did this learner reconsider her earlier erroneous interpretation, she actually tried (segment 8) to recreate the original problem situation.

The learner in Table 2 who tried to correct a typing error before she had learned how to do so had been anxious for some time to discover how to correct typos. In another case (not shown in tables), a learner had unintentionally accumulated a number of special characters ahead of the cursor. The system is always in insert state so this material was pushed along as she typed. Of course, she wanted to eliminate this unsightly mess but did not know how (the delete key would have worked). It was only much later while she was learning how to delete another kind of special character that she realized the same operation might solve her

Consolidating Procedures

The word processing domain is highly procedural. Learners must analyze basic procedures in the context of various word processing goals. This is not a matter of rote learning and passive assimilation; even the simplest procedures like word deletion or replacing a letter reveals the difficult task of identifying relevant elements of these procedures and trying to integrate them into a smooth operation. Learners' understanding of procedures works by successive approximations. Learners form general schemata or rules for those elements relevant to a procedure. These general schemata are then filled out in the course of interacting with the word processing system.

Table 5 shows an example of a learner who is trying to delete the underscoring for the three words, "... will not change." The underscoring itself looks normal but it is marked by a special underscore character which is a block of reversed video superimposed on the space immediately following the word. To delete it, the user must position the cursor "under" the character in such a way that a message "word underscore" appears on an information line at the top of the display. (It is not enough that the cursor is spatially under the reversed video block.)

The learner's attempts to coordinate her initial understanding of this delete operation demonstrate the *revelatory nature* of trying actions out: a sequence of actions and events is consolidated into a procedural concept. The learner has the correct general idea of positioning the cursor under a character and then using a delete function to delete it (evidenced in segments 1 and 2), but does not incorporate the critical feedback from the information line at the top of the screen. The procedure has been incompletely instantiated. Even though the learner has read all this, and as the example shows will read about it all again (e.g., segment 5), its significance only becomes apparent through careful and detailed attempts (segment 6) to actually integrate and exercise the procedure.

One obstacle to integrating the elements of procedures, again, is the learner's innocence. In Table 5 (segments 7 through 11), the learner tries to replace a small "t" with a capital "T" in the word "the." The learner deletes the "t" correctly, but then formulates her goal of replacing it with a "T" to be one of replacing the space at the front of the string "_he" rather than simply inserting the "T" at the beginning of the string. Of course, the "T" is in effect inserted in the existing string which now includes a space, producing the string "T_he." In segments 9 through 11 she struggles to understand this procedure by tying the

TABLE 5
Deleting a Word Underscore and Replacing a Letter

(1) *The learner is trying to delete the underscore from the second of three words "will not change." She is not locating the cursor in a way that identifies the special underscore character.*

L: What happened? The line [*underscore line*] didn't disappear, now what did I do? Was I over too many spaces? I could have been.

Still trying to delete the underscore line under "not," places the cursor under the "v" and deletes a space.

Oh, what did I do?

(2) Let me try again. I can replace the other one anyway. *Presses character delete, deleting the "c" of the third word "change." Not clear why she did this.*

What's happening?

Positions cursor immediately after the third word and "under" the underscore instruction, so that the character delete operation correctly deletes the underscore from that word.

It worked on that one, I don't understand. *Here is the problem: Underscore is represented by a special character symbol. To delete, the cursor must be positioned "under" this symbol and then deleted as any other character. The learner did not enter underscore instruction at the correct location for the second word but did so for the third. Therefore her action of locating cursor "under" the underscore character works as per instructions for the third, but not the second word. The learner does not understand what the instructions really mean or she would be able to recognize the discrepancy, and modify the instructions for the second word.*

(3) *Presses word delete key, and deletes the third and fourth words.*

E: What did you just press there?
L: I just pressed word delete.

Moves cursor to the next word and deletes it.

Oh, wait a minute, that keeps moving all of them. [*i.e., the line adjusts after material has been deleted*]

Looks in manual for information Checking out something here under [*the topic of*] word delete.

E: What is it that you're looking for?
L: I'm just trying to see . . .

(4) *"Not" is still underlined and every word in the line after "not" has been deleted.*

I got a little paranoid when I saw everything moving backward, I thought "wait a minute." Now, I realized I wanted to erase the whole thing anyway and retype it and then. . . . Because I lost a space in there and I couldn't get rid of the line under "not."

E: What were you looking for when you looked under [*the topic of*] word delete?
L: Yes, for some reason I was afraid. I saw this moving over and I saw this moving over and I was afraid that I was going to erase. I don't know I'd . . . I'd forgotten that everything was going to move over anyway as you erase, as you delete. So, I didn't want to go on to the next word, although actually I may have to erase that also. OK, I'll see, I'll see if I can type this, retype this line . . .

Types in the rest of the sentence, after underscored "not."

Oh, that's OK, alright.

(5) *Moves the cursor back to the space before the underscored word "not."*

(continued)

TABLE 5—*Continued*

E: What are you looking for now?
L: OK, I'm just looking to see what it says here again. [*I want to*] start again with the underscore . . . deleting the underscore. . . . Yes, no I'm just going over what I did before.

Still trying to delete the underscore line under "not," places the cursor under the space after the "v" and deletes a space.

Oh, what did I do?

(6) *Moves the cursor under the "t" in "not," then moves the cursor to the space after the "t." I see, OK, I didn't realize that before. I didn't realize it [the cursor] has to pass through . . . the underscore. It has to pass through the underscore from what I understand.*

E: How did you find that?
L: Um, under the, under the delete underscore instructions.

When she moves the cursor under the "t," the message "word under" appears on the screen.

I did that automatically before. It was supposed to be under the last letter of the underscore. *Presses a delete function with the cursor "under" the underscore symbol; the underscore is deleted.*

(7) *Learner moves on to another instruction for revising, this one involving replacing of a "t" with a "T" in the word "the" which is the first word of a newly revised sentence.*

(8) *She deletes the "t" in "the" to produce the string "he" with the cursor positioned under the "h." But before she tries to type the "T" she moves the cursor to the left, back under the space before the "he." Thus when she types "T" she actually inserts it in front of the space to produce "T he"; i.e., with a gap.*

E: What are you thinking?
L: OK, um, when I deleted the "t" and typed the capital "T," I created a space. Why is it doing this?

(9) *Looks in manual for help.*
E: Where are you reading now?
L: OK, I'm reading under character delete, I'm just . . . I'm trying to find out why when I retyped another character in place of the one I just deleted . . . um, I'm just wondering, there's another space after that now separating "T" and "h."

(10) *Places the cursor in the space between "T" and "h" and inserts another "T." Perhaps she is convincing herself that this really happened. Then she turns back to the manual section on deleting material.*

It says they move together.

E: Was that a particular thing you just said?
L: OK, it says, the instructions say that when you delete something the letters will move together to fill it in. OK, now that. . . . I don't understand why there's a space there as soon as I type the other one.

(11) [*Sometime later learner speculates*] When you delete, you take out. Do you add when you put in?

"addition" of text to her earlier experience deleting it. As she puts it in segment 11: "When you delete, you take out. Do you add when you put in?" Her real problem though is not recognizing that an important element of this procedure is the fact that the word processing system is always in insert mode.

A second problem, we have also seen before, that confronts this process of integrating basic procedures is that of problem tangling. In Table 5, for example, the learner had incorrectly underscored the second word of the triple (i.e., in the triple "will not change," the underscore character for "not" was originally entered at the last letter of the word, not under the interword spacing). Thus, while the learner was able to delete the underscoring for the third word "change" (segment 2), the same procedure mysteriously does not seem to work for the second word "not." The problem could be solved either by recognizing the earlier error, or by recognizing the correct feedback for locating the underscore character. Since the learner cannot untangle these problems, she cannot properly execute the procedure, which remains mysterious to her.

These examples suggest that even the simplest operations present learners with serious challenges. They must translate expository descriptions of operations into actions. They must coordinate multiple sources of information (on display, in manual, and from memory). And it is clear that the significance of the various elements of procedures (what they accomplish, what prerequisites are needed, what are relevant outcomes, etc.) only become tangible to learners in the context of their actually interacting with the system.

LEARNING BY KNOWING

Learning by reasoning and problem solving presupposes a well-defined "problem space": knowledge of what is relevant to particular goals, of how to constrain interpretations and goal-related actions, etc. Our learners understood the problem space of the conventional office, but not that of the "electronic office"—in particular, they did not understand the problem space of word processing. Nevertheless, they spontaneously referred to substantive prior knowledge from the former domain in order to understand the latter. We will refer to this as "learning by knowing"; it has often been called "metaphor" (Bott, 1979; Carroll & Thomas, 1982; Rumelhart & Ortony, 1977).

To this point, we have argued that a new user of a word processor relies without instruction on active exploration and ad hoc reasoning as learning strategies. However, not all possibilities are explored and not all hypotheses that could be reached are reached. What constrains these strategies is a sense of what could be appropriate—and this devolves from prior knowledge on the part of the learner: knowledge about devices "like" word processors (e.g., typewriters), knowledge about office routine and work in general, even knowledge culled from interacting with the word processor up to that point in time.

The Typewriter Metaphor

Office personnel learning to use a word processor typically have an extensive and fairly coherent body of knowledge regarding typewriters to which they can refer. Indeed, our learners were not able to resist referring to their prior knowledge about typewriters as a basis for interpreting and predicting experience with word processors.

One of our learners came to a halt as she read an instruction in the manual which said "Backspace to erase." It seemed that she could not interpret this instruction for, as she pointed out, backspace does not erase anything. She had irresistibly availed herself of her knowledge of how backspacing works on a typewriter, unable to even consider that this knowledge might be inappropriate for the present case. The incident had a sad ending, too. In wrestling with this problem, she accidentally incurred a "reset" condition, repositioning the cursor at the beginning of the word. Hence, when she finally elected to plunge ahead and "backspace to erase," it in fact did not work.

For a second example, recall the learner in Table 2 who was trying to move the cursor through a line of text to correct a typing mistake. Without any hesitation, she presses the space bar. She is surprised to see that this inserts a space into her text. Now, just as automatically, she presses the backspace key. This deletes the space. What is interesting in this example is first, that the space bar is expected to advance the cursor without inserting spaces, as it would do on a typewriter. Second, it is notable that when it fails to behave as anticipated, backspace is employed as an inverse operation—again just as it is on the typewriter. Neither of the expectations is thought out, rather both are immediately available in virtue of the learner's prior knowledge of typewriters. Fortunately, although the first expectation is thwarted, the second obtains: the space bar fails to provide a vehicle for cursor movement through text, but backspace succeeds in inverting the operation (including the undesired side effect).

To continue with this example (segment 5), the learner decides to abandon the goal of correcting her typing error (possibly because she cannot manage to get the cursor to the site of the error). She now wishes to advance the cursor and continue entering text. Again, with no deliberation, she keypresses the carriage return (segment 6): a blank line is inserted into the text. "Whoa!" The learner is surprised by this. Like the side effect of the space bar, it is discrepant with her expectations based on typewriters (where carriage return advances the typing point but does not insert lines)—and worse, there is no obvious predictable inverse operation available to her.

Expectations about Work

Our learners were experienced with conventional office work: typing letters, filing, etc. Their knowledge about how these routine tasks are organized in the office creates expectations in them about how analogous tasks ought to be performed in the "office of the future" (as represented by the word processor in our laboratory). Thus, one response to revising a letter task is to retype. This is striking since it is the capability of the word processor to store and retrieve documents—for revision, among other things—that is its fundamental advance over previous office technologies.

Another example of mismatched expectations is the correspondence between the typing page on the word processor and what learners expect a typing page to be from typewriting. The system ostensibly frees users from worrying about margins and formatting by doing these things automatically during printing, and having default settings. But new users can be troubled by these labor-saving features: the differences between a familiar piece of paper in a typewriter and the typing display raise many questions that are not easily answered early in learning. Learners wonder where the top and bottom, left and right margins are located on the display. They wonder how the length of the typing display corresponds to the length of a printed page (this is a relationship automatically controlled by the pagination feature). And they wonder whether error and status messages which appeared on the typing display would be part of their final product.

The learner's expectations about work transcend knowledge of how office procedures are carried out. They include motivational expectations about work-related learning and sociological expectations about power and control in work-related settings. These expectations can differ remarkably, as evidenced by comparing our learners to a college teacher learning to use a programmable calculator (Carroll & Lasher, 1981). This person was in fact, suffering many of the problems we have described above. In one particular incident, she was unable to make sense of several passages in the training manual.

Now in analogous situations our typist-learners typically concluded that the fault was their own, that they were too stupid to understand properly. However, our Ph.D. learner came to an entirely different conclusion: she decided that the manual contained misprints or other errors and could not, therefore, be used. She discarded it at that point—never considering the possibility that she was too stupid to understand in general, or even that the specific trouble was in part due to her own miscoordination of information. We believe that this manifest difference in attitudes is partly because the typist subjects identify with social powerlessness and hence expect to be victimized in work-related undertakings. However, we are basing this on a single comparison subject, and our interpretation must be weighed accordingly.

A final point we will simply make now and then return to later is that our learners seemed to expect a dichotomy between work-related learning and play. Of course work and play *are* different classes of activities for most people, but in learning it can be useful to adopt some aspects of a play orientation. Just as a casual observation, it seems that the capacity to shift gears a little and to treat work as play is characteristic of successful adult learners and problem solvers. The reluctance of our learners to do this (which was something the manual encouraged) may constitute a fairly abstract orientational learning obstacle.

Integrating Bits and Pieces

As a learning experience progresses, the learner is acquiring and organizing new bits of knowledge. The ultimate goal—and the final measure of success in the learning situation—is that of assembling these pieces into a coherent fabric, an understanding of the word processor. Along the way, any prior bit of knowledge is available for use as a basis for expectations concerning successive interactions with the system. Learners expect functional consistency from operations with similar names. One system we studied contained inconsistencies of this sort. Thus, to delete a word, one positions the cursor under the word's initial character and keypresses a word delete. However, to underscore a word, one positions the cursor under the final character of a word and keypresses the word underscore command.

This inconsistency caused one learner to misexecute one and then the other of these two operations in a dismal cycle of negative transfer as illustrated in Table 6. In two earlier episodes (not described in the table) the learner had followed explicit instructions for underscoring and deleting, and understood both. The episodes shown in segments 1–7 reveal that the learner eventually formed correct rules to cover both cases. For example, after learning how to underscore and delete on the first

TABLE 6
Learning Where to Position the Cursor for Deleting, Underscoring, and Backspacing

(1) *On Day 3 learner is about to underscore the word "solutions" but has positioned the cursor under the first letter, rather than at the correct position at the end of the word*

E: What are you doing?

L: I'm trying to code word underline [*i.e., To underline a user must press a word underline function in conjunction with a code function*]

Today I remembered which key it is [*she had trouble finding the word underscore key the day before*] but evidently I didn't hit it in the right sequence.

Not clear what reference is, but in her first experience with the function the day before, she had pressed the code key after the word underscore key, which is the wrong sequence for underscoring—but her current problem derives from having a wrong cursor position.

Why didn't it underline? Oh, I should have....

(2) E: Can you talk aloud about what you are thinking?

L: Yes. Ah, I'm thinking, I'm looking at the word "solutions" on page 3–19. I wanted to underline it. I brought the cursor back under the "s" [*first "s" of the word*] before I hit the code underline. And I think that the code underline should have been hit at the end of the word. [*She is correct: i.e., the cursor should have been at end of word, not beginning.*]

E: Why do you think that?

L: Because it only underlined one thing [*the first "s" of "solutions"*]. I think.

She is correct. She then moves the cursor to the end of word and correctly underscores

(3) *On Day 2, learner is trying to reconstruct the correct position of the cursor in order to delete a word. She had learned the day before that the correct position is at the beginning of the word*

L: They have a code word delete. [*i.e., reference to the necessity of holding a code key while pressing a key labeled "word delete"*]

E: They what?

L: Code word delete. Now what I'm trying to figure out... in these instructions they didn't tell me where the cursor should be when I do the deletion. I think probably right after the last character of the word. So we'll go see.

We're going to get the cursor down to the word we want to work on. So we are going to line advance twice. [*i.e., press function to advance the cursor down a line*] And the word we want to work on is "have." So we are going to word advance to that [*i.e., use a function which advances the cursor to the next word within a line*]

Cursor positioned at beginning of "have." Now I think probably that I want to be at the end of it to eliminate it. Uses character advance key to position cursor at end of "have."

Okay as though I had just typed it and now they have a two down [*numbered manual instruction*] they want me to code word delete. So. Find "word." I want to be sure I'm watching [*the display*] so that I can see what happens.

(4) *Pressed code plus word delete and deletes space between "have" and next word so they are concatenated*

Oh no!

E: What happened?

L: I lost the space. So I have to put the space back in. *Presses backspace which deletes the "e"*

Oh no! Now I lost the "e"!

E: What...?

L: Terrible!

E: What did you press to [*try to*] put the space back in?

L: I pressed the backspace [*which deletes*].

(5) Okay, now let's see. I tell you what I'm going to do. I going to press the "e" which I lost. [*Inserts "e" to restore "have"*] It moves over [*i.e., inserts*]. Then I'll press a space which I lost *Presses space bar to insert space between "have" and next word.*

I'm going to take the cursor and character return in to the "e" [i.e., uses function to return cursor one position left; in this case under "e" of "have"] and then I'm going to code word delete again and see what happens there.

Ah, my whole problem here is.... *Positions cursor under "e" and presses code followed by word delete which again deletes the "e." Repeats to now delete the interword space.*

No, that wasn't the answer either.

E: What did you do?

L: I pressed code word delete and all I lost was a letter [*i.e., "e"*].

E: That's not what you expected?

L: No. I expected to lose [*delete*] the whole word "have."

E: What makes you think that?

L: Well, I thought it would take the whole word out.

(6) Now maybe I coded word delete in the wrong place. So let's put the "have" back in, the "have" and the space. Um. Is the space in? I'm going to go all the way back to the beginning of "have" with the cursor.

Repositions cursor under "h" of "have." And at the beginning of "have" I'm going to put code word delete and see if it takes the whole word "have" out.

Presses code and word delete which deletes "have". Yeah. That was the proper way. So when you use that you have to be at the beginning of the word you want to delete.

(7) E: Can you think of any particular reason why you thought that? That it had to be at the end of a word rather than at the beginning?

L: Because you can't delete it unless its already there. And if you were typing on you might decide you wanted to delete something right after you typed it.

E: I see.

L: And you would do it at the end. But I see that that wouldn't work. You would have to get the cursor back to the beginning of the word if you wanted to delete the whole word.

E: Does that make sense to you now?

L: Yes. It's all right. If that's the way it works, that's fine. I still don't know why I was told to code line delete at the other one instead of coding word delete. And I'm very grateful but I don't know why I didn't lose one of those lines.

(8) *On Day 4, learner is reconstructing how to underscore a word. She tries to position the cursor at the beginning of the word, rather than correctly at the end as she learned on at least two previous occasions.*

(*continued*)

cursor under the first character of the word and then type word delete, i.e., press the word delete function, to take out the word". This generalization about deleting, was hard-won in its own right as segments 3–7 reveal. The learner spent considerable time working out the fact that she must put the cursor at the beginning of the word she wants to delete, rather than at the end.

A similar inconsistency in this system involved cursor movement. In a menu, the cursor is advanced from one line to the next by pressing a variable advance key. However, in text the cursor is properly advanced from one line to the next by means of a *line* advance key. Learners tended not to acknowledge this distinction and to flop back and forth depending on whether they had more recently been on a menu or a typing display. Of course, this reliance on immediately prior experience led to numerous errors.

The problem of prior knowledge is not a simple one. On the one hand, we might say that learners will rely on their prior knowledge, and that developers of new technologies ought to take this fact of human cognitive learning into account in designing systems and in designing the educational technologies that accompany and introduce them. However, this is paradoxical: can we reasonably expect that new technologies can be constrained by old ones in this way?

More specifically, should long-term innovations in word processors be constrained by nonoptimal properties that typewriters merely happen to have as an accident of their history? Can we even find suitable metaphors for presenting new technologies to learners? Again, to be specific, should a radical innovation in word processing be eschewed merely because there is no apparent way to couch it as an extended super-typewriter?

DESIGNING FOR EASE OF LEARNING

Learning, as we have tried to suggest, is an active process. It is inescapably directed by the learner. This fact is not altered when educational technologies—like self-instruction manuals (and the systems to which they refer)—are designed to place the learner in a relatively passive role. Rather, the learning experience becomes chaotic, frustrating, and inefficient.

Cognitive science, by focusing attention on ecologically valid learning situations of nontrivial complexity, can address the theoretical and practical issues underlying the current misfit of state-of-the-art learning technology to human learners. We close this discussion by sketching three projects this might encompass.

day, segments 1 and 2 reveal that on the third day the learner erroneously tried to underscore with cursor at the *beginning* of the word ("solutions"). Why did she assume this after learning the correct procedure earlier? The protocols are not clear in this segment, but the same problem arose on the fourth day and in this case the learner's explanation suggests a generalization based on deleting words.

This second instance of trying to underscore with the cursor at the beginning (rather than at the end) of a word is shown in segments 8–10. When we finally asked her why she did this, she suggested: "I think to give an instruction you have to be at the first character of that word. Like, in other words, to delete the word I found out you don't delete it at the end (i.e. with cursor at the end of the word). You have to get the

---

TABLE 6—Continued

L: Just sitting in the office I would just take a chance that that would underline.

Pressing word underscore with the cursor under the first letter of the word underscores that letter only, and superimposes a block of reversed video to mark the underscore character.

If it didn't I would have to go to the book and find out.

(9) E: Well, this is just a question. I think we are beginning to wrap up. In the past when you used the word underline did it actually put underlining on the screen?
L: I can't remember today [*in fact, it had underlined completely*]
E: You can't remember whether it does or doesn't?
L: Whether it did or did not. But I'm not particularly worried, because the rectangle means there is an instruction at that point and the only instruction I put in was word underline.
E: Right
L: And I think I put it in at the right place. I think to give an instruction you have to be at the first character of that word. Like in other words to delete the word I found out you don't delete it at the end. You can't type delete just after you typed the word.

You have to get the cursor under the first character of the word and then type word delete to take out the word.

(10) E: Can I ask you a question about that? For awhile we noted that when you wanted to delete a word or a line you put the cursor at the end of that respective unit, whether word or line
L: Yeah, I didn't know how to do it.
E: Why did you do that?
L: Because I figured that it was the last thing entered and that it might just erase the last thing entered. Not a very . . . oh, also I think on a line delete I did that, too. I don't remember what happened whether it took out the next line or it didn't because the carriage return was in there. I really don't know what happened.

She is referring to an earlier experience in which she tried to delete the last part of a line with the cursor incorrectly located at the end of that line. It didn't work but was sufficiently ambiguous that this may not have impressed her.

Conceptual Framework

Learners do not "absorb" knowledge: they create, explore, and integrate knowledge. New word processor technologies, and the educational technologies that support them, must take this picture of learning seriously. Prior knowledge, for example knowledge of typewriters and routine office tasks, seems to be almost accidentally relevant—sometimes transfer is positive and sometimes negative. And this is not to presume that the issues are simple; it is merely to observe that they have not been addressed seriously to date.

We should stress that we are not urging that metaphors be explicitly and discursively presented to new users (cf. Halasz & Moran, 1982). If a metaphor must be explicitly taught to a new user, it is contributing to the burden—the amount of material that must be learned—instead of relieving this burden. The best metaphor is obviously one that is implicitly and automatically suggested to the user merely by the appearance and behavior of a system. Such a metaphor maximizes the potential savings in learning effort. The well-known Query-By-Example system (Zloof, 1977) did just this by suggesting the metaphor of paper tables to users of a data base query system. The Smalltalk programming language also attempted to make use of familiar metaphors (Ingalls, 1981).

Of course, not all aspects of all systems can be as easily and elegantly fitted to metaphors. Indeed, our experience in studying the learning process in this area, inclines us to stress how easy it is to *underestimate* the subtlety, the novelty, and the complexity of the design features of computer systems. What metaphor might cover the "data stream" concept, that is the fact that the system's internal representation of objects like the "typing page" are actually linear strings of symbols? Failure to appreciate the data stream concept may indeed underlie many of the "quirks" our learners struggled with regarding insert mode, line return characters, and the like (e.g., a "blank line" on the "typing page" is represented internally as a single character). Suggesting a misleading or inconsistent metaphor through a feature of a user interface may create more learning problems than it mitigates.

Must new technology be burdened with "metaphoric compatibility" constraints? In designing the word processors of the future, will we always have to try to pretend that they are typewriters for the sake of our innocent new users? It seems to us that this is not the way to put things. For example, one can imagine the following possibility: a new office system is created—it is indeed not merely just another super typewriter (we leave open what it might be). How can it presented to new users to reap the benefits of prior knowledge and avoid the pitfalls?

A programmatic solution would be to envision a series of user inter-faces; the first very much like a typewriter (in effect concealing from the user much of the innovative function that the system has to offer). The second user interface, is richer—less strictly tied to typewriter concepts—and for users who have progressed to mastery of the initial interface. The program should be clear. No one today thinks of a typewriter as a super pencil, and no one would seriously argue that technology should stop with typewriters. However, this does not mean that the cognitive–social transition from typewriters to super word processors must necessarily be as uncoordinated as was that from pencils to typewriters (but cf. Schrodt, 1982).

Indeed, the approach we have just sketched can be elaborated somewhat. It may be too strict a constraint to expect that a single metaphor or a patently obvious metaphor (like the typewriter metaphor) will always be immediately available (or even imaginable) in new areas of technological innovation. So far, we have limited our consideration to monolithic metaphors spontaneously generated by learners as they begin to interact with a system. The possibility is open—and intriguing—that aspects of prior knowledge could be brought to consciousness and assembled into composite metaphors.

The kind of educational technology we are imagining here has simply not been developed. Accordingly, there is little more we can offer at this time. Even if one eschews an active orientation toward the construction of learning metaphors, it seems crucial to guide learners at least to the extent that they should be warned about the limits to which a metaphor can be employed. The implicit typewriter metaphor we identified in our learner's conceptualizations often caused problems for them when it was inappropriate: such cases should be ferreted out and identified for new users.

Exploratory Environments

If the picture of learning we have given here is anything close to correct, it suggests that an optimal learning environment for new users will differ from that provided by current systems. Indeed, the disparity between what exists currently and what would seem to constitute a reasonable learning environment is so great that we are only able to capture the grossest properties of what we imagine would be an optimal learning environment. By definition we will refer to this as an "exploratory environment"; our reason for choosing this term will become clearer presently.

One property of an exploratory environment is that it provides learners with *an appropriate orientation toward the task*: learners approach the task of learning to use a word processor with highly discrepant expectations about what it will be like and how difficult it will be. They—and their bosses—may understand from popular misconception that word processors are easy to learn to use and that using them will result in immediate and substantial productivity increases. This might even be true if the means of instruction is personal tutoring. However, if the means of instruction is contemporary self-study, this is far from the truth—as our studies demonstrate. Realistic expectations about the difficulty of learning to use word processing equipment would at the very least discourage attributions of self-blame on the part of learners. And this, in turn, would at the very least make learning to use these systems more pleasant.

Another aspect of realistic task orientation involves learner responsibility and control. Manuals and system interfaces implicitly attempt to place the learner in a passive role, but as we have seen learners take charge regardless. Nevertheless, the conflict between a manual/system ensemble that directs rote exercises on, say, cursor movement, and an active learner who decides in spite of this to explore techniques of typo correction is problematic: the learner will "fail" in some sense no matter what the outcome. An exploratory environment establishes and reinforces a role of responsibility and control for the learner *via* the system interface and training materials. (Some of our current research work is addressed to this and we return to it briefly in the final section of this study.)

A second property of an exploratory environment is *system simplicity*: learner problems will tangle to the extent that systems afford problem tangling. Systems should, therefore, be designed to minimize potential for tangling. However, this does not at al mean that "function" must be traded for simplicity vis-à-vis the user interface. Earlier we suggested a "staged" sequence for user interfaces. The initial user interface, on this proposal, would indeed trade function for simplicity, but it would do this by shielding the new user from potentially tangling function. In any case, new users are not the ones who complain about limitations of revealed function. Successive interfaces would increase the amount of revealed function—and therefore the potential for problem tangling—but staged in a way that would minimize the risks to learning at any given point in the process.

An alternative approach to achieving this sort of simplicity has been called "progressive disclosure" (Smith, Irby, Kimball, Verplank, & Harslem, 1982). An interface organized this way stages each function separately and places the staging sequence under the user's control. This is a more flexible approach than that of staging the entire interface as a whole and *shielding* the user from control, even awareness, of this. On the other hand, progressive disclosure, although it quite literally makes the learner "ask" for trouble, does allow such requests to be fulfilled.

Simplicity connects directly to several other properties of exploratory environments, in particular to *clarity* and *safety*. Systems are often unclear in the sense that they do not inform the user of what state they are currently in, what they are currently doing, or even what they must have just done. In one system we studied, even the command to sign-off occasioned no confirmation message at all: the system merely put up the sign-on menu (presumably for the next user). New users do not recognize that "hello" *means* "good-bye" in systems. They frequently signed on again and then asked us how they were ever going to get off of the system!

In the same system, the command to print a document elicited a confirmation message that was routed to a "message reservoir." Here the message waited for the user to request it to be displayed. The trouble is that a user might not realize what has happened and/or might not know how to display a message. This could result in the message being displayed at a time much later than that at which it was sent. Thus when one least expected it, one could learn that file such-and-such had been printed. These problems of the amount and the timing of feedback are rather easily dealt with, at least in principle: why not have more feedback and present it in a more timely fashion? (The relevant design trade off here is that the presentation of feedback might interrupt a succeeding task and thereby distract the user—but this rationale doesn't make printing any less inscrutable for the learner.)

But a further, and far less trivial, feedback problem is that the content of messages is not typically "problem-oriented." Learners do not want to read messages like "parameter omitted or not valid." They want to find out what they did wrong *in that case* with regard to their own current goals—and they would like to know what to try next to achieve those goals. This kind of situation is devastating for current Help systems. We have many times seen subjects examine a Help screen which, in fact, contained the information they needed, but which presented that information in a problem-neutral manner. Since the learners were construing their needs in a problem-oriented "vocabulary," they simply failed to see the relevance of the Help.

Addressing this problem at all would require a task-analysis-driven approach to interface design that regards *learning* as a key user task. Addressing it comprehensively would require building in some sort of "intelligence" to the system interface. Nevertheless, an exploratory environment is "clear" in the sense that it provides abundant, timely, and problem-oriented feedback to the learner.

ing, as we have described it here, is facilitated in an exploratory environment. However, in closing this section, we want to observe that this facilitation may not merely be "cognitive." Exploratory environments may enhance task oriented motivation as well. Computer games manifest many of the properties of exploratory environments, and have been argued to increase task-oriented motivation (Malone, 1980, 1981). The argument is murky, however, since the games differ from word processors in a great many irrelevant ways as well.

The game of Adventure may be an important case with respect to this both because it is so widely popular and because its "maze learning" problem scenario is analogous in many ways to learning the conceptual maze codified in a structure of interconnected menus in a word processor (Carroll, 1982b). Indeed, the similarities between Adventure and current word processing systems can be pushed quite far—which raises the question of why the game is so attractive to people. Part of the answer might be that the types of properties we have clustered into the concept of an exploratory environment—properties like feedback, safety, modularity, learner control—nurture a motivational orientation in game learners that is precluded for learners of current word processors.

Clearly, these are empirical questions that can be addressed only by developing systems that comprise exploratory environments and by studying how people manage to learn to use them. This is the direction of our own current work.

Active Learning

In the early days of cognitive psychology, it was often necessary to rail against "stimulus–response" analyses of learning that went like this: items in the world come around and get paired with responses (or dispositions to respond) in the organism (generally because the pairing led to a good effect of some sort). This is a somewhat barren analysis of human learning to be sure, and cognitive psychology succeeded in doing away with it. The solution offered by cognitive psychology then, and now, was to turn the question of "learning" into the question of "memory." This was probably a good idea; after all, successful learning ought to lead to memory and stimulus–response psychology had nothing to say about how even simple aspects of memory organization could be explained.

In turning the question around like this, however, cognitive psychology overlooked another striking problem with the stimulus–response analysis of learning: learning—in that view—is a mechanically passive matter of pairing and then incrementing the strength of pairing. The active initiatives of the learner do not figure in at all. In turning the

Safety is the capacity of the system to protect the learner from demoralizing penalty. The issue arises because, as we have seen, the learning strategies people adopt lead them into trouble with current word processors. A system that was safe to learn by doing would be one whose function was organized modularly with respect to real tasks. An error committed while correcting a typo in a menu field would not tangle with reset to alter the applicability of procedures for correcting the typo (recall Table 1). Training materials also should be organized modularly with respect to real tasks: learning by doing does not mean following out a cursor movement exercise by rote; it means typing in a letter (and "incidentally" learning to move the cursor about).

In such a system, recovering from an error might be more than a hopeless jump into an endless morass of problem tangles. Indeed, we view error recovery as a paradigmatic learning situation: the learner is highly task-oriented, primed to take action, and engaged in the system's responses. In current unsafe systems, all this is for naught since the learner is quite likely to end up lost. In a safe system, all this very constructive motivation might be effectively channeled into learning by discovery. Learners must be safe in taking action.

If the strategy of learning by thinking is to operate safely, the inferences, deductions, and abductions that people are prone to make must be correct. In some cases, this point can be codified simply: operations that have apparent natural inverses (space and backspace, line advance and line return) should indeed be inverses; they should mutually undo each other's effects; they should have predictably inverted names (Carroll, 1982a). In many other cases, designing systems that can be learned by being reasoned out is not nearly so straightforward. We simply do not understand human reasoning in these complex task environments well enough to derive from principles appropriate design strategies.

And of course, if the strategy of learning by knowing is to be safely employed then care must be taken to present a system interface which is consistent with prior knowledge: if word processors are thought of as super typewriters then, at least the initial interface should contain either nothing inconsistent with this, or if it does contain inconsistent features these should be well-marked for the new user (Carroll & Thomas, 1982). An exploratory environment is safe with respect to the strategies of learning by doing, thinking, and knowing. System operations and training materials are modular with respect to real tasks; natural inferences, deductions, and abductions entail correct expectations about the system's behavior; and prior knowledge which people regard as relevant is relevant.

These properties straightforwardly suggest the hypothesis that learn-

learning question into the memory question, cognitive psychology effectively finessed this problem: memory structures, after all, *ought* to be stable, relatively static, and so on. Reducing the analysis of memory to a set (albeit an increasingly large set) of mechanisms was viewed as an entirely proper way to scientifically approach the matter (but cf. Jenkins, 1974).

In sum, *both* stimulus–response psychology and cognitive psychology—in their approaches to the problems of analyzing learning and memory, respectively—share a basic orientation: the processes involved are "passive" with respect to the initiative of the learner–memorizer. They in fact share one other basic orientation. Neither school of psychology focused its principal empirical concern on the analysis of full-scale problems of human behavior and experience. This is as true of the classic Sperling and Sternberg brand of memory research as it is of the classic Skinnerian studies of pigeon pecking. While it may be true that in highly constrained situations or in infrahuman species active self-initiative is muted, this may not bear at all on the nature of real and complex human learning.

The treatment of learning in both stimulus–response psychology and subsequently in cognitive psychology share a picture of learning that approaches it as passive with respect to the initiative of the learner, and a methodological orientation that focuses analysis on highly constrained laboratory situations. Our examination of a more full-scale learning situation questions these premises (as has other recent work in cognitive science; Norman, 1981). Learning to use a word processor provides a study of real complex human learning that is fundamentally "active," driven by the initiatives of the learner—which are, in turn, based on extensive domain-specific knowledge and skill, and on reasoning processes which are systematic and yet highly creative.

Where do we go from here? Our examinations of current word processing systems have led us to a conception of learning, and in particular of learning to use a word processor. In the prior two sections we have summarized and projected in very general terms what we think we have learned. However, recognizing that current word processing systems might be improved from the learner's perspective by providing a conceptual framework and ensuring an exploratory environment is far short of *understanding what learning would be like in such a situation*. If the problems that learners experienced were less debilitating, we might be able to analyze learning at a finer grain and expose cognitive mechanisms that are simply lost in the confusion when people try to learn current systems. At the least, we could contrast learning in the two situations.

To address this, we are attempting to codify our suggestions for train-

ing and system design into concrete experimental prototypes. A rude approximation of this involves merely altering the training materials learners receive. The system they interact with is one we have studied previously, and one which has very little in common with exploratory environments. Nevertheless, by providing modular, problem-oriented training and training materials which make explicit the basic elements of procedures (e.g., what the goal is, what actions are required, including prerequisites, and what are the outcomes), we have been able to reduce training time without impairing learning performance (as measured by our transfer task).

These are preliminary results (our analysis is in progress) but they are encouraging. The next step for us is to exert direct control over the system interface itself. Only in this way can we seriously assess what learning may be like in an exploratory environment.

The nature of active learning remains for the most part an open question in current cognitive science. Since theory in this area is not very developed or abstract, the most promising strategy seems to be one of representatively examining a variety of accessible and realistic learning domains. Each domain must of course be probed as deeply as possible on its own terms, since we have no way of knowing antecedently which generalizations we identify will turn out to be domain-independent and which will turn out to be properties specific to particular domains or sets of domains. The current study can be placed into this programmatic framework: its chief results are its indications of what needs to be done next.

ACKNOWLEDGMENTS

We are greatly indebted to Clayton Lewis who was a full collaborator in this research and an originator of many of the ideas presented here. He was unable to participate in writing this chapter. We are also grateful to Karen Greer who helped to transcribe from tape-recordings the material presented in tables. Some of this material appeared in a slightly different form in Carroll and Mack (1983).

REFERENCES

Bott, R. A *study of complex learning: theory and methodology.* CHIP Report 82, University of California at San Diego, La Jolla, CA, 1979.

Carroll, J. Learning, using, and designing command paradigms. *Human Learning: Journal of Practical Research and Application, 1,* 31–62, 1982. (a).

Carroll, J. M. The adventure of getting to know a computer. *Computer, 15(11)*, 49–58, 1982. (b)

Carroll, J. & Lasher, M. Getting to know a small computer. Manuscript, IBM Watson Research Center, 1981.

Carroll, J. M., & Mack, R. Actively learning to use a word processor. In W. Cooper (Ed.) *Cognitive aspects of skilled typewriting*. New York: Springer-Verlag, 1983. Pp. 259–281.

Carroll, J., & Thomas, J. Metaphor and the cognitive representation of computing systems. *IEEE Transactions on Systems, Man and Cybernetics, 12*, 107–116, 1982.

Ericsson, K., & Simon, H. Verbal reports as data. *Psychological Review, 87*, 215–251, 1980.

Halasz, F., & Moran, T. Analogy considered harmful. *Proceedings of the Conference on Human Factors in Computer Systems*. National Bureau of Standards, Gaithersburg, MD, 1982.

Hayes-Roth, B., & Hayes-Roth, F. A cognitive model of planning. *Cognitive Science, 3*, 275–310. 1979.

Ingalls, D. Design principles behind Smalltalk. *Byte*, 286–298, August 1981.

Jenkins, J. J. Remember that old theory of memory? Well, forget it! *American Psychologist, 29*, 785–795, 1974.

Kinneavy, J. *A theory of discourse*. Englewood Cliffs, NJ: Prentice-Hall, 1971.

Lewis, C. *Using thinking aloud protocols to study the "cognitive interface"*. Research Report RC 9265, IBM Thomas J. Watson Research Center, Yorktown Heights, NY, 1982.

Lewis, C. & Mack, R. The role of abduction in learning to use text-processing systems. Paper presented at the annual meeting of the American Educational Research Association, New York, March 19–24, 1982.

Mack, R., Lewis, C., & Carroll, J. Learning to use office systems: Problems and prospects. *ACM Transactions on Office Information Systems, 1*, 10–30, July 1983.

Malone, T. *What makes things fun to learn? A study of intrinsically motivating computer games*. Cognitive and Instructional Sciences Series CIS-7 (SSL-80-11). Xerox Palo Alto Research Center, August, 1980.

Malone, T. What makes computer games fun? *Byte*, 258–277, December 1981.

Nisbett, R., & Wilson, T. Telling more than we can know: Verbal reports on mental processes. *Psychological Review, 84*, 231–259, 1977.

Nisbett, R., & Ross, L. *Human inference: Strategies and shortcomings of social judgment*. Englewood Cliffs, NJ: Prentice-Hall, 1980.

Norman, D. A. (Ed.) *Perspectives on cognitive science*. Norwood, NJ: Ablex, 1981.

Peirce, C. S. The logic of drawing history from ancient documents. In A. Burks (Ed.), *Collected papers of Charles Sanders Peirce*. Cambridge, MA; Harvard University Press, 1958.

Rumelhart, D., & Ortony, A. The representation of knowledge in memory. In R. C. Anderson, R. Spiro, & W. Montague (Eds.), *Schooling and the acquisition of knowledge*. Hillsdale, NJ; Erlbaum, 1977.

Schrodt, P. The generic word processor: A word-processing system for all your needs. *Byte*, 32–36, April 1982.

Smith, D., Irby, C., Kimball, R., Verplank, B., & Harslem, E. Designing the STAR user interface. *Byte*, 242–282, April 1982.

Zloof, M. Query-by-example: A data base language. *IBM Systems Journal, 16*, 324–343, 1977.

Chapter 7

The Visual Channel

It is often said that we are in the middle of an information revolution, which is likened to the industrial revolution of the last century. This is a myth. Instead, what the new technologies have brought upon us is a data explosion. Data does not become information until it informs, that is, until it can be used as the basis for learning, problem solving, and decision making. Of major importance, therefore, is the development of technology to help us extract the data that is required for the task at hand from the mass of data available, and to suppress that which is secondary, superfluous, or diversionary.

But simply providing a selective "filter" is not enough. In every transaction with a computer, the user is making decisions. We need to provide the relevant information for the task at hand, and to provide it in the most articulate, succinct, and appropriate manner possible. In doing so we exploit the human capacity for perceiving structure and organization, in short, for understanding.

The main vehicle today for delivery of information from a computer to a human being is the visual channel. This chapter deals with the visual representation, presentation, perception, and comprehension of information. The technologies with which we can carry this out will also be reviewed.

Visual Perception and Human Factors

Effective human-computer interaction requires the presentation of information so that the eye and brain can see what the presenter intended to be seen. This is not always a trivial problem, because the viewer does not perceive an image that conforms exactly to the physical image displayed on a computer screen. The visual sensations reaching the eye are translated into perceptual experience by the brain through processes such as pattern recognition. We therefore need to acquaint ourselves with the way in which man experiences and perceives such phenomena as brightness, contrast, flicker, motion, and colour.

We cannot include all the relevant material in this volume, so instead we shall provide some pointers to generally accessible literature. The student of human-computer interaction is advised to consult four kinds of sources which provide complementary insights: the literature of psychology, human factors, art appreciation and interpretation, and graphic design.

Typical of the first class are a number of chapters from Boff, Kaufman, and Thomas (1986) cited in the references, a chapter by Thompson (1985), Chapters 2 and 3 of Lindsay and Norman (1977), and the book by Gregory (1966). These authors state that perception is an *active process*. What is seen is not merely a passive response to visual input, but the result of hypothesis formation and testing conditioned by our expectations. Lindsay and Norman (1977) describe this as the combination of "data driven" and "conceptually driven" processing, what computer scientists might call "bottom up" and "top down" computation.

What kinds of hypotheses are generated? Haber and Wilkinson (1982) argue that we attempt to perceive *structure* in the images we see:

The human visual system is designed to produce organized perception. Information consisting of a variety of such spatial features as size, shape, distance, relative position, and texture is structured by the mind to represent visual scenes. These spatial features are perceived as properties of things, objects in the scene, and not merely as abstract lines or surfaces. We do not perceive lines or unattached extents; we perceive objects. All parts of each object are perceived together in one construction — not as separate, independent, and free-floating elements. And all the objects are perceived as related to each other — near, far, behind, adjoining, and so forth... .

Examples of perceived structure include the ''perceptual constancies'' that result in buildings appearing to stand still, people remaining the same size and shape, and snow remaining white, despite the fact that the retinal images may have radically different positions, shapes, and brightnesses depending upon the viewing conditions. Another central concept that emerges is that of *context*, how what is seen in one part of an image is affected by what appears in adjoining parts in space (within the current scene) and in time (in the immediate recent past). More generally, what is seen is very often not what is presented — *optical illusions* are perhaps the most dramatic example of this. Illusions are often the result of multiple possible structures and competing interpretations, as in the familiar figure-ground phenomena or the Neckar cube illusion. In structuring our screens, we must not automatically assume that our intentions can be easily translated into effective presentation and communication — we must work to achieve the desired results.

Given this framework, the student can then use the above-mentioned sources to fill in some other needed background — the basic anatomical and physiological properties of the eye and of the neural pathway to the brain, the dimensions of vision and the perception of brightness, contrast, flicker, motion, and colour. The human factors literature is complementary, focusing on the optimum characteristics of specialized kinds of displays. Typical treatments are Chapter 3 of Van Cott and Kinkade (1972), Chapter 7 of Kantowitz and Sorkin (1983), and Chapters 4 and 5 of Sanders and McCormick (1987). These consider, among other topics, the appropriate design of alphanumeric displays, visual codes and symbols, quantitative and qualitative displays of data, status indicators, signal and warning lights, and representational displays. Figure 1 reproduces a summary of visual coding methods (Sanders and McCormick, 1987, p. 101), and provides some guidelines regarding our ability to discriminate displays coded using various individual stimulus dimensions. Multiple stimulus dimensions can often be combined and used effectively together.

(Numbers refer to number of levels which can be discriminated on an absolute basis under optimum conditions.)	
Alphanumeric	Single numerals, 10; single letters, 26; combinations, unlimited. Good; especially useful for identification; uses little space if there is good contrast. Certain items easily confused with each other.
Color (of surfaces)	Hues, 9; hue, saturation, and brightness combinations, 24 or more. Preferable limit, 9. Particularly good for searching and counting tasks. Affected by some lights; problem with color-defective individuals.*†
Color (of lights)	10. Preferable limit, 3. Limited space required. Good for qualitative reading.‡
Geometric shapes	15 or more. Preferable limit, 5. Generally useful coding system, particularly in symbolic representation; good for CRTs. Shapes used together need to be discriminable; some sets of shapes more difficult to discriminate than others.‡
Angle of inclination	24. Preferable limit, 12. Generally satisfactory for special purposes such as indicating direction, angle, or position on round instruments like clocks, CRTs, etc.§
Size of forms (such as squares)	5 or 6. Preferable limit, 3. Takes considerable space. Use only when specifically appropriate.
Visual number	6. Preferable limit, 4. Use only when specifically appropriate, such as to represent numbers of items. Takes considerable space; may be confused with other symbols.
Brightness of lights	3–4. Preferable limit, 2. Use only when specifically appropriate. Weaker signals may be masked.‡
Flash rate of lights	Preferable limit, 2. Limited applicability if receiver needs to differentiate flash rates. Flashing lights, however, have possible use in combination with controlled time intervals (as with lighthouse signals and naval communications) or to attract attention to specific areas.

*Feallock et al. (1966).
†M. R. Jones (1962).
‡Grether and Baker (1972).
§Muller et al. (1955).

Figure 1: Visual Coding Methods
Some rough guidelines to facilitate the appropriate use of various visual coding methods.

The Design of Effective Visual Presentation

The literature of psychology, psychophysics, and human factors typically describes and quantifies the possibilities and limits of human visual performance. The results tell us what cannot be done, what cannot possibly work. *Graphic design* is the art of the possible, the discipline of effective visual communication. Its application is essential to the design of effective displays and usable interfaces. We cannot here provide a course on graphic design, but can introduce key concepts and provide reliable pointers to the literature.

Although out of print, Bowman (1968) provides a brilliant and systematic introduction to the visual language of effective graphic communication. He describes a vocabulary of form elements — point, line, shape, value, and texture; a grammar of spatial organization — plane, multi-plane, and continuous; an idiom of volumetric perspective — parallel, angular, and oblique; and a syntax for phrasing the image — relationship, differentiation, and emphasis. Then he discusses the visualization process in terms of the three basic steps of concept, design, and production. He concludes with an extensive design library of examples of showing *what* — natural appearance, physical structure, and organization of parts in relation to the whole; showing *how* — physical movement, system of flow in relation to component parts, and process as a succession of related events; showing *how much* — physical size, numerical quantity, trend of increase or decrease, and division of its parts in terms of the whole; and, showing *where* — natural area, environmental location, and position with respect to other individual elements.

Dondis (1973) stresses that the process of *composition* is the most crucial step in visual problem solving. She illustrates with examples combining what she defines as the basic elements of visual communication — the dot, the line, shape, direction, tone, colour, texture, scale, dimension, and movement. The compositional technique she views as most important is that of *contrast*, and she devotes some effort to its explication. She also presents a variety of purposely polarized techniques for visual communication, for example, balance and instability, symmetry and asymmetry, regularity and irregularity, simplicity and complexity, and unity and fragmentation.

A third source of design ideas is Hofmann (1965), a catalog of challenging visual design examples organized around the themes of the dot, the line, confrontation, and letters and signs.

These volumes may seem far removed from our topic, but their insights can and must be applied to the design of effective displays and usable interfaces. No designer has within the past decade argued this more forcefully and more articulately than Aaron Marcus. Marcus (1983), included as a reading, illustrates with some examples from his design practice what he calls the ''three faces of computers'':

- *interfaces*
- *outerfaces*, which are the appearances of a system that is presenting data to a user
- *innerfaces*, which are a program's appearances and interfaces to its creator and its maintainers

The examples presented by Marcus demonstrate the importance of careful selection and arrangement in using typography, signs and symbols, charts and diagrams, colour, and spatial and temporal arrangement. Along with other designers, he stresses that the application of design principles to the medium of computer displays and interactive systems is not a trivial process. The medium typically has numerous special features and restrictions such as limited spatial extent, limited availability of typefaces and point sizes, restricted graphics capability, limited numbers of colours, and highly saturated colours. Nonetheless, the basic principles of design still apply, and the designer of human-computer interfaces should enlist the participation of someone skilled in graphics to enhance the quality of the interface.

Typography at the Interface

The most basic elements of graphic design, as it affects each and every user interface, is *typography*. The craft of typography begins with the design of attractive and legible *letterforms* in a variety of *typefaces* or *fonts*, that may be either *serif* or *sans-serif*, and that are arranged in families encompassing variations in *weight*, such as *regular* and *bold*, and variations in slant, such as *roman* and *italic*. Typography includes the careful arrangement of sequences of letterforms on the page with the goal of enhancing readability. This is done by controlling parameters of individual characters, such as *point size* and *letterspacing*, of words, such as *word spacing*, and of lines, such as *line length*, *leading*, and *justification*. Finally, typography encompasses the augmentation of raw text with simple graphic elements such as *rules*, *leader lines*, and *logotypes*. Many of these typographic parameters and possibilities for variation are illustrated in Figure 2.

A line of 8 pt. type, Times Roman serif font.
A line of 8 pt. type, Helvetica sans serif font.
A line of 8 pt. type, **Helvetica bold.**
A line of 8 pt. type, *Helvetica italic.*
A line of 8 pt. type, ***Helvetica bold italic.***
A line of 9 pt. type.
A l i n e o f 9 p t . t y p e , c o n s t a n t l e t t e r s p a c i n g .
A line of 9 pt. type, with normal letter spacing.
A line of 9 pt. type, with tighter word spacing.
Two lines of 9 pt. type
of shorter line length.

A line of 9 pt. type increasing the leading.

A line of 9 pt. type flush right.

A line of 9 pt. type centred.

A rule ____

A leader line ....

Logotypes ⇒⇒⇒⇒ ΔΔΔΔΔ ∇∇∇∇∇ ⇐⇐⇐⇐⇐

Figure 2: Some Typographic Variations
A brief introduction to some of the capabilities and variations possible with typography.

The discipline of typography was always relevant to screen design, even in the days of single font fixed-width 24X80 character displays (Marcus, 1982a). Recently, with the advent of low cost ''medium resolution'' laser phototypesetters and low cost ''high resolution'' bit mapped displays, the domain of possibility has broadened considerably. The computer scientist's delight in this new freedom with type has unfortunately sometimes led to ''fontitis,'' the visual chaos resulting from an undisciplined tendency to include incredible varieties of fonts and point sizes in a single display. As the eminent graphic designer Chuck Bigelow cautioned at CHI+GI '87, "What good is all this power if you lay waste to the literate landscape?"

Rosen (1963) presents a catalog of classic typefaces whose grace and expressiveness put to shame the typical appearance of our screens and print-outs. Ruder (1967) presents a rich body of evocative examples showing some of the uses and appearances of typography within design.

Our reading by Bigelow and Day (1983) introduces some of the issues of digital typography including letterform design, representation of digital letterforms, letterform quality, legibility and readability of digital text at different resolutions, and the problem of *aliasing*. More comprehensive treatments may be found in Seybold (1984), which presents digital typesetting in the context of the entire typesetting and printing process, and Rubinstein (1987), which pays particular attention to the technology of composition and layout.

Within the literature of computer science, Witten (1985) presents the fundamentals of computer typography and some solutions to the difficult problems of line breaks, hyphenation, justification, and page makeup. Up-to-date bibliographies of computer typography may be found in van Vleet (1986) and Naiman (1985a, 1985b). Of particular interest in the latter documents is an investigation of issues related to the display of coloured text for optimal legibility.

There is also much to be learned from the literature on the legibility and readability of typography. Tinker (1963, 1965) and Huey (1968) present some classic research on the legibility of type and on the psychology of reading. Hartley (1978, 1980), Kolers, Wrolstad, and Bouma (1979, 1980), Felker (1980), and Felker et al. (1981) are more modern collections of articles on the readability of documents and structured text.

Generally, text on screens has been found to be less legible than text on paper. Gould (1986) surveys much of the relevant literature and presents the results of some experiments that fail to explain why this is so, but demonstrate some of the contributing factors. More recently, Gould et al. (1986, 1987) show that reading speeds equivalent to that on paper may be obtained through the use of high-quality anti-aliased fonts displayed with dark characters on a light background on a high resolution screen.

Pictures, Symbols, Signs, and Icons

Human-computer interfaces increasingly incorporate images as well as text. Arnheim (1969) states that images can function as *pictures*, *symbols*, and *signs*.

An image serves merely as a *sign* to the extent to which it stands for a particular content without reflecting its characteristics visually... Images are *pictures* to the extent to which they portray things located at a lower level of abstractness than they are themselves. They do their work by grasping and rendering some relevant qualities — shape, colour, movement — of the objects or activities they depict... An image acts as a *symbol* to the extent to which it portrays things which are at a higher level of abstractness than is the symbol itself... .

One trend in user interfaces, arising from advances in computer graphics, is the incorporation of increasingly realistic three-dimensional portrayals (Greenberg, 1982). Mills (1982, 1985) suggests that this by itself is not sufficient to make optimal use of the medium of computer graphics, and argues that we need also pay attention to the insights into pictorial representation and communication that arise out of art, art history, design, and the psychology of visual perception (Arnheim, 1974; Gombrich, 1961). Mills shows how man's background, history, and knowledge are embodied in his "cognitive schemata" and his capacity for metaphorical thinking, and how the choice of pictorial representation can facilitate his understanding of images and his problem solving ability. The imaginative and appropriate choice of visual representation is thus a key determinant of the success of a user interface.

Another trend is that of incorporating in the interface *icons*, images representing system commands, objects, states, or results. Many icons function as pictures. For example, a schematic pen maybe used to indicate that the user may now paint, or a short thick line can indicate that lines about to be input will be drawn with a thick stroke. Some icons function as symbols, as for example, in the use of an hourglass, watch, or "smiling Buddha" to indicate that the system is working and the user should be patient.

The design of icons is a demanding craft. Dreyfuss (1972) has catalogued the incredible variety of icons in his guide to some of the 20,000 known international graphic symbols. The AIGA, American Institute of Graphic Arts (1981), has analyzed the strengths and weaknesses of passenger/pedestrian-oriented symbols in three distinct dimensions: *semantic*, *syntactic*, and *pragmatic*:

The *semantic* dimension refers to the relationship of a visual image to a meaning. How well does this symbol represent the message? Do people fail to understand the message that the symbol denotes? Do people from various cultures misunderstand this symbol? Do people of various ages fail to understand this symbol? Is it difficult to learn this symbol? Has this symbol already been widely accepted? Does this symbol contain elements that are unrelated to the message?

The *syntactic* dimension refers to the relationship of one visual image to another. How does this symbol look? How well do the parts of this symbol relate to each other? How well does this symbol relate to other symbols? Is the construction of this symbol consistent in its use of figure/ground, solid/outline, overlapping, transparency, orientation, format, scale, colour, and texture? Does this symbol use a hierarchy of recognition? Are the most important elements recognized first? Does this symbol seriously contradict existing standards or conventions? Is this symbol, and its elements, capable of systematic application for a variety of interrelated concepts?

The *pragmatic* dimension refers to the relationship of a visual image to a user. Can a person see the sign? Is this symbol seriously affected by poor lighting conditions, oblique viewing angles, and other visual 'noise'? Does this symbol remain visible throughout the range of typical viewing distances? Is this symbol especially vulnerable to vandalism? Is this symbol difficult to reproduce? Can this symbol be enlarged and reduced successfully?

The complexity of the task of icon design is illustrated in the reading in which we excerpt some pages from AIGA (1981) showing the evaluation of possible designs for icons representing "information," "arriving flights," and "exit." We will return to the use of icons in user interfaces in Chapter 10: Interaction Styles and Techniques and in Case Study D: The Star, the Lisa, and the Macintosh.

Charts, Graphs, Maps, and Diagrams

A special class of images used increasingly in computer-generated displays are those portraying quantitative data, geographic data, and complex symbolic relationships. This is done by encoding and interpreting the data and relationships in a chart, graph, map, or diagram. The formulation and generation of intelligent varieties of these images can contribute significantly to the communicative and expressive power of computer displays.

No individual has presented this case more eloquently than Edward R. Tufte (1983). His goal is *graphical excellence*, which he defines as "the efficient communication of complex quantitative ideas":

Excellence in statistical graphics consists of complex ideas communicated with clarity, precision, and efficiency. Graphical displays should:

- show the data
- induce the viewer to think about the substance rather than about methodology, graphic design, the technology of graphic production, or something else
- avoid distorting what the data have to say
- present many numbers in a small space
- make large data sets coherent
- encourage the eye to compare different pieces of data
- reveal the data at several levels of detail, from a broad overview to the fine structure
- serve a reasonably clear purpose: description, exploration, tabulation, or decoration
- be closely integrated with the statistical and verbal description of a data set.

"Graphics *reveal* data," says Tufte. He then presents in his beautiful book "a language for describing graph-ics and a practical theory of data graphics." He concludes with humility and a healthy skepticism:

Design is choice. The theory of the visual display of quantitative information consists of principles that generate design options and that guide choices among options. The principles should not be applied rigidly or in a peevish spirit; they are not logically or mathematically certain; and it is better to violate any principle than to place graceless or inelegant marks on paper. Most principles of design should be greeted with some skepticism, for word authority can dominate our vision, and we may come to see only through the lenses of word authority rather than with our own eyes.

What is to be sought in designs for the display of information is the clear portrayal of complexity. Not the complication of the simple; rather the task of the designer is to give visual access to the subtle and the difficult — that is, *the revelation of the complex*.

Those wishing to learn about the art of "the revelation of the complex" will need to supplement the Tufte book with additional readings. The next source to consult is Cleveland (1985), which presents principles of graphical construction, a catalog of appropriate graphical methods, and a paradigm for graphical perception. The use of a theory of visual perception and experimental results on visual perception to guide the design of displays is a welcome addition to the literature.

Three valuable books with a nice "how-to" flavour are Spear (1969), Schmid and Schmid (1979), and Schmid (1983). These three books, as well as the classic by Huff (1954), include illustrations of what not to do, that is, how to lie with graphic presentation. Far more insidious, however, is the well-intentioned but ill-conceived "chartjunk" (Tufte's term) intended to enliven and entertain. Herdeg (1981), a classic catalog of lively diagrams now in its fourth edition, presents numerous examples of imaginative and appropriate work interspersed with chartjunk. Holmes (1984) is even more replete with chartjunk. The student should look at these various books and think about what makes a visual presentation effective.

The advanced student can eventually progress to the monumental works of Tukey and Bertin. Tukey (1977) focuses on the exploratory analysis of data, and the use of novel forms of graphic presentation to assist in the task. Bertin (1983) begins from a cartographic perspective, but enlarges this to a comprehensive exploration of methods of applying graphic presentation to the construction of complex yet communicative diagrams, networks, and maps.

Colour

Colour is another key component of computer-generated graphics. The appropriate use of colour is difficult. Our reactions to colour result from a complex set of physiological, perceptual, and cognitive phenomena, reviewed in our reading by Murch (1985), a paper summarizing a longer treatment (Murch, 1984). Another readable introduction to the use of colour in computer graphics, presented from a design perspective, is Marcus (1982b).

Both Murch and Marcus stress the need for restraint in the use of colour, avoiding the ''fruit salad'' appearance resulting from the undisciplined use of colour. The serious student of colour will need to review considerable material from the art and design literature, for example, Albers (1963), Birren (1969a), Birren (1969b), Chevreul (1967), Hunt (1975), Itten (1961), and Yule (1967). The computer science literature has tended to focus on issues of choosing the appropriate colour space and of automating the mapping from one space to another (Joblove and Greenberg, 1978; Meyer and Greenberg, 1980; Naiman, 1985a, 1985b; Smith, 1978). Robertson and O'Callaghan (1986) deals with the use of colour to display quantitative information. The journal *Colour Research and Application* (1986) contains the proceedings of a recent meeting covering a broad range of issues in both softcopy and hardcopy computer-generated colour.

Spatial and Temporal Arrangement

Marcus (1983) and other designers such as Ruder (1969) stress the importance of composition, and, echoing an insight from psychology, suggest the use of consistent layout and formatting conventions applied with reference to an appropriate grid. The resulting visual structure serves to guide the eye as the brain attempts to parse and interpret an image, and helps the user to navigate through the succession of displays and images presented by a system in the course of its use.

Yet achieving attractive and appropriate spatial arrangement is not the only problem. The interactive computer system medium is a dynamic one, so we require, in addition to the skills of the graphic designer, the skills of the cinematographer and animator. We can look to the language of cinema for models of how our interfaces should behave. They should enable us to include, as *global* changes to the entire screen, the *cut*, the *fade in* (*fade out*), the *dissolve*, the *wipe*, the *overlay* (superimposition), and the *multiple exposure* (image combination). *Locally*, within a region of the screen, interfaces should allow the *pop on* (*pop off*), the *pull down* (*pull up*), the *flip*, and the *spin*. Finally, they should allow, as either global or local phenomena, *reverse video*, *colour changes*, *scrolling*, *panning*, *zooming in* (*zooming out*), the *close up*, and *full motion*. With such effects, an interface can more easily be made memorable and vivid, captivating and enjoyable to use.

The Technology of Visual Displays

Once we, as interface designers, understand the kinds of images that facilitate human-computer interaction, we can then turn our attention to the technology capable of generating and displaying these images. The process occurs in four steps: 1) understanding the fundamental characteristics of images as represented on computer displays; 2) understanding the kinds of changes to images that must be supported by the technology to enable interactive applications to be effective; 3) understanding the basic technology and architecture of display systems; and, 4) understanding how to apply this technology to the generation of appropriate imagery and the dynamic changes to the imagery that are required.

The technology is advancing at breakneck speed (compare, for example, the recent paper by Sproull, 1986, to that by Baecker, 1979). The reading by Sproull (1986) is a recent overview of the technology and architecture of current visual displays. It focuses on how technological parameters and architectural design of display update processors, frame buffer memories, and video generators can either facilitate or hinder the production of the displays, picture changes, and interactive techniques that interface designers require. These techniques include the incorporation of colour and anti-aliasing, smooth scrolling and dragging, rapid pop-up menus and colour table animation.

One area ignored in Sproull (1986) is the physical and pragmatic characteristics of the resulting workstation and terminal. The last decade has seen increasing interest in the use of *flat panel displays* to overcome fundamental problems of size, weight, and power consumption inherent in the use of CRT terminals. Work has concentrated on three technologies:

- *liquid crystal displays*, in which a voltage re-orients molecules within a layer of liquid crystals sandwiched between glass plates so that light is reflected or absorbed;

- *electroluminescent displays*, in which a thin film deposited in layers on a glass plate glows orange-yellow when a voltage is applied; and,

- *plasma displays*, in which neon gas sandwiched between glass plates is ionized and thereby emits orange light.

Recent books and survey papers (Refioglu, 1983; Tannas, 1985; Aldersey-Williams and Graff, 1985; Perry, Wallich, Apt, and Baldauf, 1985) report that these technologies are capturing an increasing percentage of the market for computer displays. Electroluminescent displays in particular have recently made strong advances (Tannas, 1986). Yet the CRT continues many decades of improvement in brightness, luminous efficiency, resolution, and cost. The interested reader may want to begin with Tannas (1985), which presents a comprehensive overview of the technologies of visual displays.

Concluding Remarks

We have reviewed some of the disciplines involved in enhancing interactive computing through the use of the human visual channel. In isolation, individual factors such as typography and colour are already complicated. The issues become even more subtle, however, in the combined and interacting effects of typography, symbolism, graphics, layout, and colour. Because the contributing factors are numerous and difficult to control, and the effects of task and context profound, the human factors literature has contributed little in terms of valid and generalizable results. See, for example, such studies as Tullis (1981), Tullis (1983), Dickson, DeSanctis and McBride (1986), and Bensabat, Dexter, and Todd (1986).

Given the difficulty of the problem, good progress will probably be achieved through the multi-disciplinary collaboration of the technologist *telling us what is possible*, the psychologist *telling us what not to do*, and the designer *suggesting what to do*.

Readings

Bigelow, Charles & Day, Donald (1983). Digital Typography. *Scientific American* 249(2), August 1983, 106-119.

Marcus, Aaron (1983). Graphic Design for Computer Graphics. *IEEE Computer Graphics and Applications* 3(4), July 1983, 63-70.

American Institute of Graphic Arts (1981). *Symbol Signs: The System of Passenger/Pedestrian Oriented Symbols Developed for the U.S. Department of Transportation*, New York: Hastings House, Publishers, only pp. 60-61, 104-105, 120-121 included here.

Murch, Gerald (1985). Colour Graphics — Blessing or Ballyhoo? *Computer Graphics Forum* 4, North-Holland, 127-135.

Sproull, Robert F. (1986). Frame-Buffer Display Architectures. In *Annual Review of Computer Science*, Annual Reviews Inc., 19-46.

References

American Institute of Graphic Arts (1981). *Symbols Signs: The System of Passenger/Pedestrian Oriented Symbols Developed for the U.S. Department of Transportation*, New York: Hasting House Publishers.

Albers, J. (1963,1975). *Interaction of Colour*, Standard Edition and Revised Pocket Edition, New Haven: Yale University Press.

Aldersey-Williams, Hugh & Graff, Gordon (1985). The Flat Panel Challenge. *High Technology*, December 1985, 39-45.

Arnheim, Rudolf (1969). *Visual Thinking*, Berkeley: University of California Press.

Baecker, R.M. (1979). Digital Video Display Systems and Dynamic Graphics. *Computer Graphics* 13(2), August 1979, 48-56.

Bensabat, Izak, Dexter, Albert S., & Todd, Peter (1986). An Experimental Program Investigating Color-Enhanced and Graphical Information Presentation: An Integration of the Findings. *Communications of the ACM* 29(11), November 1986, 1094-1105.

Bigelow, Charles & Day, Donald (1983). Digital Typography. *Scientific American* 249(2), 106-119.

Birren, F. (Ed.) (1969a). *Principles of Colour*, New York: Van Nostrand Reinhold Company.

Birren, F. (Ed.) (1969b). *A Grammar of Colour: A Basic Treatise on the Colour System of Albert H. Munsell*, New York: Van Nostrand Reinhold Company.

Bertin, J. (1983). *Semiology of Graphics: Diagrams, Networks, Maps*, Madison: University of Wisconsin Press.

Boff, Kenneth R., Kaufman, Lloyd, & Thomas, James P. (1986). *Handbook of Perception and Human Performance*. 2 volumes, New York: John Wiley & Sons. See especially Chapter 4, The Eye as an Optical Instrument, by Gerald Westheimer; Chapter 5, Sensitivity to Light, by Donald C. Hood & Marcia A. Finkelstein; Chapter 6, Temporal Sensitivity, by Andrew B. Watson; Chapter 7, Seeing Spatial Patterns, by Lynn A. Olzak & James P. Thomas; Chapter 8, Colorimetry and Color Discrimination; by Joel Pokorny & Vivianne C. Smith; Chapter 9, Color Appearance, by Gunter Wyszecki; Chapter 10, Eye Movements, by Peter E. Hallett; Chapter 28, Visual Information Processing, by William G. Chase; Chapter 29, Perceiving Visual Language, by Thomas H. Carr; Chapter 33, The Description and Analysis of Object and Event Perception, by I. Rock; Chapter 34, Spatial Filtering and Visual Form Perception, by Arthur P. Ginsburg; Chapter 35, Properties, Parts, and Objects, by Anne Treisman; Chapter 36, Theoretical Approaches to Perceptual Organization, by James R. Pomerantz & Michael Kubuvy; Chapter 37, Visual Functions of Mental Imagery, by Ronald A. Finke & Roger N. Shepard; and Chapter 38, Computational Approaches to Vision, by H.G. Barrow & J.M. Tenenbaum.

Bowman, William J. (1968). *Graphic Communication*, New York: John Wiley & Sons.

Chevreul, M.E. (1967). *The Principles of Harmony and Contrast of Colours and their Application to the Arts*, New York: Reinhold Publishing Company.

Cleveland, W.S. (1985). *The Elements of Graphing Data*, Monterey, California: Wadsworth Advanced Books.

Colour Research and Application (1986). Supplement to Volume 11, New York: John Wiley & Sons.

Dickson, Gary W., DeSanctis, Gerardine & McBride, D.J. (1986). Understanding The Effectiveness of Compter Graphics for Decision Support: A Cumulative Experimental Approach. *Communications of ACM* 29(1), 40-47.

Dondis, Donis A. (1973). *A Primer of Visual Literacy*, Cambridge, Mass.: MIT Press.

Dreyfuss, H. (1972). *Symbol Sourcebook: An Authoritative Guide to International Graphic Symbols*, New York: Van Nostrand Reinhold Company.

Felker, Daniel B. (Ed.) (1980). *Document Design: A Review of the Relevant Research*, Washington, D.C.: American Institutes for Research.

Felker, Daniel B., Pickering, Frances, Charrow, Veda R., Holland, V. Melissa & Redish, Janice C. (1981). *Guidelines for Document Designers*, Washington, D.C.: American Institutes for Research.

Gombrich, E.H. (1961). *Art and Illusion: A Study in the Psychology of Pictorial Representation*, Second Edition, New York: Pantheon Books.

Gould, J.D. (1987). Why Reading is Slower from CRT Displays than from Paper: Some Experiments that Fail to Explain Why. *Human Factors*, in press, also *IBM Research Report* RC-11079, 1986.

Gould, J.D., Alfaro, L., Finn, R., Haupt, B., & Minuto, A. (1986). Reading From CRT Displays Can Be as Fast as Reading from Paper. *IBM Research Report* RC-12083.

Gould, J.D., Alfaro, L., Finn, R., Haupt, B., Minuto, A., & Salaun, J. (1987). Why Reading Was Slower from CRT Displays than from Paper. *Proceedings of CHI+GI '87*, New York: ACM, 7-11.

Greenberg, Donald (1982). An Overview of Computer Graphics. In Greenberg, Donald, Marcus, Aaron, Schmidt, Allan H., & Gorter, Vernon, *The Computer Image: Applications of Computer Graphics*, Reading, Mass.: Addison-Wesley Publishing Company, 7-75.

Gregory, R.L. (1966). *Eye and Brain: The Psychology of Seeing*, New York: World University Library.

Haber, Ralph N. & Wilkinson, Leland (1982). Perceptual Components of Computer Displays. *IEEE Computer Graphics and Applications* 2(3), May 1982, 23-35.

Hartley, J. (1978). *Designing Instructional Text*, London: Kogan Page Limited.

Hartley, J. (Ed.) (1980). *The Psychology of Written Communication*, London: Kogan Page Limited.

Herdeg, W. (1981). *Diagrams: The Graphic Visualization of Abstract Data*, Fourth Expanded Edition, Zurich: Graphics Press Corp.

Hofmann, Armin (1965). *Graphic Design Manual*, New York: Van Nostrand Reinhold Company.

Holmes, Nigel (1984). *A Designer's Guide to Creating Charts and Diagrams*, New York: Watson-Guptill Publishing Company.

Huey, E.B. (1968). *The Psychology and Pedagogy of Reading*, Cambridge, Mass.: The MIT Press.

Huff, D. (1954). *How to Lie with Statistics*, New York: W.W. Norton & Company.

Hunt, R.W.G. (1975). *The Reproduction of Colour*, Third Edition, New York: John Wiley & Sons.

Itten, J. (1961). *The Art of Colour*, New York: Van Nostrand Reinhold Company.

Joblove, George H. & Greenberg, Donald (1978). Colour Spaces for Computer Graphics. *Computer Graphics* 12(3), August 1978, 20-25.

Kantowitz, Barry H. & Sorkin, Robert D. (1983). *Human Factors: Understanding People-System Relationships*, New York: John Wiley & Sons.

Kolers, P.A., Wrolstad, M.E., & Bouma, H. (1979). *Processing of Visible Language*, Vol. 1, New York: Plenum Press.

Kolers, P.A., Wrolstad, M.E., & Bouma, H. (1980). *Processing of Visible Language*, Vol. 2, New York: Plenum Press.

Lindsay, Peter H. & Norman, Donald A. (1977). *Human Information Processing: An Introduction to Psychology*, Second Edition, New York: Academic Press.

Marcus, Aaron (1982a). Designing the Face of an Interface. *IEEE Computer Graphics and Applications* 2(1), January 1982, 23-29.

Marcus, Aaron (1982b). Colour: A Tool for Computer Graphics Communication. In Greenberg, Donald, Marcus, Aaron, Schmidt, Allan H., & Gorter, Vernon, *The Computer Image: Applications of Computer Graphics*, Reading, Mass.: Addison-Wesley Publishing Company, 76-90.

Marcus, Aaron (1983). Graphic Design for Computer Graphics. *IEEE Computer Graphics and Applications* 3(4), 63-70.

Meyer, Gary W. & Greenberg, Donald (1980). Perceptual Colour Spaces for Computer Graphics. *Computer Graphics* 14(3), July 1980, 254-261.

Mills, Michael I. (1982). Cognitive Schema and the Design of Graphics Displays. *Proceedings of Graphics Interface '82*, Toronto, Ontario, 3-12.

Mills, Michael I. (1985). Image Synthesis: Optical Identity or Pictorial Communication? *Proceedings of Graphics Interface '85*, Montreal, Quebec, 303-308.

Murch, Gerald (1984). The Effective Use of Colour, Part 1: Physiological Principles, *Tekniques* 7(4), 13-16; Part 2: Perceptual Principles, *Tekniques* 8(1), 4-9; Part 3: Cognitive Principles, *Tekniques* 8(2), 25-31; Beaverton, Oregon: Tektronix Corporation.

Murch, Gerald (1985). Colour Graphics — Blessing or Ballyhoo? *Computer Graphics Forum* 4, North-Holland, 127-135.

Naiman, Avi (1985a). High Quality Text for Raster Displays. M.Sc. Thesis, Department of Computer Science, University of Toronto, January 1985.

Naiman, Avi (1985b). Colour Spaces and Colour Contrast. *Visual Computer* 1, October 1985, 194-201.

Perry, Tekla S., Wallich, Paul, Apt, Charles M., & Baldauf, David R. (1985). Computer Display: New Choices, New Tradeoffs. *IEEE Spectrum*, July 1985, 52-73.

Refioglu, H. Ihlan (Ed.) (1983). *Electronic Displays*, New York: IEEE Press.

Robertson, Philip K. & O'Callaghan, John F. (1986). The Generation of Colour Sequences for Univariate and Bivariate Mapping. *IEEE Computer Graphics and Applications* 6(2), February 1986, 24-32.

Rosen, B. (1963). *Type and Typography: The Designer's Type Book*, New York: Van Nostrand Reinhold Company.

Rubinstein, Richard (1987). *An Introduction to Digital Typography*, Maynard, Mass.: Digital Press.

Ruder, E. (1967). *Typography: A Manual of Design*, New York: Hastings House Press.

Sanders, Mark S. & McCormick, Ernest J. (1987). *Human Factors in Engineering and Design*, Sixth Edition, New York: McGraw Hill Book Company.

Schmid, C.F. (1983). *Statistical Graphics: Design Principles and Practice*, New York: John Wiley & Sons.

Schmid, C.F. & Schmid, S.E. (1979). *Handbook of Graphic Presentation*, Second Edition, New York: John Wiley & Sons.

Seybold, John W. (1984). *The World of Digital Typesetting*, Media, Penn.: Seybold Publications, Inc.

Smith, Alvy Ray (1978). Colour Gamut Transform Pairs. *Computer Graphics* 12(3), August 1978, 12-19.

Spear, M.E. (1969). *Practical Charting Techniques*, New York: McGraw-Hill Book Company.

Sproull, Robert F. (1986). Frame-Buffer Display Architectures. In *Annual Review of Computer Science*, Annual Reviews, Inc., 19-46.

Tannas, Lawrence E., Jr. (1985). *Flat-Panel Displays and CRTs*, New York: Van Nostrand Reinhold Company.

Tannas, L.E., Jr. (1986). Electroluminescence Catches the Public Eye. *IEEE Spectrum* 23(10), October 1986, 37-42.

Thompson, Peter (1985). Visual Perception: an Intelligent System with Limited Bandwidth. In Monk, Andrew (Ed.) (1985), *Fundamentals of Human-Computer Interaction*, London: Academic Press.

Tinker, M.A. (1963). *Legibility of Print*, Ames, Iowa: Iowa State University Press.

Tinker, M.A. (1965). *Bases for Effective Reading*, Minneapolis: University of Minnesota Press.

Tufte, Edward R. (1983). *The Visual Display of Quantitative Information*, Cheshire, Conn.: Graphics Press.

Tukey, J.W. (1977). *Exploratory Data Analysis*, Reading, Mass: Addison-Wesley Publishing Company.

Tullis, Thomas S. (1981). An Evaluation of Alphanumeric, Graphics, and Color Information Displays. *Human Factors* 23(5), 541-550.

Tullis, Thomas S. (1983). The Formatting of Alphanumeric Displays: A Review and Analysis. *Human Factors* 25(6), 657-682.

Witten, Ian H. (1985). Elements of Compute Typography. *International Journal of Man-Machine Studies* 23, 623-687.

Van Cott, H.P. & Kinkade, R.G. (Eds.) (1972). *Human Engineering Guide to Equipment Design*, Revised Edition, American Institutes for Research.

van Vleet, J.C. (Ed.) (1986). *Text Processing and Document Manipulation*, Cambridge: Cambridge University Press.

Yule, J.A. (1967). *Principles of Colour Reproduction*, New York: John Wiley & Sons.

Digital Typography

Most type is now produced not by casting metal or by photography but by computer. The digital typesetter can create new letterforms with the flexibility of a scribe at up to 15,000 characters per second

by Charles Bigelow and Donald Day

The type on this page of *Scientific American* is set by a machine whose operation is digital. It is formed on the screen of a cathode-ray tube by an electron beam moving in a vertical pattern consisting of 800 lines to the horizontal inch; the motion of the beam is fast enough to generate a page of text in about 15 seconds. The resolution of the screen is much higher than that of a standard television receiver, but in other respects the two devices operate in the same way. The tiny individual picture elements—pixels—along each scan line can be made to fluoresce or remain dark by turning the beam on or off as it scans. The resulting pattern of discrete vertical strokes, which would be visible at moderate magnification, is perceived by the unaided eye as a page of smooth letterforms.

Although a digital computer is needed to control the on-off pattern of the electron beam, the type itself is digital because it is made up of discrete elements. These elements can be line strokes, pixels, colors, shades of gray or any other graphic unit from which a letterform can be constructed. Hence digital typography is not new: mosaic tiles, embroidered samplers and arrays of lights on theater marquees have long represented alphabetic characters as relatively coarse discrete arrays. These digital letterforms, however, are typographic curiosities, far from the mainstream of traditional type design and composition. The traditional letter is not digital but analogue; its final form varies smoothly with the continuous variation of some process employed in its creation, such as the pressure of a brush on paper or the contour of a punch that stamps the matrix or mold used to cast type in metal. With the development of the computer and digital electronics, typography in the past 15 years has been seeing a wholesale replacement of analogue text by digital text, which may rival the shift in the Renaissance from script to print.

It is estimated that each day in the U.S. about 10^{14} letters are reproduced; indeed, letterforms make up much of the visual texture of civilized life. Although some letters are now destined primarily to be "read," or decoded, by a machine, all letters must be read by people if the communication channel between writer and reader is to remain intact. Reading skills, however, are difficult and costly to acquire. In order to protect this educational investment the letters one reads as an adult must not be noticeably different from the letters one learned as a child, and the letterforms read by the current generation must not be significantly different from the ones created by previous generations. The transition to digital typography therefore presents a subtle question with far-reaching implications: How is it possible to take the fullest advantage of digital technology and still ensure that digital letterforms retain the quality of the traditional letters, whose beauty and legibility have contributed profoundly to literacy in our culture?

The advantages of digital typography are substantial: once letterforms are represented as discrete elements they can be efficiently encoded as discrete and distinguishable physical properties in any convenient medium, processed as bits of information by a computer, transmitted over great distances as pulses of current and decoded to reconstitute the letterforms for the person receiving the message. Indeed, once type is digitized it is effectively encoded in the binary language of the computer, and so the size, shape and subtler characteristics of letters can be readily modified by a computer program. Since some varieties of digital type can be read by machines, the semantic content of the information represented by the letters can be manipulated by a computer as well as the letterforms. Unlike analogue information, digital information is highly resistant to noise or degradation introduced during the transmission of a signal. The digital receiving device need distinguish between only two states of the signal (say on or off) in order to decode and recover the information originally transmitted.

Digital typography can be adapted to a wide variety of output devices. The composition of most daily newspapers and national magazines in the U.S. is done by cathode-ray-tube typesetters. A new generation of high-resolution laser printers has now been introduced; a highly collimated laser beam replaces the electron beam as a writing instrument, and it can either expose a typographic image on a printing plate directly from digital information or make an intermediate photographic exposure on paper or film. Lower-resolution laser printers, which are also called text setters, are employed as output devices in data processing and in the publication of forms and documents in small batch quantities. In such devices the laser beam writes out the image of the text by setting up a pattern of electrostatic charge on a belt or drum. Fine pigmented particles called toner particles are attracted to the belt or drum where the charge is created, are transferred to paper like ink from a press and are then

SAMPLES OF DIGITAL LETTERFORMS, shown at decreasing resolution from the second row to the bottom row of the illustration, are each based on the designs in the top row by Kris Holmes and one of the authors (Bigelow). The letters in each row are formed by superposing a square grid of increasing coarseness on the model letterforms at the top. If some part of the model letter coincides with the center of a square on the grid, the entire square is blackened; otherwise the square is left white. Because digital type is constructed out of discrete elements, it is ideally suited for storage, transfer and manipulation by digital electronics systems and computers. Nevertheless, it imposes a new set of constraints on typographic design: the basic letterforms must be "well tempered," that is, they must retain maximum legibility across a variety of digital displays, and so the designer must take into account many versions of the image simultaneously. The digital letters were generated by Autologic, Inc., of Newbury Park, Calif.

RNQbaeg

RNQbaeg

RNQbaeg

RNQbaeg

RNQbaeg

RNQbaeg

RNQbaeg

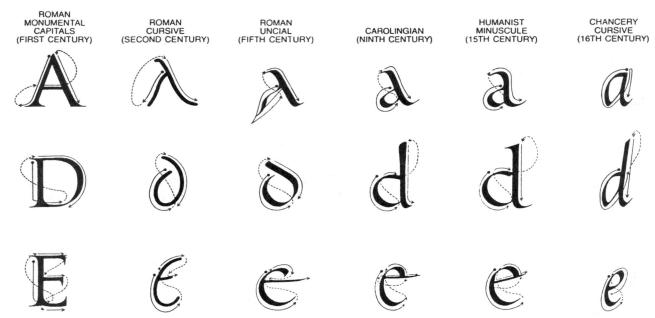

| ROMAN MONUMENTAL CAPITALS (FIRST CENTURY) | ROMAN CURSIVE (SECOND CENTURY) | ROMAN UNCIAL (FIFTH CENTURY) | CAROLINGIAN (NINTH CENTURY) | HUMANIST MINUSCULE (15TH CENTURY) | CHANCERY CURSIVE (16TH CENTURY) |

DUCTAL LETTERS are handwritten letters whose basic topology is the result of a smooth series of movements of the writing tool in the plane of the writing surface. The path of the tool is called ductus. The ductus of each letter is shown in color; the broken lines indicate the part of the ductus that is invisible in the final form of the letter, namely the path of the tool when it is not in contact with the writing sur-

ironed or fused onto the paper by heat.

There are also many devices in service whose output resolution is quite low, that is, far fewer pixels are available to approximate the form of the letter than are required for finely rendered alphabetic details. For example, the printer that is often attached to both large and personal computers is made up of a column of fine wires. The tips of the wires strike a ribbon impregnated with ink and impose a pattern of ink dots in a vertical column on the paper. As the column of wires moves across the page the tips of different wires in the column are actuated by solenoid magnets, and so the changing pattern of vertical dots on the page generates digital text. Ink-jet printers have also been developed that create letter images by directing the flight of electrically charged ink droplets toward the paper. The trajectory of the droplets is controlled by charging them electrically and then passing them through an electrostatic field [see "Ink-Jet Printing," by Larry Kuhn and Robert A. Myers; SCIENTIFIC AMERICAN, April, 1979]. Soft-copy, or transient, images of digital type on cathode-ray tubes, liquid-crystal displays and light-emitting diodes have become increasingly important as the number of personal computer work stations and word-processing devices has grown.

The capacity of all such devices to render typographic characters is best estimated by the number of pixels along the side of a square called an em square, which is equal to the printer's point size of the type in a given font. (There are approximately 72 printer's points to the inch.) The side of an em square, which is also called an em, is slightly more than the distance from the top of the ascender on a letter such as the lowercase h to the bottom of the descender on a letter such as the lowercase y. For the standard text size called pica, or 12-point type, most high-resolution digital typesetters have a resolution of from 100 to 300 lines per em; electrostatic text setters have a resolution of from 33 to 80 lines per em, and low-resolution digital output devices can vary from 10 to 30 lines per em.

The speed, versatility and low cost of digital typography have made its proliferation irresistible. Moreover, if the letterform is mapped onto a raster, or grid, of digital pixels that is sufficiently fine, the differences between the original letter and the digital letter are virtually indistinguishable. In principle it seems possible, given a fine enough digital raster, to imitate any of the traditional printed or written letterforms, no matter how refined. In practice, however, digital typography, like any other technological innovation, carries with it special problems and a new set of selective pressures.

For example, not all digital typography can begin at high resolution. There are technical limitations on the size of the dot that can currently be reproduced

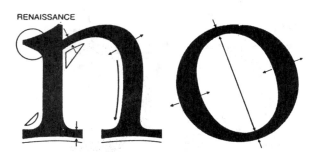

RENAISSANCE

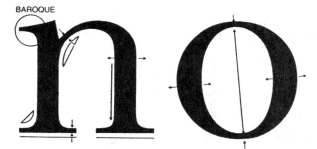

BAROQUE

EVOLUTION OF GLYPTAL LETTERS reflects the fundamental changes in the technology of letter production brought about by the invention of printing from movable type. The letter image was no longer the result of a series of strokes written "on the fly" by a scribe; instead each letter was painstakingly engraved as a single master copy onto the face of a steel punch. Early glyptal letters such as the Renaissance forms imitated scribal forms such as the Humanist minuscule, and many details (*color*) simulate the effects of a broad-edged

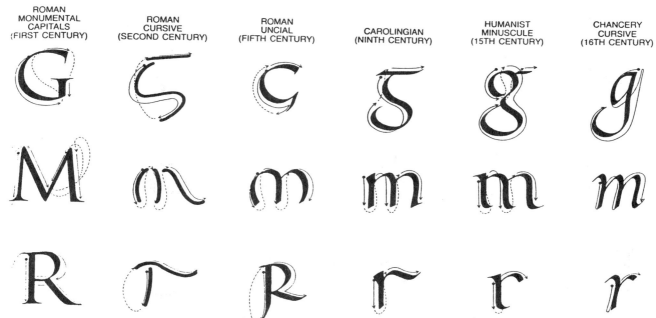

| ROMAN MONUMENTAL CAPITALS (FIRST CENTURY) | ROMAN CURSIVE (SECOND CENTURY) | ROMAN UNCIAL (FIFTH CENTURY) | CAROLINGIAN (NINTH CENTURY) | HUMANIST MINUSCULE (15TH CENTURY) | CHANCERY CURSIVE (16TH CENTURY) |

face. Alphabets such as the Roman capitals, for which a high proportion of the ductus is invisible, are called formal, whereas alphabets such as Chancery cursive, for which a high proportion of the ductus is visible, are called cursive. Much of the evolution of the Latin alphabet is the result of the interplay of the opposing tendencies between formal and cursive writing. The calligraphy was done by Holmes.

by methods such as ink-jet printing, and the attainable resolutions are too coarse to escape visual detection. Moreover, the speed and cost advantages of digital typography are reduced as the number of digital bits needed to generate the letter is increased. The number of pixels per letter increases as the square of the linear resolution of the printing device: doubling the linear resolution of the device implies a fourfold increase in the amount of information, or number of bits, that must be transmitted and processed. Although there are computational methods for compressing the data in the bit map of a letterform, the general relation between cost and resolution remains valid.

Perhaps the most challenging problem that confronts the digital-type designer is to make effective use of the enormous flexibility inherent in digital technology. For example, the text of a document could first be written at a cathode-ray-tube terminal with a reso-

lution of 10 lines per em for pica type. A proof of the same text could then be pulled from a wire-matrix printer with a resolution of 20 lines per em, circulated for correction and commentary as the output of a laser text setter with a resolution of 50 lines per em and finally set for publication on a cathode-ray-tube typesetter with a resolution of 200 or more lines per em. Similarly, when digital letters must be represented at different sizes on a machine with a fixed raster, a different bit map is required for each letter size. It is obviously desirable in such circumstances for the type designer to create a single kernel, or underlying, letterform that can generate all the forms in which the letter occurs on different machines and in various sizes.

In order to appreciate the magnitude of the problem, consider the variability of letterforms that is reflected in a single superfamily of typeface designs. For each modern design one of each of three opposing features must be speci-

fied: whether the type is roman or italic, whether it is normal weight or boldface and whether it is serif or sans-serif. (A serif is a short finishing stroke to a major writing stroke, such as the small horizontal line at the bottom of the stem in the letter T as it appears on this page; sans-serif type has no serifs.) Taken together, the three features generate eight typeface designs. Furthermore, each type alphabet typically includes characters in 16 different sizes. The total number of glyphs, or individual bit maps, necessary to accommodate a single character for a minimum superfamily of type is therefore 128; the number of glyphs necessary for a complete superfamily, which may include 128 letterforms, is 128^2, or more than 16,000.

Although digital technology imposes a new set of problems on typographic design, such problems are not without precedent; it is instructive to explore the relative stability of the letterforms

NEOCLASSICAL

pen held at an angle of approximately 30 degrees to the horizontal. In general the contrast between thick and thin elements is relatively low. In the Baroque and Neoclassical versions of the glyptal letter symmetry, harmony of structure and contrast between thick and thin

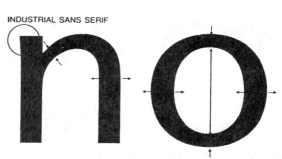

INDUSTRIAL SANS SERIF

strokes become more important than the trace of the pen. More recent designs either eliminated serifs, as in the industrial sans-serif types, or converted the serifs into independent elements, as in the industrial slab serif (not shown). The drawings were done by Holmes.

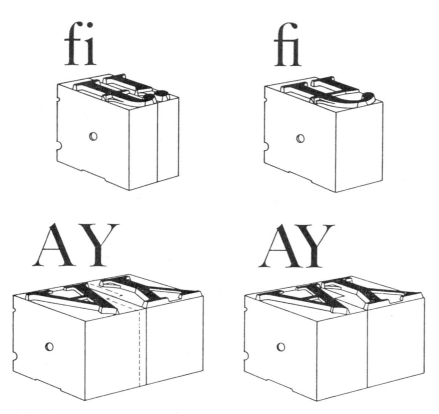

METAL TYPE is cast on a body of fixed width, and so the variant forms and spacing for different combinations of letters that are hallmarks of the fine manuscript cannot easily be emulated. In the first decades after the invention of movable type some printers cast hundreds of variant letterforms, thereby nearly canceling the advantage in time and economy afforded by the new technology. Later forms were well-tempered designs, cast on a metal body in such a way that their assembly into words would automatically lead to proper spacing. A few combinations, such as *fi*, resisted tempering and were cast on a single body of metal. Other letter combinations such as *AY* could not be properly spaced unless the type body was mortised by hand.

6 POINT
RQEN baegnov

8 POINT
RQEN baegnov

14 POINT
RQEN baegnov

18 POINT
RQEN baegnov

SCALING THE SIZE of type cannot be done proportionally even within a single typeface if optimum legibility is to be retained. In the smaller sizes from six to 12 point the letters must be wider and their stems, hairlines and serifs must be thicker than their counterparts in larger sizes. Moreover, in smaller sizes ascenders such as the stem of the lowercase *b* and descenders such as the tail of the lowercase *g* must be shorter in proportion to the height of the lowercase *n;* the counter, or interior space of a letterform, must be more open and the space between letters must be greater. The type font in the illustration is Times Roman; it has been scaled photographically to the same height of the letter *n* so that differences in design can be compared.

through typographic history and their adaptations under the pressures imposed by previous technological shifts. Two stages in the evolution of type design can be recognized following the introduction of each new technology. First, there is a period of imitation, in which the outstanding letterforms of the previous typographic generation serve as models for the new designs. Second, as designers grow more confident and familiar with the new medium, innovative designs emerge that are not merely imitative but exploit the strengths and explore the limitations of the medium. Since type is ultimately intended for the reader, however, the technology of type production is not the only influence on the final letterform; typographic design remains an art, and the successful design subtly reflects the tension between imitation and innovation.

The shapes of letters have persisted longer than any other artifacts in common use. Letter designs are still in service that are more than 2,000 years old, and many common typefaces are replicas of designs popular in the 15th and 16th centuries. The text type in this magazine, for example, was originally designed by the British typographers Stanley Morison and Victor Lardent for *The Times* of London in 1931 and is called Times Roman. It is based on French and Flemish types designed in about 1570. The basic forms of our lowercase alphabet were established in the eighth century in the monasteries and chancelleries of Charlemagne's Frankish empire. The forms of our capital letters are substantially the same as those inscribed by the Romans in the reign of Augustus Caesar. Fully half of our capital letterforms are structurally unaltered from the inscriptional forms used in Periclean Athens in the fifth century B.C.

In the scribal era the contours of the letterform were created by a continuous sequence of movements of a brush or a pen as it moved across the plane of the writing surface. During the smooth sequence of movements the writing tool was pressed against the surface or lifted from it, thereby generating the strokes that make up the letter. The sequential pattern of movements is called ductus, and it defines a characteristic topological structure for each letter of the alphabet. The evolution of writing was impelled by changes in ductus [*see top illustration on preceding two pages*] and by variations in the shape and flexibility of the writing tool. The tool was responsible for the contrast between thick and thin strokes. When the tool was an edged pen, the contrast of the letter was determined by the angle between the edge and the direction in which the pen was moving in the plane of the writing surface. When the tool was a brush or a flexible pointed pen, the contrast in the letter was determined by variations in pressure as the tool described its ductus.

An important advantage of scribal lettering is the immediate feedback between the final form of the letter and the scribe. The accomplished scribe is expert in making minor changes in the form of each letter in order to harmonize the letter with the letters adjacent to it. Moreover, to justify lines of text the scribe could insert alternative or abbreviated forms of letters and words. The great disadvantage of scribal practice, of course, is that the design of each letter must be executed in "real time": any letter that is to be read must be generated from scratch each time by hand.

When movable type was invented in Europe, it was at first modeled on scribal forms current in the 15th centu-ry, even though it was created by a radically different technology. An image of the letterform was engraved in relief onto the face of a steel punch. The punch was then hardened and struck into a blank of copper to form an intaglio, or recessed, matrix. The matrix was placed in an adjustable mold; when a molten alloy of lead, tin, antimony and copper was poured into the mold and the matrix, the design appeared in relief once again on the face of the cooled alloy. The face of the type was then inked and impressed directly onto paper. The letterform was thus created by a glyptal, or sculptural, process. The letter design was freed from the limitations of real-time execution but was constrained by the need to place it on a rigid rectangular solid. In order to imitate the scribal variations in letterform for different letter combinations a few early hot-metal typographers maintained hundreds of variant letterforms; such forms were so expensive to cast as well as to compose, however, that they nearly negated the economic advantages of movable type.

The evolution of glyptal typeface contours was guided by conceptual and perceptual forces instead of by the needs of rapid handwriting. Greater attention was given to the shape of the spaces within letters and between them. Proportion, width, weight and construction were altered independently of the underlying topology of the letter rather than being partially determined by it, as they were in the ductal letter. The designers of glyptal letters were obliged to make a different engraving for each let-

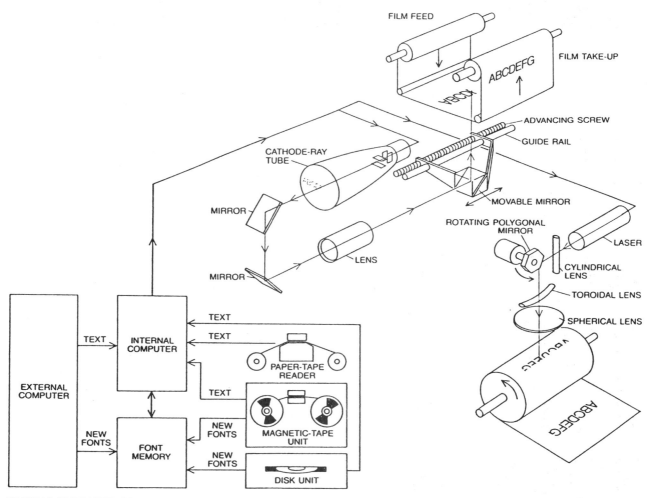

DIGITAL TYPESETTING MACHINES can store enormous numbers of type fonts for almost instant retrieval and can generate characters in almost any size at rates of up to 15,000 characters per second. The data are entered into the machine by means of punch-coded paper tape, by magnetic tape or disk or as a stream of data from an external computer. In the most recent installations the external computer organizes the text into lines, columns and pages, justifies the text if that is wanted and automatically hyphenates words where it is necessary for good spacing. Once the font, size and position of each character on the page have been specified, the data are assembled into a series of electronic pulses by an internal, "slave" computer, which drives a marking engine. In the schematic diagram two kinds of marking engine are shown. (The two devices would not both be incorporated into any real machine.) In the cathode-ray-tube typesetter an electron beam reconstructs each letter as a series of closely spaced vertical lines. The image is projected onto photosensitive film or paper. In the laser printer a laser beam takes the place of the electron beam; the laser scans horizontally across an entire page at once and generates a pattern of charge on a drum. Toner particles are attracted to the charged regions and ironed directly onto paper by heat.

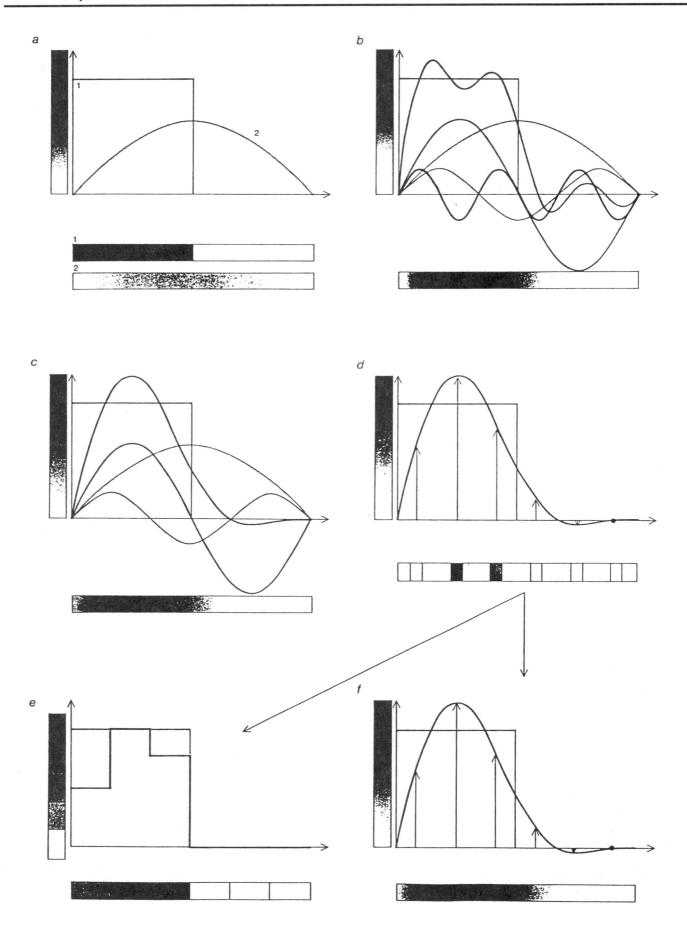

ter size, and so, like their scribal fore-bears, they could make subtle adjust-ments in spacing and stroke width for different type sizes in order to accom-modate the eye. Alternative letterforms were almost entirely eliminated, and the special demands of the new technology were met by letter designs that were felicitous in almost any combination. Nevertheless, the vestiges of the earlier ductal technology were still evident in type fonts cast in the mid-20th century: certain letter combinations such as *fi, fl, ffi* and *ffl* were cast as a ligature, that is, on a single body of metal. To achieve good spacing for combinations such as *TA* and *AY* the body of the type was often kerned, or mortised, by hand at considerable cost.

With the advent of photocomposi-tion in the mid-1950's, typogra-phy was confronted once again by a new set of technological variables. In ear-ly phototypesetters a stroboscopic light was flashed through a negative master character mounted on transparent film or glass, and from there through a lens that projected an image of the master character onto photosensitive paper or film. The size of the letter image was controlled by interchanging several lenses or by employing a zoom lens of variable focal length. A printing plate was made from the image after the pa-per or film was photographically devel-oped. Because the position of the char-acter on the paper was controlled by the lens and by a prism or mirror that moved in fine increments across a line of type, the adjustment of interletter spac-ing for special letter combinations was much simpler than the kerning of metal type. On the other hand, a significant advantage of hot-metal typography was given up. The type design could not be varied with the size of the type without preparing a new master image. The cost of additional master-image carriers and the inconvenience of inter-changing them discouraged their use.

The typographer working within the constraints of each of these technologies faced a set of problems quite similar to those now encountered by the digital type designer. For example, any typo-graphic version of the letterforms fa-miliar to the reading public is a success-ful communication system to the extent that it is able to balance two oppos-ing characteristics: discriminability and similarity of alphabetic characters. To avoid confusing the reader each letter must be rapidly and unambiguously dis-tinguishable from every other letter. On the other hand, the letterforms must also share many graphic features: if a letterform is too distinctive from the other letters in a font of type, it disturbs the flow of reading. Donald E. Knuth of Stanford University has succinctly stat-ed the goal of text-type design: "A font should be sublime in its appearance but subliminal in its effect."

Throughout the history of writing economic pressures have opposed the pressures for more readable and more beautiful typography. As always, there-fore, need must be matched to purpose. Letter quality can be sacrificed on cer-tain documents if the tradeoff is faster, cheaper or more compact reproduction. A bill of sale, for example, can be cheap to prepare and to store because it will be read infrequently by few people; the slow and expensive production of an in-scription is justified when it will be read frequently by the multitude. In the time of the Romans the basic alphabet was written rapidly in a semilegible cursive when it was employed in a papyrus doc-ument, but it was chiseled in clear im-perial capitals on a monument. Today inexpensive dot-matrix printout is less readable than the costly typography in mass-market advertising.

The effects on the reader of complex variations in letter design have not yet been quantified, but the response of the visual system to simple spatial varia-tions in light intensity has been studied for more than two decades. The simplest

variation to analyze is a visual analogue of an acoustically pure tone, whose peri-odic variation of intensity with time can be plotted as a sine or cosine wave. A train of spatial sine or cosine waves can be visualized as a ribbon compressed along its length so that its edge traces a series of ordinary sine or cosine waves. If the top side of the ribbon were shaded in such a way that the crests of the rib-bon were black, the troughs remained white and the intermediate sections were various shades of gray, then the blurred, parallel bands, or grating, of light and dark that could be seen from above the ribbon would form a spatial sinusoidal wave train.

A pure musical tone is characterized by its amplitude, or loudness, and by its frequency, or pitch. The ampli-tude of a spatial sine or cosine wave is the maximum contrast, or deviation from neutral gray, that is found in the lightest or darkest parts of the wave train, and the frequency is the number of variations from light to dark and back again within a given distance. Psycho-physicists have measured the ability of the visual system to distinguish sinusoi-dal bands of various contrasts and fre-quencies from a uniformly gray field. They have found that sensitivity to spa-tial variation of light and dark depends on the frequency of the variation; the sensitivity is greatest when the spatial frequency is approximately three cycles per degree of visual angle, and no con-trast, no matter how strong, can be per-ceived under most conditions when the frequency is greater than 60 cycles per degree. (The detection of telephone wires against the sky is one of the rela-tively unusual circumstances in which spatial frequencies that are probably higher than 60 cycles per degree can be discerned.)

What is the importance of these find-ings for reading? Although the spatial variation from black to white in letter-forms is not sinusoidal, fundamental rhythmic patterns in the letterforms are apparent. For example, as the lowercase letter *n* is scanned from left to right across its middle, the brightness of the image varies fairly smoothly from light to the dark stem of the first vertical stroke, then light again in the counter, or interior of the letterform, then dark on the second vertical stroke and finally light again to the right of the letter. Be-cause reading is often done under rather poor lighting conditions, one might ex-pect that the fundamental frequency of text letterforms has evolved to match the peak contrast sensitivity of the visu-al system.

Such a match is almost exactly what is found in the typesetting of English. In close reading the image given the most attention is projected onto the fovea, the most sensitive area of the retina. The

SPATIAL-FREQUENCY ANALYSIS can be carried out for any two-dimensional image, such as a letter, just as the graph of almost any mathematical function can be approximated by a sum of sines and cosines. A sharp-edged rectangle, for example, can be represented as a straight line parallel to the horizontal axis of the graph; the density of gray or black in the rec-tangle corresponds to the height of the line above the horizontal axis. In order to approximate the rectangle a unique set of sine and cosine waves can be superposed. The first sine wave in the approximation is shown in *a*. The spatial wave, or variation from white through shades of gray and back to white, that corresponds to the sine wave is a rather crude approximation to the rectangle. The more sine and cosine components there are in the approximation, however, the better it becomes: the five colored sine waves of various heights and wavelengths are added together along each vertical line to give the smooth red curve in *b*. In order to eliminate high-frequency noise any shape can be electronically filtered to remove components above a certain frequency. In *c* the two highest-frequency components of the red curve in *b* have been eliminated, namely the yellow and purple sine waves, and the result is the red curve in *c*. The filtered curve can be sampled by finding its height, or gray-scale value, at evenly spaced intervals along the horizontal axis (*d*). A digital approximation to the filtered curve is made by assigning a discrete shade of gray across an interval that corresponds to each sample (*e*). It can be mathematically proved that the original filtered curve can be completely reconstructed from the samples by interpolating between the sample points, provided the frequency at which the samples are taken is greater than twice that of the highest-frequency component of the filtered curve (*f*).

fovea subtends an angle of one or two degrees, and at a reading distance of 12 inches the subtended angle corresponds to a linear distance only slightly more than the length of a five-letter word set in 10-point type, the commonest type size. There are on the average about 10 spatial cycles across a five-letter word, and so the spatial frequency of the image received at the fovea is about five to 10 cycles per degree, only slightly higher than the most contrast-sensitive frequency of the visual system. There is good evidence that in fast reading word groups longer than five letters can be read in one eye fixation. The reading image is then partially projected onto the parafovea, the region of the retina surrounding the fovea.

We have tacitly assumed so far that the major patterns of black and white that make up letterforms are sinusoidal spatial waves, but it may not be apparent that the sine-wave model can support a more detailed analysis. It turns out, however, that just as the complex sound of a symphony orchestra can be analyzed as a sum of harmonics, or pure tones of various frequencies and intensities, so can almost any form be analyzed as a combination of many spatial sine and cosine waves. The result follows from a theorem of the French mathematician Jean Baptiste Joseph Fourier. In 1807 Fourier proved that by superposing one-dimensional sine and cosine waves of various phases, amplitudes and frequencies the graph of almost any function can be approximated to any desired degree of accuracy [*see illustration on page 114*].

In two dimensions the spatial sinusoidal components have an additional degree of freedom, namely their orientation with respect to some fixed direction in the plane. Fourier's theorem shows it is possible to reconstruct almost any pattern such as a letterform to any desired accuracy by superposing spatial sine and cosine waves of the proper phase, amplitude, frequency and orientation. In general the high spatial frequencies of a letter image correspond to its edges and to such details as fine serifs and the tapering of the main strokes of the letter. As we have stated, the low spatial frequencies define the fundamental rhythm of the letter, or in other words its overall pattern of light and dark. The spectrum of spatial frequencies required to represent a letter is called the bandwidth of the letter. Based solely on the maximum frequency at which the eye can detect contrast, namely 60 cycles per degree of visual angle, it might seem that completely adequate typographic reproduction could be achieved if all the spatial frequencies of a letterform above 60 cycles per degree were eliminated.

In practice high-quality digital typesetting requires that letterforms include spatial frequencies at least as high as 120 cycles per degree. One reason is that for fine detail such as the hairline at the end of a serif the acuity of the visual system may well exceed 60 cycles per degree. The main reason, however, is the relation between the spatial frequencies that make up the input letter and the process of digitizing the letter: reducing the letterform to an array of discrete units. In order to digitize a letter it must be sampled at various points. For example, if the edges of the letter were perfectly sharp, the letter could be sampled by superposing it on a grid of squares and then noting whether or not the point at the center of each square coincides with some point on the letter. If the center point of a square coincides with a point on the letter, the entire square is shaded black; if the center point does not coincide with any point on the letter, the square is left unshaded.

A perfectly sharp edge would require an infinite number of sines and cosines to represent its full spectral bandwidth. On the other hand, if the bandwidth of a letter is limited in such a way that it includes no sinusoidal component above a certain frequency, its edges must be slightly blurred. The superposition of a finite number of sinusoidal components yields a smooth transition from the black through shades of gray to white. There is nonetheless a mathematical advantage to the band-limited letter: according to results developed by Harry Nyquist at the Bell Telephone Laboratories in 1924 and 1928 and extended by Claude E. Shannon, also of Bell Laboratories, in 1949, if one knows the highest-frequency component of a band-limited signal and if samples are taken with equal spacing at any rate greater than twice the highest-frequency component, the original band-limited letter can be completely reconstructed from the sample points alone. Theoretically, therefore, a letter whose highest frequency is 60 cycles per degree of visual angle can be reconstructed solely from the measured gray values at evenly spaced sample points taken slightly more frequently than 120 times per degree of visual angle.

One difficulty with the theoretical sampling frequency is the small error introduced by the machines that scan

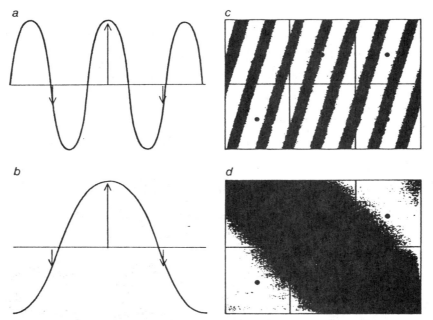

ALIASING is the commonest form of noise, or unwanted signal, found in digital typography. When the height of a wave or the gray-scale values of an image are sampled, information in the original curve or image may be lost. A reconstruction of the wave or the image from the sample points requires that the values of points between the sampled points be interpolated by finding sine and cosine components whose superposition coincides with the values of the sampled points. If the original wave or image is sampled at less than twice the frequency of its highest-frequency component, however, the highest-frequency components found by the reconstruction will have an alias frequency, lower than the highest-frequency component in the original image. In other words, spurious low-frequency components will replace the true high-frequency ones. For example, if a sine wave is sampled only 1.5 times per cycle (*a*), a reconstruction that matches the values of the samples (*colored arrows*) is a sine wave of half the original frequency (*b*). In the two-dimensional spatial wave the samples are gray-scale values taken at the centers of squares (*c*). A reconstruction of the image from the sampled values generates an alias not only of lower frequency than the original waves but also oriented in a different direction (*d*). Quantizing a letter image only compounds the errors introduced by aliasing.

and sample the input letters. Sample points may not be evenly spaced and the measured values of gray may be slightly inaccurate. A more serious problem is that, in practice, sharp band limiting is impossible. Hence in typography of the highest quality the samples are taken at a rate of at least 240 per degree of visual angle, which is theoretically sufficient to reconstruct a letter band-limited at 120 cycles per degree. Such a sampling rate is equivalent to a resolution of 200 lines per em for 12-point type, or 1,200 lines per inch.

If the letter image is sampled too sparsely, that is, at less than twice the frequency of its highest sinusoidal component, the gray-scale values of the samples can be identical with the values that would be given by a lower spatial frequency [see illustration on opposite page]. In such undersampling noise is added and information is inevitably lost. Low-frequency spatial waves that do not figure in the original wave spectrum of the letter replace the original high-frequency components; a reconstruction of the original letter from such samples would incorporate the spurious low-frequency components. The phenomenon is called aliasing, and it is the most obvious source of noise or distortion in digital typography. When the letter is converted into an array of pixels from the samples, the aliasing becomes manifest, and the amount of aliasing depends on the coarseness of the sampling.

At a high output resolution aliasing is evident only as a slight roughness in the letter contours; at medium resolution the contours become jagged, and at lower resolution the curves become polygonal and the diagonals develop dislocations. At still lower resolution the differences among straight, curved and diagonal elements is obscured and the letters become illegible. Moreover, as the resolution becomes coarser the diversity of possible letter designs is reduced; for very coarse resolutions, such as the five-by-seven or six-by-nine arrays of dots on many cathode-ray-tube terminals and dot-matrix printers, few variant designs are possible.

A less obvious but ultimately more serious consequence of undersampling is the loss of information about the proportional relations reflected in an alphabet design. In a design that has been finely tuned to the characteristics of the visual system there is a subtle interplay of proportion and thickness among the thick elements of a letterform and between thick and thin elements. The ratio of stem height to the height of the lowercase letter x and to the average width of a letter is also carefully adjusted. The outcome of such detail in design is barely perceptible in the individual letterform, but in a block of text the design becomes manifest as a visually harmonious pattern of black letterforms and white counterforms and a pleasing level of gray in the text as a whole. At a high digital resolution these proportional variations can be closely approximated, and the typographic texture appears only slightly less refined than it is in analogue typography. As the digital resolution of a letterform is decreased, however, proportional variations are rounded off, typographic elements become homogeneous and the resulting textual pattern seems crude and awkward.

When cost or the technical limits of

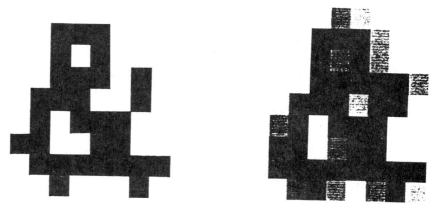

QUANTIZATION ERROR results when the shade of gray of a pixel, or minimum discrete picture element, does not match the shade of gray at the sampled point corresponding to the pixel on the original image of a letter. In most digital typography, for example, the pixel must be either black or white, which reflects the naive view that the edges of a master letterform are perfectly sharp. Actually the spatial frequencies too high to be perceived by the visual system should be filtered out before the letter is sampled and digitized. The edges of the filtered letter that results are not sharp; there is instead a continuous tone of gray that makes the transition from black to white. When the letterform is reproduced on a machine of relatively low resolution, such as a cathode-ray-tube terminal, the apparent degradation of the letter caused by the low-resolution sampling can be reduced if the pixels more accurately reproduce the shade of gray measured at each sample point. The pixels that make up the letterform at the left must be either black or white, and the design is almost illegible. The pixels that make up the same letterform can take on one of 16 gray values in the design at the right. By squinting and observing the design at the right from a distance of about 25 feet an ampersand can clearly be perceived. The digital designs were prepared by John E. Warnock of the Xerox Corporation.

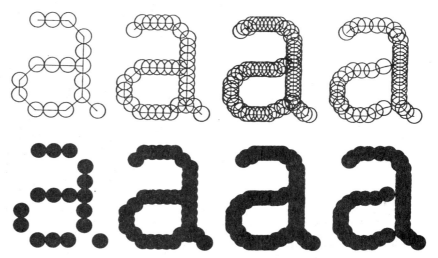

SIZE OF A WRITING SPOT in a digital printer such as a dot-matrix printer determines the smallest resolvable element of the letterform, but the position of the spot can still be adjusted to improve the image. The parallel rows of wires on the printer head can be staggered or the head can be made to pass several times across the same character. At the left a lowercase a is reproduced without overlap of the writing spot, and the result is a letter of poor quality. The overlap of the writing spot is increased to 50 percent in the second letter from the left and to 75 percent in the third one; the resulting letterforms are more continuous and the edges of the letters are better defined. As the overlap increases, however, the horizontal lines become too thick with respect to the vertical lines and the joins become too blotchy. At the right certain spots have been removed in order to lighten the horizontals and streamline the joins.

the output device require that the letterform be stored or reproduced at less than ideal resolution, there are still several strategies that can be followed to improve the image of the letter. For example, if the shade of gray measured at each sample point were preserved across the entire pixel corresponding to the point, the jagged lines would be much less apparent in the final letter than they are when the pixel must be either black or white. Some devices that have low spatial resolution can reproduce gray-shaded pixels, and so what is called quantization error between the shade of the pixel and the shade of the sample point can be made quite small. The video-terminal screen, for example, can have 256 or more gray levels for each pixel, which can help to compensate for low sampling resolution.

A second strategy for improving the image of a letterform is to store the letter in the memory of a machine in such a way as to take advantage of the overall regularity in its design. Most letters, for example, are simple and connected forms; information about the gray-scale value of the samples inside one of the stems of a letter is redundant because all the samples are black. Hence the space in the memory of a computer that would be necessary to store an arbitrarily complex set of gray-scale values for the pixels making up the stem can be reassigned to store more information about its boundaries. Letters can also be structurally coded as combinations of parts that correspond to the pen or brush strokes in the

handwritten forms. More sophisticated coding of the regularity in letterforms requires less storage in computer memory but more effort to decode it later.

One of the most versatile ways to reduce the number of samples that must be stored is to record only the positions of a few selected points along the outline of a letter. The points can then be joined by mathematically constructing lines or curves called splines, which can be computed from the outline points when the letter is retrieved from the computer memory. If only linear splines are employed, the curves of the letter are rendered as polygons; the line segments must therefore be short enough for the polygonization not to be discerned. Curved splines derived from the graphs of quadratic equations such as the circle, the ellipse and the parabola yield a better approximation to the complex outlines drawn by hand than linear splines do. Higher-order splines such as those derived from the graphs of cubic equations can give even closer approximations, but they require more computation to construct.

When the letterform is to be stored as a set of spline knots, or points, the coordinates of the points can be encoded by a device called a digitizer tablet at resolutions as high as 8,000 lines per em, much higher than the resolution of any text-output device. The outline of the character given by the splines can then be employed as a template for generating an array of pixels for any scanning pattern. The stored set of spline knots can also serve as a generic letterform from which a computer can generate a wide

variety of particular versions of the letter. For example, higher-order splines can be converted into circular arcs or straight lines on devices that generate a letter outline rather than a bit map. The contours of the letter can be scaled up or down and stretched in any direction. If the position of each spline knot is supplemented by a descriptive label that states its role in the shape of the letter with respect to other spline knots, a typeface can be automatically fitted to a particular raster without the tedious job of turning pixels on or off by hand.

Several computer programs have been written that can manipulate spline-based letterforms. The Ikarus system, developed by Peter Karow of URW Unternehmensberatung in Hamburg, is widely used in the typographic industry. A precise drawing of the outline of a letter on which the spline knots have been marked is placed on an electronic grid, and the positions of the knots are entered into computer memory with a cursor. Letter elements such as stems and serifs are identified as they are entered. The Ikarus program computes the spline outlines, and it can automatically carry out a number of design variations, such as changing the size of a letter on a fixed scanning pattern, varying the thickness of the letter strokes from light or medium to boldface and interpolating between the differing forms of the same letter in two type fonts.

Another spline-based design system called Metafont has been developed by Donald Knuth. The language employed for programming in Metafont is based

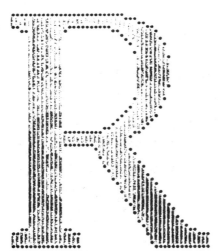  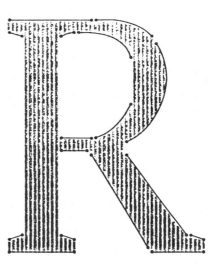

STORAGE SPACE in the memory of a computer necessary to reproduce a letter at a given resolution can be reduced in several ways. One strategy is called run-length encoding, in which only the endpoint positions of each stroke of an electron beam or a laser beam are stored instead of the gray-scale value of each pixel (*left*). Spline encoding can further reduce the memory requirements: the outline of the letterform can be specified at several critical points called spline knots. When the letter is needed, a computer can then interpolate straight lines (*middle*) or straight lines and circular arcs (*right*) between the spline knots in order to generate the endpoints for each stroke of the writing instrument. More elaborate curves such as logarithmic spirals can also be interpolated in order to more closely approximate the original letterform, but such curves trade a reduction in the computer memory for increased calculation "on the fly."

on ductal principles; once the topology of the letterform has been described the final form of the letter is determined by specifying the characteristics of a virtual "pen" that traces the skeleton of the letter. (The virtual pen must not be confused with any real pen; the computer simply represents the final shape of a letter as if it had been drawn with a real pen.) The size of the virtual pen, its angle with respect to the writing surface, the shape of its tip and other variables that can be independently specified generate quite different letter contours from the same skeleton. Other versions of Metafont are under development that describe the letterforms according to glyptal principles as well as ductal ones.

Several other systems have also been realized: FRED, a cubic spline program written by Patrick Baudelaire, and Prepress, a pixel editing program written by Robert F. Sproull, were developed for the Alto computer work station at the Palo Alto Research Center of the Xerox Corporation. A spline system based on spiral curves was developed by Peter Purdy and Ronald McIntosh of Purdy and McIntosh in Watford, England, and the ELF system, based on ductal principles, was written by David Kindersley and by Neil Wiseman of the University of Cambridge. A program and computer work station called the Letter Image Processor has been developed by the Camex Corporation in Boston.

In spite of its almost universal application and widely recognized flexibility, digital typography is only now beginning to move from the imitative to the innovative phase of its development. The sampling of letters and indeed the entire theoretical apparatus on which the sampling is based presuppose an already existing letter design. This model letter is an analogue form, and the success of the digital letter is still judged almost entirely on the degree to which it imitates the ductal or the glyptal letter. Nevertheless, the problems inherent in sampling and digitizing such a letter suggest it would be more productive to design new letterforms directly for digital technology. Moreover, recent advances in the study of vision create an opportunity for the digital-type designer to experiment with ways of adapting typography even more closely to the needs of the visual system. If letter images can be developed that more closely approximate the "language" of visual perception, the speed and efficiency of reading can be enhanced.

Creative design can best be accomplished on a synthetic system in which the type designer can interact rapidly with a computer and immediately see the effects of design changes on a screen, much as the traditional designer can immediately see and correct the mark of a pen or a brush. The system must be precise, high in resolution and capable of instantly reproducing the design in many versions, such as a spline-based outline, a bit map, a gray-scaled pixel array or a simulation of the output of a particular printer. No such machine is yet at hand, but the emerging generation of special integrated circuits for use in the graphic arts may soon make it possible to build one. When such systems become available, there will surely be a flowering of new letterforms as the digital era, like the ductal and glyptal eras before it, enters its creative phase.

a

Hamburgefons   Hamburgefons

b

Hamburgefons   Hamburgefons

c

a a a a a a

d

A pen of aspect 1/3 generated these letters.
A pen of aspect 2/3 generated these letters.
A pen of aspect 1/1 generated these letters.

e

The x-height and the heights of ascenders and descenders can be independently specified.

f

A 'slant' parameter transforms the pen motion, as shown in this sentence, but the pen shape remains the same. The degree of slant can be negative as well as positive, if unusual effects are desired. *Too much slant leads, of course, to letters that are nearly unreadable.* Perhaps the most interesting use of the slant parameter occurs when Computer Modern Italic fonts are generated without any slant.

g

The 'square root of 2' in these letters is 1.100.
The 'square root of 2' in these letters is 1.300.
The 'square root of 2' in these letters is 1.414.
The 'square root of 2' in these letters is 1.500.
The 'square root of 2' in these letters is 1.700.

VARIATIONS IN THE DESIGN of digital letterforms can be carried out automatically with the aid of several computer programs. In the Ikarus system, developed by Peter Karow of URW Unternehmensberatung in Hamburg, letters can be compressed or expanded without altering the width of their stems (*a*). The program can also correct the design automatically for different printing sizes; the required changes are much more complex than simply stretching the image in one direction (*b*). Smooth interpolations can be generated between a given letter in two different fonts. In *c* the letter at the left is Bembo and the letter at the right is Helvetica Black; the intermediate forms were constructed by the Ikarus program. Another design system called Metafont has been developed by Donald E. Knuth of Stanford University. A program written in the Metafont language alters certain characteristics of the letters by controlling the properties of a virtual pen, by means of which the computer represents the final form of the letter. For example, the shape of the tip of the pen can be controlled; it is an ellipse for which the aspect ratio, or the ratio of the vertical axis to the horizontal axis, must be specified (*d*). Samples of the effects of additional design variables on letterforms are also shown (*e, f, g*).

In concentrating on developing the computer's internal electronic communicative abilities, we have neglected the interface between the machine's display surface and the human viewer.

SPECIAL FEATURE

Graphic Design for Computer Graphics

Aaron Marcus*

Aaron Marcus and Associates

From their very beginning, all computers were computer graphics systems. In other words, they communicated with human beings by some means of graphic display or activity—communicated through flashing lights, the revolving reels of a tape drive, or the simple alphanumeric characters of a line printer. Today, however, the means for conveying information to a human being are much more complex. High-resolution displays can make use of sophisticated type fonts, three-dimensional structures, dynamic objects, and intricate color relationships.

Despite all of this increased capacity to display data, the same fundamental tasks lie before us that we as communicators have always faced: How can we attract people to information? How can we hold their attention? How can we facilitate their understanding of the information? How can we help people to remember what they have learned?

Communication between computers and people takes place in three different phases that represent the three "faces" of computers: outerfaces, interfaces, and innerfaces. Each of these faces consists of conceptual "frames" of communication that are embodied in specific displays on paper, film, or glass screens.

Outerfaces are the displays of information that are the final products of computation—texts, tables, forms, charts, maps, and diagrams, for example. All of these can be printed on paper, projected from film, or appear on a terminal screen. In daily life the people who look at this information may have very little knowledge of computers and/or the means of displaying information.

Interfaces are the frames of command/control and documentation that computer system users encounter. This human-computer connection allows the human being to understand and manipulate the functional power of the computer system. Without this "handle" on the computer tool, the device is not effective. Interfaces appear displayed on a glass screen or in printed texts and are encountered by both naive and skilled system users.

Innerfaces are the frames of command/control and documentation that computer experts confront, specifically the builders and maintainers of computer systems. Like the other faces of computer systems, innerfaces can be static or dynamic, two or three dimensional, black-and-white or polychromatic, and high or low resolution. They depict programming languages, software tools, and operating systems.

Now that significant technical advancements have been made in the high-speed display of complex computer-generated images, the time has come for graphics researchers to apply their talents to improving the communicative quality of these displays. To date, the focus of computer science and technology has been on the electronic communication that occurs prior to any display on the glass screen of a CRT or on the printed page. It is up to computer graphics specialists to modernize the forms of communication that take place between the display surface of a computer and the human viewer.

*An earlier version of this article appeared in *Proc. InterGraphics 83: Technical Session B-5*, Tokyo, Apr. 11-14, World Computer Graphics Association, Washington, DC.

Semiotics: the science of signs

To make the communication between man and machine more effective, we must pay greater attention to the semiotics[1] of computer graphics. Semiotics, the science of signs, calls attention to three dimensions of communication: syntactics, semantics, and pragmatics. In each of these dimensions, signs communicate to human viewers. The signs may vary from very representational, very obvious icons to extremely abstract, conventional symbols.

Syntactics is concerned with the visual appearance of signs and the relation of signs to each other. For example, here we would ask questions such as the following: Is a particular icon (or symbol) red or green, large or small, and near to or far from another such icon? The visual syntax of signs can be loosely or carefully structured in any particular class of communications.[2] Where informational graphics are concerned, the specifications of visual syntax are usually precise.

In the past, computer graphics has given only limited attention to semiotics— the science of signs.

Semantics deals with the relation of signs to the facts, concepts, structures, processes, and emotions being denoted by means of the signs. Here we traditionally ask, what does this sign mean? Note that semiotics applies the term "meaning" to all three dimensions of sign communication. In the past, computer graphics has given limited attention to semantics. However, there is a realm of visual rhetoric that has not been fully explored. In using rhetoric, one can take advantage of exaggeration (hyperbole), partial signs standing for complete signs (metonomy), and other specialized figures of expression.[3]

The third communication dimension, pragmatics, is concerned with how signs are produced and consumed. How expensive or difficult is it to display signs in a particular way? How legible will the signs be? How appealing will they be? These are all questions of pragmatics. Until recently, computer graphics technology has usually been applied to practical means of achieving cost-effective information displays. In a computer-intensive society, it also becomes reasonable to ask how different groups of people relate emotionally to, understand, and use visual displays of information.

Visible language and graphic design

Walk into almost any office or engineering facility today and you will find that most computer information is displayed in verbal or alphanumeric symbolism. Computer graphics, however, offers new opportunities to transform textual and tabular information into more nonverbal formats of visible language, the visual media of language expression. But what should these look like? What are the rules or principles for such transforma-

tions? Unfortunately, there is no science yet skillful enough to generally predict how this should be done. To some extent the disciplines of human factors and applied psychology can assist the person faced with the task of designing frames of information. However, a single frame, by itself, has many interrelated aspects that exceed the more limited predictions of any scientific discipline.

At this point in the development of computer graphics, it is appropriate to note the existence of a profession —graphic design—that is traditionally skilled in transforming facts, concepts, and emotions into visual analogies—a profession that is equally adept at creating visual narratives.

Graphic design is a discipline concerned with sign making with visible language. Graphic design utilizes typography, symbols (both representational and abstract), color, spatial organization or layout, and the sequencing of information frames over time in order to achieve effective communication. Information-oriented graphic designers are sensitive to the complex requirements of the senders of information, the detailed structure of the content of the message, the nature of the communication medium, and the needs of the receivers of the message.

Once the mutual contributions of graphic design and computer graphics are understood, it would seem that a symbiotic relationship could and should exist between the two disciplines. Each could contribute to the design of documents, to the user-oriented machine interface, and to the depiction of programs and control processes for the manufacturers, users, and maintainers of computer-based systems.

Computer graphics experts can design what happens behind the glass screen or before the printed document comes into existence, and graphic designers can affect the communication that takes place between the display and the human mind.

For example, graphic designers can suggest changes to the appearance of texts, tables, charts,[4] maps, and diagrams. These changes can be based in part upon precisely determined factors of legibility,[5] and the designers can also use their professional expertise to make decisions about the readability or appeal of a particular graphic image. By establishing specifications for typographic changes from a light typeface to a bold one, by determining a clear spatial layout, and by limiting the choice of colors,[6] a graphic designer can build useful, reinforcing redundancy into decisions concerning visual appearance.

Another example that illustrates the potential interaction between the two disciplines lies in the design of on-line frames and off-line pages for an information processing system.[7,8] The computer must help the user to learn complicated texts, memorize functions, make accurate decisions, and build a clear conceptual image of an information processing system. By carefully structuring words, concepts, and images,[9] these tasks are accomplished more easily in a legible and appealing verbal/visual environment. This is particularly important as computers are now used by people with varying educational, cultural, and psychological backgrounds. It is no longer appropriate to assume that one style of interface can serve all kinds of people.

Finally, in the area of program depiction and computer system visualization, graphic design can assist in making the complexities of computer structure and processing more evident and more understandable,[10,11] just as graphic design has assisted in other fields that illustrate complex subject matter—global energy interdependencies, for example.[12]

Case studies

The graphic design of outerfaces. Figures 1-3 show undesigned and designed default displays of charts and maps that were semiautomatically composed by Seedis, a large geographic database management system developed at Lawrence Berkeley Laboratory.[13] The second image illustrates superior use of available type sizes, thus making the chart legible, even in small reproduction sizes, and also clarifies the hierarchy of titling. A more clearly organized grouping of typographic elements and a use of gray areas to emphasize portions of the chart adds to the readability of Figure 2.[4]

Figures 4 and 5 show line printer and Xerox 9700 laser printer versions of 1980 US census data as they appear in reports prepared by Lawrence Berkeley Laboratory for the National Technical Information Service (NTIS).[14] The design of the tables has reduced variations of positioning and indention to a minimum and has produced a reliable design that can appear both in fixed-character-width as well as variable-character-width presentations. Size and boldness variations in the laser printer typography are used to clarify titling.

The graphic design of interfaces. The screen layouts shown in Figures 6 and 7 show undesigned and designed versions, respectively, of the on-line interface for Seedis. In the undesigned version, note the unorganized appearance of groups of type and the inconsistent use of all-capital letters versus lower case letters. In Figure 7, note the more evident order of text blocks, the use of lines of hyphens, the constant use of lower case letters, and controlled tab settings. Capital letters are used in major titling and in the menu prompt to identify the module in which the user is currently working. The screens are 80 characters wide by 24 lines deep, but information from the computer generally appears in character positions 21 through 80; the user normally begins typing at character position 1. This helps to establish visually a separation in the dialogue between human being and machine.[7,8]

Figure 8 shows a number of symbols from a high-resolution, bit-mapped interface on a Three Rivers Perq microcomputer graphics display. The interface is part of Metaform, a forms design front-end system from Intran, Inc. for the Xerox 9700 laser printer. Because the complexities of the system are made available to inexperienced computer users, pictographic light buttons use simple images to explain and reinforce the verbal mnemonics.[15] This approach is typical of newer high-resolution interfaces using nonverbal icons.[16]

The graphic design of innerfaces. A comparison of Figures 9 and 10 shows undesigned and designed versions of C language programs as they might be produced on a line printer and a phototypesetter, respectively. In the typical undesigned version (Figure 9), fixed-width characters appear in a single size and typeface. The source code is not easy to read because there is only minimal typographic hierarchy. In the variable-width version,

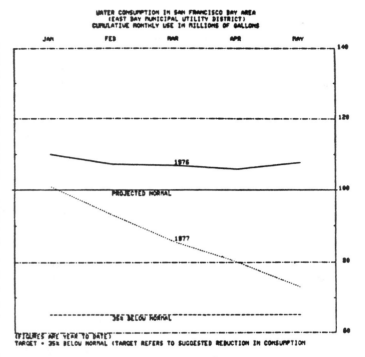

Figure 1. Generated on Seedis at the Lawrence Berkeley Laboratory, this display is a typical example of early computer-assisted chart making. Among its visual communication errors are insufficiently heavy line weight and the use of type that is too small for slide or journal reproduction.

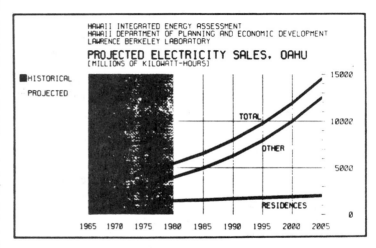

Figure 2. This figure illustrates some typical design improvements that can be achieved without the use of high-resolution characters or color. The type sizes, line weights, and gray values have been changed to emphasize the most important parts of the display.

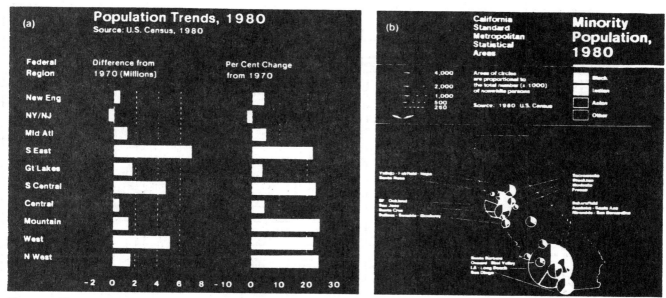

Figure 3. Chart (a) and map (b) conventions for Seedis. The graphic design specifications are relevant to high-resolution chart display on microfilm recorders and phototypesetters. Here gray-value distinctions and software-generated typography can be used to further accent features of the display. Note the systematic layout of flush-left, ragged-right groups of text elements. The images are presented in reverse to stand out on journal pages. The conventions used here are ones that could be supported by software in the Seedis information management and display context. (Reprinted with permission from *The Design Journal*, Society of Typographic Arts. Chicago, Illinois, ⊆ 1983.)

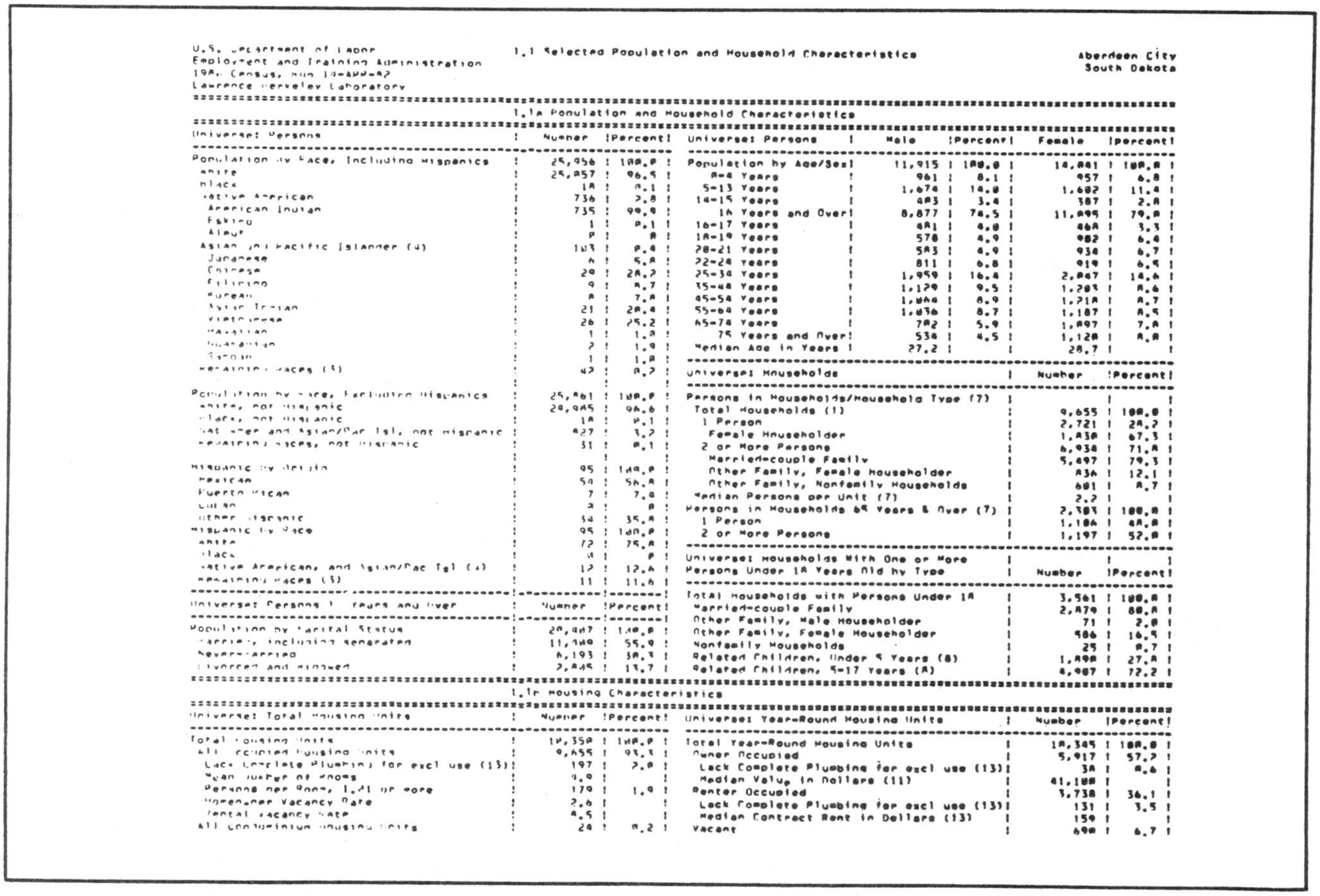

Figure 4. Typical line printer tabular output that was automatically formatted from US census data by Seedis. The layout and line headings are designed to accommodate fixed-width characters. Horizontal rules across the page are one simple means of highlighting.

U.S. Department of Labor
Employment and Training Administration
1980 Census, Run on 6 Aug 1982
Lawrence Berkeley Laboratory

Report 1A: Population Characteristics
Table: Population and Housing Characteristics

Kenai Peninsula Borough
Alaska

Population and Household Characteristics

Universe: Persons	Number	Percent
Population by Race, including Hispanics	25,282	100.0
White	23,099	91.4
Black	41	0.2
Native American	1,738	6.9
American Indian	812	3.2
Eskimo	337	1.3
Aleut	589	2.3
Asian and Pacific Islander (4)	200	0.8
Japanese	54	0.2
Chinese	10	-
Filipino	81	0.3
Korean	32	0.1
Asian Indian	2	-
Vietnamese	9	-
Hawaiian	9	-
Guamanian	1	-
Samoan	2	-
Remaining Races (3)	204	0.8
Population by Race, excluding Hispanics	24,924	100.0
White, not Hispanic	22,859	91.7
Black, not Hispanic	40	0.2
Nat Amer and Asian/Pac Isl, not Hisp (4)	1,899	7.6
Remaining Races, not Hispanic (3)	126	0.5
Population by Origin, including all races	25,282	100.0
Hispanic	358	1.4
Mexican	186	0.7
Puerto Rican	6	-
Cuban	3	-
Other Hispanic	163	0.6
Hispanic by Race	358	100.0
White	240	67.0
Black	1	0.3
Native American and Asian/Pac Isl (4)	39	10.9
Remaining Races (3)	78	21.8

Universe: Persons 15 Years and Over	Number	Percent
Population by Marital Status	18,114	100.0
Married, including Separated	11,764	64.9
Never-Married	4,494	24.8
Divorced and Widowed	1,856	10.2

Universe: Persons	Male	Percent	Female	Percent
Population by Age/Sex	13,389	100.0	11,893	100.0
0-4 Years	1,317	9.8	1,138	9.6
5-13 Years	2,172	16.2	2,072	17.4
14-15 Years	464	3.5	449	3.8
16 Years and Over	9,436	70.5	8,234	69.2
16-17 Years	513	3.8	488	4.1
18-19 Years	398	3.0	353	3.0
20-21 Years	457	3.4	351	3.0
22-24 Years	703	5.3	738	6.2
25-34 Years	2,879	21.5	2,584	21.7
35-44 Years	1,891	14.1	1,567	13.2
45-54 Years	1,298	9.7	1,085	9.1
55-64 Years	841	6.3	697	5.9
65-74 Years	375	2.8	258	2.2
75 Years and Over	81	0.6	113	1.0
Median Age in Years	27.2		26.3	

Universe: Households	Number	Percent
Total Households (1)	8,546	100.0
1 Person Households	1,683	19.7
Male Householder	1,186	13.9
Female Householder	497	5.8
2 or More Person Households	6,863	80.3
Married Couple Family	5,569	65.2
Other Family	781	9.1
Male Householder, no Wife Present	280	3.3
Female Householder, no Husband Present	501	5.9
Nonfamily Households	513	6.0
Male Householder	388	4.5
Female Householder	125	1.5
Total Households w/ Persons Age 65+ (7)	659	100.0
1 Person Households	234	35.5
2 or More Person Households	425	64.5
Total Households w/ Persons Under Age 18	4,184	100.0
Married Couple Family	3,524	84.2
Other Family	601	14.4
Male Householder, no Wife Present	189	4.5
Female Householder, no Husband Present	412	9.8
Nonfamily Households	59	1.4

Housing Characteristics

Universe: Housing Units	Number	Percent
Total Housing Units (2)	11,740	
Total Year-Round Housing Units	10,432	100.0
Condominium Units	-	-
Lack Complete Plumbing for excl use (13)	1,399	13.4
Occupied Housing Units (1)	8,546	81.9
Median Persons per Unit (7)	2.6	
Homeowner Vacancy Rate	3.2	
Rental Vacancy Rate	25.1	

Universe: Occupied Housing Units	Number	Percent
Occupied Housing Units (1)	8,546	100.0
With 1.01 or more Persons per Room	949	11.1
Owner Occupied	6,096	71.3
Lack Complete Plumbing for excl use (13)	687	8.0
Median Value in Dollars (11)	63,500	
Renter Occupied	2,450	28.7
Lack Complete Plumbing for excl use (13)	297	3.5
Median Contract Rent in Dollars (13)	300	

For meaning of symbols, see Introduction. For footnotes and definitions, see Technical Notes.

Figure 5. Typical laser printer output of census data tables similar to the ones displayed in Figure 4. This figure was also prepared by Seedis. Here, size and boldness changes are used to emphasize key elements of the page layout. This page must correspond line for line and field for field with fixed-width pages and screens for purposes of display and editing—an additional constraint upon the table's graphic design.

```
seedis
If you exit abnormally from SEEDIS, continue by typing
@restore
seedis
      Welcome to SEEDIS   VMS version 1.0
      Type  ?  for expanded menus
      Type  $  before VMS commands
(HELP,REVIEW,SUBJECT,AREA,AGG,DISAGG,
  PROFILE,DATA,DISPLAY,BUGS,NETSTAT,SHOW,QUIT): subject
Please select both data and a geographic area.
FORTRAN STOP
WELCOME TO THE SYSTEM.
YOU CAN ENTER

      EXPLAIN :TO SCAN KEYWORDS.
      SEARCH :TO LOCATE FILES CONTAINING KEYWORDS.
      QUIT :TO TERMINATE.

ENTER COMMAND OR ?COMMAND FOR MORE DETAIL.
```

Figure 6. An early undesigned Seedis welcome message. Note the scattered appearance of text groups, the inconsistency in the use of all caps and lower case, and the order of the text in which the user is told about getting out of the system even before being welcomed.

```
--------------------------------------------------
WELCOME TO SEEDIS, VERSION 2.0
--------------------------------------------------
          At any point in Seedis, you can type the following global
          commands to get these services:

Input         Description
--------------------------------------------------
?             list and describe commands in this menu
help          describe the purpose of this menu's commands
show          list and explain items to be selected
review        list current session status and history
cancel        delete current selections (depends upon context)
quit          return to previous menu
*<comment>    enter a comment in Seedis log

shortly.      Please stand by. Your menu prompt will appear

              SEEDIS: area, data, display, profile
```

Figure 7. A later designed Seedis welcome message. Note the order of text elements and the use of rules, lower case, and specific tab settings. Not all of the full-screen width (80 characters) is used for most text lines in order to improve legibility. Information on global commands is among the very first information given to the user. Also note the standard form of the menu prompt, which identifies the module (all capital letters) in which the user is currently working and the appropriate commands at this point.

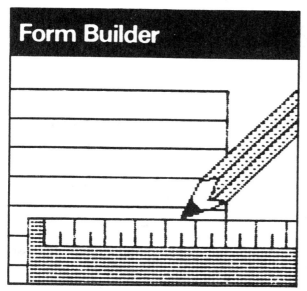

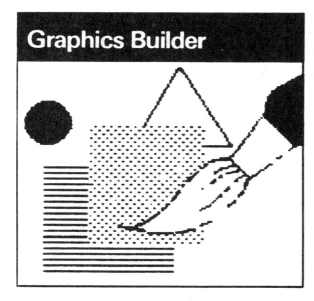
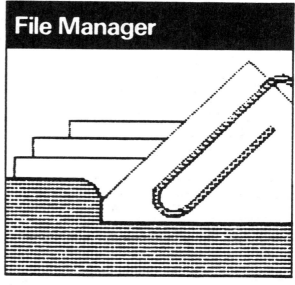

Figure 8. These illustrated, high-resolution, bit-mapped light buttons from Metaform, a forms-design front end for a laser printer, are visually complex clues to the operation of modules within the system. Instead of only verbal names or simple symbolic indicators, the icons show the cursor used in each module—e.g., pen, pencil, brush—and indicate the kind of activity. As images for an electronic "book," they correspond in some ways to the illuminated initial letters in medieval manuscripts. (Reprinted with permission from Intran, Minneapolis, Minn.)

spatial location, typographic and symbol hierarchies, and additional commentary contribute to a textual program depiction that is more legible and more readable than the one in Figure 9.[10,11]

Graphic design has improved visual communication in a variety of fields, prime examples being environmental signage,[17] diagrammatic communication,[18] and governmental documents.[19] This same expertise has relevance to improving the corporate or institutional graph-

ics of information management systems,[9,20] CAD/CAM systems,[21] and other computer graphics displays. By combining the expertise of graphic design with computer graphics, more humane as well as more cost-effective systems can emerge in the 1980's. ■

Acknowledgment

Some of the illustrations in this article originally appeared in technical memoranda from Lawrence Berkeley Laboratory.

```
#include <stdio.h>
#define MAXOP 20      /* max size of operand, operator */
#define NUMBER '0'    /* signal that number found */
#define TOOBIG '9'    /* signal that string is too big */

calc()    /* reverse Polish desk calculator */
{
        int type;
        char s[MAXOP];
        double op2, atof(), pop(), push();

        while ((type = getop(s, MAXOP)) != EOF)
                switch (type){
                case NUMBER:
                        push(atof(s));
                        break;
                case '+':
                        push(pop() + pop());
                        break;
                case '*':
                        push(pop() * pop());
                        break;
                case '-':
                        op2 = pop();
                        push(pop() - op2);
                        break;
                case '/':
                        op2 = pop();
                        if (op2 != 0.0)
                                push (pop() / op2);
                        else
                                printf("zero divisor popped0);
                        break;
                case '=':
                        printf("%f0, push(pop()));
                        break;
                case 'c':
                        clear();
                        break;
                case TOOBIG:
                        printf("%.20s ... is too long0, s);
                        break;          default:
                        printf("unknown command %c0, type);
                        break;
```

Figure 9. A typical C program in an elementary typographic form. It uses fixed-width characters of a single size and a typeface with limited horizontal spacing variation.

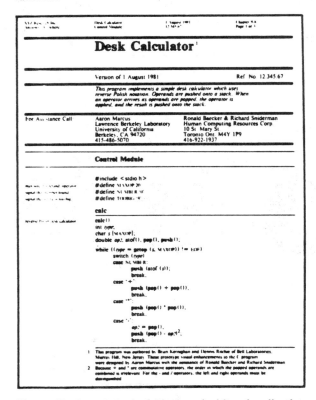

Figure 10. A prototypical black-and-white visualization that would require a high-resolution, bit-map display terminal or very high-resolution hard-copy device to produce. The actual image was generated on a computer-controlled phototypesetter, a rare but not unheard of hard-copy device. The image illustrates the potential of a graphic design approach to textual program visualization.

References

1. Umberto Eco, *A Theory of Semiotics,* Indiana University Press, Bloomington, Ind., 1976.

2. Aaron Marcus, "An Introduction to the Visual Syntax of Concrete Poetry," *Visible Language,* Vol. 8, No. 3, 1976, pp. 157-173.

3. Aaron Marcus, "Visualizing Global Interdependencies: An Application of Visual Semiotics to the Development of a Pictographic/Ideographic Narrative," *Synapse,* Vol. 1, No. 2, 1983 (in press). See also *Proc. Second Int'l Conf. Associations for the Study of Semiotics,* Vienna, 1979, Mouton, the Hague, 1983 (in press).

4. Aaron Marcus, "Computer-Assisted Chart Making from the Graphic Designer's Perspective," *Computer Graphics,* Vol. 14, No. 3, 1980, pp. 247-253.

5. Rolf Rehe, *Typography: How to Make it Most Legible,* Design Research Int'l, Carmel, Ind., 1974.

6. Aaron Marcus, "Color: A Tool for Computer Graphics Communication," *The Computer Image,* Addison-Wesley, Reading, Mass., 1982, pp. 76-90.

7. Aaron Marcus, "Designing the Face of An Interface," *IEEE Computer Graphics and Applications,* Vol. 2, No. 1, Jan. 1982, pp. 23-29.

8. Aaron Marcus, "Typographic Design for Interfaces of Information Systems," *Proc. Human Factors in Computer Systems,* National Bureau of Standards, Mar. 1982, pp. 26-30.

9. Aaron Marcus, *Managing Facts and Concepts,* Design Arts Program, National Endowment for the Arts, Washington, DC, 1983.

10. Aaron Marcus, "Paper and Glass: Graphic Design Issues for Software Documentation," *Proc. Software Documentation Workshop,* National Bureau of Standards, Mar. 1982, pp. 133-138.

11. Aaron Marcus and Ron Baecker, "On the Graphic Design of Program Text," *Proc. Graphics Interface '82,* 1982, pp. 303-311.

12. Aaron Marcus, "Visualizing Global Interdependencies," *Graphic Design* (Japan), No. 79, 1981, pp. 57-62.

13. John McCarthy et al., "The Seedis Project," publication No. PUB-424 Rev., Lawrence Berkeley Laboratory, University of California, Berkeley, Aug. 1982.

14. *Census Reports No. 1-7,* National Technical Information Service, Springfield, Va., 1982.

15. "Metaform: Technical Documentation," Intran Corporation, Inc., 4555 West 77 St., Minneapolis, Minn., 1982.

16. Kenneth N. Lodding, "Iconic Interfacing," *IEEE Computer Graphics and Applications,* Vol. 3, No. 2, Mar./Apr. 1983, pp. 11-20.

17. *Symbol Signs,* American Institute of Graphic Arts, US Department of Transportation, Washington, DC, DOT-OS-40192, Nov. 1974.

18. *Graphis: Diagrams,* Walter Herdeg, ed., Graphis Press, Zurich, 1975.

19. Bruce Blackburn, *Design Standards Manuals,* Federal Design Library, National Endowment for the Arts, Washington, DC, 1977.

20. Aaron Marcus, "A Graphic Design Manual for Seedis," technical memo, Computer Science and Mathematics Department, Lawrence Berkeley Laboratory, University of California, Berkeley, 1983 (in press).

21. Aaron Marcus, "Cad/Cam from the Graphic Design Perspective," *Proc. Symposium on Automation Technology,* Naval Postgraduate School, Monterey, Calif., Nov. 1983 (in press).

Information

1

Port

O'68

2

D/FW

ATA

IATA

Pg

NPS

BAA ✳

ADCA ✳

S/TA

TA

X'70

3

O'72

KFAI

NRR

TC

UIC

SP

5

ADV

ICAO

6

WO'72

O'64

Excerpted from American Institute of Graphic Arts (1981). *Symbol Signs: The System of Passenger/Pedestrian Oriented Symbols Developed for the U.S. Department of Transportation*, New York: Hastings House, Publishers.

Concept Description	Symbol Source	Evaluation Semantic	Syntactic	Pragmatic	Group	Symbol Design Recommendations
1 **Pair of question marks.**	Port	3	3	3	**3**	There have been no really good symbols developed to convey this message. The question mark as a symbol for Information is not completely satisfactory, but it has the potential of becoming effective and it is being widely used.
	O'68	3	4	3		
2 **Question mark.**	D/FW	4	3	3	**2**	We recommend that the question mark be used, but we feel that something more is needed to make it obvious that it is a symbol and to avoid confusion with adjacent typography.
	ATA	4	3	4		
	IATA	3	2	3		One obvious choice is to enclose the question mark in a shape, such as the circle used in the BAA symbol.
	Pg	3	3	3		
	NPS	3	3	3		
	BAA	4	4	5		**Summary:**
	ADCA	4	4	5		**Adopt Group 2 concept, with question mark inside a circle as in the BAA pictogram.**
	S/TA	3	3	3		
	TA	3	3	3		
	X'70	3	2	3		
3 **Question mark and lower case i.**	O'72	2	2	2	**3**	
4 **Lower case i.**	KFAI	2	3	3	**2**	
	NRR	2	2	2		
	TC	2	2	3		
	UIC	2	2	3		
	SP	2	2	3		
5 **Seated figure with standing figure, and question mark.**	ADV	2	1	2	**1**	
	ICAO	2	1	2		
6 **Fists pointing in various directions.**	WO'72	1	2	2	**1**	
	O'64	1	2	1		

Arriving Flights

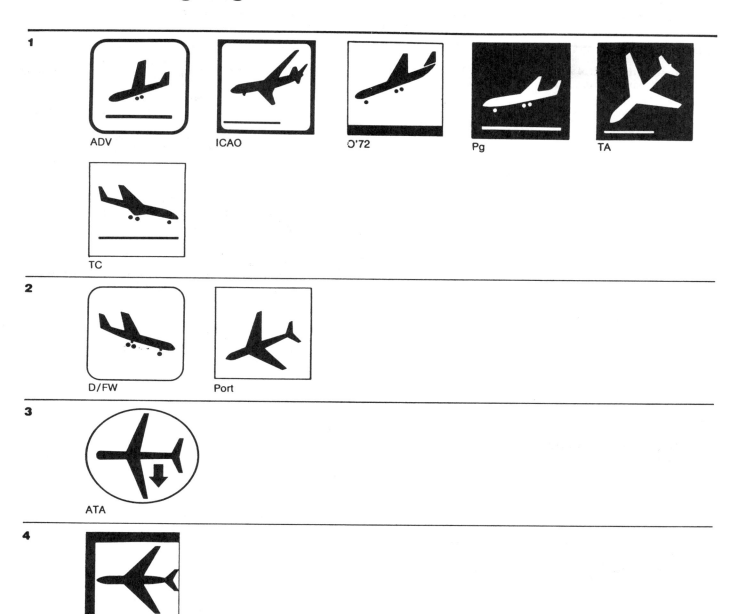

1

ADV

ICAO

O'72

Pg

TA

TC

2

D/FW

Port

3

ATA

4

FA

Concept Description	Symbol Source	Evaluation				Symbol Design Recommendations
		Semantic	Syntactic	Pragmatic	Group	
1 **Descending airplane with ground line**	ADV	3	3	3	**3**	This message causes considerable confusion. It is almost always used in conjunction with the message "Departing Flights" on approach roads and ramps. The confusion is partly verbal; you are "arriving" at the airport in another mode of transportation, but might want to "depart" in a plane, or meet someone else who is "arriving". While airport personnel understand the distinction, there seems to be agreement that the public, especially those who do not use airports regularly, have to pause to determine whether they want the "arrivals" or "departures" ramp. And it presents a danger because this point of confusion usually occurs at a critical roadway intersection.
	ICAO	3	2	3		
	O'72	3	3	3		
	Pg	3	3	3		
	TA	2	3	2		
	TC	3	3	3		
2 **Descending airplane**	D/FW	3	3	2	**2**	There is also a visual problem, because the concept of an airplane pointed at the ground, as shown in Groups 1 and 2, threateningly implies "crashing" to some people, and causes anxiety. (And, of course, in reality a plane actually lands in the opposite attitude from that shown.)
	Port	2	2	2		For these reasons, and because the real reason one takes the "arrivals" ramp is to meet an incoming passenger (not plane), we recommend that the concept be changed to "Passenger Pick-Up" and that a symbol be developed which portrays a passenger whose arm is raised in greeting or hailing an unseen person or taxi.
3 **Horizontal airplane with arrow pointing down**	ATA	2	2	2	**2**	We believe that, used in conjunction with the rising airplane for Departing Flights, this new Passenger Pick-Up concept will help relieve some of the current confusion.
4 **Horizontal airplane within box, facing inside**	FA	2	2	2	**2**	**Summary:** **Develop new symbol, showing passenger with up-raised arm.**

Exit

1

FA

2

O'72

O'76

3

UIC

KFAI

NRR

4

O'64

X'67

Pg

5

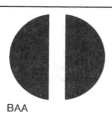

BAA

Concept Description	Symbol Source	Evaluation				Symbol Design Recommendations
		Semantic	Syntactic	Pragmatic	Group	
1 **Figure walking out of open 3-sided box**	FA	2	3	2	**1**	The word Exit, because of its mandated use in public buildings throughout the U.S., is well recognized by Americans to mean "the way out". This fact would seem to suggest the advisability of simply using the word EXIT as the symbol.
2 **Figure proceeding away from vertical bar**	O'72 O'76	2 2	3 3	2 2	**1**	Yet, unlike words such as HOTEL or TAXI, the word EXIT is little used outside of English-speaking countries. Sortie, Ausgang, Salida—all have the same meaning in other widely-used languages.
3 **Arrows penetrating opening of box and pointing out**	UIC KFAI NRR	2 2 2	3 2 2	2 2 2	**2**	The idea of Exit is a fairly abstract concept, difficult to show as an image, as can be seen from the examples shown. The Group 1 and 2 symbols are ambiguous. Groups 3 and 4 imply, to those who can read diagrams, exit from an enclosed space. But this is sometimes not the meaning intended. More importantly, the arrow implies a direction to the side, whereas in fact one usually must proceed ahead. Combining an arrow dominated symbol such as X'67 with a directional arrow pointing differently would cause considerable confusion.
4 **Arrows within boxes, pointing to opening**	O'64 X'67 Pg	2 2 2	2 2 3	2 2 2	**2**	The group 5 symbol, used at London (Heathrow) Airport, seems to us a much better direction, especially since it is complimentary to the standard No Entry symbol from the primary group. Whereas the No Entry symbol is a red ("Stop") disk with a horizontal bar (a barrier), the Exit symbol is a green ("go") disk with a vertical bar (raised barrier). To further imply the idea of passageway, the vertical bar completely bisects the green disk.
5 **Green disk, vertically bisected**	BAA	3	4	5	**4**	As with the No Entry symbol, this is abstract in concept, and would require a good deal of exposure before being understood. To overcome this problem, we recommend that, for a number of years, the symbol be combined with the appropriate word (in the U.S., with EXIT) to designate an exit. Common use of a single symbolic device with the appropriate local wording would make the message clear to both the resident and the international traveler. Additionally, after an extended period of time, the symbol would have sufficient exposure to stand on its own, without the use of any words.

Summary:
Adopt Group 5 concept of a vertically bisected green disk.

Colour Graphics — Blessing or Ballyhoo?

Gerald M. Murch *

Abstract

The human visual system's capacity and capability to process colour can be applied as a design criterion for colour information displays. This paper reviews key elements in the visual domain of colour, encompassing the visual, perceptual, and cognitive modes and develops a series of recommendations for effective colour usage based on these elements.

Keywords: Human Factors, Colour Perception, User Interface, Perceptual Ergonomics, Colour and Productivity, Colour Physiology, Colour Cognition, Colour Aesthetics

1. Introduction

Colour can be a powerful information tool. Used properly, it can enhance the effectiveness of graphics-terminal displays tremendously. However, improper use can also seriously impair information displays. So, because 85% of the display systems currently being sold are colour, it is important to establish and follow some basic guidelines for effective colour usage. Unfortunately, no one the of guidelines can cover all applications.

Up to now, colour has been used almost exclusively in a qualitative rather than a quantitative fashion, i.e., showing that one item is "different from" another rather than displaying relationships of degree. A typical example would be colour-coding each layer of a multi-layer circuit board (figure 1). Colour serves to differentiate the layers but says nothing about their relationships. A simple quantitative extension of the multi-layer circuit board might involve placing the layers in spectral order, with the first layer red, the second orange, and so on, following the popular mnemonic ROY G. BIV (red. orange, yellow, green, blue, indigo, violet).

The demands for the proper use of colour increase when colour is used quantitatively to

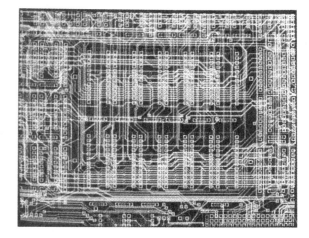

Fig. 1 The qualitative use of colour: a circuit layout in which layers are colour coded.

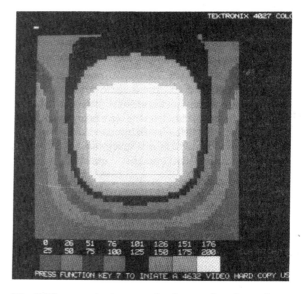

Fig. 2 The quantitative use of colour: colour is used to denote the termperature at different levels in a pipe.

show progressing change. The example in figure 2 shows a colour temperature map of a square pipe carrying a fluid at 200 temperature. The pipe is half submerged along its length in water shilled to 0. The temperature along the vertical sides of the pipe increases linearly from 0 at water level to 100 at the top. The graph shows the steady-state tem-

* Tektronix, Inc.,
P.O. Box 500,
Beaverton, Oregon 97077,
USA

North-Holland
Computer Graphics Forum, 4 (1985) 127–135

perature of interior points after solving Laplace's differential equation.

The result is a 61×61 array containing temperatures in the range of 0 to 200. The hollow center is surrounded by 3192 temperatures, displayed in colours approximating the temperatures: from white (hot) to violet (cold).

Basically, effective colour usage depends upon matching the physiological, perceptual, and cognitive aspects of the human visual system. This paper reviews some well documented aspects of these visual-system capacities and develops some basic principles that should allow us to improve graphics systems by using colour properly.

2. Physiology of Colour

In understanding how we see colour, it is important to realise that colour is not a physical entity. Colour is a sensation, like taste or smell, that is tied to the properties of our nervous system.

Figure 3 shows the light wavelengths to which the human eye is sensitive along with the corresponding colour sensed. The colour sensation results from the interaction of light with a colour-sensitive nervous system. Species having such nervous systems range from primitives through many species of fish to bumble bees, while many other species, such as dogs, do not sense colour.

Interestingly, not all colour-sensing systems function alike. Bees are insensitive to the long wavelengths that evoke the sensation of red in humans. On the other hand, bees sense ultraviolet light, which is invisible to humans. Most importantly, individuals within a species can have vastly different colour-discrimination capabilities. This

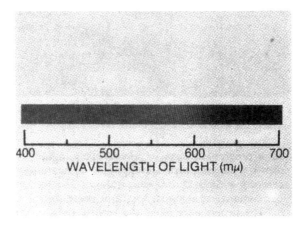

Fig. 3 The colour spectrum of human vision.

stems from differences in the eye's lens, its retina, and other parts of the visual system.

2.1. The lens

The lens of the human eye is not colour corrected. This causes chromostereopsis, an effect that causes pure colours at the same distance to appear to be at different distances. For most people, reds appear closer and blues more distant. In fact, short wavelengths — pure blue — always focus in front of the retina and thus appear defocused. This is most noticeable at night when deep-blue signs seem fuzzy and out of focus, while other colours appear sharp.[1]

Lens transmissivity also has an effect. The lens absorbs almost twice as much energy in the blue region than in the yellow or red. Also, a pigment in the retina's centre transmits yellow while absorbing blue. The net result is a relative insensitivity to shorter wavelengths (cyan to deep blue) and enhanced sensitivity to longer wavelengths (yellows and oranges).

As we grow older, lens yellowing increases, which makes us increasingly insensitive to blues. Similarly, aging reduces the transmittance of the eye's fluids, which makes colour appear less vivid and bright. Actually, age aside, there is normally a great deal of variation, with some people's eyes being very transparent and other's naturally yellowed. This alone contributes to differences in colour sensitivities between individuals.

2.2. The retina

The human retina consists of a dense population of light-sensitive rods and cones. Rods are primarily responsible for night vision, while cones provide the initial element in colour sensation.

Photopigments in the cones translate wavelengths to colour sensation. The range of sensation is determined by three photopigments — blue (445 nanometers, or nm), green(535 nm), and red (575 nm). Here, "red" is really a misnomer since maximum sensitivity at 574 nm actually invokes the sensation of yellow.

Both photopigment and cone distribution vary over the retinal surface. Red pigment is found in 64% of the cones, green in 32%, and blue in about 2%. Additionally, the center of the retina, which provides detailed vision, is densely packed with cones but has no rods. Moving outward, the number of rods increases to eventual predominance. As a result, shapes appear unclear and colourless at the extreme periphery of vision.

Because of the cone and photopigment distributions, we can detect yellows and blues further into our peripheral vision than reds and greens. Also, the center of the retina, while capable of high acuity, is nearly devoid of cones having blue photopigment. This results in a "blue blindness" that causes small blue objects to disappear when they are fixated on.

For the eye to detect any shape of a specific colour, an edge must be created by focusing the image onto the mosaic of retinal receptors. An edge is the basic element in perceiving form. It can be created by adjacent areas differing in brightness, colour, or both. Edges guide the eye's accommodation mechanism, which brings images into focus on the retina. Recent research has shown, however, that edges formed by colour difference alone with no brightness difference, such as a red circle centered on a large green square of equal brightness, are poor guides to accurate focusing. Such contours remain fuzzy. For sharply focused images, it is necessary to combine both colour and brightness differences.

Also, for photopigments to respond, a minimum level of light is required. Additionally, the response level depends on wavelength, with the visual system being most sensitive to the center of the spectrum and decreasing in sensitivity at the spectral extremes. This means a blue or red must be of much greater intensity than a minimum-level green or yellow in order to be perceived. Similarly, equal-energy reds might not appear equally intense.

Such changes in visual sensitivity as a function of wavelength make it difficult to equate colour in terms of brightness. Usually brightness is expressed in terms of luminance, a scale in which light energy is corrected for the eye's wavelength sensitivity. Unfortunately, the luminance value provides only a rough approximation of actual perceived brightness.

2.3. After the retina

The optic-nerve bundle leads from the photoreceptors at the back of the retina. Along the optic nerve path, at the *lateral geniculate body,* the photoreceptor outputs recombine.[2] Figure 4 diagrams how this recombination takes place.

Notice in figure 4 that the original retinal channels — red, green, and blue — form three new "opponent channels". One channel signals the red-to-green ratio, another the yellow-to-blue, and the third indicates brightness. Again, we find a

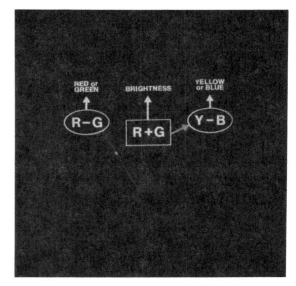

Fig. 4 Processing of colour input into opponent channels.

bias against the blue photopigments since the perception of brightness, and hence of edges and shapes, is signaled by the red and green photopigments. The exclusion of blue in brightness perception means that colours differing only in the amount of blue will not produce sharp edges.

Neural organisation into opponent channels has several other effects, too. The retinal colour zones, which link opponent red with green and opponent yellow with blue, provide an example. Opponent-colour linking includes visually experiencing combinations of opposing colours — we cannot experience reddish green or yellowish blue.

2.4. Colour blindness

The term "colour blind" is an unfortunate summarisation of the colour deficiencies besetting only about 9% of the population, and only a tiny percent of those deficiencies result in true blindness to colour.[3]

Not all of the causes of colour-deficient vision are known; however, some are related to the cones and their photopigments. A rare form occurs when blue photopigment is missing. The best known condition, however, is red-green deficiency caused by the lack of either red or green photopigments. Lack of either photopigment causes the same colour-discrimination problem; however, for people lacking red photopigment, long wave stimuli appear much darker.

A more common case is that of photopigment response functions deviating significantly from normal. In one form, the red photopigment peak lies very close to that of the green, while in another, green is shifted towards red. The net result is reduced ability to distinguish small colour differences, particularly those of low brightness. Less extreme cases of response deviation occur regularly across the population in general, which explains the common situation of two people differing on whether a given colour is blue or green.

3. Perceptual Principles

Perception refers to the process of sensory experience. Although perception is most certainly a product of our nervous system, adequate information about the "higher order" functions does not exist to describe perception in physiological terms. As a result, psychological methods must be relied on, the most valuable discipline being psychophysics. Psychophysics is a discipline that seeks to describe objectively how we experience the physical world around us.

3.1. Perception is nonlinear

Psychophysical research has shown that practically all perceptual experiences are *nonlinearly* related to the physical event. Figure 5 illustrates this by graphing perceived brightness versus light intensity. The relationship is nearly logarithmic, with perceived brightness increasing as the logarithm of stimulus intensity. We have all experienced this relationship on a more mundane level when switching intensities on a three-way lamp — the

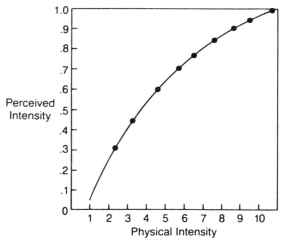

Fig. 5 Perceived brightness as a function of intensity.

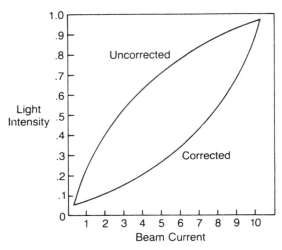

Fig. 6 "Gamma" correction as a means of increasing the number of discernible grey-scale steps on a display.

brightness increase from 50 to 100 watts appears greater than that from 100 to 150 watts.

A similar relation exists with graphics-terminal displays. The function relating beam current to display intensity known as the gamma of the display. If left uncorrected, gamma reduces the number of discriminable levels of intensity (grey levels). However, with firmware gamma correction based on perceptual principles (see Fig. 6), the terminal display can be given a full range of shades varying in perceptually even steps.

3.2. Perception of achromatic colour

White or achromatic light contains all the wavelengths to which the human eye responds. When such light strikes an object and all wavelengths are reflected equally, the colour of the object is achromatic. That is, the object appears white, black, or some intermediate level of grey.

The lightness of the object depends on the amount of light reflected. An object reflecting 80% or more appears very light; it is white. Reflection of 3% or less results in the object appearing very dark (black). Various levels of grey appear in between, with lightness toward white appearing to increase as a logarithm of reflectance.

Consider for example, black, white, and grey automobiles. Each car reflects different amounts of light and, therefore, takes on a specific achromatic colour. If the total amount of light illuminating the cars is increased, the lightness stays the same but the *brightness* increases. The white car stays white but becomes much brighter — perhaps even dazzling. Thus, lightness is a property of an object itself, while brightness depends upon the amount of light illuminating the object.

The most common example of all of this is black print on white paper. Changing illumination has little perceptual effect on the relative lightness of the paper or print since the ratio of reflectance, or contrast, remains unchanged.

The situation for a graphics-terminal display is more complex, however. Increasing the electrical signal to the display changes both lightness and brightness. Also, when the ambient light on the display is increased, an equal amount of light is added to all areas of the display; the net result is decreased contrast.

3.3. Perception of chromatic colour

Objects that reflect or emit unequal distributions of wavelengths are said to be chromatic, i.e., to have a colour. The colour we sense derives from the physical attributes of the dominant wavelengths, the intensity of the wavelengths, and the number of proportion of reflected waves. Colour identification also depends upon a multitude of learning variables, such as previous experience with the object and association of specific sensations with colour names. The sensation is also affected by the context in which the colour occurs and the characteristics of the surrounding area or the colours of other objects.

The study of the physical attributes of chromatic objects is always compounded by the experiences of the observer with colours in general. Because colour perception is subjective, many of its aspects can only be described in the psychological of hue, lightness, saturation, and brightness.

Hue is the sensation reported by observers exposed to wavelengths between approximately 380 and 700 nm. For the range between 450 and 480 nm, the predominant sensation reported is blue. Green is reported across a broader range of 500 to 550 nm, and yellow across a narrow band around 570 to 580 nm. Above 610 nm, most persons report the sensation of red. The best or purest colours — defined as those containing no trace of a second colour — would indicate pure blue at about 470 nm, pure green at 505, and pure yellow at 575 nm.

Hue, then, is the basic component of colour. It is the primary determinant for the specific colour sensation. While hue is closely related to certain wavelengths, remember that hue is a psychological variable and wavelength a physical one. Although people with normal colour vision will name a sector of the visual spectrum as red, disagreement will occur on the reddest red or where red becomes orange. Such disagreement reflects varying experiences with colour as well as the intrinsic differences in the colour mechanisms of each person's visual system.

Saturation is most closely related to the number of wavelengths contributing to a colour sensation. As the band of wavelengths narrows, the resulting colour sensation becomes more saturated — the wider the band, the less saturated the colour.

Conceptually, a scale of saturation can be envisioned as extending from a pure hue, such as red, through less distinct variants of the hue, such as shades of pink to a neutral grey in which no trace of the original hue is noticed. A measure of saturation discrimination can be obtained by starting with a neutral colour and determining the amount of pure hue that must be added in order for the hue to become detectable. Figure 7 shows the results of such a study.

In figure 7, the abscissa indicates wavelength. The ordinate shows the amount of pure hue that must be added to neutral colour for the hue to become discernible. From this graph, it becomes obvious that substantial differences exist in our ability to detect colour presence along a scale of saturation. The largest amount of colour required for detection is at the 570-nm stimulus. Such a yellow appears initially to be less saturated than any other pure hue and desaturates quickly as the wavelength distribution is broadened or as neutral colours are mixed with it.

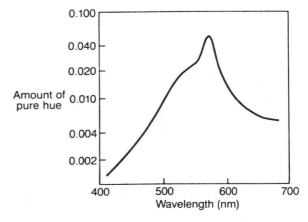

Fig. 7 Perceived saturation of different wavelengths.

Lightness, as mentioned previously, refers to the gamut of achromatic colours ranging from white through grey to black. By definition, achromatic colours are completely desaturated since no trace of hue is present.

Combining an achromatic colour with a specific hue produces a desaturated hue. Its saturation level depends on the relative amounts of each colour, and its lightness depends on the lightness of the achromatic colour used. For example, combining white with red produces a desaturated pink that is lighter than the same hue combined with grey or black.

Just as with achromatic colours, the lightness of a mixed colour also depends on the reflectance of the surface under consideration — the higher the reflectance, the lighter the colour. As might be anticipated, monochromatic colours do not all appear equal in lightness. Some hues appear lighter than others even though their reflectances are the same. If, for example, observers are shown a series of monochromatic lights of equal brightness and are asked to rate them for lightness, a relationship similar to that shown in figure 7 results. A monochromatic colour of 570 nm appears much lighter than all other wavelengths, and the lightness decreases rapidly as the extremes of the visual spectrum are approached. This means that a yellow combined with intermediate grey appears lighter than a blue-green of the same brightness combined with grey.

Brightness is another aspect of colour perception. Increasing the illumination of both achromatic and chromatic colours produces a qualitative change in appearance that ranges from dark to bright. However, separation of brightness from lightness is often difficult since brighter colours invariably appear lighter as well.

Consider broad-band light shining on a series of equal-reflectance surfaces, each reflecting a very narrow band of wavelengths. At low illumination, the surfaces are first perceived as grey. Increasing the intensity allows dark and desaturated hues to become discernible, with mid-spectrum wavelengths (555 nm) becoming visible at lower intensity levels. As the intensity increases, a broader range of hues appear, with extremely long and short wavelengths visible only at high intensities.

3.4. Colours in context

Colours are also subject to contextual effects, in which adjacent colours influence one another. For example, a colour on a dark background appears lighter and brighter than the same colour on a light background. If a test field is neutral (grey) or dark and displayed on a coloured background, the background induces colour into the test field. Red, for example, induces green into a neutral grey.

The size of a coloured area also influences its perceptual properties. In general, small areas become desaturated and can show a shift in hue. This creates problems when text is colour coded, especially with blues and yellows because they are susceptible to small-area colour loss. Also, small areas of colour can mix; red and green in smaller and smaller areas are eventually integrated by the visual system into yellow.

3.5. Individual characteristics

Thus far, perception has been described in general terms as it applies to the typical human visual system. Yet, each of us has our own perceptual idiosyncrasies that affect how we use colour on a display. For example, some people prefer highly saturated colours and others prefer muted tones.

It is important, too, to remember that colour perception changes over time. We adapt to colour with prolonged viewing. This results in an apparent softening of colours. As a result, there is a tendency to use highly saturated colours to offset adaptation. The unadapted viewer, however, sees the colours as highly saturated. Additionally, some research indicated that pure colours are visually fatiguing.

Although we are still far from developing an aesthetics of colour displays, some information has been compiled on colour combinations that go well together and those that do not. Tables 1 and 2 present data from a study in which people were asked to pick the best and worst appearing colours on different backgrounds. Choices were made for both thin lines (two pixels wide) and for larger filled panels. The tables list those combinations preferred or rejected by at least 25% of the 16 subjects participating in the study. Obviously this is a small study sample, but it does represent the start of an understanding of the complex issue of colour-display aesthetics.

4. Cognitive Principles

The least understood area of effective colour usage deals with capitalising on our modes of thinking about, and associating with, colour. This area of

Table 1

Best Color Combinations
(N = 16)

Background	Thin Lines and Text	Thick Lines and Panels
White	Blue (94%) Black (63%) Red (25%)	Black (69%) Blue (63%) Red (31%)
Black	White (75%) Yellow (63%)	Yellow (69%) White (50%) Green (25%)
Red	Yellow (75%) White (56%) Black (44%)	Black (50%) Yellow (44%) White (44%) Cyan (31%)
Green	Black (100%) Blue (56%) Red (25%)	Black (69%) Red (63%) Blue (31%)
Blue	White (81%) Yellow (50%) Cyan (25%)	Yellow (38%) Magenta (31%) Black (31%) Cyan (31%) White (25%)
Cyan	Blue (69%) Black (56%) Red (37%)	Red (56%) Blue (50%) Black (44%) Magenta (25%)
Magenta	Black (63%) White (56%) Blue (44%)	Blue (50%) Black (44%) Yellow (25%)
Yellow	Red (63%) Blue (63%) Black (56%)	Red (75%) Blue (63%) Black (50%)

Overall Frequency of Selection

Black	25%	Black	23%
White	20%	Blue	19%
Blue	20%	Red	17%
Yellow	13%	Yellow	13%
Red	11%	White	10%
Cyan	5%	Magenta	7%
Magenta	4%	Cyan	6.4%
Green	1%	Green	4%

Table 2

Worst Color Combinations
(N = 16)

Background	Thin Lines and Text	Thick Lines and Panels
White	Yellow (100%) Cyan (94%)	Yellow (94%) Cyan (75%)
Black	Blue (87%) Red (37%) Magenta (25%)	Blue (81%) Magenta (31%)
Red	Magenta (81%) Blue (44%) Green and Cyan (25%)	Magenta (69%) Blue (50%) Green (37%) Cyan (25%)
Green	Cyan (81%) Magenta (50%) Yellow (37%)	Cyan (81%) Magenta and Yellow (44%)
Blue	Green (62%) Red and Black (37%)	Green (44%) Red and Black (31%)
Cyan	Green (81%) Yellow (75%) White (31%)	Yellow (69%) Green (62%) White (56%)
Magenta	Green (75%) Red (56%) Cyan (44%)	Cyan (81%) Green (69%) Red (44%)
Yellow	White and Cyan (81%)	White (81%) Cyan (56%) Green (25%)

Overall Frequency of Selection

Cyan	24%	Cyan	23%
Green	18%	Yellow	17%
Yellow	16%	Green	16%
Magenta	11%	Magenta	12%
Red	10%	White	12%
White	8%	Blue	9%
Blue	8%	Red	7%
Black	3%	Black	2%

study falls into the domain of cognitive ergonomics.

Despite the infancy of this area of human-factors study, some initial observations prove useful in effective colour usage. An example involves the functional use of colour stereotypes: red for

warning, green for go, and yellow for attention. Since we all have experience with these meanings, maintaining the relationship maps nicely into our expectations.

In terms of colour coding graphed waveforms or measurement data, variation of hue can quickly communicate important information. Portions of the waveform or data within a certain tolerance, or range limit, can be coded green; portions approaching a limit can be yellow; and excesses can be coded red. This falls into the normal cognitive expectations.

For multiple waveform displays, where colour is simply used for quick distinction between waveforms, contrast is a big consideration. As a result, it is tempting to use red for one waveform and green for another. While this makes the waveforms readily distinguishable on the display, which is the goal, it can also bias an observer toward making some quality judgements about the waveforms — the red waveform is bad or dangerous, the green one is okay. Such biasing of the observer might not be what you intended. Thus, it is wise to consider possible biases when making colour choices and either to avoid them or to capitalise on them.

Whether or not colour graphics fulfills the great expectations rampant within the industry — i.e., whether colour graphics is a blessing or just ballyhoo — will depend on how colour is used. The simple shift from monochrome to colour graphics does not ensure an improvement in the link of human to device. Colour can improve the link, but only if the implementation follows the basic principles of human colour vision.

5. Guidelines for Effective Colour Usage

Based on the preceding discussion, some general guidelines for colour usage can be stated. They are listed here according to the area of their derivation — physiological, perceptual, or cognitive.

5.1. Physiological guidelines

Avoid the simultaneous display of highly saturated, spectrally extreme colours. Reds, oranges, yellows, and greens can be viewed together without refocusing, but cyan and blues cannot be easily viewed simultaneously with red. To avoid frequent refocusing and visual fatigue, extreme colour pairs such as red and blue or yellow and purple should be avoided. However, desaturating spectrally extreme colours will reduce the need for refocusing.

Avoid pure blue for text, thin lines, and small shapes. Our visual system is just not set up for detailed, sharp, short-wavelength stimuli. However, blue does make a good background colour and is perceived clearly out into the periphery of our visual field.

Avoid adjacent colours differencing only in the amount of blue. Edges that differ only in the amount of blue will appear indistinct.

Older viewers need higher brightness levels to distinguish colours.

Colours change appearance as ambient light level changes. Displays change colour under different kinds of ambient light — fluorescent, incandescent, or daylight. Appearance also changes as the light level is increased or decreased.

On the one hand, a change occurs due to increased or decreased contrast, and on the other, due to the shift in the sensitivity of the eye.

The magnitude of a detectable change in colour varies across the spectrum. Small changes in extreme reds and purples are more difficult to detect than small changes in other colours such as yellow and blue-green. Also, our visual system does not readily perceive changes in green.

Difficulty in focusing results from edges created by colour alone. Our visual system depends on a brightness difference at an edge to effect clear focusing. Multi-coloured images, then, should be differentiated on the basis of brightness as well as of colour.

Avoid red and green in the periphery of large-scale displays. Due to the insensitivity of the retinal periphery to red and green, these colours in saturated form should be avoided, especially for small symbols and shapes. Yellow and blue are good peripheral colours.

Opponent colours go well together. Red and green or yellow and blue are good combinations for simple displays. The opposite combinations - red with yellow or green with blue - produce poorer images.

For colour-deficient observers, avoid single colour distinctions.

6. Perceptual Guidelines

Not all colours are equally dicernible. Perceptually, we need a large change in wavelength to perceive a colour difference in some portions of the spectrum and a small one in other portions.

Luminance does not equal brightness. Two equal-luminance but different hue colours will probably appear to have different brightness. The deviations are most extreme for colours towards the ends of the spectrum (red, magenta, blue).

Different hues have inherently different saturation levels. Yellow in particular always appears to be less saturated than other hues.

Lightness and brightness are distinguishable on a printed hard copy, but not on a colour display. The nature of a colour display does not allow lightness and brightness to be varied independently.

Not all colours are equally readable or legible. Extreme care should be exercised with text colour relative to background colours. Besides a loss in hue with reduced size, inadequate contrast frequently results when the background and text colours are similar. As a general rule, the darker, spectrally extreme colours such as red, blue, magenta, brown, etc. make good backgrounds while the brighter, spectrum-centered, and desaturated hues produce more legible text.

Hues change with intensity and background colour. When grouping elements on the basis of colour, be sure that backgrounds or nearby colours do not change the hue of an element in the group. Limiting the number of colours and making sure they are widely separated in the spectrum will reduce confusion.

Avoid the need for colour discrimination in small areas. Hue information is lost for small areas. In general, two adjacent lines of a single-pixel width will merge to produce a mixture of the two. Also, the human visual system produces sharper images with achromatic colours. Thus for the fine detail, it is best to use black, white, and grey while reserving chromatic colours for larger panels or for attracting attention.

6.1. Cognitive guidelines

Do not overuse colour. Perhaps the best rule is to use colour sparingly. The benefits of colour as an attention getter, information grouper, and value assigner are lost if too many colours are used. Cognitive scientists have shown that the human mind experiences great difficulty in maintaining more than five to seven elements simultaneously; so it is best to limit displays to about six clearly discriminable colours.

Be aware of the nonlinear colour manipulation in video and hard copy. At this point, algorithms do not exist for translating the physical colours of an imaging device into a perceptually structured colour set. Video or hard-copy systems cannot match human perception and expectations on all fronts.

Group related elements by using a common background colour. Cognitive science has advanced the notion of set and preattentive processing. In this context, you can prepare or set the user for related events by using a common colour code. A successive set of images can be shown to be related by using the same background colour.

Similar colours connote similar meanings. Elements related in some way can convey the message through the degree in similarity of hue. The colour range from blue to green is experienced as more similar than the gamut from red to green.

Along these lines, saturation level can also be used to connote the strength of relationships.

Brightness and saturation draw attention. The brightest and most highly saturated area of colour display immediately draws the viewer's attention.

Link the degree of colour change to event magnitude. As an alternative to bar charts or tic marks on amplitude scales, displays can portray magnitude changes with progressive steps of changing colour. A desaturated cyan can be increased in saturation as the graphed elements increase in value. Progressively switching from one hue to another can be used to indicate passing critical levels.

Order colours by their spectral position. To increase the number of colours on a display requires imposing a meaningful order on the colours. The most obvious order is that provided by the spectrum with the mnemonic ROY G. BIV (red, orange, yellow, green, blue, indigo, violet).

Warm and cold colours should indicate action levels. Traditionally, the warm (long wavelength) colours are used to signify action or the requirement of a response. Cool colours, on the other hand, indicate status or background information. Most people also experience warm colours advancing toward them — hence forcing attention — and cool colours receding or drawing away.

While these guidelines offer some suggestions, they certainly should not be taken as binding under all circumstances. There are too many variables in colour display, colour copying, human perception, and human interpretation to make any hard and fast rules. So, by all means, experiment.

References

1.   G. Murch, *Visual Accommodation and Convergence to Multi-chromatic Display Terminals*, Proceedings of the Society for Information Display 1983.

2.   L. Hurvich, *Color Vision*, Sinaver, Sunderland, Massachusetts (1981).

3.   R. Boynton, *Human Color Vision*, Holt, Rinehart and Winston:, Amsterdam (1980).

FRAME-BUFFER DISPLAY ARCHITECTURES[1]

Robert F. Sproull

Sutherland, Sproull, and Associates, Inc., 4516 Henry Street, Pittsburgh, Pennsylvania, 15213

INTRODUCTION

The frame-buffer display is now the most popular computer output device, as a result of the rapid decline in the cost of high speed semiconductor memories and the low cost of raster-scan displays. Frame buffers are incorporated in a wide range of equipment, from home computers to engineering workstations to flight simulators. All frame buffers have the same principal role—for every picture element on the screen, to record its intensity or color and to refresh the display image continuously. However, the size, structure, and performance of frame buffers differ markedly for different applications.

A frame-buffer display has strengths and weaknesses. Its principal strength is that it can show an arbitrary image, subject only to the limits of spatial and intensity resolution provided by the display. Because the memory holds a separate digital value for each picture element, or pixel, on the screen, arbitrary images can be displayed. A potential weakness of the frame buffer is that a great many bits must be changed in order to make major changes to the picture. Thus, a key concern in the design of frame-buffer displays is to provide high-speed access to the memory for display updates.

In many applications, the frame buffer serves a second role, in addition to refreshing the display: It records an image data structure that is used by the application program. For example, an image-processing application may

[1]Notation: h = width of display, in pixels; v = height of display, in scan lines; p = number of bits recorded per pixel; d = number of bits of precision in analog intensity signal; r = display refresh rate, Hz; t_h = horizontal retrace time; t_v = vertical retrace time; n = number of rows or columns in a RAM chip; t = time to fill a memory chip; f = fraction of frame-buffer bandwidth used for refresh.

retrieve pixel values from the frame buffer, apply a filtering or convolution computation to them, and return the results to the frame buffer.

This review of frame-buffer architectures begins by describing a conventional architecture, a simple design that introduces most of the features of frame-buffer displays. We then describe how applications influence frame-buffer design and exhibit some common design problems. Following is a synopsis of architectural variations in video generation, memory structure, and processor design. The review concludes with a discussion of the state of the art and some open problems. Readers unfamiliar with frame-buffer displays are encouraged to consult Conrac (1985), Newman & Sproull (1979), Foley & van Dam (1982), Baecker (1979), or Whitton (1984) for basic information.

CONVENTIONAL ARCHITECTURES

The essential form of a frame buffer is a two-ported memory in which one port is used to read memory values at high speed for display and the other port is used by an update processor to change the display image by changing the memory contents. This memory is called a buffer because of the potentially different speeds of the accesses on the two ports. The *display port* reads the memory at very high speed in a regular pattern, synchronized to the sweep of the display's electron beam across the screen. By contrast, the *update port* makes irregular accesses and both reads and writes in the process of computing and storing the proper pixel values in the memory. Although the speed of these accesses governs the rate at which the update processor may change the image, the display will continue to function correctly even if the update rate is severely limited.

Figure 1 shows the basic frame-buffer structure. To the update processor, the frame-buffer memory behaves just like all other memory in the system. It responds to each request to read or write a byte, a word, or multiple words, as required. The display port is controlled by a *video generator*, which reads from the memory the pixel values that correspond to the raster scanning pattern used on the display. Typically, the scan starts at the upper left corner of the display, proceeds to the right along a horizontal line, and then proceeds downward, painting a series of horizontal scan lines. Each pixel value fetched from the frame-buffer memory is used to index a *video lookup table* (VLT) to obtain a digital value that is converted to an analog signal to control the intensity of the electron beam. The VLT establishes a correspondence between values stored in the frame buffer and colors on the screen.

The size and speed of the frame buffer must be chosen to match the properties of the display. If the display can show v lines, each of which is h pixels across, and each pixel can display 2^p different colors or intensities, then

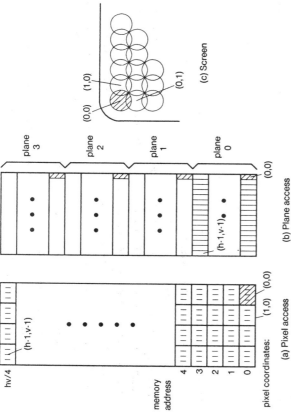

(a) Pixel access   (b) Plane access

(c) Screen

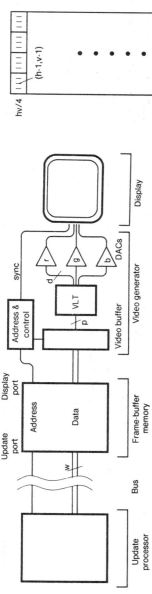

Figure 1   A conventional frame-buffer architecture consists of a dual-ported memory and a video generator. Pixel data is read through the display port, passed through a video lookup table (VLT) and digital-to-analog-converters (DAC) for red, green, and blue subchannels, and presented to the display. For monochromatic displays, only a single DAC is used. For binary displays, which show only two colors, the VLT and DAC are omitted.

the memory must contain at least vhp bits. The horizontal and vertical resolutions are influenced by the choice of display, while the number of bits stored for each pixel is partly determined by the display and partly by the application. Table 1 shows examples of typical choices.

The display port must be able to access the frame-buffer memory fast enough to refresh the display. Since cathode-ray tube displays require continual refreshing of the entire screen at rates from 30 to 70 times per second, very high memory bandwidths may be required. Table 1 shows the refresh rate, r, the number of times per second the display is scanned, and the resulting pixel time, the time available in which to display an individual pixel. The calculation of the pixel time, t_p, must allow time for the display beam's *horizontal retrace and vertical retrace*, during which no pixels are displayed. The fourth example in the table assumes a vertical retrace time $t_v = 600\ \mu s$, incurred once for each refresh, and a horizontal retrace time $t_h = 4\ \mu s$ incurred once for each scan line. Thus the pixel time is $((1/r - t_v)/v - t_h)/h$, or 10 ns for the example. If each pixel is represented in the frame buffer with eight bits, the display port must be capable of reading at 800 Mbits/s.

Meeting the bandwidth requirements of the display port is the first objective of a frame-buffer design. This usually requires that each memory cycle read

Figure 2   The two common methods by which the update processor addresses pixels in the frame buffer are (*a*) *pixel access* and (*b*) *plane access*. The bits in the frame buffer that represent the pixel at coordinates (0,0) are hatched.

values for more than one pixel, since pixel times are shorter than memory cycle times. Data read from the memory in parallel is placed briefly in a high-speed *video buffer*, from which individual pixel values are extracted as needed.

Some means must be provided to allow both ports access to the memory without undue interference. Meeting the bandwidth requirements of the display port is essential to ensure that the displayed image remains correct; the update port is usually given lower priority. To guarantee display access, the memory may be operated on a fixed schedule so that a fixed fraction of memory accesses are allocated to the display port, e.g. 1 in 2 or 2 in 3, with the remaining cycles allocated to the update port. A more restrictive method is to allow update accesses only during horizontal and vertical retrace periods, when pixels are not being displayed and the display port is idle.

How pixel values are mapped into the update processor's address space has a substantial impact on the speed with which the processor can alter the memory. The processor commonly accesses a word of memory, which contains information for more than one pixel (Figure 2). If the update port uses a *pixel organization*, one or more pixel values are packed into each word, as in Figure 2a. If p bits are recorded for each pixel, this is a packed two-dimensional array of p-bit values, indexed by the pixel coordinates (x, y). The

Table 1   Characteristics of typical raster-scan displays

Application	h	v	p	hvp	r	Pixel time
Personal computer	320	200	2	0.13×10^6	30	166 ns
Image store, full color	640	480	24	7.4×10^6	30	83 ns
Workstation, black-and-white	1152	900	1	1.0×10^6	66	11 ns
Workstation for CAD, color	1280	960	8	9.8×10^6	60	10 ns

update processor locates a pixel value by computing from its coordinates its word address in the array, reading the word, masking off the unwanted pixel values, and shifting the p bits to the right to obtain a p-bit integer. An alternative organization, the *plane organization*, is shown in Figure 2b. The memory may be viewed as storing p separate *bit-planes*, each of which is a packed array of single-bit values, one for each pixel. Hybrid organizations are also possible. For example, a memory with 24 bits per pixel may be organized as three *image planes*, each of which stores eight bits per pixel, organized for pixel access.

Many applications require mixtures of all four kinds of imagery. An engineering workstation, for example, may support all four but may emphasize geometric graphics and feedback imagery, which dominate drafting and other computer-aided design applications.

Auxiliary Data

In addition to serving as a refresh buffer, frame-buffer memories may serve as an image data structure for an application program. The best example is image-processing applications, where pixel intensities are used as input to sampling, filtering, or convolution algorithms. Likewise, most window-management software moves and scrolls windows by copying pixel values from one place on the screen to another (Pike 1983). In these cases, the update port must be able to read and write pixel values equally easily.

Some applications record more data for each pixel than just its intensity or color. This data is part of a data structure that is used by an algorithm to build or manipulate the image (Fournier & Fussell 1986). Examples are as follows:

1. Depth values, which are used in hidden-surface algorithms to find, for each pixel, the object closest to the viewer. As a new object is written into the frame buffer, it is visible at a pixel only if the depth of the new object is less than the depth of the object previously displayed at the pixel.

2. Occupancy bit. Hidden-surface algorithms based on a priority calculation can arrange to write objects into the frame buffer in depth order, with closest objects first. The occupancy bit indicates that the pixel has already been written by an object, so that any subsequent object that lies over the pixel will not affect the pixel's intensity.

3. Alpha. A scalar value, alpha, ranging between zero and one is recorded with each pixel to indicate the fraction of the pixel that an object covers. This value is used to combine images without introducing aliasing and sampling defects (Porter & Duff 1984; Duff 1985).

4. Sub-pixel mask. High-quality renderings of geometric objects require filtering, or antialiasing, in order to avoid a jagged appearance of high-contrast edges. Some algorithms compute pixel-coverage information at a higher resolution than that of the display, and record in a sub-pixel mask the parts of the pixel that are covered by an object (Carpenter 1984; Schumacker 1980).

While none of this auxiliary data is required to refresh the display, it associates data values with each pixel on the screen. As a consequence, storage for this data is often provided in the frame buffer memory itself, so that the addressing and accessing methods of the update port are available for accessing auxiliary data as well as pixel values.

REQUIREMENTS

The design of frame buffers is determined in large measure by the requirements of the application. While the size and speed of the memory must clearly match the needs of the display monitor, the update port must be designed to have sufficient memory bandwidth to change the image rapidly enough to meet the interactive performance requirements of the application. Moreover, the kinds of memory accesses permitted by the update port can have a large impact on update performance.

The kinds of images presented on the display vary among applications, and the organization of the update port varies as a consequence. The four most important categories of imagery for interactive applications are as follows:

1. Geometric graphics. Patterns of pixels representing geometric shapes such as lines, circles, polygons, and curves are written into the frame buffer. Typical applications are computer-aided design, business graphics, drafting, and technical illustration.

2. Text and window-management. Text is written onto the screen in multiple fonts, often involving special symbols. The screen is sectioned into *windows* that appear to be separate writing surfaces, often overlapping. Moving, clearing, panning, and scrolling windows are important update functions. Typical applications are workstations for engineering, document production, programming, or education.

3. Continuous-tone images. The screen is used to show continuous-tone images, either synthesized by an algorithm or sampled from a television camera or scanner. Typical applications are in graphic arts prepress, "painting" with a computer, animation, cartography, and image analysis.

4. Feedback imagery. An interactive application will often present cursors, menus, and lines on the screen as temporary feedback to assist the user's interaction with an application. These images must be displayed and removed quickly, so as not to impede interaction speed. Moreover, when a feedback image is removed, the original image must be restored.

Update Strategy

There are two techniques that an application may use to create each image in the frame buffer: It may make a global update to the image by erasing the buffer and drawing the image in its entirety, or it may make incremental updates to an existing image by changing only those pixel values required to make the new image. The choice of update strategy can influence how the frame-buffer memory is designed.

The incremental update strategy is used for most interactive applications, because only a portion of the image changes in response to a user's input actions. In a drafting application, for example, a typical update would be to write a line into the frame buffer or to erase an existing line. The rest of the image need not be changed, and redrawing the entire image would be slow.

By contrast, some applications create each image only once, or make extensive changes to an image, and so use the global update strategy. For example, flight simulators use the global update strategy because they generate a different image for each refresh of the screen in order to show motion.

Architectural Consequences

Some themes in the design of frame buffers apply to all applications, although their implications for each application may differ. The principal themes are as follows:

1. Organize the memory to provide sufficient bandwidth for both the display and update ports. While it is tempting to skimp on update port bandwidth, this will lead to poor performance because the image cannot be changed fast. If the bandwidths of the two ports are equal, then the entire image can, in principle, be changed in one frame time.

2. Organize the update port to access the pixel data that is needed. If, for example, an application often alters only a single plane of the memory at a time, a pixel access architecture is inefficient because each memory access yields all bits of a pixel rather than only the plane that needs to be changed.

3. Organize the memory so that the spatial organization of the update port accesses those pixels that often need to be changed. The conventional organization, which alters a horizontal group of pixels in one access, is inefficient for writing thin vertical lines in the frame buffer.

4. Design the update port to work in concert with the processor that will use it. It may be necessary to build into the update port functions missing from the processor, or to design a special-purpose processor to compute updates at acceptably high speeds.

Specific frame-buffer requirements differ by application and the kinds of imagery used:

1. Access by pixel and/or by plane. Displaying continuous-tone images usually requires pixel access. Geometric graphics may use either form. When an application needs to use all 2^p colors to denote different kinds of information, as in business-graphics applications, pixel access is desirable. By contrast, certain computer-aided design applications find plane access preferable, because they draw different kinds of information in separate bit-planes, e.g. wiring paths in one plane and plumbing paths in another.

2. *Plane masking*, when pixel access is provided. Masking permits the update processor to modify certain planes while leaving the contents of other planes unchanged.

3. Fast operations on rectangular regions of the screen. These operations include clearing a region to a constant color, copying pixel data from one region to another, and modifying existing pixel data. The BitBlt (or RasterOp) primitive is often used for these applications (Ingalls 1981; Newman & Sproull 1979).

4. Fast changes to the VLT to allow limited dynamics and animation (Shoup 1979).

5. A VLT structure that allows feedback images to override other imagery in the frame buffer.

6. Methods to transfer large blocks of image data from the processor's main memory to the frame buffer. These are useful when transferring continuous-tone images between a disk file and the frame buffer.

7. Double buffering for dynamic displays. To achieve a smooth transition from one frame to the next, two frame buffers are used. While one buffer is used to refresh a single frame on the display, the other is erased and filled with an image. When the refreshing and refilling processes are completed, the roles of the two buffers are switched.

8. A frame buffer larger than the screen. It is often desirable to see on the screen only a portion of a larger image stored in the frame buffer.

VIDEO GENERATION

The job of the video generator is to fetch pixel values from the display port, convert them to analog voltages, and pass the results to the display monitor, where they will control the intensity of one or more electron beams (Figure 1). The video generator also creates synchronization signals used by the display monitor to coordinate the beam's sweep across the screen with the arrival of pixel data.

The high speeds required in the video generator usually lead to a pipelined structure. Several pixel values are read from the display port in a single cycle and placed in a video buffer. While the controller is sequencing through the pixel values in the video buffer, the next read cycle on the display port may be started. Pipelining is also used in the rest of the path that the pixel data follows: looking up values in the VLT and presenting them to digital-to-analog converters.

In some designs, the video buffer is a first-in first-out queue (FIFO) large enough to contain one or more scan lines of pixel data. This design reduces the peak bandwidth required of the display port because pixels can be fetched during the entire scan-line time, even during horizontal retrace, rather than only when pixels are actively displayed. This reduces the display port bandwidth required between 17 and 25%, depending on the details of the raster-scan timing.

Video Lookup Tables

The video lookup table is a versatile device that is provided on nearly all frame-buffer displays. The table provides two principal features. First, it allows greater precision in intensity or color values than can be represented in the frame buffer directly ($d>p$ in Figure 1). Second, it allows certain kinds of dynamic displays because the table can be changed more rapidly than the contents of the entire frame buffer.

The principal uses of the VLT are summarized below:

1. The application can display 2^p arbitrary colors, because the VLT allows each of the 2^p pixel values recorded in the frame buffer to be mapped to an arbitrary color. It is common in computer-aided design applications to draw different kinds of data in separate bit planes and use the VLT to establish appropriate colors.

2. Pseudo-color can be achieved by using the VLT to produce a color coding of a scalar value recorded in pixel values. For example, if a pixel value represents temperature, the VLT can provide a mapping that shows low temperatures in blue and high temperatures in red, with appropriate colors in between.

3. Short bursts of animation can be achieved by using the VLT to select, for each frame, a subset of planes or pixel values to make visible. After each frame is refreshed, the VLT is changed to select visible pixel values for the next frame (Shoup 1979).

4. Feedback images can be presented with the help of the VLT. The feedback objects are drawn in a single plane, and the VLT is configured to show a specific feedback color whenever data is present in the feedback plane, and otherwise to show the color specified by the remaining planes. Thus the feedback image can be changed without altering the underlying picture, stored in the remaining planes.

5. The VLT can be used to select between two or more separate images stored in the frame buffer, simply by making visible only those pixel values corresponding to each image.

6. The table allows the digital values in the frame buffer to depart from a linear relationship to the voltages presented to the display. If pixel values measure intensity, then the VLT can apply *gamma correction*, which is required because the intensity of a pixel is not a linear function of the voltage delivered to the display. Alternatively, pixel values may record the logarithm of the intensity, so as to more closely model the sensitivity of the human eye; the VLT can convert these values into voltages that produce the desired intensities (Catmull 1979).

The detailed design of VLT hardware varies a great deal. One variant uses a large enough VLT to contain several different color maps. The address for the video lookup table is the concatenation of the pixel value (p bits) and q bits obtained from an auxiliary register. This register in effect selects one of 2^q color maps very quickly, so that the color map can be changed without having to change individual VLT entries.

Equipment must be provided to store values into the VLT; this is not shown in Figure 1. To avoid transient errors on the screen, the VLT is changed between frames, during vertical retrace. This interval, which varies between 600 and 1200 μs, must be sufficient for all VLT entries to be changed, since animation may require that two successive frames use completely different lookup tables.

The configuration shown in Figure 1 rapidly becomes impractical as the number of bits per pixel, p, grows. The problem is that the VLT gets so large that memories become too costly or too slow. In this case, it is common to split the video generator into separate sub-channels, one for red, one for green, and one for blue, as in Figure 3. This arrangement has less flexibility in assigning colors to pixel values than that of Figure 1. Sometimes a fourth sub-channel is added to restore some flexibility. For example, feedback images may be stored in the fourth sub-channel and may cause a single color to be displayed wherever the feedback image is present. The fourth sub-channel can be used for monochromatic images that must be changed quickly for interaction, and it can coexist with color information that does not change as rapidly, perhaps displayed in another window on the screen. An alternative sometimes used is to design the digital-to-analog converters to have an *overlay* input driven by the fourth sub-channel that forces the analog voltage to its maximum, thus displaying white on the screen.

Image Transformations

Rather than displaying the entire contents of a frame buffer on the screen, the video generator can easily select a rectangular portion of the frame buffer and

display them in sequence, the display pans to successive rectangles on successive frames, enlarging each by a factor of four.

More sophisticated image transformations are also possible. An image may be rotated as it is read from the frame buffer (Catmull & Smith 1980). A high-resolution image may be filtered as it is read from the frame buffer and may be displayed at a reduced size or lower resolution. The filtering removes "jaggies" and other aliasing effects.

Combining Images

The video generator can combine several independent images into a single video signal to be displayed (Fischer 1973; Entwisle 1977; Commodore 1986). Similar in concept to mixing several analog video signals, combination within the video generator is done digitally, usually on the pixel values themselves. Two or more images are read from one or more frame buffers, or are obtained by digitizing the video signal obtained from a camera or other video source, which results in several channels of pixel values. The video generator uses some rule to switch between the channels, so as to determine which image will be visible at each pixel. Alternatively, the channels can be mixed rather than switched, so that one image can fade into another, or one channel can control the mixing of two other channels.

In the simplest arrangement, the independent channels have a fixed priority, so that any image present in a high-priority channel will override images in lower priority channels. If a particular pixel is *transparent* in a high-priority channel, then the pixel will take on the color of a lower priority channel. A particular pixel value can be reserved to indicate transparency, or an entire bit-plane in the channel can be used to indicate transparency. If an image does not fill the entire screen, the region outside the image is considered transparent.

The most common use for combining separate image channels is to provide a cursor, whose position can be controlled easily and which does not require a full bit-plane in the frame buffer. A small frame buffer, perhaps 32 × 32 pixels, stores pixel values for a cursor (Thacker et al 1981).

The ability to combine images as the screen is refreshed, together with the panning functions discussed above, provides a range of highly dynamic effects, used frequently in video games. Typically a relatively static background image, stored in a frame buffer, is combined with a dozen or more *sprites*, small high-priority images whose positions on the screen can be controlled individually. The pixel values for these images are stored in a memory, but they are so small that not much storage is required. Wherever a sprite is transparent, lower-priority sprites or the background image is visible. Sprites can be moved very rapidly, since the position of each is controlled by horizontal and vertical positions, which are updated between frames. In order

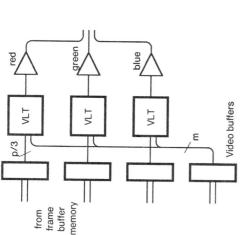

Figure 3 Three separate lookup tables are used in video generators that have more than about 12 bits per pixel. A fourth sub-channel is used for feedback imagery.

display it in a rectangular section of the screen (Kajiya et al 1975; Fischer 1973). The position of the rectangle within the frame buffer and the image on the screen can be determined independently. To implement this feature, the video generator waits until the scanning of the beam reaches a point within the screen rectangle, and then fetches from the frame buffer the corresponding pixel.

Flexible video generation of this sort permits two kinds of dynamically changing images. First, by moving only the rectangle within the frame buffer, the display appears to roam over a large image. Second, by moving only the rectangle on the screen, a fixed image appears to move on the screen, or perhaps to be dragged around in response to a user's commands. Changing the position of either rectangle can be accomplished easily between frames, since it is a matter of changing a few numbers that the video generator uses to count frame-buffer addresses and screen positions.

Normally, the sizes of the rectangle in the frame buffer and of the rectangle on the screen are identical. However, if the screen rectangle is allowed to be an integral multiple of the size of the frame-buffer rectangle, the image appears to be enlarged by the given integer (Fischer 1973). This allows the viewer to zoom in to see image detail. Zooming is usually implemented by repeating pixels within a scan line and repeating scan lines.

Crow & Howard (1981) show how rapid panning and zooming can be used to preview relatively long animation sequences. The frame buffer is divided into, say, a 4 × 4 array of rectangles, each one with 1/4 the dimensions of the entire screen. Sixteen successive frames are drawn in these rectangles. To

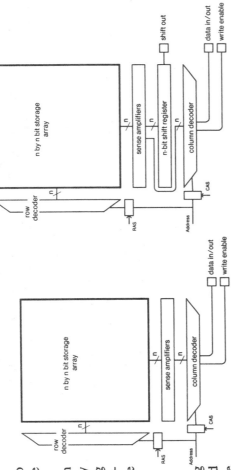

Figure 4   The internal structure of dynamic random-access memory (DRAM) chips that hold n^2 bits. (*a*) A conventional DRAM. (*b*) A video RAM, with an internal shift register.

to make video games inexpensive, sprites are supported by single-chip video generators such as the Texas Instruments TMS 9918 (see also Commodore 1986).

Applications that show overlapping windows of information on the screen can do so by combining the images of each window, using suitable priority rules. Most windowing systems combine the images into a single image using update algorithms (Pike 1983). Alternatively, the video generator may perform this function and allow windows to pan, scroll, and move around the screen rapidly (Wilkes et al 1984).

Video Input

Some frame buffers allow video input as well as video output. An analog video signal is passed through a high-speed analog-to-digital converter, and the results are written into the frame buffer. Of course, the memory must be designed to provide sufficient bandwidth. In some cases, video output is disabled while video input is being done, in order to avoid building a memory with a total bandwidth that is double the video bandwidth.

Some frame buffers allow transformed images to be rewritten into the frame buffer as they are displayed (Beg 1985). The simplest implementation returns to memory the results of the lookup performed by the VLT. This *feedback loop* is sometimes used in image-processing applications, in which the image transformation is used to compute a new image as a function of the previous one, e.g. a thresholded image.

Variations

Variations on the themes described above abound in video generators. A small amount of customization can yield enormous speed improvements for particular applications, especially when dynamic effects are required. Most of the variations are in the way image channels and sub-channels are combined and multiplexed and in the addressing used for the VLT.

MEMORY CHIP ARCHITECTURES

Because memory is the principal ingredient in a frame-buffer display, advances in frame-buffer architecture have been paced by memory chip advances in economics, performance, and structure. The decline in memory chip cost is largely responsible for the widespread use of frame buffers today. Display system designers have pressed the limits of memory chip performance in order to meet refresh and update bandwidth requirements. A recent change to the structure of memory chips, the addition of a shift register to form a "video RAM," has led to much higher bandwidths per chip. With

memory chip capacities of 256K bits and larger, the video RAM structure is essential for frame-buffer design.

Dynamic Random-Access Memory Chips

Although early frame-buffers were built using rotating disk memory, core memory, and semiconductor shift registers, it is the dynamic random-access memory (DRAM) that has made frame buffers practical. The characteristics of these parts are so critical to frame-buffer designs that we describe them briefly here.

Figure 4*a* shows the functional and physical structure of the simplest form of DRAM chip. The n^2 bits are stored in a square array of capacitors, with dimensions $n \times n$. A bit is read in two steps: First, an entire row of the memory is selected and connected to n sense amplifiers, and then a column decoder selects one of the sense amplifier outputs to transmit off the chip. Writing occurs by first connecting a row to the sense amplifiers and then using the column decoder to change a single sense bit, which is changed both in the sense amplifiers and in the row of capacitors. The two separate steps in accessing a bit are reflected in the way the chip is controlled. First, a *row address* is presented to the chip (RAS), and a row is connected to the sense amplifiers. Then a *column address* is presented (CAS), and a single sense bit is selected for reading or writing. A DRAM chip of this design reads only one bit in each memory cycle.

Although the structure shown in Figure 4*a* arose because of constraints on memory chip design, it provided display designers with an important feature called *page mode*. If several bits are to be read from the same row in succession, the row-selection step can be omitted from each memory cycle except the first. Once the sense amplifiers are connected to a given row, the column decoder can be used to read out any bits in the row. Since the row and column parts of a full memory cycle require about equal time, using page mode can almost double the bandwidth of a chip. In frame buffers, page mode is often used for display port accesses, provided the memory organization places adjacent pixels along a scan line in the same memory row.

Accessing Bits in Parallel

As the storage on a single memory chip has grown, maintaining sufficient read/write bandwidth has been problematic because the speed of the chips has not increased as much as their capacity. This effect is best demonstrated by computing the *time to fill*, t, the time required to write every bit in a memory chip using ordinary memory accesses. Table 2 shows these times for a number of DRAMs, assuming a memory cycle time of 400 ns. If the capacity of a memory chip is to be fully used, its entire contents must be read out in the time it takes to refresh a frame, i.e. the time to fill must be less than the refresh time $1/r$ (33 ms for 30-Hz displays and 17 ms for 60-Hz displays). The table shows that a 64K × 1 DRAM cannot be used efficiently with a 60-Hz display, since 26.2 ms is required to read the chip's contents, while the refresh must be completed in 17 ms. If we apportion only a fraction f of the memory's bandwidth for refresh, retaining the fraction $(1 - f)$ for update access, then the effective time to fill becomes t/f, which must be less than the frame refresh time.

By widening the data path for large DRAMs, the time to fill them is reduced. Table 2 shows that a 16K × 4 chip, which reads and writes four bits in a single cycle, provides four times the bandwidth of the 64K × 1 chip of equal capacity. The 16K × 4 chip has figured prominently in frame-buffer design, since it can support 60 Hz displays and still leave considerable bandwidth for update ($f=0.5$). However, as chip capacities grow still larger, this technique becomes impractical: to achieve performance equivalent to the 16K × 4 chip, a chip with 256K-bit capacity would require a 16-bit data path, which requires too many pins to be economical.

Video Memory Chips

A recent innovation in memory chip design is the video memory, or VRAM, which greatly simplifies frame-buffer design and increases the memory bandwidth available (Matick et al 1984). These memories contain a shift register n bits long that can be loaded in parallel from the n sense amplifiers and subsequently shifted off the chip independently of the row and column access path (Figure 4*b*). In effect, this is a dual-ported memory chip, in which the normal row/column access constitutes one port, and the shift register the other. The ports are linked only in that a row access must be used to load the shift register. The Texas Instruments TMS4161 was the first commercial video RAM; several manufacturers now offer similar 64K chips and they plan 256K and larger capacities.

The shift register in the VRAM is used for refreshing the display; in effect, it forms a large video shift register. The addressing of the memory is arranged so that a row of the memory chip contains bits that describe adjacent pixels on a scan line. The shift register is loaded at the beginning of the scan line, and then shifted to obtain the values of subsequent pixels. Since the shift register can operate at only about 30 MHz, several chips are usually operated in parallel, and a final high-speed video buffer produces values at pixel rates. If necessary, the VRAM shift register can be loaded again during a scan line to accommodate long scan lines.

The shift register in a VRAM increases the bandwidth available relative to a typical RAM chip by a factor of 6–8 in a way that directly benefits frame-buffer display designs. For display refresh, n bits are obtained with a single row access cycle, so almost 100% of the normal row/column accesses can be devoted to the update port. Only infrequently must update accesses be suspended so that a row access can reload the shift register.

Some video RAMs can use the shift register for input as well as for output. A video input port can be easily provided by such a memory simply by shifting pixel data into the shift register. This feature can also be used to clear the memory fast, by filling the shift register with zeroes and writing a row of zeroes at a time. One way to fill the shift register with zeroes is to read a row of the memory that was previously set to zero.

MEMORY ORGANIZATION

Frame-buffer memories can be organized in a variety of ways, all subject to the constraint that they provide sufficient bandwidth to refresh the display. The organizations differ principally in the way the update port is given access to pixel values. There are three important issues:

Table 2 Time to fill for different memory chip configurations

DRAM organization	Time to fill, t(ms)	t/f for $f=0.5$
4K×1	1.6	3.3
16K×1	6.6	13.1
64K×1	26.2	52.4
256K×1	105	210
16K×4	6.6	13.1
64K×4	26.2	52.4

each memory chip (Figure 4) from the mask, while supplying the data to the chip's data pin. Only those chips that are enabled will write new data.

Read-Modify-Write Access

Many algorithms for updating the frame buffer read a group of pixels, compute new values, and write the pixels back into the frame buffer. For example, an incremental update that highlights a region of the screen using "video reverse" on a black-and-white display reads each pixel in the region, flips black pixels to white and white pixels to black, and writes the new pixel values back into the memory. Often the update port is designed to permit read-modify-write access because memory chips can perform a single read-modify-write cycle faster than two separate read and write cycles.

Eliminating Word Boundaries

The processor often wishes to access a group of adjacent pixels starting at an arbitrary position along a scan line, and not be confined to accessing entire words of the frame buffer. An arbitrary access can always be broken down into a series of accesses to separate words, as shown in Figure 5a. However, by providing suitable addresses to each memory chip, it is possible to allow a single-word access by the update port to cross word boundaries in the memory and thus to access an arbitrary group of adjacent pixels, as shown in Figure 5b.

Figure 6 shows how a collection of pixels can be accessed in a single cycle because each pixel is stored in a different memory chip. The figure illustrates a frame buffer with $w=16$ bits in a word, representing 16 pixels along a scan line ($p=1$), being used to write 16 adjacent pixels starting at $x=13$. Note that each of the 16 pixels being written lies in a different memory chip, because the frame buffer uses 16 chips to write a 16-bit parallel word. Thus the write could potentially be done in a single cycle, provided each chip is given the proper address. In the example, the three high-order chips receive address 0, and the thirteen remaining chips receive address 1. These are the same addresses as would have been used in two separate writes to words 0 and 1.

To endow the update port with pixel addressing, it is necessary not only to provide proper chip addressing but also to rotate the pixel data presented by the update port in order to align it with the word structure of the memory. In the example shown in Figure 6, if the 16 bits of pixel data are presented by the update port in a word, they must be rotated 3 positions to the right so as to align the data with the appropriate chips.

This scheme can be implemented in several ways. The obvious technique is to outfit each memory chip with a multiplexor that selects between two addresses. Alternatively, both an address and its successor can be sent to all chips in two steps, but by issuing the *row address strobe* (RAS) or *column address strobe* (CAS) signals selectively, the proper address can be steered to

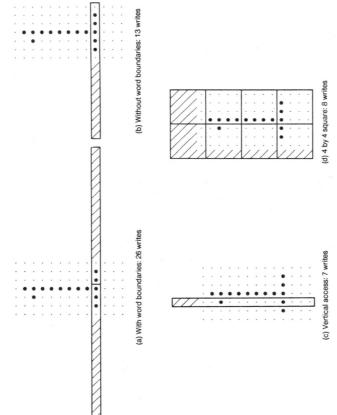

(a) With word boundaries: 26 writes

(b) Without word boundaries: 13 writes

(c) Vertical access: 7 writes

(d) 4 by 4 square: 8 writes

Figure 5   A 7 × 13 character matrix written using different frame-buffer memory organizations. (*a*) Conventional memory, with 16-pixel words aligned with horizontal scan lines. (*b*) Memory with word boundaries eliminated, or "pixel addressing." (*c*) Access to 16-pixel vertical strips. (*d*) Access to arbitrary squares, 4 × 4 pixels.

1. What pixels can be accessed in a single memory cycle?
2. What operations can be performed on the pixel values by the memory?
3. What is the correspondence between addresses supplied to the update port and pixel positions on the screen?

In order to compare different memory organizations, we shall show how a single character may be written into the frame buffer using each approach (Figure 5).

Masking

If the update port can access more than one pixel value in a single cycle, the memory may provide the ability to *mask* a write cycle, i.e. to alter some of the pixel values while leaving the remaining pixels unchanged. In this case, the processor provides data values as well as a mask to indicate which bits should be written. The mask may allow only certain bit planes to be written or may allow only certain pixels to be written, or both. In Figure 5, hatching indicates those pixels in each memory access that are masked off, i.e. that are left unchanged in the frame buffer.

A common implementation technique supplies the *write enable* signal to

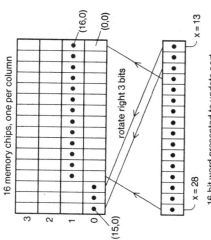

Figure 6 Chip addressing to cross word boundaries. All 16 pixels from $x=13$ to $x=28$ can be written into the frame buffer in a single cycle, because each pixel is stored in a different memory chip. Note that different chips must receive different addresses. A word presented to the update port, with the first pixel in the low-order bit, must be rotated before it can be written into the memory.

each chip (Sproull et al 1983). Or each memory chip can include an internal address incrementer invoked by an external signal, which is controlled so that selected chips will use an address one greater than the address transmitted (Gupta 1981). Bechtolsheim & Baskett (1980) describe a scheme in which the frame buffer uses a word width that is twice the update port width, so that all chips in each half-word can use the same address: a single multiplexor suffices to implement this arrangement.

Horizontal and Vertical Access

The frame buffer can be organized to allow access to horizontal and vertical lines of pixels in a single cycle (Ostapko 1984). The display port uses horizontal access to read pixel data along scan lines while the update port may offer both horizontal or vertical access, which the update processor can invoke when appropriate (Figure 5*d*). A suitable arrangement of memory chips and addressing will permit access across word boundaries (Figure 7). One advantage of this organization is its ability to rotate an image by 90° or to transpose it as it is written into the frame buffer. More elaborate arrangements allow access to horizontal lines, vertical lines, squares, and other rectangular regions (Gupta 1981; Chor et al 1982).

Square Organizations

The efficiency of the update port can be improved if the memory is organized to access a square of pixels rather than a row aligned with a scan line (Figure 5*c*). The reason for the improvement lies in the spatial extent of the objects

Figure 7 Screen layout for horizontal and vertical access to eight chips (labeled A to H). All pixels labeled A are stored in chip A. The heavy rectangles show that arbitrary horizontal and vertical access can be performed in a single memory cycle because each of the eight pixels accessed is stored in a different chip.

being written into the frame buffer. Graphical objects are no more likely to be short and wide than tall and thin, and a symmetric organization will favor all objects equally. Writing vectors of arbitrary orientation, characters, and filled objects such as polygons all benefit from the square organization. Several frame buffers based on this organization have been built (Sproull et al 1983; Walsby 1980; Page 1983; Clark & Hannah 1980).

To illustrate the performance of a square organization, consider a vector-generator that drives an 8×8 square array. Suppose that the update port is able to use page mode access to obtain 150 ns access to 8×8 squares. This will allow vectors to be drawn with 8 pixels per memory access, or about 20 ns per pixel. If lines are several pixels wide, as when antialiasing is applied, the efficiency rises even further because more than 8 pixels will be modified in a single memory access.

The square organization can be designed to allow access to an arbitrary square (Figure 8) using the techniques for eliminating word boundaries described above (Sproull et al 1983). For an 8×8 organization, this means that a 7×13 character can be written at an arbitrary position in two memory cycles. As with the horizontal and vertical organization, images may be written rotated by 90° or transposed.

A video generator for an $m \times m$ organization must be designed to accommodate the square access pattern. One technique is to read a row of squares into a video buffer that holds m scan lines and then read from the buffer the individual pixels in appropriate scan order. Two video buffers are needed, so that one can be refilled while the other is refreshing the display.

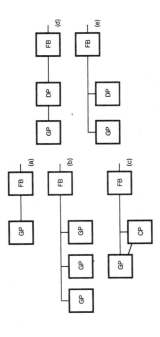

Figure 8 Screen layout using a 4 × 4 square memory organization. Sixteen memory chips, labeled A to P, store the pixels; all pixels labeled A are stored in chip A. The heavy square shows that an arbitrary 4 × 4 square can be accessed in a single memory cycle because each of the 16 pixels accessed is stored in a different chip.

With VRAMs, the shift registers in the memory chips serve as a video buffer that holds m scan lines.

UPDATE PROCESSORS

The architecture of a frame-buffer memory cannot be designed without considering the processor that is attached to the update port. In some cases, the processor and frame buffer are designed in concert to achieve high performance or low cost; in other cases, the processor is a general-purpose computer or microprocessor that accesses the frame buffer memory like all other system memory. There are also intermediate cases, such as a general-purpose processor augmented with a coprocessor designed to speed up graphics operations. In this section, we outline the different forms of processors and how they influence frame-buffer design.

General-Purpose Processors

For greatest flexibility, a general-purpose processor is often used to update a frame-buffer memory (Figure 9a). The flexibility is advantageous in several ways: Arbitrary algorithms can be used to update the frame buffer; the algorithms have access to necessary data structures in the application program; and the algorithms can build arbitrary data structures during their execution. This arrangement, though flexible, limits performance: General-purpose processors are not often suited to high-speed update algorithms, and their memory interfaces may preclude exotic frame-buffer organizations such as square arrays.

For a frame buffer to work with a general-purpose processor, its update port must provide the read and write accesses required by the processor: to words of a given width, to bytes, etc. In some cases, the frame buffer memory is an

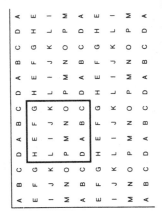

Figure 9 Alternative configurations for update processors. (a) A general-purpose processor (GP) directly addresses the frame buffer (FB). (b) Multiprocessor configuration. (c) A coprocessor (CP) handles graphics operations. (d) A display processor (DP) has exclusive access to the frame buffer. (e) Both general-purpose and display processors can update the frame buffer.

integral part of the system memory, which incorporates a display port (Thacker et al 1981).

One way to compensate for lack of facilities in a general-purpose processor is to build some processing into the update port. For example, the update port can help with addressing by allowing the processor to specify x and y addresses separately, and then providing read and write access to the addressed pixel. The update port can provide both plane and pixel access by mapping the frame buffer into the processor's address space twice, one mapping for pixel access and one for plane access. The update port can perform shifting and masking if the processor's corresponding instructions are slow (Bechtolsheim & Baskett 1980).

These measures may be less useful for high-performance processors. For example, although the MC68000 microprocessor is not particularly suited to graphics operations, the MC68020 represents a dramatic improvement. It has fast shift and rotate instructions, and its on-chip instruction cache will accommodate the inner loops of many graphics algorithms, allowing them to run dramatically faster. Shifting and masking functions in the update port thus become less valuable.

If the processor is outfitted with a data cache, special attention must be given to its interaction with the frame buffer. Data written by the processor must not be allowed to remain in the cache indefinitely; or it will not be written into the frame-buffer memory and participate in display refresh.

The principal disadvantage of using a general-purpose processor to update a frame-buffer display, its low performance, can be attacked by building multiprocessor systems. The most flexible multiprocessors use a collection of identical processors, all cooperating to solve a single problem. The frame buffer is part of the memory shared by all processors, each of which can assume all or part of the responsibility for updating the display (Figure 9b). A great many graphics algorithms decompose nicely into multiprocessing implementations suited for such hardware.

Coprocessors

A coprocessor can enhance the performance of a general-purpose processor by performing specialized graphics operations quickly. In these designs, the parent processor exercises absolute control over the actions of the coprocessor and retains its ability to access the frame buffer, so that algorithms not provided by the coprocessor can be programmed in the parent (Figure 9c).

A good example of a graphics coprocessor is a chip that contains 16-bit data paths to implement the shifting, masking, and functional combinations required to implement BitBlt (Bennett 1985). The parent processor executes a loop that generates the appropriate memory addresses, but the coprocessor is able to perform in a single read-modify-write memory cycle a set of operations that would otherwise require several instructions to implement on the general-purpose processor.

In most cases, a coprocessor uses the same memory interface as its parent processor, and the implications for update port organization are identical. However, one could build coprocessors designed for other update port organizations, such as the square array, precisely to act as an interface between a conventional processor and the update port format.

Display Processors

The job of updating a frame buffer is sometimes given to an independent *display processor*, which is connected to the update port of the frame buffer and is controlled by the host processor, which transmits drawing commands to the display processor (Figure 9d). Most display processors are designed to generate a range of geometric objects, such as lines, circles, text characters, polygons, and filled objects. Some may even include complex rendering algorithms that produce shaded images with hidden surfaces removed. Display processors were first attached to frame buffers by manufacturers to obtain products that could work with a variety of host computer systems. The host used a simple I/O channel to send commands and data to the display processor. Display processors are now being offered on single chips that include parts of the video generator and memory interface as well as graphic-generation logic.

The weakness of most display processors lies in their limited communication with the host processor and application program. Most have no access to the application program's data structures and so can neither fetch character fonts, symbol definitions, or display lists from application data structures nor write results into application data structures. Instead, the application must explicitly transmit data to and from the display processor. This weakness can

be reduced somewhat by making the frame-buffer memory large enough to hold some of this additional data. Another problem arises because most display processors prevent the host processor from having fast access to the frame buffer. Update algorithms implemented in the host processor because they cannot be accommodated by the display processor will suffer poor performance. The remedy is to allow the host access to the frame buffer as well as to the display processor (Figure 9e).

Special Display Processors

Special applications and special frame-buffer organizations usually require special-purpose processors for updates. Very high update rates required for flight simulation imagery, movie animation, or raster-scan printing require special-purpose processors. These processors are often microcoded processors with data paths customized for the update algorithms required.

The square memory organizations described above all require special-purpose processors to generate graphical data at a sufficiently high rate to warrant the exotic memory organization. A line-drawing algorithm, for example, must generate square blocks of bits and may use multiple parallel processors to achieve the necessary speed (Sproull 1982; Gupta 1981).

To obtain the highest update rates, it is necessary to have more than one processor working on the same frame buffer. These processors are built into the frame buffer itself. The Chap processor, designed to combine images at high speed for animation applications, associates a separate processor with the red, green, and blue channels (Levinthal & Porter 1984). Some designs associate a processor with each memory chip in the frame buffer (Clark & Hannah 1980; Gupta et al 1981; Gupta 1981). To obtain even greater processing bandwidths, logic to update pixel values can be integrated into the memory chip so that it can be applied to an entire row of pixels at once (Demetrescu 1985). In the extreme, each pixel has an associated processor. The best example is the "pixel planes" display that provides each pixel with a small serial computer that can decide whether a pixel lies inside a polygon, whether the polygon is hidden because it lies behind another polygon visible in the pixel, and what its red, green, and blue shade should be (Fuchs & Poulton 1981; Poulton et al 1985).

In many of these designs, the distinction between the frame buffer and the update processor becomes blurred: Each processor controls some memory, parts of which behave like a frame buffer. Issues of addressing and data manipulation pertain to both the processors and their associated memory.

PERFORMANCE EVALUATION

Since frame buffers are often designed to meet certain performance requirements, it would be useful to compare the performance of different

integration of the video buffer, video lookup table, and digital-to-analog converter on a single chip. These products are designed for workstations used in office and computer-aided-design applications, which have up to 8 Mbit frame-buffer memories and require only modest update rates. Increasing integration of frame-buffer components onto single chips drives the cost of these displays down.

For frame buffers that require extremely high update rates, special-purpose processors are increasingly used, often in multiprocessor configurations. New memory chip designs with decreased cycle times also help, e.g. static column decode, "hierarchical memories." As image-processing techniques are increasingly integrated with geometric graphics algorithms, updates are computed by digital signal-processors, either singly, in pipelines, or in arrays. As processing power increases, more update functions become feasible, such as antialiasing, wide lines, and pixel resampling that allows image copying with arbitrary scaling and rotation.

A number of challenges remain for frame-buffer designers. Surprisingly, no one has yet built a very large frame buffer (e.g. $20,000 \times 20,000$ pixels) that can be used to roam around a large image. Such a display might prove valuable in VLSI design, mapping, image interpretation, and graphic arts applications.

An open problem is how best to implement window-management systems, using a combination of hardware and software. Ideally, each application in a multiprocess computing environment has access to a complete frame buffer or to a simulation of one. The mapping from what the application deems a frame buffer to possibly overlapping windows on one or more display screens is the job of the window-management system. Individual frame buffers combined by the video generator, as in Wilkes et al (1984), can handle only a limited number of windows. One can imagine a memory-mapping scheme that would give the appearance of a separate frame buffer in each application's memory space, but in reality would be mapped to a single frame buffer. Appropriate protection would be required to prevent one application from interfering with another, and some means must be provided to inform each application about the current size of its frame buffer (window), which might change as windows are moved.

Finally, the ability to combine the outputs of several frame buffers into a single video image suggests a modular architecture for frame-buffer systems. Imagine a structure consisting of one or more modules, each consisting of a frame buffer and its associated display processor(s), all feeding a common video generator that combines the channels. Different module designs could be specialized for different types of updates: text and graphics such as used on personal computers; dynamic three-dimensional images; image-processing functions, etc. The display system could then be easily configured to meet a wide variety of application needs.

architectures. While it is relatively easy to specify the speed of each update access to a frame buffer, it is not always easy to relate this figure to overall performance. The problem lies in characterizing the kinds of updates that will be used in an application.

Part of the problem lies in the fact that each access may reference pixels that are not needed by the update. Let us define the *efficiency* of an access as the fraction of pixels accessed that are needed. When drawing a vertical line into a frame buffer that accesses 64 horizontally adjacent pixels in a single cycle, the efficiency is 1/64, or 1.6%. By contrast, when drawing a long horizontal line, the efficiency approaches 100%. In order to compare architectures, we need to know the distribution of updates that an application will require.

An example of the importance of knowing the precise character of updates comes from BitBlt. The BitBlt copy operation, when used with a conventional frame-buffer organization that accesses multiple pixels in a single cycle, requires the data to be shifted or rotated to align the source to the destination word boundaries. This would seem to suggest that a high-speed shifter is important. However, if most of the update port cycles used for BitBlt copying are for scrolling information vertically on the screen, the alignments of the source and destination data are identical, and no shifting is required. To complete the analysis, we need to know how much scrolling is done compared to other frame-buffer updates.

The little performance evaluation that has been done indicates an interesting phenomenon: While most of the graphics operations may involve short lines or small BitBlt copy operations, most of the frame-buffer memory traffic comes from long lines or large copies (Sproull et al 1983). Thus the update processor must ensure that each command is decoded and set up quickly, while the update port should cater for long lines and large copies. Note that for large copies, the spatial organization of the update port is irrelevant, since most accesses will be 100% efficient because all pixels referenced will be needed for the copy. By contrast, for line drawing, the spatial organization of the update port influences performance of lines of all lengths.

Performance evaluation would be aided if some "graphics instruction mixes," analogous to instruction mixes for general-purpose computers, were available for different applications. Mixes could be obtained by tracing graphical update commands in an application. Instruction mixes are needed to evaluate entire display systems, including software, operating-system drivers, and display processors, as well as the frame buffer.

STATE OF THE ART AND TRENDS

In early 1986, frame-buffer designs are characterized by (*a*) use of video RAM chips, (*b*) a variety of single-chip display processors available, and (*c*)

CONCLUSION

This review has emphasized three aspects of frame-buffer design:

1. The organization of memory, both on chip and off, to support the bandwidth and access pattern required to refresh a raster display.

2. The organization of the update port to provide efficient access to the frame buffer and to couple to the update processor.

3. The ability of the video generator to combine images from various sources in various ways and to transform the images as they are displayed. These facilities are especially important for making dynamic images, since changes to the frame-buffer memory itself may be slow.

Although we have touched only briefly on the design of update processors, this topic is closely related to frame-buffer design. The trend to apply more specialized processing in displays, and to place the processing closer to the memory to reduce communication overhead, means that the processors and memories must increasingly be designed together.

In a paper written in 1968, two designers observed that display systems exhibit a "wheel of reincarnation," in which functions are gradually moved from the host processor to special processing in the display, culminating in the display acquiring a program counter and becoming a processor itself (Myer & Sutherland 1968). The wheel is evident in frame-buffer design as well, but it no longer poses much of a problem for designers. Adding one or more processors to a system is now very easy, thanks to single-chip microprocessors, bit-slice ALUs, buses that support multiple processors, and so on. Today, we cheerfully add processors to improve the performance of a display.

ACKNOWLEDGMENTS

Ron Baecker, Frank Crow, Satish Gupta, Ivan Sutherland, and Bert Sutherland helped me with this review.

Literature Cited

Baecker, R. M. 1979. Digital video display systems and dynamic graphics. *Comput. Graphics* 13(2):48–56

Bechtolsheim, A., Baskett, F. 1980. High-performance raster graphics for microcomputer systems. *Comput. Graphics* 14(3):43–47

Beg, R. 1985. Image-processing system serves a variety of uses. *Comput. Des.* 24(16):99–106

Bennett, J. 1985. Raster operations. *Byte* 10(12):187–203

Carpenter, L. 1984. The A-buffer, and anti-aliased hidden surface method. *Comput. Graphics* 18(3):103–8

Conrac Corp. 1985. *Raster Graphics Handbook.* New York: Van Nostrand Reinhold. 2nd ed.

Crow, F. C., Howard, M. W. 1981. A frame buffer system with enhanced functionality. *Comput. Graphics* 16(3):63–69

Demetrescu, S. 1985. High speed image rasterization using scan line access memories. See Fuchs 1985, pp. 221–43

Duff, T. 1985. Compositing 3-D rendered images. *Comput. Graphics* 19(3):41–44

Entwisle, J. 1977. An image-processing approach to computer graphics. *Computers and Graphics* 2(2):111–17

Fischer, M. 1973. MAPS—A generalized image processor. *Comput. Graphics* 7(3):1–9

Foley, J. D., van Dam, A. 1982. *Fundamentals of Interactive Computer Graphics.* Reading, Mass: Addison-Wesley

Fournier, A., Fussell, D. 1986. On the power of the frame buffer. *ACM Trans. Graphics.* Submitted for publication

Fuchs, H., ed. 1985. *1985 Chapel Hill Conference on Very Large Scale Integration.* Rockville, MD: Comput. Sci.

Fuchs, H., Poulton, J. 1981. Pixel-Planes: A VLSI-oriented design for a raster graphics engine. 1981 (3rd Quarter):20–28

Gupta, S. 1981. *Architectures and Algorithms for Parallel Updates of Raster Scan Displays.* CMU-CS-82-111, Comput. Sci. Dept., Carnegie-Mellon Univ., Pittsburgh, Pa.

Gupta, S., Sproull, R. F., Sutherland, I. E. 1981. A VLSI architecture for updating raster-scan displays. *Comput. Graphics* 15(3):71–78

Ingalls, D. H. H. 1981. The Smalltalk graphics kernel. *Byte* 6(8):168–94

Kajiya, J. T., Sutherland, I. E., Cheadle, E. C. 1975. A random-access video frame buffer. *Proc. Computer Graphics, Pattern Recognition, and Data Structure, IEEE Comput. Soc., Los Angeles,* pp. 1–6

Levinthal, A., Porter, T. 1984. Chap—A SIMD graphics processor. *Comput. Graphics* 18(3):77–82

Matick, R., Ling, D. T., Gupta, S., Dill, F. H. 1984. All points addressable raster display memory. *IBM J. Res. Dev.* 28(4):379–92

Myer, T. H., Sutherland, I. E. 1968. On the design of display processors. *Commun. ACM* 11(6):410

Newman, W. M., Sproull, R. F. 1979. *Principles of Interactive Computer Graphics.* New York: McGraw-Hill. 2nd ed.

Ostapko, D. L. 1984. A mapping and memory chip hardware which provides symmetric reading/writing of horizontal and vertical lines. *IBM J. Res. Dev.* 28(4):393–98

Page, I. 1983. DisArray: A 16 × 16 RasterOp processor. *Eurographics 83,* ed. P. J. W. ten Hagen, pp. 367–77. Amsterdam: North-Holland

Pike, R. 1983. Graphics in overlapping bitmap layers. *ACM Trans. Graphics* 2(2):135–60

Porter, T., Duff, T. 1984. Compositing digital images. *Comput. Graphics* 18(3):253–59

Poulton, J., Fuchs, H., Austin, J. D., Eyles, J. G., Heinecke, J., et al. 1985. Pixel-planes: Building a VLSI-based graphic system. See Fuchs 1985, pp. 35–60

Schumacker, R. A. 1980. A new visual system architecture. *Proc. 2nd Interserv. Ind. Train. Equip. Conf., Salt Lake City,* pp. 1–8

Shoup, R. G. 1979. Color table animation. *Comput. Graphics* 13(2):8–13

Sproull, R. F. 1982. Using program transformations to derive line-drawing algorithms. *Trans. Graphics* 1(4):259–73

Sproull, R. F., Sutherland, I. E., Thompson, A., Gupta, S., Minter, C. 1983. The 8 by 8 display. *ACM Trans. Graphics* 2(1):32–56

Thacker, C. P., McCreight, E. M., Lampson, B. W., Sproull, R. F., Boggs, D. R. 1981. Alto: A personal computer. In *Computer Structures: Readings and Examples,* ed. D. P. Siewiorek, C. G. Bell, A. N. Newell, pp. 549–72. New York: McGraw-Hill. 2nd ed.

Walsby, A. M. 1980. Fast colour raster graphics using an array processor. *Eurographics 80,* ed. C. E. Vandoni, pp. 303–13. Amsterdam: North-Holland

Whitton, M. C. 1984. Memory design for raster graphics displays. *Comput. Graphics Appl.* 4(3):48–65

Wilkes, A. J., Singer, D. W., Gibbons, J. J., King, T. R., Robinson, P., Wiseman, N. E. 1984. The Rainbow workstation. *Comput. J.* 27(2):112–20

Catmull, E. 1979. A tutorial on compensation tables. *Comput. Graphics* 13(2):1–7

Catmull, E., Smith, A. R. 1980. 3-D transformations of images in scanline order. *Comput. Graphics* 14(3):279–84

Chor, B., Leiserson, C. E., Rivest, R. L. 1982. An application of number theory to the organization of raster-graphics memory. *23rd IEEE Symp. Found. Comput. Sci.*

Clark, J. H., Hannah, M. R. 1980. Distributed processing in a high-performance smart image memory. *Lambda* 1980 (4th Quarter): 40–45

Commodore. 1986. *Amiga Reference Manual.* Reading, Mass: Addison-Wesley

Chapter 8

The Haptic Channel

In this chapter we focus on aspects of interaction that involve physical contact between the user and the computer. Such forms of interaction may be referred to as *haptic*, which derives from a Greek word meaning *touch* or *contact*.

For the most part, our discussion will center on input. Haptic output devices are very rare. One example would be a device capable of producing output in braille. From another perspective, however, *every* input device can be considered to provide output through the tactile or kinesthetic feedback it provides to the user. In practice, the quality and appropriateness of this "feel" are often extremely important in determining a device's effectiveness and acceptance in a particular context.

The bulk of the discussion will concern manual input, since that is the most common usage and the richest source from which we can draw examples. However, it is important to remember that concepts relevant to the use of the hands generally apply to control through other parts of the body. Two examples are the use of foot pedals and tongue-activated joysticks, as used by those with physical disabilities.

Technology Makes a Difference

Each input device has its own strengths and weaknesses, just as each application has its own unique demands. With the wide range of input devices available, one of the problems that confronts the designer is that of obtaining a match between application and input technology. Part of the problem involves recognizing the

parameters which characterize the application's demands. The other is knowing how each technology being considered performs within those parameters. These topics are addressed below and in the first reading by Buxton (1986).

One way to approach these issues is to experiment with a set of representative tasks. Each task has its own idiosyncratic demands. Having enumerated such a set, we can determine the properties relevant to a particular application, and then test the effectiveness of various technologies in meeting that application's demands. This approach allows us to get a rapid match of technology to application. Furthermore, this set of representative tasks helps establish the parameters that will guide the selection process.

In the remainder of this section, we describe a basic set of generic transactions using a set of small test programs. These make an excellent implementation project for the student, and provide a good test-bed for developing an understanding of the characteristics of several input devices.

Like any other list, this one is not complete. It focuses on 2D tasks, such as those found in many graphical user interfaces. Text entry and 3D input, for example, are not emphasized. We leave it as an exercise to the reader to expand the list.

Pursuit Tracking:
In this task, illustrated in Figure 1, a moving target (a fly) moves over the screen under computer control. The operator uses a control device to track the fly's motion.

Feedback about the operator's performance is given by a tracking symbol in the form of a fly swatter. The idea is to see how many times the fly can be killed by positioning the swatter over the fly and pushing a button device.

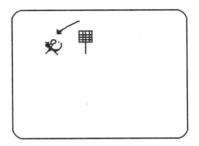

Figure 1: Pursuit Tracking

A moving target (a fly) moves over the screen. The tracking symbol is a fly swatter. When the swatter is beside the fly, the user pushes a button device to swat the fly.

The main statistic in this test is how many times the fly can be swatted in a given time interval. There are a number of parameters that should be varied in order to explore their influence on task performance. One of these is the speed that the target moves. Another is the *control:display (C:D) ratio:* the ratio between the distance the controller is moved and the corresponding distance the tracker moves on the display. For example, if the C:D ratio is 2:1, two centimeters of motion by the controller would result in only one centimeter of motion by the tracker.

A high C:D ratio is useful for fine cursor positioning, and for users who do not have well developed motor coordination (such as the aged or physically disabled). A low C:D ratio permits one to traverse the display with relatively little motion of the controller. Notice that with devices that use the same surface for both control and display, such as touch screens and light pens, the C:D ratio is almost always 1:1. This class of device, as a result, has a directness not shared by most other technologies. However, this directness can severely restrict their usefulness in a number of applications.

With the appropriate technology, the C:D ratio may be changed. Sometimes this can be done by the user. In other cases, it may be changed automatically, depending on the task. The C:D ratio need not be linear. On the Macintosh computer, for example, the C:D ratio varies, based on the speed that the controller (the mouse) is moved. In effect, the C:D ratio is governed by an "automatic transmission."

One other parameter to consider in this test is the button push that is required to swat the fly. For example, can this be activated with the same hand that is providing the spatial control? This may be difficult if a touch tablet or trackball is used. If the same limb providing the spatial control cannot be used for the button event, is another limb free in the application being tested for?

Target Acquisition:

In this task, the user must select each of a number of squares displayed on the screen, as illustrated in Figure 2. A square is selected by positioning the tracking symbol over it and signaling the system with a button event. Squares should be selected largest to smallest, left-to-right, top-to-bottom.

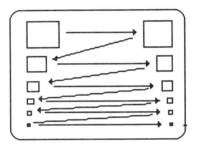

Figure 2: Target Acquisition

Select each square in turn, left-to-right, top-to-bottom. Notice how selection time is related to target size.

The main statistic to consider is the time required to select the full set of targets. Along with this, examine how target size affects the speed of target acquisition. The smaller the target the longer it will take to acquire, due to the fine motor control necessary. This is generalized more fully in the reading by Card, English and Burr (1978) as *Fitts's Law.*

Essentially, Fitts's Law states that the time to acquire a target with a continuous linear controller is a function of the distance divided by the target size. More formally, the time T_{pos} to move the hand to a target of size S which lies a distance D away is:

$$T_{pos} = K_0 + I_m \, log_2(D/S + .5),$$

where $I_m = 100[70~120]$ msec/bit and K_0 is a constant (Card, Moran and Newell, 1983, pp. 27 and 241).

As in the pursuit tracking task, issues such as C:D ratio and what button device is used will affect performance.

There are a number of variations on this basic task. Each brings to light important aspects of the input technology:

- *Homing Time:* If an application involves frequently moving between a text entry device (usually a QWERTY keyboard) and a pointing device, it is important to know the effect of this movement on performance. This is the *homing time* discussed in the Keystroke Model (Card, Moran and Newell, 1980). To illustrate the effect of homing time, have the user push a key on the keyboard (the space bar, for example), after each square is selected. Using the same tablet, for example, what is the difference in task performance using a puck or a stylus?

- *Dragging and Rubber Band Lines:* In this variation, a rubber band line is stretched from the last selected square to the tracking symbol. When the next square is selected, the rubber band line is anchored at that point, and then stretched from there. The idea is to connect the squares, one after the other.

One of the interesting questions in this version is the effect of the control sequence. Do we drag with the select-button down or up? Does it matter? Does it depend on what device is being used? What are the implications? How does this relate to dragging in general, or to interactions with pop-up or pull-down menus?

Freehand Inking:

Attempting to input a facsimile of your handwritten signature places yet another set of demands on the input technology. To evaluate the degree to which various devices lend themselves to this type of task, present the user with a screen ruled with lines of decreasing spacing. Have the user sign her name once in each space, as illustrated in Figure 3. Use a simple subjective evaluation of the quality of her signature as a means of comparing devices.

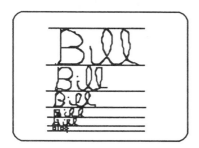

Figure 3: Freehand Inking
A device's ability to capture a good facsimile of your signature is a good measure of its effectiveness for inking and drawing tasks. Comparisons can be made for differing sizes to better understand the effect.

The attributes of this handwriting task are relevant to several other common tasks, such as those seen in drawing programs, gesture-based interfaces, and systems that utilize character recognition.

Tracing and Digitizing:

In many applications, such as cartography, CAD, and the graphic arts, it is often important to be able to trace material previously drawn, or digitize points from a map. There is wide variation in how well different devices can

perform this type of task. Relative devices such as mice and trackballs are almost useless in this regard. Even with absolute devices like tablets, for example, there is a wide variation in their ability to perform this class of task. In particular, the demands on resolution and linearity vary greatly across applications. In cartography and engineering, for example, the accuracy of the digitization is often critical and far beyond what is required in digitizing a sketch.

Constrained Linear Motion:

In some applications it is important to be able to move the tracker rapidly along a straight line path. One example is in using the scroll-bar mechanism of some systems. As another example, you might want to use the motion of a mouse in one dimension, say Y, to control one parameter, without changing the value of another parameter being controlled by motion in the other dimension, X. Different devices vary in the ease with which this can be done. X/Y thumb wheels, for example, would out-perform a mouse in the above task *if* the motion was along the primary axes.

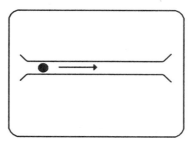

Figure 4: Constrained Linear Motion
How quickly can the ball be moved along the straight path without crossing the lines?

In the example task, illustrated in Figure 4, the tracking symbol is a ball that is dragged along a linear path defined by two parallel lines. The object is to move along the path without crossing the parallel lines. How is speed affected by the input device used and the path width? Are similar results obtained if the path is vertical or diagonal?

Constrained Circular Motion:

A variation of the previous example is to see how well the user can specify a circular motion within a constrained region. This type of control is useful in manipulating 3D objects, for example, and is described in Evans, Tanner and Wein (1981). As in the previous example, different results will be obtained from different devices, and results will also vary according to C:D ratio and the width of the path.

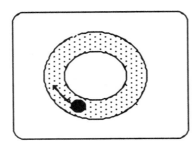

Figure 5: Constrained Circular Motion
How fast can the tracking symbol be moved around the circular shaded path without crossing the borders?

A Meaningful Taxonomy of Input Devices

The examples of the previous section highlight how different devices lend themselves to different tasks. In this section, we want to develop a categorization of input devices based on the properties that cause these differences. Our approach to this is shown in Figure 6.

		Number of Dimensions						
		1		**2**			**3**		
P o s i t i o n	Rotary Pot	Sliding Pot	Tablet	Light Pen	Joystick	3-D Joystick	M	S e n s i n g
			Touch Tablet	Touch Screen			T	
M o t i o n	Continuous Rotary Pot	Treadmill	Mouse		Trackball	Trackball	M	T y p e
		Thumbwheel						
		Tass Ferinstat		Tass X-Y Pad			T	
P r e s s u r e	Torque Sensing	Pressure Pad			Isometric Joystick		T	

" M - mechanical, T - touch .

Figure 6: Taxonomy of Input Devices.
Continuous manual input devices are categorized. The first-order categorization is what is sensed (rows) and number of dimensions (columns). Sub-rows distinguish between devices that have a mechanical intermediary (such as a stylus) between the hand and the sensing mechanism, and those which are touch sensitive. Sub-columns distinguish devices that use comparable motor control for their operation. (From Buxton, 1983.)

There is a hierarchy of criteria according to which devices are organized in this table. The table is limited, and considers only continuous, manually operated devices. Hence, the first two (implicit) organizational criteria are:

- continuous *or* discrete
- agent of control (hand, foot, *or* voice, ...)

The table is divided into a matrix whose primary partitioning into rows and columns delimit:

- what is being sensed (position, motion, *or* pressure)
- the number of dimensions being sensed (1, 2 *or* 3)

These primary partitions are delimited by solid lines. Hence, both the rotary and sliding potentiometer fall within the box associated with one-dimensional position sensitive devices (top left-hand corner).

These primary rows and columns are sub-divided by dotted lines into secondary regions. These group:

- devices that are operated using similar motor skills (sub-columns)
- devices that are operated by touch *vs* those that require a mechanical intermediary between the hand and the sensing mechanism (sub-rows)

Grouping by motor action can be seen in examining the two-dimensional devices. Since they are in the same sub-column, the table implies that tablets and mice utilize similar types of hand control and that this motor action is different from that used by joysticks and trackballs, which appear in a different sub-column.

The use of sub-rows to differentiate between devices that are touch activated and those that are not can be seen in comparing the light pen and the touch screen. While each utilizes the same basic motor control, the light pen requires the use of a stylus. Hence, the two appear in different sub-rows.

The table is useful by virtue of the structure which it imposes on the domain of input devices. First, it helps in finding appropriate equivalences. This is important in dealing with some of the problems which arose in our discussion of device independence.

The table makes it easy to relate different devices in terms of analogy. For example, a tablet is to a mouse what a joystick is to a trackball. Furthermore, if the taxonomy defined by the table can suggest new transducers in a manner analogous to the way Mendeleev's periodic table predicted new elements, then we can have more confidence in it. We make this claim and cite the "torque sensing" one-dimensional pressure sensitive transducer as an example. To our knowledge, no such device exists commercially. Nevertheless it is a potentially useful device, an approximation of which has been demonstrated by Herot and Weinzapfel (1978).

Generality and Extensibility

Choosing the input technologies to be used with a workstation generally involves balancing two conflicting demands. Each task has specialized needs that can best be addressed by a specialized technology. Yet each workstation is generally used for a multitude of tasks. Supplying the optimum device for each task is generally impossible. A compromise must be made.

Devices must be chosen to give the best coverage of the demands in their range of tasks. An important criterion in comparing devices, therefore, is the breadth of their coverage. For example, how many squares in Figure 6 can a particular device be used to fill? Graphics tablets are important in this regard, for example, since they can emulate many of the other transducers. This is demonstrated in detail by Evans, Tanner and Wein (1981). The tablet is what could be called an "extensible" device. This property of extensibility is, in our opinion, an important criterion to be considered in device selection.

Relative *vs* Absolute Controllers

One of the most important characteristics of input devices is whether they sense absolute or relative values. This has a *very* strong effect on the nature of the dialogues that the system can support with any degree of fluency. As we have seen, a mouse cannot be used to digitize map coordinates or trace a drawing, because it does not sense absolute position. Another example taken from process control is discussed in the reading by Buxton (1986). This case is known as the *nulling problem* which is introduced when absolute transducers are used in designs which use one controller for different tasks at different times.

What Our Taxonomy Doesn't Show

Perhaps the main weakness of the taxonomy presented above is the fact that it considers only the continuous aspect of devices. As the sample tasks discussed earlier in this chapter pointed out, other factors, such as the integration of button devices with continuous controllers, have a strong impact on a device's performance. This is clear, for example, in the case of trying to "pick up" and drag an object with a mouse (where the button is integrated) compared to performing the same transaction with a trackball (where it is difficult to hold down the button, which is not integrated, with the same hand that is controlling the dragging motion).

An approach to capturing this aspect of devices is found in the reading by Buxton, Hill and Rowley (1985). Here, a state-transition representation is developed which brings to light some very important, yet subtle, differences among devices. As an exercise, the reader is encouraged to compare a mouse, tablet, trackball, touch-tablet, and touch-screen in terms of their ability to make the transitions through the three states (0, 1, and 2) described in the reading. As a further exercise, try to characterize each of the sample tasks discussed at the beginning of this chapter in terms of which of these three

states a device must be able to capture before the transaction can be successfully performed.

Problems of Interfacing

The haptic channel has yet to be used to its full potential. We need more experience in its use, but obtaining this experience turns out to be rather difficult. If, for example, we want to gain some insights by comparing two devices, we may find that they are physically, electronically, and/or logically incompatible. What should be a simple comparison turns into a logistical nightmare. Let us work through an example.

Suppose that we want to compare two tablets. To make things simple, let us assume that both communicate with the host computer *via* an RS-232 interface. The first thing that we might discover is that despite the RS-232 "standard," one device has a 25-pin connector, the other has a miniature "telephone jack" connector , and the computer (an Apple Macintosh) has a 9-pin connector. We have a problem. But let us assume that all three devices have a 25-pin connector. Then, the chances are that one is female and the other male. So much for "standard" physical compatibility.

Now if we do actually get both tablets connected to the computer, we might find that there is an electrical incompatibility. We will possibly find that one device requires a powered RS-232 and the other doesn't. Some computers that use RS-232 supply power, others don't. Again, we have a problem.

But let us further assume that both devices connect physically and electrically (we won't even mention the possibility of the "null modem" problem). What we may find now is that one device communicates by request while the other must be polled, or generates interrupts. Since each of these styles of I/O can affect the design of the underlying application software, exchanging one device for the other may involve significant software modifications.

For the sake of simplicity, let us assume that both devices function by interrupt-driven I/O and the application software is set up for this. What we find next is that one encodes its data in binary-coded decimal (BCD) while the other transmits in binary digits. The number of bytes in each will differ, not to mention the fact that the data for the puck buttons will come in a different format for each device.

The point of this convoluted example is to emphasize how hard it can be to compare two similar devices that communicate using a "standard" interface. If the problems in this "simple" case are this involved, what will happen when we want to compare devices that differ even more? The lesson to be learned is that the path of least resistance will bias you *against* investigating designs that utilize alternative input techniques. The only way to counteract this bias is to take clear and definite measures in the R&D environment to set up appropriate structures and equipment to provide a test-bed for such comparative studies. This is far too uncommon in today's R&D environment, a situation that must be changed if we are to make substantive progress in this area of user interface design.

Transparent Access and the Disabled

For most users, the problems of connecting different input devices to a system, as outlined in the previous section, are an annoyance. However, for users with physical disabilities, these problems can make the difference between being able to use a computer and being denied access. This can have a major impact on the quality of life.

For most common input devices there exist special purpose transducers that permit people with different physical disabilities to supply comparable signals. A mouse may be replaced by a tongue activated joystick, or a button replaced by a blow-suck tube. It is reasonable to expect disabled persons to acquire such special purpose devices. However, it is economically unreasonable and socially unacceptable to expect them to be dependent upon custom applications in order to interact with their systems.

What is required is *transparent access* to standard applications. Existing applications should be able to be used by simply plugging in the specialized replacement transducer. The difficulties in providing transparent access are exactly the same difficulties we encountered in the preceding section when we wanted to replace one input device with another for comparative purposes. In recognizing that this is a problem ''handicapping'' all of us, perhaps the achievement of generalized transparent access will become a greater priority than it has been up to now. It is a serious problem that needs to be addressed, and is further discussed in Chapter 14: Research Frontiers and Unsolved Problems.

Device Independence and Virtual Devices

Recently there have been efforts to overcome some of the problems that stand in the way of transparent access. In particular, the concept of device independent graphics has come into common practice.

Just as machine independent compilers facilitated porting code from one computer to another, device independent programming constructs have been developed for I/O. With input, the principle idea was to

recognize that all devices more-or-less reduced to a small number of generic, or *virtual* devices. For example, an application can be written in a device-independent way such that it need not know if the source of text input is via a keyboard or a speech-recognition system. All the application need know is that text is being input. Similarly, the application need not require any information about what specific device is providing location information (in pointing, for example). All that it needs to know is what the current location is.

This idea of device independence has been discussed by Foley and Wallace (1974), Wallace (1976), Newman (1968), and Rosenthal, Michener, Pfaff, Kessener and Sabin (1982). It was refined and integrated into the standardized graphics systems (GSPC, 1977; GSPC, 1979; ISO, 1983).

Within the GKS standard (ISO, 1983), the virtual devices are defined in terms of the values they return to the application program. The virtual devices for input in GKS are:

- *locator:* a pair of real values giving the coordinate of a point in world coordinates
- *stroke:* a sequence of x/y coordinates in world coordinates
- *valuator:* a single number of type real
- *pick:* the name of a segment
- *string:* produces a string of characters
- *choice:* returns a non-negative integer defining one of a set of alternatives

For the designer of user interfaces, the main advantage of device independent graphics has been that one can experiment with different devices without normally having to modify the applications code. All that needs to be changed (from the software perspective) is the actual device driver. The application doesn't care what driver is being used for a particular device *because the standard is defined in terms of the calling protocol and the number and type of parameters returned.*

Device independent graphics, therefore, has had an important impact on our ability to rapidly prototype user interfaces. This is a subject discussed in more detail in Chapter 12: Programming Techniques and Tools, and is largely motivated by the iterative design methodologies discussed in Chapter 11: Design Principles and Methodologies.

While device independence has been a real benefit, it has also lead to some problems. The reason is that some practitioners have confused technical interchangeability with functional interchangability. Just because I can substitute a trackball for a mouse does not mean that the resulting user interface will be satisfactory. As we have seen, devices have idiosyncratic properties that make them well suited for some tasks, and not for others. Further discussion of issues relating to device-independent graphics can be found in Baecker (1980).

Conclusions

In general, input has been neglected in relation to output. The first reading (Buxton, 1986), develops many of the ideas found in this introduction. It is general in nature, and tries to tie a number of important ideas together through association. The second reading (Buxton, Hill and Rowley, 1985) can be viewed as a case study. In it, one particular technology is examined in detail: touch-sensitive tablets. The reading is included as an example of how other technologies can be studied. Finally, the third reading (Card et al., 1978) gives an example of how different technologies can be evaluated and compared quantitatively. An interesting exercise for the reader is to consider how effectively this study characterizes the devices studied, and for what tasks. In particular, is the study appropriate for all of the sample tasks discussed earlier in the Chapter? If not, what type of experiments could be designed to fill in the gaps?

Readings

Buxton, W. (1986). There's More to Interaction than Meets the Eye: Some Issues in Manual Input. In Norman, D. A. and Draper, S. W. (Eds.), *User Centered System Design: New Perspectives on Human-Computer Interaction*,Hillsdale, N.J.: Lawrence Erlbaum Associates, 319-337.

Buxton, W., Hill, R., & Rowley, P. (1985). Issues and Techniques in Touch-Sensitive Tablet Input. *Computer Graphics* 19(3), 215-224.

Card, S., English, W. & Burr, B. (1978). Evaluation of Mouse, Rate-Controlled Isometric Joystick, Step Keys and Text Keys for Text Selection on a CRT. *Ergonomics* 21(8), 601-613.

References/Bibliography

Baecker, R. (1980). Towards an Effective Characterization of Graphical Interaction. In Guedj, R.A., ten Hagen, P., Hopgood, F.R., Tucker, H. & Duce, D.A. (Eds.), *Methodology of Interaction*. Amsterdam: North Holland Publishing, 127-148.

Buxton, W. (1982). An Informal Study of Selection-Positioning Tasks. *Proceedings of Graphics Interface '82*, 8th Conference of the Canadian Man-Computer Communications Society, Toronto, May 1982, 323-328.

Buxton, W. (1983). Lexical and Pragmatic Considerations of Input Structures. *Computer Graphics* 17(1), 31-37.

Buxton, W. (1986). There's More to Interaction than Meets the Eye: Some Issues in Manual Input. In Norman, D. A. & Draper, S. W. (Eds.), *User Centered System Design: New Perspectives on Human-Computer Interaction*, Hillsdale, N.J.: Lawrence Erlbaum Associates, 319-337.

Buxton, W. (in press). Notes on Chord Keyboards. To appear in *ACM Transaction on Graphics*.

Buxton, W. Hill, R. & Rowley, P. (1985). Issues and Techniques in Touch-Sensitive Tablet Input. *Computer Graphics* 19(3), 215-224.

Buxton, W. & Myers, B. (1986). A Study in Two-Handed Input. *Proceedings of CHI '86*, 321-326.

Buxton, W., Fiume, E., Hill, R., Lee, A. & Woo, C. (1983). Continuous Hand-Gesture Driven Input. *Proceedings of Graphics Interface '83*, Edmonton, May 1983, 191-195.

Card, S., English, W. & Burr, B. (1978). Evaluation of Mouse, Rate-Controlled Isometric Joystick, Step Keys and Text Keys for Text Selection on a CRT. *Ergonomics* 21(8), 601-613.

Card, S., Moran, T. & Newell, A. (1980). The Keystroke Level Model for User Performance Time with Interactive Systems. *Communications of the ACM* 23(7), 396-410.

Card, S., Moran, T. & Newell, A. (1983). *The Psychology of Human-Computer Interaction*. Hillsdale, N.J.: Lawrence Erlbaum Associates.

Chapanis, A. & Kinkade, R. (1972). Design of Controls. In Van Cott, H. & Kinkade, R. (Eds.), *Human Engineering Guide to Equipment Design*, Revised Edition, Washington, D.C.: U.S. Government Printing Office, 345-379.

Conrad, R. & Longman, D.J.A. (1965). Standard Typewriter Versus Chord Keyboard: An Experimental Comparison. *Ergonomics* 8, 77-88.

Devoe, D.B. (1967). Alternatives to Handprinting in the Manual Entry of Data. *IEEE Transactions on Human Factors in Electronics* 8(1), 21-32.

Earl, W.K. & Goff, J.D. (1965). Comparison of Two Data Entry Methods. *Perceptual and Motor Skills* 20, 369-384.

Engelbart, D. & English, W. (1968). A Research Centre for Augmenting Human Intellect. *Proceedings of the Fall Joint Computer Conference*, 395-410.

English, W.K., Engelbart, D.C. & Berman, M.L. (1967). Display Selection Techniques for Text Manipulation. *IEEE Transactions on Human-Factors in Electronics* 8(1), 5-15.

Evans, K., Tanner, P. & Wein, M. (1981). Tablet-Based Valuators That Provide One, Two, or Three Degrees of Freedom. *Computer Graphics* 15(3), 91-97.

Fitts, P. & Peterson, J. (1964). Information Capacity of Discrete Motor Responses. *Journal of Experimental Psychology* 67, 103-112.

Foley, J.D. & Wallace, V.L. (1974). The Art of Graphic Man-Machine Conversation. *Proceedings of IEEE* 62(4), 462-470.

Foley, J.D., Wallace, V.L. & Chan, P. (1984). The Human Factors of Computer Graphics Interaction Techniques. *IEEE Computer Graphics and Applications* 4(11), 13-48.

Foley, J. & Van Dam, A. (1982). *Fundamentals of Interactive Computer Graphics*. Reading, MA: Addison-Wesley.

Friedman, Z., Kirschenbaum, A. & Melnik, A. (1984). The Helpwrite Experiment: A Human Factors Application for the Disabled, unpublished, Technion, Haifa 321000, Israel.

ISO (1983). *Information Processing-Graphical Kernel System (GKS) Functional Description.* International Standards Organization, ISO/DP 7942.

Goodwin, N.C. (1975). Cursor Positioning on an Electronic Display Using Lightpen, Lightgun, or Keyboard for Three Basic Tasks. *Human Factors* 17(3), 289-295.

Gopher, D. & Koenig, W. (1983). Hands Coordination in Data Entry with a Two-Hand Chord Typewriter. *Technical Report* CPL 83-3, Cognitive Psychology Laboratory, Dept. of Psychology, Univ. of Illinois, Champaign, Illinois 61820.

Green, R. (1985). The Drawing Prism: A Versatile Graphic Input Device. *Computer Graphics* 19(3), 103-110.

GSPC (1977). Status Report of the Graphics Standards Planning Committee. *Computer Graphics* 11(3).

GSPC (1979). Status Report of the Graphics Standards Planning Committee. *Computer Graphics* 13(3).

Guedj, R.A., ten Hagen, P., Hopgood, F.R., Tucker, H. & Duce, D.A. (Eds.) (1980). *Methodology of Interaction*, Amsterdam: North Holland Publishing.

Haller, R., Mutschler, H. & Voss, M. (1984). Comparison of Input Devices for Correction of Typing Errors in Office Systems. *Human-Computer Interaction — Interact '84*, Amsterdam: North-Holland, 177-182.

Herot, C. & Weinzapfel, G. (1978). One-Point Touch Input of Vector Information from Computer Displays. *Computer Graphics* 12(3), 210-216.

Johnstone, E. (1985). The Rolky: A Poly-Touch Controller for Electronic Music. In B. Truax (Ed.), *Proceedings of the International Computer Music Conference*, Vancouver, 291-295.

Karat, J., McDonald, J.E. & Anderson, M. (1986). A Comparison of Menu Selection Techniques: Touch Panel, Mouse and Keyboard. *International Journal of Man-Machine Studies* 25(1), 73-88.

Klemmer, E.T. (1971). Keyboard Entry. *Applied Ergonomics* 2(1), 2-6.

Knowlton, K. (1975). Virtual Pushbuttons as a Means of Person-Machine Interaction. *Proceedings of the IEEE Conference on Computer Graphics, Pattern Recognition, and Data Structures*, 350-351.

Knowlton, K. (1977a). Computer Displays Optically Superimposed on Input Devices. *The Bell System Technical Journal* 56(3), 367-383.

Knowlton, K. (1977b). *Prototype for a Flexible Telephone Operator's Console Using Computer Graphics*, 16 mm film, Bell Telephone Laboratories, Murray Hill, N.J.

Kroemer, K.H. (1972). Human Engineering the Keyboard. *Human Factors* 14(1), 51-63.

Kuklinski (1985). A Case for Digitizer Tablets. *Computer Graphics World*, May 1985, 45-52.

Lee, S.K., Buxton, W. & Smith, K.C. (1985). A Multi-Touch Three Dimensional Touch-Sensitive Tablet. *Proceedings of CHI '85*, 21-27.

Leedham, C., Downton, A., Brooks, C. & Newell, A. (1984). On-Line Acquisition of Pitman's Handwritten Shorthand as a Means of Rapid Data Entry. *Human-Computer Interaction — Interact '84*, Amsterdam: North-Holland, 145-150.

McGrath, R. (1985). PC Focus: TurboPuck, a Precision Pointing Device. *Computer Graphics World*, August 1985, 45-48.

Minsky, M. (1985). Manipulating Simulated Objects with Real-World Gestures Using a Force and Position Sensitive Screen. *Computer Graphics* 18(3), 195-203.

Montgomery, E. (1982). Bringing Manual Input into the 20th Century. *IEEE Computer* 15(3), 11-18. See also follow-up letters in the May, June, and October 1982 issues.

Newman, W.M. (1968). A Graphical Technique for Numerical Input. *Computing Journal* 11, 63-64.

Norman & Fisher (1982). Why Alphabetic Keyboards are not Easy to Use: Keyboard Layout Doesn't Much Matter. *Human Factors* 24(5), 509-519.

Noyes, J. (1983). The QWERTY Keyboard: a Review. *International Journal of Man-Machine Studies* 18, 265-281.

Ohno, K, Fukaya, K. & Nievergelt, J. (1985). A Five-Key Mouse with Built-In Dialogue Control. *SIGCHI Bulletin* 17(1), 29-34.

Owen, Sid (1978). QWERTY is Obsolete. *Interface Age*, January 1978, 56-59.

Pickering, J.A. (1986). Touch-Sensitive Screens: the Technologies and Their Application. *International Journal of Man-Machine Studies* 25(3), 249-269.

Pulfer, K. (1971). Man-Machine Interaction in Creative Applications. *International Journal of Man-Machine Studies* 3, 1-11.

Ressler, S. (1982). An Object Editor for a Real Time Animation Processor. *Proceedings of Graphics Interface '82*, Toronto, 221-223.

Richtie, G.J. & Turner, J.A. (1975). Input Devices for Interactive Graphics. *International Journal of Man-Machine Studies* 7, 639-660.

Roberts, M. & Rahbari, H. (1986). A Multi-Purpose System for Alpha-Numeric Input to Computers Via a Reduced Keyboard. *International Journal of Man-Machine Studies* 24, 659-667.

Rochester, N., Bequaert, F. & Sharp, E. (1978). The Chord Keyboard. *IEEE Computer* 11(12), 57-63.

Rosenthal, D.S., Michener, J.C., Pfaff, G., Kessener, R., & Sabin, M. (1982). Detailed Semantics of Graphical Input Devices. *Computer Graphics* 16(3), 33-43.

Schmandt, C. (1983). Spatial Input/Display Correspondence in a Stereoscopic Computer Graphic Work Station. *Computer Graphics* 17(3), 253-261.

Seibel, R. (1962). A Feasibility Demonstration of the Rapid-Type Data Entry Station. Research Report RC 845, Yorktown Heights, N.Y.: IBM Thomas J. Watson Research Center.

Seibel, R. (1972). Data Entry Devices and Procedures. In Van Cott,

H. & Kinkade, R. (Eds.), *Human Engineering Guide to Equipment Design*, Revised Edition, Washington, D.C.: U.S. Government Printing Office, 311-344.

Smyth, M. & Wing, A. (Eds.) (1984). *The Psychology of Human Movement*, London: Academic Press.

Wallace, V.L. (1976). The Semantics of Graphical Input Devices. *Proceedings of the SIGGRAPH/SIGPLAN Symposium on Graphical Languages*, 61-65.

Ward, J.R. & Phillips, M.J. (1987). Digitizer Technology: Performance Characteristics and the Effects on the User Interface. *IEEE Computer Graphics and Applications*, 7(4), 31-44.

Welford, A. (1976). *Skilled Performance: Perceptual and Motor Skills*, Glenview, IL: Scott, Foresman & Co.

Zimmerman, T.G., Lanier, J., Blanchard, C., Bryson, S. & Harvill, Y. (1987). A Hand Gesture Interface Device. *Proceedings of CHI+GI '87*, 189-192.

In our example, it is with the human's effectors (arms, legs, hands, etc.) that the greatest distortion occurs. Quite simply, when compared to other human-operated machinery (such as the automobile), todays computer systems make extremely poor use of the potential of the human's sensory and motor systems. The controls on the average user's shower are probably better human-engineered than those of the computer on which far more time is spent. There are a number of reasons for this situation. Most of them are understandable, but none of them should be acceptable.

My thesis is that we can achieve user interfaces that are more natural, easier to learn, easier to use, and less prone to error if we pay more attention to the "body language" of human-computer dialogues. I believe that the quality of human input can be greatly improved through the use of *appropriate gestures*. In order to achieve such benefits, however, we must learn to match human physiology, skills, and expectations with our systems' physical ergonomics, control structures, and functional organization.

In this chapter I look at manual input with the hope of developing a better understanding of how we can better tailor input structures to fit the human operator.

A FEW WORDS ON APPROACH

Due to constraints on space, I restrict myself to the discussion of manual input. I do so fully realizing that most of what I say can be applied to other parts of the body, and I hope that the discussion will encourage the reader to explore other types of transducers.

Just consider the use of the feet in sewing, driving an automobile, or in playing the pipe organ. Now compare this to your average computer system. The feet are totally ignored despite the fact that most users have them, and furthermore, have well-developed motor skills in their use.

I resist the temptation to discuss new and exotic technologies. I want to stick with devices that are real and available, since we haven't come close to using the full potential of those that we already have.

Finally, my approach is somewhat cavalier. I will leap from example to example, and just touch on a few of the relevant points. In the process, it is almost certain that readers will be able to come up with examples counter to my own, and situations where what I say does not apply. *But these contradictions strengthen my argument!* Input is complex, and deserves great attention to detail: more than it generally gets.

There's More to Interaction Than Meets the Eye: Some Issues in Manual Input

WILLIAM BUXTON

Imagine a time far into the future, when all knowledge about our civilization has been lost. Imagine further, that in the course of planting a garden, a fully stocked computer store from the 1980s was unearthed, and that all of the equipment and software was in working order. Now, based on this find, consider what a physical anthropologist might conclude about the physiology of the humans of our era? My best guess is that we would be pictured as having a well-developed eye, a long right arm, a small left arm, uniform-length fingers and a "low-fi" ear. But the dominating characteristics would be the prevalence of our visual system over our poorly developed manual dexterity.

Obviously, such conclusions do not accurately describe humans of the twentieth century. But they would be perfectly warranted based on the available information. Today's systems have severe shortcomings when it comes to matching the physical characteristics of their operators. Admittedly, in recent years there has been a great improvement in matching computer output to the human visual system. We see this in the improved use of visual communication through typography, color, animation, and iconic interfacing. Hence, our speculative future anthropologist would be correct in assuming that we had fairly well-developed (albeit monocular) vision.

That the grain of my analysis is still not fine enough just emphasizes how much more we need to understand.

Managing input is so complex that it is unlikely that we will ever totally understand it. No matter how good our theories are, we will probably always have to test designs through actual implementations and prototyping. The consequence of this for the designer is that prototyping tools (software and hardware) must be developed and considered as part of the basic environment.

THE IMPORTANCE OF THE TRANSDUCER

When we discuss user interfaces, consideration of the physical transducers too often comes last, or near last. And yet, the physical properties of the system are those with which the user has the first and most direct contact. This is not just an issue of comfort. Different devices have different properties, and lend themselves to different things. And if gestures are as important as I believe, then we must pay careful attention to the transducers to which we assign them.

An important concept in modern interactive systems is the notion of *device independence.* The idea is that input devices fall into generic classes of what are known as *virtual devices,* such as "locators" and "valuators." Dialogues are described in terms of these virtual devices. The objective is to permit the easy substitution of one physical device for another of the same class. One benefit in this is that it facilitates experimentation (with the hopeful consequence of finding the best among the alternatives). The danger, however, is that one can be easily lulled into believing that the technical interchangeability of these devices extends to usability. Wrong! It is always important to keep in mind that even devices within a class have various idiosyncrasies. It is often these very idiosyncratic differences that determine the appropriateness of a device for a given context. So, device independence is a useful concept, but only when additional considerations are made when making choices.

Example 1: The Isometric Joystick

An "isometric joystick" is a joystick whose handle does not move when it is pushed. Rather, its shaft senses how hard you are pushing it, and in what direction. It is, therefore, a pressure-sensitive device. Two isometric joysticks are shown in Figure 15.1. They are both made by

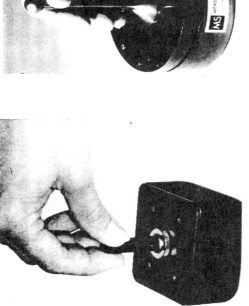

FIGURE 15.1. Two isometric joysticks. (Measurement Systems, Inc.)

the same manufacturer. They cost about the same, and are electronically identical. In fact, they are plug compatible. How they differ is in their size, the muscle groups that they consequently employ, and the amount of force required to get a given output.

Remember, people generally discuss joysticks vs. mice or trackballs. Here we are not only comparing joysticks against joysticks, we are comparing one isometric joystick to another.

When should one be used rather than the other? The answer obviously depends on the context. What can be said is that their differences may often be more significant than their similarities. In the absence of one of the pair, it may be better to utilize a completely different type of transducer (such as a mouse) than to use the other isometric joystick.

Example 2: Joystick vs. Trackball

Let's take an example in which subtle idiosyncratic differences have a strong effect on the appropriateness of the device for a particular transaction. In this example we look at two different devices. One is the springloaded joystick shown in Figure 15.2A. In many ways, it is very similar to the isometric joysticks seen in the previous example. It is made by the same manufacturer, and it is plug-compatible with respect to the X/Y values that it transmits. However, this new joystick moves when it is pushed, and (as a result of spring action) returns to the center position when released. In addition, it has a third dimension of control accessible by manipulating the self-returning, spring-loaded rotary pot mounted on the top of the shaft.

Rather than contrasting this to the joysticks of the previous example (which would, in fact, be a useful exercise), let us compare it to the 3-D trackball shown in Figure 15.2B. (A 3-D trackball is a trackball constructed so as to enable us to sense clockwise and counter-clockwise "twisting" of the ball as well as the amount that it has been "rolled" in the horizontal and vertical directions.)

This trackball is plug-compatible with the 3-D joystick, costs about the same, has the same "footprint" (consumes the same amount of desk space), and utilizes the same major muscle groups. It has a great deal in common with the 3-D joystick of Figure 15.2A. In many ways the the joystick in Figure 15.2A has more in common with the trackball than with the joysticks shown in Figure 15.1!

If you are starting to wonder about the appropriateness of always characterizing input devices by names such as "joystick" or "mouse," then the point of this section is getting across. It is starting to seem that we should lump devices together according to some "dimension of maximum significance," rather than by some (perhaps irrelevant) similarity in their mechanical construction (such as being a mouse or joystick). The prime issue arising from this recognition is the problem of determining which dimension is of maximum significance in a given context. Another is the weakness of our current vocabulary to express such dimensions.

Despite their similarities, these two devices differ in a very subtle, but significant, way. Namely, it is much easier to simultaneously control all three dimensions when using the joystick than when using the trackball. In some applications this will make no difference. But for the moment, we care about two scenarios. We look at two scenarios.

Scenario 1: We are working on a graphics program for doing VLSI layout. The chip on which we are working is quite complex. The only way that the entire mask can be viewed at one time is at a very small scale. To examine a specific area in detail, therefore, we must "pan" over it, and "zoom in." With the joystick, we can pan over the surface of the circuit by adjusting the stick position. Panning direction is determined by the direction in which the spring-loaded stick is off-center, and speed is determined by its distance off-center. With the trackball, we exercise control by rolling the ball in the direction and at the speed that we want to pan.

Panning is easier with trackball than the spring-loaded joystick. This is because of the strong correlation (or compatibility) between stimulus (direction, speed, and amount of roll) and response (direction, speed, and amount of panning) in this example. With the spring-loaded joystick, there was a position-to-motion mapping rather than the motion-to-motion mapping seen with the trackball. Such cross-modality mappings require learning and impede achieving optimal human performance. These issues address the properties of an interface that Hutchins, Hollan, and Norman (Chapter 5) call "formal directions."

If our application demands that we be able to zoom and pan simultaneously, then we have to reconsider our evaluation. With the joystick, it

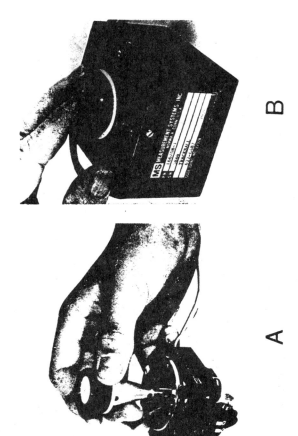

A   B

FIGURE 15.2. Comparison of joystick (A) and trackball (B). (Measurement Systems, Inc.)

is easy to zoom in and out of regions of interest while panning. One need only twist the shaft-mounted pot while moving the stick. However, with the trackball, it is nearly impossible to twist the ball at the same time that it is being rolled. The 3-D trackball is, in fact, better described as a 2+1D device.

Scenario 2: I am using the computer to control an oil refinery. The pipes and valves of a complex part of the system are shown graphically on the displays, along with critical status information. My job is to monitor the status information and, when conditions dictate, modify the system by adjusting the settings of specific valves. I do this by means of *direct manipulation*. That is, valves are adjusted by manipulating their graphical representation on the screen. Using the joystick, this is accomplished by pointing at the desired valve, then twisting the pot mounted on the stick. However, it is difficult to twist the joystick-pot without also causing some change in the X and Y values. This causes problems, since graphics pots may be in close proximity on the display. Using the trackball, however, the problem does not occur. In order to twist the trackball, it can be (and is best) gripped so that the finger tips rest against the bezel of the housing. The finger tips thus prevent any rolling of the ball. Hence, twisting is orthogonal to motion in X and Y. The trackball is the better transducer in this example *precisely because of its idiosyncratic 2+1D property.*

Thus, we have seen how the very properties that gave the joystick the advantage in the first scenario were a liability in the second. Conversely, with the trackball, we have seen how the liability became an advantage. What is to be learned here is that if such cases exist between these two devices, then it is most likely that comparable (but different) cases exist among all devices. What we are most lacking is some reasonable methodology for exploiting such characteristics via an appropriate matching of device idiosyncrasies with structures of the dialogue.

APPROPRIATE DEVICES CAN SIMPLIFY SYNTAX

In the previous example we saw how the idiosyncratic properties of an input device could have a strong affect on its appropriateness for a specific task. It would be nice if the world was simple, and we could consequently figure out what a system was for, find the optimal device for the task to be performed on it, and be done. But such is seldom the case. Computer systems are more often used by a number of people for a number of tasks, each with their own demands and characteristics. One approach to dealing with the resulting diversity of demands is to supply a number of input devices, one optimized for each type of transaction. However, the benefits of the approach would generally break down as the number of devices increased. Usually, a more realistic solution is to attempt to get as much generality as possible from a smaller number of devices. Devices, then, are chosen for their range of applicability. This is, for example, a major attraction of graphics tablets. They can emulate the behavior of a mouse. But unlike the mouse, they can also be used for tracing artwork to digitize it into the machine.

Having raised the issue, I continue to discuss devices in such a way as to focus on their idiosyncratic properties. Why? Because by doing so, I hope to identify the type of properties that one might try to emulate, should emulation be required.

It is often useful to consider the user interface of a system as being made up of a number of horizontal layers. Most commonly, syntax is considered separately from semantics, and lexical issues independent from syntax. Much of this way of analysis is an outgrowth of the theories practiced in the design and parsing of artificial languages, such as in the design of compilers for computer languages. Thinking of the world in this way has many benefits, not the least of which is helping to avoid "apples-and-bananas" type comparisons. There is a problem, however, in that it makes it too easy to fall into the belief that each of these layers is independent. A major objective of this section is to point out how wrong an assumption this is. In particular, I illustrate how decisions at the lowest level, the choice of input devices, can have a pronounced effect on the complexity of the system and on the user's model.

Example 2: Two children's toys. The *Etch-a-Sketch* (shown in Figure 15.3A) is a children's drawing toy that has had a remarkably long life in the marketplace. One draws by manipulating the controls so as to cause a stylus on the back of the drawing surface to trace out the desired image. There are only two controls: Both are rotary pots. One controls left-right motion of the stylus and the other controls its up-down motion.

The *Skedoodle* (shown in Figure 15.3B) is another toy based on very similar principles. In *computerese*, we could even say that the two toys are semantically identical. They draw using a similar stylus mechanism and even have the same "erase" operator (turn the toy upside down and shake it). However, there is one big difference. Whereas the Etch-a-

Sketch has a separate control for each of the two dimensions of control, the Skedoodle has integrated both dimensions into a single transducer: a joystick.

Since both toys are inexpensive and widely available, they offer an excellent opportunity to conduct some field research. Find a friend and demonstrate each of the two toys. Then ask the friend to select the toy felt to be the best for drawing. What all this is leading to is a drawing competition between you and your friend. However, this is a competition that you will always win. The catch is that since your friend got to choose toys, you get to choose what is drawn. If your friend chose the Skedoodle (as do the majority of people), then make the required drawing be of a horizontally-aligned rectangle. If they chose the Etch-a-Sketch, then have the task be to write your first name. This test has two benefits. First, if you make the competition a bet, you can win back the money that you spent on the toys (an unusual opportunity in research). Second, you can do so while raising the world's enlightenment about the sensitivity of the quality of input devices to the task to which they are applied.

If you understand the importance of the points being made here, you are hereby requested to go out and apply this test on every person that you know who is prone to making unilateral and dogmatic statements of the variety "mice (tablets, joysticks, trackballs, etc.) are best." What is true with these two toys (as illustrated by the example) is equally true for any and all computer input devices: They all shine for some task.

We can build upon what we have seen thus far. What if we asked how we can make the Skedoodle do well at the same class of drawings as the Etch-a-Sketch? An approximation to a solution actually comes with the toy in the form of a set of templates that fit over the joystick (Figure 15.4). The point to make here is that if we have a general-purpose input device (analogous to the joystick of the Skedoodle), then we can provide tools to fit on top of it to customize it for a specific application. (An example would be the use of "sticky" grids in graphics layout programs.) However, this additional level *generally comes at the expense of increased cost in the complexity of the control structure.* If we don't need the generality, then we can often avoid this complexity by choosing a transducer whose operational characteristics implicitly channel user behavior in the desired way (in a way analogous to how the Etch-a-Sketch controls place constraints on what can be easily drawn).

FIGURE 15.3. Two "semantically identical" drawing toys.

parameters at different stages of an operation.

Let us assume that we are implementing a system based on time multiplexing. There are two parameters, A and B, and a single sliding potentiometer to control them, P. The potentiometer P outputs an absolute value proportional to the position of its handle. To begin with, the control potentiometer is set to control parameter A. The initial settings of A, B, and P are all illustrated in Figure 15.5A. First we want to raise the value of A to its maximum. This we do simply by sliding up the controller, P. This leaves us in the state illustrated in Figure 15.5B. We now want to raise parameter B to its maximum value. But how can we raise the value of B if the controller is already in its highest position? Before we can do anything we must adjust the handle of the controller relative to the current value of B. This is illustrated in Figure 15.5C. Once this is done, parameter B can be reset by

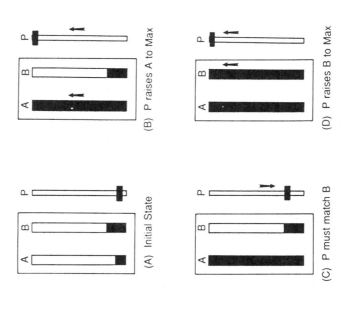

(A) Initial State

(B) P raises A to Max

(C) P must match B

(D) P raises B to Max

FIGURE 15.5. The Nulling Problem. Potentiometer P controls two parameters, A and B. The initial settings are shown in Panel A. The position of P, after raising parameter A to its maximum value, is shown in Panel B. In order for P to be used to adjust parameter B, it must first be moved to match the value of B (i.e., "null" their difference), as shown in Panels C and D.

FIGURE 15.4. Adding constraints to an input device. Templates on a Skedoodle joystick.

Example 4: The nulling problem. One of the most important characteristics of input devices is whether they supply *absolute* or *relative* values to the program with which they are interacting. Mice and trackballs, for example, provide relative values. Other devices, such as tablets, touch screens, and potentiometers return absolute values (determined by their measured position). Earlier, I mentioned the importance of the concept of the "dimension of maximum importance." In this example, the choice between absolute *versus* relative mode defines that dimension.

The example comes from process control. There are (at least) two philosophies of design that can be followed in such applications. In the first, space multiplexing, there is a dedicated physical transducer for every parameter that is to be controlled. In the second, time multiplexing, there are fewer transducers than parameters. Such systems are designed so that a single device can be used to control different

adjusting P. The job is done and we are in the state shown in Figure 15.5D.

From an operator's perspective, the most annoying part of the above transaction is having to reset the controller before the second parameter can be adjusted. This is called the *nulling problem*. It is common, takes time to carry out, time to learn, and is a common source of error. Most importantly, it can be totally eliminated if we simply choose a different transducer.

The problems in the last example resulted from the fact that we chose a transducer that returned an absolute value based on a physical handle's position. As an alternative, we could replace it with a touch-sensitive strip of the same size. We will use this strip like a one-dimensional mouse. Instead of moving a handle, the strip is "stroked" up or down using a motion similar to that which adjusted the sliding potentiometer. The output in this case, however, is a value whose magnitude is proportional to the amount and direction of the stroke. In short, we get a relative value which determines the amount of change in the parameter. We simply push values up, or pull them down. The action is totally independent of the current value of the parameter being controlled. There is no handle to get stuck at the top or bottom. The device is like a treadmill, having infinite travel in either direction. In this example, we could have "rolled" the value up and down using one dimension of a trackball and gotten much the same benefit (since it too is a relative device).

An important point in this example is *where* the reduction in complexity occurred: in the syntax of the control language. Here we have a compelling and relevant example of where a simple change in input device has resulted in a significant change in the syntactic complexity of a user interface. The lesson to be learned is that in designing systems in a layered manner—first the semantics, then the syntax, then the lexical component, and the devices—we must take into account interactions among the various strata. *All* components of the system interlink and have a potential effect on the user interface. Systems *must* begin to be designed in an integrated and holistic way.

PHRASING GESTURAL INPUT

Phrasing is a crucial component of speech and music. It determines the ebb and flow of tension in a dialogue. It lets us know when a concept is beginning, and when it ends. It tells us when to be attentive, and when to relax. Why might this be of importance in our discussion of "body language" in human–computer dialogue? Well, for all the same reasons that it is important in all other forms of communication.

Phrases "chunk" related things together. They reinforce their connection. In this section I attempt to demonstrate how we can exploit the benefits of phrasing by building dialogues that enable connected concepts to be expressed by connected physical gestures.

If you look at the literature, you will find that there has been a great deal of study on how quickly humans can push buttons, point at text, and type commands. What the bulk of these studies focus on is the smallest grain of the human–computer dialogue, the *atomic task*. These are the "words" of the the dialogue. The problem is, we don't speak in words. We speak in sentences. Much of the problem in applying the results of such studies is that they don't provide much help in understanding how to handle *compound* tasks. My thesis is, if you can say it in words in a single phrase, you should be able to express it to the computer in a single gesture. This binding of concepts and gestures thereby becomes the means of articulating the *unit tasks* of an application.

Most of the tasks which we perform in interacting with computers are compound. In indicating a point on the display with a mouse we think of what we are doing as a single task: picking a point. But what would you have to specify if you had to indicate the same point by typing? Your single-pick operation actually consists of two sub-tasks: specifying an X coordinate and specifying a Y coordinate. You were able to think of the aggregate as a single task because of the appropriate match among transducer, gesture, and context. The desired one-to-one mapping between concept and action has been maintained. My claim is that what we have seen in this simple example can be applied to even higher-level transactions.

Two useful concepts from music that aid in thinking about phrasing are *tension* and *closure*. During a phrase there is a state of tension associated with heightened attention. This is delimited by periods of relaxation that close the thought and state implicitly that another phrase can be introduced by either party in the dialogue. It is my belief that we can reap significant benefits when we carefully design our computer dialogues around such sequences of tension and closure. In manual input, I will want tension to imply muscular tension.

Think about how you interact with pop-up menus with a mouse. Normally you push down the select button, indicate your choice by moving the mouse, and then release the select button to confirm the choice. You are in a state of muscular tension throughout the dialogue: *a state that corresponds exactly with the temporary state of the system. Because of the gesture used, it is impossible to make an error in syntax, and you have a continual active reminder that you are in an uninterruptable temporary state. Because of the gesture used, there is none of the trauma normally associated with being in a mode. That you are in a mode is ironic, since it is precisely the designers of "modeless" systems that make the heaviest use of this technique. The lesson here is that it is not modes per se that cause problems.*

In well-structured manual input there is a *kinesthetic* connectivity to reinforce the *conceptual* connectivity of the task. We can start to use such gestures to help develop the role of *muscle memory* as a means through which to provide *mnemonic* aids for performing different tasks. And we can start to develop the notion of *gestural self-consistency* across an interface.

What do graphical potentiometers, pop-up menus, scroll-bars, rubber-band lines, and dragging all have in common? Answer: the potential to be implemented with a uniform form of interaction. Work it out using the pop-up menu protocol given above.

WE HAVE TWO HANDS!

It is interesting that the manufacturers of arcade video games seem to recognize something that the majority of main-stream computer systems ignore: that users are capable of manipulating more than one device at a time in the course of achieving a particular goal. Now this should come as no surprise to anyone who is familiar with driving an automobile. But it would be news to the hypothetical anthropologist that we introduced at the start of the chapter. There are two questions here: "Is anything gained by using two hands?" and "If there is, why aren't we doing it?"

The second question is the easier of the two. With a few exceptions, (the Xerox Star, for example), most systems don't encourage two-handed multiple-device input. First, most of our theories about parsing languages (such as the language of our human-computer dialogue) are only capable of dealing with single-threaded dialogues. Second, there are hardware problems due partially to wanting to do parallel things on a serial machine. Neither of these is unsolvable. But we do need some convincing examples that demonstrate that the time, effort, and expense is worthwhile. So that is what I will attempt to do in the rest of this section.

Example 5: Graphics Design Layout

I am designing a screen to be used in a graphics menu-based system. To be effective, care must be taken in the screen layout. I have to determine the size and placement of a figure and its caption among some other graphical items. I want to use the tablet to preview the figure in different locations and at different sizes in order to determine where it should finally appear. The way that this would be accomplished with most current systems is to go through a cycle of position-scale-position-... actions. That is, in order to scale, I have to stop positioning, and vice versa.

This is akin to having to turn off your shower in order to adjust the water temperature.

An alternative design offering more fluid interaction is to position it with one hand and scale it with the other. By using two separate devices I am able to perform both tasks simultaneously and thereby achieve a far more fluid dialogue.

Example 6: Scrolling

A common activity in working with many classes of program is scrolling through data, looking for specific items. Consider scrolling through the text of a document that is being edited. I want to scroll till I find what I'm looking for, then mark it up in some way. With most window systems, this is accomplished by using a mouse to interact with some (usually arcane) scroll bar tool. Scrolling speed is often difficult to control and the mouse spends a large proportion of its time moving between the scroll bar and the text. Furthermore, since the mouse is involved in the scrolling task, any ability to *mouse ahead* (i.e., start moving the mouse towards something before it appears on the display) is eliminated. If a mechanism were provided to enable us to control scrolling with the nonmouse hand, the whole transaction would be simplified.

There is some symmetry here. It is obvious that the same device used to scale the figure in the previous example could be used to scroll the window in this one. Thus, we ourselves would be time-multiplexing the device between the scaling of examples and the scrolling of this example. An example of space-multiplexing would be the simultaneous use of the scrolling device and the mouse. Thus, we actually have a hybrid type of interface.

Example 7: Financial Modeling

I am using a spread-sheet for financial planning. The method used to change the value in a cell is to point at it with a mouse and type the new entry. For numeric values, this can be done using the numeric keypad or the typewriter keyboard. In most such systems, doing so requires that the hand originally on the mouse moves to the keyboard for typing. Generally, this requires that the eyes be diverted from the screen to the keyboard. Thus, in order to check the result, the user must then visually relocate the cell on a potentially complicated display.

An alternative approach is to use the pointing device in one hand and the numeric keypad in the other. The keypad hand can then remain in home position, and if the user can touch-type on the keypad, the eyes need never leave the screen during the transaction.

Note that in this example the tasks assigned to the two hands are not even being done in parallel. Furthermore, a large population of users—those who have to take notes while making calculations—have developed keypad touch-typing facility in their nonmouse hand (assuming that the same hand is used for writing as for the mouse). So if this technique is viable and presents no serious technical problems, then why is it not in common use? One arguable explanation is that on most systems the numeric keypad is mounted on the same side as the mouse. Thus, physical ergonomics prejudice against the approach.

WHAT ABOUT TRAINING?

Some things are hard to do; they take time and effort before they can be performed at a skilled level. Whenever the issue of two-handed input come up, so does some facsimile of the challenge, "But two-handed actions are hard to coordinate." Well, the point is true. But it is also false! Learning to change gears is hard. So is playing the piano. But on the other hand, we have no trouble turning pages with one hand while writing with the other.

Just because two-handed input is not always suitable is no reason to reject it. The scrolling example described above requires trivial skills,

and it can actually reduce errors and learning time. Multiple-handed input should be one of the techniques considered in design. Only its appropriateness for a given situation can determine if it should be used. In that, it is no different than any other technique in our repertoire.

Example 8: Financial Modeling Revisited

Assume that we have implemented the two-handed version of the spreadsheet program described in Example 7. In order to get the benefits that I suggested, the user would have to be a touch-typist on the numeric keypad. This is a skilled task that is difficult to develop. There is a temptation, then, to say "don't use it." If the program was for school children, then perhaps that would be right. But consider who uses such programs: accountants, for example. Thus, it is reasonable to assume that a significant proportion of the user population *comes to the system with the skill already developed.* By our implementation, we have provided a convenience for those with the skill, without imposing any penalty on those without it—they are no worse off than they would be in the one-handed implementation. *Know your user* is just another (and important) consideration that can be exploited in order to tailor a better user interface.

CONCLUSIONS

I began this chapter by pointing out that there are major shortcomings in our ability to manually enter information into a computer. To this point, input has lagged far behind graphical output. And yet, as some of our examples illustrate, input is of critical importance. If we are to improve the quality of human-computer interfaces we must begin to approach input from two different views. First, we must look inward to the devices and technologies at the finest grain of their detail. One of the main points that I have made is that some of the most potent and useful characteristics of input devices only surface when they are analyzed at a far lower level of detail than has commonly been the case.

Second, we must look outward from the devices themselves to how they fit into a more global, or holistic, view of the user interface. All aspects of the system affect the user interface. Often problems at one level of the system can be easily solved by making a change at some other level. This was shown for example, in the discussion of the nulling problem.

That the work needs to be done is clear. Now that we've made up our minds about that, all that we have to do is assemble good tools and get down to it. What could be simpler?

SUGGESTED READINGS

The literature on most of the issues that are dealt with in this chapter is pretty sparse. One good source that complements many of the ideas discussed is Foley, Wallace, and Chan (1984). A presentation on the notion of virtual devices can be found in Foley and Wallace (1974). A critique of their use can be found in Baecker (1980). This paper by Baecker is actually part of an important and informative collection of papers on interaction (Guedj, ten Hagen, Hopgood, Tucker, & Duce, 1980).

Some of the notions of "chunking" and phrasing discussed are expanded upon in Buxton (1982) and Buxton, Fiume, Hill, Lee, and Woo (1983). The chapter by Miyata and Norman in this book gives a lot of background on performing multiple tasks, such as in two-handed input. Buxton (1983) presents an attempt to begin to formulate a taxonomy of input devices. This is done with respect to the properties of devices that are relevant to the styles of interaction that they will support. Evans, Tanner, and Wein (1981) do a good job of demonstrating the extent to which one device can emulate properties of another. Their study uses the tablet to emulate a large number of other devices.

A classic study that can be used as a model for experiments to compare input devices can be found in Card, English, and, Burr (1978). Another classic study which can serve as the basis for modeling some aspects of performance of a given user performing a given task using given transducers is Card, Moran, and Newell (1980). My discussion in this chapter illustrates how, in some cases, the only way that we can determine answers is by testing. This means prototyping that is often expensive. Buxton, Lamb, Sherman, and Smith (1983) present one such example of a tool that can help this process. Olsen, Buxton, Ehrich, Kasik, Rhyne, and Sibert (1984) discusses the environment in which such tools are used. Tanner and Buxton (1985) present a general model of User Interface Management Systems. Finally, Thomas and Hamlin (1983) present an overview of "User Interface Management Tools." Theirs is a good summary of many user interface issues, and has a fairly comprehensive bibliography.

ACKNOWLEDGMENTS

This chapter was written during a work period at Xerox Palo Alto Research Center. During its preparation I had some very helpful input from a number of people, especially Stu Card, Jerry Farrell, Lissa Monty, and Peter Tanner. The other authors of this book also made some insightful and useful comments. To them all, I offer my thanks.

References

Baecker, R. (1980). Towards an effective characterization of graphical interaction. In R. A. Guedj; P. ten Hagen, F. R. Hopgood, H. Tucker, & D. A. Duce (Eds.), *Methodology of interaction* (pp. 127-148). Amsterdam: North-Holland.

Buxton, W. (1982). An informal study of selection-positioning tasks. *Proceedings of Graphics Interface '82, 323-328.*

Buxton, W. (1983). Lexical and pragmatic issues of input structures. *Computer Graphics, 17(1),* 31-37.

Buxton, W., Fiume, E., Hill, R., Lee, A., & Woo, C. (1983). Continuous hand-gesture driven input. *Proceedings of Graphics Interface '83,* 191-195.

Buxton, W., Lamb, M., Sherman, D., & Smith, K. C. (1983). Towards a comprehensive user interface management system. *Computer Graphics, 17(3),* 35-42.

Card, S. K., English, W., & Burr, B. (1978). Evaluation of mouse, rate-controlled isometric joystick, step keys, and text keys. *Ergonomics, 8,* 601-613.

Card, S. K., Moran, T., & Newell, A. (1980). The keystroke-level model for user performance time with interactive systems. *Communications of the ACM, 23,* 396-410.

Evans, K., Tanner, P., & Wein, M. (1981). Tablet-based valuators that produce one, two or three degrees of freedom. *Computer Graphics, 15(3),* 91-97.

Foley, J. D., & Wallace, V. L. (1974). The art of graphic man-machine conversation. *Proceedings of IEEE, 62,* 462-470.

Foley, J. D., Wallace, V. L., & Chan, P. (1984). The human factors of computer graphics interaction techniques. *IEEE Computer Graphics and Applications, 4(11),* 13-48.

Guedj, R. A., ten Hagen, P., Hopgood, F. R., Tucker, H., & Duce, D. A. (Eds.) (1980). *Methodology of interaction.* Amsterdam: North-Holland.

Olsen, D. R., Buxton, W., Ehrich, R., Kasik, D., Rhyne, J., & Sibert, J. (1984). A context for user interface management. *IEEE Computer Graphics and Applications, 4(12),* 33-42.

Tanner, P., & Buxton, W. (1985). Some issues in future interface management system (UIMS) development. In G. Pfaff (Ed.), *User interface management systems* (pp. 67-69). Berlin: Springer-Verlag.

Thomas, J., & Hamlin, G. (Eds.) (1983). Graphical Input Interaction Technique (GIIT) workshop summary. *Computer Graphics, 17(1),* 5-30.

Issues and Techniques in
Touch-Sensitive Tablet Input

William Buxton
Ralph Hill
Peter Rowley

Computer Systems Research Institute
University of Toronto
Toronto, Ontario
Canada M5S 1A4

(416) 978-6320

1. Introduction

Increasingly, research in human-computer interaction is focusing on problems of input [Foley, Wallace & Chan 1984; Buxton 1983; Buxton 1985]. Much of this attention is directed towards input technologies. The ubiquitous Sholes keyboard is being replaced and/or complemented by alternative technologies. For example, a major focus of the marketing strategy for two recent personal computers, the Apple Macintosh and Hewlett-Packard 150, has been on the input devices that they employ (the mouse and touch-screen, respectively).

Now that the range of available devices is expanding, how does one select the best technology for a particular application? And once a technology is chosen, how can it be used most effectively? These questions are important, for as Buxton [1983] has argued, the ways in which the user *physically* interacts with an input device have a marked effect on the type of user interface that can be effectively supported.

In the general sense, the objective of this paper is to help in the selection process and assist in effective use of a specific class of devices. Our approach is to investigate a specific class of devices: touch-sensitive tablets. We will identify touch tablets, enumerate their important properties, and compare them to a more common input device, the mouse. We then go on to give examples of transactions where touch tablets can be used effectively. There are two intended benefits for this approach. First, the reader will acquire an understanding of touch tablet issues. Second, the reader will have a concrete example of how the technology can be investigated, and can utilize the approach as a model for investigating other classes of devices.

2. Touch-Sensitive Tablets

A touch-sensitive tablet (touch tablet for short) is a flat surface, usually mounted horizontally or nearly horizontally, that can sense the location of a finger pressing on it. That is, it is a tablet that can sense that it is being touched, and where it is being

Abstract

Touch-sensitive tablets and their use in human-computer interaction are discussed. It is shown that such devices have some important properties that differentiate them from other input devices (such as mice and joysticks). The analysis serves two purposes: (1) it sheds light on touch tablets, and (2) it demonstrates how other devices might be approached. Three specific distinctions between touch tablets and one button mice are drawn. These concern the signaling of events, multiple point sensing and the use of templates. These distinctions are reinforced, and possible uses of touch tablets are illustrated, in an example application. Potential enhancements to touch tablets and other input devices are discussed, as are some inherent problems. The paper concludes with recommendations for future work.

CR Categories and Subject Descriptors: I.3.1 [**Computer Graphics**]: Hardware Architecture: Input Devices. I.3.6 [**Computer Graphics**]: Methodology and Techniques: Device Independence, Ergonomics, Interaction Techniques.

General Terms: Design, Human Factors.

Additional Keywords and Phrases: touch sensitive input devices.

touched. Touch tablets can vary greatly in size, from a few inches on a side to several feet on a side. The most critical requirement is that the user is not required point with some manually held device such as a stylus or puck.

What we have described in the previous paragraph is a *simple* touch tablet. Only one point of contact is sensed, and then only in a binary, touch/no touch, mode. One way to extend the potential of a simple touch tablet is to sense the degree, or pressure, of contact. Another is to sense multiple points of contact. In this case, the location (and possibly pressure) of several points of contact would be reported. Most tablets currently on the market are of the "simple" variety. However, Lee, Buxton and Smith [1985], and Nakatani [private communication] have developed prototypes of multi-touch, multi-pressure sensing tablets.

We wish to stress that we will restrict our discussion of touch technologies to touch tablets, which can and should be used in ways that are different from touch screens. Readers interested in touch-screen technology are referred to Herot & Weinsapfel [1978], Nakatani & Rohrlich [1983] and Minsky [1984]. We acknowledge that a flat touch screen mounted horizontally is a touch tablet as defined above. This is not a contradiction, as a touch screen has exactly the properties of touch tablets we describe below, as long as there is no attempt to mount a display below (or behind) it or to make it the center of the user's visual focus.

Some sources of touch tablets are listed in Appendix A.

3. Properties of Touch-Sensitive Tablets

Asking "Which input device is best?" is much like asking "How long should a piece of string be?" The answer to both is: it depends on what you want to use it for. With input devices, however, we are limited in our understanding of the relationship between device properties and the demands of a specific application. We will investigate touch tablets from the perspective of improving our understanding of this relationship. Our claim is that other technologies warrant similar, or even more detailed, investigation.

Touch tablets have a number of properties that distinguish them from other devices:

• They have no mechanical intermediate device (such as stylus or puck). Hence they are useful in hostile environments (e.g., classrooms, public access terminals) where such intermediate devices can get lost, stolen, or damaged.

• Having no puck to slide or get bumped, the tracking symbol "stays put" once placed, thus making them well suited for pointing tasks in environments subject to vibration or motion (e.g., factories, cockpits).

• They present no mechanical or kinesthetic restrictions on our ability to indicate more than one point at a time. That is, we can use two hands or more than one finger simultaneously on a single tablet. (Remember, we can manually control at

most two mice at a time: one in each hand. Given that we have ten fingers, it is conceivable that we may wish to indicate more than two points simultaneously. An example of such an application appears below).

• Unlike joysticks and trackballs, they have a very low profile and can be integrated into other equipment such as desks and low-profile keyboards (e.g., the Key Tronic Touch Pad, see Appendix A). This has potential benefits in portable systems, and, according to the Keystroke model of Card, Newell and Moran [1980], reduces homing time from the keyboard to the pointing device.

• They can be molded into one-piece constructions thus eliminating cracks and grooves where dirt can collect. This makes them well suited for very clean environments (eg. hospitals) or very dirty ones (eg., factories).

• Their simple construction, with no moving parts, leads to reliable and long-lived operation, making them suitable for environments where they will be subjected to intense use or where reliability is critical.

They do, of course, have some inherent disadvantages, which will be discussed at the close of the paper.

In the next section we will make three important distinctions between touch tablets and mice. These are:

• Mice and touch tablets vary in the number and types of events that they can transmit. The difference is especially pronounced when comparing to simple touch tablets.

• Touch tablets can be made that can sense multiple points of contact. There is no analogous property for mice.

• The surface of a tablet can be partitioned into regions representing a collection of independent "virtual" devices. This is analogous to the partitioning of a screen into "windows" or virtual displays. Mice, and other devices that transmit "relative change" information, do not lend themselves to this mode of interaction without consuming display real estate for visual feedback. With conventional tablets and touch tablets, graphical, physical or virtual templates can be placed over the input device to delimit regions. This allows valuable screen real estate to be preserved. Physical templates, when combined with touch sensing, permit the operator to sense the regions without diverting the eyes from the primary display during visually demanding tasks.

After these properties are discussed, a simple finger painting program is used to illustrate them in the context of a concrete example. We wish to stress that we do not pretend that the program represents a viable paint program or an optimal interface. It is simply a vehicle to illustrate a variety of transactions in an easily understandable context.

Finally, we discuss improvements that must be made to current touch tablet technology, many of which we have demonstrated in prototype form. Also, we suggest potential improvements to other devices, motivated by our experience with touch technology.

4. Three Distinctions Between Touch Tablets and Mice[1]

The distinctions we make in this section have to do with suitability of devices for certain tasks or use in certain configurations. We are only interested in showing that there are some uses for which touch tablets are not suitable, but other devices are, and vice versa. We make no quantitative claims or comparisons regarding performance.

Signaling

Consider a rubber-band line drawing task with a one button mouse. The user would first position the tracking symbol at the desired starting point of the line by moving the mouse with the button released. The button would then be depressed, to signal the start of the line, and the user would manipulate the line by moving the mouse until the desired length and orientation was achieved. The completion of the line could then be signaled by releasing the button.[2]

Figure 1 is a state diagram that represents this interface. Notice that the button press and release are used to signal the beginning and end of the rubber-band drawing task. Also note that in states 1 and 2 both motion and signaling (by pressing or releasing the button, as appropriate) are possible.

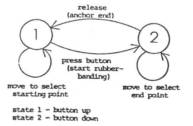

Figure 1. State diagram for rubber-banding with a one-button mouse.

Now consider a simple touch tablet. It can be used to position the tracking symbol at the starting point of the line, but it cannot generate the signal needed to initiate rubber-banding. Figure 2 is a state diagram representation of the capabilities of a simple touch tablet. In state 0, there is no contact with the tablet.[3] In this state only one action is pos-

sible: the user may touch the tablet. This causes a change to state 1. In state 1, the user is pressing on the tablet, and as a consequence position reports are sent to the host. There is no way to signal a change to some other state, other than to release (assuming the exclusion of temporal or spatial cues, which tend to be clumsy and difficult to learn). This returns the system to state 0. This signal could not be used to initiate rubber-banding, as it could also mean that the user is pausing to think, or wishes to initiate some other activity.

Figure 2. Diagram for showing states of simple touch-tablet.

This inability to signal while pointing is a severe limitation with current touch tablets, that is, tablets that do not report pressure in addition to location. (It is also a property of trackballs, and joysticks without "fire" buttons.) It renders them unsuitable for use in many common interaction techniques for which mice are well adapted (e.g., selecting and dragging objects into position, rubber-band line drawing, and pop-up menu selection); techniques that are especially characteristic of interfaces based on *Direct Manipulation* [Shneiderman 1983].

One solution to the problem is to use a separate function button on the keyboard. However, this usually means two-handed input where one could do, or, awkward co-ordination in controlling the button and pointing device with a single hand. An alternative solution when using a touch tablet is to provide some level of pressure sensing. For example, if the tablet could report two levels of contact pressure (i.e., hard and soft), then the transition from soft to hard pressure, and vice versa, could be used for signaling. In effect, pressing hard is equivalent to pressing the button on the mouse. The state diagram showing the rubber-band line drawing task with this form of touch tablet is shown in Figure 3.[4]

As an aside, using this pressure sensing scheme would permit us to select options from a menu, or

---

[1] Although we are comparing touch tablets to one button mice throughout this section, most of the comments apply equally to tablets with one-button pucks or (with some caveats) tablets with styli.

[2] This assumes that the interface is designed so that the button is held down during drawing. Alternatively, the button can be released during drawing, and pressed again, to signal the completion of the line.

[3] We use state 0 to represent a state in which no location information is transmitted. There no analogous state for mice, and hence no state 0 in the diagrams for

mice. With conventional tablets, this corresponds to "out of range" state.

At this point the alert reader will wonder about difficulty in distinguishing between hard and soft pressure, and friction (especially when pressing hard). Taking the last first, hard is a relative term. In practice friction need not be a problem (see Inherent Problems, below).

[4] One would conjecture that in the absence of button clicks or other feedback, pressure would be difficult to regulate accurately. We have found two levels of pressure to be easily distinguished, but this is a ripe area for research. For example, Stu Card [private communication] has suggested that the threshold between soft and hard should be reduced (become "softer") while hard pressure is being maintained. This suggestion, and others, warrant formal experimentation.

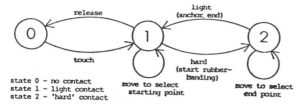

Figure 3. State diagram for rubber-banding with pressure sensing touch tablet.

activate light buttons by positioning the tracking symbol over the item and "pushing". This is consistent with the gesture used with a mouse, and the model of "pushing" buttons. With current simple touch tablets, one does just the opposite: position over the item and then lift off, or "pull" the button.

From the perspective of the signals sent to the host computer, this touch tablet is capable of duplicating the behaviour of a one-button mouse. This is not to say that these devices are equivalent or interchangeable. They are not. They are physically and kinesthetically very different, and should be used in ways that make use of the unique properties of each. Furthermore, such a touch tablet can generate one pair of signals that the one-button mouse cannot — specifically, press and release (transition to and from state 0 in the above diagrams). These signals (which are also available with many conventional tablets) are very useful in implementing certain types of transactions, such as those based on character recognition.

An obvious extension of the pressure sensing concept is to allow continuous pressure sensing. That is, pressure sensing where some large number of different levels of pressure may be reported. This extends the capability of the touch tablet beyond that of a traditional one button mouse. An example of the use of this feature is presented below.

Multiple Position Sensing

With a traditional mouse or tablet, only one position can be reported per device. One can imagine using two mice or possibly two transducers on a tablet, but this increases costs, and two is the practical limit on the number of mice or tablets that can be operated by a single user (without using feet). However, while we have only two hands, we have ten fingers. As playing the piano illustrates, there are some contexts where we might want to use several, or even all of them, at once.

Touch tablets need not restrict us in this regard. Given a large enough surface of the appropriate technology, one could use all fingers of both hands simultaneously, thus providing ten separate units of input. Clearly, this is well beyond the demands of many applications and the capacity of many people, however, there are exceptions. Examples include chording on buttons or switches, operating a set of slide potentiometers, and simple key roll-over when touch typing. One example (using a set of slide potentiometers) will be illustrated below.

Multiple Virtual Devices and Templates

The power of modern graphics displays has been enhanced by partitioning one physical display into a number of virtual displays. To support this, display window managers have been developed. We claim (see Brown, Buxton and Murtagh [1985]) that similar benefits can be gained by developing an input window manager that permits a single physical input device to be partitioned into a number of virtual input devices. Furthermore, we claim that multi-touch tablets are well suited to supporting this approach.

Figure 4a shows a thick cardboard sheet that has holes cut in specific places. When it is placed over a touch tablet as shown in Figure 4b, the user is restricted to touching only certain parts of the tablet. More importantly, the user can *feel* the parts that are touchable, and their shape. Each of the "touchable" regions represents a separate virtual device. The distinction between this template and traditional tablet mounted menus (such as seen in many CAD systems) is important.

Traditionally, the options have been:

a) Save display real estate by mounting the menu on the tablet surface. The cost of this option is eye diversion from the display to the tablet, the inability to "touch type", and time consuming menu changes.

b) Avoid eye diversion by placing the menus on the display. This also make it easier to change menus, but still does not allow "touch typing", and consumes display space.

Touch tablets allow a new option:

c) Save display space and avoid eye diversion by using templates that can be felt, and hence, allow "touch typing" on a variety of virtual input devices. The cost of this option is time consuming menu (template) changes.

It must be remembered that for each of these options, there is an application for which it is best. We have contributed a new option, which makes possible new interfaces. The new possibilities include more elaborate virtual devices because the improved kinesthetic feedback allows the user to concentrate on providing input, instead of staying in the assigned region. We will also show (below) that its main cost (time consuming menu changes) can be reduced in some applications by eliminating the templates.

5. Examples of Transactions Where Touch Tablets Can Be Used Effectively

In order to reinforce the distinctions discussed in the previous section, and to demonstrate the use of touch tablets, we will now work through some examples based on a toy paint system. We wish to stress again that we make no claims about the quality of the example as a paint system. A paint system is a common and easily understood application, and thus, we have chosen to use it simply as a vehicle for discussing interaction techniques that use touch tablets.

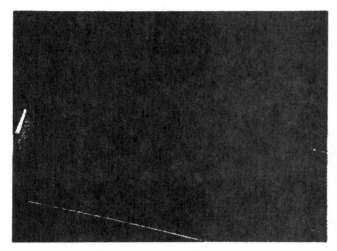

Figure 4a. Sample template.

Figure 5. Main display for paint program.

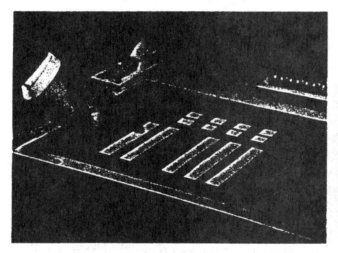

Figure 4b. Sample template in use.

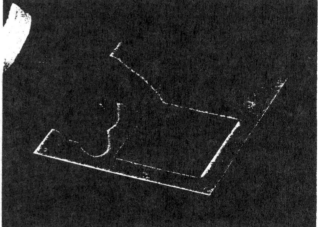

Figure 6. Touch tablet used in demonstrations.

The example paint program allows the creation of simple finger paintings. The layout of the main display for the program is shown in Figure 5. On the left is a large drawing area where the user can draw simple free-hand figures. On the right is a set of menu items. When the lowest item is selected, the user enters a colour mixing mode. In switching to this mode, the user is presented with a different display that is discussed below. The remaining menu items are "paint pots". They are used to select the colour that the user will be painting with.

In each of the following versions of the program, the input requirements are slightly different. In all cases an 8 cm x 8 cm touch tablet is used (Figure 6), but the pressure sensing requirements vary. These are noted in each demonstration.

5.1. Painting Without Pressure Sensing

This version of the paint program illustrates the limitation of having no pressure sensing. Consider

the paint program described above, where the only input device is a touch tablet without pressure sensing. Menu selections could be made by pressing down somewhere in the menu area, moving the tracking symbol to the desired menu item and then selecting by releasing. To paint, the user would simply press down in the drawing area and move (see Figure 7 for a representation of the signals used for painting with this program).

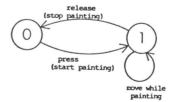

Figure 7. State diagram for drawing portion of simple paint program.

There are several problems with this program. The most obvious is in trying to do detailed drawings. The user does not know where the paint will appear until it appears. This is likely to be too late. Some form of feedback, that shows the user where the brush is, without painting, is needed. Unfortunately, this cannot be done with this input device, as it is not possible to signal the change from tracking to painting and vice versa.

The simplest solution to this problem is to use a button (e.g., a function key on the keyboard) to signal state changes. The problem with this solution is the need to use two hands on two different devices to do one task. This is awkward and requires practice to develop the co-ordination needed to make small rapid strokes in the painting. It is also inefficient in its use of two hands where one could (and normally should) do.

Alternatively, approaches using multiple taps or timing cues for signalling could be tried, however, we have found that these invariably lead to other problems. It is better to find a direct solution using the properties of the device itself.

5.2. Painting with Two Levels of Pressure

This version of the program uses a tablet that reports two levels of contact pressure to provide a satisfactory solution to the signaling problem. A low pressure level (a light touch by the user) is used for general tracking. A heavier touch is used to make menu selections, or to enable painting (see Figure 8 for the tablet states used to control painting with this program). The two levels of contact pressure allow us to make a simple but practical one finger paint program.

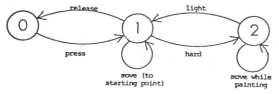

Figure 8. State diagram for painting portion of simple paint program using pressure sensing touch tablet.

This version is very much like using the one button mouse on the Apple Macintosh with MacPaint [Williams, 1984]. Thus, a simple touch tablet is not very useful, but one that reports two levels of pressure is similar in power (but not feel or applicability) to a one button mouse.[5]

5.3. Painting with Continuous Pressure Sensing

In the previous demonstrations, we have only implemented interaction techniques that are common using existing technology. We now introduce a technique that provides functionality beyond that obtainable using most conventional input technolo-

---

[5] Also, there is the problem of friction, to be discussed below under "Inherent Problems".

gies.

In this technique, we utilize a tablet capable of sensing a continuous range of touch pressure. With this additional signal, the user can control both the width of the paint trail and its path, using only one finger. The new signal, pressure, is used to control width. This is a technique that cannot be used with any mouse that we are aware of, and to our knowledge, is available on only one conventional tablet (the GTCO Digipad with pressure pen [GTCO 1982]).

We have found that using current pressure sensing tablets, the user can accurately supply two to three bits of pressure information, after about 15 minutes practice. This is sufficient for simple doodling and many other applications, but improved pressure resolution is required for high quality painting.

5.4. "Windows" on the Tablet: Colour Selection

We now demonstrate how the surface of the touch tablet can be *dynamically* partitioned into "windows" onto virtual input devices. We use the same basic techniques as discussed under templates (above), but show how to use them without templates. We do this in the context of a colour selection module for our paint program. This module introduces a new display, shown in Figure 9.

Figure 9. Colour mixing display.

In this display, the large left side consists of a colour patch surrounded by a neutral grey border. This is the patch of colour the user is working on. The right side of the display contains three bar graphs with two light buttons underneath. The primary function of the bar graphs is to provide feedback, representing relative proportions of red, green and blue in the colour patch. Along with the light buttons below, they also serve to remind the user of the current layout of the touch tablet.

In this module, the touch tablet is used as a "virtual operating console". Its layout is shown (to scale) in Figure 10. There are 3 valuators (corresponding to the bar graphs on the screen) used to control colour, and two buttons: one, on the right, to bring up a pop-up menu used to select the colour to be modified, and another, on the left, to exit.

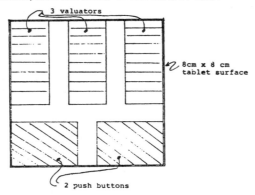

Figure 10. Layout of virtual devices on touch tablet.

The single most important point to be made in this example is that a single *physical* device is being used to implement 5 *virtual* devices (3 valuators and 2 buttons). This is analogous to the use of a display window system, in its goals, and its implementation.

The second main point is that there is nothing on the tablet to delimit the regions. This differs from the use of physical templates as previously discussed, and shows how, in the absence of the need for a physical template, we can instantly change the "windows" on the tablet, without sacrificing the ability to touch type.

We have found that when the tablet surface is small, and the partitioning of the surfaces is not too complex, the users very quickly (typically in one or two minutes) learn the positions of the virtual devices relative to the edges of the tablet. More importantly, they can use the virtual devices, practically error free, without diverting attention from the display. (We have repeatedly observed this behaviour in the use of an application that uses a 10 cm square tablet that is divided into 3 sliders with a single button across the top).

Because no template is needed, there is no need for the user to pause to change a template when entering the colour mixing module. Also, at no point is the user's attention diverted from the display. These advantages cannot be achieved with any other device we know of, without consuming display real estate.

The colour of the colour patch is manipulated by *dragging* the red, green and blue values up and down with the valuators on the touch tablet. The valuators are implemented in relative mode (i.e., they are sensitive to changes in position, not absolute position), and are manipulated like one dimensional mice. For example, to make the patch more red, the user presses near the left side of the tablet, about half way to the top, and slides the finger up (see Figure 11). For larger changes, the device can be repeatedly stroked (much like stroking a mouse). Feedback is provided by changing the level in the bar graph on the screen and the colour

of the patch.

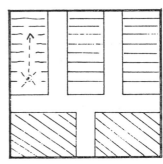

Figure 11. Increasing red content, by pressing on red valuator and sliding up.

Using a mouse, the above interaction could be approximated by placing the tracking symbol over the bars of colour, and dragging them up or down. However, if the bars are narrow, this takes acuity and concentration that distracts attention from the primary task — monitoring the colour of the patch. Furthermore, note that the touch tablet implementation does not need the bars to be displayed at all, they are only a convenience to the user. There are interfaces where, in the interests of maximizing available display area, there will be no items on the display analogous to these bars. That is, there would be nothing on the display to support an interaction technique that allows values to be manipulated by a mouse.

Finally, we can take the example one step further by introducing the use of a touch tablet that can sense multiple points of contact (e.g., [Lee, et al. 1985]). With this technology, all three colour values could be changed at the same time (for example, fading to black by drawing all three sliders down together with three fingers of one hand). This simultaneous adjustment of colours could *not* be supported by a mouse, nor any single commercially available input device we know of. Controlling several valuators with one hand is common in many operating consoles, for example: studio light control, audio mixers, and throttles for multi-engine vehicles (e.g., aircraft and boats). Hence, this example demonstrates a cost effective method for providing functionality that is currently unavailable (or available only at great cost, in the form of a custom fabricated console), but has wide applicability.

5.5. Summary of Examples

Through these simple examples, we have demonstrated several things:

- The ability to sense at least two levels of pressure is a virtual necessity for touch tablets, as without it, auxiliary devices must be used for signaling, and "direct manipulation" interfaces cannot be effectively supported.

- The extension to continuous pressure sensing opens up new possibilities in human-computer interaction.

- Touch tablets are superior to mice and tablets when many simple devices are to be simulated. This is because: (a) there is no need for a mechanical intermediary between the fingers and the tablet surface, (b) they allow the use of templates (including the edges of the tablet, which is a trivial but useful template), and (c) there is no need for positional feedback that would consume valuable display space.

- The ability to sense multiple points of contact radically changes the way in which users may interact with the system. The concept of multiple points of contact does not exist for, nor is it applicable to, current commercially available mice and tablets.

6. Inherent Problems with Touch Tablets

A problem with touch tablets that is annoying in the long term is friction between the user's finger and the tablet surface. This can be a particularly severe problem if a pressure sensitive tablet is used, and the user must make long motions at high pressure. This problem can be alleviated by careful selection of materials and care in the fabrication and calibration of the tablet.[6] Also, the user interface can be designed to avoid extended periods of high pressure.

Perhaps the most difficult problem is providing good feedback to the user when using touch tablets. For example, if a set of push-on/push-off buttons are being simulated, the traditional forms of feedback (illuminated buttons or different button heights) cannot be used. Also, buttons and other controls implemented on touch tablets lack the kinesthetic feel associated with real switches and knobs. As a result, users must be more attentive to visual and audio feedback, and interface designers must be freer in providing this feedback. (As an example of how this might be encouraged, the input "window manager" could automatically provide audible clicks as feedback for button presses).

7. Potential Enhancements to Touch Tablets (and other devices)

The first problem that one notices when using touch tablets is "jitter" when the finger is removed from the tablet. That is, the last few locations reported by the tablet, before it senses loss of contact, tend to be very unreliable.

This problem can be eliminated by modifying the firmware of the touch tablet controller so that it keeps a short FIFO queue of the samples that have most recently be sent to the host. When the user releases pressure, the oldest sample is retransmitted, and the queue is emptied. The length of the queue depends on the properties of the touch tablet (e.g., sensitivity, sampling rate). We have found that determining a suitable value requires

only a few minutes of experimentation.

A related problem with most current tablet controllers (not just touch tablets) is that they do not inform the host computer when the user has ceased pressing on the tablet (or moved the puck out of range). This information is essential to the development of certain types of interfaces. (As already mentioned, this signal is not available from mice). Currently, one is reduced to deducing this event by timing the interval between samples sent by the tablet. Since the tablet controller can easily determine when pressure is removed (and must if it is to apply a de-jittering algorithm as above), it should share this information with the host.

Clearly, pressure sensing is an area open to development. Two pressure sensitive tablets have been developed at the University of Toronto [Sasaki, et al. 1981; Lee, et al. 1985]. One has been used to develop several experimental interfaces and was found to be a very powerful tool. They have recently become available from Elographics and Big Briar (see Appendix A). Pressure sensing is not only for touch tablets. Mice, tablet pucks and styli could all benefit by augmenting switches with strain gauges, or other pressure sensing instruments. GTCO, for example, manufactures a stylus with a pressure sensing tip [GTCO 1982], and this, like our pressure sensing touch tablets, has proven very useful.

8. Conclusions

We have shown that there are environments for which some devices are better adapted than others. In particular, touch tablets have advantages in many hostile environments. For this reason, we suggest that there are environments and applications where touch tablets may be the most appropriate input technology.

This being the case, we have enumerated three major distinctions between touch tablets and one button mice (although similar distinctions exist for multi-button mice and conventional tablets). These assist in identifying environments and applications where touch tablets would be most appropriate. These distinctions concern:

- limitation in the ability to signal events,
- suitability for multiple point sensing, and
- the applicability of tactile templates.

These distinctions have been reinforced, and some suggestions on how touch tablets may be used have been given, by discussing a simple user interface. From this example, and the discussion of the distinctions, we have identified some enhancements that can be made to touch tablets and other input devices. The most important of these are pressure sensing and the ability to sense multiple points of contact.

We hope that this paper motivates interface designers to consider the use of touch tablets and shows some ways to use them effectively. Also, we hope it encourages designers and manufacturers of input devices to develop and market input devices with the enhancements that we have discussed.

---

[6] As a bad example, one commercial "touch" tablet requires so much pressure for reliable sensing that the finger cannot be smoothly dragged across the surface. Instead, a wooden or plastic stylus must be used, thus loosing many of the advantages of touch sensing.

The challenge for the future is to develop touch tablets that sense continuous pressure at multiple points of contact and incorporate them in practical interfaces. We believe that we have shown that this is worthwhile and have shown some practical ways to use touch tablets. However, interface designers must still do a great deal of work to determine where a mouse is better than a touch tablet and vice versa.

Finally, we have illustrated, by example, an approach to the study of input devices, summarized by the credo: "Know the interactions a device is intended to participate in, and the strengths and weaknesses of the device." This approach stresses that there is no such thing as a "good input device," only good interaction task/device combinations.

9. Acknowledgements

The support of this research by the Natural Sciences and Engineering Research Council of Canada is gratefully acknowledged. We are indebted to Kevin Murtagh and Ed Brown for their work on virtual input devices and windowing on input. Also, we are indebted to Elographics Corporation for having supplied us with the hardware on which some of the underlying studies are based.

We would like to thank the referees who provided many useful comments that have helped us with the presentation.

10. References

Brown, E.
Buxton, W.
Murtagh, K.
1985
Windows on Tablets as a Means of Achieving Virtual Input Devices. Submitted for publication.

Buxton, W.
1983
Lexical and Pragmatic Considerations of Input Structures. *Computer Graphics* 17.1. Presented at the SIGGRAPH Workshop on Graphical Input Techniques, Seattle, Washington, June 1982.

Buxton, W.
1985
There is More to Interaction Than Meets the Eye: Some Issues in Manual Input. (in) Norman, D.A. and Draper, S.W. (Eds.), *User Centered System Design: New Perspectives on Human-Computer Interaction.* Hillsdale, N.J.: Lawrence Erlbaum and Associates. Publication expected late 1985.

Buxton, W.
Fiume, E.
Hill, R.
Lee, A.
Woo, C.
1983
Continuous Hand-Gesture Driven Input. *Proceedings Graphics Interface '83*: pp. 191-195. May 9-13, 1983, Edmonton, Alberta.

Card, S.K.
Moran, T.P.
Newell, A.
Jul 1980
The Keystroke-Level Model for User Performance Time with Interactive Systems. *Communications of the ACM* 23.7: pp. 396-409.

Foley, J.D.
Wallace, V.L.
Chan, P.
Nov 1984
The Human Factors of Computer Graphics Interaction Techniques. *IEEE Computer Graphics and Applications* 4.11: pp. 13-48.

GTCO
1982
DIGI-PAD 5 User's Manual. GTCO Corporation, 1055 First Street, Rockville, MD 20850.

Herot, C.F.
Weinzapfel, G.
Aug 1978
One-Point Touch Input of Vector Information for Computer Displays. *Computer Graphics* 12.3: pp. 210-216. SIGGRAPH'78 Conference Proceedings, August 23-25, 1978, Atlanta, Georgia.

Lee, S.
Buxton, W.
Smith, K.C.
1985
A Multi-Touch Three Dimensional Touch-Sensitive Tablet. *Human Factors in Computer Systems*: pp. 21-25. (CHI'85 Conference Proceedings, April 14-18, 1985, San Fransisco).

Minsky, M.R.
Jul 1984
Manipulating Simulated Objects with Real-world Gestures using a Force and Position Sensitive Screen. *Computer Graphics* 18.3: pp. 195-203. (SIGGRAPH'84 Conference Proceedings, July 23-27, 1984, Minneapolis, Minnesota).

Nakatani, L.H.
Rohrlich, J.A.
Dec 1983
Soft Machines: A Philosophy of User-Computer Interface Design. *Human Factors in Computing Systems*: pp. 19-23. (CHI'83 Conference Procedings, December 12-15, 1983, Boston).

Sasaki, L.
Fedorkow, G.
Buxton, W.
Retterath, C.
Smith, K.C.
1981
A Touch Sensitive Input Device. *Proceedings of the 5th International Conference on Computer Music.* North Texas State University, Denton Texas, November 1981.

Shneiderman, B.
Aug 1983
Direct Manipulation: A Step Beyond Programming Languages. *Computer* 16.8: pp. 57-69.

Williams, G.
Feb 1984
The Apple Macintosh Computer. *Byte* 9.2: pp. 30-54.

Appendix A: Touch Tablet Sources

Big Briar: 3 by 3 inch continuous pressure sensing touch tablet

Big Briar, Inc.
Leicester, NC
28748

Chalk Board Inc.: "Power Pad", large touch table for micro-computers

Chalk Board Inc.
3772 Pleasantdale Rd.,
Atlanta, GA 30340

Elographics: various sizes of touch tablets, including pressure sensing

Elographics, Inc.
105 Randolph Toad
Oak Ridge, Tennessee
37830
(615)-482-4100

Key Tronic: Keyboard with touch pad.

Keytronic
P.O. Box 14687
Spokane, WA 99214
(509)-928-8000

KoalaPad Technologies: Approx. 5 by 7 inch touch tablet
for micro-computers

Koala Technologies
3100 Patrick Henry Drive
Santa Clara, California
95050

Spiral Systems: Trazor Touch Panel, 3 by 3 inch touch
tablet

Spiral System Instruments, Inc.
4853 Cordell Avenue, Suite A-10
Bethesda, Maryland
20814

TASA: 4 by 4 inch touch tablet (relative sensing only)

Touch Activated Switch Arrays Inc.
1270 Lawrence Stn. Road, Suite G
Sunnyvale, California
94089

Evaluation of Mouse, Rate-Controlled Isometric Joystick, Step Keys, and Text Keys for Text Selection on a CRT

Stuart K. Card*, William K. English, and Betty J. Burr

Xerox Palo Alto Research Center Palo Alto, California.

Four devices are evaluated with respect to how rapidly they can be used to select text on a CRT display. The mouse is found to be fastest on all counts and also to have the lowest error rates. It is shown that variations in positioning time with the mouse and joystick are accounted for by Fitts's Law. In the case of the mouse, the measured Fitts's Law slope constant is close to that found in other eye-hand tasks leading to the conclusion that positioning time with this device is almost the minimal achievable. Positioning time for key devices is shown to be proportional to the number of keystrokes which must be typed.

1. Introduction

An important element in the design of the man-computer interface is the method of pointing by which the user indicates to the computer his selection of some element on the computer display. This is especially important for computer-based text-editing where the user may repeatedly use a pointing device to select the text he wishes to modify or to invoke a command from a menu displayed on the screen. The choice of pointing device may have a significant impact on the ease with which the selections can be made, and hence, since pointing typically occurs with high frequency, on the success of the entire system.

English, Englebart, and Berman (1967) measured mean pointing times and error rates for the mouse, lightpen, Grafacon tablet, and position and rate joysticks. They found the mouse to be the fastest of the devices, but did not investigate the effect of distance to target. They also gave no indication of the variability of their measures. Goodwin (1975) measured pointing times for the lightpen, lightgun, and Saunders 720 step keys. She found the light pen and lightgun equally fast and much superior to the Saunders 720 step keys. However, she used only one target size and did not investigate distance. In addition, her results also show large learning effects which are confounded with the device comparisons. Both studies were more concerned with the evaluation of devices than with the development of models from which performance could be predicted. In another line of development Fitts and others (Fitts 1954, Fitts and Peterson 1964, Fitts and Radford 1966, Knight and Dagnal 1967, Welford 1968) developed and tested the relation between distance, size of target, and hand movement time. Such a relation might potentially be used to predict pointing times for devices involving continuous hand movements; however this has not been tested directly. In particular it was not known whether Fitts's Law would hold for targets of the shape and character of text strings.

The present report examines text selection performance with four devices: the mouse, a rate-controlled isometric joystick, step keys, and text keys. The study differs from the English *et al.* and Goodwin studies in that distance, target size, and learning are all simultaneously controlled and a different set of devices is measured. Also, unlike those studies, an attempt is made to give a theoretical account of the results. In particular, performance on the continuous movement devices is tested against the predictions of Fitts's Law.

*Reprint requests should be sent to Stuart K. Card, Xerox Palo Alto Research Center, 3333 Coyote Hill

2. Method

2.1. Subjects

Three men and two women, all undergraduates at Standford University, served as subjects in the experiment. None had ever used any of the devices previously and all had little or no experience with computers. Subjects were paid $3·00 per hour with a $20·00 bonus for completing the experiments. One of the five subjects was very much slower than the others and was eliminated from the experiment.

2.2. Pointing Devices

Four pointing devices were tested (see Figure 1). Two were continuous devices: the mouse and a rate-controlled isometric joystick. Two were key operated: the step keys and the text keys. The devices had been optimised informally by testing them on local users, adjusting the device parameters so as to maximise performance.

The mouse, a version of the device described in English *et al.* (1967), was a small device which sat on the table to the right of the keyboard, connected by a thin wire. On the undercarriage were two small wheels, mounted at right angles to each other. As the mouse moved over the table one wheel coded the amount of movement in the X-direction, the other the movement in the Y-direction. As the mouse moved, a cursor moved simultaneously on the CRT, two units of screen movement for each unit of mouse movement.

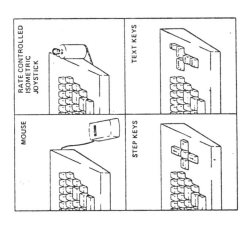

Figure 1.   Pointing devices tested.

The joystick used was a small strain gauge on which had been mounted a rubber knob 1·25 cm in diameter. Applying force to the joystick in any direction did not produce noticeable movement in the joystick itself, but caused the cursor to move in the appropriate direction at a rate $= 0·0178 \, (\text{force})^2$ in cm s^{-1}, where force is measured in Newtons. For forces less than about 4 Newtons, the cursor did not move at all, and the equation ceased to hold in the neighbourhood of 45 Newtons as the rate approached a ceiling of about 40 cm s^{-1}.

The step keys were the fimiliar five key cluster found on many CRT terminals. Surrounding a central HOME key were keys to move the cursor in each of four

the text. Pressing one of the horizontal keys moved the cursor 1 character (0.246 cm on the average) along the line. Pressing a vertical key moved the cursor one line (0.456 cm) up or down. Holding down one of the keys for more than 0.100 s caused it to go into a repeating mode, producing one step in the vertical direction each 0.133 s or one step in the horizontal direction each 0.067 s (3.43 cm s⁻¹ vertical movement, 3.67 cm s⁻¹ horizontal movement).

The text keys were similar to keys appearing on several commercial 'word processing' terminals. Depressing the PARAGRAPH key caused the cursor to move to the beginning of the next paragraph. Depressing the LINE key caused the cursor to move downward to the same position in the next line. The WORD key moved the cursor forward one word; the CHARACTER key moved the cursor forward one character. Holding down the REVERSE key while pressing another key caused the cursor to move opposite the direction it would otherwise have moved. The text keys could also be used in a repeating mode. Holding the LINE WORD or CHARACTER keys down for longer than 0.100 s caused that key to repeat at 0.133 s per repeat for the LINE key, 0.100 s per repeat for the WORD key, or 0.067 s per repeat for the CHARACTER key. Since there were 0.456 cm line⁻¹, 1.320 word⁻¹, and 0.246 cm character⁻¹ movement rates were 3.43 cm s⁻¹ for the LINE key, 13.20 cm s⁻¹ for the WORD key, and 3.67 cm s⁻¹ for the CHARACTER key.

2.3. Procedure

Subjects were seated in front of a computer terminal with a CRT for output, a keyboard for input, and one of the devices for pointing at targets on the screen. On each trial a page of text was displayed on the screen. Within the text a single word or phrase, was highlighted by inverting the black/white values of the text and the target, was highlighted by inverting the black/white values of the text and background in a rectangle surrounding the target. The subject struck the space bar of the keyboard with his right hand, then, with the same hand reached for the pointing device and directed the cursor to the target. The cursor thus positioned, the subject pressed a button 'selecting' the target as he would were he using the device in a text editor. For the mouse, the button was located on the device itself. For the other devices, the subject pressed a special key with his left hand.

2.4. Design

Text selections and targets were so arranged that there were five different distances from starting position to target, 1, 2, 4, 8, or 16, cm, and four different target sizes, 1, 2, 4, or 10 characters. All targets were words or groups of words. Ten different instances of each distance × target size pair were created, varying the location of the target on the display and the angle of hand movement to give a total of 200, randomly ordered, unique stimuli.

Each subject repeated the experiment with each device. The order in which subjects used the devices was randomised. At the start of each day, the subjects were given approximately twenty warm-up trials to refresh their memory of the procedure. All other trials were recorded as data. At the end of each block of twenty trials they were given feedback on the average positioning time and average number of errors for those trials. This feedback was found to be important in maintaining subjects' motivations. At the end of each 200 trials they were given a rest break of about fifteen minutes. Subjects normally accomplished 600 trials day⁻¹ involving about two to three hours of work. They each used a particular device until the positioning time was no longer decreasing significantly with practice (operationally defined as when the first and last thirds of a block of the last 600 trials excluding the first 200 trials of a day did not differ

significantly in positioning time at the $p < 0.05$ level using a t-test). An approximation to this criterion was reached in from 1200 to 1800 trials (four to six hours) on each device. Of the 20 subject × device pairs, 15 reached this criterion, 3 performed worse in their last trials (largely because some time elapsed between sessions), and only 2 were continuing (slightly) to improve.

3. Results

3.1. Improvement of Performance with Practice

The learning curve which gives positioning time as a function of the amount of practice can be approximated (De Jong 1957) by

$$T_N = T_1 N^{-\alpha} \qquad (1)$$

where
T_1 = estimated positioning time on the first block of trials,
T_N = estimated positioning time on the Nth block of trials,
N = trial block number, and
α = an empirically determined constant.

This form is convenient since taking the log of both sides produces an equation linear in log N,

$$\log T_N = \log T_1 - \alpha (\log N). \qquad (2)$$

Thus the ease of learning for each device can be described by two numbers T_1 and α, which numbers may be conveniently determined empirically by regressing log T_N on log N. Figure 2 shows the results of plotting the data from error-free trials according to Equation 2. Each point on the graph is the average of a block N of twenty contiguous trials from which error trials have been excluded. Only the first 60 trial blocks are shown. Since some subjects reached criterion at that point, not all continued on to further trials. The values predicted by the equation are given as the straight line drawn through the points. The average target size in each block was 4.23 cm (the range of the average target sizes for different trial blocks was 3.95 to 4.50 cm); the average distance to the target was 6.13 cm (range 5.90 to 6.42 cm).

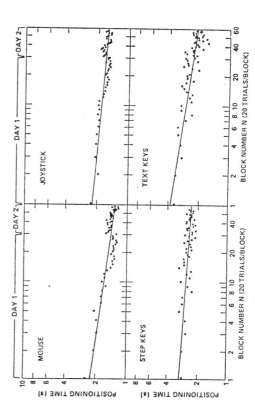

Figure 2. Learning curves for pointing devices.

The parameters T_1 and α, as determined by the regressions, are given in Table 1, along with the standard error and squared multiple correlation from the regression analysis. Practice causes more improvement in the mouse and text keys than on the other two devices. The step keys, in particular, show very little improvement with practice. Equation 2 explains 39% of the variance in the average positioning time for a block of trials for the step keys, 61% to 66% for the variance for the other devices. The fit, at least for the mouse and the joystick, is actually better than these numbers suggest. Since subjects did 30 blocks of trials on a day typically followed by a pause of a day or two before they could be rescheduled, a break in the learning curve is expected at that point and indeed such a break is quite evident for the mouse and the joystick between the 30th and 31st blocks. Fitting Equation 2 to only the first day increases the percentage of variance explained to 91% for the mouse and 83% for the joystick. In case of the step keys and text keys there is no such obvious day effect.

Table 1.   Learning Curve Parameters

DEVICE	T_1 (s)	α	Learning Curve Equation[a]	s_e (s)	R^2
Mouse	2·20	0·13	$T_N = 2 \cdot 20 \; N^{-0 \cdot 13}$	0·12	0·66
Joystick	2·19	0·08	$T_N = 2 \cdot 19 \; N^{-0 \cdot 08}$	0·08	0·62
Step Keys	3·03	0·07	$T_N = 3 \cdot 03 \; N^{-0 \cdot 07}$	0·11	0·39
Text Keys	3·86	0·15	$T_N = 3 \cdot 86 \; N^{-0 \cdot 15}$	0·16	0·61

[a] N is number of trial blocks. There are 20 trials in each block.

3.2. Overall Speed

In order to compare the devices after learning has nearly reached asymptote (as would be the case for office workers using them daily), a sample of each subject's performance on each device was examined consisting of the last 600 trials excluding the first 200 trials of a day (in order to diminish warm-up effects). The remaining analyses will be based on this subset of the data, excluding those trials on which errors occurred. Table 2 gives the homing time, positioning time, and total time for each device averaging over all the distances and target sizes. Homing time was measured from the time the subject's right hand left the space bar until the cursor had begun to move. Positioning time was measured from when the cursor began to move until the selection button had been pressed. From the table, it can be seen that homing time increases slightly with the distance of the device from the keyboard. The longest time required is to reach the mouse, the shortest to reach the step keys. Although the text keys are near the keyboard, they take almost as long to reach as the mouse. Either it is more difficult to position the hands on the text keys or, as seems likely, subjects often spent some time planning the strategy for their move in the time between hitting the space bar to start the clock and the time when they begin pressing the keys. Further evidence for this hypothesis comes from the relatively high standard deviation observed for the homing time of the text keys. While the differences in the homing times among all device pairs except the mouse vs. the text keys are reliable statistically (at $p < 0.05$ or better using a t-test), the differences are actually quite small. For example, while the step keys can be reached 0·15 s sooner than the mouse, they take 1·02 s longer to position. Thus the differences in the homing times are insignificant compared to the differences between the positioning times.

Table 2.   Overall Times

Device	Movement time for non-error trials (s)						Error rate	
	Homing Time		Positioning Time		Total Time			
	M	SD	M	SD	M	SD	M	SD
Mouse	0·36	0·13	1·29	0·42	1·66	0·48	5%	22%
Joystick	0·26	0·11	1·57	0·54	1·83	0·57	11%	31%
Step Keys	0·21	0·30	2·31	1·52	2·51	1·64	13%	33%
Text Keys	0·32	0·61	1·95	1·30	2·26	1·70	9%	28%

The mouse is easily the fastest device, the step keys the slowest. As a group, the continuous devices (the mouse and the joystick) are faster than the key-operated devices (the step keys and text keys). Differences between the devices are all reliable at $p \ll 0.001$ using t-tests.

3.3 Effect of Distance and Target Size

The effect of distance on positioning time is given in Figure 3. At all distances greater than 1cm, the continuous devices are faster. The positioning time for both continuous devices seems to increase approximately with the log of the distance. The time for the step keys increases rapidly as the distance increases, while the time for the text keys increases somewhat less than as the log of the distance, owing to the existence of keys for moving relatively large distances with a single stroke. Again the mouse is the fastest device, and its advantage increases with distance.

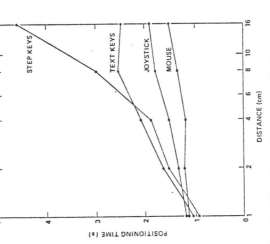

Figure 3.   Effect of target distance on positioning time.

Figure 4 shows the effect of target size on positioning time. The positioning time for both the mouse and the joystick decreases with the log of the target size. The time for the text keys is independent of target size and the positioning time for the step keys also decreases roughly with the log of the target size. Again the mouse is the fastest device, and again the continuous devices as a group are faster for all target sizes.

This finding replicates the result of Fitts and Radford (1966). In an investigation of self-initiated, discrete, pointing movements using a stylus, there was a similar marked reduction in errors as the target increased in size, but only a slight increase in error rate as the distance to the target increased.

4. Discussion

While these empirical results are of direct use in selecting a pointing device, it would obviously be of greater benefit if a theoretical account of the results could be made. For one thing, the need for some experiments might be obviated; for another, ways of improving pointing performance might be suggested. Fortunately, a first-order account for the devices of this experiment is not hard to give.

4.1. Mouse

The time to make a hand movement can be described by a version of Fitt's Law (Welford 1968),

$$T_{pos} = K_0 + K \log_2 (D/S + 0.5) \text{ s} \quad (3)$$

where

T_{pos} = Positioning time,

D = Distance to the target,

S = Size of the target,

and

K_0, K = constants.

Here the constant K_0 includes within it the time for the hand initially to adjust its grasp on the mouse and the time to make the selection with the selection button. A constant of $K \simeq 0.1 \text{ s bit}^{-1}$ (10 bits s^{-1}) appears in a large number of studies on movement. This number is a measure of the information processing capacity of the eye-hand coordinate system. For single, discrete, subject-paced movements, the constant is a little less than 0.1 s bit^{-1}. Fitts and Radford (1966) get a value of 0.078 s bit^{-1} (12.8 bit s^{-1}, recomputed from their Figure 1, Experiment 1, for the experimental condition where accuracy is stressed). Pierce and Karlin (1957) get maximum rates of 0.085 s bit^{-1} (11.7 bit s^{-1}) in a pointing experiment. For continuous movement, repetitive, experimenter-paced tasks, such as alternately touching two targets with a stylus or pursuit tracking, the constant is slightly above 0.1 s bit^{-1}. Elkind and Sprague (1961) get maximum rates of 0.135 s bit^{-1} (7.4 bit s^{-1}) for a pursuit tracking task. Fitts's original dotting experiment as replotted by Welford (1968, p. 148) gives a K of 0.120 bit^{-1} as does Welford's own study using the actual distance between the dots, the same measure of distance used in this study.

Fitts's Law predicts that plotting positioning time as a function of $\log_2 (D/S + 0.5)$ should give a straight line. As the solid line in Figure 6 shows, this prediction is confirmed. Furthermore, the slope of the line K should be in the neighborhood of 0.1 sec/bit. Again the prediction is confirmed. The equation for the line in Figure 6 as determined by regression analysis is

$$T_{pos} = 1.03 + 0.096 \log_2 (D/S + 0.5) \text{ s} \quad (4)$$

3.4. Effect of Approach Angle

The targets in text editing are rectangles often significantly wider than they are high. Hence they might present a different problem when approached from different angles. In addition, the step keys and text keys work somewhat differently when moving horizontally than when moving vertically. To test if the direction of approach has an effect on positioning time, the target movements were classified according to whether they were vertical (0 to 22.5 degrees), diagonal (22.5 degrees to 67.5 degrees), or horizontal (67.5 degrees to 90 degrees). *Analysis of variance* shows the angle makes a significant difference in every case except for the mouse. The joystick takes slightly longer to position when the target is approached diagonally. The step keys take longer when approached horizontally than when approached vertically, a consequence probably deriving from the fact that a single keystroke would move the cursor almost twice as far vertically as horizontally. By contrast, the text keys take longer to position vertically, reflecting the presence of the WORD key. The differences induced by direction are not of great consequence, however. For the joystick it amounts to 3% of the mean positioning time; for the step keys 9% for the text keys 5%.

3.5. Errors

Of the four devices tested, the mouse had the lowest overall error rate, 5%; the step keys had the highest, 13%. The differences are reliable at $p < 0.05$ or better using t-tests. There is only a very slight increase in error rate with distance. However, there is a decrease in error rate with target size for every device except the text keys (Figure 5).

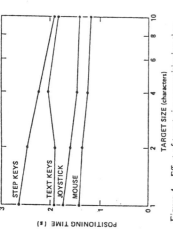

Figure 4. Effect of target size on positioning time.

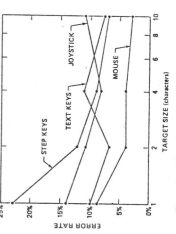

Figure 5. Effect of target size on error rate.

The equation has a standard error of 0·07 and explains 83% of the variance of the means for each condition. This is roughly comparable to the percentage of variance explained by Fitts and Radford. The slope of 0·096 bit s⁻¹ is in the 0·1 bit s⁻¹ range found in other studies. Since the standard error of estimate for K is 0·008 bit s⁻¹, the mouse would seem to be close to, but slightly slower than, the optimal rate of around 0·08 bit s⁻¹ observed for the stylus and for finger pointing.

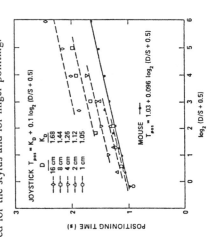

Figure 6.   Positioning time for continuous devices as a function of Fitts's index of difficulty log₂(D/S + 0·5).

The values for positioning time obtained in this experiment are apparently in good agreement with those obtained by English *et al.* Making the assumption that their CRT characters were about the same width as ours and assuming an intermediate target distance of about 8 cm, Equation 4 (plus the addition of the 0·36 s homing time from Table 2) predicts 1·87 s for 1 character targets (English *et al.* reported 1·93 s) and 1·66 s for 'word' targets of 5 characters (English *et al.* reported 1·68 s).

4.2. Joystick

Although it is a rate-controlled device instead of a position device, we might wonder if the joystick follows Fitts's Law. Plotting the average time per positioning for each distance × size cell of the experiment according to Equation 3 shows that there is an approximate fit to

$$T_{\text{pos}} = 0·99 + 0·220 \log_2 (D/S + 0·5). \qquad (5)$$

Equation 5 has a standard error of 0·13 and explains 89% of the variance of the means. The size of the slope K shows that information is being processed at only half the speed as with the mouse and significantly below the maximum rate. Closer examination gives some insight into the difficulty. The points for the joystick in Figure 6 actually form a series of parallel lines, one for each distance, each with a slope of around 0·1 bit s⁻¹. Setting K to 0·1 bit s⁻¹, we can therefore write as an alternative model

$$T_{\text{pos}} = K_D + 0·1 \log_2 (D/S + 0·5).$$

K_D is the intercept for distance D. From the figure, K_D is about 1·05 s for $D = 1$ cm, 1·12 s for 2 cm, 1·26 s for 4 cm, 1·44 s for 8 cm, and 1·68 s for 16 cm. For this model the standard error of the fit is reduced to 0·07 s, the same as for the mouse. (Since the slope was not determined by the regression, a comparable R^2 cannot be computed.) Thus the tested joystick can be thought of as a Fitts's Law device with a slope twice that for hand

movements; or it can be thought of as a Fitts's Law device with the expected slope, but having an intercept which increases with distance. The problem with this joystick is probably related to the non-linearity in the control (Poulton 1974, Craik and Vince 1963). It should be noted that for the 1 cm distance (where the effect of non-linearity is slight) the positioning time is virtually the same as for the mouse. Thus the possibility of designing a joystick with performance characteristics comparable to the mouse is by no means excluded.

4.3. Step Keys

As a first approximation one might expect the time to use the step keys to be governed by the number of keystrokes which must be used to move the cursor to the target. Since the keys can only move the cursor vertically or horizontally, the number of keystrokes is $D_x/0·456 + D_y/0·246$, where D_x and D_y are the horizontal and vertical components of distance to the target; 0·456 cm is the size of a vertical step and 0·246 cm is the size of a horizontal step. Hence positioning time should be

$$T_{\text{pos}} = K_0 + C(D_x/0·456 + D_y/0·246). \qquad (6)$$

This equation with $K_0 = 1·20$ s and $C = 0·052$ s keystroke⁻¹ has a standard error of 0·54 s and explains 84% of the variance of the means.

Since the tapping rate is around 0·15 s keystroke⁻¹, C is much too fast to be identified with the pressing of a key. It is also too fast to be identified with the 0·067 s keystroke⁻¹ automatic repetition mode. Figure 7 shows positioning time plotted against the predicted number of keystrokes. The long solid line is Equation 6 with the above parameters. The figure shows that positioning time is linear with the number of keystrokes until the predicted number of keystrokes becomes large (that is, the distance to the target is long). In these cases the user often has the opportunity to reduce positioning time by using the HOME key. Fitting Equation 6 to the first part of the graph $(D_x/0·456 + D_y/0·246 < 40)$ gives

$$T_{\text{pos}} = 0·98 + 0·074 (D_x/0·456 + D_y/0·246).$$

The equation, indicated as a short solid line on the figure, has a standard error of 0·18 s and explains 95% of the variance in the means. The reasonable slope of 0·074 s keystroke⁻¹ shows that the 0·067 s keystroke⁻¹ automatic repetition feature was heavily used.

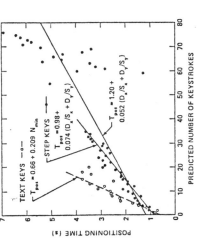

Figure 7.   Positioning time for key devices as a function of predicted number of keystrokes.

4.4. Text Keys

The text keys present the user on most trials with a choice of methods to reach the target. For example, he might press the PARAGRAPH key repeatedly until the cursor has moved to the paragraph containing the target paragraph. He could then press the LINE key repeatedly until it is on the target line, then use the WORD key to bring it over to the target. Or he might use the PARAGRAPH key to bring it over to the target, then holding, the REVERSE key down, use the LINE key to back up to the line after the target line. And finally, using REVERSE and WORD, back up until he hits the target. In fact, there are 26 different methods for moving the cursor to the target, although only a subset will be possible in a given situation. The fastest method will depend on where the target is located relative to the starting position and the boundaries of surrounding lines and paragraphs.

A reasonable hypothesis would be that positioning time is proportional to the number of keystrokes and that for well practiced subjects the number of keystrokes will be minimum necessary. To test this hypothesis each trial was analysed to determine the minimum number of keystrokes N_{min} necessary to hit the target. The average positioning time as a function of N_{min} is plotted as the open circles in Figure 7. A least squares fit gives

$$T_{pos} = 0.66 + 0.209 N_{min}.$$

The standard is 0.24 s and the equation explains 89% of the variance of the means. The keystroke rate of 0.209 s keystroke^{-1} is very reasonable, being approximately equal to the typing rate for random words (Devoe 1967). Evidently, the automatic repetition mode was little used. Examination of some statistics on the minimum numbers of keystrokes for each trial shows there was little need for it. For one thing, an average of only six keystrokes was necessary for the text keys to locate a target word. Ten or fewer keystrokes were sufficient for over 90% of the targets. For another, these keystrokes were distributed across several keys, further limiting opportunities to use the repetition mode. The PARAGRAPH key was needed on 48% on the trials, the LINE key on 85%, the WORD key on 83%, and the REVERSE key on 81%.

4.5. Comparison of Devices

Table 3 summarises the models, the standard of the fit, and the percentage of variance between the means explained by the model.

Table 3. Summary of Models for Positioning Time (T_{pos})

Device	Model (times in s)	s_e	R^2
Mouse	$T_{pos} = 1.03 + 0.096 \log_2 (D/S + 0.5)$	0.07	0.83
Joystick	$T_{pos} = 0.99 + 0.220 \log_2 (D/S + 0.5)$[a]	0.13	0.89
	$T_{pos} = K_a + 0.1 \log_2 (D/S + 0.5)$[b]	0.07	—
Step Keys	$T_{pos} = 1.20 + 0.052 (D_x/S_x + D_y/S_y)$[c]	0.54	0.84
	$T_{pos} = 0.98 + 0.074 (D_x/S_x + D_y/S_y)$[d]	0.18	0.95
Text Keys	$T_{pos} = 0.66 + 0.209 N_{min}$	0.24	0.89

[a] Least squares fit to all data points.
[d] Fit for number of keystrokes $(D_x/S_x + D_y/S_y) < 40$,
[c] Least squares fit to all data points.
[b] Fitting a separate line with slope 0.1 bit s^{-1} for each distance, where HOME key unlikely to be used.

The match of the Fitts's Law slope to the roughly $K \simeq 0.1$ s bit^{-1} constant observed in other hand movement and manual control studies means that positioning time is apparently limited by central information processing capacities of the eye-hand guidance system (cf. Welford 1968, Glencross 1977). Taking $K = 0.08$ s bit^{-1} as the most likely minimum value for a similar movement task, and $K_0 = 1$ s as a typical value observed in this experiment, it would seem unlikely that a continuous movement device could be developed whose positioning time is less than $1 + 0.08 \log_2 (D/S + 0.5)$ s (unless it can somehow reduce the information which must be centrally processed), although something might be done to reduce the value of K_0. If this is true, then an optimal device would be expected to be no more than about 5% faster than the mouse in the extreme case of 1 character targets 16 cm distant $(1 + 0.095 \log_2 (16/1 + 0.5) = 1.38$ vs. $1 + 0.08 \log_2 (16/1 + 0.5) = 1.32$ s). Typical differences would be much less. By comparison in this same case, the joystick (in this experiment) is 83% slower than the optimal device, the text keys 107% slower, and the step keys 239% slower. Even if K_0 were zero, the mouse would still be only 23% slower than the minimum. While devices might be built which improve on the mouse's homing time, error rate, or ability for fine movement, it is unlikely their positioning times will be significantly faster.

This maximum information processing capacity probably explains the lack of any significant difference in positioning time between the lightpen and the lightgun in Goodwin's experiment. Both are probably Fitts's Law devices, so both can be expected to have the same maximum 0.1 s bit^{-1} rate as the mouse (if they are optimised with respect to control/display ratio and any other relevent variables).

In interpreting these results, highly favourable to the mouse, some qualifications are in order. Of the four devices, the mouse is clearly the most 'compatible' for this task (cf. Poulton 1974, Chapter 16), meaning less mental translation is needed to map intended motion of the cursor into motor movement of the hands than for the other devices. Thus it would be expected to be easier to use, put lower cognitive load on the user, and have lower error rates. There are, however, limits to its compatibility. Inexperienced users are often bewildered about what to do when they run the mouse into the side of the keyboard trying to move the cursor across the screen. They need to be told that their mice can simply be picked up and deposited at a more convenient place on the table without affecting the cursor. Even experienced users are surprised at the results when they hold their mice backwards or sideways.

The greatest difficulty with the mouse for text-editing occurs with small targets. Punctuation marks such as a period are considerably smaller than an average character. The error rate for the mouse, which was already up to 9% for one character targets, would be even higher for these sorts of targets.

5. Summary and Conclusion

Of the four devices tested the mouse is clearly the superior device for text selection on a CRT:

1. The positioning time of the mouse is significantly faster than that of the other devices. This is true overall and at every distance and size combination save for single character targets.
2. The error rate of the mouse is significantly lower than that of the other devices.
3. The rate of movement of the mouse is nearly maximal with respect to the information processing capabilities of the eye-hand guidance system.

As a group the continuous movement devices are superior in both speed and error-rate.

For the continuous movement devices, positioning time is given by Fitts's Law. For the key devices it is proportional to the number of keystrokes.

The authors wish to thank J. Elkind, T. Moran, and A. Newell for comments on an earlier draft and E. R. F. W. Crossman for various suggestions.

Quatre dispositifs ont été évalués en fonction de la rapidité de leur utilisation pour une sélection de textes sur l'écran d'un oscilloscope. La balladeuse s'est avérée être la plus précise. On a montré que les variations dans les temps de positionnement avec la balladeuse et le levier de commande pouvaient être expliquées par la loi de Fitts. Dans le cas de la balladeuse, la pente de la droite de Fitts est proche de celle qui a été trouvée dans d'autres tâches de coordination oeil—main, ce qui semble indiquer que le temps de positionnement avec ce dispositif, est le plus court possible. Les temps de positionnement avec des touches est proportionnel au nombre de frappes nécessaires.

Es wurden vier Einrichtungen untersucht, um festzustellen, wie schnell Textstellen auf einem CRT-Display ausgewählt werden können. Die Einrichtung 'mouse' konnte in allen Fällen als die schnellste bei gleichzeitig geringster Fehlerhäufigkeit ermittelt werden. Die Ergebnisse machen deutlich, daß die Variationen der Positionierungszeiten bei den Einrichtungen 'mouse' und 'joystick' dem Gesetz nach Fitts entsprechen. Bei den Untersuchungen mit 'mouse' entsprach die gemessene Funktionskonstante des Fitt-Gesetzes den Konstanten, die bei anderen Auge-Hand-Tätigkeiten gefunden wurden. Diese Tatsache führt zu dem Schluß, daß bei dieser Einrichtung die minimal möglichen Positionierungszeiten erreicht werden. Die Positionierungszeit für Tasteneinrichtungen ist nach den Ergebnissen proportional zur Anzahl notwendiger Tastungen.

References

CRAIK, K. J. W., and VINCE, M. A., 1963, Psychological and physiological aspects of control mechanisms. *Ergonomics*, **6**, 419–440.

DEVOE, D. B., 1967, Alternatives to handprinting in the manual entry of data. *The IEEE Transactions on Human Factors in Electronics*, **HFE-8**, 1, 21–31.

DE JONG, J. R., 1957, The effects of increasing skill on cycle time and its consequences for time standards. *Ergonomics*, **1**, 51–60.

ELKIND, J. I. and SPRAGUE, L. T., 1961, Transmission of information in simple manual control systems. *IRE Transaction on Human Factors in Electronics*, **HFE-2**, 1, 58–60.

ENGLISH, W. K., ENGELBART, D. C., and BERMAN, M. L., 1967, Display-selection techniques for text manipulation. *IEEE Transactions on Human factors in Electronics*, **HFE-8**, 1, 21–31.

FITTS, P. M., 1954, The information capacity of the human motor system in controlling amplitude of movement. *Journal of Experimental Psychology*, **47**, 381–391.

FITTS, P. M., and PETERSON, J. R., 1964, Information capacity of discrete motor responses. *Journal of Experimental Psychology*, **67**, 103–112.

FITTS, P. M., and RADFORD, B., 1966, Information capacity of discrete motor responses under different cognitive sets. *Journal of Experimental Psychology*, **71**, 475–482.

GLENCROSS, D. J., 1977, Control of skilled movement. *Psychological Bulletin*, **84**, 14–29.

GOODWIN, N. C., 1975, Cursor positioning on an electronic display using lightpen, lightgun, or keyboard for three basic tasks. *Human Factors*, **17**, 289–295.

KNIGHT, A. A., and DAGNALL, P. R., 1967, Precision in movements. *Ergonomics*, **10**, 321–330.

POULTON, E. C., 1974, *Tracking Skill and Manual Control* (New York: ACADEMIC PRESS).

PIERCE, J. R., and KARLIN, J. E., 1957, Reading rates and the information rate of the human channel. *Bell System Technical Journal*, **36**, 497–516.

WELFORD, A. T., 1968, *Fundamentals of Skill* (London: METHUEN).

Chapter 9

The Audio Channel

While the audio channel is the primary medium of communication between humans, it is rarely used between human and computer. Yet this is an area in transition, and audio is a useful option in many design situations.

When considering communication with sound, speech generally comes first to mind. Case Study A: The Design of a Voice Messaging System, has already introduced us to one form of speech technology, *message store-and-forward systems*. In this chapter we continue our survey, looking at techniques for *speech synthesis, speaker recognition,* and *speech recognition.* The main reading to supplement our introduction is that by Simpson et al. (1985), which gives an excellent human factors perspective on speech-based interaction. Those interested in suppliers of speech-related technologies are referred to the magazine *Speech Technology*, and to their 1986 Buyer's Guide (Media Dimensions, 1986).

The audio channel is not restricted to speech, but can include a wide variety of audio-based interactions. We see examples of these every day, in such activities as responding to a ringing telephone or whistling for a taxi. Similarly, in computer-mediated interactions, *non-speech audio* can play an important role. Example applications are process control in factories and flight management systems in aircraft. Audio messages in such systems generally fall into one of three categories:

- alarms and warning systems
- status and monitoring indicators
- encoded messages and data

Alarms and warning systems dominate this class of communication. However, video games illustrate the potential of non-speech audio to effectively communicate higher level messages. Just compare an expert game player's score when the audio is turned off with the result when the audio is on. The significant drop in score we expect indicates that the audio conveys strategically critical information; it is more than just an acoustic "lollipop."

If audio is such a powerful and familiar mode of communication, why is it not more commonly used in human-computer interaction? Sometimes, because audio is simply inappropriate in the given context. For example, we can only be attentive to one stream of spoken instructions at a time. Consequently, in cases where we need to control more than one process simultaneously, speech alone is generally not an effective mode of communication. Like all other modes of interaction, audio has strengths and weaknesses that need to be understood. Until this understanding is more complete, audio will continue to be neglected. Finally, audio input and output have presented technical and cost effectiveness difficulties which discouraged their use in most applications. Recently, these problems have been greatly reduced, and audio is now a feasible design alternative.

Besides providing a basic review and literature pointers, we have three main objectives in this chapter:

- to put speech I/O in a realistic perspective
- to show that there is much more to the audio channel than speech input and output

- to emphasize that audio-based communication with computers (including speech) is now technologically and financially feasible

Speech Synthesis

Speech synthesis by computer is the most common used of speech in human-computer interaction. The reason is straightforward: technologies for the synthesis of understandable speech are now readily available, and even come as standard equipment on some personal computers (such as the Commodore Amiga). However, while ''understandable,'' the quality of available speech synthesis technologies varies over a broad range.

As a rule of thumb, the quality of synthetic speech varies with price. The least expensive systems sound like the popular conception of a robot, speaking in a near monotone. On the other hand, high-end systems can capture a relatively realistic range of speech qualities such as gender, inflection, and other more subtle aspects of speech. These differences can be important in many situations, since it has been shown that the demands on voice quality vary with the application (Pisoni, Nusbaum and Greene, 1985). Some of the human-factors of voice quality in text-to-speech systems are discussed in Thomas and Rosson (1984). Rosson and Cecala (1986) show that voice quality plays an important part in the acceptance of systems by users.

Speech output systems fall into three general categories:

- *Phoneme-to-speech:* systems that generate their synthesis from a phonemic description of the desired output
- *Text-to-speech:* systems that convert ASCII text directly into spoken form
- *Stored message:* systems that playback on demand a (usually digitally) pre-recorded spoken message

A large number of speech synthesizers work by implementing an electronic simulation of the vocal tract. Different phonemes can then be synthesized by adjusting the parameters of the simulation in a manner analogous to those observed in a human speaker. In principle, synthesizing speech by describing the desired phonemes to such a system can give excellent results. A good simulation affords a very fine grain of control over the output. This same fine level of control, however, also causes problems due to the large number of parameters that need to be specified.

In order to reduce complexity, many speech synthesis systems add an additional layer. Typically, this layer's input is a file containing text in a high-level language,

such as English. This text is then automatically converted into a phonemic representation, and the appropriate parameters are output to the speech synthesizer. One of the most important characteristics of such systems is the method by which the phonemic description of the text is derived. While some sort of dictionary look-up can be used, this is very expensive in time and storage. More commonly, the description is derived *by rule*. That is, the mapping is defined by a set of rules (usually specified by on the order of 200 productions). The problem with such a mapping, however, is that context and semantics cannot be utilized. Therefore, for example, such systems cannot resolve ambiguities such as how to pronounce words such as ''w-i-n-d.'' Is it what you do to a ball of string or what propels a sailboat?

The whole issue of deriving a phonemic description of a text can be avoided simply by relying upon a data base of stored utterances. If the utterances can be long, and dynamically recorded and played back, we have the basis for a voice store-and-forward messaging system, such as that discussed in Case Study A: The Design of a Voice Messaging System. However, this technology can be used for output-only situations as well.

In some systems, a set of complete messages is stored. Where the number of messages is too large for this, a set of pre-recorded words are stored, and messages are composed by splicing these words together. One example where this technique is used is with the directory information systems used by most North American telephone companies. The difficulty with this approach, however, is in achieving smooth speech by splicing together utterances recorded in isolation. With the telephone information example, different versions of each digit are stored. Which one is used depends on which digit precedes it and which digit follows it. Hence, the justification of such systems must generally be based on the need for high quality, natural sounding speech, not cost, since they are generally expensive and difficult to implement.

The reading by Kaplan and Lerner (1985), ''Realism in Synthetic Speech,'' gives a good overview of speech synthesis systems, the applicable technologies, and their use in applications. Lee and Lochovsky (1983) provide another, yet more expanded, overview.

Speaker Recognition

While not in the mainstream of speech recognition, the identification of individuals from their speech is an active area of research that has relevance to the field of human-computer interaction. The interested reader is directed to Doddington (1985), which gives a survey of this area, and has a good bibliography.

Speech Recognition

Speech recognition systems do just what their name suggests: they recognize spoken words. In this introduction, our first task is to distinguish speech recognition from natural language understanding, since the two are often confused.

Speech recognition detects words from speech. However, the recognition system does not analyze what those words mean. It only recognizes that they are words and what words they are. To be of any further use, these words must be passed on to higher level software for syntactic and semantic analysis. If the spoken words happen to be in the form of natural language (for example English), then they may be passed on to a natural language understanding system. One example of such a system is described in Biermann, Rodman, Rubin and Heidlage (1985). In what follows, we will focus only on the recognition component. Natural language understanding is discussed in Chapter 10: Interaction Styles and Techniques, and in a reading included with that chapter, Rich (1984), "Natural-Language Interfaces."

It is important to understand that the "words" that make up a vocabulary to be recognized need not be words in the normal sense. Rather, speech recognition systems typically work by matching the acoustic pattern of an acoustic signal with the features of a stored template. Within the limits of the system's resolution, these signals can be words, short phrases, whistles, or any other discernible acoustic signal or utterance. (Of course, since they are intended for speech, the pattern matching heuristics are optimized to work with the characteristic features of speech signals.)

Speech recognition systems are not yet in widespread use. Compared to synthesis, recognition is significantly more difficult. Speech input is in common use, however, in applications involving communication with the computer while the hands are otherwise occupied and when a limited vocabulary is sufficient.

Speech recognition systems vary along a number of dimensions:

- *Speaker dependent vs independent:* Does the system have to be trained separately for each different user? At this point, nearly all available systems are speaker dependent and require training.

- *Size of vocabulary:* How many words can the system recognize? Low end systems recognize tens of words while state-of-the-art high-end systems can recognize on the order of 20,000. Increasing the vocabulary can expand the utility of a system. However, it also raises the capital cost and the cost that must be invested in training the system. With some systems, the cost of this training increases with vocabulary size. With others, however, training time is a constant, independent of vocabulary size. The system developed for IBM by Jelinek (1985) is an example.

- *Isolated word vs continuous speech recognition:* One of the hardest problems in speech recognition is determining when one word ends and the next one begins. In order to side-step the problem, most systems force the user to issue single-word-at-a-time commands. Typically, words must be separated by a gap of on the order of 300 milliseconds. Since this is unnatural, speech recognition systems that require multi-word commands may requires special training on the part of the users. One perspective on this is presented in Biermann et al. (1985).

Levinson and Liberman (1981) provide a good introduction to the issues involved in speech recognition. See also the overview of the panel session on voice-based communication which took place at CHI+GI '87 (Aucella et al., 1987). These notes present a fairly broad perspective on the topic in a relatively small amount of space. The comments of Robin Kinkead, for example, provide additional perspective on some of the topics discussed above:

> Continuous versus discrete speech is a non-issue, and yet it is the most hotly debated, claimed and counter-claimed and misunderstood variable in speech recognition. Before the advent of functional large vocabulary systems, it was frequently cited as the single largest barrier to the acceptance of speech recognition by the public. The real issues of accuracy, repeatability of performance, vocabulary size, cost, flexibility, amount of training needed, ease of modification, location of microphone, complete voice control over the system, and performance in variable conditions were frequently dismissed in favour of debate over what has been shown (in studies, in use and in demonstrations) to be a minor point — whether one must speak with pauses between words or not. (Kinkead, in Aucella et al., 1987, p.42)

To get yet another perspective, the reader is referred to Bolt (1984). This book documents a number of studies undertaken at the Media Lab at MIT. One of the most interesting aspects of the systems described is how they integrate different media, not just voice, into a single system. Perhaps most impressive is that these "futuristic" interfaces were made using essentially "over-the-counter" technologies.

There are a number of interesting articles on speech recognition in a special issue of the *Proceedings of the IEEE* (November, 1985). In that issue, for example, Jelinek (1985) describes a state-of-the-art recognition system developed by IBM that has a 5000 word vocabulary. In the same issue, Levinson (1985) addresses structural issues affecting speech recognition, and Zue (1985) discusses some knowledge-based techniques.

While we are waiting for speech recognition to come of age, there is some debate as to how useful it will actually be. There are a number of studies which have investigated the use of speech in office systems. These include Allen (1983), Gould (1982), Gould and Alfaro (1984) and Gould, Conti and Hovanyecz (1983).

The Gould, Conti and Hovanyecz study investigates the potential of composing letters with a listening typewriter. Its results suggest that large vocabulary, isolated word recognition may provide the basis for a useful listening typewriter.

Perhaps as interesting to the student of human-computer interaction is the methodology used in this study. Since a practical listening typewriter was not available, the authors *simulated* one by having a subject's speech transcribed by a human, and echoed back to the subject on a CRT. The study stands as a good example of using limited resources to test the validity of an idea before making a heavy investment in its development.

Non-Speech Audio

Unless we are hearing impaired, we all use non-speech audio cues on a daily basis all of our lives. Crossing the street, answering the phone, diagnosing problems with a car engine, and whistling for the dog are all common examples. Despite the widespread use of this rich mode of interaction in other aspects of our lives, it has had little impact on our interaction with computers. This need not be so; there are significant benefits to be reaped by developing these capabilities.

Perhaps the most common application of non-speech audio has been in alarms and warning systems. To be effective, however, the meaning of each signal must be known to the intended listener. Just as in any other language, theses signals constitute a learned vocabulary. We are not born knowing the meaning of a fog horn, fire alarm, or police siren. If audio cues are to be used in interactive systems, then their design is of utmost importance. As graphic design is to effective icons (see Chapter 7: The Visual Channel), so acoustic design is to effective auditory signs, or *earcons*.

Earcon design ranges from systems built on an existing vocabulary to systems that employ a newly designed vocabulary. The former can reduce the amount of learning required to use the system. However, the extent to which existing acoustic signs can be used remains to be seen. The application of fog horn and fire alarm sounds to computer applications is rather limited. On the other hand, Gaver (1986) has presented some compelling examples which make effective use of the existing "world knowledge" of the acoustic environment. One

makes use of our association of reverberation with empty space. Gaver proposes that if there were a reverberant "clunk" when we saved a file, then the amount of reverberation would provide a good clue as to how much free space was left on the disk. Similarly, on the Apple Macintosh for example, placing a file in the "trash can" could be accompanied by an appropriate "tinny crash."

On first impression, such uses of the audio channel to provide feedback may seem frivolous or unnecessary. However, as soon as we consider the special needs of the visually impaired or those working in critical applications where such encoding can reduce the risk of error, the value of the approach is clear.

New, non-representational audio cues require more learning on the part of the user. These are to Gaver's examples what the international road-sign for *no entrance* (red disk with horizontal white bar) is to the "trash can" icon on the Macintosh computer. The former is abstract and newly learned, the latter is representational and built on existing knowledge.

Whichever approach is taken, the design must be carefully executed. The raw materials of audio design, comparable to colour and line-type in graphic design, are:

- *pitch:* the primary basis for traditional melody
- *rhythm:* relative changes in the timing of the attacks of successive events
- *tempo:* the speed of events
- *dynamics:* the relative loudness of events (static or varying)
- *timbre:* the difference of spectral content and energy over time — that which differentiates a saxophone from a flute
- *location:* where the sound is coming from

One area in which we can gain insight into the use of non-speech audio to communicate concrete concepts is musical. Examples might include the use of *leitmotiv* in Wagner's operas, or Prokofiev's use of musical themes to identify the characters of Peter and the Wolf. These examples show that humans can learn and make effective use of "abstract" audio cues. With no disrespect to Prokofiev, his is exactly the type of audio cue that has been effectively applied in the video game *Pacman*. On the other hand, the example of Wagner's operas demonstrates the need to "know the user." If you are not already familiar with the musical themes, they remain abstract references which will be lost on you.

While missing a few references in an opera is not life threatening, the same may not be true if the context is piloting an aircraft or monitoring a nuclear power plant. In the Three Mile Island power plant crisis, over 60 different auditory warning systems were activated (Sanders and McCormick, 1987, p. 155). If audio cues are to be employed, they must be clear and easily differentiable. They can be effective, but like all parts of the system, they require careful design and testing.

There is ample literature from which the designer can obtain useful guidelines about the use of non-speech audio cues. Three excellent sources are Deatherage (1972), Kantowitz and Sorkin (1983), and Sanders and McCormick (1987). Each uses the term *audio display* to describe this use of the audio channel. Figure 1 summarizes Deatherage's view on when to use audio displays rather than visual ones.

Use auditory presentation if:	Use visual presentation if:
1. The message is simple.	1. The message is complex.
2. The message is short.	2. The message is long.
3. The message will not be referred to later.	3. The message will be referred to later.
4. The message deals with events in time.	4. The message deals with location in space.
5. The message calls for immediate action.	5. The message does not call for immediate action.
6. The visual system of the person is overburdened.	6. The auditory system of the person is overburdened.
7. The receiving location is too bright or dark-adaptation integrity is necessary.	7. The receiving location is too noisy.
8. The person's job requires him to move about continually.	8. The person's job allows him to remain in one position.

Figure 1: When to Use Audio or Visual Displays. *Guidelines for determining whether to adopt the audio or the visual channel in displaying information (from Deatherage, 1972, p. 124).*

Perhaps the prime attribute of computer-generated audio output is that messages can be conveyed without making use of the visual channel. Visual messages must be seen to be understood. Audio messages are received regardless of where one is looking. This is of particular importance when the visual channel is focussed elsewhere, or when the task does not require constant visual monitoring. When the amount of information to be conveyed is high, pushing the visual channel to the limits, the audio channel can also be used to carry some of the information, thereby reducing overall load.

Recently, some researchers have been expanding upon the use of sound in interactive applications. This work, some of which is summarized in the reading by Buxton, Bly, et al. (1985), ''Communicating with Sound,'' includes the aural presentation of graphs, and the presentation of multi-dimensional statistical data. This is an area which has even more potential, and it deserves a great deal more research interest.

In the past, one of the biggest problems in exploring the use of audio signals was a logistical one. In her research, for example, Bly had to build special hardware and interface it to her computer. Some important recent developments have changed this situation dramatically. The change is a technological one resulting from the the music industry adopting a standard protocol for interfacing electronic sound synthesis and processing equipment to computers. This standard is known as *MIDI*, the Musical Instrument Digital Interface. As a result of this standard, a wide range of equipment and interfaces are now available to the researcher. In addition to the specification (IMA, 1983), an excellent general introduction to MIDI can be found in Loy (1985). Cummings and Milano (1986) give a brief introduction to MIDI and provide references to suppliers of MIDI interfaces and related hardware.

Perception and Psychoacoustics

In the preceding, we have discussed the importance of design in the use of acoustic stimuli to communicate information. One of the main resources to be aware of in pursuing such design is the available literature on psychoacoustics and the psychology of music.

Psychoacoustics tells us a great deal about the relationship between perception and the physical properties of acoustic signals. Music and the psychology of music tell us a lot about the human ability to compose and understand higher level sonic structures. In particular, the literature is quite extensive in addressing issues such as the perception of pitch, duration, and loudness of acoustic signals. It is also fairly good at providing an understanding of *masking,* a phenomenon in which one sound (for example, noise) obscures another (such as an alarm or a voice). Information at this level is available in any first-year psychology textbook. Those looking for more detailed information are referred to Scharf and Buus (1986), Scharf and Houtsma (1986), Hawkins and Presson (1986), Evans and Wilson (1977), Tobias (1970), and Carterette and Friedman (1978).

One aspect of perception not covered in the above publications is signal detection theory. This self-descriptive topic has been an important part of the classical human factors approach to audio signals. Works that address the topic at an introductory level are Sanders and McCormick (1987), Deatherage (1972), and Kantowitz and Sorkin (1983).

Under a different name, acoustic design has had a thriving life as music. While music perception is not a part of main-stream human factors, it does have something to contribute. In particular, classic psychoacoustics has dealt primarily with simple stimuli. Music, on the other hand, is concerned with larger structures. Melodic recognition and the perception and understanding of simultaneous auditory streams (as in counterpoint) is of great relevance to audio's use in the human-computer interface. As a reference to this aspect of auditory perception, we recommend Deutsch (1982, 1986) and Roederer (1975).

The audio channel is underutilized in human-computer interaction. Many users may feel that compared with other areas of research, it is just not worth developing. However, one need only consider visually impaired users to realize that the need is compelling. It becomes even more so when we come to the realization that in some (often critical) situations, all of us are visually impaired, perhaps due to the visual system being saturated, loss of light, or age. This is an area that must receive more attention. With MIDI and the widespread availability of personal computers, there is now no excuse for the omission.

Readings

Simpson, C.A., McCauley, M.E., Roland, E.F., Ruth, J.C., & Williges, B.H. (1985). System Design for Speech Recognition and Generation. *Human Factors* 27(2), 115-141.

Kaplan, G. & Lerner, E.J. (1985). Realism in Synthetic Speech. *IEEE Spectrum* 22(4), 32-37.

Buxton, W., Bly, S., et al. (1985). Communicating with Sound. *Proceedings of CHI '85*, 115-119.

References/Bibliography

Allen, R.B. (1983). Composition and Editing of Spoken Letters. *International Journal of Man-Machine Studies* 19, 181-193.

Allen, J. (1985). A Perspective on Man-Machine Communication by Speech. *Proceedings of the IEEE* 73(11), 1541-1550.

Aucella, A., Kinkead, R., Schmandt, C. & Wichansky, A. (1987). Voice: Technology Searching for Communication Needs. Panel Summary, *Proceedings of CHI+GI '87*, 41-44.

Bailey, P. (1984). Speech Communication: The Problem and Some Solutions. In Monk, A. (Ed.), *Fundamentals of Human-Computer Interaction*, London: Academic Press, 193-220.

Biermann, A., Rodman, R., Rubin, D. & Heidlage, J. (1985). Natural Language with Discrete Speech as a Mode for Human-to-Machine Communication. *Communications of the ACM* 28(6), 628-636.

Buxton, W., Bly, S. et al. (1985). Communicating with Sound. *Proceedings of CHI '85*, 115-119.

Bolt, R. A. (1984). *The Human interface: Where People and Computers Meet*, London: Lifetime Learning Publications.

Carterette, E. & Friedman, M. (Eds.) (1978). *Hearing, Handbook of Perception, Volume IV*, New York: Academic Press.

Cummings, S. & Milano, D. (1986). Computer to MIDI Interfaces. *Keyboard Magazine*, January 1986, 41-44.

Deatherage, B. H. (1972). Auditory and Other Sensory Forms of Information Presentation. In Van Cott, H. P. & Kinkade, R. G. (Eds), *Human Engineering Guide to Equipment Design, Revised Edition*, Washington: U.S. Government Printing Office.

Deutsch, D. (Ed.) (1982). *The Psychology of Music*, New York: Academic Press.

Deutsch, D. (1986). Auditory Pattern Recognition. In K.R. Boff, L. Kaufman & J.P. Thomas (Eds.), *Handbook of Perception and Human Performance*, II, New York: John Wiley & Sons, 32.1-32.49.

Doddington, G.R. (1985). Speaker Recognition - Identifying People by their Voices. *Proceedings of the IEEE* 73(11), 1651-1664.

Evans, E. & Wilson, J. (Eds.) (1977). *Psychophysics and Physiology of Hearing*, New York: Academic Press.

Fallside, F. & Woods, W. (1985). *Computer Speech Processing*, Englewood Cliffs: Prentice-Hall.

Flanagan, J.L. (1976). Computers that Talk and Listen: Man-Machine Communication by Voice. *Proceedings of the IEEE* 64(4), 405-415.

Gaver, W. (1986). Auditory Icons: Using Sound in Computer Interfaces. *Human Computer Interaction* 2(2), 167-177.

Gould, J.D. (1982). Writing and Speaking Letters and Messages. *International Journal of Man-Machine Studies*, 147-171.

Gould, J.D. & Alfaro, L. (1984). Revising Documents with Text Editors, Handwriting Recognition Systems, and Speech-Recognition Systems. *Human Factors* 26(4), 391-406.

Gould, J.D. & Boies, S.J. (1984). Speech Filing — An Office System for Principals. *IBM Systems Journal* 23(1), 65-81.

Gould, J.D., Conti, J. & Hovanyecz, T. (1983). Composing Letters with a Simulated Listening Typewriter. *Communications of the ACM* 26(4), 295-308.

Hawkins, H.L. & Presson, J.C. (1986). Auditory Information Processing. In K.R. Boff, L. Kaufman & J.P. Thomas (Eds.), *Handbook of Perception and Human Performance*, Volume II, New York: John Wiley & Sons, 26.1-26.64.

IMA (1983). *MIDI Musical Instrument Digital Interface Specification 1.0*, IMA, 11857 Hartsook St., North Hollywood, CA., 91607.

Jelinek, F. (1985). The Development of an Experimental Discrete Dictation Recognizer. *Proceedings of the IEEE* 73(11), 1616-1624.

Jusczyk, P.W. (1986). Speech Perception. In K.R. Boff, L. Kaufman & J.P. Thomas (Eds.), *Handbook of Perception and Human Performance*, II, New York: John Wiley & Sons, 27.1-27.57.

Kaplan, G. & Lerner, E. J. (1985). Realism in Synthetic Speech. *IEEE Spectrum* 22(4), 32-37.

Kantowitz, B. & Sorkin, R. (1983). *Human Factors: Understanding People-System Relationships*, New York: John Wiley & Sons.

Lee, D. L. & Lochovsky, F. H. (1983). Voice Response Systems. *ACM Computing Surveys* 15(4), 351-374.

Levinson, S. E. (1985). Structural Methods in Automatic Speech Recognition. *Proceedings of the IEEE* 73(11), 1625-1650.

Levinson, S. E. & Liberman, M. (1981). Speech Recognition by Computer. *Scientific American* 244(4), 64-76.

Loy, G. (1985). Musicians Make a Standard: The MIDI Phenomenon. *Computer Music Journal* 9(4), 8-26.

Media Dimensions (1986). 1986 Voice Processing Market Directory. *Speech Technology,* Media Dimensions Inc., 42 East 23rd St., New York, NY 10010, Mar./April 1986, 111-124.

Michaelis, P.R. & Wiggins, R.H. (1982). A Human Factors Engineer's Introduction to Speech Synthesizers. In Badre, A. & Shneiderman, B. (Eds.), *Directions in Human-Computer Interaction,* Norwood, N.J., Ablex Publishing Corp., 149-178.

Pisoni, D.B., Nusbaum, H.C. & Greene, B.G. (1985). Perception of Synthetic Speech Generated by Rule. *Proceedings of the IEEE* 73(11), 1665-1671.

Rich, E. (1984). Natural-Language Interfaces. *IEEE Computer,* 39-47.

Roederer, Juan G. (1975). *Introduction to the Physics and Psychophysics of Music,* Second Edition, New York: Springer-Verlag.

Rosson, M.B. & Cecala, A.J. (1986). Designing a Quality Voice: An Analysis of Listeners' Reactions to Synthetic Voices. *Proceedings of CHI '86,* 192-197.

Sanders, M. S. & McCormick, E. J. (1987). *Human Factors in Engineering and Design,* Sixth Edition, New York: McGraw-Hill.

Scharf, B. & Buus, S. (1986). Audition I: Stimulus, Physiology, Thresholds. In K.R. Boff, L. Kaufman & J.P. Thomas (Eds.), *Handbook of Perception and Human Performance,* Volume I, New York: John Wiley & Sons, 14.1-14.71.

Schraf, B. & Houtsma, A.J.M. (1986). Audition II: Loudness, Pitch, Localization, Aural Distortion, Pathology. In K.R. Boff, L. Kaufman & J.P. Thomas (Eds.), *Handbook of Perception and Human Performance,* Volume I, New York: John Wiley & Sons, 15.1-15.60.

Schmandt, C. (1985). Voice Communication with Computers. In H.R. Hartson (Ed.), *Advances in Human-Computer Interaction,* Norwood, N.J.: Ablex Publishing, 133-160.

Simpson, C.A., McCauley, M.E., Roland, E.F., Ruth, J.C. & Willeges, B.H. (1985). System Design for Speech Recognition and Generation. *Human Factors* 27(2), 115-141.

Thomas, J. & Rosson, M. B. (1984). Human Factors and Synthetic Speech. *Proceedings of the Human Factors Society* 2, 763-767.

Tobias, J. (Ed.) (1970). *Foundations of Modern Auditory Theory,* Volumes I & II, New York: Academic Press.

Wallich, Paul (1987). Putting Speech Recognizers to Work. *IEEE Spectrum* 24(4), 55-57.

Waterworth, J. (1984). Speech Communication: How to Use It. In Monk, A. (Ed.), *Fundamentals of Human-Computer Interaction,* London: Academic Press, 221-236.

Zue, V.W. (1985). The Use of Speech Knowledge in Automatic Speech Recognition. *Proceedings of the IEEE* 73(11), 1602-1615.

System Design for Speech Recognition and Generation

CAROL A. SIMPSON,[1] *Psycho-Linguistic Research Associates, Menlo Park, California,* MICHAEL E. McCAULEY, *Monterey Technologies, Inc., Carmel, California,* ELLEN F. ROLAND, *Rolands and Associates Corporation, Monterey, California,* JOHN C. RUTH, *McDonnell-Douglas Electronics Co., St. Charles, Missouri, and* BEVERLY H. WILLIGES, *Virginia Polytechnic Institute and State University, Blacksburg, Virginia*

This article reviews human factors research on the design of systems that use speech recognition for human control of the system or that use speech generation for the display of information. Speech technology terms are defined and the current status of the field is reviewed. Included are the performance of current speech recognition and generation algorithms, descriptions of several applications of the technology to particular tasks, and a discussion of research on design principles for speech interfaces. Finally, directions for further research are suggested. The need for better simulation techniques and performance measures is stressed, as is the importance of considering the entire system in which speech technology will function.

INTRODUCTION

Language is one of the outstanding capabilities of humans. Human-machine systems have long included written language (e.g., alphanumeric displays and keyboards), but spoken language has been used only for interpersonal communications. Automatic speech recognition and speech generation by machine now offer the promise of person-system transactions via spoken language. Speech input/output (I/O) systems accept spoken input (speech controls), or they "display" information to the user by means of the spoken word (speech displays). Automatic speech technology is of interest

within the human factors community because of its potential as a tool to help the human operator to perform certain tasks. Its potential lies in reducing or reallocating operator workload by providing an alternative I/O channel to the normally overloaded visual-manual channel. But it is only a tool, not a panacea, for the overloaded operator.

The challenge to the human factors field is to determine when, where, and how automated speech technology should be used in person-system transactions. This challenge is formidable because the technology is evolving, and guidelines for its application will depend on many variables. These variables include the characteristics of the users, the physical environment, the communications environment, the operator's workload,

the constraints imposed by the task, and the stress on the operator.

In general, the strategy for the human factors contribution to the field of speech-interactive systems is three-pronged: (1) to provide methodologies for identifying appropriate applications of speech technology. (2) to select appropriate speech recognition or generation algorithms and system characteristics, and (3) to integrate speech subsystems within the context of the user's task. The current state of the art provides some but not all of the procedures with which to implement this strategy. By their absence, the missing pieces suggest directions for future research.

TERMS AND DEFINITIONS

A human-machine control and display system is composed of a human, a machine, one or more controls, one or more displays, and an environment (Chapanis, 1976). A *voice-interactive system* is one that includes speech recognition as one form of user control or information input, and speech generation as one form of information display. There will also be systems that use one but not both of these technologies.

A superficial examination of the terminology in speech recognition and in speech generation obscures the commonality of concepts in these two technologies, which are, in many respects, mirror images of each other.

Speech Recognition Terms

From a human factors perspective, a *speech-recognition system* is composed of a human speaker, a recognition algorithm, and a device that responds appropriately to the recognized speech. The algorithm recognizes different human speech utterances and translates them into symbol strings. Those utterances could be words, phrases, or, at a lower level, syllables or *phonemes*—the vowel and consonant sounds of the language. The device assigns meaning to the symbol strings in the context of the human's task.

The term *voice recognition* is sometimes used interchangeably with the term *speech recognition*, leading to confusion with the related technology of speaker identification or voice identification. Speaker identification is the automatic identification of a given human speaker. To avoid such confusion, this paper will use the term *speech recognition* exclusively.

Speaker dependence. Speech recognition systems vary with respect to several parameters. Speaker dependence refers to the extent to which the system must have data about the voice characteristics of the particular human speaker(s) using it. *Speaker-dependent* recognition systems can recognize the speech of a particular human speaker only if examples of that person's speech have been provided. The vast majority of speech-recognition systems are speaker dependent. *Speaker-independent* systems theoretically can recognize speech spoken by any human in a particular language. Speaker-independent voice recognition is available for small vocabulary sets of from 10 to 20 utterances. In practice, recognition accuracy depends on the similarity of the speech characteristics of the group of users that use the system. So-called speaker-independent systems could be said to be *group dependent.* The less variability among speakers in the user group, the better will be the average recognition accuracy for the group using the system. Speech spoken with a foreign accent, for example, is less reliably recognized than is speech spoken with the accent for which the system has been developed. Also, in practice, it is difficult for a speaker-independent system to recognize both male and female speech (Rollins, 1984).

Speech variability. Linguists recognize at least five levels of variability in spoken language, including language families, individual languages, dialects, idiolects, and variations in the speech of individual speakers over time. The categorization of dialects themselves is multidimensional and

[1] Requests for reprints should be sent to Carol A. Simpson, Psycho-Linguistic Research Associates, 2055 Sterling Ave. Menlo Park, CA 94025.

can be made geographically, by social class, by age, and even by neighborhood (for an introduction to dialectology, see Allen and Underwood, 1971). An *idiolect* is the speech of a single individual. An ideolect varies over time as a function of physiological, psychological, and sociological factors. Similar idiolects can be grouped according to various dimensions, for example, sex, accent, or dialect.

The current practice that distinguishes between speaker-dependent and speaker-independent systems grossly simplifies the range of speaker variability. Even speaker-dependent systems will recognize people who have not enrolled the system, but the recognition accuracy will be poor. The distinction between speaker-dependent and speaker-independent systems is based largely on the engineering strategy for establishing templates. It belies the range of variability in speech and the factors that account for varying amounts of the variability, such as regional accent, sex, stress/workload, and fear. Human speech variability and large vocabulary size are two major challenges for speech-recognition systems. Advances in these areas will depend on fundamental research in linguistics at all levels of language structure (Fujimura, 1984).

Speaking mode. Another parameter of recognition systems is the speaking mode, the manner in which utterances are spoken to the system (National Research Council [NRC], 1984). *Isolated word systems* are most prevalent. With isolated word systems, the user must pause briefly (approximately 100 ms) between vocabulary items when speaking to the system. *Connected word systems* are able to recognize words within utterances spoken without artificial pauses between words. However, the individual words are spoken with the same intonation pattern that would be used if they were read from a list. The term *connected word recognition* has often been used to refer to what is here called *continuous*

speech recognition is reserved for recognition of utterances spoken with natural speech rhythm and intonation (prosodics). The final term, *continuous speech understanding* adds another dimension to the recognition task. It has been used to refer to systems that attempt to accomplish tasks using continuous speech input (see NRC, 1984).

Vocabulary size. A third parameter is vocabulary size. Speech-recognition systems with *fixed vocabulary* must be provided with samples of each word or phrase they are to recognize. They perform acoustic pattern matching at the word and phrase level and typically handle vocabularies of from 100 to 200 utterances (Kersteen and Damos, 1983). Algorithms are under development for *unlimited vocabulary* systems that analyze the speech into phonetic segments, determine the words spoken, and perhaps generate correctly spelled text.

Enrollment. A fourth parameter is the type of enrollment. Enrollment is the process of providing templates to the recognition system for the different vocabulary items. Speaker-dependent systems must be enrolled separately for each speaker who will use them if good recognition accuracy is to be obtained. Most systems provide a procedure for *user enrollment.* Some systems are more flexible than others in the permissible procedures. Speaker-independent systems, in contrast, may be designed for *vendor enrollment.* This means that the vendor develops the templates that the vendor believes will result in the best speaker-independent recognition accuracy. Some researchers have turned speaker-dependent systems into group-dependent or quasi-speaker-independent systems by means of creative enrollment procedures (e.g., Poock, Schwalm, Martin, and Roland, 1982).

Speech-Generation Terms

A speech-generation system is the mirror image of a recognition system. It is composed

of a device that generates messages in the form of symbol strings, a speech-generation algorithm that converts the symbol strings to an acoustic imitation of speech, and a human listener. A speech-generation system operates in the context of the user's task environment.

Method of generation. Speech generation systems, like recognition systems, vary with respect to several parameters. One is the method of speech generation. The two primary methods are synthesized and digitized speech. *Synthesized speech* refers to speech generated entirely by rule, without the aid of an original human recording. The term *digitized speech* applies to human speech that was originally recorded digitally, and then (usually) transformed into a more compressed data format. The most common compression techniques include, but are not limited to, Fourier Transform, Linear Predictive Coding (LPC), and Waveform Parameter Encoding. Another pair of terms used to describe these methods are *synthesis by rule* for speech synthesis and *synthesis by analysis* for digitized speech generation that uses a data compression technique (Flanagan, 1972).

Vocabulary size. Another parameter is vocabulary size. Speech generation systems can have a *fixed vocabulary* or an *unlimited vocabulary.* Fixed vocabulary systems contain a set of words or phrases that can be combined to produce messages. Unlimited vocabulary systems can produce an unlimited number of messages from normally spelled text, from phonemes, or from phonetic segments (Simpson, 1981a; 1981c). Digitized speech systems are limited to fixed vocabularies. Synthesized speech systems can have either a fixed or an unlimited vocabulary. Fixed vocabulary systems are *user programmable* only if the user can change the vocabulary items. They are *vendor programmable* if the user must rely on the manufacturer or some other third party for new vocabulary.

Voice type. Digitized speech systems can have an unlimited variety of different voices,

since they depend on human speakers for their vocabulary. However, once a particular speaker has been selected for an application, the digitized speech system, in order to sound consistent, is dependent on that same human speaker for new vocabulary. Synthesized speech systems do not depend on a human speaker for new vocabulary, but the number of different voice types than can be obtained from a given system is limited and varies currently from one to about six. Most synthesized voices can be varied under program control with respect to fundamental frequency (perceived as voice pitch) and speaking rate. Most commercially available synthesizers produce male-sounding speech although a few also produce female-sounding speech. With software control of the pronunciation of individual phonemes, some variation in dialect or accent can be obtained. For reviews of the commercially available speech-generation devices see Butler, Manaker and Obert-Thorn (1981), Sherwood (1979), Simpson (1981a), and Smith (1984).

Data rate, intelligibility, and naturalness. Three parameters often used to evaluate speech-generation systems are *data rate, intelligibility,* and *naturalness.* Data-rate terms are often confusing in the speech product literature because they can refer either to the amount of storage needed to store speech data or to the rate at which speech data are transmitted to the speech device or to the rate at which the resulting speech is actually spoken (Simpson, 1983b). The terms naturalness and intelligibility often are confused in today's product literature and, unfortunately, in the scientific literature as well. The term *intelligibility* has a very precise meaning—the percentage of speech units correctly recognized by a human listener out of a set of such units. The units may be words, sentences, individual speech sounds (called phonemes), or even the perceptual acoustic features of those phonemes. (See Kryter [1972] for a review of intelligibility testing.) *Naturalness* refers to a listener's judgment on a scale of the degree to which the speech sounds as though it were spoken by a human. Intelligibility and naturalness can be measured independently, although there are no standarized tests of naturalness (Simpson, 1983b). Further, naturalness and intelligibility are not necessarily correlated (cf. Thomas, Rosson, and Chodorow, 1984). For example, a radio announcer may sound natural in a background of static noise, but the speech may have low intelligibility. Conversely, synthesized speech warning messages that are well-known to a pilot may sound mechanical, yet pilots have rated such messages as seeming more intelligible than are human voice messages transmitted via aircraft radio (Simpson, 1983b; Simpson and Williams, 1980).

Measures of Algorithm Performance

Recognition accuracy is the most commonly used measure of performance for speech recognition algorithms. Its counterpart is speech intelligibility, which is the most commonly used performance measure for speech generation algorithms. Both measures are simply the percentage of speech utterances correctly recognized by the "listener" out of a set of such utterances presented under a particular set of listening conditions. When measuring recognition accuracy, the "listener" is the recognition algorithm. Conversely, human listeners are used to measure the intelligibility of speech generated by algorithm.

The classes of errors that occur when speech is presented to either humans or machines are the same, but human and machine performance may differ substantially. Errors fall into one of four mutually exclusive categories: (1) substitution errors (one utterance from the vocabulary is mistaken for another), (2) insertion errors (an utterance is reported that was not spoken), (3) deletion errors (an utterance that was spoken was not reported),

and (4) rejection errors (an utterance that is a legal item in the vocabulary is detected but not recognized). Rejection errors are frequently reported in the speech recognition literature. They are not reported as such in the speech intelligibility literature but occur when the subject responds with "don't know."

Both machines and humans also can make correct rejections. For machines (i.e., recognition algorithms), a correct rejection is made when the algorithm refuses to process an utterance that is not in the legal vocabulary, for example, if the user coughed or said something to another human in the work environment. Similarly, human listeners will correctly reject utterances spoken in an unfamiliar foreign language, and, under conditions of poor signal-to-noise ratio, they will also correctly reject nonsense words in their own language and often will then substitute a word that makes sense (Garnes and Bond, 1977, as reported in Bond and Garnes, 1980). This human capability (to substitute a word that makes sense) requires knowledge of syntax, semantics, and pragmatics that is well beyond that found in commercially available speech recognition systems (Fujimura, 1984; NRC, 1984).

Although intelligibility and recognition accuracy are conceptually identical, the performance of speech generation algorithms speaking to human listeners is quantitatively and qualitatively different from the performance of speech recognition algorithms "listening" to human speakers. Accordingly, the remainder of this article treats separately research on speech recognition, on speech generation, and on the integration of recognition and generation into voice-interactive systems.

SPEECH RECOGNITION RESEARCH

In the introduction, a three-pronged strategy for human factors effort in auto-

matic speech technology was stated. Two of the three levels, namely, (1) identification of speech recognition applications, and (2) selection of appropriate recognition system characteristics, will be the subject of this section on speech recognition research. The third, integration of speech subsystems within the user's task, will be discussed in the section on system integration.

Applications

Selection of test-beds for speech technology has not been systematic. Nevertheless, the application research has proven useful in helping to identify characteristics of appropriate applications, potential human-machine interaction problems, required system capabilities, and the need for an integrated systems approach to incorporating speech-recognition systems. A number of application examples (e.g., Breaux, 1977; Grady, 1982; McCauley and Semple, 1980; McCauley, Root, and Muckler, 1982; Moore, Moore, and Ruth, 1984; Poock and Roland, 1984), reviewed in NRC (1984), provide a cross section of attempted applications of speech-recognition technology.

Observations from case studies. A review of these and other case studies leads to some observations about speech recognition technology and its integration into operational systems, condensed here from the NRC (1984) report. (1) Recognition accuracy was one of the main limitations. (2) The variability in human speech under stressful conditions contributed to unacceptable performance. (3) The success of voice-interactive systems in most applications arose from their integration with other procedures or automation features. (4) Projects designed from inception to incorporate a voice-interactive system had a greater probability of success than when the capability was added to an existing system. (5) Highly connected systems that de-

pend on accurate speech recognition input tended to amplify the effects of recognition errors. (6) A staged process of voice-interactive system development, including regular checks and tests by users, was more likely to lead to successful systems. (7) Speaker enrollment (in a speaker-dependent system) was sometimes more effective when conducted in the context of the operational task. (8) Other voice-communication functions in the task environment sometimes interfered with the speech recognition task. (9) For externally paced tasks, the timing of the task sequence was disrupted by either long recognition time or recognition errors. (10) The lack of an appropriate recognition feedback mechanism tended to confuse operators regarding the status of the system.

Speech Recognition Task Selection

One compelling reason to incorporate speech recognition into complex systems is the potential for reducing the visual-manual task load. However, the decision to use speech for a particular task requires a matching of speech mode features with task characteristics (Simpson, 1984) and analysis of the advantages and constraints of the manual mode versus the speech mode in the context of the tasks to be performed (North and Lea, 1982).

The research on task selection has been conducted on two major fronts. Some researchers have aimed to develop and apply methodologies for selecting appropriate tasks for speech (North and Lea, 1982) and user-preference questionnaires for application of voice recognition and speech generation (Brown, Bertone, and Obermeyer, 1968; Cotton, McCauley, North, and Strieb, 1983; Kersteen and Damos, 1983; Williams and Simpson, 1976). Others have investigated human speech data-entry performance when simultaneous verbal and manual tasks are required (e.g., Wickens, Sandry, and Vidulich 1983).

One study determined that speech is useful primarily for complex tasks requiring cognitive and/or visual effort, whereas simple tasks involving the copying of numeric data were accomplished more quickly and accurately with keyboard entry as compared with voice entry (Welch, 1977). A series of dual-task tracking and data-entry studies (Coler, Plummer, Huff, and Hitchcock, 1977; Simpson, Coler, and Huff, 1982) conducted in the presence of helicopter noise and helicopter motion, respectively, found that, across all noise and motion conditions, tracking performance was less degraded with data entry by speech recognition than it was with data entry by keyboard. Recognition accuracy and keyboard accuracy for the no-noise and no-motion conditions were 99%. Recognition accuracy, however, declined slightly in the presence of noise and motion whereas keyboard accuracy did not. Another study found that in the presence of a simultaneous verbal task, voice data entry resulted in less decrement in tracking performance than did keyed data entry (Harris, North, and Owens, 1977). However, it has also been found that recognition error rates can increase by as much as 39% with concurrent tracking, suggesting that task stress has a sufficiently large effect on human speech production to degrade recognition accuracy (Armstrong, 1980).

Research comparing speed and accuracy of voice versus manual keyboard input has produced conflicting results, depending on the unit of input (alphanumerics or functions) and other task-specific variables. For example, one study on the use of voice input to a computerized war game concluded that the manual method of entry was faster than voice input (McSorley, 1981). Another study, conducted in the same laboratory, to assess speech recognition for operation of a distrib-uted network system, showed speech input to be superior to manual entry with regard to both speed and accuracy (Poock, 1981a). These different results were primarily attributed to task requirements, since the majority of other factors (user group composition, training, equipment, and environment) were constant. The results of these several studies suggest that the benefit to be derived from voice input and output is highly dependent on the specific task and environment.

In summary, the selection of potential tasks for speech recognition should be based on specific task requirements. Speech is not a useful substitute for manual data entry when such tasks already are being performed successfully (Welch, 1977). Speech input is likely to improve system throughput only in complex tasks that involve high cognitive, visual, and manual loading. Such limits on improvements to system throughput using the speech mode are likely to exist irrespective of any future improvements in the technology of speech itself. These characteristics and their implications will be discussed in detail in the next section on system integration. Clearly, more research is needed to better understand the complex interaction of the speech mode, voice-recognition technology, the user, and the task being accomplished.

Methods and guidelines are needed for identifying tasks that are amenable for speech recognition applications. Interview and questionnaire techniques are helpful but they are limited in predictive power because the potential user community is familiar with their job but naive with respect to the capabilities and limitations of speech technology. Finally, no analytic procedure for selecting speech tasks is likely to be accurate enough to enable detailed specification of the speech system requirements. Further work is needed on simulation techniques to establish the speech system requirements early in the system design process. This will be discussed in the next section on the second level of the research strategy, the selection of recognition system characteristics.

Selecting Speech Recognition System Characteristics

Given an appropriate task for the speech mode and given a set of performance requirements for the application system that will incorporate that speech task, the characteristics of the speech recognition system must be carefully selected. The algorithm, the human operator, and the interface that links them are all components of the speech recognition system for which the proper characteristics are to be chosen. Therefore, research on algorithm performance and on human-system performance is essential to recognition system selection. Research to date has documented a variety of factors that affect recognition system performance.

Speech recognition algorithm performance. Many factors influence recognition accuracy. They can be viewed in terms of the characteristics of the physical speech signal itself and the context in which it is spoken. Today's recognition algorithms, however, are for the most part unable to take advantage of the pragmatic and linguistic context of an utterance. And, their performance is far more fragile than humans' listening performance with respect to degradations or changes in the speech signal or the physical context in which it is spoken. Currently, speaker-dependent isolated-word systems can perform in the laboratory with vocabularies of up to 100 words with an error rate of less than 1%. However, recognizer performance demonstrated favorably in the laboratory often degrades dramatically under the effects of noise, user stress, and operational demands on the user (NRC, 1984).

User characteristics. User characteristics can affect speech recognition system perfor-mance. Successful applications of speech recognition to date usually involve a small number of carefully selected talkers who have been trained to speak distinctly and to use the equipment correctly. Doddington and Schalk (1981) reported that three-fourths of the talkers they tested had better-than-average recognition scores, indicating that a few people had a majority of the problems.

Enrollment. Enrollment is another critical element in speaker-dependent speech recognition systems. Enrollment techniques that avoid any systematic bias in the speech samples seem to be most successful. For example, recognition accuracy is better when the several tokens of each vocabulary item are sampled randomly instead of collecting all tokens of a vocabulary item in sequence (Poock, 1981b). Recognition performance is also enhanced when enrollment occurs in an acoustic or motion environment similar to that of operational conditions (Simpson et al., 1982). In a subsequent study with a different recognition system, it was found that enrollment could be done in a quiet environment for application in cockpit noise levels up to 100 dB SPL with no adverse effects on recognition accuracy (Coler, 1982). In general, performance of different commercial systems varies considerably as a function of enrollment environment (NRC, 1984). For enrollment prompts to the user, the visual mode is usually used. The use of synthesized speech to prompt enrollment has been questioned because some speakers tend to mimic the prompt (McCauley, 1984).

Adaptive recognition algorithms. Adaptive recognition algorithms for speaker-dependent systems are one method for dealing with speech variability over time for a given speaker. The algorithm alters its reference template to reflect slow changes in the user's pronunciation over time. To do this, it needs feedback on the accuracy of each recognition attempt. One study (Coler and Plummer, 1974) reported an improvement from 95% to

99.9% recognition accuracy using an adaptive algorithm.

System feedback. Feedback by the system to the user may enhance performance, either by altering the user's speech or by allowing for user error correction. Poock, Martin, and Roland (1983) found no conclusive evidence that different levels and types of feedback contributed to changes in speaking patterns or to improved recognition accuracy. However, it was shown that feedback in general affects recognition performance. Recognition performance with subjects not accustomed to feedback improved when some type of feedback was presented, and, conversely, was degraded if the feedback to which a user was accustomed was reduced. In the absence of feedback, a user may incorrectly assume that a sequence of voice commands was executed properly by the system. For example, one study (Schurick, Williges, and Maynard, in press) demonstrated that accuracy in a database entry task using speech could be increased from 70% to 97% correct with feedback and user error correction. Although there is general agreement about the need for feedback, an important issue for human factors integration is how to best provide feedback to avoid interfering with the operator's primary task and to maximize throughput.

Error correction. Speech recognition system performance can be improved with two types of error correction. The system can be designed to detect illegal input sequences automatically and to correct them to the most likely legal sequence. It can then optionally present the correction to the user for verification. For example, with syntactically constrained dialogues it has been suggested that the recognizer could select both the first- and second-choice vocabulary items by using standard parsing techniques (Spine, Maynard, and Williges, 1983). Another suggestion is the use of subject-specific confusion matrices as well as the logical "anding" of utterances when users are asked by the system to repeat (Bierman, Rodman, Rubin, and Heidlage, 1984). Although such techniques can improve recognition accuracy, they do not ultimately guarantee a semantically correct message or command. Thus, the human ought to remain in the loop, at least for critical entries.

In addition to automatic error correction, provision should be made for error correction by the user. Three documented types of user errors include failure to remember the vocabulary set, failure to follow the speech cadence restrictions, and conversing with coworkers with an active microphone. Vocabulary errors involve speaking other words outside the vocabulary, including synonyms. Cadence errors include using connected speech with discrete word recognizers. Other types of user errors are to be expected. Lack of a rapid error-correction capability can be frustrating to the user who is engaged in a dynamic, time-critical task, and it can drastically increase the time to achieve a desired system goal via speech recognition.

Environmental factors. The task environment comprises a number of factors that must be studied for their effect on human performance and therefore on speech task design. Physical, physiological, emotional, and workload factors can be expected to partially determine the success or failure of a particular speech system design. Only after the effects of these factors are known can speech systems be designed in ways that will enhance rather than hinder human performance and thus systems performance.

The major environmental factor that has been studied is the effect of background noise on recognition accuracy, but little is known of its effect on the performance of humans who are using speech recognition devices. There is qualitative information available on the effects of environmental stress on human speaking performance, but little quantitative data. Relationships between psychophysiological state and voice parameters have been investigated, including changes in laryngeal tension, rise in the fundamental frequency, pitch perturbations, and breath noises (see NRC, 1984, for references). One study manipulated task-induced stress to determine the effects of speaker stress on speech (Hecker, Stevens, von Bismark, and Williams, 1968). This study documented the variety of differences between speech spoken with and without stressful conditions as well as differences in the effects of task-induced stress on the speech of individual speakers. Because stress-related speech changes can take many forms and are neither consistent among people nor tasks, speech recognition performance may vary dramatically as a function of the work environment. This may be why most successful applications of speech recognition do not involve severe time constraints or life-threatening situations.

Human-System Performance Measurement

Although general methods for performance measurement are available for different levels of human/system performance, the measurement of speech recognition performance in a complex control and display task is more difficult and less understood. In addition to speed and accuracy of operator performance of complex tasks, it is necessary to measure variables such as operator workload and operator ability to deal with novel situations. Also, conflicts between other controls and displays and speech controls and displays have to be assessed.

Simulating Recognition Systems

By simulating speech recognition hardware, various levels of speech-recognition capability can be controlled and evaluated experimentally. Research using simulations of speech controls and displays originated with studies of how people communicate to solve problems (Chapanis, 1975). Problem solution occurred most rapidly whenever the voice link was available. Other modes were typing and handwriting. Because this study did not restrict the speech channel in vocabulary, syntax, or permissible speaking cadence, its relevance to current speech recognition capabilities is limited, but it illustrates the power of voice communication for problem solving, emphasizes the importance of further development of speech recognition technology, and demonstrates simulation of speech recognition as a research methodology.

Since those first studies, several attempts have been made to study system performance and acceptability when the speech channel is restricted in various ways to simulate the use of speech recognition hardware. One study simulated a listening typewriter, where speech was constrained either in terms of vocabulary size or speech pause requirements (Gould, Conti, and Hovanyecz, 1983). Shortcomings of the simulation included slow response time, failure to simulate misrecognition errors as well as nonrecognitions, and inconsistent restriction of discrete data entry when the spelling mode was used to enter words not in the vocabulary. However, the simulation contributes to the development of techniques to simulate speech recognition for human factors research.

Another study demonstrates the difficulty of designing a good simulation of speech recognition. The study attempted to evaluate user acceptance of various levels of recognition accuracy (Poock and Roland, 1982). Because subjects read words in a prescribed order, it was difficult to control appropriate feedback when the subject spoke the wrong word or made a detectable noise. Also, because the subjects had no real task to accomplish, they often failed to read the visual feedback provided and were unaware of errors. As a result, all levels of speech recognition accuracy tested in the simulation were judged acceptable by the subjects, probably indicating simply that they liked the concept of voice input. Avoidance of these and related problems in future simulation designs will be no trivial task.

A study by Zoltan-Ford (1984) demonstrated a simulation technique that was quite believable for subjects and provides encouraging data on successful methods for constraining users' syntax and vocabulary when they speak to a recognition system. Subjects conversing with a computer were not constrained to use any particular syntax or vocabulary. However, the computer, simulated by the experimenter, "responded" with a constrained vacabulary and syntax. The subjects imitated the "computer" and gradually adopted its vocabulary and syntax over the course of the experiment.

Future Speech Recognition Research

Simulation. Simulation techniques are needed to provide controlled variation along such dimensions as speed of recognition and feedback, recognition accuracy level, and types of recognition errors. In addition, system performance measures must be developed that integrate recognizer performance, human performance, task workload, system utility, and user acceptance.

Important issues to be addressed include the following: speed and accuracy requirements for various applications; criticality of errors, by type; appropriate forms of error correction; the need for speaker independence; the effects of large vocabulary size; and human ability to constrain speech in terms of vocabulary, syntax, and speaking patterns (NRC, 1984). Data from these simulations can be used to determine candidate tasks for speech and the speech recognition performance required for successful use of a speech database. The simulations can pro-vide samples of speech produced under various task conditions, such as noise, mental workload, stress, and various levels of recognition error rate. Finally, the simulation would provide a research environment for developing general guidelines on how speech data entry should be integrated into different task environments.

Enrollment methods and user training. Better enrollment methods are needed for speaker-dependent systems. These methods should permit enrollment of the speech recognition system in a benign environment when it is to be used in a more hostile environment. Automatic updating of speech samples while the system is in use may be a partial solution. Solution of this problem will reduce enrollment costs not only in terms of equipment operation, but also with regard to operator time, stress, and fatigue.

Better methods are needed for predicting the speech recognition performance on the basis of user characteristics. For example, the user's dialect may influence recognition performance. Research is needed on techniques for predicting low-performance users and on potential remediating methods. Training users to modify their speech patterns will be difficult because speech is a highly over-learned behavior that is difficult to modify. The extent to which training can reliably alter speaking habits, particularly under stressful conditions, has yet to be determined. This is an important research issue especially for the types of applications envisioned by the military sector.

Performance measurement. Improved performance measurement is essential for providing data for decisions about system design and effectiveness. More detailed analysis of recognition algorithm errors will permit a better understanding of the effects of different user characteristics, environmental factors, and task-related factors on recognition accuracy. Errors should be displayed in a confusion matrix format, at the task, utterance, and phoneme levels. High-fidelity quality audio recordings of subjects' utterances spoken to speech recognizers under known, controlled experimental conditions ought to be routinely made and analyzed to discover speech variability factors that affect recognition performance.

Speech recognition performance should be measured within a realistic task scenario, both within the laboratory and in the actual operational setting, including worst-case conditions. Laboratory benchmark tests using standard vocabularies, experienced users, and controlled environments, are useful for comparing recognizers but they are not sufficient for predicting actual performance in operational systems. Adequate methods for the measurement of both human and recognizer performance under realistic conditions remain to be developed. The importance of speed versus accuracy will vary with the application. Speed of command entry will not always be the primary measure of effectiveness when the user is engaged in simultaneous manual tasks. For example, performance on a primary manual task may be facilitated with the use of voice on a secondary task even though that secondary task is then accomplished at a slower but still acceptable rate. Generic measures need to be developed that can be applied to task- or mission-specific events.

Operator workload is an important measure because it can be used to compare system design alternatives. Currently, there is no single reliable method for assessing human workload in a variety of tasks (Wierwille and Connor, 1983). Although some research is being conducted in this area, an emphasis on this topic would be valuable, not only for speech recognition applications, but for many other issues in human-system interface design.

SPEECH GENERATION RESEARCH

Properly designed voice displays can potentially unload a user's visual system when performing visually demanding tasks. Examples of such tasks are reading technical maintenance or operations manuals while operating or repairing a system, looking through a microscope or other visual system to position one's work, reading flight charts while flying in busy airspace, checking multiple visual readouts while operating a nuclear power station, simultaneously controlling a robotic arm and multiple cameras on board a space station, monitoring multiple vital-sign displays during surgery, and editing text on a visual display. In such situations, not only is the user engaged in a visual task, but efficiency of task performance also depends on the user being able to maintain eye point of regard. Spoken messages, delivered by speech displays, carrying certain information might be more effective and result in more efficient overall task performance than if the same information were displayed visually.

The strategy for effective use of speech generation, like that for speech recognition, is threefold. Methodologies are needed for (1) identification of applications for speech generation, (2) selection of appropriate algorithms and system characteristics, and (3) integration of speech generation into the design of voice-interactive systems.

Applications

The most common approach for identifying applications for speech generation has been to select a particular human-machine system as a candidate for speech messages and to simulate a version of the system that uses speech messages. Usually, an existing problem such as high visual workload or poor performance is the basis for investigating the speech mode in place of the visual mode. Typically, an experiment is performed using the current system as a control condition, and various measures of task performance are used to determine the relative merits of visual and speech output for the task in question. The results of such studies support decisions regarding the utility of speech displays for that particular application, but they are difficult to generalize to other applications. However, they may suggest areas for more generic research and provide valuable input into human factors issues regarding speech display design.

General guidelines for use of speech displays. Despite the limited generalizability of results from such application-specific research, there are some general guidelines for selecting functions for speech. These are based to a small degree on experimental data, but mostly on a combination of deductive and inductive reasoning. For example, Deathridge (1972) lists general guidelines for deciding first between audio and visual displays and then for deciding between speech and nonspeech audio displays. Situations in which auditory (speech or nonspeech) rather than visual displays should be used include: (1) when warning signals are to be given, because the auditory sense is omnidirectional, (2) when there are too many visual displays, (3) when information must be presented independently of head movement or body position, (4) when darkness limits or precludes vision, and (5) when there are conditions of greater resistance of the auditory sensitivity to anoxia as compared with visual sensitivity. Situations in which speech rather than nonspeech messages should be used are: (1) when flexibility is required, (2) when the message source must be identified, (3) when listeners have no special training in coded signals, (4) when rapid, two-way information exchanges are required, and (5) when the message deals with a future

time, requiring preparation, and (6) in situations of stress, which might cause the operator to forget the meaning of coded signals. The state of the art in selecting voice functions has not really progressed beyond this philosophical stage.

Simpson (1983a) and Williges and Williges (1982) independently added the same two items to the inventory: (1) spoken information should be highly reliable, and (2) spoken information should be intended for use in the immediate future, due to its poor retainability in short-term memory.

Selection of Functions for Speech Displays

It is important to select the best functions for speech displays. These functions can be classified according to the speech acts (Searle, 1969) they represent. Simpson (in press) lists five basic types of information (i.e., speech acts) for which speech displays may be useful. These basic information types transcend specific applications. They are warnings, advisories, responses to user queries, feedback from control inputs, and commands. A sixth class, not listed, comprises spoken prompts from the system to the user to elicit user action, such as data entry. It is unlikely that any particular type of speech act will be amenable to speech output in all situations. Rather, the combination of task and user characteristics associated with a particular application will dictate the applicability of speech displays.

Warnings. Of the six types of speech acts, warnings have received most of the attention in speech display research. Results from a series of studies (summarized in Simpson and Navarro, 1984) suggest that voice warnings should be worded as short phrases containing a minimum of four or five syllables to minimize listener attention needed for what they call "perceptual copying" and to ensure high message intelligibility for unexpected mes-

sages in the presence of competing noise and speech.

The voice used for cockpit displays needs to be distinctive (Brown et al. 1968; Simpson and Williams, 1980; U.S. Dept. of Defense, 1981) in order to stand out against other human speech. A female voice for environments in which male voices prevail has frequently been suggested for warnings because of its unique voice quality (e.g., Brown et al. 1968), but there are few such environments today. There is also an accumulation of reports from pilots who have served in speech-display flight simulation studies that the voice ought not to sound too human (Simpson, 1981b; Voorhees, Bucher, Huff, Simpson, and Williams, 1983) lest it be confused with human speech. The underlying concept here is that a machine should have a machine voice as a cue to its identity when it speaks.

A main variable in the Voorhees et al. (1983) study was voice type (Simpson, Marchionda-Frost, and Navarro, 1984). Male digitized, female digitized, and a digitized version of synthesizer-generated speech were compared. Pilots reported extreme dissatisfaction with the slow speaking rate of all three digitized voices, caused by the artificial pauses that were introduced by the word-concatenation method used to generate the messages. Direct synthesized speech with more natural prosodics was judged by the same pilots as preferable to both the digitized synthesized and the digitized human female speech used in the flight simulation.

A series of studies has addressed system response time (defined below under human-system performance measurement) for synthesized voice warnings with and without preceding alerting tones or words. First, Simpson and Williams (1980) found that an alerting tone preceding a synthesized voice warning *increased* system response time,

whereas lengthening message wording with an extra word to add semantic context did not increase system response time. Hakkinen and Williges (1984) replicated these results but also found that when synthesized voice was used for multiple functions with the alerting tone as a variable only for warning messages, then an alerting tone used exclusively before warnings improved the detection of urgent messages without increasing system response time to these urgent messages. Studies of voice warning prefixes (Bucher, Karl, Voorhees, and Werner, 1984; Bucher et al., reported in Simpson and Navarro, 1984) found no difference in system response time as a function of prefix type, despite differences in actual length of the different prefixes (tone, neutral word, one of three semantic cue words). These studies support the possibility that synthesized speech is somehow distinctive, as compared with human speech, and can perform the alerting function concurrently with the information transfer function. The physical correlates of this distinctiveness remain to be determined experimentally.

Prompts. Prompts by the system to the user have been studied by Mountford and her colleagues (Mountford, North, Metz, and Graffunder, 1982). They studied different levels of verbosity for voice messages used as feedback and prompts to users of a simulated voice data-entry system for flight planning and navigation. They found that short dialogues with little prompting and terse feedback provided the best data-entry performance. Future research may well find that the trade-off between verbosity and time spent to complete voice transactions depends on the criticality of an error. The more catastrophic the effects of an error, the more willing users may be to invest the time required for more verbose prompts and feedback. More work is needed in this area.

Feedback. Feedback to discrete user control inputs is frequently mentioned as a function for speech displays. Relevant research was discussed in the section of this paper on speech recognition. In passing, it should be noted that feedback can be provided by prompts (cf. the Mountford et al. 1982, study just discussed). That is, if the system prompts the user for a reasonable next data-entry or control input, the user will assume that the system correctly received the previous input. The real-world conditions under which the user can safely make such assumptions, however, need to be understood. A variety of types of feedback should be employed, depending on the time criticality of the control input and the severity of the consequences of a speech recognition error.

Responses to user queries. User queries were studied in a computer-graphic simulation of nap-of-the-earth helicopter flight (Voorhees, Marchionda, and Atchison, 1982). Subjects could ask the helicopter to state airspeed, torque, and altitude as they attempted to fly their simulated craft through a maze on a visual display. Maze flying performance was better when subjects used voice queries and received synthesized voice responses than when they had to obtain this information from either a head-up display or conventional dial gauges.

Advisories. The advisability of using speech to provide advisories may depend on the other functions for which speech is being employed in a particular application. When advisories were given in conjunction with voice warnings, it was seen, as discussed previously (Hakkinen and Williges, 1984), that warning detection suffered, unless an alerting cue was also used. A study of pilot preferences for warning system design (Williams and Simpson, 1976) found that pilots wanted speech reserved for only the most critical (i.e., warning) information. They preferred to receive advisories visually. If speech is not being used for warnings, then its use for advisories may be appropriate. Further research is needed.

Commands. There is some research and discussion in the literature on the advisability of giving commands by automatic speech generation. Simpson and Williams (1975) argue that great caution should be exercised in the use of commands, at least in the aircraft cockpit, because pilots are reluctant to follow a command without knowing the reason for it. In partial support of this argument, a study by DuBord (1982), reported by Palmer and Ellis (1983), found that giving pilots a visual display of traffic situation information reduced their response time to a visual collision avoidance command, as compared with giving them the command without benefit of the traffic situation display. A similar effect is likely for spoken commands. On the other hand, speech commands issued as instructions, in situations that are not time critical or in conjunction with advisories, could well be useful in a variety of applications.

Simulation of human communications. The six speech acts just discussed would be performed by machines speaking qua machines to human operators. Another important speech display application is in the simulation of human speech communications; for instance, to eliminate the need for human speakers playing a role in a training situation. For example, speech generation has been proposed and evaluated for training systems for precision-approach radar controllers and for air-intercept controllers (Breaux, 1977; Grady, 1982).

Comparative display modes. Comparative speech and visual display research has addressed user preferences, response time, accuracy, and task accomplishment for speech combined with visual displays, for various speech acts.

Early voice warning research using taped messages found that pilot response time to voice warnings is faster than to visual warning displays (Lilleboe, 1963) and that a visual display augmented with a voice warning results in faster responses to emergencies than does a tone-augmented display (Kemmerling, Geiselhart, Thornburn, and Cronburg, 1969).

Another difference between the visual and speech mode may be users' tolerance for and ability to perform with false information. A study of airline pilots' preferences for design of cockpit warning systems found that pilots expressed less tolerance for false speech messages than for false visual messages (Williams and Simpson, 1976). Moreover, flight performance was poorer in the presence of false voice warnings (Simpson, 1981b) than when voice warnings gave accurate information.

A series of experiments was conducted in flight simulators to evaluate different cockpit display modes, including a large-letter LED display, a synthesized voice display, and a printed paper display (Hilborn, 1975). The airline pilot subjects who flew the simulator preferred visual displays for all but warning information. For warnings, they preferred speech messages. A large-letter LED display was preferred as a recall instrument for currently assigned heading, altitude, and airspeed information. For less time-critical information, which also must be remembered or referred to over a period of time after receipt, an in-cockpit printout was preferred.

In some situations, users may object to the speech mode for certain types of information. For example, a recent study (Stern, 1984) compared speech and visual displays for prompting and giving error messages to users of an automated teller machine. Although there were no performance differences between text and speech displays, subjects did not like spoken error messages because other customers could hear them.

For sensory-handicapped users, the selection of visual or speech displays will depend on the handicap. For systems to be used by the blind, the challenge will be to design a speech interface that will facilitate performance of those functions that are normally better accomplished using visual displays.

Selecting Speech Generation System Characteristics

Research on appropriate speech generation systems for particular applications has been done at two levels. The performance of speech generation algorithms has been assessed as a function of multiple factors that influence intelligibility. Also, human-system performance in simulations has been assessed to determine what benefits may derive from using speech displays.

Speech generation algorithm performance. Intelligibility is influenced by the physical characteristics of the speech signal and by the context in which the speech is spoken. In addition to intelligibility, comprehension and human information retention and retrieval in the speech mode must be measured.

Operational intelligibility. A recent review of research on the intelligibility of computer-generated speech (Simpson and Navarro, 1984) defines three types of context that interact with the speech signal to produce what the authors call the *operational intelligibility* of speech. The operational intelligibility of a particular algorithm is the intelligibility of its speech in a particular set of physical, pragmatic, and linguistic contexts, and it can differ considerably from basic phoneme intelligibility. Figure 1 depicts the four major factors (i.e., the physical signal and the three types of context) that contribute to operational intelligibility.

The physical speech signal can vary with

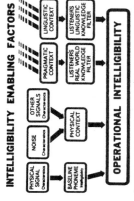

Figure 1. Factors that contribute to operational intelligibility (after Simpson and Navarro, 1984).

respect to sex and voice characteristics of the speaker, speaking rate, fundamental frequency, amplitude, accuracy of pronunciation and prosodics, accent, and dialect, among other parameters. The physical context includes aspects of the physical environment such as noise, other audio signals, vibrations, and acceleration forces. The pragmatic context is essentially the real-world situation in which the message is spoken. It includes current events, the ongoing task, time and place, past events, and logically possible future events. The effect of the pragmatic context will be filtered by the listener's knowledge of that pragmatic context. The linguistic context of a speech signal influences intelligibility by providing cues to the listener that limit the possible interpretations of the incoming speech signal. This limit on possible interpretations is a complex type of closed response set. It has long been known that as size of response set decreases, intelligibility of human speech heard in the presence of noise increases, all other factors held constant (Miller, Heise, and Lichten, 1951). Linguistic context limits the size of the response set in more complex ways than does simply limiting message set size. This is due to interactions among the constraints provided by the different levels of linguistic encoding. Simpson and Williams (1975) list

these levels and provide references to the literature on the effects of various types of linguistic context on human speech intelligibility. (For an introduction to theories and models of human speech perception see Cole, 1980.) As with pragmatic context, the effects of linguistic context are filtered by the listener's linguistic knowledge of the language being spoken.

Often the effect of factors that enable intelligibility is stronger for synthesized than for human speech (Nye and Gaitenby, 1974; Simpson, 1975). Simpson and Navarro (1984) report that with sufficient assistance from intelligibility-enabling factors, synthesized speech from commercially available devices has been found to be 100% intelligible; without such assistance it has been measured as low as 19%. Factors included as physical characteristics of the speech signal are fundamental frequency, speech rate, prosodics, intonation, learnability of the speech accent, voice type, and phonetic accuracy of the generated speech. In the section of the paper on physical context, the authors review research on effects of background noise and competing speech. Pragmatic context factors include listener familiarity with the speech accent, with the phraseology and vocabulary, and with the real-world situation in which the message will be spoken. Linguistic context factors include semantic and syntactic context and number of syllables.

The relative importance of the three types of context varies. Under ideal listening conditions, characterized by high signal-to-noise ratio, no competing speech or other audio signals, and listeners familiar with the accent of the machine speech, sentence intelligibility of synthesized speech is from 99 to 100%. Reducing the signal-to-noise ratio and leaving the other factors constant has shown little or no detriment in operational intelligibility, at least for aircraft cockpit messages (Simpson, 1984). High intelligibility (99 to 100%) has

been obtained for short, familiar phrases, heard in simulated cockpit noise, using both LPC-encoded digitized speech and synthesis-by-rule speech.

Intelligibility of digitized speech varies as a function of speaker sex. LPC-encoded and Adaptive Predictive Coding (APC) encoded female speech is more susceptible to bit errors, which might be expected during transmission, than is male speech encoded using the same algorithms. The difference is consistent across a wide range of bit error rates (Smith, 1983). Similar comparisons need to be made between female synthesized and male synthesized speech.

When linguistic context or pragmatic context, rather than signal-to-noise ratio, is reduced, substantial degradation of intelligibility occurs (Simpson and Navarro, 1984).

The excellent intelligibility reported by Simpson and Navarro (1984) was achieved at the expense of phonetic hand editing by experts in speech acoustics. The intelligibility of speech generated by text-to-speech algorithms can be poorer and depends on the particular algorithm. For example, the intelligibility of Harvard Psycho-Acoustic Laboratory (PAL) sentences (Egan, 1948) was 93.2% when spoken by one system (Pisoni and Hunnicutt, 1980) and was 87% for PAL sentences spoken by another system (Nusbaum and Schwab, 1983).

The main deficiencies of text-to-speech algorithms are phonetic errors of pronunciation for words that are exceptions to English spelling-to-sound correspondences and limitations of rules for generating correct word stress and sentence intonation. Until these deficiencies are corrected, the need for hand editing of individual speech messages (noted previously) will remain.

Comprehension. Although synthesized speech can be 100% intelligible to listeners familiar with its accent, with the phraseology, and with the pragmatically possible messages, further research is needed on com-

prehension of synthesized speech messages as compared with human speech. Luce, Feustel, and Pisoni (1983) found deficiencies in speech-processing capacity for speech synthesized by one text-to-speech system compared with human speech, when they loaded their subjects with additional short-term memory recall tasks. They interpret these results to mean that synthesized speech places increased demands on encoding and/or rehearsal processes in short-term memory and argue that synthesized speech ought not to be used for cockpit displays. However, their subjects were unfamiliar with the accent of the synthesizer prior to the experiment. The applicability of their findings to pilots' comprehension of familiar messages encoded with sentence-level linguistic context and spoken in a familiar pragmatic context remains to be determined. There is experimental evidence that pilots can store information presented by synthesized speech and later retrieve that information while flying a flight simulator under high workload (Simpson and Marchionda-Frost, 1984). Little is known about how efficiently information in synthesized speech messages can be recalled and under what circumstances listeners will become overloaded in the speech channel. General statements about performance with synthesized speech systems must be made cautiously, with attention to the particular conditions under which the results were obtained.

Voice characteristics. Desirable voice characteristics are application dependent. When an inanimate system is speaking qua machine to the user, a machine voice quality is preferred by some user populations (e.g., pilots), as has been discussed. On the other hand, when a system simulates human communications, as in an air traffic control (ATC) training system, a natural-sounding voice, using digitized human speech, is preferred (Cotton and McCauley, 1983). As with machine-sounding speech, it is important to incorporate natural prosodics into the generation process.

Voices can also be varied with respect to pitch and apparent sex of voice. Voice pitch has been suggested for indicating the urgency of a message, with higher pitch signaling greater urgency (Simpson and Marchionda-Frost, 1984). Recent research (Brokx and Nooteboom, 1982) also suggests that differences in voice pitch can help listeners track one or the other of two concurrent messages. The extent to which users can deal with multiple messages needs to be studied and may be a function of the degree of difference among voice types heard on the job.

Human-System Performance Measurement

Operational relevance. The human factors of speech generation system performance extend far beyond effects on speech intelligibility and recognition accuracy. Message comprehension, human storage and retrieval of information presented in the voice mode, and interactions between speech comprehension and human performance of other concurrent tasks are equally important. Such measures should be "operationally relevant" to the task for which a voice display is used (Simpson, 1981b). An operationally relevant measure of system performance is one that provides users and designers with information about how the system will perform in terms that are meaningful to the operator. For example, one measure of the effectiveness of a navigation computer with voice controls and displays might be a comparison of the amount of time it took a pilot, flying in turbulence in a busy ATC environment, to change a waypoint by means of voice and by means of manual keys and a visual display.

A flight-simulation study to evaluate the concept of a synthesized voice approach callout (SYNCALL) system for airline operations (Simpson, 1981b) measured flight performance in terms of percentage of time out of airline operational tolerance for flight parameters. For the less difficult types of approaches to landing, there were no differences in flight performance attributable to the SYNCALL system. But for the most visually, manually, and cognitively demanding approaches, performance with the synthesized voice system was better than when the normal procedure of pilot-not-flying callouts was used. (Pilot-not-flying callouts are callouts of altitude, airspeed, and other flight parameters that are made by the pilot who is not flying the aircraft as an aid to the pilot who is flying.) For the one approach for which SYNCALL consistently (by experimental design) made false callouts, flight performance was significantly degraded compared with performance on the same approach flown with pilot-not-flying callouts that were correct.

Measures are also needed that will predict the costs and benefits of using speech technology in terms of time saved, more efficient utilization of personnel and equipment, and safer operations. Such measures may follow a generic format but will be application specific in content.

System response time. Another operationally relevant measure is system response time. The fact that a speech message takes time to be delivered gives particular importance to what Simpson and Williams (1980) have called *system response time.* The authors defined system response time for voice warnings as the time interval starting with the onset of a warning signal and continuing until the listener has decided upon and initiated his or her first action. System response time thus includes detection, perceptual copying, comprehension, storage, retrieval, and decision making. System response time, rather than simple reaction time or human response latency, is a critical variable for voice warning display systems.

Future Speech Generation Research

Research directed toward speech displays in general will support effective design for voice-interactive controls and displays. Specific issues relevant to the design of integrated voice I/O systems are selection of voice type (human- or machine-sounding; male or female), message wording and syntax as a function of speech act, assignment of priorities to functionally different speech display messages, and methods for integrating voice and visual messages when they present the same information. Research on speech-display aspects of dialogue design must also deal with the issue of how to handle concurrent speech messages. Two cases must be handled: (1) user speaking to speech recognition device while speech display is enunciating a message, and (2) triggering more than one speech display message at a time. Speech displays also require improvements to text-to-speech generation algorithms to eliminate the need for hand editing of speech data.

The relative importance of various types of phonetic and prosodic accuracy for synthesized speech intelligibility, learnability, and comprehension is another area that requires further investigation. The degradation of operational intelligibility due to inaccurate vowels, consonants, phoneme transitions, word stress, and prosodics has not been systematically measured. Because of missing perceptual cues in synthesized speech and, to some extent, in human digitized speech in the lower bit rates, the fidelity of audio transmission systems may be more critical than it is for human speech. Just how much redundancy and what type is optimal (syntactic, semantic, phonetic) has not been determined experimentally for all types of speech acts. Also, for listener populations with possible high-frequency hearing loss, computer speech perception may present special problems just because it does not contain all of the perceptual cues of human speech. Specifications for intelligibility of speech to be used for such groups or speech to be used in high-noise environments must take this into account.

SYSTEM INTEGRATION

System integration, the third level of the research strategy, must consider the research requirements for speech recognition and generation as synergistic technologies. The human visual and manual modalities are commonly associated with perceptual and motor (input/output) characteristics. Similarly, the speech modality has identifiable human speech perception and production characteristics that will become the basis (either unwittingly or by design) for the interface characteristics of speech I/O systems.

The critical issues in human factors integration are task design specifically for the speech modality and human-system dialogue design.

Task Design

Applications using the speech modality must be designed around the characteristics of speech. Certain unique features of the speech mode preclude a one-to-one mapping of individual manual controls to speech controls, and of visual display elements to speech display messages (Cotton and McCauley, 1983; Simpson, 1984; Williges and Williges, 1982).

Speech is a discrete, single-channel, omnidirectional, well-known, semantically sophisticated encoding system for the transmission of information. It commands the user's attention and should not be allowed to deliver false information. Used for control of systems, speech can, if properly implemented, reduce the need for the user to learn computer-programming-like languages and can provide an alternative to manual input systems. Speech messages require time to be spoken and may be misunderstood by human or machine "listeners" in the presence of other, competing voice messages, aural signals, or noise. The time and single-channel constraints imposed by the speech mode must be considered in any implementation of speech displays and controls. Further, certain features of speech constrain the way in which it can be used in human-machine systems. Speech may not always provide the most rapid means of interacting with the system. The time required for an operator to execute a speech command is strongly influenced by such variables as vocabulary selection, syntax design, and especially dialogue design.

The receiver of a speech message, whether human or machine, has great difficulty in processing more than one message at a time, with the result that speech is a single-channel code in two senses: neither humans nor current machines can talk and listen accurately at the same time, and both have great difficulty in processing more than one speech message at a time. One implication of this constraint is that speech commands cannot be allowed to interfere with, or to suffer interference from, other speech messages within the system.

Speech messages have a transitory existence unless they are recorded for later playback. The limits of human memory may make it difficult for operators to remember their location in the command structure of a recognition system without the aid of feedback messages and prompts. The task conditions under which this holds true require further investigation, building on previous findings (Mountford et al., 1982).

In general, current speech recognition technology requires a vocabulary that consists of acoustically distinct words. Vocabularies and syntax must also be constrained to be compatible with current recognition technology. These limitations of the technology may be reduced by degrees in the future but cannot be expected to disappear without major advances in fundamental understanding of human speech variability and incorporation of this knowledge into recognition algorithms.

Irrespective of future advances in recognition technology, human performance limitations will dictate vocabulary and syntax constraints. To minimize human cognitive load and the time required to issue speech commands, the number of words in each command should be small. More information is needed on human memory for constrained verbal material and on the effects of such constraints on system performance. Information about the effects of harsh environments and stress on verbal versus motor memory and performance would be particularly relevant. Research in this area would lead to guidelines for establishing vocabularies that are flexible and easy to remember, and also reduce acoustic confusion and minimize awkward speech stylization. Similar guidelines are needed for developing formal grammatical rules that facilitate recognition without placing undue constraints on the user.

Human-System Dialogue Design

Careful design of all of the interchanges between the human and the system, not just the speech interchanges, will have major effects on the overall system performance. There are at least two subsets of dialogue design—the dialogue between the user and the speech system and the dialogue between the user and all of the subsystems under the user's control.

The human machine interchanges (i.e., dialogue) must be designed with regard to the total set of control and display options for all subsystems. Mission and task scenarios will have to be analyzed for speech and other audio loads, as well as for the likelihood of concurrent interfering speech messages. The properties of potential functions to be controlled by speech must be assessed, along with the priorities of all speech messages within the system. Voice commands and displays will have to be applied in ways that complement rather than conflict with other controls and displays. Future research and development efforts should address these issues.

To improve system throughput with speech, it is essential to design a speech system dialogue that facilitates rapid information transfer between human and machine. The dialogue design also should minimize the potential for error and the subsequent time required for error correction by the user. Not only the speech commands, but also such dialogue elements as prompts, system feedback, and query responses must be carefully designed and a timeline of the total dialogue evaluated. The desired type and amount of linguistic redundancy for a particular application should be determined experimentally. Syntax design should be viewed as an integral part of speech system design rather than as simply a technique for improving the performance of a marginal recognition or generation system.

Possibly the error rates obtained with current systems can be reduced if system designers provide aids to the user such as tonal prompts for cadence, menus of acceptable entries, consistent feedback, and convenient error-correction commands. The best format for these dialogue elements should be determined by further research.

New techniques are needed to capitalize on syntactic and semantic constraints in the dialogue. These techniques would improve automatic error detection and correction, thereby increasing recognition accuracy and reducing the user's burden of detecting and correcting errors.

At a higher level of dialogue design, speech controls and displays need to be carefully integrated into the total control and display system in order to preclude overloading the speech channel (Simpson, 1984). Certain types of information may be better processed if presented via speech; others may require symbolic information representation. Some basic research has addressed the issue of task/modality compatibility (Wickens et al., 1983) and provides evidence that speech is a better communication mode for some types of tasks, compared with manual input and visual output. When subjects performed two tasks simultaneously—one spatial and the other verbal—spatial task performance was better when the verbal task was accomplished using speech recognition and generation compared with the condition in which both tasks had to compete for the manual and visual channels. This basic research, however, has not involved voice-interactive dialogues. More work is needed on these compatibility issues, using realistic tasks, to support decisions about selecting appropriate tasks for speech-interactive systems with the objective of reducing operator workload. Successful speech system performance for a particular task will not guarantee successful performance of the total application system. Basic limitations of human memory and information processing must be accounted for in the design of any human-machine interface, and especially for those using speech.

Many of the problems of today's complex control and display systems, from the operator's viewpoint, may be solvable by better design at the overall system level. Speech controls and displays may play a role in those solutions, but this can be determined only after considerable analysis or simulation research to compare speech with alternative modes of control and display.

OVERALL DIRECTIONS FOR FUTURE RESEARCH

Human factors research on the design of integrated voice systems is limited, and reports are spread among conference proceedings, government technical reports, and journal articles (see for example, Cotton and McCauley, 1983; McCauley, 1984; Pallett, 1982; and Simpson, 1984). Although several new design guidelines have been suggested in these reviews, the standard references used by system design engineers, such as U.S. Department of Defense (1981) and Van Cott and Kinkade (1972), and Woodson (1981), do not incorporate the new knowledge summarized by these reviews.

If the benefits of speech technology are to be realized, a major effort in human factors research will be needed at many levels of integrated system design: task selection, determination of task-specific recognition and generation system performance requirements, human factors integration to incorporate the speech modality, speech control and display design, task environment effects, and system performance assessment.

A substantial effort in human factors research is needed to develop procedures for selecting appropriate tasks for the voice mode and for integrating voice interaction into the total system design. There is no single area that can be chosen for particular emphasis. However, all of the recommended directions for research should emphasize the total context; that is, the integrated system in which the speech I/O is to be used.

CONCLUSIONS

Although the human factors literature includes research that supports certain principles of speech system design, this knowledge has not yet been formulated as design guidelines. Human factors methodology is sufficiently developed to permit comparison of task-specific speech systems experimentally; however, it does not yet have the tools required for the generation of generic speech system design guidelines. For the near term, the simulation of speech system capabilities in conjunction with the development of im-proved system performance measures should be a productive methodology for accomplishing this work.

Speech generation algorithms may seem to be more advanced than speech recognition algorithms. Reasonably intelligible text-to-speech from standard English spelling is available commercially. The recognition counterpart, speech to text (i.e., machine conversion of human speech to correctly spelled and punctuated text), will not be available commercially in the foreseeable future and is limited to highly constrained laboratory systems. This discrepancy can be interpreted in another way, as merely illustrating the human's great superiority over human-made and machine-processed algorithms when it comes to dealing with variability in the speech signal. Humans quickly learn the strange accent of computer-generated speech, thereby compensating for the deficiencies of the algorithm that generates it. On the other hand, when humans speak to current machines, they must eliminate, as much as possible, the normal variability in their speech in order to provide the recognition algorithm with as little variability as possible in the input signal. As knowledge and understanding of the systematic variability in speech increase, recognition algorithms can be expected to perform well over a wider range of speaking contexts, and generation algorithms can be expected to provide speech that contains additional cues for the human listener. Such technology advances will enlarge the overlap between tasks appropriate for the speech mode and speech systems with characteristics that match the task requirements. However, the basic design issues discussed here will apply regardless of the state of speech technology.

For the near term, the current recognition algorithms appear adequate for use in benign environments, characterized by low to moderate noise (up to 85 dB SPL) and motion (up to 5 G), for applications that require small vocabularies and that do not place the user under severe stress. The exact limits of acceptable recognition algorithm performance when the user is under stress are not known. Therefore, great caution must be exercised with current technology for stress-inducing applications. Advances in techniques for dealing with background noise are reducing the impact of this source of variability in the utterances to be recognized.

Speech generation algorithms, on the other hand, have demonstrated acceptable performance under conditions of severe noise and high workload. This technology is ready to be applied appropriately, with careful attention to the human factors integration issues discussed here.

Together, these two technologies offer near-term potential for selected applications. The critical issues for near-term application of voice technology are primarily in the human factors domain. For the longer term, substantial efforts in both algorithm development and human factors will be required in order to extend the range of speech variability that can be accommodated by speech recognition and generation technology and hence the possible applications of speech technology.

ACKNOWLEDGMENTS

The sections of this article on speech recognition were based largely upon discussions among the authors and on material generated while they served on the Committee for Computerized Speech Recognition Technologies, Commission on Engineering and Technical Systems, of the National Research Council (NRC). The committee was sponsored by members of the Voice SubTechnical Advisory Group (SubTAG) of the Department of Defense. The committee's report, entitled "Automatic Speech Recognition in Severe Environments," was published by the National Research Council in October 1984. James L. Flanagan, AT&T Bell Laboratories, chaired the Committee. From the National Research Council, Dennis F. Miller served as Study Director, and Howard Clark was the Staff Officer. The authors gratefully acknowledge the support of the Voice SubTAG member agencies that funded the preparation of this article. The knowledge gained from our fellow committee members is gratefully acknowledged. However, the authors take full responsibility for any errors and for the opinions expressed in this article.

REFERENCES

Allen, H. B. and Underwood, G. N. (Eds.). (1971). *Readings in American dialectology*. New York: Appleton-Century-Crofts.

Armstrong, J. W. (1980). *The effects of concurrent motor tasking on performance of a voice recognition system*. Unpublished masters thesis, Naval Postgraduate School, Monterey, CA.

Bierman, A., Rodman, R., Rubin, D., and Heidlage, F. (1984). *Natural language with discrete speech as a mode for human to machine communication*. Durham, NC: Duke University, Computer Science Department.

Bond, Z. S., and Garnes, S. (1980). Misperceptions of fluent speech. In R. A. Cole (Ed.). *Perception and production of fluent speech* (pp. 115-113). Hillsdale NJ: Erlbaum.

Breaux, R. (1977). Laboratory demonstration of computer speech recognition in training. In R. Breaux, M. Curran, and E. M. Huff (Eds.). *Voice technology of interactive real-time command/control systems applications*. Moffett Field, CA: NASA-Ames Research Center.

Brokx, J. P. L., and Nooteboom, S. G. (1982). Intonation and the perception of simultaneous voices. *Journal of Phonetics, 10*, 23-26.

Brown, J. E., Bertone, C. M., and Obermeyer, R. W. (1968, February). *Army aircraft warning system study* (U.S. Army Technical Memorandum 6-68). Aberdeen Proving Ground, MD: U.S. Army Engineering Laboratories.

Butler, F., Manaker, E., and Obert-Thorn, W. (1981, June). *Investigation of a voice synthesis system for the F-14 aircraft: Final report* (Report No. ACT 81-001). Bethpage, NY: Grumman Aerospace Corp.

Bucher, N. M., Karl, R., Voorhees, J., and Werner, E. (1984, May). Alerting prefixes for speech warning messages. In *Proceedings of the National Aerospace & Electronics Conference (NAECON)* (pp. 924-931). New York: IEEE.

Chapanis, A. (1975). Interactive human communication. *Scientific American, 232(3)*, 36-42.

Chapanis, A. (1976). Engineering psychology. In M. D. Dunnette (Ed.), *Handbook of industrial and organizational psychology*. Chicago: Rand McNally.

Cole, R. A. (Ed.). (1980). *Perception and production of fluent speech*. Hillsdale NJ: Erlbaum.

Coler, C. (1982, September/October). Helicopter speech command systems: Recent noise tests are encouraging. *Speech Technology 1(3)*, 76-81.

Coler, C. R. and Plummer, R. P. (1974, May). Development of a computer speech recognition system for flight systems applications. In *Preprints of the 45th Annual Scientific Meeting* (pp. 116-117). Washington, DC: Aerospace Medical Association.

Coler, C., Plummer, R., Huff, E. and Hitchcock, M. (1977, December). Automatic speech recognition research at NASA-Ames Research Center. In *Proceedings of the Voice-Interactive Real-Time Command/Control Systems Application Conference* (pp. 143-163). Moffett Field, CA: NASA-Ames Research Center.

Cotton, J. C., and McCauley, M. E. (1983, March). *Voice technology design guides for Navy training systems: Final report for the period 23 April, 1980-2 January, 1982* (Report No. NAVTRAEQUIPCEN 80-C-0057-1). Orlando, FL: Naval Training Equipment Center.

Cotton, J. C., McCauley, M. E., North, R. A., and Strieb, M. (1983). *Development of speech input/output interfaces for tactical aircraft* (AFWAL-TR-83-3073). Wright-Patterson AFB, OH: Flight Dynamics Laboratory.

Deathridge, B. H. (1972). Auditory and other sensory forms of information presentation. In H. P. Van Cott and R. G. Kinkade (Eds.), *Human engineering guide to equipment design*. Washington, D.C.: U.S. Government Printing Office.

Doddington, G., and Schalk, T. (1981). Speech recognition: Turning theory to practice. *IEEE Spectrum, 18*, 26-32.

DuBord, M. J. (1982, June). *An investigation of response time to collision avoidance commands with a cockpit display of traffic information*. Unpublished masters thesis, San Jose State University, San Jose, CA.

Egan, J. P. (1948). Articulation testing methods. *Laryngoscope, 58*, 955-991.

Flanagan, J. L. (1972). *Speech analysis, synthesis, and perception* (2nd ed). New York: Springer Verlag.

Fujimura, O. (1984, June). The role of linguistics for future speech technology. In *LSA Bulletin 104* (pp. 4-7). Baltimore, MD: Linguistic Society of America.

Games, S., and Bond, Z. S. (1977). *The influence of semantics on speech perception*. Paper presented at the 93rd Meeting of the Acoustical Society of America, University Park, PA.

Gould, J. D., Conti, J., and Hovanyecz, J. (1983, April). Composing letters with a simulated listening typewriter. *Communications of the ACM*, 295-308.

Grady, M. W. (1982). *Air intercept controller prototype training system* (NAVTRAEQUIPCEN 78-C-0182-14). Orlando, FL: Naval Training Equipment Center.

Harris, S. D., North, R. A., and Owens, J. M. (1977, November). *A system for the assessment of human performance in concurrent verbal and manual control tasks*. Paper presented at the 7th Annual Meeting of the National Conference on the Use of On-Line Computers in Psychology, Washington, DC.

Hakkinen, M. T., and Williges, B. H. (1984). Synthesized warning messages: Effects of an alerting cue in single- and multiple-function voice synthesis systems. *Human Factors, 26*, 185-195.

Hecker, M. H., Stevens, K. N., von Bismark, G., and Williams, C. E. (1968). Manifestations of task-induced stress in the acoustical speech signal. *Journal of the Acoustical Society of America, 44*, 993-1001.

Hilborn, E. H. (1975). *Human factors experiments for data link: Final report* (FAA-RD-75-170). Cambridge, MA: Department of Transportation Systems Center.

Kemmerling, P., Geiselhart, R., Thornburn, D. E., and Cronburg, J. G. (1969). *A comparison of voice and tone warning systems as a function of task loading* (Technical Report ASD-TR-69-104). Wright-Patterson AFB, OH: U.S. Air Force, ASD.

Kersteen, Z., and Damos, D. (1983, December). *Human factors issues associated with the use of speech technology in the cockpit* (Final Tech. Report, U.S. Army Grant No. NAG2-217). (Available from J. Voorhees, U.S. Army Aeromechanics Laboratory, NASA-Ames Research Center, Moffett Field, CA 94035.)

Kryter, K. (1972). Speech communication. In H. P. Van Cott and R. G. Kinkade (Eds.), *Human engineering guide to equipment design* (pp. 161-226). Washington, DC: U.S. Government Printing Office.

Lilleboe, M. L. (1963, June). *Final Report: evaluation of Astropower, Inc. auditory information display installed in the VA-3B airplane* (Technical Report ST 31-22R-63; AD-831823). Patuxent River, MD: U.S. Naval Air Station, Naval Air Test Center.

Luce, P. A., Feustel, T. C., and Pisoni, D. B. (1983). Capacity demands in short-term memory for synthetic and natural speech. *Human Factors, 25*, 17-32.

McCauley, M. E. (1984). Human factors in voice technology. In F. A. Muckler (Ed.), *Human Factors Review: 1984*. Santa Monica, CA: Human Factors Society.

McCauley, M. E., Root, R. W., and Muckler, F. A. (1982). *Training evaluation of an automated air intercept controller training system* (NAVTRAEQUIPCEN 81-C-0055-1). Orlando, FL: Naval Training Equipment Center.

McCauley, M. E., and Semple, C. A. (1980). *Precision approach radar training system (PARTS)* (NAVTRAEQUIPCEN 79-C-0042-1). Orlando, FL: Naval Training Equipment Center.

McSorley, W. J. (1981, March). *Using voice recognition equipment to run the Warfare Environmental Simulator (WES)*. Unpublished masters thesis, Naval Postgraduate School, Monterey, CA.

Miller, G. A., Heise, G. A., and Lichten, W. (1951). The intelligibility of speech as a function of the context of the test materials. *Journal of Experimental Psychology, 41*, 329-335.

Moore, C. A., Moore, D. R., and Ruth, J. C. (1984, December). Applications of voice interactive systems—Military flight test and the future. In *Proceedings of the Sixth Digital Avionics Systems Conference* (pp. 301-308). New York: IEEE.

Mountford, S. J., North, R. A., Metz, S. V., and Graffunder, K., (1982, April). *Methodology for identifying voice functions for airborne voice-interactive control systems* (Contract No. N62269-81-R-0344). Minneapolis, MN: Honeywell Systems Research Center.

National Research Council, Committee on Computerized Speech Recognition Technologies. (1984). *Automatic speech recognition in severe environments*. Washington, DC: National Research Council, Commission on Engineering and Technical Systems.

North, R. A., and Lea, W. (1982). *Application of advanced speech technology in manned penetration bombers* (AFWAL-TR-82-3004). Wright-Patterson AFB, OH: Flight Dynamics Laboratory.

Nusbaum, H. C., and Schwab, E. C. (1983, May). *The effects of training on intelligibility of synthetic speech: II the learning curve for synthetic speech*. Paper presented at the 105th meeting of the Acoustical Society of America, Cincinnati, OH.

Nye, P. W., and Gaitenby, J. (1974). The intelligibility of synthetic monosyllabic words in short, syntactically normal sentences. In *Status report on speech research* (SR-37/38) (pp. 169-190). New Haven CT: Haskins Laboratories.

Pallett, D. (Ed.). (1982, March). *Proceedings of the workshop on standardization for speech I/O technology*. Gaithersburg, MD: National Bureau of Standards.

Palmer, E., and Ellis, S. R. (1983, October). Potential interactions of collision avoidance advisories and cockpit displays of traffic information (SAE Technical Paper Series 831544). In *Proceedings of the Second Aerospace Behavioral Engineering Technology Conference, Aerospace Congress & Exposition* (pp. 433-443). Warrendale, PA: SAE.

Pisoni, D. B., and Hunnicutt, S. (1980, April). Perceptual evaluation of MITalk: The MIT unrestricted text-to-speech system. In *IEEE International Conference Record on Acoustics, Speech, and Signal Processing* (pp. 572-575). New York: IEEE.

Poock, G. K. (1981a). *A longitudinal study of computer voice recognition performance and vocabulary size* (NPS-55-81-013). Monterey, CA: Naval Postgraduate School.

Poock, G. K. (1981b, October). To train randomly or all at once—That is the question. In *Proceedings of the Voice Data Entry Systems Applications Conference*. Sunnyvale, CA: Lockheed Missiles & Space Co.

Poock, G. K., Martin, B. J., and Roland, E. F. (1983, February). *The effect of feedback to users of voice recognition equipment* (NPS Technical Report NPS-55-83-003). Monterey, CA: Naval Postgraduate School.

Poock, G. K., and Roland, E. F. (1982, November). *Voice recognition accuracy: What is acceptable?* (NPS Technical Report, NPS55-82-030). Monterey, CA: Naval Postgraduate School.

Poock, G. K., and Roland, E. F. (1984). *A feasibility study for integrated voice recognition input into the Integrated Information Display system (IID)* (NPS Technical Report NPS-55-84-008). Monterey, CA: Naval Postgraduate School.

Poock, G. K., Schwalm, N. D., Martin, B. J., and Roland, E. F. (1982, December). *Trying for speaker independence in the use of speaker dependent voice recognition equipment* (NPS Technical Report NPS-55-82-032). Monterey, CA: Naval Postgraduate School.

Rollins, A. M., (1984). "Composite" templates for speech recognition for small groups. In *Proceedings of the Human Factors Society 28th Annual Meeting* (Vol. 2) (pp. 758-762). Santa Monica, CA: Human Factors Society.

Schurick, J. M., Williges, B. H., and Maynard, J. F. (in press). User feedback requirements with automatic speech recognition. *Ergonomics*.

Searle, J. (1969). *Speech acts*. London: Cambridge University press.

Sherwood, B. A. (1979, August). The computer speaks. *IEEE Spectrum*, pp. 18-25.

Simpson, C. A. (1975). Occupational experience with a specific phraseology: Group differences in intelligibility for synthesized and human speech. *Journal of the Acoustical Society of America, 58* (Supplement 1), 57.

Simpson, C. A. (1981a, April). Access to speech synthesis and its applications. In J. C. Warren (Ed.), *The best of the Computer Faires. Volume VI: Conference proceedings of the Sixth West Coast Computer Faire* (pp. 74-79). Woodside, CA: West Coast Computer Faire.

Simpson, C. A. (1981b). Evaluation of synthesized voice approach callouts (SYNCALL). In J. Moraal and K. F. Kraiss (Eds.), *Manned systems design: Methods, equipment, and applications* (pp. 375-393). New York: Plenum.

Simpson, C. A. (1981c, April). Programming "phoneme" voice synthesizers phonetically. In J. C. Warren (Ed.), *The Best of the Computer Faires, Volume VI: Conference proceedings of the Sixth West Coast Computer Faire* (pp. 84-90). Woodside, CA: West Coast Computer Faire.

Simpson, C. A. (1983a, December). *Advanced technology—New fixes or new problems? Verbal communications in the aviation system*. Paper presented at Beyond Pilot Error: A Symposium of Scientific Focus, sponsored by the Air Line Pilots Association, Washington, DC.

Simpson, C. A. (1983b, March). Evaluating computer speech devices for your application. In J. C. Warren (Ed.), *Proceedings of the Seventh West Coast Computer Faire* (pp. 395-401). Woodside, CA: West Coast Computer Faire.

Simpson, C. A. (1984). Integrated voice controls and speech displays for rotorcraft mission management (SAE Technical Paper Series 831523). *SAE 1983 Transactions, 92*(4), 271-280. Warrendale, PA: SAE.

Simpson, C. A. (in press). *Voice displays for single pilot IFR* (NASA Contract Report CR-172422). Hampton, VA: NASA-Langley Research Center.

Simpson, C. A., Coler, C. R., and Huff, E. M. (1982, March). Human factors of voice I/O for aircraft cockpit controls and displays. In D. Pallett (Ed.), *Proceedings of the Workshop on Standardization for Speech I/O Technology* (pp. 159-166). Gaithersburg, MD: National Bureau of Standards.

Simpson, C. A., and Marchionda-Frost, K. (1984). Synthesized speech rate and pitch effects on intelligibility of warning messages for pilots. *Human Factors, 26*, 509-517.

Simpson, C. A., Marchionda-Frost, K., and Navarro, T. N. (1984, October). Comparison of voice types for helicopter voice warning systems (SAE Technical Paper Series 841611). In *Proceedings of the Third Aerospace Behavioral Engineering Technical Conference, 1984 SAE Aerospace Congress and Exposition*. Warrendale, PA: SAE.

Simpson, C. A., and Navarro, T. N. (1984, May). Intelligibility of computer generated speech as a function of multiple factors. In *Proceedings of the National Aerospace and Electronics Conference* (84CH1984-7 NAECON) (pp. 932-940). New York: IEEE.

Simpson, C. A., and Williams, D. H. (1975, May). Human factors research problems in electronic voice warning system design. In *Proceedings of the 11th Annual Conference on Manual Control* (NASA TMX-62,464) (pp. 94-106). Moffett Field, CA: NASA-Ames Research Center.

Simpson, C. A., and Williams, D. H. (1980). Response time effects of alerting tone and semantic context for synthesized voice cockpit warnings. *Human Factors, 22*, 319-320.

Smith, C. (1983, September). Relating the performance of speech processors to the bit error rate. *Speech Technology, 2*(1), pp. 41-53.

Smith, G. (1984). Five voice synthesizers. *Byte: The Small Systems Journal, 9*(10), 337-347.

Spine, T. M., Maynard, J. F., and Williges, B. H. (1983, September). Error correction strategies for voice recognition. In *Proceedings of the Voice Data Entry Systems Application Conference*, Chicago, IL: American Voice I/O Society.

Stern, K. R. (1984). An evaluation of written, graphics, and voice messages in proceduralized instructions. In *Proceedings of the Human Factors Society 28th Annual Meeting* (Vol. 1) (pp. 314-318). Santa Monica, CA: Human Factors Society.

Thomas, J. C., Rosson, M. B., and Chodorow, M. (1984, October). Human factors and synthetic speech. In *Proceedings of the Human Factors Society 28th Annual Meeting* (Vol. 2) (pp. 763-767). Santa Monica, CA: Human Factors Society.

U.S. Department of Defense. (1981, May). *Human engineering design criteria for military systems, equipment, and facilities* (MIL-STD-1472C). Washington, DC: Author.

Van Cott, H. P., and Kinkade, R. G. (Eds.). (1972). *Human engineering guide to equipment design* (rev. ed). Washington, DC: U.S. Government Printing Office.

Voorhees, J. W., Bucher, N. M., Huff, E. M., Simpson, C. A., and Williams, D. H. (1983). Voice interactive electronic warning system (VIEWS). In *Proceedings of the IEEE/*

AIAA 5th Digital Avionics Systems Conference (83CH1839-0) (pp. 3.5.1-3.5.8). New York: IEEE.

Voorhees, J. W., Marchionda, K., and Atchison, V. (1982, March). Auditory display of helicopter cockpit information. In *Proceedings of the Workshop on Standardization for Speech I/O Technology*. Gaithersburg MD: National Bureau of Standards.

Welch, J. R. (1977, September). *Automated data entry analysis* (RADC TR-77-306). Griffiss AFB, New York: Rome Air Development Center.

Wickens, C. D., Sandry, D. L., and Vidulich, M. (1983). Compatibility and resource competition between modalities of input, central processing, and output. *Human Factors, 25,* 227-248.

Wierwille, W. W., and Connor, S. A. (1983). Evaluation of 20 pilot workload measures using a psychomotor task in a moving-base aircraft simulator. *Human Factors, 25,* 1-16.

Williams, D. H., and Simpson, C. A. (1976). A systematic approach to advanced cockpit warning systems for air transport operations: Line pilot preferences. In *Proceedings of the Aircraft Safety and Operating Problems Conference* (NASA SP-416) (pp. 617-644). Norfolk, VA: NASA-Langley Research Center.

Williges, B. H., and Williges, R. C. (1982). Structuring human/computer dialogue using speech technology. In *Proceedings of the Workshop on Standardization for Speech I/O Technology.* (pp. 143-151). Gaithersburg, MD: National Bureau of Standards.

Woodson, W. E. (1981). *Human factors design handbook.* New York: McGraw-Hill.

Zoltan-Ford, E. (1984). Reducing variability in natural language interactions with computers. In *Proceedings of the Human Factors Society 28th Annual Meeting* (Vol. 2.) (pp. 768-772). Santa Monica, CA: Human Factors Society.

Realism in synthetic speech

Synthesized speech may be intelligible, but it often sounds artificial; researchers are solving that problem

A technician at the Westinghouse Electric Corp.'s defense electronics manufacturing plant in Baltimore peers into a microscope, examining a partially completed hybrid circuit on a wafer.

"Enter defects," says a computer at the technician's side.

"Wire," the technician responds.

"Enter defect verb."

"Missing."

The dialogue continues, with the technician pinpointing the site of the missing wire and the action he takes to repair the circuit. The computer stores all this information to give the company a complete record for quality control.

Scenes like this, while still isolated, are expected to become fairly common in a few years as computers that not only listen, but also talk intelligibly and naturally, help workers to check manufactured products and help the general public to access information stored in data bases.

The system at the Westinghouse plant is one of the best money can buy today in at least one major respect—it talks intelligibly enough to guide the technician in carrying out his tasks. But intelligibility alone may not fill the needs of other potentially important applications, such as the delivery of information from a data base to a telephone caller. In this case, the realistic quality of speech is important, and that is the goal of research efforts today: synthetic speech that is not only intelligible but also sounds natural—almost human.

The speech-synthesis system employed at the Westinghouse plant and other systems that are beginning to be offered are the culmination of many years of research that began at the Joint Speech Research Unit in London in the early 1960s and continued there and at such places as the Massachusetts Institute of Technology in Cambridge, IBM Corp. in Yorktown Heights, N.Y., and AT&T Bell Laboratories in Murray Hill, N.J., as well as laboratories in Sweden, Japan, France, and elsewhere.

A fair amount of commercially available speech-synthesis systems convert text into speech rather than produce audible messages from prerecorded words. While these text-to-speech conversion systems produce acceptably intelligible speech, most lack naturalness.

Research is focusing on speech synthesis from text and the tough problem of creating speech that is not only highly intelligible but also sounds natural.

A bewildering array of variables

The problem involves such critical tasks as programming a computer for word pronunciation and intonation, as well as simulating the human vocal tract electronically to make the sounds seem natural. For a language such as English, with its vocabulary of some half a million words and its diversity of

ADVANCED TECHNOLOGY
COMPUTERS

linguistic rules, this is especially hard.

How does one program the computer, for example, to pronounce the letter combination *gh*? In the word *thorough*, *gh* has no sound; in *enough*, it is pronounced *f*; in *ghost*, it is pronounced *g*. Moreover, some words may be pronounced in more than one way, depending on the meaning intended. Consider the word *invalid*. When the accent is on the second syllable, the meaning is *not valid*. When the accent is on the first syllable of the word, it means *one who is sickly or disabled*.

Intonation is even more difficult in computer programming. The proper intonation depends on the context in which each word is used in a sentence. Take the sentence *I told you*. Depending on which of the three words is stressed with a rising intonation, the sentence takes on a different meaning.

When it comes to reproducing the vocal tract electronically, the best that researchers can hope for is close approximation. The physics of replicating such human effects on sound as the movement of lips and tongue, the vibration of vocal chords, and the reflection of sounds within the vocal tract is enormously complex.

Advanced systems turning up

Although researchers are still far from creating flawless computer speech, some advanced synthesis systems are turning up in industry [see table]. There are two distinct classes—those costing $3000 or more, which are intended for general use by groups of people, and those that generally cost less than $400, typically intended for repeated and lengthy use by an individual, such as a computer enthusiast. A typical system of the first category is the Prose 2000 text-into-speech converter, used at the Westinghouse plant in Baltimore and elsewhere. The system is available as a printed-circuit board from Speech Plus Inc., of Mountain View, Calif. [Fig. 1].

At the core of this speech synthesizer is a read-only memory

Gadi Kaplan   Senior Associate Editor
Eric J. Lerner   Contributing Editor

Defining terms

Allophone—a variant of a phoneme or basic sound
Formant—a resonant frequency in spoken sound
Morph—The smallest part of a written word with linguistic significance, such as a root—for example, *cover* in the word *coverage*
Phoneme—the basic sound unit in a language. For example, the sound of *d* in the word *dot*
Pitch—a subjective attribute of the "highness" of a sound, described in terms of a fundamental frequency and other parameters
Vocal tract—the bodily organs that produce speech, including vocal cords, larynx, mouth, tongue, nasal cavities
Vocal-tract model—the electronic part of a speech synthesizer that produces sounds

that stores extensive software, a microprocessor, and a programmable digital signal processor—an integrated circuit. This processor electronically produces sounds similar to those produced by the human vocal tract. The software [Fig. 2] does the following:

• "Normalizes" the text by converting it into a uniform written style. For example, *Mr.* is normalized as *MISTER*.

• Writes the normalized text as a string of phonemes, or basic sounds such as *b* in the word *bit*, and marks accents.

• Indicates how each phoneme should be pronounced.

• Determines how long each phoneme should be sounded and how the intonation should vary.

• Produces for each phoneme 18 time-varying acoustic parameters, such as resonance frequencies, or formants, and the bandwidths that characterize the human vocal tract during speech. These parameters, in turn, control the digital signal processor—the electronic equivalent of the human vocal tract.

Text-into-speech systems like this go a step beyond the stored-speech-synthesis systems that use digitized prerecorded speech for special purposes, such as announcements in train stations or elevators. In such systems, human speech is recorded, digitized, and permanently stored in the computer memory. Words are recreated from this stored inventory under computer control, but the vocabulary is small although speech-compression techniques allow relatively compact storage.

Many of the commercial synthesis systems today produce accented, somewhat robotic speech in converting text to speech. Sometimes the speech is hard for casual users to understand.

Coming to grips with pronunciation

Pronunciation, intonation, and electronic simulation of the vocal tract are the major concerns of researchers in the United States and elsewhere, as efforts to achieve more natural speech synthesis accelerate. The most straightforward way of handling English and its enormous vocabulary and wide swings in pronunciation is to store the entire vocabulary in a pronunciation dictionary in the computer memory, says Bishnu S. Atal, speech-synthesis researcher at AT&T Bell Laboratories in Murray Hill, N.J. The pronunciation list of the entire English vocabulary could be stored in a memory of roughly 5 megabytes, Atal believes. Other experts agree with this figure if newly coined words and proper names are excluded. At today's prices, the cost of that memory storage would come to about $400—somewhat expensive for many applications, Atal notes. But improvements in electronics—particularly very large-scale integration (VLSI) and the expected availability of memory chips that will accommodate 4 megabits per chip—would reduce the cost.

Throughout the evolution of speech synthesis, researchers in several laboratories have been trying to devise more accurate pronunciation algorithms than those of the prevailing systems.

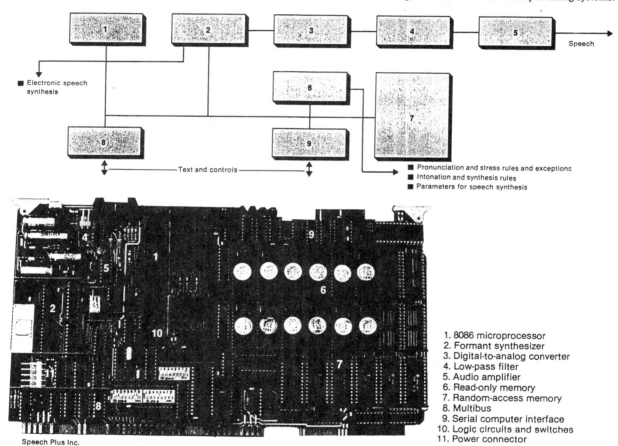

■ Pronunciation and stress rules and exceptions
■ Intonation and synthesis rules
■ Parameters for speech synthesis

1. 8086 microprocessor
2. Formant synthesizer
3. Digital-to-analog converter
4. Low-pass filter
5. Audio amplifier
6. Read-only memory
7. Random-access memory
8. Multibus
9. Serial computer interface
10. Logic circuits and switches
11. Power connector

Speech Plus Inc.

[1] An advanced system to convert written English into speech with unlimited vocabulary, the Prose 2000 from Speech Plus Inc. employs a formant synthesizer—an electronic circuit that produces sounds similar to those produced by the vocal tract when a human speaks. A read-only memory contains speech-synthesis software that includes instructions for converting text (in American Standard Code for Information Interchange format) into a stream of 18 continuously changing parameters that control the synthesizer. The converter employs a random-access memory for temporary data storage as well as multibus and serial computer interfaces, logic circuits, an 8086 microprocessor that controls the synthesizer, and other components.

One approach, originated by Jonathan Allen of the Massachusetts Institute of Technology in the late 1960s, aims at breaking written words into the smallest parts that are linguistically meaningful—called morphs—and then using algorithms to derive the correct pronunciation of the words. The morphs that make up words can be smaller words, or letter combinations such as *ly* added to an adjective to turn it into an adverb, or even single letters. For example, the morphs for the word *photography* are *photo*, *graph*, and *y*, and the pronunciation of the second *o* here is different than in either *photograph* or the isolated word *photo*. In *photography*, the second *o* is accented and sounds somewhat like the *a* in *ah*. In *photograph*, the second *o* is not accented and sounds like the *u* in *uh*, while in *photo* it has a long *o* sound.

Allen has catalogued pronunciations for some 8000 morphs, and he feels that the use of such a dictionary in a speech-synthesis system is practical even though it requires a relatively large storage, compared with that of a commercial system such as Speech Plus's Prose 2000.

The storage requirements can be reduced by using general rules for pronunciation of morphs, instead of a morph dictionary. At the Cornell University Phonetics Laboratory in Ithaca, N.Y., speech-synthesis-by-rule expert Susan Hertz has developed a set of text-into-speech algorithms including rules that analyze English words into their component morphs. Some 200 rules identify prefixes such as *sub-* and suffixes such as *-er*, and separate them from the remaining part, or root, of the word. For example, the rules divide the word *subscriber* into the prefix *sub-*, the root *scribe*, and the suffix *-er*.

There are, of course, exceptions to the rules. Hertz deals with these by building the exceptions into the rules, much like the well-known spelling rule "*i* before *e* except after *c*." For example, the general rule for pronouncing the suffix *-ed* would strip the suffix as a separate syllable (as in *lagged, picked, or booked*); it would exclude words such as *jagged*, *wicked*, and *crooked*, in which the suffix is pronounced differently.

There is a tradeoff, however, between the computer storage, required mostly for the dictionary of exceptions, and the calcula-

Representative commercial text-to-speech conversion systems

Company	Model	Cost, U.S.$	Languages	Form[1]	Voices Adult male	Voices Adult female	Voices Child	Pitch range, Hz	Speech power, watts into 8-ohm speaker	Speech mode Letters	Speech mode Words	Speech rate, words per minute
Ackerman Digital Systems Inc. Elmhurst, Ill.	Synthetalker	310	English	Board	•	•		NA	0.2		•	NA
Digital Equipment Corp. Maynard, Mass.	DECtalk	4000	English	Peripheral	•	•	•	NA	NA		•	120–350
Don't Ask Computer Software Los Angeles, Calif.	Software Automatic Mouth	125	English	Software	•			NA	NA		•	NA
First Byte Inc. Long Beach, Calif.	Smooth Talker	149	English	Software	•	•		50–300	NA	•	•	100–400
Infovox AB Danderyd, Sweden	SA 201/PC	1305	English French Spanish German Italian Swedish Norwegian[3]	Board	•	•	•	0–512	1.0	•	•	Up to 250
	SC2000	35 000	As in SA 201/PC	System	•	•	•	0–512	1.0	•	•	Up to 250
Intex Micro-Systems Birmingham, Mich.	Intex Talker	295	English	Peripheral	•	•	•	NA	1.0	•	•	120
Micromint Inc. Vernon, Conn.	Sweet Talker II	100	English	Board	•			NA	1.0		•	NA
Speech Plus Inc. Mountain View, Calif.	Prose 2000	3225	English	Board	•			50–200	2.0	•	•	50–200
	CallText 5100	10 325	English	System	•			50–200	0.5	•	•	50–250
Street Electronics Corp. Carpinteria, Calif.	Echo GP	225	English	Peripheral	•			50–500	1.0	•	•	90 or 150 (2-syllable words)
Votrax Inc. Troy, N.Y.	Personal Speech System	400	English	Peripheral	•			NA	1.0	•	•	NA
X-Com Meylan, France	Dicton III	2160	French	Peripheral	•			NA	2.0		•	NA

NA—not applicable or data not available.
1. Board: a printed circuit board that is plugged into a computer. Peripheral: a device that attaches to a computer or to another device, such as a terminal, but has its own power. Software: computer programs supplied on a floppy disk, used in common computers. System: a peripheral with built-in intelligence; may be programmable and may have more than one channel.
2. FS: formant synthesis—simulation of the formants, or resonances of the vocal tract: LPC; linear predictive coding—a mathematical representation of the vocal tract as acoustic tubes.
3. Software for each of these languages may be selected.

tions needed to implement the rules of pronouncing written English words. The greater the number of rules and the smaller the dictionary, the greater the calculation and the smaller the storage requirement, according to Allen at MIT.

Picking the right sound

But storage requirements grow with the number of individual sounds, and there is plenty of variety to deal with. A phoneme typically has several variations, called allophones, determined by the phonemes that precede and follow it, since the configuration of the human vocal mechanism—the larynx, tongue, teeth and vocal chords—changes continuously during speech.

For example, the k sound in *keep* is different from the initial sound in *count*, because the k sounds are followed by different vowels, says Dennis H. Klatt, speech-synthesis expert at MIT and originator of both the Prose 2000 and DECtalk, a rival system offered by the Digital Equipment Corp. in Maynard, Mass. The e in keep has higher-frequency components than the o in *count* because the e is produced with the tongue forward in the mouth, whereas for the o the tongue is held toward the back.

The allophonic variations of a phoneme as a result of the sounds preceding it and following it are best characterized by changes in such parameters as formants—the acoustic resonance frequencies—and their bandwidths. There are two important considerations here—the values of formants at the end of a phoneme and at the beginning of the following phoneme, and the law by which the formants change between these values. For example, in the vowel–consonant combination el (as in *elderly*), the lowest formant is changed linearly from 520 to 360 Hz—the typical values for the e and the l, respectively. But that law and similar ones are crude and lead to sounds that are unacceptably artificial; researchers are seeking to refine such rules.

For example, MIT's Klatt obtained more natural speech than that possible with these crude techniques when the formants during a transition from one phoneme to another started and ended in different values than those characteristic of the isolated phonemes. Each transition had its optimal formant start and end points. Now, after two years of painstaking analysis and synthesis, Klatt says he has compiled tables of optimized values for formants in all the consonant–vowel and vowel–consonant transitions in English. All of this is covered by six rules and several exceptions, he further notes. Such rules are included in the Prose 2000 and DECtalk systems.

Transitions between phonemes could be the key to more intelligible and natural-sounding speech synthesis. At the AT&T Bell Laboratories, Joseph P. Olive, a speech-synthesis specialist, is refining his approach. Under development for about 15 years, this approach is based on tying together transitions between phonemes, rather than the phonemes themselves. A demonstration system based on this principle is operating at the Epcot Center near Orlando, Fla. The system there uses a table of transitions, Olive explained; the table includes some 900 transitions, or about one-half the number of all possible transitions for the 43 phonemes in the English language. This is adequate for practical use, Olive added. He and his colleagues at Bell Labs have developed an experimental, improved version that he feels sounds more natural than the system that is operating at Epcot.

In addition to transitions from one sound to another, the duration of each sound must be considered. For both intelligibility and realism, each sound must have the proper duration—not too short and not too long. Duration is also important for emphasis. When emphasized, a phoneme is generally held longer than when it is without emphasis, but exactly how to relate sound length to emphasis is a problem researchers are still grappling with. It turns out that parsing information can help here.

Synthesis technique used[2]	Computer interface	Other features and comments
FS	S-100	Includes text-to-speech software on a diskette; pitch and speech rate are interdependent
FS	RS232	Interfaces with push-button telephone; has built-in diagnostics; has pitch control and other controls
NA	NA	Software only; accepts phonetic alphabet as well as English inputs
Patent applied for	NA	Software only; compatible with Macintosh computer; has pitch, speech rate, and volume controls
FS	RS232; IBM parallel and IBM bus	Compatible with IBM PC personal computer; available as a stand-alone unit (a peripheral) for $1980
FS	Per customer need	For data retrieval via a push-button telephone; serves 10 callers simultaneously; also accommodates prerecorded, stored speech
FS	Parallel Centronix-signal compatible	Has 2700-character buffer memory; has 64 levels of inflection
NA	Parallel	Compatible with Apple computers
FS	RS232C (IEEE P796)	Accepts text and phonemes in American Standard Code for Information Interchange Multibus(ASCII); has 500-character buffer storage; pitch, speech rate and other controls
FS	RS232C	For data retrieval via a push-button telephone; accepts text phonemes in ASCII characters; serves up to 5 callers simultaneously
LPC	RS232	Has 1700-character buffer storage; accepts coded phonemes
FS	RS232C	Synthesizes sound effects; has 3500-character buffer storage
LPC	RS232; multibus (IEEE P796)	Includes a buffer storage; Italian and German versions planned

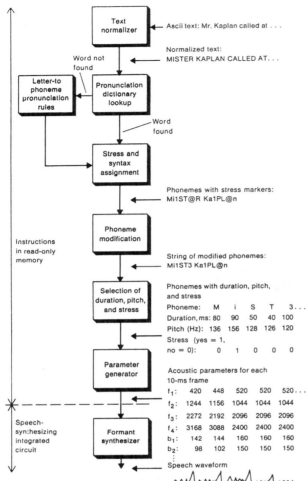

[2] *Software for conversion of text into speech first puts the text into a fully spelled-out (normalized) format, in which an abbreviation such as* Mr. *is automatically turned into* MISTER. *The software then uses a pronunciation dictionary and a set of rules to find out what phonemes—basic speech sounds—should be used. Subsequently, the software inserts stress marks; modifies the phonemes to account for preceding and succeeding sounds; and determines the duration, pitch, and stress for each sound. Finally, it generates parameters such as formants (f₁, f₂, etc.) and bandwidths (b₁, b₂, etc.) for speech synthesis.*

Klatt has developed a computer program that determines how long phonemes should be sounded based on their role in the sentence. The program requires, however, that the text given to the computer include some parsing information—such as an indication whether a word is a "content" word, such as a noun, verb, adjective, or adverb, or is merely a conjunction or preposition. Futhermore, the program requires the identification of the parts of a sentence, such as main and subordinate clauses. Based on an algorithm that uses the parsing data, the program shrinks or stretches a phoneme's length according to its role in the sentence.

Intonation, or melody, is important for stress and phrasing; Bell Labs researchers Mark D. Anderson, Janet B. Pierrehumbert, and Mark Y. Liberman have been studying how to characterize intonation. For example, when a male speaker says "Anne" in response to a question such as "Who was here?" the pitch typically goes from a high frequency of about 120 Hz down to about 70 Hz. When a male speaker asks the question "Anne?" the pitch goes up from 80 to about 140 Hz.

Modeling these and similar phenomena by quantitative rules is difficult, but some progress has been made. Intonation can now be described successfully in terms of high and low tones in pitch and the changes between them. Bell Labs researchers, after studying how high and low tones are produced in speech, have built a synthesizer that implements their findings. The Bell technique for synthesizing intonation and stress can handle any pattern of pitch, or fundamental frequency of speech, including that pertaining to a question.

Ideal intonation, however, would require the computer to be able to parse a sentence, and researchers are still far from achieving that.

Producing speech electronically

Meanwhile, Atal and his co-workers, as well as such researchers as Klatt at MIT, have been struggling to perfect the digital simulation of the human vocal tract—the key piece of hardware in a speech synthesizer. At least three techniques—formant (resonant frequency) synthesis, linear predictive coding, and waveform sampling—have evolved over the years as the main tools for production of speech. Only the first two are used in text-to-speech conversion, because they require smaller storage and slower data rates.

Formant synthesis, for example, requires a data rate of about 100 bits, based on a typical rate of 12 phonemes per second, with each phoneme characterized by an 8-bit code. By contrast, waveform sampling uses a common analog-to-digital conversion and requires about 64 000 bits per second for uncompressed speech (8000 samples per second to capture up to 4000 Hz, multiplied by 8 bits per sample).

In formant synthesis, additional hardware digitally simulates resonance and antiresonance phenomena in the vocal tract. Arranged both in series and in parallel, circuits replicate the

[3] *An electronic vocal tract in the form of an integrated circuit produces English speech by simulating resonances* (R) *and an antiresonance* (A) *of the mouth, throat, and nose. Periodic impulses simulate the flapping vocal cords when vowels are spoken. A noise source imitates the turbulence generated at the* teeth and lips when speaking such sounds as f and s. Resonances in series (top) are for voiced sounds such as those produced by the vowels and by v and z, and the parallel branch simulates voiceless speech sounds such as f and s. Arrows indicate varying inputs—control parameters for fundamental resonant and antiresonant frequencies (f₀, f₁, f₂, f₃, f₄, and f_z); bandwidths (b₁, b₂, and b₃); and amplitudes for voiced, h-like, f-like, and bypass sounds (A_V, A_H, A_F, A_B) as well as for the resonances (A₂, A₃, A₄, A₅, A₆). A passive filter (G) shapes the pulses.

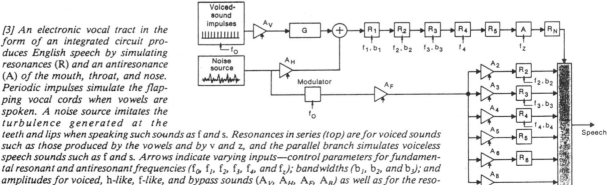

Rating the speech synthesizers

Results are now available from several evaluations of speech-synthesis systems; further reviews are underway.

Following a systematic evaluation of four text-to-speech conversion systems, Howard C. Nusbaum and David B. Pisoni —researchers at the Speech Research Laboratory of the psychology department at Indiana University in Bloomington— reported last September that "the quality of synthetic speech generated by rule will begin to approximate natural speech more closely." During tests, for example, listeners understood synthetic speech produced by Digital Equipment Corp.'s DECtalk system 97.7 percent of the time, compared with 99.4 percent for human speech, Nusbaum and Pisoni told the Fourth Voice Data Entry System Applications Conference in Arlington, Va.

Three other systems were also evaluated: MITalk-79—a research system of the Massachusetts Institute of Technology; a developmental model from Speech Plus Inc. of Mountain View, Calif., that preceded the company's Prose 2000 system; and Type-N-Talk, made by Votrax of Troy, Mich. During the tests, listeners were asked to identify words produced by the systems or spoken by humans. In an experiment called a modified rhyme test, 72 listeners were asked to choose from a list of six rhyming words the one that was actually being spoken. Words such as *tip*, *rip*, and *sip* were used.

At Michigan State University in East Lansing, researchers are investigating how intelligibility is affected by speech-synthesis techniques such as pulse-code modulation, linear predictive coding, and formant synthesis.   —G.K.

---

function of the vocal tract cavities [Fig. 3]. A periodic impulse source simulates the more or less periodic air pulses emanating from the vocal cords during such sounds as vowels. The fundamental frequency of these pulses determines the voice's pitch. A noise source in the hardware represents all other speech sounds—for example, those produced during fricatives, such as *s* or *f*. The frequency of impulses—as well as the circuit's resonant frequencies, bandwidths, and gains—are varied to reflect the varying configurations of the tongue, lips, teeth, and other parts of the vocal tract during human speech.

Introduced more than 15 years ago, linear predictive coding (LPC), by contrast, is a mathematical representation of the vocal tract as an acoustic waveguide comprising a succession of 12 to 16 uniform tubes with different areas that change dynamically during speech. Digitally represented periodical or aperiodical sound sources—for voiced and unvoiced sounds, respectively—excite the tubes, creating a series of advancing and retreating pressure waves in them. Atal and his co-workers recently replaced the LPC model that uses the common periodic pulse and white noise sources—the exitation sources— with a new LPC model that has only one source. Because it produces several pulses during each pitch period rather than the single pulse of the current model, the new, multipulse LPC model replicates the detail of vocal tract excitation better than the current one-pulse model, Atal said. As a result, the model leads to more realistic synthetic speech, he added.

In other areas of research, Klatt at MIT is seeking to synthesize the female voice, which differs from male-voice synthesis because women typically speak in a higher pitch than men. When Klatt increased the excitation frequency of a male-voice-tract model, there were undesirable jumps in the pitch of the speech. Extensive work led to a new technique in which the sound source operates at four times the sampling frequency used for the rest of Klatt's experimental speech-synthesis system, an approach that has produced "some success," he said.

Problems of this nature, many researchers agree, are what makes speech synthesis such a demanding discipline. Cecil Coker, speech-synthesis reseacher at Bell Labs, reported that one could easily spend a month on tuning or optimizing the vocal-tract parameters to make just one phoneme sound natural when preceded and followed by various other phonemes—only to discover later an additional phoneme combination in which the phoneme in question sounded artificial.

Is perfect speech synthesis necessary? Some researchers say no. Ed Bruckert, an electronics engineer with Digital Equipment and one of the designers of the DECtalk system, said he believed a system that sounded too human might scare its users. In some applications, it is in fact desirable for synthetic speech to be far from perfect, some engineers noted. A case in point, they said, is the announcement system on the train that links the departure gates at the Atlanta, Ga., airport with the main terminal. The engineers there deliberately "untuned" the speech

synthesizer, which originally sounded fairly realistic, because they felt that passengers would be more attentive to robot-sounding announcements.

But the main goal remains highly intelligible and natural-sounding speech. If most researchers have their way, many people will be able before long to pick up the telephone, dial a computer, and ask for a piece of information at random. The computer will retrieve the information from a large data base and read it over the phone—intelligibly and with feeling.

To probe further

An overview of developments before 1973, including original works of many pioneers in the field, is presented in the book *Speech Synthesis*, edited by James L. Flanagan and Lawrence R. Rabiner and published by Dowden, Hutchinson & Ross Inc., Stroudsburg, Pa., 1973.

For an elaborate description of the MITalk-79 speech-synthesis system, see "Notes on the MITalk-79 system for conversion of unrestricted English text to speech," written by Dennis H. Klatt, Sherry Hunnicutt, and David B. Pisoni, and edited by Jonathan Allen at the Massachusetts Institute of Technology. The report is available from Allen; telephone 617-253-2509.

One approach to coarticulation—the effect of a phoneme on the one preceding or following it—is outlined by Dennis Klatt in "Synthesis by Rule of Consonant–Vowel Syllables," *Working Papers of the Speech Communications Group*, vol. 2, MIT Research Laboratory of Electronics, fall 1983.

Janet Pierrehumbert summarizes her algorithms for speech intonation in "Synthesizing Intonation," *Journal of the Acoustical Society of America*, vol. 70, October 1981, pp. 985–95.

Two approaches to vocal-tract models are outlined in "Software for a Cascade/Parallel Formant Synthesizer," by Dennis H. Klatt, *Journal of the Acoustical Society of America*, vol. 67, March 1980, pp. 971-995, and in "Signal Models for Low Bit-Rate Coding of Speech" by J.L. Flanagan, K. Ishizaka, and B.L. Shipley, *Journal of the Acoustical Society of America*, vol. 68, September 1980, pp. 781–91.

A speech-research system (SRS)—a highly flexible computer system to develop text-to-speech rules for any language—is described in "From Text to Speech With SRS" by Susan R. Hertz, *Journal of the Acoustical Society of America*, vol. 72, October 1982, pp. 1155–70.

Speech analysis and synthesis in several countries are discussed in 12 papers in the proceedings of ICASSP '84, the IEEE International Conference on Acoustics, Speech and Signal Processing (IEEE publication no. 84CH1945-5).

Speech synthesizers for personal computers are discussed in "Talk To Me," by Trudy E. Bell, *Personal Computing*, September 1983, pp. 120–131.

"Perceptual Evaluation of Synthetic Speech: Some consideration of the user/system interface," by D.B. Pisoni et al. appears in the proceedings of ICASSP for 1983, pp. 535–38.   ◆

Communicating with Sound

Moderator: William Buxton, University of Toronto

Panelists: Sara A. Bly, Xerox Office Systems Division
Steven P. Frysinger, AT&T Bell Laboratories
David Lunney, East Carolina University
Douglass L. Mansur, Lawrence Livermore National Laboratory
Joseph J. Mezrich, Exxon Corporate Research Laboratories
Robert C. Morrison, East Carolina University

Overview

The *Communicating with Sound* panel for CHI '85 will focus on ways of expanding the user interface by using sound as a significant means of output. As a user's communication from the computer has progressed from large (and often smeary) printout to a teletypewriter and, finally, to the multi-window workstation displays of today, the emphasis has remained primarily on visual output. Although many user terminals and workstations have the capability of generating sound, that capability is rarely used for more than audio cues (indicating status such as an error condition or task completion) and simple musical tunes. Research shows that sounds convey meaningful information to users. With examples of such research, the panel members will demonstrate a variety of uses of sound output, discuss issues raised by the work, and suggest further directions. The intent of the panel is to stimulate thinking about expanding the user interface and to discuss areas for future research.

In the statements that follow, each panelist will describe his or her own work, including the data and audio dimensions used, the value of the research, remaining issues to be addressed, and suggestions for future research and application. A list of references is included for those who wish further reading.

from S. Bly

I am especially interested in finding ways to enhance the graphical presentations of data. I have considered three types of data that I believe are often difficult to represent and/or understand visually: multivariate, time-varying, and logarithmic. In each case, I have examined various aspects of sound that might be appropriate for the data and various encodings that map the data to sound dimensions.

For multivariate data, I used seven characteristics of an individual note: pitch, volume, duration, the fundamental waveshape, the attack envelope, the addition of a 5th harmonic, and the addition of a 9th harmonic. The pitch varied over 12 notes for each of four octaves in a piano scale, the volume varied over 12 values, and the duration ranged from 50 msec to 1050 msec. The waveshape (from sinusoidal to random), envelope (from long, slow attack to constant amplitude), and harmonics (with a varying waveshape) provided some degree of timbre control, a strong characteristic of sounds. My intent was to vary each sound dimension over a range which provided noticeable extremes, was easily audible throughout, and was computationally straightforward.

The multivariate data consisted of sets of n-tuples; thus, each n-tuple was represented by a single sound. I presented 6-dimensional data graphically, aurally, and both graphically and aurally to different groups of subjects. The results showed that the sounds did improve the subject's ability to discriminate between two data sets.

For time-varying data, I used an encoding similar to that used for multivariate data. However, since an interesting problem in time-varying data is to track two or more functions simultaneously, I varied only pitch and volume for a given function and varied the waveform across functions. This allowed a user to distinguish among functions.

For logarithmic data, I varied only the frequency of a note. For a given data value n, the output frequency, f, was calculated as $f = a \cdot 2^{b \cdot n}$, where the range of data values determines constants a and b so that the frequency range is audible. A log/linear plot could then be represented by a sequence of notes.

All the applications of sound encoding indicate the value of sound as a means of information presentation. Informally, as well as in formal tests, users were able to draw appropriate conclusions about data from aural information. Such positive results only strengthen the need for further research.

I believe that future work in using sound in the computer/human interface should include both exploration and formal studies. I suggest three areas for immediate work: exploring sound as an enhancement to time-varying data problems, exploring sound in a more straight-forward application of audio cues, and experimenting with the aspects of sound which convey the most information in a computer/human environment. In general, I believe that in problem solving, a person should have available as many resources as possible. The power of the computer, particularly with the advent of available individual workstations, has not been fully utilized. Too often, we merely mimic existing methods of problem solving rather than offer new tools and techniques. I recommend that we actively probe ways of expanding the computer/human interface.

This work was performed under the auspices of the U.S. Department of Energy by Lawrence Livermore National Laboratory under Contract W-7405-Eng-48.

from S. Frysinger and J. Mezrich

Traditional data representation techniques result in complicated, static displays when applied to multidimensional time series. We have developed a dynamic auditory and visual display system which permits the data analyst to "play" the data much like one would play a movie. For a k-dimensional time series, each "frame" of data consists of k objects in the visual display whose location is a function of data value, and k "voices" in the auditory display. The pitch of each voice is proportional to its data value. Played in sequence, such frames form a visual "dance" with a contrapuntal auditory accompaniment.

Exploratory data analysis is a common task when working with multidimensional time series data. Any set of measurements of different quantities which vary with a common index, such as time, yields multidimensional time series data. Examples include stock market data, economic indicators, well log measurements, and infrared spectrograms.

The analyst's task is to tease out relationships among the variables. In some cases the type of relationship one is looking for is known in advance. Often, however, the relationship involves complex, unpredictable interactions among the variables. The analyst examines the data to try to detect familiar patterns of interaction, and thus performs global pattern recognition. A data representation which facilitates global pattern recognition and allows the analyst to interact with the data display is needed. Our dynamic auditory and visual display system serves this need.

The auditory portion of our display is constructed by mapping each data element into a frequency value for its representative voice. Quantization at this point constrains the auditory display to three octaves of a chromatic musical scale, with the penalty of some loss of information. This choice was made because it was oberved that "melodies" on a continuous frequency scale were both unpleasnt and hard to remember; a musically quantized scale takes advantage of the analyst's years of exposure to, if not formal training in, music.

The ranges of the k voices are completely overlapped to avoid discriminatory ordering. As a consequence, crossing voices cannot be unambiguously resolved, unless the voices in the series are made to have a different waveform (which capability is provided in the working system, but not the experimental one). This is believed to favor global inspection of the data over the scrutiny of individual dimensions, although this has not been formally tested.

To test our dynamic auditory/visual display system, we set up a forced-choice classification experiment. Test data were either correlated or uncorrelated, and a transformed up-down procedure was used to determine the threshold of detectable correlation. The lower the threshold correlation, the better the data representation for correlation detection. The dynamic display system was compared in this experiment with three conventional visual display types; overlaid graphs, stacked graphs, and discretely arrayed graphs. Using four-dimensional time series (with series length an experimental parameter), the subject was presented with an uncorrelated series and a correlated series (in random order), and was required to report which series was correlated. Each subject was tested in this manner in four different sessions, one for each display type. The order of display types was varied from subject to subject, and the experiment was conducted for series of length 10, 20, and 40 samples.

For all series lengths, the threshold correlation for the dynamic display was significantly lower than those for the discrete and stacked graph displays. It was also superior to the overlaid graphs for 10 samples series, after which the two became essentially equivalent. It was observed that the overlaid graphs and the dynamic display had in common that they could be viewed globally, while the stacked and discrete graphs required local scrutiny. The experimental threshold correlation was significantly higher for the stacked and discrete graphs than for the overlaid graph and dynamic display.

While this experiment showed that auditory data representation and visual data representation could be combined to produce an effective dynamic data display system, it failed to test formally the effectiveness of auditory data representation. The accompanying visual display constitutes a confounding experimental factor.

There is clearly room for experimental inquiry in auditory data representation. Three fundamental questions tempt the experimentalist:

1. What is the set of useful auditory dimensions, what are their perceptual transfer functions, and how can displays be constructed to take advantage of them?

2. What data analysis tasks are best suited to auditory data representaion, and what types of displays best accomodate each of them?

3. How do auditory data representation and visual data representation interact, and how can this interaction be utilized to maximum advantage?

A fair number of these questions depend on more basic research in psychoacoustics, cognition, and memory, and much can be learned from the study of musical perception.

Auditory data representation, in conjunction with dynamic visual representation, has been applied to a number of economic forecasting problems. It is currently being examined for DNA sequence representation.

from D. Mansur

My purpose will be to describe the advantages and primary application areas of the use of sound in computer workstations. Applications extend from such specialized areas as computer workstations for the blind (the author's initial focus of activity) towards systems useful for all users. Many parallels can be drawn between the advantages of graphics in many of today's workstations/personal computers and similar advantages with the uses of sound. As a continually-increasing number of computers enter the market with some capacity to generate audio output (the Apple Macintosh, Xerox Dandelion, and IBM-PC to name a few), proper attention should be paid towards incorporating sound into appropriate applications.

Sound and the Hearing Process Offer Unique Advantages

Certain aspects of sound are unique and worth exploiting as an avenue for information transfer. Human hearing, and the mental processes associated with it, have evolved to where verbal communication is perhaps the greatest means for information transfer. The pattern recognition capabilities of human hearing, however, are not limited to speech but include recognition of many special characteristics of both natural and man-made sounds.

The various "dimensions" of sound have been widely discussed, where the following is a partial list of those characteristics that listeners can discern:

    pitch,
    volume,
    spatial location,
    duration,
    timbre (harmonic content),
    attack (volume rise time), and
    timing.

Many of these sound features (except spatial location) can be easily manipulated on today's workstations. Beyond these "pure" aspects of sound there are a number of higher-level processes of human hearing that may be utilized. Patterns of sound are easily recognized and remembered even in the presence of high noise levels. The parallel processing involved with hearing, like that used in vision, provides nearly instantaneous recognition of sound patterns.

Feedback Via Audio Cues

The use of "audio cues" – short-duration sound objects similar to graphical icons in the visual domain – can be advantageous for enhancing computer workstations for several reasons. The "translation distance", a term used by Smith[1] to indicate the mental effort required to go from some (visual) representation to an object's meaning, may be quite small for well-designed audio cues. Glinert and Tanimoto's comments on the value of visual icons in Pict[2] may likewise apply to audio objects. Sound icons may transmit meaningful "chunks" (single units of information) much faster than textual messages displayed visually or spoken via computer-synthesized voice. Certain audio cues may, in fact, form a universal language similar to the now-familiar international traffic signs. Furthermore, audio cues can be given a structure or hierarchy that could be made to correspond to specific sub-tasks or classes of messages on a computer system. For example, audio cues for system messages might be labeled with different tonal qualities to differentiate between fatal errors, warning messages, and messages designed to be simply informative. Further categorization labels could indicate the process that generated the signal – such as the file handler, display editor or electronic mail system.

Finally, audio cues have five other major advantages:

1) Users need not pay strict attention to audio cues – relying on subconscious processes to detect significant events – while focusing attention on more interesting tasks.

2) The user need not be within clear line-of-sight of the computer display, as with visual methods. Distance and orientation to the source of sound is completely arbitrary.

3) Well-designed audio cues may be easier to learn than certain other forms of communication such as visual icons.

4) The visual landscape on a graphical display is already cluttered, and audio cues would limit the number of distracting textual messages.

5) Sound can be used where vision is unavailable, as when the user is blind, or when he or she is away from the computer and a telephone connection is all that is available.

Application Areas – Current Work

Recently some of us here at Lawrence Livermore Laboratory have been interested in several aspects of communication with sound. Currently, one of the efforts now underway is the development of a set of guidelines for the systematic creation of audio cues. The use of motifs – short patterns or themes of musical sounds – is being explored as one means of creating the audio cues or "earcons"[3]. The author's own work is described extensively elsewhere [4,5], and concerns the creation of "sound-graphs" – sound images that are designed to convey the information content of an x-y graph to a blind or sight-impaired user. By using a continuously-varying pitch to follow changes in the y-axis values of a curve, it was found that individuals could correctly recognize key features of curves

A human-factors experiment was carried out to test subjects on their ability to make judgments concerning the slopes of lines, the classification of curves (e.g. straight lines vs. exponentials), and the detection of monotonicity, convergence and symmetry. The 13 training and 22 testing curves were presented in an average time of under 20 minutes, and yet the accuracy of recognition ranged from 79% to 95% depending on the particular curve characteristic in question.

The advantages of such a computer-generated sound-graph system for the blind are:

1) An holistic understanding of the curve is obtained very rapidly (a 3 second duration was used to sweep the curve).

2) The user is independent of other individuals and can be free to explore the data at will.

3) The data for curves can be captured from real experiments.

In addition, the cost of using a personal computer is low compared to alternatives such as having a curve verbally described to a user[6], or having tactile-graphs created (i.e. curves etched in plastic).

Additional work needs to be performed to discover the best mapping function to use when going from the linear domain of the data into the logarithmic domain[7] of human hearing. Generally, in order for a user to perceive pitch changes as occuring on some linear scale, the actual frequency must be increased in a logarithmic fashion – and it may be necessary to develop a rapid means of determining what this mapping function is for each individual.

Conclusion

Audio cues and more specialized uses of sound for information communication (such as sound-graphs) have been presented here to show the unique advantages sound has for a variety of application areas. Enhancing graphical workstations, monitoring of industrial manufacturing systems, and the representation of multi-dimensional data in sound are just some of the areas open to further exploitation.

Acknowledgments

Work performed under the auspices of the U.S. Department of Energy by Lawrence Livermore National Laboratory under Contract W-7405-Eng-48.

References

[1] Smith, D.C., *Pygmalion: A Creative Programming Environment*, PhD dissertation, Dept. of Computer Science, Stanford University, tech. report STAN-CS-75-499, 1975.

[2] Glinert, Ephraim P. and Tanimoto, Steven L., "Pict: An Interactive Graphical Programming Environment", *Computer*, vol. 17, no. 11, p. 7-25, Nov. 1984.

[3] Sumikawa, Denise A., private communication, 1984.

[4] Mansur, Douglass L., *Graphs in Sound: A Numerical Data Analysis Method for the Blind*, Lawrence Livermore National Laboratory, report UCRL-53548, June, 1984.

[5] Mansur, D.L., Blattner, M.M., and Joy, K.I., "Sound-Graphs: A Numerical Data Analysis Method for the Blind", *Proceedings, 18th Hawaii International Conference on System Sciences*, Jan. 2-4, 1985.

[6] Chang, L.A., White, C.M., and Abrahamson, L., *Handbook for Spoken Mathematics (Larry's Speakeasy)*, Lawrence Livermore National Laboratory, report UCAR-10101, Oct. 1983.

[7] Stevens, S.S., Volkmann, J., and Newman, E.B., "A Scale for the Measurement of the Psychological Magnitude of Pitch", *Journal of the Acoustical Society of America*, vol. 8, no. 3, pp. 185-190, Jan. 1937.

from R. Morrison and D. Lunney

For several years we have been working on ways to give visually impaired science students access to experimental data. We have used synthetic speech, rising and falling tones, and more complex sounds. For about three years we have been studying ways to present multivariate data as auditory patterns, and have developed a simple and potentially useful scheme for auditory presentation of infrared spectra.

In this scheme the continuous spectrum is first converted into a *stick spectrum*. The stick spectrum is mapped onto the discrete spectrum of the 96 musical notes in an eight-octave chromatic scale. The high-frequency peaks are mapped onto high-pitched notes and low-frequency peaks are mapped onto low-pitched notes. The musical notes are used to generate an auditory structure consisting of two melodic patterns and a chord. In the first melodic pattern all of the notes are played in the order of descending pitch. The time durations of the notes are controlled by the intensities of the infrared peaks: whole notes are generated for peaks with transmittances less than 0.5; half notes are generated for peaks with transmittances between 0.50 and 0.75; quarter notes are generated for peaks with transmittances between 0.75 and 0.875; and so on. The first pattern is played twice.

The notes in the second part are played in order of decreasing peak intensities: the most intense peaks are played first and the weakest are played last, and all the notes have equal durations. The second pattern is played three times; it is perceived as a quirky, syncopated piece with multiple parts, because large interval skips are not connected by the ear into a single line, but are heard as one part taking a rest while another part enters.

Finally, a chord is generated by playing all of the notes simultaneously. All notes in the chord have the same intensity and the same time duration. (The chord is almost always highly dissonant.) Because we do not use the amplitude envelope or the waveform to convey information, the user is able to select waveforms, attack rates, and decay rates at will.

In informal tests of this scheme with spectra from about a dozen simple organic compounds, we have had very few failures in matching identical patterns. We use the final chord for rapid searches; even a person who professes himself to be tone-deaf was able to match chords successfully.

This scheme for presenting infrared spectra as sound patterns has the following desirable features:

1. It allows rapid screening and matching. The final chord can be used for a rapid comparison of an unknown spectrum with a series of known spectra from a data base. If the chord does not allow selection of an exacct match of the unknown with a known compound, the other parts of the pattern can be played.

2. It produces auditory similarities from chemical similarities. For example, the peak due to the oxygen-hydrogen stretch maps into a high audio pitch, and is readily recognized in the first part of the pattern.

3. It does not depend entirely on pitch discrimination. In the first part of the pattern, the durations are controlled by the intensities of the peaks. In the second part, there is a perceived syncopated rhythmic pattern.

4. It is not limited to infrared spectra, but can also be used to display chromatograms, nuclear magnetic resonance spectra, mass spectra, etc.

The digital sound synthesizer used in this work was designed and built to our specifications. It can produce up to 64 voices from a menu of 16 arbitrary waveforms, and has six audio output channels. It is controlled by a dedicated Z80 microcomputer system, which controls frequency, amplitude, waveform, etc. in real time.

During the past decade, graph theory has been applied to the analysis of chemical data and chemical structure because there is a need to be able to visualize complex systems. Graph theory has been used to represent chemical structure, represent relationships between chemical structures, show chemical interactions, enumerate isomers, and so on. Methods of presenting graphs to blind scientists need to be developed so they can have access to these inscreasingly important graphical analyses. Such methods of presenting graphs would almost certainly include auditory presentations and probably tactile presentations.

We are also concerned that the recent trend toward interactive graphics threatens to close technical and managerial careers to visually impaired people. Unless truly effective nonvisual interfaces (tactile and auditory) can be developed, visually impaired people will once again be relegated to low level occupations. For them, it will be as if the computer revolution had never happened.

This work was supported by a grant from the U.S. Department of Education's Special Education Programs.

References

Bly, S. (1982) "Sound and Computer Information Presentation", PhD thesis, UCRL-53282, Lawrence Livermore National Laboratory and University of California, Davis.

Bly, S. (1982) "Presenting Information in Sound", *Proceedings: Human Factors in Computer Systems.*

Bly, S. (1983) "Interactive Tools for Data Exploration", *Proceedings: Computer Science and Statistics, Fifteenth Symposium on the Interface.*

Deutch, D., editor (1982) *The Psychology of Music,* Academic Press.

Gelfand, S. (1981) *Hearing, An Introduction to Psychological and Physiological Acoustics,* Marcel Dekker.

Kolata, G. (1982) "Computer Graphics Comes to Statistics", *Science,* Vol. 2, #17.

Lunney, D., R.C. Morrison, M.M. Cetera, R.V. Hartness, R.T. Mills, A.D. Salt, and D.C. Sowell (1983) "A Microcomputer-based Laboratory Aid for Visually Impaired Students", *IEEE Micro,* Vol. 3, #4.

Mansur, D.L. (1984) "Graphs in Sound: A Numerical Data Analysis Method for the Blind", MS thesis, UCRL-53548 , Lawrence Livermore National Laboratory and University of California, Davis.

Mathews, M.V. (1969) *The Technology of Computer Music,* The MIT Press, Cambridge, MA.

Mezrich, J.J, S. Frysinger, and R. Slivjanovski (1984) "Dynamic Representation of Multivariate Time Series Data", *Journal of the American Statistical Association.*

Riganati, J.P. and M.L. Griffith (1977) "Interactive Audio-Graphics for Speech and Image Characterization", *Data Structures, Computer Graphics, and Pattern Recognition,* Academic Press, Inc.

Speeth, S.D. (1961) "Seismometer Sounds", *The Journal of the Acoustical Society of America.*

Yeung, E.S. (1980) "Pattern Recognition by Audio Representation of Multivariate Analytical Data", *Analytical Chemistry.*

Part III

The Design and Implementation of Interactive Computer Systems

Part II: The User and The Usage of Interactive Computer Systems, introduced us to the human user of computer systems, to methods for modelling and evaluating her performance, and to the applied cognitive psychology that should help us understand her performance and enhance system usability. It also examined the properties of the human perceptual and motor systems which, when properly exploited, can be used for effective human-computer communication, on the design and arrangement of computer-produced and interpreted stimuli which take advantage of these properties, and on the technologies currently available to produce and mediate these stimuli. How then can we best design and implement dialogue structures and techniques to exploit these human characteristics, design principles, and available technologies? This is the topic of Part III.

We begin in Chapter 10: Interaction Styles and Techniques, with the building blocks of interactive systems, the component techniques, and approaches from which interfaces are constructed. The central concept is that of interface approach, or *style*. *Menu* systems, *command-line* dialogues, *direct-manipulation* interfaces, and *graphic interaction* techniques, although sometimes overlapping at the edges, are profoundly different ways of communicating with a computer. Our intention is to illustrate the diversity of interaction styles and techniques and the subtlety of issues that determine whether they are maximally effective in a given context.

We move in Chapter 11: Design Principles and Methodologies, to the more difficult problem of *design*. Although design is an art that can only be learned "by doing it," we introduce the reader to some of the more valuable *guidelines*, *principles*, and *methodologies* for appropriate interactive system design. Our emphasis is on presenting approaches to design that have proven themselves in real applications, some of which we also present as case studies elsewhere in this volume.

One almost universally accepted principle is the need for *prototyping* interfaces to facilitate early feedback from users on the strengths and weaknesses of a design. Another common tenet is the need for a flexible *toolkit* for easy experimentation with, and rapid change of, aspects of an interface. Although we do not like the term, the phrase *user interface management system* (UIMS) is generally used to identify the class of programming techniques, tools, and environments designed with these goals in mind. In Chapter 12: Programming Techniques and Tools, therefore, we look at prototypical UIMS's and issues in their design and implementation.

Prototypes are not systems, and neither are production versions of raw, unaugmented program code. Usable and robust systems must be supported with an infrastructure of skilled and sympathetic people, procedures, and documents. Chapter 13: Enhancing System Usability, looks at some issues involved in providing the documentation, training, on-line assistance — both computerized and human, and error handling — diagnosis, recovery, and correction, that are essential for true usability.

A system almost universally acclaimed for the quality of its user interface is the Apple Macintosh. This product did not arise in a vacuum. Case Study D: The Star, the Lisa, and the Macintosh, reviews some of the history, research, and development that occurred at Xerox Palo Alto Research Center, and then in the trio of follow-on products — the Xerox Star, the Apple Lisa, and the Apple Macintosh. In carrying out this review, we will tie together many of the themes and issues that are developed throughout Part III.

Chapter 10

Interaction Styles and Techniques

A diverse set of interactive techniques are used in various computer systems, for example, menus, form filling dialogues, help buttons, undo commands, moving cursors, programmable tracking symbols, icons, windows, scrolling text, and rubber band lines. Hundreds more could be added to this list. One goal of this chapter is to present and discuss some of the more important of the techniques that are available and to describe their strengths and weaknesses.

A way of organizing these techniques is in terms of dialogue *style*. We know intuitively, for example, that the interface to UNIX is very different from the interface to a Macintosh, and that the dialogue with Microsoft Word is not at all like that with *vi* plus *troff*. An interface with a unified and consistent set of interaction techniques can, therefore, be said to impose a certain dialogue style on the user. This concept of style is central to our ability to characterize and understand the diversity of interactive systems in use today. We do not yet have the base of experience, however, to categorize interfaces into different styles with the ease with which knowledgeable students of music and art can do so in their disciplines. Despite this problem, caused by fuzzy and overlapping categories, we shall organize our presentation of various techniques in terms of nine major general categories of interactive style:

- *Command line* dialogues, in which the user types instructions to the computer in a formally defined command language

- *Programming language* dialogues, in which the command language allows its own extensions through the definition of procedures

- *Natural language* interfaces, in which the user's command language is a significant, well-defined subset of some natural language such as English

- *Menu* systems, in which the user issues commands by selecting in sequence choices from among a menu of displayed alternatives

- *Form filling* dialogues, in which the user issues commands by filling in fields in one or more forms displayed on the screen

- *Iconic* interfaces, in which user commands and system feedback are expressed in graphical symbols or pictograms instead of words

- *Window* systems or environments, in which the user's screen is divided into a number of possibly overlapping rectangular areas, each of which handles a specific function or is itself a "virtual terminal"

- *Direct manipulation*, in which the user manipulates, through a language of button pushes and movements of a pointing device such as a mouse, a graphic representation of the underlying data

- *Graphical interaction*, in which the user is defining and modifying sketches, diagrams, renderings, and other two-dimensional and three-dimensional images and pictures

Command Line Dialogues

The most traditional method of issuing instructions to a computer is through a typed command. The space of allowable commands is described by a command language. Perlman (1984) calls these ''artificial languages,'' which he defines as ''languages created especially for precise and concise communication within a limited domain.'' Our goal, he says, should be to design these languages well enough to make them ''natural,'' that is, easy to learn and easy to use. Artificial languages (whether ''natural'' or not) have lexical, syntactic, and semantic structure. Research studies on command languages have tended to concentrate on one or another of these three aspects.

Investigators at the lexical level have looked primarily at the issue of *naming*. How does one design an optimum terminology for a command set? There is relatively little known to assist in answering this question. Perlman (1984) has investigated the mappings from concepts to names to symbols, and produced experimental evidence for the value of names that suggest the concepts they are to denote, and for the value of symbols that are compatible with the names for which they are abbreviations. Mnemonic names have been shown to be better than arbitrary names for facilitating the comprehension of computer programs (Shneiderman and Mayer, 1979). Norman (1981) has argued forcefully that the bizarre naming conventions in the UNIX command language make its interface needlessly arcane and difficult.

There remains, however, a wide latitude in the choice of command names, and in the design of their structural and semantic properties, since peoples' preferences for names, and what they consider ''natural,'' are characterized by enormous individual differences (Landauer, Galotti, and Hartwell, 1983; Furnas, Landauer, Gomez, and Dumais, 1983). There is some evidence that specific names are slightly better than general names, abbreviations, unrelated words, and pseudo-words as command names (Black and Moran, 1982; Barnard, Hammond, MacLean, and Morton, 1982a,b; Grudin and Barnard, 1984). Scapin (1982) and Jones and Landauer (1985) have shown that names generated by users are slightly better than pre-assigned names. Carroll (1982a,b) suggests that names need to be organized into paradigms, rather than being treated as if each name is an independent label, and that these paradigms need to incorporate the concept of ''congruency,'' in other words, with names chosen so that functional relations between the concepts referred to by the names are mirrored in structural relations between the names. Rosenberg (1982, 1983) has attempted to carry this work further by looking at names in terms of their ''suggestiveness'' and in terms of their ''features.'' Finally, there is an emerging body of literature that discusses and evaluates the variety of possible strategies for constructing names through abbreviations, (Ehrenreich and Porcu, 1982; Streeter, Ackroff, and Taylor, 1983; Grudin and Barnard, 1985a,b).

Even more attention has been paid to syntactic issues. A classic study focusing on the syntax of dialogues is that of Barnard, Hammond, Morton, Long, and Clark (1981). These authors carry out three studies of the problem of specifying the order of arguments in a command string, noting that there are two often conflicting methods that could be used, one based on preserving *consistency* in the position of recurrent arguments, the other preserving *compatibility* between argument order and the order of corresponding phrases in English language usage. The first study surveys and evaluates the practice of system designers in making the decision. Study II is similar but focuses instead on the stated preferences of ''naive'' subjects. The third and most extensive study is an experimental evaluation of the effect of argument order on a number of measures of subject performance on an interactive task: total time to perform the task, display viewing time, frequency of first attempt correct, whether or not the subject needed additional information, number of reversed argument errors, and number of total argument errors. It was found that positionally consistent systems with the recurrent argument in the first position are the most easily learned.

This paper illustrates both the strengths and the weaknesses of laboratory studies of human-computer interaction. The experiments are imaginative, the experimental design sound, the analysis thorough. The results are interesting and valuable but they merely scratch the surface. Do they hold for a set of 25 commands? 100 commands? Do they hold when the dialogue involves several ''almost recurrent'' arguments, in other words, two or three that appear with great regularity. Was learning really complete by the 10th message in the experiment, or would the results differ significantly if carried out to message 25? message 100? There remains a long list of unanswered questions.

An often-cited study that deals with both lexical and syntactic issues is that of Ledgard, Whiteside, Singer, and Seymour (1980). Their goal was ''to establish that a syntax employing familiar, descriptive, everyday words and well-formed English phrases contributes to a language that can be easily and effectively used.'' To do this, they developed two versions of an interactive text editor, one with an English-based command syntax, one with a more notational syntax. Groups of ''inexperienced,'' ''familiar,'' and ''experienced'' users were tested on their performance with each of the two editors, where performance was measured in terms of the percentage of the editing task completed, the percentage of erroneous commands issued, and their "editing efficiency." Their conclusion was that "performance differences strongly favored the English-based editor."

Unfortunately, the methodology used in the study is flawed. Differences between the terminology used in the two command languages are not distinguished from differences in syntax. The terminology used in the "notational" editor varies from reasonable words such as LIST and DELETE which are also used in the "English language" editor to arcane abbreviations such as "RS" and bizarre, needlessly complicated constructions such as ":/KO/;*." The syntax of the notational editor used in the study is inconsistent and the language is decidedly inferior to the state-of-the-art of such systems. Finally, the twenty minutes allotted for use of each editor is hardly sufficient to evaluate the effects of learning and to guarantee that the results obtained would persist after users became experienced with the systems. Further discussions of this paper may also be found in Klerer, et al. (1981).

Another controversial aspect of the syntax of dialogues is that of the acceptability or unacceptability of *modes*. The most outspoken opponent is Tesler, who defines a mode as follows (Smith et. al., 1982):

> A mode of an interactive computer system is a state of the user interface that lasts for a period of time, is not associated with any particular object, and has no role other than to place an interpretation on operator input.

Tesler (1981) writes:

> The most common question asked by new users, at least as often as "How do I do this?," was "How do I get out of this mode?"... .
>
> Novices are not the only victims of modes. Experts often type commands used in one mode when they are in another, leading to undesired and distressing consequences. In many systems, typing the letter "D" can have meanings as diverse as "replace the selected character by D," "insert a D before the selected character," or "delete the selected character." How many times have you heard or said, "Oops, I was in the wrong mode"?
>
> Even when you remember what mode you are in, you can still fall into a trap. If you are running a data-plotting program, the only commands you can use are the ones provided in that program. You can't use any of the useful capabilities of your computer that the author of the program didn't consider, such as obtaining a list of the files on the disk. On the other hand, if you're using a program that lets you list files, you probably can't plot a graph from the numbers that appear in the document.
>
> If you stop any program and start another, data displayed by the first program is probably erased from the screen and irretrievably lost from view. In general, "running a program" in most systems puts you into a mode where the facilities of other programs are unavailable to you...

> Many systems feature hierarchies of modes... . If you are in the editor and want to copy text from a file, you issue the *copy-from* command and it gives the prompt "from what file?" You then type a file name. What if you can't remember the spelling? No problem. Leave *from-what-file* mode, leave *copy-from* mode, *save* the edited text, *exit* from the editor to the executive, call up *file management* from the executive, issue the *list-files* command, look for the name you want (Hey, that went by too fast. Sorry, you can't scroll backwards in that mode.), *terminate* the list command, *exit* from file management to the executive, reenter the *editor*, issue the *copy-from* command, and when it prompts you with "from what file?" simply type the name (you haven't forgotten it, have you?).

Tesler condemns modes as traps leading to user confusion and frustration that must be eliminated, as they can be with the *multiple window* paradigm introduced below. Yet the elimination of *all modes*, as we hinted in our introduction to Case Study A: The Design of a Voice Messaging System, can only occur if every command is always accessible at every instant of time, a practical impossibility for dialogues and systems of any complexity. A reasonable goal is to eliminate unnecessary modes and to make those that remain as transparent and clear as possible, providing vivid feedback that reinforces the context. Towards this end, Nievergelt and Weydert (1980) presents a model of the user interface as a collection of *sites*, *modes*, and *trails*, and argues how appropriate design expressed in these terms can allow the user to obtain clear answers to the questions: "Where am I? What can I do here? How did I get here? Where can I go, and how do I get there?" We include an excerpt from this paper as a reading. Engel, Andriessen, and Schmitz (1983) presents another, complementary approach to the problem of user navigation, in their case applied to large electronic retrieval systems.

Programming Language Dialogues

When applications become advanced and command line input becomes characterized by a complex and intricate syntax, the nature of the user interface problem changes considerably. Such is the case with data base query and retrieval languages, an area which has received a great deal of attention in the literature. Reisner, Boyce, and Chamberlain (1975) and Thomas and Gould (1975) were two early human factors studies on the effectiveness of various approaches to the design of query languages. These and a number of other studies evaluating the ease of use of query languages are reviewed in Reisner (1981). Vassiliou and Jarke (1984) present a taxonomy of query languages that distinguishes them in terms of the modalities used during the interaction, such as vision, hearing, and touch, and the specific methods, such as the use of keywords, function keys, and line-by-line prompting, that are employed. Jarke and Vassiliou (1985) then apply that taxonomy in developing recommendations for the kinds of query languages that should be employed with different kinds of users.

Ultimately, these dialogue languages become most interesting when the user can program in them, when she can use the capabilities of the language and system to extend its vocabulary and repertoire of capabilities. The resulting human factors issues are closely related to those of "the psychology of programming" (see Case Study B: The Psychology of Computer Programming).

Natural Language Interfaces

Command languages are typically highly stylized and grammatically very limited artificial languages. Could the dialogue language instead be a natural language such as English? Could it be a restricted subset of English? The answer to the first question is still no, and will likely remain so for many years. The answer to the second question is yes, and there are increasing numbers of examples both in laboratory experiments and in commercial use. In looking at these systems, it is important to distinguish between *natural language* input and *speech* input, two concepts, which although often found together, can each be present without the other (see also Chapters 9: The Audio Channel and Chapter 14: Research Frontiers and Unsolved Problems).

Hayes (1985a) notes that natural language interfaces may increase the expressiveness of user input, and may allow users to gain access to systems without learning a new language, and in a way that they are likely to find comfortable and natural. Disadvantages include the verboseness of natural language and the degree of coverage provided — a system that can understand only a tiny and ill-defined subset of English will not provide an effective natural language interface. The latter point is also stressed by Rich (1984), which we include as a reading. She outlines the conditions under which "natural language" can be effective as a means of computer input and then reviews some of the more promising current technologies with which such interfaces can be constructed.

But we are still a great distance from having effective natural language communication with computers. Hayes and Reddy (1983) argue that what is required is "graceful interaction," which they define in terms of six desired skills:

- Parsing elliptical, anaphoric, fragmented, and often ungrammatical input
- Correctly interpreting utterances to allow robust communication

- Being able to explain what it has and has not done, what it can and cannot do, and what it is trying to do
- Being able to track the focus of a dialogue as it shifts
- Identifying objects from descriptions
- Generating descriptions that are appropriate to a particular context

Although Hayes and Reddy state that each ability in itself is "not much beyond the current state of the art," they acknowledge that there are as yet no gracefully interacting systems.

Dialogues Using Menus

Menu interfaces have become increasingly popular over the last decade as a means of making computers more accessible to those with little experience and/or those who use systems infrequently. Shneiderman (1986) surveys much of the research that has been carried out on the pragmatics of menu system design. This includes issues such as the use of names versus numbers versus icons as menu constituents, the design of methods such as scrolling and paging for structuring large menus, and the tradeoffs between height, breadth, and width in tree-structured menus (see Kiger, 1984; Landauer and Nachbar, 1985; Sisson, Parkinson, and Snowberry, 1986). Existing research seems to show a general preference for broad, shallow trees rather than deep, narrow ones, although the results depend on the environment in which the menus are used and on the nature and organization of the menus. The Landauer and Nachbar paper is particular interesting in that it attempts to predict selection time from various menu trees by applying "psychological laws," namely the Hick-Hyman law, which predicts choice time as a function of the number of alternatives, and Fitts's law, which predicts movement time as a function of target size and distance.

We include, as a reading, a short paper by Perlman (1985) which illustrates how straightforward psychological experiments can yield useful insights for practical application to the design of menus.

Many computer scientists view menus as a cumbersome method of finding one's way around a system, and one that is suited only to naive and casual users of a system. This is not necessarily true, as can be seen from three attempts to go beyond this, to make menu selection and traversal through large networks of menus the sole method of human-machine communication:

- The PROMIS problem-oriented system for medical guidance and for the keeping of patient medical records (Schultz and Davis, 1979; Shultz, 1986)

- The ZOG rapid response, large network, menu selection system (Robertson, McCracken, and Newell, 1981; McCracken and Akscyn, 1984)
- The *videotex* concept, in which data bases are accessed via menus over phone lines (Godfrey and Parkhill, 1980; Videotex, 1986)

ZOG is a particularly interesting system to study. It has been extensively documented in the literature, has been implemented on several computer architectures, and has been used in a variety of applications, including in the construction and maintenance of a large complex operations manual, and for the facilitation of high level planning, on the nuclear-powered aircraft carrier, the USS Carl Vinson (Newell, McCracken, Robertson, and Akscyn, 1981; Akscyn and McCracken, 1984).

Form Filling Interfaces

Perlman (1985) distinguishes between menus and forms by noting that a menu is a display of *alternatives*, in which one option or value is discriminated or selected in each cycle, and a form is a display of *requirements*, in which various options and values are specified and integrated in a single display screen. The quality of form filling interfaces depends primarily upon three factors — the extent to which the logic of the form mirrors the logic of the system for which it is structuring the input, the clarity of the design and visual presentation of the screens (see Chapter 7: The Visual Channel), and the degree to which the program accepting input into various fields on the form facilitates the keying of data that is correct and reliable (Gilb, 1975; Gilb and Weinberg, 1977). If a form directly mirrors the system the user is manipulating, such as in the display of a tax return, the the form filling interface is an example of direct manipulation (see below).

An interesting system based on the concept of form-filling interfaces is COUSIN (Hayes and Szekely, 1983; CMU, 1984; Hayes, 1985b). It supports "coarse grained semantically constrained" command interaction such as that encountered in using the command level ("shell") of an operating system, file management system, or electronic mail system. COUSIN allows the user to issue commands by filling in and modifying fields to a form, and supports the activity through extensive error detection and correction and integrated on-line help (Hayes, 1982). COUSIN is also a *user interface management system* (see Chapter 12: Programming Techniques and Tools), since it can generate and support a variety of interfaces depending upon the interface specification provided to it using a declarative interface specification language (Ball and Hayes, 1982; Hayes, 1985c; Hayes, Szekely, and Lerner, 1985).

Iconic Interfaces

One of the possible constituents of menus is the *pictogram*, or *icon* (recall our discussion in Chapter 7: The Visual Channel). Is the icon a fundamental breakthrough heralding new dimensions in computer usability, or a fad, hiding loss of productivity behind a euphoric wave of apparent "user friendliness"?

Lodding (1983) argues the former, asserting that because people find images "natural," because the human mind has powerful image memory and processing capabilities, because icons can be easily learned and recognized, and because images "can possess more universality than text," iconic interfaces can "reduce the learning curve in both time and effort, and facilitate user performance while reducing errors." Easterby (1970) stresses the advantages for international use of symbolic displays over those that are language-based. Gittens (1986) notes the ease with which graphical attributes of icons such as style and colour can be used to represent common properties of a collection of objects.

Manes (1985), on the other hand, argues the latter, asserting that icons may be confusing, wasteful of space, and totally ineffective in dealing with large numbers of similar commands, files, or concepts. Gittens (1986) notes the difficulty of finding "obvious pictographic equivalents" of computer system concepts, and of using icons to deal with the specification of large numbers of command parameters. Kolers (1969) notes that the claims for the "immediacy" and "directness" of the understanding of pictograms are exaggerated, and that recognizing even realistic icons requires "a great deal of perceptual learning, abstracting ability, and intelligence." Hemenway (1982), Jervell and Olsen (1985), and Gittins (1986), echoing a theme of Carroll's, emphasize the importance of the design of a set of interrelated icons to represent a set of related commands, and of developing a metaphor to facilitate user comprehension of a system. Yet all are concerned about the problem of overextending the metaphor, and of its breakdown when the logic of the metaphor leads to erroneous inferences about a computer system that the metaphor was intended to illuminate.

There is little experimental evidence documenting the advantages and disadvantages of icons and delimiting with precision when they can be used appropriately. Frequently cited literature (see, for example, Kolers, 1969, and Easterby, 1970) provide valuable enumerations of icon design principles and recitations of their strengths and weaknesses, but little more. Hemenway (1982) acknowledges that most of the stated advantages of icons are only speculations, with little empirical evidence backing them up. She insists, however, that icons have advantages because they are more visually distinctive than text, and because they can represent a lot of information in a little space. Icons clearly are a valuable element of modern user interfaces, but they are no panacea, no cure for bad design.

An interesting approach is that of Bewley, Roberts, Schroit, and Verplank (1983), included in Case Study D: The Star, the Lisa, and the Macintosh, which shows how human factors testing can be used to refine and improve a set of related icons.

Windows

Another much acclaimed component of modern user interfaces is the *window*. A window is a rectangular region of the screen delimited by a boundary. Each window can in principle support its own individual human-computer dialogue, thus allowing the interleaving of multiple concurrent activities at a single workstation.

Card, Pavel and Farrell (1985), which we include as a reading, document some of the categories, purposes in terms of desired tasks, and advantages and disadvantages of window-based displays. They then introduce the concept of the window working set to help in dealing with the management of the scarce resource of screen space.

Most recent and current research on windows has concerned itself with the design and implementation of window managers and window systems (see, for example, Hopgood, 1986, which contains the proceedings of a recent international workshop on window management). Particular attention is usually paid to the differences between systems based on the *overlapping window* paradigm (Pike, 1983; Myers, 1984, 1986; Goodfellow, 1986) and those based on the *tiled window* paradigm (Teitelman, 1984; Cohen, Smith, and Iverson, 1986; Gait, 1986). Bly and Rosenberg (1986) begin to analyze conditions under which tiled and overlapping windows are superior and inferior.

Unfortunately, there are very few studies like this which can guide the intelligent design of window systems and of multiple screen or window dialogues. Some interesting concepts, however, may be found in recent papers by Woods (1984) and Norman, Weldon, and Shneiderman (1986). Some video examples on the subject of windows are Xerox (1983), Bell Labs (1984), and PERQ (1985).

Direct Manipulation

The success of VisiCalc (Henderson, Cobb, and Cobb, 1983), and the excitement over the user interfaces of the Xerox Star and the Apple Lisa (discussed in Case Study D: The Star, the Lisa, and the Macintosh) have esta-

blished *direct manipulation* as a promising new interaction style. We include as a reading an excerpt from an article by Shneiderman (1983) which gives numerous examples of such interfaces. He then defines direct manipulation in terms of the following essential features (p. 64):

- Continuous representation of the object of interest.
- Physical actions (movement and selection by mouse, joystick, touch screen, etc.) or labeled button pushes instead of complex syntax.
- Rapid, incremental, reversible operations whose impact on the object of interest is immediately visible.
- Layered or spiral approach to learning that permits usage with minimal knowledge...

He argues that such systems have the following beneficial attributes:

- Novices can learn basic functionality quickly, usually through a demonstration by a more experienced user. (*Editor's Note*: Recall Nelson's Ten Minute Rule.)
- Experts can work extremely rapidly to carry out a wide range of tasks, even defining new functions and features.
- Knowledgeable intermittent users can retain operational concepts.
- Error messages are rarely needed.
- Users can immediately see if their actions are furthering their goals, and if not, they can simply change the direction of their activity.
- Users experience less anxiety because the system is comprehensible and because actions are so easily reversible.
- Users gain confidence and mastery because they initiate an action, feel in control, and can predict system responses.

Direct manipulation interfaces are indeed exciting. But we must be careful what we claim for them. Hutchins, Hollan, and Norman (1986) look more critically at the advantages cited in an earlier and similar formulation by Shneiderman (1982), and provide — in an excerpt included as a reading — a more balanced view about what actually can and cannot be asserted at this point in time about direct manipulation. The excerpt makes reference to the concepts of "semantic directness" and "articulatory directness," which are defined and discussed at length earlier in the paper. In brief, the former concept deals with the relationship between the goals of a user and the meaning of his expression in an interface language, and the ease with which he can express his intentions in that language. The latter concept deals with the relationship between the meanings of expressions and their physical form, and the ease with which a user's meanings can be translated into the form and appearance of both input and output to a computer.

Graphical Interaction

The study of graphical interaction goes back to the pioneering Sketchpad system discussed in Chapter 1: A Historical and Intellectual Perspective. Advocates of direct manipulation have, in a sense, only recently discovered what those working in interactive graphics have been trying to do for 25 years (Baecker, 1980b).

We include as a reading a more detailed paper by Baecker (1980a). It argues that the design of any interactive dialogue must be based on a careful examination of six building blocks: the display technology, the input technology, the two partners in the dialogue (the person and the machine), and the content and context of the dialogue. This is illustrated by showing the variety of solutions that must be developed as one varies the six factors in a very simple problem, that of positioning or repositioning an object on the screen. The paper then cautions us that the conventional wisdom about the desirability of device-independent interactive graphics systems which has led to the flurry of efforts in the development of *graphics standards* (Bono, 1986) is in conflict with the more important goal of providing the most congenial and fluid interface possible.

A later, related paper by Buxton (1982) stresses the importance of considering compound tasks rather than individual tasks and illustrates again, as do the earlier papers by Baecker, the diversity of solutions that can be developed for a typical user interface design problem. In this case the problem is similar to that considered by Baecker (1980a), only the issue of selecting an object to be moved receives as much emphasis as the issue of positioning it.

The reader is also referred to a recent paper by Foley, Wallace, and Chan (1984), which provides a comprehensive overview of computer graphics interaction techniques organized with respect to a taxonomy of techniques presented in the paper. Video examples of interesting interaction techniques may be found in University of Toronto (1980, 1984a,b), University of North Carolina (1981, 1983), Xerox (1984, 1985a,b,c) and Wein, et al. (1981).

Concluding Remarks

Despite the vigorous research examining particular aspects of this diversity of interaction styles and techniques, the area is resistant to simplistic solutions. Thus it has not been possible to show a general superiority among command language, menu, or natural language input (Hauptman and Green, 1983), or among command, menu, or iconic interfaces (Whiteside, Jones, Levy and Wixon, 1985), or among prefix or postfix notation (Cherry, 1986). The choice of the ''best'' interaction style is and will remain a complex function of the task, the users who are to carry out this task, the environment within which they will work, and the tools with which they are to do the job.

One interesting issue that seems to underlie much of the debate between the advocates of icons, windows and direct manipulation on the one hand, and the advocates of more traditional interaction styles on the other, is the difference between modes of problem solving: between spatial, demonstrative methods and those that are linguistic and symbolic. We must be careful to ensure that our enthusiasm for the new style of interface does not lead us to conclude that all access is best done spatially, all manipulations directly (Jones and Dumais, 1986; Streeter, Vitello, and Wonsiewicz, 1985). Most importantly, we must be conscious that there are huge individual differences in cognitive structure, in spatial ability (Streeter and Vitello, 1986), and in working style, as typified by the degree of organization on one's desk (Malone, 1982). The magnitude of these individual differences should make suspect any claims of universality or postulates of interface panaceas.

Many designers seems to feel that the issue of style has to do with making a choice between one interaction style versus another. Many real systems, however, incorporate elements from several styles in a single interface, and how to do this intelligently is a far more useful question. In a CAD system for logic design, for example, a command line and direct manipulation style might both appropriately be used. Think about the specific transaction of specifying the scope of an operator. If the elements to be operated upon are few in number and all easily visible, or have good spatial congruence, then their specification can likely best be done by *demonstration*, using direct manipulation or graphical techniques. However, if the elements to be operated upon are best described as ''all AND gates followed by an inverter,'' then a *descriptive* approach, using some form of boolean expression in a command line dialogue, will probably be more effective. The problem then becomes how to allow both types of scope specification to co-exist in a consistent and harmonious manner within the same program. More generally, a major research challenge is the development of techniques for the integration of interactive styles. This can perhaps best be done in the context of an application, where one can retain a good sense of the relationship between message content and message style (see, for example, Buxton, Patel, Reeves and Baecker, 1981).

In general, too much attention has been focused on *how* things are said to computers, and not enough on *what* is said, on the *semantics* of interaction. One exception is the paper by Rosenberg and Moran (1985), which describes a number of systems such as the Xerox Star (see Case Study D: The Star, the Lisa, and the Macintosh) that make use of *generic commands*, commands which are recognized in all contexts of a computer system. Another exception is the attention that is being paid to the design of an appropriate and meaningful *conceptual model* from which an effective *user's model* will presumably be derived (see Chapter 6: Cognition and Human Information Processing).

More effort needs to be expended on developing a taxonomy of the content of human-computer interaction. Such a taxonomy might include some of the following:

- Dialogue initiation and termination: signing on and signing off
- Dialogue mediation: "Go ahead," "Interrupt," "I'm active," "I'm waiting," wait for *X*, establish defaults, confirm critical action, request terse or verbose communications
- Context and history: "Undo," "backup state automatically," "save state," "retrieve particular state," "save," "edit," and "replay input stream"
- Communications: help, mail to system, mail to colleagues, mail to self, establish shared workspace, access tutoring system, activate system monitoring into "dribble files"

Recently, a number of investigators interested in window systems and in cooperative work have begun to investigate how system design and interaction techniques should be driven by the ways in which people work and would like to work. Cypher (1986) investigates the structure of user activities, demonstrating the various ways in which people carry out multiple, interleaved activities. He proposes the need for a powerful facility for *reminding* users of the nature and context of activities that have been interrupted (see also Malone, 1982). Miyata and Norman (1986) examine the psychological base of multiple activities, and use these insights to develop recommendations for system support for the suspension of activities, for reminding, for the resumption of activities, and for concurrent activities. Reichman (Adar) (1986) looks at the communication paradigms with which we think about interactive systems, making the distinction between systems viewed as "conversational partners" and those viewed as "patient assistants." She then uses the insights derived from this analysis to suggest how systems might better support multiwindow interaction and communication. Finally, Card and Henderson (1987) show how the identification of desirable properties to support user task switching can lead to the design of a system appropriate to these ends.

Two other important topics will be covered later in this volume. One is the need to provide easily accessible and learnable programming capabilities with which a user can alter and extend the set of capabilities presented to her by the system (Chapter 14: Research Frontiers and Unsolved Problems.) We shall also in Chapter 14 cover the topic, introduced by Buxton in Chapter 8: The Haptic Channel, of ways in which we can allow human users to employ their full vocabulary of gesture and expression to enrich their ability to communicate to the machine.

Readings

Nievergelt, J. & Weydert, J. (1980). Sites, Modes, and Trails: Telling the User of an Interactive System Where He Is, What He Can Do, and How To Get Places. In Guedj, R.A., ten Hagen, P.J.W., Hopgood, F.R.A., Tucker, H.A. & Duce, D.A. (Eds.), *Methodology of Interaction*, North Holland, 327-338, only pp. 327-332 included here.

Rich, E. (1984). Natural-Language Interfaces. *IEEE Computer*, September 1984, 39-47.

Perlman, G. (1985). Making the Right Choices with Menus. *Human-Computer Interaction — Interact '84*, Amsterdam: North-Holland, 317-321.

Card, S.K., Pavel, M., & Farrell, J.E. (1985). Window-based Computer Dialogues. *Human-Computer Interaction — Interact '84*, Amsterdam: North-Holland, 239-243.

Shneiderman, B. (1983). Direct Manipulation: A Step Beyond Programming Languages. *IEEE Computer*, Aug. 83, 57-69, only pp. 57-62 included here.

Hutchins, E.L., Hollan, J.D., & Norman, D.A. (1986). Direct Manipulation Interfaces. In Norman, D.A. & Draper, S.W. (Eds.), *User Centered System Design*, Hillsdale, N.J.: Lawrence Erlbaum Associates, 87-124, only pp. 118-123 included here.

Baecker, R. (1980a). Towards a Characterization of Graphical Interaction. In Guedj, R.A., ten Hagen, P.J.W., Hopgood, F.R.A., Tucker, H.A. & Duce, D.A. (Eds.), *Methodology of Interaction*, North Holland, 127-147.

References

Akscyn, R.M. & McCracken, D.L. (1984). The ZOG/VINSON Project: An Experiment in Direct Technology Transfer. *Proceedings of IEEE Compcon '84 Fall Conference on the Small Computer Evolution*, Silver Spring, MD: IEEE Computer Society Press, 379.

Baecker, R. (1980a). Towards a Characterization of Graphical Interaction. In Guedj, R.A., ten Hagen, P.J.W., Hopgood, F.R.A., Tucker, H.A. & Duce, D.A. (Eds.), *Methodology of Interaction*, North Holland, 127-147.

Baecker, R. (1980b). Human-Computer Interactive Systems: A State-of-the-Art Review. In Kolers, P.A., Wrolstad, M.E. & Bouma, H. (Eds.), *Processing of Visible Language 2*, New York: Plenum Press, 423-443.

Ball, E. & Hayes, P. (1982). A Test-Bed for User Interface Designs. *Proceedings of the Conference on Human Factors in Computer Systems*, Gaithersburg, Maryland, 85-88.

Barnard, P.J., Hammond, N.V., Morton, J., Long, J.B., & Clark, I.A. (1981). Consistency and Compatibility in Human-Computer Dialogue. *International Journal of Man-Machine Studies* 15, 87-134.

Barnard, P., Hammond, N., MacLean, A., & Morton, J. (1982a). Learning and Remembering Interactive Commands. *Proceedings of the Conference on Human Factors in Computing Systems*, 2-7.

Barnard, P., Hammond, N., MacLean, A., & Morton, J. (1982b). Learning and Remembering Interactive Commands in a Text-Editing Task. *Behaviour and Information Technology* 1(4), 347-358.

Bell Labs (1984). Blit. *SIGGRAPH Video Review* 13, New York: ACM.

Bewley, W.L., Roberts, T.L., Schroit, D. & Verplank, W.L. (1983). Human Factors Testing in the Design of Xerox's 8010 "Star" Office Workstation. *CHI '83 Proceedings*, 72-77.

Black, J.B. & Moran, T.P. (1982). Learning and Remembering Command Names. *Proceedings of the Conference on Human Factors in Computing Systems*, 8-11.

Bly, Sarah A. & Rosenberg, Jarrett K. (1986). A Comparison of Tiled and Overlapping Windows. *CHI '86 Proceedings*, 101-106.

Bono, P. (1986). Graphics Standards, *IEEE Computer Graphics and Applications* 6(8), August 1986, 12-16. (See also this entire issue.)

Buxton, W., Patel, S., Reeves, W. & Baecker, R. (1981). Scope in Interactive Score Editors. *Computer Music Journal* 5(3), 50-56.

Buxton, W. (1982). An Informal Study of Selection/Positioning Tasks. *Proceedings of Graphics Interface '82*, Toronto, 323-328.

CMU (1984). Cousin Interface System. *SIGGRAPH Video Review* 12, New York: ACM.

Card, S.K. & Henderson, A. (1987). A Multiple, Virtual—Workspace Interface to Support User Task Switching. *Proceedings of CHI+GI '87*, New York: ACM, 53-59.

Card, S.K., Pavel, M. & Farrell, J.E. (1985). Window-based Computer Dialogues. *Human-Computer Interaction - Interact '84*, Amsterdam: North-Holland, 239-243.

Carroll, J.M. (1982a). Creative Names for Personal Files in an Interactive Computing Environment. *International Journal of Man-Machine Studies* 16(4), 405-438.

Carroll, J.M. (1982b). Learning, Using, and Designing Filenames and Command Paradigms. *Behaviour and Information Technology* 1(4), 327-346.

Cherry, Joan M. (1986). An Experimental Evaluation of Prefix and Postfix Notation in Command Language Syntax. *International Journal of Man-Machine Studies* 24, 365-374.

Cohen, E.S., Smith, E.T. & Iverson, L.A. (1986). Constraint-Based Tiled Windows. *IEEE Computer Graphics and Applications* 6(5), 35-45.

Cypher, A. (1986). The Structure of Users' Activities. In Norman, D.A. & Draper, S.W. (Eds.), *User Centered System Design*, Hillsdale, N.J.: Lawrence Erlbaum Associates, 243-263.

Easterby, R.S. (1970). The Perception of Symbols for Machine Displays. *Ergonomics* 13(1), 149-158.

Ehrenreich, S.L. & Porcu, T. (1982). Abbreviations for Automated Systems: Teaching Operators The Rules. In Badre, A. & Shneiderman, B. (Eds.), *Directions in Human Computer Interaction*, Norwood, N.J.: Ablex Publishing Corp., 111-135.

Engel, F.L., Andriessen, J.J., & Schmitz, H.J.R. (1983). What, Where and Whence: Means for Improving Electronic Data Access. *International Journal of Man-Machine Studies* 18, 145-160.

Foley, J.D., Wallace, V.L. & Chan, P. (1984). The Human Factors of Computer Graphics Interaction Techniques. *IEEE Computer Graphics and Applications* 4(11), November 1984, 20-48.

Furnas, G.W., Landauer, T.K., Gomez, L.M., & Dumais, S.T. (1983). Statistical Semantics: Analysis of the Potential Performance of Key-Word Information Systems. *The Bell System Technical Journal* 62(6), July-August 1983, 1753-1806.

Gait, Jason (1986). Pretty Pane Tiling of Pretty Windows. *IEEE Software* 3(5), 9-14.

Gilb, T. (1975). Laws of Unreliability. *Datamation* 21(3), March 1975, 81-85.

Gilb, T. & Weinberg, G.M. (1977). *Humanized Input: Techniques for Reliable Keyed Input*, Cambridge, MA.: Winthrop Publishers, Inc.

Gittens, D. (1986). Icon-Based Human-Computer Interaction. *International Journal of Man-Machine Studies* 24, 519-543.

Godfrey, D. & Parkhill, D. (Eds.) (1980). *Gutenberg Two*, Toronto: Press Porcepic Ltd.

Goodfellow, M.J. (1986). WHIM, the Window Handler and Input Manager. *IEEE Computer Graphics and Applications* 6(5), 46-52.

Grudin, J. & Barnard, P. (1984). The Cognitive Demands of Learning and Representing Command Names for Text Editing. *Human Factors* 26(4), 407-422.

Grudin, J. & Barnard, P. (1985a). The Role of Prior Task Experience in Command Name Abbreviation. *Human-Computer Interaction — Interact '84*, 295-299.

Grudin, J. & Barnard, P. (1985b). When Does an Abbreviation Become a Word? And Related Questions. *CHI '85 Proceedings*, April 1985, 121-125.

Hauptman, A.G. & Green, B.F. (1983). A Comparison of Command, Menu-Selection and Natural-Language Computer Programs. *Behaviour and Information Technology* 2(2), 163-178.

Hayes, Philip (1982). Uniform Help Facilities for a Cooperative User Interface. *AFIPS Conference Proceedings 51*, Montvale, N.J.:AFIPS Press, 469-474.

Hayes, Philip (1985a). Introduction to the Panel on The Utility of Natural Language Interfaces. *Proceedings of CHI '85*, 19.

Hayes, Philip (1985b). Executable Interface Definitions Using Form-Based Interface Abstractions. In Hartson, E.R. (Ed.), *Advances in Human-Computer Interaction*, Norwood, N.J.: Ablex Publishing Corp., 161-189.

Hayes, Philip (1985c). The Cousin User Interface Management System. *SIGGRAPH Video Review* 18, New York: ACM.

Hayes, Philip J. & Reddy, D. Raj (1983). Steps Toward Graceful Interaction in Spoken and Written Man-Machine Communication. *International Journal of Man-Machine Studies* 19, 231-284.

Hayes, P.J., Szekely, P.A. & Lerner, R.A. (1985). Design Alternatives for User Interface Management Systems Based on Experience with COUSIN. *CHI '85 Proceedings*, New York: ACM, 169-175.

Hayes, P.J. & Szekely, P.A. (1983). Graceful Interaction through the COUSIN Command Interface. *International Journal of Man-Machine Studies* 19, 285-306.

Hemenway, K. (1982). Psychological Issues in the Use of Icons in Command Menus. *Proceedings of the Conference on Human Factors in Computing Systems*, Gaithersburg, Maryland, 20-23.

Henderson, T.B., Cobb, D.F., & Cobb, G.B. (1983). *Spreadsheet Software From: VisiCalc to 1-2-3*, Indianapolis, Ind.: Que Corp.

Hopgood, F.R.A. et. al. (Eds.) (1986). *Methodology of Window Management*, Berlin: Springer Verlag.

Hutchins, E.L., Hollan, J.D. & Norman, D.A. (1986). Direct Manipulation Interfaces. In Norman, D.A. & Draper, S.W. (Eds.), *User Centered System Design*, Hillsdale, N.J.: Lawrence Erlbaum Associates, 118-123.

Jarke, M. & Vassiliou, Y. (1985). A Framework for Choosing a Database Query Language. *ACM Computing Surveys* 17(3), September 1985, 313-340.

Jervell, H.R. & Olsen, K.A. (1985). *Behaviour and Information Technology* 4(3), 249-254.

Jones, W.P. & Dumais, S.T. (1986). The Spatial Methaphor for User Interfaces: Experimental Tests of Reference by Location versus Name. *ACM Transactions on Office Information Systems* 4(1), 42-63.

Jones, W.P. & Landauer, T.K. (1985). Context and Self-Selection Effects in Name Learning. *Behaviour and Information Technology* 4(1), 3-17.

Kiger, John J. (1984). The Depth/Breath Trade-Off in the Design of Menu-Driven User Interfaces. *International Journal of Man-Machine Studies* 20, 201-213.

Klerer, M., Hart, J., Nicholson, R.T., Fischofer, W.T., McIlroy, M.D., Kernighan, B.W., & Davenport, J.H. (1981). On Natural Language and Computer Systems. Comments on Ledgard et al. (1980), and authors' reply. *Communications of the ACM* 24(6), June 1981, 403-406.

Kolers, P.A. (1969). Some Formal Characteristics of Pictograms. *American Scientist* 57(3), 348-363.

Landauer, T.K., Galotti, K.M., & Hartwell, S. (1983). Natural Command Names and Initial Learning: A Study of Text-Editing Terms. *Communications of the ACM* 26(7), July 1983, 495-503.

Landauer, T.K. & Nachbar, D.W. (1985). Selection from Alphabetic and Numeric Menu Trees Using a Touch Screen: Breadth, Depth, and Width. *Proceedings of CHI '85*, 73-78.

Ledgard, H., Whiteside, J.A., Singer, A., & Seymour, W. (1980). The Natural Language of Interactive Systems. *Communications of the ACM* 23(10), October 1980, 556-563.

Lodding, Kenneth N. (1983). Iconic Interfacing. *IEEE Computer Graphics and Applications* 3(2), March/April 1983, 11-20.

Malone, T.W. (1982). How Do People Organize Their Desks? Implications for the Design of Office Information Systems. *Proceedings Supplement for Conference on Office Information Systems*, New York: ACM, 25-32.

Manes, S. (1985). Pushing Picture-Perfect Programs: Smash That Icon! *PC Magazine*, June 1985, 64.

McCracken, D.L. & Akscyn, R.M. (1984). Experience with the ZOG Human-Computer Interface System. *International Journal of Man-Machine Studies* 21, 293-310.

Miyata, Y. & Norman, D.A. (1986). Psychological Issues in Support of Multiple Activities. In Norman, D.A. & Draper, S.W. (Eds.), *User Centered System Design*, Hillsdale, N.J.: Lawrence Erlbaum Associates, 265-284.

Myers, Brad (1984). The User Interface for Sapphire. *Computer Graphics and Applications* 4(12), 13-23.

Myers, Brad (1986). A Complete and Efficient Implementation of Covered Windows. *IEEE Computer* 19(9), 57-67.

Newell, A., McCracken, D.L., Robertson, G.G. & Akscyn, R.M. (1984). ZOG and the USS CARL VINSON. *1980/81 CMU Computer Science Research Review*, Pittsburgh, PA: Carnegie-Mellon University, 95-118.

Nickerson, R.S. (1986). *Using Computers: Human Factors in Information Systems,* Cambridge, MA.: MIT Press.

Nievergelt, J. & Weydert, J. (1980). Sites, Modes, and Trails: Telling the User of an Interactive System Where He Is, What He Can Do, and How to Get Places. In Guedj, R.A., ten Hagen, P.J.W., Hopgood, F.R.A., Tucker, H.A. & Duce, D.A. (Eds.), *Methodology of Interaction*, North Holland, 327-332.

Norman, Donald A. (1981). The Trouble with Unix. *Datamation* 27(11), November 1981,139-150.

Norman, K.L., Weldon, L.J. & Shneiderman, B. (1986). Cognitive Layouts of Windows and Multiple Screens for User Interfaces. *International Journal of Man-Machine Studies* 25(2), 229-248.

PERQ Systems Corp. (1985). The User Interface for Sapphire. *SIGGRAPH Video Review* 19, New York: ACM.

Perlman, Gary (1984). Natural Artificial Languages: Low Level Processes. *International Journal of Man-Machine Studies* 20, 373-419.

Perlman, Gary (1985). Making the Right Choices with Menus. *Human-Computer Interaction — Interact '84*, Amsterdam: North-Holland, 317-321.

Pike, R. (1983). Graphics in Overlapping Bitmap Layers. *ACM Transactions on Graphics* 2(2), 135-160.

Reichman (Adar), R. (1986). Communication Paradigms for a Window System. In Norman, D.A. & Draper, S.W. (Eds.), *User Centered System Design*, Hillsdale, N.J.: Lawrence Erlbaum Associates, 285-313.

Reisner, P. (1981). Human Factors Studies of Data Base Query Languages: A Survey and Assessment. *ACM Computing Surveys* 13(1), 13-31.

Reisner, P., Boyce, R.F. & Chamberlain, D.D. (1975). Human Factors Evaluation of Two Data Base Query Languages — Square and

Sequel. *Proceedings of the National Computer Conference*, Montvale, N.J.: AFIPS Press, 447-452.

Rich, E. (1984). Natural— Language Interfaces. *IEEE Computer*, Sept. 1984, 39-47.

Robertson, R.M., McCracken, D.L. & Newell, A. (1981). The ZOG Approach to Man-Machine Communication. *International Journal of Man-Machine Studies* 14(4), 461-488.

Rosenberg, J. (1982). Evaluating the Suggestiveness of Command Names. *Proceedings of the Conference on Human Factors in Computing Systems*, 12-16.

Rosenberg, J. (1983). A Featural Approach to Command Names. *Proceedings of CHI '83*, 116-119.

Rosenberg, J. & Moran, T.P. (1985). Generic Commands. *Human-Computer Interaction — Interact '84*, Amsterdam: North-Holland, 245-249.

Scapin, D.L. (1982). Computer Commands Labelled by Users versus Imposed Commands and the Effect of Structuring Rules on Recall. *Proceedings of the Conference on Human Factors in Computing Systems*, 17-19.

Schultz, J.R. & Davis, L. (1979). The Technology of PROMIS. *Proceedings of the IEEE* 67(9), 1237-1244.

Schultz, J.R. (1986). A History of the PROMIS Technology: an Effective Human Interface. *Proceedings of the Conference on the History of Personal Workstations*, New York: ACM, 159-182.

Shneiderman, B. (1982). The Future of Interactive Systems and the Emergence of Direct Manipulation. *Behaviour and Information Technology* 1(3), 237-256.

Shneiderman, B. (1983). Direct Manipulation: A Step Beyond Programming Languages. *IEEE Computer*, Aug. 83, 57-62.

Shneiderman, B. (1986). *Designing the User Interface: Strategies for Effective Human-Computer Interaction*, Addison-Wesley Publishing Company.

Shneiderman, B. & Mayer, R.E. (1979). Syntactic/Semantic Interactions in Programmer Behavior: A Model and Experimental Results. *International Journal of Computer and Information Sciences* 8(3), 219-238.

Sisson, Norwood, Parkinson, Stanley R., & Snowberry, Kathleen (1986). Considerations of Menu-Structure and Communication Rate for the Design of Computer Menu Displays. *International Journal of Man-Machine Studies* 25(5), 479-489.

Smith, D.C., Irby, C., Kimball, R., Verplank, W., & Harslem, E. (1982). Designing the Star User Interface. *Byte*, April 1982, 242-282.

Streeter, L.A., Ackroff, J.M., & Taylor, G.A. (1983). On Abbreviating Command Names. *The Bell System Technical Journal* 62(6), July-August 1983, 1807-1826.

Streeter, L.A., Vitello, D. & Wonsiewicz, S.A. (1985). How to Tell People Where to Go: Comparing Navigational Aids. *International Journal of Man-Machine Studies* 22, 549-562.

Streeter, L.A. & Vitello, D. (1986). A Profile of Drivers' Map-Reading Abilities. *Human Factors* 28(2), 223-239.

Teitelman, W. (1984). A Tour Through Ceder. *Proceedings of the 7th International Conference on Software Engineering*, Silver Spring, MD.: IEEE Computer Society Press, 181-195.

Tesler, L. (1981). The Smalltalk Environment. *Byte* 6(8), August 1981, 90-147.

Thomas, J.C. & Gould, J.D. (1975). A Psychological Study of Query by Example. *Proceedings of the National Computer Conference*, Montvale, N.J.: AFIPS Press, 439-445.

University of North Carolina (1981). The Grip — 75 Man-machine Interface. *SIGGRAPH Video Review* 4, New York: ACM.

University of North Carolina (1983). University of North Carolina Sampler. *SIGGRAPH Video Review* 10, New York: ACM.

University of Toronto (1980). Newswhole. *SIGGRAPH Video Review* 1, New York: ACM.

University of Toronto (1984a). SSSP Demo. *SIGGRAPH Video Review* 12, New York: ACM.

University of Toronto (1984b). Selection-Positioning Tack Study. *SIGGRAPH Video Review* 12, New York: ACM.

Vassiliou, Y. & Jarke, M. (1984). Query Languages — A Taxonomy. In Vassiliou, Y. (Ed.), *Human Factors and Interactive Computer Systems*, Norwood, N.J.: Ablex Publishing Co., 47-82.

Videotex (1986). *Proceedings of Videotex '86*, London: Online Publishing.

Wein, M., et al, National Research Council of Canada (1981). Graphics Interactions at NRC. *SIGGRAPH Video Review* 4, New York: ACM.

Whiteside, J., Jones, S., Levy, P.S. & Wixon, D. (1985). User Performance with Command, Menu, and Iconic Interfaces. *Proceedings of CHI '85*, 185-191.

Woods, D.D (1984). Visual Momentum: A Concept to Improve the Cognitive Coupling of Person and Computer. *International Journal of Man-Machine Studies* 21, 229-244.

Xerox (1983). Smalltalk. *SIGGRAPH Video Review* 8, New York: ACM.

Xerox (1984). Mockingbird. *SIGGRAPH Video Review* 12, New York: ACM.

Xerox (1985a). Human Interface Aspects of Typefounder. *SIGGRAPH Video Review* 18, New York: ACM.

Xerox Corp. (1985b). Solidviews 1984: Interaction. *SIGGRAPH Video Review* 18, New York: ACM.

Xerox Corp. (1985c). JUNO. *SIGGRAPH Video Review* 19, New York: ACM.

SITES, MODES, AND TRAILS:
TELLING THE USER OF AN INTERACTIVE SYSTEM
WHERE HE IS, WHAT HE CAN DO,
AND HOW TO GET TO PLACES.

J. Nievergelt and J. Weydert
Informatik,
Swiss Federal Institute of Technology (ETH)
CH-8092 Zurich, Switzerland

CONTENTS

ABSTRACT

The art of designing command languages for interactive systems lags by at least a decade behind the state of the art in programming languages. Today's command languages tend to give the appearance of ad-hoc collections of individual commands, rather than of structures designed according to general principles.

Observation of the behavior of many casual users suggests that the following questions most often characterize the difficulties experienced by users unfamiliar with a given interactive system:

Where am I?
What can I do here?
How did I get here?
Where can I go, and how do I get there?

A well designed system allows the user at all times to obtain conveniently a clear answer to the above questions.

We present a framework for the design of the user interface of interactive systems, and a specific instance of a command language, based on three concepts that mirror the questions above:

Site: a neighborhood in the space of data, consisting of those data items to which the user has direct access at a given moment.

Mode: a subset of the set of commands, consisting of those commands that are active at a given moment.

Trail: a feasible time-sequence of pairs (current site, current mode).

Excerpted from Nievergelt, J. and Weydert, J. (1980). Sites, Modes, and Trails: Telling the User of an Interactive System Where He Is, What He Can Do, and How To Get Places. In Guedj, R.A., ten Hagen, P.J.W., Hopgood, F.R.A., Tucker, H.A., and Duce, D.A. (Eds.), Methodology of Interaction, North Holland Publishing Company.

In terms of these concepts many common user operations appear naturally as special cases of general features, such as:

Help: inspecting and extrapolating the user's current trail, preferably in a graphic mode.

Command macros: trail editing and re-using past trails.

An interactive system based on these concepts has been implemented in the Self-Explanatory School Computer XS-0.

1. State of the art of designing interactive dialogs

Experience with interactive systems has lead to acceptance of some guidelines for the design of command languages, such as:

- simplicity of commands
- consistency of commands
- adequate response time.
- good error recovery
- more specific principles like 'visual and tactile continuity' ([FO 74])

A statistical evaluation of the relevance (estimated by a few hundred users) of dialog qualities which result from such rules has been done by a project group of the "GMD - Institut für Software - Technologie" ([DZ 77]). Considerations such as the ones listed above apply mainly to single commands, but do not tell the designer what the overall structure of the language should be. The lack of an accepted framework for designing a command language as a whole leads to widely observed deficiencies even in systems that are carefully designed, such as:

- information access only by name

example: a programmer keeps one or more versions of the source, the listing, and the object code of a given program. When he is in a state that gives him direct access to one of these files, he should also have direct access to any of the others by means of a simple command that reflects the relationship between source, listing, and object file, without having to repeat the name of any of these files.

- incomplete specification of the dialog state

example: most systems notify the user when he has exceeded, or is about to exceed, a system limit, such as the capacity of a text file; they often fail to tell him early enough how close he is to the limit, thus making preventive action difficult.

- command structures infered from implementation

example: commands with a common special meaning are often characterized syntactically by the same first character (e.g. a '$'); this may be convenient for command analysis, but not for the user, since there is no obvious meaning which he can infer from a '$'.

This paper shows how a comprehensive approach to designing command languages can avoid pitfalls of the type above. The development of a universal model of the user-system dialog, which transcends particular applications, hardware, and syntax of commands, is the major contribution of this paper, and differentiates it from other approaches. Our model is based on a few intuitively powerful concepts rather than on a large collection of behavioral principles or interaction techniques. A brief survey of the existing literature serves to clarify this point.

The majority of contributions to the design of man-machine dialogs (or, perhaps more generally, to the user interface of interactive systems), can be classified into three categories.

General organizational principles. As an example, Bennett [BE 73] advocates the use of spatial concepts for organizing information. Such structuring principles alone emphasize some aspect of man-machine interaction, but do not constitute a comprehensive model.

Syntax of command languages. This point of view considers the question "what sequences of commands are accepted by a system, and what type of responses do they prompt?" to be of central importance. The syntactic meta-notations developed for programming languages are in general not appropriate or sufficient for defining command languages. [SH 79] is an example of the literature that studies the specification of command languages. Syntax must reflect the intended semantics at least to the extent that the syntactic structure of command sequences must assemble commands into semantically meaningful groups. This model of man-machine dialog, which imposes conditions on the relationship between syntax and semantics, leads to such principles as "naturalness of the command language" or "avoid need for memorization" (for example, [FO 74], [HA 71]).

Human engineering. These studies emphasize physiological aspects as opposed to logical ones: brightness, flicker, timing, what kind of input devices are convenient, etc. Rouse [RO 75] is an example that contains many references.

Our attempt at a universal model of man-machine interaction starts by characterizing the user's situation in the dialog. The user operates on some data by means of some commands. Which data is being affected and which commands are available is his first concern. The next section analyzes this situation.

2. The user's point of view

The casual user (as opposed to the skilled user) is the most sensitive indicator of good or bad dialog design decisions. Observation of hundreds of casual users has shown that that they are mainly concerned with knowing what kind of things they are dealing with at any given instant during the dialog, and what they can do with them. The user's situation is best characterized by asking the following three questions:

- where am I?
- what can I do here?
- how did I get here? where can I go and how do I get there?

Let's consider more closely what an adequate answer to these questions requires. As an example, assume a user is interrupted in the middle of a dialog, such as editing a text file. When he returns to his work, minutes or hours later, his first task is to identify the current state of the system. Even assuming that the state remained unchanged during his absence, the user has to convince himself of this fact. This observation must be done without altering the state. For example the user should be able to see which file is currently being affected by editor commands without leaving the editor; he should not be required to type any characters simply to find out whether or not he is in "insert mode". Many

systems allow so-called status inquiries, such as requests for a list of all available files; but often these are possible only at a certain level of the dialog, and only convey information on a few specific aspects of the dialog session.

An appropriate status display during editing might include some of the following information:

```
file: a
section: 3.1
owner: b
you have: read/write permission
      on: 1/2/78
current mode: text-edit
submode: insert
=====================================
    ...................
     .............
       ......
        .
=====================================
Press
     X to leave insert mode
     HELP for a list of active commands
```

Fig. 1) Information useful for identifying
          current state during editing

In order to be easily understood, the wealth of information which the user may want to know about the state of the dialog must be structured. We observe that the information in the example above has to do with three aspects of a dialog:

- data currently accessible (where am I?)
- commands currently available (what can I do here?)
- what happened in the past (how did I get here?), what may happen in the future (where can I go, how do I get there?)

The question "where am I?" has a clear and short answer "you are at site such-and-such" only if the environment, i.e. the collection of all available data, has a systematic structure. Organizations with long experience in providing services impose structures on their data that are appropriate for their intended use.
     Libraries, for example, have evolved subject matter classifications (such as the Dewey Decimal System) and subject, author and title indexes to structure a collection of documents in such a way that the most frequent queries are easily answered. Perhaps the single most important aspect of the conventional library catalog is the fact that it allows retrieval of a relevant document even if the user does not know its "name" (author, title, etc.). Some knowledge about the information being sought may suffice for following an access path leading to this document. In contrast to this invention of old, many of today's computer filing systems allow access to a file only via its (unique) name.

Similarly the question "what can I do here?" is most easily answered if the collection of all possible actions is structured in a meaningful way. An exhaustive list of commands is usually too long to be of great help. A casual user expects to be guided in his choice of an appropriate command through different decision levels, whereby an initially vague idea gradually becomes specified in detail. The next two sections show how this can be done.

The questions "how did I get here and where can I go?" do not require any structuring mechanism beyond those introduced for sites and modes (data and commands). They are taken care of by making time an explicitly manipulable dimension of a dialog.

3. A framework for the design of interactive dialogs

Based on the considerations of section 2, the following three concepts are introduced as the fundamental structuring tools for the design of man-machine dialogs.

3.1 Site

At any moment a user wants direct access to only a relatively small part of the data present in a system. For example, if he just compiled a program, he may want to have the source text and the compiler messages "at his finger tips". Other data should be invisible at this moment, as it would only interfere with the "active data" and make his selection of what he wants to see harder. A collection of data which is likely to be of simultaneous interest to a user for some purpose can be attached to a site. Thus it becomes a unit that can be operated upon as a whole in certain ways (such as copying); for other purposes the data attached to a site can be regarded as being hierarchically structured into subsites. A site may be identified with the set of data attached to it and a description of its type and structure. By means of this description the data becomes accessible, as the following pictures are intended to show.

Sites are linked to each other and thus form a space of sites. The topology may be that of a general network, or a restricted type of graph such as a tree; in any case it is made to reflect the semantic neighborhood relation assumed to exist on the underlying set of data. A user moves around this space of sites, can see a map of parts of it, and can edit (modify) the space when he wishes to impose a new structure over his data.

3.2 Mode

At any moment a user needs only a small part of all the commands available in the system. If he is editing a picture, for example, only graphics commands are of immediate interest. In response to a request for a list of active commands, only these and a few general commands used for mode changing should be displayed; a larger menu only makes the user's selection more difficult. Thus the set of all commands must be structured into a space of modes.

The commands grouped together in a mode must correspond to a meaningful activity in the user's mind, such as "editing". A mode may have submodes, such as "text editing", "picture editing", or "program editing". The natural relationship among these modes give the space of modes its structure, which governs the allowable transitions between the various modes.

A collection of commands which is likely to be of simultaneous use should be grouped into a mode. Thus it becomes a unit which can be operated upon as a whole in certain ways (such as enabled, disabled, protected). For other purposes the commands active in a mode can be regarded as being hierarchically structured into submodes. A mode may be identified with the set of commands active in it and a description of their effect and structure.
Modes are linked to each other and thus form a space of modes. A user moves around this space of modes, can see a map of any part of it, and may even extend the space by adding new modes and their definition in certain cases.

3.3 Trail

The order in which a user visits various sites is a relationship among the sites which is likely to be important for the current task - a relationship which may be too transient, or too special purpose, to have been imbedded into the links of the space of sites. The same can be said for the order in which modes, submodes, and commands are entered.

In order to make this relationship, which is created during a dialog, available for further use, the notion of a trail as a manipulable object is introduced.
A trail is a feasible time sequence of pairs (current mode, current site), which describes a user dialog (actual or contemplated). Trails can be named, stored, edited, and invoked (re-used).

Trails are the expansion of the first two concepts into the dimension of time. Each pair (current mode, current site) is viewed as the state of the dialog at a specific instant. By making the dimension of time manipulable it is now possible to contemplate the dialog in the past, at a given moment, or as a set of alternatives for the future.

The projection of a trail onto the spaces of sites results in the trace of the sites: the path of the cursor during an editing session is an example. The projection of a trail onto the space of modes results in a trace of modes: a history of commands entered, or a command macro, are examples.

```
Name of this site: X
================================
Owner: Y
Various attributes: ....
================================
DATA:

 1. △    2. ○    3. □

================================
Guidelines for selecting
and manipulating data
objects at this site
```

Fig. 2) The descriptor of a site gives information about the nature of its content and how to access and operate on the data

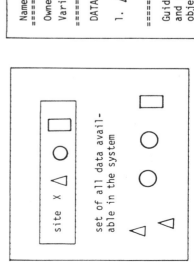

Fig. 1) A site as a collection of data objects

[SH 78] Alan C. Shaw: "On the specification of graphic command languages and their processors"
Paper for the Seillac II Workshop on the Methodology of Interaction (May 1979)

[ST 73] C.J. Stephenson: "On the structure and control of commands"
ACM Operating Systems Review, Vol. 7, No. 4, (October 1973), pp 22-26, 127-136

Acknowledgement

The self-explanatory school computer XS-0 has been the test bed for many of the ideas presented in this paper. We acknowledge the cooperation of H. Burkhart, H.P. Frei, Ch. Jacobi, B. Plattner, H. Sugaya, B. Weibel on this project ([NI 77]).

We are also grateful to A. Schmitt of the University of Karlsruhe for discussions which have given us much insight into the problem of man-machine communication; and to A.C. Shaw of the University of Washington, J. Encarnacao of the Technical University Darmstadt, and an unknown referee for useful comments on an early draft of this paper.

References

[BE 73] John L. Bennett: "Spatial concepts as an organizing principle for interactive bibliographic search" in: Interactive bibliographic search / the user-computer interface, pp 67-83
edited by D.E. Walker, AFIPS Press, Montvale, New Jersey (1973)

[DZ 77] Wolfgang Dzida, Siegfried Herda, Wolf D. Itzfeld, Helmut Schweizer: "Was ist Benuetzerfreundlichkeit?"
Der GMD - Spiegel, 3 (1977), pp 11-21

[EL 78] R.A. Ellis: "On the interactive use of a macroprocessor to generate operating system batch streams"
IEEE Transactions on Software Engineering, Vol. 4, No. 2, (March 1978), pp 146-148

[FO 74] James D. Foley and Victor L. Wallace: "The art of natural graphic man-machine conversation"
Proceedings of the IEEE, Vol. 62, No. 4 (April 1974), pp 462-471

[HA 71] Wilfred J. Hansen: "User engineering principles for interactive systems"
AFIPS Fall Joint Computer Conference, AFIPS Conference Proceedings, Vol. 39, AFIPS Press, Montvale, New Jersey, (1971), pp 523-532

[KA 76] David J. Kasik: "Controlling User Interaction"
ACM SIGGRAPH / Computer Graphics, Vol. 10, No. 2, (Summer 1976), pp 109-115

[MA 75] William C. Mann: "Why things are so bad for the computer naive user"
National Computer Conference, AFIPS Conference Proceedings, (1975), pp 785-787

[MA 73] James D. Martin: "Design of man-computer dialogues"
Prentice-Hall, Englewood Cliffs, New Jersey, (1973)

[MI 77] Lance A. Miller and John C. Thomas, Jr.: "Behavioral issues in the use of interactive systems"
Int. J. Man-Machine Studies, 9 (1977), pp 509-536

[MU 77] R. Muchsel: "Kommando-Sprachen - Wunsch und Wirklichkeit"
Angewandte Informatik, 9 (1977), pp 369-374

[NI 69] R.S. Nickerson: "Man-computer interaction: a challenge for human factor research"
IEEE transactions on Man-Machine Systems, Vol. 10, (1969), pp 164-180

[NI 77] J. Nievergelt, H.P. Frei, H. Burkhart, Ch. Jacobi, B. Plattner, H. Sugaya, B. Weibel, J. Weydert: "XS-0: A self-explanatory School Computer"
Berichte des Instituts für Informatik /Nr. 21, (August 1977) Eidgenössische Technische Hochschule Zürich

[RO 75] William B. Rouse: "Design of man-computer interfaces for on-line interactive systems"
Proceedings of the IEEE, Vol. 63, No. 6, (June 1975), pp 847-857

Natural-language interfaces eliminate the need of learning artificial programming languages, but the convenience is offset by ambiguities. Artificial intelligence provides the lingusitic tools to overcome them.

Natural-Language Interfaces

Elaine Rich, The University of Texas at Austin

Whenever two or more agents cooperate to perform a task, their ability to communicate effectively with one another is a key factor in their success. For example, several studies have shown that the time required for two people to perform a simple task like assembling a trash-can carrier can vary by more than a factor of two, depending on whether the people are allowed to talk directly to each other or whether they are constrained and can only communicate by, say, typing messages back and forth. Communication for problem solving is as important when the agents are all people as when they are all machines or some of each. Because of the importance of communication as a part of problem solving, an important part of the design of any program is its ability to communicate with its users.

There are, of course, many ways in which people can communicate with programs. Some are linguistic: they use a verbal language of some kind, be it English or an artificial command language. Others are nonlinguistic, relying instead on such techniques as pointing or drawing. This article concentrates on the use of natural languages, such as English. Such languages are attractive because they are powerful and people already know them. This power, however, causes practical difficulties in the use of natural languages as interfaces to programs. We will examine the role of natural languages in such interfaces and will ex-plore some techniques for exploiting them. Thomas and Carroll[1] and Shneiderman[2] offer interested readers more complete discussions of the whole range of human factors issues that need to be considered in interface design.

What is understanding?

The first thing to look at is the overall process by which ideas are communicated. Figure 1 illustrates what has to happen. Whenever people decide to communicate something to a program, it is because they want the program to do something (although that something may be passive, such as "remember this fact for later"). A person must generate a statement in whatever language is being used, then communicate that statement. The program must then understand the statement, by which we mean that the statement must be translated into the appropriate actions within the program. Since understanding is a translation process, a statement is understood only with respect to a particular langauge *and* set of actions. A statement has no single meaning without a target set of actions. This is important, and it is one of the main reasons that building natural-language interfaces is difficult. It cannot be done once and for all; it must be done for each program that needs an interface.

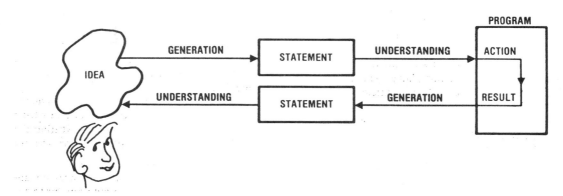

Figure 1. The language understanding process.

Sometimes the target set of actions is so simple that understanding is a trivial process of matching stored patterns of words against input sentences. The most famous example of a system such as this is Eliza,[3] which simulated a Rogerian therapist. The Eliza approach can be used in some very pragmatic contexts. For example, it was used to construct an interface to a key-word based help system.[4] But most systems needing interfaces have target sets of actions that are too complex to permit the use of this approach, in which most of the user's statement (including important words such as *not*) may be ignored.

This article treats the top half of Figure 1, namely the sending of messages from a user to a target program. This direction is more difficult from the system builder's point of view because the user, not the system, is in control. For many programs, output poses fewer problems. Although output must be considered in a complete system, we will not consider it here.

When is natural language natural?

Natural languages are not the best interfaces for all systems. Before we discuss how to build natural-language interfaces, we need to discuss when such interfaces are appropriate. Keep in mind that we are concerned here only with the use of natural language as a tool in system building. There is a whole research area that is concerned with natural language understanding for its own sake and for its implications in human cognition. We will ignore that here, however, despite its scientific significance.

We also need to remember that, when we use the term *natural-language interface,* we rarely mean that an entire natural language such as English will be used. Instead, we mean that a *subset* of a natural language will be used. Thus we must consider not just whether to use a natural language interface at all but how to choose an appropriate language subset for a particular target program. There are at least seven factors to consider in deciding whether to use a natural-language interface.

(1) Cost of the interface. The design and implementation, as well as production-mode execution time of natural-language interfaces generally cost more than those of more restricted interfaces. Some of the reasons for this will become clear later. What this means, though, is that unless there are concrete reasons to use such an interface for a particular program, it should be avoided.

(2) Ease of learning. Probably the single most attractive aspect of a natural-language interface is that is reduces to almost nothing the human effort required to learn the interface language. People already know a natural language.

This benefit is more illusory than real, though, if the interface language is not really a natural language but a run-of-the-mill, restricted language with legal statements that just happen to look like English statements (although one exception to this will be discussed below in Approach 1). Then users must learn what the boundaries are. For example, suppose that a database interface allows

Find all entries with year since 1975

but does not allow

Find all entries having year after 1975.

Clearly it is sufficient, in terms of power, to allow only one of these forms and not the other since they both produce the same query. But if only one is allowed, then the users have to learn which is which.

It was once thought that this problem could be solved by finding a *habitable* (easy to live within) subset of, say, English that users could easily learn.[5] It would contain the simple versions of desired statements. If users keyed in something only to be told that their statements were not understood, they could rephrase them to make them understood by making them simpler. This rephrasing of course assumes that users share a common notion of what constitutes simplicity. But they do not. For example, which of the above two sentences is simpler? In short, learning a natural-language interface is easier than learning an artificial one only if the natural-language subset that is chosen is broad enough to cover all (or most) of the

> **We must consider not just whether to use a natural-language interface but how to choose an appropriate subset for a particular target program.**

ways that users naturally say things. Also remember that, independent of the interface, a new operator cannot use a system without first learning what it can do. It is often fairly easy to learn a special language for a system's actions at the same time that the actions themselves are being studied.

(3) Conciseness. How long it takes to communicate something depends, at least in part, on how many symbols must be used. It takes longer to type

Please find all the articles that appeared in *Newsweek* in March that deal with Afghanistan.

than it does to type

RTR NEWSWEEK MARCH (AFGHANISTAN)

Studies have shown that, at least for some well-structured tasks like text editing, the time required for trained users to accomplish a task is a function of the number of keystrokes they must make.[6] Other studies have shown that people, when given a new task and complete flexibility in how they state their commands, will start with English-like statements and gradually get more telegraphic as they get the swing of the task or as they get bored with writing. If you give someone a series of 30 queries to write down on paper, the first is likely to look like the sentence about *Newsweek* shown above, and the last is more likely to resemble the RTR (retrieve) statement. Thus, the desire for conciseness often argues against the use of a natural language interface.

The demands of ease of learning must often be weighed against those of conciseness. In choosing an interface for a particular system, it is necessary to consider whether the primary users will be novice or casual users or whether they will be experienced, regular users.

(4) Need for precision. Many English sentences are ambiguous, in that they stand for more than one meaning. Many parts of statements are ambiguous even if the whole statements in which they occur are unambiguous—in a different context the part could have stood for something else. Consider the following statement:

Find all the articles about Cuba and Russia or China.

This request is ambiguous. It may be requesting articles about

(Cuba and Russia) or China

or it may be requesting articles about

Cuba and (Russia or China).

In fact, many English versions of logical expressions are ambiguous because the parentheses that are common in artificial, logical languages are not provided in English.

For some programs, this problem is much more serious than for others. For programs where precision is important, a natural-language interface is probably not adequate, although it may be reasonable to combine natural language and an artificial language to get the benefits of both.

(5) Need for pictures. The old adage, "A picture is worth a thousand words," says something about interfaces. Words are not the best way to describe such concepts as shapes and positions. To communicate them, other techniques, such as light pens, cursors, or digitizing pads, are better. Programs, such as many computer-aided design systems, which manipulate essentially graphical objects, may still be candidates for linguistically oriented interfaces, including those based on natural languages, but only if they are integrated with other, graphics-based, communication tools.

(6) Semantic complexity. From what has been said so far, it might make sense to conclude that natural-language interfaces are more trouble than they are worth. Are there really situations in which they are called for? The answer is yes. Could we as humans get through an ordinary day with a language like the one you use with your favorite text editor? Of course not. And the reason is that the number of different messages we need to convey is so large that no trivial language can carry the load. Natural languages are concise and efficient when the universe of possible messages is large.

The relevance of these observations to human-computer interfaces is obvious: If you have a program that can do many things and to which many messages may need to be sent, a complex language interface is necessary. Otherwise, it is not. So, for example, English offers many more options than the user of a text editor needs. But, if you had an on-line help system that could reason about a program's behavior and answer a wide range of user questions, a language with at least close to the complexity of English would be needed.[7] Many other classes of programs, such as database management systems, fall in between these two extremes, and the need for a natural-language interface must be studied carefully, with attention being given to the factors described here. As the problem-solving and reasoning capabilities of target programs grow, the gap between the power of English and the capabilities of the programs that need interfaces will narrow. Thus, although natural languages are too powerful to serve as interfaces to many existing systems, the need for them is growing.

(7) Promising more than can be delivered. The close connection between the range and complexity of a program and the range and complexity of the interface to the program exists (perhaps only implicitly) in the minds of users, but it leads them into a pitfall if there is not a good match between a program and its interface. If a program possesses a seemingly sophisticated interface, users will expect sophisticated behavior. An example occurred during work on the Ladder system (more on this later), which contained a database of facts about naval vessels. It also had an English front end. At first, users wrote queries like "What ships are in the Mediterranean?" which could be answered directly from facts in the database. Then came more sophisticated questions like "How long would it take the Constellation to get to Italy?" Procedures were then written to answer such questions from the information in the database. But then queries like "What ship should I send to Italy?" began to appear. Users expected that Ladder had the problem-solving ability to answer any question that could be stated in its input language (English).

Components of a natural-language understanding system

The process of translating statements from the language in which they were made into a program-specific form that causes appropriate actions to be performed is usually broken into three parts: words and lexicon, grammar and sentence structure, and semantics and sentence meaning.

Words and the lexicon. The first thing that must be done to understand a statement is to divide (to segment) it into its components. When statements are in a natural language, the obvious pieces to use are words. Dividing a

---

As problem-solving and reasoning capabilities of target programs grow, the gap between the power of natural and program languages will narrow.

---

sentence into words is called lexical analysis. For written English, this process is mostly trivial, by which we mean that it can be done with a single pass over the input in time that increases linearly in relation to the length of the input. Sequences of characters between spaces are words. If spoken language is used, however, this simple technique is not available, and sentences cannot usually be segmented without higher level, contextual information. In written language, it is sometimes useful to divide a statement into segments smaller than words. For example, the word *going* is composed of the root verb *go* and the suffix *-ing*. Dividing words up this way is called morphological analysis, which involves a list of the root words, a list of affixes (suffixes and prefixes), and a list of simple rules that describe how pieces are combined. An example of such a rule is that if a verb ends in *-y*, the suffix *-ed* is added by changing the final *y* to an *i*. For example, *study* plus *-ed* becomes *studied*. Unfortunately, this rule is not always enough and a list of exceptions may also be necessary. For example, *go* plus *-ed* becomes *went*.

The list of words that a particular understanding program can recognize is contained in its *dictionary* or *lexicon*. Machine-readable versions of several commercial dictionaries are currently available, but most language-understanding programs do not use them. There are two reasons for this. The first is that the vocabulary for a particular program is usually a small subset of the total available lexicon. (Remember that words that have no mapping to actions of the target program cannot be understood, whether they are in the lexicon or not.) The other reason is that the information to be associated with each word and the way that information should be represented in the lexicon vary from one program to the next depending on how the rest of the understanding system works and what the output of the understanding system should look like. Sometimes the lexicon is not actually stored explicitly as a list but, rather, is contained implicitly in the rules that describe what sentence forms will be accepted. This implicit storage will become clearer later, when several specific techniques for understanding are presented.

Design of a natural-language interface requires that a lexicon be selected, a two-step process. The first step is to isolate the concepts to be expressed. Look at what the target program can do and decide what concepts it can understand. The second thing is to select specific words to represent those concepts. It is in some sense sufficient to select a single word for each concept, but that may make it very difficult for users to know what expressions are acceptable. Selecting words that will be acceptable is important because our everyday English lexicon contains so many very similar words. A study by Furnas et al. [8] shows that, when people were asked to give a typist specific commands, in English (of the sort one could also give to a text-editing system), there was considerable disagreement in the verbs chosen for the desired actions. It is usually very cheap (in terms of understanding time) to allow synonyms for words, and doing so often substantially increases the likelihood of user constructing acceptable statements.

In selecting a lexicon for a particular task, it is useful to make the distinction between *open* lexical categories and *closed* lexical categories. Open categories can have new entries added to them regularly; closed ones are rarely, if ever, augmented. In English, noun, verb, adjective, and adverb are open categories; new entries appear daily (e.g., *laser, video*). Pronoun, preposition, and conjunction are closed categories. In interfaces to programs, the distinction between open and closed categories typically depends on the structure of the program. Users cannot add new actions to the program, but they can often add new values for the arguments to those actions, So, for example, the basic actions for a database management system might be query, add, and delete, but the keywords to be used for retrieval can change daily. The Falkland Islands may be common for a newspaper database for one period of time, although they were unheard of a year before or a year after.

Many English words are ambiguous. Consider the word *can,* for example, in the following two statements:

Can you tell me what the GNP was in 1980?
What companies make a high-quality tin can?

Whether a word is ambiguous in an English interface depends on the subset of English that is used. Whenever a large subset is used, ambiguity can seldom be avoided. Instead, it must be resolved by the context in which the ambiguous word occurs.

Grammar and the structure of sentences. Statements in a natural language are, prior to any analysis, simply flat strings of words. But they typically stand for structured ideas. A first step toward finding the meaning of a statement (i.e., understanding it) is often to assign to the statement a structure that will probably correspond in some way to the structure of its meaning. Assigning such a structure to an unstructured object is called *syntactic analysis* or *parsing*. Often parsing also serves to divide the world of possible inputs into two classes, the legal ones (sometimes called the grammatical ones), for which a complete structure (parse) can be found, and the illegal, ungrammatical ones for which the parsing process fails to find a complete structure. Of course, in interface design, we are not interested in rejecting a user's statement just because it is ungrammatical. Instead, we would like a parsing procedure that is as flexible as possible in analyzing the user's statements. Handling ungrammatical statements is dif-

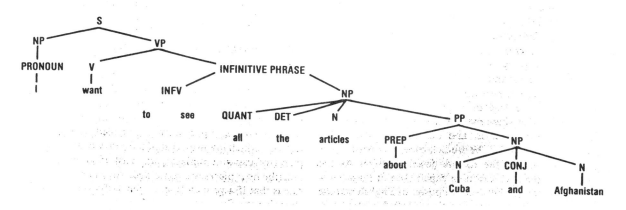

Figure 2. A syntactic parse tree which shows how the components of the statement or sentence, *S*, are formed: *NP* = noun phrase; *VP* = verbphrase; *V* = verb; *INFV* = infinitive verb; *QUANT* = quantifier; *DET* = determiner; *N* = noun; *PP* = prepositional phrase; and *CONJ* = conjunction.

ficult, although Hayes and Mouradian have made some progress on it.[9]

The parsing process must exploit a set of rules that describe the ways that higher level structures can be realized as lower level ones. For example, to parse English sentences, one might use rules such as "A sentence is composed of a noun phrase followed by a verb phrase" (S→NP VP) or "A noun phrase contains a sequence of adjectives followed by a noun" (NP→ADJ* N). A collection of such rules is called a grammar. By convention, the topmost structure, corresponding to a complete grammatical statement, is often named S.

Figure 2 shows an example of an English version of a simple database query that has been parsed by a standard English grammar. The parse tree shows how the components of the statement are formed. The subject of the sentence is I, the verb is want, and the object is to see something. Then the something is further defined.

Often the grammar is represented explicitly as a set of rules, and the parsing program refers to this set of rules. Then there are two principal ways of conducting the parsing process, and the techniques can, of course, be used in combination. The two principal approaches are bottom-up and top-down. In the bottom-up approach, the tree is constructed from the bottom, starting with the words in the statement. Intermediate constituents are formed as their components become available, and the parse is complete when the top constituent, representing a complete statement, is formed. In the top-down approach, the search for a complete parse begins at the top, with a complete statement, and lower level constitutents that could form a statement are hypothesized. The levels below them are then hypothesized, and this process continues until actual words are needed. The words are then matched against the actual input. There has been a great deal of research on parsing algorithms, much of it in the context of programming-language compilers.

An alternative technique is to encode the grammar in a transition network constructed to correspond to the allowable transitions between the constituents of a sentence. A tiny fragment of such a network is shown in Figure 3. When this technique is used, parsing is simulated by walking simultaneously through the input sentence and the network structure. Usually the arcs in the network contain extra information that tells the parser what actions it should take during the parse in order to build the desired structure by the end. Woods calls these networks augmented transition networks (or ATNs).[10]

The problem of ambiguity has already been discussed, and we saw how it could affect the process of lexical analysis. It must also be considered during syntactic analysis. Recall, for example, the request for articles about Cuba and Russia or China. It has two parses, one corresponding to each interpretation. Sometimes ambiguities such as this can be resolved during later processing since only one interpretation may make sense. Often, though, both make sense. Then the safest action is to ask the user which was intended.

Although a particular grammar defines a language to be exactly the set of sentences to which complete structures can be assigned, there is no one-to-one relationship between languages and grammars. For a given language, there are usually many different grammars. Although the different grammars may accept the same language, they may vary tremendously in their usefulness for a particular understanding program since they may assign very different structures to a particular statement. One of those structures might be similar to the final output that the understanding program should produce, while the other structures might be very different. Parsing is only one step of the total understanding process, but how it is done may make the next step, which actually produces the final output, very simple or very difficult.

Semantics and the meaning of sentences. The final step of the understanding process is to assign a meaning to the statement to be understood. In other words, we determine what action the target program is supposed to take. Assigning this meaning to a statement is called semantic processing. Actually we combine two processes that are sometimes viewed separately: semantic processing (determining what a statement means) and pragmatic processing (determining what should be done about it). To make this difference clear, let us consider the following request to a database management system:

Could you tell me all the presidents who died in office?

Literally this statement is a request for information about what the system can do. But what is intended is that the system tell which presidents died in office.

The techniques used to assign a semantic interpretation to a statement vary widely, depending on the way the rest of the intepretation process is conducted, so a discussion of them will be deferred.

Conducting a dialog. Many tasks require more than understanding individual statements by a program, so a dialog between the user and the target program occurs. Several new problems appear when we attempt to understand dialogs.

(1) User: Who is the manager of the sales division?
     System: Lucy Jones
(2) User: What is her salary?
     System: $50,000
(3) User: Her phone number?
     System: 392-7240   **(1)**

The most important problem is that in the context of a dialog, individual statements are often incomplete. Two kinds of incomplete statements are shown in the above dialog. Statement 2 contains an anaphoric reference. It uses the word her, which refers to a person already mentioned. To understand the question, it is necessary to bind

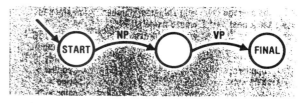

Figure 3. A piece of an augmented transition network, or ATN, in which a noun phrase, NP, is parsed with a verb phrase, VP.

her to *Lucy Jones.* Statement 3 is an incomplete statement that should be interpreted as a similar question but words identifying the information sought must be substituted into question 2 in the right slot. In this example, that means that the query, "What is her phone number?" should be constructed and answered. Although dialog issues are important if truly "natural" natural-language interfaces are to be built, they will not be dealt with further in this article; they have been discussed by Bobrow.[11] Instead, we will concentrate on the three other processes—lexical, syntactic, and semantic analysis.

At this point, the key components of any natural-language understanding program have been introduced. The next three sections describe three approaches to combining these components into an understanding program.

Approach 1: language through windows

When the number of statements that a user will need to make to the target program is not very large, one approach to the interface problem is for the system to display the available options to the user, who chooses from among those options and gradually constructs a complete statement, which then is guaranteed to correspond to actions that the target program can perform. An example of an interface built with this technique is Texas Instruments' NLX system. Figure 4 shows an example of a screen that could be presented to a user of a database system. The outlined window is *active,* and it is from this window that the next word must be selected. After each word is chosen, the screen must be updated. The selected word must be added to the bottom window in which the statement, as it has so far been formed, is recorded. Also, the windows that contain choices for later words must be updated to show those options that can form legal (grammatical and meaningful) statements in the context of what has already been said. And finally, the active marker must be moved to the window that shows the choices for the next word.

To use this window method, it is necessary to construct both a lexicon and a grammar for the language to be recognized. It is also necessary to know all of the semantic restrictions on the way elements can be combined. An important characteristic of a system like this is that only meaningful statements can be constructed. So, for example, the Connectors window contains *the average,* which the target program can compute, but it does not contain *the best,* because no code exists to compute it. Sometimes, the contents of the windows must be updated dynamically as the statement is being constructed, in order to guarantee a semantically consistent and complete statement. For example, if the statement so far were "Find all the suppliers," then only some of the Qualifiers of Figure 4 would be displayed. It does not make sense to continue that statement with *whose colors are,* assuming that, in the database, parts have colors but suppliers do not.

This approach to the design of a natural-language interface makes sense when the number of alternatives available at one time is generally small. But even in very restricted semantic domains, there may be times when a slot in a statement could take on any one of a large number of possible values. In Figure 4, these slots are listed in the Attributes window. When that window is active, the user must actually key in a value. But that value must appear in the system's lexicon, and it must be a member of a class that is available as an option (such as quantity or color).

In a window-based system, lexical analysis is trivial since most words are not even typed, but are pointed to on the screen. Parsing (syntactic analysis) is done as the user's statement is entered. In fact, the parsing process does two things at once: It builds the parse of the statement and provides the information to update the windows so that they contain the words that could complete a valid statement. The third step, semantic processing, in which the parse tree is converted to an action of the target program, is usually fairly easy and can even be done while the tree is being built. Semantic processing is usually easy because the structure of the choices presented to the user can be designed to correspond the structure necessary in the final output.

A window-based, natural-language system runs relatively efficiently because the options available to the user are so rigorously constrained. But its main usefulness occurs in domains of low semantic complexity, where there really are few options. In particular, to use this approach, it must be possible to encode, in the grammar, all the information that is required to determine whether a particular statement can be executed correctly. This decision must be made as the input is being constructed, and it must be made without appeal to the target program itself. In semantically rich domains, this is not normally possible.

Approach 2: semantic grammars

The window-based approach does not really give users control over interactions nor allow them to compose free-form statements that must then be understood by the system. Instead, the system retains control and presents a list of options to the users. When only a restricted number of statements makes sense to the system, this approach is feasible, but as the number of things that users may need to say increases, it becomes less and less practical. Another approach is then called for—one in which users compose entire statements on their own and the understanding system then translates the statements. One implementation of this approach uses what we will call a semantic grammar to drive the understanding process.

COMMANDS:	Find	Find the	Find all the
FEATURES:	**CONNECTORS:**	**QUALIFIERS:**	**COMPARISONS:**
part number	and	supplied by	between > =
part name	or	whose colors are	equal to <
quantity	of	whose price is	> < =
supplier name	the average	with shipment number	not equal to
supplier address	the lowest	whose name is	
supplier number		whose address is	**ATTRIBUTES:**
price	**NOUNS:**	who supply	< part number >
color	parts		< quantity >
	suppliers		< supplier >
	shipments		< price >
			< color >
QUERY SO FAR:			

Figure 4. A sample natural-language menu.

The basic idea behind the use of a semantic grammar is that a statement can be understood in only two steps, rather than the three previously described. Lexical analysis first separates a statement into words. Then the words are analyzed for syntax and semantics in a single step. Actually, a small third step may be required to produce the final output, but it is very simple, given the output of step 2. In many ways, a semantic grammar is a straightforward extension of the window system to allow a greater number of user options. (Historically, in fact, semantic grammars came first and formed the basis for the window approach.)

A semantic grammar, like any other grammar, consists of a set of rewrite rules. When a statement is parsed by the grammar, it is assigned a structure that is determined by the rules. The rules are designed so that the structure produced by the parser corresponds as closely as possible to the desired input to the target program. Also, the rules are designed so that the set of statements that can be parsed successfully corresponds as closely as possible to the set of actions in the target program. (Note here the similarity to the window approach.) Some statements that do not correspond to available actions may be accepted, however, if the grammar contains any rules that are not sufficiently constrained. In a complex semantic world, the grammar usually will. Example 2 shows a simplified fragment of a semantic grammar used in the Ladder system. [12] Examples of sentences that can be parsed using this grammar include "What is the speed of the Kennedy?" and "Tell me the speed of the Kennedy." These sentences in fact produce the same parse, even though one is syntactically a question and one is an imperative. Other perfectly good English sentences cannot be parsed, however, including "What is the color of the Kennedy?" and "What is today's date?"

```
S → QUERY SHIP-PROPERTY of SHIP
QUERY → what is | tell me
SHIP-PROPERTY → the SHIP-PROP |
    SHIP-PROP
SHIP-PROP → speed | length | type
SHIP → the SHIP-NAME | the fastest SHIP2
SHIP-NAME → Kennedy | Kitty Hawk |
    Constellation | . . .
SHIP2 → COUNTRYS SHIP3 | SHIP3
SHIP3 → SHIPTYPE LOCATION | SHIPTYPE
SHIPTYPE → carrier | submarine | . . .
COUNTRYS → American | British | Russian | . . .
LOCATION → in the Mediterranean | in the Atlantic | . . .
```
                                                    (2)

The categories used in the rules are different from the ones used in Figures 2 and 3. There, the categories were syntactic, noun (N), verb (V), and prepositional phrase (PP). Here, the categories have been designed specifically to correspond to the semantics of the target program and include things like ship, ship-property, and location.

When a semantic grammar is used, just as when any grammer is used, some parsing technique must be employed to apply the grammar to each input statement. Both Ladder and Planes, a semantic-grammar-based natural language interface to a database system described by Waltz, [13] use ATNs to parse.

Figure 5 shows a parse tree generated from the semantic grammar of Example 2. It also shows how the final meaning of the statement, namely a database query, can be constructed from the parse tree. Since the structure of the parse tree is so similar to the structure of the query, the query can be generated easily in either of two ways. First, actions can be attached to each grammar rule, and the actions executed when each rule is applied. Each action may use objects created by other actions in the tree. The action associated with the topmost rule ($S →$ something) puts together a complete query. The other way to construct the query is in a separate step, after the tree is formed, through a procedure that walks through the tree-performing actions associated with each link (just as in Approach 1).

Sematic grammars are useful when only a relatively small subset of a whole language needs to be recognized, but they do not capture much of the syntactic regularity of the language. As they are expanded to deal with larger and larger pieces of the language, they tend to get much larger and much more complex. Eventually their *ad hoc* character makes them unusable.

Approach 3: syntactic grammars

When a large fragment of a natural language is used as an interface, it is important to capture as much of the regularity of the language as possible in the rules used to understand it. To do so, it is necessary to capture the syntactic regularity of the language being used. This forces a return to a syntactically motivated grammar such as the one that generated the parse tree of Figure 2. Then it is possible, for example, to define the structure of a prepositional phrase once, independent of the preposition being used and the role of the phrase in the sentence. Notice how this syntactic-grammar approach contrasts with the semantic approach in which prespositional phrases may appear in several places. In the semantic grammar of Example 2, for instance, there are two uses of prepositional phrases.

When we construct a semantic grammar, we look at both sides of the translation (both the input language and the program actions) and we write grammar rules that map, as directly as possible, structures of one into structures of the other. The rules thus appear semantic in that they relate directly to the target actions. But when both sides of the translation are complex, it is difficult to consider both sides at once and to complete the translation in

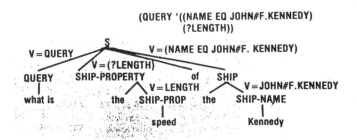

Figure 5. A semantic parse in which the categories—such as SHIP, SHIP-PROPERTY, and LOCATION—have been designed specifically to correspond to the semantics of the target program (see Example 2)

one step. Instead, we write grammar rules that can be used by a parser to assign one structure to each sentence. Typically we choose structures that capture generalities in the input language itself, independent of the target program. Then we write other rules (which may or may not be attached directly to the grammar rules) to transform the parsed structure into target actions.

As we discussed previously, several techniques are available for conducting the parsing process itself. The one that has been most often used in syntactically based natural-language interfaces (as well as in the semantically based ones of Approach 2) is the ATN. Lunar[10] and Robot[14] are examples of systems that operate this way.

Unfortunately, regardless of the parsing strategy, it is not always possible to know, as the process progresses, exactly which constituents will ultimately be needed. To see why not, consider the statement that begins with "The trash can...." Figure 6 shows two parse trees that correspond to sentences that could be started this way. The choice of the correct constituents cannot be made until more of the statement has been processed. Thus parsing must be considered a search process, which must be kept in mind to understand actions taken during the parsing process.

To minimize the number of intermediate constituents that are considered and then rejected, most parsing systems permit grammar rules to be augmented with tests that must be satisfied in order for the rules to fire. Some of these tests check syntactic properties, as in the following rule:

$S \rightarrow NP\ VP$ {where the number of NP is the same as the number of VP}

This check prevents ungrammatical statements like the following from being parsed:

I wants all the stories.

Some tests check properties that are more semantically motivated, although they are important in almost all domains of discourse. An example of this kind of check is

$VP \rightarrow VP1\ COAGENT$

$VP1 \rightarrow$ <standard verb phrase rules>

$COAGENT \rightarrow$ with NP <where NP has the animate property>

These rules permit *Mary* to be interpreted as a coagent in the sentence, "Sue went to the store with Mary." But they prevent *the best wine selection* from being a coagent in the sentence, "Sue went to the store with the best wine selection."

Still other tests may be needed to check for very specific semantic properties. For example, consider the following sentences:

Change all the entries with the editor.
Change all the entries with yesterday's date.

In the first, the prepositional phrase, *with the editor*, is part of the verb and describes how the action is to be performed. In the second sentence, the prepositional phrase, *with yesterday's date*, is part of the noun phrase and describes which objects are to be changed. To produce the correct parse requires noting that an editor can be used to make changes, but a date cannot.

So far, we have discussed only lexical and syntactic analysis. As we suggested, when we use a syntactic grammar, the third step, application of semantic rules to the parse to generate the appropriate target-program actions, is not usually trivial. There are two ways to apply semantic rules. One technique is to interleave syntactic and semantic processing and to attach to each grammar rule a set of actions that should be performed when the rule is applied. The parser must cause these actions to be executed when their corresponding rule is applied. The result of the actions executed during a successful parse should be a complete translation for the input statement. For example, actions might build up descriptions of entities and events and assign those descriptions to variables like Agent, Event, Object, or Location. Other actions might move values from one variable to another. For example, consider the two sentences:

List all the books that Smith wrote.
List all the books written by Smith.

In the first sentence, *Smith* is the agent of the action *write*. But *Smith* is also the agent of the action *write* in the second sentence, even though the word *Smith* occurs as the object of a preposition. Actions attached to the rules that recognize participles and prepositional phrases introduced with *by* can shuffle values so that the output of the understanding process will be the same for both sentences.

Remember, though, that parsing usually involves search. Some backtracking is almost always necessary. It complicates actions during parsing, since actions may need to be undone, but it suggests another way of handling syntactic and semantic processing—namely do one and then do the other. Damerau's transformational question answering (TQA) system[15] is an example of a program that separates processing. There is also another reason to separate syntactic and semantic processing: Doing so might make it possible to construct a grammar and a parser for a language, such as English, once, and to reuse it in many interfaces. This reuse is appealing because there are so many vagaries to English syntax that it is good to deal with them once and for all. For example, one can say, "List all the books that McGraw-Hill published." Or one can leave out the relative pronoun *that* and make the

Figure 6. The ambiguity of sentence or statement beginning with, "The trash can...".

equivalent statement, "List all the books McGraw-Hill published."

There have been efforts made to construct very large, general-purpose grammars of English.[16] But, unfortunately, when people tried to apply them to new tasks, they have found that the syntactic structures built with a grammar written by someone else and for another task are so difficult to use in semantic processing that it is easier to build a new system from scratch. For example, consider the following three statements:

How long is the Kennedy?
What is the length of the Kennedy?
I want to know the length of the Kennedy.

The sentences have very different syntactic structures even though they should map to the same database query. But when the entire range of things people want to say in English is considered, this syntactic variability is significant; these syntactic structures are used in other contexts for very different things. So a general-purpose parser must build different structures for the three sentences even though, in the restricted context of an interface to a database system, the three sentences should have identical interpretations.

Tools

Constructing a natural-language interface is a time-consuming task, even after the basic structure of the target-program is well understood. The lexicon, the grammar, the semantic rules, and the code that uses all of them must be built. There are, however, tools available to assist in this process. For all three approaches we have discussed, it is possible to use existing programs to do most of the understanding. That reduces the problem to the construction of the appropriate tables (lexicon, grammar, semantic rules) for those programs. Again, some help exists. There are commercially available systems that allow those tables to be built interactively, checked automatically for various kinds of consistency, and augmented by users when they run up against limits on what the system was designed, to expect. These systems can substantially reduce the bookkeeping time that would otherwise be required. Still, to construct an interface that exploits any nontrivial subset of a natural language is not a simple task.

Several techniques for constructing natural-language interfaces have been developed and are being used, but natural languages pose interpretation problems, such as ambiguity, that artificial languages usually do not share. It is because of those problems that understanding natural language statements is an artificial intelligence problem. A substantial body of knowledge, not just about language itself, but also about the domain being discussed, must be exploited to do the job. Some search is almost always required to match this knowledge against each user statement. When the domain is complex and the performance program is powerful, there is no way to avoid such a search. But for simple domains, simpler languages that lack the power of natural languages and also their problems are often better suited. ✳

References

1. J. Thomas and J. Carroll, "Human Factors in Communication," *IBM Systems J.*, Vol. 20, pp. 237-263.

2. B. Shneiderman, *Software Psychology: Human Factors in Computer and Information Systems*, Winthrop, Cambridge, Mass., 1980.

3. J. Weizenbaum, "ELIZA—A Computer Program for the Study of Natural Language Communication between Man and Machine," *Comm. ACM*, Vol. 9, No. 1, Jan. 1966, pp. 36-44.

4. S. C. Shapiro and S. C. Kwasny, "Interactive Consulting via Natural Language," *Comm. ACM*, Vol. 18, No. 8, Aug. 1975.

5. W. C. Watt, "Habitability," *American Documentation*, Vol. 19, No. 3, 1968, pp. 338-351.

6. S. K. Card, T. P. Moran, and A. Newell, *Applied Information Processing Psychology: The Human-Computer Interface*, Erlbaum, Hillsdale, N. J., 1983.

7. R. Wilensky, "Talking to UNIX in English: An Overview of an On-line UNIX Consultant," *AI Magazine*, Vol. 5, No. 1, Spring 1984, pp. 29-39.

8. G. W. Furnas et al., "Statistical Semantics: Analysis of the Potential Performance of Key-Word Information Systems," *The Bell System Tech. J.*, Vol. 62, No. 6, Part 3, 1983, pp. 1753-1806.

9. P. J. Hayes and G. V. Mouradian, "Flexible Parsing," *American J. Computational Linguistics*, Vol. 7, No. 4, 1981, pp. 232-242.

10. W. A. Woods, "Transition Network Grammars for Natural Language Analysis," *Comm. ACM*, Vol. 13, 1970, pp. 591-606.

11. D. G. Bobrow et al., "Gus, a Frame-driven Dialog System," *Artificial Intelligence*, Vol. 8, 1977.

12. G. G. Hendrix et al., "Developing a Natural Language Interface to Complex Data," *ACM Trans. Database Systems*, Vol. 3, 1978, pp. 105-147.

13. D. L. Waltz, "An English Language Question-answering System for a Large Relational Database," *Comm. ACM*, Vol. 21, No. 7, 1978.

14. L. Harris, "User Oriented Database Query with the ROBOT Natural Language Query System," *Int'l J. Man-Machine Studies*, Vol. 9, 1977, pp. 697-713.

15. F. J. Damerau, "Operating Statistics for the Transformational Question Answering System," *American J. Computational Linguistics*, Vol. 7, No. 1, 1981, pp 30-42.

16. N. Sager, *Natural Language Information Processing*, Addison-Wesley, Reading, Mass., 1981.

Elaine Rich is an assistant professor of computer sciences at the University of Texas at Austin. Her research interests include knowledge representation techniques for artificial-intelligence systems, natural-language understanding, and the use of artificial intelligence in the design of human-machine interfaces.

Rich received an AB from Brown University in 1972 and a PhD from Carnegie-Mellon University in 1979. She is a member of the ACM, the IEEE-Computer Society, the American Association for Artificial Intelligence, and the Association for Computer Linguistics.

Questions about this article can be directed to the author at Dept. of Computer Sciences, University of Texas, Austin, TX 78712.

MAKING THE RIGHT CHOICES WITH MENUS

Gary Perlman

AT & T Bell Laboratories
Murray Hill, New Jersey 07974 USA

and

Cognitive Science Laboratory
University of California, San Diego
La Jolla, California 92093 USA

Menus provide a effective way to present a limited set of options to users. System designers have to decide how many options to present in what format, and how users will indicate their choices. Two experiments are reported that manipulate (1) menu size, (2) option ordering, (3) option selector type, and (4) selector/option compatibility. The results show (a) people use simple search strategies for ordinary menu sizes, (b) people are sensitive to menu length, (c) sorted menus are easier to search, and (d) letter selectors can produce the best or worst performance depending on compatibility. Some guidelines for menu design and suggestions for further research are discussed.

A menu is a list with a limited number of options, usually words or short phrases. Often associated with menu options are unique selector strings, sometimes the index number of the option or a letter abbreviation, sometimes the option itself. Some large systems create hierarchies of menus leading to sub-menus so that large menus or inappropriate menu choices are avoided. In this paper, I present results about how menus are searched and how options in menus are selected. I conclude with some guidelines for designing menus.

EXPERIMENT 1: Menu Search

In this experiment I study how people search through menus. I vary menu size, option order, and option type to see how these factors affect how long it takes people to find menu options.

METHOD

Conditions

Subjects saw menus on a CRT terminal with keyboard connected to a mini-computer. Menus were plotted on the left side of the screen with items vertically aligned and left justified. There were two *types* of menu lists: Arabic numbers from 1 to 20, and well known names of members of categories drawn from Battig & Montague (1969) such that the letters 'a' through 't' were covered. For each menu list type, four menu lists were made up of length 5, 10, 15, and 20, using the beginning of the menu lists. Four groups, eight undergraduates each, searched sorted words, sorted numbers, random words, and random numbers, respectively. Subjects were shown only one list ordering to try to force them into the best strategy for their list. All subjects searched though four list lengths, the order of which was controlled by a Latin square.

Procedure

On each trial, one of two randomly chosen arrows '<' or '>' appeared to the left of each item, and the item to be found, the *target*, was presented at the right of the screen at a constant location. The task was to find the target and indicate when it was found by pressing the arrow key next to the target. The subjects had their left fingers on the left arrow key and their rights on the right. It was thought that this response measure would add a constant to the search time independent of the experimental factors and make sure subjects were really finding the targets. To control the amount of practice subjects had with the lists, there were 60 trials per condition so subjects had practice ranging from three trials for the 20 long lists to 12 for the five long list. Subjects rested between different list length conditions, but within a condition, trials were continuous with two second pauses between.

RESULTS

The main results are shown in Figure 1. Finding words (1.89 sec) took longer than numbers (1.56 sec) ($F(1,28) = 11.7$, $p < .01$) perhaps because the numbers were shorter or more familiar. Sorted lists (1.45 sec) were easier to search than random (2.01 sec) ($F(1,28) = 10.05$, $p < .001$). There was no interaction between list type and order.

The length of the list had a reliable effect: 5 (1.26 sec) 10 (1.57 sec) 15 (1.84 sec) 20 (2.23 sec) so it took longer to find items in longer lists ($F(3,84) = 113.86$, $p < .001$). There was an interaction between list type and length ($F(3,84) = 4.50$, $p < .01$); words took longer per list item to find than numbers. More important, there was an interaction between list order and length ($F(3,84) = 18.28$, $p < .001$); random lists had higher slopes than sorted.

The data for the first three trials (the minimum amount of practice subjects had with all list lengths) showed similar trends for all the data. People got

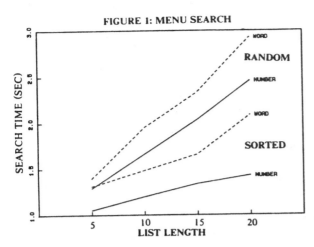

FIGURE 1: MENU SEARCH

better with practice, but it was not the only reason why they did better with the short lists with which they had more trials per item.

Error rates were lower than one percent of all trials and were nearly evenly distributed among conditions. This suggests that subjects were really finding the items and the left and right arrow key test to indicate *finding* worked properly. Reaction times for errors were non-significantly lower than correct trials. Errors did not play a large part in the experiment because subjects were instructed to be accurate.

DISCUSSION

The results of the experiment have practical applications and some interesting theoretical implications. In general, list length has a linear effect on the time it takes to find an item, and this effect is larger if the list is random. Randomness is in the mind of the person doing the searching. Usually, people searching though a list will be looking for a semantic match, not an exact match for what they have in mind. For example, a user might want to *print* a file, but the name of the command is *display*. So, in some cases, an alphabetically ordered list would not allow a fast search for what the person had in mind.

It is surprising that sorted lists show a time increase linear in list length; an optimal computer algorithm would produce a logarithmic function (Aho, Hopcroft, & Ullman, 1974). For lists of these lengths, the gains from a binary search strategy is not worth the cost of a more expensive comparison routine. An identity match is a fast operation for people while an ordinal judgement takes longer. Norman and Fisher (1981) found that alphabetic keyboards were not much easier for non-typists to learn, and this seems to be related to the findings here: making use of the ordinal information of an alphabetic keyboard is not worth the trouble because the extra computation is no match for

a simpler search and match strategy. One would expect that the comparison of numbers to be faster than words because they are shorter and their ordinal nature is much more practiced. There is some indication of this: longer lists of sorted words look like they have an increasing slope while longer lists of sorted numbers look like their's is decreasing. These trends are small and not reliable. Practically speaking, we can treat the lines as straight, though the theoretical implications of search strategies demand more experimentation.

Card (1983) concluded from his data that people search through menus with a random strategy and gradually memorize the position of the items. A fine grained analysis of the response times according to list position yielded some interesting results. For random lists, there were no reliable trends in the data suggesting that with lists they know to be random, people adopt a random strategy and perhaps try to memorize list position. This is what Card found.

For sorted lists, there was an advantage for the first few items for both words and numbers, and an advantage for the ends of number lists. With the longer sorted lists of numbers, there was an advantage for the middle of the list as well; apparently people could estimate that items were in the beginning, middle, or end of the lists and begin search in that region. This is true for lists of numbers, not words, an probably not phrases, so the practical implications must be qualified. Card found that with extensive practice, people were able to go directly to target options. This was not found in this experiment perhaps because subjects were not practiced enough.

With longer lists, people took longer to find the first list item. Even though they know that the first number is '1' and that it is at the top of all the sorted lists, they still take longer to find it. This suggests that people cannot ignore extra options added to menus.

EXPERIMENT 2: Option Selection

Once an option in a menu has been found, the next step is to select it. There are several mechanisms for selection: cursor movements, mice and joy sticks (see Card, 1983), touch screens, and even voice input, however the one most commonly used is typing a selection string, usually a character, to indicate a choice. This is primarily due to the lack of availability of more advanced technology, but selector strings can stand up to more advanced methods under certain conditions and can let users avoid moving their hands away from keyboards. When users are familiar with the available items but still want to use the menu selection scheme to abbreviate input, some selection schemes can support them and allow them to avoid menu search by using memorable selectors.

In this experiment, I recorded selection times for compatible and incompatible letter and number selectors. The experiment was motivated by an observation that menu systems using letter selectors a-z can have awkward pairings between selectors and options. Letters are attractive because there are 26 to choose from, but an ordered list of letter selectors might pair "print" with 'd' and users might type 'p' for "print." The following experiment quantifies this interference.

METHOD

Conditions

The apparatus was the same as in Experiment 1. The stimuli were eight computer terms beginning with the letters 'a' through 'h'. The terms were *assemble, buffer, compile, debug, edit, file, graph,* and *halt.* Pilot data showed that knowledge of the computer terms was not important for the task. Two types of selectors were paired with the computer terms: single letters between 'a' and 'h', and the digits 1-8. There were two compatibility conditions. A compatible letter is the first letter of the word it is paired with, and a compatible number is the ordinal alphabetical position of the initial letter of the word (e.g., 1-assemble, 4-debug). Incompatible selectors were chosen randomly so that no selectors were compatible. Incompatible letter selectors can occur when the letters 'a' through 'z' are used as menu selectors and get paired with words with different initial letters. Incompatible numbers served as a control condition.

Procedure

The left justified stimulus set of eight terms and their selectors were displayed vertically in the upper left corner for the duration of each condition. On each trial, a target word was presented at a fixed location in the lower right corner of the screen. Sixteen undergraduates were instructed to begin a trial by holding their preferred index finger away from the keyboard and then press the selector character paired with the stimulus target. Subjects saw all conditions, the presentation order of which was controlled by a Latin square. There were five trials per term per condition and about two seconds between trials; subjects were allowed to rest only between conditions.

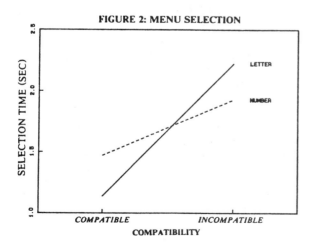

FIGURE 2: MENU SELECTION

RESULTS

The results are summarized in Figure 2. Compatible selectors were superior to incompatible $(F(1,12) = 107.9, p < .001)$. Compatible letters were the best selectors (1.14 sec) followed by compatible numbers (1.47 sec) while for incompatible selectors, the trend was reversed. Incompatible numbers (1.93 sec) were superior to incompatible letters (2.22 sec) $(F(1,14) = 52.1, p < .001)$. A 99 % Scheffe confidence interval showed all differences to be reliable.

Before each experimental condition, subjects were allowed to study the lists. Subjects spent more time (26 sec) looking at incompatible pairings than compatible (16 sec) $(F(1,15) = 14.9, p < .01)$. There was no difference in viewing times between letter and number selectors.

Errors occurred in less than one percent of the trials and most could be attributed to hitting a key next to the one they were supposed to. The remaining errors were too few for meaningful analyses. Response times for for errors were longer than for correct trials.

DISCUSSION

Norman's (1981) theory of action slips predicts that competing activations between the initial letter of a word and an incompatible selector letter should result in more errors than other conditions. Because subjects were instructed to minimize errors, there were not enough for statistical analyses. Still, the interference is manifest in the selection times. If there were no competing activations, the differences between incompatible letters and incompatible numbers would not have been observed.

The application of the results to the design of menu systems is clear. The best that can be done is to use compatible letters as selectors, but this can only be done if the designer has full control over the contents of menus. If the pairing is done automatically, such as by a program to select files, then using letter selectors can lead to the worst case, incompatible letters, and numerical selection would be preferable.

GENERAL DISCUSSION

The effects observed in the two experiments suggest that one or two seconds can be saved every time a menu selection is made. The importance of the results depends on the frequency of menu use.

A menu is particularly useful when users do not know what options are available to them or if the contents of a menu change over time. For example, the commands available in a program (e.g., a mail program) are limited to a fixed set (e.g., print, delete, answer) and so can be presented to users in a menu. These commands do not change over time, and a menu of commands useful to a new user becomes a nuisance to moderately experienced users. A menu can be used to abbreviate user keyboard inputs, but sometimes this costs menu display time or lost screen space. The objects on which commands might operate (e.g., the messages) are constantly changing, but are usually limited, and therefore suitable for menu presentation. I call this a distinction between between *static* and *dynamic* displays (Perlman, 1981).

Experiment 2 demonstrated the best single character option selectors are initial letters, but in many cases, using initial letters is not possible; there may be more than one option beginning with the same letter. Static menus are more amenable to initial letter selectors because one of two options with the same initial letter can usually be renamed with a synonym. Dynamic menus are less predictable, and numerical selectors appear to be the best compromise. This reasoning was applied to the design of a menu based interface to a programming system's (static) programs and (dynamic) files (Perlman, 1981); letters selected programs and numbers selected files.

When menus are static, they should only be displayed to novice users, or on request. Even experienced users are not familiar with all parts of complex systems, and all users occasionally need their memories refreshed. The amount of space static menus take up on the screen should be minimized; one line menus should be considered. Dynamic menus can be useful to users of all levels of expertise because their contents are unpredictable and they can provide feedback about the outcome of operations.

Users should be allowed to make a system switch modes between automatically presenting menus and only on request. The most vocal critics of menus complain about systems that automatically take over the whole screen, use simple and inefficient display drivers, and force users to use menus. These are tedious and users must be allowed to avoid them.

Menus can be compared with *forms* because both are input mechanisms. Forms are *integrators* of information while menus are used to *discriminate* among alternatives. A *form* is a series of *fields*, and so can be viewed as a menu with access to items usually controlled by cursor movements on a screen. Using character selectors to access fields on a form is an alternative that allows random access of fields. Fields are used to specify a variable value, as are menus. The difference is that any value can be entered in a field (after which validation may take place) while the options allowed by a menu is finite and can be assumed valid.

FURTHER RESEARCH

The experiments described here do not help with the overall design of systems, but their results can aid low level implementation decisions. Higher level guidelines are discussed by Shneiderman (1983). One strategy for studying user interfaces is to compare complete systems while manipulating variables of interest. The problem with that strategy is that it is so costly to do, it is not clear how the results generalize to other systems, and often the differences between systems are confounded by their complexity. Problems with isolated experiments are that they may not apply to any real systems, and the relative importance of factors may not be apparent. For practical applications, isolated experiments appear more cost effective.

Several areas of generalization for experimentation are anticipated:

Vertical lists were studied here. Would the results apply equally well to items on one line? I suspect vertical lists are easier to search, but horizontal displays usually take up less room and so might be better for static menus.

A generalization of simple lists is tabular displays and how their format affects ease of finding items. Should items cycle by rows or by columns fastest, and how important is vertical alignment of items in different columns?

All the items to be found were in the lists, but in menu systems with networks, users sometimes are looking for an option in the wrong menu. An investigation of the search times to determine an item is *not* in a list might prove useful.

Finally, for searching through menus, the usefulness of various forms of highlighting should be determined. Attributes like capitalization, reverse video, underlining, color, and intensity are but some of the possible manipulations, though using all at once might cause confusing visual displays.

ACKNOWLEDGEMENTS

I thank Anne Sutter for collecting the data. This research was conducted in part under Contract N00014-79-C-0323, NR 667-437 with the Personnel and Training Research Programs of the Office of Naval Research, and was sponsored in part by the Office of Naval Research and the Air Force Office for Scientific Research.

REFERENCES

[1]   Aho, A. V., Hopcroft, J. E., & Ullman, J. D. **The Design and Analysis of Computer Algorithms,** Reading, Massachusetts: Addison-Wesley, 1974.

[2]   Battig, W. F. & Montague, W. E. *Category Norms for Verbal Items in 56 Categories.* **Journal of Experimental Psychology Monographs,** 1969, 80:3.2.

[3]   Card, S. K. *The Evaluation of Pointing Devices.* **Digest of Papers, Compcon Spring '83,** San Francisco, 1983. New York: IEEE Computer Society Press.

[4]   Card, S. K. *Visual Search of Computer Command Menus.* in H. Bouma & D. Bouwhuis (eds.) **Attention and Performance X: Control of Language Processes,** Hillsdale, New Jersey: Lawrence Erlbaum Associates, in press.

[5]   Norman, D. A. *Categorization of Action Slips.* **Psychological Review,** 1981, **88,** 1-15.

[6]   Norman, D. A. & Fisher, D. *Why Alphabetic Keyboards Are Not Easy to Use: Keyboard Layout Doesn't Much Matter.* **Center for Human Information Processing Report 8106,** University of California, San Diego, November 1981.

[7]   Perlman, G. *The Design of an Interface to a Programming System.* **Center for Human Information Processing Report 8105,** University of California, San Diego, November 1981.

[8]   Shneiderman, B. *Design Issues and Experimental Results for Menu Selection Systems.* **CS Tech. Report 1303,** University of Maryland Computer Science Department, July, 1983.

The author's new address is:
    Wang Institute of Graduate Studies
    Tyng Road
    Tyngsboro, MA 01879
    USA

ADDITION TO EXPERIMENT 1 DISCUSSION

The appended figure shows the mean search times for the first five items in sorted lists. Note that the time to find the first item increases with list length, even though the item is always at the same location on the screen. The effect, though small, is reliable, and similar effects can be seen for other items. Also note the list end advantage for the shortest list, indicating that people start their searches of sorted lists at the beginning or end. Eye movement apparatus would be necessary to decide this.

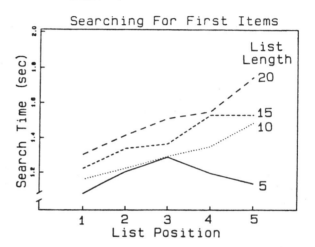

WINDOW-BASED COMPUTER DIALOGUES

S. K. Card, M. Pavel, and J. E. Farrell

Xerox Palo Alto Research Center   and   Stanford University
Palo Alto, California   Stanford, California

In recent years a number of systems have used windows as the basis for advanced user interfaces. Yet how exactly users benefit from windows or what features of windows are important for design is neither understood nor has it been studied. Current window designs are given a simple classification. Seven functional uses that have been identified for windows are described. The Window Working Set concept based on operating system theory is introduced for the an analysis of space constraints on window use.

Fig. 1. Two and one-half dimensional windows in Interlisp-D

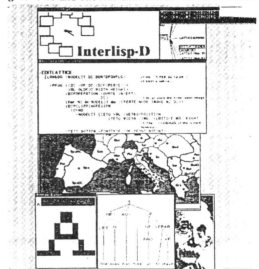

The last several years have seen substantial advances in the design of human interfaces for computing systems. These interfaces, which use techniques of computer graphics, offer substantial promise for making computers easier to use and for extending the complexity of tasks that humans can perform. But, whereas there is considerable understanding of the basic perceptual requirements of displays, how to make dials easy to read, for example, there is very little systematic understanding of the interaction between the display and the user's ability to perform cognitive tasks. Yet such tasks are a central feature of most human-machine systems and increasingly more so. The general aim of the present research is to increase our understanding of the interplay between graphical interfaces and user cognition by studying one of these techniques.

WINDOWS

Central to the new techniques for interface design are "windows." Windows allow the user to interact with multiple sources of information at the same time, as if he had a set of CRT displays of different sizes at his work-station. It is this multiplicity of contexts, together with the graphical features of the display and the ability to use graphical input devices that is the source of the power of the new interfaces.

The basic idea behind windows is simple. A window is a particular view of some data object in the computer: In Fig. 1, the time of day is displayed in one window by the hands on a stylized clock, a LISP program is presented in another window as text on a piece of paper using different typographic styles to set off its parts. Still other windows are used to display subroutine calls among LISP routines as a horizontal tree (upper right), a data structure representing the geography of Europe as a map, the bitmap pattern for the letter A from some system font in enlarged pixels to facilitate editing, the parsing of an English sentence as a tree, and an array of bit patterns encoding a photograph as as a half-tone illustration. The figure shows some of the representation potential of windows: windows can depict data structures using different textual and graphic idioms and these can coexist together on the user's display popping into and out of existence, moving about, or changing shape and size according to the exigencies of the moment.

Fig. 1 is but one way to implement the notion of a window. There are many others and arguments about which design is the best (or merely about which are not the worst) are conducted among computer scientists with considerable heat. The current designs for window systems can be broken down approximately into four categories: (1) the familiar simple TTY windows, (2) time-multiplexed windows, (3) space-multiplexed windows, and a less certain category, (4) "non-homogeneous windows."

Simple TTY Windows.

These are the the familiar single windows with automatic single direction scrolling. The user types a command that appears in the bottom line of the window. The system response also appears on the bottom line(s) of the screen after first "scrolling" the screen up. Because this method imitates the mechanical flow of paper in a teletype machine it is sometimes called a "glass teletype."

Time-Multiplexed Windows.

The concept of windows can be extended by having the content extend virtually beyond the screen in various ways. One way is to think of the screen as a resource shared by different windows at different times—time multiplexed windows. Another way is to think of sharing the space on the screen more or less constantly among different windows—space multiplexed windows. Time-multiplexed windows themselves come in at least two forms, scrolling windows and frame-at-a-time systems.

Scrollable windows. Scrolling windows are often used with text-editors. The user edits his text in a window, but has available commands that can cause the text to move up, down, or to a certain place, as if the user had a movable window he could position in front of a long scroll. This is one way of using the display to show larger amounts of text frames by showing different parts at a time.

Frame-at-a-time systems. Using a menu, the user flips back and forth among a number of frames, but only one frame is visible at a time.

Space-Multiplexed Windows

Space-multiplexed windows may be grouped according to how many dimensions of the space there are and whether the windows are independent or part of a "split."

One-dimensional windows. Fig. 2 shows the screen for a text-editor called Bravo divided vertically into a number of separate parts. Those parts below a heavy black stripe are windows open to different files (one file in the figure is the text the user is editing, another is to the references of his paper, a third is to a file containing a table in the paper). The thin line separates two separate views of the same file (one part is looking at the front and one at the end). This is an example of a "split window."

Two-dimensional windows. Fig. 3, from the Cedar system[2] shows the screen divided into separate windows in two dimensions. The windows can change in size and they can move around, but they cannot overlap.

Two-and-a-half-dimensional windows. Fig. 1 was an example of an overlapped window system. Some windows appear to have been overlaid by others. Selecting a portion of an overlapped window causes it to appear on the top of the pile. Window placement is largely determined by the user.

Split vs. independent windows. Some windows display independent information. Others are "split" into smaller windows displaying closely related information. Changes to one of these split windows may cause changes reflected in another.

Fig. 2.   One-dimensional windows in Bravo

Non-homogeneous Windows.

Instead of displaying all the information on the display at the same level of detail, the detail may change whether within the same window or across windows. Icons, bifocal windows, fish-eye windows, and zooming are techniques for accomplishing this.

Fig. 3.   Two-dimensional windows in Cedar

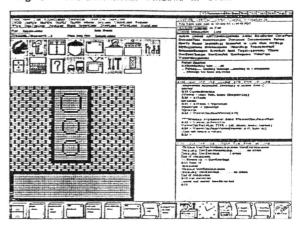

Icons. These are very small windows, generally represented on the screen by a small symbolic picture of some sort (e.g. the picture of an in-box for a mail window). The icon may be selected and expanded into a full-size window. Several icons are shown in the bottom of Fig. 3. Icons are a means for keeping reminders of a large amount of information on the screen without taking up much space.

Bifocal windows. Bifocal windows[3] are a related technique. Information is assumed to be organized hierarchically (e.g. journal, volume, issue, article). Information on one of these levels is displayed in full detail in the center. Related information, perhaps at a higher level, is displayed on the periphery in just enough detail to recognize it. Thus the user always has detailed display of some item of interest and non-detailed display of contextually related items.

Optical fish-eye window. Information in the window is compressed like the image of a convex mirror.

Logical fish-eye window. Information detail may be reduced according to its logical distance from some focal point. For example, a program listing may be completely displayed for some point of interest in the program, but only a single line devoted to other arms of a conditional statement[4].

Zooming window. Data in a window or the window itself gets larger or smaller in the manner of a zooming camera. This effect may involve changing type fonts, suppressing parts of the diagram, or even distorting parts that are salient (as on a road map).

The above is the beginning of a rough taxonomy of window designs. It shows some of the competing designs, whose relative merits we should be able to understand as a result of our analysis.

TASKS

The use of windows by a user depends heavily on the tasks the user is trying to accomplish. It is therefore impossible to accomplish an analysis of window and display design without careful consideration of the tasks for which windows are used. As a first step, we can categorize tasks by the functions windows seem to serve in accomplishing these. There are at least seven such functions:

1. More information. Window techniques may allow relatively rapid access to more information than would be possible with a single frame of the same screen size. For example, the Apple Lisa uses overlapped windows to compensate for small screen size.

2. Access to multiple sources of information. A task may require access to independently stored pieces of information. For example, a writer may need to refer back and forth to several parts of the text he is writing: a reference bibliography, a table, and possibly comments from readers and draft sections done by co-authors (see Fig. 3).

3. Combining of multiple sources of information. Information from different sources of information may need to be combined. Text from several electronic messages may need to be combined into a new message. This operation is simplified if the several sources of information are displayed simultaneously.

4. Independent control of multiple programs. A user may want to supervise or control the running of multiple programs. For example, he may use one window for the output of his program, another to control the debugger after a program error, a third to display and edit parts of the program code, a fourth to display the system stack, and others to display the state of various data structures. Several programs may run independently, each in its own window.

5. Reminding. Windows can be used to help the user keep track of information likely to be of use in the near future, but that otherwise he would need to expend some sort of effort to remember. For example, pop-up windows with menus of commands in them, a clock window giving the time, a history window containing the several commands most recently issued.

6. Command context/active forms. Windows can serve as a visible indication of a command context. They can be used to represent instances of objects. When the cursor is in the window, various commands and buttons can have different interpretations. This allows the command language to be simpler and more modular. A special case is the use of active forms. For example, in Fig. 1 there is a window containing the graph of a parse tree. Whenever the user points to a particular node in the parse tree, the user can give a command that attaches it to the cursor so it can be moved around. Because the window supplies a well-defined context for such an interpretation, this technique can be used to create, context dependent command languages. In fact, the need for typed-in commands can be eliminated.

7. Multiple representations. Windows can be used to display multiple representations for the same task. For example, in the Rabbit system[5] the user has three windows on view simultaneously, each with a different representation of his information retrieval task: a query command, a fragment of a network diagram, and specific instance. For a difficult query, the use shifts back and forth among these representations in a set of successive negotiations with the machine to satisfy his retrieval using the representation easiest at each point.

These seven functional uses of windows (as well as other functional uses that remain to be identified) warn that attempts to understand the merits of competing window designs must be clear about the function for which the windows are being used.

THE DISPLAY AS AN EXTERNAL MEMORY

Of course an analysis of windows also depends critically on an understanding of the user and how he is linked to the display. An understanding of the user must, of necessity, weave together, on the one hand, cognitive considerations of a user's goals and problem solving and, on the other hand, the perceptual and visual science issues of how he moves his eyes and what cues from the display affect his ability to locate and discover information needed for cognitive processing.

External memory

Our analysis of the effect of the human processor on window use begins with the proposition:

A fundamental constraint on users' cognitive performance arises from limitations of working memory.

The ability to do mental arithmetic is limited largely by difficulties in keeping track of the intermediate products and keeping one's place. In debugging a program, in writing a paper, in doing financial analysis of a firm, in attempting to reason about a machine, limitations on the number of mental things that can be kept track of lay a strong constraint on human cognitive capabilities.

The display of a computer provides the possibility of giving the user an *external memory* that is an extension of the user's own *internal memory*, one with which he can remember and keep track of more information than otherwise. (Of course, notes on paper scattered about a desk can serve a similar function, but they are not dynamic as with a computer display that can automatically graph in one window the data in another or always keep the listing of a program properly indented). And the computer display is not only an external memory that extends the user's internal memory, it is also (partially) shared with another active agent, the computer itself. This means that it is at once both memory and communications medium. Both the full power of the display as external memory and communications medium and the synergistic interaction between these are only realized when the display supports independent, but related, nodes or objects of memory and communication. It is for this reason that the windowing technique, with its emphasis on separate communication contexts, has become the harbinger of dramatic improvements in human-machine interfaces.

Window Working Set

The external memory i.e. the screen of the display is a resource with very definite constraints. Regardless of how advantageous it might be to display more to the human, there is only so much space. Using overlapped windows, for example, to expand the display is like placing pieces of paper on a desk. If the desk is small and the papers are numerous, the user may spend most of his time attempting to searching for his papers.

The situation is reminiscent of the design of demand paging algorithms for the virtual memory algorithms of operating systems.[6][7][8][9] Programs running on a computing system often have a virtual memory much larger than the physical memory available for the program, particularly when they run in a multiprogramming environment. During some interval of time, only a portion of the pages of the program's virtual memory are actually referenced. This set of pages is called the program's working set (to be defined more precisely later). If the number of pages in the program's working set is not greater than the number of pages actually available for the program to run, the program will run efficiently. If, however, the working set is larger, then the program will spend most of its time reading and writing pages back and forth from main memory to some secondary memory device, a condition known as thrashing.

The user might similarly be said to require during some interval of time a certain amount of screen area to present the displays he needs to accomplish his task, a window working set. If the screen size is too small he too will experience a phenomenon akin to thrashing.

Of course, in the human case there are additional complications. The user can decide he would rather not have a piece of information, possibly leading to errors later, than to churn his display to get it or he may choose an alternative, space-reduced, method of obtaining it. Nonetheless, the comparison suggests a rich set of analyses available to apply to the analysis of display space management and the effect of physical screen size. For example, an important property of program behavior is a statistical property called locality: within a short period of time, most programs tend to reference only a few pages, then move on to reference only a few other pages. This property seems likely to apply to window reference as well. Locality is a very important property in determining how much real memory is necessary to prevent a program with a certain virtual memory size from thrashing and there are technical indexes available for describing it. These could of course be applied to the analysis of window references and to the characterization of the time varying information needs of a user doing a task. An interesting possibility is that users can trade their own memory load off against using the display as an external memory. Hence it might be possible to see interesting trades between time plots of the user's internal memory load and the display loading.

WORKING SET ANALYSES OF USER BEHAVIOR

In this section we shall illustrate the usefulness of the working set idea for analyzing the space constraints operating on windows placed on the display screen. To do so we shall define the working set in terms of windows, describe a technique for data collection, and describe corresponding data analyses.

The user's interaction with a window-based interface at each instant of time is associated with a state, s. The state is identified by the particular window that is active at that time. Let S be the set of possible states. Define a reference string, R, as a list of pairs of the form

$$R = (S_1, T_1), (S_2, T_2), ..., (s_i, t_i)$$

where S_i is a random variable representing the state and T_i is a random variable representing the time when the user entered the state S_i.

The working set is then defined as a random variable $W(t, T)$ representing the set of states visited during a time interval from $t - T$ to T. More formally,

$$W(t, T) = \{s \mid S_i = s, t_i \in [t - T, t]\} \tag{1}$$

Thus the working set random variable depends only on (and can be computed from) the reference string and the working set size parameter T.

The working set notion is particularly convenient if the reference string has certain statistical properties. In particular, if the set of the states visited in a given interval T changes only slowly with time the working set provides a good

description of the number of windows that should be displayed simultaneously on the screen.

Data Collection

We have observed users performing their usual work involving windows. User behavior is videotaped and users are encouraged to talk in order to gain access to the users' goals.

Experimental Setup: The following three types of records were collected simultaneously during a session.

(1) Video monitoring of the session using two cameras aimed at a slave terminal. One camera monitored the entire screen, the other camera monitored the portion of the screen that the user was attending to.

(2) Video monitoring of the user.

(3) A record of window activities consisting of lists of active windows recorded whenever a new window was created or an old window closed.

Data Analyses

The most important goal of the analyses is to characterize the computer-user interaction and separate it from the particular task domain (e.g. editing or debugging). The data analysis began by combining the different types of information into a coherent composite protocol. Using this composite protocol enabled us to construct *reference strings* from the observations. Each reference string consisted of a list of windows that the user was working on together with the corresponding time intervals.

The first step of the analysis is determination of the recurrence of the reference string process. Recurrence is a critical property of the computer-user interaction: If each window is unique and no window is used more than once, then one can do little to improve the interface design to avoid thrashing. This is because if the user continues to use new windows, he or she will eventually reach the memory limit imposed by the size of the screen. If, on the other hand, there are windows that are used repetitively (there are recurrent states) then one may improve the efficiency of the interface by choosing an optimal set size. The proportion of recurrent windows in our example was 71.2%. This value is sufficiently high to proceed with further analyses.

Given that a significant proportion of the windows were recurrent we were then able to examine the locality of the process. An important indication of locality is captured in a inter-reference distribution h.

$$h(x) = Pr\{T_{ir} = x\} \tag{2}$$

where T_{ir} is the time interval between two consecutive references to the same window. In practice an estimate of $h(.)$ is obtained by combining inter-reference intervals for all recurrent windows. The resulting inter-reference distribution in our example is shown on Fig. 4. This plot illustrates the number of times the windows were referenced as a function of the inter-reference interval. The locality characteristics is apparent on this graph as the prominent peak at the low values of inter-reference times. Thus if a particular window is used more than once it is likely to be used two or three events later.

Encouraged by these analyses we were able to study the locality in more detail by using the working set notions. In particular, we determined the number of distinct windows $k(t, T)$ at event t referenced during T previous events. Of course k is simply the working set size

$$k(t, T) = \|W(t, T)\|. \tag{3}$$

Fig. 4.   Inter-reference distribution

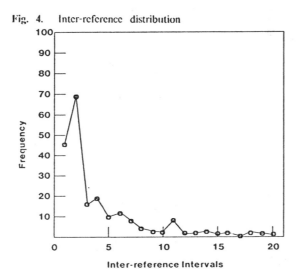

Fig. 5.   Variation of working set size with event number

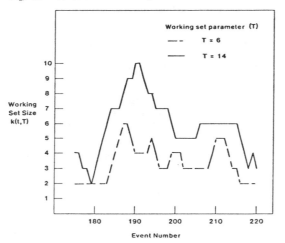

Fig. 6. Window faults as a function of working set size

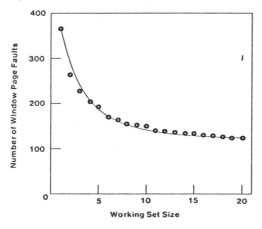

The choice of the parameter T determines the behavior of k for any particular reference string. An example of the behavior of k for two values of T is shown in Fig. 5. The interesting and potentially useful aspect of the this representation is in the relationship between the rapid changes in k and the tasks performed by the user at that time. In particular, as the user progresses through the various phases of his interaction, he may need different sets of windows. Thus the number of required windows is temporarily higher at transition between phases.

While the working set size is a useful measure of the number of windows required during various periods it is only an indirect indicator of how often a new window must be created (a *window fault*, similar to a page fault in a virtual memory system). To determine the window fault frequency or, conversely, the life-time distribution we determine from the reference string all instances when a new window is referenced based on the working set analysis. A window fault is generated whenever a window to be used is not in the working set at that time. The resulting distribution of the frequency of window faults f as a function of the working set parameter T is illustrated in Fig. 6. The locality of the string is exhibited by the rapid decay of f for small values of T. We then look at how fast the set of active windows changes over time. Whenever the change is slow (quasi-stationarity or locality holds), then the working set identifies the windows required to do the task.

DESIGN APPLICATIONS

The data presented in the previous section have been chosen to illustrate how we might begin to employ ideas from the analysis of operating systems to analyze the effect of the limited screen area resource on the use of windows. The analysis could be performed for different task domains or window system design and provides a method by which we can evaluate the advantages of particular window designs given the task demands. For example, rather than considering icons as an isolated technique, we might think of icons as external memory cues that have low space-time cost and that shift the window-fault curve favorably.

REFERENCES

[1] Newell, A. Notes for a model of human performance in ZOG. Technical Report, Department of Computer Science, Carnegie-Mellon University, Pittsburgh, Pennsylvania (1977).

[2] Teitelman, W. Technical Report, Xerox Palo Alto Research Center, Palo Alto, California, forthcoming.

[3] Spence, R. and Apperley, M. Data base navigation: an office environment for the professional. Behaviour and Information Technology 1 (1982) 43–54.

[4] Furness, G. The FISHEYE view: a new look at structured files. Internal Memorandum, Bell Laboratories, October, 1982.

[5] Williams, M. and Tou, F. Rabbit: An interface for database access, in Proceedings of the 1982 ACM Conference, 1982 (Association for Computing Machinery, New York, 1982).

[6] Denning, P. J. Virtual memory. Computing Surveys 2, 3 (1970) 153–189.

[7] Hansen, P. B. Operating System Principles (Prentice-Hall, Englewood Cliffs, New Jersey, 1973).

[8] Coffman, E. G., Jr., and Denning, P. J. Operating Systems (Prentice-Hall, Englewood Cliffs, New Jersey, 1973).

[9] Denning, P. J. Working sets past and present. IEEE Transactions on Software Engineering SE-6 (1980) 64-84.

Direct manipulation systems offer the satisfying experience of operating on visible objects. The computer becomes transparent, and users can concentrate on their tasks.

SPECIAL FEATURE

Direct Manipulation: A Step Beyond Programming Languages

Ben Shneiderman, University of Maryland

Leibniz sought to make the form of a symbol reflect its content. "In signs," he wrote, "one sees an advantage for discovery that is greatest when they express the exact nature of a thing briefly and, as it were, picture it; then, indeed, the labor of thought is wonderfully diminished."

Frederick Kreiling, "Leibniz,"
Scientific American, May 1968

Certain interactive systems generate glowing enthusiasm among users—in marked contrast with the more common reaction of grudging acceptance or outright hostility. The enthusiastic users' reports are filled with positive feelings regarding

- mastery of the system,
- competence in the performance of their task,
- ease in learning the system originally and in assimilating advanced features,
- confidence in their capacity to retain mastery over time,
- enjoyment in using the system,
- eagerness to show it off to novices, and
- desire to explore more powerful aspects of the system.

These feelings are not, of course, universal, but the amalgam does convey an image of the truly pleased user. As I talked with these enthusiasts and examined the systems they used, I began to develop a model of the features that produced such delight. The central ideas seemed to be visibility of the object of interest; rapid, reversible, incremental actions; and replacement of complex command language syntax by direct manipulation of the object of interest—hence the term "direct manipulation."

Examples of direct manipulation systems

No single system has all the attributes or design features that I admire—that may be impossible—but those described below have enough to win the enthusiastic support of many users.

Display editors. "Once you've used a display editor, you'll never want to go back to a line editor. You'll be spoiled." This reaction is typical of those who use full-page display editors, who are great advocates of their systems over line-oriented text editors. I heard similar comments from users of stand-alone word processors such as the Wang system and from users of display editors such as EMACS on the MIT/Honeywell Multics system or "vi" (for visual editor) on the Unix system. A beaming advocate called EMACS "the one true editor."

Roberts[1] found that the overall performance time of display editors is only half that of line-oriented editors, and since display editors also reduce training time, the evidence supports the enthusiasm of display editor devotees. Furthermore, office automation evaluations consistently favor full-page display editors for secretarial and executive use.

The advantages of display editors include

Display of a full 24 to 66 lines of text. This full display enables viewing each sentence in context and simplifies reading and scanning the document. By contrast, the

A portion of this article was derived from the author's keynote address at the NYU Symposium on User Interfaces, "The Future of Interactive Systems and the Emergence of Direct Manipulation," published in *Human Factors in Interactive Computer Systems*, Y. Vassiliou, ed., Ablex Publishing Co., Norwood, N.J., 1983.

Excerpted from Shneiderman, B. (1983). Direct Manipulation: A Step Beyond Programming Languages. *IEEE Computer*, August 1983, New York: IEEE Computer Society.

one-line-at-a-time view offered by line editors is like seeing the world through a narrow cardboard tube.

Display of the document in its final form. Eliminating the clutter of formatting commands also simplifies reading and scanning the document. Tables, lists, page breaks, skipped lines, section headings, centered text, and figures can be viewed in the form that will be printed. The annoyance and delay of debugging the format commands is eliminated because the errors are immediately apparent.

Cursor action that is visible to the user. Seeing an arrow, underscore, or blinking box on the screen gives the operator a clear sense of where to focus attention and apply action.

Cursor motion through physically obvious and intuitively natural means. Arrow keys or devices such as a mouse, joystick, or graphics tablet provide natural physical mechanisms for moving the cursor. This is in marked contrast with commands such as UP 6, which require an operator to convert the physical action into correct syntactic form and which may be difficult to learn, hard to recall, and a source of frustrating errors.

Labeled buttons for action. Many display editors have buttons etched with commands such as INSERT, DELETE, CENTER, UNDERLINE, SUPERSCRIPT, BOLD, or LOCATE. They act as a permanent menu selection display, reminding the operator of the features and obviating memorization of a complex command-lan-

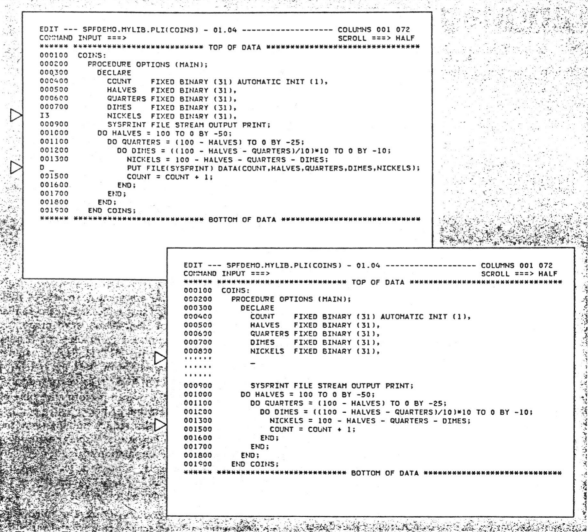

Figure 1. This example from the IBM SPF display editor shows 19 lines of a PL/I program. The commands to insert three lines (I3) and to delete one line (D or D1) are typed on the appropriate lines in the first screen display. Pressing ENTER causes commands to be executed and the cursor to be placed at the beginning of the inserted line. New program statements can be typed directly in their required positions. Control keys move the cursor around the text to positions where changes are made by overstriking. A delete key causes the character under the cursor to be deleted and the text to the left to be shifted over. After pressing an insert key, the user can type text in place. Programmed function keys allow movement of the window forwards, backwards, left, and right over the text. (Examples courtesy of IBM.)

guage syntax. Some editors provide basic functionality with only 10 or 15 labeled buttons, and a specially marked button may be the gateway to advanced or infrequently used features offered on the screen in menu form.

Immediate display of the results of an action. When a button is pressed to move the cursor or center the text, the results appear on the screen immediately. Deletions are apparent at once, since the character, word, or line is erased and the remaining text rearranged. Similarly, insertions or text movements are shown after each keystroke or function button press. Line editors, on the other hand, require a print or display command before the results of a change can be seen.

Rapid action and display. Most display editors are designed to operate at high speeds: 120 characters per second (1200 baud), a full page in a second (9600 baud), or even faster. This high display rate coupled with short response time produces a thrilling sense of power and speed. Cursors can be moved quickly, large amounts of text can be scanned rapidly, and the results of commands can be shown almost instantaneously. Rapid action also reduces the need for additional commands, thereby simplifying product design and decreasing learning time. Line editors operating at 30 characters per second with three- to eight-second response times seem sluggish in comparison. Speeding up line editors adds to their attractiveness, but they still lack features such as direct overtyping, deletion, and insertion.

Easily reversible commands. Mistakes in entering text can be easily corrected by backspacing and overstriking. Simple changes can be made by moving the cursor to the problem area and overstriking, inserting, or deleting characters, words, or lines. A useful design strategy is to include natural inverse operations for each operation. Carroll[2] has shown that congruent pairs of operations are easy to learn. As an alternative, many display editors offer a simple UNDO command that cancels the previous command or command sequence and returns the text to its previous state. This easy reversibility reduces user anxiety about making mistakes or destroying a file.

The large market for display editors generates active competition, which accelerates evolutionary design refinements. Figure 1 illustrates the current capabilities of an IBM display editor.

Visicalc. Visicorp's innovative financial forecasting program, called Visicalc, was the product of a Harvard MBA student, who was frustrated by the time needed to carry out multiple calculations in a graduate business course. Described as an "instantly calculating electronic worksheet" in the user's manual, it permits computation and display of results across 254 rows and 63 columns and is programmed without a traditional procedural control structure. For example, positional declarations can prescribe that column 4 displays the sum of columns 1 through 3; then every time a value in the first three columns changes, the fourth column changes as well. Complex dependencies among manufacturing costs, distribution costs, sales revenue, commissions, and profits can

be stored for several sales districts and months so that the impact of changes on profits is immediately apparent.

Since Visicalc simulates an accountant's worksheet, it is easy for novices to comprehend. The display of 20 rows and up to nine columns, with the provision for multiple windows, gives the user sufficient visibility to easily scan information and explore relationships among entries (see Figure 2). The command language for setting up the worksheet can be tricky for novices to learn and for infrequent users to remember, but most users need learn only the basic commands. According to Visicalc's distributor, "It jumps," and the user's delight in watching this propagation of changes cross the screen helps explain its appeal.

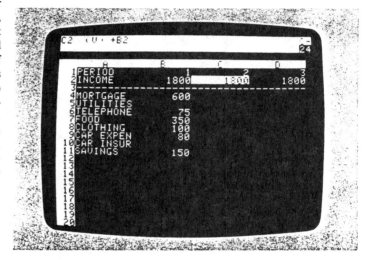

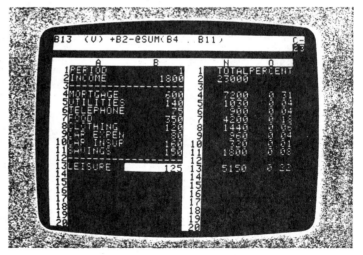

Figure 2. This simple Visicalc program display (top) shows four columns and 20 rows of home budget information. The cursor, an inverse video light bar controlled by key presses, is in position C2. The top command line shows that C2 is a value (as opposed to a text string) that has been set up to have the same value as position B2.

The second display (above) shows two windows over the home budget data with row sums to the right. The last row shows leisure dollar amounts, which are established by the top command line formula as the income minus the sum of expenses. A change to the income or expense values would immediately propagate to all affected values. (Displays reproduced by permission of Visicorp.)

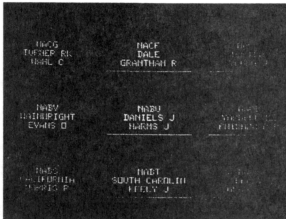

Spatial data management. The developers of the prototype spatial data management system[3] attribute the basic idea to Nicholas Negroponte of MIT.

In one scenario, a user seated before a color graphics display of the world zooms in on the Pacific to see markers for military ship convoys. Moving a joystick fills the screen with silhouettes of individual ships, which can be zoomed in on to display structural details or, ultimately, a full-color picture of the captain. (See Figure 3.)

In another scenario, icons representing different aspects of a corporation, such as personnel, organization, travel, production, or schedules, are shown on a screen. Moving the joystick and zooming in on objects takes users through complex "information spaces" or "I-spaces" to locate the item of interest. For example, when they select a department from a building floor

Figure 3. A spatial data management system has been installed on the aircraft carrier USS *Carl Vinson*. In the photo at top left, the operator has a world map on the left screen and a videodisc map of selected areas on the center screen. After some command selections with the data tablet and puck, the operator can zoom in on specific data such as the set of ships shown in the second photo. With further selections the operator can get detailed information about each ship, such as the length, speed, and fuel. (Photos courtesy of Computer Corporation of America.)

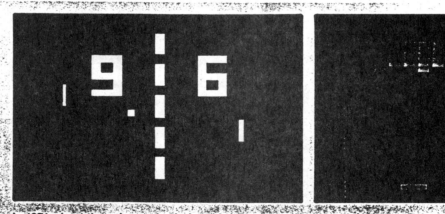

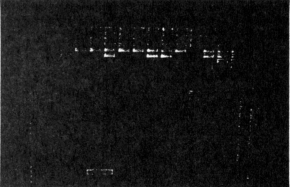

In 1971, about the only people playing video games were students in computer science laboratories. By 1973, however, millions of people were familiar with at least one video game—Pong (above left). A few years later came Breakout (above right), which, according to many designers, was the first true video game and the best one ever invented. Pong and other early games imitated real life, but Breakout could not have existed in any medium other than video. In the game, a single paddle directed a ball toward a wall of color bricks; contact made a brick vanish and changed the ball's speed.

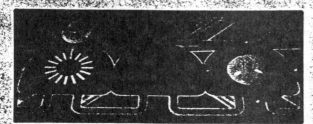

When the first arcade video game, Computer Space, went on location in a Sears store, its joystick was torn off before the end of the first day. As a result, game designers have sought controls that were both easy to use and hard to destroy. Centipede (above left) uses simple controls—a trackball and one button. On the other hand, Defender (above right) has five buttons and a joystick; novice players are confused by these relatively complex controls and usually

plan, individual offices become visible. Moving the cursor into a room brings the room's details onto the screen. If they choose the wrong room, they merely back out and try another. The lost effort is minimal, and no stigma is attached to the error.

The success of a spatial data management system depends on the designer's skill in choosing icons, graphical representations, and data layouts that are natural and easily understood. Even anxious users enjoy zooming in and out or gliding over data with a joystick, and they quickly demand additional power and data.

Video games. Perhaps the most exciting, well-engineered—certainly, the most successful—application of direct manipulation is in the world of video games. An early, but simple and popular, game called Pong required the user to rotate a knob, which moved a white rectangle on the screen. A white spot acted as a Ping-Pong ball, which ricocheted off the wall and had to be hit back by the movable white rectangle. The user developed skill involving speed and accuracy in placement of the "paddle" to keep the increasingly speedy ball from getting by, while the speaker emitted a ponging sound when the ball bounced. Watching someone else play for 30 seconds was all the training needed to become a competent novice, but many hours of practice were required to become a skilled expert.

Contemporary games such as Missile Command, Donkey Kong, Pac Man, Tempest, Tron, Centipede, or Space Invaders are far more sophisticated in their rules, color graphics, and sound effects (see sidebar below and on facing page). The designers of these games have provided stimulating entertainment, a challenge for novices and experts, and many intriguing lessons in the human factors of interface design—somehow they have found a way to get people to put coins into the sides of computers. The strong attraction of these games contrasts markedly with the anxiety and resistance many users experience toward office automation equipment.

Because their fields of action are abstractions of reality, these games are easily understood—learning is by analogy. A general idea of the game can be gained by watching the on-line automatic demonstration that runs continuously on the screen, and the basic principles can be learned in a few minutes by watching a knowledgeable player. But there are ample complexities to entice many hours and quarters from experts. The range of skill accommodated is admirable.

The commands are physical actions, such as button presses, joystick motions, or knob rotations, whose results appear immediately on the screen. Since there is no syntax, there are no syntax error messages. If users move their spaceships too far left, then they merely use the natural inverse operation of moving back to the right. Error messages are unnecessary because the results of ac-

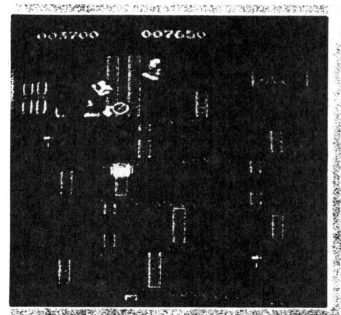

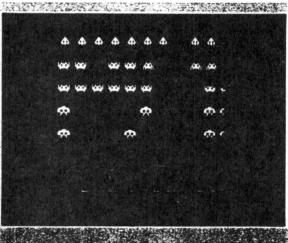

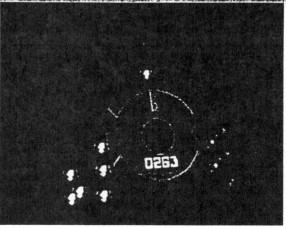

Donkey Kong, Space Invaders, and Tron (clockwise from above) exemplify the lively variety of video games now inviting the user's loose change. As of mid-1981, according to Steve Bloom, author of *Video Invaders*, more than four billion quarters had been dropped into Space Invaders games around the world—that's roughly "one game per earthling."

Video game photos reprinted courtesy of *IEEE Spectrum*. For a more complete report on the topic, see "Video Games: The Electronic Big Bang" by Tekla Perry, Carol Truxal, and Paul Wallich in *IEEE Spectrum*, Vol. 19, No. 12, Dec. 1982, pp. 20-33.

tions are so obvious and easily reversed. These principles can be applied to office automation, personal computing, and other interactive environments.

Every game that I have seen keeps a continuous score so that users can measure their progress and compete with their previous performance, with friends, or with the highest scorers. Typically, the 10 highest scorers get to store their initials in the game for regular display, a form of positive reinforcement that encourages mastery. Malone's[4] and our own studies with elementary school children have shown that continuous display of scores is extremely valuable. Machine-generated value judgments —"Very good" or "You're doing great!"—are not as effective, since the same score means different things to different people. Users prefer to make their own subjective judgments and may perceive machine-generated messages as an annoyance and a deception.

Carroll and Thomas[5] draw productive analogies between game-playing environments and application systems. However, game players seek entertainment and the challenge of mastery, while application-system users focus on the task and may resent forced learning of system constraints. The random events that occur in most games are meant to challenge the user, but predictable system behavior is preferable in nongame designs. Game players compete with the system, but application-system users apparently prefer a strong internal locus of control, which gives them the sense of being in charge.

The pleasure in using these systems stems from the capacity to manipulate the object of interest directly and to generate multiple alternatives rapidly.

Computer-aided design/manufacturing. Many computer-aided design systems for automobiles, electronic circuitry, architecture, aircraft, or newspaper layout use direct manipulation principles. The operator may see a schematic on the screen and with the touch of a lightpen can move resistors or capacitors into or out of the proposed circuit. When the design is complete, the computer can provide information about current, voltage drops, fabrication costs, and warnings about inconsistencies or manufacturing problems. Similarly, newspaper layout artists or automobile body designers can try multiple designs in minutes and record promising approaches until a better one is found.

The pleasure in using these systems stems from the capacity to manipulate the object of interest directly and to generate multiple alternatives rapidly. Some systems have complex command languages, but others have moved to cursor action and graphics-oriented commands.

Another, related application is in computer-aided manufacturing and process control. Honeywell's process control system provides an oil refinery, paper mill, or power utility plant manager with a colored schematic view of the plant. The schematic may be on eight displays, with red lines indicating a sensor value that is out of normal range. By pressing a single numbered button (there are no commands to learn or remember), the operator can get a more detailed view of the troublesome component and, with a second press, move the tree structure down to examine individual sensors or to reset valves and circuits.

The design's basic strategy precludes the necessity of recalling complex commands in once-a-year emergency conditions. The plant schematic facilitates problem solving by analogy, since the link between real-world high temperatures or low pressures and screen representations is so close.

Further examples. Driving an automobile is my favorite example of direct manipulation. The scene is directly visible through the windshield, and actions such as braking or steering have become common skills in our culture. To turn to the left, simply rotate the steering wheel to the left. The response is immediate, and the changing scene provides feedback to refine the turn. Imagine trying to turn by issuing a LEFT 30 DEGREES command and then issuing another command to check your position, but this is the operational level of many office automation tools today.

The term direct manipulation accurately describes the programming of some industrial robots. Here, the operator holds the robot's "hand" and guides it through a spray painting or welding task while the controlling computer records every action. The control computer then repeats the action to operate the robot automatically.

A large part of the success and appeal of the Query-by-Example[6] approach to data manipulation is due to its direct representation of relations on the screen. The user moves a cursor through the columns of the relational table and enters examples of what the result should look like. Just a few single-letter keywords supplement this direct manipulation style. Of course, complex Booleans or mathematical operations require knowledge of syntactic forms. Still, the basic ideas and language facilities can be learned within a half hour by many nonprogrammers. Query-by-Example succeeds because novices can begin work with just a little training, yet there is ample power for the expert. Directly manipulating the cursor across the relation skeleton is a simple task, and how to provide an example that shows the linking variable is intuitively clear to someone who understands tabular data. Zloof[7] recently expanded his ideas into Office-by-Example, which elegantly integrates database search with word processing, electronic mail, business graphics, and menu creation.

Designers of advanced office automation systems have used direct manipulation principles. The Xerox Star[8] offers sophisticated text formatting options, graphics, multiple fonts, and a rapid, high-resolution, cursor-based user interface. Users can drag a document icon and drop it into a printer icon to generate a hardcopy printout. Apple's recently announced Lisa system elegantly applies many of the principles of direct manipulation.

Researchers at IBM's Yorktown Heights facility have proposed a future office system, called Pictureworld, in which graphic icons represent file cabinets, mailboxes, notebooks, phone messages, etc. The user could compose a memo on a display editor and then indicate distribution and filing operations by selecting from the menu of icons. In another project, Yedwab et al.[9] have described a generalized office system, which they call the "automated desk."

Direct manipulation can be applied to replace traditional question-and-answer computer-assisted instruction with more attractive alternatives. Several CDC Plato lessons employ direct manipulation concepts, enabling students to trace inherited characteristics by breeding drosophilla, perform medical procedures to save an emergency room patient, draw and move shapes by finger touches, do chemistry lab projects (see Figure 4), or play games.

References

1. Teresa L. Roberts, "Evaluation of Computer Text Editors," PhD dissertation, Stanford University, 1980. Available from University Microfilms, Ann Arbor, Michigan, order number AAD 80-11699.

2. John M. Carroll, "Learning, Using and Designing Command Paradigms," *Human Learning,* Vol. 1, No. 1, 1982, pp. 31-62.

3. Christopher F. Herot, "Spatial Management of Data," *ACM Trans. Database Systems,* Vol. 5, No. 4, Dec. 1980, pp. 493-513.

4. Thomas W. Malone, "What Makes Computer Games Fun?" *Byte,* Vol. 6, No. 12, Dec. 1981, pp. 258-277.

5. John M. Carroll and John C. Thomas, "Metaphor and the Cognitive Representation of Computing Systems, *IEEE Trans. Systems, Man, and Cybernetics,* Vol. SMC-12, No. 2, Mar./Apr. 1982, pp. 107-116.

6. Moshe M. Zloof, "Query-by-Example," *AFIPS Conf. Proc.,* Vol. 44, 1975 NCC, AFIPS Press, Montvale, N.J. 1975.

7. Moshe M. Zloof, "Office-by-Example: A Business Language that Unifies Data and Word Processing and Electronic Mail, *IBM Sys. J.,* Vol. 21, No. 3, 1982, pp. 272-304.

8. Cranfield Smith et al., "Designing the Star User Interface," *Byte,* Vol. 7, No. 4, Apr. 1982, pp. 242-282.

9. Laura Yedwab, Christopher F. Herot, and Ronni L. Rosenberg, "The Automated Desk," *Sigsmall Newsletter,* Vol. 7, No. 2, Oct. 1981, pp. 102-108.

10. Ted Nelson, "Interactive Systems and the Design of Virtuality," *Creative Computing,* Vol. 6, No. 11, Nov. 1980, pp. 56 ff., and Vol. 6, No. 12, Dec. 1980, pp. 94 ff.

11. Chris Rutkowski, "An Introduction to the Human Applications Standard Computer Interface, Part 1: Theory and Principles," *Byte,* Vol. 7, No. 11, Oct. 1982, pp. 291-310.

12. Alan MacDonald, "Visual Programming," *Datamation,* Vol. 28, No. 11, Oct. 1982, pp. 132-140.

13. George Polya, *How to Solve It,* Doubleday, New York, 1957.

14. Maria Montessori, *The Montessori Method,* Schocken, New York, 1964.

15. James Bruner, *Toward a Theory of Instruction,* Harvard University Press, Cambridge, Mass., 1966.

16. John M. Carroll, J. C. Thomas, and A. Malhotra, "Presentation and Representation in Design Problem-Solving," *British J. Psych.,* Vol. 71, 1980, pp. 143-153.

17. Rudolf Arnheim, *Visual Thinking,* University of California Press, Berkeley, Calif., 1972.

18. Robert H. McKim, *Experiences in Visual Thinking,* Brooks/Cole Publishing Co., Monterey, Calif., 1972.

19. Max Wertheimer, *Productive Thinking,* Harper and Row, New York, 1959.

20. Seymour Papert, *Mindstorms: Children, Computers, and Powerful Ideas,* Basic Books, Inc., New York, 1980.

21. Ben Shneiderman, R. Mayer, D. McKay, and P. Heller, "Experimental Investigations of the Utility of Detailed Flowcharts in Programming," *Comm. ACM,* Vol. 20, No. 6, June 1977, pp. 373-381.

22. Ben Shneiderman, "Control Flow and Data Structure Documentation: Two Experiments," *Comm. ACM,* Vol. 25, No. 1, Jan. 1982, pp. 55-63.

23. Michael L. Schneider, "Models for the Design of Static Software User Assistance," *Directions in Human-Computer Interaction,* Albert Badre and Ben Shneiderman, eds., Ablex Publishing Co., Norwood, N.J., 1982.

24. Ben Shneiderman and Richard Mayer, "Syntactic/Semantic Interactions in Programmer Behavior: A Model and Experimental Results," *Int'l J. Computer and Information Sciences,* Vol. 8, No. 3, 1979, pp. 219-239.

25. Ben Shneiderman, *Software Psychology: Human Factors in Computer and Information Systems,* Little, Brown and Co., Boston, Mass., 1980.

26. Ben Shneiderman, "A Note on Human Factors Issues of Natural Language Interaction with Database Systems," *Information Systems,* Vol. 6, No. 2, Feb. 1981, pp. 125-129.

27. D. P. Ausubel, *Educational Psychology: A Cognitive Approach,* Holt, Rinehart and Winston, New York, 1968.

28. Richard W. Copeland, *How Children Learn Mathematics,* third ed., MacMillan, New York, 1979.

29. Nancy McDonald, "Multi-media Approach to User Interface," *Human Factors in Interactive Computer Systems,* Yannis Vassiliou, ed., Ablex Publishing Co., Norwood, N.J., to appear in 1983.

30. Ben Shneiderman, "A Computer Graphics System for Polynomials," *The Mathematics Teacher,* Vol. 67, No. 2, Feb. 1974, pp. 111-113.

Ben Shneiderman is an associate professor of computer science at the University of Maryland, where he is pursuing research in the design of interactive computer systems. He is the head of the recently formed Laboratory for Human-Computer Interaction within the Center for Automation Research.

Shneiderman is the author of *Software Psychology: Human Factors in Computer and Information Systems,* the coauthor of several textbooks, and the editor of three collections of papers. He has published more than 80 research journal and conference articles.

PROBLEMS WITH DIRECT MANIPULATION

Direct Manipulation systems have both virtues and vices. The immediacy of feedback and the natural translation of intentions to actions make some tasks easy. The matching of levels of thought to the interface language—semantic directness—increases the ease and power of performing some activities at a potential cost of generality and flexibility. Not all things should be done directly. Thus, a repetitive operation is probably best done via a script, that is, through a symbolic description of the tasks that are to be accomplished. Direct Manipulation interfaces have difficulty handling variables, or distinguishing the depiction of an individual element from a representation of a set or class of elements. Direct Manipulation interfaces have problems with accuracy, for the notion of mimetic action puts the responsibility on the user to control actions with precision, a responsibility that is often best handled through the intelligence of the system, and sometimes best communicated symbolically.

A more fundamental problem with direct manipulation interfaces arises from the fact that much of the appeal and power of this form of interface comes from their ability to directly support the way we normally think about a domain. They amplify our knowledge of the domain and allow us to think in the familiar terms of the application domain rather than those of the medium of computation. But if we restrict ourselves to only building interfaces that allow us to do things we can already do and to think in ways we already think, we will miss the most exciting potential of new technology: to provide new ways to think of and to interact with a domain. Providing these new ways and creating conditions that will make them feel direct and natural is an important challenge to the interface designer.

Direct manipulation interfaces are not a panacea. Although with sufficient practice many interfaces can come to feel direct, a properly designed interface, one which exploits semantic and articulatory directness, should decrease the amount of learning required and provide a natural mapping to the task. But interface design is subject to many tradeoffs. There are surely instances when one might wisely trade off directness for generality, or for more facile ways of saying abstract things. The articulatory directness involved in pointing at objects might need to be traded off against the difficulties of moving the hands between input devices or of problems in pointing with great precision.

It is important not to equate directness with ease of use. Indeed, if the interface is really invisible, then the difficulties within the task domain get transferred directly into difficulties for the user. Suppose the user struggles to formulate an intention because of lack of knowledge of the task domain. The user may complain that the system is difficult to use. But the difficulty is in the task domain, not in the interface language. Direct Manipulation interfaces do not pretend to assist in overcoming problems that result from poor understanding of the task domain.

Reassessing the Claims for Direct Manipulation

What about the claims for direct manipulation? Do these systems really meet the hopes? Alas, it is too early to tell. We believe that direct manipulation systems carry gains in ease of learning and ease of use. If the mapping is done correctly, then both the form and the meaning of commands should be easier to acquire and retain. Interpretation of the output should be immediate and straightforward. If the interface is a model of the task domain, then one could have the feeling of directly engaging the problem of interest itself. It is sometimes said that in such situations the interface disappears. It is probably more revealing to say that the interface is no longer recognized as an interface. Instead, it is taken to be the task domain itself.

But are these desirable features? Are the tradeoffs too costly? As always, we are sure that the answer will depend on the tasks to be accomplished. Certain kinds of abstraction that are easy to deal with in language seem difficult in a concrete model of a task domain. When we give up the conversation metaphor, we also give up dealing in descriptions, and in some contexts, there is great power in descriptions. As an interface to a programming task, direct manipulation interfaces are problematic. We know of no really useful direct manipulation programming environments. Issues such as controlling the scope of variable bindings promise to be quite tricky in the direct manipulation environments. Will Direct Manipulation systems live up to their promise? Yes and no. Basically, the systems will be good and powerful for some purposes, poor and weak for others. In the end, many things done today will be replaced by Direct Manipulation systems. But we will still have conventional programming languages.

On the surface, the fundamental idea of a Direct Manipulation interface to a task flies in the face of two thousand years of development of abstract formalisms as a means of understanding and controlling the world. Until very recently, the use of computers has been an activity squarely in that tradition. So the exterior of Direct Manipulation, providing as it does for the direct control of a specific task world, seems somehow atavistic, a return to concrete thinking. On the inside, of course, the implementation of direct manipulation systems is yet another step in that long formal tradition. The illusion of the absolutely manipulable concrete world is made possible by the technology of abstraction.

Earlier in this chapter we reprinted two sets of descriptions of the virtues of direct manipulation systems, claims made in the early enthusiasm of their first discovery. Now that we have examined the many aspects of directness, it is time to go back and re-evaluate those claims. Let us see what we can say about them now. First, Shneiderman (1982) pointed at three "essential features" of Direct Manipulation. Let us examine each of the three features: Shneiderman's comments in *italics*, our assessment in regular font.

1. *Continuous representation of the object of interest.*

This relates to the directness of evaluation, and as our analyses show, seems an essential aspect of a direct engagement system.

2. *Physical actions or labeled button presses instead of complex syntax.*

The feature of "physical actions" we interpret to refer to articulatory directness, and more particularly, to what one might call "mimetic directness," actions that mimic the desired changes on the objects of interest, especially movement or size changes. "Labeled button presses" must refer to semantic directness. The former clearly is important in establishing direct engagement. The latter is not. The latter operation really seems irrelevant to arguments about this form of directness, whatever the virtues for ease of learning or ease of use.

3. *Rapid incremental reversible operations whose impact on the object of interest is immediately visible.*

This is perhaps the essence of direct engagement: It reflects what we and Draper (Chapter 16) call the importance of "inter-referential I/O." The important point to us, implicitly stated in this assumption, is that the objects upon which the actions are taken are exactly the same as those upon which evaluation is made. The reversibility of the operations is desirable, but not necessary. Not all operations can have this feature in a natural way. So too with immediacy of the result: Where immediacy is a natural part of the domain, then this is essential. Otherwise, it is desirable, but may not always be necessary—as we have discussed at length within this chapter.

If we reinterpret Shneiderman's claims to be about *Direct Engagement*, then his three features fare well: They do seem to help define what is necessary to develop a direct engagement system. Now let us look at Shneiderman's six claims for the results of such a system:

1. *Novices can learn basic functionality quickly, usually through a demonstration by a more experienced user.*

This may or may not be true. We think it really derives from the fact that a good Direct Manipulation interface is invisible—the user feels as if operations are actually done directly on the task domain. And if the computer novice is already knowledgeable in the task domain, then much of what is needed to use the interface is already known.

Why might training be possible through demonstration? Well, two reasons. Lewis (Chapter 8) argues that demonstration is, in general, a superior method of instruction. Think of a demonstration as a dynamic example. In this case, then, the superiority of demonstration has nothing to do with direct manipulation. But there is a second reason. Owen (Chapter 17) points out that demonstrations with normal, command language systems, are often puzzling because the actions are not visible. That is, the expert waves hands over the keyboard and mysterious wonderful results appear on the screen. The learner often has little notion of what operation was performed. But with a typical direct manipulation (read direct engagement) system, the actions themselves are visible, and their results are both visible and also direct reflections of the operations done upon them. Whenever these cases apply, we believe the claim will be valid.

2. *Experts can work extremely rapidly to carry out a wide range of tasks, even defining new functions and features.*

We are suspicious of this claim. In fact, we would not be surprised if experts are *slower* with Direct Manipulation systems than with command language systems. We suspect that the virtues of Direct Manipulation lie elsewhere: Speed at execution is not likely to be a relevant factor. Real experts can probably type a few lines of obscure code much faster than they could move objects around a screen, position them properly, and do the necessary pointing operations.

3. *Knowledgeable intermittent users can retain operational concepts.*

This could be true, but if so it probably reflects two things: The expertise at usage really reflects expertise in the subject matter, which is probably well established and apt to fade slowly from memory, if at all; and a good semantic mapping of actions leads to slower forgetting and also easier rederivation of the operations that are forgotten. We suspect that these claims are true, but derive from aspects that would be true for many well-designed systems, not just Direct Manipulation systems.

4. *Error messages are rarely needed.*

Yes and No. Error messages are often not needed because the results are immediately visible, and because some classes of errors may not even be possible. But Direct Manipulation systems have their own problems. It is possible to make new classes of errors, some of them potentially serious. Worse, because these are apt to be errors in the task domain (but legal operations as far as the interface is concerned) they are hard to detect. Finally, Direct Manipulation systems sometimes simply don't bother with error messages, assuming that the ease of evaluation will make it obvious to the user that the desired operation was not done. It's not that the message wasn't needed, it's just that the system didn't bother to present one. This what Lewis and Norman call the "do nothing" strategy. This strategy is not always desirable (see Lewis & Norman, Chapter 20).

5. *Users can see immediately if their actions are furthering their goals, and if not, they can simply change the direction of their activity.*

The first part of the claim results from the properties of Direct Evaluation. The second part has already been discussed in our response to feature 3 of the first list. But basically, the ability to "change the direction of their activity" results from the natural reversibility of many actions. For those actions that are not so naturally reversible, the systems do not fare any differently than more conventional systems. Immediate feedback as to the outcome of an operation and "undo" commands are valuable for any system, not just Direct Manipulation systems.

6. *Users have reduced anxiety because the system is comprehensible and because actions are so easily reversible.*

This is outside the domain of our analyses and difficult to assess. A fair comparison would require two systems, both equally well-matched in capability and in semantic directness.

In conclusion, some of the claims seem too strong, some represent features of many well-designed systems, not just direct manipulation systems, and some seem to be correct. All in all, the early claims seem to fare reasonably well, although today we can bring more sophistication and depth of analysis to bear upon them then was possible at the time they were made.

References

Shneiderman, B. (1982). The future of interactive systems and the emergence of direct manipulation. *Behavior and Information Technology, 1*, 237-256.

TOWARDS AN EFFECTIVE CHARACTERIZATION OF GRAPHICAL INTERACTION

Ronald BAECKER

Associate Professor of Computer Science and Electrical Engineering
Dynamic Graphics Project, Computer Systems Research Group
University of Toronto, Toronto, Ontario, Canada

Abstract

The development of rich user-oriented interactive graphics systems has been hindered by the lack of an adequate conceptual framework for characterizing graphical input and interaction. In surveying recent work, two prevalent notions, the desirability of separating graphical input from graphical output, and the ability of any one physical device to simulate another, are emphasized; misinterpretation and misapplication of these notions are criticized. The output and input technologies, the partners in the dialogue, and the dialogue's content and context are presented as the building blocks of interactive dialogues. It is shown how these building blocks can be used to construct a number of appropriate solutions to a typical problem in graphical interaction. Outstanding solutions to some other problems are also presented. The paper concludes with a sketch of a new framework for graphical input which appears to facilitate the construction of rich interactive systems, and with some suggestions for further research.

1. Introduction

What is graphical interaction? Funk & Wagnall's Standard College Dictionary defines *interaction* as "action on each other." The Second College Edition of Webster's New World Dictionary of the American Language adds the phrase "reciprocal action or effect," where *reciprocal* is defined as "done, felt, given, etc. in return." Thus *graphical interaction* is a set of actions of a computer graphics system and its user on each other. The user provides input to the system via a set of devices; the system provides output to the user via a set of displays. These inputs and outputs must be reciprocal, that is, they must be related to one another. Graphical interaction is thus a succession of interrelated actions and reactions.

The purpose of graphical interaction is to facilitate the use of a computer, to enhance the user's powers to accomplish or to create. Towards this end, interactive graphics systems should be *user-oriented* and they should be *rich*. User-oriented design of interactive graphics systems has been explored in a recent workshop of that name [Treu 76]. The term "rich" has many meanings, including, according to Webster's", "... sumptuous ... full ... deep ... abundant ... plentiful ..."[1]

The most far-reaching and technically sound vision of the potentialities of interactive computer graphics is that of Alan Kay. He calls his dream of a "dynamic medium for creative thought," the Dynabook:

"...Imagine having your own self-contained knowledge manipulator in a portable package the size and shape of an ordinary notebook. Suppose it had enough power to outrace your senses of sight and hearing, enough capacity to store for later retrieval thousands of page-equivalents of reference material, poems, letters, recipes, records, drawings, animations, musical scores, waveforms, dynamic simulations, ... There should be no discernible pause between cause and effect. (One of the metaphors we used when designing such a system was that of a musical instrument, such as a flute, which is owned by its user and responds instantly and consistently to its owner's wishes. Imagine the absurdity of a one second delay between blowing a note and hearing it!) ... We would like the Dynabook to have the flexibility and generality of this second kind of item [items such as paper and clay], combined with tools which have the power of the first kind [items such as cars and television sets] ..."

Instruments and tools are two of the metaphors that shed light on the desirable properties of interactive graphics systems. Vehicles, games, and interpersonal dialogues are some other useful metaphors.

As Kay notes, good instruments provide immediate feedback to their user. Instruments must be crafted with care and precision -- consider the importance of the balance and feel of a violin. They must be re-engineered as components and techniques evolve and change -- consider the relationship of the harpsichord to the clavichord to the piano, a progression characterized by changes in the striking or plucking mechanism.

Kay has noted the importance of tools having power, flexibility, and generality. Tools should be as adaptable as possible -- the Swiss Army Knife is a tool of remarkable versatility. They must be robust, that is, resistant to user error -- consider the unsuitability of a saw which removes a hand from its user when it slips.

Vehicles must respond sensitively -- consider the importance of the steering of an automobile. They must respond repeatably -- otherwise how could one land an airplane. They must provide adequate feedback -- consider the multi-dimensional display of an airplane cockpit. They must be appropriate for the journey -- consider bicycling up Mt. Everest.

Some of the best interactive graphics systems are games. Games must be engrossing, captivating, even joyous -- otherwise players will lose interest. They must have rules or structure -- otherwise players will lose patience or confidence. They should challenge the players, encouraging mastery and growth.

Finally, interpersonal dialogues have many attributes which the designers of person-machine dialogues seek to emulate [Nickerson 78]. Human responses are appropriate, based on intelligent processing of messages from the other person. Human responses are sensitive, based on interpretations of subtle clues in the behavior of the other person. Human dialogue is multi-dimensional and multi-level, allowing communication to proceed along a number of paths, and threads of conversation to be started and restarted at will.

Interactive graphics systems can be instruments for expression or measurement, tools to cause effects, vehicles for exploration, games for challenge or amusement, and media for communication. They can be sumptuous and abundant rather than spartan and boring. They can entice and delight rather than oppress and shackle. How does recent research serve these ends?

---

[1] However, abundance without taste and balance results in systems that are bloated and unmanageable. Consider the differences between INTERLISP and PL/I, a symphony orchestra and a convention of high school bands, or a modern state dinner and a medieval feast.

2. Recent Research on Graphical Input and Interaction — A Critique

There have been five major streams of recent research relevant to graphical input and interaction. One stream has attempted to define architectures for graphics programming systems that would facilitate the construction of graphics application programs [Newman 74; Core 77]. A second stream has attempted to define a set of standards for graphics programming languages [Core 77]. A third stream has investigated various methodologies for graphical input programming. These include the embedding of an input sublanguage into a graphics programming language [Rovner 68,70,73], and the development of an independent control-oriented language [Newman 68,70,73; Kasik 76]. A fourth stream has proposed various sets of graphic input primitives or virtual devices [Newman 68; Cotton 72; Foley 74; Wallace 76; Deecker 77]. Finally, the fifth stream has concentrated on the effective human engineering of interactive computer systems in general and graphics systems in particular [Martin 73; Foley 74; Treu 78].

Space precludes our presenting the results of this work in detail. Instead we shall focus on two themes that pervade most current work. One theme is that of the need for separating the graphical input and output processes. The other theme is that of simulating one virtual device by any other. These two themes incorporate useful ideas, but taken to extremes they lead to misinterpretations which can hinder the development of rich user-oriented interactive graphics systems.

Recent work, motivated by the desire for device-independent, general-purpose graphics languages, and by the desire for computer graphics standards, has stressed the need for the separation of the graphical input and output processes. A strong case can be made for this point of view. Arguments include the virtues of orthogonal descriptions of complex processes, the enhancement of program portability, and an increased ability to substitute one device for another. Newman and Sproull, for example, write in [Newman 74]:

"...meddling with the output process should be avoided in the interests of device independence, even if it requires pointing by software or doing without spectacular dynamic input techniques..."

The Status Report of the Graphic Standards Planning Committee of ACM/SIGGRAPH, known as the "Core Report" [Core 77], states quite definitively:

"The conceptual framework of the Core System treats input and output devices as orthogonal concepts."

Thus recent work in graphical interaction has attempted to formalize a set of primitives for graphical input, viewed as a process separate from the graphical output process. I believe that these formalisms fail to describe the variety and richness of interaction possibilities. As Newman and Sproull imply, we *must* tamper with the output process if we are to achieve spectacular dynamic input techniques. Why is this so?

Architecturally, graphics systems come in four flavors — stand-alone single-user graphics machines, time-shared graphics systems, single-user graphics satellites, and time-shared graphics satellite systems. In a stand-alone single-user machine, immediate feedback to graphical input can be achieved by following a call to an input primitive with the code to generate the appropriate output. Since all system resources are available for this task, response time is only limited by the available computational bandwidth, and the characteristics of the display device. However, in the other kinds of graphics systems, there may be arbitrary delays between the execution of one primitive function and the execution of the next one. This may be due to the competition of other users in time-sharing, or to the complexities of host-satellite communication in remote graphics. Thus, to guarantee the integrity and responsiveness of feedback to interactive input, we must encapsulate appropriate modifications to the display file as part of the input process, despite the device-dependence and the harmful effect on portability this creates.

Work on the Core System is typical of another recent trend in the study of input and interaction. The Core Report states in [Core 77]:

"The basic goal of the Core System input primitives is to provide a framework for application program/operator interaction which is independent of the particular physical input devices that are available on a given configuration."

The primitives chosen are based most directly on the work of Foley and Wallace [Foley 74], work which is summarized in [Wallace 76] as follows:

"All input devices for interactive computer graphics can be effectively modelled in programs by a small number of virtual input devices. By specifying an appropriate set of such virtual devices, the semantics of interactive input can be defined independently of the physical form of the devices. In the service of program portability, human factors adaptability, economy, and maximal use of terminal capability, a sufficient set of virtual devices is described."

In their earlier paper [Foley 74], Foley and Wallace also wrote:

"Most important from this paper's viewpoint is the attendant flexibility of interchanging one physical device for another, thus facilitating easy experimentation and optimization of those interaction language aspects relating to visual and tactile continuity. While any physical device can be used as any one or more virtual devices, such experimentation is necessary because physical devices are not necessarily psychologically equivalent and interchangeable. To be sure, they can be substituted, but often at the cost of additional user compensation and self-training, which increases the psychological distance between man and computer. Such experimentation, which we call human factors fine tuning, would not be necessary were the design of interaction languages an exacting science rather than somewhat of an art form. But it is not..."

The fact that any virtual device *can* be simulated by any physical device does not imply that such a simulation will produce an interactive system which is congenial or effective. On the contrary, one cannot construct rich user-oriented graphical interfaces "independently of the physical form of the devices". If one input device is substituted for another, then we must, in general, redesign all aspects of the interactive dialogue to provide the most effective interface possible.

Consider an example taken from [Foley 74]. They argue that one can simulate a light pen ("pick") by successively brightening all displayed entities and noting when buttons are pushed. Yet this method is so cumbersome that it destroys the simplicity and beauty of light pen picking — pointing directly at an item, and instantaneously moving the hand to select an item through its relationship to the entire visual field, rather than by its name or description. Surely one would restructure a system to allow selection in terms of a name or a property rather than accept the awkwardness of this kind of simulation.

Another example is implicit in the Core Report. Consider the simulation of the keyboard by a tablet ("locator"). A few characters of input can be handled by a trainable character recognizer. But if the original program were heavily keyboard oriented, and the only input device were a tablet, then the correct approach would be to redesign the user interface rather than rely on an awkward and cumbersome simulation.

A third example concerns dragging, which Newman and Sproull present as a primitive and Wallace presents as a nonprimitive virtual device. The essential feature of dragging is the ability it gives the user to set the position of an object, and to make slight instantaneous adjustments based on its relationship to the visual scene. Any simulation of this capability with keyboards or buttons would be so crude as to make the result unrecognizable.

A final example deals with inking, which Newman and Sproull present as a primitive and Wallace presents as a nonprimitive virtual device. Imagine the absurdity of trying to ink or sketch with a keyboard or a button box.

Thus the search for simple methods of device simulation and substitution distracts us from the goal of crafting good user interfaces. It distracts us from studying the very difficult relationships among display technology, computational bandwidth, device kinesthetics, and response time. Its distracts us from the goal of interface optimization and suggests that we instead construct interfaces of the lowest common denominator that will function anywhere. Although portability is facilitated by device-independence, interactivity and useability are enhanced by *device dependence*. [2]

One other weakness of current attempts to formalize graphical interaction is the failure to incorporate time and the passage of time into the formalism. Foley and Wallace correctly describe boredom, panic, frustration, confusion, and discomfort as psychological blocks that often prevent full user involvement in an interaction. Appropriate response time is obviously an important factor in avoiding these blocks. Any interactive system designer or user knows how critical response time is. So why does response time not appear anywhere explicitly in our theories or descriptions of graphical interaction?

This paper now continues with a discussion of interactive dialogues, and an attempt to isolate their building blocks. We then present a collection of examples that illustrate the variety and richness of graphical interaction possibilities. These examples have all been invented in our laboratory in the last three years, although some may be similar to others invented in other laboratories. Our presentation will attempt to describe the range of possible solutions to each problem, and to explain why certain solutions are effective and others are ineffective. These explanations will usually make reference to the appropriateness of the graphical output for the particular graphical input, the response time for this output to appear, and the characteristics of the real physical device which is used for the input.

From these examples we shall try to elicit a set of characterizations of good interactive dialogues. We then present a collection of examples and mechanisms and principles that underly their construction. These principles and characterizations will then be used to provide some guidelines to the builders of graphics programming systems and some cautions to those attempting standardization. The paper concludes with a sketch of a framework for graphical input, and some suggestions for future research, both of which are rooted in extensive experience in implementing and evaluating a variety of interactive systems.

3. The Building Blocks of Interactive Dialogues

An interactive dialogue is a sequence of messages between a person and a machine. The person's messages are transmitted via a set of input devices; the machine's messages are transmitted via a set of displays. The nature of the dialogue is thus determined by the display technology, the input technology, the two partners in the dialogue (the person and the machine), and the content and context of the dialogue. Let us look at each of these factors in turn.

Most computer graphic displays belong to one of four classes: line-drawing refreshed devices, line-drawing storage devices, raster-oriented refreshed devices (digital video displays), and raster-oriented storage devices (such as plasma panels). Line-drawing refreshed devices allow the most dynamic form of interaction because subpictures can usually be inserted, deleted, and moved instantaneously. Line-drawing storage devices, such as the ubiquitous Tektronix, severely limit interaction style because they are not selectively eraseable. The plasma panel is selectively eraseable, but individual raster points cannot be updated very quickly. Digital video displays are selectively eraseable, and allow rapid updating of individual points, although current architectures do not facilitate the modification of subpictures.

There is an even greater diversity of input devices. Here are a few examples. Keyboards produce characters or character strings. Button boxes produce discretely varying values. Light pens produce pointers to subpictures. Thumbwheels produce continuously varying values. Tablets and mice produce pairs of continuous values. Some devices produce interrupts, defining events; others must be polled. All have their kinesthetic strengths and weaknesses; all can be designed and manufactured well or poorly, and can be comfortable or cumbersome to use. We shall expand on various device characteristics in the discussion that follows.

Between the input action and the displayed response there is a machine computation. Characteristics of the machine thus also affect the nature of the dialogue. By *response latency* we mean the time between the cessation of an action by the user and the initiation of a reaction by the system. This can include both time for the CPU to shift its attention to the input action, as in a time-shared graphics system, and the time to carry out whatever analysis is required before initiating a response. The response may occupy some length of time, and so by *response time* we mean the time between the cessation of the action and the completion of the reaction. Both response parameters depend upon the effective *computational bandwidth* with which the CPU can analyze the input action and produce an appropriate picture in response.

Also significant are characteristics of the user, such as those described in [Martin 73]. These include the intelligence of the user, whether he is a regular or casual user of the system, whether he is highly trained or not, whether he is strongly motivated or alienated, whether he is active or passive, and whether he is the ultimate user of the system or merely an intermediary.

Finally, it is important to consider both the content and the context of the dialogue in designing appropriate graphical interaction. Tasks requiring "linear" strategies which must be undertaken in real-time, such as air traffic control, impose different constraints than those which involve "non-linear" strategies with much backup, shifting of levels, and changing of points of view, such as computer-aided design. The input of complex curved shapes may be a very different problem depending upon whether they represent free-hand cartoon characters, borders extracted from heart X-rays, or features of maps. An emergency recovery sequence in a process control graphics system controlling a power grid will impose different requirements than a graphic simulation in a computer-aided instruction environment.

The design of interactive dialogues in general and graphical dialogues in particular is an art. I prefer to describe this art as that of "crafting a user interface". Some of the influences that play a role in this process have been described above. Now let us illustrate the process with a detailed case study.

---

[1] Another way of expressing this is as an example of the *strength* vs. *generality* issue. We are not arguing that one should never build weak, general, portable systems, but only that there are often sizeable advantages in building strong, specific systems.

4. A Problem in Graphical Interaction and Some Solutions

Consider the problem of positioning or repositioning an object -- a deceptively simple task. There are a great number of different solutions that are appropriate under various circumstances.

Solutions fall into two categories, *symbolic* or *demonstrative*. Symbolic solutions are those in which we provide a description of the object's desired position in a symbolic language. Demonstrative solutions are those in which we indicate the object's desired position by means of direct action on or modification of the picture.

With a symbolic solution, we explicitly or implicitly specify expressions which when evaluated define the object's X and Y coordinates. One method is to input directly the desired coordinates, e.g., X=250 and Y=500. Another method is to input the desired change in coordinates, e.g., add 50 to the X coordinate (i.e., move it to the right). A third method is to describe the position in terms of the position of another object or objects, e.g., place it 50 units to the right of object A and at the same height as object B.

With demonstrative solutions, we drag objects, adjust markers or pointers, or construct simple sketches which convey our intentions without the direct use of numbers or symbols. In a sketching system, we can deposit "drops of ink" with a free-hand motion of a stylus. In a graphic design system, we can grab hold of and move a particular design element until it can be seen to be touching another element in the appropriate manner. In a newspaper page layout system, we can drag rectangular areas representing half-tone pictures in a continuous motion vertically and in a discrete motion horizontally, jumping from one column of the simulated page to another. In a circuit design system, we can position circuit elements both according to a grid of possible positions and according to a perceived visual relationship with adjacent elements.

Symbolic specification is ideal for a keyboard device. We can type statements of the form "X15=250", which set's the X coordinate of object 15 to 250, or "X15=XA+50", which positions object 15 at 50 units to the right of object A. We can simulate such actions with other devices, but only with the aid of appropriately rapid modifications of the output process. For example, using a refreshed display and a tablet, we can drag object 15 to its intended destination, but we can position it exactly only if we can display its position in character string format, only if we can update this display quickly enough so the user's hand hasn't moved before he reads the position, and only if the updating is regular enough for him to relax and rely on it. If we have a digital video display and a tablet, still another solution is required -- the user would indicate with one or more pen strokes the desired position, and only then would the system move the object.

Demonstrative specification is ideal for a device such as a mouse or a tablet. We can make sketches containing positional information or drag objects to positions, adjusting our hand movement on the basis of displayed feedback. But the nature and effectiveness of the feedback depends upon the display technology and the system's response capabilities. To allow sketches, the system must echo the information from the tablet onto the display. To allow dragging, the system must move objects to keep up with the user's hand movements, which is impossible with most digital video displays, and may be difficult even with some refreshed display architectures. To allow dragging under constraints, as in a newspaper page layout system, the system must compute the effect of the constraints in synchrony with the hand movements.

For the most part, demonstrative specifications cannot be properly simulated with a keyboard or a button box. Inking becomes impossible. So does unconstrained dragging. Constrained dragging (as in the newspaper layout case where objects are moved from column to column) could be achieved by a series of keystrokes or button pushes, but may be awkward.

Interaction techniques cannot be routinely transferred from device to device. They must be crafted anew for each combination of input and output technology and system response capabilities. As an example, consider the newspaper page layout problem of moving a rectangle which represents a picture. It is constrained to column boundaries horizontally, can move freely vertically, and in both cases is not allowed to overlap or pass through items already existing on the page. (See Figure 1.)

Case 1: Tablet, refreshed display, high computational bandwidth, low response latency.

The solution is similar to that used in the NEWSWHOLE newspaper page layout system [Tilbrook 76; Baecker 76]. Move the tracking symbol into the center of the rectangle representing the picture. Select that picture by depressing a button on the cursor, then drag the rectangle with the button depressed. It jumps from column to column horizontally. It moves smoothly and continuously vertically. It stops when it runs into obstacles.

Case 2: Tablet, refreshed display, medium computational bandwidth, low response latency.

By medium computational bandwidth we mean that the system no longer has the power to drag a rectangle and compute the constraints in synchrony with hand movements. The system does have the power to move a simple tracking cross, or lay down a simple ink trail. These are intrinsically simpler operations because, unlike moving an arbitrary object or computing constraints, they *do not depend on the complexity of the picture* -- we can determine in advance whether or not they can be done rapidly enough.

One solution, therefore, is to drag the tracking cross in an unconstrained manner, and to apply the constraints later. Two signals must be given, one when the cross is near a border of the object to be moved, and one when it is near its desired position. Another solution is to lay down a trail of ink from any point on the object to be moved to its desired position. In either case, latching techniques such as in SKETCHPAD can be used so that the user need not point with extreme accuracy directly at an edge or a corner in order to signify that a particular edge or corner is intended.

Case 3: Tablet, refreshed display, low computational bandwidth, high response latency.

Here we assume that the system can move a simple tracking cross, or lay down a simple ink trail, but not smoothly. The feedback starts and stops jerkily, due, for example, to contention from other users in time-sharing. [9] Use of the tablet here can be so awkward and so unreliable that it is probably better not to use it at all, but instead to use the keyboard with a symbolic language as in case 6 below.

Case 4: Tablet, digital video display (frame buffer), medium computational bandwidth, low response latency.

Here we assume that the system can move a simple complementing cursor (tracking cross) in synchrony with hand movements. The complementing cursor inverts the color on any pixel beneath it, then restores the original value when it moves away. The solution, then, as in case 2, is to indicate two points that represent the start and end points of the move. An inking solution is possible only if the system has an independent binary frame buffer for temporary storage of ink trails so that the picture is not destroyed.

Case 5: Light pen, refreshed display, high computational bandwidth, low response latency.

Here we assume that the system supports a picking or pointing function and can also track a tracking cross. To simulate Case 1 with a light pen, we would pick up the tracking

[3] If this can happen, then the graphics support has been embedded incorrectly in the time-sharing system, or has been enfeebled due to the politics of time-sharing.

cross, drag it to the center of the rectangle, depress a button, and then drag the cross to a new position. However, a far better solution is for the user to point to an edge or a corner of an existing rectangle, and then to track the cross to the desired new position. This solution can require a great deal of CPU power. The organization of the display file and the nature of the pick function must support selection of edges or corners, or this must be simulated in software. Furthermore, tracking requires significantly more CPU power for a light pen than it does for a tablet.

Case 6: Keyboard, refreshed or digital video display, low computational bandwidth, high response latency.

If we only have a keyboard, or the tablet has been rendered impotent as in case 3 above, how do we proceed? Direct simulation of a tablet, by driving a cursor with repeated keystrokes over the picture increment by increment is a terrible solution. Rather we need construct a symbolic language with which the user can refer directly to locations on the page and to properties of objects. This language should contain statements like "R15=R17", which means that object 15 is to be moved so that its right side touches the right side of object 17; "X15=3", which means that object 15 is to be moved into column 3; "BR15=TL17", which means that object 15 is to be moved so that its bottom right corner touches the top left corner of object 17; "Y15=Y15+10", which means that object 15 is to be moved up 10 units; and, "Y15=230", which means that object 15 is to be moved to a height of 230. [4]

Case 7: Keyboard, refreshed or digital video display, high computational bandwidth, low response latency.

If we can update the picture immediately after every keystroke, then another solution becomes viable. We need not concern the user with coordinates, but can provide a set of movement direction keys and movement magnitude keys. Every time the user hits the right(left) arrow, the object moves one column to the right(left). Every time he hits the up(down) arrow, the object moves up(down) k units. Every time he hits the "increase(decrease) movement scale" key, then k is doubled(halved). These six keys would provide a very effective control console for positioning objects provide that the feedback to keystrokes is rapid enough.

The above example is intended to show in detail how, even in a simple but realistic graphical interaction problem, the solution depends upon the available display technology, input devices, and system response characteristics. It is not put forth as a complete and exhaustive discussion of the problem, which would entail considering other technologies such as the storage tube, and other aspects such as the system in which the technique is to be applied, and the user for which it is intended.

5. Other Problems in Graphical Interaction and Their Solutions

Let us now briefly pose and solve some other problems in graphical interaction. All solutions assume a tablet, a refreshed display, low response latency, and adequate computational bandwidth to provide a highly responsive form of interaction.

Problem 1: Develop a method for giving the user feedback about the state of a graphics application program, including error conditions, in as rapid and non-obtrusive a manner as possible.

Solution (designed by David Tilbrook and the author for NEWSWHOLE, and since used in all systems developed in our laboratory): Since the user is looking at the tracking symbol, or visual cursor, we change its shape to provide instantaneous feedback in a far more compelling way than is done typically with a section of the screen for error messages. Typically, our systems display a "?" when the physical cursor is not on the tablet surface, a "thumbs down" symbol when the input is meaningless, and a "smiling Buddha" symbol to encourage patience when the system is working.

Problem 2: Develop a method for translating, scaling, and cropping rectangles representing half-tone pictures in a newspaper page layout system.

Solution (designed by David Tilbrook for NEWSWHOLE): Consider each rectangle to be subdivided into nine equal rectangular regions. Translate a picture by moving the tracker into the center region, signalling by depressing a button on the cursor, dragging the rectangle to its new position, and releasing the button. Move an edge of the picture, keeping the opposite edge fixed, and stretching or shrinking the two adjacent edges, by moving the tracker into the region near that edge (Figure 2a), signalling, dragging the edge (Figure 2b), and signalling again (Figure 2c). Scale the picture, keeping one corner fixed, by moving the tracker into a corner, signalling, dragging the corner (Figure 2d), and signalling again (Figure 2e). All four edges stretch or shrink as the corner moves; the opposite corner remains fixed.

Problem 3: Develop a method for panning and zooming a camera over a scene to get a new view, assuming the display does not have hardware scaling, windowing, and clipping.

Solution (designed by the author and Greg Hill): Assume the original scene is as shown in Figure 3a. Activate the CAMERA command by pointing at a light button. This causes the scene to be redisplayed at half size with the current camera view represented as a surrounding rectangle (Figure 3b). Pan the camera by grabbing hold of the rectangle and dragging it (Figure 3c). Zoom the camera by grabbing hold of an edge or a corner of the rectangle and expanding or shrinking it (Figure 3d). When the terminate signal is given, the new scene is recomputed at full size (Figure 3e).

Problem 4: Develop a method for navigating through a hierarchical file system.

Solution (designed by the author, Greg Hill, and Martin Tuori): Activate the file system pager by pointing at a light button. The result is a display of all file names at the current level of the hierarchical structure. Pointing at an up arrow icon moves us up one level in the structure towards the root of the tree. Pointing at a down arrow icon and a particular directory name moves us down one level. Pointing at right or left arrow icons allows us to scroll forwards and backwards among the list of names in the current level of the hierarchy, since they often cannot all be displayed at once.

Problem 5: Develop a method for inputting notes to a graphical music score editor which uses traditional music notation, assuming no trainable character recognizer is possible.

Solution (designed by Bill Buxton [Buxton 78, Reeves 78]): First select the pitch for the note by moving the tracking symbol over a stationary menu of possible note positions (Figure 4a). [5] The tracking symbol then becomes a moving menu of possible note durations (Figure 4b). We position the appropriate duration over the selected pitch to complete the definition of the note (Figure 4c). Because relatively little hand movement is required,

---

[4] The syntax of this language needs improvement; it is the semantics with which we are here concerned.

[5] There are two columns of possible note positions to allow for the continuation of a chord or the initiation of a new one.

7. Towards a Suitable Formalism for Graphical Input

The preceding discussion has been directed towards the design and implementation of better interactive dialogues. In this section, we turn our attention to the tools with which such dialogues may be constructed. We shall begin with some general remarks on input devices and input languages, and then present some principles and suggestions upon which to build an input language capable of sustaining very rich interaction.

Input devices have been characterized as being of two kinds, those that cause events and those that may be sampled. [6] We shall be primarily interested in the event sublanguage of our input system, because it is there that we encapsulate a system's automatic, routine responses to input device activity. Furthermore, the event sublanguage provides the application programmer with a straightforward method of dealing with the parallelism and multi-dimensionality inherent in good interfaces. Many input devices can be activated and the system can monitor activity on all of them. With sampling, on the other hand, the application programmer must construct anew for each case a program to map input device activity into appropriate output device feedback. We must be able to sample all input devices so that we can handle extraordinary situations not covered by the event sublanguage, but our goal should be to avoid these cases by making that language as comprehensive as possible.

We must therefore provide mechanisms for activating input devices, for specifying the echo or feedback that is to result, and for specifying the response time that is required. We must also provide mechanisms for specifying any constraints on input device activity that are to be applied. Before discussing these issues in terms of specific input devices and device classes, let us examine the types of output responses that it is reasonable to provide as feedback.

Immediate feedback, as we have already stated in Section 2, must involve direct modification of the display file by the input system without resort to the application program. The input system should accomplish this by requests to the output system. What kinds of requests are reasonable and which are unreasonable? We suggest that it is reasonable to perform output which involves only local changes to the display file and which does not necessitate reinterpretation of the entire display file. The meaning of locality is based on the concept of the picture "segment", the independently manipulabl; subpicture which exists in most graphics systems. On most current refreshed vector displays and on properly designed future digital video displays [Baecker 78] it will be reasonable to provide feedback by any of the following mechanisms:

    -add a character to a sequence of characters;
    -add a point to a sequence of points (ink trail);
    -add a segment (tracker);
    -remove a segment (tracker);
    -change the tracking symbol;
    -translate the tracker;
    -translate (drag) an arbitrary segment;
    -translate a copy of the segment; [7]
    -change the intensity, texture, or colour of a segment;
    -blink a segment;
    -produce an audio response.

---

[6] The Core Report virtual devices can either cause events or be sampled, but not both, which is a design mistake.

[7] We assume that the hardware has a simple subroutining mechanism, otherwise a true copy would have to be made, necessitating interpretation of the display file.

this approach yields a remarkably fluid style of interaction.

8. Some Characteristics of Good Interactive Techniques

The above techniques work well because they adhere to a number of principles which seem to apply to the design of good interactive dialogues:

1. The feedback in response to user input, achieved by modifications of the graphical output process, is appropriate for the task at hand. Picture rectangles in NEWSWHOLE, for example, change position, size, and shape in response to user input and certain constraints.

2. The feedback occurs rapidly. One would use a different technique for placing a camera on a view surface than the one described above if the rectangle representing a field of view could not respond instantaneously to user input.

3. The feedback occurs predictably. Unpredictable response is even worse than predictably slow response, leading to frustration, tension, and anxiety.

4. The technique implemented is a powerful one, giving the user many degrees of freedom and control. The file system pager, for example, allows the user to navigate with ease anywhere in the file system.

5. The technique allows the user to focus his attention, avoiding wasted hand and eye movements. The changing tracker and note entry techniques are good examples of applications of this principle.

6. The proper visual ground or context is presented. The camera pan-zoom method redraws the scene so that the user can see the camera movements in relation to the entire visual scene.

7. It is easy to escape from or abort the action. In using the NEWSWHOLE picture mechanism, one can start or stop modification of a picture by moving the tracker in and out of the rectangle. Furthermore, critical operations can be accepted or aborted with specific signals.

8. It is difficult to make mistakes, and the system is robust enough to minimize the damage from mistakes that are made. The changing tracker technique presents diagnostic information to the user very quickly. The note entry technique helps guarantee legitimate input.

9. The techniques are natural, easy to learn, not cumbersome. Newspaper editors can begin using NEWSWHOLE within an hour after being introduced to the system.

10. As few demands as possible are made on the user's memory. In the file system pager, for example, he need not remember specific file names, and can find a file, albeit inefficiently, even if he forgets where in the file system it is located.

11. The various techniques embedded in a system share a common syntax, set of visual conventions, and interactive style. This, along with characteristics 7,8,9, and 10, allows the user to focus on the application, not the communication.

12. Finally, the techniques are very device dependent. Why should we not expect good interactive mechanisms to be so? Do we expect good device-independent flute-like instruments, chiseling tools, or flying vehicles? Do we expect works of art to be independent of the medium in which they are created?

We see input devices as clustering into four categories [Green 79], providing discrete or continuous data in single units or in sequences. A button box or an interval timer are devices that produce single discrete data items. A keyboard is a device that usually produces sequences of discrete data items. A mouse, tablet, or light pen can produce single continuous data items if it is tracking or dragging and continuous sequences if it is inking, and single discrete data items if it is pointing or selecting (picking). We have in effect defined a set of seven virtual devices -- a *signal*, a *timer*, a *selector*, a *writer*, a *tracker*, a *dragger*, and an *inker*. Let us look at the events that can occur with each device, the feedback that is needed, the response time desired, the constraints that may be applied, and the method by which each event is initiated and terminated.

A signal consists of the depression or release of a button or a contact switch or the change of state of a toggle switch. Feedback can consist of changing the state of a light associated with the button, giving an audio response, or changing the visibility status of a picture segment. Response time must be instantaneous. Constraints that may be applied include the deactivation of certain signals as legitimate inputs, and the application of a minimum delay between the appearance of two identical signals to prevent phenomena such as contact bounce. A signal is indivisible, so it is terminated as soon as it is initiated.

A timer consists of the provision of an alarm or signal after some period of time has elapsed. Feedback can consist of changing the visibility status of a particular segment, or giving an audio response. Response time must be instantaneous. Constraints that may be applied include the deactivation of the interval timer while some other event is being processed. Like the signal, the timer is indivisible.

A selector consists of pointing to a particular segment with a mouse, tablet, or light pen. Feedback consists of changing the state of the segment, for example, its intensity or blink status. Response time is limited by the number of segments whose enclosing rectangle must be compared to the mouse or stylus coordinates. [8] Constraints that may be applied include making segments visible or invisible to the selector. The selector also is indivisible.

A writer consists of a sequence of keystrokes on a keyboard. Feedback consists of echoing the characters on the display screen. The echoing must be instantaneous. Constraints that may be applied include the deactivation of certain keys as legitimate inputs, and the designation of other keys as break characters. The writer is initiated by the first keystroke, and terminated with a break character.

A tracker consists of a movement of the mouse or stylus terminated by a signal. Feedback consists of echoing the movement with a tracking symbol specified by the user. The echoing must be instantaneous. Constraints that may be applied can include the imposition of a grid of allowable positions and the designation of certain rectangular areas as protected or inpenetrable to the tracker. Other rectangular areas may be designated as special in the sense that the tracker's entering or leaving them causes an event. This is useful for implementing interactive techniques such as the NEWSWHOLE picture modification scheme and the SMALLTALK windows [LRG 78]. A tracker is initiated and terminated by various system-defined signals.

A dragger is similar to a tracker except that the segment moved is one of the currently visible picture segments rather than a special tracking symbol. Again, echoing must be instantaneous. Constraints like those on a tracker apply, as do the methods of initiation and termination.

An inker consists of a movement by the mouse or stylus which results in a sequence of coordinate pairs. These positions are displayed by the appearance of an ink trail. The trail must be laid down instantaneously. Constraints that may be applied include whether the device is sampled on an equal space or an equal time basis, and the spacing or rate of the sampling. Inking is initiated and terminated by various system-defined signals.

It should be clear that the feedback described for the above virtual devices can be provided by the display file modification techniques listed above. But what about the imposition of constraints — how is this achieved? The answer is straightforward in all cases but that of region protection, so let us examine that case now.

Regions are the minimum enclosing rectangles of segments. Assume n segments are to be protected, or are to give signals upon tracker entry or exit. Their rectangles will overlap in general as is shown in Figure 5a. Now construct an uneven rectangular mesh which covers all rectangles as is shown in Figure 5b. Each element of the mesh is now associated with zero, one, or more segments. Furthermore, each element of the mesh can be linked to each of its four neighbors in a list structured representation in which each element's storage structure has four pointers to its top, right, bottom, and left neighbors, and an additional pointer to its list of associated segments. Once this data structure is computed, it becomes straightforward to monitor for segment entry or exit by a tracker or by a dragged segment without reinterpretation of the entire display file.

As we noted in Section 2, there have been many attempts to specify ideal sets of virtual devices. The above presentation is another try to do slightly better. What distinguishes this from other attempts is the stress placed on device feedback and the introduction of constraints that determine what input is legal.

I believe that the virtual devices and echoing methods described above are adequate to handle a large percentage of desirable interaction techniques. If they are not, an escape should be provided. This escape is a method of specifying the virtual device, a routine which is to be executed whenever the virtual device is activated, and the frequency of execution of the routine that is desired. Alternatively, one can simply request that the routine be executed everytime the virtual device provides new data. It is via such escapes that tools such as graphical potentiometers and the camera pan-zoom technique could be implemented.

Finally, a graphical input language should contain mechanisms, such as those described in [Van Den Bos 78] and [Green 79], for combining the input primitives described above into richer and more powerful mechanisms. Such a combination facility must allow new events to be specified as serial or parallel combinations of old events. If parallel combination is desired, one must specify what the possibilities are and how many of the possibilities need be realized for the new event to take place. If serial combination is desired, one must specify which primitive events must occur in sequence and what timing relations must hold true for the new event to take place.

8. Summary and Conclusions

After defining graphical interaction, we developed a vision of what graphical interaction *should be* in terms of a series of metaphors. We then turned our attention to recent research to see if it is helping us design rich user-oriented interactive graphics systems. We identified two highly regarded and generally accepted themes in the current literature which needed to be questioned. We argued that the separation of the graphical input and output processes could severely restrict the interaction styles that we are able to create. We further argued that the issue of device simulation and substitution is much more complicated than it has been portrayed. It should be no surprise that we approach these issues differently — whereas most current researchers seek device-independence and portability, we strive to exploit the particular characteristics of individual devices to build the

---

[8] We assume that, with the increasing dominance of mice and tablets over light pens, and of raster over vector displays, comparison will increasingly be done by software rather than hardware, and will attempt at first to identify the segment that the user has selected.

strongest interfaces possible.

We then argued that the "crafting of a user interface" requires consideration of the display technology, the input technology, the machine, the user, and the content and context of the dialogue. We supported this argument by presenting a series of solutions to a problem in graphical interaction as we varied some of these factors. We also presented solutions to some other problems in graphical interactions, solutions which helped us to develop a number of principles that seem to apply to the construction of good user interfaces. Finally, in the preceding section, we reflected on how a language for graphical input could be made suitable for implementing graphical dialogues of the quality we had discussed.

Unfortunately, we have taken only a few small steps along the road towards the very difficult goal of a comprehensive theory or a systematic design methodology for graphical dialogues. We need to take far larger steps. We need to carry out more case studies of particular problems in graphical interaction like the one presented in Section 4. We need to accompany such case studies by building systems incorporating various design approaches and making controlled systematic observations and measurements on users. We need a methodology for carrying out such experiments. We need a language for describing graphical dialogues that is more descriptive than English. We need to record examples of design approaches and user interfaces on film, video tape, video disk, or some standard computer animation digital format, so that they can be archived, disseminated, compared, and contrasted. We computer scientists need to look closely at the literature from psychology and industrial engineering that deals with perception, memory, reaction time, problem solving, and task performance. We need to work with individuals from such disciplines to develop information processing theories of human performance in typical graphical dialogues. But even as we take our first faltering steps towards better theories of graphical interaction, we must never forget that the construction of user interfaces is and will remain a problem in *design*, and thus will always remain subject to that most intangible of qualities, good taste.

Acknowledgements

Several of the ideas in this paper were suggested or clarified by Bill Buxton, Mark Green, and Bill Reeves of the University of Toronto's Dynamic Graphics Project, and Mike Tilson of Human Computing Resources Corporation. The entire paper has benefited from their thoughtful comments. I am also indebted to Mary Lee Coombs and Dave Sherman for their help in preparing the manuscript. This work was sponsored in part by the National Research Council of Canada.

References

[Baecker 78] Ronald M. Baecker, David M. Tilbrook, and Martin Tuori, "NEWSWHOLE: A Newspaper Page Layout System", 10 minute 3/4" black-and-white video cartridge, Dynamic Graphics Project, Computer Systems Research Group, University of Toronto, 1978.

[Baecker 78] Ronald M. Baecker, "Digital Video Display Systems and Dynamic Graphics", Report to the Canadian Department of Communications, Human Computing Resources Corporation, March 1978.

[Buxton 78] William Buxton, Guy Fedorkow, Ronald M. Baecker, William Reeves, K.C. Smith, G. Ciamaga and Leslie Mezei, "An Overview of the Structured Sound Synthesis Project", *Proceedings of the Third International Computer Music Conference*, Evanston, Illinois, November 1978.

[Core 77] Status Report of the Graphic Standards Planning Committee of ACM/SIGGRAPH, *Computer Graphics*, Vol. 11, No. 3, Fall 1977.

[Cotton 72] Ira W. Cotton, "Network Graphic Attention Handling", *Online 72 Conference Proceedings*, Brunel University, Uxbridge, England, Sept. 1972, pp. 465-490.

[Deecker 77] G.F.P. Deecker and J.P. Penny, "Standard Input Forms for Interactive Computer Graphics", *Computer Graphics*, Vol. 11, No. 1, Spring 1977, pp. 32-40.

[Foley 74] James D. Foley and Victor L. Wallace, "The Art of Natural Graphic Man-Machine Conversation", *Proceedings of the IEEE*, Vol. 82, No. 4, April 1974, pp. 462-471.

[Green 79] Mark Green, "A Graphical Input Programming System", M.Sc. Thesis, Department of Computer Science, University of Toronto, 1979 (expected).

[Kasik 78] David J. Kasik, "Controlling User Interaction", *Computer Graphics*, Vol. 10, No. 2, Summer 1978, pp. 109-115.

[LRG 76] Learning Research Group, "Personal Dynamic Media", Xerox Palo Alto Research Center Report, 1976.

[Martin 73] James Martin, *Design of Man-Computer Dialogues*, Prentice-Hall, Englewood Cliffs, N.J., 1973.

[Newman 68] William M. Newman, "A System for Interactive Graphical Programming", *AFIPS Conference Proceedings (Spring Joint Computer Conference)*, Vol. 32, 1968, pp. 47-54.

[Newman 70] William M. Newman, "An Experimental Display Programming Language for the PDP-10 Computer", University of Utah, UTEC-Csc-70-104, July 1970.

[Newman 73] William M. Newman and Robert F. Sproull, *Principles of Interactive Computer Graphics*, McGraw-Hill Book Company, 1973.

[Newman 74] William M. Newman and Robert F. Sproull, "An Approach to Graphics System Design", *Proceedings of the IEEE*, Vol. 82, No. 4, April 1974, pp. 471-483.

[Nickerson 78] R.S. Nickerson, "On Conversational Interaction with Computers", appears in [Treu 78], pp. 101-113.

[Reeves 78] William Reeves, William Buxton, Robert Pike and Ronald M. Baecker, "Ludwig: an Example of Interactive Computer Graphics in a Score Editor", *Proceedings of the Third International Computer Music Conference*, Evanston, Illinois, November 1978.

[Rovner 68] Paul D. Rovner, "LEAP Users Manual", Lincoln Laboratory Technical Memorandum 23L-0009, MIT Lincoln Laboratory, December 1968.

[Tilbrook 76] David M. Tilbrook, "A Newspaper Page Layout System", M.Sc. Thesis, Department of Computer Science, University of Toronto, 1976.

[Treu 76] Siegfried Treu [Editor], "User-Oriented Design of Interactive Graphics Systems", Proceedings of the ACM/SIGGRAPH Workshop, Pittsburgh Pa., Oct. 14-15, 1976.

[Van Den Bos 78] Jan Van Den Bos, "Definition and Use of Higher-level Graphics Input Tools", *Computer Graphics*, Vol. 12, No. 3, August 1978, pp. 38-42.

[Wallace 76] Victor L. Wallace, "The Semantics of Graphic Input Devices", *Computer Graphics*, Vol. 10, No. 1, Spring 1976, pp. 61-85.

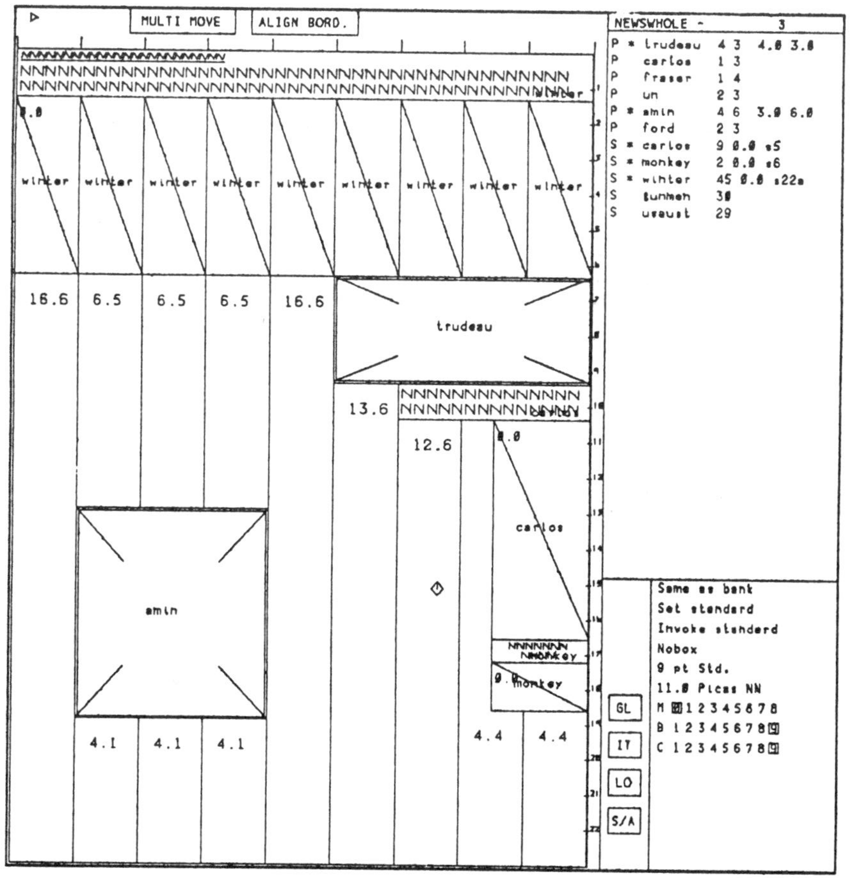

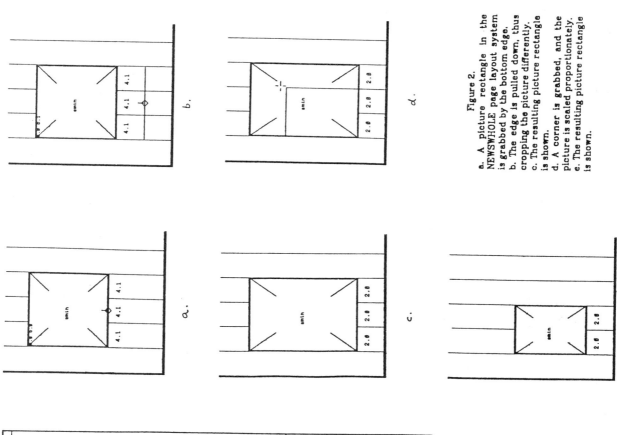

Figure 2.

a. A picture rectangle in the NEWSWHOLE page layout system is grabbed by the bottom edge.

b. The edge is pulled down, thus cropping the picture differently.

c. The resulting picture rectangle is shown.

d. A corner is grabbed, and the picture is scaled proportionately.

e. The resulting picture rectangle is shown.

Figure 1.

A typical display from the NEWSWHOLE newspaper page layout system. The left two thirds of the display represents a newspaper page, divided into nine columns. Three articles, labelled "winter", "carlos", and "monkey", are on the page, as are two pictures, labelled "trudeau" and "amin."

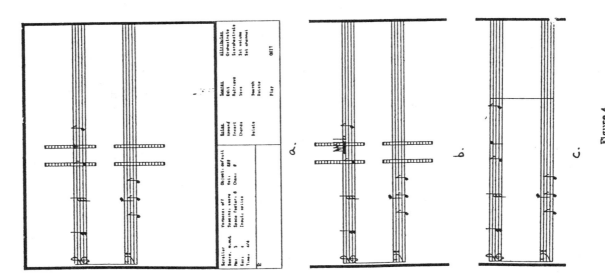

Figure 4.

a. A new note is about to be entered using the LUDWIG score editor for traditional music notation. Acceptable positions and pitches for the new note are indicated by the two ruled vertical bars.

b. The position and pitch have been selected. The tracking symbol becomes a menu of acceptable duration choices.

c. Definition of the note is complete.

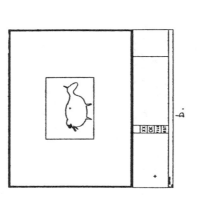

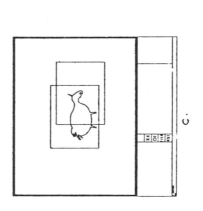

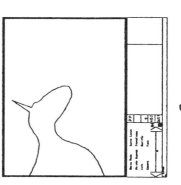

Figure 3.

a. A scene in the HAFWIT sketch editor when the CAMERA command is activated.

b. The scene is redisplayed at half size within the surrounding window.

c. The camera is repositioned.

d. The camera is given a new field of view.

e. The picture is recomputed and the new result is shown.

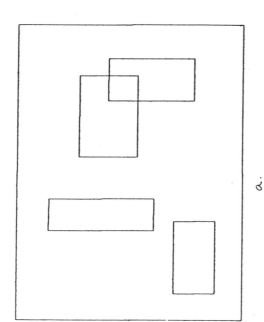

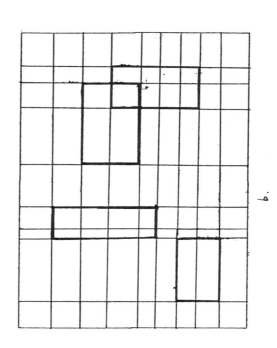

Figure 5.
a. Minimum enclosing rectangles of four picture segments.
b. Mesh which covers all picture segment rectangles, and is used
for efficient computation of segment entry and exit.

Chapter 11

Design Principles and Methodologies

The designer of an interactive system and of its user interface has available, in principle, an incredible variety of usable technologies (Chapters 7: The Visual Channel, Chapter 8: The Haptic Channel, and Chapter 9: The Audio Channel) and interaction techniques (Chapter 10: Interaction Styles and Techniques). How can these be incorporated and synthesized into a design? What is the process of user interface design? How may it be done most effectively? These are some of the questions that we shall attempt to answer in this chapter.

Answers tend to be characterizable as either *principles* or *rules*, *checklists* or *guidelines*, or *methodologies*. Principles are collections of statements which advise the designer on how to proceed, for example, "Know thy user." Guidelines are collections of tests which can be applied to an interface to determine if it is satisfactory, e.g., an average response time of less than one second. Methodologies are more-or-less formalized rules which, when followed in sequence, are intended to facilitate the process of design and lead to effective designs.

Design Principles

An early and insightful enumeration of principles for the design of interactive graphics systems is that of Hansen (1971):

- "Know the user."
- "Minimize memorization," by allowing selection of items rather than entry of data, by using names instead of numbers, by ensuring predictable

behaviour, and by providing ready access to useful system information.

- "Optimize operations," by providing rapid execution of common operations, by changing the display as little as possible in satisfying a request, by exploiting "muscle memory," and by organizing and reorganizing command parameters based on observed system usage.
- "Engineer for errors," through the provision of good error messages, by designing so that common errors are not made, by allowing actions to be reversible, by providing redundancy, and by guaranteeing data structure integrity in the face of hardware or software failure.

Foley and Wallace (1974) focus on the methods by which interface design can enable effective conversation between human and machine, and present these methods classified either as *language principles* or *psychological principles*:

The language in computer graphics communication is not one of spoken or even written words, but rather one of pictures, and of actions such as button pushes, lightpen indications, and joystick movements which serve as words.

The language and context of the conversation must be the language of the man and must be natural to him... . However, it is essential also that the language be efficient, complete, and have a natural grammar...

The second guiding principle is that the system should avoid psychological blocks that often prevent full user involvement in an interaction. The most typical of these blocks are boredom, panic, frustration, confusion, and discomfort.

Boredom is a consequence of improper pacing. The maintenance of adequate response times is the critical concern...

Panic is the consequence of unexpectedly long delays, wherein a conversational partner gives no reply to a statement or question over a prolonged period of time...

Frustration results from an inability to easily convey intentions to the computer and, consequently, eliciting either an unexpected response, or none at all. Frustration is further compounded if the unexpected response cannot be undone, or if one cannot determine what response actually took place. Frustration is caused by inflexible and unforgiving systems...

Confusion is the consequence of perceived structure being overwhelmed by detail. For example, the user may be offered many poorly defined command options at once, or may face too much undifferentiated detail in a displayed picture. The remedy for such confusion is to increase the amount of underlying structure, to improve the perception of the structure already present, or to reduce unnecessary detail...

Discomfort comes from providing an inappropriate physical environment for the graphics work station...

There are two distinct languages in the communication between the man and the graphic machine. One is the language of display by which the machine presents information regarding the state of its data and the options available for further action by the user. The other is the language of *actions* using input devices, by which the man relates his intended transformations of machine-stored data with references to objects in the displayed picture.

The goals of language design, both action and picture, are to provide a language format which is natural and which does not add to the boredom, panic, frustration, and confusion of the user. Assuming that the required response times can be achieved, that the apparatus and environment have been properly constructed, that the semantics of the intended conversation are understood, and that the suitable tutorial material can be developed, there remains a need for well-designed sequences of input actions coordinated with output pictures to permit symbiotic communication.

A number of syntactic principles of naturalness for action sequences can be abstracted from experience. The important ones, in our judgement, are sentence structure, visual continuity, tactile continuity, and contextual continuity.

An action language is sentence structured if, within a given phase or subdomain of discourse, each complete user thought can be expressed in a continuous sequence of input device manipulations with standard patterns of beginning and termination. Upon termination, the machine returns to a state from which similar action sequences, other sentences, can begin.

The essential features of this sentence structure are indivisible, complete thought; unbroken action; a well-defined "home state;" regularity of pattern. Obviously, these properties are modeled after spoken discourse...

The idea of visual continuity is that, within a given sentence, the eye should focus on a single area which moves in a continuous manner throughout the expression of the sentence...

Tactile continuity refers to the need to avoid groping or searching with hands or feet once a sentence has begun. None but a touch typist should be required to use a typewriter keyboard as an input device within the expression of a sentence...

Contextual continuity refers to the absence of unrecognized side effects resulting from a user's actions.

A third valuable enumeration appears in Baecker, Buxton, and Reeves (1979), and again in Baecker (1980):

- The nomenclature used is oriented towards and appropriate for the application.
- The techniques are refined through careful observation of their use by real users, that is, the intended users of the ultimate system.
- Screen layouts are very carefully designed and refined.
- A small but effective set of input transducers is used. Too many can lead to wasted actions; too few can lead to cumbersome interactions.
- The techniques are natural, easy to learn, not cumbersome.
- The feedback given in response to user input is iconic and is appropriate for the task at hand.
- The feedback occurs rapidly. One would use different techniques if the system could not respond instantaneously to user input.
- The feedback occurs predictably. Unpredictable response is even worse than predictably slow response, leading to frustration, tension, and anxiety.
- The technique implemented is a powerful one, giving the user many degrees of freedom and control.
- The technique allows the user to focus his attention, avoiding wasted hand and eye movements.
- The proper visual ground is presented.
- It is easy to escape from or abort the action.
- It is difficult to make mistakes, and the system is robust enough to minimize the danger from mistakes that are made.
- As few demands as possible are made on the user's memory.
- The various techniques embedded in the system share a unity of protocol — a common syntax, set of visual conventions, and interactive style. This, along with some of the other characteristics listed above, allows the user to focus on the application, not the communication.
- Finally, the techniques are very device dependent.

Other lists of principles may be found in Gould and Lewis (1985), Norman (1983), Rubinstein and Hersh (1984), and Shneiderman (1986).

Design Guidelines

Guidelines are more difficult to formulate than principles because they should be quantitative and *testable*, although in practice most published ''guidelines'' do not satisfy this criterion and are indistinguishable from what we call principles. One of the earliest formulations of guidelines is that of Engel and Granda (1975). Another, more recent one is that of Davis and Swezey (1983).

An ongoing effort is that of Smith, documented in a long series of reports and publications (Smith, 1980, 1981, 1982; Smith and Aucella, 1983; Smith and Mosier, 1984). Smith (1986) distinguishes among standards, guidelines, rules, and algorithms, defining guidelines as ''a series of generally stated recommendations for user interface software, with examples, added explanation, and other commentary, selected (and perhaps modified) for any particular system application, and adopted by agreement among people concerned with interface design.'' He argues that our present knowledge does not justify the imposition of standards for user interface software, but that intelligent and informed practice is aided by the existence of guidelines.

Smith and Mosier (1984) present 679 guidelines organized into six functional areas: data entry, data display, sequence control, user guidance, data transmission, and data protection. Examples of these guidelines are the following:

- When data entry is a significant part of a user's task, entered data should appear on the user's primary display...
- Provide displayed feedback for all user actions during data entry; display keyed entries stroke by stroke...
- The computer should acknowledge data entry actions rapidly, so that users are not slowed or paced by delays in computer response; for normal operations, delays in displayed feedback should not exceed 0.2 seconds...
- Display data consistent with standards and conventions familiar to users...
- Display complete words in preference to abbreviations...
- Minimize punctuation of abbreviations and acronyms...
- Ensure that the means of sequence control are compatible with user skills, permitting simple step-by-step actions by beginners, but permitting more complex command entry by experienced users...
- The computer should provide some indication of transaction status whenever the complete response to a user entry has been delayed...
- Design of data transmission procedures should minimize memory load on the user...
  [*Editor's Note*: ...and 670 more...]

''Principles'' and ''guidelines'' have some utility, but they are occasionally incorrect, usually vague, sometimes contradictory (Maguire, 1982), very often not at the appropriate level of specificity (Smith, 1986), and often difficult to apply to real design problems (Mosier and Smith, 1986). Norman (1983), included as a reading, correctly notes that many principles lead to conflicts when one tries to apply them in real design situations. One must therefore make a *tradeoff* between the relative importance of two or more conflicting principles. One example of this is the work of Barnard, Hammond, Morton, Long, and Clark (1981), the analysis of consistency and compatibility in command languages.

Like most experts in the field, Norman cannot resist enumerating his set of four favorite design principles and his set of five slogans that guide his work. He then shows how one can quantitatively express and analyze tradeoffs such as menu size versus display time, editor workspace versus display time, and editor workspace versus menu size. He also discusses in qualitative terms some other interesting tradeoffs such as command languages versus menus, long names versus short names for commands files, and handheld computers versus workstations.

Design Methodologies

Although principles and guidelines can assist us as we design, they do not help us to structure *the process of design*. The ideal of a design methodology is that of a procedure which when followed more or less mechanically will produce a good design. Although this ideal is unrealizable, a number of useful design methodology formulations have been developed and published.

These generally deal with design at one of two levels of generality. The higher level, which we term *application system design*, encompasses all aspect of a computer application system, hardware, software, functionality, and user interface. The lower level encompasses only the user interface defined in a relatively narrow sense.

Application System Design Methodologies

Rubinstein and Hersh (1984) describe the process of system design as occurring in five stages:

- The gathering of information, including market requirements, technical requirements, the current state of the art, existing competing products, industry standards, government regulations, and the capabilities of the system builders. The key element is carrying out a *task analysis* of the activities carried out by the users in their environment.

- System design, including specification of the *external myth* and *conceptual model* the users are to see (see also Heckel, 1982), and the *use model* describing how the system is to be used

- Implementation design and construction, first of a prototype, and then of the system itself

- Testing and evaluation, both informal and formal, of the system

- Delivery of the system, and evaluation of the reactions of the user and the marketplace to it

The process is an iterative one, with various stages repeated several times. Their view is broad and realistic, incorporating a sensitivity to the demands of the marketplace. Further details may be found in the excerpt from their book included as a reading. Rubinstein and Hersh (1987) further develop the concept of the external myth and its use in the process of design.

Shneiderman (1983) presents a somewhat more elaborate, eight stage, project lifecycle, one that stresses the need for the involvement of and the nurturing of the user community:

Initiate project and collect information.
    Organize design team.
    Obtain management, customer, and user participation.
    Determine who the users are and what tasks they perform.
    Conduct interviews with users where possible.
    Submit written questionnaires to users where possible.
    Read practical and academic literature.
    Speak with designers and users of similar systems.
    Estimate costs.
    Prepare schedule with observable milestones.
    Design the testing strategy.
Design semantic structures.
    Define high level goals and middle level requirements.
    Determine reliability and availability needs.
    Specify security, privacy, and integrity constraints.
    Design user-oriented task flow and scenarios for critical tasks.
    Organize operations into transaction units.
    Create cognitive model of data structures.
    Develop cognitive model of operations.
    Obtain management and customer agreement on goals, requirements, and semantic design.
Design syntactic structures.
    Compare alternative display formats.
    Create syntax for operations.
    Design informative feedback for each operation.
    Develop error diagnostics.
    Prepare user aids, help facilities, and tutorials.
    Write user manuals and reference guides.
    Review and evaluate design specifications and revise where necessary.
    Carry out paper and pencil pilot test or field studies with a mock-up or prototype.
Specify physical devices.
    Choose hard or softcopy device.
    Specify keyboard layout.

    Select audio, graphics, or peripheral devices.
    Establish requirements for communications lines.
    Specify system response times and display rates.
    Consider work environment noise, lighting, table space, etc..
    Carry out further pilot tests.
Develop software.
    Use dialogue management tools where available.
    Produce top-down modular design.
    Emphasize modifiability and maintainability.
    Ensure reliability and security.
    Enable user and system performance monitoring.
    Provide adequate system documentation.
    Conduct thorough software test with realistic usage load.
Integrate system and disseminate to user.
    Assure user involvement at every stage.
    Conduct acceptance tests and fine tune the system.
    Field test user and reference manuals.
    Implement a training subsystem or simulator.
    Provide adequate training and consultation.
    Follow phased approach to dissemination and provide time to make modest revisions in response to usage.
Nurture the user community.
    Provide on-site or telephone consultant where possible.
    Offer online consultant where possible.
    Develop online suggestion box and subjective evaluation questionnaire.
    Make user news available online.
    Publish newsletter for users where appropriate.
    Organize user group meetings where possible.
    Respond to user suggestions for improvements.
    Conduct subjective and objective evaluations of the current system and proposed improvements.
    Monitor usage frequencies of permissible operations.
    Track user error frequencies to guide refinement.
Prepare evolutionary plan.
    Design for easy repair and refinement.
    Measure user performance regularly.
    Improve error handling.
    Carry out experiments to assess suggested changes.
    Sample feedback from users by questionnaires and interviews.
    Schedule revisions regularly and inform users in advance.

The evolutionary plan will clearly include some repetition of various aspects of the eight stages. Shneiderman also stresses, quite correctly, that a satisfactory human interface must incorporate proper functionality, must offer reliability, availability, serviceability, security, and integrity, and must be the result of a development process which is on schedule and within budget.

Foley (1984, 1986) identifies five stages of the design process — pre-design, design, review, implementation, and fine-tuning. An important concept is that of the *design review*, in which designers, "typical users," implementors, and independent user-interface design experts carry out a final verification of the design "before implementation begins." Foley also stresses the need for a *user interface architect* to serve as a central design authority for an interface and to serve as an intermediary between the users (the clients) and the implementors (the contractors).

Wasserman has over a period of ten years evolved a comprehensive "User Software Engineering Methodology" for developing interactive information systems. It is described in Wasserman, Pircher, and Shewmake (1986), and in Wasserman, Pircher, Shewmake, and Kersten (1986), the latter included as a reading. The methodology is guided by the goals of functionality, reliability, usability, evolvability, automated support, improved developer productivity, and reusability. The methodology begins with a phase of *requirements analysis*, which includes the development of a data model, specification of the functional requirements, and identification of the user characteristics. Unlike many software engineering methodologies, it then focuses on *external design*, what the system should look like to the user. The human-computer interaction is then prototyped. At this point, the underlying relational database is designed, and a complete functional prototype may be constructed. Although rarely done, a formal specification can then be carried out to assist in the identification and correction of errors. Finally, the prototype can be fleshed out into a production system, including whatever steps of system design, implementation, and testing and verification are thought necessary (Wasserman, 1985a).

Of particular interest is the deliberate intertwining of specification, design, and implementation (see also Swartout and Balzer, 1982) which runs counter to conventional software engineering methodology. The methodology is made possible by the "Unified Support Environment," an elaborate set of supporting programming tools. The system includes the RAPID/USE subsystem (Wasserman and Shewmake, 1982; Wasserman, 1985b) for prototyping the user interface of the interactive information system being designed. We shall return to RAPID/USE, which is a User Interface Management System, in Chapter 12: Programming Techniques and Tools.

Buxton and Shniderman (1980) advance even more strongly the principle that the key to designing an effective human-computer interface is the ability to iterate upon the design:

> It is unlikely that the first implementation of any user interface is going to function as well as it could or should. Under these circumstances, an alternative is to take an iterative approach to design: keep trying until you get it right...
>
> We think of each iteration of a design as being a prototype whose purpose is to test a critical mass of the overall problem. On implementation, each prototype is tested by "guinea-pig" users whose performance is monitored.

Based on this experience, the performance of the prototype is evaluated, and the next iteration planned.

Buxton also asserts the need for powerful and flexible tools for building and prototyping systems. He introduces the concepts of menu systems, directory windows, and graphic potentiometers as essential components of a prototyping system, components which are typical of the kinds of capabilities one finds in modern development toolkits such as those discussed in the next chapter. He also suggests a number of techniques for observation of the qualities and performance of the interface and its users, including some non-verbal techniques — observation by the system, direct observation by the researcher, and observation via video taping; and some verbal techniques — a detailed session commentary by the subject ("thinking out loud"), a report of impressions by the subject, and an interrogation of the subject by the researcher after the session.

How humbling! Do we really need to "keep trying until you get it right"? Gould and Lewis (1985) develop this concept even further in an insightful and influential article included as the last reading of this chapter. Their paper recommends three fundamental principles of design, an *early focus on users and tasks*, *empirical measurement*, and, agreeing with Buxton, *iterative design*. It may appear that these principles are universally agreed upon, but the authors show, based on a survey of system planners, programmers, designers, and developers, that these tenets are neither widely held nor well understood. After elaborating the principles, Gould and Lewis illustrate them with a discussion of how they were applied to the Audio Distribution System (Gould and Boies, 1983, 1984) that is described in our Case Study A: The Design of a Voice Messaging System.

User Interface Design Methodologies

We now turn our attention to two other formulations of user interface design methodologies in the somewhat narrower sense defined above.

An early presentation of a methodology for the design of the user interface of an interactive graphics system is that given in Chapter 28 of the Second Edition of Newman and Sproull (1979). Their procedure begins with a phase of *task analysis*. This is followed by a specification of the user interface in terms of four components: the *user's model*, the *command language*, *feedback*, and *information display*:

> The user interface divides naturally into four components. One of these underlies the other three: this is the *user's model*, the conceptual model formed by the user of the information he manipulates and of the processes he applies to this information. Without this model the user can do little more than blindly follow instructions, like an

inexperienced cook following a recipe. The model enables him to develop, even with little or no knowledge of computer technology, a broad understanding of what the program is doing. With the model's help he can anticipate the effect of his actions and can devise his own strategies for operating the program. Sometimes the design of the user's model is simply a matter of simulating as closely as possible a real world system, so that the user need not develop any model of his own. This is what we would do, for example, in designing an aircraft pilot training system. This approach to the user's model does not always work, however, because simulation of the real world often proves inappropriate or difficult.

Once the user has understood the model, he needs *commands* with which to manipulate it. The system of commands we provide is called *command language* and forms the second component of the user interface. Most of us are familiar with command languages, as many of the machines we use in everyday life — the pocket calculator, the copying machine, the typewriter — have quite extensive systems of commands. That we can learn to use these machines without being conscious of learning a language is a testimonial to the care put into the design of their command languages. Ideally our computer programs should have equally natural command languages.

The third component of the user interface is *feedback*, with which the computer assists the user in operating the program. Feedback comes in many forms: acknowledgement of receipt of commands, explanatory messages, indication of selected objects, and echoing of typed characters. Some forms of feedback are provided mainly to help inexperienced users and can be ignored by experts. On the other hand, some command languages are inherently dependent on feedback; graphical positioning commands, for example, almost always require feedback on the screen in response to the movement of the positioning device.

Feedback helps the user to be sure that his commands are accurately received and fully understood by the program. It tells him little about their real effect. A fourth component, *information display*, is therefore necessary to show him the state of the information he is manipulating. Here we are concerned with organizing the displayed image to convey the information as effectively as possible. The image is a confirmation to the user that his model is correct, and we therefore design it in strict accordance with the model we have chosen. Where the model depends on realism, as in a flight simulator, we must strive for realism in the displayed image; where a more synthetic model is chosen, we may try to reinforce this model by means of well-chosen symbols and graphic imagery in the displayed information.

This subdivision into components is extremely helpful in user-interface design because it enables us both to categorize the problems arising in design and to be more thorough in addressing them. It is also possible to separate the task of user-interface design into smaller subtasks corresponding to the four components. The separation is not a clean one, however, and it is therefore not possible to design any one component independently of the rest. For example, when we design the command language, we must consider what feedback each command should provide, and these feedback techniques must

use similar output conventions to information display. As we design these components, we often return to the user's model to make minor alterations to reflect changes in the command language or in information display. Thus we must constantly shift our focus from one component to another as we proceed with the design of the user interface. Nevertheless we can apply separate strategies and design rules to each component and thus ensure that each of the four components will function satisfactorily.

Other issues enter into user-interface design and must be kept in mind by the designer. For example, throughout the design process the designer must maintain a realistic estimate of the computing and display resources available to him and must ensure that his user interface design does not overtax these resources. At the same time he must keep in mind the user's needs: these are the main driving force behind the design, and must be clearly defined at the outset.

It is therefore wise to precede the design with a phase of *task analysis* in which the user's needs are studied and a set of functional requirements drawn up. Task analysis often involves interviewing prospective users, measuring their performance, and studying their working environment; the results of these studies must then be analyzed. A written report on the task analysis often forms a starting point for the user-interface design.

Of particular value in that Chapter is the inclusion of two detailed examples of user interface specifications each intended for an identical task, that of business forms design. One example is a user interface for a system operating on a black-and-white high performance raster display with a mouse, while the other is for the unfortunately now obsolete storage tube display.

An alternative view of user interface design is that of Foley and van Dam (1982). Like Newman and Sproull, they begin with a phase of task analysis. They then formulate the remaining process of user interface design in terms of a set of four components: *conceptual design*, *semantic design*, *syntactic design*, and *lexical design*.

Concluding Remarks

We have seen a variety of principles, guidelines, and methodologies proposed to aid the designer of interactive computer systems. Despite the diversity of approach, there are three themes that seem to emerge strongly in almost all the formulations — task analysis, knowledge of the user, and iterative design.

We cannot sufficiently emphasize the need for a careful analysis of the *task* for which the system is intended. This must begin with a proper identification of the functions which are to be computerized (recall Chapter 2: The Socio/Political Environment, and see also Goransson et al., 1987). Eason (1981) notes the importance of proper task analysis, and shows how failure to do so can result in system disuse, misuse, and abuse, in user frustration and apathy, and in modification of the task the user is carrying out to fit the constraints imposed by the software. The problem of task analysis is particularly difficult, Eason (1980) argues, citing evidence on computer usage by managers, because employment of the computer alters the user's perception of her task and often leads to changes in the nature of the task. Mountford (1986) presents a method for task analysis, then shows how it may be applied in establishing the role of new technologies in existing task environments.

A variety of approaches to task analysis have been proposed over the past fifteen years, and are surveyed by Wilson, Barnard, and MacLean (to appear). The authors analyze the degree to which each technique deals with user knowledge, tries to account for "user centered dynamics" such as goals, takes into account "cognitively salient limitations" such as human memory and processing capability, and is usable.

A second universal theme is, to know the user and her characteristics, and to tailor the design accordingly. Carey (1982), for example, stresses the need to understand user differences in the nature of the task and in the conception of the task, in the user's cognitive model of the system, and in the amount and kind of prior training that the user has received.

The third theme is to acknowledge our inability to predict with accuracy what will work well in practice, and therefore to use experience with versions as a basis for successive iteration towards a better design. This philosophy is pushed to its limit in the "User Derived Interface" of Wixon, Whiteside, Good, and Jones (1983), Good, Whiteside, Wixon, and Jones (1984), and Wixon and Whiteside (1985). A system's command language is derived by extending it repeatedly on the basis of commands given by users and intercepted by hidden operators who respond to those instructions that the system is not yet equipped to handle. The articles show how a prototype electronic mail system was progressively able to handle an increasing proportion of user input. The work illustrates the extent to which a system's interface can be based on the user's "natural" way of doing things, although the dangers of too great a reliance on user preconceptions and specifications is pointed out by Wright and Bason (1982).

These three themes, however, still cannot tell us how to achieve good design. In the real world, design practice is patterned after no single methodology or conventional wisdom (Rosson, Maass, and Kellogg, 1987). Noting that design is an art as well as a science, Carroll and Rosson (1985) characterize design activity in terms of four major propositions:

- Design is a "process." It is neither a state nor an artifact that can be well described as a static entity.

- The design process is "non-hierarchical," involving both bottom-up and top-down activity.

- The design process is "radically transformational," and results in the development of interim and partial solutions that usually are not part of the final design.

- Design, in attempting to satisfy an initial set of goals, always results in "the discovery of new goals."

Given its complexity, and its mystery, how are we to proceed? The answer is implicit in the process of iterative design — *evaluation*, a topic we began in Chapter 4: Empirical Evaluation of User Interfaces. We guide the process of design by a thorough program of behavioural testing and evaluation at numerous stages in the process. One such program is that developed by the Committee on Human Factors of the National Research Council, Anderson and Reitman Olson (Editors) (1985). Participants in the Workshop on Software Human Factors characterized the software product development cycle as consisting of stages of analysis, design, and implementation, with human factors considerations prominent in each of the stages. We include as a reading their enumeration of appropriate human factors methods.

The methods cited in this reading are not the only ones possible. Long, Hammond, Barnard, Morton, and Clark (1983) propose the use of an observational technique called *social information generation*, a kind of user focus group followed by a systematic and structured analysis of participant utterances. Carroll and Rosson (1985) propose the application of *usability specifications*, which they define as "precise, testable statements of performance goals for typical users, carrying out tasks typical of their projected use of the system." Good, Spine, Whiteside, and George (1986) propose *user-derived impact analysis*, in which system usability is measured, sources of user difficulty are analyzed, and system enhancements and their likely usability improvements are proposed, some of which are then carried out. The cycle is then repeated until certain usability goals are met. Other more concrete descriptions of usability testing can be found in Eason (1984), Bury (1985), Akscyn and McCracken (1985), Yoder, McCracken, and Akscyn (1985), and Mills et al. (1986).

Ultimately, the success or failure of all of these methods may depend upon the degree to which they can be harmoniously integrated into the established software development cycles and the extent to which they can be justified economically. Grudin, Ehrlich, and Shriner (1987) and Mantei and Teorey (1987) discuss the former issue. Mantei and Teorey (1987) is also one of the first attempts to address the issue of cost/benefit analyses of human factors activities.

Readings

Norman, D. (1983). Design Principles for Human-Computer Interfaces. *Proceedings of CHI '83*, 1-10.

Rubinstein, Richard & Hersh, Harry (1984). Design Philosophy. Chapter 2 of *The Human Factor: Designing Computer Systems for People*, Burlington, MA: Digital Press, 12-22.

Wasserman, A.I., Pircher, P.A., Shewmake, D.T., & Kersten, M.L. (1986). Developing Interactive Information Systems with the User Software Engineering Methodology. *IEEE Transactions on Software Engineering* SE-12(2), February 1986, 326-345.

Gould, John D. & Lewis, Clayton (1985). Designing for Usability: Key Principles and What Designers Think. *Communications of the ACM* 28(3), 300-311.

Anderson, Nancy S. & Reitman Olson, Judith (Eds.) (1985). *Methods for Designing Software to Fit Human Needs and Capabilities*, Proceedings of the Workshop on Software Human Factors, Committee on Human Factors, Commission on Behavioural and Social Sciences and Education, National Research Council, Washington, D.C.: National Academy Press, only pp. 1-34 included here.

References

Anderson, Nancy S. & Reitman Olson, Judith (Eds.) (1985). *Methods for Designing Software to Fit Human Needs and Capabilities*, Proceedings of the Workshop on Software Human Factors, Committee on Human Factors, Commission on Behavioural and Social Sciences and Education, National Research Council, Washington, D.C.: National Academy Press.

Akscyn, Robert M. & McCracken, Donald L. (1985). ZOG and USS CARL VINSON: Lessons in System Development. In Shackel, B. (Ed.), *Human-Computer Interaction — Interact '84*, North Holland: Elsevier Science Publishers B.V., 901-906.

Baecker, R. (1980). Human-Computer Interactive Systems: A State-of-the-Art Review. In Kolers, P.A., Wrolstad, M.E. & Bouma, H. (Eds.), *Processing of Visible Language* 2, New York: Plenum Press, 423-443.

Baecker, R., Buxton, W., & Reeves, W. (1979). Towards Facilitating Graphical Interaction: Some Examples from Computer-Aided Musical Composition. *Proceedings of the 6th Canadian Man-Computer Communications Conference*, May 1979, 197-207.

Barnard, P.J., Hammond, N.V., Morton, J., Long, J.B., & Clark, I.A. (1981). Consistency and Compatibility in Human-Computer Dialogue. *International Journal of Man-Machine Studies* 15, 87-134.

Bury, Kevin F. (1985). The Iterative Development of Usable Computer Interfaces. In Shackel, B. (Ed.), *Human-Computer Interaction — Interact '84*, North Holland: Elsevier Science Publishers B.V., 743-748.

Buxton, W. & Shniderman, R. (1980). Iteration and the Design of the Human-Computer Interface. *Proc. of the 13th Annual Meeting of the Human Factors Association of Canada*, 72-81. By permission of Human Factors Association of Canada / Association Canadienne d'Ergonomie.

Carey, Tom (1982). User Difference in Interface Design. *IEEE Computer*, November 1982, 14-20.

Carroll, John M. & Rosson, Mary Beth (1985). Usability

Specifications as a Tool in Iterative Development. In Hartson, H. Rex (Ed.), *Advances in Human-Computer Interaction*, Vol. 1, Norwood, N.J.: Ablex Publishing Corp., 1-28.

Davis, E.G. & Swezey, R.W. (1983). Human Factors Guidelines in Computer Graphics: A Case Study. *International Journal of Man-Machine Studies* 18, 113-133.

Eason, K.D. (1980). Computer Information Systems and Managerial Tasks. In Bjørn-Andersen, N. (Ed.), *The Human Side of Information Processing*, North Holland: North Holland Publishing Co., 133-149.

Eason, K.D. (1981). A Task-Tool Analysis of Manager-Computer Interaction. In Shackel, B. (Ed.), *Man-Computer Interaction: Human Factors Aspects of Computers and People*, Sijthoff & Noordhoff, 289-307.

Eason, K.D. (1984). Towards the Experimental Study of Usability. *Behaviour and Information Technology* 3(2), 133-143.

Engel, S.E. & Granda, R.E. (1975). Guidelines for Man/Display Interfaces. *Technical Report* TR 00.2720, Poughkeepsie, NY.: IBM.

Foley, James D. (1984). Managing the Design of User-Computer Interfaces. *Computer Graphics '84*, National Computer Graphics Association Conference Proceedings: Volume 2, 436-451.

Foley, James D. (1986). *Managing the Design of User-Computer Interfaces*, Computer Graphics Consultants, Inc., Washington, D.C.

Foley, J.D. & van Dam, A. (1982). *Fundamentals of Interactive Computer Graphics*, Reading, Mass: Addison-Wesley Publishing Company.

Foley, J.D. & Wallace, V.L. (1974). The Art of Natural Graphic Man-Machine Conversation. *Proceedings of the IEEE* 62(4), 462-471.

Good, M., Spine, T.M., Whiteside, J. & George, P. (1986). User-Derived Impact Analysis as a Tool for Usability Engineering. *CHI '86 Proceedings*, 241-246.

Good, M., Whiteside, J., Wixon, D. & Jones, S. (1984). Building a User-Derived Interface. *Communications of the ACM* 27(10), October 1984, 1032-1043.

Goransson, Bengt, Lind, Mats, Petterson, Else, Sandblad, Bengt & Schwalbe, Patrik (1987). The Interface is Often Not the Problem. *CHI+GI '87 Proceedings*, 133-136.

Gould, John D. & Boies, Stephen J. (1983). Human Factors Challenges in Creating a Principal Support Office System — The Speech Filing Approach. *ACM Transactions on Office Information Systems* 1(4), 273-298.

Gould, John D. & Boies, Stephen J. (1984). Speech Filing — An Office System for Principals. *IBM Systems Journal* 23(1), 65-81.

Gould, John D. & Lewis, Clayton (1985). Designing for Usability: Key Principles and What Designers Think. *Communications of the ACM* 28(3), 300-311.

Grudin, Jonathan, Ehrlich, Susan F. & Shriner, Rick (1987). Positioning Human Factors in the User Interface Development Chain. *CHI+GI '87 Proceedings*, 125-131.

Hansen, Wilfred J. (1971). User Engineering Principles for Interactive Systems. *AFIPS Conference Proceedings* 39 Montvale, N.J.: AFIPS Press, 523-532.

Heckel, Paul (1982). *The Elements of Friendly Software Design*, New York: Warner Books, Inc.

Long, J., Hammond, N., Barnard, P., Morton, J. & Clark, I. (1983). Introducing the Interactive Computer at Work. The Users' View. *Behaviour and Information Technology* 2(1), 39-106.

Maguire, Martin (1982). An Evaluation of Published Reccommendations on the Design of Man-Computer Dialogues. *International Journal of Man-Machine Studies* 16(3), 237-261.

Mantei, Marilyn M. & Teorey, Toby J. (1987). CostBenefit Analysis for Incorporated Human Factors in the Software Lifecycle. Unpublished manuscript.

Mills, C.B., Bury, K.F., Reed, P., Roberts, T.L., Tognazzini, B., Wichansky, A. & Gould, J. (1986). Usability Testing in the Real World. *CHI '86 Proceedings*, 212-215.

Mosier, Jane N. & Smith, Sidney L. (1986). Application of Guidelines for Designing User Interface Software. *Behaviour and Information Technology* 5(1), 39-46.

Mountford, S. Joy (1986). A Methodology for Selecting Candidate Voice Technology Tasks. Unpublished manuscript presented at the ACM SIGCHI Workshop on Mixed Modes of Interaction, Key West, Florida, December 1986.

Newman, William M. & Sproull, Robert F. (1979). User Interface Design. Chapter 28 in *Principles of Interactive Computer Graphics*, Second Edition, New York: McGraw-Hill Book Company, 443-478. © 1979, McGraw-Hill Book Company, reprinted with permission.

Norman, D. (1983). Design Principles for Human-Computer Interfaces. *Proceedings of CHI '83*, 1-10.

Rosson, Mary Beth, Maass, Susanne & Kellogg, Wendy A. (1987). Designing for Designers: An Analysis of Design Practice in the Real World. *CHI+GI '87 Proceedings*, 137-142.

Rubinstein, Richard & Hersh, Harry M. (1984). Design Philosophy. Chapter 2 in *The Human Factor: Designing Computer Systems for People*, Burlington, MA.: Digital Press, 12-22.

Rubinstein, Richard & Hersh, Harry M. (1987). A Model for Effective Human Interface Design. Unpublished manuscript.

Shneiderman, Ben (1983). Human Engineering Management Plan for Interactive Systems. *Proceedings of the IEEE Compcon 83 Conference*, Washington, D.C., Sept. 1983, 230-238.

Shneiderman, Ben (1986). *Designing the User Interface: Strategies for Effective Human-Computer Interaction*, Addison-Wesley Publishing Company.

Smith, S.L. (1980). Requirements Definition and Design Guidelines for the Man-Machine Interface in C3 System Acquisition. *Technical Report* ESD-TR-80-122, Hanscom Air Force Base, MA: USAF Electronic Systems Division, NTIS No. AD A087 258.

Smith, S.L. (1981). Man-Machine Interface (MMI) Requirements Definition and Design Guidelines: A Progress Report. *Technical Report* ESD-TR-81-113, Hanscom Air Force Base, MA.: USAF Electronic Systems Divison, NTIS No. AD A096 705.

Smith, S.L. (1982). User-System Interface Design for Computer-Based Information Systems. *Technical Report* ESD-TR-82-132, Hanscom Air Force Base, MA.: USAF Electronic Systems Divison, NTIS No. AD A115 853.

Smith, S.L. (1986). Standards Versus Guidelines for Designing User Interface Software. *Behaviour and Information Technology* 5(1), 47-61.

Smith, S.L. & Aucella, A.F. (1983). Design Guidelines for the User Interface to Computer-Based Information Systems. *Technical Report* ESD-.-83-122, Hanscom Air Force Base, MA: USAF Electronic Systems Divison, NTIS No. AD A127 345.

Smith, S.L. & Mosier, J.N. (1984). Design Guidelines for User-System Interface Software. *Technical Report* ESD-TR-84-190, Hanscom Air Force Base, MA: USAF Electronic Systems Divison, NTIS No. AD A154 907.

Swartout, W. & Balzer, R. (1982). On the Inevitable Intertwining of Specification and Implementation. *Communications of the ACM* 25(7), July 1982, 438-440.

Wasserman, A.I. (1985a). Developing Interactive Information Systems with the User Software Engineering Methodology. *Human-Computer Interaction — Interact '84*, Amsterdam: North-Holland, 611-617.

Wasserman, A.I. (1985b). Extending State Transition Diagrams for the Specification of Human-Computer Interaction. *IEEE Transactions on Software Engineering* SE-11(8), August 1985, 699-713.

Wasserman, A.I., Pircher, P.A., & Shewmake, D.T. (1986). Building Reliable Interactive Information Systems. *IEEE Transactions on Software Engineering* SE-12(1), January 1986, 147-156.

Wasserman, A.I., Pircher, P.A., Shewmake, D.T. & Kersten, M.L. (1986). Developing Interactive Information Systems with the User Software Engineering Methodology. *IEEE Transactions on Software Engineering* SE-12(2), February 1986, 326-345.

Wasserman, A.I. & Shewmake, D.T. (1982). Rapid Prototyping of Interactive Information Systems. *ACM Software Engineering Notes* 7(5), December 1982, 171-180.

Wilson, M.D., Barnard, P.J. & MacLean, A. (to appear). Knowledge in Task Analysis for Human-Computer Systems. In Green, T.R.G., Hoc, J.M., Murray, D. & Van Der Veer, G. (Eds.), *Working with Computers: Theory Versus Outcome*, London: Academic Press.

Wixon, D., Whiteside, J., Good, M., & Jones, S. (1983). Building a User-Defined Interface. *CHI '83 Proceedings*, 24-27.

Wixon, D., Whiteside, J., Good, M., & Jones, S. (1984). Building a User-Derived Interface. *Communications of the ACM* 27(10), 1032-1043.

Wixon, D. & Whiteside, J. (1985). Engineering for Usability: Lessons from the User Derived Interface. *CHI '85 Proceedings*, 144-147.

Wright, P. & Bason, G. (1982). Detour Routes to Usability: A Comparison of Alternative Approaches to Multipurpose Software Design. *International Journal of Man-Machine Studies* 18, 391-400.

Yoder, E., McCracken, D., & Akscyn, R. (1985). Instrumenting a Human-Computer Interface For Development and Evaluation. In Shackel, B. (Ed.), *Human-Computer Interaction — Interact '84*, North Holland: Elsevier Science Publishers B.V., 907-912.

DESIGN PRINCIPLES FOR
HUMAN-COMPUTER INTERFACES

Donald A. Norman
Department of Psychology
and
Institute for Cognitive Science C-015
University of California, San Diego
La Jolla, California 92093

ABSTRACT

If the field of Human Factors in Computer Systems is to be a success it must develop design principles that are useful, principles that apply across a wide range of technologies. In the first part of this paper I discuss some the properties that useful principles should have. While I am at it, I warn of the dangers of the tar pits and the sirens of technology. We cannot avoid these dangers entirely, for were we to do so, we would fail to cope with the real problems and hazards of the field.

The second part of the paper is intended to illustrate the first part through the example of tradeoff analysis. Any single design technique is apt to have its virtues along one dimension compensated by deficiencies along another. Tradeoff analysis provides a quantitative method of assessing tradeoff relations for two attributes x_i and x_j by first determining the *User Satisfaction* function for each, $U(x)$, then showing how $U(x_i)$ trades off against $U(x_j)$. In general, the *User Satisfaction* for a system is given by the weighted sum of the *User Satisfaction* values for the attributes. The analysis is used to examine two different tradeoffs of information versus time and editor workspace versus menu size. Tradeoffs involving command languages versus menu-based systems, choices of names, and handheld computers versus workstations are examined briefly.

If we intend a science of human-computer interaction, it is essential that we have principles from which to derive the manner of the interaction between person and computer. It is easy to devise experiments to test this idea or that, to compare and contrast alternatives, or to evaluate the quality of the latest technological offering. But we must aspire to more than responsiveness to the current need. The technology upon which the human-computer interface is built changes rapidly relative to the time with which psychological experimentation yields answers. If we do not take care, today's answers apply only to yesterday's concerns.

Our design principles must be of sufficient generality that they will outlast the technological demands of the moment. But there is a second and most important criterion: the principles must yield sufficiently precise answers that they can actually be of use: Statements that proclaim

"Consider the user" are valid, but worthless. We need more precise principles.

This new field — Human Factors in Computer Systems — contains an unruly mixture of theoretical issues and practical problems. Just as it is important that our theoretical concerns have breadth, generality, and usability, so too is it important that we understand the practical problems. We are blessed with an exciting, rapidly developing technology that is controlled through the time consuming and addictive procedure called programming. There are traps for the unwary: let me tell you about them.

Tar Pits and Sirens of Technology

As with most unexplored territories, dangers await: tar pits and sirens. The former lie hidden in the path, ready to

This research was supported by Contract N00014-79-C-0323, NR 667-437 with the Personnel and Training Research Programs of the Office of Naval Research and by a grant from the System Development Foundation. Requests for reprints should be sent to Donald A. Norman, Institute for Cognitive Science C-015; University of California, San Diego; La Jolla, California, 92093, USA.

These ideas have benefited greatly by interactions with the UCSD Human-Machine Interaction project, especially Liam Bannon, Allen Cypher, Steve Draper, Dave Owen, Mary Riley, and Paul Smolensky. Comments on a draft of the paper by Danny Bobrow, Jonathan Grudin, Peter Jackson, Allen Munro, and Julie Norman resulted in major improvements of the ideas and exposition.

trap the unwary. The latter stand openly, luring their prey to destruction with bewitching sweetness. I see too many of you trapped by one or the other.

To program or not to program, that is the question. Whether it is nobler to build systems or to remain pure, arguing for abstract principles independent of the technology. Build systems and you face the tar pits, writing programs whose sole justification is to support the writing of programs, eating up work-years, eating up resources, forever making "one last improvement." When you finish, others may look and nod, saying, "yes, how clever." But will anything general be learned? Will the next technological leap pass it by? Programming can be a pit that grabs the unwary and holds them down. While in the pit they may struggle and attract attention. Afterwards, there may be no visible trace of their passing.

Alternatively, you may be seduced by the sirens of technology. High resolution screens, color, three-dimensions, mice, eye-movement detectors, voice-in, voice-out, touch-in, feelers-out; you name it, it will happen. Superficial pleasure, but not necessarily any lasting result. What general lessons will have been learned?

Damned if you do, damned if you don't. The pure in heart will avoid the struggles, detour the tar pits, blind their eyes to the sirens. "We want general principles that are independent of technology," they proclaim. But then what should they study? If the studies are truly independent of the technology, they are apt to have little applicability. How can you develop useful principles unless you understand the powers and weaknesses of the technology, the pressures and constraints of real design? Study a general problem such as the choice of editor commands and someone will develop a new philosophy of editing, or a new technological device that makes the old work irrelevant. The problem is that in avoiding the paths that contain the tar, you may never reach any destination; in avoiding temptation, you remain pure, but irrelevant. Life is tar pits and sirens. Real design of real systems is filled with the messy constraints of life: time pressures, budget limitations, a lack of information, abilities, and energy. We are apt not to be useful unless we understand these constraints and provide tools that can succeed despite them, or better, that can help alleviate them. Experimental psychology is not noted for its contributions to life; the study of human-computer interface should be.

Four Strategies for Providing Design Principles

What can we accomplish? One thing that is needed is a way of introducing good design principles into the design stage. How can we do this? Let me mention four ways.

1: Try to impress upon the designer the seriousness of the matter, to develop an awareness that users of systems have special needs that must be taken account of. The problem with this approach is that although such awareness is essential, good intentions do not necessarily lead to good design.

Designers need to know what to do and how to do it.

2: Provide methods and guidelines. Quantitative methods are better than qualitative ones, but all are better than none at all. These methods and guidelines must be usable, they must be justifiable, they must have face validity. The designer is apt to be suspicious of many of our intentions. Moreover, unless we have worked out these guidelines with skill, they will be useless when confronted with the realities of design pressures. The rules must not only be justified by reasonable criteria, they must also appear to be reasonable: designers are not apt to care about the discussions in the theoretical journals.

3: Provide software tools for interface design. This can be a major positive force. Consider the problem of enforcing consistent procedures across all components of a system. With appropriate software tools, consistency can be enforced, if only because it will be easier to use the tools rather than to do without them. We can ensure reasonable design by building the principles into the tools.

4: Separate the interface design from other programming tasks. Make the interface a separate data module, communicating with programs and the operating system through a standardized communication channel and language. Interface design should be its own discipline, for it requires sophistication in both programming and human behavior. If we had the proper modularization, then the interface designer could modify the interface independently of the rest of the system. Similarly, many system changes would not require modification of the interface. The ideal method would be for software tools to be developed that can be used in the interface design by non-programmers. I imagine the day when I can self-tailor my own interface, carrying the specification around on a micro-chip embedded in a plastic card. Walk up to any computer terminal in the world, insert my card, and *voila*, it is my personalized terminal.

I recommend that we move toward all of these things. I have ordered the list in terms of my preferences: last being most favored; first being easiest and most likely today. Each is difficult, each requires work.

There has been progress towards the development of appropriate design methods. One approach is demonstrated through the work of Card, Moran, and Newell (1983) who developed formal quantitative methods of assessing a design. Their techniques provide tools for the second of my suggested procedures. Card, Moran, and Newell emphasize the micro-processes of interaction with a computer — for example, analysis at the level of keystrokes. At UCSD, we are attempting to develop other procedures. In the end, the field will need many methods and guidelines, each complementing and supplementing the others. Let me now describe briefly the approach that we are following, then present one of our techniques — the tradeoff analysis — in detail.

The UCSD User Centered System Design Project

At UCSD we have a large and active group attempting to put our philosophy into practice. Our goal is to have pure heart and clear mind, even while feet and loins are in tar and temptation. Some of our initial activities are being presented in this conference: Bannon, Cypher, Greenspan, and Monty (1983); O'Malley, Smolensky, Bannon, Conway, Graham, Sokolov, and Monty (1983); Root and Draper (1983). Other examples have been published elsewhere or are still undergoing final development (Norman, 1983a, b, c).

The principles that we follow take the form of statements plus elaboration, the statements becoming slogans that guide the research. The primary principle is summarized by the slogan that has become the name of the project: *User Centered System Design*. The slogan emphasizes our belief that to develop design principles relevant to building human-machine interfaces, it is necessary to focus on the user of the system. This focus leads us naturally to a set of topics and methods. It means we must observe how people make use of computer systems. It brings to the fore the study of the *mental models* that users form of the systems with which they interact. This, in turn, leads to three related concepts: the designer's view of the system — the *conceptual model*; the image that the system presents to the user — the *system image*; and third, the *mental model* the user develops of the system, mediated to a large extent by the system image. We believe that it is the task of the designer to establish a conceptual image of the system that is appropriate for the task and the class of users, then to construct the system so that the system image guides the user to acquire a mental model that matches the designer's conceptual model.

The Slogans

There are five major slogans that guide the work:

- There are no simple answers, only tradeoffs.

- There are no errors: all operations are iterations towards a goal.

- Low level protocols are critical.

- Activities are structured.

- Information retrieval dominates activity.

There are no simple answers, only tradeoffs. A central theme of our work is that, in design, there are no correct answers, only tradeoffs. Each application of a design principle has its strengths and weaknesses; each principle must be interpreted in a context. One of our goals is to make the tradeoffs explicit. This point will be the topic of the second half of the paper.

All operations are iterations towards a goal. A second theme is that all actions of users should be considered as part of their attempt to accomplish their goals. Thus, even when there is an error, it should be viewed as an attempt by the user to get to the goal. Typing mistakes or illegal statements can be thought of as an approximation. The task for the designer, then, is to consider each input as a starting point and to provide appropriate assistance to allow efficient modification. In this way, we aid the user in rapid convergence to the desired goal. An important implication of this philosophy is that the users' intentions be knowable. In some cases we believe this can be done by having the users state intentions explicitly. Because many commands confound intentions and actions, intentions may substitute for commands.

Low level protocols are critical. By "protocol," we mean the procedures to be followed during the conduct of a particular action or session, this meaning being derived from the traditional meaning of protocol as "a code of diplomatic or military etiquette or precedence." Low level protocols refer to the actual operations performed by the user — button pushes, keypresses, or mouse operation — and these permeate the entire use of the system. If these protocols can be made consistent, then a major standardization takes place across all systems.

Activities are structured. User actions have an implicit grouping corresponding to user goals; these goals may be interrelated in various ways. Thus, a subgoal of a task is related to the main task in a different way than is a diversion, although both may require temporary cessation of the main task, the starting up of new tasks, and eventual return to the main one. We believe the grouping of user goals should be made explicit, both to the user and to the system, and that doing so will provide many opportunities for improved management of the interaction. For example, the system could constrain interpretation of user inputs by the context defined by the current activity, the system could remind users of where they are as they progress through a collection of tasks, or, upon request, it could provide suggestions of how to accomplish the current task by suggesting possible sequences of actions. The philosophy is to structure activities and actions so that the users perceive themselves as selecting among a set of related, structured operations, with the set understood and supported intelligently by the system (see Bannon, Cypher, Greenspan, & Monty, 1983).

Information retrieval dominates activity. Using a computer system involves stages of activities that include forming an intention, choosing an action, specifying that action to the system, and evaluating the outcome. These activities depend heavily upon the strengths and weaknesses of human short- and long-term memory. This means that we place emphasis upon appropriate design of file and directory structures, command "workbenches," and the ability to get information, instruction, and help on the different aspects of the system. We are studying various representational structures, including semantic networks, schema structures of both conventional and "additive memory" form, browsers, hyper-text structures, and other retrieval aids (see O'Malley, Smolensky, Bannon, Conway, Graham, Sokolov & Monty, 1983).

A Demonstration System

This is where we traverse the tar pits. We feel it essential that our ideas be tested within a working system, not only because we feel that the real constraints of developing a full, usable system are important design considerations that must be faced, but also because we believe that full evaluation can only take place within the bounds of a complete, working environment. Therefore, we intend to construct a test and demonstration system based around a modern workstation using the UNIX operating system. UNIX was chosen because it provides a rich, powerful operating environment. However, because UNIX was designed for the professional programmer, unsophisticated users have great trouble with it, providing a rich set of opportunities for our research.

Although we intend that our design principles will be applicable to any system regardless of the particular hardware being used, many of the concepts are effective only on high-resolution displays that allow multiple windows on the screen and that use simple pointing devices. These displays allow for a considerable improvement in the design of human-computer interfaces. We see no choice but to brave the sirens of technology. The capabilities of the hardware factor into the tradeoff relationships. We intend the demonstration systems to show how the tradeoffs in design choices interact with the technology.

Tradeoffs in Design

Now let us examine one of our proposals — tradeoffs — as a prototype of a quantitative design rule. It is well known that different tasks and classes of users have different needs and requirements. No single interface method can satisfy all. Any single design technique is apt to have its virtues along one dimension compensated by deficiencies along another. Each technique provides a set of tradeoffs. The design choices depend upon the technology being used, the class of users, the goals of the design, and which aspects of interface should gain, which should lose. This focus on the tradeoffs emphasizes that the design problem must be looked at as a whole, not in isolated pieces, for the optimal choice for one part of the problem will probably not be optimal for another. According to this view, there are no correct answers, only tradeoffs among alternatives.

The Prototypical Tradeoff: Information Versus Time

One basic tradeoff pervades many design issues:

Factors that increase informativeness tend to decrease the amount of available workspace and system responsiveness.

On the one hand, the more informative and complete the display, the more useful when the user has doubts or lacks understanding. On the other hand, the more complete the display, the longer it takes to be displayed and the more

space it must occupy physically. This tradeoff of amount of information versus space and time appears in many guises and is one of the major interface issues that must be handled. To appreciate its importance, one has only to examine a few recent commercial offerings, highly touted for their innovative (and impressive) human factors design that were intended to make the system easy and pleasurable to use, but which so degraded system response time that serious user complaints resulted.

It is often stated that current computer systems do not provide beginning users with sufficient information. However, the long, informative displays or sequence of questions, options, or menus that may make a system usable by the beginner are disruptive to the expert who knows exactly what action is to be specified and wishes to minimize the time and mental effort required to do the specification. We pit the expert's requirement for ease of specification against the beginner's requirement for knowledge.

I approach this problem by tackling the following questions:

- How can we specify the gain in user satisfaction that results from increasing the size of a menu;

- How do we specify the user satisfaction for the size of the workspace in a text editor;

- How can we specify the loss in user satisfaction from the increase in time to generate the display and decrease in available workspace;

- How can we select menu size, workspace, and response time, when each variable affects the others?

I propose that we answer the question by use of a psychological measure of *User Satisfaction*. This allows us to determine the impact of changing *physical* parameters upon the *psychological* variable of user satisfaction. Once we know how each dimension of choice affects user satisfaction, then we can directly assess the tradeoffs among the dimensions.

Example: Menu Size and Display Time

Let $U(x)$, the user satisfaction for attribute x, be given by a power function, $U(x) = kx^p$. (In Norman, 1983c, I give more details of the method. See Stevens, 1974, for a review of the power function in Psychology.) For the examples in this paper I used the method of magnitude production to estimate parameters.

User preference for menu size. The preferred amount of information must vary with the task, but informal experiments with a variety of menus and tasks suggest that for many situations, about 300 characters is reasonable: I assigned it a satisfaction value of 50. This is the size menu that can be requested for our laboratory's computer mail program ("msg"). It serves as a reminder for 26 single-letter mnemonic commands. To do the power function estimates,

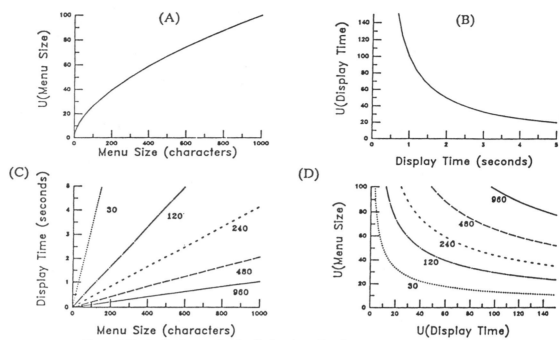

Figure 1. Tradeoff of menu size for display time. Panels A and B show User Satisfaction for menu size, $U(S) = 1.9S^{0.6}$, and display time, $U(T) = 100T^{-1}$, respectively. Panel C shows display time as a function of menu size, $T = S/\beta$, for different values of display rate, β (specified in *characters/second*). Panel D shows the tradeoff between $U(S)$ and $U(T)$ for different values of display rate (β).

I examined a variety of menus of different sizes for the message system (thereby keeping the task the same). I estimated that the menu size would have to increase to half the normal video terminal screen (1000 characters) in order to double my satisfaction. This is a typical result of psychological scaling; a substantial increase of the current value is required to make the increase worthwhile. If $U(300) = 50$ and $U(1000) = 100$, then the parameters of the power function are $k = 1.9$ and $p = 0.6$: $U(S) = 1.9S^{0.6}$.

User preference for response time. There already exists some literature on user satisfaction for response time: the judgements of "acceptable" response times given by Shneiderman (1980, p 228: the times are taken from Miller, 1968). The times depend upon the task being performed. For highly interactive tasks, where the system has just changed state and the users are about to do a new action, 2.0 seconds seems appropriate. I determined that I would be twice as satisfied with a response time of 1 second. Therefore, $U(2\ sec) = 50$ and $U(1\ sec) = 100$. For these values, the power function becomes $U(T) = 100/T$ ($k = 100$, $= -1$).

Size of menu and display time. We need one more thing to complete the tradeoff analysis: the relationship between menu size (S) and the time to present the information (T). In general, time to present a display is a linear function of S: $T = \sigma + S/\beta$, where S is measured in characters, β is the display rate in characters per second (cps) and σ is system response time.

The tradeoff of menu size for display time. Knowledge of $U(S)$, $U(T)$, and the relationship between S

and T, lets us determine the tradeoff between User Satisfaction for size of the menu and for time to display the information: $U(S)$ versus $U(T)$. If $\sigma << S/\beta$, then we can probably ignore σ, letting $T = S/\beta$. This lets us solve the tradeoff exactly. [1] If the two power functions are given by $U(S) = aS^p$ and $U(T) = bT^q$, then $U(S) = kU(T)^{p/q}$, where $k = \frac{a}{b^{p/q}}\beta^p$. The tradeoff relationship using the parameters estimated for menus is shown in Figure 1.

Maximizing Total User Satisfaction

Let overall satisfaction for the system, $U(system)$, be given by the weighted sum of the $U(x_i)$ values for each of its attributes, x_i: $U(system) = \sum \omega_i U(x_i)$, where ω_i is the weight for the *i-th* attribute. When there are only two attributes, x_1 and x_2, if we hold $U(system)$ constant at some value C, we can determine the *iso-satisfaction* line: $U(x_1) = \frac{C}{\omega_1} - \frac{\omega_2}{\omega_1}U(x_2)$. Thus, the iso-satisfaction functions appear on the tradeoff graphs as straight lines with a slope of $-\omega_2/\omega_1$, with higher lines representing higher values of $U(system)$.

If the tradeoff functions are concave downward (as are some in later figures), the maximum satisfaction occurs where the slope of the tradeoff function is tangent to the iso-satisfaction function: that is, when the slope of the tradeoff function $= -\omega_2/\omega_1$. In this case, maximum satisfaction occurs at some compromise between the two variables.

---

1. Letting $\sigma = 0$ simplifies the tradeoff relations, but this is not a necessary assumption. If system response time is slow, then σ should be reinstated: the tradeoff can still be be determined quite simply.

If the tradeoff functions are concave upward (as in Figure 1), then the *minimum* satisfaction occurs where the iso-satisfaction curves are tangent to the tradeoff functions. Maximum satisfaction occurs by maximizing one of the two attributes. The expert, for whom $\omega_T/\omega_S >> 1$, will not sacrifice time for a menu. The beginner, for whom $\omega_T/\omega_S << 1$, will sacrifice display time in order to get as big a menu as possible. For intermediate cases between that of the extreme expert or beginner, the optimum solution is still either to maximize menu size or to minimize display time, but the user might be indifferent as to which of these two was preferred. These conclusions apply to the tradeoff functions of Figure 1D regardless of display rate, as long as the curves are concave upward.[2]

These analyses say that the tradeoff solution that one tends to think of first — to compromise between time and menu size by presenting a small menu at some medium amount of workspace — actually provides the least amount of total satisfaction. Satisfaction is maximized by an all or none solution. The all-or-none preference applies only to tradeoff functions that are concave upward, such as that between menu size and display time. Later we shall see that when time is not relevant, the analysis of the tradeoff between menu size and workspace predicts that even experts will sacrifice some workspace for a menu.

Workspace

Available workspace refers to the amount of room left on the screen after the menu (or other information) is displayed. This is especially important where the menu stays on the screen while normal work continues. The tradeoff is sensitive to screen size. If we had a screen which could display 60 lines of text, using 6 lines to show the current state of the system and a small menu of choices would not decrease usability much. But if the screen could only display 8 lines at a time, then using 6 of them for this purpose would be quite detrimental.

User preference function for workspace. The user preference function for workspace clearly depends upon the nature of the task: some tasks — such as issuing a command — may only require a workspace of 1 line, others — such as file or text editing — could use unlimited workspace. Let us consider the workspace preferences for text editing of manuscripts. The most common editors can only show 24 lines, each of 80 characters: 1920 character positions. I let $U(1920) = 50$. To estimate the workspace that would double the value, I imagined working with screen editors of the sizes shown in Table 1. I concluded that I would need the size given by the two page journal

---

2. Whether a tradeoff function exhibits upward or downward concavity depends upon the choice of user satisfaction function. If both functions are power functions with one exponent positive and the other negative, the tradeoff functions are always concave upward. When both exponents are positive, the tradeoff functions are always concave downward. When the two functions are logarithmic, the tradeoff functions are always concave downward, and when they are both logistic, the tradeoff functions are both concave upward and downward, switching from one to the other as a function of the other variables (e.g., display rate). These conclusions hold whenever the two variables, x_1 and x_2, are linearly related.

spread. That is, $U(6400) = 100$. The power function parameters are $k = 0.64$ and $p = 0.6$, so that $U(w) = 0.64w^{0.6}$: the same exponent used for menu size but with a different scale factor, k. This function is shown in Figure 2.

Table 1

SIZE OF COMMON TEXTS AND DEVICES (in characters)	
TEXT OR DEVICE	APPROXIMATE NUMBER OF CHARACTER POSITIONS
Portable Computer (*Radio Shack Model 100*)	320
Home Microprocessor (*Apple II*)	960
Standard Video Display Unit	1,920
One typed manuscript page (*double spaced*)	2,600
One typed manuscript page (*single spaced*)	4,000
Journal page (*Cognitive Science*)	3,200
Double page spread	6,400
Page of Proceedings (*Gaithersberg Human Factors in Computer Systems*)	5,500
Double page spread	11,000
Newspaper page (*Los Angeles Times*)	30,000
Double page spread	60,000

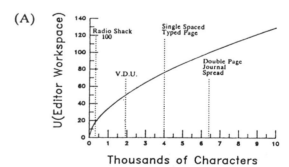

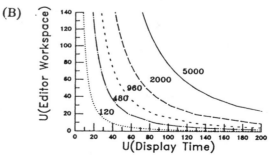

Figure 2. Panel A. User Satisfaction function for editor workspace, w: $U(w) = 0.64w^{0.6}$. Typical character sizes for various displays and texts are also shown. Panel B shows the tradeoff function of workspace against time, $U(w)$ versus $U(T)$, for different display rates, β (*characters/second*). $U(T)$ is shown in Figure 1B: $U(T) = 100T^{-1}$.

Trading workspace for display time. One penalty for increasing the size of the workspace is increased time to display the workspace. If we use the same User Satisfaction function for time as in Figure 1B, we get the tradeoff functions shown in Figure 2B. Large workspaces require very high display rates before they are satisfactory. Because these tradeoff functions are concave upward (and are very similar to the functions of Figure 1D), the same conclusions apply here as to those earlier functions: the optimum operating point is an all-or-none solution. Thus, the user either prefers a large workspace, regardless of the time penalty, or a very fast display, regardless of the workspace penalty. Here, however, the relative weights are apt to be determined by the task rather than by the user's level of skill.

Suppose the task were one in which the display changes relatively infrequently. In this case we would expect $\omega_{workspace} \gg \omega_{display\ time}$, so that the optimum solution is to have as big a workspace as possible. If the task were one that requires frequent changes in the display, then we would expect the reverse result: $\omega_{workspace} \ll \omega_{display\ time}$, so the optimum solution is to shrink the workspace to the smallest size at which the task can still be carried out, thereby minimizing display time.

Trading workspace for menu size. Adding a menu to the display decreases the amount of available workspace. Let W be the total size of the workspace that is available for use, w the workspace allocated to the text editor, and m the space allocated for a menu: $w = W - m$. We know that $U(m) = am^p$ and $U(w) = b(W - m)^q$, where $a = 2$, $b = 0.6$, and $p = q = 0.6$. This leads to the tradeoff functions shown in Figure 3.

Note that $U(editor\ workspace)$ is relatively insensitive to $U(menu\ size)$. This is because a relatively small sized display makes a satisfactory menu, whereas it requires a large display to make a satisfactory editor workspace. As a result, changing the size of the menu by only a few lines can make a large change in User Satisfaction, whereas the same change in workspace is usually of little consequence.

In some commercially available editors, the menu of commands can occupy approximately half the screen (usually 24 lines). Figure 1 indicates that for a menu of 12 lines (960 characters), $U(menu) \approx 100$. However, from Figures 2 and 3 we see that with a workspace of only 1920 characters, a menu of around 1000 characters (or of $U(menu) = 100$) reduces $U(editor\ workspace)$ from its value of 50 with no menu to 34: a reduction of almost one third. From Figure 3 we see that we would be much less impaired by the same size menu were the workspace considerably greater. In such cases, we have a clear tradeoff between the need for the menu information and the desire to have a reasonable workspace.

Maximizing total user satisfaction for menu and workspace. When tradeoff functions are concave downward (as in Figure 3), maximum satisfaction occurs where the slope of the tradeoff function is tangent to the iso-

satisfaction function. For the user who values workspace and menu equally (so that the preferred slope is -1), the optimum solution is to operate at the right hand side of Figure 3. This makes for a relatively high value of user satisfaction for the menu (which means a large menu — the exact sizes can be determined from Figure 1A) — but with little sacrifice in user satisfaction for workspace. The more expert user will have an iso-satisfaction function with a much smaller slope, and so will sacrifice menu for workspace. Similarly, the beginner will have an iso-satisfaction curve with high slope which will maximize menu size at the expense of workspace. These results are quite unlike the tradeoffs that involved time in which an all-or-none solution was optimal: here, the optimum values are compromises between workspace and editor size. Display rate and amount of total available workspace alter the point of optimum operation. The analysis provides exact numerical determination of how the optimal operating point is affected by these variables.

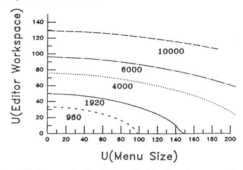

Figure 3. The tradeoff of User Satisfaction for menu size against User Satisfaction for editor workspace, for different values of total workspace, W. Horizontal lines represent constant values of $U(m)$ and, therefore, of m: the values of m can be determined from panel A of Figure 1. Similarly, vertical lines represent constant values of w: the values of w can be determined from panel A of Figure 2.

A Critique of the Tradeoff Analysis

There are a number of problems with the tradeoff analyses presented in this paper. There are two major criticisms, one minor one. Let me start with the minor one, for it represents a misunderstanding that would be good to clear up. I illustrate the misunderstanding for the variable of menu size, but the discussion applies to other variables as well:

- The functions must be wrong: *U(menu size)* continually increases as a function of *menu size*, yet when the size gets too large, the menu becomes less useful: *U(menu size)* should also decrease.

User Satisfaction for the System Is the Sum of Its Parts

This misunderstanding derives from confusing *User Satisfaction* for a single attribute with *User Satisfaction* for a system. A major philosophy of the tradeoffs analysis is that a system can be decomposed into its underlying component attributes and *User Satisfaction* for each assessed individually. The *User Satisfaction* for the entire system can only be determined from the combination of the *User Satisfaction* values for each of its components. The satisfaction for the amount of information conveyed by the menu continues to increase with size, but that the ability to find something (captured by "search time") decreases with increasing size of a menu. The overall satisfaction for the menu is given by the sum of the increasing satisfaction for the information and the decreasing satisfaction for search effort: the result is a U-shaped curve that decreases as size gets too big.

Now let me address the two major critiques:

- The tradeoff functions are arbitrary;

- How do we determine the functions when we design? It would be more useful were there a set of standards (perhaps in handbook form);

These two issues point to unsolved problems with the method. My defense is to argue that this procedure is new. The goal is to introduce the philosophy and to encourage others to help in the collection of the relevant data and in the development of the method. However, the numbers and the particular functions used here may be useful, for the tasks for which they were derived: they do mesh well with my intuitions.

The Tradeoff Functions Are Arbitrary

Although the functions used here are indeed arbitrary, three things need to be noted. First, power functions have a long tradition of satisfactory use in psychology and so are apt to be good approximations. Second, I have actually computed User Satisfaction functions using the logistic, power, and logarithmic functions; over much of the range of interest, the results differed suprisingly little, although at high data rates, the concave upward tradeoff functions became concave downward when the logistic was used for size and time, although at low data rates they were still concave upward (see footnote 2). Third, I agree that the preferred thing would be to have an experimental program to determine the exact forms and parameters of the functions. In particular, the all-or-none prediction is sensitive to the form of the User Satisfaction functions.

How Do We Determine the Functions When We Design?

Here, again, empirical work is needed. I suspect the functions will be found to vary only for a reasonably small number of classes of users, classes of tasks, and design attributes, so that it would be possible to collect typical values in a handbook. Alternatively, quick data collection methods might be devised: the magnitude estimation procedures are especially easy to apply. A handbook might be quite valuable. Before this can be done, of course, it is necessary to determine that the hypothesis is correct — that there are a relatively small number of tasks, user classes, and tradeoff variables that need be considered. Moreover, one must extend the analysis to a larger domain of problems and demonstrate its usefulness in actual design.

Some Other Examples of Tradeoffs

There are numerous other tradeoff analyses in addition to the ones presented here. Three other situations seem important enough to warrant consideration here, even though they are not yet ready for quantitative treatment. These are: (1) the comparison between command languages and menu-driven systems; (2) how to choose names for commands and files; and (3), the tradeoffs that result when moving among computer systems of widely varying capabilities, as in the differences between hand-held computers and powerful, networked workstations.

Command Languages Versus Menus

The relative merits of menu-based systems and command language systems are often debated, seldom with any firm conclusion. It is useful to compare their tradeoffs, but before we do, it is necessary to be clear about what is meant by each alternative. In this context a command language system is one in which no aids are presented to the user during the intention or choice stages, and the action specification is performed by typing a command, using the syntax required by the operating system. (The distinctions among the intention, choice, and specification stages come from Norman, 1983b.) Command languages are the most frequent method of implementing operating systems. Similarly, in this context a menu-based system is one in which all commands are presented via menus, where a command cannot be specified unless it is currently being shown on the active menu, and where the commands are specified either through short names or single characters (as indicated by the menu items) or by pointing at the relevant menu item (or perhaps at a switch or mark indicated by the item). These are restricted interpretations of the two alternatives, confounding issues about the format for information presentation and action specification. Still, because they represent common design alternatives, it is useful to compare them.

Command languages offer experts great versatility. Because of their large amount of knowledge and experience with the system, experts tend to know exactly what operations they wish performed. With a command language they can specify their operations directly simply by typing the names of the commands, as well as any parameters, files, or other system options that are required. Command languages make it easy to specify parameters (or "flags") to commands, something that may be difficult with menu-based systems.

Menus offer the beginner or the casual user considerable assistance. At any stage, information is available. Even abbreviated menus serve as a reminder of the alternatives. Experts often complain about menu-based systems because of the time penalty in requesting a menu, waiting for it to be displayed, and then searching for the desired item. Moreover, systems with large numbers of commands require multiple menus that slow up the expert. The problem is that the system is designed to give help, whether or not the user wishes it.

Two of the difficulties with menus are the delay in waiting for them to be plotted and the amount of space they occupy. Figure 1D shows that the tradeoff between amount of information and time delay is especially sensitive to information transmission rate. When transmission time becomes fast enough, there is little penalty for menus, whereas at slow rates of data transmission, the penalty is high. In similar fashion, Figure 3 shows that the tradeoff between menu size and workspace is especially sensitive to the amount of total workspace available. When sufficient workspace is available, there is little penalty for menus. Thus, slow transmission rates and small workspaces bias the design choice toward command language systems; high data rates and large workspaces bias the system toward menu-based systems.

The two systems also differ in the kinds of errors they lead to and ease of error correction. In a command language system, an error in command specification usually leads to an illegal command: no action gets performed. This error is usually easy to detect and to correct. In a menu-based system, an error in specification is almost always a legal command. This error can be very difficult to correct. If the action was subtle, the user may not even be aware it was performed. If the action was dramatic, the user will often have no idea of what precipitated it, since the action specification was unintentional.

Some of the tradeoffs associated with menu-based systems and command language systems are summarized in Table 2. Command languages tend to be virtuous for the expert, but difficult for the novice; they are difficult to learn and there are no on-line reminders of the set of possible actions. Menus are easy to use and they provide a constant reminder. On the other hand, menus tend to be slow — for some purposes, the expert finds them tedious and unwieldy — and not as flexible as command languages.

This analysis is brief and restricted to the particular formats of command language and menu-based systems that were described. There do exist techniques for mitigating the deficiencies of each system. Nonetheless, the analysis is useful, both for pointing out the nature of the issues and for being reasonably faithful to some existing systems. In the argument over which system is best, the answer must be that neither is: each has its virtues and its deficiencies.

The Choice of Names for Commands and Files

Another example of a common tradeoff is in the choice of name for a command or a file. The problem occurs because the name must serve two different purposes: as a *description* of the item and also as the string of characters that must be typed to invoke it, that is, as the *specification*; these two uses pose conflicting requirements.

Consider the properties of names when used as descriptions. The more complete the description, the more useful it can be, especially when the user is unsure of the options or is selecting from an unfamiliar set of alternatives. However, the longer the description, the more space it occu-

pies and the more difficult to read or scan the material. In addition, there are often system limitations on the length and format of names. For these reasons, one usually settles for a partial description, counting on context or prior knowledge to allow the full description to be regenerated by the user.

Table 2

TRADEOFFS BETWEEN MENU-BASED SYSTEMS AND COMMAND LANGUAGE SYSTEMS		
ATTRIBUTE	MENU-BASED	COMMAND LANGUAGE
Speed of use:	Slow, especially if large or if has hierarchical structure.	Fast, for experts; operation can be specified exactly, regardless of system state.
Prior knowledge required:	Very little — can be self-explanatory.	Considerable — user is expected to have learned set of alternative actions and command language that specifies them.
Ease of learning:	High. Uses recognition memory: easier and more accurate than recall memory. Easy to explore system and discover options.	Low. Users must learn names and syntax of language. If alternatives are numerous, learning may take considerable time. No simple way to explore system and discover options not already known.
Errors:	Specification error leads to inappropriate action: difficult to determine what happened and to correct.	Specification error usually leads to illegal command: easy to detect, easy to correct.
Most useful for:	Beginner or infrequent user.	Expert or frequent user.

Once the appropriate name has been determined, the user enters the specification stage of operation; the user must specify to the computer system which name is desired. Most users are not expert typists, and so it is desirable to simplify the specification stage. As a result, there is pressure toward the use of short names, oftentimes to the limit of single character command names. [3]

The desirability for short names is primarily a factor when specification must be done by naming. When the specification can be done by pointing, then ease of typing is no longer a factor. Nonetheless, there are still constraints on the name choice: the longer the name, the easier to find and point at the desired item, but at the cost of using a larger percentage of the available workspace, of increasing display time, and the ease of reading and search. Now names might wish to be chosen so they are visually distinct, or so that they occupy appropriate spatial locations on the display, in all cases adding more constraints to the naming

----

3. A number of systems allow for shortcuts in specification, so that one need only use sufficient characters (plus some "escape" or "wild-card" character) to make the name unique. This option poses its own naming constraints; now a name is chosen not only to be descriptive, but with the added requirement that one or two letters be sufficient to distinguish it uniquely from all other names. The typing aid introduces its own form of naming constraint.

problem. In general the descriptive requirements tend to push toward longer names, names that provide as much information as possible. The specification requirements tend to push toward shorter names, names that are easy to type.

Handheld Computers Versus Workstations

New developments in technology are moving computer systems in several conflicting directions simultaneously. Workstations are getting more powerful, with large memories, large, high resolution screens, and with very high communication bandwidths. These developments move us toward the ability to present as much information as is needed by the user with little penalty in time, workspace, or even memory space. At the same time, some machines are getting smaller, providing us with briefcase sized and handheld computers. These machines have great virtue because of their portability, but severe limitations in communications speed, memory capacity, and amount of display screen or workspace.

Just as workstations are starting to move toward displays capable of 1000 line resolution, showing several entire pages of text, handheld computers move us back toward only a few short lines — perhaps 8 lines of 40 characters each — and communication rates of 30 cps (300 baud). The major differences between workstations and handheld computers relevant to the tradeoffs discussion are in the amount of memory, processor speed and power, communication abilities, availability of extra peripherals, and screen size: in all cases, the handheld machine has sacrificed power for portability. Because the same people may wish to use both handheld machines and workstations (one while at home or travelling, the other at work), the person may wish the same programs to operate on the two machines. However, the interface design must be different, as the tradeoff analyses of this paper show.

Summary and Conclusions

The tradeoff analysis is intended to serve as an example of a quantitative design tool. In some cases it may not be possible to select an optimum design, not even for a restricted class of activities and users. In these cases, knowledge of the tradeoffs allows the designer to choose intelligently, knowing exactly what benefits and limits the system design will provide. Finally, the analyses show that some design decisions are heavily affected by technology, others are not. Thus, answers to design questions are heavily context dependent, being affected by the classes of users for whom the system is intended, the types of applications being performed, which stages of user activities are thought to be of most importance, and the level of technology being employed.

The work presented here is just the beginning. In the ideal case, the tradeoff relationships will be known exactly, perhaps with the relevant quantitative parameters provided in handbooks. This paper has limited itself to demonstrating the basic principles. Considerable development must still be done on this issue and on the other major parame-

ters and issues that affect the quality of the human-machine interaction. Much work remains to be done.

A second point of the paper is to argue for more fundamental approaches to the study of human-machine interaction. All too often we are presented with minor studies that do not lead to general application, or to studies that are restricted to a particular technology. All too often we are trapped in the tar pits of the field or seduced by the sirens of technology. If we are to have a science of design that can be of use beyond today's local problems, we must learn to broaden our views, sharpen our methods, and avoid temptation.

A major moral of this paper is that it is essential to analyze separately the different aspects of human-computer interaction. Detailed analyses of each aspect of the human-computer interface are essential, of course, but because design decisions interact across stages and classes of users, we must also develop tools that allow us to ask for what purpose the system is to be used, then to determine how best to accomplish that goal. Only after the global decisions have been made should the details of the interface design be determined.

References

Bannon, L., Cypher, A., Greenspan, S., & Monty, M.L. Evaluation and analysis of users' activity organization. *Proceedings of the CHI 1983 Conference on Human Factors in Computer Systems.* Boston, December, 1983.

Card, S., Moran, T., & Newell, A., *Applied Information-Processing Psychology: The Human-Computer* Interface. Hillsdale, N.J.: Erlbaum Associates, 1983.

Miller, R. B. Response time in man-computer conversational transactions, *Proceedings of the Spring Joint Computer Conference*, 1968, *33*. Montvale, New Jersey, pp. 267-277.

Norman, D. A. Design rules based on analyses of human error. *Communications of the ACM*, 1983a, *4*, 254-258.

Norman, D. A. Four stages of user activities. Manuscript. 1983b.

Norman, D. A. Tradeoffs in the design of human-computer interfaces. Manuscript. 1983c.

O'Malley, C., Smolensky, P., Bannon, L., Conway, E., Graham, J., Sokolov, J., & Monty, M. L. A proposal for user centered system documentation. *Proceedings of the CHI 1983 Conference on Human Factors in Computer Systems.* Boston, December, 1983.

Root, R. W., & Draper, S. Questionnaires as a software evaluation tool. *Proceedings of the CHI 1983 Conference on Human Factors in Computer Systems.* Boston, December, 1983.

Shneiderman, B. *Software Psychology: Human Factors in Computer and Information* Systems. Cambridge, Mass.: Winthrop Publishers, 1980.

Stevens, S. S. Perceptual magnitude and its measurement. In E. C. Carterette & M. P. Friedman (Eds.), *Handbook of perception* (Vol. 2). New York: Academic Press, 1974.

Design Philosophy

In applying human factors to system building, process—the set of procedures for creating the design and building the resulting system—is as important as content—the information drawn from human factors disciplines. Most of the guidelines in the following chapters relate to content: they describe qualities that systems should have. But only by understanding the human aspects of the development process and taking them into account is it possible to maximize the likelihood of producing a well human-engineered computer system.

A DESIGN PHILOSOPHY

The norm in the computer industry is to take the hardware and software environments as a "given," to build application software to perform the (presumed) desired functions, and only then to consider documentation, installation, maintenance, user training, and other "practical" issues. The priority of each of these issues depends on the organization and the people involved. Some projects are motivated most strongly by marketing considerations, others by available hardware or software, still others by the skills and interests of the developers. None of these considerations alone is sufficient. Integrated design is the formulation of a system considering all issues throughout the process. Human factors is a natural part of integrated design.

Consider the relation of error messages to a whole design, which we discuss in more detail in later chapters. Human considerations dictate provision of clear messages, phrased in familiar language. But what errors there are need not arise by accident out of the rest of the design; the design can also be manipulated to *create* the right set of errors to report. By allowing requirements for error messages to interact with those for the rest of the design, designers can maximize the effectiveness of the system by adjusting the number and kind of errors reported. It is even possible to design systems with no error states or messages. Pac-Man and other video games, for example, have virtually no error conditions. Even the *tilt* light of the old pinball machines has been eliminated.

Documentation and maintenance are two other issues that are usually left for last, to the detriment of the product. Ask yourself what the right documentation would be if the system were not otherwise constrained. And how shou d maintenance be done, ideally? Though each of these considerations will have to interact with the others, the result will be better if you bring them all to bear on the design at once. The essence of engineering is creating constructive compromises among many conflicting goals. Integrated design can occur only when all the real issues are allowed to exert an influence.

Engineering is compromise.
Integrated design is design of whole systems.

The creation of computer systems involves elements of engineering, science, and art—the practical search for results, the application of theory, and the use of skill and taste. Our design philosophy is based

Excerpted from Rubinstein, R. and Hersh, H. (1984). Design Philosophy. Chapter 2 of *The Human Factor: Designing Computer Systems for People*, Burlington, MA: Digital Press.

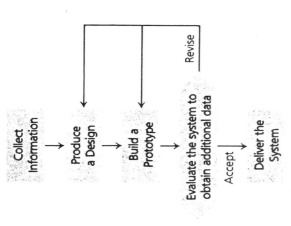

Figure 2-1. Conventional development process

A RATIONAL DEVELOPMENT PROCESS

on the view that science and art are as indispensable to design as is engineering practice.

The design of most computer systems is too complicated for one or even a few people to comprehend. One consequence of this complexity is that designers of systems are forced to break problems down into minimally interacting parts and to deal with these separately. Part of the crisis in the design of computer-based systems is that many of the important pieces are never integrated into the process. As a result, familiar ways of building computer systems work less and less well as tasks grow and change.

Consider an example from another design discipline. Architects design office buildings with a good degree of slack for "systems" such as plumbing, heating and cooling, communications, and electric wiring. It is common to have at least three feet of space above a false ceiling to ensure that mistakes can be rectified. The cost of this rule is considerable, perhaps two feet of building height for every story of building, or about 20 percent of the height of the structure. Architects have not yet devised a better way to guarantee that all constraints interact correctly in the design, but at least their rules provide workable buildings.

Design is seldom an orderly or linear process. System building occurs in a real world with constraints, interruptions, distractions, emotions, personalities, and politics. Any guidelines used for system development must operate within these complex conditions.

Figure 2-1 presents a simplified model of the development process. In this model, external information is collected and used to set the goals, bounds, and other requirements for the design. The design is then evaluated in various ways, ultimately by constructing the system and testing it. Flaws uncovered during the testing are corrected in the prototype, and the more general results of testing and evaluation are used to refine the design. The process is repeated until some criterion is reached, and finally the system is delivered. Information about market acceptance and user reactions can be used as input to the next system development cycle.

Because design is an art as well as a science, it is never a completely rational process. Inventiveness and good ideas require that the constraints on the proposed system be known early. Otherwise, the bright idea that comes is not likely to satisfy them. This is why information gathering precedes design. Then evaluation and testing allow us to improve our ideas in an orderly way.

The basic development process in no way guarantees a well human-engineered system. Systems, especially those designed by large organizations, are often sensible in each of their parts, but not so sensible when taken as a whole. If communication is poor or if differing interests are not reconciled, the individuals or teams working on different parts of the system will each do only what makes sense to them. Even when all parties cooperate, it is difficult to focus attention continually on all aspects of a large system as it develops. It is a marvel of computer technology that disparate pieces are so often assembled without producing overt conflict. The result of local sense and global nonsense is much like the drawings of M. C. Escher: each piece works and is part of the whole, but viewed from a broader perspective, things are not right. In *Belvedere* (Figure 2-2), which of the people knows that anything is wrong? Only the viewer, from his or her slight distance, is fully aware of the problem. One goal of the development process is to prevent these global problems, or at least to detect them in time to do something about them.

Our model is based on observations of two recurring impediments to well human-engineered products. The first is perspective. It is far easier to design for consistency at a local level than at a global one. We need a process that helps us to focus our attention on the global aspects of the system when necessary, and to concentrate on the details of the design without being overwhelmed.

Second, in the effort to base designs on the best available information, we must make both explicit and implicit assumptions. Explicit assumptions, such as those relating to a requirements document, can be assessed for accuracy and appropriateness. Implicit assumptions, such as those about details of the system's intended use, necessarily go unchecked. Because just being aware of potential problems can produce a dramatic improvement in human engineering, we need a process that helps make explicit as many of our assumptions as possible, so that they can be viewed objectively.

Figure 2-3 shows our elaborated development process. The chapter references in the diagram indicate where these topics are covered in detail elsewhere in the book. The major components are exactly the same as those in the basic model (Figure 2-1): information is collected, a design is created and implemented, and the system is evaluated and ultimately delivered. But the types and number of activities involved in each step are different. We will discuss the overall process here.

Information Gathering

Information gathering is the starting point, the reference point, in the development process. Once we have made the requirements and goals explicit, we can use them as constraints to guide the design. We can also use this relevant information to make many of the inevitable design tradeoffs in a rational manner, rather than at the last minute when shortage of time forces many an arbitrary decision.

As Figure 2-3 shows, a variety of information sources provide the basis for the design of computer systems. These include technical requirements, the current state of the art, products already in use, industry standards, government regulations, and the technical capabilities of the system builders.

Since the technical requirements are usually nonnegotiable, it makes sense to understand them before beginning. In addition to government regulations, the technical capabilities and skills of the builders may

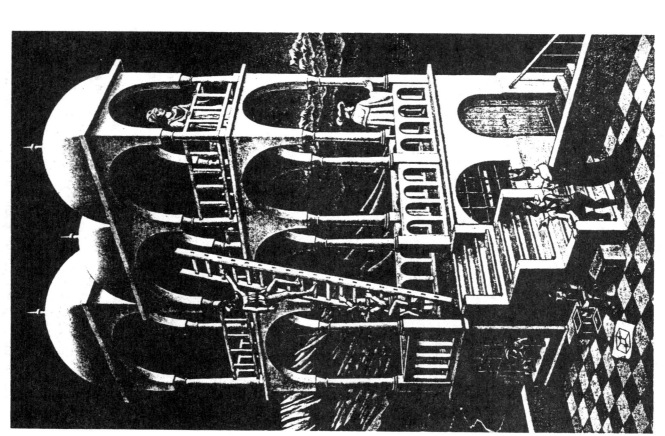

Figure 2-2. A system perspective—*Belvedere* by M. C. Escher.

limit the size and complexity of the system to be designed. But additional staffing may be possible if the right skills and job descriptions can be specified.

Market and client requirements may be provided by the sales force, professional marketing people, management, customer specifications, market surveys, or intuition about what is salable. What is the market "asking for"? Is part of the appeal of the product that it is "state of the art"? Are there particular features that competitors have already incorporated? What features or products are perceived as gimmicks? The most sophisticated design in the world fails to sell if no one wants it. Designers need a detailed written description of market requirements or, if the product is being built for an in-house user or a specific client, specifications and requirements from that source.

The specific tasks the user will perform directly influence what the system will do. A task analysis, discussed in detail in Chapter 3, aims at providing a clear picture of the users and their environment.

It is not enough to collect the information from all these sources. We also need a clear sense of the design goals and their relative importance. There may also be important process goals to consider, such as the time permitted for development, the available resources, and the total budget for the project. It is always better to identify these issues at the beginning than to have them ambush you at the end.

Design

Once the goals of the project are identified and the initial information collected and organized, the designer should have a clear picture of the requirements and constraints. From this seed grows the whole design. A well human-engineered design specifies the repertoire of functions the system will perform, how users will use the system, and how the system will fit into their lives. The design creates a user interface, that is, an external presentation of the capabilities of the system.

Figure 2-3 also shows the tasks involved in design. Although they need not be performed in a particular sequence, it is important that by the end of the initial design stage each be well defined, committed to paper, and critically assessed in relation to the initial requirements and to each other.

An external myth is chosen to support the conceptual model that the

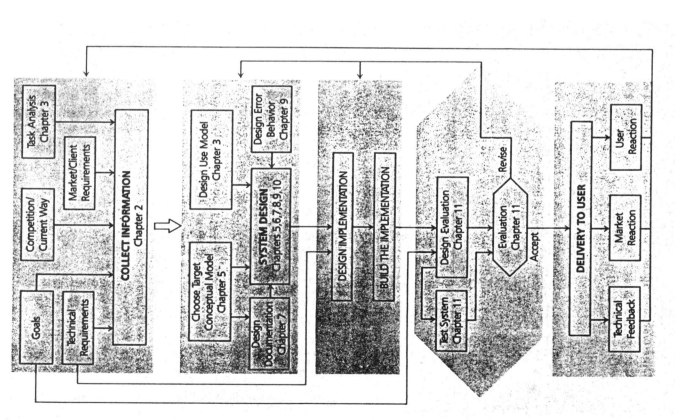

Figure 2-3. Elaborated development process

designer wants the user to build. Chapter 5 explains in detail what a conceptual model is, and why it is important in the design of systems.

Chapter 3 describes the utility of an explicit *use model*, the equivalent of a task analysis for the future. It describes how the system will be used and how it will fit into the user's life.

System design is the process of specifying the system's external behavior—the details of hardware and software that impact the user. At this stage it is essential to develop the documentation (such as the user's manual). Documentation provides an opportunity to evaluate the system long before the first line of code is written. Being able to write a coherent user's manual is a good sign that the overall design is consistent and clear. Chapter 7 discusses why the documentation should be written either before or concurrently with the design of the system.

Thinking about error behavior early makes life significantly easier for users. Since error behavior becomes part of the user's conceptual model, it is necessary to anticipate errors and to plan how users will deal with them. Chapter 9 discusses error processing in detail.

Implementation

After designing the external behavior of the system, we turn to the design of the internals, to the functions to be performed for the user. At this point the user interface is relatively fixed.

There are economic and logical arguments for doing a thorough implementation design before starting to build a system. The cost of fixing problems increases rapidly as development proceeds [Mason and Carey 1983]. Creating a complete design before coding is good software-engineering practice for systems of all sizes. This practice is one of the basic tools for preventing disasters, overruns, and schedule slippage [Brooks 1975], and applies equally well to hardware design.

Next comes the actual construction of the system. This is the part of the process that typically gets the most attention. No matter how carefully a design has been created, implementation always uncovers unspecified choices and issues that need resolution. The system design and all the information that went into it provide the basis for resolving these problems. Using the external myth, we can often answer ques-

tions of the form, "What should it do in this case?" Good management can help prevent such unforeseen issues from being decided in random or ad hoc ways.

Testing and Evaluation

Formally or informally, explicitly or implicitly, all systems are evaluated. Evaluation may be based simply on whether the product sells well. Or users may provide feedback about specific features and bugs. There may be formal evaluations that test features, performance, and user satisfaction. Evaluation creates a feedback loop that helps us improve a system in an organized way, on the basis of the goals of the project. Using this evaluation design, we test the system and assess the results to determine how the findings affect the system and how the system might be improved. Chapter 11 discusses the overall evaluation process.

Delivery

Delivery of a system implies completion of the project and gives the designer a sense of accomplishment and relief: "We've done it." But even after the system has been delivered, there is still much we can learn, as Figure 2-3 shows. Is the system effective after people learn to use it? What frustrations do users experience? What shortcuts do users invent or ask for? What gets used and what doesn't? Who is buying it (or using it)? Why?

Gathering this information can be considered either the end of a development cycle or the beginning of the next. As they learn to use the system, many people expect it to do more and more. In many environments, system development is a continuous activity.

OUR DESIGN PHILOSOPHY

Our model of development separates design from implementation because we want to understand what we are building before we start building it. Authors who write about separating *architecture* from implementation [see Brooks 1975] mean essentially the same thing. Planning pays for itself many times over, and quality requires planning.

Bibliography

[Brooks 1975]
Frederick P. Brooks, Jr.
The Mythical Man-Month
Reading, MA: Addison-Wesley, 1975.

[Mason and Carey 1983]
R. E. A. Mason and T. T. Carey
Prototyping Interactive Information Systems
Communications of the ACM, 1983, vol. 26, no. 5, pp. 347–354.

[Moran 1981]
Thomas P. Moran
The Command Language Grammar: A representation for the user interface of interactive computer systems.
International Journal of Man-Machine Studies, 1981, vol. 15, pp. 3–50.

Guideline 2. Separate design from implementation.

The model is consistent with top-down design, a topic with great currency in the literature [Moran 1981]. Top-down design is the breaking down of the whole problem into progressively smaller subproblems again and again until implementable units are reached. It is the most powerful tool available for avoiding global-inconsistency because it deals explicitly with the relation of each of the parts to the whole. Our emphasis on designing external behavior and on writing the user's manual first reflects this top-down design philosophy. Including the needs of users in the design acknowledges that the user, not the designer, is the most important component, the top, in system design.

If you work with a group or a large organization, you will not always be able to get your way on design issues. Many things are not subject to change, and enough energy and resources may not be available to change all those that are. Our goal in infusing human factors technology into design is to identify opportunities to do the things that have high payoff and to avoid those that cause the most trouble. If we can just identify properties and features at both ends of the spectrum and design accordingly, we will have made a major contribution to the design. We seek good designs, not perfect ones. It is sufficient to do a good job on those parts that make the most difference. Trying to make a design perfect can make it worse. Moreover, it frequently makes it late.

The perfect is the enemy of the good.

Developing Interactive Information Systems with the User Software Engineering Methodology

ANTHONY I. WASSERMAN, MEMBER, IEEE, PETER A. PIRCHER,
DAVID T. SHEWMAKE, STUDENT MEMBER, IEEE, AND MARTIN L. KERSTEN

Abstract—User Software Engineering is a methodology, supported by automated tools, for the systematic development of interactive information systems. The USE methodology gives particular attention to effective user involvement in the early stages of the software development process, concentrating on external design and the use of rapidly created and modified prototypes of the user interface. The USE methodology is supported by an integrated set of graphically based tools. This paper describes the User Software Engineering methodology and the tools that support the methodology.

Index Terms—Human/computer interaction, interactive information systems, rapid prototyping, RAPID/USE, software development methodology, transition diagrams, User Software Engineering.

I. SOFTWARE DEVELOPMENT METHODOLOGIES

EFFORTS to improve the quality of software systems and the process by which they are produced are at the heart of the field of *software engineering*. The key idea is to use a *software development methodology*, a systematic process for the creation of software. A methodology combines technical methods with management procedures for software development, and includes automated tools in a development support system for additional assistance [1]–[3].

The underlying philosophy is that use of a methodology can improve many aspects of the entire software development process, including a better fit to user requirements, fewer errors in the resulting system, better documentation throughout the entire process, and significantly reduced costs for system evolution.

Most methodologies give primary attention to the functions of the system being developed and the data upon which it operates. They follow a hierarchical decomposition of the problem, working from either a data-oriented or a function-oriented perspective. The user interface to the system is frequently considered only as an afterthought.

For interactive systems, though, these approaches may not work well, since user-oriented considerations must receive attention very early in the development process.

Manuscript received April 30, 1985.

A. I. Wasserman, P. A. Pircher, and D. T. Shewmake are with the Section of Medical Information Science, University of California, San Francisco, CA 94143.

M. L. Kersten is with the Centrum voor Wiskunde en Informatica, Amsterdam, The Netherlands.

IEEE Log Number 8405407.

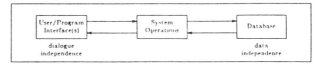

Fig. 1. Logical structure of interactive information systems.

Furthermore, user concerns and user preferences must have priority over some system-oriented considerations.

Accordingly, we created a methodology, named User Software Engineering (USE), that includes many user-oriented considerations in the framework of a software development methodology. User Software Engineering focuses on a particular type of interactive system, termed an interactive information system (IIS). An IIS may be characterized as providing conversational access to data, typically for persons who are not experts in computing.

Interactive information systems are used for applications such as airline reservations, bibliographic searching, medical record management, and banking. From a software perspective, an IIS may be seen as a human/computer dialog, a database, and a set of transactions (operations, functions), where many of the transactions involve access to or modification of a database, as shown in Fig. 1.

From a user standpoint, the interface to the IIS is often most critical and is certainly the first thing that is noticed by the user. There is growing evidence of the relationship between the quality of the user interface and the ease of use of a system [4], [5]. Accordingly, User Software Engineering gives early attention to the design of the user interface, and employs what may be termed an *outside-in* approach to software development and design. The methodology is supported by a collection of tools that support design and testing of the user interface, and the integration of the executable user interface specification with programmed actions written in programming languages and/or the data manipulation language for a relational database management system.

In the remainder of this paper, we outline first the goals of the USE methodology, and then show how systems are designed and built using the methodology and its tools, especially the RAPID/USE application development system. We shall illustrate the use of the USE methodology with the University library database example presented at the 1984 Workshop on Models and Languages for Software Specification and Design. (See *Computer*, vol. 18, no. 3, pp. 103–108.)

II. Goals of The USE Methodology

The User Software Engineering project was undertaken in 1975 with the intent of creating a methodology that would support the development of interactive information systems. The development of the User Software Engineering methodology has been guided by seven goals:

- *functionality*—The methodology should cover the entire development process, supporting creation of a working system that achieves a predefined set of requirements.
- *reliability*—The methodology should support the creation of reliable systems, so that users are not inconvenienced by system crashes, loss of data, or lack of availability.
- *usability*—The methodology should help the developer to assure, as early as possible, that the resulting system will be easy to learn and easy to use. The methodology should involve users *effectively* in the development process, particularly in its early stages.
- *evolvability*—The methodology should encourage documentation and system structuring so that the resulting system is easily modifiable and able to accommodate changes in hardware operating environments and user needs.
- *automated support*—The methodology should be supported by automated tools that improve the process of software development and the resulting system; this requirement implies the availability of both a general set of automated aids and a methodology-specific set.
- *improved developer productivity*—The methodology, with its supporting tools, should reduce the time required to create a properly functioning system.
- *reusability*—The methodology should be reusable for a large class of projects and the design products from a given application should be reusable on similar future projects.

The USE methodology, as with most other development methodologies [6], [7], follows a well-defined set of phases beginning with analysis and terminating with a validated operational system. We believe, however, that the traditional life cycle approach has several flaws when applied to the creation of interactive systems, and that evolutionary approaches involving the orderly construction of a sequence of prototype systems are frequently more effective.

III. Requirements Analysis in the USE Methodology

As with any methodology, the first step in User Software Engineering is to gain an understanding of the problem domain and specific application constraints. This section describes the requirements analysis process of User Software Engineering, showing the information that is obtained for later use. Most of the techniques used in this

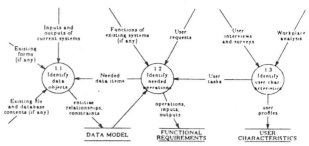

Fig. 2. Dataflow diagram showing requirements analysis in USE methodology.

process are similar to those used with other methods, and are therefore presented very briefly.

A. Aspects of Requirements Analysis

In User Software Engineering, four aspects of analysis are important: data modeling, activity modeling, analysis of user characteristics, and analysis of usage characteristics. It is largely an *informal* process, intended to gain understanding of the problem domain, the context in which a system could be developed, and the nature of the expected usage of such a system. The USE requirements analysis process is summarized in the dataflow diagram shown in Fig. 2.

We begin this phase with an object-oriented approach, identifying, informally, objects and the operations (actions) performed upon them. Conceptual data modeling techniques such as the semantic hierarchy model of Smith and Smith [8] and the entity-relationship model [9] have been used successfully for this step. These techniques are used to identify the primary entities of concern in a system, their attributes, and their relationship to one another. As these entities and relationships are identified, the operations that create and modify these entities are also identified. The USE approach resembles many other approaches in this phase, notably the Entity-Action Step of the Jackson System Development method [10].

Activity modeling is also useful for identifying entities, relationships, and operations. We have successfully used several different techniques for activity modeling, including the A-graphs of ISAC and the dataflow diagrams of Structured Systems Analysis [11], [12].

Regardless of the precise technique used, the names of entities, their attributes, and the operations are collected into a "data dictionary," so that the names may be used consistently throughout the development process. This data dictionary, part of the User Software Engineering project database, eventually obtains information about the user interface, too.

B. Levels of Abstraction in User Software Engineering

The User Software Engineering approach uses these data and activity modeling methods as a means to achieve multiple levels of abstraction based on data independence. The first level is physical data independence. The mere fact of using a database model rather than a file-oriented model provides a level of independence from the physical structure of the data on a secondary storage device; this level of independence is the traditional data independence as the term is used in the database community.

The second level of abstraction is *data-model* independence. The result of the data modeling and activity modeling is the identification of a set of abstract operations (functions, modules, transactions), with well-defined inputs and outputs. These operations, as they are refined through the development process, provide a *complete* set of operations on the database, regardless of the underlying representation or data model.

Of course, not all of the operations in an interactive information system necessarily access or modify a database. However, the same principles of abstraction can be applied, so that the nondatabase operations of the system can also be named.

In summary, all of the programs comprising the interactive information system will use the operations so defined. It should be noted that while the vast majority of these operations can be identified and specified through a typical process of requirements analysis, others will not be identified until a later phase of the software development process. For this reason, User Software Engineering does not proceed with a rigorous formal specification at this stage. The defined operations may later be refined into formal specifications following a state model approach [13]–[15].

The same ideas that provide data model independence also provide *dialog independence*, the separation of the precise syntax of the user interface to the system from the operations of the system [16].

Logical separation of the dialogue from the operations allows several different dialogs to be specified for the same system. This approach facilitates the design of multilingual programs, of different interfaces for novices and experts, for low and high speed terminals, and for different styles of interaction, such as commands versus menu selection.

These operations now provide the first version of the desired abstract operations interface to the library system. To achieve both dialog independence and data model independence, the operations invoked by a user's input to the system must be limited to those in this set.

In practice, this set would be expanded to include certain housekeeping operations, such as opening and closing the database. During the development process, "hidden" operations would also be identified. Such hidden operations are not visible to the end user, but are required by the visible operations to perform their tasks.

Thus, it is necessary to define additional abstract operations to check these values, and such operations are normally defined during the development process. As a general rule, primary attention is given to those operations that *create* or *modify* entities or their attributes in the data model, with less attention given to those operations that simply access these entities and attributes. In Parnas'

terms, and as used by SRI International's Hierarchical Design Methodology, definition of the O-functions and the OV-functions take precedence over the V-functions and the hidden V-functions.

C. *User Characteristics*

Another important aspect of requirements analysis is understanding of user characteristics, so that the interface to the IIS can be properly designed. It is important to recognize the motivation and intended skill levels for the anticipated user population, to identify the needs for various types of output documents, e.g., hard copy versus "soft" copy, and to see whether the IIS must support casual users as well as regular users. Other issues, such as discretionary use versus mandatory use, and the need for alphanumeric keyboard input, are also taken into account at this stage.

Failure to understand the intended user community may lead to poor decisions concerning the user interface and the selection of information system functions. These errors will almost certainly lead to low user satisfaction and the need to make extensive (and expensive) modifications to the implemented system.

D. *The Library Example*

The example that will be described throughout the remainder of this paper is that of a simple library system, which supports the following transactions:
1) check out a copy of a book.
2) return a copy of a book.
3) add a copy of a book to the library.
4) remove a copy of a book from the library.
5) remove all copies of a book from the library.
6) get a list of titles of books in the library by a particular author.
7) find out what books are currently checked out by a particular borrower.
8) find out what borrower last checked out a particular copy of a book.

Note that this is an informal description of the problem, and furthermore that it does not completely describe the necessary operations for a library, which would include management of information about cardholders, reservations and requests for books, and numerous additional operations.[1] Nonetheless, this example will serve adequately to explain the concepts and applications of the USE methodology.

We begin by creating a data model for the example, and use the entity-relationship model for this purpose. An abbreviated (for reasons of space) model for the library is shown in Fig. 3.

This modeling activity not only yields information that will eventually go into the database that support the application, but also provides names that may be consistently used throughout the subsequent phases of development.

---

[1]The complete example includes restrictions on the transactions and invariants on the database, which we shall take up in a subsequent section.

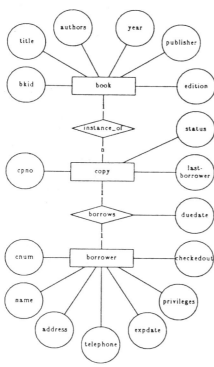

Fig. 3. Entity-relationship model for library database.

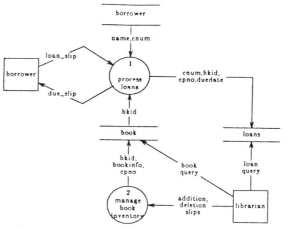

Fig. 4. "Top-level" dataflow diagram for library system.

The next step is to consider the operations that will be needed to create, access, and modify the entities and relationships in the data model. These operations are specified *informally* at this stage. While formal specification of operations is a valuable discipline, formalization can only be done successfully after a substantial amount of information has been obtained. Accordingly, the process is informal at this stage, but follows a pattern and structure that supports formalization at a later stage.

For this example, the major operations are specified by the problem statement, which is rarely the case in a practical system, where a significant amount of problem analysis and modeling is required to determine the operations that may be supported by a system. User Software Engineering, as noted, typically uses a method such as Structured Systems Analysis, and produces a set of leveled dataflow diagrams that is used to help identify the system operations. A "top-level" dataflow diagram for the library system is shown in Fig. 4.[2]

Fig. 5 shows the operations for the library system, following the problem statement. Note that names for the operations have been chosen, along with names for the inputs and outputs to the operations. The chosen input/output names correspond to the names of entities, relationships, and their attributes in the data model.

Note that operation *checkout* requires several hidden functions to check the validity of the book identification

number *bkid*, the copy number *cpno*, and the borrower card number *cnum*. These operations are *checkcard*, *checkbknum*, and *chkbkcopy*.

The problem statement for the library example provides no information about the characteristics of the users or the environment in which the system will be used. Some (not necessarily valid) assumptions may be made, however.

1) Users of the system will be library staff members, who will be regular users of the system. The terminals and printing devices with which they work will have to be located near the users' normal working locations.

2) The nature of the library and the jobs will require certain staff members to become knowledgeable in the use of the system. Some users will become quite adept in use of the system, and will wish to take advantage of any short cuts that may be built into the system. Users must be given the ability to circumvent long or repetitive messages or sequences of steps once they are comfortable with the system operation.

3) These users will not necessarily possess clerical skills, and almost certainly will not be experts in computer science or programming. These requirements imply that an effort should be made to minimize typing by the users, and that the program "lead the user" through each task.

4) There will be several different classes of users, representing several different subsystems of library management. One can easily envisage a subsystem for managing the lending of books to cardholders, and another for acquiring and removing books from the library's collection. The set of operations provided to the different classes of users may be different, but these different classes will share the same database through operations, and should be provided with similar types of user interfaces so that staff members can move from one job function to another without requiring extensive training in the use of the system.

These considerations suggest a menu-oriented interface for initial users of the system, with a command-oriented

[2]We have taken some liberties with the pure dataflow approach in this example, to provide a better match to the required transactions given in the specifications.

```
operation checkout
input bkid,cpno,cnum,duedate,MAX
output status
function
        Processes the checkout of copy cpno of book bkid to cardholder cnum, with a due date of duedate,
        only if cnum has MAX or fewer books already checked out

operation returnbk
input cnum, bkid, cpno
function
        Processes the return of copy cpno of the book with book identification number bkid by cardholder cnum

operation ins_book
input bkid, title, authors, publisher, year
function
        Inserts a new book into the catalog, with information on the book identification
        number bkid, the title, authors, publisher, and year of publication

operation del_book
input bkid, cpno
function
        Removes copy cpno of the book with book identification number bkid
        from the library; no operation performed if (bkid,cpno) pair is invalid

operation removeall
input bkid
function
        Removes all books with a given book identification number bkid from
        the library; no operation performed if the book number is invalid

operation bookbyname
input authorname
output titles
function
        Returns the set of book titles written by authorname

operation borrbooks
input borrower
output titles
function
        Returns the set of book titles presently checked out to borrower

operation lastborr
input bkid, cpno
output cnum
function
        Returns the cardholder cnum of the last person to borrow copy cpno of the book with
        book identification bkid, returns 0 if no such book

operation checkcard
input cnum
output toomany, validcard
function
        Returns true for validcard if cnum is a valid library card number and false
        otherwise; returns true for toomany if too many books are currently checked out to cnum

operation checkbknum
input bkid, cnum
output validbook, loanok
operation
        Returns true for validbook if bkid is a valid book identification and false
        otherwise; returns true for loanok if no copy of book is checked out to cnum

operation chkbkcopy
input bkid, cpno
output validcopy, statloan
operation
        Returns true for validcopy if cpno is a valid copy number for bkid and false
        otherwise; returns true for statloan if that copy is available to be checked out
```

Fig. 5. Informal description of library system operations.

option or a series of "invisible" menu options available for the experienced users.

IV. EXTERNAL DESIGN

To this point, the User Software Engineering methodology resembles many other approaches for information systems development, with its use of data abstraction and data modeling. Here, though, many other methods proceed with formalization of the functional specification, followed by architectural and detailed design, then by implementation, with a parallel activity to assure system quality and reliability.

A. Top-down Versus Outside-In Design

From the USE standpoint, this traditional emphasis on functional decomposition and top-down design works poorly in the domain of interactive information systems. In particular, the user community obtains an inappropriate perspective of the system under development, being shown what the system will do without being shown how it will appear to the user. This difference in perspective is important, as can be seen by analogy with obtaining an automobile.

Using a functional orientation, the customer (user) would be told the cost, the dimensions of the vehicle, its

horsepower, acceleration, braking, and fuel economy statistics, and would be told when it was scheduled for delivery. But the customer would not have the opportunity to
see the vehicle until it was actually delivered, and modifications to the delivered product could only be made with
great difficulty and at considerable expense. If the customer had no previous experience with automobiles, coming from a society where bicycles or rickshaws were the
common mode of transport, the user probably could not
accurately state the desired functions for this new means
of transportation. Furthermore, the customer might not
understand the technical details about the performance of
the automobile and could certainly not understand whether
the specific automobile was a good value for the price. As
a result, the manufacturer (developer) would make assumptions about the needs and desires of the customer and
hope that the customer would be satisfied with the finished
product. The customer would be extremely dependent
upon the judgment of the manufacturer, who becomes the
major determinant of customer satisfaction.

Rather than proceeding with further refinement of the
system functions, following a traditional "top-down" approach, the User Software Engineering methodology follows an "outside in" approach, in which the external interface to the system is defined.

There are two major reasons for this choice:
• It is easiest to work with the user community if the
system is defined from the user perspective rather than
from the system perspective.
• The "outside in" approach also serves the need of
functional decomposition, since logical transactions from
the user viewpoint often map directly into the previously
defined operations.

The subsequent example assumes that the user will work
at an alphanumeric terminal with a keyboard (teletype-
writer-like or video display, depending on the previous
phase).[3] For many common IIS's, the obvious choices for
a user interface are then command laguages, multiple
choice (menu selection screens), free text, or some combination of these. (Even many forms of nonkeyboard input
can be seen as equivalent to one of these.)

We then produce a preliminary design of the user interface. Our method for designing the dialog was initially
ad hoc, based on our experiences as summarized in a set
of guidelines [17]. More recently, though, we have developed and are beginning to use metrics that help evaluate
the properties of screen designs [5].

B: Concepts of USE Transition Diagrams

The user program dialog is then specified with a set of
USE transition diagrams. We began in 1977 using standard state transition diagrams, following their use in other
language processing applications [18]. We associated an

output message with each node (or state), and provided an
arc (transition) for each distinguishable class of user input
from a given state. An action could be associated with any
transition. Others have followed a similar approach [19]–
[21]. We found that state transition diagrams were a useful
mechanism for modeling interactive systems. However,
their basic form was inadequate for the range of user dialogs that one must model. For example, one could not distinguish between buffered and unbuffered input, truncate
an input string to fixed length, or terminate user input on
some character other than a carriage return. Other situations, such as immediate branching on a specific character, echo versus nonecho of user input, and branching upon
expiration of a time limit, simply could not be represented
with the basic notations.

Even worse, the complexity of diagrams quickly became
unmanageable for all but the smallest dialogs. We therefore introduced "subconversations" in a diagram as a useful structuring technique to manage the complexity of the
diagrams. A subconversation is represented by a rectangle, and works in much the same way as a subprogram
call in a programming language, suspending transitions in
the current diagram and "executing" the called diagram,
possibly repeating this process to an arbitrary depth.

In their basic form, transition diagrams are purely syntactic, having no memory and no ability to branch on the
results of actions. Both of these restrictions are unrealistic
when transition diagrams are used to model interactive information systems.

In an interactive dialog, a user frequently provides input
that is subsequently displayed or used as a parameter in
some operation. Thus, one must be able to save a user
input for additional processing. Variables are the standard
means of doing this, so the transition diagrams were extended to allow alphanumeric variables, with optional
constraints on string length and values.

Next, the sequence of a dialog is often dependent on the
results of actions. For example, if a user types in a name,
an action may look up that name in a table. A different
path must be followed if the name if found than if it is not
found. Therefore, actions must be able to return values
and it must be possible to branch in the diagram based on
those returned values.

Finally, we included cursor and screen management
symbols to be able to describe interactive dialog on a full-
screen display, not just on a line-oriented basis.

Thus, we have created an extended form of transition
diagram notation to support this class of applications [22],
and have found them to work well to specify both the user
input(s) to the system and the resulting system actions and
displays. We found transition diagrams to be preferable to
BNF, particularly for users who must comprehend the description. It is important to note that transition diagrams
provide an *executable* model of programs, with a highly
visible control flow.

As noted in [22], it is important that the descriptive notation cover a broad range of dialog styles and provide the

---

[3]Work is currently underway to extend the user interface specification
to handle bit-mapped displays and pointing devices.

Symbol	Meaning
'text'	Branch on receipt of 'text'
name	Assign user input to variable name
!	Unbuffered single key input
+	Transition without user input
@	No echo of user input
"	Time limit in seconds
&x	Transition on receipt of specific character x
list/	Accept input until character in list received
list/m	Truncate input to m characters

Fig. 6. USE transition diagram transition control symbols.

dialog designer with the flexibility to implement dialog design decisions smoothly.

This goal implies the need for a low-level specification capability, in which the dialog designer is given control over the reading and the presentation of every input character typed by the user and every output character displayed by the system. This goal is in contrast to the approach taken in some forms-oriented system, where numerous assumptions are made about the nature of human–computer interaction and about the presentation of information. While the forms-oriented systems are typically simpler to specify, the transition diagram approach envisioned for User Software Engineering is far more general. In other words, it is possible to specify the forms-oriented interfaces using the USE transition diagram approach.

C. Features of USE Transition Diagrams

The USE transition diagrams provide for input specification, output specification, and linkage to system operations.

Input may be obtained on any transition between two nodes, and may optionally be assigned to a declared variable. Input control includes control over the handling of the input, the transition conditions, and the terminator of the user input string. Input control is an important form of transition control, which determines the flow of control through a set of USE transition diagrams. The transition diagram symbols for input transition control are shown in Fig. 6.

Output may be produced at any node, and may consist of literal text, screen control information, and/or display of the contents of variables. Literal text is simply readable text surrounded by quote marks, augmented by control characters and other nonprintable symbols that may be specified as in the C programming language, e.g., "\n" for newline. Screen control information describes the placement of information on the screen, and controls the movement of a cursor representing the current row and column position. The screen control directives are intended to be mnemonic, and are shown in Fig. 7.

Variables are needed since it is frequently necessary to obtain user input, to calculate, and/or to obtain data values prior to using them in system operations or displaying them to users. Since the USE transition diagrams are intended to specify interactive information systems, the variables must support the data types typically needed for such systems, including integer, float, string, date, time, and scalar variables, as in Pascal.

cs	clear screen
rxx	to row xx
cxx	to column xx
r±n	n rows up or down
c±n	n columns left or right
h|n	row 0, column 0 (home)
rv	reverse video
sv	standard video
il	insert line
el	clear to end of line
ee	clear to end of screen
c_'text'	center text
i_'text'	insert text at current position
dc	delete character
dl	delete line
mark_a	mark the place a
tomark_a	return to the place a
t_n	move to the column marked by tab n
display (inparam, format)	
	control the formatting of a given data value

Fig. 7. Screen control directives.

lending

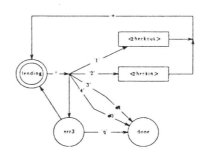

```
diagram lending entry lending exit done

tab t_0 20
tab t_1 25

node lending
        cs,r2,rv,c_'Library System',sv,
        r+2,t_0,'Please choose:',
        r+2,t_1,'1) Check out book',
        r+2,t_1,'2) Check in book',
        r+2,t_1,'3) Exit Book Lending subsystem',
        r+2,t_1,'4) Exit library system',
        r+2,t_0,'Your choice (1-4): '

node done

node err3
        r$-1,rv,bell,'Please type a number from 1 to 4',
        r$,c0,sv,'Press RETURN to continue or "q" to leave this section.'
```

Fig. 8. USE transition diagram for lending subsystem of library system.

D. USE Transition Diagrams for the Library Example

Some of the concepts described in this section can now be illustrated with USE transition diagrams from the library example. We concentrate on the lending subsystem associated with checkin and checkout of books.

The main USE transition diagram for the lending subsystem is shown in Fig. 8. This diagram shows the control flow of the dialog, along with transition control and output display information. The node with two concentric circles is the starting node, named lending. The text associated with node lending below the diagram is screen layout information. In this example, the screen is first cleared. Then the words "Library System" are centered on row 2, followed by six lines that present a "menu selection" on the screen. Note that two tabs are used for alignment of the columns in this menu display. The tabs are set at rows

checkout

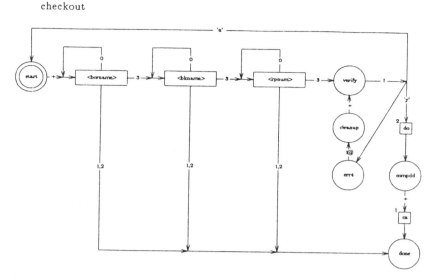

Actions

1   call checkout(cnum,bkid,cpno,duedate,today,MAX ->stat)

2   do newdate(today,loanper -> duedate)


```
diagram checkout entry start exit done

integer cnum [6:6] range 100000..999999
alpha bkid
integer cpno range 1..1000
integer MAX init 10
date duedate
scalar stat (normal, staff) init normal
integer loanper init 14

node start
        cs,r2,c_'Library System',
        r+2,c0,c_'Checkout Book'

node done

node verify
        r+2,c0,rv,'Is everything OK? (y/n) ',sv,mark_G,cl

node compdd

node err4
        r$-1,c0,rv,'Please type "y" or "n".',sv,
        r$,c0,'Type any character to continue.'

node cleanup
        r$-1,ce,tomark_G
```

Fig. 9. USE transition diagram for checkout subconversation of lending
subsystem of library system.

20 and 25, and the alignment and/or layout can be changed simply by modifying the tab stops.

The specified system will accept a single character of user input, as shown by the "!" symbol for unbuffered input, and branches accordingly. A response of "1", for example, invokes the ⟨checkout⟩ subconversation, while a response of "4" returns control to the "calling" conversation, returning the value of 0 which is then used to control flow in the calling conversation. Note that any response other than the integers from 1 to 4 causes a transition to node err3, which produces a diagnostic message at the bottom of the screen, using reverse video and an audible bell (control-G on most terminals), giving the user the option to try again or to exit the subsystem. (The help node has intentionally been omitted from this diagram, for reasons of space.)

The checkout diagram (subconversation) is shown in Fig. 9. To check out a book, it is necessary to have a valid

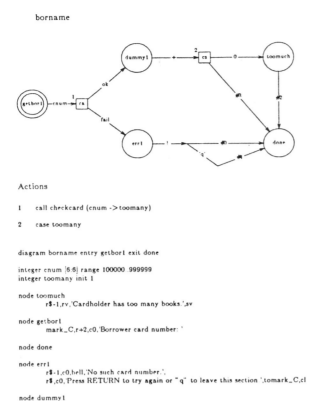

borname

Actions

1   call checkcard (cnum ->toomany)

2   case toomany

diagram borname entry getbor1 exit done

integer cnum [6:6] range 100000 .999999
integer toomany init 1

node toomuch
        r$-1,rv,'Cardholder has too many books.',sv

node getbor1
        mark_C,r+2,c0,'Borrower card number: '

node done

node err1
        r$-1,c0,bell,'No such card number.',
        r$,c0,'Press RETURN to try again or "q" to leave this section ',tomark_C,cl

node dummy1

Fig. 10. USE transition diagram for borname subconversation of checkout
       subconversation of lending system of library system.

borrower, a valid book, and a valid copy number. The checkout diagram calls upon three subconversations, borname, bkname, and cpnum, to perform those checks. In each case, the subconversation returns the value 0 if there was an error and the user wishes to try again, the values 1 or 2 for errors where the checkout operation is to be terminated, and the value 3 for a successful validation. If all three subconversations successively return the value 3, then the user is asked to verify the information, the due date is computed (**do** newdate), and the checkout operation is called.

Each of the three subconversations is similarly structured and we show the first of them, borname, as an example, in Fig. 10. Note that the transition from node getbor1 makes an assignment to variable cnum, representing the card number of the borrower. This value is passed to the checked operation (see Fig. 5), which may succeed of fail. Failure is caused by an invalid card number, and the message at node err1 asks the user to type RETURN to try again or "q" to quit. The former response yields a return value of 0, while the latter returns 1. If the checkcard operation succeeds, the value of its output parameter toomany is checked. If the value is 0, then the borrower has too many books checked out, so that the checkout operation must fail; otherwise, the checkout operation may continue (with the other subconversations). Note the paths in diagram borname that assign the values

2 and 3 as the return value of the diagram. These four values are used as the branching possibilities from the call to the borname subconversation in the checkout diagram.

In earlier versions of the library system, the validation of borrower and book information was implicit in processing the loan of a book to a borrower (the checkout operation). When that operation failed, though, there were numerous possible reasons for the failure, including improper data entry. At that point, the diagram specified that the user would be prompted to type in both the borrower and book identification again, thereby increasing the number of repetitions and the number of user keystrokes, since the user had to provide the information again regardless of the source of the problem.

It was not until the execution of the original diagram was hand simulated that this problem became obvious. In the newer versions of the checkout diagram, as shown here, the checkout operation was changed to do the data entry checking prior to the checkout operation. Once again, it is clear that premature efforts to formalize the operations completely often lead to significant amounts of rework.

This example shows how to combine diagrams for the creation of complex interactive information systems. Values can be communicated between a diagram and its subdiagram through the use of return values. Variables may also be used to store and pass values among diagrams and actions. As will be shown, these variables may be those defined in USE transition diagrams or those defined in the operations that perform the actions required in the interactive information system.

V. PROTOTYPE OF THE HUMAN/COMPUTER INTERACTION

A. *Rationale for Prototypes*

Initially (circa 1978), the transition diagrams were used simply as a specification method, since they served both the needs of the developers of the interactive system and the eventual users of the system. When used in combination with hand-drawn "mockups" of the user interface, it was possible to convey some concepts of the intended user interaction with the system.

While this approach worked moderately well, particularly for well-motivated users, it seemed that the users did not really obtain a good sense of the system from the diagrams alone. Furthermore, the developers did not obtain a good indication of the quality of the interface design of the user community's reaction to that design.

To return to the analogy with the automobile, the USE transition diagrams were equivalent to presenting the customer with a brochure describing the features of the automobile. A potential customer with some knowledge of automobiles is able to make some intelligent judgments and rule out certain types of automobiles based on that knowledge; a potential customer who has never before seen an automobile cannot immediately understand the differences (other than price and dimensions) between a Volkswagen and a Rolls-Royce.

What is needed in that case is a test drive, in which the

potential customer has the opportunity to drive the automobile and to see how it performs. The person with knowledge of the automobile will be able to investigate some of the details, while the novice will gain some of the basic concepts and increase his or her understanding of the automobile and what it can do.

The equivalent of the test drive concept in the case of User Software Engineering is an executable version of the user interface to the system—a prototype of the dialog. Without the prototype of the dialog, the user community had only a written description of the system under development. As a result, many changes to the dialog and the functions were made after implementation, with all of the usual problems attendant to evolving systems.

B. The Transition Diagram Interpreter

This observation led to the design and development of the RAPID/USE prototyping system, which contains a Transition Diagram Interpreter (TDI) [23], [24]. This Transition Diagram Interpreter[4] interprets the encoded diagrams, making it possible to allow a user to interact with a "mockup" of the user interface design.

Following the initial design of the user/prototype dialog, the transition diagram(s) are encoded in machine-processable form. This step may either be done automatically with a graphical Transition Diagram Editor (TDE) [25] or manually. We have defined a dialog specification language that supports direct encoding of the USE transition diagrams. Elements of this dialog specification language include diagrams, nodes, arcs, messages, and variables.

The Transition Diagram Editor generates this dialog description language directly, so that it is not necessary for the user to learn the exact syntax of this language (or even to see it!).

This ability to "execute" the dialog, even a portion of it, and even in the absence of operations, is of tremendous value in application of the USE methodology because it gives the user at the terminal a good understanding of the expected behavior of the IIS, and gives the developer a good understanding of the user's problems with the dialog design. It is straightforward to edit the transition diagrams or their textual equivalent as changes are needed. Most cosmetic changes to the dialog can be made in minutes, giving the user a sense of being an active participant in the design process.

For many interactive systems, the optimal design and prototyping approach is to perform the complete dialog design on a major subsystem, and then let the user community work with that interface, making changes dynamically until a workable interface design is achieved. The dialog design for that subsystem then becomes the model for other subsystems to be used by other users having similar skills, to achieve a consistent user interface throughout the system.

Not only does the executable protytpe of the interface

---

[4]"Interpreter" is actually a misnomer for the current version of this software, which compiles the dialog description language.

give the user a better sense of the planned system, but it also allows objective evaluation of the interface and helps users to think more accurately about the necessary functions for the system.

When the Transition Diagram Interpreter was first developed, the prototype was not built until the complete dialog design was complete or nearly so. Thus, the user community did not see or have the opportunity to work with the user interface until many design decisions had been made. While that process was still an improvement over the traditional means of information systems development, it did not yield as high a degree of user involvement as seemed desirable.

The development of the Transition Diagram Editor has altered the recommended process significantly, since the diagrams are executable without an intermediate encoding step. Users can work with executable versions of the user interface almost immediately, and it is often useful to have "real users" see the emerging system from the outset, occasionally with only a few screens or input opportunities.

This approach has implications for all the initial steps of the USE methodology. Rather than completing the modeling and analysis steps prior to designing the user interface, it is possible to work partly in parallel on these activities and to begin work on the user interface design well before the completion of the data and activity modeling.

In fact, the analysis, dialog design, and dialog prototyping steps can become closely intertwined. Users working with the emerging dialog design obtain a better sense of their own needs, and are therefore better able to aid in the identification of required inputs, outputs, and functions for the system. This information is then "fed back" into the analysis process, possibly causing changes in the data and/or activity models. In this way, the critical User Software Engineering goal of *effective* user involvement in the development process can be achieved.

The dialog prototyping process is iterative and partly experimental. The ability to build and quickly modify interface designs makes it practical to construct alternative interfaces and to give users the opportunity to work with all of them, stating their own likes and dislikes. Because of the dialog independence inherent in the USE approach, it is even possible to customize different interfaces for different individuals, should that be desired.

Empirical observations show that "tuning" of the dialog usually occurs through a sequence of minor changes to node descriptions and control flows. The initial versions of the dialog focus on the major functions and behave properly as long as users provide meaningful inputs. The diagrams are then modified to add nodes for errors and for user assistance (help).

C. Evaluation of the User Interface Design

The objective evaluation of the interface is made possible by the ability to keep session logs of the interaction. Two logs may be maintained: a raw input log and a transition log. The raw input log saves *every keystroke*, so that

```
diagram lending entry lending exit done

tab t_0 20
tab t_1 25

node lending
     cs,r2,rv,c_'Library System',sv,
     r+5,t_0,'Please choose:',
     r+2,t_1,'1) Check out book',
     r+2,t_1,'2) Check in book',
     r+2,t_1,'3) Exit Book Lending subsystem',
     r+2,t_1,'4) Exit library system',
     r+2,t_0,'Your choice (1-4): '

node done

node err3
     r#-1,rv,bell,'Please type a number from 1 to 4',
     r#,c0,sv,'Press RETURN to continue or "q" to leave this section.'

arc lending single_key
     on '2' to <checkin>
     on '1' to <checkout>
     on '4' to done return 0
     on '3' to done return 1
     else to err3

arc <checkout>
     skip to lending

arc <checkin>
     skip to lending

arc err3 single_key
     on 'q' to done
     else to lending

diagram checkout entry start exit done

integer cnum [6:6] range 100000..999999
alpha bkid
integer cpno range 1..1000
integer MAX init 10
date duedate
scalar stat (normal, staff) init normal
integer loanper init 14

node start
     cs,r2,c_'Library System',
     r+2,c0,c_'Checkout Book'

node done

node verify
     r+2,c0,rv,'Is everything OK? (y/n) ',sv,mark_G,cl

node compdd

node err4
     r#-1,c0,rv,'Please type "y" or "n".',sv,
     r#,c0,'Type any character to continue.'

node cleanup
     r#-1,ce,tomark_G

arc start
     skip to <borname>

arc verify single_key
     on 'n' to start
     on 'y' do newdate(today,loanper -> duedate) to compdd
     else to err4

arc compdd
     skip call checkout(cnum,bkid,cpno,duedate,today,MAX ->stat) to done

arc err4 noecho  single_key
     else to cleanup
```

Fig. 11. Textual representation of USE transition diagrams lending, checkout, and borname.

```
arc cleanup
        skip to verify

arc <borname>
        on 0 to <borname>
        on 1,2 to done
        on 3 to <bkname>

arc <bkname>
        on 0 to <bkname>
        on 1,2 to done
        on 3 to <cpnum>

arc <cpnum>
        on 0 to <cpnum>
        on 1,2 to done
        on 3 to verify

diagram borname entry getbor1 exit done

integer cnum [6:6] range 100000..999999
integer toomany init 1

node toomuch
        r$-1,rv,'Cardholder has too many books.',sv

node getbor1
        mark_C,r+2,c0,'Borrower card number: '

node done

node err1
        r$-1,c0,bell,'No such card number.',
        r$,c0,'Press RETURN to try again or "q" to leave this section.',tomark_C,c1

node dummy1

arc toomuch
        else to done return 2

arc getbor1
        on cnum call checkcard (cnum -> toomany)
                when fail to err1
                when ok to dummy1

arc err1 single_key
        on 'q' to done return 1
        else to done return 0

arc dummy1
        skip case toomany
                default to done return 3
                when 0 to toomuch
```

Fig. 11. (Continued.)

it may be serve as a scenario and be replayed later during system testing. Also, keystrokes are easily counted, giving a good measure of usability..

The transition log includes a record for each state transition. Each record includes a time stamp, the diagram name, the node name, any action called, and the user input, and the character that terminated the input. Analysis of this log permits analysis of task completion time, screen viewing times, user error patterns (if all error nodes have recognizable names), and frequency of action calls. A separate tool, rapsum, can do further analysis on the transition log, so that one can, for example, compute the percentage of nodes visited as a measure of test coverage.

RAPID/USE is designed and built specifically as part of the User Software Engineering methodology, and one can see that it supports many of the methodology's goals. It is extremely valuable in verifying and analyzing dialog designs and therefore allows a satisfactory design to be achieved at a very early stage of the IIS development process. In many respects, this use of prototypes and the availability of RAPID/USE are the major contribution of the User Software Engineering methodology.

D. Prototype User Interface for the Library Example

The textual equivalent of the USE transition diagram for the lending, checkout, and borname diagrams is shown in Fig. 11. Careful comparison of this text with the diagrams shown in Figs. 8-10 shows that the encoding of the diagrams is straightforward. The text in Fig. 11 has been generated by the Transition Diagram Editor directly from the diagrams.

The header shows the name of the diagram and the names of the entry and exit nodes. This information is followed by the declaration of the tabs, and then by the nodes and arcs of the diagram, which may be given in any order. Note that the information presented for each node

```
                    Library System

          Please choose:

              1) Check out book

              2) Check in book

              3) Exit Book Lending subsystem

              4) Exit library system

          Your choice (1-4):
```

Fig. 12. Screen layout for node lending in diagram lending.

is identicaly to the message associated with a node in the diagram above. For each node, the *arc* statement lists all of the arcs emanating from that node, along with input control and transition conditions. The arc statements provided the structural information about the diagram.

The screen shown upon entry to the borrower subsystem is shown in Fig. 12. The presentation of this screen conveys information that is not apparent from the dialog description language. When this screen design is viewed, one can see that the overall alignment is good, but that the display could be placed closer to the center of the screen by moving the last six lines of text downward by about three lines. Such a change is easily made.

VI. FROM INTERFACE PROTOTYPE TO RUNNING SYSTEM

Following completion of the dialog prototype step, the user interface has been formally specified through the USE transition diagrams, and the system operations have been specified informally. From this point, there are several possible paths that can be followed toward a complete, working system, with three major variants:

1) extend the prototype with programmed actions and database operations;

2) abandon the prototype, and proceed with a system design and implementation using a traditional programming language.

3) abandon the prototype, produce a formal specification of the entire system, and develop a production system using a different set of methods and tools.

The alternative to be taken is highly dependent on local circumstances, including the nature of the application and the structure of the organization(s) involved in the development process. Each of these approaches will be discussed, with emphasis on the first variant, extending the prototype.

A. Relational Database Design

An IIS has been characterized as providing conversational access to data. Thus, an obvious strategy for building such systems is to link a "user interface management system," such as that provided by the Transition Diagram Interpreter, with a database management system (DBMS). In following that approach, the system operations are implemented using the data manipulation language of the DBMS. Many of the commercially available "fourth gen-

eration languages" and "application generators" use this notion.

The semantic data model developed in the analysis phase must be transformed into an executable data model for some DBMS. Since there are few DBMS's that directly support these semantic data models, the most practical transformation is to a normalized relational data model. The transformation from an entity-relationship model or a semantic hierarchy model to relations is straightforward, and simply involves retaining separately the constraints that are lost in making the transformation.

The description of the operations can then be given in terms of definition and manipulation of relations and their attributes, since the database is now defined as a set of relations. All operations that affect the database can be rewritten in a relational data manipulation language, either a nonprocedural, calculus language, such as SQL/DS or QUEL [26]–[28], or a procedural algebraic language, such as that of the Troll/USE relational DBMS [29]. In this manner, the abstract operations are realized as a set of procedures on the relational database and the combination of these procedures with the dialog design provides a substantial part, if not all, of a running system.

The Troll/USE relational DBMS has been designed and developed as a central component in the toolset to support the User Software Engineering methodology. Troll/USE is a compact and efficient system providing a relational algebra-like interface, including operations at the item, tuple, and relation level. Troll/USE supports specification and checking of data types for attributes of relations, including scalar types using enumerated values as in Pascal. An especially valuable aspect of Troll/USE is its support of parameterized scripts, by which named sequences of Troll/USE data manipulation statements may be stored with formal parameters in a "library" of such scripts and may then be invoked by name with actual parameters during a Troll/USE session.

Troll/USE works on a message-passing basis, and has been used as the backend for numerous user interfaces, including the screen-oriented TBE (Troll/USE browser and editor) and the data dictionary subsystem of the Dataflow Diagram Editor developed by Interactive Development Environments, Inc. The message-passing organization makes it suitable for integration with tools in a software development environment. In this way, Troll/USE may be used both as a DBMS in support of the software development process and as the DBMS for the resulting application systems.

B. Relational Database Design for the Library Example

A relational database definition for the library example is shown in Fig. 13. Note that Troll/USE supports data types of date and variable-length string, as well as providing for user-defined scalar domains and range constraints on domains. These type definitions are enforced by the Troll/USE system to prevent undesirable operations on the database.

```
domain bookstat: scalar (onshelf, checkout);
domain loantype: scalar (regular);
domain cardtype: scalar (normal);
domain cardval: integer (100000..999999);

relation book [key bkid] of
        bkid: string;
        title: string;
        authors: string;
        publisher: string;
        year: date;
end;

relation bookcopy [key bkid,cpno] of
        bkid: string;
        cpno: integer (1..1000);
        ckoutstat: loantype;
        status: bookstat;
        lastborrower: cardval;
end;

relation borrowers [key cnum] of
        cnum: cardval;
        name: string;
        address: string;
        telephone: string;
        expdate: date;
        privileges: cardtype;
        checkedout: integer (0..100);
end;

relation loan [key cnum, bkid, cpno] of
        cnum: cardval;
        bkid: string;
        cpno: integer (1..1000);
        duedate: date;
        checkoutdate: date;
end;
```

Fig. 13. Normalized relations for library example using Troll/USE data manipulation language.

C. Implementing the IIS Operations

While the prototype of the dialog alone is useful, particularly for identifying requirements and for obtaining usable interfaces to an IIS, such a prototype does not *do* anything. Furthermore, the pure dialog prototype makes it difficult to display the dialog alternatives that may sample results, since there is no real database and no actions. The dialog prototype, as implemented with the TDI part of RAPID/USE, provides merely a "façade" for the system.

Thus, it is valuable to be able to implement some (or even all) of the actions specified for the system. The actions performed by an IIS may vary widely, from numerical computation to database management, and from language processing to application generation. Thus, the IIS developer may need access to any of several programming languages and, most importantly, to a database management system.

The logical organization of such an interactive information system is now more accurately represented as shown in Fig. 14, in which the "system operations" of Fig. 1 are partitioned into "database operations" and "computational operations." In the User Software Engineering toolset, the combinations of RAPID/USE with Troll/USE provides the mechanisms required to imple-

Fig. 14. Logical organization of interactive information systems.

ment both classes of operations. The Action Linker part of RAPID/USE serves this purpose. Routines may be written in C, Fortran 77, or Pascal.[5]

RAPID/USE operates by linking together the TDI with the actions and with libraries that provide terminal and screen handling, access to the Troll/USE DBMS, and the action routines. With that combination, the developer may gradually implement actions, adding operations, error handling, online assistance, and other features as desired.

Because the action mechanism is completely general, one could build the *entire* IIS in this way. Indeed, for systems consisting almost entirely of dialog and database manipulations, such an approach is quite easy. The RAPID/USE approach is also useful for use with programming languages having weak input/output management capabilities, since the dialog specification can be handled with TDI and the actions can be implemented in the desired programming language.

In the User Software Engineering toolset, the combination of RAPID/USE with Troll/USE provides the necessary mechanisms to implement such an IIS quickly and efficiently. Communication between the dialog description and database manipulation is accomplished with the *call* statement in the Transition Diagram Interpreter. The *database* and *library* statements in RAPID/USE dialog description files are passed to Troll/USE at execution time to define the file system location of the database and the location(s) of any libraries that contain Troll/USE scripts needed for program execution. As can be seen in the USE transition diagram for checkout above (and in its textual equivalent), there are calls to operations named checkcard, checkbknum, and checkout. Each of these operations is implemented as a parameterized script, written in the Troll/USE data manipulation language. The RAPID/USE-to-Troll/USE linkage passes the parameters from the call statement in RAPID/USE to the Troll/USE script and can similarly return values to RAPID/USE from Troll/USE.

The format of the call statement in RAPID/USE is

call operation (inparamlist → outparamlist)

The parameters are assigned to the Troll/USE global variables $0 through $9 using a positional correspondence and a call-by-reference mechanism. These global variables take

---

[5]Other languages that share linkage conventions with these languages can be easily added.

the role of formal parameters in the script. Assignments to the global variables within the called Troll/USE script are therefore reflected in changes to the output parameters (RAPID/USE variables).

Of course, not all of the IIS operations involve database manipulation, so it is important to be able to combine the dialog definition part with the computational operations as well. This situation is handled by the Action Linker portion of RAPID/USE and by the *do* statement in the dialog description.

The format of the do statement is identical to that of the call statement except that the word "call" is replaced by "do." While the linkage for the call statement may be accomplished with the Transition Diagram Interpreter, the do statement requires a more general program linkage facility.

The Action Linker accepts programmed routines written in programming languages, either in source or object form, and either as individual files or as archived libraries of routines. Source code is compiled, resulting in a collection of object files and libraries. These objects are linked incrementally, along with the object program that executes the compiled dialog description file. The dialog description file is then compiled and the resulting data structure is linked in to the object program, producing an executable program, which may be invoked in the same way as can any other object program in the environment.

The facilities of RAPID/USE and its Action Linker also support modifications to existing software built without the User Software Engineering methodology and its tools. A useful activity is to take programs that do not support the notion of *dialog independence* and to modify them to do so. That approach is now sketched out.

In many interactive programs, the input/output statements are embedded within the program, rather than separated as is done here. One could begin with existing modules and systems, and find the input and output statements to determine the information that must be communicated between the program and the "outside world." Each of the modules is then treated as an "operation" from the standpoint of User Software Engineering, and the variables that are input and output for that module become parameters passed to it from a *do* statement in the dialog description. These parameters thereby become variables in the USE transition diagrams that describe the dialog and the actions. The input and output statements in the module are then replaced with statements that make assignments to the variables. The existing modules are then combined using the Action Linker of RAPID/USE with the user interface design.

In this way, the tools supporting the User Software Engineering methodology provide direct support not only for the creation of prototypes of user/program interfaces, but also for the extension of those prototypes into running programs and the modification of existing programs.

The benefits of the RAPID/USE-Troll/USE combination are especially evident when the operations for a sys-

```
operation bookbyname (authorname)

        ans1 := book where authors # authorname;
        {ans1 is the set of books where the set of authors contains a
          string matching the given authorname}

operation checkout (bkid,cpno,cnum,duedate,MAX -> status)

        {everything already checked}
        insert loan [$0,$1,$2,$3,$4];
        bookcopy [$1,$2].lastborrower := $0;
        bookcopy [$1,$2].status := checkout;
        borrowers [$0].checkedout := borrowers[$0].checkedout + 1;
        $5 := normal;

operation ins_book (bkid, title, authors, publisher, year)

        insert book [$0,$1,$2,$3,$4];
        t3 := bookcopy where bkid = $0;
        if count (t3) = 0 then
        begin
               $5 := 1;
        end else
        begin
               $5 := max(t3.cpno)+1;
        end;
        insert bookcopy [$0,$5,normal,onshelf,999999];
        destroy t3;
```

Fig. 15. Troll/USE scripts for library system operations.

tem largely involve database manipulation. In that case, the dialog management is specified in a language well suited to that task, and the database definition and manipulation is similarly specified in a specialized language. The resulting system is built on powerful software development tools without the need for programming in a traditional programming language. Experience has shown that this approach drastically shortens the time needed to produce a running system and the amount of "code" written by the software developer, without giving up anything in performance. Furthermore, the use of the extensively tested application development tools helps to reduce the number of errors in the resulting system.

D. IIS Operations for the Library Example

This combination of tools has been used to implement the operations for the library example. Consider the library operations for displaying all of the books by a given author, for adding a book to the library, and for checking out a book. These operations have been named bookbyname, ins_book, and checkout, respectively. Each of these operations may be described as a Troll/USE procedure, involving a script of database operations that accept parameters. These three operations are shown in Fig. 15. The checkout and ins_book operations are among the most complex operations in the entire library system, yet only involve a small number of lines of code each. All of the operations for the library system, except computation of the due date for a book, are handled by 21 Troll/USE scripts totaling just 96 lines of data manipulation language with comments.

If all of the operations are described in this way, we obtain a precise *executable* specification of the operations. These executable statements, when combined with the dialog description from the USE transition diagrams, yield a running system.

VII. Formal Specification

Whether or not a functional prototype has been created, the previous steps provide sufficient information to produce a formal specification of system behavior, should one wish to do so. The transition diagrams give a formal definition of the input syntax, the output displays, and the possible sequences of state transitions, showing the points at which various operations are invoked. All that remains, then, is to give a formal specification of the behavior of the operations.

For this purpose, we follow the BASIS (Behavioral Approach to the Specification of Information System) method [30], [15], which is an abstract model approach to specification, based on the ideas of Hoare, as refined for use in the Alphard programming language [31], [32]. BASIS has five major steps: information analysis, semantic specification, verification of the design specification, implementation, and verification of the implementation. The first step, information analysis, includes the specification of the objects and transactions involved in the specification to be built. This information is derived from the requirements analysis phase (and can be done at that time).

The second step (semantic specification) includes the specification of the logical rules or properties (constraints) of the real world system. This information includes not only the operations of the system, but also the legal states of the data. If the data start out in a legal or accurate state and only legal operations are applied, then the data will be guaranteed to have semantic integrity. (This specification can be verified as the next step.)

There are three main parts of a BASIS specification of semantic integrity: the image of the object, the invariant, and input and output constraints for each operation defined on each object. The image is a list of the attributes associated with the object along with constraints on the values of these attributes for instances of the object. The invariant is composed of the interattribute constraints, if any. This invariant can be replaced by placing such constraints in the input and output constraints for the operations. The operations are defined by the input and output constraints which characterize the effects of the operations, using Hoare's notations for preconditions and postconditions. The specification of the pre and post conditions is important for three reasons: 1) the checking of particular constraints is tied to particular operations, 2) the pre and post constraints for the operations act as a guide for the implementor, and 3) they are used to prove that the specification and implementation are correct.

Formal specifications are a valuable discipline and help to eliminate the ambiguity that is often present with informal specifications. Formal specifications are rarely requested by users, though, who normally prefer that the equivalent effort be given to development of the prototype or final system. Formal specifications may be difficult to write and are not easily understood. Furthermore, most users do not yet understand that they aid in the identification and removal of errors. Thus, they have little interest in the formal specifications of the operations.

The ability to formalize one's concept of a system is an important process (even if the process is not done on every system). Thus, the formal specification step is an important part of the USE methodology. In practice, the complete formalization is rarely used, but the USE methodology is guided by the ideas inherent in the BASIS approach. Furthermore, the methods and tools used in the USE methodology are all based on formalisms, such as state transition networks and the theory of relations.

VIII. Experience

The User Software Engineering methodology has evolved since the late 1970's and has been shown to be a practical method for the creation of interactive information systems. At first, the methodology relied upon manual creation and modification of the USE transition diagrams. At that time, it was useful primarily as a specification method, rather than as a system building tool. The transition diagram specification method was used successfully on several interactive medical applications.

The envisioned implementation language was PLAIN [33], designed to support the creation of interactive information systems. PLAIN is a Pascal-based language with features for string-handling, pattern-matching, exception-handling, and relational database management, in addition to a data abstraction mechanism. While PLAIN is valuable as an implementation language, our attention was increasingly drawn to the earlier stages of the development process and to the notions of external design and rapid implementation described in this paper.

Implementation of tools to support the USE methodology directly was undertaken in 1978. The Troll/USE relational database system was designed so that it could serve both as the backend to PLAIN and as a stand-alone relational system. Design and implementation of the Transition Diagram Interpreter and RAPID/USE was begun in 1980. In both cases, an important project goal was to produce software tools that could be distributed to others. As a result, the User Software Engineering distribution was begun jointly by the University of California, San Francisco, and the Vrije Universiteit, Amsterdam, in 1981. Initially, the distribution included only the Troll/USE relational DBMS. Now, in the fourth release, the distribution includes a vastly improved version of Troll/USE, along with the third version of RAPID/USE, the Troll/USE library, the TBE browser for Troll/USE relations, and some experimental software. Approximately 100 sites are using one of the two latest versions of the distribution, divided half and half between academic and industrial users.

Commercial interest in the User Software Engineering methodology and its supporting tools led to the creation of a commercial venture, Interactive Development Environments, Inc., which markets commercial versions of this software, plus the Transition Diagram Editor and other graphical editors described in this paper.

Until 1984, experience with the methodology and tools was fragmentary, and mostly confined to the original developers of the methodology. Availability of tools and tutorial materials were necessary to transfer the technology out of the research setting. RAPID/USE has now been used for some significant applications, including the system administrator's interface for an engineering workstation, a patient record-keeping system for a health maintenance organization, a general ledger accounting system, and a customer/order management system, in addition to applications developed within our own organization and the library system described in this paper. All but the first of these applications use Troll/USE as the database support for their application.

Now that there is a substantial user community, we are forming a USE Users' Group to serve as a forum for discussing the methodology and the tools. The first meeting of this Group is scheduled for mid-1986.

IX. Evaluation

At this stage, evaluation of the methodology and tools is largely anecdotal. However, it is possible to give a subjective evaluation of the User Software Engineering methodology against the goals presented in Section II. Each of the goals is taken up in turn.

A. Functionality

Since User Software Engineering results in the creation of running systems, one could say that it covers the entire development process. In fact, though, the USE approach makes specific contributions only in the specification, design, and implementation phases, and relies heavily on integration with other approaches for analysis and testing. The identification of abstract data and abstract operations during the analysis phase supports the use of those abstract operations when one defines the external interface to the system.

B. Reliability

User Software Engineering makes a significant contribution to assuring the reliability of the interactive interface. First, the interface is formally specified and executable, making it possible to create a set of test cases to validate the interface. One can make certain that the IIS provides an error path from each node where erroneous user input may be received. The presence of these paths may be verified through inspection of the diagrams.

Second, RAPID/USE produces two logs: a *raw log* containing all of the user input from the execution of the program and a *transition log*, as described in Section V-C. The raw log may be saved and subsequently used as input to a later version of the IIS. A set of such logs can be added to a test suite for the system. The transition log can be used to obtain measures of node coverage and arc coverage for a given execution of the IIS, as well as information on user error frequency and task completion times.

A set of transition logs can assure that test coverage of the user interface was sufficient. The use of these logs, plus animation of the executing transition diagrams, is discussed at greater length in a related paper [34].

Third, the IIS is largely built upon two components: RAPID/USE and Troll/USE. These application development tools have been thoroughly tested and widely used. The amount of code to be written by the developer is relatively small, making it easier to test the program than if the equivalent system had been created *de novo* in a procedural programming language.

C. Usability

Usability of the resulting system is a key goal of User Software Engineering and the use of prototypes of the user interface may be regarded as an important contribution of the USE methodology. This notion of interface prototyping is rapidly gaining favor, and there is some preliminary evidence of this concept being introduced into other methodologies. We remain convinced by our experience that user involvement in the interface design process is a major factor in eventual user satisfaction with the system.

As noted in Section V-A, early attempts at user involvement were hindered by the lack of an executable prototype of the interface. Our own efforts to build a system for a glaucoma clinic (circa 1980) showed that transition diagrams and screen layout forms were inadequate for user understanding in the absence of the Transition Diagram Interpreter.

When end users (or surrogate end users) work with the prototype of the interface, it is possible to evaluate their experience, both objectively and subjectively. The objective information can be taken from the transition logs, while the subjective information comes from observation of the user, followed by an informal interview. Further refinement of this evaluation procedure is needed, since there is a wide variation in user skills and in motivation to use the system, especially in its early nonfunctional stages.

D. Evolvability

The separation of system specification into user interface, operations, and database is valuable for creating evolvable systems. For example, changes in the database schema typically do not affect the user interface; similarly, changes to the user interface rarely affect the database or the system operations. Thus, modifications can be isolated within the system. For example, a minor change in the user interface to a medium-sized system can often be found and corrected in a matter of seconds, with a new version of the executable user interface running within a minute.

At the same time, though, there are some difficulties with evolvability, particularly in maintaining consistent dialog styles through a set of subsystems or transaction types. Also, some changes to the specification may have far-reaching effects, requiring changes to the database, the operations, and the user interface. It is easy to make errors in the use of names for nodes, RAPID/USE variables, Troll/USE attributes, and program variables in the application code. We believe that introduction of a data dictionary can reduce the frequency of this type of problem; we have also found that multiple windows as found in many workstation environments make it easy to check for consistent use of names in different parts of the IIS.

E. Automated Support

User Software Engineering takes the position that software tools can be *integrated* into a structured software development methodology, rather than just placed into an available toolkit. While the infrastructure of the methodology is essential, it is the tools that make the methodology work. User involvement and interface prototyping are sound ideas, but they would be of little utility without the tools. The Transition Diagram Editor is an especially valuable addition to the USE toolset, reducing the need to learn the RAPID/USE syntax and eliminating some of the typing required to input the RAPID/USE language.

The USE tools are created as a set of components, many of which communicate via message passing. They are implemented on the Unix™ operating system.[6] This tool architecture supports two important aspects of tool development and use, namely

1) the ability for tools to communicate with and via a database (Troll/USE); and

2) the ability to extend tool capabilities without modifying existing tools; such extensions may be made either by the methodology's developers or by the methodology's users, since the tool interfaces are well-defined.

As with many other toolsmiths, we are continually seeking ways to provide additional automated support and to improve the existing tools. This objective continually provides many research and development projects. We are currently making modifications to Troll/USE to support long tuples ($> = 4$ kbytes); since Troll/USE already supports variable length strings, such a change will increase the usability of Troll/USE for developers and for end users.

We are also developing a "what-you-see-is-what-you-get" forms-based program for database entry, update, and retrieval. Such a tool will make it much easier to specify and to implement this important class of programs. This tool, RAPID/FORM, will generate a RAPID/USE script or executable program from a description of the form-based user interface and the associate database relations and attributes.

In summary, automated support for the USE methodology is very important, and we are pleased with the strategy that has been used for tool development and integration. Further development is aimed at simplifying the development process, and at extending the tool coverage to other aspects of that process.

™Unix is a trademark of AT&T Bell Laboratories.
6The USE tools are distributed by the University of California, San Francisco, by the Vrije Universiteit, Amsterdam, and by Interactive Development Environments, Inc., of San Francisco, which also provides support for the methodology and tools.

F. Improved Developer Productivity

Productivity is difficult to measure and has traditionally been measured in delivered source lines of code per unit of time. It is generally accepted that developers can deliver the same number of lines of code per day independent of the programming language.

By that measure, User Software Engineering can lead to a significant jump in developer productivity, since most of an interactive information system can be described either by the RAPID/USE dialog description language or by the Troll/USE data manipulation language. For a very small RAPID/USE example, we discovered that 35 lines of dialog description and data manipulation text required nearly 300 lines when reprogrammed in the C language. Furthermore, virtually none of the C language code was reusable, and it was necessary to eliminate one of the features available in the RAPID/USE version. It is apparent that creation and maintenance of 35 lines of RAPID/USE text, similar to that found in Fig. 10, is much simpler than creating and maintaining 300 lines of code in the C language.

The library example developed in this paper consists of approximately 1200 lines of RAPID/USE text, fewer than 100 lines of Troll/USE data manipulation scripts, and 30 lines of relational database definition.

It should also be noted that the RAPID/USE compiler is very fast, capable of processing more than 2000 lines of RAPID/USE input per minute on a Sun-2 Workstation or a VAX-11/750. Compilation of the library example takes approximately 30 seconds, while compilation and linking of the equivalent program in C or Pascal would take several minutes.

While we would not claim an order of magnitude improvement in productivity from User Software Engineering and its tools, such an improvement can be found for a portion of the development process, namely the design and implementation of the user interface. For the interactive systems that we have built, use of the methodology and tools has yielded an apparent factor of 3 to 4 gain in overall productivity, sharply reducing the time needed to produce a working system.

These results may be biased by our own expertise with the methodology and tools. The reported experience of others will be required before accurate estimates of productivity gains can be made. Nonetheless, initial anecdotal reports are extremely promising, and we hope that users of the USE methodology and tools will soon report on their experiences.

G. Reusability

As we continue to develop interactive information systems, consistent program schemas appear repeatedly. In the library system, we see the presence of a menu, followed by a multiway branch based on the user response. Similarly, a request for a yes-or-no response typically results in a three-way branch, corresponding to the yes case, the no case, and the error case. These "dialog schemas"

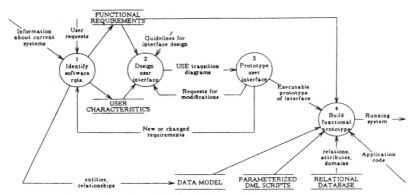

Fig. 16. Overview of the User Software Engineering methodology.

may be saved and reused in a variety of user interface designs. Similarly, entire diagrams may be reused.

We have observed that individuals and organizations develop personal styles of user interface design. These styles are captured in USE transition diagrams, which may then be repeatedly used. Further work is needed to support management of a library of reusable diagrams and dialog skeletons, but preliminary observations indicate that one can reuse part or all of a user interface design in the same way that one can reuse a piece of code.

X. Conclusion

The User Software Engineering methodology and its supporting toolset have been developed over the last ten years as an effective approach to the design and development of interactive information systems. The USE methodology has effectively integrated the design of user interfaces into a systematic development process and has created tools to support the rapid development and modification of prototypes of that interface.

The prototype variant of the USE methodology, as shown in Fig. 16, has proved to be especially valuable in improving the design of user interfaces, in constructing systems quickly, in improving the reliability of interactive information systems, and in providing users with a good framework to assist developers during the early stages of the development process.

The USE methodology supports the goals of functionality, reliability, usability, evolvability, reusability, automated support, and improved developer productivity by combining formal and informal methods for specification with extensive use of prototypes and a systematic software development process.

Current research and development on the User Software Engineering methodology is focused on extending the types of interactive media that can be supported by the specification method, on providing greater automated support for program generation, and on making the Unified Support Environment available on a large number of machines. All of these activities are intended to preserve the structure of the methodology while simplifying its use and reducing the effort needed to produce high quality interactive information systems.

References

[1] A. I. Wasserman, "Information system development methodology," *J. Amer. Soc. Inform. Sci.*, vol. 31, no. 1, pp. 5–24, 1980.
[2] ——, "Software engineering environments," in *Advances in Computers*, vol. 22, M. Yovits, Ed.   New York: Academic, 1983.
[3] M. Porcella, P. Freeman, and A. I. Wasserman, "Ada methodology questionnaire summary," *ACM Software Eng. Notes*, vol. 8, no. 1, Jan. 1983.
[4] B. Shneiderman, *Software Psychology.*   Cambridge, MA: Winthrop, 1980.
[5] D. J. Streveler and A. I. Wasserman, "Quantitative measures of the spatial properties of screen designs," in *Proc. Interact '84 Conf.* Amsterdam, The Netherlands: North-Holland, 1984.
[6] T. W. Olle, H. G. Sol, and A. A. Verrijn-Stuart, Eds., *Information System Design Methodologies: A Comparative Review.*   Amsterdam, The Netherlands: North-Holland, 1982.
[7] T. W. Olle, H. G. Sol, and C. J. Tully, Eds., *Information System Design Methodologies: A Feature Analysis.*   Amsterdam, The Netherlands: North-Holland, 1983.
[8] J. M. Smith and D. C. P. Smith, "Conceptual database design," in *Tutorial: Software Design Techniques*, 4th ed., P. Freeman and A. I. Wasserman, Eds.   Los Alamitos, CA: IEEE Comput. Soc., 1983.
[9] P. P.-S. Chen, "The entity-relationship model—Toward a unified view of data," *Trans. Database Syst.*, vol. 1, no. 1, pp. 9–36, Mar. 1976.
[10] M. Jackson, *System Development.*   London: Prentice-Hall, 1983.
[11] M. Lundeberg, G. Goldkuhl, and A. Nilsson, *Information Systems Development—A Systematic Approach.*   Englewood Cliffs, NJ: Prentice-Hall International, 1981.
[12] C. Gane and T. Sarson, *Structured Systems Analysis.*   Englewood Cliffs, NJ: Prentice-Hall, 1979.
[13] D. L. Parnas, "A technique for software module specification with examples," *Commun. ACM*, vol. 15, no. 5, pp. 330–336, May 1972.
[14] O. Roubine and L. Robinson, "SPECIAL reference manual," SRI Int., Menlo Park, CA, Tech. Rep. CSG-45, 1978.
[15] N. G. Leveson, A. I. Wasserman, and D. M. Berry, "BASIS: A behavioral approach to the specification of information systems," *Inform. Syst.*, vol. 8, no. 1, pp. 15–23, 1983.
[16] J. Roach, H. R. Hartson, R. W. Ehrich, T. Yunten, and D. H. Johnson, "DMS: A comprehensive system for managing human-computer dialogue," in *Proc. Human Factors in Comput. Syst.*, Mar. 1982, pp. 102–105.
[17] A. I. Wasserman, "User software engineering and the design of interactive systems," in *Proc. 5th Int. Conf. Software Eng.*, 1981, pp. 387–393.
[18] A. I. Wasserman and S. K. Stinson, "A specification method for interactive information systems," in *Proc. IEEE Comput. Soc. Conf. Specification of Reliable Software*, 1979, pp. 68–79.
[19] D. L. Parnas, "On the use of transition diagrams in the design of a user interface for an interactive computer system," in *Proc. 24th Nat. ACM Conf.*, 1969, pp. 379–385.
[20] R. J. K. Jacob, "Using formal specifications in the design of a human-computer interface," *Commun. ACM*, vol. 26, no. 3, pp. 259–264, Mar. 1983.
[21] D. Kieras and P. Polson, "A generalized transition network representation for interactive systems," in *Proc. CHI '83 Human Factors in Comput. Syst.*, 1983, pp. 103–106.

[22] A. I. Wasserman, "Extending state transition diagrams for the specification of human–computer interaction," *IEEE Trans. Software Eng.*, vol. SE-11, Aug. 1985.

[23] A. I. Wasserman and D. T. Shewmake, "Rapid prototyping of interactive information systems," *ACM Software Eng. Notes*, vol. 7, no. 5, pp. 171–180, Dec. 1982.

[24] A. I. Wasserman, D. T. Shewmake, and P. A. Pircher, "A RAPID/USE tutorial," Lab. Med. Inform. Sci., Univ. California, San Francisco, 1985.

[25] C. Mills and A. I. Wasserman, "A transition diagram editor," in *Proc. 1984 Summer Usenix Meeting*, June, 1984, pp. 287–296.

[26] C. J. Date, *An Introduction to Database Systems*, 3rd ed. Reading, MA: Addison-Wesley, 1982.

[27] M. R. Stonebraker and E. Wong, "The design and implementation of INGRES," *Trans. Database Syst.*, vol. 1, no. 3, Sept. 1976.

[28] D. D. Chamberlin *et al.*, "SEQUEL 2: A unified approach to data definition, manipulation, and control," *IBM J. Res. Develop.*, vol. 20, no. 6, pp. 560–575, Nov. 1976.

[29] M. L. Kersten and A. I. Wasserman, "The architecture of the PLAIN data base handler," *Software—Practice and Experience*, vol. 11, no. 2, pp. 175–186, Feb. 1981.

[30] N. G. Leveson, "Applying behaviorial abstraction to information system design and integrity," Ph.D. dissertation, Univ. California, Los Angeles, 1980. (Available as Tech. Rep. 47, Lab. Med. Inform. Sci., Univ. California, San Francisco.)

[31] C. A. R. Hoare, "Proof of correctness of data representations," *Acta Inform.*, vol. 1, no. 3, pp. 271–281, 1972.

[32] M. Shaw, Ed., *ALPHARD: Form and Content*. New York: Springer-Verlag, 1981.

[33] A. I. Wasserman, D. D. Sherertz, M. L. Kersten, R. P. van de Riet, and M. D. Dippe, "Revised report on the programming language PLAIN," *ACM SIGPLAN Notices*, vol. 16, no. 5, pp. 59–80, May 1981.

[34] A. I. Wasserman, P. A. Pircher, and D. T. Shewmake, "Building reliable interactive information systems," *IEEE Trans. Software Eng.*, vol. SE-12, pp. 147–156, Jan. 1986.

Anthony I. Wasserman (M'71) received the A.B. degree in mathematics and physics from the University of California, Berkeley, and the M.S. and Ph.D. degrees in Computer Sciences from the University of Wisconsin—Madison.

After three years in industry, he joined the University of California, San Francisco, where he is now Professor of Medical Information Science. Since 1970, he has also been Lecturer in the Computer Science Division at the University of California, Berkeley. He is also the founder and President of Interactive Development Environments, Inc. He is the architect of the User Software Engineering methodology and supporting toolset for the specification and design of interactive information systems. His research interests include software development methods, tools, and environments, human interaction with computers, and data management. He is the author of more than 60 papers and an editor of seven books, including *Tutorial: Software Design Techniques* (IEEE Computer Society), with P. Freeman, and *Automated Tools for Information Systems Design* (North-Holland), with H.-J. Schneider.

Dr. Wasserman is the Editor-in-Chief of ACM's *Computing Surveys*, and a member of the Editorial Board of several other journals, including the *International Journal of Man–Machine Studies*, *Information Systems*, and the *Journal of Systems and Software*. He is a member of the Programme Committee for the IFIP Congress '86, Vice-Chairman of IFIP WG 8.1 (Design and Evaluation of Information Systems), and a former chairman of ACM's SIGSOFT. He is a member of the Association for Computing Machinery and the IEEE Computer Society.

Peter A. Pircher was born in Lucerne, Switzerland, in 1953. He received the M.S. degree in mathematics and computer science and the Ph.D. degree in computer science from the University of Zurich, Zurich, Switzerland.

From 1980 to 1983 he was a Research Assistant and Lecturer at the University of Zurich. His research included the design of a runtime environment for an interactive Pascal programming system. In 1983, after receiving a two-year grant from the Swiss National Science Foundation, he moved to San Francisco to continue his research on programming environments. He currently works as a Research Associate in the Department of Medical Information Science at the University of California, San Francisco.

David T. Shewmake (S'85) received the B.S. degree in physics from the University of Michigan, Ann Arbor, in 1974.

He is currently completing the Ph.D. degree in medical information science at the University of California, San Francisco. His research interests are in software engineering, human factors, and medical informatics.

Mr. Shewmake is a member of the IEEE Computer Society and the Association for Computing Machinery.

Martin L. Kersten received the Ph.D. degree in mathematics and computer science from the Vrije Universiteit, Amsterdam, The Netherlands, in 1985. His dissertation was on the subject of secure programming environments.

He is currently leading a database systems project at the Centrum for Wiskunde en Informatica, Amsterdam, and holds a faculty position at the Vrije Universiteit, Amsterdam. His research interests are in database management.

Dr. Kersten is a member of the Association for Computing Machinery and the Dutch society for informatics (NGI).

Human Aspects
of Computing

Henry Ledgard
Editor

Designing for Usability: Key Principles and What Designers Think

JOHN D. GOULD and CLAYTON LEWIS

ABSTRACT: This article is both theoretical and empirical. Theoretically, it describes three principles of system design which we believe must be followed to produce a useful and easy to use computer system. These principles are: early and continual focus on users; empirical measurement of usage; and iterative design whereby the system (simulated, prototype, and real) is modified, tested, modified again, tested again, and the cycle is repeated again and again. This approach is contrasted to other principled design approaches, for example, get it right the first time, reliance on design guidelines. Empirically, the article presents data which show that our design principles are not always intuitive to designers; identifies the arguments which designers often offer for not using these principles—and answers them; and provides an example in which our principles have been used successfully.

Any system designed for people to use should be easy to learn (and remember), useful, that is, contain functions people really need in their work, and be easy and pleasant to use. This article is written for people who have the responsibility and/or interest in creating computer systems (or any other systems) with these characteristics. In the first section of this article we briefly mention three principles for system design which we believe can be used to attain these goals. Our principles may seem intuitive, but system designers do not generally recommend them, as results of surveys reported in Section 2 show. The recommendations of actual designers suggest that they may sometimes think they are doing what we recommend when in fact they are not. In Section 3 we contrast some of their responses with what we have in mind to provide a fuller and clearer description of our principles. In Section 4 we consider why designers might not actually be using our design

principles. In Section 5 we elaborate on the three principles, showing how they form the basis for a general methodology of design. In Section 6 we describe a successful example of using our recommended methodology in actual system design, IBM's Audio Distribution System (ADS), and the advantages that accrued as a result.

1. THE PRINCIPLES
We recommend three principles of design.

Early Focus on Users and Tasks
First, designers must understand who the users will be. This understanding is arrived at in part by directly studying their cognitive, behavioral, anthropometric, and attitudinal characteristics, and in part by studying the nature of the work expected to be accomplished.

Empirical Measurement
Second, early in the development process, intended users should actually use simulations and prototypes to carry out real work, and their performance and reactions should be observed, recorded, and analyzed.

Iterative Design
Third, when problems are found in user testing, as they will be, they must be fixed. This means design must be iterative: There must be a cycle of design, test and measure, and redesign, repeated as often as necessary.

2. WHAT SYSTEM DESIGNERS AND PROGRAMMERS ACTUALLY SAY
We began recommending these principles in the 1970's. Often the reaction is that they are obvious. Nevertheless, they are not usually employed in system design. Why? We wondered whether or not these principles were really obvious, or whether or not they just

seemed obvious once presented. To find out, during 1981–1982 we asked five groups of systems planners, designers, programmers, and developers to write down the sequence of five (or so) major steps one should go through in developing and evaluating a new computer system for end users. These people were attending a human factors talk, and did this just prior to its beginning. We suggested that they use an office system or point-of-sale terminal as an example. These 447 participants provide a particularly good test of how intuitive, obvious, regularly advocated, or regularly practiced our design principles are, for they are among the very people who design computer systems for people to use. Further, since they were attending a human factors talk, they would likely be biased to mention human factors issues. Each person's responses were graded independently by three or more judges (only one of whom was a human factors person), and disagreements were settled jointly.[1] Grading was very liberal: we gave credit for even the simplest mention relating to any one of our four principles, regardless how impoverished or incomplete the thought was.

Table I shows the key result. Most participants did not mention most of our four design principles. Twenty-six percent did not mention any of the four principles, and another 35 percent mentioned only one. Just 2 percent made any mention of all four. These percentages would have been much lower had we used a more stringent grading procedure.

As to the specific principles mentioned, 62 percent mentioned something about early focus on users; 40 percent mentioned something about empirical measurement, that is, behaviorally testing the system (or a simulation or prototype of it) on people (regardless of their characteristics); and 20 percent mentioned something about iterative design, that is, modifying the system based on these results.

The intent here is not to single out as "bad folks" all those people responsible for the creation of a system, whom we will collectively refer to as "designers." Principles of design are arguable, of course. Ours are not universal truths. Had human factors people, for example, been asked the same questions, the percents mentioning each principle might not have differed from those observed. Indeed, some other human factors people recommend design approaches that have little in common with what we recommend. This can be seen in several papers in recent conference proceedings covering the human factors of system design, for example, *The Proceedings of the Human Factors Society Meetings* [30] and *The Proceedings of CHI83 Human Factors in Computing Systems Meetings* [29].

Of course these survey results cannot be assumed to indicate what designers actually do, or would do, with real design tasks. They do show, however, that our principles are *not* obvious (at least before they are presented), consistent with the observation that they are

TABLE I. Summary of Six Surveys in Which 447 People Attending Classes for Systems Planners, Programmers, Designers, and Developers Briefly Wrote the Key Steps One Should Go Through in Developing and Evaluating a Computer System for End Users

Percent of respondents mentioning a given number of principles:				
Number of principles	0	1	2	3
Respondents (%)	26	35	24	16

Percent of respondents mentioning each principle:		
Early focus on users	Empirical measurement	Iterative design
62	40	20

rarely applied. Our experience is that even after hearing them, people often do not understand their full force.

3. CONTRASTS BETWEEN WHAT WE MEAN AND WHAT WAS SAID

A closer look at the survey responses reinforces the conclusion that these "common sense" design principles are not fully understood by many designers, even when they mention them. It is our experience that people sometimes lack the ability to differentiate between what we recommend and what they do.

With respect to our survey results, there are instructive distinctions between comments which we gave credit for and what we actually recommend. In many cases, these comments may *appear* similar, but they *differ significantly* in intent, how they would be carried out, and, presumably, in their impact. Thus, at the risk of appearing overly harsh, we point out some of these distinctions to clarify what we have in mind. These distinctions are often overlooked, sometimes leading designers to believe they are following the principles that we recommend when in fact they are not.

Early Focus on Users

The design team should be user driven. We recommend *understanding* potential users, versus "identifying," "describing," "stereotyping," and "ascertaining" them, as respondents suggested. We recommend bringing the design team into *direct contact* with potential users, as opposed to hearing or reading about them through human intermediaries, or through an "examination of user profiles." We recommend interviews and discussions with potential users, and actual observations, by the design team, of users on the present version of a system. Perhaps users could try to train designers to use an existing system, and thereby designers could learn a lot about the users. (Occasionally, a proposed system will be so radical that a "present system" may not exist. We still recommend talking to the intended users, and understanding how they go about their work and what their problems are.) These interviews should be conducted *prior to system design*, instead of first designing the system and then subsequently "presenting," "reviewing," and "verifying" the design with users, or "getting users to agree" to, or to "sign off" on the design.

[1] For helping us grade these surveys, we thank Lizette Alfaro, Art Benjamin, Steve Corsaro, and Jennifer Stolarz.

As part of understanding users, this knowledge must be played against the tasks that users will be expected to perform. Other disciplines have also become aware of the absence of user involvement in design. For example, the American Association for the Advancement of Science and the National Science Foundation have established a project to address the fact that too often technologies are developed for the disabled with no input from the disabled [31].

One way to increase the saliency and importance of usability issues in designers' minds is to have a panel of expected users (e.g., secretaries) work closely with them during early formulation stages. Almost no one recommended this, not even for only brief periods of time. We call this "interactive design," and we recommend that *typical users* (e.g., bank tellers) be used, as opposed to a "group of a variety of experts" (e.g., supervisors, industrial engineers, and programmers). We recommend that these potential users become part of the design team *from the very outset* when their perspectives can have the most influence, rather than using them post hoc as part of an "analysis team (of) end user representatives." Another value of this approach, especially for the design of an in-house system, is that it allows potential users to participate in the design of a system that they will ultimately use (sometimes called "participatory design").

Some respondents recommended that potential users "review," "sign off on," or "agree" to the design before it is coded. This can be useful, but does not have the full shaping force on designers' views which an earlier association would have had. Our notion is not merely "to get users to agree" to a system design, which smacks of post hoc legalese, but to create a situation in which potential users can instill their knowledge and concern into the design process from the very beginning.

Being concerned about the "human factors of noise and light levels and safety" is important, but designers must go beyond this, understanding cognitive and emotional characteristics of users as they relate to a proposed system.

Often designers build upon previous releases (e.g., of computer systems, washing machines, cars) or add a part to an existing system. Thus, there should be little difficulty in identifying users and talking with them. We have been told that when one is at the very earliest stages of design in a new area, however, it may be hard to understand who the users will be or to interact with them. When this is so, it strengthens the arguments for empirical measurement and iterative design.

Empirical Measurement

Here we emphasize two factors: actual behavioral measurements of learnability and usability, and conducting these experimental and empirical studies very early in the development process. We gave credit for *any* mention of a user test—whether or not it was early or appropriately conceived, and even if it was suggested by context alone. Several participants who received credit for mentioning "test" seemed to have in mind a

system test rather than a *user* test, for example, "test for system response, . . . , swapping time."

"Build(ing) a prototype to study *it* (emphasis ours) experimentally" (e.g., to study memory access speed, system reliability) is different from building a protytype to study how people will use and react to it and the training approaches and materials. It is not a question of "using a prototype to match against user requirements," but rather a question of finding out how easily people can learn and use that prototype. The first is an analytic question; the second is an empirical question. "Test(ing) the (completed) system—use it by ourselves" is good, but is not a substitute for testing it (and a series of previous prototypes) on the actual user audience.

"Reviewing" or "demonstrating" a prototype system for typical users and getting their reaction to it can result in misleading conclusions. What is required is a usability test, not a selling job. People who have developed a system think differently about its use [25], do not make the same mistakes, and use it differently from novices. Users should be given simple tasks to carry out, and their performance, thoughts, and attitudes should be recorded and analyzed.

Iterative Design

The person who wrote "make trial run of prototype and incorporate changes" makes no reference to behavioral evaluation and improvements. "Build prototype, code software, write documentation, and review" does not explicitly acknowledge the need to incorporate results of behavioral testing into the next version of the system. Finally, "if time permits, iterate the design . . ." is not sufficient or acceptable as a design philosophy. Even where iterative design was mentioned, many people seemed to feel that a single iteration or revision would be sufficient.

In answer to our question about the key steps in the development *process*, some people wrote *goals* for a system. Making a system "easy to use," "user friendly," "easy to operate," "simple," "responsive," and "flexible" are goals, indeed very difficult goals to reach. What is needed is a *process* to ultimately ensure meeting these goals. Almost no one mentioned establishing testable behavioral specifications (see below) early in the development process to see if, in fact, general behavioral goals are being met.

A Comment.   One might think that it has been nit-picking or even unfair to draw upon distinctions between comments that the respondents wrote rather hastily and the points that we are trying to make. However, our experience is that these comments provide a representation of how designers of all kinds of systems (whether they are programmers of computer systems, planners of educational curriculum, authors of textbooks, architects of buildings, builders of cars, or lecturers) often think and how they view ultimate users in relation to their work. They are consistent with what other designers of computer systems say when asked how they think about design [22]. But does knowing this give us greater ability to design better systems? We think it does because we can describe another way to do it and ask why this other way is not followed.

4. WHY THE PRINCIPLES ARE UNDERVALUED
Why do these principles seem obvious once you hear them, but do not seem to be recommended or followed in practice? The survey responses indicate that these principles are not regularly suggested and that they are not really obvious. Our experience is that they are seldom applied.

In this section we try to answer this question by identifying five categories of reasons. First, the principles may not be worth following. Second, there is confusion with similar but critically different ideas. Third, the value of interaction with users is misestimated. Fourth, competing approaches make more sense. Fifth, the principles are impractical. We see weaknesses in these reasons or objections, and we suggest ways of addressing them.

Not Worth Following
As we said earlier, principles of design are arguable, including these, and a variety of other design approaches have been recommended. Some designers, no doubt, understand our recommendations but question their value. Such objections will be resolved one way or the other as the recommendations are more fully tested in practice.

Confusion with Similar but Critically Different Ideas
It is our experience that designers often have difficulty differentiating between what we recommend and similar but critically different ideas. The survey results are consistent with this experience. Sometimes designers believe they are following what we recommend when in fact they are not. Sometimes designers confuse the intention to carry out user testing with the testing itself.

We hope these problems will resolve themselves over time. If designers have more interaction with users, and if they carry out more empirical evaluations of their work, we expect the value of these approaches, and their relationship to other methods, to become clearer.

The Value of Interaction with Users is Misestimated

User Diversity Is Underestimated.   Because most designers have only limited contact with users (and this is often centered on topics of the designers own expertise and not that of the users), they simply do not realize how widely users differ, and, especially, how different many users are from most designers. If dashing off a few lines of code is trivial for a designer, then that designer is not likely to imagine that this can be extremely difficult for someone else. When users do have trouble, designers are sometimes tempted to think they are "stupid." It is difficult to give fair weight to the years of training and experience that underlie one's own ability. But more important, it is almost impossible to think about whether or not someone else will have trouble if you never encounter any yourself. In observ-

ing complete novices learning to use text editors [25] or message systems [19], we have often been amazed as they encounter major problems that we did not anticipate, or when problems that seemed simple to us were impossible for them to recover from.

User Diversity Is Overestimated.   Sometimes we are told that people are so different that it makes no sense to conduct tests with only a few people. One would have to test hundreds of people and then the result would be so variable as to be useless. It is true that testing only a small sample, as is often necessary for practical reasons, cannot reveal all the problems that will arise with a design. But it is much better to identify some of the problems that some users will have than not to identify any. Further, our experience is that problems are not as idiosyncratic as is sometimes thought. The same problem, even a completely unanticipated one, often crops up for user after user.

Belief That Users Do Not Know What They Need.
This objection points up a genuine problem: Getting useful design information from prospective users is not just a matter of asking. Many users have never considered alternate or improved ways of performing their tasks and are unaware of the options available for a new design. Further, in trying to communicate, designers may unwittingly intimidate users, and users may unfortunately become unresponsive.

One way around this is to present new ideas in a way that makes it easy for users to relate them to their concerns. One approach, used with a text-editing system at Wang Laboratories (personal communication, 1980), is to write a user manual and get reactions to it, as the first stage in design. Another method is to construct detailed scenarios showing exactly how key tasks would be performed with the new system, as was done for IBM's ADS [19]. Another approach is to simulate the user interface of a proposed system [21, 23]. These approaches are valuable even if no user reaction is sought: It is extremely difficult for anybody even its own designers, to understand an interface proposal, without this level of description.

Putting the design in intelligible form is not the only difficulty in getting user reaction. Users may endorse a proposal uncritically, presuming that the technical "experts" know more than they do about their needs. In the course of extended give-and-take with designers, users may come to know too much: They may understand the technical issues so well that they can no longer detect the difficulties in comprehension that others users, who do not have the benefit of weeks of dialogue with the designers, will face.

The effect of these problems is that interacting with users during design cannot in itself ensure a good design. But at least some design issues will be defined and dealt with sooner and more effectively if user knowledge is brought to bear from the start.

Belief That My Job Does Not Require It or Permit It.
Sometimes organizational arrangements isolate designers from contact with users, or place the responsibility

for usability entirely elsewhere, with no role for others. Designers find themselves preoccupied with meeting a schedule for their individual system ingredient. There is no time for contact with users until their work is finished—which never quite happens. A rigid development process leaves no room for new approaches.

We have been told by a designer that it is sometimes difficult to get customers to commit productive users to spend sufficient time interacting on the design of a future system. When this is the case, designers can use techniques mentioned in this article that may require less time, for example, get reactions to an early user manual, help-line service, or printed scenarios of how the user interface might work.

Competitive necessity will eventually break down these obstacles and traditions. Good user-oriented systems cannot be built from local optimization of individual system ingredients. In the meantime, other ways to do the needed work can often be found. Small-scale usability evaluations can often be carried out without requiring much additional resource. Marketing or planning people are often eager to have development people participate in customer visits where their technical skills can be very helpful.

Competing Approaches

Belief in the Power of Reason. If system design were fundamentally a rational analysis of how a task should be done, then there would be no need to involve users. Why muddy the waters by getting information about existing, and probably irrational, practices? There are two problems with rational analysis as the sole basis of design. First, it leaves things out: Rational analysis does not tell you what you have to analyze. Here is an illustration. Some designers have been puzzled that word processing systems have not driven out the typewriter. Why do many offices have a typewriter and a word processor side by side? Does a word processor not handle all "document creation"? Just thinking logically about document creation is unlikely to reveal the key facts. But a few minutes of observation of real office work shows some of the things that document creation leaves out. Filling in forms is much easier with a typewriter. For very short documents, such as buck slips or telephone messages, the overhead of a typical word processor is unacceptable. One cannot discover the existence of these critical cases by armchair reflection on office work.

A second problem with relying only on reason is that systems almost always have to interact with preexisting work methods, and mismatches can be major problems. Even if a new system is intended to entirely replace former methods, there is still the problem of relating peoples' comprehension of the new ways to their established habits of thought. The problems surrounding this process are not subject to a priori rational analysis, but must be explored empirically, that is, by having actual users try out the new system under realistic conditions. Listening to users' comments is a good way to do this.

Rational analysis is, of course, important, for without it we are unlikely to create new innovative systems. Analytic approaches should be used when they are applicable, but they cannot be seen as a substitute for empirical methods.

Belief That Design Guidelines Should Be Sufficient. There is no handbook of operating characteristics for the human mind. Guidelines for user interface design do exist (e.g., [9]), and they can be useful. Certainly, for many designers, guidelines can help get the first version of a prototype system closer to the final desired version than if they were not used. However, they provide only general constraints on design. No matter how conscientious a designer is in finding and following this distilled wisdom, the resulting design may be very good or very bad.

One limitation of guidelines is that they cannot deal with choices that are highly dependent on context, as many of the important choices in interface design are. For example, a guideline cannot recommend that special purpose keys be used instead of typed commands because the choice depends on whether or not users are touch typists, whether or not it is possible for the system to distinguish commands from other entries if they are typed, whether or not the command set is extensible, and many other aspects of the situation. Existing guidelines are often based on informed opinion rather than data or established principles. Very few design choices have been investigated in a controlled way. Research cannot solve either of these problems in the foreseeable future.

Cognitive psychologists agree that human performance adapts strongly to the details of the task environment. We do not understand this adaptation well enough to predict the effects of most design choices in any one given situation, let alone form general conclusions about them. The same ignorance argues against conducting experiments to validate existing guidelines about which there is doubt. Feasible experiments could only investigate a choice in a few contexts, probably not increasing our confidence in generalizing about it very much. Psychology is not close to being able to develop significantly improved guidelines to overcome these limitations. Human factors can provide a *process* by which usable and useful systems can be designed, but cannot provide design guidelines in enough detail to determine how a system should ultimately appear to users. We feel, at present, that guidelines should be viewed as an informal collection of suggestions, rather than as distilled science. Designers will have to make many choices on their own, and be prepared to test their work empirically.

Belief That Good Design Means Getting It Right the First Time. "Getting it right the first time" seems like a laudable goal, and is, in fact, an alternative design philosophy to our own; but experience shows it is not achievable in user interface design. Certainly careful design work pays off, and the need to iterate is not a license to be sloppy. Assuming that iteration will not be needed, when laying out a schedule and choosing implementation methods, is asking for disaster in user interface design. Even the "zero defects" approach, developed by Crosby [6] for general quality control, advocates the need for evaluative testing and empirical measurement. It does not simply assert that one can, from the outset, create a design for zero defects.

"Getting it right the first time" plays a very different role in software design which does not involve user interfaces than it does in user interface design. This may explain, in part, the reluctance of designers to, relinquish it as a fundamental aim. In the design of a compiler module, for example, the exact behavior of the code is or should be open to rational analysis. Even those factors which cannot be predicted exactly, such as frequencies of data with particular characteristics, may be amenable to statistical treatment. The choice of algorithms can and should be anchored securely in a reliable analysis of the data, the transformations to be carried out, and the performance characteristics of the system. Good design in this context is highly analytic, and emphasizes careful planning. Designers know this.

Adding a human interface to the system disrupts this picture fundamentally. A coprocessor of largely unpredictable behavior (i.e., a human user) has been added, and the system's algorithms have to mesh with it. There is no data sheet on this coprocessor, so one is forced to abandon the idea that one can design one's algorithms from first principles. An empirical approach is essential. The involvement of human users escalates the need for an empirical approach well above the usual requirements for testing to make sure a system works.

When large diverse groups are involved in developing a system, we have observed a practice of "freezing the user interface" early in the development process (even prior to coding it). Apparently this reflects the need to have some aspect of the system fixed or stable as the various groups then proceed somewhat independently with their own work. But the user interface is exactly that part of the system which should be open to change. The best this approach can achieve is that a system can get *programmed* in an error-free manner, not that the resulting interface will be of high quality. It is impossible to design the system right the first time because this is based on the assumption of a perfect *forecast* of the best user interface—something which can only be determined empirically. Further, fixing the user interface early assumes nothing will be learned over the next two years, or so, of development.

When one is an outside contractor (rather than in an internal system development organization), it is often difficult to get a customer to sign a contract that includes the flexibility required in iterative design. There is, typically, insistence, we are told, on a two-stage, "preliminary design" and "final design" hierarchy, with schedule rigidity that often precludes proper accommodation of usability tests results. Ignoring the need for iterative design is perhaps even more disastrous here since geographic remoteness may further reduce required communication and observations needed to attain good usability.

Our system design philosophy is neutral vis-a-vis some other well-known strategies for program design, for example, top-down design [7], top-down testing, or structured programming [8]. Yourdon and Constantine [35] have reviewed these and other programming design strategies. The small group aspect of chief programmer teams [1] is important, we believe, in providing consistency and simplicity in overall system usage.

Impractical

Belief That the Development Process Will Be Lengthened. In a competitive world, products are always developed under time pressure. Schedules are critical. Designers sometimes fear that their schedules will not be met if behavioral testing is done. Will the development process not be lengthened by creating a prototype? Will the development process not be lengthened further by doing user tests with it? Will the development process not be lengthened even further by redesigning on the basis of the user results? We feel that these questions reflect two underlying assumptions. The first is that usability work must be added to the end of the development cycle, as opposed to overlapped with it. The second is that responding to tests must be time consuming.

With respect to this first assumption, one can do user testing before a system is built, and continue this work throughout the development process. One can create paper and pencil tasks that test critical features of the interface such as the syntax of commands. IBM's "Query-by-Example" [36] was evaluated by asking users to write down the queries they would construct to answer questions given to them in English [33]. This was done before a single line of code was written. It was therefore done without the benefit of system feedback [33] which was studied in later experiments [3, 5]. More comprehensive testing can be done by constructing a simulated system. For example Gould, Conti, and Hovanyecz [21] did extensive testing of a "listening typewriter," a device that would use speech recognition to give real-time visual feedback during dictation, by using a human typist in the computer feedback loop. Kelley [23] used a computerized simulation of a calendaring system in which the experimenter could invisibly enter the user-system dialogue whenever the computerized system would not give an appropriate response. Here, again, both of these simulations were done before a line of code was written for the real systems. Once a running prototype exists, experimental tests with real users can be conducted, followed by empirical (field) studies of training, user interface, and reading materials used together.

It is our personal experience and observation that building simulated or informal prototypes, rather than delaying or lengthening system development, actually helps get a new project off the ground, gives it something tangible for others to see, and stimulates thought and progress.

We have been told that with some new systems the main issue is sometimes one of technical feasibility or capability of the technology to perform in a certain way. "How can this be explored without building a box?" we have been asked. The answer is that is exactly what was done in the Thomas and Gould [33], the Gould, Conti, and Hovanyecz [21], and the Kelley [23] simulation studies. While some aspects of new technology may be difficult to simulate we have never encountered a design problem in which at least some important aspects could not be usefully simulated.

With respect to the second assumption, that responding to the user test results must be time consuming and expensive, it is possible to build a system so that one can do this quickly and easily. The implementation is structured so that the user interface can be changed without changing the implementation of underlying services. In a sense, the system becomes its own prototype, in that it is easy to construct and evaluate alternative designs. IBM's ADS, discussed in more detail below, has this structure.

Even when these approaches are taken, there is no denying that user testing still has a price. It is nowhere near as high as is commonly supposed, however, and it is a mistake to imagine that one can save by not paying this price. User testing will happen anyway: If it is not done in the developer's lab, it will be done in the customer's office. Brooks [4] has pointed out that everyone builds a prototype. The only question is whether or not, in the case of vendors, they also market it as a product, or in the case of in-house development, they give it to their users. The price is poor quality, extra (unanticipated) customer expense, and extra (and unanticipated) vendor costs. Changes that must be made after the product is delivered are, of course, much more expensive than those made even late in development. They must be done piecemeal, and under more constraints of compatibility, in that changes have to be minimized to avoid disrupting users. Fixes are likely to be superficial, and quality will continue to suffer. Heavy reliance on initial customer feedback, rather than early empirical simulations, prevents innovation because too many constraints then exist, making fresh substantially different approaches impossible.

Belief That Iteration Is Just Expensive Fine-Tuning. Our philosophy is not just a trivial expensive matter of "fine-tuning," but a basic design philosophy to be contrasted with other principled design philosophies. An iterative design philosophy may seem expensive, but with the present state of understanding about user interface design, it is the only way to ensure excellent systems. The three principles we outlined can be extended and coordinated to form an overall approach to user interface development, as is partially done in the next section.

Belief in the Power of Technology to Succeed. We have been told that technical people have a lot of faith in the "power of technology" to succeed. People will buy it in spite of the user interface. This has been true at the high end of computer systems, and was true in the case of the automobile industry. But as the American automobile industry found out, other manufacturers will make the necessary accommodations to users. We belive the same thing will happen in the computer industry. Just because there is a speech recognition system, a touch screen, a wireless terminal, or a picture phone is no longer a guarantee that these will succeed. Increasingly, with computer systems the product *is* the user interface. This reinforces the points we are trying to make. More and better students are becoming involved with the human factors of computer systems, and they will be developing new methodologies and providing a stream of findings on usability, which may very well exert powerful effects in the marketplace.

5. AN ELABORATION OF THE PRINCIPLES
To carry out our suggestions, we roughly divide the activities required in explaining our recommended principles into an initial design phase and an iterative development phase, although there is no sharp dividing line separating them.

Initial Design Phase

Preliminary Specification of the User Interface. This is only one of several activities that need to be attacked early. Here are others.

Collect Critical Information About Users. Some of what is needed, such as literacy level or how long users stay at one job (both of which affect training requirements), can sometimes be gathered second-hand, from surveys or consultants. But direct contact with potential users is essential to flesh out the basics. Reluctance or willingness on the part of the users to read manuals, tolerance for delay or effort, and expectations about what a new system should provide are examples of factors that are unlikely to come through in second-hand descriptions of users but which designers need a feel for. Perhaps more important, one does not know what one needs to know about a user until one sees the user in person. These contacts are almost always full of surprises.

Sometimes there is a (understandable) tendency for designers to want to look up in a book what the characteristics of a class of users (e.g., bank tellers) are (an extension of the guidelines approach), and build a system from these. We have tried to find an example of a system whose user set is so narrow and so well specified that general user characteristics, such as reading level, age, and so forth, would be an adequate basis for design. We have not found any. To the extent that the scope of users and tasks becomes broader, understanding the user becomes all of psychology (cognitive, behavioral, anthropometric, attitudinal, etc. characteristics), and general descriptive data will be of even less value.

As noted earlier, one of the surprises may be how difficult seemingly easy operations may really be for users. Direct contact with users, both in this phase and in later behavioral testing, can make designers aware of just where these difficulties are cropping up.

There is an analogy between the sort of insight into users and their needs that a designer must have and the sort of insight into the needs of a particular industry that a software developer must have. Just as "insider" knowledge is essential to develop really useful software for banking, say, or insurance applications, so an "inside" view of user requirements is essential to create a superior user interface. For most designers the only way to get this inside view is by close consultation with users.

Such consultation is greatly facilitated if the users can see and react to a real "users'-eye-view" of the proposed system. This can be done by preparing a users manual for review, as has been done at Wang for a word processor (personal communication, 1980), by presenting detailed usage scenarios, as was done for ADS [19], or possibly by presenting a description of how a user would interact with the system, as was done at Apple for the Lisa computer system [34]. Even if it is not used in user consultations, preparing such a users view can be helpful in focusing design energy on interface issues. It can also form the basis for behavioral specifications and tests.

Develop Behavioral Goals. The plan for a new system always includes performance and capacity targets for the hardware and software, for example, memory size and access rates, and calculation times. These need to be supplemented by targets which specify how well the *user* must be able to perform using the system. For example, one might specify that 80 percent of a sample of representative users must be able to master specified basic operations on a word processor in half an hour. With such goals in place it is possible to consider whether or not proposed design features or design changes will contribute to the goals. Without such goals, it is easy for such issues as implementation convenience or memory requirements to dominate the design to the detriment of usability. Thus, when viewed properly, a major reason for behavioral targets is that they provide a management tool to assure that system development proceeds properly.

Behavioral goals should be testable, that is, there should be a clear procedure for determining whether or not a design meets the goals. This will mean that the statement of the goals must cover at least the following points.

1. A description of the intended users must be given, and the experimental participants to be used to represent these users in tests should be agreed upon: for example, typists supplied by temporary employment agencies in Los Angeles (30 percent of whom have English as a second language).

2. The tasks to be performed, and the circumstances in which they should be performed, must be given. For example, a test scenario might specify that the participant will be given a manuscript and asked to use a prototype copier to make five copies on legal size paper

(not presently in the copier), collated and stapled. No assistance would be available except a telephone "hot line."

3. The measurements of interest, such as learning time, errors, number of requests for help, or attitude, and the criterion values to be achieved for each, must be given. Most systems are improvements on older ones, and in these cases it is relatively easy to specify the behavioral criteria, for example, learning time. But it is harder to establish the appropriate values these criteria must take on, and this may have to be done iteratively. In the case of an altogether new system, where the functions have not previously been implemented, specifying the criteria correctly the first time may also be hard, and iteration will be required.

Any specifications, including behavioral goals, influence the design process in complicated ways. Rigid enforcement of specifications is often impossible, but even when they are violated, specifications help to focus design attention and effort in the right places. The process of creating and agreeing on a good set of specifications can be valuable in itself. This process can help clarify the validity of various measures of usability.

Organize the Work. The user interface of a system is a complex entity with diverse parts. The software, the workstation from which the software is operated, the training procedure (if any) in which users participate, the reference manuals or materials, all work or fail to work together to create the conception with which the user ultimately deals. Unfortunately these interacting pieces are usually designed separately. Definers, designers, implementers, application writers, and manual writers constitute large groups in themselves, and are often separated by geography or organization. They often become part of the development process at different times, and thus must accept what earlier participants have already solidified. The picture can be even worse when significant work, such as writing user manuals, is vended out to third parties. It appears that superior quality can be attained only when the entire user interface, including software, manuals, etc., can be designed by a single group, in a way that reflects users' needs, and then evaluated and tuned as an integrated whole. This approach was followed with ADS, as discussed below.

Iterative Development Phase
With testable behavioral goals, and ready access to user feedback, continuous evaluation and modification of the interface can be undertaken. But it will only be feasible if an implementation strategy that permits early testing of design features and cheap modification of the evolving implementation has been planned. Such a strategy has to include fast flexible prototyping and highly modular implementation. These virtues can be combined: The ADS system was essentially self-prototyping, in that the final implementation, in fact, has the structure of a prototyping tool, with table-driven interface specification. This approach solved two problems often associated with prototyping. First, little work was

invested in a separate prototyping system that was then discarded. Second, once design features were prototyped there was no further work needed to incorporate them in the final implementation since the prototype and final implementation were the same.

Experience shows that iterative design should not be thought of as a luxury tuning method that puts finishing touches on a design (at great expense). Rather, it is a way of confronting the reality of unpredictable user needs and behaviors that can lead to sweeping and fundamental changes in a design. User testing will often show that even carefully thought out design ideas are simply inadequate. This means that the flexibility of the implementation approach has to extend as far into the system as possible. It also means that designers have to be prepared for evaluation results that dictate radical change, and must have the commitment to abandon old ideas and pursue new ones. Prototype testing can identify system problems with reliability and responsiveness. These two factors are absolutely necessary for a good user interface and interact with other usability factors.

We have already mentioned methods to determine whether or not behavioral targets are being met. When behavioral targets are not being met, how does one find a remedy? This is usually a very tough problem. Often user comments are the best source of ideas since they may reveal why particular errors are occurring. For example, user comments can quickly show that particular wording on a screen or in a manual is unfamiliar and is being misinterpreted. It may be desirable to collect comments while the user is working with the system since impressions given after a task is complete are often sketchy and may gloss over difficulties that were eventually overcome. The "thinking-aloud" technique, borrowed from cognitive psychology [10, 24, 27] can be useful in such cases. Of course such methods may not be appropriate in assessing whether or not a behavioral goal is being met since the process of collecting comments may interfere with or artificially improve users' performance with the system. But the problem of determining *whether or not* behavioral goals are being met is different from deciding *why* they are not being met, and what to do about it. Different methods are needed for these two aspects of the evaluation process.

A Comment. Some readers may feel that our recommendations are "not science." They may be disappointed that we do not, for example, enthusiastically describe recent developments in cognitive psychology as being able to predict design details for a new user interface or for user reading material. However, design by its very nature is not just science, but also involves engineering, history and custom, art, and invention. Our recommended approach is the best way to develop the scientific aspects of the human factors of system design. This is so for two reasons. First, the methodologies available are sufficiently rigorous and conform to the traditional scientific approach. Within the framework we outline, the methodologies range from pure observation, analysis, and hypothesis testing of

ethologists to psychophysics so precise that no manmade system can measure as accurately. Second, the approach we recommend ensures that real situations and problems will be studied, in their full complexity. This enables talented designers, human factors people, and management to identify and concentrate on the critical problems that must be solved to produce superior usability.

6. A CASE STUDY—IBM'S AUDIO DISTRIBUTION SYSTEM

As compared to the methods of science, much less is known and written about the processes of technology development [11]. Generally, the development process for most systems is (understandably) kept confidential, or at least not often written about. The exceptions, such as the interviews with designers of Lisa [26] can be very instructive. We offer here a short summary of the development of the IBM Audio Distribution System, called ADS, emphasizing the action of the design principles we have presented. In practice, actual development of a system follows any design philosophy only approximately, regardless of how formal or precisely mandated it is. Goals evolve as new ways of doing things are figured out and new useful functions are identified. ADS was no exception.

ADS is a computer-based message system that allows users to send and receive messages using a touch-tone phone as a terminal [19, 20]. Such functions as reviewing previously received messages, creating and using distribution lists, inquiring as to whether or not a message has been heard by the recipient, and changing passwords are all performed by choices and commands entered on the pushbutton telephone. ADS was intended to be used by people with no other exposure to computers, with minimal training. Ease of learning and use were paramount among design goals. Evidence to date indicates that it is very easy to learn. Customers report new users are often able to learn ADS with no training. The principles presented in this article partially evolved from the experience gained in meeting these goals.

Early Focus on Users

The target population was identified very early: managers and professional people. It was known that these people typically do not use computers themselves and do not have computer terminals. They travel frequently, and work in many different places, so access to the system away from the office is important. These considerations led to an emphasis on the use of an ordinary pushbutton telephone as a terminal, even though it was clear that restricted keypad and lack of visual output would be tough constraints.

It was also recognized that these people would be discretionary users, in that they would not be required to use ADS, but would only use it if it seemed sufficiently easy and useful to do so. They indicated that they would spend little time or effort learning a system. This led to very great effort directed toward making the user interface as self-explanatory as possible, and matching the functions as closely as possible to user needs.

The initial set of functions designed into ADS were quite different from those which eventually emerged [19, 20]. Initially the system was thought of mainly as an enhanced dictation system, in which dictated memos could be filed and retrieved, and routed to a transcription center. Secondarily, ADS was initially thought of as an "electronic mail" communication system for relatively brief spoken messages. Laboratory experiments began to indicate that dictating was not as efficient a composition system as originally thought, and that speaking was a potentially superior composition method [12, 13, 15, 16, 19, 20]. Only after a prototype was in use was it determined that the spoken message communication features of the system were the really useful ones, however. The dictation transcription feature was then deemphasized.

This example illustrates several points we have tried to make. First, initial interaction with users did not start as early with ADS as we would now suggest it should. As a result, the first command language was cumbersome. Second, even when early interactions with users did take place, they often could not say what would be useful new functions for them. Almost no one envisioned how useful noninteractive voice communication would be. Third, giving potential users simulations and prototypes to work with enhanced the quality of feedback they gave. Empirical prototype studies identified, for example, which functions were actually used. Fourth, the architecture (or programming technology), and the designers' motivation, was flexible enough to allow iterative design.

The prototype system led to extensive interaction between users and designers. Users were free with suggestions about what they did not like (such as pushing a lot of keys to accomplish basic functions, having to remember the digits for specific commands, for example, 71 to Record, the necessity to read documentation or spend time for training, and what they thought should be added). Having a Pending Message Box to remind the sender and recipient that an action is needed was based on a user suggestion.

Empirical Measurement

Throughout the development of the system, a great many different forms of user testing were used. Most concentrated on the ability or inability of test users to learn to perform a given set of functions with a given form of training or prompting. Some tests used simple paper-and-pencil methods, in which users had to write down the keys they would use to perform a task. Other tests involved watching users use a keypad, writing down and video-taping what they did; still others involved memorization and recall studies of various command possibilities; laboratory experiments on spoken message quality [28]; and experiments on impression formation [32]. Studies of new users almost always evaluated a combination of training, reading materials,

and user interface. Versions of prototype systems in actual usage were demonstrated to visitors and at technical meetings for several years. This provided useful feedback. This work was carried out by Stephen Boies, John Conti, John Gould, Nancy Grischkowsky, Don Nix, and John Thomas. These tests led directly to many changes in the wording of messages, the organization of commands, the style of training, and other aspects of the system [19].

Later, a simple but flexible simulation tool in which a subset of keys on a computer terminal modeled the pushbutton telephone keypad was developed. Prompts and messages were automatically shown on a screen where an experimenter could read them to the test user. The action of the simulator was easily changed without programming. The experimenter could edit a set of tables that determined what would happen when a given key was pressed in a given state of the system. These tables were designed and implemented by Stephen Boies and John Richards, and an illustration is given in Table II.

Iterative Design

This simulator proved so useful that it was eventually incorporated as the actual user interface of the system itself. That is, the operation of the ADS system now marketed by IBM is controlled by tables identical to those used in "programming" the simulator. This means that sweeping changes to the user interface of the actual system can be made with no reprogramming whatsoever, simply by editing the control tables.

Once in place, this feature of the system was exploited to the full. When the system was prepared for release as an IBM product, user testing was continued until very late in the development cycle since changes were so easy to incorporate. It proved possible to include three separate user interfaces, designed for different user classes, in the product, since specifying an interface was so well isolated from the rest of the product.

What were some of the changes that all this flexibility made possible? One is a good example of the small but critical corrections that are so hard to spot in advance of testing. In one well-tested version, R (the 7-key) was used for RECORD and T (the 8-key) was used for TRANSMITting a message. This was satisfactory, and was in general use for over a year. As part of a major redesign to add new functions, it was felt that S (the 7-key) for SEND and T (the 8-key) for TALK provided a more natural-sounding command set. What could be more natural? Several months of informal user testing revealed a problem: When using this new command set users tried to SEND a message before TALKing it. (In the other case, users almost never tried to TRANSMIT a message before RECORDing it.) "I want to SEND a message to Smith," a user would reason. It was not clear that they had to TALK a message before SENDing it because SEND seemed to mean the whole action of composing and transmitting a message, at least for many novice users. Changing S for SEND to T for

TABLE II. An Example of a "Standard Table"

TNEUT	HEAD	LVL1 + LVL0, TNEUT, 0, 0, 3000	NEUTRAL MODE
	LINE	0, 0, NONE, EMPTY, 0, 0	NOT USED IN THIS TABLE
	LINE	1, 0, NONE, EMPTY, 0, 6	NOT USED IN THIS TABLE
	LINE	2, 0, COSLINE, TCUST, 0, 12	CUSTOMIZE MODE
	LINE	3, 0, NONE, TDISC, 0, 0	FAST DISCONNECT
	LINE	4, 0, COSLINE, XGET, 0, 0	GET MODE
	LINE	5, 0, COSLINE, XLIST, 0, 0	LISTEN AND EDIT
	LINE	6, 0, NONE, EMPTY, 0, 6	UNDEFINED KEY
	LINE	7, 0, COSLINE, XRECD, 0, 0	RECORD MODE
	LINE	8, 0, COSLINE, XXMIT, 0, 0	TRANSMIT MODE
	LINE	9, 0, NONE, EMPTY, 0, 0	NOT USED IN THIS TABLE
	LINE	*, 0, NONE, EMPTY, 0, 5	STAYS IN NEUTRAL: OK
	LINE	OPER, 0, NONE, EMPTY, 0, 6	NOT USED IN THIS TABLE
	LINE	#, 0, NONE, QNEUT, 0, 0	TELL USER WHAT TO DO
	LINE	DELAY, 0, NONE, QNEUT, 0, 0	TELL USER WHAT TO DO
	LINE	EOM, 0, NONE, EMPTY, 0, 0	NOT USED IN THIS TABLE

Note: Lines beginning with LINE 1 through LINE # correspond to the keys on a pushbutton telephone. If a user presses one of these keys, the corresponding LINE is executed in the table. For example, if a user presses 2 (i.e., the C-key) to customize his or her profile, LINE 2 is executed. That is, system message 12 is played out ("Customize"), a routine called COSLINE is called to initialize some variables, and control is transferred to a table called TCUST. If the user fails to push any key within 30 seconds (i.e., the 3000 centiseconds specified in HEAD) after arriving in this table, then LINE DELAY is executed. This will transfer control to a table called QNEUT which in turn will select a helpful prompt for the user, based on what is appropriate for the user to do.

TRANSMIT fixed the problem. Note that TRANSMIT is a less common, more technical term: Guidelines would probably rule against it (although some recent evidence is consistent with it; [2]). But the empirical method made the right call over our rational analysis.

Another example had to do with users making modifications to a message they were listening to. ADS asked users whether or not they wanted to add a comment at the beginning of the message, add a comment where they had stopped listening, or erase the message and start over. Some new users had trouble with this concept. For example, the wording "add a comment . . ." made sense if they were listening to a message from someone else, but not if they were listening to a message they were composing themselves. On the other hand, ". . . start over" made sense for messages they were composing themselves. Yet all three alternatives were important for both cases, for example, users needed to "insert" in their own messages (rather than "annotate" or "comment"). After testing many alternative wordings on many first-time users (which gave insight into the problem), ADS tables were "reprogrammed" to play out a slightly different prompt depending on whether users were listening to a message from someone else or one that they had composed themselves. This was easy to do at the level of the tables but required a fundamental algorithm modification so that ADS would distinguish between these two types of messages.

In the earliest stages of ADS, there were no specific behavioral goals. It was intended that the system be "easy to use," "useful," etc. We had not yet developed the principled type of thinking outlined in this article. With time, however, one behavioral goal was to create a system which required no user training. For several years, informal tests on possible user interface changes were motivated by this goal, and each major prototype revision reflected this goal. The command language was reorganized and emphasis on documentation was modified greatly. Informal feedback from customers and users indicates that a majority of new users learn ADS with no training, which is radically different from what was found for the earliest ADS prototype and for new users of most computer systems today.

Beyond ADS

It may seem that ADS is an unfair example of the application of our design ideas. The very simple terminal, with limited input and output, lent itself very well to table-driven design, with the flexibility that it provides. It was developed by a small group of people, several of whom had behavioral expertise. Could the same approaches work with a more typical system?

We believe they can. The key lesson of the ADS experience is not the implementation strategy—that is the secondary lesson. The most important lesson is the unpredictability of good design: The large number of features of the final design that were not and could not have been anticipated in the initial design. These features were only discovered and incorporated because of the focus on users and user testing in the design process.

The implementation strategy played a supporting role: It made it possible to respond to user feedback quickly and cheaply. Further, it gave *real control* of the user interface to the people who had responsibility for usability. No longer did they have to get systems experts to devote extensive time to making simple changes in the user interface. While table-driven implementation may not be possible in some cases, the underlying idea can still be used. One approach is to identify the system functions and a set of high-level interface services that control such things as the positioning of information on a screen, collecting user responses, and the like. All these are embodied in a set of routines or macros. The interface designer can now program the interface at a high level and make changes freely without reprogramming any of the underlying services.

7. CONCLUSIONS

Computer systems are hard for most people to learn and use today. We believe that if systems were designed using the three principles we have mentioned, they would receive much higher usability marks. Survey data show that these principles (early focus on users, empirical measurement, and iterative design) are not intuitive. There is one case history, and parts of others, which indicate that the principles lead to usable systems.

Acknowledgments. For their comments on an earlier version of this manuscript, we thank Karen Assunto, Dick Berry, Stephen Boies, Jack Carroll, Robin Davies, John Hughes, John Karat, Jeff Kelley, Emmett McTeague, John Richards, Bob Taylor, and John Thomas. Some of our ideas were developed as a result of working on the ADS project and were influenced by Stephen Boies. Others were developed or sharpened while conducting a study group on human factors at IBM in 1979. Other members of that group were Jack Carroll, Web Howard, John Morrisey, and Phylis Reisner.

REFERENCES

NOTE: References 14, 17, and 18 are unreferenced in the text.

1. Baker, F.T., and Mills, H.D. Chief programmer teams. *Datamation*, (Dec. 1973), 58–61.
2. Black, J., and Moran, T. Learning and remembering command names. In *Proceedings of the Human Factors in Computer Systems Meetings*. (Gaithersburg, Md.), ACM, Washington, D.C., 1982, 8–11.
3. Boyle, J.M., Bury, K.F., and Evey, R.J. Two studies evaluating learning and use of QBE and SQL. Tech. Rep. HFC-39, IBM GPD Human Factors Center, San Jose, Calif., 1981.
4. Brooks, F.P. *The Mythical Man-Month: Essays on Software Engineering.* Addison-Wesley, Reading, Mass., 1975.
5. Bury, K.F., and Boyle, J.M. An on-line experimental comparison of two simulated record selection languages. In *Proceedings of the Human Factors Society Annual Meeting*, (Seattle, Wash.), R.E. Edwards, (Ed.), 74–78, 1982. (Available from the Human Factors Society, Box 1369, Santa Monica, Calif. 90406).
6. Crosby, P.B. *Quality is Free.* New American Library, New York, 1979.
7. Dijkstra, E.W. *Structured Programming: Software Engineering Techniques*, NATO Scientific Affairs Division, Brussels 39, Belgium, Apr. 1970, 84–88.
8. Dijkstra, E.W., and Hoare, D. *Structured Programming.* Academic Press, N.Y., 1973.
9. Engel, S., and Granda, R. Guidelines for man/display interfaces. Tech. Rep. TR00.2720, IBM, Poughkeepsie Lab., N.Y., 1975.
10. Ericsson, K.A., and Simon, H.A. Verbal reports as data. *Psychol. Rev. 87*, (1980), 215–251.
11. Gomory, R.E. Technology development. *Science 220*, (1983), 576–580.
12. Gould, J.D. An experimental study of writing, dictating, and speaking. In *Attention and Performance VII*, J. Requin, (Ed.), Erlbaum, Hillsdale, N.J., 1978, 299–319.
13. Gould, J.D. How experts dictate. *J. Exp. Psychol.: Hum. Percept. Perform. 4*, 4 (1978), 648–661.
14. Gould, J. D. Experiments on composing letters: Some facts, some myths, and some observations. In *Cognitive Processes in Writing.* L. Gregg, and I. Steinberg, (Eds.) Erlbaum, Hillsdale, N.J., 1980, pp. 98–127.
15. Gould, J.D. Composing letters with computer-based text editors. *Hum. Fact. 23*, (1981). 593–606.
16. Gould, J.D. Writing and speaking letters and messages. *Int. J. Man Mach. Stud. 16*, (1982). 147–171.
17. Gould, J.D., and Boies, S.J. How authors think about their writing, dictating, and speaking. *Hum. Fact. 20*, (1978), 495–505.
18. Gould, J.D., and Boies, S.J. Writing, dictating, and speaking letters. *Science 201*, (1978), 1145–1147.
19. Gould, J.D., and Boies, S.J. Human factors challenges in creating a principal support office system—The speech filing system approach. *ACM Trans. Office Inform. Syst. 1*, 4 (1983), 273–298.
20. Gould, J.D., and Boies, S.J. Speech filing—An office system for principals. *IBM Syst. J. 23*, (1984), 65–81.
21. Gould, J. D., Conti, J., and Hovanyecz, T. Composing letters with a simulated listening typewriter. *Commun. ACM 26*, 4 (1983), 295–308.
22. Hammond, N., Jorgensen, A., MacLea A., Barnard, P., and Long, J. Design practice and interface usability: Evidence from interviews with designers. In *Proceedings of the CHI83 Human Factors in Computing Systems* (Boston, Mass., Dec. 1983). ACM, N.Y., 40–44.
23. Kelley, J.F. Natural language and computers: Six empirical steps for writing an easy-to-use computer application. Ph.D. dissertation, Johns Hopkins University, 1983. (Available from University Microfilm International; 300 North Zeeb Rd. Ann Arbor, Mich. 48106).
24. Lewis, C.H. Using the "thinking aloud" method in cognitive interface design. IBM Res. Rep. RC-9265, Yorktown Heights, N.Y., 1982.
25. Mack, R., Lewis, C.H., and Carroll, J. Learning to use word processors: Problems and prospects. *ACM Trans. Office Inform. Syst. 1*, 3 (1983), 254–271.
26. Morgan, C., Williams, G., and Lemmons, P. An interview with Wayne Rosing, Bruce Daniels, and Larry Tesler. *Byte*, 1983, 90–113.
27. Newell, A., and Simon, H.A. *Human Problem Solving.* Prentice-Hall, Englewood Cliffs, N.J., 1972.
28. Nix, D. Two experiments on the comprehensibility of pause-depleted speech. IBM Res. Rep. RC-6305, Yorktown Heights, N.Y., 1976.
29. *Proceedings of the Human Factors in Computing Systems Meetings.* (Washington, Mar. 1981; Boston, Dec., 1983) (Available from ACM, Box 64145, Baltimore, Md. 21264).
30. *Proceedings of the Human Factors Society Meeting*, (Seattle, Wash, Oct. 1982; Norfolk, Va., Oct., 1983) (Available from the Human Factors Society, Box 1369, Santa Monica, Calif. 90406).
31. *Science.* New Project Explores Disability Research, 233, (1984), 157.
32. Thomas, J.C. Office communications studies: I. Effects of communication behavior on the perception of described persons. IBM Res. Rep. RC-7572, Yorktown Heights, N.Y., 1979.
33. Thomas, J.C., and Gould, J.D. A psychological study of query-by-example. In *Proceedings of 1975 National Computer Conference.* (1975), 439–445.
34. Williams, G. The Lisa computer system. *Byte* (1983), 33–50.
35. Yourdon, E., and Constantine, L.L. *Structured Design.* Yourdon, New York, 1976.
36. Zloof, M.M. Query by example—A data base language. *IBM Syst. J. 4*, (1977), 324–343.

CR Categories and Subject Descriptors: H.1.2 [**Models and Principles**]: Users/Slash Machine Systems—*human factors*; D.2.2 [**Software Engineering**]: Tools and Techniques—*user interfaces*; D.2.9 [**Software Engineering**]: Management—*software quality assurance (SQA)*
   General Terms: Human Factors
   Additional Key Words and Phrases: systems development, principles of design

Authors' Present Addresses: John D. Gould, IBM Thomas J. Watson Research Center, P.O. Box 218, Yorktown Heights, NY 10598. Clayton Lewis, Department of Computer Science, ECOT 7-7 Engineering Center, Campus Box 430, Boulder, CO 80309.

Methods for Designing Software to Fit Human Needs and Capabilities

Proceedings of the Workshop on Software Human Factors

Nancy S. Anderson and Judith Reitman Olson, Editors

Committee on Human Factors
Commission on Behavioral and Social Sciences and Education
National Research Council

At present, software for specific applications and user-computer interfaces are aggressively developed in industry, but they are designed largely with only the designer's intuition as guide and often without empirical testing with end users. Two observations made in a popular software magazine point out the resulting problem:

The computer systems and software we have today are too damn complicated for the end user. There is too much to learn, too many fiddly details, too much jargon, too much said that shouldn't be and not enough said that should be . . . (A. Johnson-Laird, Software News, April 1982).

Data processing still has one ongoing problem to solve: the end user's dissatisfaction with today's systems. The entire industry has been grappling with this problem of ergonomics, or the interface between human and machine. In the case of data processing, ergonomics involves the development of "user-friendly" systems which can be operated by the user at the terminal and which generate results that the user can understand and utilize (M. Parks, Software News, February 1983).

Because of such difficulties, some industry and academic research groups are developing an interest in gathering and building appropriate guidelines from basic research and incorporating these guidelines and observations of users' behavior into the design process. A new field has emerged called software psychology or the psychology of human-computer interaction. It is in a very exciting state--a relatively new amalgam of

experimental/cognitive psychology, computer science, business, and engineering.

The field is growing in a variety of sectors. There are more human factors groups in industry than ever before. Approximately 50 universities in this country and abroad have PhD programs in human-computer interaction, which are housed in psychology, computer science, social sciences, engineering, business, and English departments (Mantei and Smelcer, 1984). Many more schools offer one or more courses in the area. The Association for Computing Machinery has a Special Interest Group for Computer-Human Interaction (SIGCHI). The Human Factors Society has a group called the Computer Systems Technical Group, which is concerned with human factors aspects of interactive computing systems, the data processing environment, and software development. Consumer demand for computers is increasing at a rapid pace, and many schools are acquiring computers for tutoring and the word-processing and mathematical tools that they provide. The systems that sell are those that provide the right usability and functionality--that provide the right design for the end user.

THE NEED FOR NEW METHODS

Designing systems to fit the end user is a difficult process. The field is searching for new methods. Classical experimental designs (e.g., controlled factorial designs) may not be appropriate for industrial settings in which cost-effectiveness and timeliness are major concerns. However, tests of single, intuition-driven designs with users, measuring their performance and satisfaction, do not advance our general knowledge about designs and do not indicate why certain features are good or bad.

There are, however, hybrid methods being used in industry, and new, more complex laboratory tests being constructed to assess users' performance in and/understanding of complex systems. These methods are described below, along with their advantages and disadvantages and where they fit into the product development cycle. Each method is annotated with references to a few key articles that report its use.

Excerpted from Anderson, N.S. and Reitman Olsen, J. (Eds.) (1985). *Methods for Designing Software to Fit Human Needs and Capabilities*, Proceedings of the Workshop of Software Human Factors, National Research Council, Washington, D.C.: National Academy Press.

THE PRODUCT DEVELOPMENT CYCLE

Software products are typically developed in three general stages:

1. Analysis--the product's functionality and initial hardware/software constraints are determined, analysis is made of the product's projected costs and benefits, and a development schedule is projected.
2. Design--the product is designed, first at the level of functional specifications and later in complete detail, then coded and tested, ending with a running system.
3. Implementation--the product is distributed and installed in its final locations, and users are trained and then operate the equipment.

At all three stages human factors considerations appear:

1. In assessing users' needs and capabilities during the analysis phase;
2. In designing and redesigning the system with human factors principles of usability, and in testing prototypes with end users during the design stage; and
3. In monitoring use of the system after its implementation, gathering information for redesign to correct errors or to add new, useful features.

In what follows the methods appropriate to each of these stages are described. These methods, or their variants, are useful for both laboratory research and industry. They may be used in the slower, more controlled environment of the laboratory, where research is designed to study people's performance on complex tasks. And they contribute equally to design and evaluation in industry, where timeliness is frequently considered to be more important than the ability to generalize from the results.

HUMAN FACTORS METHODS IN RESEARCH AND PRODUCT DESIGN

ANALYSIS: GATHERING IDEAS

The ideas behind products typically arise from three major sources: from the redesign of an existing product, from an identified need in the marketplace, and from a new technological capability that provides a useful new function to users. Information about the success of existing products can be obtained either by asking their users for their opinions and uses of the systems or by gathering unobtrusive data about their use. Information about a new product can come from reports of needs from potential users.

Reports from Users

Questionnaires and interviews are the most common methods for gathering information about the success of a product or the needs for new functions or a new product. Both questionnaires and interviews are good methods for eliciting information about how a person goes about his or her work, what aids or tools he or she uses or desires, what kind of knowledge or training is required to do the work, what difficulties he or she reports about the work, where the work originates and where it goes, what interactions are necessary with other people to do the work, and how the user thinks the work process could be improved. Questionnaires are more rigid in format than interviews, since interviews can go where the interviewee leads, often uncovering unanticipated new information. The principal disadvantage of interviews, however, is that they are time-consuming; only one person can be interrogated at a time. By aggregating information from a number of interviewees or questionnaires, one can construct a general picture of users' needs and construct some tentative system concepts for helping the users do their work (Kelley and Chapanis, 1982; Rosson, 1983).

Diaries provide a similar form of informal data gathering and are used to uncover the needs and capabilities of the potential users of a new product. Data about work can be gathered in detail over a long period of time, especially about how much time particular kinds of activities take and their sequential dependencies. Because a shorter time elapses between the occurrence of an event and its report, diaries give a more accurate record of actual activity than retrospective reports in questionnaires and interviews (Mantei and Haskell, 1983).

A common marketing technique for gathering information about existing or potential users' needs is the *focus group*. Instead of interviewing a single user at a time, groups of users who are either similarly trained or who share common goals are first told about some potential capabilities of a system, then asked to discuss how they might find uses for these capabilities. Occasionally active brainstorming from these sessions generates very good ideas. The same kind of method is used to collect opinions about an existing product and to ask for suggestions for improvements. Often designers will gather expert users of a system and ask their opinion about how to improve the system or how to design a new, computer-based tool for aiding their work (Al-Awar et al., 1981). The advantage of such methods is that the participants stimulate each others' thoughts, uncovering ideas or suggestions they may not have thought of individually. That is also its disadvantage: a participant's true opinions can be swayed by group pressure.

Inferring Needs from Natural Observation

One of the main drawbacks of the methods listed above is that they rely on users' perceptions of their needs and capabilities. Sometimes new products meet needs unforeseen by their users; sometimes users, either consciously or unconsciously, distort their daily work activities and feelings about existing working conditions. In such cases, it may be better to collect information, not by asking users, but by watching their behavior and inferring their needs and capabilities from their activities.

Two methods are often used to collect information about users' behavior in natural work settings. In the case of *activity analysis*, an observer watches and records certain behaviors of the workers. The data may be collected by direct observation or by analyzing video or film recordings. Individual samples of categorized activities are aggregated into activity frequency tables, graphs, or state transition diagrams. Such performance analyses are particularly useful in assessing the changes made in work by comparing activity before and after a new system or design change is implemented (Hartley et al., 1977; Hoecker and Pew, 1980).

Logging and metering techniques involve observations of what a user does with a system, but the measurement is embedded directly into the software. These procedures can include a simple record with a time-stamp of every interaction that a user makes with the computer, or it can involve a complete hard copy representation of a sequence of particular display frames. Powerful logging and metering software can also categorize certain recognizable events and summarize their times. For example, one could summarize such events as time to complete a task, user and/or system response time, and frequencies and types of errors.

Logging and metering procedures are typically embedded in the operational software. Where there are limits to the access to such software, one can connect a second computer in tandem to the first and direct data about the user's activities to it, in essence providing a "passive tap." In this way, logging does not interfere with system response times, and information about the user inputs and the system responses can be recorded in detail for future use (see Whiteside et al., 1982; Goodwin, 1982).

DESIGN: THE INITIAL DESIGN

Designers go through two stages in constructing an initial design, either implicitly, driven by intuition or experience, or explicitly, using some or all of the detailed tools described below. First, the designers decide what the user is going to do, conducting an informal or formal task analysis. Second, they specify what the interface will look like and what the dialog will consist of. There are a variety of methods that apply to this stage, where designers use informal or formal guidelines, consult end users, or have some theory-based judgments to draw on.

Determining What the User Needs to Do

The most common form of analyzing the user's activities is called a *task analysis*. Task analysis is the process of analyzing the functional requirements of a system to ascertain and describe the tasks that people perform. It focuses both on how the system fits within the global task the user is trying to perform (e.g., prepare a report of a projected budget) and what the user has to do to use the system (e.g., access the application program, access the data files, etc.).

Task analysis has two major aspects: the first specifies and describes the tasks, and the second, and more important, analyzes the specified tasks to determine such system or environmental characteristics as the number of people needed, the skills and knowledge they should have, and the training necessary. The first step involves decomposition of tasks into their constituent subtasks and annotating each subtask for its essential elements and their interdependencies. The second step involves examination of the actual tasks and interdependencies, assessing how difficult each is, what knowledge is required, where the information resides, etc. Results of task analyses are used not only in writing functional specifications for a particular application, but also for assigning work to groups of workers, arranging equipment in an efficient configuration, determining task demands on people, and developing operating procedures and training manuals (see Bullen and Bennett, 1983; Bullen et al., 1982).

Specifying the Initial Design

An initial system or interface design is constructed next. With the global tasks the user has to perform specified as above, the designer groups the subtasks according to logical function from the perspective of the user but tempered by system/hardware constraints. Then the actual interface or system details come from three sources: design guidelines or principles, intuitions of the designer sometimes aided by intuitions of the users themselves, and theory-based judgments.

In generating an initial design, the designer can address existing *design guidelines* for general prescriptions of how to specify particular components of the interface. For example, if the interface has a menu, the guideline may prescribe that the alternatives should be listed by order of frequency of use or cluster them according to functional similarity, rather than displayed alphabetically or randomly. Current design guidelines (e.g., Woodson and Conover, 1966; Van Cott and Kinkade, 1972) include prescriptions about such topics as the readability of type fonts, the brightness levels of display screens, keyboards designed to fit hand shape and function, and rules for making abbreviations and symbols (see also Schneiderman, 1982; Smith, 1982).

Current guidelines, however, are more concerned with perceptual and performance characteristics than with the cognitive properties of the interaction. Thus, they would prescribe appropriate type fonts, but not what words these fonts should express to the user to suggest the appropriate analogy for performing the task on the system. There are several major caveats in the use of design guidelines: the prescriptions or recommendations contained may have been derived from situations or research not applicable to the system being designed; new or unaccounted for variables may interact in unanticipated ways; and current guidelines do not always publish the source of the recommendation, whether it was generated by a controlled laboratory study or derived from the collected wisdom of experience. Guidelines have to be applied with care.

Though design guidelines have their flaws, they are very useful in placing a particular new design in a setting of conventional wisdom. Often the designer, skilled in interacting with systems and cognizant of the end tasks that are being supported in this design, cannot foresee the difficulties the new user will have with the system. Design guidelines provide suggestions to the designer that will in many cases be better than those based solely on intuition. (For a recent version of guidelines, see Smith, 1984.)

The *skills and knowledge of users* themselves can be used to advantage by incorporating users in the design team. Users can provide some critical insights about how they think of the task and thus the system (e.g., what kinds of information should be accessible when, what the screens should look like to mimic the original, a noncomputer version of the task, what commands ought to be called). They know the procedures and terminology and, with proper support, can contribute to the design and layout of forms and menus as well as act as critics of the design. Gould and Lewis (1985) and Miller and Pew (1981) provide examples of the involvement of users in the design process. Other ways in which the sophisticated user can be involved in the design of software systems can be found below in the section on prototype testing with users.

A third source of information about the original design specification is psychological theories. *Theory-based judgments* can constrain aspects of a design or suggest promising areas of investigation. For example, theories of color contrast can provide insight into the appropriateness of certain combinations used in screen high-lighting or predict the readability of a new monochrome display color. Because Fitt's Law accounted for movement time for placing a cursor in a desired position with a mouse and for placing the appropriate finger on a desired key location, two conclusions follow: the invention of a faster pointing devices was unlikely to increase performance and the design of keyboards with larger peripheral key caps would increase the accuracy of keying (Card et al., 1978; Card et al., 1980b).

Part of the difficulty in constructing a design and analyzing its usability has to do with how the interface is specified. Verbal descriptions of how a system works are particularly unsuited for conveying the flow of an interaction and the choices the user has at each point. Several specification languages or formats have been explored recently not only to serve as a way of conveying to those who actually build or code the system what it will do but also as a way of concretely specifying the system to analyze its usability.

One way to specify the interaction is to use an interactive tool kit called a *human-computer dialog management system*. This system guides the definition of the interaction language that describes the actions of the user and the system and the screen formats displayed at each moment. Hartson et al. (1984), Jacob (1983), and Wasserman (1982) provide good examples of this kind of interface definition.* A second format for displaying

what the system does at each state is a *state transition diagram*, recently used as a description of a system's workings in Kieras and Polson (1983).

DESIGN: FORMAL ANALYSIS OF THE INITIAL DESIGN

Once an initial design is specified, even if it is a partial design, it can be subjected to several kinds of scrutiny. The goal in this analysis stage is to make the initial design as good as possible before it is made into the prototype for user testing. Three methods aid in this process: structured walk-throughs, decomposition, and task-theoretic analytic models.

Structured walk-throughs involve construction of tasks that a user carries out on a simulated system. The user tries out the system by going through the task, step by step, screen by screen, command by command. This can be done with the design as specified in a number of different formats, using an experimental simulation of a prototype or even with the experimenter presenting paper and pencil figures of the screens, menus, and commands in the appropriate sequence. The technique helps to identify confusing, unclear, or incomplete instructions, illogical or inefficient operations, unnatural or difficult procedures, and procedural steps that may have been overlooked because they were implicitly rather than explicitly defined. Gould et al. (1983), Ramsey (1974), Ramsey et al. (1979), and Weinberg and Friedman (1984) provide examples of the use of structured walk-throughs.

A second kind of formal analysis, called *decomposition*, is proposed in Reitman et al. (1985). In this analysis, the major components of the design are separated and analyzed for their impact on cognition. The picture displayed on the screen, for example, is assessed for how it helps or hinders the user's ability to perceive meaningful relationships or the system model. The commands are assessed for their load on long-term memory, how easy they are to remember, and how confusable they are among each other. For each component, a second design alternative is constructed to fit within the general guidelines of usability. Then, through discussion and debate, the design team decides which alternative of each component is the better design. This method encourages careful scrutiny of the proposed design and often encourages designers to specify better interfaces before the first prototype is built.

---

*This is also a system that allows rapid embodiment of the functioning of a new, developing system and thus is a

The third kind of formal techniques invoke *task-theoretic analytic models*. These models provide representations and analyses that assess, for example, which parts of a metaphor aid performance and which do not (Douglas and Moran, 1983) and how big the user's short-term memory load is at each step of the interaction (Kieras and Polson, 1985). Prime examples of these techniques include metaphor analysis (Carroll and Thomas, 1982; Carroll and Mack, 1982), assessment of mental models (deKleer and Brown, 1983; deKleer and Brown, in press; and others in Gentner and Stevens, 1983), development of production rule systems that represent the user's knowledge of the task (Kieras and Polson, 1985), object/action analysis (called "external/internal task mapping" by Moran, 1983), the GOMS model (Card et al., 1980b; 1983), and formal grammar notation systems (Reisner, 1981a, 1984; Blesser and Foley, 1982).

These task analytic models are very useful tools. However, none of them yet encompasses all of the cognitive aspects of the interaction; each focuses on one or more important aspects. These methods require training to use and often take a long time. However, they all have the advantage of being based on sound theories of human behavior and can provide important analysis of usability before any coding of software or running of subjects is contemplated. There is a trade-off, then, between time spent in analysis and time spent testing users in the laboratory or the field. The hope embodied in this approach is that as the science of user-interface design grows, analytic tools will improve to the point of making the actual user testing of designed systems merely a last, short check of a good, finished design.

DESIGN: BUILDING A PROTOTYPE

Three methods provide simulations or quick versions of significant aspects of a new system so it can be tried by actual users. The methods are called facading, the Wizard of Oz technique, and rapid prototyping.

Facading is the technique of quickly and inexpensively building a simulation of the external appearance (i.e., the "facade") of a system's interface. Its advantages are that it is quick and relatively easy; the target system's underlying complexity and/or final computational capability is "finessed." To be maximally beneficial, the facade must embody some level of the functional capability of the final target system. It does not just generate a series of static snapshots of the system but rather includes the control structure, flow, or connectivity of the final system. Hanau and Lenorovitz (1980) and Lenorovitz and Ramsey (1977) provide good examples of the use of this technique.

A variant of the facading technique is the *Wizard of Oz* technique. Instead of having the computer embody the simulated system, hidden human operators intercept user commands and provide output back to the user. Often the technique is used to test a new interface language: the hidden human operator intercepts the new commands, translates them into the real system commands, and, after receiving output from the real computer system, retranslates them back to the tested end-user (see Gould et al., 1983; Gould and Boies, 1978; Ford, 1981; Kelley, 1983; Wixon et al., 1983).

Rapid or *fast prototyping* are terms applied to the more formalized building of a prototype in a hurry. The speed of building a running system depends mainly on the underlying supporting software, which makes the specific prototype programmable from existing modules. Ideally, the prototype programming language separates elements of the dialog from the actual implementation software. For example, the designer can specify the placement of the command input line or the menu choices variously without having to program new modules to execute these different input formats. One of these, the "dialog management system," is under development by Hartson and his colleagues (Hartson et al., 1984; Yunten and Hartson, 1984); another system is described in Wasserman (1982) and Wasserman and Shewmake (1982). Another project that uses rapid prototyping methods is reported in Hayes et al. (1981).

DESIGN: PROTOTYPE TESTING WITH USERS

When a prototype of some form has been built, actual users are then brought in to use the system and report their opinions about it. These tests can vary greatly in how well controlled their designs are and how representative the set of tested users are of the final population of users. Moreover, users are asked to perform several kinds of tasks, some testing the normal, frequent tasks that regular users will be expected to perform, others testing those subtasks thought to be especially difficult either for the system (e.g., those producing long system response times) or for the user (e.g., the longest sequence of commands for a particular type of task). Prototype tests differ in what kinds of data are taken from the user--times and errors, thinking aloud protocols, or attitudes.

Experimental Designs

Field tests to evaluate systems are fashioned after laboratory tests common in the academic field of experimental psychology. In general, they require the comparison of at least two systems, systems that differ in only one component or variable. Measures are designed to reflect the performance attributable to the effects of that variable, and subjects are chosen to be representative of the population of end users. Of particular importance are various techniques for controlling irrelevant variables. For example, one must ensure that measures of intelligence of the test subjects do not differ across both conditions, affecting the results in addition to the effects of the independent variables.

Often the rules of good experimental design are violated in the interest of proceeding quickly. Subjects who are different from the end users but more available may be tested; comparisons may be made between two systems that differ on more than one variable; measures may be taken that are less sensitive than those that will directly test why performance on one system is better or worse than another; occasionally only one system is tested and performance on it is measured against some predetermined standard (e.g., a 10-minute rule for time to learn a system). The closer the test is to good experimental design, the more quickly the findings can advance knowledge about the important aspects of good human-computer interface. However, as is often the case in development, the goal is not ultimate knowledge but rather global assessment of the adequacy of a particular interface or system. A compromise design procedure is described in Reitman et al. (1984). The use of experimental design is found in Ledgard et al. (1981), Reisner et al. (1975), Reisner (1977, 1981b), and Willges and Willges (1982).

One variant from controlled experimental evaluation that has been found useful in the development of inter-

designs involve capturing data at several time intervals, typically of durations measured in weeks or months. Sometime during the data capturing intervals, a change or a modification of a system is introduced; the data being captured are expected to reflect the impact of this change. Some of these quasi-experimental designs allow for comparisons with a control group. These designs are hard to control, since the investigator must typically take existing groups of users, giving one the change and the other no change. Inherent differences in existing groups is a major worry in evaluating the results. A complete description of this technique can be found in Cook and Campbell (1979); Koltum (1982) and Rice (1982) provide good examples of this method.

Selection of Tasks to Perform

There are two reasons one has users try out a prototype system: to identify points of difficulty for the user so that those points can be redesigned and to measure standard use of the system, so that later changes in hardware can be assessed or so those concerned with the staffing of a large operation of users can determine how many people will be needed. For the first purpose, tasks are selected that stress the system and the user, generally called critical incidents. For the second purpose, tasks are selected to estimate basic characteristics of the system's use, called benchmark tests.

In terms of *critical incidents*, the goal is to set up situations or tasks that have been shown historically to tax the user and/or the system and are sufficiently important that they can make the difference between success or failure on task or system performance. One might, for example, require the user to access items distant from what is being presented on the current screen or to perform a long command sequence, to determine the loads of this part of the design on the user's ability to imagine the stored information's underlying structure or the mnemonic characteristics and grammatical rules implied by the command sequences. The goal is to set up situations in which the data will tell the designers something about the limits of human or system performance. These tasks are illustrated in the work of Al-Awar et al. (1981), Kelley and Chapanis (1982), and Flanagan (1954).

In *benchmark* tests, the goals are quite different. The designer wants to measure the likely performance times and errors expected in normal use. The tasks are not designed to tax the system or the user, but rather to be representative of the kinds of frequent tasks the system will normally support. Typically, tasks are constructed to measure the expected amount of time it takes a new user to learn a system, the amount of time it takes the user to perform a set of predefined tasks, and the amount of time it takes the system to respond to a user's request. A good study that illustrates the use of this method is that of the evaluation of eight text editors by Roberts and Moran (1983). A study of database interfaces using benchmarks was done by Mantei and Cattell (1982).

Kinds of Data Collected

There are four major kinds of data collected in tests of systems: the time it takes to perform a task, the frequency and kinds of errors, the goals and intentions of the users, and the attitude of the user.

The amount of time a task takes (either how long an entire task takes or how long each successive keystroke takes) reflects the time it takes the user to perceive inputs, categorize and plan appropriate actions, and execute proper responses. Error frequencies and types reflect the difficulties users have with these processes and often point to the cause of the error (whether the error response is similar to one in a similar plan, was generated from confusion with a similar screen, has a label that sounds the same as another, etc.) A simple analysis of users' *times and errors* is found in Reisner et al. (1975) and Reisner (1977). A comprehensive analysis of users' times is found in Card et al. (1980b, 1983). Other uses of times and errors can be found in Boies (1974), Rosson (1984), Sheppard and Kruesi (1981), and Thomas and Gould (1975).

A more thorough, complicated kind of data to collect during evaluation involves the user's *thinking aloud* while performing the task. Typically the user is video- and sound-recorded while he or she is performing the tasks. The recording captures what is said and done, what is displayed on the screen, what sections of the documentation are being examined, what parts of the task instructions the user is reviewing, etc. The most complete protocols ask the subjects to verbalize their intentions, what their goals are, and what current plans they have about reaching their goals. Other behavior is directly observable; thoughts and plans typically are not. This method has been used by Mack et al. (1983), Carroll and Mack (1982), and Card et al. (1980a) in their studies of skilled text editing. More complete descriptions of the technique and its advantages and disadvantages can be found in Lewis (1982), Olson et al. (1984), and Ericsson and Simon (1980).

A third kind of data collected in evaluation sessions is the *users' opinions* about the system's ease of use and functionality. A common instrument used to scale users' global attitudes about the system is the evaluation component of Osgood et al.'s (1957) Semantic Differential (see Good, 1982, for an example of its use). Questionnaires and interviews also tap users' reactions to particular components of the system. One problem with users' reports, however, is that they are typically distorted by their experience with other, similar systems. Or a user may have difficulty separating components of the system such; for example, a user who has a very difficult time using a system may report that he or she likes it a great deal, recognizing how much easier it is to perform the task on a computer compared with previous manual methods.

Redesign

Typically as the prototype of the original design is tested, errors are found and revisions suggested. The methods appropriate to the initial design are appropriate also at the stage of redesign. This part of the design process iterates through "fixing" and "testing" until either an acceptable level of performance is reached or the deadline for developing the system is reached.

IMPLEMENTATION: MONITORING CONTINUED PERFORMANCE

Just as data were collected in the original conception and analysis phase of product development, data are collected on the system as implemented. At this stage, activity analyses, diaries, logging and metering, and questionnaires and interviews are all appropriate methods for assessing whether the product as designed is performing as predicted in the final environment. If problems are found in the field, either small corrections are made in the code (e.g., changing what a command is called is easy to change in the code but can have an enormous impact on the ease of use), or a redesign is called for, sending the product design process back to prototype development or fully back to the top of the cycle.

OTHER METHODS

Three additional methods are worth mentioning, though they do not fit neatly into the scheme above. They include the dialog specification procedure, experimental programming, and case studies.

The *dialog specification method* is a global procedure that cuts across the first several steps outlined above. It is a procedure that prescribes a method for developing an interactive dialog with a system and sets a design standard. The method includes task analysis and flow charting of user activities as well as standard means of communicating the specific design requirements to the programmer. The design standard describes acceptable screen layouts, interactive devices and how they are to be used, acceptable command language syntax, etc., down to a level of detail compatible with the specificity of the range of applications to which it is intended to apply. For example, if all designs concerned telephone management applications, the specification would deal only with the range of tasks in this domain. These specifications are built from human factors principles as well as accumulated data from user testing. Pew et al. (1979) describe this method more fully.

Experimental programming is similarly a more global method for designing systems and interfaces. It is a more flowing, adaptive technique involving users, designers, and programmers (sometimes all in the same person). Someone builds a prototype of a new system with some fraction of the functionality and some fraction of the user interface in place. This prototype is then used by a variety of programmer/users who generate suggestions for new features and suggestions for revisions for existing functions. As many suggestions as possible are incorporated into the prototype; the good features

survive, poor features disappear. Occasionally, when new features are incompatible with the old, a competing prototype is built. Sometimes someone merges the most popular ideas from both. This method is very informal. The only rules for its application are that everyone's opinion get a fair hearing and that anyone in the community can implement a change.

This method allows for progressively better understanding of the application as well as the computation and interface requirements. Its weakness lies in its casual nature and that it relies on the opinion of users, most of whom are programmers; its strength lies in its exploratory, evolutionary, democratic nature. One well-known product that benefited from experimental programming is the EMACS text editor (Stallman, 1980), which pioneered such concepts as user-customization, on-line documentation, and a particular command style. In addition, Teitelman (1972) used experimental programming to develop the concept called DWIM ("Do What I Mean"), which included a set of facilities that automatically corrected predictable errors.

A third global technique goes under the rubric of *case studies*. Case studies involve observation and analysis of a singe user, group, or project. The information collected may range from informal, subjective impressions to detailed quantitative data. Because case studies involve no comparison or control group, they are not very useful in inferring causality. As a result they are not appropriate for building a data base of basic research results from which to construct theories and principles. They can, however, be extremely useful for gaining insights when one is first investigating an area of interest and for providing concrete demonstrations of the use of new methods and tools.

An example of a case study in which new insights were gained about a domain involved the use of the Ada system. The purpose of the study was to understand the problems that are likely to arise when the system is first introduced into an organization (Bailey et al., 1982). A second case study involved a demonstration of new methods for designing systems to be embedded in special purpose hardware, such as airplanes and tanks (Britton et al., 1981). The documentation and related products produced by this case study provide examples that others may use in trying to apply the methods to their own software projects. Brooks (1975) documents the use of a case study in a large computer programming project. And, the case study by Baker (1972) was extremely influential in leading the structured programming revolution. Others include Gould and Boies (1978, 1983, 1984), and Heninger (1980).

ADVANCES AND SUCCESSES

Over the last 10 years, it has become clear that research on the issues surrounding human-computer interaction is worth doing. The design of the human-computer interface makes a marked difference in users' performance. Software products exist that embody well-designed interfaces derived from human factors input: the Xerox STAR, Apple LISA, and MACINTOSH work stations and the Rolm and IBM mail systems are examples. In addition, major changes in the design of the telephone directory assistance system, as well as original designs of telecommunication control devices, were a result of human factors studies.

Human factors research has also shown the usefulness of some important generic display and control devices: the partitioning of screens into windows, icons for the control of operations and the display of objects, better help messages, and better defined response and function keys. In addition, more is known about users' limitations and adaptability.

Human factors design is also influencing documentation and training for software use (Felker, 1980). Because software is more available to a variety of users, there is an increased awareness by the public of the need to make software easy to learn and use.

FUTURE METHODS

Although we have catalogued a variety of methods to be used in the software design and research process, some needs for information are still unmet. The research needs fall roughly into three categories of needs: new theories, new representations, and new data collection and analysis methods.

THEORIES

Three particular kinds of theories are seen as needed. *Automation theories* would tell us what should be automated and what should be assigned to the human processor. Such theories would also prescribe an appropriate mix of automation and human control. Some seeds of theories are suggested in the field of supervisory control and in office analysis techniques, but a more explicit theory is needed to prescribe the best mix of human and computer processing.

Theories of individual differences would tell us about the different kinds of computer support required and desired by different user populations. Special continuing interest focuses on the differences between naive or casual users and expert or dedicated users.

Theories of standardization would tell us about which aspects of a system should be standardized for all users (as in the basic control devices in an automobile) and which can be customized for adaptation by and for specific users.

In addition, two taxonomies are needed: a characterization of the kinds of tasks for which software can be built (so that design prescriptions can be tied, perhaps, to particular classes of tasks) and a characterization of the kinds of users that use software applications (related to the theories of individual differences described above). The partial taxonomy of human-computer interface tasks advanced by Lenorovitz et al. (1984) provides a baseline for this effort.

REPRESENTATION

Many of our analyses outside the testing of a working system with real end users require some specification of what the system can do, what the user knows about how the system works, and how the user conceives of the task. There is thus a need for better representational schemes than those now being used. One such scheme would describe a complex system so that documentation and training could be better designed. Another would represent exactly how a system works--the interface, dialog, communication, or transaction--so that the design could be both analyzed for its fit to users' needs and capabilities and conveyed to those who have to program it.

CONCLUSION

The field of software human factors is rising in its research needs faster than the scientific data base is growing. Additional basic research is clearly needed. Educational programs are now training future researchers and practitioners in this field. Data in laboratories and industry need to be collected more systematically and disseminated more widely. As a compendium of current methods, their descriptions and evaluations, and references to existing literature that use these methods, this report should then help coalesce the field and move it toward fruitful work in the future.

REFERENCES

Al-Awar, J., Chapanis, A., and Ford, W.R.
1981   Tutorials for the first time computer user. IEEE Transactions in Professional Communication. PC-24(1):30-37.

Bailey, J., Basili, V., Gannon, J., Katz, E., Kruesi, E., Sheppard, S., and Zelkowitz, M.
1982   Monitoring an Ada Software Development Project. Ada Letters 2(July-August):58-61.

Baker, F.T.
1972   Chief programmers team management of production programming. IBM Systems Journal 11:56-73.

Blesser, T., and Foley, J.D.
1982   Towards specifying and evaluating the human factors of user-computer interface. Pp. 309-314 in Proceedings of the Human Factors of Computing Systems. New York: Association of Computing Machinery.

Boies, S.J.
1974   User behavior on an interactive computer system. IBM Systems Journal 13:2-18.

Britton, K.H., Parker, R.A., and Parnas, D.L.
1981   A procedure for designing abstract interfaces for device interface modules. Proceedings of the 5th International Conference on Software Engineering. Orlando, Fla: IEEE.

we need techniques for inferring what a user currently understands of a system, a method for extracting the appropriate information from the user and for displaying the resulting understanding or "mental model." These techniques are as useful in basic research on the performance of complex tasks as they are in the applied design process. (A report of the Committee on Human Factors' workshop on mental models in the use of information systems is scheduled for publication in 1985.)

DATA COLLECTION, MEASURES, AND ANALYSES

Although we have a rich variety of measures to collect from users interacting with a system, we have no direct measures of the user's affect nor do we collect any of the neurophysiological responses that accompany intense work, frustration, and satisfaction. In addition, there is a need for better hardware tools for collecting logging and metering information without slowing the system that the user normally interacts with. More specific methods are needed for analyzing the mountain of data that comes from protocol analysis, not only in deducing how the user is satisfying his or her task goals and subgoals, but also in deducing ongoing memory and perceptual loads on the user and how the user compensates for them in performing the task. Our task analysis methods need to be expanded to include more cognitive aspects of the user's performance, his or her memory, language, and perceptual aspects.

Research methods considered most likely to produce high payoff in the near future include:

o Representations of the users' understanding of a system;

o Representations of a dialog to convey the design to programmers;

o More comprehensive task analyses that include memory, perceptual, and language considerations as well as timing and error predictions; and

o Hardware advances that allow the collection of logging and metering data for tapping the current use of a system.

Brooks, F.P.
1975 The Mythical Man Month: Essays on Software Engineering. Reading, Mass.: Addison-Wesley.

Bullen, C.V., and Bennett, J.L.
1983 Office Workstation Use by Administrative Managers and Professionals. IBM Research Report RJ 3890.

Bullen, C.V., Bennett, J.L., and Carlson, E.D.
1982 A case study in office workstation use. IBM Systems Journal 21(3):351-369.

Card, S.K., English, W.K., and Burr, B.J.
1978 Evaluation of mouse, rate-controlled isometric joystick, stop keys, and text keys for text selection on a CRT. Ergonomics 21:601-631.

Card, S., Moran, T., and Newell, A.
1980a Computer text-editing: an information processing analysis of a routine cognitive skill. Cognitive Psychology 12:32-74.

1980b The keystroke level model for user performance with interactive systems. Communications of the ACM 23:396-410.

1983 The Psychology of Human Computer Interaction. Hillsdale, N.J.: Lawrence Erlbaum.

Carroll, J.M., and Mack, R.L.
1982 Metaphor, computing systems and active learning. IBM Research Report RC 9636.

Carroll, J.M., and Thomas, J.C.
1982 Metaphor and the cognitive representation of computing systems. IEEE Transactions on Systems, Man, and Cybernetics 12:107-116.

Cook, T.D., and Campbell, D.T.
1979 Quasi-Experimentation: Design and Analysis Issues for Field Settings. Chicago: Rand McNally.

deKleer, J., and Brown, J.S.
1983 Assumptions and ambiguities in mechanistic mental models. In D. Gentner and A.S. Stevens, eds., Mental Models. Hillsdale, N.J.: Lawrence Erlbaum.

in press A qualitative physics based on confluences. In B. Moore and J. Hobbs, eds., Formal Models of the Common-Sense World. Norwood, N.H.: Ablex.

Douglas, S.A., and Moran, T.P.
1983 Learning text editing semantics by analogy. Pp. 207-211 in Proceedings of the Conference on Human Factors in Computing Systems. New York: Association of Computing Machinery.

Ericsson, K.A., and Simon, H.A.
1980 Verbal reports as data. Psychological Review 3:215-251.

Felker, D.C., ed.
1980 Document Design: A Review of the Relevant Research. American Institute for Research. Technical Report 75002-4/80, Washington, D.C.

Flanagan, John C.
1954 Critical incident technique. Psychological Bulletin 51:327-358.

Ford, William R.
1981 Natural Language Processing by Computer--A New Approach. Ph.D. dissertation. Department of Psychology, Johns Hopkins University.

Gentner, D., and Stevens, A.L. eds.
1983 Mental Models. Hillsdale, N.J.: Lawrence Erlbaum.

Good, M.
1982 An ease of use evaluation of an integrated document processing system. CHI 82. Pp. 142-147 in Proceedings of Human Factors in Computing Systems. New York: Association of Computing Machinery.

Goodwin, N.C.
1982 Effect of interface design on usability of message handling systems. Pp. 69-73 in Proceedings of the Human Factors Society. 26th annual meeting, Seattle, Wash.

Gould, J.D., and Boies, S.J.
1978 Writing, dictating, and speaking letters. Science 201:1145-1147.

1983 Human factors challenges in creating a principal support system--the speech filing approach. ACM Transactions on Office Information Systems 1(4):273-298.

1984 Speech filing--an office system for principals. IBM Systems Journal 23(1):65-81.

Gould, J.D., and Lewis, C.
1985 Designing for usability of key principles and what designers think. Communications of the ACM 28:300-311. New York: Association of Computing Machinery.

Gould, J.D., Conti, John, and Hovanyecz, Todd
1983   Composing letters with a simulated listening typewriter. Communications of the ACM 26:295-308.

Hanau, P.R., and Lenorovitz, D.R.
1980   A prototyping and simulation approach to interactive computer system design. Pp. 23-25 in Proceedings of the 17th Design Automation Conference, Minneapolis, Minn.

Hartley, C., Brecht, M., Pagersy, P., Weeks, G., Chapanis, A., and Hoecker, D.
1977   Subjective estimates of work tasks by office workers. Journal of Occupational Psychology 50:23-36.

Hartson, H.R., Johnson, D.H., and Ehrich, R.W.
1984   A human-computer dialogue management system. Pp. 57-61 in Proceedings of INTERACT '84, London. Amsterdam: Elsevier Science Publications.

Hayes, P., Ball, E., and Reddy, R.
1981   Breaking the man-machine communication barrier. Computer 14(3):19-30.

Heninger, K. L.
1980   Specifying software requirements for complex systems: new techniques and their application. IEEE Transactions on Software Engineering. SE-6(1):2-13.

Hoecker, D.G., and Pew, R.W.
1980   User Input to the Design and Evaluation of Computer-Assisted Service Delivery. Report #4358. Cambridge, Mass.: Bolt Beranek and Newman Inc.

Jacob, R.J.K.
1983   Using formal specifications in the design of the human-computer interface. Communications of the Association of Computing Machinery 26(4):259-270.

Johnson-Laird, A.
1982   Most software more complicated than needed. Software News 2(4):47.

Kelley, J.F.
1983   Natural Language and Computers: Six Empirical Steps for Writing an Easy-to-Use-Computer Application. Ph.D. dissertation, Department of Psychology, Johns Hopkins University.

Kelley, J.F., and Chapanis, A.
1982   How professional persons keep their calendars: implications for computerization. Journal of Occupational Psychology 55:241-256.

Kieras, D.E., and Polson, P.A.
1983   A generalized transition network representation for interactive systems. CHI-83. Pp. 103-106 in Proceedings of the Conference on Human Factors in Computing Systems. New York: Association of Computing Machinery.

1985   An approach to formal analysis of user complexity. International Journal of Man-Machine Interaction. In press.

Koltum, P.L.
1982   Evaluation of a Teaching Approach for Introductory Computer Programming. Ph.D. dissertation, Department of Computer Sciences, University of North Carolina.

Ledgard, H., Singer, A., and Whiteside, J.A.
1981   Directions in Human Factors for Interactive Systems. New York: Springer-Verlag.

Lenorovitz, D.R., and Ramsey, H.R.
1977   A dialogue simulation tool for use in design of interactive computer systems. Pp. 95-99 in Proceedings of the Human Factors Society Annual Meeting. Santa Monica, Calif: Human Factors Society.

Lenorovitz, D.R., Phillips, M.D., Ardrey, R.S., and Kloster, G.V.
1984   A taxonomic approach to characterizing human-computer interfaces. In Human-Computer Interaction, G. Salvendy, ed., Proceedings of the First USA-Japan Conference on Human-Computer Interaction. Amsterdam: Elsevier Science Publications.

Lewis, C.
1982   Using the "thinking aloud" method in cognitive interface design. IBM Research Report RC #9265.

Mack, R.L., Lewis, C. and Carroll, J.M.
1983   Learning to use word processors: problems and prospects. ACM Transactions on Office Information Systems 1:254-271.

Mantei, M., and Cattell, R.G.G.
1982   A study of entity-based data base interfaces. ACM SIGCHI Bulletin 14(1).

Ramsey, H.R.
1974   Plans: human factors in the design of a computer programing language. CHI 83. Pp. 39-41 in Proceedings of the Human Factors Society Annual Meeting. Santa Monica, Calif.: Human Factors Society.

Ramsey, H.R., Atwood, M.E., and Willoughby, J.K.
1979   Paper simulation techniques in user requirements analysis for interactive computer systems. Pp. 64-68 in Proceedings of the Human Factors Society Annual Meeting. Santa Monica, Calif.: Human Factors Society.

Reisner, P.
1977   Use of psychological experimentation as an aid to development of a query language. IEEE Transactions on Software Engineering SE-3(3):218-229.

1981a   Formal grammar and human factors design of an interactive graphics system. IEEE Transactions on Software Engineering SE-7(2):229-240.

1981b   Human factors of data-base query languages: a survey and assessment. Computing Surveys 13:13-31.

1984   Formal grammar as a tool for analyzing ease of use: some fundamental concepts. In J. Thomas and M. Schneider, eds., Human Factors in Computer Systems. Norwood, N.H.: Ablex.

Reisner, P., Boyce, R.F., and Chamberlain, D.D.
1975   Human factors evaluation of two data base query languages: SQUARE and SEQUEL. Pp. 447-452 in Proceedings of the National Computer Conference. Arlington, Va.: American Federation of Information Processing Societies Press.

Reitman, J.S., Whitten, W.B.,II, and Gruenenfelder, T.M.
1985   A general user interface for entering and changing tree structures, nested menus, and decision trees. In Proceedings of NYU Symposium on User Interface Design. Norwood, N.H.: Ablex.

Rice, Ronald E.
1982   Human Communication Networking in a Teleconferencing Environment. Ph.D. dissertation, Department of Computer Sciences, Stanford University.

Mantei, M., and Haskell, N.
1983   Autobiography of a first-time discretionary microcomputer user. CHI 83. Proceedings of the Conference on Human Factors in Computing Systems. New York: Association of Computing Machinery.

Mantei, M., and Smelcer, J.B.
1984   Listing of doctoral programs in human-computer interaction. ACM SIGCHI Bulletin 16(2):12-40.

Miller, D.C., and Pew, R.W.
1981   Exploiting user involvement in interactive system development. Pp. 401-405 in Proceedings of the Human Factors Society Annual Meeting. Santa Monica, Calif: Human Factors Society.

Moran, T.P.
1983   Getting into a system: external-internal task mapping analysis. CHI-83. Pp. 45-49 in Proceedings of the Conference on Human Factors in Computing Systems. New York: Association of Computing Machinery.

Olson, G.M., Duffy, S.A., and Mack, R.L.
1984   Thinking-out-loud as a method for studying real-time comprehension processes. Pp. 253-286 in D.E. Kieras and M.A. Just, eds., New Methods in Reading Comprehension. Hillsdale, N.J.: Lawrence Erlbaum.

Osgood, C.E., Suci, G.J., and Tannenbaum, P.H.
1957   The Measurement of Meaning. Champaign-Urbana: University of Illinois Press.

Parks, M.
1983   Productivity tools enable users to obtain better (not more) code. Software News 3(2):22-23.

Pew, R.W., Rollins, A.M., and Williams, G.A.
1979   Generic Man-Computer Dialogue Specification: An Alternative to Dialogue Specialists. Bolt Beranek and Newman Inc., Cambridge, Mass.

Polson, P., and Kieras, D.E.
1985   A quantitative model of learning and performance of text editing knowledge. CHI-85. In Proceedings of the Conference on Human Factors in Computing Systems. New York: Association of Computing Machinery.

Roberts, Teresa L., and Moran, Thomas P.
1983   The evaluation of text editors: methodology and empirical results. Communications of the ACM 26:265-283.

Rosson, Mary Beth
1983   Patterns of experience in text editing. CHI-83. Pp. 171-175 in Proceedings of the Conference on Human Factors in Computing Systems. New York: Association of Computing Machinery.

1984   Effects of experience on learning, using, and evaluating a text editor. Human Factors 26:463-475.

Sheppard, S.B., and Kruesi, E.
1981   The effects of the symbology and spatial arrangement of software specifications in a coding task. General Electric Company Information Systems Programs Report TR-81-388200-3. Arlington, Va.: General Electric.

Shneiderman, B.
1982   Systems message design: guidelines and experimental results. In A. Badre and B. Scheiderman, eds., Directions in Human-Computer Interaction. Norwood, N.H.: Ablex.

Smith, S.L.
1982   User-system interface design for computer-based information systems. Mitre Corporation Report ESD-TR-82-132. Bedford, Mass.: Mitre Corporation.

Smith, S.L., and Mosier, J.N.
1984   Design guidelines for user-system interface software. Mitre Corporation Report ESD-TR-84-190. Bedford, Mass.: Mitre Corporation.

Stallman, R.M.
1980   EMACS Manual for ITS users. AI Lab Memo 554. Masschusetts Institute of Technology, Cambridge, Mass.

Sullivan, M.A., and Chapanis, A.
1983   Human factoring: a text editor manual. Behaviour and Information Technology 2:113-125.

Teitelman, W.
1972   Do what I mean: the programmer's assistant. Computers and Automation 21(4)8-11.

Thomas, J.C., and Gould, J.D.
1975   A psychological study of query by example. In Proceedings of the National Computer Conference. Arlington, Va.: American Federation of Information Processing Societies Press.

Van Cott, H., and Kinkade, R.G., eds.
1972   Human Engineering Guide to Equipment Design. Prepared by the American Institutes for Research for the U.S. Department of Defense. Available from the U.S. Government Printing Office, Washington, D.C.: U.S. Department of Defense.

Wasserman, Anthony I.
1982   The user software engineering methodology: an overview. Pp. 591-628 in A.A. Verrijn-Stuart, ed., Information System Design Methodologies. Amsterdam: North Holland Press.

Wasserman, Anthony I., and Shewmake, David T.
1982   Rapid prototyping of interactive information systems. Software Engineering Notes 7(5):171-180.

Whiteside, J., Archer, N., Wixon, D., Good, M.
1982   How do people really use text editors? Pp. 29-40 in Proceedings of the SIGOA Conference on Office Information Systems, Philadelphia.

Wienberg, G.M., and Friedman, D.P.
1984   Reviews, walk-throughs, and inspections. IEEE Transactions on Software Engineering SE-10(1).

Williges, R.C., and Williges, B.H.
1982   Modeling the human operator in computer based data entry. Human Factors 24:285-299.

Wixon, D.R., Whiteside, J.A., Good, M.D., and Jones, J.R.
1983   Building a user defined interface. CHI-83. Pp. 24-27 in Proceedings of the Conference on Human Factors in Computing Systems. New York: Association of Computing Machinery.

Woodson, W.E., and Conover, D.W.
1966   Human Engineering Guide for Equipment Designers. 2nd ed. Berkeley: University of California Press.

Yunten, T., and Hartson, H.R.
1984   A Supervisory Methodology and Notation (SUPERMAN). In H.R. Hartson, ed, Advances In Human-Computer Interaction. Norwood, N.H.: Ablex.

Chapter 12

Programming Techniques and Tools

It should be clear by now that user interface design is an important and difficult problem. While we have seen a number of techniques and technologies that can be used in user interface design, there is little in the way of theory that we can apply *a priori* to achieve workable (much less optimal) results.

In Chapter 11: Design Principles and Methodologies, a number of design methodologies were discussed. While these help us focus on critical issues and possible solutions, virtually all of them involve some degree of *iteration* in the design process. Where theory is not complete, we must resort to experimentation.

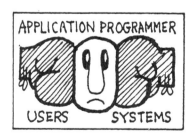

Figure 1: Caught in the Middle.
Typically, today's programmer is caught between the demands of the user and the inadequacy of the tools available for meeting these demands. The programmer needs help (figure by Aaron Marcus, Aaron Marcus and Associates, Berkeley, CA.).

All of this puts the applications programmer in an untenable situation (see Figure 1). On the one hand, there are the demands of the end user. While the programmer may want to explore a number of different avenues towards meeting these demands, the inadequacy of the tools generally available (such as programming languages, editors, and debuggers) makes it unfeasible or uneconomical to attempt any but the simplest or most obvious alternatives.

User Interface Management Systems

Much recent effort has been directed towards the development of improved tools to support user interface design, implementation (including rapid prototyping), maintenance, and evaluation. Collectively, these tools have come to be known as *User Interface Mangement Systems (UIMS's)*. One way of conceptualizing the UIMS is shown in Figure 2.

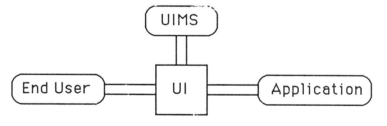

Figure 2: The UIMS in Context.
A UIMS can be thought of as a set of tools to support the design, implementation, maintenance, and evaluation of the user interface.

Think of the user interface as the software that sits between the functional part of the application and the end user. The UIMS is a set of tools that is used in managing or administering the user interface, much in the way a DBMS is used in administering a data base.

555

There is a great need for the tools that UIMS's are trying to provide. However, UIMS's vary greatly in design, style and utility. Consequently, a major objective of this chapter is to present some meaningful measures according to which different UIMS's can be compared. We do this by introducing a conceptual model of a generic UIMS and discussing some of the important issues relevant to its various components. This discussion is largely based on an earlier paper by Tanner and Buxton (1985). The chapter readings then present a few representative UIMS's in more detail for comparison and analysis.

The Beginnings of a Model

Virtually all UIMS's consist of two main modules. The first is a preprocessor which is used to design and implement the user interface. This we will call the *Specify/Maintain Module*. The second is the module that arbitrates all interactions between the user and the application during run-time. This we will call the *Interaction Handler*. These two components are illustrated in Figure 3.

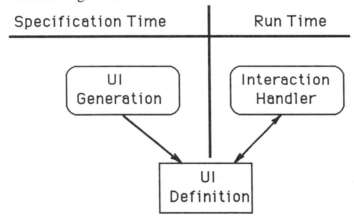

Figure 3: Main Modules of a typical UIMS.
During run-time, all interaction between the user and the application is arbitrated by the Interaction Handler. The nature of this arbitration, the user interface, is governed by the User Interface Definition. This definition is generated and maintained by a separate module, the Specify/Maintain Module.

How the Interaction Handler arbitrates between the end user and the application at run-time is governed by the *User Interface Definition*. This is what is specified by the Specify/Maintain Module.

The nature of the UI Definition is one of the most important features in characterizing UIMS's. This is a data structure or knowledge base which must be shared by both the Interaction Handler and Specify/Maintain modules. The majority of existing UIMS's define the UI as a finite-state automaton, and the UI Definition is a table containing the state-transition information. This is the case, for example, in a very early system built by

Newman (1968), and the more recent RAPID/USE system described in Wasserman and Shewmake (1982) and in the reading by Wasserman (1985).

A benefit of the state-transition approach is that the technology is fairly well understood. However, this type of automaton can run into problems when any degree of concurrency must be dealt with, with large systems, and in some styles of graphical interaction (such as many direct manipulation type interfaces). A radically different approach is that described in the reading by Myers and Buxton (1986). Here, the user interface is defined in terms of rules and constraints.

Another key dimension along which UIMS's vary is *when* the UI can be specified and/or modified. On most systems, the interface definition takes place previous to run-time, probably before compile time. On other systems, especially those that run in interpreted environments (such as Smalltalk and LISP), execution of the application can be suspended and the user interface can be modified on the spot. This *suspended-time* UI editing has a major impact on the utility of the UIMS in rapid prototyping. Some examples of systems that permit this type of suspended time editing are Trillium (Henderson, 1986), Sassafras (Hill, 1986, 1987a,b), and the Peridot system, described in the reading by Myers and Buxton (1986) and in Myers (1987a.b).

Glue Systems and Module Builders

To better understand and compare existing and future UIMS's, it is useful to further sub-divide what we have, up to now, been calling the "Specify/Modify Module". The resulting new form of our model is illustrated in Figure 4. Here, we view UI as being constructed from components, or *Interaction Modules*, which are drawn from an existing repertoire, or *library*. We will call the tool that is used to assemble the UI from these interaction modules the *Glue System*. The interaction modules, themselves, are created for the library by a separate set of tools which we will call the *Module Builder*.

It is important to note that most UIMS's do not have specific components that correspond directly to these modules. Nevertheless, we think that it is important to make a strong distinction between these functions. If for no other reason, we do so to force the reader to consider the relative strengths and weaknesses of any UIMS being designed or evaluated in terms of performing these two tasks.

Should the person who defines the modules also define the presentation level of the UIMS using the Glue System? Do these two tasks require the same skills? If not, then should special tools not be designed to suit the specialized skills of the different people involved?

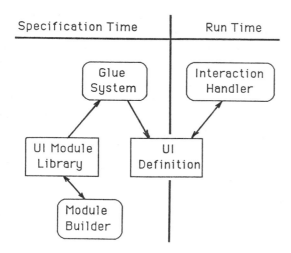

Figure 4: Interaction Modules and Glue System.
Typically, a UI is constructed using existing components, or interaction modules. This can be done by the Glue System. The interactive modules come from an existing library which is generated by another tool, the Module Builder.

Where do most changes take place: in the module definition, or in their use? Where should the emphasis be, therefore, for the most productivity gain to be realized? These are questions the reader should consider. The systems described in the readings provide a good range of approaches to use as case studies.

Trillium (Henderson, 1986), *Menulay*, described in the reading by Buxton, Lamb, Sherman, and Smith (1983), and *Action* (Tanner and Evans, 1979) are examples of systems which are primarily glue systems. The power and range of such systems are largely a function of the range and power of the interaction library, and the interactive style used in assembling the UI. Direct Manipulation, menus, and command languages have all been used to perform the glue task. Regardless, to be effective, these systems must provide the intended user with an effective and appropriate environment for specifying or modifying the UI.

Other UIMS's reported in the literature are less well suited to the glue function of user interface management. Rather, they are optimized to facilitate the task of specifying the low-level aspects of the UI, as would be required to specify interaction modules for the UI Module Library.

Tiger (Kasik, 1982) and *SYNGRAPH* (Olsen and Dempsey, 1983) are examples of such systems. This type of system typically provides a special language for defining interaction modules and dialogues. A fair degree of programming expertise is generally required to use such systems. The advantage, on the other hand, is that such systems are quite general. The interaction programmer is not restricted to the set of interactive tech-

niques that some user interface manager has provided in a library. The UIMS provides tools to create one's own library.

Handling Graphic Design

Sub dividing the Specify/Modify Module of the UIMS can be extended one more step (see Figure 5). Designing the presentation level of the UI includes the graphic design and layout of icons (which may be used as light buttons and tracking symbols), and other graphics segments used for lexical and semantic feedback. The layout function is naturally handled by the glue system. However, like the design of interaction modules, the design of icons requires a special environment.

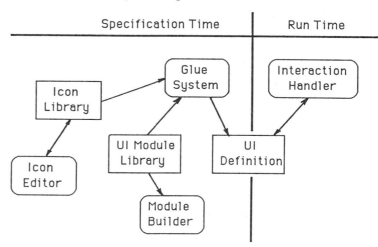

Figure 5: Adding Graphic Design Modules.
Special tools should be provided so that a graphic designer can create icons and other graphics.

The *Icon Editor* would store graphics in a standard format in a special library, which could be accessed by the glue system. One implication of this structure is that a standard format for the graphics (such as GKS metafiles) must exist.

Evaluation and Post-Processing

The UIMS model developed thus far has two main parts, the pre-processor and run-time modules. Yet UIMS's must facilitate an iterative approach to design (Buxton and Sniderman, 1980), and this requires support for the following three stages:

- design and implementation
- testing
- evaluation

The Specify/Maintain and Run-Time modules handle the first two of these phases. To fully assist an iterative process and the rapid prototyping of interfaces, the UIMS must be enhanced to include tools that can be used in the evaluation phase.

One approach to doing so is illustrated in Figure 6. Here, the Interaction Handler generates a log file of time-stamped data recording all interactions that occur during the test phase.

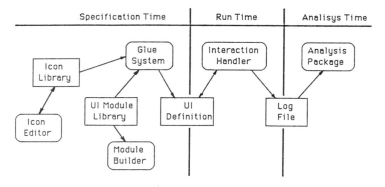

Figure 6: Supporting the Evaluation Phase.
The Interaction Handler generates a log file recording a time-stamped record of all interactions of a test session. This data is then analyzed by a specialized Evaluation Module.

Tools to assist in the analysis of this data must also be provided in a complete, integrated UIMS. Preliminary work in this area suggests that such tools have great potential in UI design (Buxton, 1982; Buxton et al., 1983). However, it is in this evaluation phase where most existing UIMS's are least effective.

Example UIMS's

The student of the UIMS's can well begin by looking at six typical systems. Descriptions of all but the first are included as readings. TIGER (Kasik, 1982) is an early second generation UIMS that has been used in generating large CAD applications for Boeing Corp. The system is real, and has a powerful language for defining the low-level details of the user interface. A video of this system is Boeing (1984).

The second system is RAPID/USE by Wasserman (1985). This is an example of a UIMS with which the interface is specified as a state-transition network. While the UIMS uses graphical techniques, it is only capable of generating text-based interfaces. The system is in wide use, is well documented and supported, and runs under the UNIX operating system. The reading may be viewed as a companion piece to that included in Chapter 11: Design Principles and Methodologies.

The University of Toronto UIMS, described in the reading by Buxton, Lamb, Sherman, and Smith (1983) and a video (U. of T., 1984), is a prototype UIMS. It's importance lies in the power of its ability to function as an interactive glue system for prototyping graphical user interfaces. The system is also able to support multi-handed input and is capable of generating itself. This last point is worth noting. One can reasonably ask, "Why would a UIMS itself use interactive techniques that it is not capable of generating itself?"

The Trillium system described in Henderson (1986) was designed to rapidly prototype controls for photo-copy machines, rather than large interactive systems. It has powerful glue-system capabilities. One important point about the system is that it has suspended-time editing of the UIMS. That is, while using the interface being prototyped, the designer can suspend execution, make a change in the interface, and then step back into execution mode. This is facilitated by careful object-oriented implementation in an interpretive environment.

MacApp (Schumucker, 1986) is a commercial system for facilitating the development of applications for the Apple Macintosh computer. It greatly improves the ease with which one can use the large library of interactive modules available on the Macintosh. The approach differs from the other systems looked at. In essence, MacApp provides ready-made generic applications which the user "clones" and modifies to his special needs.

Finally, the Peridot system described in Myers and Buxton (1986; see also Myers, 1987a,b) is an example of a "semi-intelligent" UIMS. The user of Peridot "programs" an interface by sketching what the interface should look like and demonstrating how it should work. One of the more interesting things about Peridot is that it has the power to do automatic inferencing. In particular, it can often guess what constraints should be in effect (but always asks for confirmation, just to be sure).

Summary

As with any "hot" area of research, the field of UIMS's is changing rapidly. The literature is growing. A couple of references exist, however, that give fairly good over-views of the field. In particular, the reader is directed to Thomas and Hamlin (1983), Pfaff (1985), Olsen (1987), and the three special issues of the ACM Transactions on Graphics (TOGS, 1986). Some video examples of interesting UIMS's are TRW (1984), U. of T. (1984), CMU (1984), Boeing (1984), and Hayes (1985).

Readings

Wasserman, A.I. (1985). Extending State-Transition Diagrams for the Specification of Human-Computer Interaction. *IEEE Transactions on Software Engineering* 11(8), 699-713.

Buxton, W., Lamb, M. R., Sherman, D. & Smith, K. C. (1983). Towards a Comprehensive User Interface Management System. *Computer Graphics* 17(3), 35-42.

Henderson, A. (1986). The Trillium User Interface Design Environment. *Proceedings of CHI '86*, 221-227.

Schumucker, K.J. (1986). MacApp: An Application Framework. *Byte* 11(8), August 1986, 189-193.

Myers, B. & Buxton, W. (1986). Creating Highly-Interactive and Graphical User Interfaces by Demonstration. *Computer Graphics* 20(3), 249-258.

References/Bibliography

Ball, E. & Hayes, P. (1980). Representation of Task-Specific Knowledge in a Gracefully Interacting User Interface. *Proceedings of the First Annual Meeting of the American Association for Artificial Intelligence*, 116-120.

Ball, E, & Hayes, P (1982). A Test-Bed for User Interface Designs. *Proceedings of the Conference on Human Factors in Computer Systems*, Gaithersburg, Maryland, 85-88.

Boeing (1984). Tiger System Demonstration. *SIGGRAPH Video Review* 12, New York: ACM.

Borufka, H.G., Kuhlmann, H.W. & ten Hagen, P.J.W. (1982). Dialogue Cells: A Method for Defining Interactions. *IEEE Computer Graphics and Applications* 2(5), 25-33.

Buxton, W. (1982). An Informal Study of Selection-Positioning Tasks. *Proceedings of Graphics Interface '82*, Toronto, 323-328.

Buxton, W. (1983). Lexical and Pragmatic Considerations of Input Structures. *Computer Graphics* 17(1), 31-37.

Buxton, W., Lamb, M. R., Sherman, D. & Smith, K. C. (1983). Towards a Comprehensive User Interface Management System. *Computer Graphics* 17(3), 35-42.

Buxton, W. & Sniderman, R. (1980). Iteration in the Design of the Human-Computer Interface. *Proceedings of the 13th Annual Meeting, Human Factors Association of Canada*, 72-81.

CMU (1984). Cousin Interface System. *SIGGRAPH Video Review* 12, New York: ACM.

Cardelli, L. & Pike, R. (1985). Squeak: a Language for Communicating with Mice. *Computer Graphics* 19(3), 199-204.

Carson, G.S. (1983). The Specification of Computer Graphics Systems. *IEEE Computer Graphics and Applications* 3(6), 27-41.

Durham, I., Lamb, D. & Saxe, J. (1983). Spelling Correction in User Interfaces. *Communications of the ACM* 26(10), 764-773.

Feldman, M.B. & Rogers, G.T. (1982). Toward the Design and Development of Style-Independent Interactive Systems. *Proceedings of the Conference on Human Factors in Computer Systems*, 111-116.

Foley, J.D. & Wallace, V.L. (1974). The Art of Graphic Man-Machine Conversation. *Proceedings of IEEE* 62(4), 462-470.

Garrett, M.T. & Foley, J.D. (1982). Graphics Programming Using a Database System with Dependency Declarations. *ACM Transactions on Graphics* 1(2), 109-128.

Green, M. (1981). A Methodology for the Specification of Graphical User Interfaces. *Computer Graphics* 15(3), 99-108.

Green, M. (1985). Design Notations and User Interface Management Systems. In Pfaff, G. (Ed.), *User Interface Management Systems*, Berlin: Springer Verlag, 89-107.

Green, M. (1985). The University of Alberta User Interface Management System. *Computer Graphics* 19(3), 205-213.

Guest, S.P. (1982). The Use of Software Tools for Dialogue Design. *International Journal of Man-Machine Studies* 16(3), 263-285.

Hanau, P.R. & Lenorovitz, D.R. (1980). Prototyping and Simulation Tools for User/Computer Dialogue Design. *Computer Graphics* 14(3), 271-278.

Hanusa, H. (1983). Tools and Techniques for the Monitoring of Interactive Graphics Dialogues. *International Journal of Man-Machine Studies* 19, 163-180.

Hartson, H.R., Johnson, D.H. & Ehrich, R.W. (1984). A Human-Computer Dialogue Management System. *Human-Computer Interaction — Interact '84*, Amsterdam: North-Holland, 379-383.

Hayes, Phillip (1985). The Cousin User Interface Management System. *SIGGRAPH Video Review* 18, New York: ACM.

Henderson, A. (1986). The Trillium User Interface Design Environment. *Proceedings of CHI '86*, 221-227.

Hill, R. (1986). Supporting Concurrency, Communication, and Synchronization in Human-Computer Interaction — The Sassafras UIMS. *ACM Transactions on Graphics*, 5(3), 179-210.

Hill, R. (1987a). Supporting Concurrency, Communication, and Synchronization in Human-Computer Interaction. Ph.D. Thesis, Department of Computer Science, University of Toronto.

Hill, R. (1987b). Event-Response Systems: A Technique for Specifying Multi-Threaded Dialogues. *Proceedings of CHI+GI '87*, 241-248.

Jacob, R.J.K. (1983). Using Formal Specifications in the Design of a Human-Computer Interface. *Communications of the ACM* 26(4), 259-264.

Jacob, R.J.K. (1985). A State Transition Diagram Language for Visual Programming. *IEEE Computer* 18(8), 51-59.

Johnson, S.C. (1980). Language Development Tools on the Unix System. *IEEE Computer* 13(8), 16-21.

Kasik, D.J. (1982). A User Interface Management System. *Computer Graphics* 16(3), 99-106.

Mason, R. & Carey, T. (1983). Prototyping Interactive Information Systems. *Communications of the ACM* 26(5), 347-354.

Myers, B.. (1987a). Creating User Interfaces by Demonstration. Ph.D. Thesis, Department of Computer Science, University of Toronto.

Myers, B. (1987b). Creating Dynamic Interaction Techniques by Demonstration. *CHI+GI '87 Proceedings*, 271-278.

Myers, B. & Buxton, W. (1986). Creating Highly-Interactive and Graphical User Interfaces by Demonstration. *Computer Graphics* 20(3), 249-258.

Newman, W.M. (1968). A Graphical Technique for Numerical Input. *Computing Journal* 11, 63-64.

Olsen, D.R. (1983). Automatic Generation of Interactive Systems. *Computer Graphics* 17(1), 53-57.

Olsen, D. R., Buxton, W., Ehrich, R., Kasik, D., Rhyne, J. & Sibert, J. (1984). A Context for User Interface Management. *IEEE Computer Graphics and Applications* 4(12), 33-42.

Olsen, D.R. & Dempsey, E.P. (1983). SYNGRAPH: A Graphical User Interface Generator. *Computer Graphics* 17(3), 43-50.

Olsen, D.R., Dempsey, E.P. & Rogge, R. (1985). *Computer Graphics* 19(3), 191-197.

Olsen, D. (Ed.) (1987). Whither (or Wither) UIMS? *Proceedings of CHI+GI '87*, 311-314.

Parnas, D.L. (1969). On the Use of Transition Diagrams in the Design of a User Interface for an Interactive Computer System. *Proceedings of the 24th National ACM Conference*, 379-385.

Pfaff, G. (Ed.) (1985). *User Interface Management Systems*, Berlin: Springer Verlag.

Roach, J., Hartson, R., Ehrich, R., Yunten, T. & Johnson, D. (1982). DMS: A Comprehensive System for Managing Human-Computer Dialogue. *Proceedings of the Conference on Human Factors in Computer Systems*, Gaithersburg, Maryland, 102- 105.

Rubel Software (1983). *BLOX Graphics Builder*, Rubel Software, One Soldiers Field Park 605, Cambridge, Massachusetts 02163.

Schmucker, K.J. (1986). MacApp: An Application Framework. *Byte* 11(8), August 1986, 189-193.

Schulbert, A.J., Rogers, G.T. & Hamilton, J.A. (1985). ADM — A Dialog Manager. *Proceedings of CHI '85*, 177-183.

Sheil, B. (1983). Power Tools for Programmers. *Datamation* 29(2), 131-144.

Sibert, J.L., Hurley, W.D. & Bleser, T. (1986). An Object-Oriented User Interface Management System. *Computer Graphics* 20(4), 259-268.

Swartout, W. & Balzer, R. (1982). On the Inevitable Intertwining of Specification and Implementation. *Communications of the ACM* 25(7), 438-440.

Tanner, P.P. & Buxton, W. (1985). Some Issues in Future User Interface Management System (UIMS) Development. In Pfaff, G. (Ed.), *User Interface Management Systems*, Berlin: Springer Verlag, 67-79.

Tanner, P.P. & Evans, K.B. (1979). ACTION, a Graphics Aid to Interacting with Models and Simulations. *Proceedings of the 6th Conference of the Canadian Man-Computer Communications Society*, Ottawa, 49-61.

Tanner, P.P., MacKay, S.A., Stewart, D.A. & Wein, M. (1986). A Multitasking Switchboard Approach to User Interface Management. *Computer Graphics* 20(4), 241-248.

Thomas, J. & Hamlin, G. (Eds.) (1983). Graphical Input Interaction Technique Workshop Summary. *Computer Graphics* 17(1), 5-30.

TOGS (1986). ACM Transactions on Graphics: Special Issues on User Interface Software, Part I — 5(2), Part II — 5(3), and Part III — 5(4).

TRW (1984). Rapid Prototyping Using Flair. *SIGGRAPH Video Review* 12, New York: ACM.

U. of T. (1984). Towards a Comprehensive UIMS. *SIGGRAPH Video Review* 12, New York: ACM.

Van den Bos, J., Platsmejer, M.J. & Hartel, P.H. (1983). Input-Output Tools: A Language Facility for Interactive and Real-Time Systems. *IEEE Transactions on Software Engineering* 3, 247-259.

Wasserman, A.I. (1985). Extending State-Transition Diagrams for the Specification of Human-Computer Interaction. *IEEE Transactions on Software Engineering* 11(8), 699-713.

Wasserman, A.I. & Shewmake, D.T. (1982). Rapid Prototyping of Interactive Information Systems. *ACM Software Engineering Notes* 7(5), 171-180.

Wasserman, A.I. & Shewmake, D.T. (1985). The Role of Prototypes in the User Software Engineering (USE) Methodology. In Hartson, H.R. (Ed.), *Advances in Human-Computer Interaction*, Norwood, N.J.: Ablex Publishing.

Wong, P.C.S. & Reid, E.R. (1982). FLAIR — User Interface Design Tool. *Computer Graphics* 16(3), 87-98.

Yunten, T. & Hartson, H.R. (1985). A Supervisory Methodology and Notation (SUPERMAN) for Human-Computer Development. In Hartson, H.R. (Ed.), *Advances in Human-Computer Interaction* , Norwood, N.J.: Ablex Publishing.

Extending State Transition Diagrams for the Specification of Human–Computer Interaction

ANTHONY I. WASSERMAN, MEMBER, IEEE

Abstract–User Software Engineering is a methodology for the specification and implementation of interactive information systems. An early step in the methodology is the creation of a formal executable description of the user interaction with the system, based on augmented state transition diagrams. This paper shows the derivation of the USE transition diagrams based on perceived shortcomings of the "pure" state transition diagram approach. In this way, the features of the USE specification notation are gradually presented and illustrated. The paper shows both the graphical notation and the textual equivalent of the notation, and briefly describes the automated tools that support direct execution of the specification.

This specification is easily encoded in a machine-processable form to create an executable form of the computer–human interaction.

Index Terms–Executable specifications, interactive information systems, rapid prototyping, software development methodology, transition diagrams, user interfaces, User Software Engineering.

I. INTRODUCTION

AN interactive system can be seen as having two components: the user interface to the system and the operations performed by the system. The user interface provides the user with a language for communicating with the system. The interface can take many forms, including multiple choice (menu selection), a command language, a database query language, or natural language-like input. In all cases, however, the normal action of the program is determined by user input, and the program may respond in a variety of ways, including results, requests for additional input, error messages, or assistance in the use of the system.

The user interface is often the principal determinant of system success, especially for those interactive systems where usage (or purchase) is discretionary. Yet for many systems used on alphanumeric terminals, design of the user interface is often an afterthought, with the design based on system-oriented, rather than user-oriented, concerns.[1]

The User Software Engineering project was undertaken in 1975 with the idea of combining concerns about user involvement in the design of interactive information systems with those of software engineering. The outcome of the effort is the creation of a methodology [1], [2] with a set of automated tools to support the methodology [3]–[7]. User participation is very important at the early stages of the meth-

Manuscript received February 8, 1984; revised February 20, 1985. This work was supported by corporate research grants from Nippon Electric Company and from Alcoa Foundation.

The author is with the Section of Medical Information Science, University of California, San Francisco, CA 94143.

[1] Interfaces for graphics-based systems and especially video games are based on the value of pictorial display and interaction. Therefore, more attention is given to the nature of the user interface.

odology, where users (or user surrogates) can provide useful information to help the development process. For example, the initial analysis phase includes not only traditional data and activity modeling, but also identification of user characteristics, e.g., ability to type, intensity of anticipated usage, motivation and education of users, etc. Attention is also given to the environment in which the system will be used, so that the system can fit in with the user's work pattern, and can be tailored to any constraints on terminal types or transmission rates.

The second step of the USE methodology is *external design*, which involves design of the user interface(s) to the proposed system. The analysis step serves to identify major functions and required inputs and outputs, at least at a high level. The concern of external design is to determine how the user can request those functions and how the output will be displayed. Thus, instead of top-down or bottom-up design, the USE methodology uses an "outside-in" design.

The third step is the creation of an executable version of the user interface defined at the previous stage, so that the user and developer can jointly explore, both objectively and subjectively, the usability of the original design, and to make modifications as needed. This ability to rapidly create system prototypes, presenting the user view of the evolving system, is a key aspect of User Software Engineering. Clearly, there is iteration among the first three steps until one or more acceptable interfaces are found.

In the remainder of this paper, we describe the notation used to specify this user interface in the USE methodology. We are not concerned here with the methodological process of defining the user interface, with the succeeding steps of the methodology that lead to a finished system, or with evaluation of the user interface.

II. USER INTERFACE DEFINITION WITH TRANSITION DIAGRAMS

In searching for an appropriate notation for describing user interfaces to interactive systems, we established several requirements, including the following:

1) Formalism: The notation had to serve as a formal definition of the interface.

2) Completeness: The notation had to be self-contained, including user input, system output, and linkage to system operations (application code).

3) Comprehensibility: The notation had to be comprehensible both to system developers and to users (or their representatives).

4) Flexibility: The notation had to accommodate a broad variety of dialog styles. In other words, the notation could not make assumptions about the nature of human–computer interaction, but had to give the designer of the dialog as wide a selection of possibilities as possible. This decision implies the need for a "low-level" approach to dialog specification.

5) Executability: The notation had to be directly executable to support prototyping, development, and testing of interactive information systems.

We observed that the interactive system and its actions are driven by raw or transformed user input. Accordingly, an effective specification technique for programming languages can be used effectively for specifying user interfaces. One can write down the grammar of the user input, and associate program actions with the successful recognition of "words" or "phases" in the grammar.

We decided to adapt transition diagrams for this purpose [8]. Transition diagrams have been used for a variety of language translators, including an early Cobol compiler [9], and are used as the formal specification of the MUMPS programming language [10]. (Transition diagrams have also been selected by others as an appropriate notation for specifying interactive programs [11]–[15].)

A transition diagram is a network of nodes and directed arcs. Each arc may contain a token, corresponding to a character string in the primitive alphabet (such as ASCII), or the name of another diagram. If the path is blank, it will be traversed as the default case, i.e., if all other paths leaving a given node fail. Scanning of the diagram begins at a designated entry point and proceeds until reaching an exit node or a dead end (no successful match on the paths from a given node). An operation may be associated with any path; traversal of the path causes the associated operation to occur.

Intuitively, one can see that paths may contain arbitrary strings and that the state transitions can invoke arbitrary operations. The distinguished inputs then lead to different states from which other input symbols may cause yet additional actions.

We began by using a simple transition diagram model to design and build several small interactive systems. This model contained just three different symbols, as follows:

*1) node—*shown by a circle, representing a stable state awaiting some user input. Each node within a diagram has a unique name, and an output message may be displayed when a node is reached. One node is designated the *starting node*, designated by two concentric circles, and there is a single exit point.

*2) arc—*shown by an arrow, connecting nodes to one another. Each arc represents a state transition based on some input. The input is designated either by a string literal, such as "quit," or by the name of another diagram, enclosed within angle brackets, such as <diag2>. One arc emanating from each node may be left blank, in which case it becomes the *default* transition, and is taken only when the input fails to match that specified on any of the other arcs. We shall assume for the moment that there is no ambiguity concerning which arc to take for a given input at a given node.

*3) operation—*shown by a small square with an associated integer. An action may be associated with a transition to represent an operation that is to be performed whenever a spe-

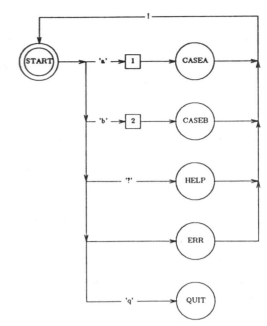

node START
    '   RAPID/USE Tutorial Example Program',
    '   Please choose: ',
    '   a - Case a',
    '   b - Case b',
    '   ? - Help',
    '   q - Quit',
    '   Your choice: '

node HELP
    'Valid commands are "a" and "b" ',
    'Press any key to continue'

node CASEA
    'You are at CASEA',
    'Press any key to continue'

node CASEB
    'You are at CASEB',
    'Press any key to continue'

node ERR
    'Sorry, but you made an error -- please try again.',
    'Press any key to continue'

node QUIT
    'Thank you -- good bye'

Fig. 1. A USE transition diagram.

cific arc is traversed. The same action may be associated with more than one arc.

A very simple diagram is shown in Fig. 1. The diagram begins at START, where it waits for input. Input is a string terminated by a carriage return. There is a transition to one of five nodes based upon the input. The input of "a" causes action 1 to be performed during the transition to CASEA; the input of "b" causes action 2 to be performed during the transition to CASEB, the input of "?" causes a transition to HELP, and the input of "q" causes a transition to QUIT; anything other than "a", "b", "q", or "?" causes a transition to ERR.

The text beneath Fig. 1 shows the message displayed when a transition is made to that node. Thus, this figure is a very simple instance of a menu-selection dialog, with the START node used to present a menu, and the five other nodes representing two system commands, a quit command, a help command, and an error case.

We quickly recognized some significant shortcomings with this simple model, including the following.

1) Output Specification: It was important to specify formatting and layout of system output, rather than just describing the message itself.

2) Display of Input Information: It was not possible to include as part of an output specification any text that had been recognized as input from the user. Yet such display is a major component of many interactive programs.

3) Input Processing: Some interactive dialogs accept a line of user input, followed by a terminator, such as a carriage return, before performing an operation or making a transition, while others respond on a single key stroke or the recognition of a specific key, such as a function key. The simple model we were using accepted only a variable length string, followed by a carriage return.

4) Diagram Complexity: Complex dialogs result in very complex diagrams, greatly reducing their comprehensibility and increasing the likelihood of errors in drawing or maintaining the diagrams.

5) Alternative Displays Based on Operations: The logical flow of an interactive program is often dependent upon the result of an operation, e.g., success or failure in a table lookup. Such a situation could not be represented with the simple transition diagram model.

6) Time Limits: It was not possible to make a transition after a fixed amount of time as needed to produce a remainder message.

We therefore sought to develop a transition diagram-like notation that would overcome these shortcomings. We also wanted to define a textual representation of these diagrams to facilitate their encoding for creating an executable version of the user interface. We shall henceforth refer to these diagrams as USE transition diagrams.

We now take up the approaches to these shortcomings that were introduced in USE transition diagrams.

III. Output Specification

A node is used to display a message. In its simplest form, a message may simply be a text string, such as shown in Fig. 1. In practice, though, more power is needed for output specification.

A. Cursor Control

First, it is useful to take advantage of screen-oriented displays, specifying the exact or relative position on a screen at which a message should be placed. Thus, one might want to specify that the message begin on row 12 at column 25, or that it begin two-lines below the previously written message. We can specify the message as

r12, c25, 'Good morning, fearless leader'

It is often desirable to center a message on a line. Rather than counting spaces to find the correct starting point, the symbol "c_" may be used to denote the center, so that the specification

r12, c_ 'Good morning, fearless leader'

would cause the message to be centered on line 12.

We adopt the convention that the upper left hand corner of the screen is (0, 0) and the last row and column are each designated by "$". Thus, a message to be written at the beginning of the last line could be addressed with r$, c0. A relative movement is designated with "+" and "−," so that one could write

r + 2, c25, 'Your request...'

In many cases, a message may contain an entire screen full of information, so that the message could contain an arbitrary mixture of text and positioning directives. One could write, then,

cs, r5, c5, 'Please choose one of the following:',
r + 2, c10, '1) deposit',
r + 2, c10, '2) withdraw',
r + 2, c10, '3) help',
r + 2, c10, '4) quit',
r$, rv, 'Your choice...', sv

to specify a screen filled with text.

Note that screen-oriented directives are used in this example.

cs	clear screen and go to home position (r0, c0)
rv	use reverse video (if available)
sv	return to standard video

Additional screen-oriented directives provide needed cursor control. In all cases, these directives may be included in an output specification.

hm	go to home position (0, 0)
nl	start a new line (r + 1, c0),
cl	clear to end of line on current row
ce	clear to end of screen from current line
dc	delete the character at the current position, then shift subsequent characters on line to left
dl	delete entire line (current row) and scroll lower lines (if any) upward
is_'text'	insert the text beginning at the current position
il	open a blank line at the current position and move lower lines down

B. Reuse of Messages

Second, we may want to reuse a message. Common examples of this situation are error messages, screen headings, and on-line assistance. The structure of a message is identical to that of a node specification, so that a message may include cursor movement information, text strings, and variable names. We define a message name, then refer to it by that name whenever we want to display that message. Conceptually, we would define

message prompt
    r$, rv, 'Your choice...', sv

and we then write

cs, r5, c5, 'Please choose one of the following:',
r + 2, c10, '1) deposit',
r + 2, c10, '2) withdraw',
r + 2, c10, '3) help',
r + 2, c10, '4) quit',
prompt

The appearance of the message name "prompt" causes the substitution of the text associated with the message definition of "prompt."

C. Tab Settings

The layout of the previous example is dependent upon the alignment of four lines of text, requiring the inclusion of the directive "c10" in four different places. Changing the placement of these lines requires changing four occurrences of the column directive in this message, and potentially other dependent column directives in other messages that might be concurrently displayed. Flexibility and the ability to modify layouts rapidly suggests the need to associate *tabs* with column settings.

We introduce the tab definition and allow a column to be associated with a specific tab declaration, as follows.

```
tab t_0 5
tab t_1 10

cs, r5, t_0, 'Please choose one of the following:',
r + 2, t_1, '1) deposit',
r + 2, t_1, '2) withdraw',
r + 2, t_1, '3) help',
r + 2, t_1, '4) quit',
prompt
```

In this way, the alignment may be changed with only one change to the definition, namely the column associated with the tab definition.

D. Partitioned Screens

Another problem in controlling a display is to be able to partition the screen into two or more parts and to move freely between them. For example, we may wish to use the bottom two lines of the screen for error messages, regardless of what has been placed on the remainder of the screen. In that case, we would like to "mark" a position on the screen, move to another position, and then return to the marked position.

The directives "mark" and "tomark" provide part of this capability. The upper and lower case letters may be used as names of marks and then referenced. Named marks may be included as part of the output specification. The nodes

```
node one
      r + 1, 'Your reply: ', mark_A
node error
      tomark_A, cl,
      r$, mark_E, rv, 'Please type a number from 1 to 5',
      sv, tomark_A
```

allow an erroneous reply to be cleared, and an error message to be displayed on the bottom line (in reverse video), after which the cursor returns to the point at which the reply is wanted. Note also that mark_E is set to the beginning of the error line so that some other node could be defined

```
node clean_err
      mark_B, tomark_E, cl, tomark_B
```

to remove the error message at a subsequent point. The removal should not be done in node one, since it would disappear from the screen before the user had a chance to read it.

This screen partitioning is a first step toward the multiple window interfaces employed in systems such as Smalltalk-80 and Interlisp [16], [17]. We return to this point later.

IV. VARIABLES IN DIAGRAM SPECIFICATION

Output messages are often dependent upon previous input or upon computed results. Data entry systems must display and/or reformat information input by a user, as well as passing that data to operations. Programs involving multiple screens typically redisplay data given on one screen on a subsequent display. For example, a bank teller program may obtain account information, and then display the account holder's name or account number later in the interactive dialog. Thus, the limitation of fixed text in the output specification is inadequate, and we must introduce *variables*. We adopt the convention that a variable may be assigned the string received on a specific input, or be assigned a value as the result of an action. The variable name is shown on one or more arcs in a diagram. When such an arc is traversed, the input string is assigned to that variable.

Thus, the appearance of a variable name on an arc emanating from a node means that the input is assigned to that variable.

If there were a message such as

```
cs, r10, c10, 'Please type your name:'
```

the resulting input could be assigned to a variable called "name," and could subsequently be displayed as follows:

```
r0, c40, 'User--', name
```

within a node or another message.

As with variables in programming languages, we wish to define constraints on their values. We define four kinds of constraints:

1) data type: string, integer, float, scalar, date, time

2) string length: minimum and maximum length (both optional)

3) range of values: lexicographic or numeric ranges, depending on type (both optional)

4) display format: used as default format for displaying values of the variable.

Thus, all of the following are variable definitions:

```
string name
string licenseplate [1:7]
string longstring [50:*]
string a_to_c_word range 'a'..'c'
integer count
integer testresult [2:2] range 30..50
scalar weekday (monday, tuesday, wednesday, thursday,
      friday)
float flt display ("r7.2")
date sunbday init '19820222
time lunch init @123000
```

The numbers in square brackets delimit the length of the input in characters. The range constraint specifies a restriction on the *value* of the variable, where the range for "integer" is given by integer values and the range for "string" is given by the ASCII collating sequence. An asterisk "*" may be used to denote the absence of a fixed limit. The syntax for the display format is similar to that used for the *printf* function in the Unix™ standard I/O library, and has been extended to support the display of scalars, month (numeric and text), day, year, weekday, hours, minutes, and seconds, as well as left, right, and center adjustment of displayed variables.

Variables may be assigned by appearing on a transition, so that user input meeting the constraint(s), if any, causes the transition and makes the assignment. In Fig. 2, the transition from step1 to step2 causes the variable "restname" to be assigned the user input string.

Once a variable has been assigned a value, it may subsequently be used in messages and in actions. As with variables in other programming notations, it may also be assigned a new value.

V. INPUT PROCESSING

The basic transition diagram model assumes that the input to determine transitions along an arc is a variable length string terminated by a carriage return. Also, there *must* be some input to cause a transition. All of these assumptions are unnecessarily restrictive, in addition to being unrealistic for the practical design of interactive systems. Therefore, extensions to the transition diagram model are needed for these cases.

First, though, we observe that the input character set must be extended beyond the typical set of 95 ASCII printable graphics, to accommodate control characters, function keys, and other inputs that may be received from a modern terminal keyboard. We use the following symbols to represent the extended input character set.

esc	escape
cr	carriage return (default)
bs	backspace
lf	line feed
del	delete
tab	tab character (ctl_i)
ctl_{A-Za-z}	any control character, such as ctl_D, for any letter
f{0-9}	function keys f0 through f9
↑	up arrow
↓	down arrow
←	left arrow
→	right arrow
home	home key

Thus, in the same way that one can write a string literal on an arc, one can write any of these symbols, treating them as "reversed words" and prohibiting the use of variables with these names.

A. Buffered versus Unbuffered Input

As noted, the assumption of inputs terminated by carriage returns is very restrictive, and fails to represent many of the most common uses of interactive systems. While we use that assumption as a default, we need mechanisms for overriding that case.

First, a single keystroke may be used to determine the appropriate branch, without a terminating character. This ap-

Fig. 2. Assignment to a variable.

proach is commonly found in multiple-choice (menu selection) applications, not only with keyboard input, but also with touch screens and mouse input. Indeed, single keystroke (or equivalent) processing is a key aspect of many highly interactive systems. Rather than buffering the input, it must be processed immediately.

Thus, the two forms of input processing must be distinguished, which cannot be done with the simple model of transition diagrams. We introduce the "!" symbol to denote this immediate transition, which we term a *single key* transition. The appearance of the "!" followed by a character on an arc means that a single "character" input is used to cause a transition. Fig. 3 gives an example of this case.

B. Specific Character Recognition

A similar problem arises when it is desired to make a transition based on the recognition of a particular character, whenever it appears in the user input. This is termed a *special key* transition, and is shown by preceding the key with an ampersand ("&") on the arc. The ampersand indicates the immediate transition, without waiting for a terminator, rather than accepting input until a terminator is received.

Note that "single key" and "special key" transitions are difficult. In a command-oriented system, it may be possible to interrupt a command or any other input by typing a specific key, such as control-C or "?". It is only the "special key" concept that permits this interruption, unless *all* input is handled as "single key."

We have also considered the case in which a specific key, such as an escape or a function key, can be globally used to terminate a diagram and perhaps return to a specific node in a specific diagram. From a notational standpoint, it is necessary to have an explicit arc from every node where such an input could be received. (It is straightforward to implement this idea in software, though.) Without such an explicit arc, a diagram (or, as we shall see, a set of diagrams) may have unconstrained flow of control (the *goto* problem); furthermore, such branching in a set of diagrams raises traditional programming language questions about the scope of variables.

C. Truncating Input String Length

The default case in transition diagrams is to accept a string of any length until a carriage return is received. We wish first to consider strings of fixed length (frequently length 1), and also strings terminated by something other than a carriage return. Consider the very common case of asking a user for a "yes" or "no" response. The decision can normally be made by examining the first character of the user input, so that a variety of different response can be handled similarly. Even in this simple case, the truncation greatly simplifies the problem of decoding input, which might be any of "N," "n," "NO," "No," or "no," excluding numerous possibilities from languages other than English. Note that the *length* option is different from the single_key option in that the length trun-

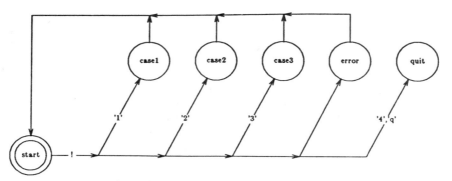

Fig. 3. Transition diagram illustrating immediate transition.

cation is only applied after the input termination character (normally the carriage return) is received.

D. Nonstandard Terminators

The carriage return default may be overridden with the *until* option. In the *vi* text editor for the Unix operating system, for example, insertion mode is terminated with the "escape" character. In other applications where the input may extend over several lines, the carriage return must be treated as a normal input character, with the terminator switched to a different character. Thus, one might wish to describe that all input received prior to an escape character will be assigned to a variable named inputstr.

The until feature may be combined with the length feature, so that an input string may be truncated to a fixed length regardless of the terminator. Fig. 4 illustrates the notation used in the USE transition diagram for nonstandard terminators and/or fixed length strings. This information precedes the input string(s) and is denoted by the slash symbol "/". A list of zero or more alternative terminators is given to the left of the "/" and the length, if fixed, is given to the right. The fragment of the diagram shown in Fig. 4 indicates that input is read until an escape or a tab character is received, and then truncated to eight characters. The resulting string is assigned to variable instring. These extensions to input processing, the extended character set, single key input, special key transitions, alternate terminators, and input string truncation, allow the description of a much greater set of interactive dialogs than was previously possible.

VI. DIAGRAM DECOMPOSITION

The added expressiveness given by the output specification notation, the inclusion of variables, and the extensions to input processing made it possible to describe most interactive systems using alphanumeric display terminals. The USE transition diagrams could be used with a means for specifying the actions, and thereby serve as a specification method.

One important aspect of specifications, though, is comprehensibility. We found that it was very easy to create large complex diagrams that could not easily be written or understood. Diagram complexity arose initially from the desire to provide error handling and help facilities in the interactive dialog. By following our own guidelines for designing inter-

Fig. 4. Nonstandard terminators in USE transition diagrams.

active systems [18], we were led to provide a help arc and an error arc from each node where user input could occur (virtually all). Accordingly, the number of nodes and arcs proliferated. The situation was even worse if one wanted to provide a *different* message on the second occurrence of an error than on the first.

At first, we simply adopted the strategy of drawing a set of diagrams with no error handling and no interactive help facilities so that the diagram presented the "normal" flow of dialog. Yet this was also inadequate as we attempted to model increasingly complex dialogs and systems.

A. Subconversations

The solution taken was to introduce a hierarchy of diagrams, so that any diagram could "invoke" another diagram. A connected set of nodes could be named, and could be "called" from another diagram. This idea of a "subconversation" was useful because it also modeled a commonly occurring situation in interactive systems: a set of "transaction types." Accordingly, a fourth symbol was added to the node, arc, and action:

4) subconversation—shown by a rectangular box, with an associated diagram name. When an arc enters a subconversation box, traversal of that diagram is suspended, and control is transferred to the starting node of the diagram named in the subconversation box. The new diagram is then traversed until its exit point is reached, at which point control returns to the "calling" diagram, and the subconversation box is exited.

A simple example of this situation is shown by the diagram structure of Fig. 5, where there are subconversations for "deposit," "withdraw," and "balance." The capability for any node to have multiple exits is retained in the subconversation by permitting a diagram to return a value to the invoking diagram so that the branch upon exit from the subconversation may be determined by the return value. The returned value is denoted by a nonnegative integer preceded by the "#" symbol in the invoked diagram. If more than one arc emanates from a subconversation box, the associated return value used to determine the branch can appear on each arc. We adopt

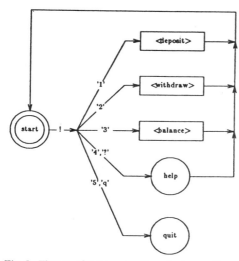

Fig. 5. The use of subconversations for transactions.

Fig. 6. Returning values from subconversations.

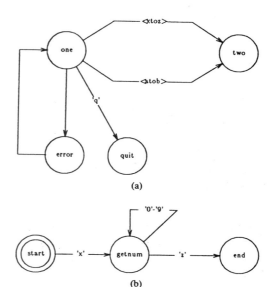

Fig. 7. (a) Using diagram names for arc traversal. (b) Use of a subconversation for string recognition.

the convention that such values may only be returned to the immediate caller, i.e., one level of invocation. This use is shown in Fig. 6.

B. Transitions Described by Diagrams

Until now, we have assumed that all inputs are described either by a string literal (a directly named sequence of characters) or by an input string that is immediately assigned to a variable. In some cases, though, it is useful to use a diagram to describe the syntax that causes a transition. Rather than using a string literal or a variable name on an arc, one can use the name of a diagram. That diagram, and any additional levels invoked from that diagram, must be successfully traversed to cause the given arc to be traversed. This situation is shown in Fig. 7; in Fig. 7(a), the diagram name <xtoz> is associated with an arc connecting nodes "one" and "two," while Fig. 7(b) shows the diagram xtoz. Note that <atob> is another possibility for the traversal from "one" to "two," which can also be tried.

This use of subconversations allows recognition of a string composed of several components, possibly of indeterminate length, without overly complicating the higher level diagram. As before, the called diagram could be inserted into the higher level diagram, without altering the effect. In this case, though, it becomes possible to hide the structure of the recognized string. This construct is also useful for allowing several different strings to cause the same transition, which is frequently needed for dialogs supporting novice and expert interfaces, for example.

C. Decomposing Messages and Actions

Another important option is the ability to decompose messages and/or actions. Suppose that we want to perform action 2 on one arc, actions 2 and 3 in response to another input, and actions 1 and 2 in response to yet another input. To do so, one must create an intermediate node to permit the actions to be specified independently. Yet we do not want to require additional input to cause the second action to occur. Simi-

larly, one may wish to display two separate messages in response to a single input without waiting for additional input from the user.

In both of these cases, one must make an automatic transition from one node to another. This case, called the *skip* case, is denoted by a "+" on an arc; of course, no string, return value, or diagram name can appear on such an arc.

D. User Interfaces as a Hierarchy of USE
Transition Diagrams

The use of subconversations is both an aid to diagram decomposition and a notational convenience. There are, however, several distinct advantages to their use.

1) Any diagram may be referenced from other diagrams in a dialog and thereby reused; this supports the creation of libraries of diagrams that can be integrated into systems.

2) A higher level diagram can often be designed without making decisions about the actual input text; this approach allows decisions about the dialog to be deferred and isolated, and therefore changed easily.

3) Subconversations help to break up a diagram that has a large number of nodes; to aid comprehension, diagrams should contain fewer than 10 nodes.

4) Subconversations help to illustrate the structure of a dialog; many dialogs are naturally hierarchical and the subconversation mechanism allows this hierarchy to be shown in the diagrams.

VIII. SEMANTIC ASPECTS OF USE TRANSITION DIAGRAMS

Until now, transitions between nodes in diagrams have been driven by the *syntax* of the user input. The extensions have either been structural, e.g., subconversations, or directed to finer input control, e.g., unbuffered input. Even the introduction of variables into diagrams did not alter this situation. However, it now becomes necessary to introduce *semantic* dependencies into USE transition diagrams.

A. *Returning Values from Actions*

We previously noted that the direction of a dialog is often dependent upon the result of an action. For example, in a banking system, the user (a teller) would be asked to input a customer account number. A subsequent action would be to look up this account number in the bank's customer account database. The next message presented to the teller would depend on the success of the search.

To achieve this effect, it is necessary to associate a return value with the *action*, and then to branch on that value. This is easily accomplished in our notation by indicating one or more arcs emerging from an action box, with arcs labeled with alternate return values, following the same approach used for subconversations. This situation is shown in Fig. 8. One path, labeled 1, leads to node found, while the other path, labeled 2, leads to node notfound. Note that the continuation from an action may be either unconditional, as we have previously seen, or conditional based on a return value. In the unconditional case, there may be a returned value, but it will not affect the transition following the action.

B. *Time Limits*

In modeling interactive systems with state transition diagrams, we found no convenient way to express time, since transitions are linked to user input. In practice, though, one often expects user input within a fixed amount of time, with an unexpected delay indicating a problem. Thus, it is desirable to be able to effect a transition on the expiration of a predefined time limit. In this way, it is possible to branch to another node, from which a reminder or help message can be displayed.

We thus introduce the *alarm* transition, and denote that transition by writing the time limit on the appropriate arc, e.g., 30''. The alarm transition is made if no input is received from the user before the time limit expires.

VIII. AN EXTENDED EXAMPLE

To this point, all of the examples of the USE transition diagram specification method have dealt with "toy" examples, intended to denote the overall style and scope of the specification method. In this section, we show a small part of a much larger example, a data dictionary system to support a variant of Structured Systems Analysis [19]. This example not only shows a broad range of the features of the USE specification method for interactive systems, but represents a running application system in everyday use. Because of space limitations, though, only three of the 31 diagrams representing the system are shown, and the display is limited to the diagrams themselves (with the associated text and action calls),

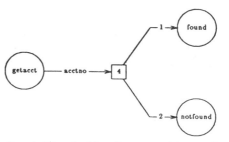

Fig. 8. Branch determined by value returned from action rules.

omitting the description of the actions on which they operate.

The data dictionary is represented by a set of relations, specified in the Troll/USE data definition and manipulation language, and shown in Fig. 9 [5], [20].

The first diagram, the main diagram for the data dictionary system, is shown in Fig. 10(a). Three features are worth noting in this diagram.

1) The action box numbered "2" is a call to the database script "startup." If this action succeeds (return "ok"), then control flows to node "start;" otherwise, control flows to "nodb" and "x" and the program terminates.

2) The center of activity is node "select," which provides a menu-like interface to the user, providing the user with the ability to enter the subconversations "add," "modify," "delete," and "query." The "select" node also provides for terminating the program, asking for help, and handling unexpected input (the "error" node).

3) The structure found in this diagram is generic for transaction-oriented interactive programs. Many interactive information systems exhibit the same structure, and this diagram can be easily modified to suit other applications. (Note the similarity to Fig. 5.)

The subconversation "add" is shown in Fig. 10(b), and has much the same structure as does the top-level diagram, asking the user to specify the type of entry to be placed in the data dictionary. (Clearly, this dialog has been designed to minimize typing and to present a screen-oriented interface to the user.)

Note that the subconversations "add_element" through "add_message" all return the value 0 if the item is successfully inserted in the data dictionary. This return value is used to direct control flow to node "inserted," which displays the message "successful insertion" before prompting the user for another entry.

The "add" subconversation then invokes "add_process" when the user wishes to define a new process and store information about that process in the data dictionary. Several aspects of the diagram shown in Fig. 10(c) are worth noting.

1) Three different kinds of actions are performed in this diagram. The actions "checkpro," "inspro," and "delparams" operate on the database shown in Fig. 9, as indicated by the use of the "call" to the actions. The action "CallEdit" is to an executable program, to be written in a high level programming language; it is, in fact, a call to the *vi* editor for a file to hold the process description for the given process. Finally, there is a case statement, denoted by the "cs" action box, which controls branching after the "checkpro" action is per-

```
relation data_element [key name] of
    name: string;
    el_descrip1,el_descrip2,el_descript3,el_descrip4,el_descrip5: string;
    el_type: string;
    el_constraints: string;
    el_notes: string;
    el_count: integer;
end;

relation data_store [key name] of
    name: string;
    store_notes: string;
    store_count: string;
end;

relation data_flow [key name] of
    name: string;
    flow_notes: string;
    flow_count: integer;
end;

relation process [key name] of
    name: string;
    proc_module: string;
    proc_notes: string;
end;

relation proc_params [key name, param_name] of
    name: string;
    param_name: string;
    param_type: scalar(inparam,outparam);
end;

relation message [key name] of
    name: string;
    msg_descript: string;
    msg_number: integer;
end;

relation allnames [key name] of
    name: string;
    name_type: scalar (element,store,flow,proc,msg);
end;

relation flow_parts [key name, component] of
    name, component: string;
end;

relation store_parts [key name, component] of
    name, component: string;
end;
```

Fig. 9. Relational database schema for data dictionary.

formed. The USE transition diagram notation does not allow two consecutive action boxes, so it is necessary to interject the dummy node "hack1" between the call to "checkpro" and the case statement.

2) Three different values may be returned to "add," representing successful insertion of the information (0), an error in insertion (1), or user cancellation of the insertion (2). Referring back to Fig. 10(b), we note that the "add" diagram does not presently distinguish between the latter two cases.

3) The arc "skip" feature, denoted by "+", is used several times, when actions and/or displays are performed without intervening user input. Without the skip feature, it would be necessary to combine information that is logically separate or to require user input in the interim.

4) The message "main.lastline" is used, allowing the dialog designer to define some standard message formats in the main diagram and then use them throughout the dialog. This feature improves consistency of the interface design for the user.

IX. EXECUTABLE SPECIFICATIONS

As described in the introduction, a critical step in applying the User Software Engineering methodology is to create an executable version of the user interface. To this end, we have designed and built a system called RAPID/USE, which consists

of two components: the transition diagram intepreter (TDI) and the action linker [3], [21]. The TDI was designed to accept an encoding of the USE transition diagrams that resembles the diagrams and messages as much as possible.[2] This encoding, called a *dialog description* or a *script*, is transformed into tables by TDI. In this way, one can draw the diagrams and quickly transform them to an executable form. The encoding may be achieved either by editing the textual representation of the diagrams, or by using a graphical tool, the transition diagram editor [22], to draw the USE transition diagrams interactively, and to have the TDI dialog description generated automatically.

Input to TDI consists of one or more diagram descriptions, each representing a transition diagram. Each diagram may have five types of statements.

1) Diagram name statement—identifies the diagram, its entry node and exit node.

2) Variable definition statements—permit the use of names to describe strings of alphanumeric or numeric characters, along with range constraints on their values.

3) Message definition statements—permit the use of names to describe messages that are to be called from multiple points in the diagram.

4) Node definition statements—define the node names for the diagram, along with the associated messages and screen control for each node.

5) Arc statements—describe the structure of the diagram and its transition conditions.

The Action Linker part of RAPID/USE allows programmed actions to be associated with the transitions. Routines may be written in C, Fortran 77, or Pascal. (Linkage to other languages can also be provided.)

The syntax for the nodes is virtually identical to that shown in Fig. 10(a)-(c). The description for the arcs is given by the name of the starting node, followed by all of the possible branches and actions emanating from that node. Fig. 11 shows the TDI text for the diagram shown in Fig. 10(a). An inspection of this text will show that it is a direct encoding of the diagram itself. This encoding is done automatically by the transition diagram editor, and may also be done manually by someone without access to the graphical editor. Thus, RAPID/USE is used both for building and validating user interfaces (TDI) and for building functioning systems (TDI + Action Linker).

X. FURTHER EXTENSIONS TO DIALOG SPECIFICATIONS

The USE transition diagrams, as described so far, cover a very broad range of the interactive dialogs that are suitable for user interfaces on "intelligent" alphanumeric display terminals. Furthermore, both the diagrams and the accompanying TDI notation are independent of the physical characteristics of any specific terminal. Thus, these diagrams may serve as a general descriptive technique for interactive systems.

With recent advances in computer terminals and worksta-

[2] The present distribution of RAPID/USE supports all of the transition diagram features described in Sections III-VII except for some restrictions on transitions described by diagrams (Section VI-B).

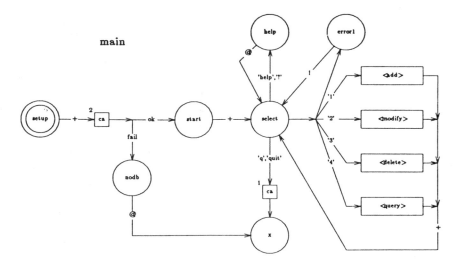

Actions

1   call shutdown
2   call startup

diagram main entry setup exit x

database 'usedddb'
library '../scripts'

tab t_0 15
tab t_1 20

message header
    cs,r2,c0,c_'USE Data Dictionary'

message lastline
    r$,c0,'Hit any character to continue.'

node setup

node select
        tomark_A,ce,r+3,t_0,'Please choose ',
        r+2,t_1,'1: Add a dictionary entry.',
        r+2,t_1,'2: Modify a dictionary entry.',
        r+2,t_1,'3: Delete a dictionary entry.',
        r+2,t_1,'4: Query data dictionary',
        r+2,t_1,'help: Information on use of program',
        r+2,t_1,'quit: Exit USE/Data Dictionary',
        r+2,t_0,'Your choice: '

node help
        cs,r$-3,c0,'For more information about a command, enter',
        r$-2,c0,'the command number, press return and then type "help" or "?"',
        r$,c0,'Hit any key to continue'

node nodb
        cs,r$,c0,'Could not open database directory'

node start
        header,mark_A

node x
        cs

node error1
        r$-1,c0,rv,bell,'Please type a number from 1 to 4.',sv,
        lastline

(a)

Fig. 10. (a) Top-level USE transition diagram of data dictionary system.

add

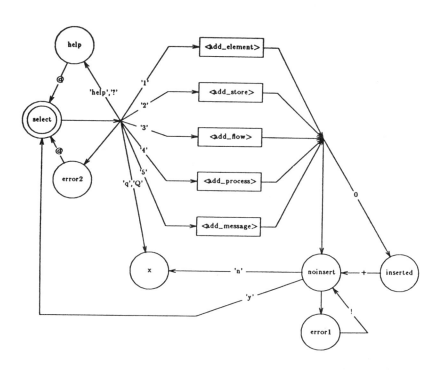

diagram add entry select exit x

tab t_0 10
tab t_1 15

node error1
       r$,c0,rv,'Please type " y " or " n " ',sv,tomark_E

node select
       main.header,
       r4,c0,c_'Add entry to dictionary',
       r+2,t_0,'Please select type of data entry: ',
       r+1,t_1,'1: data element',
       r+1,t_1,'2: data store',
       r+1,t_1,'3: data flow',
       r+1,t_1,'4: process',
       r+1,t_1,'5: message',
       r+2,t_0,'Your choice (1-5): '

node help

       cs,r0,c0,c_'USE/Data Dictionary',
       r12,c0,c_'Add new entry',
       main.lastline

node x

node inserted
       r$-4,c0,'Successful insertion'

node error2
       r$-1,cs,rv,bell,'Please type a number from " 1 " to " 5 " ',sv,
       r$,c0,'Hit any character to continue.'

node noinsert
       r+2,c0,'Another entry (y/n)? ', mark_E

(b)

Fig. 10. (*Continued.*)   (b) The "add" subconversion of data dictionary system.

add_process

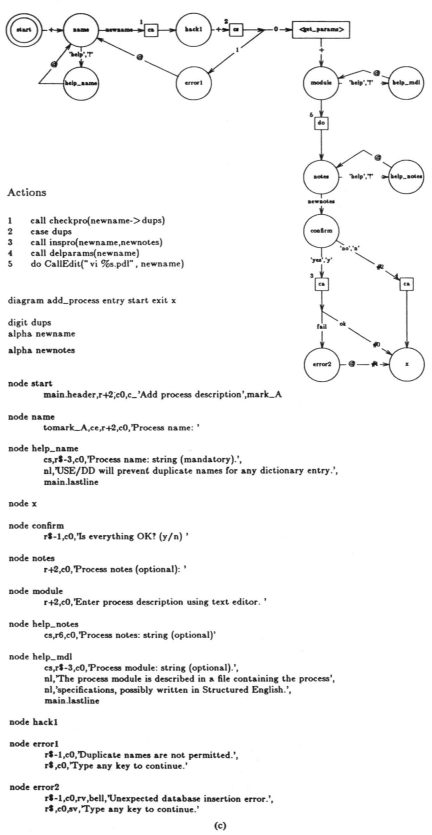

Actions

1   call checkpro(newname->dups)
2   case dups
3   call inspro(newname,newnotes)
4   call delparams(newname)
5   do CallEdit(" vi %s.pdl" , newname)

diagram add_process entry start exit x

digit dups
alpha newname

alpha newnotes

node start
        main.header,r+2;c0,c_'Add process description',mark_A

node name
        tomark_A,ce,r+2,c0,'Process name: '

node help_name
        cs,r$-3,c0,'Process name: string (mandatory).',
        nl,'USE/DD will prevent duplicate names for any dictionary entry.',
        main.lastline

node x

node confirm
        r$-1,c0,'Is everything OK? (y/n) '

node notes
        r+2,c0,'Process notes (optional): '

node module
        r+2,c0,'Enter process description using text editor. '

node help_notes
        cs,r6,c0,'Process notes: string (optional)'

node help_mdl
        cs,r$-3,c0,'Process module: string (optional).',
        nl,'The process module is described in a file containing the process',
        nl,'specifications, possibly written in Structured English.',
        main.lastline

node hack1

node error1
        r$-1,c0,'Duplicate names are not permitted.',
        r$,c0,'Type any key to continue.'

node error2
        r$-1,c0,rv,bell,'Unexpected database insertion error.',
        r$,c0,sv,'Type any key to continue.'

(c)

Fig. 10. (*Continued.*) (c) The "add_process" subconversation of data dictionary system.

```
arc setup.
    skip call startup
             when ok to start
             when fail to nodb

arc select
    on 'q','quit' call shutdown to x
    on '4' to <query>
    on '2' to <modify>
    on '3' to <delete>
    on '1' to <add>
    on 'help','?' to help
    else to errorl

arc help noecho single_key
    else to select

arc <modify>
    skip to select

arc <delete>
    skip to select

arc nodb noecho single_key
    else to x

arc start
    skip to select

arc <add>
    skip to select

arc <query>
    skip to select

arc errorl single_key
    else to select
```

Fig. 11. Fragment of dialog description syntax from Fig. 10(a) using RAPID/USE syntax.

tions, one is naturally drawn to determine if these ideas can be extended to such devices. Many such extensions seem feasible; in this section, we sketch out suitable strategies for these extensions. Since all of them now become minor refinements of previously discussed concepts, the treatment here is brief.

Modern bit-mapped displays are capable of displaying both textual and graphical output, of partitioning the display into two or more (possibly overlapping) regions (windows), and of either monochromatic or color display. Such displays often have a special pointing device, such as a mouse, that allows "picking" (selecting one of several buttons) and cursor movement.

One can immediately see that the notion of output specification, as associated with nodes in USE transition diagrams, may be extended to accommodate many of these concepts. For example, many pictures may be drawn by using a graphical language such as PIC [23] and simply allowing the output specification language for transition diagrams to include calls to PIC. Similarly, color definitions (or pixel values) can be associated with output nodes or with items displayed within a node, just as reverse video and standard video were used in Section III.

The problem with respect to drawing objects is not so much to draw them, but rather to be able to refer to them subsequently. Graphical interaction often involves the selection of an item, command, or icon with a pointing device. Thus, any object that might be referenced by such a device must be identifiable.

A transition diagram based strategy can only succeed if there is a way to associate placement of objects on the display with the placement of the pointing device. To achieve this, the pointing device must transmit more information than the input signal alone.

For a mouse, the "pick" buttons on top of the device may be specified and handled in the same manner as for a function button or any other single key input, as described in Section V. In other words, one could write "pick(1)" on an arc to indicate a transition from one node to another on receipt of that input. However, that transition would also require an action routine which would need information concerning the current screen position of the pointing device. This information is necessary to associate the pointing device with a displayed object, or to indicate a position at which text or additional objects should be placed.

Extension to multiple windows can also be accomplished. Windows may be edfined independently of the diagrams, and then any transition diagram may be associated with a specific window. When a subconversation is invoked, that may cause the appearance of a new window, either at a predetermined place or at a place indicated by the location of a pointing device on the screen. This approach can work for both "persistent" windows and for "popup" windows.

Once multiple windows are introduced, then the extension to multiple concurrent dialog is also possible. This extension is handled most easily by using the location of the pointing device to determine the active dialog, but other possibilities exist as well.

In general, then, many extensions for bit-mapped graphics, multiple windows, pointing devices, and concurrency can be made within the framework of USE transition diagrams as described here. Such extensions would provide a formal basis for describing a yet larger class of interactive systems.

It is clear, though, that there are practical limits to these extensions. Even with the extensions described here, the notations would be tedious. Many sophisticated users would prefer to do "reverse specification," interactively designing the windows, icons, and user interface, and to generate the formal specification of the interaction from there.

It is important to note that transition diagrams represent a sequence of finite states, so that they become unsuitable as a representation scheme when one attempts to describe continuous input devices, such as found in many video games and drawing systems. Alternative approaches must be devised to represent continuous input.

XI. EVALUATION

In Section II, five requirements were established for a user interface notation: formalism, completeness, comprehensibility, flexibility, and testability. We conclude by evaluating USE transition diagrams against these requirements.

Formalism: Transition diagrams are a specification method for formal grammars, and have long served as a means for unambiguous specification of programming languages. The extensions made for USE transition diagrams retain that formalism, yielding an unambiguous method for dialog specification. When used in combination with formal specifications for the related actions, e.g., preconditions and postconditions, one has a formal specification methodology.

Completeness: The basic form of transition diagrams, while complete from the standpoint for specifying a formal grammar, was far from complete for specifying interactive dialogs. The extensions described here greatly extend the scope of user interaction that can be described with the diagrams, and are quite thorough for dialogs involving alphanumeric keyboards and displays, including special purpose keys and screen-oriented display. We have sketched out approaches for additional extensions that are appropriate for a broader range of terminal, yet even these extensions are incomplete. We continue to search for effective descriptive techniques for broader classes of dialogs.

Comprehensibility: Transition diagrams were selected in preference to Backus–Naur form as a notation for dialog description largely on the basis of relative comprehensibility. Our own empirical evidence supports this decision. At the same time, though, additional extensions to the notation would have a negative effect upon comprehensibility. Furthermore, we have observed that understandability of the diagrams is enhanced by the use of sample screens, either using TDI or hand drawn screens, to show the typical displays from specific nodes.

Flexibility: There are three major "styles" of interactive dialogs on alphanumeric terminals: command oriented, menu selection (multiple choice), and natural language. We found that all three of these styles were easily handled with USE transition diagrams. Furthermore, we saw that we could define *multiple interfaces* to the *same* set of actions. Thus, one could build a menu selection *and* a command oriented interface to a system, where the menu selection might be more appropriate for the novice user, with the command approach designed for the experienced user. Similarly, one could build multilingual programs, carrying out the same set of computations in each case, but providing the user interface in two or more different languages, such as French and English.

The flexibility of the USE transition diagrams comes with a tradeoff against simplicity. Many interactive dialogs are "forms-oriented," in which the user fills in one or more entries on a screen designed to look like a form. Such systems are often specified with a "what-you-see-is-what-you-get" form layout program, as found in numerous commercially available user interface management and application generation systems. The USE transition diagram notation for such a form can be quite complex, involving a node, a transition, and possibly an action for every user input on the form.

The reason for this complexity is that the creators of the forms design system have made numerous standard decisions about the nature of the interface for their users, and hence do not need the generality provided by the USE specification method. The low-level degree of control available with the transition diagram approach is "overkill" for this class of interface, and thus requires the developer to specify in detail many features that are implicit in the form-oriented approach.

As a practical matter, we have designed and written a forms-oriented program to provide a general interface to a Troll/USE relational database. It is instructive to note that this forms-oriented program *generates* the transition diagram language used by the Transition Diagram Interpreter, from which an executable program is created. Thus, the transition diagram

notation is sufficiently flexible to handle the forms-oriented approach.

Executability: The ease of machine processing of the USE transition diagrams allows informal testing of a set of alternative interfaces, so that potential system users may be presented with an executable version of an interface design and the users and dialog designers can jointly evaluate the design. The structure of RAPID/USE allows direct linkage of the executable dialog with programmed actions, so that the prototype of the dialog can be directly extended to produce a fully operational system. Thus, RAPID/USE serves the needs for prototyping *and* development.

Much of the work in program testing is based on coverage of program paths; these notations are easily carried over into interface testing by describing coverage of dialog paths. The formal description of the input language, as given by the USE transition diagrams, is most useful for defining a set of test cases that allow testing of the user interface. Indeed, RAPID/USE contains logging facilities that support analysis of dialog designs, and includes the "rapsum" subsystem to generate summaries of a session with TDI.

In summary, the USE transition diagram method is a general method for the specification of human–computer interaction. It can be viewed as a pictorial programming language, encompassing many of the issues of control flow and scope of variables found in traditional programming languages. When combined with the use of the Transition Diagram Interpreter to create executable and easily modifiable versions of user interfaces, one can quickly iterate on designs of a user interface, yielding a design that is satisfactory from the user standpoint, while formalizable and implementable from the developer standpoint. The USE transition diagrams can thereby provide effective methods and tools for the engineering of interactive systems.

ACKNOWLEDGMENT

I am grateful to my colleagues who have contributed to the ideas presented in this paper. S. Stinson validated the basic ideas of using state transition diagrams for modeling interactive information systems. D. Shewmake and P. Pircher built the Transition Diagram Interpreter and the RAPID/USE system. C. Mills and P. Pircher built the Transition Diagram Editor used as a front-end to RAPID/USE. M. Kersten built the Troll/USE relational database management system. Their help has been invaluable.

REFERENCES

[1] A. I. Wasserman, "The user software engineering methodology: An overview," in *Information System Design Methodologies: A Comparative Review*, A. A. Verrijn-Stuart, Ed. Amsterdam, The Netherlands: North-Holland, 1982, pp. 591–628.

[2] ——, "USE: A methodology for the design and development of interactive information systems," in *Formal Models and Practical Tools for Information System Design*, H.-J. Schneider, Ed. Amsterdam, The Netherlands: North-Holland, 1979, pp. 31–50.

[3] A. I. Wasserman and D. T. Shewmake, "Rapid prototyping of interactive information systems," *ACM Software Eng. Notes* vol. 7, no. 5, pp. 171–180, Dec. 1982.

[4] A. I. Wasserman, D. D. Sherertz, M. L. Kersten, R. P. van de Riet, and M. D. Dippé, "Revised report on the programming language

PLAIN," *ACM SIGPLAN Notices*, vol. 16, no. 5, pp. 59–80, May 1981.

[5] M. L. Kersten and A. I. Wasserman, "The architecture of the PLAIN data base handler," *Software–Practice and Experience*, vol. 11, no. 2, pp. 175–186, Feb. 1981.

[6] A. I. Wasserman, "The unified support environment: Support for the user software engineering methodology," in *Proc. IEEE Comput. Soc. SoftFair Conf.*, July 1983, pp. 145–153.

[7] A. I. Wasserman and M. L. Kersten, "A relational database environment for software development," Lab. Medical Inform. Sci., Univ. California, San Francisco, Tech. Rep. 65, 1983.

[8] A. I. Wasserman and S. K. Stinson, "A specification method for interactive information systems," *Proc. IEEE Comput. Soc. Conf. Specification of Reliable Software*, 1979, pp. 68–79.

[9] M. E. Conway, "Design of a separable transition-diagram compiler," *Commun. ACM*, vol. 6, no. 7, pp. 396–408, July 1963.

[10] J. T. O'Neill, Ed., *MUMPS Language Standard*, ANSI Standard XII.1, Amer. Nat. Standards Inst., 1977.

[11] D. L. Parnas, "On the user of transition diagrams in the design of a user interface for an interactive computer system," in *Proc. 24th Nat. ACM Conf.*, 1969, pp. 379–385.

[12] B. E. Casey and B. Dasarathy, "Modeling and validating the man-machine interface," *Software*, vol. 12, no. 6, pp. 557–569, June 1982.

[13] R. J. K. Jacob, "Using formal specifications in the design of a human-computer interface," *Commun. ACM*, vol. 26, no. 3, pp. 259–264, Mar. 1983.

[14] P. Bieleski, "Flowcharting revisited (obsolete techniques vs. unexploited techniques)," in *Conference Papers: 8th New Zealand Comput. Conf.*, 1983, pp. 123–139.

[15] D. Kieras and P. Polson, "A generalized transition network representation for interactive systems," in *Proc. CHI '83 Human Factors in Comput. Syst.*, 1983, pp. 103–106.

[16] A. Goldberg and D. Robson, *Smalltalk-80: the Language and its Implementation.* Reading, MA: Addison-Wesley, 1983.

[17] W. Teitelman and L. Masinter, "The INTERLISP Programming Environment," *Computer*, vol. 14, no. 4, pp. 25–33, Apr. 1981.

[18] A. I. Wasserman, "User software engineering and the design of interactive systems," in *Proc. 5th Int. Conf. Software Eng.*, 1981, pp. 387–393.

[19] T. DeMarco, *Structured Analysis and System Specification.* Englewood Cliffs, NJ: Prentice-Hall, 1979.

[20] M. L. Kersten and A. I. Wasserman, *Troll/USE Reference Manual*, Lab. Medical Inform. Sci., Univ. California, San Francisco, 1984.

[21] A. I. Wasserman and D. T. Shewmake, "The role of prototypes in the user software engineering (USE) methodology," in *Advances in Human-Computer Interaction*, H. R. Hartson, Ed. Norwood, NJ: Ablex, 1985, pp. 191–210.

[22] C. Mills and A. I. Wasserman, "A transition diagram editor," in *Proc. 1984 Summer Usenix Meeting*, June 1984, pp. 287–296.

[23] B. W. Kernighan, "PIC-A language for typesetting graphics," *ACM SIGPLAN Notices*, vol. 16, no. 6, pp. 92–98, June 1981; see also *Proc. SIGPLAN/SIGOA Symp. Text Manipulation*.

Anthony I. Wasserman (M'71) received the A.B. degree in mathematics and physics from the University of California, Berkeley, and the M.S. and Ph.D. degrees in computer sciences from the University of Wisconsin–Madison.

After three years in industry, he joined the University of California, San Francisco, where he is now Professor of Medical Information Science. Since 1970, he has also been Lecturer in the Computer Science Division at the University of California, Berkeley. He is also the founder and President of Interactive Development Environments, Inc. He is the architect of the User Software Engineering methodology and supporting toolset for the specification and design of interactive information systems. His research interests include software development methods, tools, and environments, human interaction with computers, and data management. He is the author of more than fifty papers and an editor of seven books, including *Tutorial: Software Design Techniques* (IEEE Computer Society), with P. Freeman, and *Automated Tools for Information Systems Design* (Amsterdam, The Netherlands: North-Holland), with H.-J. Schneider.

Dr. Wasserman is the Editor-in-Chief of ACM's *Computing Surveys*, and a member of the Editorial Board of several other journals, including the *International Journal of Man-Machine Studies, Information Systems*, and the *Journal of Systems and Software*. He is a member of the Programme Committee for the IFIP Congress '86, Vice-Chairman of IFIP WG 8.1 (Design and Evaluation of Information Systems), and a former chairman of ACM's SIGSOFT. He is a member of the Association for Computing Machinery and the IEEE Computer Society.

TOWARDS A COMPREHENSIVE
USER INTERFACE MANAGEMENT SYSTEM

W. Buxton, M. R. Lamb,
D. Sherman & K. C. Smith

Computer Systems Research Group
University of Toronto
Toronto, Ontario
Canada M5S 1A4

ABSTRACT

A UIMS developed at the University of Toronto is presented. The system has two main components. The first is a set of tools to support the design and implementation of interactive graphics programs. The second is a run-time support package which handles interactions between the system and the user (things such as hit detection, event detection, screen updates, and procedure invocation), and provides facilities for logging user interactions for later protocol analysis.

The design/implementation tool is a preprocessor, called MENULAY, which permits the applications programmer to use interactive graphics techniques to design graphics menus and their functionality. The output of this preprocessor is high-level code which can be compiled with application-specific routines. User interactions with the resulting executable module are then handled by the run-time support package. The presentation works through an example from design to execution in a step-by-step manner.

CR Categories and Subject Descriptors: D.2.2 [Software] Tools and Techniques - User Interfaces; H.1.2 [Information Systems] User/Machine Systems - Human Information Processing; I.3.4 [Computer Graphics] Graphics Utilities - Software Support; I.3.6 [Computer Graphics] Methodology and Techniques - Interactive Techniques.

General Terms: Human-Computer Dialogue, Interaction Management.

Additional Keywords and Phrases: Dialogue Design and Specification, and Dialogue Run-Time Support.

1. INTRODUCTION

Traditionally, interactive graphical programs have been written using conventional programming languages, low-level tools, and often *ad hoc* techniques. The cost of doing so has been time, frustration, and quality of end product.

A *user interface management system* (UIMS) is intended to reduce this cost. The objective is to free the applications programmer from low-level details so as to be able to concentrate on higher applications-specific aspects of the user interface. A UIMS typically consists of a package of tools which support the implementation, debugging and evaluation of interactive human-computer dialogues.

An analogy can be drawn between a UIMS and a data base management system (DBMS). The DBMS mediates between programmer and data, enforcing a consistency of technique among all programmers in accessing that data. It provides portability because only the lowest-level DBMS routines are hardware-dependent. Similarly, the UIMS mediates between the applications programmer and the input events, encouraging a consistency both of graphical layout representation and of input processing mechanisms.[1]

This paper presents a UIMS developed at the Computer Systems Research Group, University of Toronto. The system comprises a set of tools for designing and implementing menu-based dialogues and for providing run-time support for more general event-driven interactive programs. The module for designing/implementing menu-based dialogues has the property of permitting hand-written programs to be integrated with code automatically synthesized from the programmer's specifications.

1.1 The Need for a UIMS

Our current understanding of human-computer interaction is extremely limited. We cannot sit down and design an interface for an application and know, *a priori*, how well it will perform. We must accept at the outset, therefore, the inevitable intertwining of specification, design, and implementation (Swartout & Balzer, 1982). Design then becomes an iterative process, each iteration consisting of three phases: *design, implementation* and *evaluation* (Buxton & Sniderman, 1980). The motivation to develop improved tools can therefore be seen as a desire to increase the number of iterations that we can afford to pass through in this loop. The hoped-for consequence will be an improvement in the quality of the user interfaces which we produce.

The UIMS presented herein aids in the *design* and *implementation* phases by providing the following set of tools: a graphics package; sketch editors; a standardized graphics communications protocol; table-driven run-time support of the user dialogue; and, most recently, a graphical layout and interaction specification preprocessor which generates C language programs. Underway are the development of interaction analysis tools to aid in the *evaluation* phase of the cycle.

---

1. This is not to imply that data-base management is independent of the user interface. Rather, the tools applied to each of these free the applications programmer so that their mutual influence can be better taken into consideration.

Each of the modules of the existing system has limitations. However, when viewed together, the various pieces begin to shed some light on what would comprise a comprehensive set of tools for the user interface designer. In presenting our experience in a longitudinal way, it is hoped that we will make some contribution towards the realization of such a comprehensive set of tools.

1.2 U of T UIMS Structure

In its current state, our UIMS consists of two main modules. The first is a preprocessor which enables the program designer, using interactive graphics techniques, to design and specify the graphical layout and functionality of menu-based user interfaces. It is with this module that the applications programmer establishes the relationships between what the user sees, does, and hears, and the application-specific semantics underlying the program being implemented.

The second main module is the run-time support package. It handles things such as event and hit detection, procedure invocation, and updating the display - all according to the schema specified using the preprocessor. An important aspect of this implementation is that the code executed by the run-time module can be generated automatically (complete with comments) from the data specified to the preprocessor.

The applicability of the current implementation of the preprocessor is restricted to menu-based interaction. Within this domain, however, it is quite flexible, and supports various types of displays (colour or monochrome) and sound output. The run-time support package is more general and does not depend upon the preprocessor. It is designed for supporting event-driven software and a variety of input devices. These two packages do not stand alone. They are just two components in a more general "kit" of prototyping tools to support iterative and experimental programming (Deutsh & Taft, 1980). In discussing these tools, we find it useful to distinguish between *general design tools* and *programmers' packaged units*.

The general design tools facilitate the specification of graphical information and functional relationships, the writing of application-specific code and the debugging of successive versions of applications programs. Many of these tools are standard components in modern operating systems. Besides the two modules mentioned above, our inventory of such tools includes: (1) the UNIX[2] operating system, with its highly sophisticated command interpreter, C language compiler, hierarchical file system and many utilities; (2) the GPAC device-independent graphics package (Reeves, 1975); (3) routines to save and retrieve pictures stored as standard format metafiles; (4) text editors; (5) graphical sketch editors; and (6) interactive symbolic debuggers.

Programmers' packaged units are ready-made modules which can be integrated into applications software. They are documented and tested *building-blocks*. They are generally packaged versions of blocks of code which are observed to be reccuring and of general utility. Our library of such modules, therefore, is continually expanding. Representative of such packaged units are: (1) specialized iconic cursors which can be used as meaningful tracking symbols; (2) directory windows which permit graphical user reference to any file of a given type; (3) a graphical potentiometer with a "knob" which the user can "slide" up and down to change the value of a program parameter; (4) a graphical piano keyboard which audibly plays the notes pointed to; (5) routines to manipulate lightbuttons within the above menu-driven system (e.g, to flash, deactivate and highlight individual menu items); and (6) an audio support package, which drives a digital sound synthesizer (Buxton, Fogels, Fedorkow, Sasaki & Smith, 1978). Many of these

2. UNIX is a trademark of Bell Laboratories.

modules will be illustrated in examples which follow.

2. EVOLUTION OF OUR UIMS

Our UIMS has evolved over several years, in parallel with the development of innovative software for graphics applications. It is implemented in the C programming language on a PDP-11/45, which was acquired in 1975 and runs UNIX version 6.

First came GPAC, a device-independent graphics package (Reeves, 1975), onto which successively higher levels were built. Interaction techniques, specialized cursors and directory windows followed, in 1976-78. As part of the Structure Sound Synthesis Project, the table-driven run-time support package of the UIMS was put together in 1979. Finally, in 1982, MENULAY, the graphical menu layout and function specification preprocessor was built.

2.1 Table-driven run-time support system

With the development of a number of menu-based interactive programs in the late 1970's, it became apparent that the user interfaces all had a large number of common features, but that each programmer implemented them with a "personal" touch. So personal, in fact, that the code was difficult for others to understand or support. Accordingly, we began to develop a more uniform methodology which not only captured the best ideas of these various approaches, but also made them available in a fully-documented and well-supported environment. The basis of our new methodology was an externally-controlled, table-driven system which supported event-driven interactions. The programmer supplied the system with the applications-specific routines and information about what types of events were active when, and what and how such events were to affect the program's behaviour. At run-time, then, responses to user interactions (such as event and hit detection, display updates, and procedure invocation) were handled by this package.

The present package, an extension of that developed in 1979, is primarily oriented towards screen and menu-based systems. It is capable of supporting event-driven interactions that go well beyond simple light-button selection (examples are: Buxton, Sniderman, Reeves, Patel & Baecker, 1978; and Buxton, Patel, Reeves & Baecker, 1982). The tables used by the system have nine user-specified fields per entry. These fields include:

the name of a user-specified procedure which is to be invoked upon the detection of a specified input event;

the input event which is to trigger that procedure;

fields to contain (variable) parameters of that procedure;

the x and y hit area for procedures triggered by pointing events;

any text (or the name of a graphics file containing a picture) to be displayed;

the x and y co-ordinates of the item to be displayed;

the item's size and colour.

The system also supports dummy table entries for setting various parameters, such as whether subsequent hit-areas are to have boxes drawn around them or not. As well, it provides for functions to be invoked in special cases arising in menu-based systems: (1) if the user misses all of the light-buttons, (2) when entering or (3) when exiting from the menu.

Finally, the package provides easy-to-use routines for setting-up and switching among the menus, or "states" of the application-defined system.

While this package was of value, it was still a tedious task to specify the data which made up the tables. This was especially true during the early stages of development, when the graphic design, functionality, and syntax of the user interface were continually being revised due to experimentation. Consequently, we were motivated to develop another tool which would facilitate the specification and modification of these data. The result was the preprocessor, MENULAY, described in the next section.

3. MENULAY AND MAKEMENU

3.1 Concept

The preprocessor which serves as the front end of our UIMS is known as MENULAY. The package is designed to enable the user interface designer (who is not necessarily the applications programmer) to specify rapidly and naturally the graphical and functional relationships within and among the displays making up a menu-based system. Specifications made using the package are converted into the C programming language and compiled through the use of a companion program MAKEMENU. The resulting code can be linked with application-specific routines.

MENULAY enables the designer to define user interfaces which are made up of networks of menus. These may be structured in a hierarchic manner, or in an arbitrary fashion. Furthermore, the method of interacting with these menus is open, and up to the designer. A prime objective of the tool is to minimize the bias imposed by the path of least resistance, which may favour one interaction technique over another. MENULAY is a product of itself. It therefore gives the user interface designer a feel for the nature of the interaction sequences being specified, while at the same time indicates the range of tools available.

3.2 Functional Flow

The entire sequence as set out in Figure 1 can be performed by the

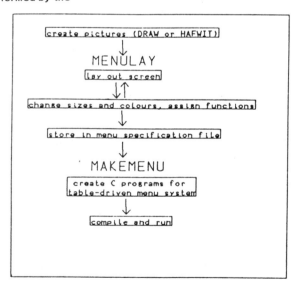

Figure 1. A typical Sequence for Constructing an Interactive Dialogue

applications designer in an interactive graphics environment. A graphics tablet and four-button puck are used for all input to MENULAY (except for such character-oriented input as the typing of the names of application-specific functions to be called upon hit detection). The MAKEMENU program creation and compilation options are also specified graphically.

3.3 Automatic Code Generation

MENULAY's elegance lies in the automatic conversion into C language programs of the graphical interface specified by the applications designer. This conversion is performed by MENULAY's companion program, MAKEMENU. The programs generated from MENULAY's compact specification files are syntactically correct, complete and internally documented with liberal comments. They are designed for compilation with the same table-driven support system on which MENULAY itself is built. Because these programs are in C, however, they can be adapted when required by using a text editor. Where necessary, these changes can be recorded automatically, and repeated whenever the menu specification files are changed[3].

Where the applications designer specifies names of application-specific functions, the programs generated by MAKEMENU contain unresolved external references ("hooks"). By writing functions with the required names and referencing the appropriate file names when MAKEMENU is called, the applications programmer can add any amount of application-specific programming to the layout and sequence information specified by the designer. The two sets of code (computer-generated and programmer-authored) are completely compatible, and can share global variable names, external function references, and so on.

Work is presently underway on a decompiler which will be able to reverse the MAKEMENU process. This decompiler, called UNEMEKAM, will convert a C program which makes use of the table-driven menu software into a menu specification file which can be edited graphically using MENULAY.

3.4 Command Hierarchy

MENULAY has one main command level, containing seven basic commands. These are *layout*, *size*, *colour*, *function*, *get save*, *tryout* and *exit* These are illustrated in Figure 2.

Figure 2. MENULAY Commands

Layout allows the designer to create textual items (e.g., light buttons) on the screen; add pictures either taken from the system library of graphical icons or created by the user with a sketch editor; change the position of any item; and delete items from the screen (see Figure 3).

Size enables the designer to change the scale of any item on the screen, either by "sliding the knob" on a graphical potentiometer or by typing in a scale factor, as shown in

---

3. Hand-coding changes to MAKEMENU output obviously causes problems in "unmaking" menus. Using the facility is a concession to reality: the state-of-the-art does not yet permit us to make a totally comprehensive UIMS.

Figure 4.

Colour allows one to specify (or change) the colour of any item on the end-user's screen (see Figure 5). This is independent of the device on which the designer is using MENULAY; the high-resolution display we most commonly use, for example, does not support colour graphics.

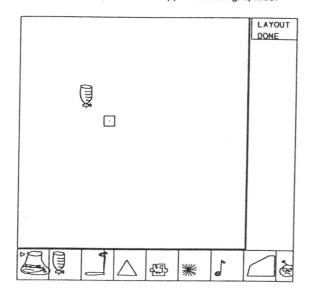

Figure 3. MENULAY – Laying Out the Display Graphics

Figure 4. MENULAY – Changing the Size of an Item (the stand) with a Graphical Potentiometer

Function enables the designer to specify what will happen when the end-user points to light buttons. The light buttons may be text or pictures. The designer may also specify a function to be invoked if the user activates an input event without pointing to any one light button. In addition, it is possible to specify functions to be called when the menu being designed is entered and exited. This is shown in Figure 6.

The function names may be taken from MENULAY's library of utility functions or be written by the applications

Figure 5. MENULAY – Assigning Colours to the Items on the Screen

programmer before compilation of the program. The writing of these functions is done entirely independently of (and either before or after) the creation of the menu specification file with MENULAY.

Function also allows programs of up to 50 characters – such as short *print* statements – to be typed directly into MENULAY. MAKEMENU takes care of creating a new function name for the function table to enable the code typed in by the user to be loaded.

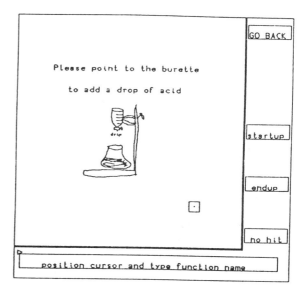

Figure 6. MENULAY – Assigning Function Names to the Active Items (Light-Buttons)

Get (and *save*) allow the user to retrieve from (and store into) a menu specification file the details of the layout and functional relationships which the designer has specified. The menu specification file is extremely compact and is thus a very efficient storage format. Each item of the menu screen is referenced by x and y coordinates, hit area, size, colour, function, text (if a textual item) or standard graphics format file name (if a graphical icon).

Tryout gives the user the opportunity to invoke *makemenu*, the code generation program, by specifying graphically the options and files he wishes to access (see Figure 7).

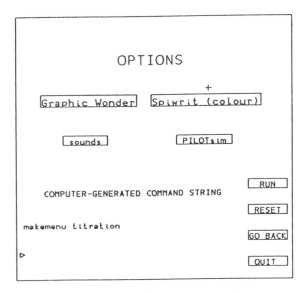

Figure 7. MENULAY – Generating 'C' Code to Implement Specified Interface (by invoking MAKEMENU)

Once the program has been compiled, *tryout* then runs it for the user.

Exit is used to exit the program. The user is given a new menu with "YES" and "NO" options to confirm that he does indeed wish to exit.

MENULAY has levels of use: "novice" and "expert". In *novice* mode, only the basic commands (as set out above) are accessible. All input is done through one button on the cursor puck, and instructions are given at various points in the program. In *expert* mode, the other three buttons on the puck can be used to perform special functions (e.g., displaying a grid while positioning items; flipping from one menus of pictures or colours to another; assigning a function name which is identical to the text in the menu item), and fewer instructional diagnostics are displayed. The system maintains on disk a profile for each user (a file called "userpro"), initially tagging each person as "novice" and upgrading them based on experience with the system and on specific request.[4]

From any point within MENULAY (except during *layout*, where typing text causes the creation of light buttons containing the text typed), the user can access the UNIX shell (command interpreter) by typing at the terminal. (When this happens, the MENULAY screen fades and the user's scroller is reset to the full screen until the user returns to MENULAY.) This means that the full range of terminal-based commands can be accessed instantly without leaving MENULAY. For example, any calculations which the designer wishes to make in the course of the graphical layout specification can be made by invoking the on-line desk calculator. Similarly, the applications designer who is also a programmer may compose a function by invoking the text editor. Or the designer may send the programmer comments about the implementation by electronic mail before there's a chance to forget them.

3.5 Applications

MENULAY has already been used to construct the user interface for each of the following programs: (1) MENULAY itself; (2) the DRAW sketch editor, which is used to generate light-button graphics; (3) a computer-assisted instruction (CAI) program which teaches children about birds and their nests[5] (see Figure 8);

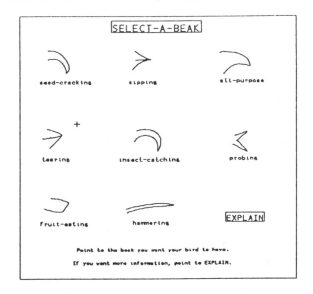

Figure 8. Beak Selection Sequence from 'Land Birds and Their Nests'

and (4) a graphical piano keyboard and musical notation editor (Kuzmich, in preparation: see Figure 9).

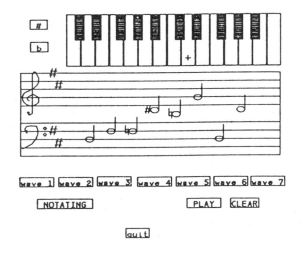

Figure 9. 'Melody Manipulations' music notation editor and teaching tool

It can be used to assemble, in minutes, sequences of frames for CAI in virtually any area of instruction where graphics is helpful. It has also proven useful for laying out

5. "Land Birds and Their Nests", designed by Young Naturalist Foundation, Toronto, Canada, and programmed by CSRG (in press).

figures such as Figure 1 of this paper. Appendix I presents a walk-through of a CAI example.

It is notable that since graphical icons for the user's screen are referenced by file name, these pictures can be changed without even having to recompile the applications program. Thus, a program could be fully constructed by an applications designer who is not a graphic artist, and an artist brought in later to revise the pictures.

4. UNIFORMITY AND PORTABILITY

It is important that a UIMS be portable in a number of senses. The system described satisfies these criteria theoretically and we are in the process of proving its portability in practice.

4.1 Output Device Independence

At the most primitive level, a user interface management system must support a number of different output devices with different characteristics. In the case of MENULAY and MAKEMENU, for example, the device independence is achieved by using the GPAC graphics package with such varied devices as a high-resolution vector display with 16 intensity levels and a low-resolution 16-colour raster display. The run-time support package (without MENULAY as of yet) has also been made to run on various alphanumeric terminals.

4.2 Input Device Independence

The UIMS must also be able to support alternative input techniques. The primary input device used in MENULAY at present is a graphics tablet with a four-button puck and the typewriter keyboard. A set of Allison sliders[6] are also used, but are only available through pre-programmed packages. Other pointing devices (such as mice, light-pens, or touch-screens) could be used in place of the tablet with the provision of the appropriate GPAC device driver. The run-time support package, however, can be driven by virtually any event-generating device that has a GPAC driver.

4.3 Language Independence

At a further level of portability, the UIMS should be structured to facilitate the ability to generate code in different programming languages. The output of MENULAY is a metacode which is translated into high-level language by MAKEMENU. To output code in a different language would involve rewriting this program and providing run-time support in a compatible format.

4.4 Machine Independence

At a higher degree of portability is the capacity to transfer a system such as MENULAY either to a more powerful machine than the PDP-11/45 (e.g., a VAX-11/780) or a less powerful one (e.g. an APPLE microcomputer).

As has been noted, MENULAY and MAKEMENU are written in C (a standardized language which is relatively portable) and use GPAC, a device-independent graphics package (which is itself written in C). Provided the necessary hardware drivers are available, GPAC and thus MENULAY/MAKEMENU could be transferred at reasonable cost to any system which will support UNIX and C.

4.5 Applications Program Portability

In contrast with MENULAY, the applications programs generated by MAKEMENU can be ported even to systems which do not support UNIX. With a cross-compiler and a basic graphics package, for example, applications programs such as computer-assisted instruction frames could be compiled to run on many microcomputers.

---

6. This device is a continuous belt slider. It is a treadmill with a 9 by 1.5 cm surface exposed which is used as a motion-sensitive input device. The mechanical section was developed by Allison Research Inc., 2817 Erica Place, Nashville, Tenn. 37204. The electronics used here were developed in house.

5. COMPARISON WITH OTHER SYSTEMS

Other UIMSs do exist, and have had an influence on the evolution of our system. The most distinguishing feature of MENULAY is its natural way of integrating graphical design specification with human-written applications programming. By way of comparison, we review briefly three systems: TRW's FLAIR; Olsen's automatic code generation design; and Kasik's TIGER.

5.1 FLAIR

FLAIR (Functional Language Articulated Interactive Resource) (Wong & Reid, 1982), is a user interface dialogue design tool which enables a system designer to construct graphically a user dialogue for an applications program. It is largely driven by voice input and incorporates text picture construction and editing (at the graphical primitive level) as well as dynamic frame layout. Its high-level features include the ability to define and control a menu hierarchy, graph and map generation, an on-line calculator and relational data base access for graphical entity storage and retrieval.

FLAIR is more advanced than MENULAY in its use of multiple input techniques and in its ability to permit the applications designer to specify a wide range of end user interactions. However, we are in the process of extending MENULAY's capabilities to permit the specification of a much wider range of user interactions.

FLAIR contains a powerful set of internal utilities, but appears to be rather limiting in its integration with application-specific code. FLAIR is a language and package unto itself, with no apparent "hooks" into other programming languages. This suggests that if the FLAIR "language" does not permit the applications programmer to program a certain algorithm conveniently, then that algorithm will be inaccessible. MENULAY, on the other hand, creates menu specification files that are converted into fully-documented C programs which, as noted earlier, are automatically integrated with any code the programmer may have written for the specific application.

5.2 Olsen's Model for Automatic Code Generation

Olsen (1982) describes research into the automatic generation of interactive graphical systems to facilitate faster and cheaper generation of interactive user interfaces. This work has not yet progressed beyond the design stage.

Olsen points out the useful distinction between these *design* of the application program interface and thes *writing* of the program itself. He observes that it is the design aspect of the program creation which is suited to automatic program generation. This is because of the high cost in time and effort of hand-coding and the increased reliability of automatically generated software.

Olsen envisages the use of Pascal procedure definitions for the characterization of interactive commands in the applications program. We feel that MENULAY is a significant improvement over this idea in that the command menus and interaction relationships are specified in the very way in which the end user will interact with the applications program, i.e. by pointing. Olsen does not address the possibility of having the specification technique use the same devices and interfaces as those the end-user will ultimately face.

5.3 TIGER

Kasik (1982), describes a UIMS which, like our UIMS, takes care of the bookkeeping associated with screen layout, interrupt handling and the definition of interactive dialogue sequences. This UIMS, called TIGER, has as its core the language TICCL, which permits the applications programmer to concentrate on the logical functions which he wishes to perform rather than the physical, low-level steps which must be taken to accomplish the task.

TICCL can be used to describe algorithms which combine graphical primitives in response to user interactions as well as to define user interaction sequences. TICCL code operates at a higher level than the Pascal code which is used for the non-graphical portion of the applications programming.

TICCL is useful as a mechanism for specifying user interaction at a higher level than is otherwise available to its designers. Such a language combined with a higher level package such as MENULAY would permit even more flexibility in user interface prototyping. While TIGER does not currently incorporate a module comparable to MENULAY, TICCL is a powerful language, and could support such a tool.

To the extent TICCL is used for constructing graphical primitives from user interactions, it is more advanced than our table-driven menu system for which MENULAY acts as preprocesor. On the other hand, we feel that our programmers' packaged units, together with the flexibility of GPAC and its integration into programmers' C code, provide a useful alternative set of interaction response tools.

6. FUTURE DIRECTIONS

6.1 Protocol Analysis

The recording of sequential data about end-user interactions is essential to the evaluation of the interaction techniques used in an applications program. With a menu-driven system based on cursor and tablet, this data consists of a time-stamped record of each user input, recording the x and y tablet co-ordinates of the cursor and the input event which was activated.

We are in the process of developing tools for the analysis of this data, stored in a so-called "dribble file". As part of the process of developing the interaction sequences for an applications program, the designer will ask an end-user to spend a session with the program. Afterwards the new tools will facilitate the analysis of the "dribble file" for that session in a number of ways. First, they will allow the designer to "play back" the user interactions in real time, so as to get a feel for the flow of the user-computer dialogue. Second, they will draw for the designer a "spiderweb" which superimposes graphically all of the hand motions of the user in his interaction with the program (see Figure 10). The spiderweb makes it easy to spot the

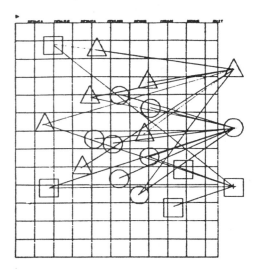

Figure 10. Tracing of Coordinates of Events Recording a User's Session

points at which the user is being forced to repeatedly make

hand motions that are uncomfortable or excessively long.

To function properly, the dribble file data must be recorded at every user input. This implies that the recording be done at the level of event recognition, and that the information always be available unless the programmer has specified otherwise. To do so, however, requires special support in the event-detection mechanism of the graphics package used. Furthermore, the event recognition routines themselves should be able to function in a mode which permits input from sources other than the physical input devices. The stored data files should be able to be used as the source of input events.

6.2 Window Management

MENULAY presently generates code which operates within a single window on the screen. While multiple *frames* or *levels* within a program can be created very easily, multiple *windows* can not.

It is intended to expand the capabilities of the table-driven menu system (and therefore of MENULAY) to permit the designation of multiple windows by the applications designer. Windows would have attributed to them specific cursor tracking symbols, background colours, and input events. As at present, specific light buttons (text or graphical) will be locatable at any place within a particular window.

7. ACKNOWLEDGEMENTS

MENULAY and MAKEMENU are the highest level of a user interface management system which is built on years of work at the Computer Systems Research Group. We acknowledge with thanks the contributions of Ron Baecker and Leslie Mezel, former directors of the Dynamic Graphics Project; Bill Reeves, author of the GPAC graphics package; and other major contributors to our inventory of graphical tools and techniques: Tom Duff, Greg Hill, Tom Horsley, Sanand Patel, Rob Pike, David Tilbrook, Mike Tilson and Martin Tuori.

We also gratefully acknowledge the helpful comments made by the referees and by Dave Kasik.

Interactive graphics research at the Computer Systems Research Group has been funded for many years by the National Sciences and Engineering Research Council, and more recently by the Social Sciences and Humanities Research Council.

8. REFERENCES

Buxton, W., Fogels, A., Fedorkow, G., Sasaki, L. & Smith, K. C. (1978). An Introduction to the SSSP Digital Synthesizer. *Computer Music Journal* **2(4)**, 28 - 38.

Buxton, W., Patel, S., Reeves, W. & Baecker, R. (1982). Objed and the Design of Timbral Resources. *Computer Music Journal* **6(2)**, 32 - 44.

Buxton, W., Sniderman, R., Reeves, W., Patel, S. & Baecker, R. (1978). The Evolution of the SSSP Score Editing Tools. *Computer Music Journal* **3(4)**, 14 - 25.

Buxton, W. & Sniderman, R. (1980). Iteration and the Design of the Human-Computer Interface. *Proceedings of the 13th Annual Meeting of the Human Factors Association of Canada*, pp 72 - 81.

Deutsh, L & Taft, E. A. (1980). Requirements for an Experimental Programming Environment. *Technical Report CSL-80-10*, XEROX PARC.

Kasik, D. (1982). A User Interface Management System. *Computer Graphics*, **16(3)**, 99 - 106.

Kuzmich, N. (in preparation). Melody Manipulations. **Music**

Dept., Faculty of Education, University of Toronto.

Olson, D. (1983). Automatic Generation of Interactive Systems, *Computer Graphics* 17(1), 53 - 57.

Reeves, W. (1975). *A Device-Independent Interactive Graphics Package* M.Sc. Thesis, Dept. of Computer Science, University of Toronto.

Swartout, W & Balzer, R. (1982). An Inevitable Intertwining of Specification and Implementation. *Communications of the ACM* 25(7), 438 - 440.

Wong, Peter C.S., and Eric R. Reid (1982). FLAIR - User Interface Dialog Design Tool, *Computer Graphics*, 16(3), 87 - 98.

APPENDIX 1: A Walkthrough of a CAI application

The following is a brief account of an applications designer's use of MENULAY to create a lesson to help teach chemistry titration. The time taken in this instance was less than ten minutes.

The designer begins by typing "draw" to invoke the DRAW program and then uses the graphics tablet to input free-hand pictures of a burette, a beaker and a stand. Each picture is scaled down in size by pointing to the command "SIZE" and then sliding the "knob" on the displayed potentiometer (like that in Figure 4). The "knob" is slid by positioning the cursor over it and holding down the main button on the cursor puck while sliding it up or down. Each picture is stored in a disk file (by pointing to the command "SAVE", and typing in or pointing to the file name).

Next, MENULAY is invoked (by selecting "EXIT" and then "MENULAY" from a new menu), whereupon an explanation is displayed together with MENULAY's command menu. The user selects "LAYOUT" and sees the newly created pictures in a menu at the bottom of the screen. Selection of the burette causes a copy of it to be tracked as the cursor. It is anchored in the work area by pressing or releasing the main button on the cursor puck (see Figure 3). The same is done to the beaker and the stand. Typing at the keyboard causes that text to be displayed at the current cursor position. Any item in the work area (whether text or graphics) can be repositioned by pointing to it and dragging it to a new position, again anchoring it either by releasing the button or, if it was released immediately upon pointing, by pressing the button again.

To change the scale of any item, the user selects "SIZE" in the main menu (displayed in Figure 2), selects the item, and then changes its size, again with a graphical potentiometer (see Figure 4). To set or change the colour of any item, the user selects "COLOUR" in the main menu and chooses a tint from the menu at the bottom of the screen. This tint is tracked (as shown in Figure 5) until another tint is selected. Any items pointed to are assigned the currently tracked colour. The colour of each item is displayed next to the item if the hardware device does not support colour graphics.

The designer specifies that the function named *drip* is to be invoked when the end-user points to the burette (by selecting "FUNCTION", selecting the burette, and typing "drip": see Figure 6). The entire set of interface specifications is now stored in a file (by pointing to "SAVE" and typing a file name.

Finally, the user selects "TRYOUT" and then chooses Spiwrit (a colour raster screen) as the display device (see Figure 7) and references "drip.c", an application-specific C source file. This causes the interaction specifications to be automatically converted into C language programs which are compiled and linked with the application-specific code. The resulting binary file is then executed (see Figure 11).

Figure 11. Running the Titration Simulation

Here is the source code for the *drip* routine - the only code which the programmer had to write:

```
#include "/u0/dave/master/menuglobal.h"
#define beaker picture("beaker");
int drops 0;

drip()
{
        type("Added a drop of liquid...");
        sound(DRIPPING);
        drops = drops + 1;

        if(drops == 3)
        {
                type("Wow! It changed colour!");
                resetcolour(beaker, PINK);
                sound(BUZZING);
        }
}
```

The Trillium User Interface Design Environment

D. Austin Henderson, Jr.

Intelligent Systems Laboratory
Xerox Palo Alto Research Center
Palo Alto, California 94304

Abstract

Trillium is a computer-based environment for simulating and experimenting with interfaces for simple machines. For the past four years it has been use by Xerox designers for fast prototyping and testing of interfaces for copiers and printers. This paper defines the class of "functioning frame" interfaces which Trillium is used to design, discusses the major concerns that have driven the design of Trillium, and describes the Trillium mechanisms chosen to satisfy them.

Introduction

As machines become more complex, the design of their user[1] interfaces becomes more difficult. A good methodology for improving these machine interfaces is "cut and try": build the interface, try it out on all interested parties (most particularly the end users), discover what its difficulties are, modify the design, and repeat. This empirical approach works best if the total time around this implementation cycle is short — the shorter the better. The goal is so-called "fast prototyping." At Xerox, we wanted to explore speeding up the design cycle by using a computer-based design environment for prototyping and simulating interfaces. The approach to be taken was to build a computer-based "construction set" populated with pieces appropriate for rapidly assembling our class of "functioning frame" interfaces.

Historical Background

Five years ago at Xerox, the cycle time for interface design and experiment was, for the most part, so long that one or two cycles was the norm for our products. These products were "simple" machines, copiers and printers, with "simple" interfaces: mechanically-based control panels with lights, buttons and mimic presentations of the machine and its parts; typewriter-based recursive-decent menu systems; and display-based graphic interfaces. However, the functionality of the products was growing, and the interfaces (including display-based graphic interfaces) were becoming more complex. Given this increasing complexity, the production of good interfaces was becoming more and more difficult to guarantee.

As a result, a few design sites had included programmers in their design teams, and testing was done on simulations of the interfaces, rather than on final product itself. This reduced the design cycle time from months to weeks and was clearly improving the quality of product interfaces. However, it was observed that, although formal passes around the cycle would involve operability testing, often it was the case that the designers themselves, on first seeing and using their interface would immediately know how to improve it. The resulting desire to "fix" it before spending the resources to test it would shorten the cycle still more. Most of the effort in this shortened cycle was in the programming necessary to create the interface simulations.

To tighten the design loop any further, we clearly needed to remove the programming from the cycle. Fortunately, the availability of personal computers capable of running modern symbolic programming environments provided the opportunity to experiment

---

1. In this paper, the word "user" refers to the person who interacts with the interface designed using Trillium. The word "designer" refers to the person who interacts with Trillium itself. The word "operator" is avoided because it carries the connotation that the role of the person interacting with the machine is the "machine's operator," when interfaces for a broader class of users (repair persons, installers, sales persons) may all be appropriate for design using Trillium.

with doing just that. In response to this opportunity, a user interface design environment called Trillium was built [Henderson, 1983]. The rest of this paper discusses Trillium, examining a few of the key issues which influenced its design[2].

"Functioning Frame" Interfaces.

It will be helpful to ground the discussion in an example of the class of interfaces that Trillium is designed to design. Figure 1 shows a single frame from an interface for a simple copier. This frame is one of many making up the interface. It is composed of a decorative border, a collection of controls, and an area summarizing the description of the job. The number pad controls the count of the number of copies that should be made when the Start button is pressed. The buttons in each of the columns control other features of the job. Buttons are "pushed" by using the mouse. The buttons are back-lit (simulated by inverting the screen), with the lights "coming on" to indicate which particular choice has been made. There are also some restrictions on the settings of the features. For example, no more than 99 copies can be made in any given job and the copier does not make one-sided copies from two-sided originals. When these restrictions are violated, the interface takes some appropriate action to notify the user (in one case by refusing to take the expected action).

The frame in Figure 1 is one of many in this interface, through which the operator must move while using the machine. It shares a number of common features with the other frames, such as the artwork defining the border, the graphics defining the controls, and the displays comprising the summary area.

The term "Functioning Frame" will be used to describe interfaces like the one just described — the interfaces that Trillium can simulate. The key features of this class are:

- frame based control panels
- active controls and displays presented in two-dimensional
- concurrently active controls
- controlled movement among multiple frames

Other interfaces of this class include keyboard-driven menu systems and simple window-based editors.

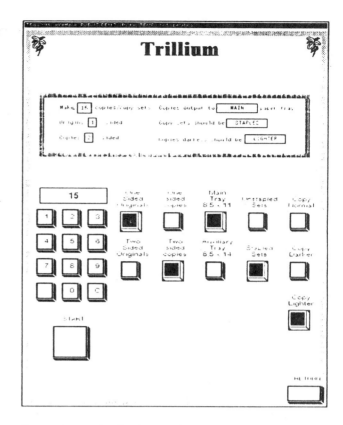

Figure 1: A single frame from an interface for a multi-functional office machine.

Design environments for Functioning Frame interfaces.

A fast prototyping environment for functioning frame interfaces should have the follow characteristics:

From the context of Trillium's conception (see Historical Background above):

1. Design should not require programming: Programming admits specifying much more than interfaces, and is therefore much more fine-grained than is needed for specifying just interfaces. Some formalism for specifying the design which is more specialized to design and reflects design abstractions is needed.

2. Design should be fast: The time required to go around the design/try cycle should be kept as short as possible. Design changes should be immediately affectable, and the ramifications of those changes immediately experienced. A short cycle maintains the designer's focus, and permits more exploration of the design space.

---

2. There are many of these design issues, arising out of the task which it addresses, the technology on which it is built, and the skills and interests of users who employ it. This short paper can focus on only a few of the most important. Also, there are other design environments which address different sets of these issues. A longer paper (in preparation) will explore these in much greater detail and will discuss the relationship of Trillium of other design environment.

3. The environment should support the design of the interface's behavior as well as its presentation: Interfaces are active entities. Fast prototyping must enable experimenting with the behavior of the interface as well as with its visible presentation (looks).

From the nature of the interfaces to be designed[3]:

4. The environment should support two-dimensional controls and displays: The interfaces being designed are based on both physical and electronic displays and controls. These controls must be presented simultaneously and be concurrently active. This will require good graphic support.

5. The environment should support multiple views (presentation and behavior) of the machine: Interfaces break down the presentation of the functionality of the machine into parts, not all of which may be visible at once. For example, on a display-based multi-functional office machine, separate sections may be provided for copying and sending mail. Also, the interface may have different modes: similar presentations of the machine that behave in different ways. For example, when the user is entering an identification code, the number pad buttons control change significance and the other buttons cease to function.

6. The environment should support moving among the views of the machine: The interface may have to supply its user with some way to move around amongst these different views: going deeper into a more detailed description of the job, backing out to a higher level, moving over to another view.

7. Designs should make a clear distinction between machine state and presentation (controls and displays): That the machine behaves implies that it has some sort of internal state. Presentating these states to the user is one of the important functions of the interface. An interface may choose to present this state in many different ways. Also, many different controls may affect the same part of the state. It is therefore important to make a distinction between the state of the machine and its presentation.

8. Designs should support restrictions on, and interactions between, parts of the state of the machine: Certain states may be illegal. Certain changes may occasion other changes. Means for expressing these, and the actions that should be taken when these are detected must be provided. Certain changes may occasion other changes. Means for expressing these dependencies must also be provided.

From the design process:

9. The environment should recognize similarity among the pieces of the interfaces: An interface is made up of many individual pieces for describing controls, presentation and the interactions between parts of the state. Segments are similar to one another, but are different along distinguishable dimensions. (In Figure 1, the buttons are all similar, but each has its own label and effect). The environment should support and make full use of this concept of "similarity through controllable diversity."

10. The environment should support the construction and use of new design abstractions, particularly composition and specialization: The designers at a site develop their own local ways for describing these segments of interfaces. In addition. these design abstractions evolve. A design environment with a fixed set of design abstractions is a conservative force, restricting the designer to describe interfaces with unchangeable terminology. In contrast, an evolving set of abstractions supports a design community in extending its own language of, and thinking about, designs. Two of the simplest mechanisms for creating new abstractions are composition and specialization. Particular configurations when used repeatedly take on a life of their own, with the whole having its own characteristics that determine the characteristics of its parts. Specialization comes from the recognition of a particular configuration of a more general abstraction as having a separate importance of its own.

11. The environment should support incomplete specifications: Given a changing set of design abstractions, it is important for a designer to be able to create an instance of a design abstraction without knowing all the details of its definition. Then those details should be available from that instance for modification as the design progresses.

12. The environment should support sharing of common parts of the interface: There is much that is shared between different parts of any interface of any size. (In the example, the border and the Return button are the same in all frames. Also, the graphic used in all the buttons is the same.) While copying parts provides easy construction, it does not support easy modification of these shared parts.

---

3. Not all interfaces need all of these capabilities. But the environment must enable designers to create interfaces with these alternative characteristics, if for no other reason than to establish that the chosen interface is preferable.

Describing an interface in Trillium

A Trillium interface is composed of a collection of frames. Figure 1 portrays one frame of many in the interface of a multi-functional office machine, one of which is presented at any given time while the interface is operating. Each frame is composed of a collection of items, each of which is of some itemtype. In Figure 1, the collection of controls and displays which supports entering the number of copies is a single item -- a NumberPad. Each itemtype has a set of characteristics. The number pad has a *Placement*, a *Cell*, an *InitialValue*, and so on – 13 in all. Each characteristic has a value type from which Trillium determines how to manipulate values of that characteristic. The value type of *PrintBackground* is "grayshade" which indicates that the designer will want a shade editor to manipulate values of this characterisitc. Specific items are defined by supplying values for some of these characteristics; values not supplied by the designer are filled in with the characteristic's default value. The graphic which is the value of the *Picture* characteristic of the NumberPad is defaulted to *SimpleButtonBitmap*.

The style is that of a child's construction set; the set has pieces (items) of the same kind (itemtype). However, unlike the pieces in a construction set each of which it unchangeable, Trillium items are variable along certain dimensions (the characteristics). It is as though the rods in the set, for example, instead of coming in fixed lengths (and color, etc.), were adjustable in length (and color, etc.). Items are assembled within a frame to create both presentation and behavior. A designer uses the editing tools in Trillium to create, modify and experiment with operator interfaces. Thus the copier frame of Figure 1 is created by laying out a NumberPad, five SetOfVerticalButton's, and then adding some other pieces which constraint the values set by those items. This involves shifting rapidly between editing the interface (designing) and trying it out (operating) to evaluate the effect achieved. This process is supported by interactive window-based editors, as shown in Figure 2.

Itemtypes are either primitive or composite. An item of a composite itemtype defines a sub-assembly of other items; the composite item is expanded into these sub-items. A NumberPad has as subitems twelve buttons of various itemtypes, a PrintRegion, and a NumericInitializer; a button has as subitems a Picture depicting the button, a LineOfText for its label, and a sensor detecting when that area· of the screen is "touched" with the mouse The substance of the

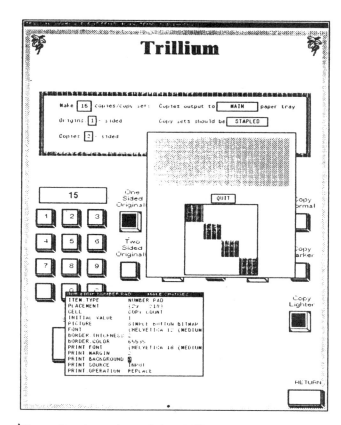

Figure 2:   A portion of the Trillium screen containing an editor for a NumberPad showing its characteristics and their values, and a shade editor being used to modify one of those values.

composite itemtype, therefore, is an explicit description of how the characteristics of the composite item determine the number and individual characteristics of the sub-items of which it is composed. A (little) language of composition is used in making the descriptions. A NumberPad is described in this language as having a characteristic named LabelFont (among others) for controlling the font used in labelling the buttons, and as being composed of (among the other subitems) ten NumberButtons, each of which has, as the value of its characteristic for controlling the label, just exactly the value of the LabelFont characteristic of the NumberPad. Figure 3 shows part of the cascade of items resulting from the expansion of a NumberPad. Trillium also includes editors for manipulating the descriptions of itemtypes, as weel as some simple tools for inferring the description of a composite itemtype from an example - a set of items which together would be the expansion of an item of the new composite itemtype.

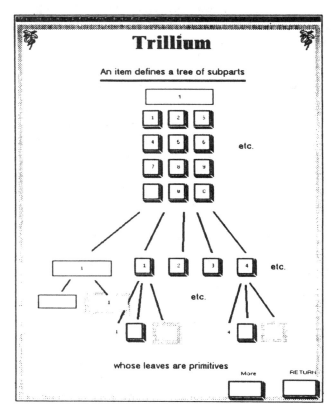

Trillium

An item defines a tree of subparts

etc.

etc.

etc.

whose leaves are primitives

More   RETURN

Figure 3: Part of the cascade of items resulting from the expansion of a NumberPad.

The Trillium Machine

The presentation and behavior of a Trillium interface is defined by the behavior of the items that make up its frames. A composite item derives all its presentation and behavior from its sub-items; primitive items have their presentation and behavior built in. The primitive itemtypes have built into them (as functions in the underlying programming language, Interlisp-D) the visible and behavioral description of the interface. This presentation and behavior is actually realized by an interpreter of the interface, the "Trillium machine." As it "runs" the interface, the Trillium machine need only look at the primitive sub-items resulting from the expansion of all the items in the frame currently being presented.

While running the interface, the Trillium machine creates and modifies a data structure representing the state of the machine being simulated. The state of the machine is given by two things: the frame stack - a push-down stack of frames which have been traversed to get to the current (top of stack) frame; and a collection of cells, each of which has a name and holds a value (a state variable).

The primitive items are divided into six kinds: each kind has a different protocol to which it must respond. The behavior of the interface is determined by the responses of the primitive items to the messages in these protocols.

The first three kinds of primitive item deal with the presentation of the machine:

artwork: the static graphics of the interface. Borders are artwork, as are the pictures which give the illusion of a button.

sensors: items which sense activity in the "world" around the interface, and take some action as a result; actions change the state of the machine, either by changing the frame stack (push - go deeper, pop - go back, or move - go sideways to another frame) or by attempting to change the value of cell. There are sensors which detect the mouse button being pushed within a certain rectangular region of the display; and others which detect the passage of time.

displayers: items which reflect the values of cells onto the display. The Lights "behind" buttons are displayers, as is the PrintRegion in the NumberPad and the PrintRegions making up the summary area.

The second three kinds deal with the behavior of the machine:

initializations: items defining actions to be taken on entry to a frame. The cell referenced by the NumberPad is initialized by a SetInitialValue which is a sub-item of that NumberPad.

inhibitors: items defining restrictions on the values which a cell may take. The cell referenced by the NumberPad has a NumericChecker on it which refuses values over 99; the Sidedness.of.Output cell has an Interaction inhibitor on it which prevents it from taking the value 1 when the Sidedness.of.Input cell has value 2.

implications: items defining actions which must be carried out to propagate effects. The Sidedness.of.Input cell has a ConditionalPropogator implication on it which sets the value of the Sidedness.of.Output cell to 2 whenever the value of Sidedness.of.Input cell is changed to 2.

The Trillium Machine runs a frame by looking at all the primitive items in the frame — the items which are the leaves of the tree of the expansion of composites (see Figure 3).

The Trillium Machine works as follows:

- on entry to a frame:
    - run each initialization (initializes the machine state for that frame).
    - run each artwork (sets up the static graphic background for the frame).
    - run each displayer (presents the values of the cells).
    - until the state indicates that it is time to change frames, repeatedly:
        - run each sensor (senses the world) and actions are taken (responds to the sensors).
- to take an action, either:
    - call for a frame change — push (go deeper), pop (go back), or move (go sideways); this is done by setting the indicator in the state which is tested in the sensor loop (see above), or
    - attempt to change the value of a cell:
        - do nothing if the new value is the same as the value that is there (prevents useless changes, and breaks loops in propagating values among mutually constrained cells).
        - run each inhibitor associated with the cell (check that the value is acceptable).
        - set the new value into the cell (the change is finally made).
        - run each displayer associated with the cell (presents the new value of the cell).
        - run each implication associated with the cell (propagates effects of the change by taking further actions).

Trillium's Language of Design

Because presentation and behavior are determined entirely by the assembly of items of particular itemtypes, the language of design within Trillium is determined by the collection of itemtypes. One advantage of this is that the language can evolve by creating and modifying itemtypes. To support such evolution, designers are given tools to create new composite itemtypes. Also, new primitive itemtypes can be added by the supporters (programming in Interlisp-D), thus extending the very nature of the interfaces being described (eg. to handle new input devices - dials, or output devices - color display). This evolution of the terminology of design reflects conceptual development within the design community. For example, over time, the notion of NumberPad might change to reflect new requirements on design, such as that the layout of the buttons be variable to permit the NumberPad embedding in physical spaces of differing shape and size.

Sharing parts of a design

To share information, any frame can be given other frames, called superframes, which act as its backdrop. Superframes can have items of all kinds in them, so they impart behavior as well as presentation. Thus the frame of Figure 1 contains the buttons and the number pad, and has two superframes: the Border frame which contains the artwork around the edge, and the ChangeFrameButton label Return (this insures that it is consistently in the same place in all frames); and the Summary frame, containing the PrintRegions and artwork of the summary.

The sharing of graphical information (such as bitmaps) and reference infomration (such as colors) is accomplished with the use of service frames. These frames are used solely for storing information about shared items, and are not seen by the user during the operation of the interface. By changing these referenced items, all the items which refer to them are indirectly changed in concert, thereby maintaining consistency.

Trillium as a design environment for Functioning Frame interfaces

The criteria set out earlier for a design environment for Function Frame interfaces can now be matched against Trillium's structure and capabilities:

1. Design should not require programming: In most cases, it doesn't. Items are just placed appropriately, and they interact through the cells they reference. The behavior is built into the primitive items into which they expand.

2. Design should be fast: Creating new items takes at most minutes. The elapsed time from completion of a bit of design to experimenting with the effect is the time taken to move the finger on the mouse from the design button to the one that requests that the interface be run.

3. The environment should support the design of the interface's behavior as well as its presentation: Five of the six kinds of primitive item have active behavior built in. Composites have whatever behavior their sub-items have. Interacting behaviors (eg. the interactions of the various functions of a NumberPad) result in the higher level abstractions encompassing more complex behaviors.

4. The environment should support two-dimensional controls and displays: It does because the presentation primitive kinds (artwork, sensors and displayers) do so (see more below, concerning the embedding of Trillium in interlisp-D.)

5. The environment should support multiple views (presentation and behavior) of the machine: Frame support different views of the same collection of cells.

6. The environment should support moving among the views of the machine: The frame stack supports motion among frames.

7. Designs should make clear distinction between machine state and presentation (controls and displays): The presentation primitive kinds (artwork, sensors and displayers) are distinct from the behavior primitive kinds (initiations, inhibitors and implications)

8. Designs should support restrictions on, and interactions between, parts of the state of the machine: The inhibitors and implications do this.

9. The environment should recognize similarity among the pieces of the interfaces: Items are instances of itemtypes. Itemtypes capture similarity through their different characteristics.

10. The environment should support the construction and use of new design abstractions, particularly composition and specialization: Composite itemtypes capture constrained sets of sub-items as forming interesting abstractions. Specialization is achieved by having a more general item be the sole sub-item of the specialization, masking some of the variability by setting the values of some of the characteristics of the more general abstraction within the expansion process.

11. The environment should support incomplete specifications: Characteristics of itemtypes have default values which are used in items when values are not explicitly specified by the designer. When initially created (as opposed to copied), all of the characteristics have default values. The designer creates an item to learn what its characteristics are, and then by experimenting with the values, discovers the range of its functionality.

12. The environment should support sharing of common parts of the interface: Superframes may be shared among other frames. Service frames provide for sharing of information in terms of which other items are defined.

In addition to meeting these criteria, the acceptance and use of Trillium within Xerox argues that it is a successful design environment for Functioning Frame interfaces. Trillium is in use at more than half a dozen sites within Xerox located on two continents. Most of the interfaces for the next generation of machines has been affected by experiments using Trillium. Some of them have been entirely designed using the tool. In one case, automatic transportation of interface designs out of the (Lisp-based) Trillium design environment into the final (non-Lisp) product has even been achieved[4].

In short, the design of Trillium has been driven by the needs of fast prototyping, the interfaces to be designed, and the design process itself. By restricting attention to only the "Functioning Frame" interfaces, Trillium provides designers with a powerful tool for fast prototyping. This tool is in use with Xerox for designing interfaces for copies and printers. The ability to fast prototype has changed the quality of interfaces produced by both permitting early experience with the interface to expose problems with the design, and by permitting exploration of more of the space of possible designs.

Acknowledgements

Although originating from research at Xerox PARC, Trillium is now used, maintained and enhanced by the Trillium Community, an informal confederation of designers, supporters, trainers, researchers and management from many organizations within Xerox, all of whom are responsible for making Trillium what it is today. Also, my thanks to Bill Anderson for commenting on an earlier draft of this paper.

References

Henderson, D. Austin, Jr., Trillium: A design Environment for Copier Interfaces, videotape, CHI'83, Boston, MA. December, 1983.

---

4. Trillium is written in Interlisp-D, running on the Xerox 1100 series processors. Interlisp-D provides interactive graphics, symbolic representation, and an "escape clause" to programming when appropriate Trillium itemtypes are not available.

O·B·J·E·C·T-O·R·I·E·N·T·E·D L·A·N·G·U·A·G·E·S

MACAPP: AN APPLICATION FRAMEWORK

BY KURT J. SCHMUCKER

This application can significantly reduce Macintosh program development time

ONE FASCINATING and potentially far-reaching use of object-oriented programming is in the design of an application framework for a personal computer or workstation. Several examples of such frameworks exist, such as the Lisa Toolkit, discussed in "Software Frameworks" by Gregg Williams (December 1984 BYTE), and more are being designed all the time. This article examines one specific application framework for the Macintosh, MacApp—The Expandable Macintosh Application from Apple.

The average end user does not generally use or even know about application frameworks. They are tools for developers who design the software for end users. In theory, an application framework can be developed for any personal computer. However, they are especially useful on those with a well-defined user-interface specification.

WHAT IS MACAPP?

The MacApp framework is basically a complete, self-contained application that implements most of the Macintosh user-interface standard. It has

menus that pull down and windows that scroll and can be moved about the screen, it works correctly with desk accessories and with Switcher, and it prints on the Imagewriter and the LaserWriter. The only things missing from a complete application are the contents of the windows and the items on the menus. An application framework is only the shell of a real application—a shell that you can easily customize into a true application. This customization process differentiates an application framework from a set of merely useful subroutines.

For example, let's examine the way in which an application framework supports undoing commands. MacApp knows that after you choose a menu command, the Undo command should reverse the effect of the command. But a general application framework can't know how to undo, or do, all the commands. These operations are accomplished with the dynamic binding present in an object-oriented language. The application framework "knows" about command objects and it knows that when a command is to be performed or undone,

it should send the message DoIt or UndoIt to the current command object. The application framework defines the basic skeleton of the application, but it leaves the specifics—for example, the actual details of undoing the Double Space command—to the command object. To build a specific application from this framework, you need to design only the objects that perform these specific actions and then install them into the framework.

The framework knows in general what a Macintosh application is supposed to do. It knows how to make the menus work, how to give up control when a desk accessory is activated, how to scroll windows, and so on—all the things that are common to

(continued)

Kurt J. Schmucker, director of educational services for Productivity Products International (Severna Park Mall, H & R Block Office, 575 Richie Highway, Severna Park, MD 21146), teaches seminars on object-oriented programming. Kurt has written three books on computer science, including the forthcoming Object-oriented Programming for the Macintosh *(Hayden, 1986).*

Macintosh applications. The framework knows that the most recent command should be undone when you choose the Undo menu item and that the current selection should be highlighted when you activate a window. However, it doesn't know how to reverse the actions of particular commands or how to highlight the current selection. The *objects* you install in your customization of the application framework determine these actions. For example, to undo the last command, the application framework sends the message UndoIt to the current command object. The dynamic binding of this UndoIt message to a method at run time invokes the routine you have designed to handle undoing this particular command. The application framework proceeds without knowing what that command, or that selection, really is.

The application framework is more than just a skeleton with a fixed number of pluggable slots for commands and selection. Using the techniques of object-oriented programming, you can override every major decision (and many minor ones). Any application on this framework can take control at any decision point in the program by overriding the preprogrammed method to perform a user-written application-specific method.

To give it this flexibility, the application framework is set up as a group of classes, or class library, that you can use and specialize while developing a new application. If you want your application to behave in some unique, specific way, you can add some new objects into the framework to provide this behavior. If you don't want anything unusual, the application framework will handle the application correctly as is.

THE BASIC STRUCTURE OF MACAPP

The class library that is MacApp contains more than 30 different classes and over 450 methods. (Figure 1 shows the inheritance structure of these classes.) However, if you understand the operation of just three of these classes—TApplication, TDocument, and TView—and seven of their methods, you will be able to build your own application on top of the MacApp framework. The class TApplication takes care of things that are the responsibility of the application as a whole. This includes launching the application, setting up the menu bar, deciding which documents to display in the ''Open Which Document?''

(continued)

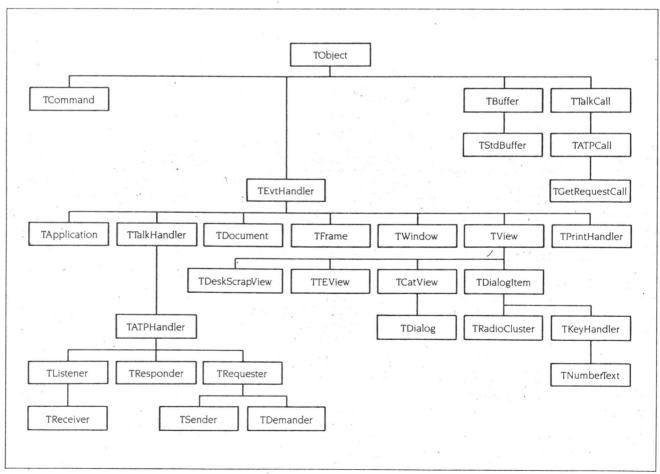

Figure 1: *The inheritance tree of the MacApp classes.*

dialog box, and so on. You design your own special subclass of TApplication, overriding whatever methods you choose in order to specialize any of these behaviors. One behavior you must always override is the type of document that holds your application's data (the method DoMakeDocument).

The class TDocument processes commands like Save and Close, which are specific to each of the documents that are open at any one instant. (MacApp applications can usually deal with multiple documents being open at once.) Two behaviors that you must override in your subclasses of TDocument are the types of windows that display the data stored in the document (the method DoMakeWindows) and the contents of the windows (the method DoMakeViews). (The DoMake-something MacApp methods are the ones you *must* override.)

The class TView takes care of everything inside your windows—drawing the images, highlighting the selection, handling mouse interaction with those images, and other things. TView knows when a portion of the window needs to be redrawn and when the selection should be highlighted. It doesn't know exactly how to do these things. It relies on you to override the methods that supply these behaviors in your subclasses of TView. These methods are Draw, Highlight-Selection, and DoMouseCommand.

DEVELOPING AN APPLICATION

To develop a MacApp application, you must design your own subclasses of TApplication, TDocument, and TView. It is traditional in MacApp programming to name these new subclasses so that you can easily determine their respective superclasses. Therefore, I have used the names TSmallApplication (a subclass of TApplication), TSmallDocument (a subclass of TDocument), and TSmallView (a subclass of TView). The application is called SmallApplication, and its entire source code requires only 87 lines of Object Pascal. (For a discussion of Object Pascal and other object-oriented languages, see my article "Object-oriented Languages for the Macintosh" on page 177.) Two printouts of screen shots from SmallApplication are shown in figures 2 and 3. [Editor's note: *The entire source listing for SmallApplication is available in a variety of formats. See page 405 for details.*] Let's look at two representative methods from this application—the DoMakeViews method of the class TSmallDocument and the Draw method of TSmallView.

DoMakeViews is one of the methods MacApp needs to access one of the classes designed specifically for SmallApplication. I call this kind of method a MacApp *hook* method. Listing 1 contains the full text of SmallApplication's DoMakeViews method. This method generates, initializes, and installs one instance of TSmallView. MacApp sends the message DoMakeViews precisely so it can obtain one of these and use it to draw inside the window. If this method seems rather short, that is a common characteristic of object-oriented programs, especially those

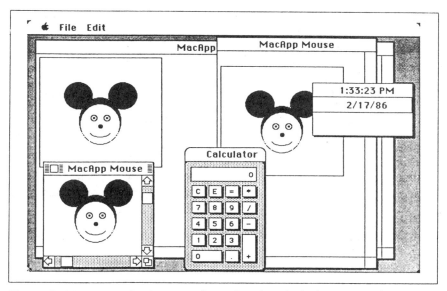

Figure 2: *SmallApplication—the smallest MacApp application.*

Figure 3: *MacApp applications typically work with multiple documents and always work correctly with desk accessories, even multiple ones.*

Listing 1: *The full text of* DoMakeViews.

```
PROCEDURE TSmallDocument.DoMakeViews(forPrinting: BOOLEAN); OVERRIDE;
VAR smallView: TSmallView;
BEGIN
   NEW(smallView);                { Create a new instance of TSmallView }
   smallView.ISmallView(SELF);    { Send new view object its init message }
   SELF.fSmallView := smallView;  { Install this view object in document }
END;
```

Listing 2: A *procedure that overrides* TSmallView's Draw *method to draw a picture of a mouse.*

```
PROCEDURE TSmallView.Draw(area: Rect); OVERRIDE;

   FUNCTION MakeRect(top, left, bottom, right: INTEGER): Rect;
   VAR r: Rect;
   BEGIN
      SetRect(r, left, top, right, bottom);
      MakeRect := r;
   END;

BEGIN
   PenNormal;
   PaintOval(MakeRect(74, 72, 139, 127));    { Outline of the mouse head }
   EraseOval(MakeRect(84, 74, 138, 125));    { Outline of the mouse face }
   FrameOval(MakeRect(109, 84, 129, 115));   { Mouse mouth (part 1 of 2) }
   EraseRect(MakeRect(109, 84, 123, 115));   { Mouse mouth (part 2 of 2) }
   FrameOval(MakeRect(98, 87, 107, 96));     { Left eye }
   FrameOval(MakeRect(98, 104, 107, 113));   { Right eye }
   PaintOval(MakeRect(101, 90, 104, 93));    { Left pupil }
   PaintOval(MakeRect(101, 107, 104, 110));  { Right pupil }
   PaintOval(MakeRect(111, 97, 117, 103));   { Nose }
   PaintOval(MakeRect(53, 52, 91, 90));      { Left ear }
   PaintOval(MakeRect(53, 110, 91, 148));    { Right ear }

   FrameRect(MakeRect(20, 20, 170, 180));    { A bounding rectangle }

END;
```

designed to be overridden for many different purposes. Instead of hard coding many decisions, the designer of a class will make each such decision a method. You can change such a decision by creating subclasses and overriding the appropriate method.

The Draw method of the TSmallView class is a method for which MacApp cannot possibly provide a generic version. You can't draw anything in a window that would be useful to all Macintosh applications. In such cases, MacApp provides a stub method that does nothing, a *null* method. You don't have to override a null method like you do a hook method, but if you don't override this one, part of your application may appear to do nothing. The code in listing 2 overrides TSmallView's Draw method to draw a picture of a mouse. If you continue this process for five

other methods, you will have developed SmallApplication, an application that draws a picture of a mouse. SmallApplication is a stand-alone Mac application that works correctly on 128K-byte and 512K-byte Macs, the new Mac Plus, and the Mac XL. It works with Switcher and with any number of desk accessories, prints on the Imagewriter and the LaserWriter, supports multiple documents, and allows you to resize and move windows and use menus. As trivial as the application itself may seem, it does illustrate the flexibility of the MacApp framework.

THE BENEFITS AND COSTS OF USING MACAPP

Early studies indicate that MacApp can reduce application development time by a factor of four or five. MacApp also decreases the amount of source code you need, again by a

factor of four or five. It maintains consistency with respect to the Macintosh user-interface standard and provides error handling and an interactive debugging facility, which are useful during development. It provides a conceptual framework that lets you concentrate on your application rather than on Macintosh internals.

Some feel that these gains are at the expense of performance in the finished application and of a large amount of additional memory. In fact, many MacApp programs actually run faster than their non-MacApp versions, despite the run-time overhead of messaging. MacApp applications are usually somewhat larger than their non-MacApp versions—about 10K to 15K bytes. But for most end-user applications, this is not a large penalty when weighed against the decrease in development time. ∎

Creating Highly-Interactive and Graphical User Interfaces by Demonstration

Brad A. Myers
and
William Buxton

Dynamic Graphics Project
Computer Systems Research Institute
University of Toronto
Toronto, Ontario, M5S 1A4
Canada

ABSTRACT

It is very time-consuming and expensive to create the graphical, highly-interactive styles of user interfaces that are increasingly common. User Interface Management Systems (UIMSs) attempt to make the creation of user interfaces easier, but most existing UIMSs cannot create the low-level interaction techniques (pop-up, pull-down and fixed menus, on-screen "light buttons", scroll-bars, elaborate feedback mechanisms and animations, etc.) that are frequently used. This paper describes Peridot, a system that automatically creates the code for these user interfaces while the designer *demonstrates* to the system how the interface should look and work. Peridot uses rule-based inferencing so no programming by the designer is required, and Direct Manipulation techniques are used to create Direct Manipulation interfaces, which can make full use of a mouse and other input devices. This allows extremely rapid prototyping of user interfaces.

CR Categories and Subject Descriptors: D.1.2 [**Programming Techniques**]: Automatic Programming; D.2.2 [**Software Engineering**]: Tools and Techniques - *User Interfaces*; I.2.2 [**Artificial Intelligence**]: Automatic Programming - *Program Synthesis*; I.3.6 [**Computer Graphics**]: Methodology and Techniques.

General Terms: Human Factors.

Additional Key Words and Phrases: Programming by Example, Visual Programming, User Interface Design, User Interface Management Systems, Graphical User Interfaces, Direct Manipulation.

1. Introduction

This paper discusses Peridot, a new User Interface Management System (UIMS) currently under development, that can create graphical, highly interactive user interfaces. Peridot stands for <u>P</u>rogramming by <u>E</u>xample for <u>R</u>eal-time <u>I</u>nterface <u>D</u>esign <u>O</u>bviating <u>T</u>yping. It is implemented in Interlisp-D [Xerox 83] on a Xerox DandeTiger (1109) workstation, and allows the user interface designer to create user interfaces by *demonstrating* what the user interface should look like and how the end user will interact with it. This approach frees designers from having to do any programming in the conventional sense, and allows them to design the user interface in a very natural manner. The general strategy of Peridot is to allow the designer to *draw* the screen display that the end user will see, and to perform actions just as the end user would, such as moving a mouse, or pressing a mouse button or keyboard key. The system attempts to guess (or *infer*) the relationship of that action to existing elements of the user interface based on context, and asks the designer if the guess is correct. If so, a piece of code is generated by the system that will handle this action for the end user. If incorrect, other reasonable guesses are tried, or the designer can explicitly specify the relationship.

The guesses are encoded as simple condition-action rules, and the generated code is put into small parameterized procedures to help ensure a structured design of the resulting system. The screen displays and interactions depend on the values of the parameters to the procedures. The procedures created by Peridot can be called from application programs or used in other user interface procedures created by demonstration.

Many user interface designers now draw, typically on paper, scenarios (or "story boards") of how the user interface (UI) will look and act. Unfortunately, it is difficult to get a feeling for how a system works from the paper descriptions, and customers of the user interface are not able to investigate how the system will work. Peridot enhances the design process by supporting extremely rapid prototyping with little more effort than drawing the scenarios on paper. In addition, the user interfaces produced by Peridot are expected to be efficient enough for use in the actual end systems.

Another motivation for this style of specifying user interfaces is that it should be possible to allow non-programmers to design *and implement* the interfaces. This will allow professional UI designers (sometimes called "User Interface Architects" [Foley 84]) and possibly even end users, to design and modify user interfaces with little training and without conventional programming. Virtually all textual UI specification methods are too complicated and program-like to be used by non-programmers [Buxton 83].

The *Direct Manipulation* style of user interfaces [Shneiderman 83][Hutchins 86], where the user typically uses a mouse to select and manipulate objects on the screen, has become very popular (and possibly even predominant) for modern computer systems. Unfortunately, there are virtually no tools available to help develop the low level interaction techniques that support these interfaces, so almost all are laboriously programmed using conventional programming languages. It is well documented in the literature how expensive this process is [Williams 83][Smith 82]. This limits the amount of prototyping possible, and therefore the quality of the interfaces. Existing tools to help build user interfaces, called User Interface Management Systems (UIMSs) [Thomas 83][Olsen 84][Pfaff 85], have not provided a powerful and flexible way to conveniently generate the interaction techniques for these styles of interfaces. In particular, few systems have allowed Direct Manipulation techniques to be used to create the interfaces [Shneiderman 86].

All UIMSs are restricted in the forms of user interfaces they can generate [Tanner 85]. Peridot is only aimed at graphical, Direct Manipulation interfaces. For example, Peridot should be able to create interfaces like those of the Apple Macintosh [Williams 84]. Peridot does not help with textual command interfaces or with the coding of the semantics of the application. The set of interfaces it will produce is rich enough, however, to be very interesting and of practical use for commercial systems.

In summary, the goals of Peridot are that:

1) interaction techniques for Direct Manipulation interfaces should be supported,

2) the system should be easy to use for the designer and require little or no training,

3) the designer should not have to write programs,

4) the interface should be visible at all times as it is developed and changes should be immediately apparent,

5) the *behavior* of the interface should also be created in a Direct Manipulation manner and it should run in real time (points 4 and 5 provide for extremely rapid prototyping), and

6) the system should create run-time code that is efficient enough for use in actual application programs.

This paper presents the design and implementation of the demonstrational aspects of Peridot. A longer report providing more detail and covering other aspects is in preparation [Myers prep]. Throughout this paper, the term "designer" is used for the person creating user interfaces (and therefore using Peridot). The term "user" (or "end user") is reserved for the person using the interface created by the designer.

2. Background and Related Work

Tanner and Buxton [Tanner 85] present a model of User Interface Management Systems that identifies a number of separate parts (see Figure 1). Peridot is aimed mainly at the "module builder" aspects, but it also covers the "system glue" and "run-time support" components.

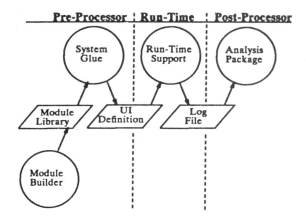

Figure 1.
Model for User Interface Management Systems (from [Tanner 85]).

The "module builder" creates a library of specific interaction techniques. Some systems, such as the Macintosh ToolBox [Apple 85] and the routines that come with most modern window managers [Myers 84][Tesler 81], are essentially the library portion by itself. Using a library has the advantage that the final UI will look and act similarly to other UIs created using the same library, but clearly the styles of interaction available are limited to those provided. In addition, the libraries themselves are often expensive to create. A few UIMSs, such as Syngraph [Olsen 83] and Squeak [Cardelli 85], are designed to help with the creation of the interaction techniques that make up the library, but the indirect and abstract methods used by these programs have proved difficult to use. Peridot attempts to make this process more direct.

Many (probably most) UIMSs concentrate on combining ("gluing") the modules together after they have been created, since it is often non-trivial to write the programs that coordinate the interaction techniques. This is evidenced by the need for the MacApp system to help write programs that use the Macintosh ToolBox. Some, such as Menulay [Buxton 83] and Trillium [Henderson 86], allow the designer to see the design as it is created, but most require that the specification be in a textual language (e.g. [Hayes 85][Jacob 85]). Although a number of modern UIMSs allow the layout of the screen to be specified in a Direct Manipulation manner, virtually all still require the interaction to be specified in an abstract, indirect way, such as using state transition networks. Peridot allows Direct Manipulation to be used for both.

The power in Peridot comes from the use of a new approach to user interface design. The principles of *Programming by Example* and *Visual Programming* have been adapted to allow the designer to demonstrate the desired user interface graphically. These principles are defined, and a comprehensive taxonomy of existing systems that use them is presented, in [Myers 86]. "Visual Programming" (VP) refers to systems that allow the specification of programs using graphics. "Programming by Example" (PBE) systems attempt to infer programs from examples of the data that the program should process. This inferencing is either based on examples of input-output pairs [Shaw 75][Nix 86], or traces of program execution [Bauer 78][Biermann 76b]. Some systems that allow the programmer to develop programs using specific examples do not use inferencing [Halbert 81 and 84][Lieberman 82][Smith 77]. For example, SmallStar [Halbert 84] allows users to write programs for the Xerox Star office workstation by simply performing the normal commands and adding control flow afterwards. Visual Programming systems, such as Rehearsal World [Gould 84], have been successful in making programs more visible and understandable and therefore easier to create by novices.

Peridot differs from these UIMSs and programming systems in that it applies Programming by Example and Visual Programming to the specific domain of graphical user interface specification. Tinker [Lieberman 82] has similar aims, but it does not provide inferencing, and code is specified in a conventional, textual manner in LISP. Early inferencing systems were rather unsuccessful since they often guessed the wrong program and it was difficult for the programmer to check the results without thoroughly studying the code [Biermann 76a]. In limited domains, PBE has been more successful, for example, for editing in the Editing by Example system [Nix 86]. Other systems that are relevant to the design of Peridot are those, such as [Pavlidis 85], that try to "beautify" pictures by inferring relationships among the picture elements (such as parallel and perpendicular) and modifying the picture to incorporate them.

3. Sample of Peridot in Action

The best way to demonstrate how easy it is to create a user interface with Peridot is to work through an example. Due to space limitations, we will take a simple interaction: a menu of strings. The operations discussed in this example will be further explained in the following sections. First, however, we present the Peridot screen.

When using Peridot, the designer sees three windows and a menu (see Figure 2). The menu, which is on the left, is used to give commands to Peridot. The window at the top shows the name of the current procedure, the name of its arguments, and *examples* of typical values for those arguments. The window in the center shows what the user will see as a result of this procedure (the end user interface), and the window at the bottom is used for prompting the designer and for messages. For debugging Peridot itself (and for the very few designers that will be interested), the system can be configured to display the generated code in a fourth window. Currently this code is presented in LISP, but creating a more readable form is possible in the future. The displayed procedure and the picture are always kept consistent, so if the picture is edited, the code is changed, and when the code changes, the picture is also updated. It is not necessary for the designer to view or use the code to perform any operations in Peridot.

Figure 3 shows the steps that can be used to create a procedure that handles a menu with a grey drop shadow. First, the designer types the name for the procedure, ("MyMenu"), the name for the parameters ("Items"), and an example of a typical value for each parameter (the list: ("Replace", "Move", "Copy", "Delete", "Delete All", "Help", "Abort", "Undo", "Exit")). Next, the designer draws a grey box for the shadow and then a black box for the background slightly offset from it (see Figure 3a). These commands are given using the Peridot command menu and a mouse. The system guesses that the black box should be the same size as the grey one and at an offset of 7 in X and Y. The designer confirms that this is correct. Next, (in Figure 3b)

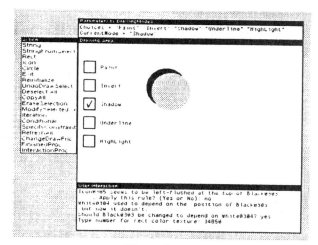

Figure 2.

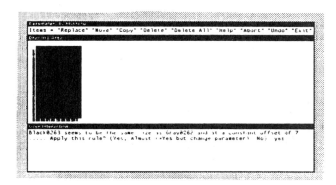

Figure 3a.

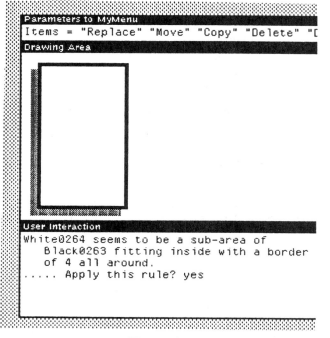

Figure 3b.

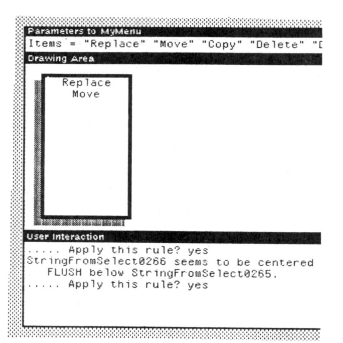

Figure 3c.

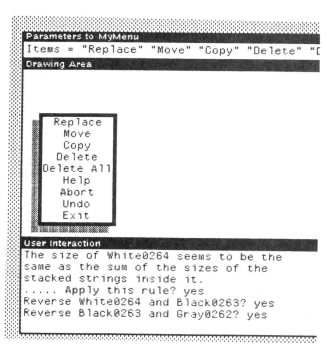

Figure 3e.

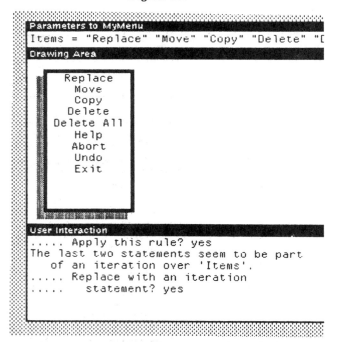

Figure 3d.

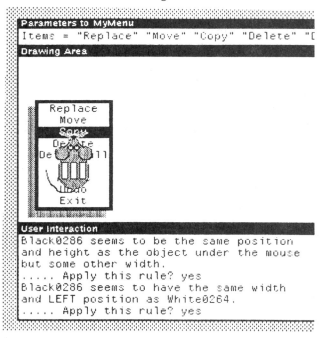

Figure 3f.

A sequence of frames during the definition of a menu interaction technique. (The pictures for 3b-3f have been expanded to be more readable.) In 3a, the shadow and background are drawn (and the system infers that they should be the same size). In 3b, a white area is nested inside the background, and in 3c the first two elements of the parameter are copied to the top of the white rectangle. Peridot notices that they are stacked vertically, and that they are part of an iteration. The rest of the iteration is executed in 3d. The size of the white rectangle is then changed to be just big enough to include all the strings and the system changes the black and grey rectangles accordingly 3e. In 3f, the interaction is being defined using the "simulated mouse."

a white box inside the black one is drawn, and the system adjusts it to be a constant 4 pixels all around, after confirmation from the designer. Next, (in Figure 3c) the first item in the argument ("Replace") is copied to the top of the white rectangle, and the system asks if it should be centered at the top. Peridot makes this assumption because the string was placed approximately centered in the box, as shown in Figure 3c. If the string had been placed left-justified in the box instead, then Peridot would have asked if the string should be left-justified. The system asks the designer to confirm every assumption because sometimes the placing is ambiguous. Next, the second string, "Move", is copied below "Replace" and the system guesses that it is also centered. Since the first two elements of a list have been placed on the screen, the system guesses that the entire list might be desired, so it asks the designer if there should be an iteration to display all elements of the list. After the designer confirms this (in Figure 3d), the system executes the rest of the iteration and changes the code to be a loop. Finally, (in Figure 3e) the designer adjusts the size of the white rectangle to be approximately the size of the strings, and the system asks if the rectangle should be adjusted to fit exactly around all the strings. The sizes of the black and grey rectangles are then automatically adjusted to be proportional to the size of the white rectangle. This completes the presentation aspects of the menu (Figure 3e). It should be remembered that the code being generated does not depend on the specific example values for the parameter; any list of strings will work correctly.

To specify the *interaction* (behavior) of the user interface for the menu, the designer uses an icon that represents the mouse. First, this "simulated mouse" is moved over one of the menu items, and then the designer draws a black rectangle over that item in INVERT drawing mode (see Figure 3f). Peridot infers that the box should be the same height and Y position as the string, and the same width and X position as the white box. The designer then moves the simulated mouse off to the side and erases the black rectangle. Peridot infers that the box should be erased when the mouse is no longer over an object. The designer can perform this action on another string, or explicitly specify an iteration, and the code that handles highlighting is completed. Now the designer "presses" one of the simulated mouse's buttons and specifies, using a Peridot command, that the object under the mouse is returned. From this, the system infers that the procedure should be exited upon button press. The MyMenu procedure is now complete.

Although the textual description of the designer's actions is clumsy, only about ten actions had to be performed to create this procedure (plus confirming Peridot's 12 guesses). Once created, the picture or interaction can be edited, and the menu can used as part of other user interfaces.

4. General Principles of Peridot

One problem with all demonstrational systems is that the user's actions are almost always ambiguous. The system cannot usually know *why* the person did a particular action. This is especially true when the system attempts to infer a general case from a particular example. For instance, when an item is selected, does the user mean that particular item, an item with a similar name, an item at that particular place on the screen, an item with the

same type as the selected one, or an item with some other property? Early inferencing systems attempted to solve this problem by guessing and requiring the user to go back later and check the generated code. Non-inferencing systems, such as Halbert's system for the Xerox STAR workstation [Halbert 81 and 84], require the user to explicitly specify why objects were chosen. Peridot, on the other hand, tries to guess what the designer intends by an action, but, to avoid the problems of earlier systems, it always asks the designer if each guess is correct. It is expected that the guesses will usually be correct, which will save the designer from having to specify a great deal of extra detail and from having to know a programming language to express those details. In addition, it is easy to check for errors since the results of all actions and inferences are always immediately visible on the screen.

Any graphical user interface is composed of two parts: the *presentation* or layout, which defines what pictures are on the screen, and the *interaction* or behavior, which determines how these pictures change with user actions. As shown in the previous example, these are specified separately in Peridot. The pictures that Peridot currently supports are: rectangles filled with various grey shades, text strings, filled circles, and static pictures drawn with other programs (e.g. icons)[1].

Peridot uses inferencing in three different ways. First, it tries to infer how various objects in the scene are related graphically. When the designer draws an object, it usually has some implied relation with other objects that have already been drawn. For example, a box might be nested inside another box, or a text string centered at the top of a box. If the picture was simply a static background that never changed, it would not be important for the system to notice these relationships. In Peridot, however, the pictures usually depend on the parameters to the procedure that generate them. For example, the size of the box around a menu might depend on the number of items in the menu and the width of the largest item. Peridot must therefore infer the meaningful relationships among objects from the drawings that the designer produces. This object-object inferencing is described in section 5.1.

The second type of inferencing used by Peridot is to try to guess when control structures are needed. For example, when the designer displays the first two elements of a list, Peridot infers that the entire list should be displayed and will generate an iteration. Conditionals are also inferred for special cases and exceptions. For example, a check-mark might be displayed to show the current value of a set of choices (as in Figure 2). Iterations and conditionals are discussed in sections 5.2 and 5.3 respectively.

The final type of inferencing used by Peridot is to try to guess when actions should happen during the execution of an interaction. For example, a highlight bar might be displayed when the left mouse button goes down. This type of inferencing is described in section 6.

---

[1] Straight and curved lines, and individual pixels should be easy to add in the future, if needed.

5. Specifying the Presentation of a User Interface

When specifying the presentation of a user interface, the designer is mainly interested in placing graphics on the screen. During this process, however, Peridot is constantly watching the objects to see what object-object relationships there are, and whether some objects drawn would properly be part of an iteration or conditional.

The designer may draw an object on top of another object. Depending on the drawing function in use, the second object may obscure parts of the first object. This is obvious in Figure 3e, where the black rectangle obscures some of the grey rectangle, the white rectangle obscures part of the black one, and the text obscures part of the white one. For this reason, Peridot never changes the order for drawing objects (although the designer is allowed to do this, of course). The calculation order may be changed, however, if a property of an object to be drawn later is needed. For example, in Figure 3e, the width of the strings are needed to calculate the width of the white rectangle even though the rectangle must be drawn first. Peridot insures that the calculation is done in the correct order before the drawing commences.

5.1. *Inferring Object-Object Relationships*

The object-object relationships that are inferred deal with the position and size properties of the objects. The other properties (color, value, font, etc.) are assumed to be constant unless the designer explicitly specifies that they should depend on some other object or parameter. In the example of section 3 above, the colors of the rectangles were constant, but the values for the strings were explicitly specified to depend on the parameter "Items" (by selecting "Replace" and "Move" in the parameter window and using the "StringFromSelect" menu command).

Each object-object relationship that can be inferred is represented in Peridot as a simple *condition-action rule*. Each rule has a test that determines if the relationship is appropriate (the *condition*), a message to be used to ask the designer whether the rule should be applied, and an *action* to cause the objects to conform to the rule. The Appendix lists some sample rules from Peridot. The rules are currently expressed in LISP so the designer will not be able to add new rules. It is very easy, however, for a LISP programmer to modify the rule set.

Since the rules specify very low level relationships (e.g. that a string should be centered inside a box), there appear to be a small number of rules required to handle existing interfaces. In an informal survey of a number of Direct Manipulation interfaces, about 50 rules seemed to be sufficient. In order to allow for human imprecision, however, some leeway must be given to the designer as to the placement and size of objects, so the drawings will not be exact. For example, the designer may want one box to be inside another box with a border of 3 pixels all around, but actually draw it with a border of 5 on one side and 2 on another. Therefore the tests in Peridot for whether to apply a particular rule have thresholds of applicability. Unfortunately, this means that the same drawing may pass more than one test. The *conflict resolution strategy* is simply to order the tests based on restrictiveness (the most demanding tests are first) and based on the heuristically determined likelihood of their being appropriate. This ordering is changed based on the types of the objects being tested, since, for example, it is much more likely for a text string to be centered at the top of a box than for another box to be.

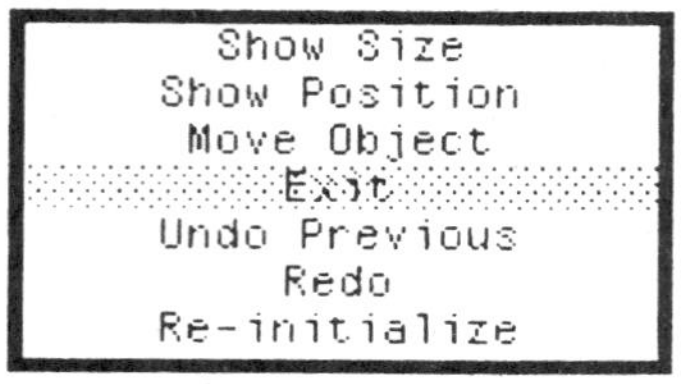

Figure 4.
The grey rectangle is the same height and Y position as the string "Exit" and the same width and X position as the white rectangle.

When the designer draws an object and a rule's test succeeds, Peridot queries the designer whether to apply the rule using the rule's message (see the lower window in Figures 3a-3f). If the system has guessed wrong, the designer answers "no" and the system will try to find a different rule that applies. If the system is correct, the designer may still want to modify parameters of the rule. For example, the system may decide that a box is inside another box with a border of 13 pixels all around, and the designer may decide to use 15 pixels instead. Of course, it may be the case that no rule is found or that the appropriate rule is skipped because the designer has been too sloppy in the original drawing and the rule's test fails. In this case, the designer will usually modify the drawing so that the test will succeed, but it is also possible to explicitly pick a rule to apply.

Most rules in Peridot relate one object to one other existing object[2]. The designer can explicitly specify two objects to apply rules to, but normally the relationships are inferred automatically when an object is created. In this case, the other (existing) object is found by searching through all the other objects in a certain order. When defining the *presentation* of the user interface, the order is: (1) the selected object (the designer can explicitly select an object to apply the rules to), (2) the previous object that was created, and (3) the objects in the vicinity of the new object. When defining the *interaction* portion of the user interface, the order for checking is: (1) the selected object, (2) the object under the simulated pointing devices (see section 6), and (3) the objects in the vicinity of the new object. The system stops searching when an object and a rule are found that completely specifies all of the positional and shape properties of the new object.

Occasionally some of an object's properties may depend on one object and other properties depend on a different object. For example, the highlight bar in a menu may have the same height and "y" value as the string, but the same width and "x" as the surrounding box (see Figure 4). To handle this case, there are rules in Peridot that only define some of the properties of objects. These rules are marked as "incomplete" so that Peridot knows to try additional rules on other objects to handle the rest of the properties (in the Appendix, rule "Rect-same-size" is incomplete).

---

[2] There are a small number of special rules that test a *group* of objects. This is necessary, for example, to make the size of a box depend on the sum of the sizes of all the items inside it.

Peridot will infer relationships among objects no matter how they are created. Therefore, the same rules will be applied whether an object is created from scratch, by copying some other object, or by transforming an existing object. Since Peridot generalizes from the *results* of the operations, and not *traces* of the actions like many previous Programming by Example systems, it provides much more flexibility to the designers and allows user interfaces to be easily edited. For example, if the designer makes an error when drawing an object or wants to change an existing object, he can simply correct it and Peridot will automatically apply the rules to the new version.

The relationships that Peridot infers can be thought of as *constraints* [Borning 79][Olsen 85] between the two objects. Although the relationships are inferred in one direction (e.g. object R2 depends on object R1), the reverse dependency is also remembered so the relationships can be automatically reversed, if necessary. For instance, the width of the white rectangle in the example of section 3 originally depended on the width of the black rectangle (Figure 3b). When it is later changed to depend on the width of the widest string (Figure 3e), Peridot automatically reverses the constraint with the black rectangle so *black* rectangle's width depends on the *white* rectangle, and similarly for the grey and black rectangles.

Usually, the first object tested is the correct one to apply rules to and the first rule whose test succeeds covers all of the properties of the object. Even when multiple comparisons are required, however, the rule checking occurs without any noticeable delay. If the delay were to increase in the future, this would still not be a problem since the rules are checked at design time (not when the user interface is used by end users), so some delays are acceptable. The advantage of using inferencing rather than requiring the designer to explicitly specify the relationships is that much less knowledge is required by the designer. This is because the designer does not have to know how to choose which of the 50 possible relationships apply and what the parameters to those relationships are.

5.2. *Inferring Iterations*

A recognized problem with all Direct Manipulation systems is that repetitive actions are tedious. For example, if a procedure takes a list of strings to be displayed, the designer does not want to have to individually demonstrate where to display each one. Therefore, Peridot watches the designer's actions to try to infer when two previous actions might be part of a loop. If they appear to be, it queries the designer as to whether a loop is intended. If so, the statements are replaced with a loop statement, and the rest of the loop is executed. As an example, if the designer copies the first two strings from a list of strings and displays them stacked vertically (as in Figure 3c), Peridot asks the designer if the rest of the strings should be displayed in the same manner. If the designer agrees, Peridot calculates how to display the rest of the strings in a similar manner as the first two (as in Figure 3d) and the code for the procedure is automatically changed.

Clearly, this assumes that the objects will be related in some linear fashion, and it will not handle some types of layouts. For example, it will not handle the items of the menu being spaced exponentially, or only displaying every third menu item. Our claim is that these unusual layouts are extremely rare in *real* user interfaces and Peridot will have good coverage without them.

Currently, Peridot infers iterations when the first two elements of a list are displayed[3]. Other objects may also be involved in the iteration, however. For example, in Figure 2, there are black boxes and white boxes for each string taken from the list. Peridot therefore will also include these in the iteration.

5.3. *Inferring Conditionals*

Conditionals are important in user interfaces for specifying *exceptions* and *special cases*. As an example of an exception, a procedure might display a list of strings vertically. However, if one of the strings is a list, then the first element of the list might be the string to be displayed, and the rest of the list might be a sublist to select from after this element is selected. With special cases, the designer wants something extra to happen when certain conditions are met. For example, a check mark may signal the current value from a set of choices, as in Figure 2.

For conditionals, the designer needs a way to specify what to look for to signal the condition (the "IF" part) and what action or actions to perform (the "THEN" part). Peridot supports this by having the designer specify the general case as described above, and giving the "Conditional" command to Peridot. The designer then selects the item that is an exception or special case. For an exception, Peridot tries to infer why it is different, and for a special case, it tries to infer when the graphic should occur. The conditions that are noticed are:

- one value has a different type (e.g. a list versus an atom, or a number rather than a string),
- one is an empty string, or
- numerical properties such as equal to, greater than, or less than zero.

Alternatively, the designer can specify that the value of a parameter should determine whether the conditional should apply. For example, the parameter CurrentMode in Figure 2 determines when to display the check mark.

After Peridot knows the "IF" part, it then allows the designer to demonstrate the "THEN" part, if it is not already displayed, using the same techniques as for any other picture.

Naturally, after a conditional statement is specified, Peridot re-executes the code to insure that the picture is consistent with the new procedure. This causes any additional places where the condition applies to be displayed correctly, which should help the designer spot any errors in the conditional.

6. Specifying the Interaction for a User Interface

One of Peridot's primary innovations is to allow the interaction portion of a user interface to be specified by demonstration. This operates in a similar manner to the presentation component. The major change is the addition of input devices which can determine when actions should take place and the parameters for those actions.

---

[3] It will be easy to also allow the designer to explicitly specify that an iteration should occur for some integer number of times, where the integer may be constant or depend on the value of some variable.

(a)   (b)

Figure 5.
A simulated "mouse" pointing device with three buttons. The device can be moved by pointing at the "nose" (using a real pointing device), and the buttons can be toggled by pressing over them. In (b), the center button is pressed over the word "replace".

Ideally, the designer would simply use the various input devices in the same manner as the end user, but this has three main problems. First, all of the end user's devices may not be available to the designer (for example, in designing the user interface for a flight simulator). Second, some of the input devices are also used for giving commands to Peridot, so disambiguating actions meant for Peridot from those that the end user will perform is difficult. Third, it may be difficult to keep the input device in the correct state (e.g. with a button held down or at a certain location) for the entire time it takes to specify the actions. Therefore, Peridot uses *simulated* devices by having a small icon for each input device (see Figure 5). The designer can move these and toggle "buttons" to indicate what the end user will do with the real input devices.

In addition, it is necessary to have a mode in which the designer can demonstrate what will happen using the *actual* input devices. Although often more clumsy, this is necessary when there are time dependencies, such as with double-clicking or with animations that should happen at a particular speed[4]. In this case, there will be "start watching" and "stop watching" commands to tell Peridot when actions signify what the end user will do and when they are Peridot commands.

When specifying the interaction portion of the user interface, the designer typically moves a simulated input device or changes the status of one of its buttons, and then performs some operation, such as moving an object or drawing a new object. Peridot then creates a conditional statement that is triggered when the input device state or position changes. Of course, there will always be ambiguities (e.g. is the new position significant because it is over an object or because it is no longer over the previous object?) so the designer is always queried to confirm Peridot's guess. Iterations (e.g. perform this until a button is hit), exceptions, and special cases are all be supported for controlling the interaction.

Just as what the end user *sees* is always visible to the designer, what the end user will *do* can also be executed at any time. The designer simply enters execution mode, and the procedure so far is executed. The designer can either use the simulated or the real devices while in execution mode.

---

[4] It is also intended in the future to allow designers to specify timing dependencies by constraining actions to a clock as in Rehearsal World [Gould 84].

7. Current Status

The design and implementation of Peridot are not complete as of the time of this writing (May, 1986). The inferencing mechanisms in Peridot are working, and the presentation component is mostly complete: object-object inferencing is working, iterations are inferred, as shown in Figures 2 and 3, and conditionals are designed but not implemented, although they are expected to be a straightforward extension. For the interaction component, the correct inferences are being made, but the code generation is not implemented.

8. Future Work

In addition to finishing the implementation of the parts of Peridot that are described here, other aspects of Peridot will be developed. Connections with application programs will use "active values," which behave like continuously evaluated procedures. These can be updated by either the interface or the application and the other will be immediately notified so it can make the appropriate updates.

The designer can easily edit the presentation of an interface after it has been created, but it is a difficult unsolved problem how to allow editing of the interaction component. To support multiple input devices operating in parallel [Buxton 86], multiple processing for procedures and constraints will be added. In addition, multiprocessing and constraints should allow animations and complex echoing and feedback to be specified using Peridot. Peridot will also be tested with a number of different user interface designers to ensure that the same guesses about relationships apply to different people.

9. Conclusions

Although not yet completed, Peridot already is capable of producing a variety of graphical, highly interactive user interfaces. Both the presentation (layout) and interaction (behavior) of these Direct Manipulation interfaces can be created in an extremely natural, Direct Manipulation manner. For example, Peridot can now create light buttons (as in Figure 2), menus (Figure 3), and toggle switches. Automatic inferencing is used to free the designer from having to specify most of the properties of objects. Constant feedback through queries, and continuously making the results of actions visible, helps insure that all inferences are correct. When fully implemented, Peridot should be able to handle the user interfaces of state-of-the-art graphical programs, such as those on the Apple Macintosh and other Direct Manipulation systems, including Peridot's own user interface. Extremely rapid prototyping should be possible, as well as generation of the actual code used in the final user interfaces. Peridot should also be easy enough to use so that even end users will be able to modify the user interfaces of programs. In its present form, Peridot has already demonstrated that the application of rule-based inferencing and Programming by Example techniques to User Interface Management Systems has tremendous potential.

Appendix: Sample rules

This appendix shows the form of three rules used in Peridot. The rules are shown in a LISP-like form, with the arithmetic presented in the normal infix notation to make it more readable. The TEST part determines whether the rule should be applied, the MSG is used to ask the designer for confirmation, the ACTION enforces the rule, and the SPECIFIES field tells which of the graphical properties of the object are covered by the rule. The actual rules in Peridot are slightly more complicated.

```
Rect-same:
    TEST:      (AND ((abs (R1.left - R2.left)) < THRESHHOLD)
                    ((abs (R1.bottom - R2.bottom)) < THRESHHOLD)
                    ((abs (R1.width - R2.width)) < THRESHHOLD)
                    ((abs (R1.height - R2.height)) < THRESHHOLD) )
    MSG:       (CONCAT R1.name
               " seems to be the same size and position as "
               R2.name ".")
    ACTION:    (SETQ R2.left "Fetch R1.left")
               (SETQ R2.bottom "Fetch R1.bottom")
               (SETQ R2.width "Fetch R1.width")
               (SETQ R2.height "Fetch R1.height")
    SPECIFIES: ALL

Rect-same-size-with-same-offset:
    TEST:      (AND ((abs (R1.left - R2.left)) < BigTHRESHHOLD)
                    ((abs (R1.bottom - R2.bottom)) < BigTHRESHHOLD)
                    ((abs (R1.width - R2.width)) < SmallTHRESHHOLD)
                    ((abs (R1.height - R2.height)) < SmallTHRESHHOLD)
                    ((abs ( (abs (R1.left - R2.left)) -
                       (abs (R1.bottom - R2.bottom)) )) < SmallTHRESHHOLD) )
    MSG:       (CONCAT R1.name " seems to be the same size as "
               R2.name " and at a constant offset of "
               (SETQ offset (ave ((abs (R1.left - R2.left)) -
                                  (abs (R1.bottom - R2.bottom)))))
               ".")
    ACTION:    (SETQ R2.left (CONCAT "Fetch R1.left + " offset))
               (SETQ R2.bottom (CONCAT "Fetch R1.bottom + " offset))
               (SETQ R2.width "Fetch R1.width")
               (SETQ R2.height "Fetch R1.height")
    SPECIFIES: ALL

Rect-same-size:
    TEST:      (AND ((abs (R1.width - R2.width)) < THRESHHOLD)
                    ((abs (R1.height - R2.height)) < THRESHHOLD) )
    MSG:       (CONCAT R1.name " seems to be the same size as "
               R2.name " but in an unrelated place.")
    ACTION:    (SETQ R2.width "Fetch R1.width")
               (SETQ R2.height "Fetch R1.height")
    SPECIFIES: (width height)
```

ACKNOWLEDGEMENTS

First, we want to thank Xerox Canada, Inc. for the donation of the Xerox workstations and Interlisp environment. This research was also partially funded by the National Science and Engineering Research Council (NSERC) of Canada. For help and support with this paper, we would like to thank the SIGGRAPH referees, and Bernita Myers, Peter Rowley, Ralph Hill, and Ron Baecker.

REFERENCES

[Apple 85] Apple Computer, Inc. *Inside Macintosh*. Addison-Wesley, 1985.

[Bauer 78] Michael Anthony Bauer. *A Basis for the Acquisition of Procedures*. PhD Thesis, Department of Computer Science, University of Toronto. 1978. 310 pages.

[Biermann 76a] Alan W. Biermann. "Approaches to Automatic Programming," *Advances in Computers*, Morris Rubinoff and Marshall C. Yovitz, eds. Vol. 15. New York: Academic Press, 1976. pp. 1-63.

[Biermann 76b] Alan W. Biermann and Ramachandran Krishnaswamy. "Constructing Programs from Example Computations," *IEEE Transactions on Software Engineering*. Vol. SE-2, no. 3. Sept. 1976. pp. 141-153.

[Borning 79] Alan Borning. *Thinglab--A Constraint-Oriented Simulation Laboratory*. Xerox Palo Alto Research Center Technical Report SSL-79-3. July, 1979. 100 pages.

[Buxton 83] W. Buxton, M.R. Lamb, D. Sherman, and K.C. Smith. "Towards a Comprehensive User Interface Management System," *Computer Graphics: SIGGRAPH'83 Conference Proceedings*. Detroit, Mich. Vol. 17, no. 3. July 25-29, 1983. pp. 35-42.

[Buxton 86] William Buxton and Brad Myers. "A Study in Two-Handed Input," *Proceedings SIGCHI'86: Human Factors in Computing Systems*. Boston, MA. April 13-17, 1986.

[Cardelli 85] Luca Cardelli and Rob Pike. "Squeak: A Language for Communicating with Mice," *Computer Graphics: SIGGRAPH'85 Conference Proceedings*. San Francisco, CA. Vol. 19, no. 3. July 22-26, 1985. pp. 199-204.

[Foley 84] James D. Foley. "Managing the Design of User-Computer Interfaces," *Proceedings of the Fifth Annual NCGA Conference and Exposition*. Anaheim, CA. Vol. II. May 13-17, 1984. pp. 436-451.

[Gould 84] Laura Gould and William Finzer. *Programming by Rehearsal*. Xerox Palo Alto Research Center Technical Report SCL-84-1. May, 1984. 133 pages. A short version appears in *Byte*. Vol. 9, no. 6. June, 1984.

[Halbert 81] Daniel C. Halbert. *An Example of Programming by Example*. Masters of Science Thesis. Computer Science Division, Dept. of EE&CS, University of California, Berkeley and Xerox Corporation Office Products Division, Palo Alto, CA. June, 1981. 55 pages.

[Halbert 84] Daniel C. Halbert. *Programming by Example*. PhD Thesis. Computer Science Division, Dept. of EE&CS, University of California, Berkeley. 1984. Also: Xerox Office Systems Division, Systems Development Department, TR OSD-T8402, December, 1984. 83 pages.

[Hayes 85] Philip J. Hayes, Pedro A. Szekely, and Richard A. Lerner. "Design Alternatives for User Interface Management Systems Based on Experience with COUSIN," *Proceedings SIGCHI'85: Human Factors in Computing Systems*. San Francisco, CA. April 14-18, 1985. pp. 169-175.

[Henderson 86] D. Austin Henderson, Jr. "The Trillium User Interface Design Environment," *Proceedings SIGCHI'86: Human Factors in Computing Systems*. Boston, MA. April 13-17, 1986. pp. 221-227.

[Hutchins 86] Edwin L. Hutchins, James D. Hollan, and Donald A. Norman. "Direct Manipulation Interfaces," *User Centered System Design*, Donald A. Norman and Stephen W. Draper, eds. Hillsdale, New Jersey: Lawrence Erlbaum Associates, 1986. pp. 87-124.

[Jacob 85] Robert J.K. Jacob. "A State Transition Diagram Language for Visual Programming," *IEEE Computer*. Vol. 18, no. 8. Aug. 1985. pp. 51-59.

[Lieberman 82] Henry Lieberman. "Constructing Graphical User Interfaces by Example," *Graphics Interface, '82*, Toronto, Ontario, March 17-21, 1982. pp. 295-302.

[Myers 84] Brad A. Myers. "The User Interface for Sapphire," *IEEE Computer Graphics and Applications*. Vol. 4, no. 12, December, 1984. pp. 13-23.

[Myers 86] Brad A. Myers. "Visual Programming, Programming by Example, and Program Visualization; A Taxonomy," *Proceedings SIGCHI'86: Human Factors in Computing Systems*. Boston, MA. April 13-17, 1986. pp. 59-66.

[Myers prep] Brad A. Myers. *Applying Visual Programming with Programming by Example and Constraints to User Interface Management Systems*. PhD Thesis, Department of Computer Science, University of Toronto, Toronto, Ontario, Canada. In progress.

[Nix 86] Robert P. Nix. "Editing by Example," *ACM Transactions on Programming Languages and Systems*. Vol. 7, no. 4. Oct. 1985. pp. 600-621.

[Olsen 83] Dan R. Olsen and Elizabeth P. Dempsey. "Syngraph: A Graphical User Interface Generator," *Computer Graphics: SIGGRAPH'83 Conference Proceedings*. Detroit, Mich. Vol. 17, no. 3. July 25-29, 1983. pp. 43-50.

[Olsen 84] Dan R. Olsen, Jr., William Buxton, Roger Ehrich, David J. Kasik, James R. Rhyne, and John Sibert. "A Context for User Interface Management," *IEEE Computer Graphics and Applications*. Vol. 4, no. 2. Dec. 1984. pp. 33-42.

[Olsen 85] Dan R. Olsen, Jr., Elisabeth P. Dempsey, and Roy
    Rogge. "Input-Output Linkage in a User Interface Manage-
    ment System," *Computer Graphics: SIGGRAPH'83 Confer-
    ence Proceedings*. San Francisco, CA. Vol. 19, no. 3. July
    22-26, 1985. pp. 225-234.

[Pavlidis 85] Theo Pavlidis and Christopher J. Van Wyk. "An
    Automatic Beautifier for Drawings and Illustrations," *Com-
    puter Graphics: SIGGRAPH'85 Conference Proceedings*. San
    Francisco, CA. Vol. 19, no. 3. July 22-26, 1985. pp. 225-234.

[Pfaff 85] Gunther R. Pfaff, ed. *User Interface Management Sys-
    tems*. Berlin: Springer-Verlag, 1985. 224 pages.

[Shaw 75] David E. Shaw, William R. Swartout, and C. Cordell
    Green. "Inferring Lisp Programs from Examples," *Fourth
    International Joint Conference on Artificial Intelligence*.
    Tbilisi, USSR. Sept. 3-8, 1975. Vol. 1. pp. 260-267.

[Shneiderman 83] Ben Shneiderman. "Direct Manipulation: A
    Step Beyond Programming Languages," *IEEE Computer*.
    Vol. 16, no. 8. Aug. 1983. pp. 57-69.

[Shneiderman 86] Ben Shneiderman. "Seven Plus or Minus Two
    Central Issues in Human-Computer Interfaces," *Proceed-
    ings SIGCHI'86: Human Factors in Computing Systems*.
    (closing plenary address) Boston, MA. April 13-17, 1986.
    pp. 343-349.

[Smith 77] David Canfield Smith. *Pygmalion: A Computer Pro-
    gram to Model and Stimulate Creative Thought*. Basel,
    Stuttgart: Birkhauser, 1977. 187 pages.

[Smith 82] David Canfield Smith, Charles Irby, Ralph Kimball,
    Bill Verplank, and Erik Harslem. "Designing the Star User
    Interface," *Byte Magazine*, April 1982, pp. 242-282.

[Tanner 85] Peter P. Tanner and William A.S. Buxton. "Some
    Issues in Future User Interface Management System
    (UIMS) Development," in *User Interface Management Sys-
    tems*, Gunther R. Pfaff, ed. Berlin: Springer-Verlag, 1985.
    pp. 67-79.

[Tesler 81] Larry Tesler. "The Smalltalk Environment," *Byte
    Magazine*. August 1981, pp. 90-147.

[Thomas 83] James J. Thomas and Griffith Hamlin, eds.
    "Graphical Input Interaction Technique (GIIT) Workshop
    Summary." ACM/SIGGRAPH, Seattle, WA. June 2-4, 1982.
    in *Computer Graphics*. Vol. 17, no. 1. Jan. 1983. pp. 5-30.

[Williams 83] Gregg Williams. "The Lisa Computer System,"
    Byte Magazine, February 1983, pp. 33-50.

[Williams 84] Gregg Williams. "The Apple Macintosh Com-
    puter," *Byte Magazine*. February 1984. pp. 30-54.

[Xerox 83] Xerox Corporation. *Interlisp Reference Manual*.
    Pasadena, CA. October, 1983.

Chapter 13

Enhancing System Usability

Having looked at the kinds of human-computer dialogue that are easily realizable with today's technology, and some of the methods of analyzing a problem and developing a design solution, as well as examples of the development and prototyping tools that can aid this process, we next examine a number of seemingly unglamorous topics that are often overlooked and hence doom a system to failure. In an insightful article, oriented towards time-sharing systems but applicable to the broader class of interactive systems, Nickerson (1981) considers the question of why "interactive systems are sometimes not used by people who might benefit from them." He suggests a number of reasons:

- Functionality. The system doesn't do what it should do.

- Accessibility-availability. Users don't have immediate access to the system on a continuing basis.

- Start-stop hassle. Initializing or terminating a session involves cumbersome overhead.

- System dynamics and response time. The system is slow and subject to unpredictable delays.

- Work-session interrupts. The system is unreliable and crashes frequently and/or unpredictably.

- Training and user aids. Users are given little useful assistance in learning the system, and little help when they get into trouble.

- Documentation. Tutorial and reference documentation is unclear, inaccurate, incomplete, poorly organized, and/or out of date.

- Command languages. The system's dialogue language is unnatural, difficult to learn, and/or difficult to use.

- Consistency and integration. The system presents a variety of subsystems with conflicting conventions and command languages.

- User conceptualization of system. It is difficult for the user to form a correct and useful *user's model* of the function and structure of the system.

We have already discussed the issues of appropriate functionality (Chapter 11: Design Principles and Methodologies), command languages (Chapter 10: Interaction Styles and Techniques), consistency and integration (Chapter 10), and mental models (Chapter 6: Cognition and Human Information Processing). Problems of accessibility, start-stop hassles, and work session interrupts are becoming somewhat rarer as time sharing terminals are replaced with personal computers and workstations. More fundamentally, system designers and implementors now generally realize that usable, robust systems require a process of testing and polishing, a process often known as *quality assurance* (Ross, 1978). This is no simple matter, for we must shake down and assure not only the program code but all the supporting elements to be described in this chapter. Only then will we deliver systems that are not only usable in principle, but in practice.

We begin this chapter with a brief discussion of system dynamics and response time. We then focus on the procedures and mechanisms available to help users get started with a system, and to keep them going when, as is inevitable, they run into trouble. In other words, we shall examine what Norman and Draper (1986) term the "information flow" among the systems, documents, and users of a system, including not only manuals but also other people, system displays, system messages, and prompts.

System designers and developers can assist beginning users in a number of ways:

- By providing effective teaching and training for new users
- By providing usable and useful documentation
- By designing systems that facilitate active learning through exploration

System designers and developers can also assist users who are having difficulty in a number of ways:

- By designing for human error
- By facilitating user self help by enhancing communication among the community of users, and by providing a good on-line help capability
- By providing, where possible, an intelligent tutoring system (see Chapter 14: Research Frontiers and Unsolved Problems)
- By crafting systems that motivate the user to enjoy and appreciate her experience with the system

In the words of Brown (1986):

> ...we must widen our focus from designing for the avoidance of trouble to design for the *management of trouble* — of both a communicative and an operative nature. From this perspective, the notion of *repair*, as a fundamental mechanism of natural communication, becomes a crucial construct for interface design; that is, we need to design user-system interaction that supports human participants in using the particular context of the interaction, including the larger social setting, to aid in the recognition and repair of misunderstandings.

System Dynamics and Response Time

One of the chief determinants of user satisfaction with interactive computer systems is response time. A second determinant is the variability in response time. A sluggish system produces user anxiety and frustration. Similar effects are produced by systems with irregular and unpredictable response characteristics.

Increasing the system response rate, however, does not always lead to increased user performance. Task characteristics and individual user characteristics interact with response time issues in complex patterns that are not yet fully understood. The interested reader is referred to Shneiderman (1986) for a comprehensive survey of the existing literature and experimental results.

An interesting and relevant result is presented by Myers (1985a,b). He asserts, and demonstrates through an experiment, that there are advantages to the use of a "percent-done progress indicator," a graphical technique which allows a user to monitor the progress of her computation in qualitative, and where possible, quantitative terms.

Teaching and Training Users

New users beginning work with a system typically require assistance to get started. This can be done through *teaching* them the relevant principles of operation, and/or through *training* them in the skills required for successfully carrying out the desired tasks.

Yet there are many obstacles to the realization of this simple idea. New users may be *novice* or *expert* in a particular technology, such as word processing, and the approaches required for teaching them will need to be dramatically different. Users also bring different kinds of expertise to bear upon a situation. Consider, for example, the different needs of a skilled touch typist and a skilled computer programmer in learning a new word processor. Depending upon their motivation and upon their readiness to tackle certain kinds of tasks, users may also be receptive or closed to absorbing instruction, no matter how relevant it is or how competently it is presented.

Schneider (1985) presents an insightful discussion of the training of a high performance skill, which he defines as "one for which (1) more than 100 hours of training are required, (2) substantial numbers of individuals fail to develop proficiency, and (3) the performance of the expert is qualitatively different from that of the novice." He cautions that many training programs are based on implicitly assumed fallacies:

- Practice will result in near-optimal performance.
- Training should be in a form similar to the final execution of the skill.
- Skill learning is intrinsically motivating and enjoyable.
- One should train for highly accurate performance.
- Initial performance is a good predictor of one's ultimate performance.
- Once a learner has a conceptual understanding of a system, she will develop proficiency in the operational setting.

In place of these, he proposes a new set of working guidelines to promote the training of high performance skills:

- Present information in a consistent manner.
- Allow numerous trials of critical skills.
- Do not overload short-term memory; do minimize memory decay.
- Vary aspects of the task that vary in the operational setting.
- Maintain active participation of the trainee.
- Maintain high motivation of the trainee.
- Present information in a context that illustrates several points at once.
- Intermix training of various component skills.
- Train under slightly speeded-up conditions.
- Train strategies that minimize the workload of the operator.
- Train skills for time-sharing under situations of high workload.

Documentation

Nickerson (1981) bewails the abysmal quality of most current documentation, and notes that as a result many users are reluctant or unwilling to use it. Yet users will inevitably need to consult documentation. Mantei and Haskell (1983) illustrate this in their "autobiography of a first-time discretionary microcomputer user." More than half of the problems encountered by an individual in learning a new system had to do with the documentation, and particularly with its perceived incompleteness and its lack of "user orientation."

As in the case of training, part of the problem arises from the varied expertise possessed by users and from the differing needs posed by various tasks. The result is that there is a large class of useful document types, including tutorial guides for beginner users, principles of operation manuals, and reference manuals and command summaries for experts. Improving the organization, form, and content of these kinds of documents would substantially improve the user interface of many systems. Experimental evidence supporting this position has been presented by Foss, Rosson, and Smith (1982) and by Sullivan and Chapanis (1983). del Galdo, Williges, Williges, and Wixon (1986) show how "critical incident" evaluation can be used to suggest improvements to documentation.

Wright (1981, 1983, 1984a) is an articulate advocate of the value of documentation, developing principles to better guide its development. Wright (1977, 1980) stresses that usability should be the criterion for designing written technical information, and surveys research findings relevant to achieving this goal. Wright (1983), included as a reading, summarizes a "user-oriented"

approach to creating computer documentation. Central to her approach is an analysis of how readers search through documents, how they understand what they find in documents, and how they apply their understanding.

The interested reader should consult Hartley (1978) and Felker et al. (1981) for detailed and thoughtful presentations of the document design process. Felker (1980) present another survey of relevant research findings. Clement (1984) discusses the creation of documentation as a specific kind of text design. Hartley (1981), Hartley (1984), and Wright (1984b) focus particularly on issues of typography, design, and presentation. An interesting collection of papers on "designing usable texts" is that of Duffy and Waller (1985).

Minimalist Design and Active Learning

Carroll has arrived at a novel philosophy to solve the problems of developing suitable documentation and training materials. He defines this philosophy of "minimalist design" as follows (Carroll, 1984):

> The appropriate orientation to the training problem of the future will be directing and supporting the natural learning styles and strategies of users, i.e., giving them less to read if they don't want to read or letting them try real tasks immediately, if they want to do that. This is the essence of minimalist design, and the following are its principles:
> - Slash the verbiage...
> - Force coordination of the system and the training...
> - Expect every possible error...
> - Focus on real tasks and activities...
> - Let the learner lead...

Two experimental approaches incorporating this philosophy, the *minimal manual* and the *training wheels processor* are described in Carroll (1985), included as a reading. Further details may be found in Carroll and Carrithers (1984a,b), Carroll and Kay (1985), and Carroll et al. (1986). An approach similar to training wheels is the "excursions" process developed by Darlington, Dzida, and Herda (1983).

The theory of user behaviour motivating minimalist design is that of "active learning" and "guided exploration" (Carroll et al., 1985). Carroll and his co-workers argue and present experimental evidence that learning is enhanced when users explore, when they set their own goals and problems, and when they solve these problems at their own initiative and in their own way. Yet more structured practice is often valuable (Charney and Reder, 1986), particularly in introducing new concepts and in keeping the user out of dead ends.

One conclusion we can draw is that there is a diversity of learning situations and styles, and user documentation and support materials must be rich enough to reflect this diversity. Another conclusion is that there is a need for ongoing research into the phenomena of active learning. An interesting recent contribution of this kind is a study of the "instructionless learning" of a programmable toy (Shrager and Klahr, 1986). Their work illustrates the roles of hypothesis formation, experiment, and evaluation of results in the process of active learning. These methods allow the learner, despite making many errors, to synthesize an understanding of the syntax, semantics, and principles of operation of the toy's command language.

Designing for Human Error

Even highly motivated, highly skilled users make errors. It is imperative that systems be designed with this in mind.

Norman (1983) suggests the development of system design rules based on an analysis of the classes of errors made by people using the system. He defines an *intention* as the "highest level specification of a desired action," a *mistake* as "an error in the intention," and a *slip* as "an error in carrying out the intention." After characterizing various classes of slips, such as "mode errors," "description errors," "unintentional activation," and "capture errors," he suggests procedures to minimize their occurrence.

Another theoretical formulation is that of Rouse and Rouse (1983), who classifies errors as occurring in one of six component activities of a user's task:

- Observation of the system state
- Choice of a hypothesis
- Testing of the hypothesis
- Choice of a goal
- Choice of a procedure to achieve the goal
- Execution of the procedure

Lewis and Norman (1986), included as a reading, notes that many situations typically thought of as user "errors" might more appropriately be considered failures by the system to understand. Support for this hypothesis is also advanced by Davis (1983a). Lewis and Norman then proceed to suggest methods for minimizing the possibility of errors or failures to understand, methods of detecting errors, and methods for correcting errors.

Shneiderman (1982a,b) counsels us on the importance of the proper wording of error messages, stressing that they should be:

- Brief
- As specific as possible

- Comprehensible, not cryptic
- Positive, constructive, and helpful, rather than critical and negative in tone
- "User-centered," stressing the user's ability to control the system

Experimental evidence supporting these guidelines is presented in Shneiderman (1982b). Similar advice is given by Golden (1980) and Dwyer (1981).

The most comprehensive and insightful analysis is that of Dean (1982), who summarizes as follows:

Set human goals for messages. We should first commit ourselves to certain goals. A major goal is to be tolerant of "user errors." We have to decide how much error-correction the program will do. By anticipating the kinds of mistakes humans will make, we can identify the messages needed to account for those mistakes, as well as for error-free operation.

Apply psychology in writing messages. We have an idea how people think and feel around computers. We ought to provide messages that match their expectations, that help them fit the pieces together the first time they read the messages, and that put them at ease. First decide what meaning to convey, then select the information to convey that meaning, and choose the language to present it.

Write messages for the audience and the situation. People want messages to suit their situation. To determine what information to put in a message in each situation, first analyze what things people will need to know, then determine whether they already know or can learn those things from the context. If not, the message must provide them, either explicitly or implicitly.

Playact to evaluate the messages for usability. We should evaluate messages for usability before coding begins to avoid big surprises later, when it is harder to repair things. We can either "play the program" or have people who represent real users interact with a prototype while we observe them. This exercise in imagination is a must.

Edit the messages for appropriate language. Wording of messages is secondary to the point they make and to the information that is selected to make the point. But the language of messages must be edited for appropriate language: good writing, familiar terminology, standard conversational English, similarity among messages of the same type, standard punctuation.

Design the computer program or system to produce the messages. With messages written and evaluated, we can design the program or system to produce them and avoid the trap of compromising human requirements for the sake of program convenience. Perhaps the more challenging problems of computer science today lie not in inventing new function, but in making existing function easier to use.

Test the messages along with the running code. Messages should be evaluated for usability again after the program or system is working. People actually use it in realistic situations and observe what's what.

Help for Users

Many modern computer systems attempt to provide some sort of *on-line help* or *interactive help* system. Borenstein (1985a) defines such a system as "any software that has as its primary function the task of providing the user with information that will assist him in the use of some other software system." The design of software systems is a relatively neglected art leading Borenstein to describe help systems as generally being "uniformly unappealing." He then develops a systematic taxonomy of help systems consisting of seven dimensions:

- Access initiative, from the human user and/or from the computer

- Access mechanisms, which are either key word help, menu help, contextually invoked help, graphically invoked help, natural language help requests, and spoken help requests (Note the parallels here to Chapter 10: Interaction Styles and Techniques.)

- Access complexity, as determined by a host of syntactic and pragmatic issues

- Presentation methods, including references to printed manuals and the use of multiple windows on screens

- Presentation source, such as an on-line manual, a network of help texts, or a relational data base; and, more fundamentally, whether text is retrieved verbatim from a data structure or computed "on the fly"

- Text quality, as measured in terms of criteria such as readability, organization, formatting and headings, chunk size, and voice and orientation

- Integration, both in terms of the help databases and in terms of the methods of access to them

Given the complexity of this taxonomy, it is not surprising that help systems built to date have been characterized by an incredible variety (Relles, 1979; Sondheimer and Relles, 1982; Houghton, 1984; Borenstein, 1985a). Video examples of on-line help systems are Borenstein (1985b) and Symbolics (1985). Three of the more interesting experimental systems are those of Relles and Price (1981), Relles, Sondheimer, and Ingargiola (1981), and Borenstein (1985a,b). O'Malley et al. (1983) propose a database of on-line help information as part of a comprehensive "integrated structured manual." Experimental results pertaining to the use of help systems have been reviewed recently in Borenstein (1985a) and Shneiderman (1986).

Some of the new experimental results of Borenstein (1985a) are particularly interesting:

- Borenstein asserts, based on his experience which appears to be similar to that of Relles, that "implementing a moderately sophisticated help system integrating several different help access mechanisms is actually a relatively simple and straightforward programming task."

- It is important to invest this effort. In Borenstein's case, his help system made up half the difference between a standard and typically bad help system and a human tutor. This was the case with both novice and expert users.

- Perhaps surprisingly, the most important factor determining the quality of the help system was the quality of the texts stored in the help data base. Once again, we see the importance of good expository writing and good documentation.

Borenstein's work presents some clues as to ways to improve the quality of on-line help. Two other important directions are enhancing the information flows among individuals, as we shall discuss below, and adding more intelligence to the help system. This latter idea leads to the topics of *intelligent help systems*, *intelligent tutoring systems*, and, more generally, *intelligent interfaces*, which we shall address in Chapter 14: Research Frontiers and Unsolved Problems.

The Norman and Draper (1986) emphasis on information flows leads to a number of novel approaches to helping users. Owen (1986) suggests that a system might occasionally offer unsolicited tidbits of factual information to the user in order to advance her knowledge about the system. O'Malley (1986) notes that users typically prefer to consult other people, and presents the need for integrated information delivery systems which help users to formulate questions and help themselves. Bannon (1986) also notes the importance of interpersonal communication and the role of the expert in helping users, and suggests that systems need to be designed to facilitate these kinds of interactions. The need to "support" users and/or customers has long been recognized commercially by successful companies, but there is very little literature on this important aspect of real computer use (however, see Lang, Auld, and Lang, 1982).

Human Motivation

No matter how helpful the error messages are and how sophisticated the help systems are, the ultimate determinant of success or failure is often the degree to which we can motivate the user. This of course depends upon the socio-political framework within which the user will work (see Chapter 2: The Socio/Political Environment), and upon other factors such as dialogue style (Chapter 10: Interaction Styles and Techniques) and input technology (Chapter 8: The Haptic Channel).

Malone (1980,1982) has suggested that we have much to learn in this regard from computer games, and asks us to consider the concepts of challenge, fantasy, and curiosity. Carroll (1982), included as a reading, attempts a somewhat deeper comparison between those playing the game of Adventure and those learning a text editor. He suggests that both must deal with similar problems — disorientation, illusiveness, emptiness, mystery messages, slipperiness, side effects, paradox, and *laissez-faire*. The difference, he argues, is that an exploratory environment has a number of desirable characteristics not shared by most word processors — responsiveness, benchmarks, acceptable uncertainty, safe conduct, learning by doing, opportunity, taking charge, and control.

Individual Differences

The most profound problem facing the designer of any of the usability enhancing subsystems discussed in this chapter is that of individual differences. Users vary in intelligence, in training, and in expertise. They are naive or expert, casual or regular, alienated or motivated, passive or active, each to a greater or lesser extent. Any such characterization depends upon the task, the context, the user's prior experience, and, as we have seen above, his motivation. Since users differ significantly in terms of what might be termed "cognitive style" (Robertson, 1985), there are no universal solutions that will make all or even most of them happy (compare, for example, Stevens, 1983, to Rushinek and Rushinek, 1986). There is wide debate about the characteristics and prevalence of "computer anxiety" (Gilroy and Desai, 1986; Howard and Smith, 1986), and about the nature of mental work load and stress (LeMay and Hird, 1986). There is not even agreement (Potosnak et al., 1986) about the desirability of interfaces tailored to specific classes of users or adapting to individual users (see Chapter 14: Research Frontiers and Unsolved Problems).

The problems of the *novice user* are particularly acute and require careful attention (Paxton and Turner, 1984; Allwood, 1986). There is a need for more studies such as Kiesler, Sproull, and Eccles (1986) investigating why computers are typically more attractive to boys than to girls. We must broaden our perspective to encompass the full range of psychological and sociological determinants and influences on computer use. If we are to understand why introducing novices to computers has recently been described as "encountering an alien culture" (Sproull, Kiesler, and Zubrow, 1984), then we need to understand in a far deeper sense than we now do what Sproull, Kiesler, and Zubrow call the "culture of computing" and how it affects the quality and spirit of human-computer interaction.

Readings

Wright, Patricia (1983). Manual Dexterity: A User-Oriented Approach to Creating Computer Documentation. *Proceedings of CHI '83*, December 1983, 11-18.

Carroll, John M. (1985). Minimalist Design for Active Users. In B. Shackel (Ed.) (1985), *Human-Computer Interaction — Interact '84*, Amsterdam: North-Holland, 39-44.

Lewis, Clayton & Norman, Donald A. (1986). Designing for Error. In Norman, Donald A. & Draper, Stephen W. (Eds.), *User Centered System Design*, Hillsdale, New Jersey: Lawrence Erlbaum Associates, 411-432.

Carroll, John M. (1982). The Adventure of Getting to Know a Computer. *IEEE Computer* 15(11), November 1982, 49-58.

References

Allwood, Carl Martin (1986). Novices on the Computer: A Review of the Literature. *International Journal of Man-Machine Studies* 25(6), 633-658.

Anderson, John R. & Skwarecki, Edward (1986). Designing Computer System Messages, The Automated Tutoring of Introductory Computer Programming. *Communications of the ACM* 29(9), September 1986, 842-849.

Bannon, Liam J. (1986). Helping Users Help Each Other. In Norman, Donald A. & Draper, Stephen W. (Eds.), *User Centered System Design*, Hillsdale, New Jersey: Lawrence Erlbaum Associates, 399-410.

Borenstein, Nathaniel S. (1985s). *The Design and Evaluation of Online Help Systems*, Pittsburgh: Carnegie-Mellon University, 1-54.

Borenstein, Nathaniel S. (1985b). ACRONYM. *SIGGRAPH Video Review* 19, New York: ACM.

Brown, John Seely (1986). From Cognitive to Social Ergonomics and Beyond. In Norman, Donald A. & Draper, Stephen W. (Eds.), *User Centered System Design*, Hillsdale, New Jersey: Lawrence Erlbaum Associates, 457-486.

Carroll, John M. (1982). The Adventure of Getting to Know a Computer. *IEEE Computer* 15(11), 49-58.

Carroll, John M. (1984). Minimalist Training. *Datamation*, November 1, 1984, 125-136. © by Cahners Publishing Co., reprinted with permission.

Carroll, John M. (1985). Minimalist Design for Active Users. In Shackel, B. (Ed.), *Human-Computer Interaction — Interact '84*, Amsterdam: North-Holland, 39-44.

Carroll, John M. & Carrithers, Caroline (1984a). Training Wheels in a User Interface. *Communications of the ACM* 27(8), August 1984, 800-806.

Carroll, John M. & Carrithers, Caroline (1984b). Blocking Learner Error States in a Training-Wheels System. *Human Factors* 26(4), August 1984, 377-389.

Carroll, John M. & Kay, Dana S. (1985). Prompting, Feedback and Error Correction in the Design of a Scenario Machine. *CHI '85 Proceedings*, April 1985, 149-153.

Carroll, John M., Mack, Robert L., Lewis, Clayton H., Grischkowsky, Nancy L. & Robertson, Scott R. (1985). Exploring Exploring a Word Processor. *Human-Computer Interaction* 1, 283-307.

Carroll, John M., Smith-Kerker, Penny L., Ford, Jim R. & Mazur, Sandra A. (1986). The Minimal Manual. IBM Research Report RC 11637 (#52295), Yorktown Heights, New York.

Charney, D.H. & Reder, L.M. (1986). Designing Interactive Tutorials for Computer Users. *Human-Computer Interaction* 2(4), 297-317.

Clement, Darlene (1984). The Role of Documentation in Human-Computer Interaction. In Salvendy, G. (Ed.), *Human-Computer Interaction*, Amsterdam, Netherlands: Elsevier Science Publishers, 203-206.

Cohill, Andrew M. (1985). Retrieval of HELP Information for Novice Users of Interactive Computer Systems. *Human Factors* 27(3), 335-343.

Darlington, Jared, Dzida, Wolfgang, & Herda, Siegfried (1983). The Role of Excursions in Interactive Systems. *International Journal of Man-Machine Studies* 18, 101-112.

Davis, Richard (1983a). User Error or Computer Error? Observations on a Statistics Package. *International Journal of Man-Machine Studies* 19, 1983, 359-376.

Davis, Richard (1983b). Task Analysis and User Errors: A Methodology for Assessing Interactions. *International Journal of Man-Machine Studies* 19, 561-574.

Dean, M. (1982). How a Computer Should Talk to People. *IBM Systems Journal* 21(4), 1982, 424-453. © 1982, International Business Machines Corp.; reprinted with permission.

Duffy, Thomas M. & Waller, Robert (1985). *Designing Usable Texts*, Orlando, Florida: Academic Press, Inc.

Dwyer, Barry (1981a). Programming for Users: A Bit of Psychology. *Computers and People*, January-February 1981, 11-14.

del Galdo, Elisa M., Williges, Robert C., Williges, Beverley H., & Wixon, Dennis R. (1986). An Evaluation of Critical Incidents for Software Documentation Design. *Proceedings of the Human Factors Society — 30th Annual Meeting*, 19-23.

Felker, Daniel B. (Ed.), (1980). *Document Design: A Review of the Relevant Research*, Washington, DC: American Institutes for Research.

Felker, Daniel B., Pickering, Frances, Charrow, Veda R., Holland, V. Melissa & Redish, Janice C. (1981). *Guidelines for Document Designers*, Washington, DC: American Institutes for Research.

Foss, Donald J., Rosson, Mary Beth & Smith, Penny L. (1982). Reducing Manual Labor: An Experimental Analysis of Learning Aids for a Text Editor. *Proceedings of the Conference on Human Factors in Computer Systems*, 332-336.

Gilroy, Faith D. & Desai, Harsha B. (1986). Computer Anxiety: Sex, Race and Age. *International Journal of Man-Machine Studies* 25(6), 711-719.

Golden, Donald (1980). A Plea for Friendly Software. *ACM SIGSOFT, Software Engineering Notes* 5(4), October 1980, 4-5.

Hartley, James (1978). *Designing Instructional Text*, New York: Nichols Publishing.

Hartley, James (1981). Eighty Ways of Improving Instructional Text. *IEEE Transactions on Professional Communication* 24(1), March 1981, 17-27.

Hartley, James (1984). Space and Structure in Instructional Text. In Easterby & Zwaga (Eds.), *Information Design*, John Wiley & Sons, 497-515.

Howard, Geoffry S. & Smith, Robert D. (1986). Computer Anxiety in Management: Myth or Reality? *Communications of the ACM* 29(7), 611-615.

Houghton, Raymond C., Jr. (1984). Online Help Systems: A Conspectus. *Communications of the ACM* 27(2), 126-133.

Kiesler, Sara, Sproull, Lee & Eccles, Jacquelynne S. (1983). Poolhalls, Chips, and War Games: Women in the Culture of Computing. *Psychology of Women Quarterly* 9, 451-462.

Lang, Kathy, Auld, Robin & Lang, Terry (1982). The Goals of Methods of Computer Users. *International Journal of Man-Machine Studies* 17, 375-399.

LeMay, Moira & Hird, Eric (1986). Operator Work Load: When is Enough Enough? *Communications of the ACM* 29(7), 638-642.

Lewis, Clayton & Norman, Donald A. (1986). Designing for Error. In Norman, Donald A. & Draper, Stephen W. (Eds.), *User Centered System Design*, Hillsdale, N.J.: Lawrence Erlbaum Associates, 411-432.

Magers, Celeste S. (1983). An Experimental Evaluation of On-line HELP for Non-Programmers. *CHI'83 Proceedings*, 277-281.

Malone, Thomas W. (1980). What Makes Things Fun to Learn? A Study of Intrinsically Motivating Computer Games. *Technical Report* CIS-7 (SSL-80-11), Palo Alto, CA.: Xerox Palo Alto Research Center.

Malone, Thomas W. (1982). Heuristics for Designing Enjoyable User Interfaces: Lessons from Computer Games. *Proceedings of the Conference on Human Factors in Computing Systems*, 1982, 63-68. Also in Thomas, John C. & Schneider, Michael L. (Eds.), *Human Factors in Computing Systems*, Norwood, N.J.: Ablex Publishing Corp., 1-12.

Mantei, Marilyn & Haskell, Nancy (1983). Autobiography of a First-time Discretionary Microcomputer User. *CHI '83 Proceedings*, 286-290.

Myers, Brad (1985a). The Importance of Percent-Done Progress Indicators for Computer-Human Interfaces. *CHI '85 Proceedings*, 11-17.

Myers, Brad (1985a). Percent Done Indicator. *SIGGRAPH Video Review* 19, New York: ACM.

Nickerson, Raymond S. (1981). Why Interactive Computer Systems are Sometimes not Used by People Who Might Benefit From Them. *International Journal of Man-Machine Studies* 15, 469-483.

Norman, D. (1983). Design Rules Based on Analyses of Human Error. *Communications of the ACM* 26(4), April 1983, 254-258.

Norman, Donald A. & Draper, Stephen W. (Eds.), (1986). *User Centered System Design*, Hillsdale, New Jersey: Lawrence Erlbaum Associates.

O'Malley, C., Smolensky, P., Bannon, L., Conway, E., Graham, J., Sokolov, J., & Monty, M.L. (1983). A Proposal for User Centered System Documentation. *CHI '83 Proceedings*, 282-285.

O'Malley, Claire E. (1986). Helping Users Help Themselves. In Norman, Donald A. & Draper, Stephen W. (Eds.), *User Centered System Design*, Hillsdale, New Jersey: Lawrence Erlbaum Associates, 377-398.

Owen, David (1986). Answers First, Then Questions. In Norman, Donald A. & Draper, Stephen W. (Eds.), *User Centered System Design*, Hillsdale, New Jersey: Lawrence Erlbaum Associates, 361-376.

Paxton, Anne Lee & Turner, Edward J. (1984). The Application of Human Factors to the Needs of the Novice Computer User. *International Journal of Man-Machine Studies* 20, 137-156.

Potosnak, Kathleen M., Hayes, Philip J., Rosson, Mary Beth, Schneider, Michael L., & Whiteside, John A. (1986). Classifying Users: A Hard Look at Some Controversial Issues. *CHI '86 Proceedings*, 84-88.

Relles, Nathan (1979). The Design and Implementation of User-Oriented Systems. *Computer Sciences Technical Report* #357, University of Wisconsin-Madison, July, 1979.

Relles, Nathan & Price, Lynne A. (1981). A User Interface for Online Assistance. *5th International Conference on Software Engineering*, 1981, 400-408.

Relles, Nathan, Sondheimer, Norman K. & Ingargiola, Giorgio (1981). A Unified Approach to Online Assistance. *Proceedings of the National Computer Conference*, 1981, 383-388.

Robertson, Ivan T. (1985). Human Information-Processing Strategies and Style. *Behaviour and Information Technology* 4(1), 19-29.

Ross, D.T. (1978). Quality Starts with Requirements Definition. In Hibbard, P.G. & Schuman, S.A. (Eds.), *Constructing Quality Software*, North Holland Publishing Company, 397-402.

Rouse, William B. & Rouse, Sandra H. (1983). Analysis and Classification of Human Error. *IEEE Transactions on Systems, Man, and Cybernetics* 13(4), 539-549.

Rushinek, Avi & Rushinek, Sara F. (1986). What Makes Users Happy? *Communications of the ACM* 29(7), 594-598.

Schneider, Walter (1985). Training High-Performance Skills: Fallacies and Guidelines. *Human Factors* 27(3), 285-300.

Shneiderman, Ben (1982a). Designing Computer System Messages. *Communications of the ACM* 25(9), September 1982, 610-611.

Shneiderman, Ben (1982b). System Message Design: Guidelines and Experimental Results. In Badre, Albert & Shneiderman, Ben (Eds.), *Directions in Human/Computer Interaction*, Norwood, N.J.: Ablex Publishing Corp., 55-78.

Shneiderman, Ben (1986). *Designing the User Interface*, Don Mills, Ontario: Addison-Wesley.

Shrager, Jeff & Klahr, David (1986). Instructionless Learning about a Complex Device: The Paradigm and Observations. *International Journal of Man-Machine Studies* 25(2), 153-189.

Sondheimer, Norman K. & Relles, Nathan (1982). Human Factors and User Assistance in Interactive Computing Systems: An Introduction. *IEEE Transactions on Systems, Man, and Cybernetics* 12(2), 102-107.

Sproull, Lee S., Kiesler, Sara & Zubrow, David (1984). Encountering an Alien Culture. *Journal of Social Issues* 40(3), 31-48.

Stevens, G.C. (1983). User-Friendly Computer Systems? A Critical Examination of the Concept. *Behaviour and Information Technology* 2(1), 3-16.

Sullivan, Marc A. & Chapanis, Alphonse (1983). Human Factoring a Text Editor Manual. *Behaviour and Information Technology* 2(2), 113-125.

Symbolics (1985). The Document Examiner. *SIGGRAPH Video Review* 19, New York: ACM.

Wright, Patricia (1977). Presenting Technical Information: A Survey of Research Findings. *Instructional Science* 6, 93-134.

Wright, Patricia (1980). Usability: The Criterion for Designing Written Information. In Kolers, Paul A., Wrolstad, Merald E. & Bouma, Herman (Eds.), *Processing of Visible Language* 2, New York: Plenum Press, 183-205.

Wright, Patricia (1981). Five Skills Technical Writers Need. *IEEE Transactions on Professional Communication* 24(1), March 1981, 10-16.

Wright, Patricia (1983). Manual Dexterity: A User-Oriented Approach to Creating Computer Documentation. *CHI '83 Proceedings*, 11-18.

Wright, Patricia (1984a). Designing the Documentation that Explains How It Works. *Design Studies* 5(2), April 1984, 73-78.

Wright, Patricia (1984b). Informed Design for Forms. In Easterby & Zwaga (Eds.), *Information Design*, John Wiley & Sons, 545-577.

MANUAL DEXTERITY

<u>a user-oriented approach to creating computer documentation.</u>

Patricia Wright

MRC Applied Psychology Unit

Cambridge, U.K.

This paper will not advocate a list of firm recommendations about document design because it is recognised that design decisions will vary with many factors. Instead, the present discussion will emphasize that when making these decisions it is necessary for designers to take account of how readers will use the information provided. In order to help them do this, a simple framework is proposed which outlines the rudiments of how people interact with technical documents.

The advantages of this framework will be illustrated by using it to motivate design decisions at two decision levels. At a "macro" level the document designer must make broad decisions about the contents and format of the manual. At a "micro" level the designer must select particular combinations of linguistic, graphic and typographic options which will help readers locate, understand and implement the information given in the manual.

KEYWORDS: design, documentation, manuals, usability, writing.

INTRODUCTION

Complaints about computer manuals are widespread (e.g. Howard, 1981). Yet there are many facets of language and its presentation which could enhance the effectiveness of documentation. So the puzzle is why these factors are sometimes overlooked by writers. Even more puzzling is why some of the nonsenses that occur are not spotted and corrected during the process of design.Various principles for writing computer documentation have been put forward (e.g. Morgan, 1980; Barnum, 1981)but on their own these may not be sufficient. Writers may also need a perspective that motivates the application of particular principles at local points in the text. Such a perspective could come from an appreciation of how people use computer manuals.

HOW READERS INTERACT WITH DOCUMENTS: A SIMPLE FRAMEWORK

Although computer documents serve a variety of readers, nevertheless there are some common activities which all readers undertake. We will concentrate on three:

(1) SEARCHING: Readers have to locate the information within the documentation that is of specific relevance to their present needs.

(2) UNDERSTANDING: Readers have to understand this information, both its literal meaning and the inferences intended by the writer.

(3) APPLYING: Readers usually have to implement their understanding.That is to say, after consulting the manual, readers usually carry out procedures which they anticipate will satisfy the query that led them to turn to the documentation in the first place.

These three broad categories will be briefly expanded in order to make clear their design implications. But for the present, the point to note is that the design of the documentation, the information it gives and the way it presents it, may support or hamper any of these three reader activities. Furthermore, design options which support some activities may be detrimental to others. For example, including full details about all minor changes to the system may help readers' interpret the text once it has been found, but may make the search task considerably more onerous. So it is important to evaluate design options against the full spectrum of readers' needs. In this sense the emphasis in the following discussion will be firmly on "usability" rather than "legibility" or "readability".

HOW READERS SEARCH

IGNORING DOCUMENTS: Outside the computer domain it is a common complaint among technical writers that their readers do not trouble to read the documentation with any care. This behaviour has been noted when people are filling in forms, where they do not always follow the instructions (Matthews, Jacobson and Jones, 1982) and when they are consulting tables, where they do not always read the description given (Wright and Threlfall, 1980). Explanations for readers behaving in this way may be thought to range from sloth and apathy, to haste and time pressure. But recent research suggests that there is another set of contributing factors, namely people's expectations (Wright, Creighton and Threlfall, 1982).

Sometimes people anticipate that there is nothing new that they need to know about the system or product. At other times they may recognise that they need certain information, yet nevertheless believe that there are quicker ways of finding out than by reading the documentation. (e.g. they may prefer to play with the instrument itself, if it is something like a pocket calculator, or they may refer to ask "someone who knows" if it is a complex interaction with which they are totally unfamiliar.) When people were presented with a list of 60 "new brand" products and invited to say how much of the instructions they would read, there was considerable agreement among people that for some products NONE of the instructions would be read. So choosing not to read documentation must be seen as a deliberate strategy rather than as a careless mistake. With reference to the simple framework outlined earlier, the search task can only begin if readers formulate a target. Sometimes they do not do this.

DESIGN IMPLICATIONS OF UNWILLINGNESS TO READ: This notion that documentation may only be read by those who are looking for answers to questions has several implications for document design. One is that it would be helpful if writers knew what these questions were that readers were trying to answer. There is as yet no theory of readers to which one can turn to answer this question; although psychologists are becoming increasingly concerned with the related issue of how people know they do not know (Glucksberg and McCloskey, 1981) and what they need to know in order to formulate a question (Miyake and Norman, 1979). Document designers, at least for the present, will

need to use empirical techniques to find out how their readers formulate questions. This point will be taken up later in a discussion of design procedures.

Another implication of the evidence that people turn to documentation when they have a question that they are trying to answer, is that computer manuals need to be designed so that people can locate information speedily. At the macro-level this means providing adequate contents lists, indexes, page headings and section headings. At the micro level it means enhancing the usability of each of these elements. There are a number of relevant research studies relating to many of these components (e.g. see the review by Felker, 1980 and the guidelines proposed by Hartley, 1981); but this would seem to be a domain where enlightened common sense can go a long way.

Contents lists become more usable when text and page numbers are fairly close together. Once readers are turning from the contents list to the text, then they will find it easier to locate a particular section if the page numbers are in arabic (1,2,3) and are situated on the outside edge of the page.

Many readers prefer to leaf through a document rather than use a contents list or index. In a study of the use of manuals by military personnel, Sticht (1977) reported that contents lists and indexes were used only 25% of the time where their use was relevant. In contrast, the activity of leafing through was used more than 90% of the time. Here again the location of page headings on the outside edge of the page can be helpful, because readers will often let the curled pages fall through their thumb rather than open each page fully. Obviously if page headings are devoted to the title of the manual, or to the manufacturer's name, they are so uninformative that their location is of no consequence. But if document designers appreciated how important the search component was when people were using their manuals, then perhaps the "access structures" (Waller, 1979, 1982) that they provide for readers would be improved.

Soft-copy documentation can pose some special problems for designers, in relation to the kinds of access structures which can be made available. Some of these special problems arise from the limitations of space on the screen. This spatial limitation may lead the designer to reconstruct information that would be printed as a list (contents lists, indexes) and reform it as a hierarchy. When presenting these tree structures to readers only one level is exposed at a time. One risk with this form of display is that it may require searchers to make decisions about the search target which they are unprepared for, or may not know how to meet. A general discussion of the problems that people have in handling menu structures for viewdata systems and their implications for designers will be found in Young and Hull (1982, 1983).

Other problems arise from the typographic limitations of many screen displays (Reynolds, 1979; Twyman, 1982). Whereas a printed manual has recourse to type that varies in size, weight and font, a screen presentation may be limited to upper and lower case with perhaps some reverse video. Among the consequences that follow from this is the fact that other means have to be found (e.g. explicit numbering of sections) to signal the relative status of different sections of the text. Moreover the reading of lengthy texts on a VDU screen appears to be something which many readers prefer not to do, probably because they do it more slowly than reading text printed on paper (Muter, Latremouille, Treurniet and Beam, 1982).

HOW READERS UNDERSTAND

It is important at the outset to appreciate that there are different kinds of understanding that people can acquire from reading a document. In terms of the implications for document designers probably the two most common kinds of understanding relate to the distinction between declarative and procedural knowledge. This distinction is by no means absolute. Several psychologists have argued that there exists an interaction between them, with procedures when carried out generating feedback which in turn refines both declarative and procedural knowledge (e.g. Hayes-Roth, Klahr and Mostow, 1981; Anderson, 1982). Nevertheless the distinction has been found relevant to describing individual differences. Coombs, Gibson and Alty (1982) noted a tendency for those who were less successful as novice programmers to use descriptive knowledge when procedural knowledge would have been more appropriate.

The distinction between declarative and procedural knowledge has implications for document designers, both with respect to the content and the format of the information in a manual. Many of the people who turn to a manual will be looking for answers to questions about what to do, rather than seeking an understanding of why they should do it. This suggests that there is value in visually differentiating the two kinds of information if they are both included in the same section. Indeed often the two classes may be best served by quite different presentation techniqes.

An expository text (e.g. giving a description of system capabilities) may be easily understood when written in a conventional prose style. This is not the case for a text which explains how to carry out certain procedures. Procedural information becomes easier for readers to follow if the writer abandons the sentence style of prose paragraphs and instead presents the information as a list of steps (Frase, 1981). Even flow diagrams may be more helpful than prose if contingencies have relevance to the procedure.

Not only will macro-level decisions about the general form of the documentation be influenced by considerations of how people understand what they read, so too will a number of design decisions at the micro-level. Readers probably find it easier to acquire declarative knowledge if the writer provides a succinct, broad-brush overview of the general principles relevant in that domain. This will help them formulate appropriate schemata for interpreting the text (see below). For lengthy procedural sequences an outline of the major subsections may also be helpful, but usually the information which readers will find most critical concerns the details of the steps to be undertaken (e.g. whether spaces are important, whether upper or lower case characters should be used).

SCHEMATA: There is considerable evidence that readers seek to integrate what they read with knowledge that they already have. Anything which helps readers activate the appropriate past know_ledge is therefore going to be helpful. The options available to writers include titles, summaries and opening statements.

Although "schema" (plural "schemata") is a term used in somewhat different ways by different theorists, it refers to an active organisation of past experience that may well be hierarchically organised and which generates expectancies. As an example of the hierarchic structure, consider the instruction "Load the source disc in drive B". This specifies a superordinate goal which can only be followed if readers have schemata from which they can construct the subgoals of opening and closing the disc drive, of removing the disc from its protective cover and inserting it into the drive in the appropriate orientation. By relying on a schema that the reader already has, writers can reduce the amount of information that they need to give.

Helping readers create appropriate schemata becomes an important task for document designers. This involves macro-level decisions. Thematic titles can help, so too can overviews whether provided verbally or by diagrams. The choice will inevitably vary with the specific content being communicated and with the selection of linguistic and typographic options for other functions. Undoubtedly the sequence in which information is presented can make a critical contribution to schema formation (Kieras, 1980). More will be said about this when discussing text structure.

Writers also need to be aware that readers may adopt inappropriate schemata and so may be drawing inferences from the text which were not intended. This risk can be heightened by the use of examples, metaphors and analogies. These can all be helpful for readers who are trying to acquire either declarative or procedural knowledge. Nevertheless, readers can easily overgeneralise from the example given, and so attribute an unintended correspondence between the analogy and the referent of the explanation (Rummelhart and Norman, 1981). One safeguard against this may be for writers to define explicitly the dimensions of similarity which they intend the reader to use, rather than use blanket statements of the kind "A word processor is very like a typewriter".

TEXT STRUCTURE: Through schemata readers are able to bring to bear the prior knowledge that they have about the subject matter. Of course people also have knowledge about language and the structure of documents. Just as people expect short stories to have a beginning, a middle and an end, so they have expectations about the structure of technical documents. To give a personal example, when we first linked up a printer to our new micro we wanted to check if it worked. We had some text on disc, so we needed only to print it out. The relevant manual had two chapters each of 12 pages explaining the numerous print options available. But we just wanted to know the command for Print. Our expectation was that it would be near the front of the first chapter. It turned out to be near the bottom of page 9 of the second chapter. Undoubtedly it would help if readers' expectations about document structures were matched by writers' design decisions.

Gilliland (1972) has characterized a dozen different paragraph structures, most of which can be found in computer manuals. Readers' knowledge of possible text structures can be exploited by document designers in several ways. For example, there is evidence that people tend to remember the points they consider to be important in a text; and they tend to consider as important, the information given early in a paragraph (Kieras, 1981). Here macro-level decisions about text organization tend to shade into micro-level decisions about order of mention and sentence structure.

There are numerous factors relating to the choice of words and sentence structures which designers need to be able to take account of at the micro level of decision making. A useful summary of these is given by Felker, Pickering, Charrow, Holland and Redish (1981). Unfortunately, knowing what characteristics the text should have is no guarantee that a writer can achieve this. Editing one's own writing is a perceptual task hampered by blindspots.

At this micro-level, software support is becoming available which can help writers monitor whether their writing conforms to the criteria they intended (Coke, 1982). The extent to which such support systems will come to bias a writer's choice at the macro-level remains to be seen. Software may also offer valuable support when it comes to chores such as compiling indexes. Bethke (1979) has suggested that the creation of an index can itself be a design tool, since it can highlight errors of terminology and organisation within a manual. How well writers can make use of such a tool is not yet known.

The argument that text structure needs to be conveyed explicitly to the reader by means of appropriate typographic signals has been strongly made by Hartley (1978). He has illustrated how the use of space, both vertical and horizontal, can make technical materials (such as a college prospectus) easier for readers to understand. It seems unlikely that software support will become available for decisions about presentation and display options, because the determinants of the required groupings tend to be semantic (or prag-

matic), rather than definable from text characteristiscs.

MENTAL MODELS: Readers may start with schemata about the topic and expectations about the structure of the text, but during the course of reading they also build up a mental representation of the information given in the document. This information may take various forms. In some instances it may correspond to a network of propositions. These propositional representations preserve much of the information given in the surface structure of the text. (Students reading for a quiz may choose to learn this way). Alternatively readers may adopt some form of analog representation (possibly but not necessarily mental imagery) in which the gist rather than the details are represented (Johnson-Laird, 1980).

Research has shown that analog models may be easier for readers to achieve, but sometimes at the cost of accuracy (Mani and Johnson-Laird, 1982). There is also evidence that as people read, they try to integrate successive sentences into a single coherent model (Baker and Anderson, 1982). In some circumstances, when readers recognise the importance of the information but are unable to satisfactorily integrate it at the time of first reading, they may mentally represent it in propositional form (Ehrlich and Johnson-Laird, 1982). This illustrates that no strict cleavage exists between the two forms of representation. For document designers the issues are twofold: how can they influence the mental representations that people choose, and in what directions should such influence be exercised?

There is no doubt that macro level decisions about the use of diagrams and other graphic forms have a considerable impact on how readers choose to represent what they read. People who studied a recipe written as a prose paragraph tended to reproduce it as prose, whereas those who had studied a formatted list of instructions tended to reproduce that format (Hartley, 1982). Similar observations have been made of people studying flowcharts (Wright and Reid, 1973). In fact, there is evidence that readers encode many of the display characteristics of the material that they read; they can subsequently use this information when searching through a document (Rothkopf, Fisher and Billington, 1982). (e.g. people tend to remember that the information they now want was at the top of a right-hand page somewhere near the end of a chapter.) From this it follows that the more "landmarks" designers are able to provide for readers, the easier it is for readers to know where they are in the text on subsequent readings. The advantage accrues both to search and understanding processes.

As to what forms of representation should be encouraged, this may well vary within different sections of a manual. Sometimes literal accuracy is required. The details of an operational sequence to be followed exactly may come in this category. Dixon (1982) has explored how readers create action plans for carrying out procedures which depend upon some contingency arising ("If the file space gets below 50K then change the logged disc drive to B"). He has shown that people find it easier to carry out such instructions when the action information ("change the logged disc drive to B") precedes the contingency information ("if the file space gets below 50K"). Earlier work had shown that sentences are usually easier to understand if the main clause precedes the subordinate clause (Clark and Clark, 1968). Dixon demonstrated that the advantage of retaining the Action-Condition sequence was separable from, and operated in addition to, the other syntactic effects.

A different kind of mental model relates to the aspect of language which linguists term "register". People do not speak in the same way to their parents, their colleagues and to strangers, even if they are intending to convey the same message. Halliday (1978) has stressed that any utterance, besides its strictly informative content, also conveys a message about the relation between the listener and hearer, or reader and writer. Certainly most of us have had the experience of reading documents whose tone we found unhelpful, perhaps it was too patronising or too aggressive. It would certainly seem that readers form mental models of the writer(s).

Although there are several studies of the politeness conventions which operate in conversation (Clark and Lucy, 1975; Clark and Schunk, 1980), nothing comparable exists for written language. It therefore seems premature to discuss how this can be monitored and modified during the process of document design. In a sense it was a recognition of this problem of how to capture the tone of a text which led Flesch (1948) to devise the index of "Human Interest" to accompany his "readability" index. This may have been a useful start but it is certainly not an end point. The reader's image of the writer may be influenced by macro decisions concerning such factors as the use of graphics, the length of paragraphs, perhaps even the size of the paper and the quality of the print, just as much as by micro-level decisions about the use of personal pronouns and short, active sentences.

HOW READERS APPLY THEIR UNDERSTANDING

Once readers have found the section in the manual which seems to answer their question, and once they have understood what the writer was trying to say, it might be thought that everyone's problems are over. This is not necessarily the case. The readers of computer manuals are usually trying to accomplish some task, in relation to which the activity of consulting the manual was a diversion. Consequently the information found will usually be transformed into an action or sequence of actions that are realated to the original task. Here several new classes of problems may be encountered. One is the problem of reference. It is by no means rare to find that a procedure which has been carefully understood does not in fact apply to the system on which the reader is working because progress in developing the hardware and the software so often seems to outstrip progress in developing the documentation.

Another class of problems relates to the memory demands being made upon the reader. If the procedures are lengthy then it will be helpful if document designers can divide them into meaningful sub-stages and number them. It hardly needs research to confirm that it helps readers if procedural steps are given in the order in which they should be carried out. In an unpublished study with Ann Lickorish, we asked 14 people to carry out a fairly simple text-editing manipulation. The instructions for how the text was to be changed either focussed on the change to be made ("Underline the third letter of the first word to the right of the word above the word FRAME"), or were resequenced in the order in which the reader had to apply the search sub-goals: "Find the word FRAME; Find the word above it; Find the word to the right of this; Underline the third letter". Because the task was set up so that people switched between the instructions and the text to which these applied, people sometimes made mistakes. With the action focus, 46% of attempts were wrong first time, compared with 16% when the instructions were resequenced. From the work of Bransford on the problems that people have concatenating information across sentences (Bransford, 1979), we doubt that the effect is primarily due to sentence length rather than sequencing. We are currently exploring how to bend the English language to check our doubts.

Yet a totally different class of problems arises when the reader, having carried out what was believed to be the appropriate procedure, finds that something unexpected happens. Relatively little is known about this aspect of readers' interaction with documentation. In the text editing task just described, the software asked people to try again if they made a mistake. We noticed a tendency for people to error-check from the end of the sequence. They tended to assume that they had got to the correct place but then had performed the wrong operation. We have plans to check how far this retracing occurs, but meanwhile this strategy of reader interaction has implications for document design. If certain steps in a procedure are more likely to be error-prone than others, then making this explicit may help readers to check these point first.

Of course it may not be self-evident just which steps in a procedure are likely to be most error prone. This could imply the need to obtain some empirical data. So finally we must address the broad question of design procedures. Which techniques are best suited to creating manuals that can be easily used by readers who want to search for, understand and apply information.

DOCUMENT DESIGN PROCEDURE

Compared with the many decades of research on reading, studies of the processes of writing and information design have only just begun. Already it is evident that the physical medium of composition can have important consequences. Gould (1981) showed that people using line-oriented text editors took 50% longer to write letters than did those using longhand, without there being any apparent gain in quality. Yet there were cost-benefits from an organisational viewpoint. The longhand letters took longer to produce because they involved additional secretarial time. The cost benefits of the different media and different design procedures seem likely to vary with different kinds of documents.

A four stage model of the process of document design has been proposed by Duffy (1981). The four stages are: 1.analysis, 2.planning, 3.development, 4.evaluation. The simple framework of how readers interact with the document, may offer heuristic assistance during several of these stages.

From the initial analysis phase comes a specification of the function of the document, the context in which it will be used and relevant audience characteristics. An explicit consideration of how readers will be searching,understanding and applying the information from the manual may help to determine what questions need to be answered before writing can begin.

It is during this early pre-writing stage that it often becomes necessary to find compromise solutions which will adequately satisfy the needs of readers, the characteristics of the system being written about, and the realities of the production constraints (time, budget) which apply to the documentation. Hammond, Jorgensen, Maclean, Barnard and Long (1983) have shown how the priorities set at the initial stages of system design may not always give adequate weight to the user's requirements.

During the planning phase decisions are taken about content and presentation variables, i.e. decisions at the macro-level of design. Here it is necessary to check the mapping between structure and function. For example, a heading may serve a variety of functions but may need to be worded or located differently for these different purposes. It is increasingly accepted that the structure of written material should be determined by its function. The framework which has been outlined of how readers interact with documentation, helps to make explicit what the reader's functional requirements are.

In the development phase the writer works through the micro-level decisions which arise from the previous macro-level decisions. Again a detailed specification of just what readers are doing as they interact with the text can indicate where difficulties are likely to arise. This is particularly so for difficulties due to reader strategies or cognitive limitations (Wright, 1980). Formative evaluation (obtaining feedback to guide design decisions) may be a necessary part of this development process. The text has to be monitored for adequacy and coherence. Ways of doing this include drawing upon expert opinions and empirically pilot-testing the materials.

Finally a summative evaluation is undertaken, to establish whether the manual which has been created really can be easily used by the intended audience. There are many empirical techniques available, each with its strengths and weaknesses (see the review by Wright, 1983). So it is usually desirable to adopt several converging techniques, rather than just relying on one evaluation procedure. One major difficulty in undertaking any assesment of the overall quality of a manual is that the evaluation criteria are not obvious. It may be unrealistic to hope for zero difficulty for all readers, but how much error is too much? In part the answer necessarily depends upon the cost-benefit of removing the trouble spots. Where patterns of errors are found or communalities exist, then revision is likely to be worth-while. The aim of this stage of the design process is not the attainment of perfection but simply the avoidance of some of the catastrophies and nonsenses with which computer manuals abound.

One limitation of trouble-shooting methodologies is that they tend to give information about problems at the micro-levels rather than the macro-levels, or at least the temptation is to interpret the data this way. If a sentence is misunderstood it is reworded rather than replaced by a diagram or some non-sentential structure. This may be one of the reasons why revisions are sometimes no better, and may even be worse, than the originals (Duffy, Curran and Sass, 1983). One way of reducing this limitation is by having ready access to experts from different disciplines.

In spirit, Duffy's model is very similar to that proposed by Redish, Felker and Rose (1981). Perhaps the major difference is that Redish et al. bring out more forcefully the cyclic interactions among some of these stages. It would be a mistake to imagine that they represent a simple linear sequence. In particular the summative evaluation may indicate trouble spots which need revision, and such revisions will need further evaluation.

Both Duffy and Redish et al. place great emphasis on the need for preparatory work before writing starts, and the need for empirical procedures for collecting data during the preparatory and the evaluation stages. The notion that complex documentation, such as a computer manual, can be adequately produced by a single individual has been challenged (Felker, 1980; Wright,1981). There is an obvious need for skills in domains as diverse as language, graphic design and behavioral testing. Much of the present discussion has sought to show that understanding something of the psychology of readers could be helpful too.

Macdonald-Ross and Waller (1976) suggest that the production of technical documents needs people who can function as "transformers", much as radio and television programs have producers. It is part of the producer's job to know what expertise is needed, where to get it and how to co-ordinate it. Accepting such a suggestion will clearly have implications for the organisation and management of writing teams. In the short term it will not make the production task cheaper; in the long term, given the deleterious effects of dissatisfied customers, it is certainly likely to be a good investment. Happily, there are indications that some organisations are seriously concerned to improve the ease with which their computer manuals can be used (e.g. Bethke, Dean, Kaiser, Ort and Pessin, 1981). It is hoped that the present discussion of how readers interact with documents can contribute to such endeavours. It offers to those who design computer documentation a framework that can help transform manual labour into manual dexterity.

REFERENCES

Anderson, J.R. (1982) Acquisition of cognitive skill. Psychological Review, 89, 369 - 406.

Baker, L. and Anderson, R.I. (1982) Effects of inconsistency on text processing: evidence for comprehension monitoring.Reading Research Quarterly, 17, 281 -294.

Barnum, C. (1981) A view from the lectern: What's wrong with technical writing today? Byte, 6, 409 - 412.

Bethke, F.J. (1979) The index as editor. Journal of Technical Writing and Communication,9, 281 - 286.

Bethke, F.J., Dean, W.M., Kaiser, P.H., Ort, E. and Pessin, F.H. (1981) Improving the usability of programming publications. IBM Systems Journal, 20, 306 - 320.

Bransford, J.D. (1979) Human Cognition:Learning, Understanding and Remembering. Belmont, Ca: Wadsworth.

Clark, H.H. and Clark, E. (1968) Semantic distinctions and memory for complex sentences. Quarterly Journal of Experimental Psychology, 20, 129 - 138.

Clark, H.H. and Lucy, P. (1975) Understanding what is said from what is meant: a study in conversationally conveyed requests. Journal of Verbal Learning and Verbal Behavior, 14, 56 - 72.

Clark, H.H. and Schunk, D.H. (1980) Polite responses to polite requests. Cognition, 8, 111 - 143.

Coke, E. (1982) Computer aids for writing text. In D.H. Jonassen N.J.: Educational Technology Publications.

Coombs, M.J., Gibson, R.and Alty, J.L. (1982) Learning a first computer language: strategies for making sense. International Journal of Man-Machine Studies, 16, 449 -486.

Dixon, P. (1982) Plans and written directions for complex tasks. Journal of Verbal Learning and Verbal Behavior, 21, 70 - 84.

Duffy, T.M. (1981) Organising and utilising document design options. Information Design Journal, 2, 256 - 266.

Duffy, T., Curran, T.E. and Sass. D. (1983) Document design for technical job tasks: an evaluation. Human Factors, 25, 143 - 160.

Ehrlich, K. and Johnson-Laird, P.N. (1982) Spatial descriptions and referential continuity. Journal of Verbal Learning and Verbal Behavior, 21, 296 - 306.

Felker, D.B. (1980) Instructional Research. In D.B. Felker (ed) Document Design: a review of the relevant research. Washington, D.C.: American Institutes for Research Technical Report 75002 - 4/80.

Felker, D.B., Pickering, F., Charrow, V.D., Holland, V.M. and Redish, J.C. (1981) Guidelines for Document Designers. Document Design Project, American Institutes for Research, Washington, D.C.

Flesch, R.F. (1948) A new readability yardstick. Journal of Applied Psychology, 32, 221 - 233.

Frase, L.T. (1981) Writing, text and the reader. In C.H. Frederiksen and J.F. Dominic (eds) Writing: the nature, development and teaching of written communication, volume 2, process development and communication. Hillsdale, N.J.: Lawrence Erlbaum Associates.

Gilliland, J. (1972) Readability. London: Hodder and Stoughton.

Glucksberg, S. and McClosky, M. (1981) Decisions about ignorance: knowing that you do not know. Journal of Experimental Psychology: Human Learning and Memory, 7, 311 - 325.

Gould, J.D. (1981) Composing letters with computer-based text editors. Human Factors, 23, 593 - 606.

Gregg, L.W. and Steinberg, E.R. (eds) Cognitive processes in writing. Hillsdale,N.J.:Lawrence Erlbaum.

Halliday, M.A.K. (1978) Language as Social Semiotic: the social interpretation of language and meaning. London: Edward Arnold.

Hammond, N. Jorgensen, A., Maclean, A., Barnard, P. and Long, J. (1983) Design practice and interface usability: evidence from interviews with designers. Proceedings of CHI'83,Boston.

Hartley, J. (1978) Designing Instructional Text. London: Kogan Page

Hartley, J. (1981) Eighty ways of improving instructional text. IEEE Transactions on Professional Communication, 24, 17 - 27.

Hartley, J. (1982) Information mapping: a critique.Information Design Journal,3, 51-58.

Hayes-Roth, F., Klahr, P. and Mostow, D.J. (1981) Advice taking and knowledge refinement: an iterative view of skill acquisition. In J.R. Anderson (ed) Cognitive Skills and their Acquisition. Hillsdale, N.J.: Lawrence Erlbaum Associates.

Howard, J. (1981) What is good documentation? Byte, 6, 132 -150.

Kieras, D.E. (1980) Initial mention as a signal to thematic content in technical passages. Memory and Cognition, 8, 345 - 353.

Johnson-Laird, P.N. (1980) Mental models in cognitive science.Cognitive Science,4,71-115.

Macdonald-Ross, M. and Waller, R.H. (1976) The transformer. Penrose Annual, 69, 141 - 152.

Mani, K. and Johnson-Laird, P.N. (1982) The mental representation of spatial descriptions. Memory and Cognition, 10, 181 - 187.

Matthews, C., Jacobson, M. and Jones, R. (1982) Common sense, skill and research in forms design. Information Design Journal,3, 87-95.

Miyake, N. and Norman, D.A. (1979) To ask a question one must know enough to know what is not known. Journal of Verbal Learning and Verbal Behavior, 18, 357 - 364.

Morgan, C. (1980) What's wrong with technical writing today? Byte, 5, p6,8,10.

Muter, P., Latremouille, S.A., Treurniet, W.C. and Beam, P. (1982) Extended reading of continuous text on television screens. Human Factors, 24, 501 - 508.

Redish, J.C., Felker, D.B. and Rose, A.M. (1981) Evaluating the effects of document Design Principles. Information Design Journal, 2, 236 - 243.

Reynolds, L. (1979) Teletext and Viewdata - a new challenge for the designer. Information Design Journal, 1, 2 - 14.

Rothkopf, E.Z., Fisher, D.G. and Billington, M.J. (1982) Effects of spatial context during acquisition on the recall of attributive information. Journal of Experimental Psychology: Human Memory and Cognition, 8, 126 - 138.

Rummelhart, D.E. and Norman, D.A. (1981) Analogical processes in learning. In J.R. Anderson (ed) Cognitive Skills and their Acquisition. Hillsdale, N.J.: Lawrence Erlbaum Associates.

Sticht, T.G. (1977) Comprehending reading at work. In M.A. Just and P.A. Carpenter (1977) Cognitive Processes in Comprehension. Hillsdale, N.J.: Lawrence Erlbaum.

Twyman, M. (1982) The graphic presentation of language. Information Design Journal,3, 2-22.

Waller, R.H. (1979) Typographic access structures for educational texts. In P.A. Kolers, M.E. Wrolstad and H. Bouma (eds) Processing of Visible Language 1. N.Y.: Plenum Press.

Waller, R.H. (1982) Text as diagram: using typography to improve access and understanding. In D.H. Jonassen (ed) The Technology of Text. Englewood Cliffs, N.J.: Educational Technology Publications.

Wright, P. (1980) Usability: the criterion for designing written information.In P.A. Kolers, M.E. Wrolstad and H. Bouma (eds) Processing of Visible Language 2. N.Y.: Plenum Press.

Wright, P. (1981) Five skills technical writers need. IEEE Transactions on Professional Communication, 24, 10 - 16.

Wright, P. (1983) Is evaluation a myth? Assessing text assessment procedures. In D.Jonassen (ed) The Technology of Text, vol 2. Englewood Cliffs, N.J.:Educational Technology Publications.

Wright, P., Creighton, P. and Threlfall, S.M. (1982) Some factors determining when instructions will be read. Ergonomics,25, 225 - 237.

Wright, P. and Reid, F. (1973) Written information:some alternatives to prose for expressing the outcomes of complex contingencies. Journal of Applied Psychology, 57, 160 - 166.

Wright, P. and Threlfall, S.M. (1980) Readers' expectations about format influence the usability of an index. Journal of Research communication Studies, 2, 99 - 106.

Young, R.M. and Hull, A.H. (1982) Cognitive aspects of the selection of viewdata options by casual users.Proceedings of 6th International Conference on Computer Communication. London.

Young, R.M. and Hull, A.H. (1983) Categorisation structures in hierarchical menus. Proceedings of 10th International Symposium on Human Factors in Telecommunications. Finland.

MINIMALIST DESIGN FOR ACTIVE USERS*

John M. Carroll

Computer Science Department
IBM Thomas J. Watson Research Center
Yorktown Heights, NY 10598 USA

Recent studies in computer human factors indicate that novice learners of office systems are "active", preferring self-initiated problem solving to rote drill and practice as a learning strategy. But in high-function systems users may need help in exploring basic functions without being distracted by advanced material. Two experimental approaches to this problem are outlined: The MINIMAL MANUAL attempts to support active learning by providing concise instruction focussed on easy-to-understand goals. The TRAINING WHEELS WORD PROCESSOR encourages exploration of basic functions by disabling the more advanced functions that can distract and confuse novices.

Over the last two years, we have been studying the plight of the first time user of computer word processing equipment ([5], [6], [11] [12]). In our studies, participants were asked to learn basic text entry and revision skills, including the use of menus for formatting and printing, and the interpretation of system messages. We asked participants to "think aloud" as they progressed; that is, to verbalize their thoughts, plans, and concerns regarding the learning task. Learning in this situation appears to be very frustrating. System interfaces are inscrutable to the novice and the accompanying training materials provide little help in penetrating these mysteries.

0.1 Troubles with manuals. Contemporary self-study manuals tend to consist of rather extensive exposition augmented by narrowly focussed exercises and practice drills. However, even though our learners desperately needed this training, they could not use it very successfully in this form. We believe that one reason for this is that people prefer to be active learners. New users we have observed tend to "jump the gun" when introduced to new word processing topics -- including signing on the system. They plunged right into the topic without reading the manual fully or in some cases at all. A second reason, we believe, is that people *cannot* be passive in this learning situation. Learners who tried attentively to follow out the instructions step by step frequently committed small errors that totally side-tracked them. Manuals cannot anticipate the variety of potential learner errors, and accordingly cannot support error recognition, diagnosis, and recovery processes adequately. Even small errors can seriously derail learners, forcing them to resort to active, self-initiated, learning strategies in order to recover. Third, even when learners both attentively followed the manual and avoided the pitfalls of small errors, they often did not know what they had done or why, exclaiming "What did we do?".

Rote descriptions and practice are resisted, and even when complied with, prove difficult to follow and assimilate. But perhaps more important, they are not adequate for communicating the detailed procedural and declarative knowledge needed for understanding and solving problems in a complex task domain like text editing. Learners resort to more heuristic reasoning processes like abduction (generating hypotheses on basis of very limited information) and adduction (verifying hypotheses within these same limitations of information) rather than through more principled reasoning processes (like deduction or induction). These processes produce conclusions that are less constrained, but which open up the possibility of discovering knowledge on the basis of impoverished information.

0.2 Troubles with systems. Analogous problems can be cited with respect to the interface itself. Contemporary systems require new users to master novel and complex design elements that are not always obvious or intuitive. When learners try to find information relevant to their current situation, or to interpret their current situation at all, they frequently focus on considerations that are non sequiturs from the perspective of the system. Conversely, they quite often fail to respect the seemingly arbitrary distinctions that, from the system's perspective, are crucial. One participant, who finally succeeded in executing an operation after more than one try, wondered whether her earlier failures were somehow due to her having hit the ENTER key "in the wrong way". To an experienced user this is a nonsensical possibility, but new users do not know enough to rule out interpretations which seem obviously wrong to an experienced user.

Mistaken interpretations like this create confused concepts -- the user ends up making distinctions that have no real consequence. The cases in which users fail to respect the system's actual fine distinctions are worse, for in these cases there *are* very frustrating consequences. One system we studied has multiple ways of deleting material and of moving the cursor. But the key that moves the cursor on the typing page display, causes an error condition when employed on a menu display. Conversely, the key that cancels menus is invalid if used on the typing page display. Participants in our studies tended, at least at first, not to see these distinctions.

The problems occasioned by users drawing unwarranted distinctions and of failing to recognize actual distinctions also interact to produce tangled -- and very nearly undiagnosable -- hybrids. And this does not by any means exhaust the inventory of problems we have identified. From all this, one might be moved to recommend that learners be discouraged from *any* thinking at all. For it is their reluctance (and inability) to passively accept the system *as it is* that causes most of the learning difficulty we have observed. Nevertheless, the novices we have studied are active learners. They do not passively read or follow along rote exercises. They try things out according to self-generated agendas of needs and goals. They construct theories on the fly to explain what the system does. And they spontaneously anchor much of this active reasoning in their prior knowledge (e.g., of typewriters). (See [2], [7] and [10]).

0.3 The minimalist design program. In sum, the problem seems to be that novices try to learn systems by exploration, although this strategy is perhaps not advisable -- that is, from a more expert perspective -- and, as our studies make painfully clear, is not supported by either the interface design or the manual design of current systems. One can take a hard line here about novice explorers getting what they "deserve" or paying their "dues", but one can also face the facts: we can design systems and training to be pretty much any way we want, but human preferences and propensities are fixed constraints. With this sentiment in mind, I want to outline two projects currently underway: one attempts to provide a manual design that could better support our novice explorers, the second attempts to provide a "training" interface design that might also afford better support for the active learning strategies we have documented.

In both cases, I will be describing designs that were developed iteratively in conjunction with human factors testing with real users (office temporaries). Moreover, as will become clearer below, both the training manual and the training interface were also originally conceived of and then designed in direct response to our empirical studies of people trying to learn to use commercial word processors. Hence, both should be regarded as codified *results* of human factors research, generally and in their particulars. Finally, both projects have involved extensive empirical testing. (See also [9]).

1. The Minimal Manual.

Impressed by the frustration and failure we observed when novices attempted to learn to use commercial word processing systems by means of the commercial self-study books that accompany them, Bob Mack, Clayton Lewis and I embarked on a series of studies of "minimalist" training instruments. At the very beginning of this stream of work, we observed a learner who was given essentially *no* training material whatsoever. Her learning was quite chaotic, but she noticed far more information on the display than her typical self-study counterpart. However, she made only halting and non-convergent progress in learning to use the system [1].

We retreated from this extreme "training" procedure in our subsequent work. In one effort, we have trained operators to use the word processing function of office systems using Guided Exploration "cards" [8]. We ended up with a set of about 20 cards (drastically less than the 150 or so pages of self-study manual). In all of this work, a guiding principle has been that learners simply will not read, and that in particular they will not read purely expository materials or be led through purely rote practice exercises (as opposed to *doing* task-oriented

things). Guided exploration via the cards was a mixed success. Learning by guided exploration is sometimes quite chaotic -- and in their own statements, our learners have often expressed a desire for more structure.

Where can we go next? One possibility is to move toward a manual that incorporates elements of the Guided Exploration approach. That is, we might re-introduce the structure of a manual, but in doing so try also to codify some of the principles we have concluded were helpful to our guided exploration learners. The Minimal Manual was constructed for the core function of a commercial word processor. (For details, see [3]). However, while it addresses the same topics as the commercially developed self-study manual that accompanies the system, its design differs in several key ways:

1.1 Less to read. First, the Minimal Manual is less than a quarter as massive as other primers, 45 pages in all. We achieved this by eliminating all repetition, all summaries, reviews, and practice exercises, the index and the troubleshooting appendix. All material not related to doing things was eliminated or radically cut down (the welcome to word processing overview, descriptions of the system status line, details on the system components, the chapter entitled "Using the display information while viewing a document.", etc.). Novice learners do not read manuals effectively or reliably, hence it may be better to spare them the details and include only critical specifics.

As is now well-known, real operators must schedule their training around a host of other work activities. Designers of self-study primers have responded to this by organizing small, independent modules. The problem is -- as we learned in our prior work -- these modules are in fact not nearly small enough. Learners get lost within them. In the Minimal Manual, topics average less than 3 pages (a fifth the typical length).

1.2 Greater task orientation. Manuals often include chapters like "Using the display information while viewing a document", which no word processing tyro would ever really *decide* to undertake. The creation of a real document is often delayed until halfway through the manual. Yet the creation of a real document is the overriding goal that novices bring to this learning situation.

The Minimal Manual seeks to be more task oriented in that its topics (modules) are directed at real work activities instead of merely rote exercise. Chapter headings are task oriented, the Table of Contents serves as a simple index that even a computer naive person can understand as being meaningful: "What is this thing all about?", "Typing something", "Printing something on paper", "Revising something you have typed", etc. Realistic and open ended work exercises are included, under the heading "On Your Own" (see 1.3 immediately below). One reason to include such exercises is to maintain and foster the connection between training and real work. After all, operators must try to learn to use office application systems in the midst of also trying to do their actual work.

1.3 More learner initiative. The learner is cast in a more active role by the Minimal Manual. Its step-by-step exercises give only abbreviated specifications of procedures, leaving some of the detail for the learner to discover or infer. For example, when the arrow cursor keys are introduced in Chapter 4, explicit practice with the down arrow key is followed by the general statement that the other keys work analogously, and by the invitation to "Try them and see." Or again, when the coded Cancel key is first introduced, as a general error recovery, it is explicitly stressed that the user must "use Cancel by holding down the Alternate Shift key while pressing the Cancel key" (Chapter 1). Our earlier work showed that failing to code such keys is a common error. Later in the Minimal Manual, Cancel is still suggested as a general error recovery, but in a more abbreviated form: "If you make a mistake, press Alternate + Cancel and start again." (Chapter 7).

The learner must fill in the steps -- by referring back in the Minimal Manual, by remembering, or by experimenting. In addition, explicitly *non*-step-by-step exercises, labeled "On Your Own," have been incorporated into the manual at the end of most of the topic modules (e.g., Chapter 4): "As you can see on page 4:3, more deletions, insertions, and replacements are suggested for the Smith Letter document. Practice your revision skills by trying some of these. When you have practiced enough, print out Smith Letter (refer to Chapter 3 for help with printing)."

In our prior work, we have found that self-study books are sometimes so complete that learners spend all of their time with their noses in the book. They may not coordinate what they are supposedly learning with what is actually happening on the display. The Minimal Manual attempts to encourage the learner to attend to the display by posing questions to learners regarding prompts. Thus, instead of merely saying that the system will prompt for a document name, and to type the name and press Enter, the Minimal Manual asks the learner "Can you find this prompt on the display?: "Type document name; press Enter." or gives a contingent instruction "Make sure that the word processor is prompting you: "Type document name; press Enter".

1.4 More error recovery information. Despite these reductions in massiveness, there is one category of information that has been greatly increased in the Minimal Manual. This is error recovery information. Most self-study primers do not provide learners with suggestions as to what they can to do if the step-by-step procedure doesn't seem to work out as it should. If novices are going to explore on their own (willingly or in response to prior errors) they are going to make mistakes and get lost. When this happens, they need help in getting back on course. Error recovery information is a distinct category of information in the Minimal Manual.

Specific error recovery information addressed the chief errors we had inventoried. For example, we had found that learners had trouble with the diskette name concept and often typed an incorrect diskette name when prompted, which had the effect of leaving the system hung up. The system in fact had a specific recovery procedure for this problem, but the commercially developed training manual failed to mention it, and learners did not manage to find it in the ancillary documentation. The Minimal Manual included the specific error recovery information for this error. Another error that was typical for learners was pressing the Cancel key without holding

down the Alternate Shift. Cancel is perhaps the best general error remedy the system offers, but has an entirely different meaning when used without the Alternate Shift, and one which leads to complex side effects. We referred to the key as "Alternate + Cancel" throughout the Minimal Manual, to stress the correct key combination -- and we referred to it frequently (to remind learners of its use in error recovery).

1.5 Reference use after training. People using training manuals also use them for reference. This makes sense since part of the learning that goes on when someone works through a training manual is the learning of the book itself. Nevertheless, learners are frustrated in trying to extend training manuals to a new use as reference manuals because all of the explanations, side-tracks, and drills of the manual become camouflage for the kernel information being sought. Learners we have observed often cannot successfully use their self-study materials as reference aids when they try to cross the bridge from "training" to "using". The Minimal Manual should be more extensible for use as a reference both because it is briefer overall and because it is pitched more explicitly at real components of real work (see 1.2 above).

Finally, the "On Your Own" sections of the Minimal Manual often suggest open ended exercises that refer back to other topic modules, thereby encouraging learners to make use of the training manual for reference. This strategy is based on accepting the fact that learners are going to try to use their training books for reference in any case. Our response is to design the books, therefore, to *train* learners in using them for reference.

1.6 Empirical verification. We have tested the Minimal Manual in two large studies. The first study (designed by Jim Ford, Penny-Smith Kerker, and Georgia Gibson) involved 49 learners who used one of five training methods (including two variations of the Minimal Manual) for up to seven full working days. In this study, the Minimal Manual proved to be 40% faster than the other manuals for the basic topic areas it covered -- and to produce learning achievement at least as good as the other methods. The Minimal Manual only covered basic topics, where the commercial manuals covered advanced topics as well. In a later phase of the experiment, Minimal Manual learners were transferred to the advanced topics sections of a commercial manual. Notably, they still were 40% faster, but in this comparison their performance on learning achievement tests was better by a factor of ten. In sum, this experiment provides evidence that the Minimal Manual design is substantially more effective than comparable state-of-the-art commercial manual designs.

A second experiment is being completed now (with Sandra Mazur) in which 32 learners used either the Minimal Manual or a commercially developed alternative. This study is focussing on each learner in detail for 6 hour sessions. Our goal is to analyze the advantages of the approach more finely than mere time and performance studies afford. We know the approach works, but we still have much to learn about why it works and how it can be optimized.

2. The Training Wheels Word Processor.

The minimalist training materials we have designed face a paradox in the fact that the system function they attempt train against is often rather "maximal". That is, contemporary office application systems are capable of many advanced functions. But advanced functions can create problems for the learner who is not ready for them. How can these problems be avoided? Our approach is to limit the learner to only simple functions, and to make advanced functions unavailable.

2.1 Learning simple things first. Why would anyone want to do this? Put directly, learning something that is simple is easier and less frustrating than learning something that is complicated. This should not sound either trivial or paradoxical. Reading Dick and Jane books facilitates reading Russell and Wittgenstein, even though the former is simple and the latter complicated. Indeed, even in the domain of word processing the general training strategy has been to first address simple function and only then more complicated function. It is merely an extension of this strategy to suggest that we first *provide* simple function and only then provide more complicated function.

How can this be done? This question is not simple. There are possibly as many ways to limit function as there are to provide it in the first place. But one simple and direct method suggests itself immediately. One can "close off", or disable, the function of a full system, providing a message like "X is not available in the Training Wheels System.", with X being whatever advanced function a novice ought not to get into at first. This was the approach taken in the design of the Training Wheels Word Processor (as implemented by David Boor). (For details, see [2], [3] and [4]).

Most basically, one wants a word processor to type in documents, to edit documents already typed in, and to print. From this bare bones perspective, functions like Spelling Aids, Format Changing, Menu Skipping, Save-keys, Pagination, and Merging Data, are extras. In a word, this is the design of the Training Wheels System. One loads the system in the same way as one would the full system. One sees the same Home Menu, the first menu that comes up. But then the limitations begin to emerge. From the Home Menu, one can *only* select "a", for Document Tasks. The other choices merely elicit the system response "X is not available on the Training Wheels System"., with X being choices like Program Diskette Tasks, Data Diskette tasks, Merge Data, etc.

2.2 Positive transfer of learning. Notice how this addresses three problems of the novice explorer. First, the need for a training manual has been vastly reduced. (We developed a single Guided Exploration-type card as basic instructional material for the Training Wheels System.) Second, the sometimes reckless novice can safely explore. Menu choices can be tried and tested without fear of inadvertently getting into things like Program Diskette Tasks -- which will be confusing to the first time user, but which are a choice on the Home Menu (and an important set of functions for more skilled users).

Third, the novice -- while "protected" from the consequences of reckless exploration -- *has* seen the choices,

seen the full menus, and even tested the operations involved in making the choices. And all at no cost in terms of side-tracks and the frustration of getting lost. In psychological jargon, these common interface elements provide a basis for "high positive transfer" between the Training Wheels System and the full system interface. For when this novice graduates to the full system, the same displays will appear and the same keys can be pressed. However, instead of the disabled function messages, the full function will be engaged.

To make this point, let us briefly tour the Training Wheels System. After loading the system, the Home Menu appears. The only route open at this point is choice "a", Document Tasks. Having arrived at the Document Tasks Menu, the user can select "a" to create a document, "b" to edit a document, "d" to print a document, or "f" to return to the Home Menu. Printing can only be selected if the user has immediately before selected create or edit. Otherwise, a disablement message comes up: *"Print Document" is only available after a "Create" or a "Edit" document.* We return to this specific disablement below.

All three of Create, Edit, and Print evoke a prompting sequence to elicit from the user a document name and then a work diskette name (just as they do on the full system). When these have been specified, either the Create or Edit Document Menu or the Print Menu appears, depending on what was originally requested by the user. However, none of the menu options on either of these two menus is active in the Training Wheels System. Indeed, the only productive thing the user can do on these menus is to press Enter. In the case of the Create or Edit Document Menu, this brings up the Typing Area, and allows the user to enter data. In the case of the Print Document menu, this causes the specified document to be sent to the printer for printing on paper, and returns the Document Tasks Menu to the display.

Typing Area function can also be complex. Its complexity derives not from a diversity of menu selections and branching, but from a diversity of special function keys, Word Underscore, Required Backspace, Center, etc. These function keys are very useful, indeed necessary, to the skilled user of word processing equipment, but they can confuse the novice. They sometimes perform a powerful function without apparently altering the displayed document (e.g., Required Backspace). None of these function keys are active in the Training Wheels System. The user can type regular alpha-numeric characters and line returns, and can delete by backspacing. But nothing else works.

So far, a stripped down word processing system has been sketched in which nearly everything is disabled and labelled as such by messages of the type "X is not available in the Training Wheels System". It has been argued that the sheer reduction of complexity is a plus for novices, and further that there should be a positive transfer of learning due to the fact that the menus, messages, and prompts that *can* be reached are identical to those of the full system -- and the fact that the disablement messages themselves, by specifically saying "not available in the Training Wheels System", invite the new user to understand that these disabled keys *will* be available in another version of the system, the non-Training Wheels version. These points can be sharpened by examining the specific error states that the Training Wheels System "saves" its novice users from.

2.3 Common error states are unreachable. The Training Wheels System also blocks several error states which seem to be characteristic problems for novices, based on our observational studies. We have already referred to the pervasive tendency of new users to recklessly try menu choices like Program Diskette Tasks (from the Home Menu) only to encounter trouble in returning to where they started their exploratory excursion. We might call this the Exotic Menu Choice error. As noted, the Training Wheels System eliminates this sort of error by responding: *(Program Diskette Task) is not available on the Training Wheels System.* A second typical error is the Print First error. Users really want to achieve something real with system, and fast. It is typical that a new user requests a print on Document Tasks *before* creating any documents to print. The system prompts for a document name and then for a diskette name -- but of course the user has no document name to give, because there is no document to print. As noted earlier, this error cannot be committed on the Training Wheels System because it is impossible to request a print before creating or revising. One gets the disablement message: *"Print Document" is available only after a "Create" or a "Edit" document.*

Perhaps a more frustrating case is the Parameter Loop error. On menus like Create or Edit Document and Print Document, there is a highlighted prompt: "Type id letter; press Enter". From these menus, a user need not choose any menu parameter at all, and indeed there is another message on the display "When finished with this menu, press Enter". However, the latter message is not highlighted and new users never seem to see it. They do see the former message however, and they invariably type a letter to specify a parameter. Having done so, they are now prompted "Type Your Choice; press Enter". Two problems now occur. First, people type "Your Choice" -- which is taking things too literally and leads to a tangle of errors. Second, they correctly enter a choice -- only to again be presented with the highlighted prompt "Type id letter; press Enter". Very frequently, new users *again* go through the your-choice business, redundantly respecifying the original menu parameter, or altering another parameter. This can go on and on, hence the name Parameter Loop. This error state is unreachable in the Training Wheels System because *all* of the parameters on the Print Document and the Create or Edit Document menus are disabled. On these menus, users either press Enter to go on, or Cancel to go back. Nothing else works.

Another troubling problem for novices is the Alternate Shift Error. The full system has a dangerous Utility key. "Dangerous" because it brings up the Utility Menu when pressed, anywhere. Novice users have particular difficulty with understanding the concept of transfer of control [13], and the Utility key abruptly transfers control to the Utility Menu. Thus, a user who presses Utility in the Typing Area is whisked away from the document he or she was working on to a menu offering seemingly inscrutable choices. The problem is further complicated

when the Utility Menu is dismissed (by making a choice and pressing Enter), since control is returned to the state from which Utility was originally called. However, the user has quite typically forgotten all about this state and is as confused by its return as by its original disappearance. This error is relatively easy to make because Utility is the nonalternated variant of Cancel, and users trying to Cancel often get Utility by failing to hold down the Alternate Shift key. The Alternate Shift Error state is unreachable in the Training Wheels System because the Utility key is disabled.

A fifth error is the Print Queue error. Sensibly enough, the full system allows multiple print jobs to be queued. Novices of course lack the concept of a "queue" (they lack the term as well). Moreover, because they often fail to operate the Message key -- either at all or at the appropriate times, novices get inconsistent feedback from the system regarding the success their print jobs. We have found that it is extremely typical that new users issue multiple print requests, not even realizing that multiple prints have been requested. When they (finally) get paper output, they conclude that the print was a success, and they go on to other things. However, the queued prints -- the ones they have not yet put on paper -- remain in the print queue. This leads to several further problems. For example, if the user now requests another print of an entirely new document, and then goes on to put it on paper, the output will be what was queued and not what was just requested. Or, if the user now attempts to edit the document that is in fact queued to print, an inscrutable error message comes up: "(document name) in use." Novice users just don't know what is happening in these cases. The Print Queue error state is unreachable in the Training Wheels System because its print queue can hold only one document. A user who requests a second print gets a message: *Only one document at a time can be printed on the Training Wheels System.*

Another inaccessible error state is the Diskette Name error. In the course of creating, revising, and printing a document, the user is prompted by the system to specify a document name and a diskette name, in that order. The typical case is that the user has one data diskette which is named WORK. Hence, to the prompt "Type diskette name; press Enter", the user should type in the name WORK. New users have trouble with these prompt sequences. They often type the document names incorrectly, and have to retype. However if they mistype the diskette name, say WROK instead of WORK, the system now prompts "Insert diskette WROK". Of course, the user has no diskette WROK to insert. The Diskette Name error state is unreachable in the Training Wheels System because it only accepts the name WORK as a response to the diskette name prompt. Entering any other name evokes the message: *Diskette "WROK" is not available on the Training Wheels System.*

2.4 Conclusion and working plans. The Training Wheels System (1) makes many error states unreachable for novice users, (2) encourages positive transfer of learning to the full function system by maintaining common interface elements, and (3) provides a new sort of solution to the problem of learning by exploration, namely the solution of encouraging -- not penalizing -- such learning effort. The Training Wheels System can be a real "exploratory environment" [1] for learning -- responsive to users (in virtue of its many disablement messages), forgiving of errors (by blocking them), and encouraging active learning strategies. And it can as well be a real step toward mastering the full function of an office application system.

Beyond these considerations, the Training Wheels System might be useful on other grounds as well. First, it could be a very convenient level of word processing function for temporary office personnel. Imagine the situation in which an office temp is required for a single day in an office which is equipped with several word processors. The permanent secretarial staff are advanced well beyond the Training Wheels level of function, but the one-day temp is starting from scratch. This person can be assigned a Training Wheels System with which no very serious errors can be made, and with which something useful can be accomplished, even if not the more skilled jobs involving tables and format changes. Another possible case is the office principle, that recalcitrant discretionary user. These people -- conventional wisdom suggests -- have no taste for manuals or start-up time of any kind. Perhaps a system that is so simple that errors are virtually all blocked, that can reduce its training manual to a single card -- even at the cost of more limited function, is just the environment this class of new user might need to break into the regular use of word processing -- and other electronic office -- equipment. (These possibilities were suggested by David Boor.)

Finally, the Training Wheels System can be part of a new approach to to training. Instead of following through a single manual with a single system, we might imagine the Training Wheels System, with rather spare training materials, as the first module of a training program that could involve several "staged" manual-system interfaces. As a specific case, the Training Wheels System affords all of the function necessary to complete Chapters 1-3 of the Minimal Manual discussed in Section 1 above. The two could be conjoined into a single training program in which the first stage consisted of the Training Wheels System, with its Guided Exploration card or with Chapters 1-3 of the Minimal Manual, followed by the full system, with Chapters 4-15 of the Minimal Manual. Indeed, one could imagine breaking the training into many more stages -- with the possibility of reducing the overall volume of printed material much further than even the Minimal Manual.

We have carried out several experimental evaluations of the Training Wheels System. In the first two studies we asked 24 learners to use either the Training Wheels System or the complete commercial system to learn to type and print out a simple document. In one study we asked learners to learn by the book, to follow the manual in learning, and in the other study we asked them to learn by doing, that is to focus on getting the job done. The results of these studies were quite encouraging: learners using the Training Wheels System got started faster, produced better work, and spent less time not only on the errors that our design blocked, but on the errors we did not block -- indicating a generalized facilitation of

learning. Moreover, the magnitude of these advantages increase over the course of the experiment. Lastly, the Training Wheels learners performed better on a system concepts test we administered after the experiment [4].

Minimalist design gambles on the expectation that if you give the learner *less* (less to read, less overhead, less to get tangled in), the learner will achieve *more*. The early results on Minimalist design are in, and they are encouraging. Furthermore, these early results were not costly in terms of development time: the Minimal Manual and the Training Wheels Word Processor, were designed and implemented at a cost of less than a man-month [3]. It is surprising when both users and developers can get more for less, but it makes for a happy ending.

Note. I am grateful to Clayton Lewis for his comments.

References.
[1] Carroll, J.M. The adventure of getting to know a computer. *Computer,* 15 (1982) 49-58.
[2] Carroll, J.M. Presentation and form in user interface architecture. *Byte,* 8 (1983) 113-122.
[3] Carroll, J.M. Designing MINIMALIST training materials. IBM Watson Research Center (February 1984).
[4] Carroll, J.M. and Carrithers, C. Training wheels in a user interface. *Communications of the ACM,* (1984).
[5] Carroll, J.M. and Mack, R.L. Actively learning to use a word processor. In W.E. Cooper (ed.) *Cognitive aspects of skilled typewriting,* (Springer-Verlag, New York, 1983).
[6] Carroll, J.M. and Mack, R.L. Learning to use a word processor: By doing, by thinking, and by knowing. In J.C. Thomas and M. Schneider (eds.), *Human factors in computing systems.* (Ablex, Norwood, NJ, 1984).
[7] Carroll, J.M. and Mack, R.L. Metaphor, computing systems, and active learning, IBM Watson Research Center (October 1982).
[8] Carroll, J.M., Mack, R.L., Lewis, C.H., Grischkowsky, N.L., and Robertson, S.R. Learning to use a word processor by Guided Exploration, IBM Watson Research Center (January 1984).
[9] Carroll, J.M. and Rosson, M.B. Usability specifications as a tool in iterative development. In H.R. Hartson (ed.), *Advances in Human-Computer Interaction,* (Ablex, Norwood, NJ, 1984).
[10] Carroll, J.M. and Thomas, J.C. Metaphor and the cognitive representation of computing systems. *IEEE Transactions on Systems, Man, and Cybernetics,* 12 (1982) 107-116.
[11] Lewis, C.H. and Mack, R.L. The role of abduction in learning to use text-processing systems. American Educational Research Association, Annual Meeting (March 1982).
[12] Mack, R.L., Lewis, C.H., and Carroll, J.M. Learning to use word processors: Problems and prospects. *ACM Transactions on Office Information Systems,* 1 (1983) 254-271.
[13] Miller, L.A. Programming by non-programmers. *International Journal of Man-Machine Studies,* 6 (1974) 237-260.

Designing for Error

CLAYTON LEWIS and DONALD A. NORMAN

```
longjmp botch: core dumped
Fatal error in pass zero
awk: syntax error near line 1
awk: bailing out near line 1
cp: asd: No such file or directory
```

The above messages illustrate the surface of the difficult problem of dealing with error. The messages all result from the fact that the user has done something that the system cannot respond to. The result is for the system to produce an error message, much like the five examples shown above.

The difficulty with error messages is well known. Shneiderman (1980) and du Boulay and Matthew (1984), among others, have pointed out that the format and tone of these messages are often offensive, especially for beginners, leading them to believe that they, personally, have performed some serious misdeed due to their own incompetence. Moreover, even if a user tries to correct the fault that is being signaled, the information provided them is not always sufficient to allow them to find the problem. Indeed, the messages are often presented in such a way as to encourage the sorts of false explanations described by Lewis in Chapter 8.

*The examples that opened this chapter were all real. The "longjmp botch" message comes courtesy of the "more" program in 4.2BSD UNIX, discovered (repeatedly) by D. Norman (see Draper & Norman, 1984). Note that the error message does not even say which program has had the difficulty, so that if many procedures are being used at the same time (as is often the case), the user does not even have any idea of which routine has caused the problem, how to recover, or how to avoid the difficulty in the future. The "Fatal error in pass zero" message comes from a compiler heavily used by students. It is discussed in du Boulay and Matthew (1984). The "awk" errors are two of the more famous exit lines of the UNIX program "awk" when it finds the situation hopeless. You might think that "awk" was being helpful by identifying itself and then indicating roughly where in the file the difficulty occurred. You would be wrong. The two errors both resulted from specifying a nonexistent file (the command used was "*awk asd*." "Awk" is perfectly capable of determining that its difficulty came from the fact that the file "asd" did not exist. Instead, it gives the erroneous and misleading error messages appropriate had the file existed with a non-intelligible first line. Other UNIX programs, such as "cp" (the copy command) do better. The command sequence "*cp asd*" yields the last error message in the list: meaningful and useful. Even it could have done better, however, by aiding the user to make the correction rather than simply quitting, forcing the user to retype the sometimes lengthy command line for what might have been an error in a single character.*

Why are these situations called "errors"? In fact, what is really meant is that the system can't interpret the information given to it. By convention, this is called an error, a fault generated by the user. This is a rather arrogant point of view coming from a system designed to serve its users. A more appropriate point of view should really be that of apology:

I am very sorry, but I seem to have gotten confused. Could you help me out?

After all, if User Centered Design is to be taken seriously, then the interaction with a system is to be thought of as a cooperative endeavor: The task is not to find fault and to assess blame but rather to get the task done. Failures to understand are commonplace and normal. Conversation is riddled with speech errors, from incomplete sentences to erroneous choice of words. But certainly we do not expect the people with whom we talk to respond to our speech errors with:

Your sentence was not grammatical. Say it again. (But do it right this time. Please.)

In conversation, minor speech errors get repaired so automatically that the speaker often does not even realize they were made. And when the utterance cannot be understood, the listener can ask for correction of only the single word or phrase that caused the trouble:

I'm sorry—where should I put the glass?

In the normal conversational situation, both participants assume equal responsibility in understanding. If there is a failure to understand, both take responsibility for repairing the difficulty. The analogous statement in a computer system would be something like this—the response that we classify later in this chapter as "Let's talk about it":

I can't find the filename you mention:
/csl/norman/HCIbook/LewisNorman/designingForError
Do you mean:
*   1: DesigningForError*
*   2: design-notes*
Please type which number or specify a new name:

Consider the last three error messages in the opening example of the chapter. Those responses would have the user retype that entire, lengthy file specification (49 characters long!) simply for failure to capitalize the "d" in the last term of the expression. If the system took some of the responsibility, talking about the difficulty rather than assigning blame, the result would be a much more cooperative endeavor.

Although we do not believe it possible to design systems in which people do not make errors, we do believe that much can be done to minimize the incidence of error, to maximize the discovery of the error, and to make it easier to recover from the error. The focal theme of this chapter is to examine ways of treating a person's error in such a way that discovery and recovery are simple, natural, and even pleasant.

The ideal situation would be one in which the error recovery was so graceful that it was not noticed

DEALING WITH ERROR

We would prefer not even to use the term "error." Misunderstandings, problems, confusions, ambiguities: Any other term would be preferable. The very term "error" assigns blame, yet as we just pointed out, the system is just as much to blame for its failure to understand as is the user for a failure to be perfectly, unambiguously, precise. Nonetheless, the term and the concept is with us. So for the while we should learn to deal with "error" as gracefully as possible.

We can do several things with error. One is to try to devise systems that eliminate or minimize errors. Another is to try to make it easier to deal with error when it exists, first by providing clear indication of the problem and its possible causes and remedies, second by providing tools that make correction easier. Finally, because many errors—sometimes serious ones—go undetected for surprisingly long times (because the actions being performed are legal and even sensible under other circumstances), the system should provide the kind of information that helps the user understand the implications of the actions being followed. For all of these procedures it is useful first to start with an understanding of error.

Understanding Error

Several theoretical analyses of errors exist (Norman, 1981a, 1983b; Reason & Mycielska, 1982). These analyses have been useful, but for current purposes we simply need to note the major categories of errors and the major difficulties that are associated with them. We divide errors into two major categories: *mistakes* and *slips*. The division occurs at the level of the intention: A person establishes an intention to act. If the intention is not appropriate, this is a *mistake*. If the action is not what was intended, this is a *slip*. It is of course possible to perform both a mistake and slip simultaneously; form an erroneous intention, and then carry it out improperly.

Slips can be analyzed and categorized into their causes. Interestingly enough, many forms of slips do not occur with beginners: The highly practiced, automated behavior of the expert leads to the lack of focused attention that increases the likelihood of some forms of slips. Slips are usually not as serious a problem as mistakes, and within mistakes, the greatest problems seem to result from misinterpretation or misdiagnosis of the situation. There are several consequences that follow from misdiagnosis, perhaps the most obvious being that the behavior that follows is then likely to be inappropriate for the situation. Worse, misinterpretation hampers detection of the effort, and even serious errors may go undetected for hours (and in the case of program bugs, sometimes for years). Detection of misdiagnosis is hampered by several factors, including the prevalence of the explanations discussed by Lewis in Chapter 8. We return to these later when we consider how people detect error.

MINIMIZING ERROR

Although we do not believe that it is possible to design systems that eliminate error, much can be done to minimize it. One factor is simply good system design, including the physical layout of the components and displays of the interface, intelligent choice of command names, and so on. These topics are well covered in standard human factors procedures and numerous studies of command names: We will not pursue them further. Another factor comes from providing good explanatory tools, a good conceptual model, a system image that matches that model. (This topic is of central concern for most of the chapters within this section of the book.) In similar fashion, the more effort that the person must exert to bridge the Gulfs of Execution and Evaluation (Chapters 3 and 5), the more room for errors of understanding and of interpretation. Some errors can be reduced through careful choice of representation: Thus, some task representations rule out whole classes of errors present with other representations.

Avoiding Error Through Appropriate Representation

Consider the problem of specifying a nonexistent file, the problem that led to the last three error messages in the opening illustration of the chapter. Why might a nonexistent file be specified? Here are reasons: The intended file perhaps didn't really exist; it might exist, but its name might be misremembered or misspelled; the file name might be correct, but the user might be working in the wrong directory. We could imagine many ways of providing better information about which files existed and what their names were. We could imagine spelling correctors or intelligent search procedures that would correct for some errors and for some instances of improper directories. And we could imagine improved error messages and error correcting techniques.

But note that the class of errors results from the representational format chosen by the system: Files are represented by typed strings of characters, thus requiring exact specification of the character string. If

a different representational format for files were used, the entire class of errors would no longer exist. Thus, if files were indicated by icons on the screen and specification were done by pointing at an icon, it would not be possible to point at a nonexistent file. Directory errors would be noted by the physical absence of the desired icon and by the surrounding context, and spelling errors would no longer be a factor. The representational system has the *intrinsic* property of foreclosing a whole class of errors found with other forms of representation. (File selection by pointing at icons is really a form of menu selection, and the same comments therefore apply to any system in which files are specified through menu options.)

Note that we are not attempting to advocate file specification through the use of menus or icons over other forms of specification. We are simply pointing out that every choice of representation provides a set of intrinsic properties, sometimes eliminating whole classes of errors that are troublesome with other representations. But every design decision is a tradeoff, and this form of representation makes difficult some desirable operations, such as specifying a file from within a program (without user intervention) or specifying a class of files, such as "all files whose names start with 'test.doc'." Moreover, some old problems remain, although in slightly different form. Thus, although one cannot specify a nonexistent file or misspell a file name when files are specified by pointing, it is still quite possible to point at the wrong file.

Avoiding False Understandings

Some difficulties arise through false understanding of the system's properties. As a result, this class of errors can be minimized by giving more information. Some false understandings arise because people can generalize more from a single experience than is really appropriate. The positive side of this is to increase the efficiency of learning. The negative side is to make false inferences.

We can illustrate this point through an example given to us by a student during a class discussion of an early draft of this book. Student S commented that he often learned system commands in the "indirect" manner discussed by Owen in Chapters 9 and 17. Thus, when he first moved to a UNIX system, he could not figure out how to "delete" a file. But one day he watched someone "rm" a file, and decided that in UNIX, "delete file" was referred to as "remove file, with "remove" abbreviated as "rm." This is a positive example of

done by Norman (1983b): We summarize here the major findings of that study. There are several categories of slips, but the most relevant for system design are mode errors, capture errors, and description errors. Let us examine each briefly.

Mode errors suggest the need for better feedback. A large class of errors are classified as mode errors: doing the operation appropriate for one mode when in fact you are in another. Modes will be with us as long as we wish to be able to do more operations than it is sensible to have special keys for. Most complex devices end up having them, be they digital watches, aircraft automatic pilots, or text editors. Even "modeless systems" have modes, but disguised. *Smalltalk*, the text editor *Emacs*, the *Macintosh* operating systems: all have numerous states where the first operation performed changes the interpretation of subsequent keypresses or mouse clicks. Avoiding modes entirely is not practical, but one can minimize modes. Feedback is essential so that the user can tell in what mode the system is in: Make sure that the modes are distinctively marked.

Description errors suggest the need for better consistency. A description error occurs when there is insufficient specification of the action, and the resultant ambiguity leads to an erroneous act being performed. The name emphasizes the fact that the description of the action was correct, but insufficiently specified, so the act that got done in error matched many characteristics of the correct one. One class of description errors occurs when a person attempts to rederive an action sequence and does so improperly, forming a sequence appropriate for an action different from the one intended. This occurs primarily through a lack of consistency in command structure, so that the appropriate structure for one command is not the same for another, even, though the commands appear to be related and share a common description of purpose, action, and even part of the command format. The basic concept involved here is that when people lack knowledge about the proper operation of some aspect of a machine, they are apt to derive the operation by analogy with other, similar aspects of the device. The "derivation" may be unconscious, and it can influence behavior without the person realizing that it is happening.

Capture errors suggest the need for better feedback. A capture error occurs when there is overlap in the sequence required for the performance of an infrequent and a frequently performed action, and in the course of attempting the infrequent one, the more common act gets

learning indirectly: One observation resulted in a general rule. In class it was pointed out that this was a false generalization: There might actually be many different ways of deleting files, and "rm" might only be one special way. There isn't, but on one exposure, S really was taking a risk by making such a generalization.

S agreed, and gave this second example of just that problem. He learned the UNIX mail system by watching someone else use it. The person read his mail and left the mail system with the command "x" (for "exit"). S thereafter read his mail in the same way. However, he noticed that although he would "delete" many of the messages as he read his mail, on each new use those "deleted" messages were still present. Eventually, he sent a message to the system administrator, explaining that there was an error in his mail program. The administrator, obviously skilled with the mail program, suggested that S was using the wrong command to terminate the mail session: He should have been using the command "q" for "quit." The command "x" is the abnormal exit, one that aborts without updating records. The normal way to terminate the mail program is with "q": it updates all the mail files.

Note that S made the same form of inference in both the "rm" and the mail system examples. In one case it was correct, but in the other case erroneous. In neither case did S entertain the notion that there might be several versions of the command.

These are examples of learning by induction, a procedure that is both powerful and problematic. When learning is accomplished in this manner, its success depends critically upon getting the right sequence of examples (see especially the work of VanLehn & Brown, 1980, and Winston, 1975). This implies that the problems faced by the learners won't be solved by such things as improvements in the system image. Rather, we need to contrive ways to get users to try some alternatives— and just the right alternatives at that.

Minimizing Errors That Result From Slips

Analysis of slips can yield suggestions for the design of systems that minimize the incidence of this class of errors. One such analysis was

shows it to be wrong. [1] As we argue later, this cognitive hysteresis appears to result from a bias to search only for confirming evidence, the danger of partial explanations, and the similarity between the actual and the perceived event. Developing a system that can provide sufficient information to help in effective diagnosis and in getting out of the cognitive hysteresis should be a major design consideration.

How Should the System Respond?

Now let us get to the heart of the matter: How should the system respond when it can not interpret the information given to it by the user? There are two goals here: one is to figure out what is intended so that the system can proceed with its operations; the other is to warn when something inappropriate has taken place (or is about to take place). Let us first examine this latter goal, that of providing a signal to the user thus signifying that something has gone wrong.

One basic response that helps signal the occurrence of difficulty is to construct the system in such a way that difficulties prevent continued operation. We call this property a *forcing function*: something that prevents the behavior from continuing until the problem has been corrected. This guarantees self-detection. Suppose you get into your automobile and start to drive away, but without ever starting the engine (the error does actually occur). This error cannot go undetected—the car simply will not move. This is a forcing function and the error is self-correcting. The fact that something is wrong is brought forcefully to attention. Forcing functions are sometimes carefully constructed by the designer, but can often fall out of the system operation naturally— as in the example of the automobile keys.

Note that the forcing function is not to be thought of as an error message. Rather, the sequence of operation is so designed that the one simply cannot proceed, but the observation occurs naturally, in the normal course of events. No error bells or messages need occur in the automobile example. Starting the engine is a natural prerequisite to driving the automobile. The lack of movement serves as the indication that something has gone wrong. It is not always possible to develop such natural sequences. Thus, removing the ignition keys from the

done instead. One possible way of avoiding this class of error is to minimize overlapping sequences, but this may not be possible, especially when the infrequent action sequence is simply a modification of the frequent one. A second way of avoiding the error is to try to catch it where it occurs. The error occurs at the critical place where the sequences deviate, so it is here that the problem must be faced. If the system knows what the intention of the user is (perhaps by requiring the user to indicate the overall intention), it could be designed so that at the critical choice point the proper path was flagged or in some other way brought to the attention of the operator. In addition, sufficient feedback about the state of the system should be provided to offer reminders as to the deviation from the intention. A major issue here is simply to know the critical place at which the errors occur so that remedial action can be built into the system at that critical point.

DETECTING ERROR

Detecting an error is the first step toward recovery. Early detection of error is extremely important. Delayed detection obviously wastes time and effort as the user works through steps that will not be effective because of an earlier error. As steps pile up, the diagnosis of the error becomes harder: The more that has happened, the more places there are to look for something wrong. This is especially a problem for the new user, who cannot partition what has been done into the surely right and the possibly wrong—the "bootstrapping" problem discussed in the Introduction to this section of the book. And in most systems the repair aids, "undo's or inverse operations, often can only be applied right after the error, or within a small number of steps of it. Making errors show up clearly and quickly is a key design goal.

Slips are easier to detect than mistakes. In a slip, the action that was performed differs from the action intended: Detection occurs by comparing the outcome with the intention. In a mistake, it is the intention that is wrong, so if the person compares the outcome with the intention, it matches, so the person is apt to say, "yup, things are going just fine." As a result, it can be remarkably difficult to discover an error. Slips, mind you, are not always easy to discover. A major problem in the discovery of slips is the problem of levels: The level at which actions take place in the world differ from the level at which the intention is formed. Detection of misdiagnosis is hampered by a *cognitive hysteresis*—the tendency to stick with a decision even after the evidence

---

[1] We use the term *cognitive hysteresis* because it takes less information to reach a particular interpretation of the situation than it does to give up that interpretation. Indeed, it sometimes appears that people can form judgments of a situation rapidly, but that it takes an enormous amount of information, time, and energy to cause them to discard that initial judgment. The psychological terms "set" and "functional fixation" refer to related concepts.

automobile at the end of the trip is not on a natural sequence of prerequisite events. As a result it is not uncommon to leave the keys in the car. (Requiring the use of the keys to lock the auto doors may seem inconvenient to some, but it does provide a natural forcing function, making it impossible to lock one's only set of keys in the car: an event that happens with some frequency in cars that can be locked without the use of keys.)

Forcing functions guarantee detection of a problem, but not proper identification of it. Failure to load the proper floppy diskette into a computer has a forcing function: The program will not work properly. However, the user may be only aware of the fact that something went wrong, but unaware of the cause. Determining the cause requires more feedback from the system.

In the early days of the UNIX text editor Ed it was possible to spend hours on the terminal editing a file, then quit—failing to save the work in permanent storage (the computer disk). As a result, all the work would be lost. (The event happened more frequently than might be expected.) The solution was to add a forcing function: An attempt to quit without first saving the text will fail. In the UNIX vi text editor (a grandchild of Ed) the failure is accompanied by the message: No write since last change (:quit! overrides). This response is both a forcing function and an explanation, describing why the command has not been executed, and stating how the command can be done, if that is really what is desired. On many small business and personal computers, it is still possible to stop editing without saving the work by removing the diskette. The Macintosh computer attempts to prevent this with a forcing function: The diskette cannot normally be removed unless the application has been terminated properly. This still does not prevent the user from simply turning off the power, however.

A forcing function is simply one of many responses the system can make when it senses difficulties. In fact, we identify six possible responses: *Gag, Warn, Do Nothing, Self Correct, Teach Me,* and *Let's Talk About It.* In the next sections we discuss these six kinds of responses.

Gag. The automobile that will not move unless the key is in the ignition provides a good illustration of the technique we call *gag.* "Gag" is a forcing function, one that deals with errors by preventing the user

from continuing, thus preventing the user from expressing impossible intentions. Some systems deal with error by locking the keyboard, preventing further typing until the user has "reset" the terminal. This is an effective gag, but one that at times appears to use brute strength when a friendly reminding would do: If the goal is to antagonize the user, this method works well.

A more successful illustration of "gag" comes from a tutorial language system called FLOW, developed by Raskin (1974). In this system, commands are typed in and processed one character at a time. If the user attempts to key a character that does not have a continuation into a legal command, the character is not accepted. You just can't type anything that isn't a legal command in the given context.

FLOW was an elementary programming language, designed by Raskin for beginning computer users from the fine arts, students who normally cringed at the thought of mathematics or computers. Raskin used to demonstrate this system by closing his eyes and pounding upon the keyboard, gleefully pointing out that not only did no system error messages appear, but that at the end, there would be a legal, syntactically correct program. (Of course the program was meaningless.) The result, explained Raskin, was that his students were not afraid to experiment. The lack of error message associated with syntax and text entering increased their confidence. (An excellent tracing program that stepped through the program line-by-line, showing which statement was being executed and what result would occur, helped the understanding of the semantics of the language.)

"Gag" transfers the users' concern from trying to do things to trying to say them: The front-line problem is typing something the system will accept. Rather than letting the user try out various intentions, which may not work, the system intervenes to block the expression of the intention, perhaps before it is fully formulated. This may interfere with learning, especially learning through experimentation. But, as in Raskin's FLOW system, it can also relieve the frustrations associated with low-level typing errors, allowing the user to concentrate upon the major themes to be learned.

Warn. Several types of warnings are possible. In many automobiles, a buzzer warns when the seatbelts are not fastened, but the auto can be operated even if the warning is ignored. In some computer systems, similar warnings tell of files that are not write-protected, or other conditions that are not set up in normal fashion. Here, the philosophy is to note the occurrence of a potentially dangerous situation, to tell the user, but then to let the user decide how to respond. "Gag" forces itself on the user: "Warn" is less officious.

The Macintosh interface uses a related approach. Here, the menus show all possible actions, including ones that are not legal at the current state. The user is warned of the illegal actions: The commands not available at the moment are signaled by being shaded in gray as a warning that they cannot be selected at the moment. The user is not forced: The user can still attempt to select the command. In some sense, "warn" is presenting the error message before the fact, and as such might also be considered as an error-preventing procedure rather than as an error message.

Do nothing. Some direct manipulation interfaces use the *do nothing* approach. If you attempt an illegal action it just doesn't work. Nothing special happens, and you are left to infer that you tried something forbidden. The lack of movement after the attempt to drive an automobile without starting the engine is an example of a "do nothing" response. In the *Pinball Construction Set* (Budge, 1983), if you try to change the color of an object whose color can not be changed, you can go through all the motions, but nothing happens. "The paint won't stick" is how one user characterizes it. Note that the users of neither the automobile nor the construction set consider the "do nothing" response to be an error message. It is simply the way the system works: In the real world, some operations don't work on some objects. The pinball world is similar: Not all operations have effects. One could argue the merits of the "do nothing" strategy, but in this particular type of situation it seems to be very effective, both in conveying the error and in avoiding any disruption or ill feeling on the part of the user.

The "do nothing" method relies on visibility of the effects of its operations to convey the gap between intentions and outcomes. "Do nothing" is mostly seen in direct manipulation systems. But it isn't linked to the direct manipulation concept in any fundamental way, except that if it is to be effective, the lack of action must be readily apparent: In the terms used in earlier chapters of this book, the Gulf of Evaluation must be small or nonexistent.

"Do nothing" is the simplest error technique and, when used properly, seems to have some important advantages. The user stays focused on the domain of actions and their effects, rather than being drawn out to process error messages. The user may have to do some experimenting to discover why what was tried didn't work, but this has its good side: The user is kept in a mode in which trying things out seems reasonable.

"Do nothing" also seems superior to "warn" in situations as complex as the *Pinball Construction Set.* Thus, even though when the user invokes the paint brush, the system knows that the intention is to color some objects, but when the display is complex with a large number of objects, an attempt to "warn" which objects were colorable and which not might result in a display that was visually more confusing than revealing.

Self correct. Another approach is for the system to try to guess some legal action that might be what the user would like to do. Simple spelling correction is an example of this approach. The ultimate in such systems is probably *DWIM: Do What I Mean,* the corrector available on the InterLisp system (Teitelman & Masinter, 1981). Note that automatic correction facilities, such as DWIM are only acceptable when there is a good "undo" facility, so if DWIM does something inappropriate, it is easy to "undo" it. As the designer of the system (Teitelman) once put it: "If you have made an error, you are going to have to correct it anyway. So I might as well have DWIM try to correct it. In the best case, it gets it right. In the worst case it gets it wrong and you have to undo it: but you would have had to make a correction anyway, so DWIM can't make it worse."

DWIM becomes a way of life, a fundamental part of InterLisp that changes the way people think of the system. DWIM is powerful enough that it is used deliberately. Because DWIM remembers corrections given it, one can deliberately introduce a new term that will cause

Not all system designers seem aware of the requirement that "do nothing" can be used only where there is good feedback. Thus, in the Berkeley 4.2BSD UNIX system, the "remote copy" command, "rcp," copies files between computers. It requires a minimum of two arguments. If only one argument is given, the command fails, but with no indication. If two arguments are given, but neither refers to a legal file, the command still appears to work. "rcp" follows the "do nothing" philosophy of error message, much to the frustration of the user. UNIX does not provide automatic display of the state of its file system, so in this case the "do nothing" philosophy is inappropriate. (The normal copy command, "cp," does not misbehave in this way: It responds to a non-existent file with a message, as shown by the last example at the start of the chapter.)

the system to call upon DWIM, then tell DWIM that it means whatever it is that was really wanted, and forever after type a simple term instead of a more complex one, letting DWIM "correct" the term, simplifying the typing. DWIM has even been used to introduce Algol-like notation to Lisp: When the user typed in Algol expressions, DWIM "corrected" it to Lisp syntax. DWIM also can be annoying, for it can sometimes get carried away, correcting things that ought not to be corrected. Some users swear by DWIM, some swear at it. As an error correcting facility, DWIM seems superb. Its negative features result from the overgeneralization of its facilities. Although DWIM can be asked to query the user before making changes (and it can be turned off entirely), the problem is that the user wants some of the features, but not all, and this is not easy to arrange.

DWIM—and presumably other "intelligent" error correction systems, can sometimes be too smart, frustrating the user. Here is one user's description of the problem:

One especially annoying thing that DWIM can do is this: You are composing Lisp code and in true Lisp tradition, you want understandable variable and function names. Suppose you define and call a function "(get-next)." DWIM sees the expression and helpfully decides that you have made a typing error: You clearly mean to subtract "next" from "get" but forgot both the spaces and also the proper Lisp notation that requires the action to be listed first. So, DWIM politely, elegantly transforms your name "(get-next)" into the Lisp code "(minus get next)." When you try to run the program, you get an error message: "get" was discovered to be an unbound variable, found while Lisp was executing IDIFF, the routine for taking differences between integers. The problem, of course, is the hyphen in the function name. Using hyphenated names is common practice in other Lisp environments, but is to be avoided in InterLisp. There the convention is to capitalize initial letters, so the function would be called "GetNext" instead of "get-next." One learns these conventions after being burned a few times, but the first few times it happens, it can be very difficult to debug. Remember you never thought you mentioned a variable "get" and perhaps you didn't do any subtraction. Worse yet, maybe you did do some subtraction, and so you waste much time trying to fix the place in your program where you were subtracting. Argghhhh!

Simpler instances of "self correct" can be found. Some operations

are insensitive to the order of arguments, yet the command insists upon a particular ordering. This requirement could be weakened, or at the least, the system could try all orders and ask the user if it was OK. Calling the text editor upon a nonexistent file is usually treated through a "self correct" philosophy. Most editors interpret this as wanting that file to exist—a guess that is often correct, and when not, not costly to repair. "Self correct" can probably be used a lot more than it is. There are numerous simple cases where not much intelligence is required to determine what the user might really have meant, if only the designer would have thought to try.

Let's talk about it. Some systems respond to problems by initiating a dialog with the user: We call this strategy "Let's talk about it," and we consider it a major step forward toward true interaction. A good example is the way that many Lisp systems respond when they get into trouble: a message describing the problem to the best of the system's ability, but then, automatic entry into the "Lisp Debugger" allows the user to interact with the system and explore the various candidates for trouble. For the class of experienced users for whom such systems are designed, there is a high likelihood that the user can simply fix the problem and proceed. Here we have shared responsibility between user and system to explore the problem and come up with a solution.

Teach me. And finally, there is the response we call "Teach me," the system that queries the user to find out just what a particular phrase or command might have meant. In the best of these systems, for example, *Clout* (a natural language inquiry system for the *Microrim* relational database system), when the system finds a word it does not understand, it asks the user for a definition. Any words in the definition that are not understood are then themselves asked about. This continues until all the terms have been defined. The new terms are then retained by the system so that the same phrases can be used in the future.

The Problem of Level

One major problem associated with error messages is to convey just where the problem is. It is often the case that the system detects an error, the user recognizes that an error has been made, but there is still considerable difficulty in determining just what the error is. A major factor is the existence of numerous levels of intentions. The situation that led to the "longjmp botch" error with which we opened this chapter illustrates the problem. It was first found while formatting files on the terminal, using a program that internally invoked "more," the screen-display program. "More" got into trouble and collapsed most ungracefully, displaying the message *longimp botch: core dumped.* What is a "longimp botch?" Why is the user being told this? Of what use is this information?

One problem with this message is that it is presented at the lowest level of program execution whereas the user is thinking at a fairly high level of intention. The user is formatting a file, unaware that "more" is even involved. But the error message does not give any hint as to what level the trouble is at: The user assumed it was a problem either with the text file or with the formatter.

Suppose a task is performed, but the end result is not satisfactory. Why not? The reason could lie at any level. There are many places for error, many places where intentions could fail to be satisfied. If the operation were carried out manually, one step at a time, then it might be relatively easy to detect the place where the problem lies. But in many situations this is not possible: All we know is that the intention has not been satisfied. Many of us have experienced this problem, spending hours "fixing" the wrong part of a program or task because we did not have the information required to judge the level at which the problem had occurred. The question, however, for the system designer is: What information is most useful for the user?

The question is very difficult to answer. For the system programmer who is trying to debug the basic routines, the statement *longimp botch* might be very useful—just the information that was needed. The problem is not that the error message is inappropriate; the problem is that sometimes it is appropriate, other times not.

One approach to the levels problem is to know the intention. If the program knew it was being used by a person who was intending to format a file, it could make one set of responses. If it knew it was being used by someone trying to track down a problem, it could make another set. However, although knowing user intentions and levels often helps, it does not guarantee success. In studies of human errors there are found numerous cases where knowledge of the intention would not help. Consider the following example:

X leaves work and goes to his car in the parking lot. X inserts the key in the door, but the door will not open. X tries the key a second time: It still doesn't work. Puzzled, X reverses the key, then examines all the keys on the key ring to see if the correct key is being used. X then tries once more, walks around to the other door of the car, walks around to the other door of the car to try yet again. In walking around, X notes that this is the incorrect car. X then goes to his own car and unlocks the door without difficulty.

It is easy to generate a large collection of examples like this, some involving cars, others apartments, offices, and homes. The common theme is that even though people may know their own intentions, they seem to tackle the problem at the lowest level, and then slowly, almost reluctantly, they pop up to higher levels of action and intention. If the door will not unlock, perhaps the key is not inserted properly. If it still won't work, perhaps it is the wrong key, and then, perhaps the door or the lock is stuck or broken. Determining that the attempt is being made at the wrong door seems difficult. Now perhaps the problem is the error messages are inappropriate: The door simply refuses to open. It would be better if the door could examine the key and respond "This key is for a different car." Can programs overcome this problem? (See Chapter 16 by Draper for one possible direction—a solution based on the notion of "responsibility.")

The "Let's Talk About It" strategy provides a possible solution to the problem of levels. Suppose the message indicating difficulty was always presented at the highest level, indicating that there has been a problem and its seriousness. Then, let the user be given tools to explore the problem to whatever depth is desired. Let the user be able to trace down the levels, to see where the original mismatch occurred, how that level was reached, and the state of the system at each level. The programmer can explore in detail: The experienced user can explore until the basic problem is clear, and the uninterested can remain uninterested. Such exploratory tools will require some skills to be constructed, but the multiwindow, run-time support for Lisp Machines (and even Macintosh Pascal and Basic) offer suggestions of how to proceed. But this kind of constructive interaction with the system has the possibility of solving the levels problem along with the error message problem.

The Failure to Detect Problems

Often actions will accomplish a legal effect, and so cannot be detected as errors by the system, but are still problems in that they neither advance the user towards the goal nor do what the user intended. As we saw in the chapter by Lewis (Chapter 8), the users' ability to detect such states is unreliable. Word-processor learners can explain away even disastrous errors: They adjust their idea of what should be happening to fit what appears to be happening. Our studies of error bring out the same phenomenon: Serious failures may not be detected even though the available evidence appears (in hindsight) to be fully adequate. Norman (1984b, 1986) proposes three hypotheses that may account for these difficulties in detecting errors: relevance bias, partial explanation, and overlap between model and world.

Relevance bias. People seem to have an apparent bias toward seeking confirmatory evidence when evaluating a hypotheses, though looking for disconfirming evidence is often more useful (Johnson-Laird, 1983). This bias may be forced by the need to select evidence to consider from a large pool, too large to permit full examination. In selecting evidence one has to make judgments of relevance. But judgments of what is relevant must be based on what one thinks is happening: in short, based on one's hypotheses. If confirming evidence is more likely to look relevant to a hypothesis than disconfirming evidence, the bias toward confirmation can be reinterpreted as a bias toward relevant-seeming evidence.

An example discussed by Lewis (Chapter 8) seems to fit Norman's analysis. When the learner searched for a page number and found a line number instead, the learner was satisfied, even though the label on the number made no sense in this context. The message looked relevant because it contained a number. And because it looked relevant, its very presence lent support to the hypothesis that it was what was wanted.

Partial explanation. The second conjecture is that errors are not detected because people accept crude agreement between what they expect and what they see. The example just discussed shows this mechanism at work as well. The learner interpreted the number in a way that accounted for the number, but not for the rest of the message. As noted, the rest of the display message indicated that the number was a line number, not a page number, but the learner did not require a complete interpretation. Like relevance bias, acceptance of partial explanations can be seen as a necessary response to limitations in processing capacity. One simply could not function if everything in the environment had to be fully interpreted.

Overlap of model and world. The final suggestion is that error detection is impeded by the fact that one's model of the world is likely to agree to a great extent with the way the world really is, even if the

model is wrong in part. If one's model were too far off it would have to be adjusted. As a result of this rough agreement, finding points of disagreement is hard. Most things that one does will produce the results predicted by one's model, which is thus supported.

CORRECTING ERROR

If an error is detected the user needs to recover from it. Some existing systems provide general (or intended to be general) "undo" facilities, so that one can back up to an earlier state after making an error. Other systems aim to structure their operations so that they have natural inverses: Erasing a line is the inverse of drawing, and vice versa. It seems clear that, at the very least, *undo* is a desirable element of a system. It allows users to experiment more freely, it reduces anxiety and tension, and it permits ready recovery of many simple errors. Implementation of *undo* is nontrivial, however. An "undo" command that recovers from the last command is relatively easy, but many operations that the user thinks of as a single event can launch several different actions, only the last of which will be recoverable from with a single-step undo. But as soon as we go beyond recovery of the last operation, numerous technical and conceptual issues arise that have not yet been solved. Even single-step undo routines can be expensive of resources if one wishes to be able to recover from any command, including writing and reading from files and accidental or erroneous exits from the program.

Nievergelt has argued strongly for the essential kind of information a user must have in order to recover from error (Nievergelt & Weydert, 1980). Essentially, the user needs to know what the current state of the system is (*sites*), where one came from (*trails*) and what the possible alternatives are (*modes*). He bases the design of his experimental system around these three concepts: sites, modes, and trails.

The "Let's Talk About It," Teach Me," and the "Self Correct" strategy of dealing with problems seem like important directions to pursue. Certainly human-to-human communication makes very heavy use of these techniques.

CONCLUSION

In this chapter we have examined some of the ways that a system designer can deal with error. We think that error is the natural result of a person attempting to do a task. An error results for several reasons, including accidental mishaps, slips of action, and sincere mistakes. In many cases, the erroneous action represents the person's best

reducing effort and trauma by all concerned parties. When we fail to understand what a person has said we ask for correction. But we act as a cooperative team and minimize the effort required to deal with the error. Basically, we assume the person is trying to tell us something, so that even errors or local incoherence are still informative attempts. We treat understanding as a cooperative endeavor, requiring effort from both speaker and listener.

If we think of interaction with a computer as a cooperative endeavor we see that each side has certain talents. The person is good at setting goals and constructing intentions. The computer is great on the details. Let the two work together, with the person in charge. And let the computer go out of its way to make things easy for the user, to make corrections easy, to go that extra step toward understanding that makes conversation with an intelligent colleague so fruitful.

References

Budge, B. (1983). *Pinball construction set* (Computer program). San Mateo, CA: Electronic Arts.

Draper, S. W., & Norman, D. A. (1984). Software engineering for user interfaces. In *Proceedings of the 7th International Conference on Software Engineering* (pp. 214-220). Silver Spring, MD: IEEE.

du Boulay, B., & Matthew, I. (1984). Fatal error in pass zero: How not to confuse novices. *Behaviour & Information Technology, 3,* 109-118.

Johnson-Laird, P. N. (1983). *Mental models.* Cambridge, MA: Harvard University Press.

Nievergelt, J., & Weydert, J. (1980). Sites, modes, and trails: Telling the user of an interactive system where he is, what he can do, and how to get places. In R. A. Guedj, P. ten Hagen, F. R. Hopgood, H. Tucker, & D. A. Duce (Eds.), *Methodology of interaction* (pp. 327-338). Amsterdam: North-Holland.

Norman, D. A. (1981a). Categorization of action slips. *Psychological Review, 88,* 1-15.

Norman, D. A. (1983b). Design rules based on analyses of human error. *Communications of the ACM, 4,* 254-258.

Norman, D. A. (1984b). *Working papers on errors and error detection.* Unpublished manuscript, University of California, San Diego, Institute for Cognitive Science, La Jolla, CA..

attempt at the desired action. It is this case that most interests us, for here is where the spirit should be one of genuine cooperation. The user tried, and got it wrong. Think of the input not as an error, but as the user's first iteration toward the goal. The system should do its best to help. If it can figure out what was intended, so much the better. If not, it should explain gracefully where its problem is, perhaps making suggestions. It should not require retyping a long sequence or redoing a long set of operations when only one detail was in error. Human conversation does not require such correction.

Sometimes the responses of the person are not easily detected as being in error. That is, they are legal operations, but not appropriate for the situation. This is a more difficult case, for only the most intelligent of systems can detect this situation, and probably not even then. The solution here is to provide sufficient feedback and exploratory aids that the person is aware of the actions and of the system state. It should be easy for the user to examine the system, to find the consequences of actions, and to modify those actions. Undo facilities are desirable, but undo with the extra information that allows for intelligent use of the facility, including knowledge of how the operation got to its current state and what alternatives exist.

At times the best strategy is for the system simply to provide warnings, or not to respond at all. Sometimes it is possible to correct the error without further input from the person, although because the system too can make errors, this should only be done with consultation and permission. More important, it is often possible to avoid whole classes of error simply by reformulating the problem, eliminating aspects that would otherwise have caused trouble. This chapter does not attempt to be comprehensive in its treatment. The chapter is meant to provide the spirit of the enterprise: that error should be considered a normal part of operation, not an exception.

There already exists a system that accepts erroneous statements gracefully, usually managing to interpret actions correctly in spite of error, other times providing elegant correction procedures. The system?—human speech. Normal speech contains many errors and corrections, yet people have evolved such skillful procedures for correction that the listener seldom notices either the errors or the corrections. In a conversation, we do not complain of "syntax errors," even though there are many. Even simple errors of meaning can be tolerated if it is clear what was meant. When a speaker detects an error, the erroneous part of the utterance can be corrected while leaving the surrounding material unchanged.

Norman, D. A. (1986). New views of information processing: Implications for intelligent decision support systems. In E. Hollnagel, G. Mancini & D. Woods (Eds.), *Intelligent decision aids in process environments.* New York: Springer-Verlag.

Raskin, A. J. (1974). The flow-language for computer programming. *Computers and the Humanities, 8,* 231-237.

Reason, J., & Mycielska, K. (1982). *Absent minded? The psychology of mental lapses and everyday errors.* Englewood Cliffs, NJ: Prentice-Hall.

Shneiderman, B. (1980). *Software psychology: Human factors in computer and information systems.* Cambridge, MA: Winthrop.

Teitelman, W., & Masinter, L. (1981, April). The Interlisp programming environment. *Computer,* pp. 25-33.

VanLehn, K., & Brown, J. S. (1980). Planning nets: A representation for formalizing analogies and semantic models of procedural skills. In R. E. Snow, P. A. Federico, & W. E. Montague (Eds.), *Aptitude, learning, and instruction: Vol. 2. Cognitive process analyses of learning and problem solving* (pp. 95-137). Hillsdale, NJ: Lawrence Erlbaum Associates.

Winston, P. H. (1975). Learning structural descriptions from examples. In P. H. Winston (Ed.), *The psychology of computer vision* (pp. 157-209). New York: McGraw-Hill.

Making text editors more like computer games may seem ridiculous on the surface, but these "games" use basic motivational techniques— something designers of application systems have overlooked.

The Adventure of Getting to Know a Computer

John M. Carroll
IBM Thomas J. Watson Research Center

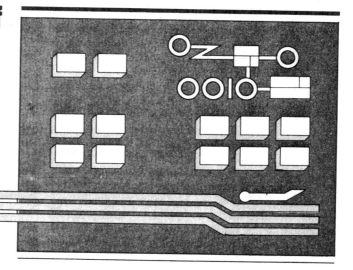

It is suppertime, and most everyone in the computing center has already gone home. But framed against one bright gray wall sits a lone explorer. In his mind, he is deep underneath the surface of the earth in a dark and dangerous cave—but he is entering into a world of color, imagination, action, and general amazement. He is playing Adventure. On the screen is a cryptic message: "The bird was unafraid when you entered, but as you approach, it becomes disturbed and you cannot catch it." He stares intently, his thoughts are almost tangible, leaping between his head and the screen. He is going over every variation of every possibly relevant parameter of the situation, and he will do this over and over again until he has wrung out *at least* 470 points. It's just a game.

The very next morning, someone else is sitting in the same chair, directly in front of the same console, staring into the very same tube. Despite the background bustle, this person also sits quietly mesmerized by the cryptic message on the screen: "Task not applicable at this time." Like her predecessor, this person is silently examining her knowledge and her hypotheses about the system: "What is a task?" "Does 'not applicable' mean I don't need to do this or that I have to do it, but not this way?" "If I sit here and wait for some time to pass, will it work then?"

But unlike her predecessor, this person is not navigating a cave far below the surface of the earth—she is trapped between two menus in a text editing facility. Also unlike her Adventure counterpart, she will probably not win all 470 points, at least not for a long time, because she can resolve the task-not-applicable problem more quickly than the other can resolve the bird problem—she simply

decides that "Task not applicable at this time" means nothing very much at all and goes on. She gets to the next menu, or the prior menu, or she just turns the machine off and starts fresh—the lessons, whatever they might have been in the prior session segment, are sacrificed. The goal, after all, is to learn how to get a letter typed out—this is no game!

Here we have two people, a player of Adventure, a well-known and popular computer game, and a user who is trying to learn an application system. Despite their obvious differences, they have much in common: both are struggling to cope with an unfamiliar environment, and both are experiencing certain types of learning difficulties. To a large extent, these difficulties are inevitable characteristics of human-computer interaction and as such are potential problems in any system. In Adventure, however, problems are turned into challenges; whereas in application systems, they are burdens—even severe learning obstacles at times. This difference may partially explain why people master computer games with no useful (practical) goal, while they fail to become even accomplished novice users of application systems like text editors.

Studies of office personnel learning to use text editors show that the type of learning environment affects how the user perceives the system and how easily he learns to use it.[1-3] A computer game like Adventure has a conceptual, mazelike learning approach, which I call an exploratory environment, that makes the player *want* to overcome the problems, even invent ways to use them to his advantage. The application system, on the other hand, has a more passive, prescribed environment that seems to frustrate more than help. What I hope to show in this article is that by examining the similarities and differences between the Adventure player and the inexperienced user, we can find some insights to use in designing application systems that are easier for the user to learn.

The common basis

Computers are freeing us from paper and pencil. For example, Adventure is quite similar to the paper-and-pencil game, Dungeons and Dragons, but games like Adventure are masters at keeping track of the sorts of details that would render paper and pencil versions unbearably tedious. Players don't have to wait to find out what happens to them in the course of a move; they don't have to throw dice; they don't have to write things on bits of paper. They just get the good stuff.

Text editors, and other application systems, are in some ways even better.* They relieve people of having to scrawl things on paper—even people who are writing a letter! Once in the system, text can be revised, manipulated, or printed out. Repetitive tasks, like mass mailing, can be automated by the use of variables: once input, forever done. Using a text editor can help a child learn to write more fluently and more quickly, and it can make an adult feel more comfortable and confident about writing.[5,6] Moreover, learning to use a text editor is easy—at least relative to learning to write or type. Text editing is really only a step away from typing and actually reenforces this skill.

But although text editors are potentially "easy" to learn to use, people are still having tremendous difficulty learning to use them. In most cases, they are learned in-

---

*Malone[4] distinguishes sharply between application tools (e.g., text editors) and puzzles, which include computer games like Adventure. But his distinction rests on an error. He says, "... in the case of text editors, the central problem is not how to use editing commands, but how to improve the document being edited." In studies of those learning to use text editors, we at the research center have *never* come across a subject who thought of the task in these narrow terms. The problem our learners spontaneously—and quite stubbornly—orient to is "how does this system work?"

Table 1.
Typical problems faced by new users and Adventure players.

Disorientation	The user/player doesn't know what to do in the system environment
Illusiveness	What the user/player *wants* to do is deflected towards other, perhaps undesired, goals.
Emptiness	The screen is effectively vacant of hints as to what to do or what went wrong.
Mystery messages	The system provides feedback that is useless and/or misleading.
Slipperiness	Doing the "same thing" in different situations has unexpectedly different consequences.
Side effects	Taking an action has consequences that are unintended and invisible, but cause trouble later.
Paradox	The system tells the learner/player to do something that is clearly inappropriate.
Laissez-faire	The system provides no support or guidance for overall goals (e.g., "winning," "typing a letter").

completely and after significant confusion and error. A variety of severe problems beset people who are learning to use contemporary text editors.[1-3, 7] From these, I have selected eight specific problems that are shared by a person learning to use an application system and a person playing Adventure. These learning problems, which are summarized in Table 1, may seem bizarre and exotic to those unfamiliar with text editors, but they are fairly typical with respect to both learners and systems.

These problems are an unpalatable potpourri of troubles. People have difficulty getting started at all because they are *disoriented* by the screen display, by the manual, and by the bad fit of both to their own expectations. The system is unresponsive to what they do (*illusiveness*); the screen is *empty* and/or unchanging. When information does appear on the screen, it is, for them, like a *mystery message*—and often useless. It may stay on the screen too long and confuse later work; it may flash momentarily, or be located in a remote part of the display, and be missed. Subtleties of command interpretation and command architecture make the causal connection between commands and functions appear unpredictable (*slippery*) or *paradoxical*. Invisible *side effects* of user actions intensify this impression. Finally, the system's *laissez-faire* structure allows the new user to become lost in a maze of mystery messages, commands, and side effects.

Disorientation. Computing systems are often very alien to the backgrounds of new users. When a novice enters a computing environment, the first reaction is disorientation. Learners my colleagues and I have studied spend interminable amounts of time just trying to sign on—and then trying to figure out what happened when they did sign on. Suppose they manage to log into the local system, and even to enter the text editing environment. They see at the top of the screen:

EDIT: 'TEXT SCRIPT A1' TABS: 1 6 11 16 21 26 31

In the middle of the screen, at the left:

EOF:

And at the bottom of the screen, at the right:

YKTVMV RUNNING

"OK, now what?" the users ask, and naturally, help is not available in this initial state.

Likewise, the player enters an environment like Adventure with no idea of what will be there. Presumably *some* sort of adventure will occur, but from the start, he doesn't know what sort of adventure or where to find it. The first message from the game to the player is simply

> You are standing at the end of a road before a small brick building. Around you is a forest. A small stream flows out of the building and down a gully.

Where is the adventure? In the building? Surely not in the stream. Perhaps in the forest . . . The answer just isn't there.

Illusiveness. Computing systems, even the ones data processing professionals consider elementary, are complex. The new user may sign on with a goal, like typing a memo. But very quickly that goal is all but lost in a morass of decisions and subgoals that develop and must be confronted during the session's interaction. First, the user might find out that what he calls "typing in a letter," is known to the system only as Create Document or Input Mode. ("Ah-ha," the user thinks, "so *that's* what I wanted to do!") But first, he must dispose of the Create Document Menu, which asks for a "document name"; whether the document will be "shared access" or "private"; what "retention period" is desired; which "Document Format Source" is to be invoked; and what "Charge Number" will be used. By the time the user has dealt with all these matters, he will be lucky indeed to remember the content of the letter!

Adventure is again closely parallel. Because the task situation of the game changes constantly from one instant to the next, the overall goal of winning (like typing a letter) evolves endlessly into a succession of more immediate, lower level goals. At one point, a player's goal is FIND TREASURE, but he then stumbles into a maze—the new goal is GET OUT. Suddenly, a little dwarf attacks with knives, and the player's goal becomes KILL DWARF. Note that *the player* has not done anything to change the game situation. From the player's perspective, while trying to accomplish *X,* something unforeseen occurred that changed things, impelling him to accomplish *Y.*

Emptiness. To protect the user from what's going on inside the application system, designers typically opt to display little or nothing to define what has just happened or what is now happening. Frequently during a learning session, the new user is staring at a blank, or at least static, screen. For example, when each new command is issued, the display is typically cleared of prior commands. The learner is thus deprived of any trace of the session, which he may need in planning further action. Indeed, many actions that a user initiates have no visible consequence on the screen at any time—although inside the system they are being executed. This lack of response is often true for both appropriate and inappropriate commands. Wildly wrong keypresses, for example, those that have no meaning anywhere in the system, may only trigger a reset condition, which is signalled by a tiny light on the side of the screen (where learners often fail to notice it). Maybe you're right; maybe you're wrong; maybe you're making progress; and maybe you're not—but the machine's not telling.

Here, the Adventure parallel breaks down just a bit. For although the screen per se is frequently empty and static in Adventure, the game does put forth some response to every user action—albeit brief and cryptic: "You can't be serious!" or "I don't understand that!" Moreover, the language that the system employs is extremely vivid; the world that Adventure constructs is one of extraordinary visual intensity, even though the scenario of the game is in caves, which in the real world are dimly lit places of limited color. In Adventure, when you kill a dwarf, "The body vanishes in a cloud of greasy black smoke." When you enter a room, it seems to light up:

You are at the east end of the two-pit room. The floor here is littered with thin rock slabs, which

make it easy to descend the pits. There is a path bypassing the pits to connect passages from east to west. There are holes all over, but the only big one is on the wall directly over the west pit where you can't get to it.

Even when the ambient light is low and things are shadowy, the descriptions are still vividly intense.

Mystery messages. System messages are designed to be succinct and precise, but even when they are they may be of little use to the new user. Quite often messages that the system delivers to the user are puzzles rather than prompts, problems rather than assistance. For example, one system says "Task not valid at this time," which is really too vague to be helpful. The message is also a bit jargony, since few new users have figured out what a "task" is, and it stays on the screen almost permanently, worrying the user about a continuing error. One subject we studied interpreted the message as meaning that her request could not be completed at that time and thought that if she waited, it would later work all right. "Task not applicable in this situation," would be somewhat of an improvement, but it, too, is jargony and conveys only that *something* is amiss.

Adventure is full of these mystery messages. For example, early in the game one approaches a little bird.

The bird was unafraid when you entered, but as you approach, it becomes disturbed and you cannot catch it.

Now even a player who has barely managed to get this far in the game knows that the bird must be captured or taken along somehow, but something is still *not* being said—just the something that the player needs to know.

Slipperiness. Computing systems require that commands be entered exactly. A slight deviation in spelling or syntax renders a command meaningless, or worse, changes the meaning to something unintended and entirely different. Commands also frequently function differently when issued in different system states. The learner, then, may not notice a slight misspelling amid all the disorienting confusion, and he typically cannot recognize the difference between relevant system states. From the user's viewpoint, and from the player's as well, the very same action mysteriously elicits unpredictably different consequences when employed on different occasions. In one text editor, a buttonpress command, "Cancel," is used to escape from many situations (for example, menus). Learners invariably try to use Cancel to escape from a typed page display, for example, when they have completed a memo and want to store it or print it out. However, Cancel does nothing; instead, the mystery message "Task not valid at this time." appears. To escape from the typed page situation, the user must employ a different command entirely.

Adventure is also slippery. Early on, the adventurer comes upon a rod, which he can wave, but a mystery message says, "Nothing happens." Only when he waves the rod in a certain place in the cave does something happen: a crystal bridge appears at the great fissure. Another example is the Pirate's treasure, which does not materialize in the cave until all other treasures are collected. Adventure is slippery because of its probabilistic aspects. When a dwarf attacks a player, he thinks, "If I am prudent and lucky enough to have an axe with me, I can throw the axe at the dwarf. Having done all this, I might kill the dwarf and save myself, or I might miss and have to make a death-defying attempt to retrieve the axe and try again." Success in killing a dwarf depends on doing the right things, but also on random luck. The game is slippery here; the player can do everything right and still end up dead.

Side effects. Each command causes a variety of effects, only some of which are visible to the user. Nevertheless, the other, invisible, effects of a command can become relevant to the user's goals later on. Quite often the inexperienced user or the Adventure player can do something that seems harmless enough—perhaps even right—at the time but that later produces a negative side effect. For example, printing a document may cause it to become inaccessible for re-editing (while it is on the print queue). To the new user, this side effect is unpredictable, and the system may give no hint that it has occurred. So when the learner asks to have the file again for reformatting, the mystery message "Document Unavailable" comes up. Sometimes users believe that someone else has appropriated their document. Sometimes they believe that the machine has temporarily lost the document. They never guess that *they* caused this undesirable situation.

In Adventure a player encounters a magic rod, which he generally picks up and takes along. Later he encounters a little bird. However, he cannot now catch the bird. As the message (given above) indicates, the bird is now afraid. What the player doesn't know is that while he is holding the rod, the bird is afraid. This is an odd side effect of the rod and an unpredictable obstacle to progress in the game. As a tricky consolation, the game allows him to kill the little bird (which he is inclined to do after not being able to capture it):

The little bird is now dead. Its body disappears.

But side effects from this action will occur: killing the bird will make progress impossible later in the game.

Paradox. New users come to a system with a rich, and often idiosyncratic, body of knowledge and experience. They use this background to interpret each message and instruction that is presented to them. When prior knowledge is generalized correctly, it can be useful, but it can also be trouble. Often new users and players are presented with actions or choices that seem clearly wrong. Consider an instruction manual that says "Backspace to erase." The typical learner, probably thinking of typewriters, reads this as a paradox. Backspace doesn't erase on a typewriter; it just moves the typing point back. Indeed, I have watched learners come to a complete standstill during an exercise and stare vacantly at this instruction. The paradox—real though it may be to the novice—is only apparent, because if the user throws intuition to the wind and backspaces anyway, he finds that backspace does delete prior text. In the same system, CHAR DEL can

also delete blank *lines*—since the system views them as characters in the data stream.

Adventure is a game about collecting treasures, yet at one point the player encounters a troll who demands one treasure be given up in payment for crossing his bridge, which the player rightly suspects will lead to more treasures. How can this be? Of course, the lucky player can foil the troll and avoid giving up a treasure, but even so, he is faced with the immediate paradox. Another example is that, at the end of the game, the player must decide whether or not to blow up the cave through which he has so carefully navigated.

Laissez-faire. Systems are finally *tools*, and as such they are intended to be used. Although initially the user may be led through programmed learning exercises, ultimately the user will direct the system. Except for truly intelligent systems, the system must play a limited role in directing and supporting the user's goals. Thus situations will inevitably occur in which each command issued is correct in the short term—but also perfectly useless since the command fails to advance the user's overall goals. Indeed, these situations are commonplace of novices.

Not only is laissez-faire inevitable, but it is also a bit cruel. Computer systems, like anything complex, can be conceptual mazes—I have often observed learners wandering hopelessly and without end. The system just accepts each new command, letting the lost learner race onward to nothing at all. The game scenario in Adventure is quite literally maze learning, and Adventure doesn't merely *allow* the player to wander; it traps and compels him to wander. For example, one region of the Adventure cave consists of "twisty little passages all alike."

Remedial actions

Having defined these problems, we can now look for ways to treat them. The first approach that comes to mind is using common sense. A serious common-sense analysis of the new user's plight may provide some insight, but as the past bears out, it alone is not likely to solve the problem. The more fundamental point is that people want to *do* things with computers and, particularly when they are learners, they make errors. These errors tangle up the "pure" forms of the problems in Table 1 and are impossible to anticipate (or to diagnose) by mere common sense. The bottom line is that people do not, and possibly cannot, learn passively—although many current system designs incorporate this learning approach.

Common sense. I have presented the learning problems in their extreme form, which may not be something we have to live with. Indeed, we should be able to resolve the extreme cases fairly quickly. For example, messages can be purged of gratuitous jargon merely by adding some common sense to the design process. In one system, menus are defined as displays containing "items." Subsequently, an item is called a "parameter" in a menu. Now this label would be reasonable if parameters were not always items, but they are. To complicate things further, the command that moves the cursor between items/parameters in a menu is VAR ADV (Variable Advance)—even though all variables are parameters. What we have, then, is item-parameter-variable, three terms instead of one. Even worse, the system recognizes only parameter and variable, which are the two terms learners don't know.

Getting this kind of common sense into system design is evidently easier said than done, but for the sake of argument, suppose we could. I'm not certain that even then we could resolve the troublesome usability concomitants of these problems. Systems are complex, and any action we take will have side effects. Perhaps these side effects can be made more visible to the user, but they will be there, nonetheless. To resolve emptiness, we need to strike a balance between empty or static screens and screens so cluttered with explanation and aids that they are potentially confusing. However, we cannot simply "solve" this problem.

The problems of laissez-faire and illusiveness have a certain inevitability that is, surprisingly, somewhat desirable. If the application system is to be a tool and not a task master, then endless wandering is always possible, at least until we can anticipate user goals. And any task involving complex and dynamic goal elaboration has a certain degree of illusiveness. However, Bandura and Schunk[8] and Csikszentmihalyi[9] argue that these problems may be beneficial. The possible short-term goals that can emerge from the interaction of agent and environment are crucial in motivating a user and keeping him oriented to a task.

Allowing for user error. Many problems in Table 1 have a hybrid form that develops through interaction with user error. Thus, pure slipperiness is probably something that a serious understanding of psychological consistency can ease considerably.[10] But slipperiness can also be apparent, that is, caused by error. In learning the text editor referred to above, users often picked up use of the Cancel key quickly. Although in many situations, Cancel is essentially an undo or escape key, it can also be a Request if the Code key is not held down. Since Cancel and Request are the same physical key, whose function depends on whether or not the Code key is held down, we can see how new users could get into trouble. Suppose a user wishes to escape from an environment. All he needs to do is press the Code key and then the Cancel/Request key. But what if he presses Code too late and actually issues a Request?

Request causes the cursor to move to the Request line and allows the user to issue a request. However, the user who struck Request by mistake didn't want any of this, so he hits Cancel, which he supposes is the right thing to do. Unfortunately, Cancel in this context cancels only the request. Hence, after the failed Cancel and the successful Cancel the user is looking at the original screen. In his opinion, Cancel has failed twice. Later, he will probably learn about environments and will realize that thinking of Cancel only as escape is reckless. But for now the user simply concludes that Cancel is slippery—sometimes it works and sometimes it doesn't.

Even if we managed to get large quantities of common sense into the design process and to solve the troubles associated with all the problems in Table 1, we would still have to deal with the pervasive difficulties that result from interactions of systems characteristics and learner error. Naturally, we cannot reasonably envisage any application system that can prevent learners from making errors of the Cancel/Request sort. Therefore, if people are always going to make errors we need to motivate them to be active problem solvers *as they are learning*.

Active learning. Why is laissez-faire a problem for new users? Why would anyone faced with these disorienting, illusive, slippery, secretive, and paradoxical mystery makers even hope to be given guidance in their personal goals? One user I observed believed that the screen's Reset/Help light, which came on when she entered illegal characters or keypresses, was the machine telling her that in its view she needed some help: "It thinks I need help," she said. This perception was doubly unfortunate, since not only was the machine not worrying about her progress towards high-level goals, but also when she inadvertently got the light to go off by trying Help uncoded (Reset), she concluded that the machine felt she was now on the straight and narrow again. Too bad.

One answer to the laissez-faire puzzle is that while the systems are indeed fraught with troubles for the learner, they also implicitly promise to be traditional environments: the exercises of their self-instruction manuals promise this; their reference-book Help facilities promise this; and even their jargon, paradoxes, side effects, slipperiness, and all-around inscrutability promise this. However, the systems are *not* like traditional learning environments. These depend crucially on the special design skills of a human teacher, while the systems are notoriously stupid without even rudimentary problem-solving capabilties. Also, traditional learning environments fail most decisively to encourage active learning.[11]

Exploratory environments

So how does Adventure come off so well for people even though it causes all the problems we've discussed? Part of the answer is surely that Adventure is recreation whereas application systems are work. In our culture, we sharply isolate work from recreation, and we consequently may have quite different response modes to these two situations. Adventure is dealing in fantasies, while application systems are dealing in accounting, word processing, and the like. Text editors are not about dragons or treasure; they are about documents, printers, and libraries. (I may not be totally secure in this argument, since Adventure is often played by programmers, and other computer professionals and hobbyists, while application systems are typically learned and used by nonprogrammer adults. Possibly, these differences make comparison of the two experiences invalid, but to be certain, we would need a more empirical study, perhaps of secretaries learning Adventure.)

This contrast between work and play should not be viewed as monolithic, however; indeed, we can learn much about work by examining play environments. We can see how particular aspects of recreation and work co-exist in complex human activities and experiences and can use that knowledge to structure work environments that are based on the organization of play. What Adventure does *not* share with a typical application system makes it compelling to learn, even though it has some of the same problems that application systems suffer. This difference is what I call the *exploratory environment* (Table 2).

Ironically, Adventure is a parody of applications systems *because* it presents the learner with an exploratory environment. Consequently, the Adventure player is not frustrated by the laissez-faire problem, but rather *expects* it. Neither is the player frustrated, or beaten into passivity, by the other problems in Table 1; rather he fights back, actively extracting each secret from the game.

The key is motivation. In an exploratory environment the learning experience belongs to the learner. Extrinsic authority, like a teacher, manual, or system, is absent, making the learner the sole control.* Since extrinsic penalties are ruled out, the usual sort of learning anxiety

just can't arise. Extrinsic rewards are also ruled out, which is not necessarily a bad thing.[16] Rather, the environment affords, encourages, and even demands conceptual and empirical experiment. We can have no unengaged learner in such an environment, and this motivational orientation overcomes the cognitive learning problems in Table 1.

Responsiveness. Even though the screen display is often empty and static, Adventure tends to provide *some* reaction for every user action; it is not always helpful or supportive but it is at least some reaction. The player cannot issue a command that will fail to elicit some message (however mysterious) from the system. If you issue a command that is syntactically and situationally correct, you will see some sensible consequences immediately. If you issue a command that is *incorrect,* you will still see some consequence—even if it is only "Huh?" This may not seem like a lot, but it keeps players responding. The one thing that a learner cannot seem to overcome is the silent treatment. Informing the learner of consequences *on the occasion of learning* can help him recognize when to engage this learning in the future.[17,18]

For a prime example of *un*responsiveness, pick any text editor. Even a major command like Print often elicits nothing from the system. On one text editor, a print message is sent to the user but held in a message reservoir. The unsophisticated user doesn't recognize what has happened and quite often doesn't realize that anything has been printed. If the user fails to examine the print message when it is sent and waits—or simply discovers it later—he might end up getting a print confirmation message for File 1, having just created or even printed File 2.)

Benchmarks. Adventure allows the player to assess his progress in skill and achievement. The continuum from novice to seasoned expert is finely and intricately segmented. At any point in an Adventure session, the player may get a score, reflecting the success he has had in dispatching the various tasks of the game scenario. This score is also a basis for classifying the player at the end of an adventure. The challenge of such clear mappings of personal progress increases the learner's task-oriented motivation.[4,11,19]

Again, we have a contrast because application systems eschew benchmarks. For example, when a user first signs on, the text editor does not display any message like "You have successfully signed on"; rather, it immediately brings up the task selection menu. The sign-on challenge, "do you want to use the system and are you authorized to do so?" is replaced by the task challenge, "What do you want to do?" The shrewd user will of course recognize that a new menu *is* a benchmark, but then again the shrewd user isn't the one who needs to know. Perhaps the saddest case of this sort is signing off from the first session. When a user successfully signs off, the *sign-on* menu comes up immediately. Again the experienced user knows that the system is saying good-bye and hello, but the new user is quite apt to see it only as another request to fill in an inscrutable menu, which he then does—inadvertently signing back on again. Is there no end to this misery?

---

*The consensus on learner control at the moment seems to be that it improves task-oriented motivation and may reduce anxiety but often slows down learning rate. Students tend to choose the easy problems over the difficult ones.[12-15] However, I caution against applying these conclusions to the context presented here. First, learner control as a real-world issue in instructional design may have quite a different complexion from what it has in these studies, which are very limited in scope. The most extensive study only tracked learning for 15 days of half-hour sessions. Second, most of these studies focused on learning unintegrated material by rote or on refining arithmetic skills. This focus is quite different from what is involved in learning to use application systems and in playing Adventure—namely, acquiring integrated conceptual structures. Finally, these studies focus exclusively on children, who would most likely be pretty bad at designing the character of their own instructional environments. Results from this type of study might be quite irrelevant to adult learning.

Table 2.
Typical characteristics of an exploratory environment.*

Responsiveness	When you do something, you get some feedback (at least informational).
Benchmarks	You can tell where you are within a given episode or session. You have the means for assessing achievement and development of skill.
Acceptable uncertainty	Being less than fully confident of your understanding and expertise is OK.
Safe conduct	You cannot do anything *too* wrong.
Learning by doing	You *do* so that you can learn to do: you design a plan; you do not merely follow a recipe.
Opportunity	Most of the things you learn to do work *everywhere.* You can reason out how to do many other things.
Taking charge	If progress stagnates, something new is suggested or happens spontaneously.
Control	*You* are in control, or at least have the illusion of being in control.

*The properties in Table 2—and for that matter in Table 1— are clearly a nonexhaustive, somewhat arbitrary set of contrasts and similarities. I make no claim to the contrary. I can't call on any substantive psychological theory of either computer games like Adventure or text editors to clarify my list, since no theory really exists. Hence, even if I'm basically right about the learning benefits of so-called exploratory environments, I may be overlooking the role psychological factors play and may have the right conclusions for the wrong reasons.

Acceptable uncertainty. In Adventure, having low, even virtually no, confidence in one's strategy or understanding of the game's inner workings doesn't matter a bit. In fact it adds to the fun, to the uncertainty, and to the indeterminacy (as the player's mental model of the game shifts and changes dynamically). Indeed, the game's interface is written with the obvious expectation that players will often be struggling. In contrast, the interface and training for a real application system presumes and implies that the user will succeed perfectly on the first try. No wonder our subjects have exclaimed, "It makes me feel stupid!!"

The new user of a text editor gets messages on various wavelengths that the experience is *not* fun. Unfortunately, the general context in which work is performed in our society quite typically presupposes a disjoint relation to fun. True, the system is not to blame but it doesn't do even a little to change this learning bias. Training materials are stuffy, stilted, and oriented towards "correct performance," never towards personal growth and discovery.

People often prefer to be uncertain, at least of their actual possibilities of success or failure. Weiner[20] found that people prefer goal-driven activities in which their probability of success is near 0.5. Berlyne[21] argues extensively that the conceptual conflict due to the uncertainty of outcome is a fundamental source of curiosity. In other words, games like Adventure keep players interested by keeping them uncertain.

Safe conduct. The intolerance with which application systems view diffidence suggests to learners that mistakes will be costly. Text editor learners we have studied invariably ask whether they might accidentally destroy something during an exercise. The policy of our research group is to tell them "no" to put them at ease, but with no trouble at all, a new user can obliterate all the files. The machine itself is saying "look out!" through its interactions with them. For example, in one editor, the user may enter DEL/ anywhere in a file to delete the current line—anywhere, that is, except the end-of-file line. If the user enters DEL/ here, the whole file will be deleted. One user who did this, quickly issuing a FILE command in panic, compounded the problem by saving a consequently empty file instead of his whole day's work.

In Adventure, players cannot really do anything too wrong. The pirate may get your treasure, the dwarves may indeed get you, but the game flow will survive. Players can't accidentally destroy their game, and they know it. This property of Adventure is what Moore and Anderson[11] called the "autotelic principle." This principle states that in initial stages of learning, the learner should be protected from the consequences of mistakes. Early learning should be enjoyed as much as possible for its own sake, and costly mistakes spoil this.

Learning by doing. In Adventure, if you want to know about it, you do it. A miniscule part of its total instruction is what we call "passive." The player customizes an exploratory foray, actively carries it out, and draws what conclusions he can. Nothing comes for free, and almost nothing comes passively. Empirical data support this concept also. Animals in maze learning experiments learn faster and more thoroughly when they actively traverse a maze than when they are passively carted around the maze. A person learns the layout of a new town much faster if he is the driver (active), rather than rider (passive).

Current training programs for application systems rely heavily on traditional passive modes of instruction, such as reading and classes. Fortunately, largely because of the desire to reduce costs, self-instruction approaches are becoming prevalent—but even these are passive. The learner merely follows instructions and does not exert any prerogative as to what to do or how to do it. Moreover, self-instruction approaches apparently fail anyway, and the new user's co-workers end up providing the instruction. When learners were restricted to the self-instruction materials, they had severe and wide-ranging learning problems. A learner who succeeded in following an exercise passively often asked, "What did I do?" upon completing it.

Opportunity. By providing a command architecture that affords action, Adventure supports a learn-by-doing orientation. Virtually all canonical Adventure commands can be issued anywhere in the system. Quite typically, a player can deduce a command, or a proper course of action, on the basis of other experience with the game, like treasure taking and escape. Consequently, the player can always do something; maybe he can't win, maybe he can't do what he wants, and maybe he can't do anything that seems particularly rewarding or useful—but he can do something. Moore and Anderson[11] describe this extendable consistency as a "productive principle."

Things are grimmer with application systems. Much more often than you would think, novice users find themselves in a part of the system from which only *one* command can deliver them, and they don't know that command. Being in this situation cannot really be described, and it isn't pleasant to watch. Of course, they can always switch the machine off and escape to a clean start, but this strategy isn't elegant, and it nullifies at least some of the potential for learning from the previous segment of the session. A "flatter" command architecture might be useful here, since the system is really a myriad of small compartments, each with its own special meanings for commands.

Taking charge. Problems like those in Table 1 can often cause a temporary conceptual paralysis. When the consequences of the user's actions are routinely uninterpretable, he is encouraged to simply stop taking action at all. Adventure does not allow this to happen. If the player founders even a bit, the game will actively intervene:

Adventure: You are in a maze of twisty little passages, all alike.
Carroll: (about 100 moves ensue)
Adventure: Do you need help getting out of the maze?
Carroll: Yes.

Adventure: I am prepared to give you a hint, but it will cost you 4 points. Do you want the hint?
Carroll: Yes.
Adventure: You can make the passages look less alike by dropping things.

Indeed, the game may do more than merely suggest new possibilities. It may actually reconfigure the player's immediate situation. Thus, an explorer who is aimlessly wandering the caves carrying treasure may suddenly be robbed by the cave's Pirate:

There are faint rustling noises in the darkness behind you. Out from the shadows behind you pounces a bearded pirate! "Har, Har," he chortles, "I'll just take all this booty and hide it away with me chest deep in the maze." He takes your treasure and disappears in the gloom.

The player doesn't ask for this and doesn't want it; it just happens. The chance of being attacked by marauding dwarfs also increases when the player is stuck.

Control. The player learns by doing or can always do something in Adventure, but more important is that the player *directs* what goes on—as the chief instigator. Perhaps this illusion of overall control is what fundamentally drives the aggression fantasies of games like Adventure. Imagine an adventure in which the player is a base camp and can only send up mail and provisions and give advice to the real explorer—who may or may not take it. That scenario just wouldn't do. Zimbardo[22] showed that even the illusion of control can increase motivation to perform a task.

An important distinction about learners of application systems is that not only are they not in control but they are *made to feel* that way. In harsher terms, they are made to feel incompetent. Within the first ten minutes a new user is staring at a message, "Parameter omitted or not valid." She is a very bright woman; she even knows what *parameter* means. However, she does not know what it means here, and indeed it can mean any of the several things displayed on the screen. She explores various of these and concludes that parameter must be the boxlike character directly above the cursor, which identifies a free-key field. She is, of course, wrong, and any illusions she might have had about being in control have been discouraged. (Maybe system designers like to use words like parameter and default so that *they* can feel they're in control.)

So there you have it: people seem to like learning in exploratory environments. Of course most of my evidence is in anecdote and, as such, does not make the case that applications systems ought to be modeled on computer games. Indeed, I am not arguing that they should be. Adventure, for example, has no "undo" key. However, our studies of people learning to use text editors strongly indicates that some such function would substantially ease many of the difficulties learners experience. I am merely trying to say that something might be learned from a study of what's going on in computer games like Adventure and new insights could be applied to the design of application systems. At the very least, we could get some additional perspective on what makes application systems

difficult. We might even find new design techniques that make them easier to learn to use. Only a fool looks a gift horse in the mouth.

Implications

The properties that define exploratory environments transform the problems in Table 1—shared by Adventure *and* typical application systems—into challenges for the learner. Now the difference between a challenge and an obstacle can be fine, but as writers like Malone[4,23] and Moore and Anderson[11] extensively argue, it hinges on the character of the learning environment. If the learner's motivation is task oriented and if the learner feels in control of the situation, then obstacles can become challenges. (Malone, in fact, examined computer games from this perspective, but focused on explicitly pedagogical skill games, like Breakout and Darts, rather than on conceptual maze learning games like Adventure.[4])

This transformation of obstacles into challenges can happen in an exploratory environment. The player is immediately apprised whenever he manages to do something. Through explicit functions, the learner is kept informed of his progress and achievement—but he also always knows that it doesn't matter too much if he does make mistakes. A dynamic world is presented in which the learner not only *can* act—without worry about untoward consequence—but *must* act: the learner's exploration is what this world is about.

A person traversing an exploratory environment *expects* laissez-faire and illusiveness; regards paradox, side effects, and slipperiness as intriguing potential keys to the inner logic of the environment; and is unperturbed by disorientation, emptiness, and mystery messages. Each new problem is an intimate and preemptive invitation to learn. In such an environment, the learning truly belongs to the learner.

In any case, if we assume that learners will always make some errors—no matter how good our cognitive solutions to interface design are—then the issue becomes one of motivating learners to actively solve the problems they encounter.

The game metaphor. Adventure may provide a metaphor from which to construct interface concepts for application systems.[24,25] The logic for this is straightforward: the game is similar to the application systems, but the *potential* "troubles" shared by both are *real* troubles only in the systems, not in the game. So why not look at why the two differ and try to make the systems more like the game? We could really go overboard: text editors that award points, or tell you that you're "dead" if you try to print an empty file—but why be silly? To really exploit the game metaphor in making application systems easier to learn will clearly require a considerable and systematic research effort in software psychology and system design. It is serious business.

To get an inkling, in a very small way, of what the metaphor could come to, we may only have to ask people to explore a conventional text editor as if it were an

Adventure-like maze. In ongoing work at the research center, my colleagues and I have been attempting to project the "typewriter metaphor" to ground the subject's understanding of the task and the "game metaphor" to ground the subject's task-oriented motivation. We instructed one typist to read the following instructions on exploring a computer maze:

We are studying how people learn to use small computing systems. We are interested in how a person goes about such a learning task when *no formal instruction at all* is provided. What we want you to do is to interact just as you please with the computer, to explore its capacities, and to learn to do interesting things with it (HINT: this computer is in many ways a sort of super-typewriter). This, should you decide to accept, is your mission.

We want to emphasize several aspects of this learning task. Most importantly, you should not worry about doing the "wrong" thing. In this situation, the only wrong thing you can do is nothing. The most important thing to do is explore: the computer is in many ways like a maze and you have to find out how to get around (getting lost a little on the way is inevitable). This mazelike quality also means that you should be willing to change your goals from time to time. We have found that in the course of trying to do X, a person very often stumbles onto Y—but you have to be willing to give up on X for the moment!

This super-typewriter-maze idea may sound like a video game in disguise. In fact, we would like you to think of this learning experience as a sort of game. The more you explore of the computer-maze, the higher your "score." If you get stuck, we will answer direct and specific questions. Don't waste your questions, for we will answer only 10 (ten) throughout the entire session. But by all means ask for help when you really need it (otherwise you'll be holding yourself back from further exploration). If you can get by without a question—Bravo!

Because we want to learn how people approach this sort of learning task, we will ask you to try to "think aloud" (as thoughts occur to you, just speak them out loud). To help this along, from time to time we will ask you "What are you thinking just now?" and the like. (You'll get used to it.) In the service of thinking aloud, feel free to ask "rhetorical" questions: we won't charge you for telling us what questions are on your mind—unless you ask us to answer them!

Finally, here are two HINTS.

1. Try these keys for interesting results: CODE, ENTER, HELP, RESET, REQST, VAR ADV (we will show you where each of these keys is on the keyboard).

2. The computer "believes" that your Operator Name is your first name.

These instructions were presented instead of the normal training materials we had used with other subjects.

The trade-off here is that while the normal-case subjects were passively led through a series of exercises that presented them with knowledge about the system, our explorer subject was forced to be active, to discover knowledge about the system, or learn nothing. The other important difference is that while normal-case subjects were run in a 16-hour learning procedure, our explorer subject was run for only four hours.

In many ways, the explorer's experience was comparable to that of our other subjects. She failed to notice an indicator light, then tried unsuccessfully to type in a reset condition, and became frustrated. She failed to hold down the Code key consistently and was then surprised at the "inconsistency" of the system. She wrongly generalized Cancel and Enter as commands that get you to the next menu—even though they in fact do, but only occasionally and as side effects, etc., etc., etc. These similarities are not really surprising. The system is difficult to learn to use—as work with normal-case subjects made clear. We would have had quite a finding indeed if simply taking away the training materials had made learning easier.

The character of what the explorer did was somewhat different from that for normal-case subjects. The explorer used Help more in her 4-hour session than any of our other subjects had in 16 hours. This difference is important, since the training manual explicitly tells learners how to use Help, and encourages its use. One of the four training modules we used for our prior subjects was concerned centrally with the use of Help. Her use of Help—and of all the information displayed on screens—was qualitatively different too. She read it.

Our normal-case subjects, who had the manual to more or less lead them by the hand, often didn't "see" the screen displays. The most striking case was a subject who, after three days of working with the system, insisted that she had never seen the sign-on menu; her reason was that in trying to passively follow the manual, she had been trying not to look at the screen! The explorer got into areas of the system that the training manual prevented other subjects from discovering. She learned about text blocks, document archiving, margin changes (line format changes), and document duplication. Of course, she also had new problems: because she read the screen information, she was really hurt when it was incomplete, turgid and jargony, or misleading.

Nonconclusions

Generally speaking, simple answers do more harm than good in behavioral science. Luckily, from this vantage point, we cannot generate any simple answers from this discussion. My analysis is fully consistent with the view that an Adventure metaphor for application systems could make them easier to learn to use. But the indications for this are still indirect and our confidence must be qualified accordingly. And even if the empirical and theoretical issues were resolved sharply and favorably, we would still not know to what degree such a metaphor should be implemented in the actual development of interface designs and instructional materials.[26,27] In guideline definition, we still have so far to go that it's hard to tell when we've taken a step. ■

Acknowledgments

I am grateful to Norman Brenner, Colette Daiute, Fred Damerau, Clayton Lewis, Robert Mack, Don Nix, and John Thomas for helpful comments on earlier versions of this paper. Clayton Lewis, in particular, said several things that totally changed the paper. The original Adventure game was written by Willie Crowther at MIT. It was later revised and extended by Don Woods at the Stanford AI Lab.

References

1. J. M. Carroll and R. Mack, "Learning To Use a Word Processor: By Doing, by Thinking, and by Knowing," to appear in *Human Factors in Computer Systems,* J. Thomas and M. Schneider, eds., Ablex, Norwood, New Jersey.

2. J. M. Carroll and R. Mack, "Actively Learning to Use a Word Processor," manuscript, 1982b, to appear in *Cognitive Aspects of Skilled Typewriting,* W. Cooper, ed., Springer-Verlag, New York.

3. R. Mack, C. Lewis, and J. Carroll, *Learning To Use Office Systems: Problems and Prospects,* manuscript, 1982.

4. T. W. Malone, *What Makes Things Fun To Learn? A Study Of Intrinsically Motivating Computer Games,* Xerox PARC Report CIS-7, 1980, p. 55.

5. C. A. Daiute, "Where Has All the Paper Gone?" *Electronic Learning,* Jan. 1982.

6. J. D. Gould, "Composing Letters with Computer-Based Text Editors," *Human Factors,* Vol. 23, 1981, pp. 593-606.

7. R. Bott, *A Study of Complex Learning: Theory and Methodology,* CHIP report 82, University of California, La Jolla, 1979.

8. A. Bandura and D. Schunk, *Cultivating Competence, Self-Efficacy, and Intrinsic Interest Through Proximal Self-Motivation,* Stanford University, 1980.

9. M. Csikszentmihalyi, *Beyond Boredom and Anxiety,* Jossey-Bass, San Francisco, 1975.

10. J. M. Carroll, "Learning, Using, and Designing Command Paradigms," *Human Learning: J. Practical Research and Application,* Vol. 1, 1982, pp. 31-62.

11. O. K. Moore and A. R. Anderson, "Some Principles for the Design of Clarifying Educational Environments," *Handbook of Socialization Theory and Research,* D. Goslin, ed., Rand McNally, New York, 1969.

12. M. D. Fisher, et al., "Effects of Student Control and Choice on Engagement in a CAI Arithmetic Task in a Low-Income School," *J. Educational Psychology,* Vol. 67, 1975, pp. 776-783.

13. J. P. Fry, "Interactive Relationship Between Inquisitiveness and Student Control of Instruction," *J. Educational Psychology,* Vol. 63, 1972, pp. 459-465.

14. J. B. Hansen, "Effects of Feedback, Learner Control, and Cognitive Abilities on State Anxiety and Performance in a Computer-Assisted Instruction Task," *J. Educational Psychology,* Vol. 66, 1974, pp. 247-254.

15. E. R. Steinberg, "Review of Student Control in Computer-Assisted Instruction," *J. Computer-Based Instruction,* Vol. 3, 1977, pp. 84-90.

16. M. R. Lepper, D. Greene, and R. E. Nisbett, "Undermining Children's Intrinsic Interest with Extrinsic Rewards: A Test of the Overjustification Hypothesis," *J. Personality and Social Psychology,* Vol. 28, 1973, pp. 129-137.

17. E. M. Abernathy, "The Effect of Changed Environmental Conditions upon the Results of College Examinations," *J. Psychology,* Vol. 10, 1940, pp. 293-301.

18. J. A. McGeoach, *The Psychology of Human Learning,* Longmans Green, New York, 1942, pp. 501-505.

19. E. L. Deci, *Intrinsic Motivation,* Plenum Press, New York, 1975.

20. B. Weiner, *Human Motivation,* Rand McNally, Chicago, 1980.

21. D. E. Berlyne, *Structure and Direction in Thinking,* John Wiley & Sons, New York, 1965.

22. P. G. Zimbardo, *Cognitive Control of Motivation,* Scott, Foresman & Co., Glenview, Illinois, 1969.

23. T. W. Malone, "What Makes Computer Games Fun?" *Byte,* Dec. 1981, pp. 258-277.

24. J. M. Carroll and J. C. Thomas, "Metaphor and the Cognitive Representation of Computing Systems," *IEEE Trans. Systems, Man, and Cybernetics,* Vol. SMC-12, 1982, pp. 107-116.

25. H. G. Petrie, "Metaphor and Learning," *Metaphor and Thought,* A. Ortony, ed., Cambridge University Press, New York, 1979.

26. H. A. Simon, *Sciences of the Artificial,* 2nd ed., MIT Press, Cambridge, Massachusetts, 1981.

27. J. C. Thomas and J. M. Carroll, "Human Factors in Communication," *IBM Systems J.,* Vol. 20, 1981, pp. 237-263.

John M. Carroll has been a research staff member in the Computer Science Department of the IBM Thomas J. Watson Research Center in Yorktown Heights, New York, since 1977. His research is in the analysis of basic cognitive skills and capacities that underly complex human behavior and experience. He is the author of *Toward A Structural Psychology of Cinema* and of 45 technical papers including, "The Psychological Study of Design," "Creative Analogy and Language Evolution," "Human Factors in Communication," and "Structure in Visual Communication." He was also coeditor of *Talking Minds* (in press), the proceedings of an interdisciplinary conference held at the Watson Research Center.

Carroll is a member of the Linguistics Society of America and the Psychonomic Society. He received a BA in mathematics and a BA in information science from Lehigh University in 1972 and a PhD in experimental psychology from Columbia University in 1976.

Case Study D

The Star, the Lisa, and the Macintosh

We have seen in Chapter 13: Enhancing System Usability that the concept of a user interface must be defined very broadly to include not only the dialogue structures, presented in Chapter 10: Interaction Styles and Techniques, but also a system's documentation, error messages, help structures, training materials, and user support system. Even doing all this, however, is no guarantee that a product will succeed, as we shall now see.

The Xerox Star

It should be clear from many of the preceding chapters that, in the 1970's, the Xerox Palo Alto Research Center (PARC) was an environment of enormous creativity. It was the site of pioneering work in the design of new personal workstations, in the invention of interactive techniques to exploit their capabilities and facilitate their use, and in the development of an applied cognitive psychology to help guide appropriate design. These activities finally resulted in the announcement, in April 1981, of the 8010 Star Information System, ''a new personal computer designed for offices ... intended for business professionals who handle information'' (Smith, Irby, Kimball, Verplank, and Harslem, 1982, 1983). Star was probably the first comprehensive direct manipulation system intended for a business application in an office environment.

Star was greeted with much enthusiasm, particularly because it codified and made available, for the first time in a commercial product, many of the user interface ideas developed or refined at PARC in the 70's:

- A familiar *user's conceptual model* employing icons and windows on a simulated ''desktop.''
- The ability to see and point rather than to remember and type on a keyboard.
- The use of *property* or *option* sheets to specify the appearance of objects.
- *What you see is what you get* (WYSIWYG).
- *Universal* or *generic* commands (Rosenberg and Moran, 1984), that is, a few commands such as MOVE, COPY, and DELETE that can be used throughout the system.
- A relatively high degree of consistency and simplicity.
- *Modeless* interaction (Tesler, 1981).
- A certain amount of user tailorability.

Further details about these principles may be found in Smith, Irby, Kimball, Verplank, and Harslem (1982, 1983), which is included here as a reading. A more technical description of the interface components appears in Smith, Harslem, Irby, and Kimball (1982). Other relevant papers are Thacker et al. (1982), which describes the prototype Alto computer on which much of the underlying research and development was done; Harslem and Nelson (1982), which describes the Star development environment and process; Lipkie, Evans, Newlin, and Weisman (1982), which describes the graphics implementation; and Purvy, Farrell, and Klose (1983), which describes the Star's records processing capability.

The high quality of the Star user interfaces was only partly due to inspired design based on a decade of creative and relevant research and development (Pake, 1985; Perry and Wallich, 1985). Another factor was the extensive use of prototyping of ideas, pencil-and-paper analyses, and human factors experiments with potential users. Some of these experiments are described in Bewley, Roberts, Schroit, and Verplank (1983) which is also included as a reading.

How did Star fare in the marketplace? It was not a smashing commercial success. One can hypothesize a number of reasons for this:

1) It was a pioneering system both in terms of its user interface and of its orientation towards the "knowledge worker" as the intended user. Often the technological trailblazer only paves the way for a second or third product to be successful. Xerox was simply too early; the "knowledge worker" market did not exist in 1981.

2) Including a proportional share of the "file servers" and "print servers" that were part of the network, each individual Star cost an amount approaching $15,000. At that time, this was considered too expensive relative to the perceived benefit.

3) The Star possessed very limited functionality relative to the customers and purposes for which it was intended. In discussing what he calls "the office automation (OA) mirage," Hammer (1984) writes:

> The following list indicates the actual relative importance of various aspects of an OA system:
> 1. Functionality
> 2. Functionality
> 3. Nothing
> 4. Functionality
> 5. Everything else
>
> The questions that will guide the perplexed through the OA maze (and that would have saved many a vendor from extinction) are these: who will use this product, what will they use it for, and why will they be better off for using it? This acid test can be used to explain otherwise puzzling phenomena. For example, the Xerox Star (8010) was widely hailed upon its introduction as the harbinger of a new age. The Star was positioned as a management/professional workstation; it used a high-resolution screen and employed a user interface based on icons and a mouse. It was intended to advance OA beyond secretarial word processing to the manager and professional. It sank like a stone. Even a casual inspection of the Star's functionality would have predicted this result. The Star did not provide any management/professional applications worthy of the name. It had a host of adequate administrative support applications and a very good word processor, but nothing that would address the business needs of its intended users. (In fact, the one market in which the Star has achieved some success is in the high end of word processing.) The reports in the press were enthusiastic to the point of sycophancy, but even they should have aroused

suspicion, for they focused exclusively on the Star's interface, not on its capability.

> Vendors have learned a lesson about ease of learning, ease of use, friendly interfaces, and the like, but unfortunately it is the wrong lesson. They have been roundly (and appropriately) chastised for the often unusable interfaces that their systems presented to users; it has finally sunk in that expressing oneself in JCL is an unnatural act. From this, the vendors have reached the imaginative conclusion that a good user interface covers all sins. They have forgotten two laws of nature: first, people buy systems for functions, not for interfaces; and secondly, when a vendor talks about interface, it means he has nothing else to say.
>
> In reality, user interface is a second-order factor. All other things being equal, the system with the better interface is to be preferred. But a system with better functionality will almost always win over one with a better interface....

4) The Star lacked an open architecture, a set of technical and administrative mechanisms to encourage third party software developers to create new software for the system. The CUStomer Programming (CUSP) system that was supplied (Purvy, Farrell, and Klose, 1983), a record processing language that for some time was not even a full programming language, was not suitable for the development of applications. Xerox was for a long time unwilling to license to third parties the tool they themselves had used for their programming, the Mesa development environment (Mitchell, Maybury, and Sweet, 1978; Horsley and Lynch, 1979; Lauer and Satterthwaite, 1979; Johnson and Wick, 1982).

5) The Star was perceived as slow. Roberts and Moran (1983) show that, despite the system's long response time, it was one of the two best of nine text editors evaluated, in terms of the average time required to carry out a set of benchmark tasks. However, it is the *perception* of human users, and not any abstract *reality*, that is the ultimate determinant of user satisfaction.

6) It may be that the skills and methods applicable to the marketing and sale of photocopiers were not directly applicable or quickly adaptable to the sale of office automation workstations for knowledge workers.

The Apple Lisa

It is said that Steven Jobs, Apple's founder and Chairman, was incredibly impressed with the bit-mapped displays and the applications running on them that he saw in a visit to Xerox PARC in 1979 (Perry and Wallich, 1985, p. 72). The result was that, early in 1983, Apple introduced the Lisa, a product similar to the Star in terms of its user interface (but see Marcus, 1984, for a discussion of some fine distinctions). There were a number of important differences between the two products:

- Star was much more ambitious than Lisa in providing networking and distributed computing.

- At roughly $10,000, Lisa was somewhat less expensive than Star.

- Lisa was positioned somewhere between an office system and a personal productivity tool, one that could be used by individuals for such tasks as editing documents, building forecasting models with spreadsheets, and managing small data bases.

Williams (1983) describes the design and the user interface of the Lisa. Morgan, Williams, and Lemmons (1983) discuss the design process. Apple's ongoing attempts to upgrade and revitalize the product are documented in Williams (1984a,b), Redhed (1984) and a video (Apple, 1983). An illuminating observational study of users learning the Lisa is that of Carroll and Mazur (1986). In contrast to the other glowing accounts of Lisa's usability, this study shows that even a highly crafted and successful user interface can still have significant weaknesses.

The Apple Macintosh

Because of its cost, its confused product positioning, and its inadequate base of software and applications, Lisa also was not successful, and was withdrawn within three years. Finally, in January of 1984, Apple introduced the Macintosh at a price of approximately $2,500. Why, in contrast to the Star and the Lisa, did the Macintosh succeed so well?

1) The Mac did not need to trailblaze. Star and Lisa had prepared the ground in terms of the user interface. Numerous companies, including IBM, had opened up the market for professional personal computers.

2) Since the Mac was in a sense a second generation Lisa, Apple had the opportunity to learn from experience and eliminate many of the bugs (Tognazzini, 1985). There were a number of user interface improvements along the way from Star to Lisa to Mac.

3) The product was very aggressively priced.

4) Although initial product functionality was quite limited, a partially open architecture, a powerful developer's toolkit (Apple, 1985), and an aggressive program of third party software development soon led to the widespread availability of a great variety of significant software product offerings (McCroskey, Mellin, and Ritz, 1985).

5) The excellent graphics and the availability of a reasonably priced 300 dot per inch laser printer (the Laserwriter) allowed the Macintosh to achieve early domination in the emerging market of *desktop publishing*. Again, Apple's timing was better than Xerox's. Although Xerox had done the pioneering work on the

computer-controlled laser printer (Pake, 1985; Perry and Wallich, 1985), Apple was able to commercialize a high quality implementation of the concept at a reasonable price.

6) Apple was able to draw upon a number of years of successful experience in the personal computer business, and upon attendant marketing expertise, distribution channels, and skills in sales and support.

Williams (1984c) and Webster (1984) describe the design and the user interface of the Macintosh. Lemmons (1984), Markoff and Shapiro (1984), and Guterl (1984) discuss the design process. Jennings (1984) is a critical evaluation of the functionality and user interface of the Macintosh Finder, which provides the Macintosh equivalent of the command level interface to the operating system in a traditional computing environment.

Conclusion

The message is simple. The best user interface work in the world may be wasted if it is not coupled with a product that offers significant functionality at a reasonable price, is introduced in a timely fashion, and is well marketed to an appropriately targeted group of customers. Furthermore, if there must be a tradeoff between functionality and the user interface, functionality must be given the higher priority.

Readings

Smith, D.C., Irby, C., Kimball, R., Verplank, W. & Harslem, E. (1983). Designing the Star User Interface. In Degano, P. & Sandewall, E. (Eds.), *Integrated Interactive Computing Systems*, Amsterdam: North-Holland Publishing Company, 297-313. Originally appeared in *Byte* 7(4), April 1982, 242-282.

Bewley, W.L., Roberts, T.L., Schroit, D., & Verplank, W.L. (1983). Human Factors Testing in the Design of Xerox's 8010 "Star" Office Workstation. *Proceedings of CHI '83*, 72-77.

References

Apple Computer Company (1985). *Inside Macintosh*, Volumes I, II, III, Addison-Wesley Publishing Company, Inc.

Apple Corp. (1983). Lisa. *SIGGRAPH Video Review* 8, New York: ACM.

Bewley, W.L., Roberts, T.L., Schroit, D., & Verplank, W.L. (1983). Human Factors Testing in the Design of Xerox's 8010 "Star" Office Workstation. *Proceedings of CHI '83*, 72-77.

Carroll, J.M. & Mazur, S.A. (1986). Lisa Learning. *IEEE Computer* 19(10), November 1986, 35-49.

Guterl, F. (1984). Design Case History: Apple's Macintosh. *IEEE Spectrum*, December 1984, 34-43.

Hammer, M. (1984). The OA Mirage. *Datamation*, February 1984, 36-46. © by Cahners Publishing Co., reprinted with permission.

Harslem, E. & Nelson, L.E. (1982). A Retrospective on the Development of Star. *Proceedings of the 6th International Conference on Software Engineering*, September 1982, 377-383.

Horsley, T.R. & Lynch, W.C. (1979). Pilot: A Software Engineering Case Study. *Proceedings of the 4th International Conference on Software Engineering*, IEEE Computer Society, September 1979.

Jemmings, M.S. (1984). Evaluating the Macintosh Finder. *Byte*, December 1984, Guide to the Apple, A94-A101.

Johnsson, R.K. & Wick, J.D. (1982). An Overview of the Mesa Processor Architecture. *Proceedings of the Symposium on Architectural Support for Programming Languages and Operating Systems*, Palo Alto, CA., March 1982.

Lauer, H.C. & Satterthwaite, E.H. (1979). The Impact of Mesa on System Design. *Proceedings of the 4th International Conference of Software Engineering*, IEEE Computer Society, September 1979.

Lemmons, P. (1984). An Interview: The Macintosh Design Team. *Byte*, February 1984, 58-80.

Lipkie, D.E., Evans, S.R., Newlin, J.K., & Weisman, R.L. (1982). Star Graphics: An Object-Oriented Implementation. *Computer Graphics* 16(3), July 1982, 115-124.

Marcus, Aaron (1984). Corporate Identity for Iconic Interface Design: The Graphic Design Perspective. *IEEE Computer Graphics and Applications* 4(12), 24-32.

Markoff, J. & Shapiro, E. (1984). Macintosh's Other Designers. *Byte*, August 1984, 347-356.

McCroskey, M., Mellin, M. & Ritz, R. (1985). *The Book of Macintosh Software*, Arrays Inc., The Book Division, Van Nuys, CA, 1985.

Mitchell, J.G., Maybury, W., & Sweet, R.E. (1978). Mesa Language Manual. *Technical Report* CSL-78-1, Xerox Corp., Palo Alto Research Center, Palo Alto, CA., February 1978.

Morgan, C., Williams, G., & Lemmons, P. (1983). An Interview with Wayne Rosing, Bruce Daniels, and Larry Tesler: A Behind-the-Scenes Look at the Development of Apple's Lisa. *Byte*, February 1983, 90-114.

Pake, George E. (1985). Research at Xerox PARC: A Founder's Assessment. *IEEE Spectrum* 22(10), 54-61.

Perry, Tekla S. and Wallich, Paul (1985). Inside the PARC: The 'Information Architects.' *IEEE Spectrum* 22(10), 62-75.

Purvy, R., Farrell, J., & Klose, P. (1983). The Design of Star's Records Processing: Data Processing for the Noncomputer Professional. *ACM Transactions on Office Automation Systems* 1(1), 3-24.

Redhed, D.D. (1984). The Lisa 2: Apple's Ablest Computer. *Byte*, December 1984, Guide to the Apple, A106-A114.

Roberts, T.L. & Moran, T.P. (1983). The Evaluation of Computer Text Editors: Methodology and Experimental Results. *Communications of the ACM* 26(4), 265-283.

Rosenberg, J. & Moran, T.P. (1984). Generic Commands. *Human-Computer Interaction — Interact '84*, Amsterdam: North-Holland, 360-364.

Smith, D.C., Harslem, E., Irby, C., & Kimball, R. (1982). The Star User Interface: An Overview. *Proceedings of the AFIPS 1982 National Computer Conference* 50, June 1982, 515-528.

Smith, D.C., Irby, C., Kimball, R., Verplank, W. & Harslem, E. (1982). Designing the Star User Interface. *Byte* 7(4), April 1982, 242-282.

Smith, D.C., Irby, C., Kimball, R., Verplank, W. & Harslem, E. (1983). Designing the Star User Interface. In Degano, P. & Sandewall, E. (Eds.), *Integrated Interactive Computing Systems*, Amsterdam: North-Holland Publishing Company, 297-313. Originally appeared in *Byte* 7(4), April 1982, 242-282.

Tesler, L. (1981). The Smalltalk Environment. *Byte*, August 1981, 90-147.

Thacker, C.P., McCreight, E.M., Lampson, B.W., Sproull, R.F. & Boggs, D.R. (1982). Alto: A Personal Computer. In Siewiorek, D., Bell, D.G. & Newell, A.(Eds.), *Computer Structures: Principles and Examples*, McGraw-Hill, 1982.

Tognazzini, Bruce (1986). Usability Testing in the Real World. In Mills, C.B. et al., *CHI '86 Proceedings*, 212-215.

Webster, B.F. (1984). The Macintosh: System Review. *Byte*, August 1984, 238-251.

Williams, G. (1983). The Lisa Computer System. *Byte*, February 1983, 33-50.

Williams, G. (1984a). Apple Announces the Lisa 2. *Byte*, February 1984, 84-85.

Williams, G. (1984b). Update on Apple Macintosh and Lisa 2. *Byte*, May 1984, 339.

Williams, G. (1984c). The Apple Macintosh Computer. *Byte*, February 1984, 30-54.

Designing the Star User Interface

David Canfield Smith, Charles Irby, Ralph Kimball, Bill Verplank, Eric Harslem

Office Systems Division
Xerox Corporation
Palo Alto and El Segundo, California
U.S.A.

The Star user interface adheres rigorously to a small set of design principles. These principles make the system seem familiar and friendly, simplify the human-machine interaction, unify the nearly two dozen functional areas of Star, and allow user experience in one area to apply in others. In a companion paper[17] we presented an overview of the features in Star. Here we describe the principles behind those features and illustrate the principles with examples. This discussion is addressed to the designers of other computer programs and systems – large and small.

INTRODUCTION

In April 1981, Xerox announced the 8010 Star Information System, a new personal computer designed for offices. Consisting of a processor, a large display, a keyboard, and a cursor control device, it is intended for business professionals who create, analyze and distribute information.

Star is a multifunction system combining document creation, data processing, and electronic filing, mailing and printing. Document creation includes text editing and formatting, graphics editing, mathematical formula editing, and page layout. Data processing deals with homogeneous relational data bases that can be sorted, filtered and formatted under user control. Filing is an example of a network service utilizing the Ethernet local-area network.[13, 9] Files may be stored on a work station's disk, on a file server on the work station's network, or on a file server on another network. Mailing permits users of work stations to communicate with one another. Printing utilizes laser-driven raster printers capable of printing both text and graphics.

As Jonathan Seybold has written, "This is a very different product: Different because it truly bridges word processing and typesetting functions; different because it has a broader range of capabilities than anything which has preceded it; and different because it introduces to the commercial market radically new concepts in human engineering."[15]

THE IMPORTANCE OF AN APPROPRIATE ARCHITECTURE

Before describing Star's user interface, we should point out several aspects of the Star architecture that are essential to it. Without these elements, it would have been impossible to design an interface anything like the present one.

The Star hardware was modeled after the experimental Xerox "Alto" computer[19]. Like Alto, Star consists of a Xerox-developed high bandwidth MSI processor, local disk storage, a bit-mapped display screen having a 72 dot-per-inch resolution, a pointing device called the "mouse," and a connection to the Ethernet network. Stars are higher performance machines than Altos, being about three times as fast, having 512K bytes of main memory (versus 256K bytes on most Altos), 10 or 29M bytes of disk memory (versus 2.5M bytes), a 10¼"×13¾" display screen (versus 10¼"×8"), and a 10M bits-per-second Ethernet (versus 3M bits). Typically Stars, like Altos, are linked via Ethernets to each other and to shared file, mail and print servers. Communication servers connect Ethernets to one another either directly or over phone lines, enabling internetwork communication.

A Star work station showing the processor, display, keyboard and mouse

- **Display** – The most important ingredient of the user interface is the bit-mapped display screen. Both Star and Alto devote a portion of main memory to the screen: 100K bytes in Star, 50K bytes (usually) in Alto. Every screen dot can be individually turned on or off by setting or resetting the corresponding bit in memory. It should be obvious that this gives both computers an excellent ability to portray visual images. We believe that all impressive office systems of the future will have bit-mapped displays. Memory cost will soon be insignificant enough that they will be feasible even in home computers. Visual communication is effective, and it can't be exploited without graphics flexibility.

- **Memory bandwidth** – There must be a way to change dots on the screen quickly. Star has a high memory bandwidth, about 90 MHz. The entire Star screen is repainted from memory 39 times per second, about a 50 MHz data rate between memory and the screen. This would swamp most computer memories. However since Star's memory is double ported, refreshing the display does not appreciably slow down processor memory access. Star also has separate logic devoted solely to refreshing the display. Finally, special microcode has been written to assist in changing the contents of memory quickly, permitting a variety of screen processing that would not otherwise be practical.[8]

- **Mouse** – People need a way to quickly point to items on the screen. Cursor step keys are too slow; nor are they suitable for graphics. Both Star and Alto use a pointing device called the "mouse." First developed at Stanford Research Institute,[6] Xerox's version has a ball on the bottom that turns as the mouse slides over a flat surface such as a table. Electronics sense the ball rotation and guide a cursor on the screen in corresponding motions. The mouse possesses several important attributes:

  It is a "Fitts's Law" device. That is, after some practice you can point with a mouse as quickly and easily as you can with the tip of your finger. The limitations on pointing speed are those inherent in the human nervous system.[7, 3]

that affect the user's understanding of the system's behavior. Many of these issues are highly subjective and are therefore often addressed in an *ad hoc* fashion. We believe, however, that more rigorous approaches to user interface design can be developed....

"These design methodologies are all unsatisfactory for the same basic reason: they all omit an essential step that must precede the design of any successful user interface, namely *task analysis*. By this we mean the analysis of the task performed by the user, or users, prior to introducing the proposed computer system. Task analysis involves establishing who the users are, what their goals are in performing the task, what information they use in performing it, what information they generate, and what methods they employ. The descriptions of input and output information should include an analysis of the various *objects*, or individual types of information entity, employed by the user....

"The purpose of task analysis is to simplify the remaining stages in user interface design. The *current task description*, with its breakdown of the information objects and methods presently employed, offers a starting point for the definition of a corresponding set of objects and methods to be provided by the computer system. The idea behind this phase of design is to build up a new *task environment* for the user, in which he can work to accomplish the same goals as before, surrounded now by a different set of objects, and employing new methods."

Prototyping is another crucial element of the design process. System designers should be prepared to implement the new or difficult concepts and then to *throw away* that code when doing the actual implementation. As Frederick Brooks says, the question "is not *whether* to build a pilot system and throw it away. You *will* do that. The only question is whether to plan in advance to build a throwaway, or to promise to deliver the throwaway to customers. ... Hence *plan to throw one away; you will, anyhow.*"[2] The Alto served as a valuable prototype for Star. Over a thousand Altos were eventually built. Alto users have had several thousand work-years of experience with them over a period of eight years, making Alto perhaps the largest computer prototyping effort ever. Dozens of experimental programs were written for the Alto by members of the Xerox Palo Alto Research Center. Without the creative ideas of those systems Star in its present form would have been impossible. In addition, we ourselves programmed various aspects of the Star design on Alto, but all of it was "throwaway" code. Alto, with its bit-mapped display screen, was powerful enough to implement and test our ideas on visual interaction.

Some types of concepts are inherently difficult for people to grasp. Without being too formal about it, our experience before and during the Star design has led us to the following classification:

Easy	Hard
concrete	abstract
visible	invisible
copying and modifying	creating from scratch
choosing from a list	filling in a blank
recognizing	generating
editing	programming
interactive	batch.

The characteristics on the left were incorporated into the Star user's conceptual model. The characteristics on the right we attempted to avoid.

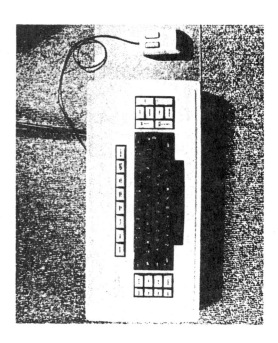

The Star keyboard and mouse.
Note the two buttons on top of the mouse.

It stays where it was left when you are not touching it. It doesn't have to be picked up like a light pen or stylus.

It has buttons on top which can be sensed under program control. The buttons let you point to and interact with objects on the screen in a variety of ways.

• **Disk** – Every Star and Alto has its own rigid disk for local storage of programs and data. This enhances their personal nature, providing consistent access to information regardless of how many other machines there are on the network or what anyone else is doing. Larger programs can be written, using the disk for swapping.

• **Network** – The Ethernet network lets both Stars and Altos have a distributed architecture. Each machine is connected to an Ethernet. Other machines on the Ethernet are dedicated as "servers" – machines which are attached to a resource and provide access to that resource.

STAR DESIGN METHODOLOGY

We have learned from Star the importance of formulating the fundamental concepts (the user's conceptual model) *before* software is written, rather than tacking on a user interface *afterward*. Xerox devoted about thirty work-years to the design of the Star user interface. It was designed *before* the functionality of the system was fully decided. It was designed *before* the computer hardware was built. We worked for two years before we wrote a single line of actual product software. Jonathan Seybold put it this way, "Most system design efforts start with hardware specifications, follow this with a set of functional specifications for the software, then try to figure out a logical user interface and command structure. The Star project started the other way around: the paramount concern was to define a conceptual model of how the user would relate to the system. Hardware and software followed from this."[15]

In fact, before we even began designing the model, we developed a methodology by which we would do the design. Our methodology report[10] stated:

"One of the most troublesome and least understood aspects of interactive systems is the *user interface*. In the design of user interfaces, we are concerned with several issues: the provision of languages by which users can express their commands to the computer; the design of display representations that show the state of the system to the user; and other more abstract issues

PRINCIPLES OF THE STAR USER INTERFACE

The following are the main goals we pursued in designing the Star user interface. We will discuss each of them in turn.

- Familiar user's conceptual model
- Seeing and pointing versus remembering and typing
- What you see is what you get
- Universal commands
- Consistency
- Simplicity
- Modeless interaction
- User tailorability

I. FAMILIAR USER'S CONCEPTUAL MODEL

A "user's conceptual model" is the set of concepts that a person acquires over time to explain the behavior of a system, whether it be a computer system, a physical system, or a hypothetical system. It is the model developed in the mind of the user that enables him to understand and interact with the system. The first task for a system designer is to decide what model he wants for users of his system. This extremely important step is often neglected or done poorly. The Star designers devoted several work-years at the outset of the project discussing and evolving what we considered to be an appropriate model for an office information system: the metaphor of a physical office.

Physical-Office Metaphor

The designer of a computer system can choose to pursue familiar analogies and metaphors or to introduce entirely new functions requiring new approaches. Each option has advantages and disadvantages. We decided to create electronic counterparts to the physical objects in an office: paper, folders, file cabinets, mail boxes, and so on — an electronic metaphor for the office. We hoped that this would make the electronic "world" seem more familiar, less alien, and require less training. (Our initial experiences with users have confirmed this.) We further decided to make the electronic analogues be *concrete objects*. Documents would not exist only as file names on a disk; they would be represented by pictures on the display screen. They would be selected by pointing to them with the mouse and clicking one of the mouse buttons. Once selected, they would be moved, copied or deleted by pushing the MOVE, COPY or DELETE key. Moving a document became the electronic equivalent of picking up a piece of paper and walking somewhere with it. To file a document, you would move it to a picture of a file drawer, just as you walk with a physical piece of paper to a physical file cabinet.

The reason that the user's conceptual model should be decided *first* when designing a system is that the approach adopted *changes the functionality of the system*. An example is electronic mail. Most systems provide electronic mail draw a distinction between *messages* and *files* to be sent to other people. Typically, your one program sends messages and a different program handles file transfers, each with its own interface. But we observed that offices make no such distinction. Everything arrives through the mail, from one-page memos to books and reports, from intraoffice mail to international mail. Therefore, this became part of Star's physical-office metaphor. Star users mail documents of any size to one another, from one page to many pages. Messages are just short documents, as in the real world. User actions are the same whether the recipients are in the next office or in another country.

A physical metaphor can simplify and clarify a system. In addition to eliminating the artificial distinctions of traditional computers, it can eliminate commands by taking advantage of more general concepts. For example, since moving a document on the screen is the equivalent of picking up a piece of paper and walking somewhere with it, there is no "send mail" command. You simply move it to a picture of an out-basket. Nor is there a "receive mail" command. New mail appears in the in-basket as it is received. When new mail is waiting, an envelope appears in the picture of the in-basket. This is a simple, familiar, nontechnical approach to computer mail. And it's easy once the physical-office metaphor is adopted!

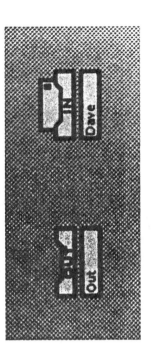

In-basket and out-basket icons.

The in-basket contains an envelope, indicating that mail has been received.

(Note: Most of the illustrations in this paper are taken directly from the Star screen.

Therefore the text in them appears at screen resolution.)

While we want an analogy with the physical world for familiarity, we don't want to limit ourselves to its capabilities. One of the raisons d'être for Star is that physical objects do not provide people with enough power to manage the increasing complexity of the "information age." For example, we can take advantage of the computer's ability to search rapidly by providing a search function for its electronic file drawers, thus helping to solve the long-standing problem of lost files.

Icons, Windows and the "Desktop"

Every user's initial view of Star is the "Desktop," which resembles the top of an office desk, together with surrounding furniture and equipment. It represents your working environment – where your current projects and accessible resources reside. On the screen are displayed pictures of familiar office objects, such as documents, folders, file drawers, in-baskets and out-baskets. These objects are displayed as small pictures or "icons."

You can "open" an icon to deal with what it represents. This enables you to read documents, inspect the contents of folders and file drawers, see what mail you have received, etc. When opened, an icon expands into a larger form called a "window," which displays the icon's contents. Windows are the principal mechanism for displaying and manipulating information.

The Desktop "surface" is displayed as a distinctive grey pattern. This is restful and makes the icons and windows on it stand out crisply, minimizing eye strain. The surface is organized as an array of one inch squares, 14 wide by 11 high. An icon may be placed in any square, giving a maximum of 154 icons. Star centers an icon in its square, making it easy to line up icons neatly. The Desktop always occupies the entire display screen; even when windows appear on the screen, the Desktop continues to exist "beneath" them.

The Desktop is the principal Star technique for realizing the physical-office metaphor. The icons on it are visible, concrete embodiments of the corresponding physical objects. Star users are encouraged to think of the objects on the Desktop in physical terms. Therefore, you can move the icons around to arrange your Desktop as you wish. (Messy Desktops are certainly possible, just as in real life.) Two icons cannot occupy the same space (a basic law of physics). Although moving a document icon to a Desktop resource such as a printer involves transferring the document icon to the same square as the printer icon, the printer immediately "absorbs" the document, queuing it for printing. You can leave documents on your Desktop indefinitely, just as on a real desk, or you can file them away in folders or file drawers. Our intention and hope is that users will *intuit* things to do with icons, and that those things will indeed be part of the system.

(a) Star models the real world accurately enough. Its *similarity* with the office environment preserves your familiar way of working and your existing concepts and knowledge.

(b) There is sufficient *uniformity* in the system. Star's principles and "generic" commands (discussed below) are applied throughout the system, allowing lessons learned in one area to apply to others.

The model of a physical office provides a simple base from which learning can proceed in an incremental

stand out: (1) conscious thought deals with concepts in the short term memory,[1] and (2) the capacity of the short term memory is limited.[14] When everything being dealt with in a computer system is visible, the display screen relieves the load on the short term memory by acting as a sort of "visual cache." Thinking becomes easier and more productive. A well-designed computer system can actually improve the quality of your thinking.[16] In addition, visual communication is often more efficient than linear communication: "a picture is worth a thousand words."

A subtle thing happens when everything is visible: *the display becomes reality*. The user model becomes identical with what is on the screen. Objects can be understood purely in terms of their visible characteristics. Actions can be understood in terms of their effects on the screen. This lets users *conduct experiments* to test, verify and expand their understanding – the essence of experimental science.

In Star we have tried to make the objects and actions in the system *visible*. Everything to be dealt with and all commands and effects have a visible representation on the display screen or on the keyboard. You never have to remember that, for example, CODE+Q does something in one context and something different in another context. In fact, our desire to eliminate this possibility led us to abolish the CODE key. (We have yet to see a computer system that has a CODE key that doesn't violate the principle of visibility.) You never invoke a command or push a key and have nothing visible happen. At the very least, a message is posted explaining that the command doesn't work in this context, or it is not implemented, or there is an error. It is disasterous to the user's model when you invoke an action and the system does nothing in response. We have seen people push a key several times in one system or another trying to get a response. They are not sure whether the system has "heard" them or not. Sometimes the system is simply throwing away their keystrokes. Sometimes it is just slow and is *queuing* the keystrokes; you can imagine the unpredictable behavior that is possible.

Property and Option Sheets

We have already mentioned icons and windows as mechanisms for making the concepts in Star visible. Another mechanism is Star's "property and option sheets." Most objects in Star have properties. A "property sheet" is a two-dimensional form-like environment that displays those properties. Below is the character property sheet. It appears on the screen whenever you make a text selection and push the PROPERTIES key. It contains such properties as type font and size; bold, italic, underline and strikeout face;

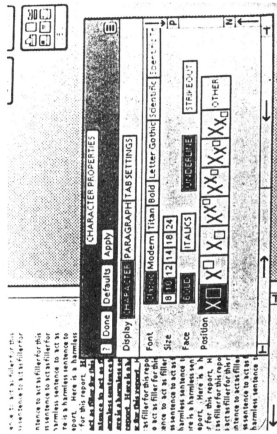

fashion. You are not exposed to entirely new concepts all at once. Much of your existing knowledge is embedded in the base.

Additional user models

In a functionally rich system, it is probably not possible to represent everything in terms of a single model. There may need to be more than one model. For example, Star's records processing facility cannot use the physical-office model, because physical offices have no "records processing" worthy of the name. So we invented a different model, a record file as a collection of *fields*. A record may be displayed as a row in a *table* or as filled-in fields in a *form*. Querying is accomplished by filling in a blank example of a record with predicates describing the desired values, which is philosophically similar to Zloof's "Query-by-Example".[21]

Of course, the number of different user models in a system must be kept to a minimum. And they should not overlap; a new model should be introduced only when an existing one does not cover the situation.

II. SEEING AND POINTING VERSUS REMEMBERING AND TYPING

Visibility

A well-designed system makes everything relevant to a task visible on the screen. It doesn't hide things under CODE + key combinations or force you to remember conventions. That burdens your memory. During conscious thought, the brain utilizes several levels of memory, the most important being the "short term memory." Many studies have analyzed the short term memory and its role in thinking. Two conclusions

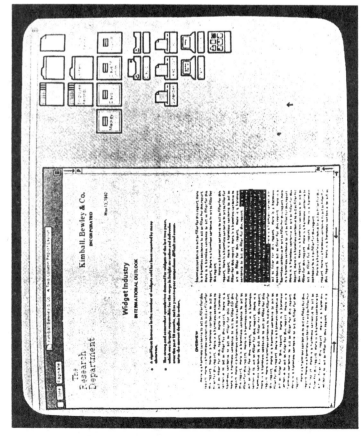

A Desktop as it appears on the screen.

It contains icons that this user commonly uses, including a document to serve as a "form pad" source for blank paper.

There is also an open window displaying a document.

and superscript/subscript positioning. Instead of having to remember the properties of characters, the current settings of those properties, and, worst of all, how to change those properties, property sheets simply *show everything on the screen. All* the options are presented. To change one, you point to it with the mouse and push a mouse button. Properties in effect are displayed in reverse video.

This mechanism is used for *all* properties of *all* objects in the system. Star contains a couple of hundred properties. To keep you from being overwhelmed with information, property sheets display only the properties relevant to the type of object that is currently selected (e.g. character, paragraph, page, graphic line, formula element, frame, document or folder). This is an example of "progressive disclosure": hiding complexity until it is needed. It is also one of the clearest examples of how an emphasis on visibility can reduce the amount of remembering and typing required.

Property sheets may be thought of as an *alternate representation* for objects. The screen shows the visible characteristics of objects, such as the type font of text characters or the names of icons. Pro-perty sheets show the underlying structure of objects and make this structure visible and accessible.

Invisibility also plagues the commands in some systems. Commands often have several arguments and options that you must remember with no assistance from the system. Star addresses this problem with "option sheets." An "option sheet" is a two-dimensional form-like environment which displays the arguments to commands. It serves the same function for commands that property sheets do for objects.

III. WHAT YOU SEE IS WHAT YOU GET

"What you see is what you get" (or WYSIWYG) refers to the situation in which the display screen portrays an accurate rendition of the printed page. In systems having such capabilities as multiple fonts and variable line spacing, WYSIWYG requires a bit-mapped display, for only that has sufficient graphic power to render those characteristics accurately.

WYSIWYG is a simplifying technique for document creation systems. All composition is done *on the screen.* It eliminates the iterations that plague users of document compilers. You can examine the appearance of a page *on the screen* and make changes until it looks right. The printed page will look the same. Anyone who

has used a document compiler or post-processor knows how valuable WYSIWYG is. The first powerful WYSIWYG editor was Bravo, an experimental editor developed for Alto at the Xerox Palo Alto Research Center.[12] The text-editor aspects of Star were derived from Bravo.

Trade-offs are involved in WYSIWYG editors, chiefly having to do with the lower resolution of display screens. It is never possible to get an *exact* representation of a printed page on the screen since most screens have only 50 to 100 dots per inch (72 in Star), while most printers have higher resolution. Completely accurate character positioning is not possible. Nor is it usually possible to represent shape differences for fonts smaller than eight points in size since there are too few dots per character to be recognizable. Even 10-point ("normal" size) fonts may be uncomfortably small on the screen, necessitating a magnified mode for viewing text. WYSIWYG requires very careful design of the screen fonts in order to keep text on the screen readable and attractive. Nevertheless, the increase in productivity made possible by WYSIWYG editors more than outweighs these difficulties.

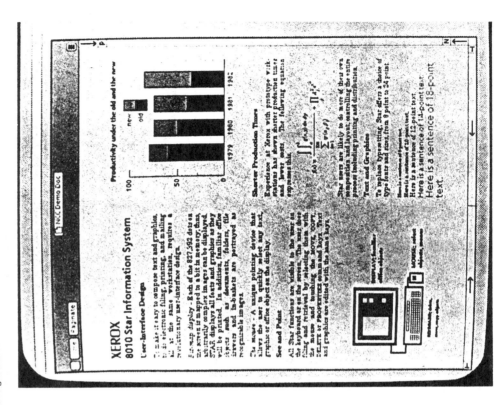

A Star document showing multi-column text, graphics, and formulas.

This is the way the document appears on the screen, and this is the way it will print (at higher resolution, of course).

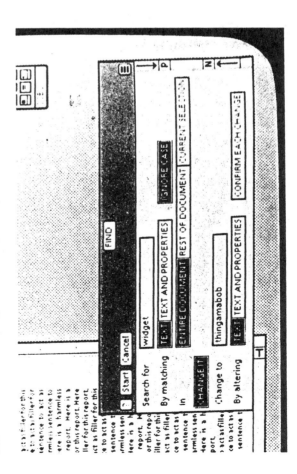

IV. UNIVERSAL COMMANDS

Star has a few commands that can be used throughout the system: MOVE, COPY, DELETE, SHOW PROPERTIES, COPY PROPERTIES, AGAIN, UNDO and HELP. Each performs the same way regardless of the type of object selected. Thus we call them "universal" or "generic" commands. For example, you follow the same set of actions to move text in a document, to move a line in an illustration, or to move a document in a folder: select the object, push the MOVE key, and indicate a destination. (HELP and UNDO don't use a selection.) Each generic command has a key devoted to it on the keyboard.

These commands are far more basic than the commands in other computer systems. They strip away the extraneous application-specific semantics to get at the underlying principles. Star's generic commands derive from fundamental computer science concepts because they also underly operations in programming languages. For example, much program manipulation of data structures involves moving or copying values from one data structure to another. Since Star's generic commands embody fundamental underlying concepts, they are widely applicable. Each command fills a variety of needs, meaning fewer commands are required. This simplicity is desirable in itself, but it has another subtle advantage: it makes it easy for users to form a model of the system. What people can understand, they can use. Just as progress in science derives from simple, clear theories, so progress in the usability of computers is coming to depend on simple, clear user interfaces.

MOVE is the most powerful command in the system. It is used during text editing to rearrange letters in a word, words in a sentence, sentences in a paragraph, and paragraphs in a document. It is used during graphics editing to move picture elements such as lines and rectangles around in an illustration. It is used during formula editing to move mathematical structures such as summations and integrals around in an equation. It replaces the conventional "store file" and "retrieve file" commands; you simply move an icon into or out of a file drawer or folder. It eliminates the "send mail" and "receive mail" commands; you move an icon to an out-basket or from an in-basket. It replaces the "print" command; you move an icon to a printer. And so on. MOVE strips away much of the historical clutter of computer commands. It is more fundamental than the myriad of commands it replaces. It is simultaneously more powerful and simpler.

Much simplification comes from Star's object oriented interface. The action of setting properties also replaces a myriad of commands. For example, changing paragraph margins is a command in many systems. In Star you do it by selecting a paragraph object and setting its MARGINS property.

V. CONSISTENCY

Consistency asserts that mechanisms should be used in the same way wherever they occur. For example, if the left mouse button is used to select a character, the same button should be used to select a graphic line or an icon. Everyone agrees that consistency is an admirable goal. However, it is perhaps the single hardest characteristic of all to achieve in a computer system. In fact, in systems of even moderate complexity, consistency may not be well defined.

The Dimensions of Consistency: An Example of Consistent Inconsistency

A question that has defied consensus in Star is what should happen to a document after it has been printed. Recall that a user prints a document by selecting its icon, invoking MOVE, and designating a printer icon. The printer "absorbs" the document, queuing it for printing. What happens to that document icon after printing is completed? There are two plausible alternatives:

1. The system deletes the icon.
2. The system does not delete the icon, which leads to several further alternatives:
   2a. The system puts the icon back where it came from (i. e. where it was before MOVE was invoked).
   2b. The system puts the icon at an arbitrary spot on the Desktop.
   2c. The system leaves the icon in the printer. You must move it out of the printer explicitly.

The consistency argument for the first alternative goes as follows: when you move an icon to an out-basket, the system mails it and then deletes it from your Desktop. When you move an icon to a file drawer, the system files it and then deletes it from your Desktop. Therefore, when you move an icon to a printer, the system should print it and then delete it from your Desktop. Function icons should behave consistently with one another.

The consistency argument for the second alternative is: the user's conceptual model at the Desktop level is the physical-office metaphor. Icons are supposed to behave similarly to their physical counterparts. It makes sense that icons are deleted after they are mailed, because after you put a piece of paper in a physical out-basket and the mailperson picks it up, it is gone. However, the physical analogue for printers is the (Xerox) office copier, and there is no notion of deleting a piece of paper when you make a copy of it. Function icons should behave consistently with their physical counterparts.

There is no one right answer here. Both arguments emphasize a dimension of consistency. In this case, the dimensions happen to overlap. We eventually chose alternative 2a for the following reasons:

Model dominance – The physical metaphor is the stronger model at the Desktop level. Analogy with physical counterparts *does* form the basis for people's understanding of what icons are and how they behave. Argument 1 advocates an *implicit* model that must be learned; argument 2 advocates an *explicit* model which people already have when they are introduced to the system. Since people use their existing knowledge when confronted with new situations, the design of a system should be based on that knowledge. This is especially important if people are to be able to *intuit* new uses for the features they have learned.

Pragmatics – It is dangerous to delete things when users don't expect it. The first time a person labors over a document, gets it just right, prints it, and finds that it has disappeared, he is going to become *very nervous*. Not to mention angry. We also decided to put it back where it came from (2a instead of 2b or 2c) for the pragmatic reason that this involves slightly less work on the user's part.

Seriousness – When you file or mail an icon, it is not deleted entirely from the system. It still exists in the file drawer or in the recipients' in-baskets. If you want it back, you can move it back out of the file drawer or send a message to one of the recipients asking to have a copy sent back. Deleting after printing, however, is final: if you move a document to a printer and the printer deletes it, that document is gone for good.

Paradigms

One way to get consistency into a system is to adhere to *paradigms* for operations. By applying a successful way of working in one area to other areas, a system acquires a unity that is both apparent and real. Paradigms that Star uses are:

● **Editing** – Much of what you do in Star can be thought of as editing. In addition to the conventional text, graphics and formula editing, you manage your files by *editing filing windows*. You arrange your working environment by *editing your Desktop*. You alter properties by *editing property sheets*. Even programming can be thought of as *editing data structures*.[16]

● **Information retrieval** – A lot of power can be gained by applying information retrieval techniques to information wherever it exists in a system. Star broadens the definition of "database." In addition to the traditional notion as represented by its record files, Star views file drawers as databases of documents, in-baskets as databases of mail, etc. This teaches users to think of information retrieval as a general tool applicable throughout the system.

● **Copying** – Star elevates the concept of "copying" to a high level: that of a paradigm for creating. In all the various domains of Star, you *create by copying*. Creating something out of nothing is a difficult task. Everyone has observed that it is easier to modify an existing document or program than to write it originally. Picasso once said, "The most awful thing for a painter is the white canvas. ... To copy others is necessary."[20] Star makes a serious attempt to alleviate the problem of the "white canvas" by making copying a practical aid to creation. For example, you create new icons by copying existing ones. You create graphics by copying existing graphic images and modifying them. In a sense you can even type characters in Star's 216-character set by "copying" them from keyboard windows.

These paradigms *change the very way you think*. They lead to new habits and models of behavior that are more powerful and productive. They can lead to a *human-machine synergism*.

Classes and Subclasses

Star obtains additional consistency by using the class and subclass notions of Simula[4] and Smalltalk.[11] The clearest example of this is classifying icons at a higher level into "data icons" and "function icons." Data icons represent objects on which actions are performed. Currently the three types (i.e. subclasses) of data icons are documents, folders and record files. Function icons represent objects that perform actions. Function icons are of many types, with more being added as the system evolves: file drawers, printers, in- and out-baskets, printers, floppy disk drives, calculators, terminal emulators, etc.

In general anything that can be done to one data icon can be done to all, regardless of its type, size or location. All data icons can be moved, copied, deleted, filed, mailed, printed, opened, closed, and a variety of other operations applied. Most function icons will accept any data icon; for example, you can mail any data icon using an out-basket. This class concept in the user interface design reduces the artificial distinctions that occur in some systems.

VI. SIMPLICITY

Simplicity is another principle with which no one can disagree. Obviously a simple system is better than a complicated one if they have the same capabilities. However the world is never as (ahem) simple as that. Typically, a trade-off exists between easy novice use and efficient expert use. The two goals are not always compatible. In Star we have tried to follow Alan Kay's maxim: "simple things should be simple; complex things should be possible." To do this, it was sometimes necessary to make common things simple at the expense of uncommon things being harder. Simplicity, like consistency, is not a clear-cut principle.

One way to make a system appear simple is to make it uniform and consistent, as we discussed above. Adhering to those principles leads to a simple user's model. Simple models are easier to understand and work with than intricate ones.

Another way to achieve simplicity is to minimize the redundancy in a system. Having two or more ways to do something increases the complexity without increasing the capabilities. The ideal system would have a minimum of powerful commands that obtained all the desired functionality and that did not overlap. That was the motivation for Star's "generic" commands. But again the world is not so simple. General mechanisms are often inconvenient for high-frequency actions. For example, the SHOW PROPERTIES command is Star's general mechanism for changing properties, but it is too much of an interruption during typing. Therefore, we added keys to optimize the changing of certain character properties: BOLD, ITALICS, UNDERLINE, SUPERSCRIPT, SUBSCRIPT, LARGER/SMALLER (font), CENTER (paragraph). These significantly speed up typing, but they don't add any new functionality. In this case we felt the trade-off was worth it because typing is a frequent activity. "Minimum redundancy" is a good but not absolute guideline.

In general it is better to introduce new general mechanisms by which "experts" can obtain accelerators than to add a lot of special one-purpose-only features. Star's mechanisms are discussed below under "User Tailorability."

Another way to have the system as a whole appear simple is to make each of the parts simple. In particular, the system should avoid overloading the semantics of the parts. Each part should be kept conceptually clean. Sometimes this may involve a major redesign of the user interface. An example from Star is the mouse. The mouse has been used on the Alto for eight years, and before that it was used on the NLS system at SRI.5 All of those mice have three buttons on top. Star has only two. Why did we depart from "tradition"? We observed that the dozens of Alto programs all had different semantics for the mouse buttons. Some used them one way, some another. There was no consistency between systems. Sometimes there was not even consistency within a system. For example, Bravo uses the mouse buttons for selecting text, scrolling windows, and creating and deleting windows, depending on where the cursor is when you push a mouse button. Each of the three buttons has its own meaning in each of the different regions. It is hard to remember which button does what where.

Thus, we decided to simplify the mouse for Star. Since it is apparently quite a temptation to overload the semantics of the buttons, we eliminated temptation by eliminating buttons. Well then, why didn't we use a one-button mouse? Here the plot thickens. We did consider and prototype a one-button mouse interface. One button is sufficient (with a little cleverness) to provide all the functionality needed in a mouse. But when we tested the interface on naive users, as we did with a variety of features, we found that they had a lot of trouble making selections with it. In fact we prototyped and tested six different semantics for the mouse buttons: one one-button, four two-button, and a three-button design. We were chagrined to find that while some were better than others, *none of them* was completely easy to use, even though, a priori, it seemed like all of them would work! We then took the most successful features of two of the two-button designs and prototyped and tested them as a seventh design. To our relief, it not only tested better than any of the other six, everyone found it simple and trouble-free to use.

This story has a couple of morals:

- The intuition of designers is error-prone, no matter how good or bad they are.

- The critical parts of a system should be tested on representative users, preferably of the "lowest common denominator" type.

- What is simplest along any one dimension (e.g. number of buttons) is not necessarily conceptually simplest for users. In particular, minimizing the number of keystrokes may not make a system easier to use.

VII. MODELESS INTERACTION

Larry Tesler defines a *mode* as:

"A mode of an interactive computer system is a state of the user interface that lasts for a period of time, is not associated with any particular object, and has no role other than to place an interpretation on operator input."18

Many computer systems use modes because there are too few keys on the keyboard to represent all of the available commands. Therefore, the interpretation of the keys depends on the mode or state the system is in. Modes can and do cause trouble by making habitual actions have unexpected results. If you do not notice what mode the system is in, you may find yourself invoking a sequence of commands quite different from what you had intended.

Our favorite story about modes, probably apocryphal, involves Bravo. In Bravo the main typing keys are normally interpreted as commands. The "i" key invokes the Insert command, which puts the system in "insert mode." In insert mode, Bravo interprets keystrokes as letters. The story goes that a person intended to type the word "edit" into his document, but he forgot to enter insert mode first. Bravo interpreted "edit" as the following commands:

E(verything) – select everything in the document
D(elete) – delete it
I(nsert) – enter insert mode
t – type a "t".

The entire contents of the document were replaced by the letter "t." This makes the point, perhaps too strongly, that modes should be introduced into a user interface with caution, if at all.

Commands in Star take the form of noun-verb. You specify the object of interest (the "noun") and then

See and Point

All Star functions are visible to the user on the keyboard or on the screen. The user does filing and retrieval by selecting them with the mouse and touching the MOVE, COPY, DELETE or PROPERTIES command and keys. Text and graphics are edited with the same keys.

Star users are likely to do more of their own composition and layout, controlling the entire ...

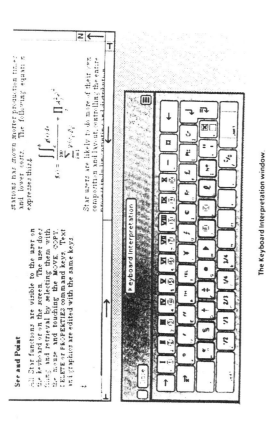

The Keyboard Interpretation window.

This serves as the "source" of characters that may be entered from the keyboard.

The character set shown here contains a variety of office symbols.

invoke a command to manipulate it (the "verb"). Specifying an object is called "making a selection." Star provides powerful selection mechanisms, which reduce the number and complexity of commands in the system. Typically you will exercise more dexterity and judgment in making a selection than in invoking a command. The object (noun) is almost always specified before the action (verb) to be performed. This helps make the command interface modeless; you can change your mind as to which object to affect simply by making a new selection before invoking the command. No "accept" function is needed to terminate or confirm commands, since invoking the command is the last step. Inserting text does not even require a command; you simply make a selection and begin typing. The text is placed after the end of the selection.

Note that the noun-verb command form does not by itself imply that a command interface is modeless. Bravo also uses the noun-verb form; yet it is a highly modal editor (although the latest version of Bravo has drastically reduced its modality). The difference is that Bravo tries to make one mechanism (the main typing keys) serve more than one function (entering letters and invoking commands). This inevitably leads to confusion. Star avoids the problem by having special keys on the keyboard devoted solely to invoking functions. The main typing keys only enter characters. (This is another example of the simplicity principle: avoid overloading mechanisms with meanings.)

Modes are not necessarily bad. Some modes can be helpful by simplifying the specification of extended commands. For example, Star uses a "field fill-in order specification mode." In this mode you can specify the order in which the NEXT key will step through the fields in the document. Invoking the SET FILL-IN ORDER command puts the system in the mode. Each field you now select is added to the fill-in order. You terminate the mode by pushing the STOP key. Star also utilizes temporary modes as part of the MOVE, COPY and COPY PROPERTIES commands. For example, to move an object you select it, push the MOVE key which puts the system in "move mode," and then select the destination. These modes work for two reasons. First, *they are visible*. Star posts a message in the Message Area at the top of the screen indicating that a mode is in effect. The message remains there for the duration of the mode. Star also changes the shape of the cursor as an additional indication. You can always tell the state of the system by inspection. Second, *the allowable actions are constrained during modes*. The only action that is allowed – except for actions directly related to the mode – is scrolling to another part of the document. This constraint makes it even more apparent that the system is in an unusual state.

VIII. USER TAILORABILITY

No matter how general or powerful a system is, it will never satisfy all its potential users. People always want ways to speed up often-performed operations. Yet, everyone is different. The only solution is to design the system with provisions for user extensibility built in. The following mechanisms are provided by Star:

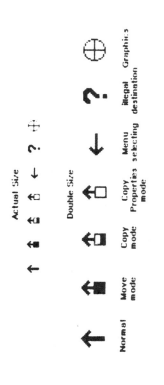

Some of the cursor shapes used by Star to indicate the state of the system.
The cursor is a 16×16 bitmap that can be changed under program control.

- You can tailor the appearance of your system in a variety of ways. The simplest is to choose the icons you want on your Desktop, thus tailoring your working environment. At a more sophisticated level, a work station can be purchased with or without certain functions. For example, not everyone may want the equation facility. Xerox calls this "product factoring."

- You can set up blank documents with text, paragraph and page layout defaults. For example, you might set up one document with the normal text font being 10-point Classic and another with it being 12-point Modern italic. The documents need not be blank; they may contain fixed text and graphics and fields for variable fill-in. A typical form might be a business-letter form with address, addressee, salutation and body fields, each field with its own default text style. Or it might be an accounting form with lines and tables. Or it might be a mail form with To, From and Subject fields, and a heading tailored to each individual. Whatever the form or document, you can put it on your Desktop and make new instances of it by selecting it and invoking COPY. Thus each form can act like a "pad of paper" from which new sheets can be "torn off."

Interesting documents to set up are "transfer sheets," documents containing a variety of graphic symbols tailored to different applications. For example, you might have a transfer sheet containing buildings in different sizes and shapes, one devoted to furniture, animals, geometric shapes, flow chart symbols, circuit components, logos, or a hundred other possibilities. Each sheet would make it easier to create a certain type of illustration. Graphics experts could even construct the symbols on the sheets, so that users could create high-quality illustrations without needing as much skill.

- You can tailor your filing system by changing the sort order in file drawers and folders. You can also control the filing hierarchy by putting folders inside folders, to any desired level.

- You can tailor your record files by defining any number of "views" on them. Each view consists of a filter, a sort order, and a formatting document. A filter is a set of predicates that produce a subset of the record file. A formatting document is any document that contains fields whose names correspond to those in the record file. Records are always displayed through some formatting document: they have no inherent external representation. Thus, you can set up your own individual subset(s) and appearances(s) for a record file, even if the record file is shared by several users.

- You can define "meta operations" by writing programs in the CUStomer Programming language CUSP. For example, you can further tailor your forms by assigning to fields computation rules expressed in CUSP. Eventually, you will be able to define your own commands by placing CUSP "buttons" into documents.

- You can define abbreviations for commonly-used terms by means of the abbreviation definition/expansion facility. For example, you might define "sdd" as an abbreviation for "Xerox Systems Development Department." The expansion can be an entire paragraph, or even multiple paragraphs. This is handy if you create documents out of predefined "boilerplate" paragraphs, as the legal profession does. The expansion can even be an illustration or mathematical formula.

- Every user has a unique name by which he is identified to the system, usually the user's full name. However, you can define one or more *aliases* by which you are willing to be known, such as your last name only, or a shortened form of your name, or a nickname. This lets you personalize your identification to the rest of the network.

SUMMARY

In the 1980's the most important factors affecting how prevalent computer usage becomes will be reduced cost, increased functionality, improved availability and servicing, and perhaps most importantly of all, progress in user interface design. The first three alone are necessary but not sufficient for widespread use. Reduced cost will allow people to *buy* computers, but improved user interfaces will allow people to *use* computers. In this paper we have presented some principles and techniques that we hope will lead to better user interfaces.

User-interface design is still an art, not a science. Many times during the Star design we were amazed at the depth and subtlety of user-interface issues, even such supposedly straightforward issues as consistency and simplicity. Often there is no one "right" answer. Much of the time there is no scientific evidence to support one alternative over another, just intuition. Almost always there are trade-offs. Perhaps by the end of the decade, user-interface design will be a more rigorous process. We hope that we have contributed to that progress.

REFERENCES

[1] Arnheim, R., *Visual Thinking* (University of California Press, Berkeley, California., 1971).

[2] Brooks, F., *The Mythical Man-Month* (Addison-Wesley, Reading, Massachusetts, 1975).

[3] Card, S., English, W. and Burr, B., Evaluation of Mouse, Rate-Controlled Isometric Joystick, Step Keys, and Text Keys for Text Selection on a CRT, *Ergonomics*, 21, 8 (1978) 601-613.

[4] Dahl, O.-J. and Nygaard, K., SIMULA–An Algol-Based Simulation Language, *Communications of the ACM*, 9, 9 (1966) 671-678.

[5] Engelbart, D. and English, W., A Research Center for Augmenting Human Intellect, *Proceedings of the AFIPS 1968 Fall Joint Computer Conference*, 33 (1968) 395-410.

[6] English, W., Engelbart, D. and Berman, M. L., Display-Selection Techniques for Text Manipulation, *IEEE Transactions on Human Factors in Electronics*, HFE-8, 1 (1967) 21-31.

[7] Fitts, P.M., The Information Capacity of the Human Motor System in Controlling Amplitude of Movement, *Journal of Experimental Psychology*, 47 (1954) 381-391.

[8] Ingalls, D., The Smalltalk Graphics Kernel, *Byte*, 6, 8 (1981) 168-194.

[9] Intel, Digital Equipment and Xerox Corporations, *The Ethernet, A Local Area Network: Data Link Layer and Physical Layer Specifications*, version 1.0, Office Products Division, Xerox Corporation (1980).

[10] Irby, C., Bergsteinsson, L., Moran, T., Newman, W. and Tesler, L., *A Methodology for User Interface Design*, Office Products Division, Xerox Corporation (1977).

[11] Kay, A. and the Learning Research Group, *Personal Dynamic Media*, Xerox Palo Alto Research Center Technical Report SSL-76-1 (1976). A condensed version is in *IEEE Computer*, (March 1977) 31-41.

[12] Lampson, B., Bravo Manual, *Alto User's Handbook*, Palo Alto Research Center, Xerox Corporation (1976 and 1978). Much of the design and all of the implementation of Bravo was done by Charles Simonyi and the skilled programmers in his "software factory."

[13] Metcalfe, R. and Boggs, D., Ethernet: Distributed Packet Switching for Local Computer Networks, *Communications of the ACM*, 19, 7 (1976) 395-404.

[14] Miller, G., The Magical Number Seven, Plus or Minus Two: Some Limits on Our Capacity for Processing Information, in: Miller, G., *The Psychology of Communication* (Basic Books, New York, 1967). An earlier version appeared in *Psychology Review*, 63, 2 (1956) 81-97.

[15] Seybold, J., Xerox's 'Star', *The Seybold Report*, Seybold Publications, 10, 16 (1981) Media, Pennsylvania.

[16] Smith, D. C., *Pygmalion, A Computer Program to Model and Stimulate Creative Thought* (Birkhäuser Verlag, Basel, Switzerland, 1977).

[17] Smith, D. C., Irby, C., Kimball, R. and Harslem, E., The Star User Interface: An Overview, *Proceedings of the AFIPS 1982 National Computer Conference*, 50, (1982), 515-528.

[18] Tesler, L., private communication; but see his excellent discussion of modes in The Smalltalk Environment, *Byte*, 6, 8 (1981) 90-147.

[19] Thacker, C. P., McCreight, E. M., Lampson, B. W., Sproull, R. F. and Boggs, D. R., Alto: A Personal Computer, in: Siewiorek, D., Bell, C. and Newell, A. (eds.), *Computer Structures: Principles and Examples*, (McGraw-Hill, 1982).

[20] Wertenbaker, L., *The World of Picasso* (Time-Life Books, New York, 1967).

[21] Zloof, M. M., Query-by-Example, *Proceedings of the AFIPS 1975 National Computer Conference*, 44 (1975) 431-438.

Human Factors Testing in the Design of Xerox's 8010 "Star" Office Workstation

William L. Bewley, Teresa L. Roberts, David Schroit, William L. Verplank

Xerox Office Systems Division

Abstract

Integral to the design process of the Xerox 8010 "Star" workstation was constant concern for the user interface. The design was driven by principles of human cognition. Prototyping of ideas, paper-and-pencil analyses, and human-factors experiments with potential users all aided in making design decisions. Three of the human-factors experiments are described in this paper: A *selection schemes* test determined the number of buttons on the mouse pointing device and the meanings of these buttons for doing text selection. An *icon* test showed us the significant parameters in the shapes of objects on the display screen. A *graphics* test evaluated the user interface for making line drawings, and resulted in a redesign of that interface.

1. Introduction

The Xerox 8010 office workstation, known as Star during development, is meant for use by office professionals. In contrast to word processors which are largely used by secretarial and administrative personnel, or computer systems which are largely used by technically-trained workers, Star had to be designed for casual users who demand extensive functionality at a small training cost. Since the background of the targeted users was very different from that of Star's designers, the designers' intuitions could not always be used as the criteria for an acceptable system.

Recognizing that design of the Star user interface was a major undertaking, the design team approached it using several principles, derived from cognitive psychology:

- There should be an explicit user's model of the system, and it should be familiar (drawing on objects and activities the user already works with) and consistent.

- Seeing something and pointing to it is easier for people than remembering a name and typing it. This principle is often expressed in psychological literature as "recognition is generally easier than recall" [Anderson].

- Commands should be uniform across domains, in cases where the domains have corresponding actions (e.g., deleting a word from text, deleting a line from an illustration, and deleting information from a database).

- The screen should faithfully show the state of the object the user is working on: "What you see is what you get."

Even given these principles, the design space is enormous, and many proposed designs turned out to be unsatisfactory. Further tools were needed for designing Star than just a set of principles to start from. Once a design was proposed, it had to be tested, which we did in several ways.

First, the general user interface was prototyped in an environment which made it easy to modify. Care was spent on the user illusion, but not on all the underpinnings necessary to provide an integrated, robust system. This prototype was used by Star designers and others to get a "feel" for what they were proposing.

Sometimes a prototype was not appropriate to answer questions arising in the design, so various analyses were performed. For instance, Card, Moran, and Newell's Keystroke Level Model [Card] was used to study the number of user actions and amount of time required to perform large office tasks, given a proposed command language. This helped identify bottlenecks and annoyances in the procedures that would be necessary to perform the tasks.

Finally, in certain domains where neither analysis nor informal use of prototypes was sufficient to validate or invalidate proposed designs, the Functional Test Group (which also did much of the user interface analysis) performed formal human-factors experiments. Those experiments are the topic of this paper.

In the rest of the paper, we first present the basics of the Star user interface, to give the reader the context of the tests which were run. Then we describe three representative experiments which we performed. Finally, we discuss what sort of things were tested successfully and what sort of things were not tested, significant features of the testing we did, and the effect the testing had on the success of Star's user interface.

2. Background description of Star

The Star user interface has been extensively described in papers which also address the design philosophy and process [Seybold, Smith1, and Smith2]. Here we describe only enough of Star to motivate the user interface tests we will be covering.

Star is run on a powerful personal computer. It has a 17" diagonal, high-resolution, bitmapped screen which can display arbitrarily complex images; a keyboard which has a moderate number of function keys to the left, right, and above the main typing array; and a pointing device (the mouse). Figure 1 shows these elements graphically.

Central to the user interface is the office metaphor. Familiar office objects, such as documents, folders, and file drawers, are represented on the screen by small pictures called *icons*. Data icons, such as documents, are mailed, filed, and printed by moving them to icons representing outbaskets, file drawers, and printers, respectively, so individual commands are not needed for these operations. When the content of an object needs to be seen, such as for editing, the icon is *opened* to take up a large rectangular area.

on the screen called a *window*.

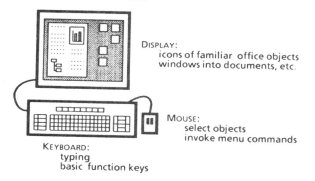

DISPLAY:
icons of familiar office objects
windows into documents, etc.

MOUSE:
select objects
invoke menu commands

KEYBOARD:
typing
basic function keys

Figure 1. Elements of the Star Workstation

Star documents include text, graphics, typeset mathematical formulas, and tables, all freely intermixed. All appear on the screen exactly as they will appear when they are printed (within the limits of the display resolution), and all can be edited interactively.

The user performs a Star action by first selecting the object of the action by pointing to it with the mouse; it videoinverts to give feedback that it is selected. After making a selection, the user presses the function key indicating the desired command. Most Star actions can be performed with only four function keys: Delete, Move, Copy, and Show Properties. These are applied to all kinds of Star objects from characters and paragraphs to data-driven barcharts and icons. The function of Delete is clear. Move and Copy, in addition to allowing rearrangement and replication of objects, perform printing, mailing, and filing functions, as mentioned above.

The Show Properties key brings up a *property sheet*. Each Star object has a set of properties displayed on its property sheet. For instance, the properties of a character are its typeface, size, position with respect to the baseline, and so forth. The properties of a folder (a collection of documents and other folders) include its name and the sort order of its contents. The properties of a data-driven barchart include information on the desired orientation and shading of the bars, the number of ticks on the axis, and, of course, the data. The property sheets appear when asked for, let the user select desired property settings, and then disappear when no longer needed. They offer an immense flexibility of options for Star objects, without cluttering either a command language or the screen.

3. Selection Schemes Tests

The goal of the two selection schemes tests was to evaluate methods for selecting text. The schemes are various mappings of one, two, or three mouse buttons to the functions needed for indicating what text is to be operated on. The kinds of selection behavior needed are (1) *Point*: indicating a point between two characters, to be used as the destination of a Move or Copy, or the position where new typed text will be inserted; (2) *Select*: selecting some text, possibly in increments of a character, word, sentence, paragraph, or the whole document; and (3) *Extend*: extending the selection to include a whole range of text.

Selection Scheme Test 1

The first test compared six selection schemes. These schemes are summarized in Figure 2, schemes A through F. The six selection schemes differ in the mapping between mouse buttons and the three operations. As one example of the differences among schemes, in two schemes, A and B, different buttons are used for Point and Select, while in the remaining four schemes the first button is used for both Point and Select.

Methodology. Using a between-subjects paradigm, each of six groups (four subjects per group) was assigned one of the six schemes. Two of the subjects in each group were experienced in the use of the mouse, two were not. Each subject was first trained in the use of the mouse and in basic Star editing techniques. Next, the assigned scheme was taught. Each subject then performed ten text editing tasks, each of which was repeated six times. Dependent variables were selection time and selection errors.

Selection time. Mean selection times are shown in Figure 3. Among these six schemes, scheme F was substantially better than the others over all six trials (p < .001).

	Scheme A	Scheme B	Scheme C	Scheme D	Scheme E	Scheme F	Scheme G
Button 1	Point	Point	Point C Drawthrough	Point C, W, S, ¶, D Drawthrough	Point C, W, S, ¶, D Drawthrough	Point C Drawthrough	Point C, W, S, ¶, D
Button 2	C Drawthrough	C, W, S, ¶, D Drawthrough	W, S, ¶, D Drawthrough		Adjust	Adjust	Adjust
Button 3	W, S, ¶, D Drawthrough						

Key: Point: Selects a point, *i.e.*, a position between adjacent characters. Used as destination for Move or Copy. If the button doesn't also make a text selection, Point is also used to indicate a destination for type-in.

C, W, S, ¶, D: Selects a character, word, sentence, paragraph, or whole document, by repeatedly clicking the mouse button while pointing at something that's already selected.

Drawthrough: The user holds the button down and moves the mouse. The selection extends from the button-down position to the button-up point. The selection is extended in units of whatever was previously selected.

Adjust: The user clicks the mouse button to extend the selection from the existing selection to the button-up point. The selection is extended in units of whatever was previously selected.

Figure 2. Description of the Selection Schemes

Scheme A	Scheme B	Scheme C	Scheme D	Scheme E	Scheme F	Scheme G
12.25	15.19	13.41	13.44	12.85	9.89	7.96

Figure 3. Mean Selection Time (Secs)

Selection Errors. There was an average of one selection error per 4 tasks. The majority (65%) were errors in drawthrough: either too far or not far enough. The frequency of drawthrough errors did not vary as a function of selection scheme. "Too Many Clicks" errors, *e.g.*, the subject clicking to a sentence instead of a word, accounted for 20% of the errors, with schemes which employed less multiple-clicking being better. "Click Wrong Mouse Button" errors accounted for 15% of total errors. These errors also varied across schemes, with schemes having fewer buttons being better.

Selection Scheme Test 2

The results of the first test were interpreted as suggesting that the following features of a selection scheme should be avoided: 1) drawthrough, 2) three buttons, and 3) multiple-clicking. The second selection scheme test evaluated a scheme designed with these results in mind. Scheme G is also described in Figure 2. It is essentially Scheme F with the addition of multiple-clicking. It avoids drawthrough and uses only two buttons. Multiple-clicking is used because, although 20% of the errors in the first test were attributable to errors in multiple-clicking, Star's designers felt that a selection scheme must provide for quick selection of standard text units.

The same methodology was used for evaluating the new scheme as was used for the rest, except that only one user was experienced with the mouse and three were not.

Results. The mean selection time for the new scheme was 7.96 sec, the lowest time so far. The frequency of "Too Many Clicks" errors in Scheme G was about the same as the frequency observed in the first selection scheme test.

Conclusions. The results of the second test were interpreted as indicating that Scheme G was acceptable for use in Star, since (1) selection time for Scheme G was shorter than for all other schemes, and (2) the advantage of providing quick selection of standard text units through multiple-clicking was judged sufficiently great to balance the moderate error rate due to multiple-clicking errors.

4. Icon Shape Test

A series of tests was used in helping to decide what the icons should look like so that they would be readily identifiable, easy to learn, and distinguishable. The purpose of the tests was to give some feedback to the icon designers about probable user response to designs. We did not intend that the tests alone be used to decide which set of icons was best, but rather to point up difficulties and preferable design directions.

We did not test icons as commands. These tests did not consider the issues of whether iconic representation and implicit commands are better than typed names and typed commands or whether a small set of "universal" commands (Delete, Move, Copy, Show Properties) applied uniformly across domains (text, graphics, printing, mailing) are superior to a large number of commands specialized to each domain.

Methodology and Results

Four different sets of 17 icons were designed by four different designers (see Figure 4). Five subjects were assigned to each set for a total of 20 subjects. A series of paper-and-pencil tests was used to assess familiarity (Naming Tests); two response-time tests using a computer and display measured recognizability and distinguishability (Timed Tests); finally, subjects were asked for their opinions (Rating Tests).

Naming Tests. First the experimenter showed the icons one at a time, each on a 3×5" card, and asked for "a short description of what you think it is." Then the entire set was presented and the subjects were allowed to change their descriptions. Next, names and short descriptions were given and the subject was asked to "point to the symbol that best fits each description." Finally, with all the names available, the subject was asked to put "one of the names next to each symbol."

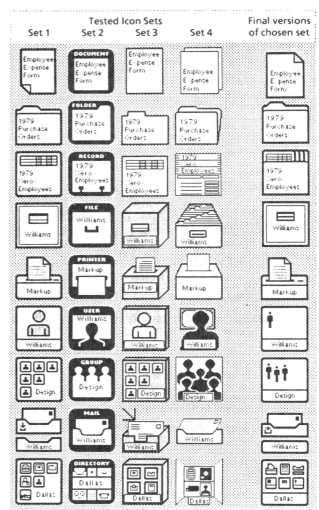

Figure 4. Four sets of icon designs were tested (only nine of the seventeen in each set are shown here). Set 1 was chosen and modified as shown at the right.

Since Set 2 had each icon named already, the naming tests showed the obvious value of having labels on icons. The three sets without labels were misinterpreted about 25% of the time on first sight. A few specific icons were revealed as most difficult: Printer (Sets 3 and 4), Record File (1, 3, 4), Directory (3, 4), Group (1, 3). For example, the Group from Set 1 was described as "cemetery plots -- to purge information" and as "keyboard -- pushbuttons".

Timed Tests. The two timed tests used a Xerox Alto computer with the icons displayed on the screen as they would be in Star. For the first timed test, we used a procedure suggested by Pew and Green [Green]. The subjects were given the name of an icon and told that it may or may not appear on the display. When an icon appeared they responded as quickly as possible by pressing a YES- or a NO-button depending on whether they thought the one presented was the one named. This test showed no significant differences among the icon sets. We concluded that the short training involved in the Naming Tests was adequate for any of the sets.

In the second timed test, we asked the subjects to point as quickly as possible to the named icon in a randomized display of all the icons. Results of this test, combined with the naming results, are shown in Figure 5. This test showed some significant differences

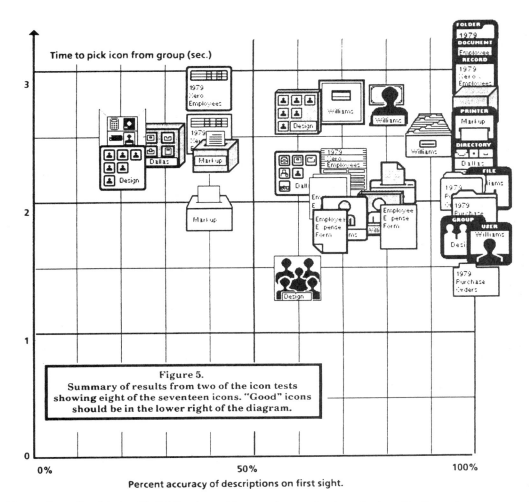

Figure 5.
Summary of results from two of the icon tests
showing eight of the seventeen icons. "Good" icons
should be in the lower right of the diagram.

Percent accuracy of descriptions on first sight.

among sets and icons. Over all, subjects with Set 2 took roughly 0.5 seconds longer than subjects with the other sets to find icons (2.5 vs 2.0), and subjects took more than a second longer to find the Document and Folder than to find the other icons (3.0 vs. 2.0).

Rating Tests. At the end of the tests, subjects were asked to say whether any of the icons in their set were "easy" or "difficult ... to pick out of the crowd". Subjects' opinions corresponded fairly well with their performance.

When shown all four sets and asked to choose a best icon for each type, subjects usually chose on the basis of which was most realistically depicted or because of the labels. Over-all preference was given to Set 2 ("most helpful") or to Set 4 ("more different shapes"). The opinions strongly reflect the tasks given in the tests; considerations beyond the tests would have been difficult for the subjects to judge.

Conclusions

The naming tests pointed out the value of labels (in Set 2), but the YES-NO response-time test indicated that, once learned, there was little difference among the sets for recognition. The pointing test, where distinguishability was important, showed that the sets with more visual variety (Sets 1, 3, and 4) were more successful. The most useful results from the icon tests were recommendations about specific icons; those with problems were redesigned.

The final choice of icon designs included a variety of concerns beyond those that could be addressed by the tests. For example, to give the user feedback that a particular icon is selected, its image is inverted (everything white becomes black and vice versa). Set 1, which has every icon predominantly white, was considered the

best at showing selection. Finally, an important consideration in choosing the icon designs was how refined the set was graphically. With some redesign, Set 1 was the final choice for Star.

5.   Graphics Tests

Unlike the two tests just described, the goal of the graphics testing was much less clearcut. We simply wanted to find out how easy the user interface was to learn, and where the difficulties were.

The Star graphics functionality, described in detail in [Lipkie], involves a structured graphics approach to making line drawings. Lines and rectangles, like other Star objects such as icons and characters, are objects that can be selected, moved, copied, and altered. According to the original user interface at the time of the tests, selection of graphics objects followed the text paradigm closely (see Figure 6): clicking the left mouse button once at an object (such as a line) selected one point on the object (an end of the line); a second click of the left button enlarged the selection so that it included the whole object. Because of this richness in selecting, few function keys were able to perform many functions. For instance, a user could lengthen, shorten, and rotate ("stretch") a line by selecting only one end and pressing the Move key. The same key moved the entire line if the whole line were selected (by clicking twice). Creation of new lines was done with the Copy key, with a special accelerator when only an end of a line was selected that aided in making connected lines. Captions could be added to the illustration by copying into the picture a "text frame," a rectangular area which was capable of containing text. Prototype examples of all graphics objects could be obtained from a system-supplied document called a "graphics transfer sheet."

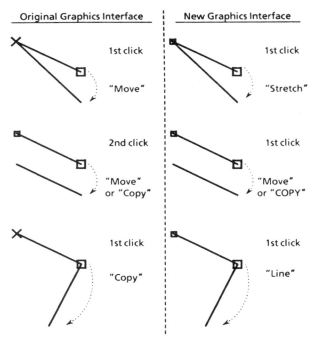

Figure 6. Graphic selections and commands. The new scheme simplified selection by eliminating multiple-clicking and adding graphics-only commands (Stretch and Line).

Methodology

This experiment used a small number (3) of inexperienced subjects, since we were looking for qualitative behavior, rather than statistical significance in these tests. The subjects had already been through a prototype of Star's on-line introduction to the general functions, so they had a background in the use of Star, and we knew roughly how they fit into the spectrum of Star users. For this test the subjects read hardcopy graphics training which consisted of explanatory material, interspersed with exercises done on the machine. At the end of the training, the subjects were asked to create some illustrations, both from scratch and by modifying existing illustrations. The test was self-paced. Time and performance were the dependent variables.

About five weeks later, two of the three subjects returned to do some exercises to show how much of the training they had retained.

The entire study (taking up to one day for the test, and one hour for the follow-up) was videotaped. Cameras showed both the user and the screen, along with the time of day.

Results

Both during the test and follow-up, evaluators recorded the times spent in each part of the training and exercises, plus critical incidents in the use of the system. These critical incidents were later catalogued into problems with the prototype implementation, with the design of the user interface, with the training, and with the design of the experiment. They were also prioritized according to how pervasive and persistent they were.

The design problems were described to the Star design group, and were reinforced by showing the designers clips of the videotape. There were two major user-interface problems: First, the multiple clicking that distinguished selection of the end of an object from selection of the whole object was far too error-prone. Selection should be made at one level only. This necessitated addition of a function key for the Stretch function, since the Move key could no

longer do double duty. Secondly, the Copy method of making a new line was too awkward. Since making a new line is central to graphics, it was felt that a function key should be dedicated to this operation.

Redesign. Both of these changes to the user interface involved adding new function keys. But at that time the number of keys on the Star keyboard was frozen, and all had assigned meanings. The suggested solution was to change the meanings of the function keys across the top of the keyboard, since (a) they were already being changed in another context, and (b) they were normally just accelerators for text functions and had no use in the graphics context. The new meanings of the keys would be displayed on the screen whenever they were in effect. There were eight keys there, but only two were needed to solve the problems found by testing. However, the inventive designers quickly found uses for most of the rest.

After this redesign, the graphics user interface was presumably easier to use. But the new design added complication to Star in general by allowing function keys to change their meaning in a way much more obtrusive than before. We did not know whether the overall effect was an improvement or not, so the test was repeated to compare the new scheme with the old.

Retest. The second graphics test fixed several problems in the experiment design, and used early versions of the customer training materials. It was run similarly to the first, with three subjects learning the old user interface and four learning the new one. The results of the repeated test of the old user interface were very similar to those of the original test. Both versions took similar amounts of time in the training portion, but at the end the users of the new interface were quicker at making illustrations and finished more of the tasks (see Figure 7). New problems were identified, of course, but they were relatively easy to fix, so the new user interface was the one adopted for the product.

	Old Interface	New Interface
Time per training module (min.)	32 ± 12	42 ± 12
Time per task (min.)	18 ± 5	9 ± 5

Numbers are given as $M \pm SD$, where M is the mean over all the users and SD is the standard deviation.

Figure 7. Quantitative Comparison of Graphics Interfaces

6.   Summary and Conclusions

The three experiments described here run the gamut from formality to informality, depending on the purposes of the tests and the costs of the experiments. In general, we were able to be most formal and careful when the topic of the experiment was well-defined and when the experiments could be kept short. As the questions to be settled became less well-defined, on the other hand, experiments took on a flavor of "fishing expeditions" to see what we came up with. Particularly when we addressed problems relating to use of a general Star function and the relationship of that function to the rest of Star, the experiments required large amounts of training. This was very costly both in setting up the tests and in execution; a consequence was that fewer subjects were used. Finally, extremely vague questions, such as whether icons in general provide a better user interface than typing commands, were not tested at all; icons were shown to be an acceptable user interface, and that result sufficed for our purposes.

Important points we found in our experimentation are the following:

(1)   Videotaping was a very important tool. First of all, the cameras allowed us to see and hear the subject without being in the same room. Secondly, it was a record of all activity, so we didn't need to take perfect notes during the

experiment. Third, the designers were more convinced by the videotapes than by our dry numbers that people were having trouble with their system.

(2) All tests were flexible enough to allow the experimenters to observe why results were coming out the way they were For example, verbal protocols were elicited in many of the tests and formal or informal interviews followed all the tests. This was important in helping us suggest design improvements.

Star was a mammoth undertaking. "The design effort took more than six years. ... The actual implementation involved from 20 to, eventually, 45 programmers over 3.5 years producing over 250,000 lines of highlevel code." [Harslem] By the time of the initial Star release, the Functional Test Group had performed over 15 distinct human-factors tests, using over 200 experimental subjects and lasting for over 400 hours (Figure 8). In addition, we applied a standard methodology to compare Star's text editing features to those of other systems [Roberts]. The group averaged 6 people (1 manager, 3 scientists, and 2 assistants) for about 3 years to perform this work.

The impact of Functional Testing on the Star product has been a pervasive set of small and large changes to the user interface. The amount of difference these changes made is, of course, impossible to assess, but the quality of Star's user interface is well known. It has won an award as the "friendliest" computer system of 1982, as judged by *Computing* magazine. Imitators, led by Sidereal, Apple's Lisa, and VisiCorp's VisiON, are starting to have a major impact on the marketplace. We can only take this as a ratification of Star's design process, a rich blend of user interface principles, functional analysis, and human interface testing.

Test Topic	No. Sub	Tot. Hrs	Impact
Selection Schemes	28	64	Lead to new design; validated new scheme
Keyboard (6 layouts)	20	40	Led to design of keyboard
Display	20	10	Specified display phosphor and refresh rate
Tab-indent	16	16	Caused redesign of Tab and Indent functionality
Labels	12	6	Caused change in property sheet and keyboard labels
Property Sheets	20	40	Identified potential interface problems and redesigns
Fonts	8	6	Led to decision on screen-paper coordination
Icons	20	30	Led to design of icons
Initial Dialogue	12	36	Led to design of training facility and materials
HELP	2	6	Validated HELP design ideas
Graphics	10	65	Led to redesign; validated new design
Graphic Idioms	4	16	Contributed to redesigns
J-Star Labels	25	25	Led to design of keyboard labels for Japanese-Star

Figure 8. Partial listing of Star-1 Functional Tests

Acknowledgments

The tests described here were carried out by the staff of the Functional Test Group consisting of W. Bewley, C. McBain, L. Miller, T. Roberts, D. Schroit, W. Verplank, and R. Walden. Able assistance was provided by M. Beard, W. Bowman, N. Cox, A. Duvall, W. Judd, J. Newlin and D. Silva. Star user-interface design was the result of a long process of innovation at Xerox PARC and elsewhere; however immediate credit should go to Eric Harslem, Charles Irby, Ralph Kimball, and David C. Smith.

References

[Anderson] Anderson, J. R. *Cognitive psychology and its implications.* W. H. Freeman and Company, San Francisco, 1980.

[Card] Card, S. K., Moran, T. P., and Newell, A. The Keystroke-Level Model for user performance time with interactive systems. *Communications of the ACM, 23,* 7, (July 1980), 396-410.

[Green] Green, P. and Pew, R. W. Evaluating pictographic symbols: an automotive application. *Human Factors, 20,* 1, (Feb. 1978), 102-114.

[Harslem] Harslem, E., Nelson, L. E. A retrospective on the development of Star. *Proc. of the 6th International Conference on Software Engineering,* Tokyo, Japan, (Sept. 1982), 377-383.

[Lipkie] Lipkie, D. E., Evans, S. R., Newlin, J. K., Weissman, R. L. Star graphics: an object-oriented implementation. *Computer Graphics, 16,* 3, (July 1982), 115-124.

[Roberts] Roberts, T. L. and Moran, T. P. The evaluation of text editors: methodology and empirical results. *Communications of the ACM, 26,* 4, (April 1983)

[Seybold] Seybold, J. W. The Xerox Star, a "professional" workstation. *The Seybold Report on Word Processing, 4,* 5, (May 1981), 1-19.

[Smith1] Smith, D. C., Irby, C., Kimball, R., Verplank, W., Harslem, E. Designing the Star user interface. *Byte, 7,* 4, (April 1982), 242-282.

[Smith2] Smith, D. C., Harslem, E., Irby, C., Kimball, R. The Star user interface: an overview. *Proceedings of the AFIPS 1982 National Computer Conference, 50,* (June 1982), 515-528.

Chapter 14

Research Frontiers and Unsolved Problems

In the preceding chapters we have discussed issues that affect the current practice of user interface design. But even if all these issues were resolved, the field of human-computer interaction would have passed only from its infancy to its adolescence.

There are a number of papers worth examining which present views of the current state of the art, and analyze where we might go in the future in order to reach maturity. One, by Nickerson (1976), is included as a reading. This paper enumerates a number of characteristics of human-human dialogues and argues that most of these could and should be part of human-computer interactions. This discussion is a good starting point for thinking about future directions.

Another interesting paper, Shneiderman (1986), proposes seven basic issues as the main challenges in user-interface research today. These are:

- Studies of ''natural'' interaction styles
- Research on appropriate input techniques
- Development of guidelines for creating meaningful patterns in screen organizations
- Studies of user behaviour under various response times
- Development of strategies for preventing user errors
- Design of systems that deal appropriately with individual differences and the needs of classes of users such as novices, women, and the elderly
- Development of ''explanatory and predictive theories, practical philosophy and generative guidelines''

Another view of future research agendas and priorities from a somewhat broader perspective is that of Shackel (1984a, 1984b). Nine principal research gaps and needs are proposed as the main priorities until about 1990:

- Theory, especially in cognitive ergonomics
- Cognitive/software interface
- User variables and models of users
- Measurement methods
- Knowledge for usability design
- Procedures and tools for designers
- Work organization and system operation
- Standardization issues
- Organizational and social issues

Shackel goes on to discuss the likelihood of such long term developments as:

- The passing of paper
- Reduction of writing
- The victory of voice
- The *wired* society

A third viewpoint is that of Gaines and Shaw (1986a,b). This two-part article includes a thoughtful survey of the development of user interface research and design, and tries to characterize what is required to reach the ''6th generation'' user interface. Their thesis is that the development of computing has been characterized by a series of breakthroughs in technology. Each breakthrough, they argue, goes through a similar cycle of developing maturity. They place user interface design at a phase which most requires the development of deep theories, and they express concern about the dangers of viewing the problem from a narrow, rather than an overall systems perspective.

One topic which is currently receiving considerable debate is methodology, and how art and science should come together in developing an improved design practice. Perhaps nowhere is this debate better aired than in a series of articles which discuss the relative merits of "hard" versus "soft" approaches to science. The first of these (Newell and Card, 1985) grew out of Newell's keynote address at the CHI '85 Conference. The main position of this paper is that "hard" science will drive out "soft" science (which is claimed to be too prevalent). Carroll and Campbell (1986) present a rebuttal to this argument, stating that the position of Newell and Card is overly restrictive in terms of what approaches and methodologies are viewed as acceptable science. This criticism was, in turn, answered by another article by Newell and Card (1986). This debate is an interesting and important one, and is valuable reading for anyone interested in the issue of future directions.

There are many views on where we are right now, how we got to this point, and where we should go next. The articles cited above express diverse views. Doing a detailed comparative critique of them is a recommended and valuable exercise for any serious student of user interface design, To supplement these papers, we present in the rest of this chapter a discussion of some areas of research which we feel will be of particular importance over the next five years. These are topics worthy of consideration by anyone embarking on a new program of research, or looking for a good thesis topic:

- *Character and gesture recognition:* interfaces that accept printed and sketched characters and symbols, and freehand gestures.

- *Multi-modal interfaces:* interfaces that involve video, speech, and sound.

- *Extensible interfaces:* interfaces that accept both demonstrative and symbolic input, and that may be extended by their users.

- *Intelligent interfaces:* Work in artificial intelligence can be applied to allow us to construct interfaces that are, for example, more flexible, more tolerant of user error, more helpful, and able to tutor their users when it is appropriate.

- *Interfaces for the disabled:* for the blind, the deaf, the aged, or those with any other sensory/motor disability.

- *Cooperative work:* systems that involve multiple users, often in different physical locations, working jointly on a single, or related problems.

Character and Gesture Recognition

The graphics tablet and stylus have been in use since at least 1964 (Davis and Ellis, 1964). Interactive graphics displays have been in use since at least 1963 (Sutherland, 1963). Despite the existence of these tools, communication with stylus and display bears little resemblance to the way we communicate with pencil and paper, chalk and blackboard. We all write letters, understand basic proofreading symbols, and can make sense of a teacher's diagrammatic annotations on the blackboard. But with very few exceptions, today's user interfaces make little or no use of these skills.

This is all the more interesting, since many early interactive systems utilized character and gesture recognition techniques. The earliest example that we could find is Dimond (1957). Sutherland (1963) used light-pen gestures extensively in SKETCHPAD. As early as 1969, Coleman had developed a system for revising text documents using proofreading symbols. Much of this early work is reviewed by Munson (1968). A more recent comprehensive review and bibliography can be found in Suen, Berthold and Mori (1980).

While these techniques are neglected, they are technically and economically feasible today, and deserve a great deal more attention than they are getting.

One of the problems with character and gesture recognition is that we tend to lump together all of the different approaches. In fact, there is probably as much stylistic difference between a system that recognizes block-printed characters and one that recognizes proofreading symbols as there is between a menu system and one that uses direct manipulation. Consequently, we will give a brief overview of the different classes of recognition systems, with pointers to the appropriate literature.

In looking at the problem of character recognition, we are confronted with the range of *styles* of writing and the range of *penmanship* in executing any of these styles. Figure 1 illustrates five different writing styles that might be used as input to a recognition system. The examples are presented in order of increasing difficulty. Upper-case block characters constrained to being printed in specified boxes are the easiest to recognize. Mixed cursive and discrete script is the hardest. Ehrich and Koehler (1975) and Tappert (1982, 1984) are all good examples of work in the difficult area of cursive script recognition. An excellent review of the field can be found in Ehrich (1978).

Even within a particular style of writing, penmanship varies a great deal. This type of variation, illustrated in Figure 2, adds greatly to the technical problems in building a robust recognition system. Since both involve pattern recognition, it should come as no surprise that character recognition has much in common with speech

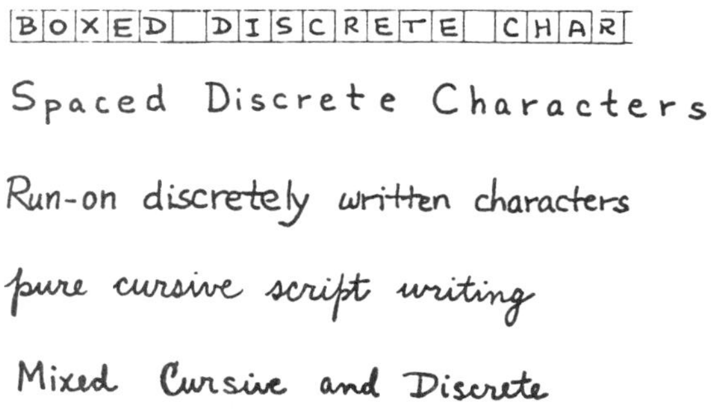

BOXED DISCRETE CHAR

Spaced Discrete Characters

Run-on discretely written characters

pure cursive script writing

Mixed Cursive and Discrete

Figure 1: Handwriting Types.
Different types of handwriting present different levels of difficulty in automatic recognition. The examples are presented in order of increasing difficulty. (From Tappert, 1984).

recognition (see Chapter 9: The Audio Channel). In particular, performance of many systems improves if the recognizer is trained for the specific user's script. A good introduction to a trainable character recognizer can be found in Appendix VIII of the first edition of Newman and Sproull's *Principles of Interactive Computer Graphics* (1973).

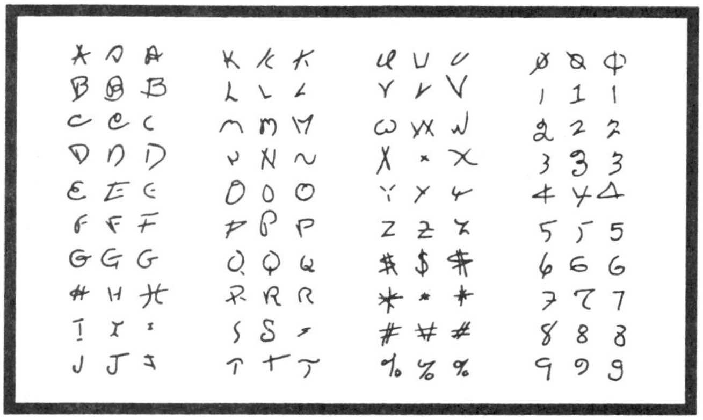

Figure 2: Variation of Printed Characters.
Even when restricted to discrete character recognition, variability in penmanship makes the problem very difficult. The figure shows the range of characters that, nevertheless, can be recognized by a commercial system (from Ward & Blesser, 1985).

Essentially, if one is only trying to understand *what* characters are input, character and handwriting recognition merely provide an alternative to the QWERTY keyboard. Without wanting to down-play the importance of this (especially, for example, as a means of recognizing Asian languages that do not lend themselves to the Western keyboard), it is important to recognize that the technique really comes into its own when other features are also extracted. Ward and Blesser (1985), for example, describe a commercially available system, which

can be seen in the Pencept (1985) video, that can recognize discrete characters as well as their *size* and *position*. This can be of value, for example, in annotating drawings, or where size and position of the characters has significance. In many cases there will be a bigger payoff and smaller investment with a system that recognizes discrete characters with position and size, than from a system that "just" recognizes cursive script.

One of the shortcomings of using character recognition to input ASCII text is one of human speed. A relatively poor typist can enter text faster than can be done using even cursive script. In such cases, reasons other than speed must justify the use of character recognition techniques.

There is another perspective on this issue of speed, however. The characters being recognized need not come from our standard alphanumeric symbol set. If we can increase the power, or *semantic loading*, of each gesture, we can often reap dramatic improvements in bandwidth. (The analogy here would be with function keys: Pushing a function key takes the same basic motor action as, but generally carries a lot more power than, depressing an alphanumeric key on the keyboard.) Figure 3 illustrates this. It shows a symbol set used in a system to transcribe music (Buxton, Sniderman, Reeves, Patel and Baecker, 1979). The symbols represent a powerful form of shorthand. Each basic symbol represents a particular note duration. These symbols are "written" on the musical staff using a tablet and a stylus. Based on where the symbols are placed, the system automatically determines the desired pitch and point of time when the specified note should start.

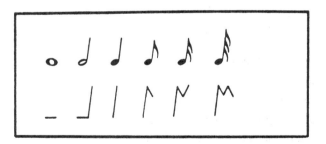

Figure 3: Shorthand Symbols for Music.
Characters need not come from standard alphabets. Application-specific shorthand symbols can be used effectively. One such set used for music transcription is shown. The symbols indicate note duration. Pitch and entry time information was determined by where the symbols were drawn. (From Buxton, Sniderman, Reeves, Patel and Baecker, 1979).

We need not invent our own shorthand symbols, however. One approach which shows promise in certain contexts is to use common Pitman shorthand. There is a significant base of expertise in the notation, and experts are able to transcribe text at rates of over 120 words per minute. This area has been investigated by Leedham, Downton, Brooks and Newell (1984) and Leedham and Downton (1986). There are a number of problems remaining, however, before a practical system can be developed. One problem is that what is captured by shorthand is a type of phonemic representation of the text which must itself be translated into standard text. This is a difficult problem. Dye, Newell and Arnott (1984) and Downton and Brooks (1984) are two sources discussing some of the issues involved.

In recent years, there has been a growing interest in *gesture* recognition systems. These are systems whose capabilities go well beyond the recognition of simple alphanumeric or shorthand symbols. One example would be a system that could recognize the annotations that a proofreader might make on a document. Coleman (1969) is an early example of such a system. Another would be a system that could recognize the "chalk-talk" dialogues that a coach might employ on a blackboard in explaining plays to a football team.

Rhyne and Wolf (1986) present a recent example in which this type of annotation is used to interact with a spreadsheet. Buxton, Fiume, Hill, Lee, and Woo (1983) present another example in the form of a prototype sketch editor. Wolf (1986) and Wolf and Morrel-Samuels (1987) present a study investigating people's ability to use such annotations. See Konneker (1984) for yet another.

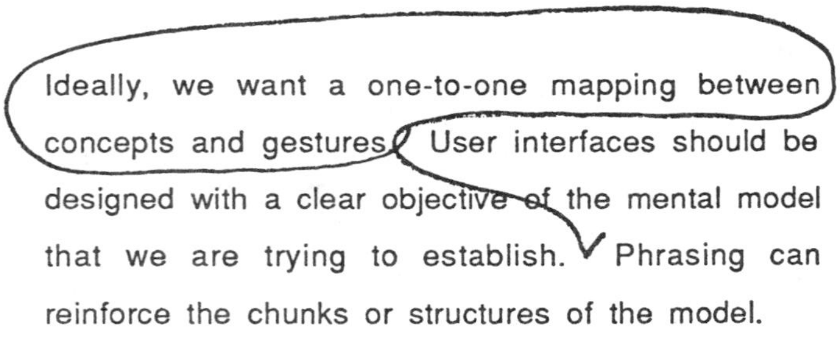

Ideally, we want a one-to-one mapping between concepts and gestures. User interfaces should be designed with a clear objective of the mental model that we are trying to establish. Phrasing can reinforce the chunks or structures of the model.

Figure 4: Proofreader's Gesture.
Although it is a single continuous line, the proofreader's move gesture gives three pieces of information: the command move, what is to be moved, and where it is to be moved. Compared to conventional text editing, the gesture is generally known and it is virtually impossible to make a mistake in syntax in giving the command. (From Buxton, 1986).

Gestural languages go beyond character recognition in that they include messages such as motion, scope and location. Consider the example of the proof-reader's *move* symbol, shown in Figure 4. All three linguistic components of the transaction are articulated in a single continuous gesture: the verb (move), the direct object (the text to be moved), and indirect object (where the text is to be moved to). Because of the continuous nature of the gesture, it is virtually impossible for the

operator to make an error in syntax. The entire transaction is articulated in a single gesture, or *chunk* (Buxton, 1986).

If character and gesture recognition systems are going to be employed, there are some important considerations that must be kept in mind. First, the kinesthetics of this class of transaction virtually require that a stylus be used, rather than a puck or a mouse. There is another technological bottleneck, as well. Despite the (relatively) long existence of graphics tablets, most are not up to the demands of precision character recognition. One of the most valuable pieces of advice in this section is: If you want to investigate this style of interaction, chose your tablet and stylus carefully. Linearity, resolution, and minimal tip-switch travel are critical parameters to consider. Ward and Phillips (1987) presents a good discussion of some of these hardware issues.

From the examples discussed, it should be clear that character and gesture recognition systems cover a broad range of styles. There are a number of situations in which these types of techniques can and should be used to good effect. Many of these techniques were explored before the required resources were generally available or cost effective. But viable commercial systems are now beginning to become available. As a result, it is hoped that this approach to interaction will begin to reach its full potential.

Multimedia, Multimodal Interfaces

The user interface of today makes very little use of the breadth of human motor-sensory potential or of the range of technologies available. We stare at tiny screens and poke at cramped keyboards. In the systems that are hyped as being the most "user friendly," we drag tiny mice a few inches one way or the other on our desks. But we cannot speak. The systems are silent. We cannot gesture. Our expressions, our eye movements, and our body language are ignored. The systems have limited data and even more limited intelligence. Compared to what both we and the machines are capable of, our dialogues are impoverished.

Negroponte (1970), Baecker (1980a,b), Buxton et al. (1983), and Bolt (1984,1985), among others, have suggested this need not be so. There are numerous techniques which could be incorporated into interfaces, to the enrichment of our dialogues and our communicative possibilities. These include:

●Large display surfaces, such as provided by large format screens and video projection, that better permit us to make use of spatial relationships in what we are viewing and which increase the amount of information that falls within the range of our gaze.

- Voice input and output, and the use of non-speech audio output (Schmandt, 1985; Chapter 9: The Audio Channel, of this book).

- Large capacity video storage with random access available from the emerging compact video disk (CD-V) technologies.

- Large scale digital data storage with random access available on the emerging CD-ROM technologies (Lambert & Ropiequet, 1986).

- Improved browsing and navigational tools, for example using spatial relationships, as with the Spatial Database Management System (Herot, 1984) or the Rooms System (Card and Henderson, 1987).

- The use of the visual channel for *input*: Here a video camera captures body movement which is used as input by exploiting pattern recognition and machine vision techniques (Kruger, 1983, 1985).

- The ability to communicate through eye movements that are tracked and interpreted by the computer (Bolt, 1981, 1984).

- The ability to use these and other techniques *in combination*, to support rich, congenial, and appropriate multi-dimensional and multi-modal dialogues.

These are no longer "blue sky" fantasies. In fact, prototype systems demonstrating virtually all of these approaches have been built, many by the Architecture Machine Group at MIT. Bolt (1984) describes much of this work. One of the most striking things about the systems he describes is that they were virtually all built using technology that was available "over the counter" several years ago. This work was ahead of its time, and deserves far more serious attention than it has received. Work from the Architecture Machine Group, and others, that deserves particular attention includes:

- *Put That There* (Bolt, 1980; a video MIT, 1984b): a system that effectively combined voice recognition, a limited English language understanding capability, manual gesturing (especially pointing), voice synthesis, and large format graphics presentation.

- *Gaze Oriented Dynamic Windows* (Bolt, 1981): a system that detected and adapted its behaviour to the locus of the user's gaze.

- *The Movie Map* (Lippman, 1980): a system which attempted to aid one in navigating through and understanding new spaces by giving contextually adaptive information.

- *The Movie Manual* (Baker and Gano, 1982; a video MIT, 1984a): a form of dynamic book that made effective use of concepts from hypertext, computer graphics, animation, and video disk technologies in supporting education and training functions.

- *VIDEOPLACE* (Kruger, 1983, 1985): one of the first systems to demonstrate that computers can "see" and that this ability to process video images in real-time can be used as the basis for very effective human-computer interaction.

- *Spatial Database Management System (SDMS)* (a video Herot et al., 1981; Herot, 1984) *and SDBMS* (McCann, Taylor, and Tuori, in press): systems that make powerful use of spatial metaphors as a means of organizing complex data.

- *Phone Slave* (Schmandt and Aarons, 1984a,b): a system which shows how a "semi-intelligent" voice messaging system can be built by combining two technologies: the telephone and the computer.

Besides the book by Bolt (1984), which provides additional discussion of the "Put That There" and "Gaze Oriented Dynamic Windows" work, the interested reader is strongly recommended to read *Artificial Reality,* which describes Krueger's terrific work (Krueger, 1983).

One final point need be made about this body of work. As pointed out by Lippman in a panel at SIGGRAPH '87, these systems succeed not because a "friendly front end" has been grafted onto a bad system, but because they embody creative and imaginative design of the *entire system.*

Extensible Interfaces

One problem that nearly all systems suffer from is that their interfaces are not modifiable or extensible in the hands of knowledgeable users. This limitation means that even interfaces that are easy to learn and use can eventually become cumbersome. They don't grow with the individual user nor can they be easily adapted to the individual differences of different users.

Consider, for example, a user of Macwrite on the Macintosh computer. To begin or conclude a typical text editing session, a highly repetitive series of mouse movements and button pushes must be executed. This sequence of actions may feel increasingly slow, sluggish and annoying as the user becomes more skilled. The solution would be to allow sequences to be encapsulated as "macros" invokable by a single action on the keyboard or using the mouse. Where appropriate, the macro would have a single "argument" or "parameter" such as a filename or file icon.

Good examples of the use of such techniques are in Micrcosoft Excel (Microsoft, 1985) and Lotus 1-2-3 (LeBland and Cobb, 1985), where the macro capability is widely used and is one of the prime factors accounting for the products' success.

An established technique for computer scientists in programming environments, the use of macros is not common in most applications. This may largely be due to the contrast in interaction style used in direct manipulation based applications, compared to the command-line style interfaces in which macro facilities are generally found. However, just as traditional macros generally record a series of keystrokes, so can systems record a series of mouse gestures. The notion of macros and extensibility must be separated from the stylistic biases of past implementation. Further research needs to be undertaken to develop techniques, such as graphical programming, and programming by example (Myers, 1986), that will provide functionality and extensibility in a manner which is consistent with, and a direct extension of, the user's existing mental model. diSessa (1986; see also a video, Abelson, 1985) is a good example demonstrating that this is attainable within the context of today's direct manipulation systems. Other videos demonstrating programming by example are Atari (1984) and Xerox (1985).

Intelligent Interfaces

If we place ourselves in the user's shoes for a moment, then we can be excused for asking what seems a perfectly reasonable question: "If these machines are so smart, and artificial intelligence is all it is cracked up to be in the press, then why must I continue to adapt to this system rather than have it adapt to me?" Indeed!

Todays user interfaces are not even half-witted. They are downright intolerant, insensitive and stupid. Yet they cannot be allowed to remain so. Negroponte, quoted in Chapter 1: A Historical and Intellectual Perspective, was one of the earliest to suggest that there was an alternative, and to argue for *individual* or *idiosyncratic* interfaces that respond differently and appropriately to different users. Rissland (1984), in a paper included here as a reading, defines what she feels is needed in terms of *services*, *style*, and *understandability*.

Intelligent User Interfaces (IUIs) should provide certain *services* to its users, such as:

- carry out menial tasks (e.g. set terminal characteristics);
- automate routine tasks (e.g. doing back up of active files, often);
- provide assistance with more complex tasks (e.g. file transfer protocols);
- provide easy access to tools (e.g. DBMS packages);
- provide status information (e.g. on the progress of tasks like file formatting);
- provide on-line assistance and documentation (e.g. HELP and manuals).

- allow multi-tasking.

IUIs should provide these services in a *style* that:

- is helpful and forgiving (e.g. "infinite" UNDO/REDO capabilities);
- encourages experimentation (e.g. in a safe "mock-up" or hypothetical session);
- minimizes errors (e.g. failsafe questioning on undoable actions like DEL);
- allows user to manipulate objects and tasks directly (e.g. halt the printing of a long file if there is a mistake on the first page);
- allows him to see directly the results of his actions (e.g. "WYSIWYG");
- doesn't get in the way;
- is under the user's control;
- "idiosyncratic," that is, adapts to the user's style, preferably without his having to give explicit directions, when possible;
- unambiguous and consistent (e.g. or rather counterexample, the use of control-C, Y, and Z in many systems);
- has a repertoire of good presentation services (e.g. window systems).

IUIs should be *understandable*, that is:

- learnable through conceptual models and not just by rote;
- aid the transition from novice to expert (e.g. by selectively disclosing more of its internal workings, enabling control to become direct);
- allow the user to "macro-ize" and customize tasks (e.g. user-defined composite functions).

One of the keys to providing intelligence in interfaces is *user modelling*. This concept involves the system's construction of a representation of the user's knowledge, skills, and/or behaviour in such a way that it can adapt its behaviour to that particular user's individual characteristics. Rich (1983) describes three dimensions of user models:

- one model of a single, canonical user vs a collection of models of individual users.
- models specified explicitly either by the system designer or by the users themselves vs models inferred by the system on the basis of the user's behaviour.
- models of fairly long-term user characteristics such as areas of interest or expertise vs models of relatively short-term user characteristics such as the problem the user is currently trying to solve.

She then develops a technique for building effective user models using *stereotypes*, collections of user traits that typically occur together, a technique further extended and applied by Chin (1986). Other interesting developments in user modelling are reported by Zissos and Witten (1985) and Wahlster and Kobsa (1986).

The attempt to embed intelligence in interfaces is in its infancy, and is most often applied in one of two specific domains. The first is intelligent help systems (Rissland, 1984; Croft, 1984; Mason, 1986; Chin, 1986; Quinn and Russell, 1986). The second, intelligent tutoring systems, to be discussed below. A third interesting example is in a new class of music system, where the computer's accompaniment of a musician is based on what the instrumentalist is playing live (Buxton, 1986).

The goal of intelligent automated tutor has been viewed by many as a remote possibility, at best only achievable in the research laboratory. It turns out, however, that for restricted problem domains an intelligent tutor does not require that all problems in artificial intelligence be solved before it can be realized. Perhaps the most compelling example is Carnegie-Mellon's successful construction of an automated LISP tutor that teaches introductory programming automatically and successfully (Anderson and Skwarecki, 1986). Sleeman and Brown (1982) is an edited collection of papers introducing the state-of-the-art in intelligent tutoring systems. A more recent survey of the field is Dede (1986). An even more recent, more critical survey is Carroll and McKendree (1987). Wenger (1987) is a new comprehensive reference text on the subject.

There is no universal agreement on the desirability or short term feasibility of building significant intelligence into interfaces (Nickerson, 1976, included as a reading). Robertson (1985) stresses the need for a cognitive psychology of human information processing strategies and style. McKendree and Carroll (1986; see also Carroll and McKendree, 1987) suggest that we carry out in-depth studies of human advisory protocols before we attempt to design advisory systems; in doing so, they argue that advisers carry out a variety of significantly different tasks, including *informing*, *defining*, *indexing*, and *structuring*. Greenberg and Witten (1985; see also Witten, Greenberg, and Cleary, 1983, and Trevellyan and Browne, 1987) note that there are disadvantages as well as advantages to adaptive and changing interfaces — they may seem to be inconsistent and may cause the user additional effort in adapting to the changing system. These writers then proceed to assemble empirical evidence that in at least one context, that of tree-structured menu access to a telephone directory, an adaptive interface leads to better user performance *and* strong user preference.

Interfaces for the Handicapped

Ideally, the introduction of computer-based technologies should have a major positive impact on employment opportunities and quality of life for the physically dis-

abled. In many ways, this is what is happening. Optical character recognition technologies, coupled with speech synthesis, provide reading machines for the visually impaired. Voice input technologies permit those with motor disabilities to interact with their environment in a way never before possible. And portable terminals with modems enable those with restricted hearing to make use of the telephone.

While we would expect things to continue to improve, some trends in computer and user interface design are actually eliminating gains previously made. One example is due to the increasing popularity of *direct manipulation* systems. How, for example, does one provide a blind person access to any of the Macintosh applications? Similarly, how does someone with severe motor-control problems interact with a system that relies so heavily on accurate pointing, dragging and selection?

Access to computer systems for those with physical disabilities is typically dependent upon the use of specialized transducers that compensate for the individual's specific disability. However, we must repeat a statement made in Chapter 8: The Haptic Channel. Interfacing non-standard I/O transducers to today's computers is just too hard ("standard" interfaces, such as RS-232 notwithstanding). Those with physical disabilities have enough problems without being saddled with the need to go through costly custom conversions before they can use a computer. A major challenge of the industry is to get to the point where *transparent access* is the norm for the bulk of disabled users. That is, we must reach the state where software and hardware can be operated using specialized transducers without any special modifications or customization of computer hardware or software. This means that future computers must permit the connection of arbitrary transducers using standardized ports. Similarly, user interface management system technologies (as discussed in Chapter 12: Programming Techniques and Tools) must be designed to easily support user interfaces being adapted to match the capabilities of users with specific disabilities.

These issues, and others, are discussed in more detail in the reading by Bowe (1987). See also Buxton (1986). Both are directed at encouraging designers to maintain consideration of the needs of the physically disabled throughout the design process.

Interfaces for Cooperative Work

In nearly all of our discussion of human-computer interaction, our frame of reference has been the dialogue between a single user and a system. Electronic mail, group dynamics, and conferencing have played some part in the discussion. However, the focus has not generally been on how computers can be used to enhance our ability to work in groups, or to foster cooperative or shared decision making. This, however, is an area of growing importance.

The potential of the computer to enhance human communication was perhaps first realized in the 1960's by Engelbart (1968). This typically occurs in one of five ways — through *computer mail*, *electronic bulletin boards*, *computer conferencing*, *cooperative authoring*, and *cooperative work and problem solving*. Computer mail is the sending of messages, via a computer system or network, from one user to another user or group of users. Electronic bulletin boards are repositories for messages typically organized by subject matter and intended to be read by anyone interested in that subject. Computer conferencing systems provide a vehicle for the recording and dissemination of messages on a particular topic and commentaries on these messages organized chronologically as the conference dialogue unfolds. Cooperative authoring systems support two or more individuals jointly authoring a document. Systems for cooperative work allow people to act together in carrying out activities, or in solving a problem through the medium of a computer system, whether they be in the same room or at remote locations. Thus, cooperative work systems subsume all the other categories as special cases.

The cooperative work perspective opens up a host of new issues and problems. An early effort of this kind was the work of Engelbart (1968) in developing a system for computer messaging, conferencing, and cooperative authoring. Other more recent efforts are those of Turoff (1972), Turoff and Hiltz (1982), Sarin and Greif (1985) and Stefik et al. (1987). Much of the current research on cooperative work is described in the proceedings of an 1986 conference on the topic (Grief, 1986).

What is required is a new theoretical framework in which to characterize and describe such systems. One approach is that of Malone (1985; see also Malone, in press). He defines an ''organizational interface'' as ''the parts of a computer system that connect human users to each other and to the capabilities provided by computers.'' He suggests (Malone, 1985) that we need to look at organizational interfaces from at least four different perspectives — *information processing*, *motivational*, *economic*, and *political*, and that these perspectives will assist in the development of useful design-oriented theories.

We also need to enhance our understanding of human behaviour, as individuals transact with computer messaging and work systems. Hiltz and Turoff (1981) have documented the growth in abilities and expectations as users gained more experience with a computerized conferencing system. Turoff and Hiltz (1982) have shown that, in at least one controlled case, computerized conferences effectively support group communication and decision making — the quality of the decision reached was just as good as that reached by a face-to-face meeting, but it was harder to reach a consensus via the computerized conference. In another experiment, they showed the value of data display and analysis of options being considered by the group in assisting consensus formation. For further results from their almost two decades of work, the reader is referred to Hiltz and Turoff (1978), Kerr and Hiltz (1982), and Hiltz (1984).

Kiesler, Siegel, and McGuire (1984) have also studied how computerization affects group efforts to reach consensus. They discovered that communication efficiency was reduced over face-to-face participation, that group members participated more equally using computer communication, that computer-mediated groups showed significantly higher choice shift, and that people in computer-mediated groups were more uninhibited than when they were in face-to-face groups. In a more detailed follow-on field study in a Fortune 500 company, Sproull and Kiesler (1985) found evidence that ''electronic mail reduced social context cues, provided information that was relatively uninhibited, self-absorbed, and undifferentiated by status, and provided new information.''

Conclusions

While computers have the potential to bring dramatic positive benefit to our lives, there is nothing inherent in the technology that will cause them to do so. In fact, the opposite is an equally plausible scenario. The development of these systems cannot be left to chance. What computers are, and how they are used and will be used by individuals and societies, can and should be subject to careful, thoughtful, and imaginative design. This volume has addressed many of the design issues that we feel are important, but, for every topic covered, there were several left out. Making the technology realize its potential requires a major initiative and represents a significant challenge. Hopefully the topics and studies covered in this volume will help lay the foundation for meeting that challenge.

Readings

Nickerson, R.S. (1977). On Conversational Interaction with Computers. *User-Oriented Design of Interactive Graphics Systems*, New York: Association for Computing Machinery, 101-113.

Bolt, Richard A. (1985). Conversing with Computers. *Technology Review* 88(2), February/March 1985, 35-43.

Rissland, Edwina (1984). Ingredients of Intelligent User Interfaces. *International Journal of Man-Machine Studies* 21, 377-388.

Bowe, F. (1987). Making Computers Accessible to Disabled People. *Technology Review* 90(1), January 1987, 52-59,72.

References — General

Carroll, J.M. & Campbell, R.L. (1986). Softening Up Hard Science: Reply to Newell and Card. *Human-Computer Interaction* 2(3), 227-249.

Gaines, B.R. & Shaw, M.L.G. (1986a). From Timesharing to the Sixth Generation: The Development of Human-Computer Interaction. Part I. *International Journal of Man-Machine Studies* 24, 1-27.

Gaines, B.R. & Shaw, M.L.G. (1986a). Foundations of Dialogue Engineering: The Development of Human-Computer Interaction. Part II. *International Journal of Man-Machine Studies* 24, 101-123.

Newell, A. & Card, S. (1985). The Prospects for Psychological Science in Human-Computer Interaction. *Human-Computer Interaction* 1, 209-242.

Newell, A. & Card S. (1985). Straightening Out Softening Up: Response to Carroll and Campbell. *Human-Computer Interaction* 2(3), 251-267.

Shackel, B. (1984a). Designing for People in the Age of Information. *Proceedings of Interact '84*, Vol. 1, 6-15.

Shackel, B. (1984b). Information Technology — a Challenge to Ergonomics and Design. *Behaviour and Information Technology* 3(4), 263-275.

Shneiderman, Ben (1986). Seven Plus or Minus Two Central Issues in Human-Computer Interaction. *Proceedings of CHI '86*, 343-349.

Character and Gesture Recognition

Anderson, R.H. (1968). *Syntax-directed recognition of handprinted two-dimensional mathematics*, Ph.D. Thesis, Harvard University.

Blackwell, F.W. & Anderson, R.H. (1970). An On-Line Symbolic Mathematics System Using Hand-Printed Two-Dimensional Notation. RAND Memo RM-6018-PR.

Brown, R. (1964). On-Line Computer Recognition of Hand-Printed Characters. *IEEE Transactions on Computers* EC-13 (12), 750-752.

Buxton, W. (1986). Chunking and Phrasing and the Design of Human-Computer Dialogues. H.-J. Kugler (Ed.), *Proceedings of the IFIP 10th World Computer Congress*, Dublin, Ireland, September 1-5, 1986, Amsterdam: Elsevier Science Publishers B.V. (North-Holland), 475-480. © IFIP, 1986.

Buxton, W., Fiume, E., Hill, R., Lee, A. & Woo, C. (1983). Continuous Hand-Gesture Driven Input. *Proceedings of Graphics Interface '83*, 191-195.

Buxton, W., Sniderman, R., Reeves, W., Patel, S. & Baecker, R. (1979). The Evolution of the SSSP Score Editing Tools. *Computer Music Journal* 3(4), 14-25.

Coleman, M.L. (1969). Text Editing on a Graphic Display Device Using Hand-Drawn Proofreader's Symbols. In M. Faiman & J. Nievergelt (Eds.) *Pertinent Concepts in Computer Graphics,*

Proceedings of the 2nd University of Illinois Conference on Computer Graphics, Urbana: University of Illinois Press, 282-290.

Davis, M.R. & Ellis, T.O. (1964). The Rand Tablet: A Man-Machine Graphical Communication Device. *FJCC*, p.325.

Dimond, T.L. (1957). Devices for Reading Handwritten Characters. *Proceedings of the Eastern Computer Conference*, 232-237.

Doster, W. & Oed, R. (1984). Word Processing with On-Line Script Recognition. *IEEE Micro* 4(5), 36-43.

Downton, A.C. & Brooks, C.P. (1984). Automated Machine Shorthand Transcription in Commercial Applications. *Human-Computer Interaction — Interact '84,*, Amsterdam: North-Holland, 151-156.

Duda, R.O. & Hart, P.E. (1968). Experiments in the Recognition of Hand-Printed Text, II: Context Analysis. *FJCC,* p.1139.

Dye, R., Newell, A.F. & Arnott, J.L. (1984). An Adaptive Editor for Shorthand Transcription Systems. *Human-Computer Interaction — Interact '84,*, Amsterdam: North-Holland, 157-161.

Ehrich, Roger W. (1978). Handwriting Recognition. In J. Belzer, A.G. Holzman, and A. Kent (Eds.), *Encyclopedia of Science and Technology* 9, New York: Marcel Dekker, Inc., 180-198.

Ehrich, R.W. & Koehler, K.J. (1975). Experiments in the Contextual Recognition of Cursive Script. *IEEE Transactions on Computers* 24(2), 182-194.

Groner, G.F. (1966). Real-Time Recognition of Hand Printed Text. *FJCC,* 591.

Hornbuckle, G.D. (1967). The Computer Graphics User/Machine Interface. *IEEE Transactions on Human Factors in Electronics* 8(1), 17-20.

Irani, K. B., Wallace, V. L., and Jackson, J. H. (1970). Conversational Design of Stochastic Service Systems from a Graphical Terminal. In Parslow and Green, (Eds.) *Proceedings of the 1970 International Symposium on Computer Graphics,* 91-101.

Konneker, L.K. (1984). A Graphical Interaction Technique Which Uses Gestures. *Proceedings of the IEEE First International Conference on Office Automation,* New Orleans, 51-55.

Leedham, C.G. & Downton, A.C. (1986). On-Line Recognition of Pitman's Handwritten Shorthand: An Evaluation of Potential. *International Journal of Man-Machine Studies* 24(4), 375-393.

Leedham, C.G., Downton, A.C., Brooks, C.P. & Newell, A.F. (1984). On-Line Acquisition of Pitman's Handwritten Shorthand as a Means of Rapid Data Entry. *Human-Computer Interaction — Interact '84,*, Amsterdam: North-Holland, 145-150.

Munson, J.H. (1968). Experiments in the Recognition of Hand-Printed Text, I: Character Recognition. *FJCC,* 1125.

Newman, W. & Sproull, R. (1973). *Principles of Interactive Computer Graphics,* First Edition, New York: McGraw-Hill Co.

Pencept Inc. (1985). Software Control at the Stroke of a Pen. *SIGGRAPH Video Review* 18, New York: ACM.

Rhyne, J.R. & Wolf, C.G. (1986). Gestural Interfaces for Information Processing Applications. Computer Science Technical Report RC 12179, Yorktown Heights, N.Y.: IBM T.J. Watson Research Center.

Suen, C., Berthold, M, & Mori, S. (1980). Automatic Recognition of Hand-Printed Characters — The State of the Art. *Proceedings of IEEE* 68(4), 469-487.

Sutherland, I. (1963). SKETCHPAD: A Man-Machine Graphical Communication System. *SJCC*, p.329.

Tappert, C.C. (1982). Cursive Text Recognition by Elastic Matching. *IBM Journal of Research and Development* 26(6), 765-771.

Tappert, C.C. (1984). Adaptive On-Line Handwriting Recognition. *IEEE 7th Int. Conference on Pattern Recognition*, 1004-1007.

Teitelman, W. (1964). Real Time Recognition of Hand-Drawn Characters. *FJCC*, 559.

Ward, J.R. (Ed.)(1987). Issues Limiting the Acceptance of User Interfaces Using Gesture Input and Handwriting Character Recognition. Panel summary, *Proceedings of CHI+GI '87*, 155-158.

Ward, J.R. & Blesser, B. (1985). Interactive Recognition of Hand-printed Characters for Computer Input. *IEEE Computer Graphics and Applications* 5(9), 24-37.

Ward, J.R. & Phillips, M.J. (1987). Digitizer Technology: Performance Characteristics and the Effects on the User Interface. *IEEE Computer Graphics and Applications* 7(4), 31-44.

Wolf, C.G. (1986). Can People Use Gesture Commands? *ACM SIGCHI Bulletin* 18(2), 73-74.

Wolf, C.G. & Morrel-Samuels, P. (1987). The Use of Hand-Drawn Gestures for Text-Editing. *IBM Technical Report* RC 12523 (#56294) 2/19/87. To appear in *IJMMS* (in press).

Multimedia Interfaces

Backer, D.S. & Gano, S. (1982). Dynamically Alterable Videodisc Displays. *Proceedings of Graphics Interface '82*, Canadian Man-Computer Communications Society, Toronto, 365-371.

Baecker, R.M. (1980a). Towards a Characterization of Graphical Interaction. In Guedj, ten Hagen, Hopgood, Tucker & Duce (Eds.), *Methodology of Interaction*, Amsterdam: North Holland, 127-147.

Baecker, R.M. (1980b). Human-Computer Interactive Systems: A State-of-the-Art Review. In Kolers, Wrolstad & Bouma (Eds.), *Processing of Visible Language* 2, New York: Plenum Press, 423-443.

Bolt, Richard A. (1980). "Put-That-There": Voice and Gesture at the Graphics Interface. *Computer Graphics* 14(3), 262-270.

Bolt, Richard A. (1981). Gaze-Orchestrated Dynamic Windows. *Computer Graphics* 15(3), 109-119.

Bolt, Richard A. (1984). *The Human Interface: Where People and Computers Meet*, Boston: Lifetime Learning Publications.

Card, S. & Henderson, A. (1987). A Multiple, Virtual-Workspace Interface to Support User Task Switching. *Proceedings of CHI+GI '87*, 53-59.

Herot, C. et al. (1981). Spatial Data Management System. *SIGGRAPH Video Review* 2, New York: ACM.

Herot, Christopher F. (1984). Graphical User Interfaces. In *Human Factors and Interactive Computer Systems*, Vassilion (Ed.), Norwood, NJ: Ablex Publishers, 83-103.

Kruger, Myron W. (1983). *Artificial Reality*, Reading, MA: Addison-Wesley.

Kruger, Myron W., Gionfriddo, Thomas., & Hinrichsen, Katrin (1985). VIDEOPLACE — An Artificial Reality. *Proceedings of CHI '85*, 35-40.

Lambert, S. & Ropiequet, S. (Eds.) (1986). *CDROM: The New Papyrus*, Redmond, WA.: Microsoft Press.

Lippman, Andrew (1980). Movie-Maps: An Application of the Optical Videodisc to Computer Graphics. *Computer Graphics* 14(3), 32-42.

MIT (1984a). The Movie Manual Project. *SIGGRAPH Video Review* 13, New York: ACM.

MIT (1984b). Put That There. *SIGGRAPH Video Review* 13, New York: ACM.

McCann, C.A., Taylor, M.M. & Tuori, M.I. (in press). ISIS: The Interactive Spatial Information System. *International Journal of Man-Machine Studies*, 40 pages.

Negroponte, Nicholas (1970). *The Architecture Machine: Towards a More Humane Environment*, Cambridge, Mass.: The MIT Press.

Schmandt, C. & Aarons, B. (1984a). A Conventional Telephone Messaging System. In *International Conference on Consumer Electronics Digest of Technical Papers*, Rosemont IL.

Schmandt, C. & Aarons. B. (1984b). Phone Slave: A Graphical Telecommunications Interface. In *Society for Information Display 1984 International Symposium Digest of Technical Papers*, San Francisco, CA.

Schmandt, Christopher (1985). Voice Communication with Computers. In H.R. Hartson (Ed.), *Advances in Human-Computer Interaction*, Norwood, N.J.: Ablex Publishers, 133-159.

Stults, B. (1986). *Media Space*, Systems Concepts Lab Technical Report, Xerox Palo Alto Research Center.

Extensible Interfaces

Abelson, H. (1985). Boxer: Applications of a Personal Computing Environment. *SIGGRAPH Video Review* 18, New York: ACM.

Atari (1984). Video Games by Example. *SIGGRAPH Video Review* 12, New York: ACM.

diSessa, A.A. (1986). Notes on the Future of Programming: Breaking the Utility Barrier. In Norman, D. & Draper, S. (Eds.), *User-Centered System Design*, Hillsdale, N.J.: Lawrence Erlbaum, 201-218.

LeBlond, G.T. & Cobb, D.F. (1985). *Using 1-2-3*, Second Edition, Indianapolis, Indiana: Que Corporation.

Microsoft (1985). *Microsoft Excel User's Guide*, Bellevue, WA: Microsoft Corp.

Myers, B.A. (1986). Visual Programming, Programming by Example, and Program Visualization; A Taxonomy. *Proceedings of CHI '86*, 59-66.

Xerox Corp. (1985). Programming by Example. *SIGGRAPH Video Review* 18, New York: ACM.

Intelligent Interfaces

Anderson, J.R. & Skwarecki, E. (1986). The Automated Tutoring of Introductory Computer Programming. *Communications of the ACM* 29(9), 842-849.

Buxton, W., Dannenberg, R., & Vercoe, B. (1986). The Computer as Accompanist. *Proceedings of CHI '86,* 41-43.

Carroll, John M. & McKendree, Jean (1987). Interface Design Issues for Advice-Giving Expert Systems. *Communications of the ACM* 30(1), 14-31.

Chin, D.N. (1986). User Modeling in UC, the UNIX Consultant. *Proceedings of CHI '86,* 24-28.

Croft, Bruce W. (1984). The Role of Context and Adaptation in User Interfaces. *International Journal of Man-Machine Studies* 21, 283-292.

Dede, Christopher (1986). A Review and Synthesis of Recent Research in Intelligent Computer-Assisted Instruction. *International Journal of Man-Machine Studies* 24(4), 329-353.

Greenberg, S. & Witten, I.H. (1985). Adaptive Personalized Interfaces — A Question of Viability. *Behaviour and Information Technology* 4(1), 31-45.

Mason, M.V. (1986). Adaptive Command Prompting in an On-Line Documentation System. *International Journal of Man-Machine Studies* 25(1), 35-51.

McKendree, J. & Carroll, J.M. (1986). Advising Roles of a Computer Consultant. *Proceedings of CHI '86,* 35-40.

Negroponte, Nicholas (1970). *The Architecture Machine: Towards a More Humane Environment*, Cambridge, Mass.: The MIT Press.

Nickerson, R.S. (1977). On Conversational Interaction with Computers. *User-Oriented Design of Interactive Graphics Systems*, New York: ACM, 101-113.

Quinn, Lisa & Russell, Daniel M. (1986). Intelligent Interfaces: User Models and Planners. *CHI '86 Proceedings*, 314-320.

Rich, E. (1983). Users are Individuals: Individualizing User Models. *International Journal of Man-Machine Studies* 18, 199-214. Reprinted by permission of Academic Press, London.

Rissland, Edwina (1984). Ingredients of Intelligent User Interfaces. *International Journal of Man-Machine Studies* 21, 377-388.

Robertson, Ivan T. (1985). Human Information-Processing Strategies and Style. *Behaviour and Information Technology* 4(1), 19-29.

Sleeman, D. & Brown, J.S. (1982). *Intelligent Tutoring Systems*, London: Academic Press.

Trevellyan, R. & Browne, D. (1987). A Self-Regulating Adaptive System. *Proceedings of CHI+GI '87,* 103-107.

Wahlster, Wolfgang and Kobsa, Alfred (1986). Dialogue-Based User Models. *Proceedings of the IEEE* 74(7), 948-960.

Wenger, Etienne (1987). *Artificial Intelligence and Tutoring Systems*, Los Altos, CA.: Morgan Kaufmann Publishers.

Witten, Ian H., Greenberg, Saul, & Cleary, John (1983). Personalizable Directories: A Case Study in Automatic User Modelling. *Proceedings of Graphics Interface '83*, 183-189.

Zissos, Adrian Y. & Witten, Ian H. (1985). User Modelling for a Computer Coach: A Case Study. *International Journal of Man-Machine Studies* 23, 729-750.

Interfaces for the Handicapped

Bowe, F. (1987). Making Computers Accessible to Disabled People. *Technology Review* 90(1), 52-59, 72.

Buxton, W. (Ed.) (1986). Human Interface Design and the Handicapped User. *Proceedings of CHI '86*, 291-297.

IBM (1985). *Directory of Services and Specialized Equipment for the Physically Impaired,* Kingston, N.Y.: IBM Corporation, Department 63C/028, Kingston, N.Y. 12401.

Kane, R.M. & Yuschik, M. (1987). A Cas Example of Human Factors in Product Definition: Needs Finding for a Voice Output Workstation for the Blind. *Proceedings of CHI+GI '87,* 69-73.

Ladner, R., Day, R., Gentry, D., Meyer, K. & Rose, S. (1987). A User Interface for Deaf-Blind People. *Proceedings of CHI+GI '87,* 75-80.

Vanderheiden, G., Bengston, D., Brady, M. & Walstead, L. (1984). *International Software Registry,* Madison, Wisconsin: Trace Research and Development Center, Waisman Center, 1500 Highland Ave., Madison, Wisconsin, 53705-2280.

Verburg, G., Field, D., St. Pierre, F. & Naumann, S. (1987). Towards Universality of Access: Interfacing Physically Disabled Students to the Icon Educational Microcomputer. *Proceedings of CHI+GI '87,* 81-87.

Interfaces for Cooperative Work

Engelbart, D.C. (1963). A Conceptual Framework for the Augmentation of Man's Intellect. In Howerton & Weeks (Eds.), *Vistas in Information Handling*, Vol. 1, Washington, D.C.: Spartan Books, 1-29.

Engelbart, D.C. & English, W.K. (1968). A Research Center for Augmenting Human Intellect. *AFIPS Conference Proceedings* 33, 395-410.

Greif, I. (Ed.)(1986). *Proceedings of CSCW '86,* Conference on Computer-Supported Cooperative Work, Austin TX: MCC.

Hiltz, S.R. & Turoff, M. (1978). *The Network Nation: Human Communication via Computer*, New York: Addison-Wesley.

Hiltz, S.R. & Turoff, M. (1981). The Evolution of User Behavior in a Computerized Conferencing System. *Communications of the ACM* 24(11), 739-751.

Hiltz, S.R. (1984). *Online Communities: a Case Study of the Office of the Future*, Norwood, N.J.: Ablex Publishers.

Kerr, E.B. & Hiltz, S.R. (1982). *Computer-Mediated Communication Systems: Status and Envaluation,* New York: Academic Press.

Kiesler, S., Siegel, J., & McGuire, T.W. (1984). Social Psychological Aspects of Computer-Mediated Communication. Research Papers Series, Carnegie-Mellon University.

Malone, T.W. (1985). Designing Organizational Interfaces. *Proceedings of CHI '85,* 66-71.

Malone, T.W. (in press). Computer Support for Organizations: Toward and Organizational Science. In Carroll, J. (Ed.), *Interfacing Thought: Cognitive Aspects of Human-Computer Interaction,* Cambridge, MA.: MIT Press.

Sarin, S. & Greif, I. (1985). Computer-Based Real-Time Conferencing Systems. *IEEE Computer* 18(10), 33-45.

Sproull, L. & Kiesler, S. (1985). *Reducing Social Context Cues: Electronic Mail in Organizational Communication,* Carnegie Mellon University, November 1985.

Stefik, M., Foster, G., Bobrow, D.G., Kahn, K., Lanning, S. & Suchman, L. (1987). Beyond the Chalkboard: Computer Support for Collaboration and Problem Solving in Meetings. *Communications of the ACM* 30(1), 32-47.

Turoff, M. & Hiltz. S.R. (1982). Computer Support for Group Versus Individual Decisions. *IEEE Transactions on Communications* COM-30(1), 82-91.

Turoff, M. (1972). Party-Line and Discussion: Computerized Conferencing Systems. *Proceedings, First International Conference on Computer Communications,* Washington, 161-171.

Turoff, M. (1978). Development and Field Testing of an Electronic Information Exchange System: Final Report on the EIES Development Project, New Jersey Institute of Technology, 1978.

ON CONVERSATIONAL INTERACTION WITH COMPUTERS

R. S. Nickerson

Bolt Beranek and Newman Inc.

Cambridge, Massachusetts 02138

Several properties of conversations are considered as they relate to person-computer interaction. Some of the ways in which existing computer systems support interactions that have some features in common with interperson conversations are noted. Exception is taken to the notion, however, that person-computer interactions should, ideally, resemble person-person conversations in all respects.

Among the various ways in which people communicate with each other, probably none is more effective than conversing person to person. Perhaps for this reason, developers of interactive computer systems have shown a great interest in recent years in what has often been referred to as conversational computing, or, more generally, as a conversational mode of person-computer interaction. Presumably, such terms are intended to connote interactions between people and computers that resemble conversations between persons in nontrivial ways. But a conversation between persons is an uncommonly complex form of behavior. It has many dimensions, and one cannot always be sure which of them a writer has in mind when he refers to an interaction between a person and a computer as having a conversational character.

In another paper [35] I have listed what appear to me to be some of the more obvious characteristics of interperson conversations. That list is reproduced in Table 1. One of the purposes of this paper is to consider a few of the ways in which some of these characteristics are realized, or partially realized, in existing systems. No attempt has been made to produce a comprehensive review of existing systems; most of the system features that are cited for illustrative purposes are drawn arbitrarily from systems with which I happen to have some acquaintance. A second purpose of the paper is to question whether realization of the possibility of person-computer interactions that are like interperson conversations in all, or even most, respects is a goal for which system developers should strive.

Bidirectionality
Mixed initiative
Apparentness of who is in control
Rules for transfer of control
Sense of presence
Nonverbal communication
Intolerance for silence
Structure
Characteristic time scale
Wide bandwidth
Informal language
Shared situational context
Common world knowledge
Shared special knowledge
History
Peer status of participants

Table 1.
Some Characteristics of Conversations

Bidirectionality

Bidirectionality--the two-way flow of information--is a fundamental property of a conversation. Without it, one has, at best, some kind of monologue. Bidirectionality should not be thought of as an all-or-none property, however. A conversation can be more or less bidirectional, or, what is the same thing, more or less unidirectional, to the extent that one or the other party monopolizes it. It seems likely, however, that there is a limit to how unidirectional a conversation can become before it loses the character of a conversation and is perceived as something else.

Interactive systems, by definition, permit interactions that are bidirectional to some degree. In many cases, the bidirectionality is minimal, however, and the information flows much more freely in one direction than in the other. This is not to imply that systems that are grossly asymmetrical in this regard are necessarily poorly designed systems. On the contrary, it is easy to think of applications of computer systems in which one wants the computer to do most of the "talking", and perhaps of others in which one would want it primarily to "listen". Such interactions might best be characterized, however, as something other than conversational.

Mixed Initiative

This characteristic of conversations is similar to that of bidirectionality, but goes somewhat beyond it. Not only is there a two-way flow of information between participants, but each participant, on occasion, takes the conversational lead. He not only responds to what the other says, but he feels free to volunteer information that is not requested, and sometimes asks questions of his own.

There are many computer systems that permit an interaction in which the computer takes control momentarily in a preplanned fashion, in order to ask the user for information that is needed to set a program parameter value, or to select from among a set of branching options. Some systems also demand explicit confirmation of certain commands before executing them. The types of commands for which confirmation is usually required are those that will trigger expensive operations such as report generation [17] or will result in actions, such as file destruction, that could have unpleasant consequences if executed in error [15, 30]. HERMES [33], a computer-mediated mail system, for example, demands confirmation of the SEND command, which causes a message to be dispatched to its addressees, and of its DELETE and ERASE commands, which effect, respectively, the deletion of specified header fields and the erasure of message files. (In addition to demanding confirmation of potentially disastrous commands, some systems provide the capability of undoing the effects of commands such as file deletion, at least for a period of time following execution of the command [31].

Some programs have the capability of monitoring certain aspects of the behavior of a user and of making suggestions regarding how he might want to modify that behavior. Stewart [41] gives an example of this type of capability in a straightforward statistical analysis program. In his example, the program notes that the user has six times in a row asked for the calculation of Spearman rho correlation coefficients, Kendall tau correlation coefficients, and Pearson's product moment correlation coefficients, whereupon it asks if all three of these coefficients are necessary, and points out that if they are not, some time could be saved by calculating only one of them. It also asks the user if he has considered the possibility of other, perhaps more appropriate, analyses of his data.

While these and other examples of computer-initiated communicative acts illustrate mixed initiative capabilities of a rudimentary sort, there are few, if any, systems that permit the kind of give-and-take of initiative that characterizes interperson conversations. One pioneering effort in the development of mixed-initiative systems that permit a give-and-take that is somewhat characteristic of interperson conversations was the SCHOLAR system developed by Carbonell [7]. Carbonell's intent was to develop a computer-assisted instruction system that would be able both to ask questions of the user and to answer questions that the user asked of it. Carbonell's work has been extended by his colleagues, and, at the present time, several SCHOLAR-based systems exist [e.g. 16,21]. These systems support a relatively rich mixed-initiative interaction over a limited range of discourse.

Apparentness of Who
is in Control

While control passes back and forth between the participants in conversation, usually it is clear to both parties who is in control--whose turn it is to speak--at any given moment. When the possibility of ambiguity on this point arises, one of the participants is likely to take some explicit action to resolve it. If, for example, the individual whose turn it is to speak wants to delay speaking for an appreciable time, he is likely to inform the other participant of the anticipated delay.

Occasional uncertainty about who is waiting for whom has been reported to be a source of frustration for users of some interactive systems. Suppose, for example, that the user has made a request of the computer and has no idea how long the reply may be delayed. As time passes and nothing happens, he may begin to wonder if he entered the request incorrectly, or if the computer is waiting for additional input. Developers of the JOSS system anticipated this type of problem, and equipped the user's console with a red and a green light, one of which was always on during an interactive session; one of the lights indicated that the console was being controlled by the user, the other that it was being controlled by the machine [2].

In some full-duplex systems, the user can always determine who is in control by virtue of the fact that the system does not echo the user's input except when it is the user's turn to "speak". Many systems also provide explicit control cues of various sorts. The PROPHET system, for example, does a carriage return or a space (depending on the type of terminal) to signify that it has parsed the user's input [9]. Each of the various user programs that runs under the TENEX system informs the user that it is waiting for an input by typing (or displaying) a control character (unique to that program) at the leftmost position of the next available line on the page or display [5].

Rules for Transfer of Control

The transfer of control from one participant in an interperson conversation to the other may be effected in a variety of ways: usually the speaker spontaneously relinquishes the floor to the listener; however, the listener may signal the desire to take the floor, or he may simply interrupt the speaker, and take it by force, as it were.

As in person-person conversations, control is usually assumed by one of the participants in a person-computer interaction by virtue of the fact that the other participant has voluntarily relinquished it. Some systems permit only this type of transfer. The inability to have listener-initiated transfers is an unfortunate limitation, however, a fact that is being recognized by an increasing number of system designers. Many interactive systems now provide the user with the capability to interrupt the machine, although few provide the machine with the capability to interrupt the user.

The desirability of providing the user with an interrupt capability is obvious. Suppose, for example, that the user has asked the computer to generate a lengthy table of numbers by invoking a user-defined procedure, and that by the time the first few values of the table have been typed, it is clear that the procedure is not free of bugs. The user should not be forced to wait until the table has been completed before regaining control of the interaction. Or, suppose the computer has begun to type a lengthy message that, for whatever reason, the user finds uninformative or uninteresting. He should be able to say,

in effect, "That's enough of that", and to recapture control. Many systems provide such user-initiated interrupt capabilities.

The desirability of providing the computer with the capability to interrupt the user is perhaps somewhat less apparent. Although one can easily imagine situations in which the user could be spared some wasted time and effort if the machine could inform him that he is making an error or doing something inefficiently while he is in the act of making or doing it. The HERMES system [33] will sometimes interrupt a user's attempt to complete a nonsensical command, or to do other inadmissible things. It also will, under certain conditions, interrupt a user to tell him that new mail has just arrived at his mailbox. Interruptions for the latter purpose can occur only when the user is at a "prompt" which is to say, when it is his turn to say something, but he has not yet begun to do so. It is important to note that the sole purpose of HERMES-initiated interruptions is to give the user some presumably helpful information, that the interruption is always very brief, and that control is transferred back to the user immediately after he has been given the information that he needs.

An important difference between people and computers that is relevant to the provision of interrupt capabilities is the fact that one need not, yet at least, be concerned about the emotional or cognitively-disruptive effect on the machine of interrupting it in the middle of a sentence. More generally, there is no need to worry about implementing subtle and tactful ways of requesting that it relinquish its control of the interaction to the user. It is not safe to assume, however, that the user will be equally indifferent to the ways in which control is taken away from him.

Sense of Presence

Each participant in a conversation tends to be aware at any given time of the degree to which the other participant is paying attention to what he says. Signals confirming one's attentiveness are conveyed from one participant to the other in a variety of ways.

A source of frustration that has been cited by users of interactive systems is the uncertainty they sometimes have, when the computer's response is unexpectedly delayed, as to whether the computer is working on their problem, off attending to other demands, or dead. Techniques that would provide the user, either automatically or on request, with something analogous to the "sense of presence" that characterizes interperson conversations would contribute to the smoothness of person-computer interactions.

Under some conditions, the SCHOLAR system, after waiting more than a certain number of seconds for a response from the user, outputs an inquiry along the lines of: "Are you still there? I'm waiting" [7]. The user would like to be able to ask a similar question of the computer on occasion and obtain to that particular question an immediate response. We should not assume, however, that the implementation of such techniques would necessarily maximize the user's contentment; one might expect a user to become somewhat disgruntled upon learning that the computer was ignoring him for awhile in order to attend to other demands, just as a participant in a conversation might be displeased to lose the attention of the other participant to competing activities.

Nonverbal Communication

Nonverbal behavior serves at least two purposes in conversations: sometimes it conveys information that relates to the substance of the conversation, as when the nodding of the head is used to indicate agreement with, or understanding of, an assertion; at other times it conveys other types of information as when a frown is used to indicate annoyance with the speaker, or "uh-huh's" are interjected into a long talk-spurt in a phone conversation to assure the speaker of the listener's continuing attention.

It seems unlikely that anyone would argue that the computer must be given the ability to communicate nonverbally in the same way that people do. It would seem important, however, that it be given the means of conveying to the user the type of information that people sometimes convey to each other in nonverbal ways. In particular, it should be able to do something analogous to saying "uh-huh" at appropriate times to assure the user that he continues to have its attention.

Some system designers have shown a sensitivity to this issue and have provided what Foley and Wallace [20] have called some form of placebo to assure the user of the continuing attention of the machine. Jacks' DAC-1 system [27], for example, provides continuous feedback regarding the progress of a program by displaying a sequence of numbers on the scope. The SELMA system of Irani, Wallace, and Jackson [26] constructs large pictures--which require considerable time to complete--piece by piece so the user is aware that the computer is working on his problem.

Smith [40] has suggested that for every action by the user of an interactive system, there should be a noticeable reaction by the computer to define the transaction. In particular, he suggests that if the computer's substantive output is to be delayed, the computer should make some quick intermediate response to acknowledge the user's input. But "delayed" and "quick" are in need of definition: how long need a delay be to justify making an intermediate response, and how quickly should the latter be made? The data that would provide objective answers to these questions have not been gathered, but some opinions have been expressed. Cheriton [15], for example, suggests that, ideally, some feedback should be given to the user within two seconds, and that at the outside one should not have to wait more than ten seconds for some reassurance when the substantive response is to be delayed for a longer time.

Intolerance for Silence

People engaged in conversations show a strong intolerance for silence when it cannot be accounted for. Failure of one's partner in a phone conversation to say something when he is expected to so do, for example, is likely to evoke an inquiry as to whether he is still on the line. This clearly is related to the "sense of presence" notion, but perhaps goes somewhat beyond it. Unaccountable silence during a conversation can be awkward even when--perhaps especially when--the presence of the partner whose turn it is to speak is not in doubt.

Although data on the issue are sparse, it has been suggested that a primary source of user dissatisfaction with delays is uncertainty regarding the reasons for the delays and how long they will last [8, 34]. If this conjecture is valid, it suggests that person-computer interactions could be enhanced by providing the computer with the capability to inform the user whenever there is to be a delay that is longer than its context would lead one to expect, and, if possible, to give him an estimate of how long the delay is likely to be. The ability to provide this information on request would also be a desirable feature. The TENEX operating system [31] provides information on request that lets the user know what to expect by way of system response times, on the average, but it does not tell him how long any given delay is likely to be. Whenever the user types a particular control character, the system reports the current "load average", a number that represents the current demand on the machine.

Structure

Conversations have beginnings, endings, and what is in between. And one typically does not initiate or terminate conversations in arbitrary ways, but according to established protocol. So much is also true of person-computer interactions. The structure in the latter case is probably somewhat more formal and less flexible than in the case of person-person conversations. For any given interactive system there usually is only one acceptable way of initiating an interaction and only one acceptable way of terminating it.

There is another way in which the structure of a person-computer interaction may differ from that of a person-person conversation. Often, during the course of a single work session, the user will interact with several systems. He may, upon entering a computer network from a remote terminal, communicate first with a control program whose function it is to attach him to the appropriate host computer. Once routed to the specified host, he will interact with the executive program on that machine. He may then specify one of several software systems that he wishes to use. So far, the process is analogous in some respects to the placing of a phone call in which one first talks perhaps with a long-distance operator, then with a company switchboard operator, and finally with the individual with whom he really wishes to carry on a conversation. The difference is in the closing procedure. Whereas to terminate a phone conversation, one simply observes the sign-off protocol that is appropriate vis-a-vis the person with whom one had the real conversation and then hangs up, in the case of person-computer interaction, it may be necessary (although this is not invariably true) to sign off explicitly at each level. That is to say, the termination procedure is the inverse, in a sense, of the initiation procedure: the user first logs out of the lowest order system, the effect of which is to pop him up to the next level in the hierarchy, whereupon he logs out at that level, and so on.

It would not be difficult to let the user, in effect, say good-bye only once, and have the logging out at the higher levels follow automatically from the termination of the interaction with the lowest level system. There are advantages, however, to doing it the way it is typically done inasmuch as the user may wish to go only part way up the tree and then come back down another branch during the same work session. This is somewhat analogous to terminating a phone call by returning to a switchboard to transfer to another extension rather than hanging up and breaking the higher level connection. What would

probably be a convenience to the user would be to follow the telephone analogy further than it currently is followed by permitting him, upon completing his interaction with a particular subsystem, either, in effect, to hang up and thereby terminate the connection at all levels or to return to the switchboard, as it were, to make use of another subsystem.

Characteristic Time Scale

Among the most distinguishing aspects of interperson conversations are their temporal characteristics. In particular, although data on the subject are sparse, those that exist suggest that control typically is transferred from one participant to the other at an average of once every four or five seconds.

The temporal characteristics of person-computer interaction have received relatively much attention from system developers and investigators. This is probably due, in part, to the fact that measurements of some temporal parameters can be made automatically by the system in ways that do not interfere with the interaction [1, 23, 28].

Response times of both systems and users have been the primary foci of attention. Some investigators have attempted to study the effects of problem-solving performance of controlled variations in system-response dynamics [3, 22, 24, 29]. The most general conclusion to be drawn from these studies is that user behavior does seem to be affected by system response time in a variety of ways. However, exactly what the effect of an increase in system delay will be appears to depend somewhat on the nature of the task that is being performed.

Measured user response times have varied considerably from user to user, from system to system, and from task to task. Sackman and Citrebaum [39] summarized data from five studies of interactive computing that were done between 1965 and 1967. The mean user response time (time between completion of the computer's output and the next user input) in these studies varied from 20 to 71 seconds; medians varied from 9 to 13 seconds. To the extent that these data are representative of person-computer interaction in general, they suggest that such interactions are considerably less fluent than are interperson conversations. These data are relatively old, and one could undoubtedly find examples of interactions involving currently existing systems for which the average user response times were less than those reported; however, it seems safe to assume that person-computer interactions still lack, for the most part, the temporal fluency that characterizes conversations between persons.

In the case of systems that rely primarily on typed input from the user, the temporal characteristics of the interaction are determined in part by the user's typing skill. It cannot be assumed, however, that increasing the typing skill of all users, or developing interactive languages that require the typing of fewer keys, would simply reduce the user's response time. Brown and Klerer [4] have shown that the introduction of consoles permitting the input of entire words of a command language like that of BASIC with a single key stroke could have the effect of increasing system response time or of decreasing the number of users that a given system could simultaneously service. This is because in a time-sharing system the time that one user takes to key in lengthy command strings is used to advantage by the computer to service other users.

Wide Bandwidth

Most of the methods that people currently use to get information into computers in interactive situations have relatively narrow bandwidths. Most systems rely on keyboard input devices such as typewriters and teletypewriters. And, even in the hands of skilled typists, the information-transfer rates that can be sustained with these devices are low compared to what can be accomplished with speech.

To refer to speech as a high-bandwidth communication mode is not to suggest that the information-transfer rate in interperson conversations is always high. Evans [19] makes the point that some conversations between people accomplish the transfer of very little information indeed, involving, as they do, the exchange of a series of platitudes about the weather, the price of food, politics, and so forth. A similar point has been made by other writers. I recall reading an essay--the writer's name escapes me--the point of which was that the real message that is being conveyed by many verbal exchanges is that the parties to the exchange are not angry at each other. It is expected that when friends or acquaintances come in contact with each other, they will speak. What they say may be more or less irrelevant, provided only that it is calculated not to offend. Failure to speak, however, may be interpreted as a snub.

The importance of being able to use speech for communication in situations in which there is a genuine need for information exchange, as, for example, when two persons are attempting to solve a problem cooperatively, has been explored in a series of experiments by Chapanis and his colleagues [11-14, 36]. What is not clear from this work is whether the utility of speech has any basis other than the greater bandwidth it represents. One wonders if speech would show the same advantages, for example, if compared with typing by highly skilled typists who had a large amount of practice using typed messages as a means of real-time communication. And how would it compare with other higher-bandwidth input methods involving, perhaps, sophisticated graphics terminals with touch-panel capabilities?

How seriously a typewriter or other keyboard input device limits person-computer interaction probably depends not only on the skill level of the user, and the purpose of the interaction, but also on the detailed nature of the dialog that is necessary to accomplish the task. This fact is illustrated by the contrasting results of two attempts to implement interactive medical history-taking systems. Evans [19] reports that narrow-bandwidth was no impediment to his history-taking program, inasmuch as the program had been designed to require from users the same small set of responses that he had found were required by most doctor-conducted interviews: "Yes", "No", "Don't know", and, occasionally, "Don't understand". (Evans also reports that users in this situation were annoyed neither by the slow--10 characters per second--rate of the teletypewriter as a device for outputting text, nor by the noisiness of the device.) In contrast is the experience of Castleman et al.[10] who, after trying to have patients interact directly with the computer for the purpose of medical history-taking, decided--because of the excessive length and variability of the time spent by patients at the terminal--to employ a skilled typist to act as an intermediary between the patient and the machine. The patient answered questions on a paper questionnaire, and the typist transferred the information from the questionnaire to the computer through the remote terminal. These investigators considered this modification to their original plan to have been a successful one, inasmuch as the typist required only about 5% of the terminal time that patients had been using.

A careful comparison between Evans' system and that of Castleman et al., with respect to the types of responses they required from patients and the details of the interactive session, could provide some useful hints concerning the factors that determine the bandwidth that a communication channel should have in order to support an effective person-computer interaction. We should note in passing, however, that the taking of a medical history typically does not involve a conversation in the usual sense of that word. It is more in the nature of an interrogation and, consequently, may be accomplished very efficiently even if the interrogatee is constrained by a very limited response repertory.

System developers have made use of various tricks to increase effectively the bandwidth of typewriters as input devices. One such trick is to give the computer the ability to recognize a command on the basis of the typing of its first few letters [18, 31, 32, 33]. One of the ways in which this feature works in practice is as follows. The user types as many characters as he thinks are necessary to identify a command uniquely, whereupon he presses one of two control keys. If the computer cannot recognize the command because not enough characters have been typed to identify it uniquely, it asks for more characters. If the command can be recognized, the computer either types the rest of it (or causes it to appear on a display if a video terminal is being used) or goes on to the next step in the dialog, depending on which control character was struck.

Another way of increasing the effective bandwidth of a typewriter-video display combination is described in a planning document for an interactive system that is to be used by U.S. Department of Agriculture personnel [37]. The interaction between person and computer in this case takes place through a series of "frames", or formatted displays. Each input frame requires a formatted input from the user. The inputs in many cases are expected to be highly predictable, a fact on which the system capitalizes in the following way. Striking of a "default" key produces the single most likely (as prespecified) character in the "current character position" (at which a cursor is pointing on the display). Thus, for many of the more predictable entries, the input would be accomplished by the repetitive pressing of a single control key. The principle could be generalized so that an entire word or phrase could be evoked by a single key press.

Informal Language

One of the most striking characteristics of conversational language is its lack of precision and formal rigor. Not only do we typically talk in incomplete and grammatically incorrect sentences, we often say something quite different from what we mean. The question, "Can you reach the butter?", if interpreted literally calls for a "yes" or "no" answer. However, when directed to one's companion at the dinner table, it is clearly intended not to elicit a "yes" or "no" response, but, instead, butter-passing behavior. Indeed, we often say precisely the opposite of what we mean, not to be deceptive, but, strangely, to emphasize our meaning as, for example, when one says, "That's wonderful", when the message one wishes to convey is that it is really horrible.

No existing computer system can accommodate anything like the informality that characterizes the language of interperson conversations. It seems to be widely assumed that if a computer could be given this ability it would be a good thing. The assumption can be--has been--challenged, however [e.g. 25]. The great advantage of natural language as computer input is the fact that most people know how to use it moderately well. But one might argue that people do not communicate effectively <u>because</u> of the vagueness of natural language, but in <u>spite</u> of it. In contrast to natural languages, computer languages, even those that have been designed for non-programmer users, are precise to a fault--perversely literal, one might say. Consequently, they impose a discipline on the computer user that person-person communication does not. Whether, on balance, this discipline is a good or bad thing is a debatable point. Hill [25] has argued that not only is it a good thing for person-computer communication, but that some measure of it could improve person-person communication, at least in certain instances, as well. The problem of learning to program, after all, is less that of learning to talk to a computer than that of learning to talk <u>precisely</u> to one's self.

It is not necessary to espouse the notion that the language in which person-computer interaction takes place should be as unconstrained as that of interperson conversation, however, in order to recognize the desirability of removing some of the constraints that many current languages impose on users. BASIC's limitation of variable names to a single letter or to a single letter followed by a number is an obvious example of an unnecessary and frustrating constraint. The inability of most systems to recognize synonyms for words in its command vocabulary is another. The inability to recognize simple spelling errors as errors and to correct them is still another. As is the failure to provide the user with a straightforward means of defining abbreviations for frequently used terms.

Such limitations are not essential, given the current state of the art, and one can find examples of systems that have removed one or more of them by implementing features that add flexibility to the language and increase its adaptability to the individual user's tastes and preferences. Not all interactive algebraic languages have BASIC's single-letter constraint on variable names. There are systems (e.g., HERMES, INTER-LISP, PROPHET) that can recognize and correct some spelling errors, as well as syntactic errors in command language usage, and that permit the use of abbreviations [32, 33, 38, 42].

There undoubtedly is a need to develop computer languages that are more convenient to use than any that currently exist--which may mean making them more similar to natural languages in some respects--but whether the goal of making it possible to communicate with a computer in an unconstrained natural language is a desirable one is not clear. The assumption that the preferred mode of interaction with a computer is via natural language--or something that approximates it as closely as possible--has led some system developers to endow their systems with certain characteristics that are calculated to convey the impression of a natural-language capability when, in fact, one does not exist. Thus, for example, a system might be given the ability to refer to the user by name, to insert folksy prattle into its output, and to project a "Hello, I'm your friendly and clever computer" image in other ways. It is at least a plausible conjecture that such superficial hints at intelligence and natural-language ability can have the effect of making the interaction less, rather than more, natural than it otherwise might be, especially when the user discovers the fact that the sophistication he had been led to expect from the computer really is not there. A design principle that might be worth adopting is that of taking pains to make the system appear to be exactly as intelligent as, or at least no more intelligent than, it really is.

Cheriton [15] notes the importance, both of the user's image of the system (the model he forms from what he sees at the interface, which constitutes the window through which he sees the system) and of the user's attitude towards the system (his emotional response to it). Conservatism in image building may go against the instincts of the system developer who wants his system to be appreciated, but it should help avoid the problem of the user becoming disillusioned when a system does not live up to expectations that were ill-founded in the first place.

Perhaps one of the major arguments in favor of increasing the informality of interactive languages is that people tend to think in terms of informal language. The argument has weight if one assumes that it would be advantageous to the user if he could talk to the computer in a way that is similar to that in which he talks to himself. Without necessarily going this far, some investigators have emphasized the importance of a high degree of correspondence between the way in which commands are expressed in the interactive language and the way in which one would naturally describe the operations one wishes the computer to perform. As one measure of command-language efficiency, Treu [43] proposes the amount of "mental work" that a user is required to do in order to represent in terms of the system's command language the actions that he desires the computer to carry out. As a step toward defining an approach to making such measurements he distinguishes between "action primitives" (the verb-object pairs that identify, in terms of basic system-independent operations, what the user wants done) and "system commands" (the instantiations of these action primitives in terms of a specific command language). Mental work ("think time") is involved both in the selection and sequencing of the action primitives that define a particular problem solution, and in translating them into the appropriate system commands. Treu proposes an analytic approach to identifying and measuring components of both of these processes.

Shared Situational Context

The importance of a shared situation--perceptual or conceptual--as a source of extralinguistic cues that can help disambiguate what is being said in a conversation is difficult to overestimate. Each participant in a face-to-face conversation naturally assumes that the other participant is, for the most part, aware of the same aspects of a situation that he is. One does not feel compelled, for example, to tell one's partner that the car in which they are both riding is moving before making a comment whose interpretation would depend upon knowledge that the car is in motion. Many effective conversations would be meaningless to a third-party eavesdropper who did not share the situational context of the participants.

An appreciation of a situational context is an exceedingly difficult thing to give a computer. Consequently most of the information that people get from the situation to disambiguate their verbal communication must be provided explicitly in person-computer interactions.

For this reason such interactions are bound to be somewhat more formal and explicit than interperson conversations for some time to come.

An interesting exception to this rule may be found in the use of graphics terminals, especially as more innovative techniques for using such terminals as input devices are developed. The graphics display may be thought of as a shared situation, in a sense. It is a surface on which both user and computer can draw, erase, and modify things, and view the results of their combined efforts. It permits the construction of a context in which pointing makes sense, and in which relationships can be seen so they need not be described explicitly. This is not to say that interactions between people and computers that take place via graphics terminals will necessarily resemble person-person conversations more than those that do not involve such terminals. They do, however, represent exciting possibilities for the development of new and innovative interactive techniques. But the excitement stems at least as much from ways in which the resulting interactions may differ from person-person conversations as from how they may resemble them.

Common World Knowledge

It is clear that conversations, as we know them, could not occur if it were not for the fact that the participants share a great deal of "common knowledge" about the world. How to represent world knowledge within the computer and to make use of it in person-computer interactions are problems that have been receiving considerable attention from researchers in the area of machine intelligence. These problems are far from being solved, and the world knowledge that is possessed by most of the interactive systems that currently exist is miniscule compared with that possessed by their users.

What one does find in many systems is knowledge about a mini-world, namely the particular mini-world about which the computer and user can communicate. The interaction between user and computer then is facilitated to the extent that the user understands and, in a sense, shares this view. The point may be illustrated with another reference to HERMES. This system has a model of the message world with which it deals. This model involves such things as messages, addresses, senders, filters, templates, address lists, and so on. If one is to use the system effectively, one should conceptualize the message world in terms of these entities. Moreover, in addition to sharing the same model of the mini-

world of interest, it can be most helpful if the user and computer have a common view about the current state of the world. Thus, for example, given one state of the world, the user could cause the system to print his oldest unseen message by typing a single character; if the user could not assume that state, he would have to type PRINT (to distinguish this output option from other possibilities) and specify the desired message by date and sender, or in some other explicit way.

Shared Special Knowledge

The special knowledge that people bring to conversations and that helps them disambiguate what is being said includes knowledge about each other and about special information (e.g., by virtue of being members of the same family, profession, neighborhood) that they may share.

Some initial attempts have been made to provide interactive computer systems with at least rudimentary models of their users (e.g.[6]). The term "friendly terminal", as it has sometimes been used, connotes a terminal that can adapt to the level of expertise, and perhaps the style and preferences, of the user. It might permit the user to designate abbreviations for frequently used terms, and it might provide prompting in an effort to anticipate and prevent errors that this user tends to make.

Some system builders have envisioned systems that will have the ability to develop very sophisticated models of their users. Such systems would presumably be able to serve as extensions of their users' memories, to implement their problem-solving and decision-making capabilities, and generally to augment their cognitive performance in a variety of ways. But this is speculation, and whether, or when, personalized systems with these capabilities will appear remains to be seen.

History

Most conversations occur between people who have conversed--perhaps many times and possibly on the same topic(s)--before. This fact is bound to condition conversations in a variety of ways. In particular, a conversation between people who have conversed more or less daily for an appreciable time is likely to be quite different in both substance and tone from one involving people who are interacting for the first time.

Most interactive systems provide some help to the user in maintaining continuity from one interactive session to the next. Most provide a file storage capability, for example, and usually this includes the ability to store the current status of an incomplete work session in such a way that one can return to the system at some later date and pick up precisely where one left off. No existing system, however, is capable of showing the same effects from repeated interactions with the same person as may be seen in interperson conversations.

Peer Status of Participants

It was suggested in the earlier paper [35] that the most satisfying conversations usually involve intellectual peers. This was not to suggest that conversations do not occur between people who differ greatly in intellectual capabilities, but only that they tend to be more difficult in this case.

There is no computer system in existence yet that can carry on a conversation with a human being as an intellectual peer. While the development of such a capability represents a challenge if one is motivated to produce a system that can pass Turing's [44] intelligence test, one might argue that giving a computer the ability to function as a person's peer is precisely the wrong thing to do if one wants to maximize the utility of person-computer interaction. Rather than two peers engaged in a conversation, perhaps what one wants is an interaction involving two participants that complement each other in a way that two persons never could. There are some things that computers do far better than people, and, at the present time at least, some things that people do far better than computers. The most satisfying interactions between people and computers, one might predict, would be those in which each participant does what he (it) does best.

Concluding Remarks

In conclusion, there are two contentious remarks that I would like to make regarding the notion of conversational interaction between persons and computers. The first is that the differences between the person-computer interactions that take place today and interperson conversations are far greater than the similarities between them. The second is that interperson conversation may be, in some respects, an inappropriate and misleading model to use as a goal for person-computer interaction.

On the whole, most interactions that take place between people and computers today still have much in common with the command-and-execute mode of interaction with desk calculators. The commands are

more sophisticated and their execution more complicated, but the command-and-execute format is apparent all the same. The user issues commands in the form of action-object, verb-predicate, procedure-argument pairs, and the computer carries out the commands. The communication between the person and the computer in this case can certainly be interactive and effective, but it is not--in the usual sense of the word--a conversation. The very term "command language", which is commonly used to denote the linguistic medium of such interactions, is antithetical to the notion of a conversation. In fact, it implies a grossly asymmetrical interaction inasmuch as the commands it refers to flow in one direction only. Cheriton [15] makes this point by explicitly distinguishing between the command language (in which the user specifies commands to the computer) and the system response language (in which the system responds to the user's commands).

With respect to the appropriateness or inappropriateness of interperson conversation as a model for person-computer interaction, the position taken here is that whether an interaction resembles a conversation is irrelevant to the more important question of whether it is satisfying to the user and effective in helping him realize his goals. Satisfying and effective interactions may resemble conversations in some respects; they may differ from them markedly in others.

Person-computer interactions are, by definition, bidirectional. A mixed-initiative dialog is characteristic of many systems to a small degree, and of a few systems to a moderate degree. Undoubtedly, there are advantages to be gained by extending this capability, at least for certain types of applications. Apparentness of who is in control is a highly desirable feature and one that is easy to implement. The ability to interrupt the computer is a convenience to the user and a capability that many systems provide. A sense of presence is a desirable characteristic that is not well implemented in many systems. In general, there is a need for better methods to inform the user regarding how attentive the system is being to his demands at any time. Cues and prompts to signal the user regarding such things as receipt of an input, change of control, machine state, waiting for input have been implemented on many systems and undoubtedly benefit the user. Minimization of unaccounted for "silences" and delays of unpredictable duration would eliminate major sources of user annoyance. Development of new methods of increasing the effective bandwidth of input techniques should be a goal of system builders. All of these features, if implemented or extended, would tend to increase the conversational character of person-computer interactions.

On the other hand, one can imagine a variety of ways in which it might be desirable for person-computer interaction to lack the symmetry that one typically expects of interperson conversations: one might want the computer to know a great deal more than the user about some things and virtually nothing about others, to respond more or less instantaneously to all requests while being infinitely tolerant of delays originating with the user, to be much more precise than a person in its use of language, to be interruptable at all times but very circumspect in its decisions concerning whether or when to interrupt the user, never to terminate an interaction on its own initiative, and so on. One also surely wants the computer to do things that no human participant in a conversation can be expected to do: produce complex graphical displays on demand, search large data bases and output the results in various organized ways, purge its memory of obsolete, erroneous or otherwise useless facts, store new items of information for later precise detailed recall.

The model that seems appropriate for this view of person-computer interaction is that of an individual making use of a sophisticated tool and not that of one person conversing with another. The term "user" is, of course, often used to denote the human component in a person-computer interaction, as it has been in this paper. It is, to my taste, preferable to the term "partner", not only because it seems more descriptive of the nature of the relationships that existing systems permit, and that future systems are likely to, but because it implies an asymmetry with respect to goals and objectives that "partner" does not. "User" is not a term that one would normally apply to a participant in a conversation.

Acknowledgment

This paper was prepared under Contract No. MDA903-76-C-0207 with the Defense Advanced Research Projects Agency. I am grateful to Catherine Hausmann, Austin Henderson, Richard Pew, Ann Rubin, Albert Stevens, and John · Swets for helpful comments on an early draft.

References

1. Abrams, M.D., Lindamood, G.E., & Pyke, T.N., Jr. Measuring and modeling man-computer interaction. Proceedings of First Annual SIGME Symposium on Measurement and Evaluation, 1973, 136-142.

2. Baker, C.L. JOSS: Introduction to a helpful assistant. The RAND Corporation RM-5058-PR, August 1966.

3. Boehm, B.W., Seven, M.J., & Watson, R.A. Interactive problem-solving-- An experimental study of "lockout" effects. Proceedings Spring Joint Computer Conference, Interactive Problem Solving, 1971, 206-210.

4. Brown, T. & Klerer, M. The effect of language design on time-sharing operational efficiency. International Journal of Man-Machine Studies, 1975, 7, 233-247.

5. Burchfiel, J.D., Leavitt, E.M., Shapiro, S., & Strollo, T.R. TENEX user' guide. Bolt Beranek and Newman Inc., 1975.

6. Burton, R.R. & Brown, J.S. A tutoring and student modelling paradigm for gaming environments. Proceedings of ACM-SIGCUE Joint Symposium, Computer Science and Education, Feb. 197

7. Carbonell, J.R. AI in CAI: An artificial intelligence approach to computer-assisted instruction. IEEE Transactions on Man-Machine Systems, 1970, MMS-11, 190-202.

8. Carbonell, J.R., Elkind, J.L., & Nickerson, R.S. On the psychological importance of time in a time-sharing system. Human Factors, 1968, 10, 135-142.

9. Castleman, P.A., Russell, C.H., Webb, F.N., Hollister, C.A., Siegel, J.R., Zdonik, S.R., & Fram, D.M. The implementation of the PROPHET system. AFIPS Conference Proceedings, 1974, 43, 457-468.

10. Castleman, P.A., Whitehead, S.F., Sher, L.D., Hantman, L.M., & Massey, L.D., Jr. An assessment of the utility of computer aids in the physician's office. Bolt Beranek and Newman Inc. Report No. 3096, 1974.

11. Chapanis, A. The communication of factual information through various channels. Information Storage and Retrieval, 1973, 9, 215.

12. Chapanis, A. Interactive human communication. Scientific American, 1975, 232, 34-42.

13. Chapanis, A., Ochsman, R.B., Parrish, R.N., & Weeks, G.D. Studies in interactive communication: I. The effects of four communication modes on the behavior of teams during cooperative problem-solving. Human

Factors, 1972, 14, 487-509.

14. Chapanis, A., Parrish, R.N., Ochsman, R.B., & Weeks, G.D. Studies in interactive communication: II. The effects of four communication modes on the linguistic performance of teams during cooperative problem solving. Human Factors, in press.

15. Cheriton, D.R. Man-machine interface design for timesharing systems. Proceedings, Annual Conference of the Association for Computing Machinery, Houston, Texas, October 20-22, 1976, 362-366.

16. Collins, A.M., Warnock, E.H., & Passafiume, J.J. Analysis and synthesis of tutorial dialogues. In G.H. Bower (Ed.), The psychology of learning and motivation, Vol. 9. New York: Academic Press, 1975.

17. Ebeling, H.W. The CHIMP manual. MIS Department, Bolt Beranek and Newman Inc., May 1974.

18. Engelbart, D.C., Watson, R.W., & Norton, J.C. The augmented knowledge workshop. AFIPS Conference Proceedings, National Computer Conference, 1973, 9-21.

19. Evans, C. What I have learnt about computer communication and what computers have taught me about human communication. Paper presented at NATO Advanced Study Institute Conference, Mati, Greece, September 5-18, 1976.

20. Foley, J.D. & Wallace, V.L. The art of natural graphic man-machine conversation. IEEE Proceedings, Special issue on Computer Graphics, April 1974, 462-471.

21. Grignetti, M.C., Gould, L., & Hausmann, C. NLS-SCHOLAR: Modifications and field testing. ESD-TR-358, November 1975.

22. Grignett, M.C. & Miller, D. Modifying computer response characteristics to influence command choice. Proceedings of IEE Conference on Man-Computer Interaction, London, UK, Sept. 1970, 201-205.

23. Grignett, M.C., Miller, D., Nickerson, R.S., & Pew, R.W. Information processing models and computer aids for human performance. BBN Report No. 2352, March 1972.

24. Grossberg, M., Wiesen, R.A., & Yntema, D.B. An experiment on problem solving with delayed computer responses. IEEE Transactions on Systems, Man, and Cybernetics,

25. Hill, I.D. Wouldn't it be nice if we could write programs in ordinary English--or would it? Computer Bulletin, 1972, 16, 306-312.

26. Irani, K.B., Wallace, V.L., & Jackson, J.H. Conversational design of stochastic service systems from a graphical terminal. Proceedings of 1970 International Symposium on Computer Graphics, R.D. Parslow & R.E. Green (Eds.). New York: Plenum, 1971, 91-107.

27. Jacks, E.L. A laboratory for the study of graphical man-machine communication. Proceedings, 1964 AFIPS Fall Joint Computer Conference. Montvale, N.J.L. AFIPS Press, 1968, 363-386.

28. Martin, T.H. & Parker, E.B. Designing for user acceptance of an interactive bibliographic search facility. Interactive bibliographic search: The user/computer interface. D.E. Walker (Ed.). AFIPS Press, 1971, 45-52.

29. Morefield, M.A., Wiesen, R.A., Grossberg, M., & Yntema, D.B. Initial experiments on the effects of system delay on on-line problem-solving. M.I.T. Lincoln Laboratory Technical Note TN-1969-5, 1969.

30. Muchnick, S.S. The command interpreter and command language design of the COM-SHARE COMMANDER II system. Proceedings, Annual Conference of the Association for Computing Machinery, Houston, Texas, Oct. 20-22, 1976, 367-372.

31. Myer, T.H. & Barnaby, J.R. TENEX executive language: Manual for users. Bolt Beranek and Newman Inc., 1971. Revised by Plummer, W.W., 1973.

32. Myer, T.H. & Dodds, D.W. Notes on the development of message technology. Proceedings of the Berkeley Workshop on Distributed Data Management and Computer Networks (LBL-5315). Published by Lawrence Berkeley Laboratory, Univ. of California and U.S. Energy Research and Development Administration, Wash., D.C., May 1976.

33. Myer, T.H. & Mooers, C.D. HERMES users' guide. Preliminary Draft, Bolt Beranek and Newman Inc., June 3, 1976.

34. Nickerson, R.S. Man-computer interaction: A challenge for human factors research. Ergonomics, 1969, 12, 501-517.

35. Nickerson, R.S. Some characteristics of conversations. Paper presented at NATO Advanced Study Institute Conference on Man-Computer Interaction, Mati, Greece, 5-18 Sept. 1976.

36. Ochsman, R.B. & Chapanis, A. The effects of 10 communication moves on the behavior of teams during cooperative problem-solving. International Journal of Man-Machine Studies, 1974, 6, 579-619.

37. Pew, R.W. & Rollins, A.M. Dialog specification procedures. BBN Report No. 3092, U.S. Dept. of Agriculture, August 1975.

38. Rubin, A.D. & Risley, J.F. The PROPHET system--An experiment in providing a computer resource to scientists. BBN paper to be submitted to MEDINFO, 1976.

39. Sackman, H. & Citrebaum, L. Online planning towards creative problem solving. Englewood Cliffs: Prentice Hall, 1972.

40. Smith, S.L. An on-line model of traffic control in a communication network. MITRE Report No. MTR-281B, March 1974.

41. Stewart, T.F.M. The specialist user. Paper presented at NATO Advanced Study Institute Conference on Man-Computer Interaction, Mati, Greece, 5-18 September 1976.

42. Teitelman, W., Hartley, A., Goodwin, J., Lewis, D., Bobrow, D., Jackson, P., & Masinter, L. Interlist reference manual. Xerox, Palo Alto Research Center, Palo Alto, Calif. 94304. 1974.

43. Treu, S. Interactive command language design based on required mental work. International Journal of Man-Machine Studies, 1975, 7, 135-149.

44. Turing, A.M. Computing machinery and intelligence. Mind, 1950, 59, 433-460.

Computers are learning
how to carry on a normal conversation
by capturing the richness of dialogue, gestures, and
glances. The interface between people and
computers will be much friendlier
as a result.

Conversing with Computers

BY RICHARD A. BOLT

WHEN I see an advertisement heralding a certain computer or program as "conversational," I just don't believe it. To me, conversation is speaking back and forth, pointing out this or that—a lively dialogue that involves glancing about and following the other person's glances as well as using gestures to describe, indicate, and emphasize. Whether the topic is trivial or weighty, conversation means a strong sense of another's presence in a setting we both share.

If you have used a computer at all lately, you know why I'm skeptical about claims that they are "conversational" in this rich sense. Yet I believe that such a relationship between people and computers will come about, and in fact I have been trying to help make it happen. For the past eight years I have been working in M.I.T.'s Architecture Machine Group laboratory, founded in 1968 on the basis of Nicholas Negroponte's optimism about the future of human-machine communication. My role is to combine a background in computers with insights from cognitive psychology to improve the interface where people and computers meet.

The rationale for making computers truly conversational is, to borrow a phrase from Professor Negroponte, to provide "supreme usability." This means making the computer as easy and as interesting to talk to as another person, for the novice or occasional user as well as the computer veteran. Despite vaunted claims of "user friendliness," even today's most advanced computer systems—in industry, homes, or the military—are too often excruciatingly difficult and frustrating to use. Of course, many research groups are actively following a variety of paths to make computers friendlier. But at the risk of seeming immodest, what sets our laboratory apart is the zest with which we are bringing many disciplines to bear on the problem.

Our goal is not simply a utilitarian one of enabling a manufacturer, for example, to produce so many more widgets per unit of time. Rather, we

*Somewhere along the way
we've lost the expectation that interacting
with computers can be as natural as
carrying on a conversation.*

want to enhance the quality of the human-computer interface in its own right. We are convinced that using a computer should be a pleasurable, even exhilarating, experience. Whatever else computers are, they should be fun.

This is in many ways a radical idea. Many people have long since adopted the notion that computers are for "getting the job done." They can be improved, certainly, but they will basically remain tools that you put up with for the sake of the task at hand. Somewhere along the way we've lost the expectation that interacting with computers can be as natural as ... carrying on a conversation. We've been forced, largely by commercial vendors, to be thankful for small advances toward user friendliness. But our group believes we shouldn't mistake microsteps for real progress. Our sights are set on the root meaning of "to converse": to *keep company with*. It is this conviviality that is now so egregiously absent from our experience with computers yet so vital to our sense of ourselves.

Put-That-There

Personal computers are now on the market that let you point at items on display, either by putting your finger on a touch-sensitive screen or by manipulating a "mouse," a small device on a cord that controls a cursor on the display screen. There are computers that let you speak to them, comparing your message with stored samples of your speech. Some such recognizers handle only discrete speech—that is, phrases spoken one word at a time. Others can handle normal speech in which words are strung together with no pauses in between.

But computers that let you use both gesture and speech are not yet offered by commercial vendors. The expressive power of speech and gesture combined clearly exceeds that of either alone—hence the importance of using both to communicate with computers. We have made a start toward this goal.

For example, several years ago I originated an exercise called "Put-That-There." The setting for Put-That-There is a special room that becomes a computer terminal you enter rather than sit at. Called the Media Room, it is about the size of a personal office: eight feet high, ten feet wide, and roughly thirteen feet long. The front wall is entirely display screen on which images can be created by a projector located behind the screen (*see page 39*).

The user sits at the center of the room wearing a microphone wired to an automatic speech recognizer. The recognizer is of the "connected-speech" type and has a vocabulary of 120 words. The user also wears a wristwatch band to which a small plastic cube is attached. This cube works in concert with a similar but larger cube mounted on a pedestal close to the chair. Both cubes generate magnetic fields when activated. From the relative position of the two magnetic fields, an associated computer calculates the position and orientation in space of the smaller cube, making it effectively a wrist-borne "pointer."

In Put-That-There, you create objects on the display screen simply by talking and pointing. You can name them, change their color and shape, move them about, and delete them. For example, you might say, "Create a large green circle . . . there"—while pointing with your raised arm at some spot on the screen. The system responds by putting up a large green circle at the spot you indicated. Next you might change the color of the circle by pointing at it and saying, "Make that red."

Instead of manipulating simple shapes on a plain background, you might manage color-coded ships against a map of the Caribbean. You can say, "Put a large blue tanker (pointing) there." Or "create a yellow freighter southeast of Haiti." Then you name the ship: "Call that (pointing to the freighter) the *Flying Cloud*."

The information you give by either hand movements or speech need not be perfect. Put-That-There requires only that gestures and speech, when considered together, converge upon what the user intended. Suppose you point to some spot on the map and issue the command, "Put the green freighter there"—but you mumble a bit on the phrase "green freighter," so the match with the prerecorded phrase is only marginal. A speech recognizer would ordinarily declare it a miss. Your pointing, too, is a bit wobbly, hitting the freighter but sweeping by some other ship's image as well. In other words, the data taken separately from either mode are ambiguous. Combined, though, the evidence gains strength. "Green freighter" is a plausible interpretation of what you intended to say, as you did in fact point toward the freighter, though you hit other items as well. The system, able to weigh the evidence from both modes, draws the reasonable conclusion that you probably did intend to move the green freighter. This ability to use pronouns and adverbs instead of names and descriptions—and to point at the objects—reduces the usual problems of automatic speech recognition. It's like being able to identify one clown out of a crowd of them, not by saying "the tall clown with the purple nose and the green jacket," but by pointing and exclaiming "him!"

Vendors of automatic speech recognizers typically claim that their products are at least 99 percent accurate. But such levels of accuracy are achieved only under optimal testing conditions, including low noise levels, trained speakers, and specially selected vocabularies. Performance under more realistic conditions may reach only about 65 percent. Obviously what matters is the *effective* level of communication—not the narrow issue of speech recognition but the broader and more fruitful one of speech interpretation.

The Put-That-There system takes the situation into account when interpreting speech. Suppose you say, "Create a blue freighter there," and the speech recognizer misses the command "create." On the basis of syntax alone, the missing word could be "create" or it could be "move." The system resolves that uncertainty by knowing whether a blue freighter already exists. If one doesn't, the system properly infers that the missed word must be a create command, not a move command, and so it puts a blue freighter at the indicated spot.

Chris Schmandt and Eric Hulteen, who programmed Put-That-There, did their utmost to avoid making the user repeat words unnecessarily. Suppose the user says, "Move *Flying Cloud* northwest of Haiti." If the word "northwest" is missed, the system simply asks, in its synthesized voice, "What direction?" It does not demand that the entire command be repeated. Computer visionary Alan Kay, in an interview in *Psychology Today*, characterized interacting with the Put-That-There system as being "like dealing with a friendly, slightly deaf butler. . . . From the standpoint of your expectations, you are willing to deal with it." Indeed, our aim is to make the user feel that despite inevitable lapses in word recognition, the system is doing its best to understand the user's intent. Achieving such user confidence is a big factor in any system's acceptance.

Telling Glances

Developmental psychologists tell us that one of the first things a child learns is to follow the mother's

A computer can determine a user's interests by tracking eye movement. In his classic studies, Alfred Yarbus asked people to examine repeatedly a painting (upper left). Before each trial, he gave the observer a question to answer afterward. Here, the observer's "looking patterns" differed markedly with each question. (From *Eye Movements and Vision*, Alfred Yarbus, 1967. Used with permission of Plenum Publishing Corp.)

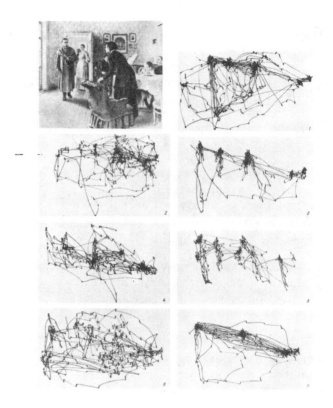

line of gaze as she speaks about things. For example, the child hears the sound "kitty" while following the mother's gaze to that lively, furry creature. Similarly, we can tell where someone's visual attention is directed by watching the eyes. By contrast, we cannot directly determine "where" a person is listening; people's ears don't angle about like a rabbit's do. But interestingly enough, psychologists have found evidence for a link between eye position and auditory attention: we tend to listen in the direction we are looking.

This conversational strategy of watching where the other person is looking—as a way of tapping into what that person is paying attention to—can help a computer. By monitoring which part of the display screen the user is looking at, the machine can better understand what the user is interested in and is trying to communicate.

In a complementary sense, the computer's graphic

I envision a "self-disclosing" computer system that need not tell you how to operate it or what services it can provide.

display externalizes what the computer is offering to talk about—putting it "out there," visibly, for the user to react to. This tends to focus the user's speech upon what is "on the table" for discussion, which in turn greatly simplifies speech recognition by putting implicit limits upon the range of vocabulary likely to be used. At the same time, the display provokes the user's looking, pointing, and speaking: "What's this? Where does that come from?"

In his influential book *The Nature of Managerial Work*, Henry Mintzberg of McGill University characterizes the managerial world of the modern executive as one of brevity, variety, and fragmentation. Executives spend little time on any one activity and must deal with a great number and variety of problems in the course of a day. They must be in up-to-the-minute touch with rapidly changing situations yet not succumb to "information overload." We can mimic electronically this salvo of events that confront executives—events demanding various degrees of attention and decision—to see how they might be better managed.

In the exercise called "Gaze-Orchestrated Dynamic Windows," we simulate the spirit of such a volatile situation in graphics on the Media Room's display screen. We do this by creating a composite of many television episodes—a collection of up to 40 moving images playing simultaneously. Some episodes appear just as others are ending. The stereo soundtracks of all the episodes are also piped in, creating a kind of "cocktail party" mélange of voices and sounds. We then exploit the selective visual attention of our hypothetical manager to orchestrate this complex, dynamic display—that is, we let the user's eyes help sort out what he or she wants.

The user sitting in the Media Room wears glasses that have a miniature eye-tracking system mounted in the frame. The device, developed by the Denver Research Institute, shines a tiny beam of infrared light onto the cornea and traces the reflection. This provides a constant measure of the position of the wearer's eye with respect to the glasses. We also mount on the frame a small location-sensing cube—the same kind worn on the wrist in Put-That-There—to detect the position of the frame within the room. The measurements of eye position in the glasses and frame position in the room combine to reveal where the user is looking on the display screen.

Whenever the system finds that the user is looking steadily at a particular image, it turns off the sound-tracks of all other episodes. If the user persists in looking at this episode for a few seconds or so, the system "zooms in" to fill the screen with that image. To recover the many deleted images, the user simply moves a joystick mounted on the arm of the chair. The net effect is to allow users to filter out all but the information of immediate interest, while enabling them to return at will to the more complex environment. We think this offers a way to exploit people's natural processes of selective visual attention to help them focus on the most relevant events in the midst of near-overwhelming complexity.

Computers as Good Hosts

Computers that know where on a display the user is looking and can capture speech and gesture suggest the possibility of "self-disclosing" systems: computers that tell about themselves. I don't mean simply that the computer would be "manual-free," although that would be a blessing unto itself. The reams of printed material that accompany some personal computers sometimes seem to weigh more—both physically and intellectually—than the hardware. Rather, I envision a self-disclosing system that need not tell you how to operate it at all or what services it can provide.

This computer would be instrumented to respond to your presence and normal behavior. It would have a full-color graphics display and eye-tracking capability for determining where on its display you are looking. You would be able to point at it and speak to it, and the computer would communicate back with synthesized or recorded speech as well as text on its display. It would disclose its contents—its information base—according to the interests you exhibit through your actions, and would do so at a speed that matches your own.

This system would interact with its user just as one person would interact with another. Suppose you breed guinea pigs and are showing someone the badges and ribbons your cavies have won, which are displayed in your trophy room. As a good host you try not to dominate things but remain alert to the cues your guest gives off: what is he looking at, what does he say, what message is his "body language" sending? Suppose the guest, surveying a wall full of ribbons, asks, "What are those?" You respond: "Those are the ones we won over the years at the Westfield Fair and Exposition." A certain trophy

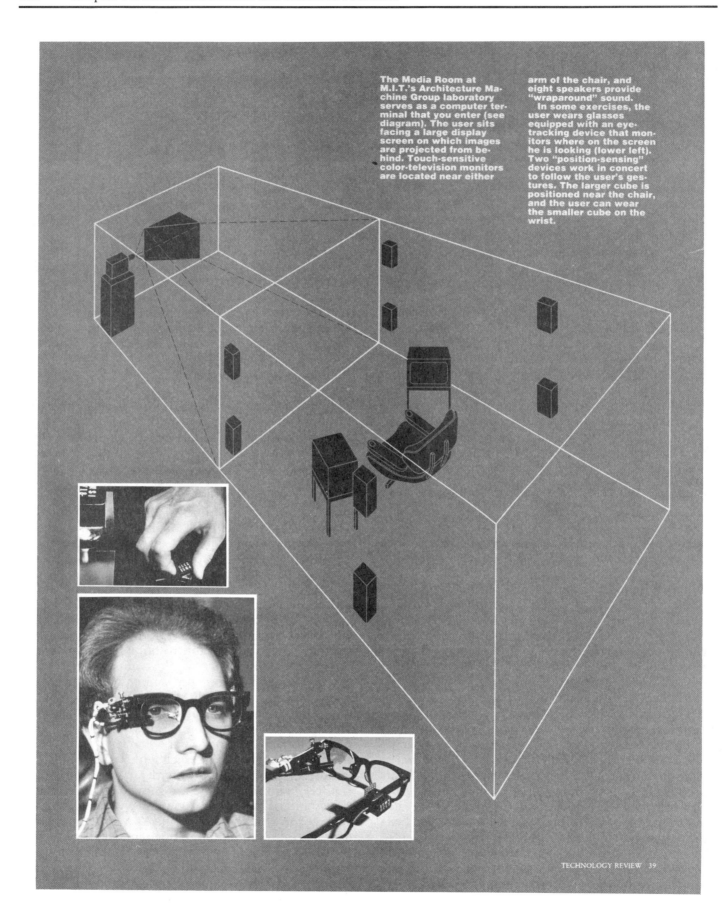

The Media Room at M.I.T.'s Architecture Machine Group laboratory serves as a computer terminal that you enter (see diagram). The user sits facing a large display screen on which images are projected from behind. Touch-sensitive color-television monitors are located near either arm of the chair, and eight speakers provide "wraparound" sound.

In some exercises, the user wears glasses equipped with an eye-tracking device that monitors where on the screen he is looking (lower left). Two "position-sensing" devices work in concert to follow the user's gestures. The larger cube is positioned near the chair, and the user can wear the smaller cube on the wrist.

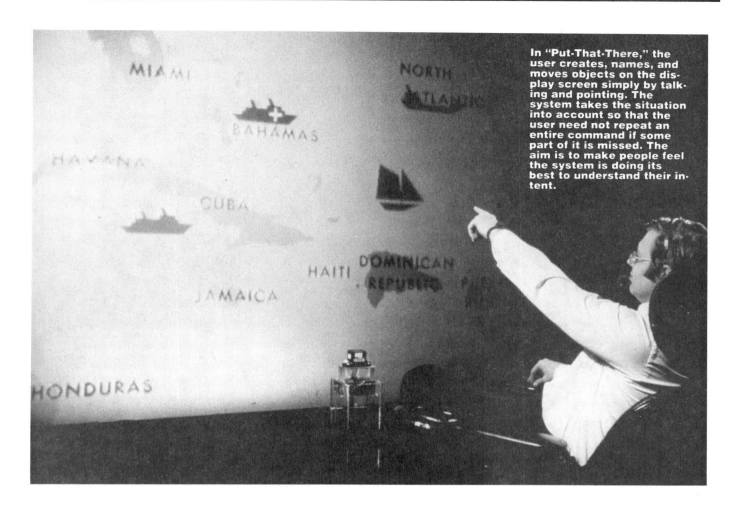

In "Put-That-There," the user creates, names, and moves objects on the display screen simply by talking and pointing. The system takes the situation into account so that the user need not repeat an entire command if some part of it is missed. The aim is to make people feel the system is doing its best to understand their intent.

catches your guest's eye. You take it from the shelf and offer it for closer inspection. Your guest reads the inscription and inspects the detail. Then his eyes turn elsewhere, a cue for you to relieve him of the trophy and go on to something else. Next your guest's eyes range over a set of distinctive badges. "What are those?" he asks—the very question he uttered a moment before. But it has become a *different* question, changed by the direction in which he is looking.

Consider now that our self-disclosing computer is showing such a collection of items. The computer's display sets the topic, just as did the real-life artifacts of the trophy room. The computer—like the human—can determine where its guest is looking, listen to his speech, detect his gestures. The system can then zoom in upon the item or area of interest to discuss it.

Such a computer can act very skillfully in deciding what and how much to tell about the subject at hand, again by taking its cues from the user's eyes. There is evidence that the eyes reveal the pattern of an observer's curiosity along very specific lines. In his classic eye-tracking studies in the Soviet Union during the 1960s, Alfred Yarbus asked people to examine a copy of the famous nineteenth-century painting by Ilya Repin entitled "They Did Not Expect Him." The scene is of a young man just returned from political exile to the midst of his startled family. Before looking at the picture for three minutes, each observer was asked one of a number of questions: What are the ages of the people? What are the material circumstances of the family? What was the family doing before the young man arrived? The observers' "looking patterns" differed markedly depending upon their goals as set by the question.

Of course, the computer must be able to tell the difference between a protracted stare stemming from the fact that the viewer is puzzled by something and blank staring stemming from saturation. But that is not likely to be difficult: researchers studying eye movements have found that eye patterns when interest is saturated differ from those when curiosity is live. Furthermore, pupil diameter varies with tension, interest, and suspense. These cues, coupled with what viewers say, can help a machine make reasonable inferences about when to move on. The machine can also gauge the effectiveness of its presentation by checking whether viewers look in the right places when it tells them about a display. If viewers fail to look at a relevant spot, the computer can reemphasize or recast its explanation.

In "Gaze-Orchestrated Dynamic Windows," a salvo of images and sounds mimics the type of rapidly changing environment that business executives must confront. The system exploits people's natural processes of selective visual attention to help them focus on the most relevant events in the midst of near-overwhelming complexity.

Give-and-Take

This kind of interchange between human and computer is a process of mutual self-disclosure. The computer is disclosing itself—or, more specifically, its contents—on the basis of the user's disclosing of himself or herself explicitly in speech and gesture and implicitly by eye movements. It is an ongoing two-way process.

What drives this conversation? What keeps it going and gives it direction? It is primarily the *curiosity* of the user as it interacts with the built-in *reactivity* of the system. For example, psychologists have shown that people are attracted to things that are visually rich and complex. People are also driven by so-called epistemic curiosity: we want to know the why and what of things. In its response to these "simple" levels of curiosity, the system obligingly tries to follow whatever leads its users give. The computer's "personality" is that of the convivial yet reserved person: it responds in a lively way but doesn't push itself on the user.

The system can readily sense the difference between a politely curious inquirer and a "serious" one—the difference, for example, between the tourist who strolls through Westminster Abbey taking it

all in and the scholar who studies it. Both might spend the same time looking, but their ways of observing provide a clue to how organized and comprehensive a guide's exposition must be—technical for the scholar, lucid but light for the tourist.

When a user has an even more compelling reason to communicate with the system, the computer can respond in kind. For instance, if you are a graduate student who must know all about colonial architecture in New England by final exams next Wednesday, you can instill motivation in the system by asking it, "Tell me about colonial architecture." Now the computer goes directly into a kind of superordinate "teaching" mode, in sharp contrast to its previously relaxed, reserved posture. The system may go slowly now and then to let you digest information when it senses that your rate of uptake has faltered. But it assumes more responsibility for shaping the exchange than in the more leisurely mode. All the while, whether the overall mode is relaxed or purposeful, the moment-to-moment conversational initiative drifts to and fro between human and computer, much as the "attack" passes back and forth between two fencers. Thus, the actions of the user and the system are mutually determined, either party by turn driving or being driven.

The hardest job will be fostering a view of the computer interface as a comfortable place where people and machines truly "keep company."

Users' sophistication—their style of looking and the questions they ask—can also help determine how the computer will respond. For instance, novices and expert chess players look at board positions differently. And of two people interested in antiques, one may have a "trained eye" for detecting the fine points of a collectible while the other examines the item in a less disciplined way. Such differences in looking style, though subtle, can enable a computer to infer what should be shown and said next.

Keeping Company

In person-to-person conversation, we speak not to some disembodied spirit but to someone right before us. One of the benefits of this direct presence is that we can look the person in the eye—for example, we can shift our gaze from an object under discussion to the eyes of the person with whom we're speaking. Beyond the sense of engagement this creates, eye contact can signal that we wish to shift the discourse to a personal level: to talk "to" the person rather than "with" them about external matters. Given that conversationality is a positive value in human-computer communications, how might we establish the ability to look the machine "in the eye"?

Patrick Purcell and some of his students at M.I.T. have been experimenting with a kind of computer "persona." Next to the Media Room's display screen is a video monitor that bears the face of a person—in this case, Professor Purcell himself. When you speak to the system—for example, to command it to display the art and architecture slides stored on its videodisc—this image speaks back to you. You ask: "I'd like to see some examples of Romanesque." The face on the monitor responds with synthesized speech, "Early or late?" The lips on the image are synchronized to the phonetics of the synthesized speech in a convincingly lifelike way.

This exercise was originally done somewhat tongue-in-cheek, with the modest goal of providing a more cordial, congenial channel for output messages than the line of print or the disembodied voice. The persona doesn't—yet—track the user's eyes and thus can't tell whether he or she is paying attention. With eye-tracking powers added, the persona could become a specific spot for the user to look at to establish "eye contact" with the machine.

Many of these technologies to support friendlier and richer human-computer interactions already ex-

ist, at varying levels of refinement. Devices that recognize and synthesize speech have improved markedly in recent years. Reliable touch-sensitive screens that enable users to point at data on display are on the market. Body-sensing equipment for capturing various levels of gesture is developing apace. For example, researchers in our laboratory are working on a glove that will allow the computer to discern a user's hand and finger movements. What has not existed is the appreciation of such technologies as essential parts of a computer's instrumentation.

Eye tracking offers a good example. Unobtrusive tracking systems that can be situated as much as six feet from the user have been available for several years. But they cost about $100,000, which prohibits them from serious consideration as system components. Part of the high cost is due to the proverbial chicken-and-egg dilemma. The systems are currently sold one at a time to research laboratories as measurement tools, not in large quantities to become part of well-equipped computer systems. Growing demand and high-volume production would help lower costs. But the fact that eye tracking can become a system component has not yet really struck home. There is a vague sense that tracking may be useful, but no real conviction.

This situation could change with new developments in digital cameras, microprocessors, and tracking technology. As tracking systems become more compact, they will become embedded in terminals as an integral part of new systems. In the long run, the price of a tabletop or personal computer will less and less reflect the memory and processing elements. Rather, it will reflect the costs of the electromechanical accoutrements that capture the user's intentions.

More difficult than developing the hardware for capturing multiple human modes of conversation, however, will be creating the machine intelligence to interpret human outputs and map appropriate responses. This effort will involve computer science, psychology, linguistics, artificial intelligence, and cognitive science—with scientists from all disciplines contributing to the necessary insights and inventions.

But hardest of all will be fostering a view of the computer interface as a comfortable place where people and machines truly "keep company." The world of computers outside the home—where the largest number of computer consumers still resides—contains two classes of users. There are those people who actually operate computers, and there are those who decide whether to adopt a particular kind of computer. The latter users are usually indifferent to the subjective experience of those who actually interact with machines.

Most organizations operate according to the ethos that those lower in the hierarchy should not be too comfortable, and that the tools provided for them should be "cost-effective." If one tool is a computer that is excruciating to use, so much the worse for the employee. Unless they are computer buffs, people higher up in an organization usually avoid computers and hence do not understand the feelings of frustration and lack of control they can engender.

The world of home computers is different. People who buy those machines are normally the users, and they put a high stake on their subjective experience at the interface. For them, the flavor of "keeping company" *is* the bottom line. Yet the loudly trumpeted home-computer revolution seems to have stalled. People perceive word-processing and spreadsheets as helpful and games as entertaining baby-sitters for the kids, and that's about all. Only when home computers provide a real help—and good company—will the true revolution begin. Then, inexorably, people in the workplace will come to expect and even demand the kind of conviviality they are accustomed to at home. That vision is seductive.

RICHARD A. BOLT is a principal research scientist in M.I.T.'s Media Laboratory, where he is acting head of its Human-Machine Interface Group. He is the author of The Human Interface, *(Lifetime Learning Publications, a subsidiary of Van Nostrand Reinhold, 1984).*

Ingredients of intelligent user interfaces

EDWINA L. RISSLAND

Department of Computer and Information Science, University of Massachusetts, Amherst, Massachusetts 01003, U.S.A.

In this paper, we discuss certain general features of intelligent user interfaces, such as the sources of knowledge needed by an interface to be considered intelligent, and characteristics desirable in an interface. We illustrate these ideas by examining two examples of interfacing between a user and a system: on-line HELP and tutoring. We conclude by briefly surveying some of the challenges to designers of interfaces.

1. Introduction: questions and issues

Interfaces between humans and machines have been around for a long time, one could say as long as there have been computational tools and users to use them. However, in the last few years, there has been an emerging realization that the interface can, and should, be viewed as more than a simple "membrane", such as a screen separating the user and his computing environment, and more than a simple "gateway", which includes physical aids (like mice) through which user input and tool output pass. The interface is not merely characterized by physical attributes but rather encompasses a larger context that includes aspects like the user's intentions. Schematically, this is the difference between indicating the scope of the interface as a box *around both user and machine* rather than as a line or a zone between them.

The interface provides not only access to tools but also an environment in which to use them. The goodness of the interface is often judged by the degree of support it offers the user and the "gracefulness" and "friendliness" of the interchange (Ball & Hayes, 1980). It seems we have far too many examples of bad interfaces [e.g. the "horror" stories in Hayes (1980) and Schneider & Thomas (1983)]. Thus it is no longer a question of whether the interface should offer support but rather a question of how and how much it should.

In fact, the pendulum has swung the other way from the simple, passive gateway model: we now tend to imbue the interface with great amounts of intelligence and power. Some want the interface to act as an intelligent agent or intermediary which, when it understands our goals can effect them, much as a lieutenant carries out the orders of higher officers; others would be happy to have the interface act in a more reasonable and forgiving manner, for instance by accepting more "natural" input (Walker, 1976), being tolerant to typos and other errors (Hayes, 1980; Norman, 1983), and presenting output in nicer formats like those of sophisticated graphics and windows. Regardless of how much intelligence, agency or support one wants in an interface, or exactly how one defines the scope of an interface, one must tackle certain questions.

Some such questions are the following.

(a) What makes an interface intelligent, friendly, efficient, etc. for the naive, occasional, expert user? What are desirable (and undesirable) characteristics of an interface?

(b) What sources of knowledge must an interface have access to in order to be what we want? In particular, what is the role of domain-, task-, tool-, user- and context-specific knowledge?

(c) How should the interface interact with an individual or a class of users? What is the role of user modelling?

(d) What styles and "modalities" of interaction should be in the kitbag of an interface? In particular, what are the role of graphics, natural language, video, audio—input and/or output?

(e) Should an interface take initiative or control? Where should the burden of control lie? Or rather, how should it be shared?

(f) How and how much should the interface adapt and learn? In response to what? To what ends?

(g) How should interfaces be evaluated? Can we say what qualities exemplify "good" taste or feel?

(h) Are there heuristics for good interface design? Can we move interface design further along the spectrum from art to science?

These are the sort of questions which one can ask. As yet, we really do not know complete answers. We probably do not even know how best to phrase some of the questions. Still, we must begin to attack these issues consciously.

This article is an attempt to underscore certain themes and issues in intelligent user interfaces (IUIs). It reflects concerns often expressed in other papers in this issue, all of which grew out of a recent NSF-sponsored workshop† under the direction of this author. In particular, this article focuses on the issue of the knowledge that an IUI possesses. The various types of knowledge we discuss can be seen in the IUIs discussed in the other articles of this issue, for instance, in Croft's article on his POISE system. Our list of knowledge sources is probably not exhaustive and it certainly is not exclusive. Our hope is that what we present here can be used as an initial check-list to inventory knowledge in an interface.

Our discussion here is not concerned with system performance in the tasks it is doing for the user. For instance, response time is vital for satisfying the user, but it is not here considered part of the IUI. Similarly, applications programs ought to interact intelligently with users; our concern is to provide the programs and the tools to make that possible. But there is no way for the IUI itself to insure that systems and applications programs do so.

2. Sources of knowledge to an interface

For an interface to be *intelligent*—that is, able to satisfy or address some of the desiderata implicit in the above questions—it must have access to many different sources of knowledge. In this section, we "bullet" some of these types of knowledge and give examples of what we include in each category.

† Supported by National Science Foundation under Grant No. IST-8212238.

(a) *Knowledge of the user*—his expertise, style, preferences, history. In teaching programming, a novice with one week of experience needs different support and "handling" from one with one semester: the one-week novice has no in-depth programming experience on which to draw. Such a difference in expertise has implications, for instance, as to how one provides explanations and system level support. With regards to cognitive or working "style", the one-week novice may not have a programming style at all, the one-semester novice may, and the one-week novice may attempt to transfer one from other domains, for better or worse.† An interface must meet different demands for different classes of users like new users, occasional users, computer professionals or users new to a tool (such as a text editor); user groups may differ in the professions they represent, such as lawyers or chemists. In addition, an individual user may have his own idiosyncrasies (e.g. use of a keypad rather than control characters in a text editor like EMACS (Stallman, 1984)).

(b) *Knowledge of the user's tasks*—context, purpose, ultimate use of the result. In a business environment, a secretary probably has different purposes and contexts from a manager. The secretary's purpose might be to satisfy management and the context might be the tasks completed since coming to work that day; the manager's goal might be to beat all competitors (inside or outside the company) and context might be a new market initiative. The secretary's goal might be to get a report prepared so as to look "pretty"; the manager's might be to prepare it ASAP. Another contrasting pair of tasks would be the preparation of a legal brief and of a proposal budget.

(c) *Knowledge of the tools* (*available and being used*)—protocols for invocation and use, default parameters, side-effects, resources needed, costs for usage. Different tools like text editors, spreadsheet programs and communication programs require different protocols and parameters, such as those concerning terminal characteristics and transmission rates. To match the user with an appropriate tool and then facilitate its usage, the IUI should take care of many details, especially those that are nitty-gritty and boring, certainly for users not interested in them (such as a secretary or manager as opposed to a systems hacker).

(d) *Knowledge of the domain* (*of the user's task*)—epistemological knowledge such as its structure and representation, measures of importance, conceptual hierarchies, domain-specific concepts. A lawyer using a legal retrieval tool such as LEXIS or WESTLAW (Sprowl, 1976) puts different burdens on the interface from an engineer using a mathematical tool such as MACSYMA. To intelligently help the lawyer to accomplish a task such as retrieving cases, the interface must know something about the body of the case law being searched, at the very minimum relevant keywords and classification schemes; and, better, the inherent structure of case law. For instance, to help the lawyer who has retrieved too few or too many cases to reformulate the query, the interface would need to know about such things as jurisdictional partitions of the case base (e.g. U.S. Supreme Court decisions, U.S. Circuit Court of Appeals, etc.) as well as syntactic details of queries. For the mathematician or engineer, the IUI should know about the content and representation of mathematical knowledge such as the specification of functions through formulae, graphs or tables.

(e) *Knowledge of interaction modalities*—graphics input and output display (including visual metaphors such as icons, and management of color, menus and windows), video, audio (including spoken input and synthesized output), language (natural, command, etc.), pointing devices (such as a mouse, touch sensitive areas). How the interface passes on and receives information for its use depends on the ways it can do so. An interface that can "talk" or "see" can accept and present information differently from one that cannot. For instance, an interactive Fourier transform program that accepts sketch input will not require the user to specify algebraically the function to be transformed.

(f) *Knowledge of how to interact*—when to intervene, look over the user's shoulder, adapt, enter and leave tutoring or coaching modes, how long to wait for user responses. There are many ways to interact. Along one dimension there are the extremes of giving constant feedback/monitoring and of not: for instance, whether to inform the user that a background job, such as printing a file, has been queued, that there will be a long wait or not, that the job is about to be done, etc. When the system is slow or flaky, a user might well like to be given some status information without actively seeking it; on the other hand, when there is no real concern about time or reliability, there may not be much point in that.

(g) *Evaluation knowledge*—how to judge effectiveness of the interaction, act on gripes. An interface ought to be able to know how it is doing: is it helping or hindering the user? Is it slowing or speeding task accomplishment? For instance, if the IUI is not presenting status reports and the user requests them, then perhaps the interface

† Although a novice has a lot of real-world experience, it could be detrimental to learning. For instance, using non-technical plans as programming plans can introduce bugs (Bonar, 1984).

Knowledge of user
Lawyer: occasional, non-expert user of LEXIS
Technical writer: EMACS and TEX hacker
Secretary: unsure novice, except for MAIL

Knowledge of user's tasks
Lawyer: research for appeals brief
Technical writer: prepare camera-ready copy for science magazine
Secretary: Fill-out purchase order, ASAP

Knowledge of tools
Lawyer: primary is LEXIS, others include WESTLAW
Technical writer: EMACS, TECO, TEX, RUNOFF, R
Secretary: POISE, SPELL, MAIL

Knowledge of domain
Lawyer: copyright law, Federal courts
Technical writer: medical (oncology) research, Chicago manual of style
Secretary: NSF and university regulations

Knowledge of modalities
Lawyer: IBM PC without graphics
Technical Writer: screen-based display
Secretary: mouse-sensitive, manipulatable icons

Knowledge of how to interact
Lawyer: OK to volunteer terse assistance
Technical writer: do not interrupt in EMACS, only notify of MAIL upon exit
Secretary: intervene immediately when error detected, verbose tutorial style is best

Knowledge of evaluation
Lawyer: no missed cases, citations in order
Technical Writer: no lost text, long error-free editing sessions
Secretary: few control-Ys, completion by end of day

FIG. 1. Sources of knowledges: some examples.

ought to take that as an indication that it could be more effective by doing the reporting automatically; on the other hand, if the user consistently aborts the presentation of such messages, perhaps they ought not to be sent.

To endow an interface fully in each of these areas of knowledge is probably to ask too much. But requiring some knowledge in each area and a lot in those particularly relevant to the particular IUI is probably a good goal. (Of course, determining relevance is another problem itself. One approach might be to empirically determine what types of knowledge match particular desiderata for IUIs based, for instance, on task or domain.) Figure 1 shows what might be included in the various sorts of knowledge.

3. Examples: on-line HELP and tutoring

In this section we briefly show how the above seven sources of knowledge enter into two types of interfaces geared to the non-expert user.

3.1. ON-LINE HELP

The design of an on-line HELP facility illustrates the many sources of knowledge needed by an interface if it is to offer support in the form of explanations to its users.

To "parse" the user's request for help, that is, determining what he needs help on (e.g. after he has invoked the HELP facility, with the use of a HELP key) requires several types of knowledge. The parsing is easy if the user knows what he wants to know about (not the usual case!). For instance, the user might not phrase his request in the facility's dialect (e.g. asking about "quit", when the command is called "exit"). Two of the most frequently used ways to handle such communication is with stylized keyword input or heirarchical menu arrangements of topics and subtopics, e.g. the VAX/VMS HELP system (DEC, 1978), less frequently used are natural language (e.g. Wilensky, 1982). Another is by analyzing what the user is doing and volunteering advice (Finin, 1983; Shrager & Finin, 1982). *To parse the user's request thus takes as a minimum knowledge of the thing to be explained and the medium of the interchange; that is, knowledge of the tool, interaction modalities and perhaps knowledge of the domain and the user.*

To build a response to the user's request, the help facility must access knowledge needed to explain the request. At the very least, this involves knowledge of the feature being explained and how to present the response to the user. To make the response intelligent in the sense of custom-tailoring, the help facility needs at least to have knowledge of the user and his tasks. *Thus, to compose its response, the HELP facility needs domain-, task- and user-knowledge.*

One approach to custom-tailoring on-line HELP is to embed in the explanations examples which are customized to the user, in addition to using "canned" examples harvested from an expert's knowledge of the subject to be explained. Examples can be customized through modifications to already existing examples. *Such an enhancement to HELP, of course, requires a good base of domain- and user-knowledge, as well as recent history of user–system interaction.*

To deliver the response to the user, the help facility needs again to know about its interaction modalities, at the very least about what constitutes a unit (e.g. screenful) of response and how to handle multiple units. The delivery of information might well be handled by an intermediary graphics or natural language generation module. More importantly, the HELP facility needs to know how to present and interact with the

user; for instance, when to present explanations in a command-scrolling mode (e.g. in which the user is queried at appropriate intervals whether he wants "More", an "Example", another "Topic" or to "Quit" at appropriate intervals) or in a tutorial mode (in which the material is presented in a tutorial interchange). *Thus, to deliver the response, the HELP facility needs to have knowledge of modalities, the user and how to interact.*

My research group is currently building a HELP facility which makes strong use of examples (Rissland, Valcarce & Ashley, 1984). It builds upon our past work on example generation (Rissland, 1980, 1981; Rissland & Soloway, 1980) and the structure of knowledge in complex domains such as mathematics and law (Rissland, 1983, 1984b). Basically the HELP cycle is to present a unit of information to the user (e.g. a graphics demo, a screenful of text or examples) and to ask the user if he wants more, an illustrative example, etc.

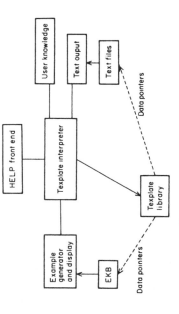

Fig. 2. Modules in on-line HELP.

The HELP facility we are building, shown schematically in Fig. 2, uses the following modules and sources of knowledge.

(a) *HELP front end* which parses the user's request by using keywords, command names, actual key strokes, and a synonym dictionary and presents HELP's response.

(b) *Texplate-interpreter* which controls what the user sees next and assembles the text and examples to be presented.

(c) *User-profile knowledge* including rough measures of expertise and details about how many and which examples have been presented in the current invocation of HELP.

(d) *"Texplate"-library* which is a collection of scripts indexed by the feature to be helped with and represented as a text and example template.

(e) *Textfiles* containing chunks of text used in composing HELP responses.†

(f) *Examples knowledge base (EKB)* of pre-existing examples and ways to modify them.

(g) *Example generator* which oversees the generation of examples through instantiation and modification to meet constraints arising from the user's profile.

---

† There is deliberate sharing of text and examples between HELP, an on-line introductory tutorial, and the on-line manual (Rissland, 1984a).

Our system is being built to handle two sets of tools: (1) those for rank beginners using an environment called "Interactive Ladybug" which integrates Pascal type programming constructs with LOGO-like control of a graphic object (the "ladybug") (Levine & Woolf, 1984); and (2) a subset of the VAX/VMS command language (DEC, 1978), specifically dealing with directory commands such as DIR, PURGE, and SET PROTECTION.

3.2. TUTORING

To be effective, tutoring requires that the tutor have knowledge not only about the subject but also about the tutee and how to interact with him. For a student trying to learn a body of material such as geography, knowledge of the user's task is not a major factor (other than that the task is implicitly taken to be the gaining of increased understanding). Knowledge of tools is also secondary unless the tutorial interchange is directed towards tool usage, in which case it is really domain knowledge for the tutor. If such a tutor were embedded in an IUI with the purpose of helping a user doing tasks other than learning a body of knowledge, it would need access to such tool and task-knowledge as well.

The recently-built tutoring system MENO (Woolf, 1984) provides an excellent example of the many sources of knowledge needed for tutoring (and of course, interfacing) with a user in a cycle of "talking, listening, reacting and thinking". MENO works in an interleaved manner with a surface language generator, MUMBLE (McDonald, 1982). It is envisioned that these two componets would be embedded in a larger tutoring environment which would contain at least two other components: a language understander for tutee input and a critic, such as that of Bonar (1984) or Soloway (Johnson & Soloway, 1984), to find student misconceptions and evaluate performance.

The tutoring component involves tutoring-specific knowledge and makes decisions about *what* to say and *how* to say it. The surface language generator takes specifications from the tutoring component and realizes them into syntactically correct text. The specifications are built from pedagogical approaches (e.g. "tutor" or "hack" a misconception) and which have been embedded into domain-specific but non-linguistic elements. Figure 3 shows a schematic of the processes in such a tutoring system environment.

The tutoring component can be best described as a set of decision-makers which execute successive refinements on a "virtual utterance". At the highest level of refinement, the pedagogic level, a restriction is made about the overall approach for the discourse. At the second level of refinement, the strategic level, the pedagogy is focused into an expository strategy. At the final level of refinement, the tactical level, a determination is made about how to implement the strategy. These decisions are encoded into states built into the system and traversed by an iterative function which follows a chain from state to state. The procedure is highly parameterized and its effect is accentuated by meta-rules which can cause jumps other than the default transitions.

The MENO tutoring component thus has a vast store of *domain- and user-specific knowledge as well as knowledge of how to interact (tutor)*. When the complete tutoring environment is considered, there is the additional knowledge of interaction modalities (in this case, natural language). Woolf has not addressed the evaluation knowledge to judge the equality of the interaction from an IUI point-of-view; rather, her critic module makes evaluations of the correctness of the user's knowledge and is thus another source of domain-specific knowledge.

4. Some desiderata for intelligent interfaces

There are obviously many things required of an interface; different users will have different needs, depending on the tasks they have, the tools available, their training and expertise, and even their tastes. In this section, our purpose is to continue the discussions of others like Hayes who suggests the desireability of "flexible parsing, robust communication, focus tracking, natural output, an explanation facility, and personalization" (Hayes, 1980), Norman, who on the basis of analyzing human errors, suggests having "mode-less" interaction or distinctively marked modes, functionally organized menus, making operations with serious and irreversible consequences difficult to accomplish, etc. (Norman, 1983), and McCracken & Akscyn who suggest "direct manipulation of data, semi-automatic operation, low learning overhead and a safe, exploratory environment" (see their article in this issue).

We divide the desiderata into several categories: (1) services; (2) style; and (3) understandability.

IUIs should provide certain *services* to its users, such as:

(a) carry out menial tasks (e.g. set terminal characteristics);
(b) automate routine tasks (e.g. doing back up of active files, often);
(c) provide assistance with more complex tasks (e.g. file transfer protocols);
(d) provide easy access to tools (e.g. DBMS packages);
(e) provide status information (e.g. on the progress of tasks like file formatting);
(f) provide on-line assistance and documentation (e.g. HELP and manuals);
(g) allow multi-tasking.

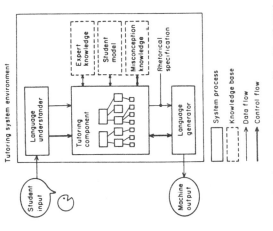

FIG. 3. Tutoring system environment (from Woolf, 1984).

IUIs should provide these services in a *style* that:

(a) is helpful and forgiving (e.g. "infinite" UNDO/REDO capabilities);
(b) encourages experimentation (e.g. in a safe "mock-up" or hypothetical session);
(c) minimizes errors (e.g. failsafe questioning on undo-able actions like DEL *.*);
(d) allows user to manipulate objects and tasks directly (e.g. halt the printing of a long file if there is a mistake on the first page);
(e) allows him to see directly the results of his actions (e.g. "WYSIWYG");
(f) doesn't get in the way;
(g) is under the user's control;
(h) "idiosyncratic", that is, adapts to the user's style, preferably without his having to give explicit directions, when possible;
(i) unambiguous and consistent (e.g. or rather counter-example, the use of control-C, Y, and Z in many systems);
(j) has a repertoire of good presentation services (e.g. window systems).

IUIs should be *understandable*, that is:

(a) learnable through conceptual models and not just by rote;
(b) aid the transition from novice to expert (e.g. by selectively disclosing more of its internal workings, enabling control to become direct);
(c) allow the user to "macro-ize" and customize tasks (e.g. user-defined composite functions).

Many of these desiderata are not independent. For instance, one can argue that if a system is consistent, it will then tend to be learnable and understandable. One can argue that consistency and selective self-disclosure of its model will make the IUI easier to learn than one which is "simple" but inconsistent. Also, adaptiveness, which is sometimes called "responsiveness", is probably more important than "speed" for the IUI to exhibit "good" feel for the user. One should not confuse being "invisible" with being "non-obtrusive"; the latter seems to be much more important and contributes to the IUI not getting in the way.

5. Some (nagging) problems and issues

In this section, we present some themes which permeate discussions on interfaces. Understanding such issues is critical to progress; even though they are typically not "solvable" in the sense of having one "right" answer.

5.1. OMNISCIENCE

It is easy to think of interfaces at the extrema of the intelligence spectrum: totally "dumb" or "super-human". The "problem of omniscience" refers to pushing the interface ever further towards the high end of the spectrum; for instance, by shifting to it more and more of the knowledge of the tools and users for which it is intermediary.

Yes, the interface must have access to many sources of knowledge, some of which we outlined above, but it is not useful to load all the problems of intelligence into the interface, as if the interface contained a "hidden homunculus" (Dennett, 1978; McDermott, 1976). Where the critical boundary is for off-loading too little or too much intelligence onto the interface is not settled: in fact, it probably changes in response to many factors (user, goals, tasks, knowledge domain, etc.).

5.2. CONTROL: SHARING THE BURDENS

In many ways, control *is* the issue. What complicates this aspect of IUIs is that there is not one answer here any more than for the other issues. Sharing the burden of control is a matter of more or less.

One factor control depends on is the user. For instance, a novice user does not need, and probably does not want, to have control of setting up his own resource management; the hacker does. There is an analogy here with driving a car: many automobile operators do not ordinarily care about the oil temperature of the engine (as opposed to a racecar driver); but when things go wrong, they do care.

A rule of thumb concerning what should be controllable might be, "if you use it, you should be able to control it" which could be interpreted to mean "if you do not use it (and it is important), then maybe the interface ought to take responsibility for it". Hence shared burdens. What is being taken care of by the interface or explicitly by the user changes depending on factors such as change in the environment and change in the user. However, the locus of control *is* the interface.

5.3. CHANGE: ADAPTATION AND LEARNING

Everyone expects the "ideal" interface to change over time, specifically, to get "better". But how to do this?

It will not happen by magic: adaptation and learning are not alchemy. They require care and thought about sources of knowledge and adaptive and learning mechanisms. Again, the effecting of change can be shared between the user and the interface.

Many kinds of learning are possible in an interface, just as in AI learning systems (Carbonell, Michalski & Mitchell, 1983). Some learning can happen by the interface *being told* by the user. For instance, declaring certain personal abbreviations or macros. Even this simplest kind of learning can have vast effects on the felicity of the interface for a user. There is nothing wrong in telling someone what you want, when you know what that is and it's easy for you. For instance, setting up a "demon" to notify you whenever you receive a mail message from your boss is easy and is probably a good thing. An interface should also be able to learn by *being shown*. In some interfaces, what the user does is kept (in a buffer) and if the user says "remember what I just did", the interface can. The MXEC interface of Selfridge and Ash (Ash, 1981) is capable of these two kinds of learning.

Some learning is appropriate for adaptive mechanisms such as fine-tuning of parameters; some is appropriate for symbolic, "AI", learning. However, to give the interface a capacity to change is only part of the problem. Equally important is what sort of changes and to what ends. Each of the sources of knowledge provides an arena for change. While we do have some wish lists for learning ("it ought to learn my preferences...", "it ought to learn new tasks...", "it ought to adapt to system parameters...") progress has not gone very far, yet. Nevertheless, to be intelligent the interface must be capable of change and without giving it the capacity to change we are dooming it to be less useful than it might be and in fact, probably brittle, pre-obsolescent, and over-narrow.

5.4. EVALUATION

Many of the discussions about interfaces are similar to those about what is art, or what is *good* art. That is, a central issue is how to judge an interface and how to determine what makes one interface better than another. In answer to the question, "Would you use it again?", why do some interfaces merit a "yes" and others a "no".

Again there are no definitive answers, although there are methodologies to address the more objective evaluative criteria such as time for task accomplishment and rates of user errors; two evaluation methodologies are "keystroke-level model" analysis (Card, Moran & Newell, 1980), and use of "benchmark" tasks [e.g. for the evaluation of text editors (Roberts & Moran, 1983)]. For more subjective criteria like "gracefulness" or "clumsiness", evaluation measures are less well-defined but no less important. As Norman has argued, one could develop measures based on desiderata such as those given above, and hopefully this would contribute to a science of interface engineering. The evaluation issue is very complex since one has to ask evaluative questions from different points of view, especially with respect to different types of users, tasks, domains, etc. However, without good evaluation techniques, judgement of IUIs is nearly impossible.

6. Conclusions

In this article, we have discussed issues involved in intelligent user interfaces and have posed some questions and desiderata which we hope will be useful to designers and which can serve as foci for future discussions. In particular, we have listed seven sources of knowledge for an IUI:

1. knowledge of the user;
2. knowledge of user tasks;
3. knowledge of tools;
4. domain-specific knowledge;
5. knowledge of interaction modalities;
6. knowledge of how to interact; and
7. evaluation knowledge.

We have concluded with discussion of four difficult and important problems: (1) omniscience; (2) control; (3) change; and (4) evaluation.

This paper is based upon work supported by the National Science Foundation under Grant No. IST-8304023.

References

ASH, W. L. (1981). MXEC: Parallel processing with an advanced macro facility. *Communications of the ACM*, 24(8), 502-509.

BALL, E. & HAYES, P. (1980). Representation of task-specific knowledge in a gracefully interacting user interface. In *Proceedings AAAI-80*, Stanford University, August.

BONAR, J. (1984). Understanding plans of novice programmers. *Ph.D. Dissertation*, Department of Computer and Information Science, University of Massachusetts, Amherst.

CARBONELL, J. G., MICHALSKI, R. S. & MITCHELL, T. M. (1983). Machine learning: a historical and methodological analysis. *The AI Magazine*, IV(3), 69-80.

CARD, S. K., MORAN, T. P. & NEWELL, A. (1980). The keystroke-level model for user performance time with interactive systems. *Communications of the ACM*, 23(7), 346-410.

DEC (1978). *VAX/VMS Command Language User's Guide*. Digital Equipment Corporation. Order No. AA-D023B-TE, Massachusetts.

DENNETT, D. C. (1978). *Brainstorms*. Vermont, Virginia: Bradford Books.

FININ, T. W. (1983). Providing help and advice in task oriented systems. In *Proceedings IJCAI-83*, Karlsruhe, West Germany.

HAYES, P. (1980). Computers with natural communication skills. In *Computer Science Research Review 1979-1980*, Carnegie-Mellon University, Pittsburgh, Pennsylvania.

JOHNSON, L. & SOLOWAY, E. M. (1984). PROUST: knowledge-based program debugging. In *Proceedings Eighth International Software Engineering Conference*, Orlando, Florida.

LEVINE, L. & WOOLF, B. (1984). Do I press return? In *Proceedings ACM-SIGCSE Symposium on Computer Science and Education*, Philadelphia, February.

MCDERMOTT, D. (1976). Artificial intelligence meets natural stupidity. *SIGART Newsletter 57*, 4-9.

MCDONALD, D. D. (1982). Natural language generation as a computational problem: an introduction. In BRADY, Ed., *Computational Theories of Discourse*. Cambridge, Massachusetts: M.I.T. Press.

NORMAN, D. L. (1983). Design rules based on analyses of human error. *Communications of the ACM*, 26(4), 245-258.

ISSLAND, E. L. (1981). *Constrained Example Generation*. Department of Computer and Information Science, University of Massachusetts, Amherst, (COINS TR 81-24).

RISSLAND, E. L. (1983). Examples in legal reasoning: legal hypotheticals. In *Proceedings IJCAI-83*, Karlsruhe, West Germany, August.

RISSLAND, E. L. (1984a). Steps along the on-line assistance spectrum. Proceedings Sixth Annual Conference of the Cognitive Science Society, Boulder, Colorado, June.

RISSLAND, E. L. (1984b). The structure of knowledge in complex domains. In CHIPMAN, S., SEGAL, J. & GLASER, R., Eds, *Thinking and Learning Skills: Research and Open Questions*. New York: Lawrence Erlbaum, New Jersey.

RISSLAND, E. L. & SOLOWAY, E. M. (1980). Overview of an example generation system. *Proceedings AAAI-80*, Stanford University, August.

RISSLAND, E. L., VOLCARCE, E. M. & ASHLEY, K. D. (1984). Explaining and Arguing with Examples *Proceedings AAAI-84*, University of Texas, Austin, August.

ROBERTS, T. L. & MORAN, T. P. (1983). The evaluation of text editors: methodology and empirical results. *Communications of the ACM*, 26(4), 265-283.

SCHNEIDER, M. & THOMAS, J. C. (1983). INTRODUCTION: the humanization of computer interfaces. *Communications of the ACM*, 26(4), pp. 252-253.

SHRAGER, J. & FININ, T. W. (1982). An expert system that volunteers advice. In *Proceedings AAAI-82*, Pittsburgh, Pennsylvania.

SPROWL, J. A. (1976). *A Manual for Computer-Assisted Legal Research*. Chicago: American Bar Foundation.

STALLMAN, R. M. (1984). EMACS: the extensible, customizable, self-documenting display editor. In BARSTOW, D., SHROBE, H. & SANDEWALL, E., Eds. *Interactive Programming Environments*. New York: McGraw-Hill. (Also available as M.I.T. AI Lab. Memo 519a, 1981.)

WALKER, D. E, Ed. (1976). *Speech Understanding Research: Final Report*. Stanford Research Institute, Menlo Park, California.

WILENSKY, R. (1982). Talking to UNIX in English: an overview of UC. In *Proceedings AAAI-82*, Pittsburgh, Pennsylvania, August.

WOOLF, B. P. (1984). Context sensitive text planning in tutorial discourse generation. *Ph.D. Dissertation*, Department of Computer and Information Science, University of Massachusetts, Amherst.

Making Computers Accessible to Disabled People

BY FRANK BOWE

IN Fairfax, Va., Rick Pilgrim, who has a spinal-cord injury that prevents him from moving even his head, works as a systems analyst for the National Institutes of Health. Thirty miles away, Kevin Riley, who has a similar injury, works as a programmer for IBM. Telecommuting—using a modem-equipped personal computer in the home to receive, process, and send information back to the workplace—promises to allow severely disabled individuals to work at demanding jobs. These same technologies can permit severely disabled children to "go to school" without leaving their homes. Speech synthesizers that read print and instantly transform it to speech now give people who are blind or have dyslexia access to worlds of information previously unavailable.

However, a major problem remains before computer technology can fulfill its promise of allowing people to overcome the limitations of severe physical handicaps and learning disabilities. The technology must be designed to be fully accessible to—that is, easily usable by—people who are handicapped. Today computers are not set up to accommodate the input and output devices that many disabled people require. This means that special keyboards and other aids often require custom solutions for use with each computer, making the devices expensive and limiting their availability. If options for different users were incorporated into the design of all computers, the lives of millions of disabled individuals could be greatly enhanced.

The concept of accessibility is most familiar in the design of buildings. We see accessible architecture in the form of automatic doors and entrances level with exterior landscaping in airports, at hotels, on college campuses, and in libraries. These designs seem natural to us: they do not look as though they were created specifically for individuals who are handicapped. Most people do recognize ramps and lifts, lowered public telephones and drinking fountains, Brailled elevator buttons, and bathroom grab bars as designs with a special purpose. But whether striking or unobtrusive, architectural accessibility has opened up hundreds of thousands of buildings to use by people with disabilities.

What is startling is how recent all these changes are. Congress did not enforce a requirement that federal buildings be accessible until it passed the Re-

habilitation Act of 1973, and the government did not extend the requirement to structures erected with federal grant monies until 1977. Each step was actively opposed by many architects who believed that the requirements would detract from the aesthetics of their designs, by builders who feared higher construction costs, and by universities and other institutions that insisted they could not afford to retrofit their buildings. Indeed, the American Council on Education fought the act for almost a year. Said University of Missouri vice-president A.G. Unklesbay in disgust: "This law requires us to spend untold millions to prepare facilities that almost certainly will never be used." But despite such opposition, the concept of accessibility has now become an accepted tenet of architecture.

Quiet persuasion, militant protest, and litigation by people who are disabled, as well as an altruistic desire to assist handicapped individuals on the part of others, have helped architectural accessibility gain acceptance fairly quickly. Yet progress would undoubtedly have been much slower had not the concept proven valuable to people who are not handicapped. For each wheelchair user who traverses a ramp, ten other people without disabilities also take advantage of it: parents with baby carriages, bicycle riders, furniture movers, and pedestrians who simply find it easier to walk up a ramp than to climb stairs. In fact, easier access to buildings is so convenient for everyone that architects and engineers have a hard time explaining why they did not always build this way.

Even the issue of costs has sometimes worked to the advantage of those who have complied with the new laws. When university enrollments began to sag in the early 1980s as the "baby bust" generation came of college age, college chancellors discovered with delight that the changes they had made so reluctantly turned out to be critical in attracting the large, previously untapped population of disabled students. Today the American Council on Education estimates that 7.4 percent of the nation's 1.6 million college freshmen are disabled, up from 2.6 percent

FRANK BOWE, formerly executive director of the American Coalition of Citizens with Disabilities, is the author of Personal Computers and Special Needs *(Sybex Computer Books, 1984) and* Changing the Rules *(TJ Publishers, 1987). Dr. Bowe, who is deaf, writes frequently about technology and social issues.*

in 1976. One-half million handicapped students now attend colleges and universities as a direct result of the enhanced accessibility of buildings and facilities.

Efforts to make information technologies more usable by and affordable to people who are disabled would have a similar effect. Such efforts would not only allow a major segment of our society to communicate more easily and participate fully in productive work but would also benefit all other users as well.

Disability Is Universal

Disability is something that happens to people in the normal course of their lives. On one level, we all know that: our grandparents lose vision, hearing, and manual dexterity as they age. Yet exposure to telethons that focus on handicapped children leads people to believe that disability is most often something "those people are born with." This is a myth we must explode: five of every six disabled individuals become impaired during their working or retirement years. In other words, anyone can become disabled at any time, and most of us become temporarily disabled at some point during our lives.

In the United States, about 36 million of some 240 million people have disabilities. About half of Americans 75 and over are handicapped, usually with vision and hearing impairments. Almost three in ten Americans aged 65 to 74 are disabled. One-tenth of the school-age population—4 million children—is disabled. And about 13 million persons of working age (16 to 64) are handicapped, or one in eight.

Because ramps and lifts have become so prevalent, people often assume that physical disabilities are the most common. Yet only about 500,000 Americans use wheelchairs. In contrast, some 8 million Americans of all ages have learning disabilities, including dyslexia, an impairment that interferes with reading the printed word. Dyslexia is undiagnosed in many adults and is a major factor contributing to illiteracy.

A total of 6.5 million Americans do have restricted mobility in their upper and/or lower limbs, often caused by arthritis. Another 3.5 million individuals have disorders of the central nervous system, including cerebral palsy, muscular dystrophy, multiple sclerosis, paraplegia, and quadriplegia. Some 6 million people are seriously hearing-impaired, including 2 million who are deaf. About 5 million Americans are retarded, and some 2 million are severely mentally ill, usually from schizophrenia or psychosis. Just under 1.7 million people have poor vision or are legally blind. And about 1 million have epileptic conditions that cause periodic seizures.

The most common handicaps among children and youth are learning disabilities and mental retardation; impaired mobility affects just 150,000 school-age children. Many children have speech disorders owing to hearing loss, cerebral palsy, or other conditions, but deafness and blindness are relatively rare until people reach advanced age.

Another popular assumption about disabled individuals is that the government "takes care of those people." However, only 2 million handicapped Americans of all ages live in institutions. Like many other attitudes toward disability, this one has its roots in truth: institutionalization was a common response to disability until the late 1970s. Indeed, the United States historically preferred to keep disabled individuals out of sight: the 13 colonies forbade them to immigrate unless relatives or others agreed to assume full responsibility for their care. Later, large hospitals for disabled people were erected, mostly in rural areas far removed from central communities.

The idea of deinstitutionalization gained momentum as disabled individuals demanded to become part of mainstream society and the costs of institutional care soared (they now average more than $85,000 per year). Today the vast majority of disabled people lives in the community. More than half resides in private homes or apartments with spouses, another 25 percent lives with other family members, and one in twelve lives alone. Only about 5 percent of disabled individuals lives in hospitals, nursing homes, or other institutional settings.

The Retrofit Solution

The architects who built America's cities were not concerned about making them accessible, since disabled people would not be living in and using the facilities. Similarly, there was no apparent reason for engineers to extend the concept of accessibility to sophisticated machinery in the mid-1970s, when high technology remained the preserve of the few. So in technology we have repeated the pattern we followed in architecture: we have designed for people with full possession of their faculties, only to discover later that we had inadvertently excluded large numbers of disabled individuals.

When Congress first passed the Rehabilitation Act, computers were still obscure and frightening machines for most Americans. These room-sized contraptions were kept in locked areas, attended by professional programmers, and intolerant of even slight errors on data-entry cards. The Apple II personal computer appeared just about the time handicapped activists stormed the U.S. Department of Health, Education, and Welfare in April of 1977 to demand enforcement of the act passed four years earlier. Yet not until 1980 and 1981, when the Apple IIe and the IBM PC were introduced, did the idea that the computer could become a commodity for the masses take hold. Dramatically lowered costs were largely the reason for the change, but so, too, was the blossoming idea of "user friendliness": that computer hardware and software could be designed specifically for non-programmers.

People with disabilities were quick to grasp the potential of the personal computer to help them surmount the obstacles of everyday life. In Fort Wayne, Ind., after a motorcycle accident left him blind, Bill Grimm wrote special software that linked an Apple IIe to a small speech synthesizer that read aloud the text on his computer screen. In Shreve, Ohio, Barry Romich built extra-large keyboards so friends with cerebral palsy could use IBM PCs to write. And in Rockville, Md., John Yeh wrote machine code allowing him to use the telephone despite his deafness.

These were all retrofit solutions, or "patches" in computer jargon—analogous to placing wooden ramps beside stairs. Custom-designed alterations were expensive, and the number of people who could afford the technologies was limited.

Some computer technologies designed to help people who are disabled have since become more affordable and therefore come into more common use. For example, speech synthesizers, some now selling for as little as $100, can convert many kinds of text to artificial speech. Personal computers can also be equipped with software that translates from English to Braille for printing. But even these advances have their limitations. Most popular word-processing and business software uses the PC operating system in a way that prevents a speech synthesizer from capturing the output. Thus, many blind and dyslexic individuals are restricted to software designed specifically to be used with a speech synthesizer, reducing the choice from tens of thousands of programs to a few dozen. Moreover, most synthesizers cannot read pictorial symbols (or icons) and graphics.

People with conditions that limit finger mobility, such as cerebral palsy, quadriplegia, and severe arthritis, can use a light pen, joystick, or large keyboard to give the computer commands. Again, however, such keyboard substitutes work with very few commercial programs. Moreover, to make the computer think that input is coming from the standard keyboard, an "emulator" must be attached between the keyboard and the operating system. The emulator has to be custom-designed for each of the many PC models, including those produced by the same company, because there is no standard configuration now in use. The situation is similar to that of a remote-control device for a TV. Viewers can change channels by touching keys or using the remote control; an emulator in the TV allows it to respond to both kinds of input. Yet the remote-control unit cannot be used with a set of a different model. The retrofit solution helps, but it doesn't help enough.

Furthermore, because computers are not now designed to accommodate special needs, adaptations such as those allowing someone with cerebral palsy to use a PC can cost as much as $20,000. That cost could drop significantly if the problems of fitting different components together did not require custom solutions.

In some cases, educators have created problems by needlessly designing software to teach some disabled children at the expense of others. Some of this software is excellent, and most is readily affordable by schools. For example, talking software teaches blind children to count, and touchpads enable children with cerebral palsy to answer questions posed on the screen. But these one-dimensional changes create barriers for other disabled students: deaf children cannot hear the talking programs. The new aids also sometimes help keep handicapped children segregated from other children. That effect runs counter to the mandate of federal law, which requires schools to integrate disabled children into regular classrooms whenever possible.

Some problems with inaccessible technology occur because decision makers don't understand the consequences of their decisions. When Drexel University in Philadelphia required all its freshmen to purchase Macintosh computers, the school apparently did not realize it was sending the message that "no blind person need apply here"—a move of questionable legality. The original Macintosh required the use of icons, which voice synthesizers cannot read. The Macintosh also used a mouse input device, which blind people cannot point effectively. Had the university chosen another machine without those restrictions, such as the IBM PC or a compatible, these problems would not have arisen. Apple has redesigned the Mac to permit keyboard entry of commands previously available only by mouse, and is doing research on the problem of enabling voice synthesizers to read icons. But such products are not yet on the market, and Drexel's action erected barriers to the disabled that need never have existed.

Designing for Access

How does one design hardware and software to be more easily usable by people with disabilities? The key concept is "transparency"—designing the parts of the PC to work together smoothly without the need for artificial aids. For example, the operating system of a transparent PC might not need an emulator because it would not distinguish between input from a keyboard and that from a joystick or other device. Users could therefore adopt whatever format for the machine that most suited their needs. Nor would the PC and its software "know" that the output was going to a voice synthesizer instead of a screen. This capacity would allow people needing a synthesizer to choose any software on the market.

The second critical idea is "redundancy": designing hardware and software to provide output simultaneously to both the screen and synthetic speech at the user's option. If a software package throws up icons onto the screen, it should provide text as well. The text might be hidden until someone blind or dyslexic asks for it, but it would be available. Redundancy would allow users to choose how they want to use a system, while transparency would allow the hardware and software to work together smoothly with any option.

The third requirement is to ease physical access to machines. There is no good reason, for example, for locating on/off switches at the rear of a PC. There is no excuse for requiring users to press two keys simultaneously to activate a command when the keyboard and software can just as easily be designed to accept sequential keying.

These three concepts apply not only to PCs but to copiers, printers, telephones, and other technologies as well. The idea is to acknowledge the fact that different people have different needs. IBM and Xerox discovered the importance of this concept when they tried selling their big copiers in Japan: few companies wanted to buy them because they were too high and their controls were located toward the back. Like Americans using wheelchairs, Japanese of short stature couldn't reach the controls. The retrofit solution? The U.S. companies suggested that the Japanese use stools. Of course, the better solution would have been to lower the control panel.

AT&T has offered redundancy as a solution to disabled people who are not dextrous enough to use coin telephones. An individual dials "O," says the word "special," and is connected to an operator who charges the call to the person's credit card. Newer phones are more obviously redundant: users can insert their credit cards directly, bypassing the coin slots altogether. Entrex Electronics even introduced a telephone in 1984 that permits users to "answer" simply by saying "phone": the unit behaves exactly as if the user had lifted the receiver.

In California, Steven Wozniak, co-founder of Apple Computer and now president of a company called Cloud Nine, is trying to build transparency into remote-control devices so they will function with any television, stereo, or compact-disc player. It's an exciting and potentially far-reaching advance in making technologies accessible.

The Prognosis

What are the chances that we will make our technologies as accessible as our buildings? In architecture, nothing much happened until the government made accessibility a requirement in state- and federally assisted projects.

The Rehabilitation Act of 1973 could be used to mandate that government-assisted employers provide accessible technology. Section 504 requires any program or activity that receives federal grants to provide access for disabled people that is "equally effective" to that offered to nondisabled individuals. Section 504 also requires programs receiving federal aid to supply "auxiliary aids" so that individuals who are disabled may participate. Some lawyers argue that Congress did not intend to include personal computers, which had not even been invented in 1973, in the law's purview. Litigation will be needed to resolve that question, but none is now pending.

Section 501 of the same act requires federal agencies to make "reasonable accommodations," including providing equipment and other assistance, to disabled employees so they can perform work for which they are qualified. And in Section 503, Congress mandated that the federal government's 30,000 prime contractors and 75,000 subcontractors take affirmative action and make reasonable accommodations in hiring disabled employees. But it is unclear whether these provisions mean that agencies and private employers must purchase technology that is specifically designed to accommodate the needs of handicapped workers.

When Congress reauthorized the Rehabilitation Act in October 1986, it did call upon the General Services Administration (GSA) to develop guidelines for all federal agencies in purchasing accessible PCs and other office automation equipment. The act requires the GSA to work with electronics companies and representatives of disabled consumers in writing the guidelines. Unfortunately, federal agencies often are free to accept or reject the GSA's suggestions. The agency has until October 1988 to develop the guidelines for fiscal-year 1989, so the effect of the new law will be unclear for some time.

If federal agencies do comply with GSA-issued requirements, the effect on making technology more accessible to disabled consumers would be dramatic. The U.S. government is the world's largest buyer of office automation equipment. In 1986 agencies purchased $845 million in hardware, software, and related products. By 1991, according to one market-research firm, government agencies will spend $1.3 billion on office automation. Virtually every computer manufacturer would want to respond by making its products more accessible.

Some disabled consumers are working through

large organizations such as the Boston Computer Society to pressure computer manufacturers to modify their equipment. These groups could extend the pressure to manufacturers of all kinds of commodity electronics. Such consumer activism could prove to be an important supplement to government regulation, and there have been some encouraging early results. IBM hastily redesigned one of its products after shipping the first units when it realized that the device could not be used by some blind people. Xerox has added sharp contrast to the lettering on its Marathon copiers to help people with poor vision read the controls. The company also elegantly designed paper trays so that people with severely limited hand dexterity can use them easily.

Another hopeful sign is the emerging dialogue among representatives of government, industry, and disabled consumers. In February of 1984, representatives of these groups met in the Indian Treaty Room in the White House to discuss what could and should be done to make computer hardware and software more accessible. Many of the companies that attended this meeting, including Apple, Honeywell, AT&T, and Digital, are examining their product lines to determine how to redesign the next generation. These companies will have to make such concerns an ongoing part of their work, since the pace of change in electronics is so rapid that efforts to make one product more accessible would have little permanent effect.

The costs of such efforts will vary widely but need not be severe. Programming a keyboard to accept sequential keying costs nothing. A chip that allows a computer to give voice output costs only about $5. Writing code to instruct hardware and software to send information to that chip may be a lengthy and costly procedure, but possibly only the first time each manufacturer makes the effort.

Yet industry has begun to realize that equipment developed to meet the special needs of disabled consumers is more attractive and practical for everyone. Companies are working to develop computers that understand human speech not in response to the needs of people who are deaf and blind: they are doing it because many executives are reluctant to use keyboards. Workers who use their hands for other tasks, such as quality inspectors on factory assembly lines, will also find computers that recognize the human voice invaluable.

Similarly, the idea of transparency is attractive to many nondisabled users who want to be able to link hardware and software from different vendors. For example, companies are trying to develop transparency for "local area networks": office systems in which a series of computers, printers, and other devices work together.

The idea of redundancy also appeals to many nondisabled users. Some people prefer to listen to information rather than to read it. Some like to use a mouse while others shun the rodent. Some people prefer the mouse for spreadsheets but find it awkward for word processing. Redundancy allows users to choose different options in different situations. The concept is simply an extension of user friendliness: it permits users to "do it their way."

The Promises

Designing electronics to accommodate diverse needs will allow tens of millions of disabled Americans to participate fully in community life. The personal computer will be able to see for blind people, remember for those who are retarded, hear for those who are deaf, and move for individuals with physical limitations.

Computers that can recognize the speech of different people—the next major advance in making this technology accessible—will revolutionize the lives of many disabled people. These machines will probably use the new Intel 80386 chips, which partition vast amounts of memory so that the computer can run several software programs at once (called "multi-tasking.") These chips are expected to allow programmers to design software that understands tens of thousands of words, allowing desktop computers to print what they hear as they hear it. This will enable deaf individuals to talk on the telephone, participate in meetings, even overhear gossip. The machines will also enable blind and physically disabled people to enter words and data without keying.

Such speaker-independent systems are probably still five to ten years away. IBM's experimental Tangora system now recognizes thousands of words and displays them instantly on the screen, but it and other such systems can understand only the voice that trains them. Commercial speech-recognition systems now cost about $7,000 to $9,000, but as with all other electronics, the cost will probably drop by about 20 percent a year as they are mass-produced.

There will always be a need for special computer components and software, just as accessible buildings do not meet the needs of all disabled people. Individuals who are both blind and deaf and many who are retarded, for example, will need extraordinary measures to permit them to use electronics in everyday life. But these exceptions will be relatively few. When society makes a commitment to making new technologies accessible to everyone, the focus will no longer be on what people cannot do, but rather on what skills and interests they bring to their work. That will be as it always should have been. □

Guide to Further Reading

Where does the reader go from here? We can suggest some books, journals, periodicals, and conferences, although this list is only a beginning.

Books

Two books that present general, highly readable introductions to the principles of effective user interface design are Rubinstein and Hersh (1984) and Heckel (1982). Nickerson (1986) is an articulate review of many aspects of human-computer interaction in the context of how computers are applied and used. Shneiderman (1986) covers from a somewhat different perspective some of the topics covered in this book.

At a more advanced level, a number of books focus more precisely on topics and themes begun in this book. Sauter, Chapman, and Knutson (1986) survey and recommend solutions to many of the health concerns that have developed around the use of VDT's. Westin, Schweder, Baker, and Lehman (1985) provide a guide to managing the people, organizational, and regulatory aspects of office technology. Ray and Ravizza (1985) is a valuable introduction to the methods of behavioural observation and experimentation for those with little background in the area. Van Cott and Kinkade (1972) is a classic reference on human factors as it applies to equipment design. Boff, Kaufman, and Thomas (1986) is an encyclopedic compendium of survey articles covering many aspects of perception and human performance that are crucial to the effective use of computer systems. Card, Moran, and Newell (1983) is a comprehensive and

deep introduction to one family of models of the human user of computer systems. Norman and Draper (1986) and Carroll (1987) are the two most useful references for those wanting to think more deeply about the cognitive aspects of human-computer interaction. Bolt (1984) is an inspiring presentation giving a sense of how our interactions with computers may eventually be qualitatively different form what they are now.

Journals

The major journals reporting results on human-computer interaction are the International Journal of Man-Machine Studies (1969-present), Behaviour and Information Technology (1983-present), Human-Computer Interaction (1983-present), Human Factors (1959-present), and Cognitive Science (1977-present).

Periodicals

Other useful regular sources of information are the ACM SIGCHI Bulletin (1982-present), and the Report Store's Hufact™ Quarterly (1987-present).

Conferences

The major conferences at which recent results are presented and published are the annual ACM CHI conference (1982-present), the IFIP Interact conference (1984-present), the British Computer Society HCI conference (1985-present), the International Conference on Human-

Computer Interaction (1985-present), and the annual meeting of the Human Factors Society (1957-present).

References

Boff, K.R., Kaufman, L., & Thomas, J.P. (1986). *Handbook of Perception and Human Performance*, 2 Volumes, New York: John Wiley & Sons.

Behaviour and Information Technology (1982-present). Volumes 1-6, published quarterly by Taylor & Francis, Inc., 242 Cherry Street, Philadelphia Pennsylvania 19106 USA.

Bolt, Richard A. (1984). *The Human Interface: Where People and Computers Meet*, Boston: Lifetime Learning Publications.

Card, S.K., Moran, T.P., & Newell, A. (1983). *The Psychology of Human-Computer Interaction*, Hillsdale, N.J.: Lawrence Erlbaum Associates.

Carroll, J. (Ed.). *Interfacing Thought: Cognitive Aspects of Human-Computer Interaction*, Cambridge, MA.: MIT Press.

CHI (1982-present). The annual Conference on Human Factors in Computing Systems is sponsored by the Special Interest Group on Computers and Human Interaction (SIGCHI) of the Association for Computing Machinery (ACM), 11 W. 42nd Street, New York, N.Y., 10036. The 1988 meeting will be held from May 15 through 19 in Washington, D.C. The Proceedings are published as a special issue of the SIGCHI Bulletin, and will in the future be distributed by Addison-Wesley Publishing Company.

Cognitive Science (1977-present). Volumes 1-11, published bimonthly by Ablex Publishing Company, 355 Chestnut Street, Norwood New Jersey 07648 USA.

HCI (1985-present). The annual conference on People and Computers is sponsored primarily by the British Computer Society. The 3rd meeting was held from September 7 through 11, 1987, in Exeter, England. The contact address is B.I.S.L., 13 Mansfield Street, London W1M 0BP. The proceedings are published.

Heckel, Paul (1982). *The Elements of Friendly Software Design*, New York: Warner Books.

Hufact™ Quarterly (1987-present). This "current awareness resource" is published quarterly by the Report Store, 910 Massachusetts Street, Suite 503S3, Lawrence Kansas 66044 USA.

Human Computer Interaction (1985-present). Volumes 1-2, published quarterly by Lawrence Erlbaum Associates, Inc., 365 Broadway, Hillsdale New Jersey 07642 USA.

Human Factors (1959-present). Volumes 1-29, published bimonthly by The Human Factors Society, Inc., P.O.Box 1369, Santa Monica California 90406 USA.

Human Factors Society Annual Meeting (1957-present). The proceedings are published by The Human Factors Society, Inc.,

P.O.Box 1369, Santa Monica California 90406 USA. The 31st meeting was held from October 19 through 23, 1987, in New York City.

Interact (1984-present). The IFIP conference on Human-Computer Interaction is sponsored primarily by the International Federation of Information Processing (WG 8.2).. The 2nd meeting was held from September 1 through 5, 1987, in Stuttgart, Germany. The contact address is IPA/IAO, Fraunhofer-Institut fur Produktionstechnik, Nobelstrasse 12, P.O. Box 80 04 69, 7000 Stuttgart 80, F.R. Germany. The proceedings of the first conference were published by North-Holland.

International Conference on Human-Computer Interaction (1985-present). This conference is sponsored by the International Commission on Human Aspects of Computing, Geneva, Switzerland. The 2nd meeting was held from August 10 through 14, 1987, in Honolulu, Hawaii. The proceedings are published.

International Journal of Man-Machine Studies (1969-present). Volumes 1-26, published bimonthly by Academic Press Inc. (London) Limited, High Street, Foots Cray, Sidcup Kent DA14 5HP England.

Nickerson, Raymond S. (1986). *Using Computers: Human Factors in Information Systems*, Cambridge, Mass.: MIT Press.

Norman, D.A. and Draper, S.W. (Eds.), *User Centered System Design: New Perspectives on Human-Computer Interaction*, Hillsdale, N.J.: Lawrence Erlbaum Associates.

Ray, William J. & Ravizza, Richard (1986). *Methods Toward a Science of Behavior and Experience*, Second Edition, Belmont, CA.: Wadsworth Publishing Company.

Rubinstein, Richard & Hersh, Harry (1984). *The Human Factor: Designing Computer Systems for People*, Burlington, Mass.: Digital Press.

Sauter, S.L., Chapman, L.J. & Knutson, S.J. (1985). *Improving VDT Work: Causes and Control of Health Concerns in VDT Use*, Madison: University of Wisconsin. Distributed by The Report Store, 910 Massachusetts St., Suite 503, Lawrence Kansas 66044 USA.

Shneiderman, Ben (1986). *Designing the User Interface: Strategies for Human-Computer Interaction*, Reading, Mass.: Addison-Wesley Publishing Company.

SIGCHI Bulletin (1982-present). This quarterly is published by the Special Interest Group on Computers and Human Interaction (SIGCHI) of the Association for Computing Machinery (ACM), 11 W. 42nd Street, New York, N.Y., 10036.

Van Cott, H. & Kinkade, R. (Eds.) (1972). *Human Engineering Guide to Equipment Design*, Revised Edition, Washington, D.C.: American Institutes for Research.

Westin, A., Schweder, H., Baker, M & Lehman, S. (1985). *The Changing Workplace: A Guide to Managing the People, Organizational and Regulatory Aspects of Office Technology*, White Plains, NY: Knowledge Industry Publications, Inc.

Evaluation and Feedback Form

The authors would like to hear your reactions to and comments on this book. As with any situation in human-computer or human-book interaction, we can only improve the product through an iterative design process based on observations of real users. So please photocopy these 2 pages, write down your suggestions, and mail the result to:

Ronald Baecker and William Buxton
Department of Computer Science
University of Toronto
Toronto Ontario M5S 1A4 Canada.

Briefly describe how you used this book.

Briefly describe your background and experience in human-computer interaction prior to reading this book.

Briefly describe what you do in life and the role of human-computer interaction in your work.

What did you most like about this book?

What did you most dislike about this book?

What general suggestions do you have to improve the Second Edition?

Which readings do you feel should be omitted, and why?

What papers do you feel should be included, and why?

Any other comments or suggestions?

Subject Index

Note: The level of indexing detail is greater for the original material than for the readings.

Name Index